CW01475983

The Wiley International Handbook of Correctional Psychology

The Wiley International Handbook of Correctional Psychology

Edited by

Devon L. L. Polaschek, Andrew Day, and Clive R. Hollin

WILEY Blackwell

Registered Office(s)
John Wiley & Sons, Inc., 111 River Street, Hoboken, NJ 07030, USA
John Wiley & Sons Ltd, The Atrium, Southern Gate, Chichester, West Sussex, PO19 8SQ, UK

Editorial Office
111 River Street, Hoboken, NJ 07030, USA

For details of our global editorial offices, customer services, and more information about Wiley products visit us at www.wiley.com.

Wiley also publishes its books in a variety of electronic formats and by print-on-demand. Some content that appears in standard print versions of this book may not be available in other formats.

Library of Congress Cataloging-in-Publication Data

Names: Polaschek, Devon L. L., editor. | Day, Andrew (Andrew John Dallin), editor. | Hollin, Clive R., editor.
Title: The Wiley international handbook of correctional psychology / edited by Devon L.L. Polaschek, Andrew Day, and Clive R. Hollin.
Description: Hoboken, NJ : John Wiley & Sons, Inc., 2019. | Includes bibliographical references and index. |
Identifiers: LCCN 2018042659 (print) | LCCN 2018044144 (ebook) | ISBN 9781119139966 (Adobe PDF) | ISBN 9781119139973 (ePub) | ISBN 9781119139683 (hardcover)
Subjects: LCSH: Criminals–Rehabilitation. | Criminal behavior. | Criminal psychology.
Classification: LCC HV9275 (ebook) | LCC HV9275 .W495 2019 (print) | DDC 364.601/9–dc23
LC record available at https://lccn.loc.gov/2018042659

Cover image: © Lou Levit/Unsplash.com
Cover design by Wiley

Set in 10/12.5pt Galliard by SPi Global, Pondicherry, India

Printed in Singapore by C.O.S. Printers Pte Ltd

To Harry Love and Paul Gendreau for their distinct contributions to correctional psychology in Aotearoa/ New Zealand (DLLP)

To Kevin Howells, the spiritual leader of correctional psychology in Australia (AD)

To James McGuire, psychologist extraordinaire (CRH)

The contributions to the book represent creative and systematic work that was undertaken to increase the stock of knowledge on this topic.

Contents

About the Editors

Devon L. L. Polaschek is Professor of Psychology and Joint Director of the New Zealand Institute of Security and Crime Science at the University of Waikato (Te Whare Wānanga o Waikato) in Hamilton, New Zealand. She has a longstanding interest in correctional psychology practice, and in training psychologists and other staff to be more effective in their work with offenders. Her research publications span the psychology of violent and sexual offending, high-risk offenders, psychopathy, the working alliance, treatment change, treatment outcome, and parole. She is a former Fulbright Scholar, recipient of the New Zealand Psychological Society's Hunter Award for lifetime excellence in scholarship, research, and professional achievement in Psychology, and Fellow of the Association of Psychological Science.

Andrew Day is Enterprise Professor in the School of Social and Political Sciences at the University of Melbourne and Adjunct Professor in the Indigenous Education and Research Centre at James Cook University. He has research interests in areas of offender rehabilitation, violent offenders, and juvenile justice. He is widely published in the field of forensic psychology and criminal justice.

Clive R. Hollin is Emeritus Professor of Criminological Psychology at the University of Leicester, UK. He wrote the best-selling textbook *Psychology and Crime: An Introduction to Criminological Psychology* (2nd ed., 2013); his latest books are *The Psychology of Interpersonal Violence* (2016) and *Reducing Interpersonal Violence: A Psychological Perspective* (2018). In all, he has published 23 books alongside over 300 other academic publications and was for 20 years lead editor of the journal *Psychology, Crime, & Law*. Alongside various university appointments, he has worked as a psychologist in prisons, the Youth Treatment Service, special hospitals, and regional secure units. In 1998, he received The Senior Award for Distinguished Contribution to the Field of Legal, Criminological and Forensic Psychology from The British Psychological Society.

Notes on the Contributors

Ronald H. Aday, PhD is a Professor of Sociology and Director of the Graduate Program in Gerontology at Middle Tennessee State University. An international scholar on the topic of aging and health issues in the field of correction, Aday has contributed significantly to the public policy debate on older offenders. His research on older prisoners has spanned more than 4 decades, resulting in more than 65 refereed articles and book chapters. He is the author of *Aging Prisoners: Crisis in American Corrections* (2003) and co-author of *Women Aging in Prison*. He is also the co-author of a forthcoming book near completion on the *Life of Women Lifers*.

Geraldine Akerman is a chartered and HCPC (Health and Care Professions Council) Registered Forensic Psychologist, EuroPsych, and Associate Fellow of the British Psychological Society. She sits on the British Psychological Society's Division of Forensic Psychology Executive Committee and the National Organisation for the Treatment of Abusers Research Committee. She is a Trustee for the Safer Living Foundation. Geraldine has academic publications on offense-paralleling behavior, managing deviant sexual fantasies and offending, and ex-service personnel in prison and edited a book on enabling environments. Geraldine currently works as a therapy manager at HMP Grendon in the UK.

Alfred Allan qualified in law and psychology and is registered with clinical and forensic endorsements in Australia. Professor Allan has taught law, psychology, and professional ethics in South Africa and Australia. He is a member of the inaugural Psychologists Board of Australia, a director and the Chair of the Standing Committee on Ethics of the International Association for Applied Psychology (IAAP), and a Fellow of the Australian Psychological Society (APS). He is on the editorial committee of *Psychiatry, Psychology and Law* and the editorial board of *Philosophy, Ethics, and Humanities in Medicine*, and *Ethics & Behavior*.

Danyal Ansari, BA (Hons), is currently undertaking training as a Clinical Associate in Applied Psychology and is employed with NHS Greater Glasgow & Clyde. His work focuses on providing cognitive behavioral therapy for individuals experiencing common mental health problems. He has previously worked with individuals with intellectual and developmental disability, and with autism, where he provided clinical and forensic input to the service.

Rebecca L. Bauer is a licensed Psychologist who received her PhD in counseling psychology from Texas Tech University. She previously worked as a staff psychologist for the Federal Bureau of Prisons. Currently, she is in private practice conducting forensic evaluations. Her research interests include correctional mental health.

David P. Bernstein is an endowed Chair of Forensic Psychotherapy (Section Forensic Psychology) in the Faculty of Psychology and Neuroscience at Maastricht University, the Netherlands. He has served as President of the Association for Research on Personality

Disorders, Vice President of the International Society for the Study of Personality Disorders, and Vice President of the International Society for Schema Therapy.

Astrid Birgden is a Consultant Forensic Psychologist and Adjunct Clinical Associate Professor at Deakin University, Australia. Dr. Birgden has developed policy and service delivery to correctional services (sex offenders and drug-related offenders), disability services (forensic disability clients), and in problem-solving courts (family violence court and drug court). Dr. Birgden's international work includes designing a practical intervention in a torture prevention project for police and military personnel in Sri Lanka and Nepal (EU funding), and training correctional officers regarding sexual and drug-related offenders in the Caribbean (EU funding). She has published on offender rehabilitation, therapeutic jurisprudence, and human rights.

Erica Bowen is Professor of Violence Prevention Research at the University of Worcester, UK. Erica is a Registered Forensic Psychologist (Health and Care Professions Council) and a Chartered Psychologist and Associate Fellow of the British Psychological Society. Her research for the past two decades has focused on understanding and preventing intimate partner violence in adult and adolescent relationships. Erica has developed innovative interventions including a serious-game-based primary intervention to combat adolescent dating violence, and a brief intervention for preventing domestic violence in adult relationships used primarily for non-court mandated clients.

Sarah Brown is a Professor of Forensic Psychology in the Centre for Advances in Behaviour Science at Coventry University, UK. She has been conducting research related to sexual aggression for over 20 years and has been working at Coventry University since 1999. Sarah is the Chair-Elect of NOTA, the National Organisation for the Treatment of Abusers. She is an Associate Editor of _Child Abuse and Neglect_ and a member of the editorial board of _Sexual Abuse_ and the _Journal of Sexual Aggression_, having been the Editor of the latter journal from 2008 to 2014. Sarah is a member of the Advisory Board of the new Centre for Expertise on Child Sexual Abuse that is funded by the UK Home Office and was launched in 2017.

Shelley L. Brown is an Associate Professor of Forensic Psychology in the Department of Psychology at Carleton University in Canada, which she joined in 2006, after a 10-year research career with Correctional Service of Canada. She completed a PhD in 2002 at Queens University on dynamic risk assessment among adult male offenders. Since then her main research focus has been improving gender responsive services for girls and women in the criminal justice system using a mix of quantitative and qualitative approaches. The Criminal Justice Section of the Canadian Psychological Association awarded Shelley (jointly with Kelley Blanchette) a significant contribution award for their work on female criminal conduct.

Sharon Casey, PhD, holds a conjoint appointment at Deakin University, Australia, in the School of Psychology. She is widely published in many areas of forensic psychology and has a particular interest in offender rehabilitation. Her research interests include substance use, juvenile offending, and scale development and validation. She has worked extensively with correctional agencies both in Australia and overseas in the development, provision, and evaluation of offender rehabilitation programs and the provision of staff training.

Nick Chadwick, MA, is a PhD candidate in forensic psychology at Carleton University, Ottawa, Canada. He has conducted research projects on the use and implementation of evidence-based practices in community supervision as well as the utility of dynamic risk assessment and incorporating offender change in the prediction of recidivism.

Maartje Clercx studied psychology at Maastricht University, the Netherlands. She then obtained her master's degree in forensic psychology from Maastricht University as well. She is mainly interested in juvenile and adult psychopathy, and has worked for Dr. Lieke Nentjes and conducted research on the comprehensive assessment of psychopathic personality in collaboration with Professor David Cooke. Currently she is working as a junior researcher at Maastricht University, where she mainly concentrates on the randomized controlled trial of Professor David Bernstein. Maartje is currently working toward finding a suitable PhD position, preferably on the topic of psychopathy.

David J. Cooke is a Consultant Forensic Clinical Psychologist and former Head of the Forensic Clinical Psychology service in Glasgow, UK. He is a Visiting Professor in the Faculty of Psychology at the University of Bergen in Norway and an Adjunct Professor in the Faculty of Law at La Trobe University, Melbourne, Australia. He undertakes research on psychopathic disorder, the risk management of violent offenders, and the impact of institutional settings on violent and disturbed behavior. He has published widely in the field and he serves on a number of editorial boards and expert groups.

Raymond R. Corrado is a Professor in the School of Criminology at Simon Fraser University, Canada, a visiting Fellow at Clare Hall College and the Institute of Criminology, University of Cambridge, UK, and founding member of the Mental Health, Law, and Policy Institute at Simon Fraser University. He is on the editorial boards of six major criminology and forensic mental health journals, has co-edited nine books, and published over 150 articles, book chapters, and reports on youth/juvenile justice, violent young offenders, mental health, adolescent psychopathy, Aboriginal victimization, child/adolescent case management strategies, and terrorism. He received his PhD from Northwestern in Chicago.

Michael Daffern is Professor of Clinical Forensic Psychology with the Centre for Forensic Behavioural Science, Swinburne University of Technology, and Consultant Principal Psychologist with the Victorian Institute of Forensic Mental Health (Forensicare), Australia. He divides his time between teaching, clinical practice, and research, the focus of which is the assessment and treatment of violent offenders.

Jason Davies is Professor of Forensic and Clinical Psychology in the Department of Psychology, Swansea University & ABMU Health Board, South Wales, and a Consultant Forensic and Clinical Psychologist. He has worked in high, medium, low secure, and community-based forensic mental health services in the UK. His clinical and research interests include psychological treatment, outcome measurement, personality, staff supervision, and service development. He has published on mental health, forensic psychology, and rehabilitation, including three books (two edited, one authored): *Research in Practice for Forensic Professionals* (2011), *Supervision for Forensic Professionals* (2016), and *Individual Psychological Therapies in Forensic Settings: Research and Practice* (2017).

Simon Davies completed his LLB and BSc (psychology and criminology) at Victoria University of Wellington, New Zealand, in 2012, where he is currently a PhD student completing his postgraduate diploma in clinical psychology. His PhD research examines the predictive validity of risk assessments conducted by probation officers with high-risk men on parole. Previously his research has examined the skills and techniques used by probation officers during supervision to help reduce recidivism, and the effectiveness of parole supervision. His broader research interests include risk assessment, community supervision, reintegration, and application of the scientific method to all aspects of the criminal justice system.

xvi Notes on the Contributors

Sara Del Principel has an MA in Criminology, Law, and Society from George Mason University, during which she worked as a Graduate Research Assistant for the Center for Advancing Correctional Excellence (ACE!) on various research projects aimed at utilizing evidence-based practices to enhance the field of corrections and maximize the positive reentry of individuals on probation. Since completing her MA, Ms. Del Principe has worked as a Crime Analyst with two local police departments.

Kevin S. Douglas is Professor of Clinical-Forensic Psychology at Simon Fraser University, Canada, and current President of the American Psychology-Law Society. His research and professional activities include violence risk assessment and management; dynamic risk factors; mental disorder and violence; and psychopathy. He is lead author on the latest revision of the Historical-Clinical-Risk Management-20 (HCR-20) violence risk assessment measure, published in 2013. Dr. Douglas has authored over 160 journal articles, books, or book chapters, and has received approximately $5 million of research funding, from the US National Science Foundation and the Social Sciences and Humanities Research Council of Canada, among others.

Clare-Ann Fortune, PhD, PGDipClinPsyc, is a Senior Lecturer in Clinical Forensic Psychology at the School of Psychology, Victoria University of Wellington, New Zealand. She is a registered Clinical Psychologist and teaches on the Forensic Psychology and Clinical Psychology programs at Victoria University of Wellington. Her research interests focus on risk assessment, offender rehabilitation, and factors impacting the competency of young people involved in the justice system. She has published papers on strength-based approaches to offender rehabilitation, risk assessment, and young people who have engaged in sexually abusive behaviors.

Paul Gendreau, OC, PhD, trained at University of Ottawa and Queen's University, Ontario, Canada. After working at Kingston Penitentiary, Ontario, from 1961, he held a series of academic appointments at Canadian universities, and remains an Emeritus Professor at the University of New Brunswick. He has published extensively on "what works" with offenders, program implementation, effects of prison life, and the use of statistics in knowledge cumulation. In 2007, Dr. Gendreau was appointed an Officer of the Order of Canada "for achievement and merit of a high degree, especially service to Canada or to humanity at large."

Claire Goggin holds a PhD in psychology from the University of New Brunswick, Canada, and is now an Assistant Professor at St. Thomas University, New Brunswick. Her research interests include correctional program evaluation, the effects of imprisonment; empirical research methodologies and statistics, particularly meta-analysis; and knowledge cumulation and transfer. Recent projects include an examination of inscription practices in selected scientific disciplines; a meta-analysis of the effects of imprisonment on offender recidivism and emotional wellbeing; an examination of the relationship between rates of homicide and capital punishment in Canada between 1920 and 1949; and a prospective study of the socialization process among police officers.

Sheilagh Hodgins, PhD, FRSC, is currently Professor at the Département de Psychiatrie, Université de Montréal and the Institut Universitaire de Santé Mentale de Montréal, Canada, and a Visiting Professor at the Department of Clinical Neuroscience at the Karolinska Institutet, Sweden. Professor Hodgins has been studying and publishing her research findings on the antisocial behavior of persons with severe mental illness for many decades. Presently, she is working on prospective, longitudinal studies in Canada and in Sweden that aim to unravel the complex interplay between genetic and environmental factors that impact the developing brain to promote antisocial and aggressive behavior.

Tom Hogan is a Training and Program Specialist at Central Connecticut State University's Institute for the Study of Crime and Justice. Over the past 30 years he has accumulated a diverse array of Community Corrections experience: as a Probation Officer, a Chief Probation Officer, and as a Best Practices specialist for a large community-based correctional treatment agency. He has trained and coached hundreds of probation, parole, and treatment workers in the use of motivational interviewing and cognitive behavioral skills. His work with justice-involved clients has appeared in journal articles and been presented at national correctional conferences.

Richard C. Howard started his academic career researching neurophysiological substrates of personality disorder while working at an English high secure forensic hospital, Broadmoor, in the 1970s. Since then, he has worked in a variety of academic settings in several countries, most recently at the University of Nottingham in the UK. He has authored or co-authored almost 100 scientific papers and book chapters. His particular interest is in the relationship between violent offending and personality disorder, and he co-edited, with M. McMurran, *Personality, Personality Disorder and Violence* (2009). He is affiliated to the Institute of Mental Health in Nottingham, and resides in Wiesbaden, Germany.

Joseph T. Hunter is a fourth-year doctoral student in Robert D. Morgan's Forensic and Correctional Psychology laboratory in the Counseling Psychology program in the Department of Psychological Sciences at Texas Tech University. Joe's current research interests focus on the treatment of justice-involved persons with mental illness and the assessment and treatment of persons at risk for criminal justice involvement within the community.

Lawrence Jones is a Forensic and Clinical Psychologist whose career has included working in the community, at HMP Wormwood Scrubs, and at Rampton High Secure Hospital, UK, where he is now the Head of Psychology. He is a former Chair of the Division of Forensic Psychology and teaches on the Sheffield and Leicester Clinical Psychology doctorate courses and the Nottingham Forensic Psychology Doctorate. He has published in a range of areas, including therapeutic communities, working with people with personality disorder diagnoses who have offended sexually, iatrogenic responses to intervention, motivation, offense paralleling behavior (OPB), and trauma-informed care.

Marije Keulen-De Vos, PhD, is a senior researcher at Forensic Psychiatric Center de Rooyse Wissel in the Netherlands. She also manages the development and implementation of evidence-based care pathways for offenders. She received her doctorate degree in clinical psychology from the University of Maastricht, the Netherlands. She is an expert on schema therapy. Recently, she has adapted schema therapy for offenders with an intellectual disability. Her research focuses on forensic treatment, emotional states, intellectual disability, and sex offenders. Since 2017, she has been President of the Dutch chapter of the Association for the Treatment of Sexual Abusers.

T. Glen Kilgour trained as a Clinical Psychologist at Waikato University, graduating in the early 1990s. He has worked in the New Zealand Department of Corrections since 1995 in a variety of roles, including Principal Psychologist and, currently, a Principal Adviser in the Office of the Chief Psychologist. His interests include reducing violence, program evaluation, group therapy, young offenders, leadership, staff development, and science fiction.

Marissa Kiss is a PhD candidate in the Department of Sociology and Anthropology, and has an MA in sociology from George Mason University (2012), where she is currently a researcher at the Institute for Immigration Research. She previously worked as a Research Analyst at National Opinion Research Center at the University of Chicago, and as a Research Associate at the Center for Advancing Correctional Excellence (ACE!) at George Mason University, where she managed two large-scale research projects, including Your Own Reintegration System, a guided goal-setting and manualized treatment program used by supervising officers to facilitate reentry.

Sanja Klein, BSc, received her bachelor degree in psychology from the Justus-Liebig-University in Giessen, Germany, where she is currently a graduate student, majoring in clinical psychology. She has been working closely with Professor Hodgins for 4 years and has completed research internships at University College London, UK, and Charité Berlin, Germany.

Gabrielle Klepfisz completed a bachelor's degree in psychology at Monash University, Australia, in addition to her fourth-year honors, during which she investigated violent offender treatment change. She has continued this research as a doctoral candidate in the Doctor of Psychology (Clinical and Forensic) at Swinburne University of Technology. Ms. Klepfisz has worked as a research assistant both in Australia and in Canada. She has gained clinical experience working with individuals in community and inpatient forensic settings as well as with various mental health concerns, including psychosis, depression and suicidality, anger, social and generalized anxiety, obsessive compulsive disorder, hoarding disorder, and past sexual/physical abuse.

Daryl G. Kroner, PhD, is a Professor at the Department of Criminology and Criminal Justice at Southern Illinois University (SIU). He has more than 20 years of experience in the field as a correctional psychologist. During this time, he worked at maximum, medium, and minimum facilities delivering intervention services to incarcerated men. Dr. Kroner has consulted on prison management and release issues, including with the Council of State Governments Justice Center and the UK's National Offender Management System. He is also a fellow of the Canadian Psychological Association. In collaboration with Dr. Jeremy Mills, he has developed several instruments, including the Measures of Criminal Attitudes and Associates (MCAA), Depression, Hopelessness, and Suicide Scale (DHS), Criminal Attribution Inventory (CRAI), Transition Inventory (TI), and the Measures of Criminal and Antisocial Desistance (MCAD). In collaboration with Drs. Morgan and Mills, Dr. Kroner co-authored *A Treatment Program for Justice Involved Persons with Mental Illness* (2017). In 2008, Dr. Kroner joined the Department of Criminology and Criminal Justice at SIU. Current research interests include risk assessment, measurement of intervention outcomes, interventions among offenders with mental illness, and criminal desistance.

William Lindsay, PhD, is a Fellow of both the British Psychological Society and the International Association for the Scientific Study of Intellectual Disabilities. As an author of over 200 scientific articles and book chapters, his research interest included the fields of cognitive behavioral therapy for people with intellectual disabilities and forensic psychology. He has served as associate editor for the *Journal of Applied Research in Intellectual Disabilities* and the *Journal of Intellectual and Developmental Disabilities*. Sadly, Bill passed away in 2017 before this booked was published.

Caleb D. Lloyd, PhD (Carleton University, Ottawa, Canada) is a Senior Lecturer with the Centre for Forensic Behavioural Science at Swinburne University of Technology, Melbourne, Australia. He directs a program of research on offender change in corrections and the community, with an aim to conduct theoretically informed research with clear practical applications for the correctional system.

Caroline Logan is a Forensic Clinical Psychologist. She is Professional Lead for Psychology in the Specialist Services Network, Greater Manchester Mental Health NHS Foundation Trust (GMMH), UK. Dr. Logan is also an Honorary Research Fellow at the University of Manchester in the UK, where she is also the Associate Director of a post-graduate master's degree course in forensic mental health. Dr. Logan has worked in forensic and correctional services for over 20 years, as both a clinician and a researcher, focusing on personality disorder (including psychopathy) and its relationship to risk of harm to self and others, subjects on which she has published two books and a number of articles.

Lydie R. Loth is currently a Senior Data Analyst for the Public Safety Performance Project juvenile justice team at the Pew Charitable Trusts. In this role, she provides technical assistance to state agencies involved in addressing issues of juvenile offender recidivism, public safety, and the controlling of criminal justice system costs through data-driven and research-based policies. She received her doctorate in Criminal Justice from the University of Cincinnati in 2018. Her research interests include correctional program evaluations, employment opportunities for inmates and ex-offenders, and juvenile justice.

Nina MacLean is a doctoral candidate in the Department of Psychological Sciences at Texas Tech University. Her research interests include unconscious biases in forensic evaluations and the development of strategies to mitigate bias to increase objectivity.

Sarah M. Manchak is an Assistant Professor in the School of Criminal Justice at the University of Cincinnati. She received her doctoral degree in experimental psychopathology from the University of California, Irvine, in 2011. Prior to that, she earned her master's degree in forensic psychology at John Jay College of Criminal Justice. Her research seeks to inform policy and interventions for offenders with mental illness and individuals at risk for violence, self-harm, and antisocial behavior. Her prior research includes an examination of client–therapist relationships in mandated treatment and how probation and mental health agencies communicate and collaborate.

Liam E. Marshall, PhD, RP, ATSAF, received his degrees (BAH, MA, PhD) in developmental psychology from Queen's University in Kingston, Ontario, Canada. He has been providing treatment for and conducting research on offenders and mentally ill offenders for more than two decades. Liam has more than 100 peer-reviewed publications, including four books, is a board member and reviewer for many international journals, and has made numerous international conference presentations on offender and mental health issues. He has delivered trainings for therapists who work with sexual and violent offenders in 22 countries. Liam was recently (2016) invested as a Fellow of the Association for the Treatment of Sexual Abusers (ATSA) for his significant contribution to the prevention of sexual violence. He is currently a researcher and clinician at Waypoint and Director of Rockwood Psychotherapy & Consulting.

Tina Maschi, PhD, LCSW, ACSW, is an Associate Professor at the Fordham University Graduate School of Social Service in New York City. She is internationally known for her social work research and practice efforts, which are at the intersection of aging, trauma, health, and justice. Dr. Maschi is a practitioner scholar with over 100 peer reviewed journal publications, book chapters, and books, including *Forensic Social Work* (2009). Dr. Maschi also has published in the area of older adults involved in the criminal justice system, particularly related to life-course trauma and stress and resilience among older adults before, during, and after prison.

Jeff Mathesius is a PhD student in the School of Criminology at Simon Fraser University, Canada. His research interests include sexual offending/sexual offenders, onset of delinquency, serious and violent juvenile offenders, temperament, mental health, and developmental/life-course criminology. He has published in various criminological and psychological journals, including *Psychological Assessment, Journal of Criminal Justice*, and *Sexual Abuse: A Journal of Research and Treatment.*

James McGuire is Emeritus Professor of Forensic Clinical Psychology at the University of Liverpool, UK. He has worked in intellectual disability services and in a high-security hospital, has carried out research in probation services, prisons, youth justice, addictions units, and other settings on aspects of psychosocial rehabilitation with offenders, and designed and evaluated a number of intervention and staff training programs. He has published widely on these and related issues, and has acted as a consultant to criminal justice agencies in a number of countries.

Mary McMurran, PhD, is Emeritus Professor at the University of Nottingham, UK, and Visiting Professor at Cardiff Metropolitan University, UK. Her research interests include the treatment of people with personality disorders; the treatment of alcohol-related aggression and violence; forensic case formulation; and enhancing engagement in treatment. She has written over 200 academic articles, books, and book chapters on these topics. She is a HCPC (Health and Care Professions Council) Registered Forensic and Clinical Psychologist, a Fellow of the British Psychological Society, and in 2005 was recipient of the Division of Forensic Psychology's Lifetime Achievement Award. She has worked as a Clinical and Forensic Psychologist in HM Prison Service and the UK's National Health Service. She is currently a member of the Parole Board for England and Wales.

Damon Mitchell, PhD, is a Professor of Criminology and Criminal Justice at Central Connecticut State University. As a criminal justice consultant, he has developed and delivered training workshops related to forensic assessment and treatment, and conducted evaluations of criminal justice programs. He is co-editor of and a contributor to *Forensic CBT: A Handbook for Clinical Practice* (with R. C. Tafrate, 2014) and also a contributor to *Cognitive Therapy of Personality Disorders—Third Edition* (2015). His most recent book, *CBT with Justice-Involved Clients: Interventions for Antisocial and Self-Destructive Behaviors*, was published in 2018 (co-edited with R. C. Tafrate and D. J. Simourd).

Robert D. Morgan is the John G. Skelton, Jr. Regents Endowed Professor in Psychology, Chairperson for the Department of Psychological Sciences, and Director of the Institute for Forensic Science at Texas Tech University. Dr. Morgan's research and scholarly activities include treatment and assessment of justice-involved persons with mental illness, effects of incarceration including in restricted housing units, and forensic mental health assessment. His research has been funded by the National Institute of Mental Health, the National Institute of Justice, and the Center for Behavioral Health Services & Criminal Justice Research. He provides forensic mental health services at the request of courts, defense, and prosecution, and consults with state and private correctional agencies to inform practice.

Mark E. Olver, PhD, is a Full Professor and Registered Doctoral Psychologist at the University of Saskatchewan, in Saskatoon, Canada, where he is involved in program administration, graduate and undergraduate teaching, research, and clinical training. Mark's research interests include offender risk assessment and treatment, young offenders, psychopathy, and the evaluation of therapeutic change. He is the co-developer of the Violence Risk Scale-Sexual Offense version (VRS-SO) and he provides training and consultation services internationally in the assessment and treatment of sexual, violent, and psychopathic offenders.

Rob Paramo is a UK trained Registered Forensic Psychologist. He now lives and works in Wellington, New Zealand. He has worked for the Department of Corrections in frontline and national office roles for the past 8 years. His passion for rehabilitation programs started 17 years ago as a therapist working on sex offender programs. Since this time, he has worked supervising, managing, and later supporting nationally delivered programs in both HM Prison Service and NZ Corrections. His areas of interest include programs for complex and high-risk sexual and violent offenders, as well as program development, evaluation, and quality systems.

Adrienne M. F. Peters is an Assistant Professor in the Department of Sociology at Memorial University of Newfoundland and a Research Associate with the Centre for Public Safety and Criminal Justice Research, Canada. Her research areas include young offender intervention programming and rehabilitation; serious–/violent youth offending; mental health and delinquency; youth and sexual offenses; youth justice legislation and policy; offender rehabilitation and reentry; evidence-based policing; and collaborative crime reduction strategies. She is the Principal Investigator of a Social Sciences and Humanities Research Council-funded project titled *A Longitudinal Study of the Reoffending Outcomes of Serious-Violent, Gang-Involved, Mentally Disordered, and Sexual Offenders Supervised on Specialized Youth Probation.*

Karen Salmon is a Clinical Psychologist who held an academic appointment at the University of New South Wales (Sydney, Australia) for 10 years, before returning to New Zealand and Victoria University of Wellington in 2007. Karen Salmon's research focuses on the role of adolescent autobiographical memory in the development of child and adolescent psychopathology and in psychological wellbeing. For example, she has investigated the influence of everyday conversations between adults and children on the children's memory for their emotional experiences and on their developing emotion competence, and currently is focusing on the role of specific memory biases in children and adolescents' psychological functioning.

Terri Scott is a PhD candidate working under the supervision of Dr. Shelley Brown at Carleton University, Canada, where she has completed a bachelor of arts (honors) in criminology with a concentration in psychology and a master's in psychology (forensic). She has been a researcher with the federal government for the past 15 years. Her PhD dissertation is focused on determining gender-specific predictors of crime, including both strength and risk factors among juvenile offenders through meta-analysis, as well as a validation study of a gender-informed risk assessment tool for adjudicated youth, the Youth Assessment Screening Instrument (YASI).

Ralph C. Serin is a Professor of Psychology at Carleton University, Ottawa, Canada, and Director of the Criminal Justice Decision Making Laboratory. His current research reflects parole decision-making, dynamic risk assessment, offender change, and crime desistance.

Jennifer L. Skeem is the Mack Distinguished Professor and Associate Dean of Research in Social Welfare, and Professor of Public Policy at the University of California, Berkeley. Her research is designed to inform legal decision-making about people with emotional and behavioral problems. Her current work addresses a recent surge of interest in the use of risk assessment to inform criminal sentencing, including how this practice may affect racial and economic disparities in imprisonment. She is author of about 120 articles and chapters and editor of two books and past President of the American Psychology-Law Society.

Peter Sturmey is Professor of Psychology at The Graduate Center and the Department of Psychology, Queens College, City University of New York, where he is a member of the behavior analysis doctoral program. He specializes in autism and other developmental disabilities, especially in the areas of applied behavior analysis, dual diagnosis, evidence-based practice, and staff and parent training. Professor Sturmey has published 25 edited and authored books, over 200 papers, and 50 book chapters, and made over 250 presentations nationally and internationally, including recent presentations in Canada, Brazil, and Italy.

Tamara Sweller is a Forensic Psychologist with Corrective Services New South Wales, Australia. She is a clinician in the Custody-Based Intensive Treatment program for sexual offenders at Long Bay Correctional Complex. She is also completing a PhD through Swinburne University of Technology.

Raymond Chip Tafrate, PhD, is a Professor in the Criminology and Criminal Justice Department at Central Connecticut State University. He co-chairs the Forensic Issues and Externalizing Behaviors special interest group for the Association for Behavioral and Cognitive Therapies and frequently consults with criminal justice agencies regarding difficult-to-change problems such as anger dysregulation and criminal behavior. His research has been presented throughout North America, Europe, Asia, and Australia. His most recent books are: *Forensic CBT: A Handbook for Clinical Practice, Anger Management for Everyone* (co-edited with D. Mitchell, 2014) and *CBT with Justice-Involved Clients: Interventions for Antisocial and Self-Destructive Behaviors* (co-edited with D. Mitchell and D. J. Simourd, 2018).

Armon J. Tamatea is a Clinical Psychologist of Māori (*Rongowhakaata; Te Aitanga-A-Maahaki*) and English descent who served as a clinician and Senior Research Advisor for the Department of Corrections (New Zealand) before being appointed Senior Lecturer in Psychology at the University of Waikato. He has worked extensively in the assessment and treatment of violent and sexual offenders, and contributed to the design and implementation of an experimental prison-based violence prevention program for high-risk offenders with psychopathy. His research interests include New Zealand gang communities, psychopathy, and culturally informed approaches to offender management.

Jayne L. Taylor is a Clinical Psychologist working within the Adult Forensic Service of the Specialist Services Network, Greater Manchester Mental Health NHS Foundation Trust (GMMH), UK. She is also Honorary Lecturer at the University of Manchester in the UK. Since her arrival at GMMH in 2002, Dr. Taylor has specialized in the treatment of women with complex difficulties who are at risk to themselves or others, across settings and security levels. She is currently the Lead Psychologist for the Women's Service in the Adult Forensic Service, and teaches at universities across the region.

Faye S. Taxman, PhD, is a Professor in the Criminology, Law and Society Department and Director of the Center for Advancing Correctional Excellence at George Mason University. Dr. Taxman has published more than 190 articles, including "Tools of the Trade: A Guide to Incorporating Science into Practice," and is co-author of *Implementing Evidence-Based Community Corrections and Addiction Treatment* (with S. Belenko, 2012). The American Society of Criminology's Division of Sentencing and Corrections has recognized her as Distinguished Scholar twice. She has also received the Rita Warren and Ted Palmer Differential

Intervention Treatment award. She received the Joan McCord Award in 2017 from the Division of Experimental Criminology.

Stephanie A. Van Horn is a doctoral candidate in counseling psychology at Texas Tech University. Ms. Van Horn's research interests include correctional rehabilitation program evaluation, measurement invariance in risk assessments, the effects of incarceration on women offenders, and gender-specific challenges to successful community reentry.

Kate Walker is a Research Fellow in the Centre for Advances in Behavioural Science (CABS) at Coventry University, UK. Her main research focus is desistance from intimate partner violence and the behavioral changes associated with this process, and the development and evaluation of primary and tertiary interventions for the prevention of violence and interpersonal aggression in adult and adolescent populations. She has recently developed, implemented, and delivered a solution-focused brief therapy intervention for partner-violent men and women, both in prison and in the community. Her research also focuses on non-consensual sharing of sexually explicit media (image-based sexual abuse).

Glenn D. Walters, PhD, is a Professor in the Department of Criminal Justice at Kutztown University in Kutztown, Pennsylvania, where he teaches classes in corrections, criminological theory, research methods, and substance abuse and crime. Prior to this he worked as a Clinical Psychologist and Drug Treatment Coordinator for the Federal Bureau of Prisons. Dr. Walters has published over 300 book chapters and peer-reviewed journal articles and 19 books and monographs. His current research interests include offender therapy and assessment, the drug–crime relationship, causal mediation analysis, and the development of an overarching psychological theory of criminal behavior.

Kayla A. Wanamaker is a PhD candidate at Carleton University in Ottawa, Canada, working under the supervision of Dr. Shelley Brown in the Gender and Crime Lab. Her dissertation work is focused on determining whether there are gender-specific crime trajectories, incorporating both strength and risk factors that remain stable over time, and includes a validation study of a gender-responsive risk assessment tool. Kayla is also a Research Analyst at Public Safety Canada, examining the importance of effective training in community supervision and how it may aid in the reduction of recidivism rates among male and female offenders.

Nick J. Wilson has been working as a Clinical Psychologist for the New Zealand Department of Corrections for the past 18 years, and is currently Principal Adviser, Psychological Research, with responsibility for the provision of specialist training, expert witness testimony, and research in the area of risk assessment and offender management and treatment (i.e., development of the Dynamic Risk Assessment Offender Re-entry (DRAOR) and Structured Dynamic Assessment Case-Management-21 (SDAC-21) tools). Dr. Wilson has a long-standing interest in criminal psychopathy and personality disorder, its assessment and treatment, and has conducted research and provided clinical services and training in this area since 2000.

Stephen C. P. Wong, PhD, is Adjunct Professor at the Department of Psychology, University of Saskatchewan, Canada, and the Swinburne University of Technology, Melbourne, Australia, and is Fellow of the Canadian Psychological Association. His research focuses on the assessment and treatment of violent, sexual, and psychopathic offenders. He is the lead author of the Violence Risk Scale (VRS), the Violence Risk Scale: Sexual Offender Version (VRS:SO), and the Violence Reduction Program (VRP). He has published extensively in the areas of risk assessment, treatment, and psychopathy; he also consults internationally with forensic mental health and criminal justice organizations.

Part I
Correctional Psychology in Context

1

Correctional Psychology: A Short History and Current Standing

Devon L. L. Polaschek
University of Waikato (Te Whare Wānanga o Waikato), New Zealand

Andrew Day
James Cook University and University of Melbourne, Australia

Clive R. Hollin
University of Leicester, UK

Correctional psychology is much practiced, but rarely defined. Contemporary correctional systems have employed psychologists for many years now, but it is by no means easy to describe the professional roles of those who work in correctional settings.[1] Additional challenges have arisen that followed the introduction of legislation that defines psychologists as allied health practitioners (Allan, 2013), given that some, if not most, of the work that correctional psychologists do does not fall neatly into the category of a health service. It is also the case that correctional practice does not always closely align with the academic research and teaching of psychology that underpins it (Brodsky, 2007; Clements et al., 2007). And, to complicate matters even further, the term *correctional psychology* has a number of different meanings; it not only refers to professional psychologists who practice in corrections, but also to the wider application of psychology *to* corrections, and the use of psychological research to inform correctional policy and practice. The term is defined, in part, by public and correctional staff perceptions about what psychology is, and its perceived utility in the correctional system, as well as perceptions more generally about the status and utility of science, what causes crime, and what works to reduce it. Unsurprisingly then, correctional psychologists are sometimes uncertain about their professional identity, and may find themselves practicing in environments that are hostile to their ways of working.

This Handbook represents the efforts of many people who have expertise in correctional psychology, and, collectively, their contributions help define what correctional psychology represents in practice, and identify how it can contribute to more effective correctional service delivery. We recognize at the outset the importance of compiling a resource that will inspire and support the next generation of psychologists who want to make a difference, as well as reminding experienced practitioners that this is an exciting and important field.

Today's correctional systems can be understood in terms of their primary role to administer sentences that are handed down by the criminal courts. But although correctional psychology

---

The Wiley International Handbook of Correctional Psychology, First Edition. Edited by Devon L. L. Polaschek, Andrew Day, and Clive R. Hollin.

has sometimes been defined as applying only to convicted offenders (e.g., Morgan, Beer, Fitzgerald, & Mandracchia, 2007), correctional agencies have a secondary mandate to safely contain people who are remanded in various forms of custody while they await trial or sentencing. Correctional psychology has also often been defined primarily in relation to work that occurs in prisons (Biere & Mann, 2017; Gendreau & Goggin, 2013; Magaletta, Patry, Dietz, & Ax, 2007), despite correctional systems in most countries having responsibility for the administration of both custodial and community sentences.

It is also instructive to reflect on what it is that correctional psychologists actually do in practice, even though this varies in emphasis across jurisdictions. In the USA, for example, Dvoskin and Morgan (2010) have proposed that the role typically involves three main activities: (a) the treatment of mentally disordered offenders and the provision of mental health treatment; (b) the rehabilitation of offenders for the purposes of reducing criminal risk and improving community safety; and (c) the smooth and safe running of the correctional system itself. In other Western countries, there are clearer boundaries between those who work with mentally disordered offenders—which remains for the most part the province of mental health systems—and those who work to rehabilitate offenders for risk reduction purposes (Soothill, Rogers, & Dolan, 2008). A further consideration is the extent to which correctional psychologists practice directly with offenders or are responsible more widely for the application of psychology by other parts of the correctional system (e.g., in the selection or training of prison officers or by advising on prisoner management or sentence compliance). Contributions in each of these areas can assist the correctional system to achieve its legislative mandate, which can be best understood in terms of the broad aims of containing, punishing, and reforming offenders, with the main differences between jurisdictions lying largely in the emphasis placed on each (see Table 1.1). Importantly though, all three aims are linked to outcomes that are potentially measurable in terms of human behavior. So, while psychology does not generate all of the knowledge needed for correctional systems to achieve these respective aims, it clearly has something to contribute to each.

We start by providing a brief overview of the history of correctional practice, which serves to remind us of how different systems can be, depending on how human behavior is understood. This approach helps us to position current practice in the broader context of community responses to antisocial behavior and law-breaking, and takes us into the modern era, with its focus on the development of psychological rehabilitation programs.

A Brief History of Correctional Trends

Punishment

In any society, the dominant explanation for the causes of an offender's wrongdoing will play a role in determining how that society deals with the individual offender. One of the oldest explanations for criminal behavior lies in possession by evil spirits and demons. In Christianity at least, this belief in demonic possession sat alongside, not unsurprisingly, a corresponding belief in the omniscient power of God. These twin beliefs formed the basis for the practice of *trial by ordeal.* Given that God would always intervene on behalf of the innocent—the principle of *judicium Dei,* a judgment by God in favor of the guiltless—it was believed that in a trial, which literally threatened life and limb, the innocent would emerge unscathed while the guilty would suffer or die.

Table 1.1 Examples of the Purposes, Objectives, and Missions of Several Western Correctional Systems, as Enshrined in Legislation

---

Federal Correctional System, Canada

The purpose of the federal correctional system is to contribute to the maintenance of a just, peaceful, and safe society by

a carrying out sentences imposed by courts through the safe and humane custody and supervision of offenders; and

b assisting the rehabilitation of offenders and their reintegration into the community as law-abiding citizens through the provision of programs in penitentiaries and in the community.

(Corrections and Conditional Release Act, 1992)

Corrective Services, New South Wales, Australia

This Act has the following objects:

a to ensure that those offenders who are required to be held in custody are removed from the general community and placed in a safe, secure, and humane environment,

b to ensure that other offenders are kept under supervision in a safe, secure, and humane manner,

c to ensure that the safety of persons having the custody or supervision of offenders is not endangered,

d to provide for the rehabilitation of offenders with a view to their reintegration into the general community.

Crimes (Administration of Sentences) Act 1999 No. 93

New Zealand Department of Corrections

The purpose of the corrections system is to improve public safety and contribute to the maintenance of a just society by

a ensuring that the community-based sentences, sentences of home detention, and custodial sentences and related orders that are imposed by the courts and the New Zealand Parole Board are administered in a safe, secure, humane, and effective manner; and

b providing for corrections facilities to be operated in accordance with rules set out in this Act and regulations made under this Act that are based, amongst other matters, on the United Nations Standard Minimum Rules for the Treatment of Prisoners; and

c assisting in the rehabilitation of offenders and their reintegration into the community, where appropriate, and so far as is reasonable and practicable in the circumstances and within the resources available, through the provision of programmes and other interventions; and

d providing information to the courts and the New Zealand Parole Board to assist them in decision-making.

(New Zealand Corrections Act 2004)

For example, this reasoning underpinned trial by ordeal through fire or water in tenth-century Saxon Europe, until it was banned by the Church in 1215 AD. In "ordeal by fire" the accused was forced to grasp a red-hot iron or to walk over red-hot metal; in "ordeal by water" the accused was forced to pluck by hand a stone from boiling liquid, or to drink poisoned water, or to be submersed in water. Another form of trial, "trial by combat," was common in sixteenth-century Europe. In this type of trial, also based on *judicium Dei*, the protagonists fought each other until one of them was dead or unable to continue, leaving the victor to be declared the winner of the dispute. In some ways, this was a very efficient system, since it bound together both trial and sentence, in a sense, and was completed in a very short time.

As time passed, so trial by ordeal and trial by combat were discarded in favor of the now familiar trial by jury. A trial by jury is part of a Western system of law in which if the accused is found guilty by their peers then a sentence will be passed in accordance with the law. A sentence may seek to achieve several outcomes, such as delivering retribution and punishment or otherwise seeking to correct criminal behavior. The various aims of sentencing are not mutually exclusive: it could be argued, however wrongly, that punitive retribution can have a corrective effect on the criminal's future actions, but equally, other components of the sentence may be intended to achieve a corrective outcome. The notion of retribution—for instance—has its origins in the principle of *lex talionis* ("the law of retaliation"), sometimes understood as an "eye for an eye." In earlier times, the victim or family often inflicted this retaliation. But in time, the rise of the state as the dominant form of social organization led to that state formally exacting compensation for criminal offenses against its citizens, and often taking away the right of individuals to do so. This compensation could be tangible, usually in the form of financial recompense to the victim, or in some other type of direct harm to the offender, generally involving physical pain or social humiliation.

In the eighteenth and nineteenth centuries it was a free-for-all when it came to punishing offenders. Those who had committed less serious offenses were publically humiliated by being shackled to the *pillory*, a wooden device that immobilized the offender by locking their hands and legs. Offenders were typically held for a few hours but sometimes remained fettered for several days. A similar device, the *stocks*, held the offender's ankles; the German *pranger* chained the victim's neck to leg restraints fastened around the ankles, although sometimes a short chain was used to force the offender into a painful half-kneeling posture. The pillory, also used for other corrective sentences, such as public floggings, was situated in a public place, such as a market square, and passers-by would amuse themselves and others by throwing rotten fruit and vegetables at the hapless offender. If the offense had been serious then stones would be thrown and the offender could be physically attacked and even mutilated. In most European countries, the use of the pillory and the stocks was abolished by the middle of the nineteenth century; England and Wales abolished stocks and pillories in 1837.

Punishment for serious crimes could also involve physical injury such as mutilation, mainly cutting off body parts and removing eyes, or flogging, or branding with a red-hot iron. Those criminals who were sent to prison had to endure harsh regimes characterized by punishments such as immobilization through the use of body irons, long periods of solitary confinement (including wearing masks so prisoners could not see each other), hard manual labor, and physical exhaustion through hours spent on the treadmill. The practice of oakum-picking involved prisoners in untwisting lengths of old rope to return it to its constituent strands—damaging their fingers in the hours spent picking at the coarse material—then unrolling these strands to produce loose fibers. The fibers were sold to ship-builders where they were mixed with tar to seal the lining of wooden boats. Oakum-picking has left its legacy in the expression "money for old rope." Treadmills also were adopted into prisons in the United Kingdom in the early 1800s, to ameliorate prisoner idleness and sometimes also to pump water or grind grain; prisoners were forced to climb the "steps" on these large wooden wheels for 6 hours or more each day.

In addition to imprisonment and the poorhouse, capital punishment was used liberally. Pettifer (1939/1992) stated that in mid-eighteenth-century England there were over one hundred crimes, including offenses such as damaging property, and theft, which were punishable by death. There were various methods of execution in use which included burning, hanging, and *peine forte et dure* ("strong and hard pain") in which the offender was crushed to death. In Britain, France, and other European countries, the more fortunate criminals were spared death, but suffered penal deportation to the colonies: most notably, Maryland and Virginia in the United States, Australia, and India.

Application of Enlightenment Philosophy to Sentencing

The first theoretical doubts about the utility of harsh punishment in reducing crime emerged in the mid-1700s through the influence of the *classical* school of philosophers, associated with the Enlightenment philosophers and theorists—including John Locke (1632–1704), Sir Isaac Newton (1642–1727), David Hume (1711–1776), and Immanuel Kant (1724–1804)—and it became a dominant force in Europe and America in the late eighteenth and the nineteenth centuries. A basic tenet of Enlightenment philosophy was that the origins of human action arise as each individual exercises their reason and free will (Paternoster, 2010). The specific application of the principles of Enlightenment philosophy to crime, in particular the notion of free will, was made by the Italian mathematician and economist Cesare Bonesana Marchese di Beccaria (1738–1794) and the English philosopher and jurist Jeremy Bentham (1748–1832).

The classical explanation of criminal behavior is very different to *judicium Dei*. It holds that a crime is the consequence of the individual's free and rational decision with regard to the likely balance between personal gain and loss; when the former outweighs the latter, a crime follows. The Enlightenment philosophers argued for a *utilitarian* view of criminal law where the purpose of punishment should have wider benefits rather than just inflicting pain. Punishment, from this perspective, could potentially have four aims: (a) to prevent crime; (b) if prevention is not possible, to encourage the criminal to commit a less serious crime; (c) to reduce the harm caused by the crime; (d) to prevent crime at the lowest possible financial cost.

In direct contrast to the belief of the day, utilitarianism viewed excessive punishment as unnecessary and even counter-productive with regard to reducing crime. Instead, the level of punishment should be in proportion to the severity of the crime (see von Hirsch, 1993). The logic underpinning proportionality is that if every crime meets an equally harsh punishment, then punishment cannot have a selective effect according to the type of crime and its severity. If sexual abuse and murder were both punishable by death, for example, then the rapist or child abuser would have nothing to lose by murdering their victim to reduce the likelihood of detection. However, if punishment is proportional to the crime, such that murder results in a more severe penalty than a sexual offense, then punishment may have a deterrent or corrective effect. The application of the principles of utilitarian philosophy brought about extensive changes to the legal systems in eighteenth-century Europe; many are still evident today. For example, the principle of *mens rea*, guilty intent, is at the heart of Western criminal law and is close to the notion of free will. Thus, we accept that for most crimes, given due allowance for age and mental capacity, criminals understand that they are doing wrong, and therefore should be held responsible for their criminal acts. If they do not, there may be grounds for acquittal or detention in a mental hospital. In addition, we agree with proportionality in the administration of punishment, and in most cases, we hold that extremely punitive acts are not tolerable in the name of justice.

The deterrent value of punishment is very much part of modern-day criminological thinking (Kennedy, 2009). Many people take it as self-evident that punishing the individual can influence that person's future behavior, and that administration of punishment may have wider benefits for the majority. Thus, in theory we have *specific deterrence*—the experience of punishment is held to have a corrective effect in that it deters the individual offender from committing further crimes—and *general deterrence*, where knowing that there is a risk of punishment if caught deters law-abiding members of society from involvement in illegal activities. Unfortunately, the evidence for either of these cherished effects is, at best, weak overall (Nagin, 2013; Paternoster, 2010).

In modern criminal justice systems, the twin aims of retribution and deterrence are addressed through either taking something of value away from the offender or by imposing conditions which the individual is anticipated to dislike. In the former case there may be removal, for example, of an individual's tangible assets or their access to their children; alternatively, criminals may lose their liberty: either partially, through the imposition of a curfew with electronic monitoring, or completely by imprisonment – or they may be expected to work without pay for a set number of hours (e.g., chain gangs, and more recently, community work). Finally, in some parts of the world the death penalty remains available as the definitive personal loss.

As with any approach to criminal justice there are questions to be raised on both a philosophical and a practical level. Is there really such a thing as free will and, if so, does everyone have the same capacity to exercise it (see Honderich, 1993)? Why do some people, but not others, choose to commit criminal acts? Is it the case that we obey the law simply because of fear of punishment and not because of higher levels of moral reasoning? From a psychological perspective, the view that an individual freely commits a crime following rational consideration of the outcomes is rather limited in scope. If we follow Roshier (1989) then "the goal of our rationality is personal satisfaction; rational self-interest is the key motivational characteristic that governs our relationship with crime and conformity" (pp. 14–15). Thus, the criminal becomes no more than a hedonist, estimating the gains and losses of their actions in their personal equation of avoiding pain and gaining profit. Lilly, Cullen, and Ball (2002) have called this account the "criminal as calculator."

Modern Historical Trends in Imprisonment

Following on from sentencing approaches based on *lex talionis,* as the state took over responses to criminal transgressions, imprisonment was used to hold people who failed to pay fines. Over time, prisons came to be used not just *as* punishment, but *for* punishment; for example, by the Romans more than 2,500 years ago. However, mass imprisonment may not have occurred until late in the 1700s, when growing public unhappiness about public torture and hangings led to the need for alternatives. Transportation in old hulks to the colonies was used for some time, but from the late 1700s, hard labor was becoming popular as an alternative, and proved to be invaluable in constructing essential infrastructure; for example, in the confederate south after the US civil war, and in many parts of the "colonies."

The Advent of Correctional Reform

The history of rehabilitation for criminals in Britain can be traced back to the influence in prisons of the great social reformers of the eighteenth century such as John Howard (1726–1790) and Elizabeth Fry (1780–1845). Now prisons aimed to reform prisoners' lives, and accordingly regimes changed from an emphasis on harsh punishment to include constructive activities such as education and training for employment. It is hard to overemphasize what a fundamental shift this was. Punishing people is based on an assumption that people have what is needed to reform themselves, but now there was a shift to providing resources to help people correct themselves.

For example, in the northern United States, the development of the Pennsylvania system—also known as "separate confinement"—soon after the American Revolution isolated prisoners from each other but not from visitors and staff who taught them to read and write, and provided moral instruction. Prisoners also worked at various activities alone in their cells, in silent reflection (Rubin, 2017). However, the Pennsylvania system had limited influence on correctional practices of the day, and was superseded by the Auburn system, named for the opening of Auburn State Prison in New York in 1817. The Auburn system took much less space. Its rehabilitative philosophy was based on strict routines of industry, obedience, and complete silence (and so was known as the "congregate" or "silent" system; Randol, 2014). But as before, it became evident quite soon that Auburn-style prisons had considerable productivity potential, and their labor was much valued (Charleroy, 2013).

In practice, it is likely that many prisons were hybrids of various reform philosophies just as they are today (i.e., they have always been theoretically eclectic in their approach to "what works"). These hybrid philosophies are revealed when we consider the early, and often challenging, role of physicians. For example, well before the advent of psychologists in prisons, Charleroy (2013) noted that the Minnesota State Prison physician was responsible not only for keeping the prisoners physically healthy enough to work in prison factories but also for their "mental and behavioral reform" (p. 24).

Developing and Applying Psychology to Criminal Behavior and its Remediation

The history of psychology's involvement with the correctional system is a fascinating one which includes many important figures.[2] The approach taken here focuses more on the theories and research themselves and how these were applied both to understanding criminal behavior (i.e., "What are the causes of crime"?) and to understanding how to reduce it ("What makes interventions effective?" "What is needed for offenders to change?") Interestingly, psychology has had much more to say about the second than the first. Although replete with etiological theories for various forms of the human condition, relatively few have been applied to criminal behavior specifically. This state is in marked contrast to disciplines like sociology, which has a proud history of crime- and criminality-specific theories.

Psychoanalytic Theory

The use of psychological approaches with offenders broadly followed the development of the discipline of psychology as a helping profession and the progression of psychological theory: beginning with psychoanalysis and psychodynamic psychotherapy, moving to behavior modification and behavior therapy, and so to cognitive behavioral and cognitive therapies. Much of its early history reflects a plethora of approaches that parallel the development of psychological therapies for other problems and conditions. At least with offenders, it was not until the 1970s and 1980s that systematic research began to identify that approaches often designed to improve the wellbeing of people did not necessarily reduce their offending risk, nor actually even improve their wellbeing in some cases.

It is generally taken that therapeutic psychology as a distinct specialism has its origins in psychoanalytic theory and the work of Sigmund Freud (1856–1939) and his followers such as Alfred W. Adler (1870–1937), Abraham A. Brill (1874–1948), and Carl Jung (1875–1961). The early theorists applied psychoanalytical concepts such as the pleasure principle (Aichhorn, 1925/1955), the reality principle (Alexander & Healy, 1935), and sublimation (Healy & Bronner, 1936) in formulating explanations of antisocial and criminal behavior. Psychologically based explanations of criminal behavior influenced by psychoanalytic theory continued to appear throughout the 1940s (e.g., Abrahamson, 1944; Friedlander, 1947), eventually progressing to accounts founded on theoretical constructs such as self-concept (Reckless & Dintz, 1967), self-esteem (Bennett, Sorensen, & Forshay, 1971), and transactional analysis (Jesness, DeRisi, McCormick, & Wedge, 1972). The earliest therapeutic work with delinquents within a psychoanalytic tradition (e.g., Aichhorn, 1925/1955) rested on the assumption that delinquent behavior was the product of a failure in psychological development, which is, perhaps ironically, not too different from today's developmental life-course theories (see Chapter 21). But therapists of those times were perhaps more optimistic about the ability of psychotherapy alone to correct this developmental failure. The use of group and milieu therapies with offenders—including group counseling, psychodrama, reality therapy, transactional analysis, and therapeutic communities—became increasingly widespread during the 1940s, 1950s, and 1960s (Lester & Van Voorhis, 2004a, 2004b). Psychodynamic or psychoanalytic treatment was also used unsuccessfully by the early psychopathy clinician Cleckley (1988) and his colleagues (Salekin, 2002).

By and large, psychoanalytic and psychodynamic therapy approaches have shown little evidence of effectiveness with offenders, either in personal development or risk-reducing terms. In comparison with a modern understanding of what makes for effective intervention, they lack a number of the key features associated with effectiveness. However, the theories themselves are also limited in that they locate the origin of the individual's behavior entirely *within the person*, and not only that, but at an unconscious level; how we act is an expression of our inner conflicts and needs. The practice of forensic psychotherapy remains today, although perhaps as a niche specialty more familiar in psychiatry than in psychology (Cordess, 2001). Psychoanalytic theory today is largely irrelevant to correctional rehabilitation psychology because it did not provide a model of change that was useful with offenders.

Learning Theories

Currently, criminal and correctional psychology assumes primarily that criminal behavior is learned, and that its remediation also requires learning. Therefore, psychology is relevant not only for what it offers to understanding the development of criminal behavior, but also for providing the empirical scaffold for how best to change people's antisocial behavior. After psychoanalytic theory, relevant psychological theory focuses entirely on developments in learning theory, of which the next major stage began with the Nobel Prize-winning Russian physiologist Ivan Pavlov (1849–1936), and then B. F. Skinner (1904–1990) with the development of learning theory.

Pavlov, while conducting laboratory research using dogs as subjects, realized that the dogs' salivation was the result of a *learned* association between sound (a clanking food pail) and food: this type of learning became known as *classical conditioning*. Pavlov's work had a profound impact on other early American behaviorists, such as John B. Watson (1878–1958), as they moved away from searching for internal causes of behavior as the psychoanalysts had done, to concentrate on the way in which the environment shapes our actions.

A related notion, that the likelihood of an individual repeating a given behavior is related to its consequences, was formulated by Edward Thorndike (1874–1949) in his law of effect (Thorndike, 1911). However, it was B. F. Skinner whose experimental work with pigeons and rats led to the formulation of the principles of *operant learning* (Skinner, 1938, 1953). The basis of operant learning is that a behavior's consequences directly determine whether it becomes part the individual's behavioral repertoire (acquisition) and stays being part of it over time (maintenance). Thus, a behavior *operates* on the environment to produce changes which, for the individual concerned, may be either reinforcing or punishing: if a behavior keeps occurring at a steady rate or with increasing frequency, it is, by definition, being *reinforced* by its environmental consequences; a behavior which decreases over time is, by definition, being *punished* by its consequences.[3] The relationship between a behavior and its consequences is termed a *contingency*. There are two types of reinforcement contingency: *positive reinforcement* in which the behavior is followed by a reward (e.g., money); and *negative reinforcement* where the behavior results in the removal of an aversive consequence (e.g., decrease in noise). There are also two punishment contingencies: *positive punishment* in which some aversive consequence is added to the environment of the individual (e.g., something that causes pain); and *negative punishment* where something valued is removed from the individual's environment as a consequence (e.g., money through fines).

Differential reinforcement theory (Jeffery, 1965) viewed *criminal* behavior as an operant behavior: maintained by the consequences it elicits for the individual criminal. A large number of crimes entail some form of stealing and so produce the obvious reward of material and financial gain. In other cases, the consequences of crime may be social gain such as peer group approval (Short, 1968). Thus, material, financial, and social rewards act to *positively* reinforce the criminal behavior. Negative reinforcement contingencies may also maintain criminal behavior. Stealing has a strong association with unemployment (Nagin, Farrington, & Moffitt, 1995) so that in this context its consequences may be the avoidance of loss of accommodation or of a family break-up, or of hunger. In the same way, violent behavior may be negatively reinforced in that it may effectively put an end to an argument or curtail a victim's resistance.

Operant conditioning research helps to establish why punishment delivered by the criminal justice system can be retributive (i.e., punishing in the sense that it harms people) but without deterring them from future crime (as we signaled above). Research on the conditions in which punishment is effective not just in harming people but in reducing behavior shows that it requires conditions that could never be met by the criminal justice system. Punishment only has the potential to reduce the future occurrence of a behavior if at least these five conditions are met: (a) it is delivered at maximum intensity (b) immediately after the behavior occurs; (c) it must happen *every time* the behavior occurs; (d) there must be no escape from it; and (e) it does not occur alongside a number of reinforcing consequences (Bonta & Andrews, 2017).

Criminals may experience immediate punishment for some criminal acts (e.g., getting bitten by a dog during a burglary) but for the most part criminal behavior is initially reinforced in various ways, with either no punishment, or low-intensity punishment that is distal to the behavior and easily avoided. If it recurs, we can assume both that it is being reinforced, but also that the aversive consequences of the behavior, if any, have failed to control or eliminate the act.

So as psychoanalytic or psychodynamic therapeutic methods faded from correctional practice they were replaced by methods of change based on learning theory, such as token economies, response cost procedures,[4] and time out (Lester, Braswell, & Van Voorhis, 2004). Operant or classical conditioning-based techniques were also used with individual offenders; most notably to alter sexual arousal patterns in sexual offenders (Laws & Marshall, 1990, 1991), and occasionally with other habit patterns such as repetitive fire-setting (Jackson, Glass, & Hope, 1987).

These methods of behavior change were particularly used with success with young offenders (Hollin, 1990a; Kirigin, Braukmann, Atwater, & Wolf, 1982). However, like any approach, they can be applied more or less effectively and ethically. The application of these techniques in closed institutions, particularly prisons, generated criticism on the grounds that they were being used to control institutional behavior rather than to address criminal behavior. Over time they mostly disappeared, despite some evidence of effectiveness in reducing recidivism (Gendreau & Ross, 1979). There was a recent revival of interest among prison administrators as part of the "accountability agenda" (Gendreau, Listwan, Kuhns, & Exum, 2014).

The third major development in learning theory saw a shift in the role of cognitions and emotions in the acquisition and maintenance of behavior, and the development of an understanding of the importance of observation and imitation in learning. Although some of the concepts informing social learning theory had been around for some time (e.g., Miller & Dollard, 1941), it was Albert Bandura who framed the contemporary form of social learning theory in psychology (Bandura, 1977). While operant theory maintains that behavior is acquired through reinforcement and punishment from the environment, social learning theory extends the ways that new behaviors may be acquired with the addition of learning through observation by imitating the actions of other people. Those whose behavior is imitated are referred to as *models*: the process of learning through observation is enhanced if the model is someone the observer regards as competent at what they are doing or perceives to be of high status. Social learning theory (SLT) also extends the notion of reinforcement by introducing the concept of *motivation*. Bandura (1977) described three aspects of motivation: (a) *external reinforcement* in the form of rewards from the environment, as in operant theory; (b) *vicarious reinforcement*, when an individual is motivated by seeing another person's behavior being reinforced or punished; (c) *self-reinforcement*, which occurs when an individual is motivated by the delivery of their own reinforcement (e.g., a sense of pride or achievement in their own behavior).

SLT has been applied to criminal behavior by psychologists (Nietzel, 1979) and sociologists (Akers, 1973). And in fact Bandura (1973) originally developed SLT specifically for explaining aggressive behavior. The acquisition of criminal behavior can be explained by observational learning of behaviors modeled within the family, the peer group, or in television or films. Once acquired, criminal behavior may be motivated by the tangible or social rewards it garners, but also by enhancing the criminal's self-image and by seeing how others are rewarded for acting illegally.

As SLT grew in influence, so it precipitated interest in the role of cognition and emotion in criminal behavior. The adoption of the term *cognitive behavioral* signified a clear departure from interventions based solely on operant learning, and ultimately opened the door on crime-supportive thinking as a focus in rehabilitation. The term refers both to the application of developments in cognitive and social cognitive psychology, and to the adaptation of cognitive therapy as it was developed as a method of treating mental health problems (e.g., Beck, Rush, Shaw, & Emery, 1979).

Three strands emerged in the application of cognitive psychology to criminal behavior. The first considered aspects of social cognition such as empathy, social problem-solving, moral reasoning, and social perception (Ross & Fabiano, 1985). The second strand concerned social information processing and its application to the development of aggressive delinquent behavior (e.g., Dodge & Crick, 1990). The third strand used decision-making in viewing the criminal as a rational decision-maker (e.g., Cornish & Clarke, 1986).

The place of emotion in criminal behavior is best exemplified by the work of Raymond Novaco on the relationship between anger and violence (e.g., Novaco, 1975, 2006). Novaco's theory seeks to explain how a combination of social and individual factors can lead to angry violence. A sequence of events begins with the individual's perception and appraisal of environmental cues, such as the actions of other people, which may lead to a heightening of physiological and psychological arousal. The heightened arousal leads, in turn, to an intensified hostile appraisal of the situation, thereby increasing the likelihood of a provocative act as the individual confronts the source of their anger. If the other people involved respond in kind, there is an escalation toward violence. Anger Control Training aims to help offenders to identify the specific triggers for their anger and to gain awareness of their own angry thoughts and behaviors. Once this level of self-appraisal has been attained, the offender develops strategies, including learning coping skills and social problem-solving skills (see below), in order to gain control over his or her anger (Novaco, 2011, 2013).

Social skills training (SST) was one of the first interventions based on SLT, incorporating techniques such as modeling and role-play with feedback. The practice of SST with both juvenile (Henderson & Hollin, 1983; Hollin, 1990b) and adult offenders (Howells, 1986) became widespread during the 1980s. As SLT gained in scope and influence, so new therapeutic techniques were developed and, as in generations before, were applied to criminal populations. *Social problem-solving training* is illustrative of this new approach. It typically consists of helping the individual to progress through the five stages of: (a) awareness of the problem; (b) defining the problem; (c) generating solutions to the problem; (d) deciding on the best, most acceptable, solution; (e) implementing the solution and checking efficacy (D'Zurilla & Goldfried, 1971). This technique has been used successfully with a range of offenders, including sex offenders, psychopathic offenders, and young offenders (McMurran & McGuire, 2005), and is a component of many multimodal programs (e.g., Polaschek & Kilgour, 2013).

In some cases, social skill training has been developed into a comprehensive curriculum of diverse social skills needed for lawful survival. The Skillstreaming component of Goldstein's (1988) Aggression Replacement Training (ART) represents this type of more comprehensive approach. ART has been used in a wide range of applications, with children and with adolescent and adult offenders (Goldstein, Nensen, Delaflod, & Kalt, 2004), along with its more evolved form, the Prepare Curriculum (Goldstein & Glick, 1987).

A limitation of these various interventions is that they may only influence one or several factors of many that may maintain ongoing offending. Criminal behavior is usually the product of a complex interaction between many different factors, and so similarly its remediation is more likely with more complex intervention responses.

Multimodal Rehabilitation Approaches

There have been numerous attempts to construct large-scale models of criminal behavior: some using findings from longitudinal research (e.g., Farrington, 2002); others focusing on a specific type of act such as violence (e.g., Nietzel, Hasemann, & Lynam, 1999). These large-scale models seek to integrate myriad individual and social factors associated with criminal behavior. Examples include Farrington's Integrated Cognitive Antisocial Potential (ICAP) model (e.g., Farrington, 2003; Chapter 12), and the General Personality and Cognitive Social Learning model of criminal conduct (Andrews & Bonta, 2003, 2006, 2010). Both models draw together influences from a variety of criminological theories and research studies to identify how people develop a relatively higher or lower propensity for crime, and then, which factors are most relevant in how that disposition interacts with situational factors to evoke a criminal event. The upshot of examining these models is that they include a variety of factors that can serve as a basis for deciding what to focus on in an intervention.

The most influential model of how to design, target, and deliver programs from a correctional standpoint is the Risk-Needs-Responsivity (RNR) model. First promulgated as just three principles by Andrews, Bonta, and Hoge (1990), it represents a deceptively simple codification of key findings from myriad studies and meta-analyses on the effects on recidivism of correctional interventions. The meta-analysis reported by Garrett (1985) proved to be the forerunner of many such aggregation studies: McGuire (2002) commented on the "30 meta-analytic reviews published between 1985 and 2001" alone (p. 13). Syntheses of the findings from the meta-analyses became known as "*What Works*" (McGuire, 1995). Each study's program characteristics (e.g., who are the targeted offenders, which risk factors is it attempting to change, how long is it, and what sort of staff run it?) are coded and the myriad resulting coded characteristics are correlated with recidivism outcomes. The mean size of those correlations (i.e., the effect size) determines how important that characteristic is in predicting recidivism. To the extent that same characteristic is changeable, it becomes "grist to the mill" for improving program outcomes. The latest version of the model (Bonta & Andrews, 2017) has 15 principles, grouped into three categories: *overarching* (e.g., programs are more likely to be effective if they are guided by a psychological theory); *core* principles and key clinical issues (see below), and lastly, *organizational* (e.g., more effective programs are community based, and have a supportive management context). The three best known of the 15 are in the core principles and clinical issues cluster: the Risk, Need, and Responsivity principles. They state that programs are more likely to reduce recidivism if they: (a) work with higher risk rather than low-risk offenders, providing them with relatively intensive interventions (the *risk* principle); (b) focus intervention goals on reducing the strength of changeable characteristics that are themselves predictive of recidivism; these characteristics are called criminogenic needs. The most strongly predictive of recidivism are antisocial personality (e.g., impulsivity, irritability), antisocial cognition, and association with antisocial peers (the *need* principle); (c) encourage change by the use of cognitive social learning and behavioral strategies (e.g., social skills training, cognitive restructuring; the *general responsivity* principle); and (d) are designed to enhance participants' engagement in the program, and in the targeted behavioral change: the *specific responsivity* principle (e.g., cultural and gender relevance, literacy, how relevant and interesting the program seems). Participants who enter programs under coercion may need initial approaches that start by acknowledging their resistance to engaging (Bonta & Andrews, 2017).

Another important principle of the RNR model is the use of *core correctional staff practices*. Program effect sizes are larger when staff form a positive relationship with participants, characterized by interpersonal warmth, a collaborative approach, humor, fairness, respect and liking, and when they structure their interactions to include skill learning, with prosocial modeling, effective use of authority—including frequent use of approval and other forms of reinforcement for prosocial behavior, and occasional use of disapproval for antisocial behavior—and advocate for and provide brokerage to other services and resources on an individualized basis (Bonta & Andrews, 2017).

Finally, quality and integrity of intervention or service implementation are important for effectiveness. Markers of these features include: staff selected for relationship skills who are trained and supervised in their service work, printed or otherwise documented manuals, procedures for monitoring the intervention process, and a specific model that the program follows (Bonta & Andrews, 2017).

The RNR model is often mistaken as an etiological model, or a program theory. It is neither. It is an intervention framework, meaning that it is intended for use as a guide to which interventions and services are more or less likely to work. For correctional systems, often managing thousands of offenders, it is very useful to be able to identify whether an existing or new intervention is *likely* to reduce recidivism, and if not, what could be done to change that.

Jurisdictions in Canada, the United Kingdom, Australia, New Zealand, and pockets of the United States adopted the RNR model, recognizing its potential to reduce imprisonment costs by reducing reconviction rates. The result has been to take the model out of the hands of psychologists and translate it for widespread implementation, leading to problematic practices in some key respects that, in turn, threaten its continued acceptance despite its evidence base (see Polaschek, 2012, for more detail).

First, instead of being understood as a guide, it has been treated as a prescriptive model. A great diversity of interventions has been part of the evidence base, from imprisonment (0% effect on recidivism, Cullen, Jonson, & Nagin, 2011) to employment and education programs, and various punishment-based services and responses (e.g., "scared straight," intensive supervision probation). Effective interventions emerging from this melting pot include forms of contingency management, therapeutic communities, and probation supervision. When many people think of the RNR model, they think of a group-based manualized cognitive behavioral treatment program. Why? This very narrow response to the evidence has led to a perception that it is the model itself that is rigid and inflexible, when in reality there remains enormous room, still largely unexplored, for innovation and expansion within the model's aegis (e.g., programs for indigenous offenders).

Second, insufficient psychologist workforce and the relatively high cost of psychologists have led to the employment of cheaper, more variably trained staff. They are often prepared for the work with a block of on-the-job training from the employer. Because of their presumably more limited skills, and sometimes also little professional supervision, the programs they are given to run are often very prescriptively specified so as to prevent integrity drift. The result may be that the program cannot adhere to the responsivity or core correctional practice principles (e.g., each five- to ten-minute block is specified, leaving no room to vary the treatment process). There are examples of large-scale roll-outs that have been striking failures (Bonta & Andrews, 2017).

Third, psychologists themselves don't necessarily understand the RNR model, leading them to promulgate inaccuracies about it. Some of the responsibility for such misunderstandings could be laid at the feet of the authors of RNR, who started writing up the foundations of the model in a time and place when we could assume that everyone working as a psychologist or facilitator of rehabilitation programs did so for the benefit of the offender, as well as that of the wider community (e.g., Andrews & Kiessling, 1980). But many newer psychologists have not read the original material, and may only know the RNR model third-hand.

Fourth, the RNR model is erroneously described as "deficit-based" or "only focused on avoidance goals." This represents a misunderstanding of its roots in how effective behavior change occurs. The best way to change behavior is to teach more adaptive or prosocial behavior that achieves similar outcomes for the person who carries it out. Targeting criminogenic needs for change at the level of the actual intervention invariably requires teaching offenders helpful and prosocial skills that are often useful far beyond the original issue, and indeed, useful for most people. For example, better problem-solving, relationship-building and communication skills and how to remain calm and get distressed less easily are skills that can all lead to other positive outcomes besides not going back to court (Coupland, 2015). This idea of substitution goes back at least to early behaviorism (Miltenberger, 2004), and in the RNR model, is incorporated into the core process of "building up rewards for non-criminal alternatives" (Andrews, Bonta, & Wormith, 2011, p. 741).

Over time the RNR model has been used to support the widespread development of offending behavior programs. As programs became more widely used, so organizational practice (e.g., practitioner training, managing intervention integrity, and collecting monitoring and evaluation data) inherent in implementing and delivering effective programs rose to prominence (Gendreau, Goggin, & Smith, 2002). As offending behavior programs became established, so they became more specialized. Some programs, such as *Think First* (McGuire, 2005) were refined to develop the cognitive skills of offenders generally (Hollin & Palmer, 2009), while other programs were intended for specific types of offenders or offenses such as violence (McGuire, 2008a; Polaschek, 2006) and sexual offending (Mann & Fernandez, 2006; Marshall & Hollin, 2015). Despite the possibilities, the RNR model still has rarely been used to justify the development of more effective employment programs or programs for reintegrating offenders back into the community. But newer developments include the use of the RNR model to capitalize on interactions between prison or probation officers and offenders (see Chapter 44). The RNR model is more than a quarter-century old, but by no means is its potential fully explored. In fact, it is surprising how much we still don't know about what works with whom, to reduce recidivism.

Correctional Psychology in the Modern Era

The development of modern psychological services in correctional settings has been strongly influenced by the emergence of convincing bodies of empirical research on both psychologically based risk assessment and the psychology of criminal risk reduction. Led by Canadians, this work has been adopted by researchers and practitioners in the United Kingdom, United States, Australia, and New Zealand. As noted above, since the 1980s a group of practicing and academic psychologists, sometimes referred to as the "Canadian school"[5] (Cullen, 2002; e.g., Don Andrews, James Bonta, Paul Gendreau, Steve Wormith, and others), have been primarily responsible for the dissemination of what is essentially a human service intervention approach to correctional service delivery. The extent to which offender rehabilitation is now seen as a core activity for corrections (Wormith et al., 2007) can be largely attributed to the influence of their work over the last quarter-century, with the combined contributions of these researchers also embracing sexual offending, psychopathy, the quality of correctional environments, and understandings of criminal responsibility. Their work has created a strong empirically developed psychology that is oriented to working with offenders in correctional systems to assess and reduce reconviction risk, and many organizations and individual psychologists have adopted this work as a frame for their practice.

As we noted at the start of this chapter, correctional psychologists in some jurisdictions also have a key role to play in the delivery of mental health services. This is especially true in the

United States, where there is a legislative imperative to do so (Dvoskin and Morgan, 2010), where key Supreme Court decisions handed down in the mid-1970s (*Estelle v. Gamble*, 1976; Diamond, Wang, Holzer, Thomas, & Cruser, 2001) mandated that mental health services be provided in custodial settings. As a consequence, psychologists quickly came to be important providers of these services.

In other parts of the world, however, a much smaller part of the work of psychologists in corrections is dedicated toward the amelioration of mental suffering and dysfunction as an end in itself (Richards-Ward & McDaniel, 2007). Although mental health services are recognized to be important, they are not always considered to be the responsibility of correctional services. In other words, the health of offenders, whether mental or physical, remains the responsibility of the same services that look after the health of non-offenders. For example, England and Wales have significant National Health Service input into the management and treatment of prisoners with mental illness. In Canada, some mental health services are provided within the prison system (e.g., regional psychiatric centers where corrections-employed psychologists are part of the teams), but others come from state mental health systems (Wormith et al., 2007). It is likely that those jurisdictions with correctional systems that have a strong focus on mental health have taken on the responsibility to ensure that prisoners with mental health difficulties have the same access to mental health care as the rest of the community, and that any deleterious effects of imprisonment on mental health are remediated (Olver, Preston, Camilleri, & Helmus, 2011). The reason that the treatment of mental disorder is not considered mainstream correctional psychology is, of course, because it doesn't typically account significantly for criminal behavior (Bonta, Blais, & Wilson, 2014), and the amelioration of criminal risk in those with mental disorders appears to be achieved best by the same RNR-focused approaches as for other offenders (Skeem, Steadman, & Manchak, 2015; Skeem, Winter, Kennealy, Eno Louden, & Tatar, 2014).

The situation in the United States is somewhat distinct, even allowing for the wide variety of jurisdictions within the country. For one thing, the United States has an imprisonment rate that outstrips its nearest Western European neighbor by a factor of almost three (Walmsley, 2013, cited in Gendreau et al., 2014). A second distinctive aspect is that health services are largely privatized and often linked to employment, making them difficult for many to access. Magaletta and Verdeyen (2005) proposed a descriptive framework to make sense of the three main service roles of *clinical* psychologists in US federal corrections: mental health services (MHSs), mental health treatment programs (MHTPs) and correctional treatment programs (CTPs). According to Magaletta and Verdeyen (2005) MHSs are psychiatric services for seriously mentally ill prisoners, and are provided by clinical staff, using traditional diagnostic systems, with treatments delivered directly by trained clinicians and mainly on a one-to-one basis. When clinical psychologists carry out these services, the main professional adjustments needed are to work within the constraints of a prison environment and deal with psychological conditions that have a higher base rate than occurs in other settings (e.g., antisocial personality disorder). At the other end of direct service provisions are CTPs, which Magaletta and Verdeyen described as primarily psycho-educational group interventions that aim to teach skills that reduce criminogenic need. The CTP role would seem to be most like that of offender rehabilitation-oriented services in other countries. Occupying the middle ground are MHTPs, which target change in "diagnosable, psychopathological conditions that are empirically linked to, and supported as criminogenic need and risk factors" (Magaletta & Verdeyen, 2005, p. 40). Three examples of these are: (a) substance abuse disorders, linking to impulsivity; (b) when "the behavioral manifestation of the pathological condition itself may be criminal (e.g., pedophilia)" (p. 40); or (c) when criminal activities themselves may be criteria for diagnostic inclusion (e.g., in antisocial personality disorder). Interestingly, a survey of the work that US federal prison psychologists do showed that the roles drew on nine core bodies of knowledge, none of which appeared to be related to rehabilitating offenders, with many being related to mental health, prisoner management, and humane containment issues (Magaletta et al., 2007).

Although some characteristics of the US federal workforce are distinctive, across a number of countries, surveys also show that psychologists in correctional systems undertake myriad tasks beyond those related to offender rehabilitation and mental health service delivery. These include the training and supervision of less qualified staff in program or service delivery, program design and evaluation, training and education of policy-makers, monitoring of suicidal prisoners and prisoners in segregation, critical incident stress debriefing, reception screening and cell placement, release planning, and so on (Bartol & Bartol, 2015; Day & Collie, 2013; Dvoskin & Morgan, 2010; Gendreau & Goggin, 2013; International Association for Correctional and Forensic Psychology, 2010; Magaletta et al., 2007, 2011; Olver et al., 2011; Richards-Ward & McDaniel, 2007; Towl, 2010, Towl & Crighton, 2007). Indeed, in a number of parts of the world, prisons directly employ psychologists, which has led to them being drawn into institutional and management roles (e.g., hostage negotiation, staff selection; Bartol & Bartol, 2015) that may have little to do with the types of correctional psychology described above.

What is Correctional Psychology?

In examining the sheer diversity of tasks psychologists have undertaken, it also quickly becomes clear that any simple definition of correctional psychology, as currently practiced, will lack coherence. Magaletta and Verdeyen's (2005) framework is useful in drawing attention to the need for an overall organizing framework for practice within the US federal system. But its scope and emphasis less accurately reflect practice in other countries, and it has additional limitations for defining correctional psychology internationally. We are not the first to have noted this problem (Brodsky, 2007; Clements et al., 2007; Magaletta et al., 2007). As is evident from our discussion thus far, correctional psychology's development has been driven more by system needs than by any consistent recognition among academics or professional bodies that this is an important area of application for psychology. Although pockets of academic research relevant to correctional practice exist in many different places, to date much of the literature about correctional psychology as a professional entity has primarily developed from the bottom up, with the evidence to support practice following after. The result is two serious interlinked problems. First, it can be difficult to identify a coherent training path for people who want to work in corrections as psychologists; and second, there is currently no conceptual framework to organize bodies of psychological knowledge that are relevant to policy and practice across the entire correctional system. And so, in the remainder of this section, we identify three main bodies of psychological knowledge that we see as particularly relevant to achieving the goals of correctional agencies. It will be obvious that these are nonetheless overlapping and interrelated.

The first: psychiatric and psychological knowledge about the causes, diagnosis, and treatment of mental disorders can contribute to the safe, humane, and secure containment of prisoners, as well as help to improve rehabilitation outcomes. Psychologists with a high level of expertise in these bodies of knowledge will usually be clinically trained, with additional training in how to assess and intervene in correctional settings, such as high-security custody units (Magaletta et al., 2007).

In applying clinical psychology beyond the need to keep people safe and well in correctional settings, we often refer to theories, research, and practice approaches that originate in clinical psychology, but have utility in understanding, assessing, and formulating criminal behavior in a way that can inform the design and implementation of rehabilitation. Some may dispute the use of the term *clinical* to define this body of knowledge, but clinical psychology has made significant contributions to the treatment of a wide range of behavioral problems, and the potential application to offending behavior is clear, especially since the development of SLT. *Clinical correctional psychology* thus blends together—with varying degrees of success—clinical psychology imported from mental health settings, with psychological theory and research about the onset, development, and maintenance of criminal behavior, as well as the impact of correctional settings on mental health. Crucially, cognitive behavioral clinical psychology offers a strong functional approach to assessing, formulating, and intervening with human behavior regardless of its nature (Sturmey, Ward-Horner, Marroquin, & Doran, 2007), which makes it immediately useful with criminal behavior. The adoption of the scientist-practitioner model of clinical training also emphasizes the importance of research that is carried out in the practice setting, in relation to the need to ensure that those services that are provided to offenders are evidence-based.

A third broad area of knowledge that is applicable to correctional psychology practice is criminology. Criminological psychology has been defined by Hollin (2013) as "psychological knowledge applied to the study of criminal behavior and the various agencies charged with its management" (p. 22). Criminological psychology therefore seeks to apply foundational information about the phenomenon of crime and the array of characteristics of those engaged in it. It covers a basic understanding of criminal development, and of those theories that contribute to understanding crime and how crime can be prevented. Criminological psychology knowledge is likely to be useful for all correctional staff. Indeed, it is from criminological psychology that the corrections-wide approach developed by Andrews and Bonta came (published as the first edition of *The Psychology of Criminal Conduct* in 1994). Notably they combined a knowledge of the psychology of crime with an analysis of key processes of social influence and behavior change. Those who without this knowledge base do psychological work with offenders often are not able to identify, for example, common risk factors for crime, nor distinguish them from other needs that are not linked to crime, and may use methods of intervention that have been proven ineffective, or misjudge the volume of intervention needed to effect longstanding change.

The Evidence Base: Next Steps

Advances in the evidence base that informs effective correctional practice have been significant over the past three decades. Despite this progress, many gaps in knowledge remain, with relatively small amounts of money invested in research in this domain. Biere and Mann (2017) pose the thought-provoking question of why a hotel chain like the Marriott—similar to a prison system in providing continuous safe housing and a range of services to thousands of people every day—employs more than 1000 people simply to collect and analyze data for the purposes of better understanding and higher achievement of core outcomes, but when public money is involved, there appears to be no equivalent incentive to improve performance. In fact, as Gendreau, Smith, and Thériault (2009) note, despite the evidence we have, too much correctional practice remains based on whimsy and rhetoric and is endorsed by senior managers without critical or specialist knowledge.

An example of this poor practice lies in the phenomenon of pink prison cells. Genschow, Noll, Wänke, and Gersbach (2015) describe how, despite the absence of evidence, the myth grew that pink cells calmed aggressive prisoners, leading to a proliferation of pink prison cells. Genschow et al. showed empirically that pink cells have no effect on aggression: whether this finding will influence those administrators and practitioners who rely on "common sense," anecdote, and personal experience remains to be seen. Latessa, Cullen, and Gendreau (2002) provided a scathing litany of similar unsupported theories such as offenders "need to get back to nature," "treat offenders as babies and dress them in diapers," "offenders need to have a pet in prison," "offenders need acupuncture," "offenders need a better diet and haircut," and "male offenders need to get in touch with their feminine side."

It is notable that these "commonsense" evidence-free solutions are too often based on the equally implausible meta-premise that simple solutions exist for complex problems: magic bullets. Those who espouse quackery believe that the exercise of (their) common sense, personal values, and experience trumps empirical knowledge, and this leads to expensive and potentially damaging correctional practice. As Latessa et al. (2002) stated, "quackery is proudly displayed, as its advocates boldly proclaim that they have nothing to learn from research conducted by academics 'who have never worked with a criminal'" (p. 43). The fact that practice without an evidence base can flourish in the correctional system is of concern on two fronts. First, it questions the probity of those running the system: if the medical treatment of physically ill people employed unproven, unscientific practices instigated at the whim of a practitioner or manager there would, quite rightly, be a public outcry. Second, when the inevitable conclusion is reached that some particular form of quackery has no effect on offending, its failure is taken as evidence that rehabilitation of offenders is a failed enterprise. What is perhaps most puzzling about this argument is that unpacking it usually reveals that what is meant is that if evidence-based rehabilitation doesn't work all of the time with all types of offenders, then we would be better to return to something we know works almost none of the time, and is inevitably more expensive, such as imprisonment (Cullen et al., 2011).

Despite the progress that has been made, calls for simplistic, expensive approaches that have already proven ineffective persist, and politicians and media tend to support these views rather than debunk them, because their predominant formats of communication do not allow for nuance or complexity. Some governments have developed quite skilled ways to deal with the gap between the louder forms of public sentiment and what the scientific evidence calls for. For instance, just prior to the New Zealand 2017 national election, the conservative-led government suggested it would provide military-based boot camps for the most severe young offenders. In a national radio interview, the prime minister was challenged about the empirical evidence base showing that boot camps are ineffective in reducing recidivism (Wilson, MacKenzie, & Mitchell, 2005). He replied that "it has never been tried before with these kids in New Zealand" (English, 2017, August 14). This of course, is an interesting comment because one of the major contributions of previous research is to establish whether there is a pattern of results that can be used to predict the future without having to research the exact instantiation of that future. But behind the media interviews was a different story. Boot camps are based on deterrence theory. But the details of the proposed policy showed that in addition to classic boot camp elements, components based on more rehabilitative and reintegration support approaches were planned (e.g., access to specialized alcohol and drug treatment services, educational skills, and personal case managers simultaneously working with the offender's family/whānau to support successful reintegration [New Zealand National Party, 2017]). So, it would seem that the then government was actually engaging in "tough talk," but planning to follow an evidence-based "walk," at least to a limited extent.

Even in systems where evidence-based practices have been implemented for a sustained period, political forces remain more influential in determining their ongoing success. For example, the United Kingdom, where a rehabilitation ethos has been strong over 25 years, has backed away from it in the past few years, due to a complex combination of financial ideology, a growing "us and them" punitive public sentiment, and enthusiasm for simplistic solutions. Canada suffered a similar fate under its conservative government (Gendreau et al., 2014). And New Zealand provides an interesting example in another way. In 2009 the then prime minister openly acknowledged that "prisons are a moral and fiscal failure."[6] Under that same prime minister, the prison population increased by 20% in little more than two years (from 2015 to 2017) to a per capita rate around 217, with almost a third being prisoners held on remand,[7] and 56% being indigenous people. Although the situation in New Zealand deteriorated quickly, it is expected to take many more years to "wind it back" to levels commensurate with other OECD (Organisation for Economic Co-operation and Development) countries.

Introduction to the Handbook

We have argued in this chapter that correctional psychology is not easy to define, given variations in how it has developed in different parts of the world and how it is currently practiced, and needs to be understood as developing from a broader historical context in which responses to criminal behavior have changed dramatically. Nonetheless, there are core activities relating to the assessment and treatment of mental disorder, the provision of interventions that aim to rehabilitate offenders, and an array of other organizationally relevant tasks that can help to define the role. These can be understood in relation to several semi-distinct bodies of knowledge that make different but substantial contributions to correctional work focusing on offenders: clinical psychology, both pure (diagnostically focused and contributing to health provision) and applied (focused on identifying and changing problematic psychological characteristics that underpin criminal risk); and criminology—theories and empirical research on crime itself—which, when combined with psychology, has application across the whole sector. For correctional systems to make the most of psychological knowledge, it needs to be used by a wide variety of staff who share a common basic understanding of the key principles and concepts, and their application. Systems will run more smoothly and are likely to be more effective and efficient if the staff share such an understanding.

With that vision in mind, the contents of this Handbook are by no means exhaustive, but cover a wide variety of core knowledge that is helpful in developing such a shared understanding across professions and workforces. Parts I–IV will be relevant to a wide range of correctional professionals. In the opening block of chapters—*Correctional Psychology in Context*—this chapter is followed by two concerned with ethical issues: Allan considers more generally the challenges of behaving ethically in a context where different normative systems are often in conflict, and Birgden outlines the processes by which revisions to the American Psychological Association's ethical code led it to be associated with torture at the US military prison at Guantanamo Bay, Cuba.

Next is a series of chapters on *The Roles of Psychology in Managing Prisons and Offenders.* Morgan and colleagues examine the effects of imprisonment on people; then Cooke reviews his leading work on assessing and reducing prisoners' violent behavior through environmental evaluation and change, and Wilson and Kilgour follow this chapter with one on managing more directly prisoners' difficult behavior. Logan and Taylor cover the equally serious issue of how to manage suicide and self-harm among prisoners, and Gendreau and Goggin report on the use and misuse of segregation and punishment in prisons. The next two chapters are relevant to increasing concern about vulnerable offender populations: senior citizens in prison (Aday and Maschi), and those with intellectual disabilities (Lindsay and Ansayi). Part II concludes by considering the challenges for prisoners' families and children, the difficulties of parenting from prison, and the roles of visits (Fortune and Salmon).

The group of chapters that follows—*Foundational Knowledge of Offending and Offenders*—is an introduction to information useful for a wide variety of correctional staff in understanding the criminal behavior of people with particular problems or offending histories. It covers those who have committed violent (Polaschek) and family violence (Walker and Bowen) offenses, serious and violent young offenders (Corrado, Peters, and Mathesius), sexual offenses (Brown), severe mental illness (Hodgins and Klein), personality disorders (McMurran and Howard); indigenous offenders (Tamatea and Day), women (Scott, Brown, and Wanamaker), and research on the processes involved in moving away from a criminal lifestyle (Polaschek).

Part IV: *Intervention: Theory, Design, Implementation, and Evaluation* begins with two chapters by Casey that review the implications of theories of crime, and of behavior change for program design. Next, Paramo considers the ever-challenging issue of program integrity and the wide variety of factors that can influence it. The final two chapters in Part IV discuss key approaches and their limitations in establishing empirically whether interventions are effective: in-program change (Daffern, Klepfisz, Sweller, and Day) and recidivism outcomes as indicators of "what works" (Polaschek).

Part V begins with a comprehensive section on *assessment*. Chapters on risk assessment cover structured professional judgment (Douglas), how to combine risk estimates and clinical information together into an "explanatory story" that communicates both assessment and management information (Kroner), and dynamic risk approaches (Olver and Wong), and concludes with case formulation and planning for treatment (Sturmey, McMurran, and Daffern) and a summary of issues in correctional assessment (Day).

The next block—*treatment: specific populations and problems*—outlines approaches for a range of offending types and contexts, including violent (Polaschek) and sexual offenders (Marshall), intimate partner violence (Bowen and Day), and alcohol-related offending (McGuire) and drug misuse (Casey and Day). Next are chapters on a number of *treatment modalities*—individual vs. group treatment (Davies) and communal living (Akerman)—and specific *approaches*—motivational interviewing (Tafrate, Hogan, and Mitchell), CBT (Hollin), criminal thinking-based approaches (Walters), and Schema Therapy (Bernstein, Keulen-de Vos, and Clercx), finishing with an overview of new directions for intervention (Jones).

Finally, Part VIII deals with *community interventions*. Kiss, Del Principe, and Taxman open with reentry approaches and interventions, which leads into community supervision practices (Davies and Polaschek), how to understand, assess, and use dynamic risk factors in community supervision (Serin, Lloyd, and Chadwick), and effective approaches to probationers with mental illnesses (Manchak, Loth, and Skeem). Taxman closes this section with a chapter that argues for taxonomizing community treatment to enhance offender placement and clarify how programs facilitate change. Our concluding chapter raises some current issues in assessment, treatment, role identities, and emerging areas of application.

Conclusions

In summary, the idea of using correctional strategies informed by psychological theory and research to reduce crime has come relatively recently in the long history of crime and punishment. But then, psychology is a relatively young discipline, and throughout its development, its relevance to crime and corrections has been evident (Biere & Mann, 2017). In a relatively short period, much has been learned about the parameters of effective correctional practice and fresh advances continue to be made. At a time when questions are still being asked about the effectiveness of punishment in reducing crime (Hollin, 2002) and hence about the effectiveness of sentencing (McGuire, 2008b), there is a strong case for effective correctional practice. Indeed, there is a case to be made for a wider influence of psychology across the criminal justice system (Dvoskin, Skeem, Novaco, & Douglas, 2012). Just as there is no unvarying set of purposes to which psychology can be applied in corrections, there also is no coherent body of academic knowledge or training that leads to its application. The upside of all this untidiness is that there are many interesting roles and tasks within corrections that can be informed by psychology, the science of human behavior, and mental processes, with new ones emerging all the time. Perhaps the most important thing for the future development of correctional psychology is to foster strong collaborations between the leading edge of correctional operations and translational psychological researchers with connections to the institutions that train the next generation of correctional practitioners.

Notes

1 This chapter is written largely from a Western perspective, drawing mainly on European traditions of philosophy, law, and psychology.
2 Readers interested in this approach are referred to Biere and Mann (2017) and Cullen (2005).
3 In contrast to its everyday usage, in operant theory the term *punishment* refers to any contingency that reduces behavior, not to the administration of physical pain. That is, hurting someone—physically or otherwise—is one such contingency, but taking away their access to sources of reward would be another.
4 Response cost procedures are a form of negative punishment, where undesirable behaviors are reduced by the removal of a reinforcer. For example, a therapist turns away from an offender (withdrawing attention, potential praise) in group treatment whenever s/he says something antisocial.
5 Actually, Wormith et al. (2007) have suggested that there are three main Canadian university-affiliated research influences which account for a significant proportion of this evidence base: the "Canadian school" (above); a West Coast group based at the University of British Columbia with Robert Hare; and a group based at Queens University and the Penetanguishene Mental Health Centre in Ontario, with principal researchers Vernon Quinsey and the late Marnie Rice and Grant Harris. Of course, significant practice-related research work has also come from the Correctional Service of Canada and Public Safety Canada throughout that period.
6 www.odt.co.nz/opinion/editorial/prisons-moral-and-fiscal-failure.
7 http://www.prisonstudies.org/country/new-zealand.

References

Abrahamson, D. (1944). *Crime and the human mind.* New York, NY: Columbia University Press.
Aichhorn, A. (1925). *Verwahrloste jungend.* Wien: Internationaler Psychoanalytischer Verlag. (Trans. Wayward youth) (1955). New York, NY: Meridian Books.

Akers, R. L. (1973). *Deviant behavior: A social learning approach.* Belmont, CA: Wadsworth.

Alexander, F., & Healy, W. (1935). *Roots of crime.* New York, NY: Knopf.

Allan, A. (2013). Ethics in correctional and forensic psychology: Getting the balance right. *Australian Psychologist*, 48, 47–56.

Andrews, D. A., & Bonta, J. (2003). *The psychology of criminal conduct* (3rd ed.). Cincinnati, OH: Anderson.

Andrews, D. A., & Bonta, J. (2006). *The psychology of criminal conduct* (4th ed.). Newark, NJ: Matthew Bender.

Andrews, D. A., & Bonta, J. (2010). *The psychology of criminal conduct* (5th ed.). Newark, NJ: Matthew Bender.

Andrews, D. A., Bonta, J., & Hoge, R. D. (1990). Classification for effective rehabilitation: Rediscovering psychology. *Criminal Justice and Behavior*, 17, 19–52.

Andrews, D. A., Bonta, J., & Wormith, J. S. (2011). The Risk-Need-Responsivity model: Does the Good Lives Model contribute to effective crime prevention? *Criminal Justice and Behavior*, 38, 735–755.

Andrews, D. A., & Kiessling, J. J. (1980). Program structure and effective correctional practices: A summary of the CaVIC research. In R. R. Ross, & P. Gendreau (Eds.), *Effective correctional treatment* (pp. 439–463). Toronto, Canada: Butterworth.

Bandura, A. (1973). *Aggression: A social learning analysis.* Englewood Cliffs, NJ: Prentice Hall.

Bandura, A. (1977). *Social learning theory.* New York, NY: Prentice Hall.

Bartol, C. R., & Bartol, A. M. (2015). *Introduction to forensic psychology: Research and application* (4th ed.). Thousand Oaks, CA: Sage.

Beck, A. T., Rush, A. J., Shaw, B. F., & Emery, G. (1979). *Cognitive therapy of depression.* New York, NY: Guilford.

Bennett, L., Sorensen, D., & Forshay, H. (1971). The application of self-esteem measures in a correctional setting. *Journal of Research in Crime and Delinquency*, 8, 1–10.

Biere, D. M., & Mann, R. E. (2017). The history and future of prison psychology. *Psychology, Public Policy, and Law*, 23, 478–489.

Bonta, J., & Andrews, D. A. (2017). *The psychology of criminal conduct* (6th ed.). London, UK: Routledge.

Bonta, J., Blais, J., & Wilson, H. A. (2014). A theoretically informed meta-analysis of the risk for general and violent recidivism for mentally disordered offenders. *Aggression and Violent Behavior*, 19, 278–287.

Brodsky, S. L. (2007). Correctional psychology and the American Association of Correctional Psychology: A revisionist history. *Criminal Justice and Behavior*, 34, 862–869.

Charleroy, M. L. (2013). *Penitentiary practice: Healthcare and medicine in Minnesota State Prison, 1855–1930.* (Unpublished doctoral dissertation). University of Minnesota, Minneapolis.

Cleckley, H. M. (1988). *The mask of sanity: An attempt to reinterpret the so-called psychopathic personality* (5th ed.). St Louis, MO: Mosby.

Clements, C. B., Althouse, R., Ax, R. K., Magaletta, P. R., Fagan, T. J., & Wormith, J. S. (2007). Systemic issues and correctional outcomes: Expanding the scope of correctional psychology. *Criminal Justice and Behavior*, 34, 919–932.

Cordess, C. (2001). Forensic psychotherapy. In C. R. Hollin (Ed.), *Handbook of offender assessment and treatment* (pp. 297–329). Chichester, UK: Wiley.

Cornish, D. B., & Clarke, R. V. G. (Eds.) (1986). *The reasoning criminal: Rational choice perspectives on crime.* New York, NY: Springer-Verlag.

Corrections and Conditional Release Act. S.C. 1992, c. 20. Canada.

Crimes (Administration of Sentences) Act 1999 No 93. New South Wales, Australia.

Coupland, R. B. A. (2015). An examination of dynamic risk, protective factors, and treatment-related change in violent offenders. (Unpublished doctoral dissertation). University of Saskatchewan, Saskatoon, Canada.

Cullen, F. T. (2002). Rehabilitation and treatment programs. In J. Q. Wilson, & J. Petersilia (Eds.), *Crime: Public policies for crime control* (pp. 253–289). Oakland, CA: ICS Press.

Cullen, F. T. (2005). The twelve people who saved rehabilitation: How the science of criminology made a difference. *Criminology*, 43, 1–42.

Cullen, F. T., Jonson, C. L., & Nagin, D. S. (2011). Prisons do not reduce recidivism: The high cost of ignoring science. *The Prison Journal*, 91, 48S–65S.

Day, A., & Collie, R. M. (2013). An Australasian approach to offender rehabilitation. In L. A. Craig, L. Dixon, & T. A. Gannon (Eds.), *What works in offender rehabilitation: An evidence-based approach to assessment and treatment* (pp. 408–420). Chichester, UK: Wiley.

Diamond, P. M., Wang, E. W., Holzer, C. E., Thomas, C. M., & Cruser, D. A. (2001). The prevalence of mental illness in prison. *Administration and Policy in Mental Health*, 29, 21–40.

Dodge, K. A., & Crick, N. R. (1990). Social information processing bases of aggressive behavior in children. *Personality and Social Psychology Bulletin*, 53, 1146–1158.

Dvoskin, J., & Morgan, R. D. (2010). Correctional psychology. In I. B. Weiner, & W. E. Craighead (Eds.), *The Corsini encyclopedia of psychology* (4th ed., Vol. 1) (pp. 417–420). Hoboken, NJ: Wiley.

Dvoskin, J. A., Skeem, J. L., Novaco, R. W., & Douglas, K. S. (2012). What if psychology redesigned the criminal justice system? In J. A. Dvoskin, J. L. Skeem, R. W. Novaco, & K. S. Douglas (Eds.), *Applying social science to reduce reoffending* (pp. 291–302). Oxford, UK: Oxford University Press.

D'Zurilla, T. J., & Goldfried, M. R. (1971). Problem solving and behavior modification. *Journal of Abnormal Psychology*, 78, 107–126.

English, B. (2017, August 14) *Military camp scheme 'has never been tried before'—PM/Interviewer: G. Espiner*. Radio New Zealand Morning Report. Retrieved from www.radionz.co.nz/news/political/337115/military-camp-scheme-has-never-been-tried-before-pm

Farrington, D. P. (2002). Key results from the first forty years of the Cambridge study in delinquent development. In M. D. Krohn, & T. P. Thornberry (Eds.), *Taking stock of delinquency: An overview of findings from contemporary longitudinal studies* (pp. 137–174). New York, NY: Kluwer Academic/Plenum.

Farrington, D. P. (2003). Developmental and life-course criminology: Key theoretical and empirical issues—The 2002 Sutherland Award address. *Criminology*, 41, 221–255.

Friedlander, K. (1947). *The psychoanalytic approach to juvenile delinquency*. London, UK: Routledge & Kegan Paul.

Garrett, C. G. (1985). Effects of residential treatment on adjudicated delinquents: A meta-analysis. *Journal of Research in Crime and Delinquency*, 22, 287–308.

Gendreau, P., & Goggin, C. (2013). Practicing psychology in correctional settings. In I. B. Weiner, & R. K. Otto (Eds.), *The handbook of forensic psychology* (4th ed.) (pp. 759–793). Hoboken, NJ: Wiley.

Gendreau, P., Goggin, C., & Smith, P. (2002). Implementation guidelines for correctional programs in the "real world.". In G. A. Bernfeld, D. P. Farrington, & A. W. Leschied (Eds.), *Offender rehabilitation in practice: Implementing and evaluating effective programs* (pp. 228–268). Chichester, UK: Wiley.

Gendreau, P., Listwan, S. J., Kuhns, J. B., & Exum, M. L. (2014). Making prisoners accountable: Are contingency management programs the answer? *Criminal Justice and Behavior*, 41, 1079–1102.

Gendreau, P., & Ross, B. (1979). Effective correctional treatment: Bibliotherapy for cynics. *Crime & Delinquency*, 25, 463–489.

Gendreau, P., Smith, P., & Thériault, Y. L. (2009). Chaos theory and correctional treatment: Common sense, correctional quackery, and the law of fartcatchers. *Journal of Contemporary Criminal Justice*, 25, 384–396.

Genschow, O., Noll, T., Wänke, M., & Gersbach, R. (2015). Does Baker-Miller pink reduce aggression in prison detention cells? A critical empirical examination. *Psychology, Crime & Law*, 21, 482–489.

Goldstein, A. P. (1988). *The Prepare Curriculum: Teaching prosocial competencies*. Champaign, IL: Research Press.

Goldstein, A. P., & Glick, B. (1987). *Aggression replacement training: A comprehensive intervention for aggressive youth*. Champaign, IL: Research Press.

Goldstein, A. P., Nensen, R., Delaflod, B., & Kalt, M. (Eds.) (2004). *New perspectives on aggression replacement training: Practice, research, and treatment*. Chichester, UK: Wiley.

Healy, W., & Bronner, A. F. (1936). *New light on delinquency and its treatment*. New Haven, CT: Yale University Press.

Henderson, M., & Hollin, C. (1983). A critical review of social skills training with young offenders. *Criminal Justice and Behavior*, 10, 316–341.

Hollin, C. R. (1990a). *Cognitive-behavioral interventions with young offenders*. Elmsford, NY: Pergamon Press.

Hollin, C. R. (1990b). Social skills training with delinquents: A look at the evidence and some recommendations for practice. *British Journal of Social Work*, 20, 483–493.

Hollin, C. R. (2002). Does punishment motivate offenders to change? In M. McMurran (Ed.), *Motivating offenders to change: A guide to enhancing engagement in therapy* (pp. 235–249). Chichester, UK: Wiley.

Hollin, C. R. (2013). *Psychology and crime: An introduction to criminological psychology* (2nd ed.). London, UK: Routledge.

Hollin, C. R., & Palmer, E. J. (2009). Cognitive skills programmes for offenders. *Psychology, Crime & Law*, 15, 147–164.

Honderich, T. (1993). *How free are you? The determinism problem*. Oxford, UK: Oxford University Press.

Howells, K. (1986). Social skills training and antisocial behaviour in adults. In C. R. Hollin, & P. Trower (Eds.), *Handbook of social skills training, Vol. 1: Applications across the life span* (pp. 185–210). Oxford, UK: Pergamon Press.

International Association for Correctional and Forensic Psychology (2010). Standards for psychology services in jails, prisons, correctional facilities and agencies. *Criminal Justice and Behavior*, 37, 749–808.

Jackson, H. J., Glass, C., & Hope, S. (1987). A functional analysis of recidivistic arson. *British Journal of Clinical Psychology*, 26, 175–185.

Jeffery, C. R. (1965). Criminal behavior and learning theory. *Journal of Criminal Law, Criminology, and Police Science*, 56, 294–300.

Jesness, C. F., DeRisi, W., McCormick, P., & Wedge, R. (1972). *The youth center research project*. Sacramento, CA: California Youth Authority.

Kennedy, D. M. (2009). *Deterrence and crime prevention: Reconsidering the prospect of sanction*. London, UK: Routledge.

Kirigin, K. A., Braukmann, C. J., Atwater, J., & Wolf, M. M. (1982). An evaluation of Achievement Place (Teaching-Family) group homes for juvenile offenders. *Journal of Applied Behavior Analysis*, 15, 1–16.

Latessa, E. J., Cullen, F. T., & Gendreau, P. (2002). Beyond correctional quackery-professionalism and the possibility of effective treatment. *Federal Probation*, 66, 43–49.

Laws, D. R., & Marshall, W. L. (1990). A conditioning theory of the etiology and maintenance of deviant sexual preference and behavior. In W. L. Marshall, D. R. Laws, & H. E. Barbaree (Eds.), *Handbook of sexual assault: Issues, theories, and treatment of the offender* (pp. 209–229). New York, NY: Plenum.

Laws, D. R., & Marshall, W. L. (1991). Masturbatory reconditioning with sexual deviates: An evaluative review. *Advances in Behaviour Research and Therapy*, 13, 13–25.

Lester, D., Braswell, M., & Van Voorhis, P. (2004). Radical behavioral interventions. In P. Van Voorhis, M. Braswell, & D. Lester (Eds.), *Correctional counseling and rehabilitation* (5th ed.) (pp. 61–83). Cincinnati, OH: Anderson.

Lester, D., & Van Voorhis, P. (2004a). Early approaches to group and milieu therapy. In P. Van Voorhis, M. Braswell, & D. Lester (Eds.), *Correctional counseling and rehabilitation* (5th ed.) (pp. 85–110). Cincinnati, OH: Anderson.

Lester, D., & Van Voorhis, P. (2004b). Psychoanalytic therapy. In P. Van Voorhis, M. Braswell, & D. Lester (Eds.), *Correctional counseling and rehabilitation* (5th ed.) (pp. 41–60). Cincinnati, OH: Anderson.

Lilly, J. R., Cullen, F. T., & Ball, R. A. (2002). *Criminological theory: Context and consequences* (3rd ed.). Thousand Oaks, CA: Sage.

Magaletta, P. R., Patry, M. W., Dietz, E. F., & Ax, R. K. (2007). What is correctional about clinical practice in corrections? *Criminal Justice and Behavior*, 34, 7–21.

Magaletta, P. R., Patry, M. W., Gross, N. R., Butterfield, P. M., McLearen, A. M., Patterson, K. L., & Norcross, J. C. (2011). Clinical practice in corrections: Providing service, obtaining experience. *Psychological Services*, 8, 343–355.

Magaletta, P. R., & Verdeyen, V. (2005). Clinical practice in corrections: A conceptual framework. *Professional Psychology: Research and Practice*, 36, 37–43.

Mann, R. E., & Fernandez, Y. M. (2006). Sex offender programmes: Concept, theory, and practice. In C. R. Hollin, & E. J. Palmer (Eds.), *Offending behaviour programmes: Development, application, and controversies* (pp. 155–177). Chichester, UK: Wiley.

Marshall, W. L., & Hollin, C. R. (2015). Historical developments in sex offender treatment. *Journal of Sexual Aggression*, 21, 125–135.

McGuire, J. (Ed.) (1995). *What works: Reducing reoffending*. Chichester, UK: Wiley.

McGuire, J. (2002). Integrating findings from research reviews. In J. McGuire (Ed.), *Offender rehabilitation and treatment: Effective programmes and policies to reduce reoffending* (pp. 3–38). Chichester, UK: Wiley.

McGuire, J. (2005). The Think First programme. In M. McMurran, & J. McGuire (Eds.), *Social problem solving and offending: Evidence, evaluation and evolution* (pp. 183–206). Chichester, UK: Wiley.

McGuire, J. (2008a). A review of effective interventions for reducing aggression and violence. *Philosophical Transactions of the Royal Society B*, 363, 2577–2597.

McGuire, J. (2008b). What's the point of sentencing? In G. Davies, C. Hollin, & R. Bull (Eds.), *Forensic psychology* (pp. 265–291). Chichester, UK: Wiley.

McMurran, M., & McGuire, J. (Eds.) (2005). *Social problem solving and offending: Evidence, evaluation and evolution*. Chichester, UK: Wiley.

Miller, N., & Dollard, J. (1941). *Social learning and imitation*. New Haven, CT: Yale University Press.

Miltenberger, R. G. (2004). *Behavior modification: Principles and procedures* (3rd ed.). Belmont, CA: Wadsworth Thomason Learning.

Morgan, R. D., Beer, A. M., Fitzgerald, K. L., & Mandracchia, J. T. (2007). Graduate students' experiences, interests, and attitudes toward correctional/forensic psychology. *Criminal Justice and Behavior*, 34, 96–107.

Nagin, D. S. (2013). Deterrence in the twenty-first century. In M. Tonry (Ed.), *Crime and justice in America: 1975–2025* (pp. 199–264). Chicago, IL: University of Chicago Press.

Nagin, D. S., Farrington, D. P., & Moffitt, T. E. (1995). Life-course trajectories of different types of offenders. *Criminology*, 33, 111–139.

New Zealand Corrections Act 2004, No 50.

New Zealand National Party (2017, August). Youth Justice Policy Announcement. Retrieved from https://d3n8a8pro7vhmx.cloudfront.net/nationalparty/pages/8079/attachments/original/1502665477/Youth_Crime_-_Policy_Document.pdf?1502665477

Nietzel, M. T. (1979). *Crime and its modification: A social learning perspective*. Oxford, UK: Pergamon Press.

Nietzel, M. T., Hasemann, D. M., & Lynam, D. R. (1999). Behavioral perspective on violent behavior. In V. B. Van Hasselt, & M. Hersen (Eds.), *Handbook of psychological approaches with violent offenders: Contemporary strategies and issues* (pp. 39–66). New York, NY: Kluwer Academic/Plenum.

Novaco, N. W. (2011). Anger dysregulation: Driver of violent offending. *Journal of Forensic Psychiatry & Psychology*, 22, 650–668.

Novaco, N. W. (2013). Reducing anger-related offending: What works. In L. A. Craig, L. Dixon, & T. A. Gannon (Eds.), *What works in offender rehabilitation: An evidence-based approach to assessment and treatment* (pp. 211–236). Chichester, UK: Wiley.

Novaco, R. W. (1975). *Anger control: The development and evaluation of an experimental treatment.* Lexington, MA: D. C. Heath.

Novaco, R. W. (2006). Anger dysregulation: Its assessment and treatment. In T. A. Cavell, & K. T. Malcolm (Eds.), *Anger, aggression, and interventions for interpersonal violence* (pp. 3–54). Mahwah, NJ: Lawrence Erlbaum.

Olver, M. E., Preston, D. L., Camilleri, J. A., & Helmus, L. (2011). A survey of clinical psychology training in Canadian federal corrections: Implications for psychologist recruitment and retention. *Canadian Psychology*, 52, 310–320.

Paternoster, R. (2010). How much do we really know about criminal deterrence? *The Journal of Criminal Law and Criminology*, 100, 765–823.

Pettifer, E. W. (1992). *Punishments of former days.* Winchester, UK: Waterside Press (Original edition published by the author in 1939.).

Polaschek, D. L. L. (2006). Violent offender programmes: Concept, theory, and practice. In C. R. Hollin, & E. J. Palmer (Eds.), *Offending behaviour programmes: Development, application, and controversies* (pp. 113–154). Chichester, UK: Wiley.

Polaschek, D. L. L. (2012). An appraisal of the Risk-Need-Responsivity model of offender rehabilitation and its application in correctional treatment. *Legal and Criminological Psychology*, 17, 1–17.

Polaschek, D. L. L., & Kilgour, T. G. (2013). New Zealand's special treatment units: The development and implementation of intensive treatment for high-risk male prisoners. *Psychology, Crime & Law*, 11, 511–526.

Randol, B. (2014). Auburn system. In J. S. Albanese (Ed.), (Ed. in Chief) *The Encyclopedia of Criminology and Criminal Justice* (pp. 1–4). Oxford, UK: Wiley Blackwell.

Reckless, W. C., & Dintz, S. (1967). Pioneering with self-concept as a vulnerability factor in delinquency. *Journal of Criminal Law, Criminology, and Police Science*, 58, 515–523.

Richards-Ward, L. A., & McDaniel, C. (2007). Corrections in Aotearoa/New Zealand: Current issues and future challenges. In R. K. Ax, & T. J. Fagan (Eds.), *Corrections, mental health, and social policy: International perspectives* (pp. 174–206). Springfield, IL: Charles C Thomas.

Roshier, B. (1989). *Controlling crime: The classical perspective in criminology.* Milton Keynes, UK: Open University Press.

Ross, R. R., & Fabiano, E. A. (1985). *Time to think: A cognitive model of delinquency prevention and offender rehabilitation.* Johnson City, TN: Institute of Social Sciences and Arts.

Rubin, A. (2017). Pennsylvania prison system. In K. R. Kerley (Ed.), *The encyclopedia of corrections* (pp. 1–5). Oxford, UK: Wiley.

Salekin, R. T. (2002). Psychopathy and therapeutic pessimism: Clinical lore or clinical reality? *Clinical Psychology Review*, 22, 79–112.

Short, J. F. (Ed.) (1968). *Gang delinquency and delinquent subcultures.* New York, NY: Harper & Row.

Skeem, J. L., Steadman, H. J., & Manchak, S. M. (2015). Applicability of the Risk-Need-Responsivity model to persons with mental illness involved in the criminal justice system. *Psychiatric Services*, 66, 916–922.

Skeem, J. L., Winter, E., Kennealy, P. J., Eno Louden, J., & Tatar, J. R. (2014). Offenders with mental illness have criminogenic needs, too: Toward recidivism reduction. *Law and Human Behavior*, 38, 212–224.

Skinner, B. F. (1938). *The behavior of organisms.* New York, NY: Appleton-Century-Crofts.

Skinner, B. F. (1953). *Science and human behavior.* New York, NY: Macmillan.

Soothill, K., Rogers, P., & Dolan, M. (Eds.) (2008). *Handbook of forensic mental health.* Cullompton, UK: Willan.

Sturmey, P., Ward-Horner, J., Marroquin, M., & Doran, E. (2007). Structural and functional approaches to psychopathology and case formulation. In P. Sturmey (Ed.), *Functional analysis in clinical treatment* (pp. 1–21). Burlington, MA: Academic Press.

Thorndike, E. L. (1911). *Animal intelligence: Experimental studies.* New York, NY: Macmillan.

Towl, G. (2010). Psychology in the National Offender Management Service for England and Wales. In J. R. Adler, & J. M. Gray (Eds.), *Forensic psychology: Concepts, debates and practice* (pp. 529–542). Abingdon, UK: Willan.

Towl, G., & Crighton, D. (2007). Psychological services in English and Welsh prisons. In R. K. Ax, & T. J. Fagan (Eds.), *Corrections, mental health, and social policy: International perspectives* (pp. 87–106). Springfield, IL: Charles C Thomas.

von Hirsch, A. (1993). *Censure and sanctions.* Oxford, UK: Clarendon Press.

Wilson, D. B., MacKenzie, D. L., & Mitchell, F. N. (2005). Effects of correctional boot camps on offending. A Campbell Collaboration systematic review. Retrieved from https://campbellcollaboration.org/media/k2/attachments/Wilson_Bootcamps_review.pdf

Wormith, J. S., Althouse, R., Simpson, M., Reitzel, L. R., Fagan, T. J., & Morgan, R. D. (2007). The rehabilitation and reintegration of offenders: The current landscape and some future directions for correctional psychology. *Criminal Justice and Behavior*, 34, 879–892.

2

Being Ethical Psychologists in Correction Settings

Alfred Allan

Edith Cowan University, Australia

Psychology's Morality and Codes

The profession cannot tell psychologists what their personal values should be, but it can require psychologists to adhere to what it considers right and good behavior (psychology's morality) in their professional practice. The profession must therefore conceptualize its morality and explain it to psychologists. The conceptualization process started with the work of the early psychologists, and particularly the drafters of the first American Psychological Association (APA) code (Allan, 2015). These drafters invited the members of the APA in 1948 "to describe a situation they knew of first-hand, in which a psychologist made a decision having ethical implications, and to indicate what the correspondents perceived as being the ethical issues involved" (APA, 1953, p. vi). They then analyzed the data to identify psychology's ethical principles and used them to formulate minimum behavioral standards to guide psychologists in situations they might *frequently* encounter in their professional activities.

Most, if not all, modern codes use a similar set of principles because psychologists in other countries either applied the APA's principles or identified similar principles while developing their codes (Allan, 2011). An ad hoc committee of the International Union of Psychological Science and the International Association of Applied Psychology furthermore confirmed the existence of these principles during an extensive international consultation process (see, e.g., Gauthier, Pettifor, & Ferrero, 2010). The same principles therefore underpin the standards of most codes even though the wording used in them might differ to reflect the public morality and law of the relevant jurisdiction (Allan, 2010). Psychologists must generally obey these standards because they represent the profession's minimum behavioral requirements. Drafters, however, for practical reasons draft standards dealing with issues most psychologists regularly encounter and understand that psychologists working under exceptional circumstances and/ or in uncommon settings might find them insufficient (Allan, 2011). They therefore explicitly state the aspirational principles of psychology's morality for two reasons. First, they want psychologists working in niche areas to use them to develop practice guides or codes of

The Wiley International Handbook of Correctional Psychology, First Edition. Edited by Devon L. L. Polaschek, Andrew Day, and Clive R. Hollin.
© 2019 John Wiley & Sons Ltd. Published 2019 by John Wiley & Sons Ltd.

conduct that reflect the unique moral challenges they might encounter (see, e.g., IACFP Practice Standards Committee, 2010). Second, they want psychologists to internalize and use these principles in higher-level moral decision-making while solving novel and/or uncommon moral problems (see Allan, 2015 for a more comprehensive discussion).

Principles

Drafters of codes recognize at least three principles, but they often subdivide them into more principles and use different nomenclature to describe them. I will structure my overview of the principles by distinguishing between eight overlapping principles; namely, responsibility, respect for humanity, respect for autonomy, justice, non-maleficence, beneficence, integrity, and fidelity.

Responsibility

This principle requires psychologists to honor their legal and moral responsibilities in the course of their professional practice. Correctional psychologists' responsibilities will generally be toward society, their employers, the profession, and those to whom they provide assessment or intervention services (i.e., clients).

Public morality and law define psychologists' *responsibility to society*, but legal norms generally carry more weight because states with their considerable power determine and enforce them. All psychologists therefore have a responsibility to know the law that applies in the jurisdictions, settings, and roles they work in. They must know the registration (or licensing) legislation that regulates their professional behavior and other applicable legislation that for those working in corrections might include correctional, parole, and mental health acts. Psychologists' specific legal responsibilities depend on the jurisdiction and organization they work for and their specific roles within the organization.

Psychologists' *responsibility to their employers and colleagues* emanate from the employment contracts they sign that require them to obey their employers' organizational rules and lawful orders from superiors. Psychologists must therefore understand the terms of their employment contracts before they sign them because they could be subject to disciplinary proceedings and civil or criminal action if they fail to obey these rules and lawful orders. They must also fully understand the implications of employers' explicit rules (e.g., policies, procedures, and standing orders). Psychologists encountering situations where they feel uncertain about the interpretation of organizational rules or where it appears to them that implicit rules exist must ask their employers to clarify the situation in writing.

Psychologists' exact responsibility in organizations depends on their specific roles and therefore the obligations of assessors might differ from those of therapists in the same organization. Psychologists increasingly also work within teams that consist of non-psychology colleagues whose professional obligations or ethos might differ from psychology's morality because their professions serve different functions and pursue different aspirations. Psychologists should accept that these colleagues' moral decisions might sometimes be different from theirs but be equally sound. Psychologists whose colleagues, however, put pressure on them to behave contrary to psychology's morality must clarify the differences that exist, and work with their colleagues to find the mutually acceptable and constructive outcomes most beneficial to all interested parties.

Psychologists' *responsibility to their profession and the discipline* include ensuring that they do not harm members of the public or bring psychology into disrepute. Psychologists working in corrections must by necessity treat offenders differently from how they would treat clients in other settings. They should therefore try to reduce the risk that prisoners' experiences in prison could discourage them from consulting psychologists outside prison or allowing family members to consult psychologists by explaining to prisoners how and why they treat them differently. They can do this by explaining to prisoners, and repeating such explanations when required, that their legal and/or organizational obligations require them to deviate from what psychologists might typically do in other roles or settings.

Psychologists frequently give prisoners explicit or implicit undertakings that create specific *client responsibilities*. They must, however, take care that these client responsibilities do not clash with their social, organizational, and professional responsibilities. They must therefore be so familiar with their normative responsibilities in their specific work settings and the hierarchy of these responsibilities that they can explain the situation to interested parties at the outset of relationships and thereafter when required. Psychologists must avoid unnecessary multiple relationships because managing and resolving unavoidable conflicts of interest flowing from them can be very difficult and unsatisfactory. Psychologists should therefore avoid any role that requires them to participate in disciplinary decisions except as witnesses (see, e.g., Weinberger & Sreenivasan, 1994).

Respect for Humanity

This principle requires psychologists to behave in an aspirational manner in contrast to the rigid observance of obligations required by the responsibility principle. The humanity principle, which also underlies human rights law (Allan, 2013), can be traced back to the notion that humans' capacity of self-awareness and self-reflection and their ability to make rational and considered decisions give them an intrinsic worth (humanity) that sets them apart from animals and other objects. Kant (1785/2001) and later philosophers argued that people must respect other people's humanity and their own. They further argued that people cannot reduce their humanity by behaving in an objectively abhorrent manner and that they cannot give consent to others to disrespect their humanity (see, e.g., *Wackenheim v. France*, 2002) in the absence of other overarching justifying moral reasons.

People often find it difficult to respect the humanity of people who disregard their own humanity and those of others, for example, offenders who sexually abused and humiliated their victims. This principle, however, requires psychologists to respect humanity as such and therefore the humanity of *all* people they interact with professionally irrespective of their behavior or the esteem in which psychologists hold them. The word respect derives from the Latin word *respicio* that figuratively means "to have regard for, care for, consider" (Simpson, 1971, p. 518). Psychologists can show regard for others in many ways, but I will focus on two aspects here, namely respect for others' self-worth (frequently referred to as dignity in the philosophical literature) and their privacy.

People respect others' self-worth by being attentive and responsive to them and their needs. They therefore disrespect others' humanity by failing to acknowledge them (e.g., ignoring them when they enter into a room), or addressing them in a disrespectful manner (e.g., not using appropriate titles or using diminutive forms of their names), or labeling them (e.g., psychopaths or schizophrenics). They might also disrespect people's self-worth by making demeaning statements about them and/or their circumstances. Allan and Davidson (2013) argued people show respect to others' self-worth by treating them the way that people of their culture and society consider courteous (Tamatea & Day, Chapter 18). Researchers found psychological support for this principle by demonstrating that people who experience discourteous behavior present with higher levels of psychological distress (Cortina, Magley, Williams, & Langhout, 2001; Lim & Cortina, 2005), which in turn adversely affected their physical health (Lim, Cortina, & Magley, 2008). Psychologists cannot protect offenders from others' discourteous behavior, but if they act courteously toward prisoners and colleagues they not only show respect for their self-worth but also act as role models of respectful behavior in their work settings.

Psychologists use prisoners for their own ends when they provide non-beneficial services to them merely to satisfy their own personal needs. They do this at a concrete level (e.g., trainee psychologists administering psychological tests merely to satisfy registration requirements) or at an intangible level such as where they spend unnecessary time with low-risk and need prisoners to avoid spending time with high-risk and need prisoners who they find difficult to work with.

People respect others' privacy by recognizing their right to be left alone and control access to their personal information. They further respect people's privacy by keeping private information they collect confidential and only using and/or disclosing it for the primary purpose for which it was collected. They should therefore only use or disclose information for secondary purposes with the explicit consent of the owner of the information, or when justified by overriding ethical, legal, or organizational considerations. Psychologists might find it particularly difficult to respect the privacy of offenders when employers may legitimately ignore it by covertly collecting and sharing private information. Psychologists might therefore receive unsolicited information about clients and/or find their employers expect a level of intrusiveness and disclosure from them beyond what their professional rules accept. They must nevertheless diligently endeavor to optimize prisoners' privacy by only collecting the information they strictly require to provide the relevant services and obtaining informed consent from them before collecting or accessing their private information. Psychologists may, however, access offenders' files without their consent to prepare reports that serve society's interests (i.e., risk assessment reports), but not for other assessment and treatment reports (Inmate Welfare Committee, 2003). They should therefore refrain from using covertly collected information, for example transcripts of telephone conversations made without prisoners' consent. Psychologists working in settings where their employers may legitimately order them to use covertly collected information for the protection of the organization or society should limit their violation of people's right to privacy to a minimum. They should further urge their employers to inform prisoners and those conversing with them that their conversations might be recorded and used for security purposes.

Respect for Autonomy

Psychologists respect people's autonomy by not using them as means for their own ends and by recognizing their right to make decisions pertaining to their own lives. Researchers (see, e.g., Ryan & Deci, 2000) provide psychological data to support the importance of this ethical principle by suggesting that ignoring people's autonomy affects their mental health.

Psychologists also disregard prisoners' autonomy if they fail to give them opportunities to make free, voluntarily, and informed decisions about matters of importance to them. Psychologists might find it difficult to give prisoners options in settings where society legitimately restricts their rights of self-determination and liberty. They should, nevertheless, endeavor to maximize their prisoners' choices within the legal and organizational limitation placed on them by engaging them in shared decision-making processes where they and prisoners explore their limited options. Psychologists can do this by adopting a collaborative attitude and assisting prisoners to identify the options available to them and exchanging views about the advantages and disadvantages of each option. They might not agree about the best option, but prisoners will at least have an opportunity to express their views and will understand psychologists' positions even though they may not accept them. Psychologists should generally accept prisoners' choices, but they might sometimes find themselves in situations where they must actively restrict prisoners' autonomy (e.g., where they must restrain them because they pose a risk of harming themselves). They must always do this in the least restrictive and intrusive manner, explain the reasons for their decisions to prisoners, and give them opportunities to express their views if practical.

People must be competent to make autonomous decisions and psychologists should therefore routinely screen prisoners' capacity to make legally binding decisions to ensure the lawfulness of their choices. Psychologists who question prisoners' legal capacity must either assess their capacity comprehensively or refer them to suitably qualified peers if they cannot undertake such assessments themselves. Psychologists should optimize the autonomy of prisoners whose legal capacity to make binding decisions might be restricted by their mental or physical health. They must where practical provide relevant information to prisoners with diminished legal capacity and allow them an opportunity to express their wishes even though their assent will not be lawful. Psychologists working with prisoners whose legal capacity fluctuates must try to contract with them when they deem them legally competent.

Non-Maleficence

Both law and ethics recognize the non-maleficence principle, and psychologists generally find it easy to relate to this principle that requires them to avoid doing reasonably foreseeable harm to others. Psychologists cannot avoid all foreseeable harm because there might be situations when harm will follow irrespective of the option they exercise. They might, for example, find that by preventing harm to one person or group they cause harm to others, such as where their warning to employers that clients intend harming other prisoners leads to the punishment of their clients. They could also find that by preventing one type of harm they cause another form of harm. Psychologists authorizing the placement of suicidal persons in observation cells might reduce their risk of successful suicide but cause a deterioration of their mental health and/or harm their professional relationships with them. Ethicists refer to this as *double effect* and most of them argue that the negative consequences in these cases will be justified provided psychologists' intentions were benevolent.

I will briefly discuss the three most common ways that psychologists cause foreseeable harm to others. First, they might cause harm by practicing carelessly, that is below the standard of care that can be expected of reasonable and competent (i.e., knowledgeable, skilled, and experienced) psychologists working in the specific settings. This *reasonable psychologist test* implies that psychologists working in corrections should be adept at identifying and managing self-harm risks because society expects institutions such as correctional and mental health facilities to prevent suicides (see, e.g., Allan et al., 2006). Second, otherwise competent psychologists might cause harm by practicing beyond the limits of their competence. Psychologists must in particular refrain from undertaking tasks that require specialist competence they lack, because the *reasonable specialist test* applies when people undertake specialist activities. Third, psychologists might cause harm if physical or mental impairments cause them to practice carelessly or incompetently. Impaired psychologists' inability to recognize an escalation of prisoners' risk of harming others could, for example, lead to situations where those prisoners injure their psychologists or other staff or prisoners. Impaired psychologists might also find it difficult to maintain their professional boundaries, leading them to manipulate and/or exploit others, or to be manipulated and/or exploited by prisoners.

Psychologists should engage in continuous career-long supervision to prevent them from inadvertently working beyond their competence and/or while impaired (see, e.g., Andersen, Van Raalte, & Brewer, 2000) and should resist employers' expectation that they should undertake tasks beyond their competence. Psychologists find it difficult to approach employers about these issues but the non-maleficence principle requires them to do so either individually, as a group, or through employers' organizations such as unions. Employers should respond positively to such reports because their legal and moral duty to prevent harm requires them to prevent psychologists from practicing carelessly, working beyond their competence, and/or working when impaired. Employers should therefore make it possible for their employees to develop the competencies they require to fulfill their professional duties, prevent impairment among psychologists working for them, and ensure timely detection of any impairment that occurs and manage it effectively. They should further create internal and external supervision opportunities for their employees. Psychologists should in turn use supervision sessions to explore their functioning and vulnerabilities irrespective of how threatening this might be at times.

Beneficence

This principle requires psychologists to balance the benefits, risks, and costs in all situations in a way that will be most beneficial to all interested parties depending on the circumstances. Psychologists in situations where they must do something that will harm others' rights, interests, or wellbeing must do so in the least intrusive and restrictive way, taking into account the normative restrictions placed on them. Psychologists who conclude that they must warn authorities that their clients pose a risk to other prisoners should try to minimize the negative impact on their clients by telling them what they intend doing, but only if they do not place themselves at risk. Psychologists should further anticipate, and guard against, potential harm to those they provide services to, and take proactive steps to prevent such harm from materializing, even in situations not covered by their duty of care under the non-maleficence principle. They should, for example, while obtaining consent to provide services, explain to clients what the possible negative consequences could be if they refuse to participate in assessment or group activities. Psychologists must, however, avoid using coercive methods or manipulation to encourage them to follow their advice.

Justice

Psychologists must in the course of their professional practice treat people fairly. This principle arguably takes on special significance for prisoners who find themselves in heavily regulated and restrictive environments. The distributive justice element of the justice principle obliges psychologists to monitor the accessibility of their services to those who need them and to take reasonable steps to remedy limitations they identify. Psychologists can often not do much more in this regard than point the limitations they identify out to their employers.

The procedural justice element requires psychologists to be fair when they make decisions that affect the interests of others. Psychologists working in corrections make many decisions that might significantly influence peoples' legal and moral rights, interests, and mental health (Beijersbergen, Dirkzwager, Eichelsheim, van der Laan, & Nieuwbeerta, 2014). These include decisions about their risk of harming themselves or others, and offenders and employers expect psychologists to make *independent and unbiased* decisions and they should therefore avoid any perceptions or actual conflicts of interest or bias. Psychologists often find themselves in conflicting positions when they adopt multiple roles with the same prisoners, such as therapist and risk assessor. The non-maleficence principle requires treating psychologists to routinely assess clients' risk of harming themselves or others in order to make decisions about their and other prisoners' protective status. Treating psychologists should, however, refrain from undertaking purposeful assessments aimed at informing decisions about prisoners' security classification or parole specifically required to protect the public and therefore justified primarily by their social responsibility. Employers, clients, and even some practitioners (for psychiatrists' opinions see, e.g., Taylor, Graf, Schanda, & Völlm, 2012) feel that treating psychologists' intimate knowledge of their clients might make them more accurate assessors of their risk to harm others, but this closeness leads to ethical problems. Psychologists in dual relationships could for instance be privy to information they would otherwise not have had access to, making their decisions unfair (Greenberg & Gould, 2001; Greenberg & Shuman, 1997, 2007). Their closeness with prisoners might also impair their decision-making ability and lead to unsafe decisions, as was pointed out in an independent review of a murder committed by Anthony Rice while a parolee in the United Kingdom (Her Majesty's Inspectorate of Probation, 2006). The Inspector found that the "the psychologist's assessment that Anthony Rice was ready to move direct from Category B to Category D (open prison) conditions, was a misjudgement … The fact that this assessment was being made by the psychologist who was also delivering treatment may be a factor in this case" (paragraph 10.1.6). Treating psychologists can make useful contributions, but should rather do so by recording their observations in the prisoner's notes or providing their insights to assessors in the form of written reports with prisoners' consent.

Psychologists should *consistently follow the same process* when they make decisions that might influence people's legal and moral interests and should generally take into account the previous decisions they made in similar circumstances. They must record the reasons for deviating from process or precedents when they feel compelled to do so.

They must during the decision-making process collect all *relevant and reasonably accessible information* that might influence their decisions from all representative sources. They must therefore allow offenders opportunities to contribute material and respond to what other people have said, and must avoid using information obtained from anonymous sources if feasible. They must report their reasons for not collecting specific information and/or restricting offenders' involvement in the process.

Psychologists must only use *trustworthy information* when meeting their social obligations and while they can use hearsay information when they develop intervention plans, they should avoid using such information as evidence when they for example do parole assessments. They must use reliable methods and instruments if they collect information (see, e.g., *Ewert v. Canada*, 2018). Psychologists working in countries that lack valid instruments to access offenders from specific groups must identify the best instrument available in the circumstances and obtain their consent before they use it. Psychologists should not use such unreliable instruments without the consent of the examinees unless they can justify proceeding on the basis of legal-organizational rules. Decision-makers must always assess the reliability of the evidence they use and record their conclusions in their professional notes and reports they might prepare.

They must identify the *relevant decision-making criteria* applicable, which can range from organizational policies to legislative requirements. Psychologists' decisions frequently involve an element of discrimination and they might discriminate unfairly against people if they fail to apply the relevant criteria when they make decisions about them.

Decision-makers must *articulate their decisions clearly* and must be able to justify them by *clarifying their analysis of the information and explaining their reasoning*. Their justifications should go beyond merely listing the reasons for the decision to a demonstration of how they analyzed and weighed the relevant information at the hand of the relevant criteria.

Decision-makers should ideally convey their decisions to those affected before submitting them and allow them *opportunities to respond* to them. Psychologists could invite peers to review disputed decisions even though their employers or some other bodies might provide a formal review process.

Integrity

Psychologists must be accountable, honest, and transparent in all spheres of their professional behavior. Psychologists contracting with prisoners must therefore, for example, acknowledge the limits of confidentiality and not give undertakings they anticipate, or should reasonably anticipate, they might not be able to honor. Psychologists should explain to prisoners how and why they treat clients in prison differently from elsewhere to dispel any unrealistic unspoken expectations prisoners might hold if they had experience with psychologists working outside prison settings. They should also be honest with their employers about limitations in their competencies and/or impairments they suffer that might impact on their ability to provide competent services. They must furthermore be honest in what they capture in their prisoners' records and put in reports (Allan & Allan, 2016).

Fidelity

Both lawyers and ethicists require people in positions of trust to demonstrate a higher degree of trustworthiness than generally required of people. They consider psychologists as people in positions of trust because people must trust psychologists in order to benefit from their experience, knowledge, and skills. People generally consult psychologists while experiencing crises that make them feel emotionally vulnerable and helpless and they might therefore be incapable of protecting themselves from being taken advantage of. They often increase their vulnerability by consulting psychologists because doing so requires them to share very sensitive information. Psychologists' knowledge and experience might also give them insights into their clients' situation, personal dynamics, and vulnerabilities that allow them to make self-serving suggestions that could bring them undue benefits if clients accept them (Allan, 2016). Lay people furthermore generally lack the knowledge required to judge the quality of advice they receive from psychologists and must trust them to give competent and sound advice.

People who use psychologists' services trust they will be competent, cautious, and unimpaired. Psychologists must therefore, inter alia, avoid relationships and/or boundary crossings that might impair their ability to provide effective and objective services, or could lead them to harm or exploit clients.

Addressing Moral Uncertainty

Psychologists confronted with moral (i.e., right and good) issues in their professional practice should search for solutions among the standards of their codes and, if necessary, apply the ethical principles. The principles carry equal weight and psychologists might sometimes identify several courses of action that can each be justified by a different principle (e.g., when they must decide whether to disclose clients' confidential information against their will [autonomy] to protect them [non-maleficence]). They might also find that the same principle requires them to behave in a manner that will affect people differently (e.g., reporting clients' threats to harm other prisoners could protect the targets, but harm those clients). Psychologists should, preferably in consultation with colleagues, analyze the information in their possession and decide which principle (or combination of principles) appears to provide the optimally right and good solution in the specific circumstances and should be applied.

Psychologists' knowledge of their profession's ethical principles might not always help them achieve certainty about moral issues because their personal values and the norms of other groups they belong to also influence their moral beliefs. People could therefore experience moral discomfort if they feel one or more sets of their external normative obligations require them to participate in, or accept, behavior that conflicts with their personal values or that another set of external norms requires of them. They might for example find that their organizational rules require them to violate the privacy of clients when their ethical principles and/ or personal values require them to protect their privacy. Psychologists confronting situations that cause them moral uncertainty should identify the reasons for this discomfort in consultation with objective and trustworthy senior colleagues.

Public Morality

The problem might be at the *public morality* level, in other words the composite and shared beliefs of the majority of members of a specific society regarding what is right and good behavior. Many psychologists follow their public mores as intuitively and unconsciously as they apply the grammar rules of their native languages. Public morality across societies appears to be grounded on a set of about five or six moral foundations, but societies differ in the relative weight they give to the different foundations and therefore some societies might differ from others regarding what they define as right and good behavior (Graham & Haidt, 2012). In societies where public morality and religion still overlap, the public mores will generally be well-defined and monistic (i.e., intolerant of other views). People in secular societies, in contrast, often hold pluralistic moral views and people from different socioeconomic and educational backgrounds may therefore differ from each other. Public morality in secular countries generally evolves over time in response to circumstances in their societies. The majority of people in many societies currently appear risk averse (Rose, 1998) and supportive of a strong ethic of care that leads them to accept, for example, indeterminate and mandatory sentences, while a minority of people appear to support policies based on an ethic of justice. Public morality can also change rapidly in response to changes in society, as has been happening during the twenty-first century in response to the increase in incidents of global terrorism. Secular societies also tolerate public debates allowing people to express opposing moral views, and these arguments might contribute to the uncertainty some psychologists experience about what they should do in their professional capacity. Psychologists in their professional capacity should, however, behave in accordance with their codes that summarize *psychology's morality* and usually reflect the public morality and law of the relevant jurisdiction. They must in particular obey the minimum behavioral standards of their codes if they do not want to face regulatory and/or legal sanctions.

Organizational Rules

Psychologists who feel unsure because they believe their *organizational rules* require them to violate the standards of their codes must clarify these conflicts and try to find constructive resolutions that will allow them to adhere to their professional obligations, or will minimize deviations from their professional obligations. They might need to involve professional bodies or unions in such negotiations.

Psychologists must always, subject to what I say below, adhere to the law and, when ordered to undertake tasks that appear to violate people's fundamental rights, such as their right to privacy, must ensure that the organization acts within the law and follows the correct legal process, such as obtaining the necessary warrants. Those who conclude their employers expect them to behave unlawfully should obtain legal advice and make their position clear to management in writing, and where appropriate use the legal remedies available to them, which I discuss below.

Psychologists might find it more difficult to change organizational norms and practices they find wrong, but can try to use their professional and personal status to bring about change while conforming with their legal, organizational, and professional obligations. Psychologists trying to change norms within organizations must particularly refrain from acting as advocates for a specific client, but they may use legitimate methods to try to bring about change for groups or classes of people. Some psychologists who fail to change their organizations might decide to leave; others might feel that they will abandon people who need their services by leaving and that it will be more useful for them remain while pursuing their aspirational professional and personal values as far as systems allow them. Psychologists should be guided by the non-maleficence principle when they make this decision and take the option that will minimize the risk of harm to them personally and to others close to them.

Law

Psychologists must follow clear legal directives because *law* reflects what society expects of them. Law, however, generally reflects society's minimum standards, and psychologists might find that their ethical principles require a higher standard of moral behavior from them than law does. Law in most countries, for instance, allows psychologists to engage in sexual relationships with former clients; the profession expects them to abstain from such relationships as long as those clients might be vulnerable and generally prohibits such relationships for a period after the professional contact has ended. Psychologists should always follow their aspirational ethical principles if they can do so within the spirit of the law, but they might sometimes conclude that their legal obligations require them to do something they consider contrary to their professional obligations and/or public morality.

Psychologists facing a conflict between their legal and professional obligations should recognize that psychology's morality reflects what the majority of psychologists consider right, good, and in the interest of people, while law reflects what society considers as important and therefore protects (for a discussion of this issue in medical ethics see Foster & Miola, 2015). Psychologists as individuals and collectives can in democratic societies use their constitutional rights to advocate for changes to the law, but meanwhile they must obey the law in their professional capacity.

Psychologists who believe their legal obligations deviate from public morality face an age-old problem, namely whether law can be immoral and, if it can be, who, especially in pluralistic societies, decides when this might be the case. Many lawyers and philosophers recognized this problem, and since the eighteenth century two broad schools of thought have developed. The natural law school's supporters argued that law can be immoral, but since most of them currently do not support the notion of divine law they find it difficult to identify an alternative universal set of moral obligations. Supporters of the positivist school said that judges and legislators must in their administration of law identify and apply public morality, but the behavior of judges in Nazi Germany prior to and during World War II demonstrates the weakness of this approach because they applied law that most people outside Germany considered wrong and bad.

The modern versions of these schools, while coming from different premises, nevertheless appear to accept that law should adhere to fundamental societal values. The set of values most Western lawyers accept can be traced back the set of rights lawyers started developing during the reformation to define the relationship between states and their citizens (Witte, 2007). This set of rights evolved over the years and became particularly prominent in the middle of the twentieth century after the atrocities prior to and during World War II. Modern authors refer to these values as human rights because they reflect states' obligation to respect the humanity of their citizens (for a more comprehensive discussion see, e.g., Allan, 2013; Corbin, 1919).

The United Nations' (UN, 1948) *Universal declaration of human rights* provides a description of these rights, but to accommodate cultural differences some countries developed regional human rights instruments. Many states ratified these declarations and other international human rights instruments, such as the UN's *Declaration on the protection of all persons from being subjected to torture and other cruel, inhuman or degrading treatment or punishment* (1975). This binds states, but citizens of member countries might be able to exercise them by using the UN's Human Rights Council complaint procedure[1] or that of similar regional organizations.

States can, however, give their citizens better remedies by incorporating these rights, or variations of them, into their constitutions and/or specific human rights legislation and/or their general legislation, thereby making them enforceable claim rights (Feinberg, 1973; Hohfeld, 1919). Citizens may therefore use their domestic legal systems to test the moral rightness of legislation and its application (for prisoners' position see Mackay, 2015). Citizens of states that adopted certain international or regional conventions might also be able to approach international tribunals. Many European countries, for example, adopted the *European convention on human rights* (Council of Europe, 1950) and by doing this they allow external bodies, in this case the European Court of Human Rights, to review their legislation and the judgments of their courts.

Personal Values

Many psychologists' moral uncertainty comes from their personal values (i.e., their evolving schemata and scripts regarding what constitutes right and good behavior). People's unique experiences, personalities, and learning, and external (e.g., cultural) influences shape their values and, though they mostly operate at an unconscious level, they influence people's automatic and deliberate decision-making (see, e.g., Haidt, 2001; Reynolds, 2006).

Psychologists must therefore first exclude the possibility that their absolutistic views might cause their unhappiness with their legal and/or organizational and/or professional obligations and that they might be trying to force their values onto others whose values, decisions, and behavior might be equally sound as theirs. They should preferably adopt Hinman's (2013) pluralistic principles to decide whether the behavior in question should be prohibited, tolerated, or adopted for the good of society. The *principle of fallibility* requires people to appreciate that even with the best of intentions their judgments might be flawed. They must therefore examine their own values for possible inadequacies and be open to learn from other people. The *principle of understanding* requires people to develop a full understanding and appreciation of the meaning of moral norms and values of other people before judging them. The *principle of tolerance* requires psychologists to accept the inevitability of moral differences among people and that as a rule people should be allowed to pursue their own morality. The principle of *standing up to evil*, however, requires psychologists to recognize that some behavior might be so wrong and/or bad that they should not tolerate it. Psychologists who feel entitled to advocate for changes that reflect their values can do so as members of professional bodies and/or as citizens of countries, but they must do so within the legal and profession regulatory framework to avoid sanctions.

Conclusion

Psychologists must accept that the plurality of values and norms that govern their professional behavior will sometimes cause them moral uncertainty. I argue that they should primarily look toward psychology's ethical principles for guidance, but I appreciate that psychologists whose personal values lean toward an ethic of care might feel that the responsibility principle forces them to adopt an ethic of justice (see Day, 2014). Psychologists working for government departments charged with the exercise of justice must accept this, but the other principles require them to meet their legal and organizational responsibilities in the most humane, benevolent, fair, and transparent way, while they respect prisoners' autonomy and avoid causing them unnecessary harm or betraying their trust. They must therefore try to find the balance between the principles in a way that optimizes the interests of prisoners and to ensure they remain objective and can, when necessary, stand up for what they consider to be right and good. This could be difficult for individuals and therefore psychologists should ideally become members of professional bodies and engage in ongoing supervision.

Acknowledgments

The author thanks Maria Allan, Sunny Gianatti, Crista McDaniel, and Christa Strauss for their comments on previous drafts of this chapter.

Note

1   See   http://www.ohchr.org/EN/HRBodies/HRC/ComplaintProcedure/Pages/HRCComplaint ProcedureIndex.aspx.

Key Readings

Allan, A. (2015). Ethics in psychology and law: An international perspective. *Ethics and Behavior*, 25, 443–457.

Haag, A. M. (2006). Ethical dilemmas faced by correctional psychologists in Canada. *Criminal Justice and Behavior*, 33, 93–109.

IACFP Practice Standards Committee (2010). Standards for psychology services in jails, prisons, correctional facilities, and agencies: International Association for Correctional and Forensic Psychology (formerly American Association for Correctional Psychology). *Criminal Justice and Behavior*, 37, 749–808.

Konrad, N., Völlm, B., & Weisstub, D. N. (Eds.) (2013). *Ethical issues in prison psychiatry* (Vol. 46). Dordrecht, the Netherlands: Springer.

References

Allan, A. (2010). Introduction. In A. Allan, & A. W. Love (Eds.), *Ethical practice in psychology: Reflections from the creators of the APS Code of Ethics* (pp. 1–11). Chichester, UK: Wiley.

Allan, A. (2011). The development of a code for Australian psychologists. *Ethics and Behavior*, 21, 435–451.

Allan, A. (2013). Are human rights redundant in the ethical codes of psychologists? *Ethics and Behavior*, 23, 251–265.

Allan, A. (2015). Ethics in psychology and law: An international perspective. *Ethics and Behavior*, 25, 443–457.

Allan, A. (2016). *An international perspective of law and ethics in psychology* (3rd ed.). Somerset West, South Africa: Inter-Ed.

Allan, A., & Allan, M. M. (2016). Psychologists' collection and management of clients' information: An ethico-legal perspective. *Psychiatry, Psychology and Law*.

Allan, A., & Davidson, G. R. (2013). Respect for the dignity of people: What does this principle mean in practice? *Australian Psychologist*, 48, 345–352.

Allan, A., Packman, W. L., Dear, G. E., O'Connor Pennuto, T., Orthwein, J., & Bongar, B. (2006). Ethical and legal issues for mental health professionals working with suicidal prisoners. In G. E. Dear (Ed.), *Preventing suicide and other self-harm in prison* (pp. 213–232). London, UK: Palgrave-Macmillan.

American Psychological Association (1953). *Ethical standards of psychologists*. Washington, DC: Author.

Andersen, M. B., Van Raalte, J. L., & Brewer, B. W. (2000). When sport psychology consultants and graduate students are impaired: Ethical and legal issues in training and supervision. *Journal of Applied Sport Psychology*, 12, 134–150.

Beijersbergen, K. A., Dirkzwager, A. J. E., Eichelsheim, V. I., van der Laan, P. H., & Nieuwbeerta, P. (2014). Procedural justice and prisoners' mental health problems: A longitudinal study. *Criminal Behaviour and Mental Health*, 24, 100–112.

Ewert v. Canada. (2018). SCC 30. Retrieved from https://scc-csc.lexum.com

Corbin, A. L. (1919). Legal analysis and terminology. *The Yale Law Journal*, 19, 163–173.

Cortina, L. M., Magley, V. J., Williams, J. H., & Langhout, R. D. (2001). Incivility in the workplace: Incidence and impact. *Journal of Occupational Health Psychology*, 6, 64–80.

Council of Europe. (1950). European convention on human rights. Retrieved from http://www.echr.coe.int/Documents/Convention_ENG.pdf

Day, A. (2014). Competing ethical paradigms in forensic psychiatry and forensic psychology: Commentary for a special section of legal and criminological psychology. *Legal and Criminological Psychology*, 19, 16–18.

Feinberg, J. (1973). *Social philosophy*. New York, NY: Prentice Hall.

Foster, C., & Miola, J. (2015). Who's in charge? The relationship between medical law, medical ethics, and medical morality? *Medical Law Review*, 23, 505–530.

Gauthier, J., Pettifor, J., & Ferrero, A. (2010). The universal declaration of ethical principles for psychologists: A culture-sensitive model for creating and reviewing a code of ethics. *Ethics and Behavior*, 20, 179–196.

Graham, J., & Haidt, J. (2012). Sacred values and evil adversaries: A moral foundations approach. In M. Mikulincer, & P. R. Shaver (Eds.), *The social psychology of morality: Exploring the causes of good and evil* (pp. 11–31). Washington, DC: American Psychological Association.

Greenberg, L. R., & Gould, J. W. (2001). The treating expert: A hybrid role with firm boundaries. *Professional Psychology: Research and Practice*, 32, 469–478.

Greenberg, S. A., & Shuman, D. W. (1997). Irreconcilable conflict between therapeutic and forensic roles. *Professional Psychology: Research and Practice*, 28, 50–57.

Greenberg, S. A., & Shuman, D. W. (2007). When worlds collide: Therapeutic and forensic roles. *Professional Psychology: Research and Practice*, 38, 129–132.

Haidt, J. (2001). The emotional dog and its rational tail: A social intuitional approach to moral judgment. *Psychological Review*, 108, 814–834.

Her Majesty's Inspectorate of Probation. (2006). An independent review of a serious further offence case: Anthony Rice. Retrived from http://news.bbc.co.uk/2/shared/bsp/hi/pdfs/10_05_06_probation.pdf.

Hinman, L. M. (2013). *Ethics: A pluralistic approach to moral theory*. Boston, MA: Wadsworth.

Hohfeld, W. N. (Ed.) (1919). *Fundamental legal conceptions as applied in judicial reasoning: And other legal essays*. New Haven, CT: Yale University Press Retrieved from http://archive.org/details/fundamentallegal00hohfuoft

IACFP Practice Standards Committee (2010). Standards for psychology services in jails, prisons, correctional facilities, and agencies: International Association for Correctional and Forensic Psychology (formerly American Association for Correctional Psychology). *Criminal Justice and Behavior*, 37, 749–808.

Inmate Welfare Committee, William Head Institution v. Canada. (2003). FC 870. Retrieved from https://www.canlii.org/en/ca/fct/doc/2003/2003fc870/2003fc870.html?resultIndex=1

Kant, I. (1785/2001). Fundamental principles of the metaphysics of morals. In A. W. Wood (Ed.), *Basic writings of Kant* (pp. 143–221). New York, NY: The Modern Library.

Lim, S., & Cortina, L. M. (2005). Interpersonal mistreatment in the workplace: The interface and impact of general incivility and sexual harassment. *Journal of Applied Psychology*, 90, 483–496.

Lim, S., Cortina, L. M., & Magley, V. J. (2008). Personal and workgroup incivility: Impact on work and health outcomes. *Journal of Applied Psychology*, 93, 95–107.

Mackay, A. (2015). Human rights protections for people with mental health and cognitive disability in prisons. *Psychiatry, Psychology and Law*, 22, 842–868.

Reynolds, S. J. (2006). A neurocognitive model of the ethical decision-making process: Impliciations for study and practice. *Journal of Applied Psychology*, 91, 737–748.

Rose, N. (1998). Governing risky individuals: The role of psychiatry in new regimes of control. *Psychiatry, Psychology and Law*, 5, 117–195.

Ryan, R. M., & Deci, E. L. (2000). Self-determination theory and the facilitation of intrinsic motivation, social development, and well-being. *American Psychologist*, 55, 68–78.

Simpson, D. P. (1971). *Cassell's new Latin-English dictionary* (5th ed.). London, UK: Cassell.

Taylor, P. J., Graf, M., Schanda, H., & Völlm, B. (2012). The treating psychiatrist as expert in the courts: Is it necessary or possible to separate the roles of physician and expert? *Criminal Behaviour and Mental Health*, 22, 271–292.

United Nations (1948). *Universal declaration of human rights*. New York, NY: Author Retrieved from http://www.ohchr.org/EN/UDHR/Pages/Introduction.aspx

United Nations. (1975). *Declaration on the protection of all persons from being subjected to torture and other cruel, inhuman or degrading treatment or punishment adopted by General Assembly resolution 3452 (XXX) of 9 December 1975.* Retrieved from http://www.cirp.org/library/ethics/UN-torture

Wackenheim v. France, Communication No 854/1999, U.N. Doc. CCPR/C/75/D/854/1999. (2002). Retrieved from http://www1.umn.edu/humanrts/undocs/854-1999.html

Weinberger, L. E., & Sreenivasan, S. (1994). Ethical and professional conflicts in correctional psychology. *Professional Psychology: Research and Practice, 25,* 161–167.

Witte, J. (2007). *The reformation of rights: Law, religion and human rights in early modern Calvinism.* Cambridge, UK: Cambridge University Press.

3

The American Psychological Association's Misuse of the Role of Psychologist-as-Organizational-Consultant to Torture: Where Was the "Bright Line" Position?

Astrid Birgden

Deakin University, Australia

The correctional psychologist has a dual role as organizational consultant and service provider (see Birgden & Perlin, 2009). The psychologist-as-organizational-consultant ordinarily promotes appropriate staff selection and development, a safe and humane correctional environment, and a positive organizational culture. The psychologist-as-treatment-provider ordinarily delivers offender assessment (of mental health, risk of reoffending, treatment needs, parole eligibility, and malingering), treatment (of substance abuse, sexual and violent offending, antisocial values and attitudes, and suicide prevention), and management (of case coordination, responding to institutional violence and sexual assault, and crisis intervention). As detailed in the American Psychological Association's[3] (APA) Ethics Code (APA, 2010a), the psychologist follows ethical principles of: beneficence (safeguarding welfare and rights) and non-maleficence (doing no harm); justice (not engaging in unjust practices); respect for rights and dignity (respecting privacy, confidentiality, and autonomy and not supporting prejudice by others); integrity (applying evidence-based techniques); and fidelity and responsibility (establishing trusting relationships with both individuals and the community and managing conflicts of interest that may result in harm). The focus of this chapter will primarily be on fidelity and responsibility, particularly in avoiding a conflict of interest. From a human rights perspective, while offenders are rights-violators they are also rights-holders, and therefore there is an imperative for the psychologist to act as a duty-bearer in ensuring that offenders' dignity, respect, and autonomy are upheld at all times (Ward & Birgden, 2007a, 2007b).

In correctional services, psychologists are placed in a difficult position in which they must balance community and offender rights, while being part of an organization that engages in punishment (Ward & Birgden, 2007a). If the punishment is justifiably proportionate to the crime and protected by due process in law, and the correctional psychologist does not "add" to the punishment, then the ethical application of the dual role is not compromised. A report

The Wiley International Handbook of Correctional Psychology, First Edition. Edited by Devon L. L. Polaschek, Andrew Day, and Clive R. Hollin.
© 2019 John Wiley & Sons Ltd. Published 2019 by John Wiley & Sons Ltd.

regarding the mistreatment of offenders with mental disability in US jails and prisons by correctional staff (Human Rights Watch, 2015) detailed a litany of actions that were unjustifiable, such as neglect or "deliberate indifference," inadequate treatment, inappropriate institutional responses to rule-breaking and disciplinary systems, and the use of solitary confinement (and limited caged exercise), physical force and cell extractions, physical and mechanical restraint, and chemical agents and stun devices, and retaliatory and abusive cultures (e.g., Rikers Island, NY, and Orleans Parish Prison, NOLA). While an offender may threaten harm to self and others, under the US constitution and international human rights law, force cannot be applied unless as a last resort, and never as punishment (Human Rights Watch, 2015). This means that if a psychologist engages in, directs, supports, facilitates, trains, consults, or ignores unjustifiable acts, their actions (or inaction) would be unethical. If the organization places unethical expectations on the psychologist, protests may be seen to be "whistle blowing," and so compromising the career path. In this scenario, it would be expected that the APA acts as a protective mechanism to support ethical practice by its members.

This chapter provides a case example of where the APA, together with the US Department of Defense (DoD) and the Central Intelligence Agency (CIA), endorsed unethical expectations of psychologists who were working as organizational consultants. However, this example has implications for correctional psychology more broadly. The history dates back to 2002 when, based on legal advice provided by the US Office of Legal Counsel, President Bush adopted a position in 2003 that prohibition on torture did not apply to a President during wartime, meaning that US domestic policy was considered outside the reach of international human rights law.[4] The legal Yoo/Bybee memos,[5] determined that interrogations that were "cruel, inhuman or degrading" (including biological experimentation) should *not* be considered torture and were *not* forbidden if used against non-US citizen detainees outside of the United States (e.g., Guantanamo Bay in Cuba). US military psychologists were subsequently supported by the APA in applying "enhanced interrogation techniques" (or torture) subsequent to the events of September 11, 2001, and the ongoing "Global War on Terrorism" and were disengaged from the role of psychologist-as-treatment-provider. As human rights principles were not upheld by the APA in support of either role, this could be understood as a slide down a slippery ethical slope (Opotow, 2007).

US military psychologists were engaged in interviewing detainees. Rather than applying sophisticated psychological techniques in building rapport and establishing a trustworthy relationship, enhanced interrogation techniques were reverse engineered versions of a Survival, Evasion, Resistance, Escape (SERE) technique, originally designed to help US prisoners-of-war to withstand torture. These techniques included waterboarding, "walling," forced stress positions, and the deliberate deprivation of necessities such as sleep and warmth. As is now known, these techniques were illegally applied in detention centers in Guantanamo Bay Naval Base in Cuba, Abu Ghraib Prison in Iraq, Bagram Airbase in Afghanistan, and "black sites" operated by the CIA in Europe and elsewhere. Supported by the DoD and the CIA, enhanced interrogation techniques were specifically designed to break the will of the detainee and provide intelligence information (Hoffman et al., 2015). As a consequence, the use of such techniques resulted in serious violations of the human rights of non-US citizen detainees outside of the domestic criminal justice system. Acting disingenuously, the APA leadership enabled these violations by making misleading public pronouncements that the APA's tight ethical guidelines in theory would prevent torture, while ensuring its loose guidelines in practice allowed psychologists to engage in torture without fear of violating the APA Ethics Code (Hoffman et al., 2015). The APA ought to have guided the profession in ensuring international human rights law obligations were met.

The Hoffman Report

In 2014, the APA contracted Sidley Austin LLP to conduct an independent review of the allegations that the APA allowed psychologists to participate in enhanced interrogation techniques. This review of 50,000 documents included interviews and access to meeting minutes and e-mail correspondence and became known as the Hoffman Report (Hoffman et al., 2015). The 547-page report was subsequently accepted by the APA and was made public on its website in July 2015.[6] In sum, the Hoffman Report found that:

- there was collusion between key APA officials and DoD officials in order to adopt and maintain APA ethical guidelines that did not restrict DoD policies and procedures;
- the extent and nature of this collaborative relationship was kept secret by Behnke (Director, APA Ethics Committee), others who worked with him, and members of the APA Task Force;
- the collaboration could "easily" be described as improper and dishonest.

Most notably, the investigators noted that:

We found little evidence of analyses or discussions about the best or right ethical position to take in light of the nature of the profession and the special skill that psychologists possess regarding how our minds and emotions work—a special skill that presumably allows psychologists to be especially good at both healing and harming … Although APA officials insisted at the time, and for years after, that all their actions were based on independent ethics and policy judgments about how to provide appropriate ethical guidance for psychologists who worked in this area, we found that this was not the case. (Hoffman et al., 2015, p. 11)

and

We have heard from psychologists who treat patients for a living that they feel physically sick when they think about the involvement of psychologists intentionally using harsh interrogation techniques … The prospect of a member of their profession using that same training and skill to intentionally cause psychological or physical harm to a detainee sickens them. We find that perspective understandable. (Hoffman et al., 2015, p. 70)

Hoffman et al. (2015) explored in detail the issues regarding the APA's relationship with the military, revision of the Ethics Code (2002), the Presidential Task Force on Psychological Ethics and National Security (PENS) Report (APA, 2005), and the subsequent APA handling of ethics complaints against military psychologists. While stopping short of stating that the APA had enabled torture (although Elkin, 2016, has argued that the APA did enable torture), broadly the conclusions of the Hoffman Report regarding the APA leadership were as follows:

- The APA's principal motives were to "curry favor" with the DoD with the aims to: (a) create a good public relations response to negative media coverage that expressed concern about ethical issues by establishing an unequivocal position which supported the DoD position; and (b) keep the growth of psychology unrestrained by supporting rather than restricting military psychologists (and not lose these lead roles to psychiatrists). Conflicts of interest regarding personal relationships between DoD and APA staff were virtually ignored.[7]

- Key APA officials (principally Behnke) colluded with important DoD officials (principally Banks, Army Colonel) to have the APA issue loose, high-level ethical guidelines that did not constrain the DoD within its existing interrogation guidelines. APA officials ought to have had strong suspicions about enhanced interrogation techniques but were substantially indifferent to potentially abusive interrogation techniques; described as an "ostrich" defense.
- The revision of the APA Ethics Code in 2002 was not influenced by APA attempts to assist the government's interrogation efforts, but the potential problem of the Nuremberg defense—"I was just following orders"—was ignored.
- The close and collaborative relationship with the DoD influenced the composition of the PENS Task Force, key ethical statements in the PENS Report, and subsequent public APA statements and policies.
- APA officials, principally Behnke, engaged in secret collaboration with DoD officials to defeat efforts by the APA Council of Representatives[8] to introduce and pass resolutions (see below) that would have definitively prohibited psychologists from participating in interrogations.
- The handling of the ethics complaints against prominent military psychologists had been improperly managed with a focus on protection from censure (this concerning issue will not be detailed in this chapter).

APA leaders subsequently apologized for colluding with the DoD and the CIA to issue guidelines that supported torture (APA, 2015a) and wrote to the international psychology community outlining the steps taken to address the issues raised in the Hoffman Report (APA, 2015b).

The Timeline of Events

Some of the information provided in this chapter has relied upon the APA timeline,[9] which commences with a Joint Statement with the American Psychiatric Association Condemning Torture in 1985. However, in light of the Hoffman Report, the APA timeline is considered biased and therefore it is supplemented with information provided by the Coalition for an Ethical Psychology.[10] As the information is detailed and complex, it has been divided sequentially into three interrelated phases that commenced with changes to the APA Ethics Code, followed by the PENS Report, and culminated in ethically minded psychologists redressing the imbalance.

Phase 1: The APA Ethics Code

The revision of the APA Ethics Code set the scene for a slide down a slippery ethical slope. In 2002, the APA Council of Representatives accepted revision of the Ethics Code (effective June 1, 2003) that included permitting psychologists to follow law (adding regulations or other governing legal authority) even when these conflicted with ethical obligations. Ethical Standard 1.02 was revised to address a perceived conflict between ethics and law, but for the first time, an unresolvable conflict would allow the psychologist to follow workplace obligations over professional ethical obligations. This revision was in response to forensic and clinical psychologists receiving subpoenas, and military and correctional psychologists being ordered to disclose confidential patient records (Hoffman et al., 2015). However, both revisions immediately raised ethical concerns among psychologists regarding a loophole to engage in torture and avoid ethical sanctions. Nonetheless, Hoffman could not conclude that these changes were the result of governmental collusion.

But there were still pertinent problems. In 2005, the APA Council of Representatives directed that the APA Ethics Committee explore adding language to the APA Ethics Code consistent with basic principles of human rights, but the Ethics Committee rejected this request and "Behnke engaged in a wide variety of actions to intentionally delay and obstruct efforts to amend 1.02 [as it] was of importance to national security psychologists" (Hoffman et al., 2015, p. 42). The Ethics Committee was also asked to produce an ethics casebook that Behnke had promised the PENS Task Force in 2005 would be completed within 4–6 months (Hoffman et al., 2015). It was not until 2011 that a 30-page document was produced, providing links to eight policy documents, although by 2016 this was no longer available and rendered out-of-date and invalid.[11] To the investigators, Behnke indicated that he had not developed the ethics casebook because yearly resolutions from 2006 by the APA Council of Representatives (see below) had provided the necessary guidance; but in contrast, an e-mail from Behnke in January 2011 indicated that he planned: "To post this text quietly, very quietly, on the Ethics webpage" (Hoffman et al., 2015, p. 41). Hoffman opined that there was never a real desire to create an ethics casebook, because it would require the same specificity successfully avoided in the PENS Report.

In a petition referendum at the 2008 APA Annual Conference (see below), it was requested that identified changes be included in the APA Ethics Code, especially 1.02 (APA Presidential Advisory Group, 2008). In 2009, the APA Council of Representatives directed a change and the APA finally amended the APA Ethics Code to state that "Under no circumstances may this standard be used to justify or defend violating human rights," effective June 1, 2010 (APA, 2010b). Prior to this, "in keeping with basic human rights" was an aspirational introduction, absent within the enforceable section of the Ethics Code. The amendments occurred 8 years after the initial revision of the Ethics Code.

Phase 2: The APA PENS Report

A key aid to the slide down a slippery ethical slope was the APA PENS Report (APA, 2005) that allowed US domestic law, US community rights, and psychologist-as-organizational-consultant to trump international human rights law, detainee rights, and psychologist-as-treatment-provider (Birgden & Perlin, 2009). At this time, concern raised by human rights organizations as early as 2002 was being corroborated by researchers, government reports, and legal briefs. While there were "clear and strong indications that such abuse had in fact occurred … based on strategic goals the APA intentionally decided not to make enquiries or express concern … thus effectively hiding its head in the sand" (Hoffman et al., 2015, p. 11). The PENS Task Force was suggested by Koocher (then APA President) and was formed in response to a 2004 *New York Times* article by Lewis (2004) and "as reaction to the threat that a pro-human-rights division in APA would push for an aggressive resolution in the Council of Representatives that would likely be very negative for DoD and intelligence psychologists" (Hoffman et al., 2015, p. 17). The PENS Task Force was to explore the ethical aspects of psychologists' involvement in national security-related investigations (Soldz et al., 2015).

Unusually, the identity of the PENS Task Force members was withheld from APA members, but Hoffman et al. (2015) provided the definitive list as follows: Moorehead-Slaughter (the non-voting chair who was found to have taken direction from the DoD psychologists), Behnke, six military/DoD psychologists (Banks, Schumate, James, Gelles, Lefever, and Fein), two military "observers" (Newman and Gravitz), only three non-military psychologists (Thomas, Arrigo,[12] and Wessells), APA observers (Mumford, Kelly, and Brandon), and Koocher as a Board liaison member. Koocher was described as taking aggressive positions[13] against the three non-DoD members when they queried whether psychologists could ethically support interrogations, raised the Geneva Convention and other international law, and requested specificity regarding permissible interrogation techniques. Arrigo's suggestion to include the American Medical Association's medical ethicist on the Task Force was rejected (Hoffman et al., 2015). The Task Force members are listed here as the majority of them are identified in analysis in other parts of this chapter.

Of most concern, the "E for ethics" in the PENS Report was virtually ignored. The composition of the PENS Task Force, the content of the PENS Report (APA, 2005), and the APA's adoption of its policy, public communication, and response to valid criticisms were never based on ethical analysis (Elkin, 2016; Hoffman et al., 2015). The PENS Task Force consisted of members with military experience rather than academics equipped to critically analyze the evidence and/or ethicists to debate the moral issues: "The question of whether psychologist participation in interrogations was ethical was never seriously discussed by the task force" (Soldz, 2008, p. 600).

As noted by Birgden and Perlin (2009), while the PENS Report (APA, 2005) recommended that "psychologists do not engage in, direct, support, facilitate, or offer training in torture or other cruel, inhuman, or degrading treatment" (p. 1) and "psychologists are alert to acts of torture and other cruel, inhuman, or degrading treatment and have an ethical responsibility to report these acts to the appropriate authorities" (p. 4), it was also considered "… consistent with the APA Ethics Code for psychologists to serve in consultative roles to interrogation and information-gathering processes for national security-related purposes, as psychologists have a long-standing tradition of doing in other law enforcement contexts" (p. 1). In effect, the PENS Report recommended that psychologist-as-organizational-consultant to interrogators (deemed appropriate) be demarcated from psychologist-as-treatment-provider to detainees (deemed inappropriate). Acknowledging that engaging in such consultative and advisory roles entailed a delicate balance of ethical considerations, the PENS Report argued that psychologists were in a unique position to assist in ensuring that these processes were safe, legal, ethical, and effective; oft repeated wording directly mirroring DoD military documents that had been initially devised by Colonel Banks as a key military liaison (Hoffman et al., 2015). To the *New York Times* journalist (Lewis, 2006), Behnke indicated that psychologists made an important contribution against terrorism. A year later the APA argued to the US Select Committee on Intelligence that psychologists had an important contribution to make in eliciting information to protect national security by building rapport and relationships (APA, 2007). Crucially, consensus was not reached within the PENS Task Force on whether international human rights law or domestic US law prevailed. Note that the APA is a UN-accredited non-government organization (NGO) and so is bound to honor international law (Altman, 2008). Without irony, an APA press release indicated that as "an association dedicated to human welfare and an UN-accredited NGO, the APA has long held a clear and unequivocal position on human rights, which applies to the treatment of detainees" (APA, 2009a). As the policy shift toward detainee rights only commenced in 2009, one wonders whether the APA ought to have been stripped of its NGO status for failing to honor international law, as required.

Once the PENS Report (APA, 2005) was completed, the APA Board of Directors convened an emergency session to make it official APA policy. Ordinarily the APA Council of Representatives formally endorsed policy, and it was falsely claimed that the APA Council of Representatives had done so (Pope, 2011). Hoffman et al. (2015) concluded that this urgency was in order to produce a press release setting forth strict ethical guidelines for participation in interrogations— to manage public relations and to curry favor so the DoD could promptly use the report for its own purposes. When reading the Hoffman Report, it becomes evident that there was an extremely close working relationship between APA members and the military; "the APA must end its affair with the US military ... stand on its own feet as an association dedicated to human rights" (Elkin, 2016, p. 106).

In my opinion, the relationship could have been described as a "military-psychology complex."[14] The ethical violation was that the APA leadership treated the military as its client and the detainees as a means to its own ends. APA leaders appeared to have been captured by a sense of retribution at the time, where the efficacy of interrogation became subordinate to revenge, humiliation, and punishment (Janoff-Bulman, 2007), described as a morally corrupt position (Soldz, 2008). In stark contrast, the American Psychiatric Association (2006) had unambiguously banned participation and consultation of their members. This ban then meant that the DoD preferred psychologists over psychiatrists (Hoffman et al., 2015). Meanwhile, that the APA was "violating human rights and sidestepping international and national laws and professional ethics will be remembered as wrong in the harsher light of time" (Opotow, 2007, p. 460) and a "bright line" position forbidding psychologists (Olson & Soldz, 2007) was long overdue.

Phase 3: Redressing the Ethical Imbalance

After the release of the PENS Report (APA, 2005), critics within the APA membership acted to redress the imbalance away from community rights and psychologist-as-organizational consultant and toward detainee rights and psychologist-as-treatment-provider (see Olson & Soldz, 2007; Olson, Soldz, & Davis, 2008; Pope, 2011; Soldz, 2008, 2009; Soldz et al., 2015; Tolin & Lohr, 2009). Between 2005 until 2008, the APA Council of Representatives put forward resolutions at each APA Annual Convention attempting to ban psychologists from participating in interrogations in US detention centers, with active thwarting from the APA leadership. In a nutshell, critics of the APA leadership were of the view that:

> APA's refusal to strictly limit—if not prohibit—the involvement of psychologists in national security interrogations on ethical grounds created an indelible stain on the entire profession, and a warped and improper definition of what it means to be a psychologist. (Hoffman et al., 2015, p. 4)

Information summarized in Table 3.1 shows that between 2005 and 2008 resolutions were tabled yearly by some APA members, with the APA leadership either responding to or ignoring the resolutions.

In the heated debate prior to the member vote in 2008, Resnick (ex-APA President) argued against the resolution as too broad in its definition. He argued that it harmed vulnerable populations and placed ethical psychologists at risk by prohibiting them from working in settings inconsistent with international law and the US Constitution, such as jails and prisons, psychiatric hospitals, and forensic units[15] (APA, 2008). An alternative viewpoint is that psychologists

Table 3.1 APA Member Resolutions and Outcomes

Tabled resolution	APA response	Outcome
2005		
That any departure from the APA Ethics Code, under direction of authority, is to be in accordance with "basic human rights."	No response.	No change.
2006		
That psychologists should not engage in cruel/inhumane treatment/punishment and should report unethical acts.	Issued a press release reaffirming the Joint Statement with the American Psychiatric Association Condemning Torture 1985 document regarding an "unequivocal position" against torture and abuse.	Did not define "cruel/ inhumane," did not exempt "pain & suffering" from sanction if not causing lasting harm, only expressed "grave concern" if human rights were violated rather than "prohibition," and it remained unresolved whether domestic and international law, or ethics and law, conflicted.
2007		
That there be an "absolute prohibition" of torture/ interrogation.	APA Council of Representatives rejected an outright ban but prevented hooding, forced nakedness, stress positions, dogs, and so on but only if this caused significant pain and suffering or lasting harm.	Reflects Yoo/Bybee memos' language (see below). The conflict between ethics and law remained unresolved. Meanwhile, the Coalition for an Ethical Psychology was formed to ensure the independence of psychological ethics from government and other vested interests, combining research with activism.[a]
2008		
That psychologists be prohibited from any techniques considered torture as defined in international law and psychologists were not to work in settings where the detainee was outside the protection of international or US law (i.e., unethical use of psychologist-as-organizational-consultant).	This resolution was a "petition resolution"[b] and required members to vote for the first time in the APA's 120-year history (Hoffman et al., 2015).	The resolution was supported. Of 150,000 members, 14,949 (10%) voted, of whom 6,157 (41%) did not support protecting the human rights of detainees. Of concern was that the word "unlawful" was inserted and the word "ethical" was absent. The ethical conflict in the APA Ethics Code therefore remained.

[a] See http://ethicalpsychology.org.
[b] The complete petition resolution can be found at: http://www.apa.org/news/press/statements/work-settings. aspx.

may work in such settings as long as they engage in ethical behaviors as finally resolved by the APA in 2014 (see below).

The APA leadership notified members that President Bush had been informed that, since the APA had become aware that there had been credible reports of torture and cruel, inhuman, or degrading treatment and punishment of detainees, there had been a "significant" change in policy that limited the roles of psychologists in certain unlawful detention settings where human rights were being violated (APA, 2008). Psychologists would now ostensibly be limited to working directly for detainees, working for an independent third party protecting human rights, or providing treatment to military personnel (i.e., psychologist-as-treatment-provider). However, this stance continued to be unenforceable in the APA Ethics Code (Pope, 2011). APA staff noted that since the word "ethics" was absent, it suggested no consequences for violating the policy, and e-mail correspondence between a DoD psychologist (James) and the DoD group noted that "… victory had been achieved and the resolution would have no practical effect, because the word 'unlawful' had been inserted … James said [to us] with some pride that the 'other side' simply hadn't done its homework" (Hoffman et al., 2015, pp. 43–44). However, as we now know, the actions of military psychologists were unlawful.

The 2008 resolution had still not been enforced by the APA leadership, as noted by the UN Special Rapporteur on Torture (Tolin & Lohr, 2009), and the Council of Representatives had voted to suspend the rule that the resolution was to be endorsed at the following Annual Conference (Faberman, 2009). Despite statements from the APA Board of Directors that information had emerged on the public record that some psychologists were not committed to ensuring that interrogations were safe and ethical and the role of such psychologists was "reprehensible" and "cast a shadow" over the profession (APA, 2009b), psychologists as behavioral science experts were part of the High-Value Detainee Interrogation Group (Department of Defense, 2013).

An open letter to the APA in June 2009 from the Coalition for an Ethical Psychology, Psychologists for Social Responsibility, Amnesty International USA, Physicians for Human Rights, and other organizations highlighted the APA's:

> Grievous mismanagement [in] providing ethical cover for psychologists' participation in detainee abuse [and the unacceptable minimization of] the greatest ethical crisis in our profession's history [placing a] terrible stain on the reputation of American psychology. (Soldz, 2009, pp. 1–2)

Among other things, the open letter requested that the 2008 resolution be fully implemented as an enforceable section of the APA Ethics Code and that section 1.02 of the APA Ethics Code be removed to disallow the "Nuremberg Defense" and the PENS Report be entirely annulled. Finally, in 2014, almost a decade after the PENS Report was produced, ethical guidance for the military-psychology complex, underpinned by international human rights law, was adopted. A further vote in 2015, led by Division 32, banned APA members from participating in military and national security interrogations altogether (Elkin, 2016).

The Ethical Debate: Lessons for Correctional Psychologists

Because of the dual role that the correctional psychologist experiences in managing the fine balance between offender and community rights within the organization, awareness of the intersection between politics, law, and psychology is necessary. In this instance, the uncritical APA policy response to the sociopolitical environment ultimately resulted in support for torture. The Hoffman Report sheds light on the APA's resounding failure to ethically balance the dual role of psychologist-as-organizational-consultant (for the US community) and psychologist-as-treatment-provider (for detainees); fidelity and responsibility is required in both roles. Indeed, in an ethics opinion piece in 2002, Gravitz (PENS Task Force observer and CIA contractor) opined "that one of the Ethics Code's stated goals is 'the protection of the individuals and groups with whom psychologists work, the latter including the national interest'" (Hoffman et al., 2015, p. 50). It is worth, then, considering each of these roles in more detail, and how they may apply to correctional psychologists.

Psychologist-as-Organizational-Consultant

Psychologists-as-organizational-consultants chaired Behavioral Science Consultation Teams (BSCTs or "biscuits") in developing and teaching interrogation strategies. Concerns about the role of military psychologists in the use of snarling dogs, nudity, forced standing, sleep deprivation, pornography, and so on were originally raised by the International Committee of the Red Cross in 2004 (see Pope, 2011). A CIA declassified document subsequently indicated that military psychologists were involved in "breaking detainees down," while simultaneously providing assurances that techniques such as waterboarding were not causing lasting psychological harm, and that psychologists were not providing support for illegal interrogations (Pope, 2011). In 2014, the US Senate Select Committee on Intelligence found that two clinical psychologists (Mitchell and Jessen) had aided the CIA in initiating a program of "brutal" interrogation techniques that violated US values, law, and treaty obligations. Neither psychologist had experience in conducting interrogations, specialized knowledge of al-Qa'ida, a background in counter-terrorism, or any relevant cultural or linguistic expertise (Council on Foreign Relations, 2014). In addition to the violation of fidelity and responsibility, these practices also appeared to have infringed upon the remaining ethical principles in terms of do good but do no harm, apply an evidence base, be competent, and respect the rights and dignity of the detainees regarding race, ethnicity, culture, national origin, religion, and so on.

In the eyes of the APA, the role of the psychologist-as-organizational-consultant was to monitor the safety of the interrogator as well as assist with the implementation of effective interrogation techniques (Hoffman et al., 2015). When visiting Guantanamo Bay, Levant (APA President) issued a press release and was quoted as saying that the APA would:

> ...continue to provide our expertise and guidance for how psychologists can play an appropriate and ethical role in national security investigations ... ensure that psychologists add value and safeguards to such investigations ... that protects the safety of all involved. (Soldz, 2006)

Likewise, in 2008, Kazdin (APA President) and Anderson (APA Chief Executive Officer) informed the US Attorney-General and others that military psychologists could promote effective and ethical interrogation techniques to prevent acts of violence as well as safeguard the welfare of interrogators and detainees (APA, 2008). Despite mounting evidence that psychologists had participated in torture at Guantanamo Bay and elsewhere, and in an attempt to distinguish psychologists from other professions, Behnke (2006), Director of the APA Ethics Committee, stated that the:

APA frames a role that psychologists have unique training to fill: the role of observing interrogations in order to guard against "behavioral drift" on the part of interrogators. Behavioral drift, which may arise in high stress situations where there is insufficient ethical guidance or oversight, involves a deviation from professionally and ethically acceptable behavior and so may lead to coercive interrogation techniques. Psychologists, as experts in human behavior, are trained to observe and intervene to prevent behavioral drift. (p. 67)

Psychologist-as-Treatment-Provider

In contrast, the APA gave very little consideration to psychologist-as-treatment-provider as the detainee was not considered to be the "client." For example, PENS Task Force members discussed the client as the interrogator, national security agencies, and the government, and that detainee rights were subordinate to that of national security (Hoffman et al., 2015). Shockingly, Koocher commented on the PENS Task Force listserv that "… the goal of such psychologists' work will ultimately be the protection of others (i.e., innocents) by contributing to the incarceration, debilitation, or even death of the potential perpetrator, who will often remain unaware of the psychologists' involvement."[16] Correctional psychologists could find themselves in a similar position, where their client is the organization and there is an expectation that community protection and staff safety will override offender rights.

A PENS ethical guideline referred to Standard 3.04 (Avoiding Harm), which also applied to detainees. However, because physical and psychological distress was not equated to "harm," the guideline lacked specificity and was unenforceable, and so did not serve alone to protect detainees from harm (Hoffman et al., 2015). In contrast, do no harm was a central focus of the American Psychiatric Association (2006) policy position on torture.

Conclusion

APA leaders showed little interest in preventing behavioral drift in psychologists and other military personnel toward torture. In an interview with the investigators, one of the psychologists who had initiated the program of "brutal" interrogation techniques (Mitchell) stated that he believed that his actions were ethical because he was giving less weight to the potential harm to the detainee in order to gather information to prevent a terrorist attack against the potential harm to the community caused by a terrorist attack (Hoffman et al., 2015). The APA failed to adequately balance two important values in its response: the need to assist the government to obtain important intelligence information regarding future threats to the US community, and not intentionally causing physical or psychological harm to detainees in custody outside the US criminal justice system (Hoffman et al., 2015). That is, the psychologist-as-organizational-consultant and psychologist-as-treatment-provider balance. As we now know, the role of the psychologist in such an ethically charged sociopolitical context is a very difficult one to balance, and with a weighting toward the US community by APA leaders, harm was inevitably inflicted upon detainees. In effect, the APA supported US community rights by trumping detainee rights and used detainees as a means to meet the APA's ends for funding and kudos: clearly an unethical position. The APA prioritized the protection of psychologists (including those who engaged in unethical behavior) over the protection of the universal community; described as "third-party beneficence" by Hoffman et al. (2015).

In debating the PENS Report, the non-military APA Task Force member (Wessell) argued that it was important for the APA to go beyond the narrow US government definitions of torture in setting ethical guidelines for psychologists:

> What kind of damage [will be done] to APA if we say we do not support human rights as defined in the Geneva Conventions and other conventions? What about [the] damage to our national security? If we engage in human rights violations, the message that sends to other countries [is damaging to our national security]. They therefore become our enemies and attack ... The standards [on international human rights] are not an issue for debate at this point ... [The] APA Code commits us to human rights. Does American law trump international law? As a professional society, do we have commitments in [the] human rights direction? If we aspire to these things, can we throw international human rights away? APA is diverse but the diversity is not represented here ... We would damage ourselves as an association if we support American law when it contradicts international law. DoD has defined a set of standards not congruent with international law. If we endorse that, we damage our credibility ... As a professional association, at a moment of national panic, [we must] take a high standard. (Hoffman et al., 2015, pp. 22–23)

What has this example of a slippery slope into unethical professional behavior got to do with the role of correctional psychologists? A psychologist may be pressured by the organization to engage in practices that violate the APA Ethics Code, in inflicting physical or psychological harm to an offender in the quest to meet organizational requirements for safety and community protection (i.e., the organization is the client and the offender is a means to an ends). The psychologist will have to choose between ethical action (refusing to comply and reporting) or unethical inaction (complying and failing to report). Coyle (2008) correctly observed that the "need to operate within an ethical context is universal and is also one of the defining features of good prison management" (p. 4). To reiterate, just because an individual is an offender does not mean that his or her basic dignity as a human being is forfeited, and human rights violations ultimately occur through lack of respect for the individual's rights and dignity (Ward & Birgden, 2007b). There is no "bright line" at which torture can be set, but there can be a "bright line" forbidding torture outright in order to prevent a behavioral drift toward disrespectful and punitive offender management; the slippery ethical slope. As the 2014 APA resolution finally resolved:

> Psychologists shall not knowingly engage in, assist, tolerate, direct, support, advise, facilitate, plan, design, or offer training in torture or other cruel, inhuman, or degrading treatment or punishment under any and all conditions, nor shall they participate in any procedure where such treatment is threatened. Psychologists may not enlist others to employ these techniques in order to circumvent this policy's prohibition. Moreover, psychologists shall not provide knowingly any research, instruments, or knowledge that facilitates the practice of torture or other forms of cruel, inhuman, or degrading treatment or punishment. (APA, 2014)

Fallenbaum (member, Psychologists for an Ethical APA) articulated the consequences of APA policy in providing "cover" for those who had engaged in torture:

> The moral issue of our time has landed on the doorstep and we cannot turn away. When a governing authority opts out of the rule of law, psychologists need to speak out for human rights. Psychologists working within unjust settings deserve a professional organization that protects them against participating in and legitimizing unethical and illegal behavior. (Members of the APA Presidential Advisory Group, 2008, p.18)

Notes

1   The APA is 122 years old with 54 divisions and 120,000 members (Hoffman et al., 2015).
2   In stark contrast, international human rights law is unequivocal that torture is a human rights violation. The UN Convention against Torture (1987) is clear that torture is a human rights violation (Article 1.1) and there are no exceptional circumstances to justify torture whatsoever, whether state of war, threat of war, or internal instability (Article 2).
3   Released by President Obama in 2009.
4   There was an immediate public response expressing shock and condemning such practices from the European Federation of Psychologists' Association (http://www.efpa.eu/news/efpa-deeply-shocked-by-conclusions-of-hoffman-report-about-involvement-of-apa-officials-and-us-psychologists-in-torture, 13 July 2015), the British Psychological Society (www.bps.org.uk/news/british-psychological-society-statement-apa-hoffman-review, 14 July 2015), and the Australian Psychological Society (www.psychology.org.au/apsmatters/16July2015/ed, 16 July 2015). However, it appears no preventive action had been taken by any of these organizations to influence APA policy in a collegial manner prior to the Hoffman Report, and none have signed the petition to annul the PENS Report (see below).
5   The interrelationships between individuals are so complex and interwoven that they will not be detailed here; it would require a large "family tree" (see Hoffman et al., 2015; Soldz et al., 2015, for a list of key roles 2003–2006).
6   The APA Council of Representatives is the legislative body that has authority over the affairs of the APA, including the power to review the actions of any board, committee, division, or affiliated organization. It allows members to have a voice in policy developments. See http://www.apa.org/about/governance/council/index.aspx.
7   See APA timeline: http://www.apa.org/news/press/statements/interrogations.aspx.
8   See alternative timeline: http://ethicalpsychology.org/timeline.
9   See http://www.apa.org/ethics/programs/statement/national-security-comments.aspx.
10   Dr. Arrigo, later joining the Coalition for an Ethical Psychology, broke ranks from the Task Force, describing at an APA Conference in 2007 the process as having been neither balanced nor independent, that it was conducted in haste and secrecy, and that she felt that Koocher had exerted strong control over decisions and censured dissidents. See http://www.democracynow.org/2007/8/20/apa_interrogation_task_force_member_dr.
11   Other examples of aggression available on the PENS listserv include calling the head of the American Psychiatric Association "an idiot full of sound and fury" (quoting Shakespeare) and describing Arrigo as having "personal biases" and a "troubled upbringing" because her father had been involved in torture (Hoffman et al., 2015).
12   The military-industrial complex denotes the network of contracts and flows of money and resources between government, military, and industry—in this instance, consultancy, training delivery, and research opportunities for psychologists.
13   Directly reflecting forensic settings issued by Department of Defense. See http://ethicalpsychology.org/timeline, DoD offers talking points against APA members' referendum initiative, August 22, 2008.
14   See http://ethicalpsychology.org/timeline, PENS Koocher: non-traditional clients, May 5, 2005.

Key Readings

Hoffman, D. H., Carter, D. J., Lopez, C. R. V., Benzmiller, H. L., Guo, A. X., Latifi, S. Y., & Craig, D. C. (2015). *Independent review relating to APA ethics guidelines, national security interrogations and torture: September 2015.* Chicago, IL: Sidley Austin LLP Retrieved from http://www.apa.org/independent-review/revised-report.pdf

Olson, B., & Soldz, S. (2007). Positive illusions and the necessity of a bright line forbidding psychologist involvement in detainee interrogations. *Analyses of Social Issues and Public Policy*, 7, 45–54.

Opotow, S. (2007). Moral exclusion and torture: The ticking bomb scenario and the slippery ethical slope. *Peace and Conflict: Journal of Peace Psychology*, 13, 457–461.

Soldz, S., Raymond, N., Reisner, S., Allen, S. A., Baker, I. L., & Keller, A. S. (2015). *All the President's psychologists: The American Psychological Association's secret complicity with the White House and US intelligence community in support of the CIAs "enhanced" interrogation program*. Retrieved from http://cryptocomb.org/wp-content/uploads/2015/04/All-the-Presidents-Psychologists.pdf

References

Altman, N. (2008). The psychodynamics of torture. *Psychoanalytic Dialogues*, 18, 658–670.

American Psychiatric Association. (2006). *Position statement on psychiatric participation in interrogation of detainees*. Retrieved from http://www.cja.org/article.php?id=888

American Psychological Association (2005). *Report of the American Psychological Association Presidential Task Force on Psychological Ethics and National Security*. Washington, DC: Author Retrieved from https://www.apa.org/pubs/info/reports/pens.pdf

American Psychological Association. (2007). *Statement of the American Psychological Association: Submitted to the United States Senate Select Committee on Intelligence*. Retrieved from https://www.apa.org/news/press/statements/senate-2007.pdf

American Psychological Association. (2008). *Letter to the Attorney-General*. Retrieved from http://www.apa.org/news/press/statements/attorney-general.pdf

American Psychological Association. (2009a). *APA applauds new executive orders signaling a fundamental change in the rights and treatment of detainees*. Retrieved from http://www.apa.org/news/press/releases/2009/01/guantanamo.aspx

American Psychological Association. (2009b). *An open letter from the Board of Directors*. Retrieved from http://www.apa.org/news/press/statements/open-letter-membership.pdf

American Psychological Association. (2010a). *Ethical principles of psychologists and code of conduct*. Retrieved from http://www.apa.org/ethics/code/index.aspx

American Psychological Association. (2010b). *American Psychological Association amends Ethics Code to address potential conflicts among professional ethics, legal authority and organizational demands*. Retrieved from http://www.apa.org/news/press/releases/2010/02/ethics-code.aspx

American Psychological Association. (2014). *Policy related to psychologists' work in national security settings and reaffirmation of the APA position against torture and other cruel, inhuman, or degrading treatment or punishment*. Retrieved from http://www.apa.org/about/policy/national-security.aspx

American Psychological Association. (2015a). *Letter to APA members*. Retrieved from https://www.apa.org/independent-review/letter-members-apology.pdf

American Psychological Association. (2015b). *Letter to colleagues in the international community*. Retrieved from http://www.apa.org/independent-review/international-letter.pdf

APA Presidential Advisory Group (2008). *Report of the APA Presidential Advisory Group on the implementation of the petition resolution*. Retrieved from http://www.apa.org/ethics/advisory-group-final.pdf

Behnke, S. (2006). Ethics and interrogations: Comparing and contrasting the American Psychological, American Medical and American Psychiatric Association positions. *Monitor on Psychology*, 37, 66–67.

Birgden, A., & Perlin, M. (2009). "Where the home in the valley meets the damp dirty prison": A therapeutic jurisprudence role for forensic psychologists in corrections: Special issue. *Journal of Aggression and Violent Behavior*, 14, 256–263.

Council on Foreign Relations. (2014). *Senate Intelligence Committee: Study on the Central Intelligence Agency's detention and interrogation program.* United States Select Committee. Retrieved from https://fas.org/irp/congress/2014_rpt/ssci-rdi.pdf

Coyle, A. (2008, May 14). *Managing prisons in a time of change.* Address presented at senior management seminar, Department of Corrections, Wellington, New Zealand.

Department of Defense. (2013). Department of Defense: Directive: No. 3115.13: DoD support to the High-Value Detainee Interrogation Group (HIG). Retrieved from http://www.esd.whs.mil/dd/

Elkin, D. N. (2016). The American Psychological Association and the Hoffman Report. *Journal of Humanistic Psychology, 56*, 99–109.

Faberman, R. K. (2009). A stronger vision for APA. *Monitor on Psychology, 40*(4), 68 Retrieved from http://www.apa.org/monitor/2009/04/vision-apa.aspx

Hoffman, D. H., Carter, D. J., Lopez, C. R. V., Benzmiller, H. L., Guo, A. X., Latifi, S. Y., & Craig, D. C. (2015). *Independent review relating to APA ethics guidelines, national security interrogations and torture: September 2015.* Chicago, IL: Sidley Austin LLP Retrieved from http://www.apa.org/independent-review/revised-report.pdf

Human Rights Watch (2015). *Callous and cruel: Use of force against inmates with mental disabilities in US jails and prisons.* New York, NY: Human Rights Watch Retrieved from https://www.hrw.org/report/2015/05/12/callous-and-cruel/use-force-against-inmates-mental-disabilities-us-jails-and#02889c

Janoff-Bulman, R. (2007). Erroneous assumptions: Popular belief in the effectiveness of torture interrogation. *Peace and Conflict: Journal of Peace Psychology, 13*, 429–435.

Lewis, N. A. (2004, November 20). Red Cross finds detainee abuse in Guantánamo. *New York Times.* Retrieved from http://www.nytimes.com/2004/11/30/politics/red-cross-finds-detainee-abuse-in-guantanamo.html

Lewis, N. A. (2006, June 7). Military alters the makeup of interrogation advisers. *New York Times.* Retrieved from http://www.nytimes.com/2006/06/07/washington/07detain.html?fta=y

Members of the APA Presidential Advisory Group (2008). *Report of the APA Presidential Advisory Group on the implementation of the petition resolution.* Retrieved from http://www.apa.org/ethics/advisory-group-final.pdf

Olson, B., & Soldz, S. (2007). Positive illusions and the necessity of a bright line forbidding psychologist involvement in detainee interrogations. *Analyses of Social Issues and Public Policy, 7*, 45–54.

Olson, B., Soldz, S., & Davis, M. (2008). The ethics of interrogation and the American Psychological Association: A critique of policy and process. *Philosophy, Ethics, and Humanities in Medicine, 3*, 1–15.

Opotow, S. (2007). Moral exclusion and torture: The ticking bomb scenario and the slippery ethical slope. *Peace and Conflict: Journal of Peace Psychology, 13*, 457–461.

Pope, K. S. (2011). Are the American Psychological Association's detainee interrogation policies ethical and effective? Key claims, documents, and results. *Zeitschrift für Psychologie/Journal of Psychology, 7*, 459–481.

Soldz, S. (2006, August). The folks who brought us brainwashing and ECT try to clean up: Psychologists, Guantanamo, and torture. *Counterpunch.* Retrieved from http://www.thewe.cc/weplanet/news/americas/us/us_psychologists_doctors_medics_and_torture.htm

Soldz, S. (2008). Healers or interrogators: Psychology and the United States torture regime. *Psychoanalytic Dialogues, 18*, 592–613.

Soldz, S. (2009). *Open letter in response to the American Psychological Association Board.* Retrieved from http://www.commondreams.org/newswire/2009/06/29/open-letter-response-american-psychological-association-board

Soldz, S., Raymond, N., Reisner, S., Allen, S. A., Baker, I. L., & Keller, S. L. (2015). *All the President's psychologists: The American Psychological Association's secret complicity with the White House and US intelligence community in support of the CIAs "enhanced" interrogation program.* Retrieved from http://cryptocomb.org/wp-content/uploads/2015/04/All-the-Presidents-Psychologists.pdf

Tolin, D., & Lohr, J. (2009). Psychologists, the APA and torture. *Clinical Science: Society for the Science of Clinical Psychology: Section III of the Division of Clinical Psychology of the American Psychological Association: Newsletter, Fall*, 4–10.

United Nations (1987). *Convention against torture and other cruel, inhuman or degrading treatment or punishment.* Retrieved from https://www.ohchr.org/en/professionalinterest/pages/cat.aspx

Ward, T., & Birgden, A. (2007a). Accountability and dignity: Ethical issues in forensic and correctional practice. *Aggression and Violent Behavior*, 14, 227–231.

Ward, T., & Birgden, A. (2007b). Human rights and clinical correctional practice. *Aggression and Violent Behavior*, 12, 628–643.

Part II

The Roles of Psychology in Managing Prisons and Offenders

4

The Effects of Imprisonment

Robert D. Morgan, Stephanie A. Van Horn,
Nina MacLean, Joseph T. Hunter, and Rebecca L. Bauer

Texas Tech University, USA

As of 2015, there were over 10 million people incarcerated worldwide, with over 2.2 million imprisoned in the United States alone (Walmsley, 2013). By and large, incarceration rates have increased across the globe (Walmsley, 2013), and questions remain regarding the effects of imprisonment on inmate physical and mental health, and general wellbeing. In this chapter, we review a range of effects on inmate functioning, including prison overcrowding, inmate relationships with correctional officers and staff, length of incarceration, and victimization. We also review the iatrogenic effects of incarceration as it pertains to post-release functioning, including known criminal risk variables such as vocational outcomes and social support networks, but also criminal recidivism more directly. We will conclude this chapter by examining special considerations associated with incarceration, such as the differential effects on female and other minority status inmates, on inmates with severe and persistent mental illnesses, and the effects resulting from the use of administrative segregation.

Individual Effects of Incarceration

Much has been written about the effects of incarceration (see Toch, 1992a, 1992b) with issues of prisonization, decompensation (loss of functioning), victimization, and stigma remaining as primary concerns.

Prisonization

It is hoped by society that the undesirable experiences associated with incarceration will serve as a deterrent from committing additional criminal acts (Gendreau, Cullen, & Goggin, 1999); however, incarceration may be counter-productive in that it can also be criminogenic (Gendreau et al., 1999). Imprisonment is believed to be criminogenic when prisonization occurs: that is, when inmates take on the "folkways, mores, customs, and general culture of the penitentiary" (Clemmer, 1940, p. 270). Although some prisonization is necessary for offenders to successfully transition to the prison environment (e.g., adopt a new language characterized

The Wiley International Handbook of Correctional Psychology, First Edition. Edited by Devon L. L. Polaschek, Andrew Day, and Clive R. Hollin.
© 2019 John Wiley & Sons Ltd. Published 2019 by John Wiley & Sons Ltd.

by prison slang), when inmates begin to integrate the dogmas and mores of the prison subculture (i.e., anti-institutional beliefs, attitudes, behaviors) incarceration becomes increasingly
criminogenic. Specifically, prisonization is associated with increased antisocial attitudes
(Thomas, Petersen, & Cage, 1981), and may contribute to increased recidivism (Clemmer,
1950; see also Smith, Goggin, & Gendreau, 2002, and Spohn & Holleran, 2002).

Of particular concern with regard to prisonization or the criminogenic properties of prison is
when incarceration is used with offenders at low risk for reoffending. Specifically, incarceration
of low-risk offenders has been shown to increase criminal recidivism (Smith, 2009). Length of
incarceration is also of concern with regard to prison producing criminogenic effects for some
offenders. As previously noted, incarceration rates have exploded worldwide, with "get tough"
crime policies and legislation leading to longer prison sentences. Although such policies (e.g.,
longer prison sentences) aimed to deter crime, they have actually proven to, at best, have no
appreciable reduction effect, and at worst, to actually increase recidivism (Crayton, 2013;
Gendreau, Goggin, Cullen, & Andrews, 2000; Sherman, Smith, Schmidt, & Rogan, 1992;
Smith et al., 2002; Snodgrass, Blokland, Haviland, Nieuwbeerta, & Nagin, 2011).

Decompensation

Decompensation refers to reduced levels of physiological and psychological functioning as a
result of incarceration. It has long been assumed that the cruel and harsh realities of prison life
(Toch, 1992b) were responsible for universal harm among prisoners (Cohen & Taylor, 1972;
Mitford, 1973); however, findings from more recent research have challenged these earlier
conclusions.

Physiological effects

Although research examining the physiological effects of incarceration is much less prominent
than research examining psychological effects, much has been learned. Despite speculation
that stress associated with incarceration may increase inmates' likelihood of contracting an
infectious disease (Pridemore, 2014), empirical findings indicate that physiological symptoms
(e.g., blood pressure) decrease over the course of incarceration (Paulus & Dzindolet, 1993).
This finding is consistent with others that examined the effect of long-term incarceration
without indication of physical deterioration among inmates (Bonta & Gendreau, 1990).
Although inmates reported increased physical health concerns during the course of their incarceration (Heigel, Stuewig, & Tangney, 2010), a study of long-term incarceration suggested
that the physical health of inmates correlated with age rather than being a function of incarceration (Dettbarn, 2012).

Psychological effects

Research findings on the mental health effects of incarceration have been mixed. Historically,
it was generally accepted that incarceration adversely affected inmates' psychological functioning (Cohen & Taylor, 1972; Mitford, 1973); however, research has since shown that
psychological functioning can actually improve over the course of incarceration (see Bonta &
Gendreau, 1990; Bukstel & Kilmann, 1980). Although some continue to speculate that
mental health of inmates deteriorates in prison (see Haney, 2003), empirical findings continu-
ously illustrate improvements in mental health functioning of inmates (Harding & Zimmermann, 1989; Hassan et al., 2011; Taylor et al., 2010; Zamble & Porporino, 1990). In fact,
although inmates experience an increase in psychiatric symptoms (i.e., anxiety and depression)

immediately following incarceration, these symptoms typically dissipate after a period of adjustment (MacKenzie & Goodstein, 1985). Longitudinal studies further indicate decreased negative affect (i.e., depression, anxiety, hopeless) over time, with increased self-esteem (Zamble, 1992), and a meta-analytic review of 15 studies corroborated these findings (Walker et al., 2014). Thus, imprisonment is not necessarily psychologically harmful, and some individual differences (e.g., age, coping abilities, presence of mental illness) likely influence an offender's ability to adjust to incarceration (Bukstel & Kilmann, 1980; Gendreau & Bonta, 1984; Gendreau & Thériault, 2011).

Mental illness remains one variable of particular interest when considering the adjustment of inmates to prison life; however, when examining effects of incarceration, researchers have typically focused on inmates without mental illness to the exclusion of inmates with severe mental illness. The findings from research on non-mentally ill inmates should not be generalized to offenders with mental illness (OMI), as their overall experience as an inmate can be significantly different (Abramsky & Fellner, 2003). Despite speculation that incarcerating OMI contributed not only to significant deterioration in mental health functioning, but also to poorer institutional functioning and increased criminal risk, upon further scrutiny, this does not appear to be the case. Specifically, it appears that length of incarceration is negatively associated with OMI's mental health functioning, but length of incarceration is not associated with increased criminogenic risk such as antisocial attitudes (e.g., criminal thinking; Bauer, Bolanos, & Morgan, 2012).

Disruption of prosocial support system

Through the process of incarceration, offenders' relationships with close relatives and friends are often harmed (Austin & Hardyman, 2004; Kenemore & Roldan, 2006). Social support from prosocial friends and neighbors may also be disrupted (Rose & Clear, 2003). This disruption of the social support system appears to be the result of prison location (i.e., distance from the support system), visitation procedures such as limited visitation hours, and prison policies (e.g., limits on telephone calls; Austin & Hardyman, 2004). Over time, these factors may weaken the relationship of the inmate with their support system, thereby negatively impacting the likelihood of success upon community reentry (Andrews et al., 1990; Hanrahan, Gibbs, & Zimmerman, 2005).

Victimization

Victimization in prison has long been a concern for prisoners, family members, correctional staff, and policy-makers alike. Victimization is prominent in popular media portrayals of life in prison (see for example *The Shawshank Redemption, American Me, American History X*). Importantly, victimization has become an increased focus for advocacy groups and researchers, in part due to a report published by Human Rights Watch that suggested that the prevalence of coerced sex in male prisons in the United States was between 20 and 33% (Mariner, 2001). The publication of this report prompted development of the Prison Rape Elimination Act of 2003, which mandated government funding for researchers to examine sexual victimization in prison with the ultimate goal of reducing its frequency. This is an important step; however, victimization in prison includes a wide range of behavior beyond unwanted sexual contact, including physical assault, intimidation, and theft or destruction of property.

It is commonly accepted that official reports underrepresent the actual prevalence of victimization (Wolff, Blitz, Shi, Siegel, & Bachman, 2007). Using self-report data of experience of physical assault by another inmate, Wolff, Blitz, and colleagues (2007) found a 6-month prevalence rate of approximately 21% in both male and female facilities; however, rates varied significantly by size of facility, with assaults by another inmate occurring more frequently in smaller facilities. Assaults by a staff member occurred more frequently in larger facilities, and were more prevalent in male facilities (24.6%) than female facilities (8.3%). Sexual assault in prisons appears to be less common. A meta-analysis of the victimization literature estimated a 1.9% lifetime prevalence rate (Gaes & Goldberg, 2004), and a large-scale survey of prisons in one state revealed a 6-month prevalence rate of 1.5% for sexual assault by another inmate in male prisons and 3.7% in a female prison. Sexual assault by a staff member was similar in both male and female facilities (2.1%; Wolff, Shi, Blitz, & Siegel, 2007).

Correlates of physical or sexual assault may indicate risk factors that prison administrators can use to help identify inmates at greater risk for victimization. In terms of sexual assault, prior diagnosis of a mental disorder, sexual victimization before the age of 18, and higher levels of education have all been associated with increased likelihood of sexual assault, as have sexual orientation and small physical stature (Wolff, Shi, et al., 2007). Other correlates of victimization by another inmate (broadly defined here as theft, property damage, threatened with violence, and assault) include younger age, history of violent misconduct, and propensity for risk taking (Gonsalves, Walsh, & Scalora, 2012; Kerley, Hochstetler, & Copes, 2009; Wooldredge & Steiner, 2013). Looking specifically at victimization by staff, being young, African American, and convicted for a violent crime were all associated with increased likelihood of sexual victimization in male prisons; increased education was associated with increased likelihood of sexual assault in female prisons (Wolff, Shi, et al., 2007).

The consequences of prison victimization can be long lasting and include increased antisocial behavior including crime, substance abuse, depression, and hostility (Zweig, Yahner, Visher, & Lattimore, 2014). Given the detrimental effects of victimization, it is incumbent upon prison administrators to ensure the safety of the inmates in their care. Using what is known about risk factors for victimization to develop actuarial risk assessments to identify those at greatest risk would be an important step in curtailing victimization in jails and prisons.

Stigma

Offenders are stigmatized because of their criminal record, which is compounded if they have served time in prison (Brown, 2011). This is particularly true for vocational outcomes as former inmates will experience significant stigma and bias when seeking employment (Fletcher, 2001; Pettit & Lyons, 2009), which ultimately creates a barrier to successful community reintegration (Brown, 2011; Shivy et al., 2007; Varghese, Hardin, Bauer, & Morgan, 2009). Specifically, offenders typically experience a challenge in both finding and maintaining employment (Tripodi, Kim, & Bender, 2010). These difficulties are often related to lack of opportunity in job-related experience or skill (Winnick & Bodkin, 2008), inability to develop a professional network, and limited connection to employers while incarcerated (Tripodi et al., 2010). Laws also may restrict those with a criminal record from certain jobs (Harris & Keller, 2005). For example, an offender's ability to participate in some healthcare positions, child-related services, and security positions will be limited (Holzer, Raphael, & Stoll, 2003). As a result of stigma and biases, offenders are less likely to receive a job interview (Pager & Quillian, 2005), and are offered menial jobs with low pay (Irwin, 2005). Although stigma reduces the likelihood of employment for ex-offenders, those who belong to multiple disadvantaged groups (e.g., African American, mentally ill) experience exceptional hardship in securing employment (Batastini, Bolanos, & Morgan, 2014; Pager & Quillian, 2005).

Effects of Incarceration on Racial and Ethnic Minorities

Racial and ethnic disparities in the US criminal justice system have been well documented (Petersilia, 1985; Sampson & Lauritsen, 1997), and incarceration appears to affect racial and ethnic minorities differently as well. Black inmates are more likely than White inmates to experience physical or sexual victimization by a staff member (Wolff, Shi, & Blitz, 2008), whereas White inmates are more likely to experience victimization by another inmate (Wolff et al., 2008; Wooldredge & Steiner, 2012), and to experience property crimes (Wooldredge & Steiner, 2012). Hispanic inmates reported above average victimization by both staff and other inmates (Wolff et al., 2008).

Racial and ethnic differences have been noted on rates of inmate misconduct; however, determining the extent to which misconduct is affected by the prison environment and the extent to which engagement in misconduct is a function of pre-existing attitudes accepting of antisocial behavior is a complex endeavor. The application of general strain theory (GST) to institutional misconduct suggests the interaction of individual characteristics, prison environment, and coping skills provides a more thorough framework from which to examine prison adjustment as compared to any one of those variables on its own (Blevins, Johnson Listwan, Cullen, & Jonson, 2010). Empirical studies have lent support to the need for a nuanced understanding of misconduct by demonstrating that individual characteristics supportive of antisocial attitudes and behaviors are more predictive of severe misconduct (e.g., assault or escape) than moderate misconduct (e.g., refusal to participate in rehabilitative programming, stealing; Walters & Crawford, 2013), and that environmental strain has a significant association with misconduct independent of individual characteristics indicative of proclivity for antisocial behaviors such as type of offense and gang membership (Morris, Carriaga, Diamond, Leeper Piquero, & Piquero, 2012). That being said, there is a lack of empirical data examining the relationship between strain, race and ethnicity, and prison misconduct.

Looking solely at the relationship between race/ethnicity and prison misconduct, a study of inmates in state prisons found that Black inmates were more likely than White inmates to engage in both violent and non-violent misconduct (Steiner & Wooldredge, 2015). The race/misconduct relationship was mediated by Black to White inmate ratio, and cynicism toward prison staff. Specifically, race was not as predictive of misconduct in institutions with higher ratios of Black to White inmates; however, in institutions where the inmates were more distrustful of staff, the relationship between race and misconduct was stronger (Steiner & Wooldredge, 2015). Not all studies have supported the relationship between race and violent misconduct, and some have instead found no differences between Black and White inmates (Berg & DeLisi, 2006; Camp, Gaes, Langan, & Saylor, 2003). Berg and DeLisi (2006) found Hispanic and Native American inmates in male facilities were more likely to engage in violent misconduct than non-Hispanic or non-Native American inmates, and female African American and Native American inmates were more likely to engage in violent misconduct than their White, African American, or Asian counterparts. White inmates appear significantly more likely to engage in alcohol or drug-related misconduct (Harer & Steffensmeier, 1996). Overall, it appears that race and ethnicity may be associated with propensity for misconduct; however, little is known about the theoretical or causal relationship between those constructs. Furthermore, additional examination is needed to tease apart the effects of pre-existing antisocial proclivities and environmental strain on institutional misconduct, and how race/ethnicity may moderate these relationships.

The negative effects of incarceration on post-release employment appear to be worse for Black ex-offenders than for White ex-offenders. For example, Black confederate job applicants were less likely to be interviewed for a job than their White counterpart confederate applicants, even when they had identical criminal records (Pager, Western, & Sugie, 2009). This effect appears to differ by application modality; no racial or ethnic differences in hiring were noted when applications were completed online; however, both Black and Hispanic ex-offenders were less likely to have favorable hiring outcomes than White ex-offenders (Decker, Ortiz, Spohn, & Hedberg, 2015). Although the disparity between racial/ethnic minority status and employment opportunity has been noted independent of criminal history (Pager, 2003), the effect is more pronounced when criminal record is included. Among confederates without a criminal record, 25% of Black applicants were contacted for an interview compared to 31% of White applicants (Pager et al., 2009). Among confederates with a criminal record, the discrepancy was even more pronounced; White applicants were more than twice as likely (22%) to be contacted for an interview as Black applicants (10%; Pager et al., 2009). Overall, employers appear particularly reluctant to interview applicants of racial or ethnic minority status who also have a criminal history.

Effects of Incarceration on Women

There is a paucity of research examining the effects of incarceration on women. As a result, assessment measures and treatment programs for female offenders tend to be based on modified versions of tools and programs that were developed for male offenders (Blanchette & Brown, 2006); however, just as incarceration appears to have differential effects on racial and ethnic minorities, so it does on women offenders.

In general, the maintenance of relationships with their children appears to be especially important for women offenders (Jiang & Winfree, 2006; Wright, Salisbury, & Van Voorhis, 2007). Approximately 64% of incarcerated women in the United States reported living with their children before their arrest or incarceration (Glaze & Maruschak, 2008). Although up to 90% of women inmates reported having had some contact with their children, up to 58% reported having never had a personal visit with their children since being incarcerated. Barriers to visitation include prison location, administrative policies such as inflexible visiting schedules, prohibitions on physical conduct, and other aspects of the prison environment (e.g., lack of privacy, visiting spaces that may be intimidating to young children, long waiting periods; Austin & Hardyman, 2004; Casey-Acevedo & Bakken, 2002). Empirical evidence also supports the importance of parental contact during incarceration. Women who were in contact with their children by phone evidenced a 27% reduction in rule violations compared to women who were not in contact with their children. In a separate study, as parenting stressors increased (e.g., concerns about contact with their children, competence as a parent), so did mothers' anxiety, depression, and severity of institutional misconduct (Houck & Loper, 2002).

Looking at social support more broadly, a recent study found that visitation from family and friends was the only predictor of misconduct in women above and beyond shared predictors between male and female inmates (Celinska & Sung, 2014). This may be particularly problematic for women as the limited number of women's correctional facilities contributes to increased travel time and expense for family and friends (Monroe, 2012). In general, the relationship between access to social support from family and friends and misconduct appears to be particularly salient for incarcerated women compared to incarcerated men; however, conclusions regarding other hypothesized predictors of misconduct cannot yet be drawn given the inconsistent findings of the limited number of studies examining these relationships.

In terms of gender differences in victimization, female prisoners were more likely to be victims of theft (Wolff & Shi, 2009). After theft, female prisoners' most frequent victimization experiences were physical assault (i.e., slapped, kicked, or bit), followed by someone threatening the safety of a loved one. Comparatively, male prisoners' most frequent victimization experiences were being threatened with a weapon followed by physical assault. Women were also more likely to report instances of physical victimization to staff than their male counterparts (Wolff & Shi, 2009). Women prisoners were more likely than male prisoners to experience unwanted sexual touching by another inmate, although rates of sexual assault or rape by another inmate were similar for men and women, as were rates of any sexual victimization by a staff member (Wolff & Shi, 2008). Although sexual assault or rape was not common, male prisoners were more likely than female prisoners to report these incidents to staff when they were victimized by a staff member (Wolff & Shi, 2008).

Special Considerations

Overcrowding

Prison overcrowding is a global concern. Nearly 81% of the 204 countries that provide occupancy statistics are currently operating above 80% capacity, the level at which prison administrators report crowding begins to affect how facilities operate (Klofas, Stojkovic, & Kalinich, 1992). Further, a staggering 57% are operating at or above 100% capacity (World Prison Brief, n.d.). As the United States prison population began to experience rapid growth in the 1970s, the effects of crowding on inmates became a growing concern for scholars and administrators alike (Gaes, 1994; Haney, 2006).

In terms of physiological effects, prison crowding has been linked to increased rates of tuberculin infection (MacIntyre, Kendig, Kummer, Birago, & Graham, 1997), increased blood pressure and heart rate (Bonta & Gendreau, 1990), and physical illness complaints in inmates housed in open dormitories as opposed to those housed in single or double person cells (Cox, Paulus, & McCain, 1984). In fact, there appears to be widespread agreement that crowding in prisons is related to increases in physiological markers of stress and subjective experience of distress (Bonta & Gendreau, 1990; Gaes, 1985, 1994; Haney, 2006). Unfortunately, *how* that stress manifests itself physically in terms of illness, and whether the effects are short or long term, is still unclear.

The degree to which crowding affects inmate conduct (e.g., assault, homicide, suicide, disciplinary infractions) is another area of concern for correctional staff. Several studies demonstrated that as crowding increases, so do disciplinary infractions (Megargee, 1977), assault rates (Cox et al., 1984; Gaes & McGuire, 1985; Nacci, Teitelbaum, & Prather, 1977; Wooldredge, Griffin, & Pratt, 2001), suicides (Cox et al., 1984; Dye, 2010; Huey & McNulty, 2005), and homicides (Cox et al., 1984). Other studies, however, found no statistically or practically significant effect of crowding on various measurements of inmate misconduct (Bonta & Kiem, 1978; Bonta & Nanckivell, 1980; Camp et al., 2003; Ekland-Olson, Barrick, & Cohen, 1983), and two studies found an inverse relationship between crowding and inmate misconduct (Tartaro, 2002; Walters, 1998). Meta-analyses have found no effect (Bonta & Gendreau, 1990), or small effects of crowding on institutional misconduct (Franklin,

Franklin, & Pratt, 2006). Although no direct relationship between overcrowding and adverse outcomes has been established, crowding and inmate conduct is complex, and future research should focus on identifying moderating variables (e.g., negative life events, other sources of stress, adaptability; Gaes, 1994) so as to more precisely define this.

Segregated housing

Of the approximately 1.5 million adults incarcerated in state and federal prisons across the United States (Glaze & Herberman, 2013), an estimated 81,622 are detained in restricted housing units (Stephan, 2008). Much has been written about potential adverse and harmful effects of administrative segregation (AS; see Grassian, 2006; Haney, 2009; Kupers, 2008). Specifically, it has been reported by some that inmates subjected to AS experience a myriad of mental health concerns and symptoms, including appetite and sleep disturbance, anxiety including panic, depression and hopelessness, irritability, anger and rage, lethargy, psychosis, cognitive rumination, cognitive impairment, social withdrawal, and suicidal ideation, as well as self-injurious behaviors (see Haney, 2003, 2008, 2009 for a summary of this literature). This body of literature suggests that long-term placement in AS (often times defined as greater than 3 months; see Kupers, 2008) is harmful and can cause "lasting emotional damage" (p. 1006). Consequently, Grassian (1983) coined the term SHU (Security Housing Unit) Syndrome. This syndrome represents a constellation of symptoms and mental health deficits that are alleged to result from long-term placement in segregated housing.

Not all studies, however, have borne out the adverse effects of placement in AS. When examining brief periods of segregation, almost no deleterious effects have been found (see Bonta & Gendreau, 1995; Gendreau & Bonta, 1984; Suedfeld, Ramirez, Deaton, & Baker-Brown, 1982; Zinger, Wichmann, & Andrews, 2001). Even more compelling are the results from O'Keefe, Klebe, Stucker, Sturm, and Leggett (2010) obtained from the most sophisticated segregation study to date. Contrary to the researchers' hypotheses, results indicated that AS confinement of 1 year was generally not associated with the onset of psychological symptoms or cognitive impairment for mentally ill and non-mentally ill inmates; nor did inmates with mental illness fare worse in administrative segregation than their non-mentally ill peers.

Given these conflicting findings it is not surprising that the use of segregation in corrections has become a global debate and a heavily litigated issue. To clarify the competing perspectives, Morgan and colleagues (2016) report on the results of two independent meta-analytic reviews that examined the effect AS has on inmates' physical and mental health functioning, as well as behavioral outcomes. Collectively, the findings from these reviews indicated small to moderate effects across all domains of interest: tentatively suggesting that AS may not produce any more negative effects than those produced by incarceration more generally. Notably, these results do not support the popular contention that AS is responsible for producing devastating and lasting emotional damage.

Staff Relationships

The staff in correctional settings can have a significant impact on the overall environment and, consequently, the experience of inmates. Correctional staff have multiple, often competing, roles: custody and control (i.e., supervising, disciplining, inspecting, observing, and also at times offering guidance), and caregiving (see Liebling, Price, & Shefer, 2011).

Although it is ideal for custody staff members to balance their multiple roles, research has shown a tendency to rely most heavily on disciplinary action due to a close identification with security and custody roles (Williams, 1983). This role imbalance often results in additional punishment or harsh treatment even in times of inmate need (Appelbaum, Hickey, & Packer, 2001; Marzano, Ciclitira, & Adler, 2012). However, it should be noted that more punitive approaches to corrections are not necessarily the result of callousness by the individuals, but rather a result of unclear role expectations and lack of training in this regard (Liebling et al., 2011). For example, a study on attitudes of prison staff toward care concerns, such as self-harm among offenders, showed custody staff felt strain in balancing care and security roles, and felt uncomfortable and inadequately prepared to address care concerns (Short et al., 2009). Adherence to traditional security roles may also contribute to the perception that many offenders use "non-genuine" health concerns as a tool of manipulation, resulting in correctional staff anger and resentment toward offenders (Short et al., 2009; Towl & Forbes, 2002), subsequently leading to feelings of isolation and helplessness for offenders (Towl & Forbes, 2002).

Implications for Psychologists

Psychologists (and other mental health professionals) have an important role in mitigating potentially harmful effects of incarceration. Although rehabilitation is a primary focus for correctional psychologists, providing basic mental health services (e.g., symptom management, prison adjustment; Morgan, 2003) is a necessary obligation in the United States (see *Estelle v. Gamble*, 1976). Thus, psychologists are at the forefront of examining inmate functioning to ensure that iatrogenic effects are not occurring, and must provide psychological services in the event an inmate is experiencing a negative reaction to their incarceration.

Beyond direct services, psychologists in some jurisdictions have an important role with regard to correctional officer training. As previously noted, correctional officers struggle with the varied and complex roles they serve when managing inmates, and additional training on the responsibilities in these various roles is increasingly needed. Furthermore, correctional officers are the front line defense not only for security, but also for identifying inmates in crisis; thus, psychologists need to help train officers to help equip them with the knowledge and tools to identify and respond appropriately when a crisis does occur.

Lastly, although results of empirical studies suggest that incarceration produces limited iatrogenic effects, inmate responses to incarceration are individualized. It is incumbent upon correctional psychologists to identify at-risk inmates, and to provide preventive or therapeutic services aimed at minimizing harmful effects of incarceration. Thus, psychologists should engage in research designed to further identify who is at greatest risk for prison maladjustment such as acting out (e.g., violence) or who will experience mental health decompensation. Psychologists should also focus efforts on developing preventive, as well as therapeutic, mental health programming, for inmates identified as at risk for prison maladjustment. As one example, one of the authors co-developed *Escaping the Cage: A Mental Health Treatment Program for Inmates Detained in Restrictive Housing* (Batastini, Morgan, Kroner, & Mills, 2014). Escaping the Cage is, in part, a preventive program designed to limit possible adverse effects resulting from placement in segregated housing, and is one example of preventive mental health programming that should be offered to inmates at risk for decompensation.

Conclusion

Increasing incarceration rates are a global problem with issues of prisonization, decompensation (loss of functioning), victimization, and stigma as primary concerns. These issues are even more concerning when recognizing that subgroups of inmates are differentially impacted, such as women, inmates of minority status, and inmates suffering from serious mental illness. Given effects of incarceration, including effects that impact transitional difficulties during community reentry, psychologists (and other mental health professionals) are needed not only on the front lines, but also in training correctional officer staff to mitigate the harms that can occur from incarceration. This is necessary to ensure a safe and humane environment for those detained in correctional facilities.

Key Readings

Andrews, D. A., Zinger, I., Hoge, R. D., Bonta, J., Gendreau, P., & Cullen, F. T. (1990). Does correctional treatment work? A clinically relevant and psychologically informed meta-analysis. *Criminology*, 28(3), 369–404.

Bonta, J., & Gendreau, P. (1995). Reexamining the cruel and unusual punishment of prison life. In T. J. Flanagan (Ed.), *Long-term imprisonment: Policy, science, and correctional practice* (pp. 75–94). Thousand Oaks, CA: Sage.

Morgan, R. D. (2003). Basic mental health services: Services and issues. In T. Fagan, & R. K. Ax (Eds.), *Correctional mental health handbook* (pp. 59–71). Thousand Oaks, CA: Sage.

O'Keefe, M. L., Klebe, K. J., Stucker, A., Sturm, K., & Leggett, W. (2010). *One year longitudinal study of the psychological effects of administrative segregation*. Colorado Springs, CO: Colorado Department of Corrections Retrieved from http://www.ncjrs.gov/pdffiles1/nij/grants/232973.pdf

Toch, H. (1992b). *Mosaic of despair: Human breakdowns in prison* (Rev. ed.). Washington, DC: American Psychological Association.

References

Abramsky, S., & Fellner, J. (2003). *Ill equipped: US prisons and offenders with mental illness*. New York, NY: Human Rights Watch.

Andrews, D. A., Zinger, I., Hoge, R. D., Bonta, J., Gendreau, P., & Cullen, F. T. (1990). Does correctional treatment work? A clinically relevant and psychologically informed meta-analysis. *Criminology*, 28(3), 369–404.

Appelbaum, K. L., Hickey, J. M., & Packer, I. (2001). The role of correctional officers in multidisciplinary mental health care in prisons. *Psychiatric Services*, 52(10), 1343–1347.

Austin, J., & Hardyman, P. L. (2004). The risks and needs of the returning prisoner population. *Review of Policy Research*, 21(1), 13–29.

Batastini, A. B., Bolanos, A. D., & Morgan, R. D. (2014). Attitudes toward hiring applicants with mental illness and criminal justice involvement: The impact of education and experience. *International Journal of Law and Psychiatry*, 37, 524–533.

Batastini, A. B., Morgan, R. D., Kroner, D. G., & Mills, J. F. (2014). *Escaping the cage: A mental health treatment program for inmates detained in restrictive housing*. Unpublished treatment manual.

Bauer, R. L., Bolanos, A. D., Morgan, R. D. (2012, March). Incarceration of long-term incarceration for persons with mental illness. In Morgan, R. D. (Chair), *Mental illness in criminal justice settings: Identifying needs and custodial concerns*. Symposium presented at the 2013 Annual Conference of the American Psychology-Law Society, Portland, OR.

Berg, M. T., & DeLisi, M. (2006). The correctional melting pot: Race, ethnicity, citizenship, and prison violence. *Journal of Criminal Justice, 34*, 631–642.

Blanchette, K., & Brown, S. L. (2006). *The assessment and treatment of women offenders: An integrative perspective*. West Sussex, UK: Wiley.

Blevins, K. R., Johnson Listwan, S., Cullen, F. T., & Lero Jonson, C. (2010). A general strain theory of prison violence and misconduct: An integrated model of human behavior. *Journal of Contemporary Criminal Justice, 26*, 148–166.

Bonta, J. L., & Gendreau, P. (1990). Reexamining the cruel and unusual punishment of prison life. *Law and Human Behavior, 14*, 347–372.

Bonta, J. L., & Gendreau, P. (1995). Reexamining the cruel and unusual punishment of prison life. In T. J. Flanagan (Ed.), *Long-term imprisonment: Policy, science, and correctional practice* (pp. 75–94). Thousand Oaks, CA: Sage.

Bonta, J. L., & Kiem, T. (1978). Institutional misconducts in a jail setting: Preliminary findings and a note of caution. *Crime and/et Justice, 6*, 175–178.

Bonta, J. L., & Nanckivell, G. (1980). Institutional misconducts and anxiety levels among jailed inmates. *Criminal Justice and Behavior, 7*, 203–214.

Brown, C. (2011). Vocational psychology and ex-offenders' reintegration: A call for action. *Journal of Career Assessment, 19*(3), 333–342.

Bukstel, L. H., & Kilmann, P. R. (1980). Psychological effects of imprisonment on confined individuals. *Psychological Bulletin, 88*, 469–493.

Camp, S. D., Gaes, G. G., Langan, N. P., & Saylor, W. G. (2003). The influence of prisons on inmate misconduct: A multilevel investigation. *Justice Quarterly, 20*, 501–533.

Casey-Acevedo, K., & Bakken, T. (2002). Visiting women in prison: Who visits and who cares? *Journal of Offender Rehabilitation, 34*, 67–83.

Celinska, K., & Sung, H. (2014). Gender differences in the determinants of prison rule violations. *The Prison Journal, 94*, 220–241.

Clemmer, D. (1940). *The prison community*. Boston, MA: Christopher.

Clemmer, D. (1950). Observations of imprisonment as a source of criminality. *Journal of Criminal Law & Criminology, 41*, 311–319.

Cohen, S., & Taylor, L. (1972). *Psychological survival: The experience of long-term imprisonment*. Harmondsworth, UK: Penguin.

Cox, V. C., Paulus, P. B., & McCain, G. (1984). Prison crowding research: The relevance for prison housing standards and a general approach regarding crowding phenomena. *American Psychologist, 39*, 1148–1160.

Crayton, A. L. (2013). Long-term incarceration and public safety: Predicting the recidivism risk of long-term prisoners. *Dissertation Abstracts International Section A: Humanities and Social Sciences, 73*(7A), Abstract retrieved from PsycINFO. (Accession No. 2013-99010-440).

Decker, S. H., Ortiz, N., Spohn, C., & Hedberg, E. (2015). Criminal stigma, race, and ethnicity: The consequences of imprisonment for employment. *Journal of Criminal Justice, 43*, 108–121.

Dettbarn, E. (2012). Effects of long-term incarceration: A statistical comparison of two expert assessments of two experts at the beginning and the end of incarceration. *International Journal of Law and Psychiatry, 35*, 236–239.

Dye, M. H. (2010). Deprivation, importation, and prison suicide: Combined effects of institutional conditions and inmate composition. *Journal of Criminal Justice, 38*, 796–806.

Ekland-Olson, S., Barrick, D. M., & Cohen, L. E. (1983). Prison overcrowding and disciplinary problems: An analysis of the Texas prison system. *The Journal of Applied Behavioral Science, 19*, 163–176.

Estelle v. Gamble, 429 US 97, 103 (1976).

Fletcher, D. (2001). Ex-offenders, the labour market and the new public administration. *Public Administration, 79*, 871–891.

Franklin, T. W., Franklin, C. A., & Pratt, T. C. (2006). Examining the empirical relationship between prison crowding and inmate misconduct: A meta-analysis of conflicting research results. *Journal of Criminal Justice, 34*, 401–412.

Gaes, G. G. (1985). The effects of overcrowding in prisons. *Crime and Justice: An Annual Review of Research*, 6, 95–146.

Gaes, G. G. (1994). Prison crowding research reexamined. *The Prison Journal*, 74, 329–363.

Gaes, G. G., & Goldberg, A. L. (2004). *Prison rape: A critical review of the literature*. Washington, DC: National Institute of Justice.

Gaes, G. G., & McGuire, W. (1985). Prison violence: The contribution of crowding versus other determinants of prison assault rates. *Journal of Research in Crime and Delinquency*, 22, 41–65.

Gendreau, P., & Bonta, J. (1984). Solitary confinement is not cruel and unusual punishment: People sometimes are! *Canadian Journal of Criminology*, 26, 467–478.

Gendreau, P., Cullen, F. T., & Goggin, C. (1999). *The effects of prison sentences on recidivism*. Ottawa, Canada: Solicitor General Canada Retrieved from https://www.prisonpolicy.org/scans/e199912.htm

Gendreau, P., Goggin, C., Cullen, F. T., & Andrews, D. A. (2000). Effects of community sanctions and incarceration on recidivism. *Forum on Corrections Research*, 12(2), 10–13 Retrieved from http://www.csc-scc.gc.ca/research/forum/e122/e122c-eng.shtml

Gendreau, P., & Thériault, Y. (2011). Bibliotherapy for cynics revisited: Commentary on a one year longitudinal study of the psychological effects of administrative segregation. *Corrections & Mental Health: An Update of the National Institute of Corrections*. Retrieved from www.nicic.gov

Glaze, L. E., & Herberman, E. J. (2013, December). Correctional populations in the United States, 2012. *Bureau of Justice Statistics Bulletin*. Retrieved from https://www.bjs.gov/content/pub/pdf/cpus12.pdf

Glaze, L. E., & Maruschak, L. M. (2008, August). Parents in prison and their minor children. *Bureau of Justice Statistics Special Report*. NCJ 222984. Retrieved from https://www.bjs.gov/content/pub/pdf/pptmc.pdf

Gonsalves, V. M., Walsh, K., & Scalora, M. J. (2012). Staff perceptions of risk for prison rape perpetration and victimization. *The Prison Journal*, 92(2), 253–273.

Grassian, S. (1983). Psychopathological effects of solitary confinement. *The American Journal of Psychiatry*, 140, 1450–1454.

Grassian, S. (2006). Psychiatric effects of solitary confinement. *Washington University Journal of Law and Policy*, 22, 325–383.

Haney, C. (2003). Mental health issues in long-term solitary and "supermax" confinement. *Crime & Delinquency*, 49(1), 124.

Haney, C. (2006). The wages of prison overcrowding: Harmful psychological consequences and dysfunctional correctional reactions. *Journal of Law & Policy*, 22, 265–293.

Haney, C. (2008). A culture of harm: Taming the dynamics of cruelty in supermax prisons. *Criminal Justice and Behavior*, 35, 956–984.

Haney, C. (2009). The social psychology of isolation: Why solitary confinement is psychologically harmful. *Prison Service Journal*, 181, 12–20.

Hanrahan, K., Gibbs, J. J., & Zimmerman, S. E. (2005). Parole and revocation: Perspectives of young adult offenders. *The Prison Journal*, 85(3), 251–269.

Harding, T., & Zimmermann, E. (1989). Psychiatric symptoms, cognitive stress and vulnerability factors. A study in a remand prison. *The British Journal of Psychiatry*, 155, 36–43.

Harer, M. D., & Steffensmeier, D. J. (1996). Race and prison violence. *Criminology*, 34, 323–355.

Harris, P. M., & Keller, K. S. (2005). Ex-offenders need not apply the criminal background check in hiring decisions. *Journal of Contemporary Criminal Justice*, 21, 6–30.

Hassan, L., Birmingham, L., Harty, M. A., Jarrett, M., Jones, P., King, C., ... & Thornicroft, G. (2011). Prospective cohort study of mental health during imprisonment. *The British Journal of Psychiatry*, 198, 37–42.

Heigel, C. P., Stuewig, J., & Tangney, J. P. (2010). Self-reported physical health of inmates: Impact of incarceration and relation to optimism. *Journal of Correctional Health Care*, 16, 106–116.

Holzer, H. J., Raphael, S., & Stoll, M. A. (2003). *Employment barriers facing ex-offenders*. Washington, DC: The Urban Institute.

Houck, K. D. F., & Loper, A. B. (2002). The relationship of parenting stress to adjustment among mothers in prison. *American Journal of Orthopsychiatry*, 72, 548–558.

Huey, M. P., & McNulty, T. L. (2005). Institutional conditions and prison suicide: Conditional effects of deprivation and overcrowding. *The Prison Journal*, 85(4), 490–514.

Irwin, J. (2005). *The warehouse prison: Disposal of the new dangerous class*. Los Angeles, CA: Roxbury Press.

Jiang, S., & Winfree, L. T. Jr. (2006). Social support, gender, and inmate adjustment to prison life: Insights from a national sample. *The Prison Journal*, 86, 32–55.

Kenemore, T. K., & Roldan, I. (2006). Staying straight: Lessons from ex-offenders. *Clinical Social Work Journal*, 34(1), 5–21.

Kerley, K. R., Hochstetler, A., & Copes, H. (2009). Self-Control, prison victimization, and prison infractions. *Criminal Justice Review*, 34(4), 553–568.

Klofas, J., Stojkovic, S., & Kalinich, D. (1992). The meaning of correctional crowding: Steps toward and index of severity. *Crime & Delinquency*, 38, 171–188.

Kupers, T. (2008). What to do with the survivors? Coping with the long-term effects of isolated confinement. *Criminal Justice and Behavior*, 35, 1005–1016.

Liebling, A., Price, D., & Shefer, G. (2011). Who is the prison officer? In *The Prison Officer* (2nd ed.). New York, NY: Willan.

MacIntyre, C. R., Kendig, N., Kummer, L., Birago, S., & Graham, N. M. (1997). Impact of tuberculosis control measures and crowding on the incidence of tuberculosis infection in Maryland prisons. *Clinical Infectious Diseases*, 24, 1060–1067.

MacKenzie, D. L., & Goodstein, L. (1985). Long-term incarceration impacts and characteristics of long-term offenders: An empirical analysis. *Criminal Justice and Behavior*, 12, 395–414.

Mariner, J. (2001). *No escape: Male rape in US prisons*. New York, NY: Human Rights Watch.

Marzano, L., Ciclitira, K., & Adler, J. (2012). The impact of prison staff responses on self-harming behaviours: Prisoners' perspectives. *British Journal of Clinical Psychology*, 51, 4–18.

Megargee, E. I. (1977). The association of population density, reduced space, and uncomfortable temperatures with misconduct in a prison community. *American Journal of Community Psychology*, 5(3), 289–298.

Mitford, J. (1973). *Kind and unusual punishment*. New York, NY: Knopf.

Monroe, A. (2012). Effects of prisoner location on visitation patterns. *McNair Scholars Research Journal*, 8, 41–52.

Morgan, R. D. (2003). Basic mental health services: Services and issues. In T. Fagan, & R. K. Ax (Eds.), *Correctional mental health handbook* (pp. 59–71). Thousand Oaks, CA: Sage.

Morgan, R. D., Gendreau, P., Smith, P., Gray, A. L., Labreque, R. M., MacLean, N., ... & Mills, J. F. (2016). Quantitative syntheses of the effects of administrative segregation on inmates' well-being. *Psychology, Public Policy, and the Law*, 22, 439–461.

Morris, R. G., Carriaga, M. L., Diamond, B., Leeper Piquero, N., & Piquero, A. R. (2012). Does prison strain lead to prison misbehavior? An application of general strain theory to inmate misconduct. *Journal of Criminal Justice*, 40, 194–201.

Nacci, P. L., Teitelbaum, H. E., & Prather, J. (1977). Population density and inmate misconduct rates in the federal prison system. *Federal Probation*, 41, 26–31.

O'Keefe, M. L., Klebe, K. J., Stucker, A., Sturm, K., & Leggett, W. (2010). *One year longitudinal study of the psychological effects of administrative segregation*. Colorado Springs, CO: Colorado Department of Corrections Retrieved from http://www.ncjrs.gov/pdffiles1/nij/grants/232973.pdf

Pager, D. (2003). The mark of a criminal record. *American Journal of Sociology*, 108, 937–975.

Pager, D., & Quillian, L. (2005). Walking the talk? What employers say versus what they do. *American Sociological Review*, 70, 355–380.

Pager, D., Western, B., & Sugie, N. (2009). Sequencing disadvantage: Barriers to employment facing young Black and White men with criminal records. *The Annals of the American Academy of Political and Social Science*, 623, 195–213.

Paulus, P. B., & Dzindolet, M. T. (1993). Reactions of male and female inmates to prison confinement: Further evidence for a two-component model. *Criminal Justice and Behavior*, 20, 149–166.

Petersilia, J. (1985). Racial disparities in the criminal justice system: A summary. *Crime and Delinquency*, 31, 15–34.

Pettit, B., & Lyons, C. J. (2009). Incarceration and the legitimate labor market: Examining age-graded effects on employment and wages. *Law & Society Review*, 43(4), 725–756.

Pridemore, W. A. (2014). The mortality penalty of incarceration evidence from a population-based case-control study of working-age males. *Journal of Health and Social Behavior*, 55, 215–233.

Prison Rape Elimination Act, 42 USC §§ 15602–15609 (2003).

Rose, D., & Clear, T. (2003). Incarceration, reentry, and social capital: Social networks in the balance. In J. Travis, & M. Waul (Eds.), *Prisoners once removed* (pp. 313–341). Washington, DC: Urban Institute Press.

Sampson, R. J., & Lauritsen, J. L. (1997). Racial and ethnic disparities in crime and criminal justice in the United States. *Crime and Justice*, 21, 311–374.

Sherman, L. W., Smith, D. A., Schmidt, J. D., & Rogan, D. P. (1992). Crime, punishment, and stake in conformity: Legal and informal control of domestic violence. *American Sociological Review*, 57(5), 680–690.

Shivy, V. A., Wu, J. J., Moon, A. E., Mann, S. C., Holland, J. G., & Eacho, C. (2007). Ex-offenders reentering the workforce. *Journal of Counseling Psychology*, 54, 466–473.

Short, V., Cooper, J., Shaw, J., Kenning, C., Abel, K., & Chew-Graham, C. (2009). Custody vs care: Attitudes of prison staff to self-harm in women prisoners—A qualitative study. *Journal of Forensic Psychiatry & Psychology*, 20, 408–426.

Smith, P. (2009). The effects of incarceration on recidivism: A longitudinal examination of program participation and institutional adjustment in federally sentenced adult male offenders. *Dissertation Abstracts International*, 69, 4445.

Smith, P., Goggin, C., & Gendreau, P. (2002). *The effects of prison sentences and intermediate sanctions on recidivism: General effects and individual differences*. Ottawa, Canada: Public Safety Canada Retrieved from http://publications.gc.ca/Collection/JS42-103-2002E.doc

Snodgrass, G. M., Blokland, A. A. J., Haviland, A., Nieuwbeerta, P., & Nagin, D. S. (2011). Does the time cause the crime? An examination of the relationship between time served and reoffending in the Netherlands. *Criminology*, 49, 1149–1194.

Spohn, C., & Holleran, D. (2002). The effect of imprisonment on recidivism rates of felony offenders: A focus on drug offenders. *Criminology*, 40, 329–358.

Steiner, B., & Wooldredge, J. (2015). Racial (in)variance in prison rule breaking. *Journal of Criminal Justice*, 43, 175–185.

Stephan, J. J. (2008). *Census of state and federal correctional facilities, 2005*. US Department of Justice, Office of Justice Programs, Bureau of Justice Statistics. Retrieved from http://www.bjs.gov/content/pub/pdf/csfcf05.pdf

Suedfeld, P., Ramirez, C., Deaton, J., & Baker-Brown, G. (1982). Reactions and attributes of prisoners in solitary confinement. *Criminal Justice and Behavior*, 9, 303–340.

Tartaro, C. (2002). The impact of density on jail violence. *Journal of Criminal Justice*, 30, 499–510.

Taylor, P. J., Walker, J., Dunn, E., Kissell, A., Williams, A., & Amos, T. (2010). Improving mental state in early imprisonment. *Criminal Behaviour and Mental Health*, 20, 215–231.

Thomas, C. W., Petersen, D. M., & Cage, R. J. (1981). A comparative organizational analysis of prisonization. *Criminal Justice Review*, 6, 36–43.

Toch, H. (1992a). *Living in prison: The ecology of survival*. Washington, DC: American Psychological Association.

Toch, H. (1992b). *Mosaic of despair: Human breakdowns in prison* (Rev. ed.). Washington, DC: American Psychological Association.

Towl, G., & Forbes, D. (2002). Working with suicidal prisoners. In G. Towl, L. Snow, & M. McHugh (Eds.), *Suicide in prisons* (pp. 93–101). Malden, MA: Blackwell.

Tripodi, S. J., Kim, J. S., & Bender, K. (2010). Is employment associated with reduced recidivism? The complex relationship between employment and crime. *International Journal of Offender Therapy and Comparative Criminology*, 54, 706–720.

Varghese, F. P., Hardin, E. E., Bauer, R. L., & Morgan, R. D. (2009). Attitudes toward hiring offenders: The roles of criminal history, job qualifications, and race. *International Journal of Offender Therapy and Comparative Criminology*, 54, 769–782.

Walker, J., Illingworth, C., Canning, A., Garner, E., Woolley, J., Taylor, P., & Amons, T. (2014). Changes in mental state associated with prison environments: A systematic review. *Acta Psychiatrica Scandinavica*, 129, 427–436.

Walmsley, R. (2013). *World prison population list* (10th ed.). London, UK: International Centre for Prison Studies.

Walters, G. D. (1998). Time series and correlational analyses of inmate-initiated assaultive incidents in a large correctional system. *International Journal of Offender Therapy and Comparative Criminology*, 42, 124–132.

Walters, G. D., & Crawford, G. (2013). In and out of prison: Do importation factors predict all forms of misconduct or just the more serious ones? *Journal of Criminal Justice*, 41, 407–413.

Williams, T. A. (1983). Custody and conflict: An organizational study of prison officers' roles and attitudes. *Australian & New Zealand Journal of Criminology*, 16, 44–55.

Winnick, T. A., & Bodkin, M. (2008). Anticipated stigma and stigma management among those to be labeled 'ex-con.'. *Deviant Behavior*, 29, 295–333.

Wolff, N., Blitz, C. L., Shi, J., Siegel, J., & Bachman, R. (2007). Physical violence inside prisons: Rates of victimization. *Criminal Justice and Behavior*, 34, 588–599.

Wolff, N., & Shi, J. (2008). Patterns of victimization and feelings of safety inside prison: The experience of male and female inmates. *Crime & Delinquency*, 57, 29–55.

Wolff, N., & Shi, J. (2009). Type, source, and patterns of physical victimization: A comparison of male and female inmates. *The Prison Journal*, 89, 172–191.

Wolff, N., Shi, J., & Blitz, C. L. (2008). Racial and ethnic disparities in types and sources of victimization inside prison. *The Prison Journal*, 88, 451–472.

Wolff, N., Shi, J., Blitz, C. L., & Siegel, J. (2007). Understanding sexual victimization inside prisons: Factors that predict risk. *Criminology & Public Policy*, 6, 535–564.

Wooldredge, J., & Steiner, B. (2012). Race group differences in prison victimization experiences. *Journal of Criminal Justice*, 40, 358–369.

Wooldredge, J., & Steiner, B. (2013). A bi-level framework for understanding prisoner victimization. *Journal of Quantitative Criminology*, 30, 141–162.

Wooldredge, J., Griffin, T., & Pratt, T. (2001). Considering hierarchical models for research on inmate behavior: Predicting misconduct with multilevel data. *Justice Quarterly*, 18, 203–231.

World Prison Brief. (n.d.). Highest to lowest-occupancy level (based on official capacity). Retrieved from http://www.prisonstudies.org/highest-to-lowest/occupancy-level?field_region_taxonomy_tid=All

Wright, E. M., Salisbury, E. J., & Van Voorhis, P. (2007). Predicting the prison misconducts of women offenders: The importance of gender-responsive needs. *Journal of Contemporary Criminal Justice*, 23, 310–340.

Zamble, E. (1992). Behavior and adaptation in long-term prison inmates: Descriptive longitudinal results. *Criminal Justice and Behavior*, 19, 409–425.

Zamble, E., & Porporino, F. (1990). Coping, imprisonment, and rehabilitation: Some data and their implications. *Criminal Justice and Behavior*, 17, 53–70.

Zinger, I., Wichmann, C., & Andrews, D. A. (2001). The psychological effects of 60 days in administrative segregation. *Canadian Journal of Criminology*, 43, 47–83.

Zweig, J. M., Yahner, J., Visher, C. A., & Lattimore, P. K. (2014). Using general strain theory to explore the effects of prison victimization experiences on later offending and substance use. *The Prison Journal*, 95, 84–113.

5

Violence and the Pains of Confinement: PRISM as a Promising Paradigm for Violence Prevention

David J. Cooke
University of Bergen, Norway

I have lain in prison for nearly two years. Out of my nature has come wild despair; an abandonment to grief that was piteous even to look at; terrible and impotent rage; bitterness and scorn; anguish that wept aloud; misery that could find no voice; sorrow that was dumb. I have passed through every possible mood of suffering. (Oscar Wilde, *De Profundis*, p. 4)

Introduction

The keystone of forensic practice is violence prevention. Through the care, treatment, supervision, and management of individuals the forensic practitioner endeavors to minimize the likelihood and the severity of harm directed at self or others. This is true whether the client is in the community or within an institution. While it is often difficult to evaluate the true rate of aggression in forensic institutions, available studies suggest that it is a constant and a significant problem (Nijman, Merckelbach, Allertz, & à Campo, 1997).

The reduction of violence, self-harm, and suicidal behaviors are all World Health Organization (WHO) priorities (Krug, Dahlberg, Mercy, Zwi, & Lozano, 2002). This prioritization is not surprising given that the costs of violence are both high and wide-ranging in nature. They include the direct costs of injury, illness, and absenteeism. Costs also include the less obvious costs created by impaired work performance, the need for higher staffing levels, increased staff turnover, recruitment difficulties, and the need for more rigorous security standards. Costs may be long lasting. In violent institutions inmates are less likely to engage in regime activities and, on their release, they face an increased risk of recidivism as a consequence of being held in a criminogenic environment (Bowers et al., 2008; Noll, 2015). The costs do not stop there. The costs also include the more intangible costs of loss of reputation, the impaired motivation and morale of staff, and impaired organizational creativity and innovation, as well as political costs (Cooke, 1991, 1997; Cooke & Johnstone, 2010, 2012; Noll, 2015). Institutional violence is costly.

The Wiley International Handbook of Correctional Psychology, First Edition. Edited by Devon L. L. Polaschek, Andrew Day, and Clive R. Hollin.

Institutional Violence Prevention

The focus of this chapter is violence prevention. I will describe attempts to evaluate the environment of prisons and forensic psychiatric hospitals: in particular, attempts to identify the situational risk factors that serve to heighten the likelihood of violence. The focus is practical. The focus is on how complex institutions designed to contain the distressed, the disordered, and the difficult can be reorganized to prevent violence. I will consider different strategies for violence prevention; I will describe the evolution of an approach—Promoting Risk Interventions by Situational Management (PRISM)—which applies the thinking of structured professional judgment to the institution rather than to the individual inmate of the institution. I will then describe the process whereby an evaluation of the institution can lead to interventions designed to create an institutional experience that enhances violence prevention. I will conclude with a discussion of avenues for future work.

The WHO makes clear that violence can be prevented (WHO, 2010); critically, this is not a matter of faith but a matter of evidence. The public health perspective, which flows from organizations such as the WHO, recommends two broad strategies of prevention—the "high-risk" and the "population" strategies. The high-risk strategy is the strategy usually favored in forensic practice; a risky individual is identified then s/he is contained, treated, supervised, or otherwise managed. By way of contrast, the population approach intervenes at the level of the population, or the level of the large group; effective population strategies for the prevention of violence would include reducing the availability of alcohol or access to weapons, changing cultural norms and expectations, and developing the life skills of children and adolescents (WHO, 2010). A classic example of the population strategy applied to a health outcome is the use of the price mechanism to control alcohol consumption: the reduction of the average consumption of the population leading directly to a disproportionate reduction in the number of at-risk heavy drinkers at the upper tail of the consumption distribution (Rose, 1992). Population strategies directed toward prevention are more likely to be effective than high-risk strategies when the risk factors for the outcome of interest are relatively weak in their effect. This is the case for violence (Cooke & Johnstone, 2010). Rose (1992) propounded the prevention paradox; in essence, if a large number of people are exposed to a weak risk it will, in fact, generate more cases than if a small number of people are exposed to a strong risk. Under these circumstances—the circumstances that apply in forensic practice—"the high-risk preventative strategy is dealing only with the margin of the problem" (Rose, 1992, p. 60).

On Approaches to Violence Risk Management

In forensic practice the high-risk strategy reigns supreme—and for good reason. The past three decades have witnessed significant strides, not only in our ability to evaluate the risks that an individual might pose, but also in our ability to manage those risks. Perhaps most notable has been the evolution of structured professional judgment (SPJ) approaches to violence risk assessment (e.g., HCR-20; Douglas, Hart, Webster, & Belfrage, 2013). SPJ guides have been developed for the whole gamut of violent acts—sexual, spousal, child abuse, elder abuse, stalking, and extremism (Otto & Douglas, 2010). SPJ procedures require the assessor to consider a number of risk factors known through research or clinical understanding to be associated with violence risk. A multimodal approach to assessment is adopted: Information about risk factors is gathered through interview, document review, and formal psychometric testing.

If risk factors are present the assessor has to determine whether they are relevant to future violent offending; relevant either because they are in some sense causally linked to future violence or because they may adversely affect the risk management plan. The assessor is required to formulate an account of why the individual may be at risk of engaging in violence, consider what form that violence might take, and, finally, describe risk management strategies designed to counter the risk. SPJ approaches fit the clinical task. They provide a common language for practitioners of many disciplines to analyze cases and plan effective interventions; they have revolutionized forensic practice. Critically, they place clinical skill and clinical knowledge at the center of decision-making about risk.

It must be acknowledged that the focus of the SPJ guides has been on risk factors of individuals (e.g., history of violence, substance misuse disorder, personality disorder, major mental illness, sexual ideation, etc.). This is not surprising. Clinical psychologists and other mental health professionals, by dint of training and experience, emphasize the individual over the environmental. To some extent, however, this emphasis represents a form of fundamental attribution bias (Ross, Amabile, & Steinmetz, 1977); that is, there is the tendency, when explaining the behavior of others, to emphasize their personal characteristics and downplay the external factors; the opposite of what we do when explaining our own behavior. This is perhaps because awareness of our own situational factors is greater and they are thus easier to take into account. One consequence of this bias is termed the *individualistic fallacy*, the fallacy of assuming that individual-level outcomes can be explained exclusively by individual-level variables. Silver (2000) observed that the individualistic fallacy is a problem for most research on violence risk generally, and research on mental disorder and violence risk, in particular. Ignoring institutional factors can result in researchers failing to estimate individual-level effects accurately (Silver, 2000). With all the focus on individual risk factors there has been a systemic failure to appreciate, evaluate, and manage situational factors. This problem is not peculiar to forensic practice. The interplay between the individual's characteristics and his/her situation has long been a source of debate and dispute in psychology. Perhaps, most notably, Mischel (e.g., 2004) provided serious critiques of trait psychology in which he argued that the features of the situation in which a person resides have as much—if not more—influence on their behavior than their personal attributes.

Clearly, focusing merely on individual risk factors misses an important source of uncertainty in risk assessment (e.g., Cooke, 1989, 1991, 2010). Both aspects have importance, both for practice and for theory. Toch (1997) summarized the challenge:

> … the goal is the reduction of violence through the creation of a climate that understands its own occasions for violence and begins to defuse them. When one accomplishes this goal, residual violence will be "person centered," and can be addressed as such. (p. 189)

On the Pains of Confinement

Prisons and forensic hospitals are complex systems within which sets of risk factors are interactive; these processes engender circumstances that create violence. It has long been recognized that context, including the pains of confinement—so vividly portrayed by Oscar Wilde in *De Profundis*—affects behavior (Folger & Skarlicki, 1998; Liebling & Arnold, 2012; Perline & Goldschmidt, 2004; van der Laan & Eichelsheim, 2013; Wilde, 1996). A sizeable empirical literature confirms the association between particular risk factors and violence in prisons (e.g., Byrne & Hummer, 2007; Cooke, 1989; Dilulio, 1987; Gadon, Johnstone, & Cooke, 2006; Grant & Jewkes, 2015; Toch, 1982; Wortley, 2002). Theories of prison violence such as the deprivation model, the management model (e.g., Dilulio, 1987), general strain theory (Morris, Carriaga, Diamond, Piquero, & Piquero, 2012) and the procedural justice paradigm (Bierie, 2013) have incorporated situational factors into their explanatory frameworks. More importantly, situational crime control has been shown to be effective in institutional contexts (e.g., Cooke, 1989; Wortley, 2002).

Space precludes a more detailed review; however, I will outline Bierie's (2013) study as it provides a powerful exemplar of situational thinking and analysis. Bierie (2013) examined the impact and saliency of the system for processing the complaints of inmates in the Federal Bureau of Prisons on subsequent inmate violence; he subjected monthly panel data—drawn over a 7-year period from all federal prisons in the USA—to detailed analysis. The results are telling. Inmate violence was not predicted by the outcome of the decision (whether the complaint was denied or upheld). Rather, it was associated with both late replies and the rejection of complaints on administrative grounds; for example, rejection because the prisoner did not complete the complaint form correctly or rejection because of inadequate compliance with the specific language required by the Bureau standards. Bierie's (2013) analysis, through the lens of the procedural justice paradigm, is helpful because it provides a nuanced account of the link between a failing complaints system and violent acts by focusing upon the psychological processes that may drive these acts. Within the procedural justice paradigm, the distinction is made between the desirability of the outcome (was the complaint upheld?) and whether the process was construed as just. Four aspects of the process influence the perception of whether a decision is construed as just. First, was the person's point of view heard before the decision? Second, was everyone treated equally—was the process fair? Third, were the outcomes proportionate? Fourth, and finally, was there access to a review or appeal process?

Rejecting complaints because they do not conform to some bureaucratic standard, or indeed, delivering delayed decisions violates many, if not all, of the core aspects of procedural justice. It is not surprising that failures in the complaint system are linked to violent outcomes with disturbed, distressed, or difficult people. How can this type of analysis be put into action? How can it assist violence prevention?

A Structured Professional Approach to the Evaluation of Institutional Risk

A number of professional experiences heightened my awareness of the impact of situational variables on men at high risk of violence. These experiences included first, working in a radical regime for men characterized as the most violent in the Scottish Prison system—the Barlinnie Special Unit—second, being present as a member of the command team at four major prison riots, and third, attending a 3-day conference held in camera 9 months after the cessation of these riots; a conference attended by 10 of the prisoners who had been central to the riots and hostage takings (Cooke, 1989, 1997; Cooke & Johnstone, 2010, 2012).

My colleague Lorraine Johnstone and I identified a clear need to complement the SPJ guides developed to consider individuals; it was clear that the SPJ paradigm could apply to institutions as well as to individuals (Cooke & Johnstone, 2010; Johnstone & Cooke, 2008). Our overarching aim was to develop evidence-based practice guidelines that could be implemented in forensic settings—forensic hospitals and prisons—and help staff to reflect on what could be done to reduce the incidence of violence. We called these guidelines PRISM (Johnstone & Cooke, 2008). We take the prism analogue from optics. A prism splits white light into its constituent elements and allows these colors to be analyzed and evaluated. Our PRISM takes the whole organization and considers the constituent elements that affect the incidence of violence within the organization; it helps to break down complexity in order that change can be approached in manageable chunks.

Having identified the need, we developed PRISM in four steps guided by the principles of evidence-based practice. First, we performed a systematic review of the literature on situational risk factors for interpersonal violence that occurs in prisons and forensic psychiatric hospitals. We were immediately struck by the paucity of any systematic consideration of this class of risk factors (Gadon et al., 2006). Thus, in the second step, we obtained evidence from inmates and from staff through semi-structured interviews. This was revealing. Not only did we gather evidence about the aspects of the institution which should be considered, but also, we struck a rich seam of explanations about why such factors might serve to promote violent incidents; for example, factors that engendered a sense of injustice, that entailed disrespectful treatment, that promoted a sense of uncertainty or a sense of frustration, and conditions that could be regarded as deprivation, were viewed as serving to promote violence risk (Cooke & Wozniak, 2010).

Third, we used the information derived in the first two steps to develop the PRISM protocol. We distilled and refined the information using rational criteria. We considered that five conceptual domains captured the essential features of 22 risk factors; history of violence, physical environment, organizational factors, staff features, and patient/prisoner care and management. Consistent with the SPJ approach, we defined each risk factor; we specified the range of information sources that should be considered; and we explained how scenario planning techniques could be applied to envision future hazards and described how these scenarios could be used to formulate a risk management plan (See Cooke & Johnstone, 2010, for a detailed account).

The *History of Institutional Violence* domain focuses on the nature, frequency, and pattern of violence in the past 2 years; this allows the establishment of a baseline and a benchmark against which to compare an institution with itself over time, but also, with other comparable institutions. Evidence from this domain provides invaluable information for the scenario planning process used to envision what form future violence might take in that institution.

The *Physical and Security* domain focuses on both the quality of the built environment (e.g., structural quality, cleanliness, noise, temperature, space) and security; is the built environment fit for purpose and does it conform to health and safety and human rights concerns? What is the quality of supervision and control imposed; does it match the level of risk imposed or not? Security that is either too rigorous or too lax can serve to promote violence, the first through a need to save face, the second because of the anxiety generated.

The *Organizational Factors* domain is a broad domain as it is concerned with the strengths and weaknesses of the institution being considered, but also it is concerned with the wider organization in which the institution is embedded (e.g., health authority or prison system). The focus is on the management of violence; is there someone in charge of relevant policies, practices, and procedures, is the management focused on zero tolerance of violent behavior, and is conflict and change within the organization managed systematically and effectively?

The *Staff Features* domain is perhaps the most salient domain when it comes to violence management. It focuses on the strengths and weaknesses of the staff complement; are skilled staff recruited and retained, do staff numbers match the demands of the regime, is the skills/ experience mix correct, do staff receive relevant training for the management of potentially violent individuals, do staff engage and communicate professionally with those in their care, and do they receive required levels of support to do their jobs?

The final domain, the *Case Management* domain, is focused on the services available to potentially violent inmates: does the institution have a systematic approach to the evaluation of individual risks and needs, are quality intervention programs available, and more broadly, to what extent do inmates have access to positive experiences including education, recreation, or contact with family? The fourth step in the development of the current version of PRISM was to field test it in a multiple case study analysis of five Scottish prisons (Johnstone & Cooke, 2010).

The PRISM Process

How does a PRISM evaluation work in practice? PRISM was designed to engender an action-orientated and collaborative approach (Cooke & Johnstone, 2010; Johnstone & Cooke, 2008). The assessment process was designed not only to be sufficiently flexible to cope with the diversity of the institutions being considered, but also to be flexible enough to meet the evolving challenges faced by institutions, from the radicalization of prisoners to the use of drones to deliver drugs and weapons into prisons (Liebling & Arnold, 2012). We strove to avoid the process being viewed as "an inspection." The first stage in the process is to recruit a multidisciplinary team from the institution. The team members are trained to acquire the relevant information (a multimodal, multiple informant approach is used), to evaluate that information, to assess its relevance for future violence, to speculate systematically about what might happen in the institution in the future, and most critically, to propose and implement changes designed to obviate perceived hazards. This collaborative approach increases "buy-in" across the institution. Buy-in increases the likelihood of change (see below). It is critical that risk interventions should be both realistic and achievable. It is essential that proposed changes fit with the capacities and capabilities of the institution and are implemented within a realistic time frame. Some changes can be implemented immediately, within current resources; others require long-term planning and the acquisition of suitable resources.

From Risk Factors to Risk Processes

PRISM provides a template or process for handling information. That information has to be evaluated. As can be seen from the above, identifying those risk factors that are present is not the end point; rather it is the first step. If we are to implement positive change, the interesting question is not *what?* but *why?* Why does a particular institutional practice or structure promote, or indeed, diminish the likelihood of violence? For example, why does poor staff training, the absence of a clear violence policy, or the lack of a risk-needs assessment process increase the likelihood of violence? Answering the why question is a key step for both action and for theory. As Bunge (2006) remarked: "The hallmark of modern science is the search for mechanisms behind facts, rather than the mindless search for data and statistical correlation among them" (p. 119).

Theory can assist. Wikström (2014) has proposed situational action theory (SAT) as a way of integrating personal and contextual variables: "People do what they do because of who they are and the features of the environments in which they take part. What kinds of people are in what kind of settings explains what kind of actions are likely to happen." (p. 75) Thus at the heart of this theory is neither the person *nor* the setting but rather the "perception-choice process"; it is this process which leads to action, a process that is underpinned by both the individual's propensities and his/her situation. An individual who suffers from psychopathic personality disorder, for example, may have a higher propensity for violence than prisoners in general, so that the deterrents to violence require more rigor for such prisoners. By way of contrast, a prisoner with a low propensity for violence would need to be exposed to much more intrusive situational factors before they act violently.

As noted above, developing a proper formulation and an understanding of the perception-choice therefore requires consideration of "why?" and "how?" and not merely "what?" (Cooke, 2010; Cooke & Wozniak, 2010). By way of illustration, consider van der Laan and Eichelsheim's (2013) analysis of a Dutch institution for juvenile offenders. These authors highlighted a series of risk processes that influenced the institutional behavior of the inmates: the failure of staff to provide social support that might buffer stress, the capricious enforcement of rules, and the failure to engender a sense of safety within the institution. By way of further illustration, Liebling and Arnold (2012), contrasting the functioning of a specific prison over a 12-year period, described risk processes in graphic terms:

> The study found a decline in already low levels of trust, with dramatic effects on the prison's inner life. Relationships between prisoners were fractured, more deeply hidden than in the original study, and the traditional prison hierarchy, formerly easily visible in long-term prisons, had dissolved. Longer sentences, fears of radicalization, confusion about prison officer power, and high rates of conversion to Islam, reshaped the dynamics of prison life, raising levels of fear. (p. 413)

How can the perception-choice process be understood in practice? The PRISM assessment starts by considering 22 risk factors as they apply to the institution under study; but as noted above, this is where the process starts—not where it ends. PRISM is a framework for analysis but it is essentially practical; it must lead to action. Once the risk factors have been mapped out, the detailed conceptual work starts; the professional skill and knowledge of the PRISM team comes to the fore. In essence, a formulation must be derived. In clinical practice a formulation is an organizational framework on which to hang our knowledge of the institution—and its functioning—to facilitate the generation of an understanding of the likely mechanisms that drive violence—or other negative outcomes—and which can be used to generate interventions designed to impact on violent behavior (Hart & Logan, 2011). The formulation is based both on case-specific factors and also upon knowledge—clinical, professional, and empirical knowledge—about the underlying processes that drive risk for violence in any institution. Formulation is not an algorithmic or mechanical process but rather it is a process that depends upon applying psychological knowledge and psychological theories and hypotheses to the problem of concern (Hart & Logan, 2011). Self-evidently, organizations are complex and many factors can singly, and in combination, set the conditions that amplify the risk of institutional violence. The task of the PRISM team is to use the data systematically collected to underpin the formulation of risk.

The analytic approach leans on the thinking that underpins quasi-experimental methods (e.g., Shadish, Cook, & Campbell, 1999) and systematic case study methods (Yin, 2009). Yin (2009) captured the challenge well: "Data analysis consists of examining, categorizing, tabulating, testing, or otherwise recombining evidence, to draw empirically based conclusions. Analyzing case study evidence is especially difficult because these techniques still have not been well defined" (p. 126). Techniques familiar to other fields, including pattern matching, logic models, and cross-case synthesis of findings, are powerful tools that allow the evaluation of alternative interpretations of phenomena being considered (Yin, 2009). The range of analytic strategies available is beyond the scope of this chapter; however, two approaches to formulation of PRISM cases may illustrate the general principles. These approaches can be characterized first, as looking for themes that undergird the risk factors, and second, seeking out putative root causes.

The empirical work that led to the development of the PRISM allowed us to identify the risk factors that should be considered in the general case; however, when it comes to understanding the individual institution it is necessary to move from a simple account of which risk factors are present toward an analysis of why any particular risk factor—or more commonly combinations of risk factors—impact on the violence level in the institution of concern. This is the basis of the formulation.

As noted above, there are many ways of viewing and evaluating data derived from systematic case studies. One useful step is the refining and reduction of the number of risk factors in order to simplify the formulation and facilitate the development of a risk management plan. The 22 risk factors can be thought of—by analogue—to be surface markers of underlying latent traits, or what we term *risk processes* (Cooke, 2010, Cooke & Wozniak, 2010). Risk processes can be considered to be theoretical constructs that can be instantiated by the risk factors; but critically, they are constructs that explain how and why the risk factors act to generate the risk of future violence. SPJ approaches are generally predicated on a decision theory framework that posits that the decision to be violent is a choice. "The decision may be made quickly, based on bad information, and with little care and attention—that is, it may be a bad decision or a decision made badly—but it is a decision nonetheless" (Hart & Logan, 2011, p. 94). Risk processes are about cause: Risk processes are the nexus between the environment and psychological state that leads to the decision to be violent. In Wikström (2014) terms, the risk processes affect the "perception-choice process." Thus, once a risk factor has been identified, it is important to deconstruct it by asking the questions: why and how? Why does this risk factor affect the decision to be violent? Does the risk factor drive, destabilize, or disinhibit the individual so that their decision to be violent is more likely? (Cooke, 2010). The key elements of the relevant risk factors are generally underpinned by a limited set of risk processes that influence the decision to be violent. The identification of key risk processes simplifies and clarifies understanding. As noted above, both the literature and experience indicate that common themes that promote violence include a sense of injustice, a sense of disrespect, a sense of uncertainty, loss of agency, loss of trust, and the affiliative need to be violent to achieve gang membership or peer acceptance (Cooke & Wozniak, 2010).

In our case study of the causes of the riot in Barbados (Cooke & Wozniak, 2010), for example, it was clear that a fundamental risk process was the sense of injustice that prevailed among the inmates. What created this sense? There were many sources. These included government policies that failed to implement a parole system and that tolerated remand periods of up to 4 years for minor offenses; "justice delayed is justice denied." Risk factors internal to the prison included an ethos that violence was acceptable; the failure to sanction members of staff who perpetrated violence; the arbitrary use of complete lockdown in response to a localized infraction, and physical conditions that were unsanitary, restricted, overcrowded, and lacking in basic facilities.

Of course, in the complexity of institutional life, many risk factors influence more than one risk process; for example, inadequate staff training could engender perceptions of disrespectful treatment, and feelings of uncertainty and frustration; aspects of the physical layout and resources could engender perceptions of injustice, deprivation, and being disrespected. The task of formulation is to capture and understand these fundamental risk processes.

From Evaluation Through Scenarios Toward Interventions

In line with modern SPJ approaches, the PRISM adopts a scenario planning approach. That is, the PRISM process envisions descriptions of possible future violence in the particular institution, based on the formulation. Scenarios are short narratives designed to encapsulate the essence of the complex of information; these narratives guide systematic thinking about the topography of future violence in the institution of concern; critically, they provide guidance for interventions designed to obviate risk (Hart & Logan, 2011). Scenario planning has a long history in the management of uncertain and negative futures; it is well suited to the analysis of complex organizations.

When it comes to planning interventions it frequently becomes clear that there is a natural hierarchy of relevant risk factors; by targeting the risk factors that represent root causes it may be possible to effectively impact a number of other relevant risk factors. To illustrate, if the risk factor *Leadership and management on violence-related issues* is problematic then it could lead to many other risk factors being problematic: for example, *Security measures, Policies and procedures on violence, Staff training and competencies, Staff approach, style and accessibility, Staff morale, Individualized assessment for risks/needs,* and *Interventions for violence reduction.* Thus, by focusing on a putative root cause, for example, improving the quality of management focused on violence-related issues in the institution, it can be possible to influence a complex of risk factors and, thereby, enhance violence prevention.

Having developed a detailed formulation of risk processes that operate within an institution and envisioned possible violent outcomes, the next step is to develop an action plan. PRISM is sufficiently flexible to be applied for a range of purposes, from critical incident review, through ongoing review of current practice, to strategic planning for new services. What might interventions look like? I will briefly consider several real case examples to illustrate action plans.

Thinking About Situational Interventions

The pilot version of PRISM was used to provide a critical incident review to the government of Barbados following the total loss of Her Majesty's Prison (HMP) Glendairy, Barbados, as a result of rioting and arson in 2005. This review led directly to a program of work drawing on international perspectives but tailored to fit both the resources and the culture of Barbados (Cooke & Johnstone, 2012; Cooke & Wozniak, 2010). This program of work was designed to improve staff training, including leadership training, human rights training, staff–inmate communication, systems for evaluating risk/needs of prisoners, and the implementation of offending behavior programs for selected inmates. Specifically, frontline staff felt alienated and disempowered; leadership training designed to reduce the overly hierarchical and constrained management style was recommended. The implementation of appropriate information systems was recommended to counter the identified problem that little systematic information was held about prisoners. This lack led to capricious decision-making. It is vital that recommended interventions are tailored to fit the resources and cultures of the country. Recommendations have to be implementable to be effective; evolution rather than revolution is more likely to lead to permanent change.

In a well-functioning UK high secure forensic psychiatric hospital, a number of improvements were implemented following a routine review based upon PRISM. These included improvements in the violence recording system—clearer operational definitions and identification of potential motivators and precipitants—the provision of more opportunities for patients to have quiet time, the improvement of furniture layouts to limit blind spots, and the encouragement of staff to use clinical supervision to reflect on their interactional style and thereby consider the best ways to engage with specific patients. Similar interventions were implemented in a Scandinavian high secure facility.

When five Scottish prisons were evaluated in a multiple case study, a range of interventions were developed. These included the refinement of violence-recording measures, a review of the complaint procedures, staff training focused on violence prevention, a communications strategy regarding security and control, improved policies and procedures on violence issues, and better individualized violence risk assessment (Johnstone & Cooke, 2010).

A notable illustration of the use of PRISM proactively—for strategic planning—is the work carried out in Denmark to plan the transfer of the high secure hospital to a new facility some 80 km from its original base. A PRISM process was carried out some 18 months prior to the move. It provided a framework for the development of the new regime including, but not limited to, the development of systematic risk assessment processes for individual patients; clear policies on security procedures including fire, hostage-taking, fights, and bomb threats; staff training focused on de-escalation skills; and the development of meaningful patient activities. This proactive approach has been deemed to be effective in terms of establishing a new institution using evidence-based approaches (Susanne Møller-Madsen, personal communication, May 25, 2015). A key finding from the studies carried out so far is that while interventions need to be tailored to the specific needs and structures of the organization being considered, there are clear commonalities that can allow best practice to be transferred among organizations.

The Application of the PRISM Process

To my knowledge, PRISM has been used to evaluate a wide range of forensic psychiatric and prison settings in the United Kingdom, Norway, Sweden, Denmark, New Zealand, Singapore, and Barbados. There are a number of published studies reporting on the application of PRISM. The approach has been used to evaluate the functioning of five prisons in Scotland (e.g., Cooke, Wozniak, & Johnstone, 2008; Johnstone & Cooke, 2010), the prison in Barbados (Cooke & Wozniak, 2010), high-security prisons in New Zealand (Wilson & Tamatea, 2010), and a prison for young offenders in England (Cregg & Payne, 2010). However, because of the sensitive nature of the evaluations, the majority of case studies are not published; they are used as action documents.

A number of recent case studies highlight the applicability of PRISM in different types of secure services; I will describe these studies briefly to further illustrate the diversity of settings that can be evaluated. Nötesjö and Asare (2016) reported on four case studies in Sweden. Statens institutions Styrelse (SiS) is a government organization that provides compulsory care for young people with severe psychosocial difficulties and for adults with severe substance abuse across some 36 institutions distributed the length and breadth of Sweden. Difficulties with institutional violence had been identified. Following PRISM assessments, the most salient difficulties identified across the four institutions were the mismatch between formal records and other reports of violence, major gaps in risk assessment processes, and poor adherence to policies and procedures. Senior SiS management valued the assessments: PRISM is now being implemented in other SiS institutions.

De Villiers (2016) described a 13-bedded learning disability assessment and treatment ward in Scotland which had a consistently high level of physical aggression and staff injury. The unit was in crisis; staff withdrew care from a patient who engaged in frequent violence; members of staff were afraid to come to work. De Villiers' PRISM evaluation found the physical environment was unsafe, the management structure was unclear, and the organizational ethos accepted that staff could be abused and assaulted regularly; staff felt alienated and undervalued, and professional relationships were fractured—their morale was low—policies and procedures were available but rarely implemented. Closure of the unit was mooted.

Perhaps the most salient indicator of the organization's dysfunction was the initial refusal of senior management to accept the PRISM report, and their attempts to have the report altered. Eventually, critical risk factors were addressed by (a) implementing processes to improve on-site staff conflicts, (b) ensuring that staff engaged with clinical supervision, (c) streamlining management decision-making, and (d) the improvement of the physical fabric of the institution. De Villiers (2016) reported that violence levels are now much reduced and that new unsettled patients have been admitted without a return to previous high levels of violence.

Lehany (2016) described the implementation of the PRISM process in a 15-bedded medium secure service in New Zealand (NZ). This was a proactive assessment based on the desire to avoid violence by systematically evaluating current practices and conditions, to ensure that best practice was in place. The primary aim of the intervention was to ensure that violence was prevented by making violence reduction a key goal for all staff. Given the ethnic mix of the unit (Māori, Pacific, and NZ European cultures) there was a need for cultural sensitivity. The assessment took place in the context of increasing levels of reported assaults in mental health services in New Zealand. The primary recommendation of the PRISM report was the physical refurbishment of the unit, along with enhanced staff training, improved skills sharing with other units and other professional groups, and developments in rehabilitation programs.

In England and Wales, the National Offender Management Service has responded to the increasing problem of institutional violence by piloting the application of PRISM across both the public and the private sector. Fifteen sites have been evaluated. A thematic review is being conducted to determine the lessons that can be learned at the organization level as well as those that can be learned at the level of the individual prison. It is anticipated that the pilot will inform any wider use of PRISM. (J. Tew, personal communication, October 3, 2016). These brief accounts hopefully highlight both the diversity of applications and the diversity of contexts that the PRISM process has been applied in—so far.

Achieving Organizational Change

The *raison d'être* of a PRISM evaluation is organizational change. As I just described, organizational changes may range from the development of a clear policy on how violent events are dealt with, or the implementation of a proper recording system for violent incidents, through improvement in inmate activities, increases in staff–inmate communication, enhanced contact with visitors, to the building of new facilities. How can these changes be achieved?

There is no magic formula or recipe book for effective organization change. Change management is a vast and specialized topic (e.g., Blake & Bush, 2008) which cannot be done justice in this brief chapter. Each organization is— in its own way—unique; effective interventions should be based on the systematic analysis and best judgment of those who work in the institution. However, reflecting on experience with a wide range of institutions—in a number of countries—there are several broad principles that can be derived.

First, the conditions for change should be set from the outset of the PRISM process through the careful selection of the team that will complete the process. It is important to select a range of stakeholders from all parts of the organization. Experience suggests that even merely starting the PRISM process can kick-start change by directing the organization's attention to the issue of violence—and the impact of situational factors. To illustrate this point, Wilson and Tamatea (2010) implemented PRISM in three maximum security units in Auckland prison in New Zealand, units that were troubled by serious and high-profile assaults. They trained staff in the PRISM process, but it was a number of months before they could complete the evaluation; they found that having directed the unit staff's attention to the power of environmental factors, the staff had spontaneously injected greater flexibility and variety into the quality of life of the unit; they had improved the staff mix and implemented an active management approach to challenging prisoners.

Second, it is essential that the PRISM team from the institution own the process; care must be taken in ensuring that the process is not perceived as an inspection—a process to assign blame—but rather it is a forward-facing process designed to consider how the institution might do things better. The PRISM process is designed to be collaborative and action-orientated. It is heartening that independent users of PRISM have found it effective in that regard (e.g., Lehany, 2016; Nötesjö & Asare, 2016; Susanne Møller-Madsen, personal communication, May 25, 2015; Wilson & Tamatea, 2010). Wilson and Tamatea (2010), for example, reported that staff found the use of scenario planning to be emblematic of the shift from a culture of blame to a forward-facing and proactive stance. Nötesjö and Asare (2016) found that the approach "made sense" to staff; such perceptions increase the likelihood of engagement with change.

Third, if change is to be achieved it is critical that proposed risk interventions be realistic and achievable, that the interventions fit with both the capacities and the capabilities of the institution. Clearly, there will be changes that can be implemented quickly and within current resources (Wilson & Tamatea, 2010), whereas other changes will require planning and the acquisition of resources (Cooke & Wozniak, 2010).

Fourth, while it might be tempting to focus on the most obvious changes, or the changes that are easiest to implement, it is important to focus effort on the changes that can produce the biggest potential benefits. Tackling root causes can often achieve disproportionate impact.

Fifth, staff are the lynchpin of an effective institution; managing staff is the key to effective change. It is vital to focus on both the technical changes and the human changes. Organization changes often trigger feelings of loss, anxiety, and bewilderment in staff members. It is important that staff see the point of the changes and that the processes and reward system support rather than oppose changes; training in the required skills should be provided—and critically—role models must actively model the changes they require of their staff. In essence, effective change will only come about if staff—at all levels—are engaged and able to realign their own personal mental models about why inmates might be violent.

There is no magic formula or recipe book for effective organizations; PRISM helps the process of analysis and the evolution of case-specific solutions, be it in a prison following a riot, a high secure hospital facing relocation some 80 km away, or the planning of a new prison for sex offender treatment.

How Is the PRISM Process Viewed in Practice?

Evaluations have demonstrated high levels of user satisfaction with the PRISM approach (Cregg & Payne, 2010; Johnstone & Cooke, 2010; Wilson & Tamatea, 2010). Describing work in a forensic inpatient unit in Wellington, New Zealand, Lehany (2016) reported that the staff found the PRISM process to be helpful because it provided a clear and specific focus on unit practice and unit safety, and additionally, staff appreciated being consulted. Nötesjö and Asare (2016) reported that PRISM has ecological validity, making sense to both staff and clients alike. Other professionals involved have commented that the protocol provides a framework within which a broad range of issues can be explored and where multiple staff perspectives can be acknowledged and interwoven to produce an outcome relevant to progressing change. Cregg and Payne (2010) concluded that the PRISM assessment of a juvenile custodial setting: "… brought about the design of a number of child-appropriate interventions that have been recognized as innovative for managing violence by key stake-holders" (p. 178). Managers of institutions have reported that having an evidence-based evaluation has allowed them to procure additional resources (e.g., staff, training, improved buildings) from funding agencies including government bodies (e.g., Nötesjö & Asare, 2016; Susanne Møller-Madsen, personal communication, May 25, 2015).

The Future Challenges for Situational Approaches

The evolution of SPJ approaches to the violence risk management of the individual offender has revolutionized forensic practice. How might the scope of situational approaches to risk management be expanded and refined? I consider that there are three areas ripe for development.

First, the PRISM approach may generalize beyond interpersonal violence. The risk processes identified above—such as a sense of injustice, sense of being disrespected, or sense of fear—are likely to impact on other signs of institutional malfunction: self-neglect, self-harm, suicidal behavior, absconding, and so on. Lösel (2012), for example, noted "mutual respect, humanity, support, relationship-orientation and trust play an important role in the prevention of conflicts, suicides and other problems" (p. 84). While there is currently a paucity of evidence on the impact of situational factors on self-neglect, self-harm, and suicidal behavior, there is some evidence that implicates such factors (see also Logan and Taylor, Chapter 7). For example, studies by Bonner (2006) and Marzano, Hawton, Rivlin, and Fazel (2011) suggest that people residing outside normal prison wings may be at elevated risk of self-harm. Nijman and à Campo (2002) described lack of stimulation and interaction with others in secure psychiatric settings as being provoking factors for self-harming behavior. Ramluggun (2013) reported a cluster of staff factors associated with an elevated risk of self-harm: inadequate training, lack of management support, and interdisciplinary conflict. Bowers et al. (2008) concluded that the availability of qualified nursing staff and intensive programs of patient activities served to mitigate the risk of self-harm during inpatient care.

Second, the PRISM approach may generalize not just to other adverse outcomes but also to other types of settings. The risk processes are unlikely to be peculiar to the settings—prisons and forensic hospitals—where the PRISM approach was developed. Conceptually it appears likely that these risk processes will lead to problems wherever they are found. Closed settings (e.g., psychiatric hospitals, care homes, children's homes, prisons, and other residential settings) are high-risk environments for such behaviors (Richter & Whittingon, 2006). The problem in the field is the lack of empirical data; this lack is perhaps founded on the fundamental attribution bias which assumes that for inmates of closed institutions their problems are a consequence of their failings, not the consequence of the institutional environment.

Third, there is a need to develop a taxonomy of risk processes and a taxonomy of risk management strategies. Having reviewed the available studies, there are key risk processes (e.g., disrespectful treatment, fear) that typically serve to potentiate the decision to be violent across many institutional settings. Similarly, while responses need to be tailored to the individual institution, there are common strategies that can be adapted. The wheel does not require reinvention.

Violence prevention is the keystone of forensic practice. Although long neglected there is now a growing awareness of the import of identifying and understanding the situational factors which contribute, not only to institutional violence, but also to other indicators of institutional distress. It is hoped that the PRISM process makes a contribution toward understanding and managing these factors: disturbed, distressed, and disordered people are not violent merely because of who they are but because of where they are, and how they are treated. The PRISM process can also improve organizational resilience; that is, the organization's capacity to both survive and thrive in challenging conditions; its capacity to resist operational hazards: in this case, violent incidents (Burnard & Bhamra, 2011).

Key Readings

Cooke, D. J. (1989). Containing violent prisoners: An analysis of the Barlinnie Special Unit. *British Journal of Criminology*, 29, 129–143.

Cooke, D. J., & Wozniak, E. (2010). PRISM applied to a critical incident review: A case study of the Glendairy prison riot. *International Journal of Forensic Mental Health Services*, 9, 159–172.

Gadon, L., Johnstone, L., & Cooke, D. J. (2006). Situational variables and institutional violence: A systematic review of the literature. *Clinical Psychology Review*, 26, 534–548.

Rose, G. (1992). *The strategy of preventative medicine.* Oxford, UK: Oxford Medical Publications.

Wilson, N. J., & Tamatea, A. (2010). Beyond punishment: Applying PRISM in a New Zealand maximum security prison. *International Journal of Forensic Mental Health Services*, 9, 192–204.

Wortley, R. (2002). *Situational prison control. Crime prevention in correctional institutions.* Cambridge, UK: Cambridge University Press.

References

Bierie, D. M. (2013). Examining complaints among federal inmates (2000–2007). *Psychology, Public Policy, and Law*, 19, 15–29.

Blake, I., & Bush, C. (2008). *Project managing change: Practical tools and techniques to make change happen.* London, UK: Pearson Education.

Bonner, R. L. (2006). Stressful segregation housing and psychosocial vulnerability in prison suicide ideators. *Suicide and Life-Threatening Behavior*, 36, 250–254.

Bowers, L., Whittington, R., Nolan, P., Parkin, D., Curtis, S., Bhui, K., ... & Simpson, A. (2008). Relationship between service ecology, special observation and self-harm during acute in-patient care: City-128 study. *The British Journal of Psychiatry*, 193, 395–401.

Bunge, M. (2006). *Chasing reality: Strife over realism*. Toronto, Canada: University of Toronto Press.

Burnard, K., & Bhamra, R. (2011). Organisational resilience: Development of a conceptual framework for organisational responses. *International Journal of Production Research*, 49, 5581–5599.

Byrne, J. M., & Hummer, D. (2007). Myths and realities of prison violence. *Victims and Offenders*, 2, 77–90.

Cooke, D. J. (1989). Containing violent prisoners: An analysis of the Barlinnie Special Unit. *British Journal of Criminology*, 29, 129–143.

Cooke, D. J. (1991). Violence in prisons: The influence of regime factors. *The Howard Journal of Criminal Justice*, 30, 95–109.

Cooke, D. J. (1997). The Barlinnie Special Unit: The rise and fall of a therapeutic experiment. In E. Cullen, L. Jones, & R. Woodward (Eds.), *Therapeutic communities for offenders* (pp. 101–120). London, UK: Wiley.

Cooke, D. J. (2010). Personality disorder and violence. Understand violence risk: An introduction to the special section personality disorder and violence. *Journal of Personality Disorders*, 24, 539–550.

Cooke, D. J., & Johnstone, L. (2010). Somewhere over the rainbow: Improving violence risk management in institutional settings. *International Journal of Forensic Mental Health Services*, 9, 150–158.

Cooke, D. J., & Johnstone, L. (2012). A look through the PRISM. *The Psychologist*, 25, 604–607.

Cooke, D. J., & Wozniak, E. (2010). PRISM applied to a critical incident review: A case study of the Glendairy prison riot. *International Journal of Forensic Mental Health Services*, 9, 159–172.

Cooke, D. J., Wozniak, E., & Johnstone, L. (2008). Casting light on prison violence: Evaluating the impact of situational risk factors. *Criminal Justice and Behavior*, 35, 1065–1078.

Cregg, M., & Payne, E. (2010). PRISM with incarcerated young people: Optical illusion or reflection of reality. *International Journal of Forensic Mental Health Services*, 9, 173–179.

de Villiers, J. 2016 *When the ward is the patient: A case study*. Paper presented at the International Asssociation of Forensic Mental Health Services, New York.

Dilulio, J. J. (1987). *Governing prisons*. New York, NY: The Free Press.

Douglas, K. S., Hart, S. D., Webster, C. D., & Belfrage, H. (2013). *HCR-20*³ *Assessing risk for violence*. Burnaby, Canada: Simon Fraser University.

Folger, R., & Skarlicki, D. (1998). A popcorn model of workplace violence. In R. W. Griffin, A. O'Leary-Kelly, & J. M. Collins (Eds.), *Dysfunction behavior in organizations: Violence and deviant behavior* (pp. 1–42). Stamford, CT: JAI Press.

Gadon, L., Johnstone, L., & Cooke, D. J. (2006). Situational variables and institutional violence: A systematic review of the literature. *Clinical Psychology Review*, 26, 534–548.

Grant, E., & Jewkes, Y. (2015). Finally fit for purpose: The evolution of Australian prison architecture. *The Prison Journal*, 95, 223–243.

Hart, S. D., & Logan, C. (2011). Formulation of violence risk using evidence-based assessments: The structured professional judgment approach. In P. Sturmey, & M. McMurran (Eds.), *Forensic Case Formulation* (pp. 81–106). Chichester, UK: Wiley.

Johnstone, L., & Cooke, D. J. (2008). *PRISM: Promoting Risk Intervention by Situational Management. Structured professional guidelines for assessing situational risk factors for violence in institutions*. East Kilbride, UK: Authors.

Johnstone, L., & Cooke, D. J. (2010). PRISM: A promising paradigm for assessing and managing institutional violence: Findings from a multiple case study analysis of five Scottish prisons. *International Journal of Forensic Mental Health Services*, 9, 180–191.

Krug, E. G., Dahlberg, J. A., Mercy, J. A., Zwi, A. B., & Lozano, R. (2002). *World report on violence and health*. Geneva, Switzerland: World Health Organisation.

Lehany, G. (2016). *International perspectives: PRISM in New Zealand*. Paper presented at the International Association of Forensic Mental Health Services, New York, NY.

Liebling, A., & Arnold, H. (2012). Social relationships between prisoners in a maximum security prison: Violence, faith, and the declining nature of trust. *Journal of Criminal Justice*, 40, 413–424.

Lösel, F. (2012). What works in correctional treatment and rehabilitation for young adults. In F. Losel, D. Farrington, & A. Bottoms (Eds.), *Young adult offenders: Lost in transition* (pp. 74–112). Abingdon, UK: Routledge.

Marzano, L., Hawton, K., Rivlin, A., & Fazel, S. (2011). Psychosocial influences on prisoner suicide: A case-control study of near-lethal self-harm in women prisoners. *Social Science & Medicine*, 72, 874–883.

Mischel, W. (2004). Towards an integrative science of the person. *Annual Review of Psychology*, 55, 1–22.

Morris, R. G., Carriaga, M. L., Diamond, B., Piquero, N. L., & Piquero, A. R. (2012). Does prison strain lead to prison misbehavior? An application of general strain theory to inmate misconduct. *Journal of Criminal Justice*, 40, 194–201.

Nijman, H. L., & à Campo, J. M. (2002). Situational determinants of inpatient self-harm. *Suicide and Life-Threatening Behavior*, 32(2), 167–175.

Nijman, H. L. I., Merckelbach, H. L. G. J., Allertz, W. F. F., & à Campo, J. M. L. G. (1997). Prevention of aggressive incidents on a closed psychiatric ward. *Psychiatric Services*, 48(5), 694–698.

Noll, T. (2015). Prison violence (editorial). *International Journal of Offender Therapy and Comparative Criminology*, 59(4), 335–336.

Nötesjö, G. A., & Asare, F. (2016). *Institutional violence in Swedish compulsory care: Results form a multiple case study using PRISM* Paper presented at the International Asssociation of Forensic Mental Health Services, New York.

Otto, R. K., & Douglas, K. S. (2010). *Handbook of violence risk assessment*. New York, NY: Routledge.

Perline, I. H., & Goldschmidt, J. (2004). *The psychology and law of workplace violence: A handbook for mental health professionals and employers*. New York, NY: Charles C Thomas.

Ramluggun, P. (2013). A critical exploration of the management of self-harm in a male custodial setting: Qualitative findings of a comparative analysis of prison staff views on self-harm. *Journal of Forensic Nursing*, 9(1), 23–34.

Richter, D., & Whittingon, R. (2006). *Violence in mental health settings: Causes, consequences, management*. London, UK: Springer.

Rose, G. (1992). *The strategy of preventative medicine*. Oxford, UK: Oxford Medical Publications.

Ross, L. D., Amabile, T. M., & Steinmetz, J. L. (1977). Social roles, social control, and biases in social-perception processes. *Journal of Personality and Social Psychology*, 35(7), 485–494.

Shadish, W. R., Cook, T. D., & Campbell, D. T. (1999). *Experimental and quasi-experimental designs for generalized causal inference*. Boston, MA: Houghton Mifflin.

Silver, E. (2000). Race, neighborhood disadvantage, and violence among persons with mental disorders: The importance of contextual measurement. *Law and Human Behavior*, 24(4), 449–456.

Toch, H. (1982). The disturbed disruptive inmate: Where does the bus stop? *The Journal of Psychiatry and Law*, 10, 327–349.

Toch, H. (1997). *Corrections: A humanistic approach*. Guilderland, NY: Harrow and Heston.

van der Laan, A., & Eichelsheim, V. (2013). Juvenile adaptation to imprisonment: Feelings of safety, autonomy and well-being, and behaviour in prison. *European Journal of Criminology*, 10(4), 424–443.

Wikström, P. O. H. (2014). Why crime happens: A situational action theory. In G. Manzo (Ed.), *Analytical sociology: Actions and networks* (pp. 74–94). Chichester, UK: Wiley.

Wilde, O. (1996). *De Profundis*. Mineola, NY: Dover.

Wilson, N. J., & Tamatea, A. (2010). Beyond punishment: Applying PRISM in a New Zealand maximum security prison. *International Journal of Forensic Mental Health Services*, 9, 192–204.

World Health Organisation (2010). *Violence prevention: The evidence*. Geneva, Switzerland: Authors.

Wortley, R. (2002). *Situational prison control: Crime prevention in correctional institutions*. Cambridge, UK: Cambridge University Press.

Yin, R. K. (2009). *Case study research: Design and methods* (4th ed.). Thousand Oaks, CA: Sage.

6

Managing Difficult and Disruptive Prisoners

Nick J. Wilson and T. Glen Kilgour
Department of Corrections, New Zealand

Around 20 years ago as a junior correctional psychologist, one of us—Nick Wilson—was asked by prison staff to assist with the management of a young prisoner we will call "Simon" (not his real name). Nick knew that staff were desperate because asking a psychologist for assistance was their last resort! Aged just 18, Simon was refusing to return to a mainstream unit after 12 months of solitary confinement. There was a long-standing "battle" going on between custodial staff and Simon, with both sides accusing the other of assault and bad behavior, resulting in a large number of misconduct reports and complaints. Simon had also upset staff by smearing feces on his cell walls, and he was not well liked by custodial staff, as reacting to his behavior had become a major part of their work day.

When Nick arrived at the cell door to speak with Simon it was clear from observing his empty cell that his only remaining possessions were the clothes he wore and one blanket, with escalating punishment having been the only strategy used by the prison. Staff consulting with Nick murmured that they had run out of punishment options unless they broke the prisoner's arm! Nick spoke with the staff about the "ego rewards" Simon was gaining from his refusal, especially when there were no other rewards available for compliance considering his deprived environment.

Nick's recommendations were to enrich Simon's environment and to agree to reasonable requests, in order to stop the battle of wills. This advice was received with skepticism because it was seen as letting the prisoner win and rewarding him for prior non-compliance. However, in the absence of any other way forward, the desperate staff followed this approach and agreement was later gained from Simon to move back to a mainstream unit. The extreme and challenging behavior by Simon soon reduced and staff found him easier to manage, although he continued to be vigilant to unfair treatment.

This story about Simon illustrates many of the issues that difficult and disruptive prisoners, or indeed offenders in general, bring to those tasked with their care. Challenging behavior can be complex but it always has a function. However, it is easy for staff to personalize the interactions, and to become frustrated and punitive in response. The aim of this chapter is to provide understanding and guidance about how to manage prisoners, such as Simon, who can negatively define our days.

Definitional Issues

The definition of "difficult and disruptive prisoners" is plagued with problems. Prisoners described as difficult and disruptive may be involved in a wide range of concerning behaviors: from undermining the security and safety of the prison environment through covert actions (e.g., oppositional behavior, introducing banned substances, running a "shop"[1]), through to inciting others to riot, religious radicalization of others, self-harm, threats, or physical aggression toward other prisoners or staff. Complicating this is the lens (or lenses) through which these behaviors are examined and understood. The development and function of difficult and disruptive prisoner behaviors needs to be understood from a number of perspectives, including developmental (e.g., family of origin values and teachings, other prior socialization events, offense history), personality (e.g., antisocial, psychopathic, paranoid, borderline, or other significant traits or syndromes), mental health (e.g., history of head injury, substance abuse, serious psychopathology), and environmental (e.g., institutional setting, managerial regime, custodial officer behavior, access to programs, and prosocial support). A full review of all these considerations is beyond the scope of this chapter. However, we also direct the reader's attention to Chapters 5 and 7.

There have been relatively few attempts to formally describe and categorize disruptive prisoner behaviors. Cooke (1998) developed the Prison Behaviour Rating Scale (PBRS) in an attempt to provide a reliable procedure for use among adult prisoners. The PBRS recorded prison officers' judgments of prisoner behavior to help classify disruptive prisoners into one or more of three broad categories: Antiauthority; Anxious-Depressed; and Dull-Confused, with the hope to inform appropriate placement decisions. Those classified as antiauthority also had higher scores for psychopathic personality, more prior criminal behavior, were likely to be held in higher security, and typically had a higher risk of reoffending after release. The link between psychopathy and prison misconduct has been confirmed through meta-analysis (Walters, 2003), although the results across studies are viewed as weak to moderate depending on whether the focus is general versus violent misconduct ($r = .29$ to $r = .17$). These results also indicate that psychopathy ratings (using the Psychopathy Checklist—Revised [PCL-R], Psychopathy Checklist: Screening Version [PCL:SV], and Psychopathy Checklist: Youth Version [PCL:YV]) for patterns of past socially deviant behavior are associated with misconduct more strongly than for items related to antisocial personality traits. This stronger relationship with patterns of past behavior rather than personality traits is consistent with the general literature on risk prediction and psychopathy (Guy, Edens, Anthony, & Douglas, 2005; Walters, 2003). Interestingly, while we are sure that the custodial staff involved would have classified Simon as antiauthoritarian, Nick's assessment also found a high level of anxiety contributing to his behavior.

Environmental and contextual circumstances may also trigger or maintain difficult and disruptive prisoner behavior, with ample evidence to suggest that the prison environment exerts significant control over the management and expression of the behavior of prisoners. King, Steiner, and Breach (2008), for example, outlined the historical context, environmental circumstances, and subcultural contributions—both of prisoners and of prison staff—in the development of a normative expectation of violence within a Californian "supermax" prison. Particular concerns included the expectation that such a facility, or indeed most high-security settings, are designed to manage "the worst of the worst." Design of these facilities aimed to eliminate contact between staff and prisoners as well as between prisoners. This isolation supported normative expectations of violence for what is a typically paranoid population, with lengthy periods of social isolation increasing mental health difficulties, including predisposition to anger, violent fantasy, and an inability to self-manage emotion. We have also found in our own clinical experience working with prisoners in high-security settings over 20 years that such rigid and deprived environments amplify the worst personality aspects and dysfunctional automatic behavioral responses. In contrast, sometimes the best initial intervention may be as simple as placing the disruptive prisoner into a less deprived and less punitive environment. However, this can be complicated by the prisoner's own negative expectations of what prison should be like and their own self-perceptions (e.g., "real men do their time in maxi").

It doesn't, however, require a "supermax" prison to "cook" bad behavior, even among non-prisoner populations. Zimbardo's famous experiment in the early 1970s randomly assigned university students to roles of prisoner and prison officer. The behavior of some individuals from both groups deteriorated across several days, showing the impact of context and role expectations within an extreme custodial environment. Zimbardo himself acknowledged getting caught up in his role as "Prison Superintendent"; coming to "talk, walk and act like a rigid institutional authority figure more concerned about the security of 'my prison' than the needs of the young men entrusted to my care" (Zimbardo, 2004, p. 15). While Zimbardo (2004) emphasized only the role of situational factors such as deindividuation and dehumanization, other sources point out that extreme behavior "flows" from extreme institutions. It appears that some prison guards even self-select to work in maximum security; so the scenario is less about good people going bad than it is about an institution that expects bad behavior from its prisoners finding a ready and reactive staff cohort (Konnikova, 2015).

Examining the effects of prison on recidivism, it appears not only that there is a lack of deterrent effects from incarceration but also that prisons—especially "gratuitously painful ones"—are criminogenic (Cullen, Jonson, & Nagin, 2011). Cullen et al. encouraged policy-makers to take a step back from the hubris around harsh sentencing policy and, particularly for high-risk offenders subject to incarceration, provide evidence-based rehabilitation programs to help offset the iatrogenic nature of prison environments. In summary, tough prisons make tough prisoners.

Such observations lead to concerns over whether difficult and disruptive behavior is a function of *prisoner* characteristics or *prison* characteristics. This difference in functional focus has contributed to the development of progressive measures such as the Promoting Risk Intervention by Situational Management (PRISM; Johnstone & Cooke, 2008), which examines situational and environmental risk factors for violence within institutional environments (Chapter 5). However, the best approach in our opinion to these functional differences is most likely found somewhere in the continuum between these poles of individual and prison factors. In general, difficult and disruptive behavior is complex and requires consideration of multiple factors and approaches as with PRISM rather than simple single-factor management regimes.

The remainder of this chapter will therefore address the broadly non-compliant and hostile or aggressive behavior by prisoners that is typical of those held in higher security custodial settings. While our focus will be on individual prisoner characteristics, especially personality and how psychology can inform prisoner management, the interaction with the prison setting and custodial practices are acknowledged.

Prevalence of Behavior

The disruptive and difficult prisoners we described earlier in our chapter are believed responsible for a high proportion of violence toward other inmates or staff (68%) and property damage (73%; Coid, 1998). More recent research on the frequency of misconduct prison aggression indicates 25% of prisoners in Florida prisons were aggressively defiant with 11% of this defiance involving physical aggression (Cunningham & Sorensen, 2010). This is in keeping with other US prison studies indicating around a 22% base rate of prison violence (Edens, Buffington-Vollum, Keilen, Roskamp, & Anthony, 2005).

Much disruptive behavior, however, may go unreported. Liebling, Price and Shefer (2011) in studying UK prisons describe discretion and flexibility in the imposition and application of prison rules whereby prison staff may ignore and not report difficult behavior. In our own prison experience, how "disruptive" prisoner behavior is managed in terms of perceived fairness and whether a particular misconduct is formally recorded can be highly variable. The response to the disruptive behavior can be dependent on a number of features including, for example, the experience of the prison officer and their prior relationship with the prisoner. Reliable estimates of less serious difficult prisoner behavior are therefore hard to find when based only on official records. However, estimates of prevalence and consequences of more serious, dangerous prison behavior, such as serious assaults resulting in the hospitalization of other prisoners and staff, are easier to quantify and are far lower in prevalence (2.9 per 1,000 inmates and 0.8 per 1,000 inmates, respectively) than the routine disruptive or difficult behaviors encountered by staff on a daily basis (Cunningham & Sorensen, 2010).

We found from interviewing staff and prisoners involved in serious assaults (see below) that many instances of non-violent institutional misconduct were not recorded. Even violence between prisoners was sometimes not recorded, or was minimized and viewed as "sparring"[2] or "fighting" (Kilgour, Paramo, & Wilson, 2013). This selective recording was particularly marked in higher security institutional settings and probably reflective of the staff normalization of prisoner misconduct and because the high base rate of these behaviors would otherwise create a high recording workload (Wilson & Tamatea, 2013).

Effects on Staff

Besides the impact of the actual incidents of difficult and disruptive behavior, what are the costs of managing these volatile prisoners? Gadon, Johnstone, and Cooke (2006) noted costs from prison violence that were both proximal (i.e., disability, illness, absenteeism, counseling, sick pay, loss of experienced staff, and staff turnover) and distal (e.g., reduction in staff morale and motivation, diminished loyalty). The impact of physical injuries to staff members who are assaulted by difficult and disruptive prisoners is easily observed; however, as discussed, actual prisoner staff assaults are lower than the more frequent, sometimes daily, experience of threats, abuse, and oppositional behavior from prisoners. Managing difficult and disruptive prisoners can result in emotional exhaustion, intense stress, depersonalization and avoidance of prisoners, high levels of intrusion, and hyper-reactivity: all factors enhancing the risk of post-traumatic stress disorder (PTSD) symptoms (Boudoukha, Altintas, Rusinek, Fantini-Hauwei, & Hautekeete, 2013).

We have similarly encountered the presence of PTSD symptoms when administering the PRISM in some maximum security units (Wilson & Tamatea, 2010). This study assessed the functionality and applicability of this situational risk assessment tool for New Zealand prison conditions. This was to be done by applying the PRISM within three dedicated maximum security units situated at Auckland Prison. These blocks were selected in the wake of a number of high-profile serious assaults that involved prisoner-on-prisoner and prisoner-on-staff violence. The blocks in the study held 179 prisoners, most of Māori ethnicity (70%), with a mean age across units of 30 years (range 17–56), serving long sentences, usually for violence (m = 6 years), many on life imprisonment for murder (26%, n = 46). One of the maximum security units in the PRISM study was the scene of a very serious assault where an officer was stabbed in the neck and almost died from blood loss. When interviewed about safety in the unit, staff regularly referred to this incident and it clearly generated intrusive thoughts, resulting in stress, prisoner avoidance, and hyper-reactivity; yet the incident occurred some 2 years prior to the interviews, and most staff interviewed were either not working in the unit at the time or had not observed the assault. In summary, the damage associated with violent behavior in prisons is considerable and the potential benefits of prediction and prevention are significant.

Assessing Violence Risk

Explanations of why some prisoners are disruptive and violent often identify internal factors such as mental illness (e.g., paranoid schizophrenia and auditory hallucinations; Monahan et al., 2001), antisocial personality types like psychopathy or antisocial personality disorder (Lykken, 1995), or criminogenic needs such as procriminal attitudes and beliefs (Bonta & Andrews, 2017). The variables most frequently associated with chronically disruptive prisoners include offense factors such as violent index offenses, younger age, and sentences of 5 years or more (Ditchfield, 1990).

Personality disorders (antisocial personality disorder, paranoid; narcissistic, borderline personality disorder) have been strongly linked to pervasive and serious misconduct behavior (Coid, 1998; Coyle, 1987). A large prisoner sample from New York identified a chronic subgroup with a high rate of misconducts, the majority of whom had been diagnosed as psychopathic using the Psychopathy Checklist—Revised (Toch, Adams, & Grant, 1989). Widely used structured risk assessment instruments (e.g., Historical-Clinical-Risk Management-20 [HCR-20], Webster, Douglas, Eaves, & Hart, 1997; Level of Service/Case Management Inventory [LS/CMI], Andrews, Bonta, & Wormith, 2004) have made important contributions to the assessment of interpersonal violence with an exclusive focus on individual internal factors and, of course, promote individual intervention to reduce or manage violence in prison.

The effectiveness of actuarial structured measures (scores relate to community reconviction) for predicting violence risk over the longer term are well proven and these approaches have been shown to be more effective than unstructured clinical judgment (Bonta & Andrews, 2017). However, there has been little attempt to bring a structured approach to the assessment of violence risk over short-term periods in institutions. Structured assessment has demonstrated some potential to assist in the prediction and management of acute violence risk within institutionalized settings such as forensic hospitals and prisons where the risk of violence to staff or between detainees can be significant. One of the few attempts to achieve this has been the Dynamic Appraisal of Situational Aggression (DASA; Ogloff & Daffern, 2006), which aims to predict violence risk over the next 24 hours based on behavior occurring in the previous 24 hours.

Risk assessment over the short term necessitates a shift from focusing on relatively static or historical (e.g., criminal history variables) and stable (i.e., relatively consistent patterns of behavior, including those generated by personality issues) toward more dynamic and changeable behavioral indicators. As an example, an individual might have a history of prior aggression, a number of stable personality attributes, and a mental health disorder that all contribute to a high risk for future violence over a 5-year period; however, knowing this might be little use in the short-term prediction of this individual's aggressive behavior within a new prison environment. For any practical utility, staff need to know which of the higher risk individuals they are managing could "blow" on a day-to-day basis in order to know when to intervene, but also to avoid over-managing other individuals (i.e., moving from "blanket" to individualized management approaches).

There might be a number of acute (short-term) indicators that suggest a particular individual might be at imminent risk of committing an aggressive act. The DASA draws together some of these well-known acute dynamic risk variables (i.e., irritability, impulsivity, unwillingness to follow directions, sensitivity to perceived provocation, being easily angered when requests are denied, negative attitudes, verbal threats) in a user-friendly format, and provides a structure for their observation and measurement by floor staff. Although initially designed for use by nursing staff in forensic settings, the DASA has since been adapted for prison-based settings and recently piloted in a number of prison units within New Zealand to examine dynamic prediction of acute staff safety risk (Kilgour & Wilson, 2015).

Custody staff using the DASA in the New Zealand study were universally complimentary about the measure during a trial period (Kilgour & Wilson, 2015). Used on a selective basis, where staff targeted those for whom the most concern was held (a "top five" approach), the DASA appeared to have little additional impact on the workload for staff—being integrated into existing reviews of prisoners' behavior—and had some strong potential to inform knowledge and capability around risk management. In particular:

- Training on the DASA appeared to be easily accomplished with staff within a group format and is quickly understood by untrained staff through guidance from staff with prior experience of the measure.
- Once familiar with the DASA, staff completed it within a brief time period on a select group of prisoners (new prisoners or identified management concerns) as part of daily debriefing.
- The DASA over-predicted risk (false positives) but rarely missed predicting actual aggression in the short term. Some apparent false positive predictions may have been a consequence of prison staff actively managing their prisoners differently because of the use of the tool.

The use of structured actuarial measures may help us to understand the specific or broader contributions to violence but also needs to be complemented with a functional analysis of risk for individual prisoners. In our project to assist New Zealand Corrections in improving staff safety we interviewed prisoners and the staff they had assaulted about each violent incident (Kilgour et al., 2013). We wanted to identify any patterns or key risk factors that could predict such violence or improve post-violence management. In total 17 prisoners and 16 staff were interviewed (Kilgour et al., 2013) and functional analyses of 18 assaults were undertaken, with themes and commonalities across assaults identified. A common antecedent to assaults on staff was a perception by prisoners of unfair treatment by staff in response to requests, or believing that staff members were indifferent, dismissive, or antagonistic to their particular concerns. An example was a prisoner who tried and failed all day to arrange a phone call to organize an escorted temporary release for a family member's funeral. He described feeling ignored and "mucked around" by several staff so when being locked down for the night he assaulted the first available officer. Few prisoners interviewed placed the blame squarely on staff or other external factors for their assaultive behavior, recognizing that their approach to situations or conflicts could also be changed. However, prisoners also thought staff did not communicate well about why requests could not be actioned. Most staff (65%) reported that they believed they had a good relationship with the prisoner who assaulted them, yet this pre-existing trust or friendship did not work as a protective factor or reduce acute situational hostility in the circumstance of the assault. Staff also identified difficulties coping with the stress from managing and interacting with disruptive and difficult prisoners. While the assaulted staff generally felt well supported by prison management and health and safety support structures after these attacks, they struggled with returning to work in high-security settings, with some reporting PTSD symptoms.

Qualitative thematic analysis of the interview results found three general functional pathways or functional sequences for staff assaults that supported a more comprehensive approach to the prevention and management of assault risk. Pathways were:

- "Slow burn"—escalating frustration and anger from perceived unfair treatment. This slow build-up of anger and frustration is not typical of these prisoners who, while experienced criminals, are usually compliant, although not overly friendly, in prison. The trigger was therefore mainly external and involved an issue of great personal importance to the prisoner. The officer who was assaulted was not usually the initial antagonist but rather someone who was seen as also treating them unfairly, even if this was a slight problem. After the assault, the prisoner calmed quickly and did not present a continued risk to staff, although they were often managed as such.
- "Fast burn"—characterized by impulsive/reactive prisoners with significant personality and or mental health issues. Assaults were perpetrated by volatile, entitled prisoners with a "hair trigger" to situations where their desires were blocked; or they were paranoid, contributing to immediate hostile attributions if they perceived unfair treatment or challenge. They often calmed quickly after the assault and were surprised by ongoing custodial responses to manage them. However, they continued to be an ongoing risk because they rapidly experienced anger at often innocuous treatment, with little or no consideration of consequences for themselves or their victims.
- "Planned attack"—instrumental violence to intimidate/manipulate staff and management. A typical example was an assault for the purpose of getting reclassified and moved to another unit, or assault to facilitate an escape. This was the smallest subgroup of the three pathways. The antecedents of violent assaults by individuals in this group were difficult to predict due to the lack of observable deterioration in their mood or other observable behavior, with often long periods of covert planning.

Managing Difficult and Disruptive Behavior

We now turn to what can be done to manage difficult and disruptive prisoner behavior, and the reader should keep in mind "Simon's" story in terms of his management issues within the limitations of the prison environment.

One of the typical issues in getting prison staff to consider a different management approach with disruptive and difficult prisoners with personality disorder is getting them to understand that those in *Diagnostic and Statistical Manual of Mental Disorders, Fourth Edition* (DSM-IV) Cluster A (odd: schizoid, paranoid, schizotypal) and Cluster B (dramatic: antisocial, borderline, histrionic, and narcissistic) are inherent rule-breakers and challengers (Craissati et al., 2011). This rule-breaking orientation may have differing expression depending on the particular personality pathology (e.g., impulsivity, anti-authoritarian attitudes and beliefs, avoidance). The intuitive response of any prison officer, when faced with a rule-breaker, is to try to exert more control. This is partly why personality-disordered offenders tend to be placed in high-security settings and stay there far longer than most, often to the end of sentence. Unfortunately, higher security management simply provides the difficult and disruptive prisoner with more rules to break! Paradoxically, the prison officer may then be in the position of trying to manage too many rules and the security regime may become inconsistently enforced, reinforcing the attribution of these prisoners that they are unfairly treated. The recommendation is to act in a counter-intuitive way: cut down the enforcement of prison rules to a bare and essential minimum—those which best manage risk—and then enforce them with consistency. However, it is equally important to have a positively oriented system—such as therapy—to provide a pathway out of higher security environments for prisoners, including building their self-management strategies and their ability to achieve goals toward personal prosocial values.

The Role of Prison Officers

Although correctional officers are in essence the key personnel in any prison setting, research traditionally neglected them as a resource (Fox, 2010), or unduly maligned them (DiLulio, 1987) as brutish figures who continued the unfair treatment prisoners have suffered from society and the "system." There was little examination of variables such as the ability of staff to detect disruption at an early stage through extensive face-to-face contact, and to maintain good consistent relations with prisoners.

While at one level it is attractive to put behavior contingencies in place that lead prisoners to take more responsibility for their behavior, the reality is that, in the main, prisons accommodate a high density of violent antisocial people (Hare, 1998). Prisoners are unlikely to take an interest in behavior change, or to take more responsibility for self-management, if their main focus is on survival due to fears of victimization. What is not disputed is that adherence to custodial rules and a civil disposition toward others is part of rehabilitation, and is more likely to occur when rules are applied consistently and fairly. The key question or puzzle is how to ensure compliance with prison management regimes without "an iron fist" which may result in abuse of power and worsening staff–prisoner relations (Konnikova, 2015).

Recognition and utilization of the prison officer role within this dynamic, however, has not been ignored entirely, and one of the key developments has been in the area of the prison officer's role in therapeutic interventions. In the United Kingdom, for example, Liebling and Price (2001) observed that "officers in the modern prison deliver (and help to deliver) professional treatment and development programs for sex offenders, violent offenders, drug users and others, and arguably have developed a strengthened 'treatment intervention' role over recent years" (p. 45). This is a sign of the increasing recognition of the critical role of prison staff as change agents rather than simply the owners of security and institutional compliance. This is certainly our experience in working in prisons in New Zealand where the success of treatment has been amplified by the effort and interest of a prison officer encouraging a prisoner who they often know better than the psychologist does.

A common core of factors defining "role-model" prison officers in the United Kingdom has included verbal persuasion, appropriate use of authority, human relations skills, leadership abilities, direct and honest talk, ability to maintain boundaries across contexts, moral courage, a sense of purpose, patience, and empathy, and a professional orientation (Liebling et al., 2011). Prison officers were able to gain compliance and cooperation without resorting to punishment control contingencies through use of an established relationship and a working alliance that acknowledged shared prosocial goals. Staff understood the need to balance care and control, and also recognized that a variety of different approaches might be required across the management of different individual prisoners (Liebling et al., 2011).

This transition of officers from their traditional roles toward a more therapeutic orientation may not be straightforward. In one example, Fox (2010) outlined this uneasy transition in the implementation of the dangerous and severe personality disorder (DSPD) treatment program within Her Majesty's Prison (HMP) Whitemoor in the United Kingdom in the late 1990s and early 2000s. Fox (2010) observed that "reconciling the often-contradictory tasks of control and treatment is perhaps the greatest stumbling block to introducing treatment-oriented reforms in a prison" (p. 222). Officers can become concerned about compromise to the principles of good order and discipline and "tended to vacillate uneasily between the role of quasi-therapist and gaoler . . ." (p. 225). Education about treatment processes appeared to help lessen this discomfort as DSPD staff developed an increased understanding about personality disorder and schema-focused therapy, and was further reinforced as officers began to see the benefit of treatment to enhancing secure control. This in our opinion was one of the key reasons prison staff quickly saw the advantages of the DASA use in New Zealand. Of course, a related problem when working with personality-disordered offenders is that we might not typically expect any immediate or short-term benefits given the entrenched nature of behaviors of the prisoners concerned. Officers might rightly take a skeptical or cautious approach to adopting new strategies or accepting apparent changes in prisoner behavior.

Fox (2010) observed a series of processes, and shifts in perception and behavior among custody staff that helped to resolve these types of issues. These included clever use of interpersonal skills, application of therapeutic strategies or goals, specific interventions to avoid burnout, and increasing explicit professional communication.

Prison officers have been shown to be quick studies with this type of approach. For example, Antonio, Young, and Wingeard (2009) observed that a brief, 2-hour training on reinforcing positive behavior for all new prison staff—including corrections officers, therapy staff, managers, and administrators—had a positive effect on staff ownership and promotion of a good social environment, role-modeling positive behavior and correcting inappropriate behavior within the prison environment. Notably, corrections officers consistently rated themselves as the most responsible for these activities compared with other staff, and their ratings became stronger following training.

Designing and Implementing Effective Programs with Difficult and Disruptive Prisoners in High/Maximum Security Settings

Treating difficult and disruptive prisoners, however, poses significant challenges. These include balancing the security requirements of pulling together a cohort of dangerous prisoners into a program room, the practicalities of introducing a therapeutic regime into physical environments often poorly designed for such interventions (e.g., rooms too small, too noisy, etc.), staff engagement, support and training, and soliciting an organizational "tolerance" for the frequent setbacks in working with such a population. The dilemma for many of these prisoners and the staff managing them is that their repeatedly aggressive behavior results in the need to maintain them at the highest levels of security. This retention in maximum and high security provides prisoners with limited opportunities to learn the types of self-regulation skills required to sustain sufficient periods of settled or compliant behavior to reduce their security classifications. Prisoners being released directly from these higher security environments are then unprepared for the complex and unstructured environments of everyday life. The staff assault survey (Kilgour et al., 2013) mentioned earlier reinforced these observations, with both prisoners and staff identifying the lack of formal and intensive rehabilitation available in higher security restricting the opportunities for prisoners to begin to learn how to manage their problem behavior.

To address this issue, we piloted an intensive High Risk Personality Program (HRPP) for offenders in a high-security environment over 11 months (44 weeks) during 2007. Prisoners were selected for their high-risk status, relatively high rates of institutional misconduct, often recent serious staff assaults, severe personality disturbance, and high levels of case complexity. Of 12 participants, 11 completed this lengthy period of therapy with significant reductions in institutional misconduct during therapy and subsequent placement beyond the treatment unit (Wilson & Tamatea, 2013). Custodial staff noted improvements in participants' conduct, compliance, and attitude during and following the program, with 80% reducing their security classification during a 6-month follow-up. Despite these results, the high cost of the program meant it was unable to be immediately continued. However, ongoing serious assaults on staff and other prisoners helped to maintain a consistent cohort of difficult and disruptive prisoners in high and maximum security and, beginning in 2014, the HRPP was re-piloted across two prison sites: for maximum security prisoners in Auckland Prison and high-security prisoners in Christchurch Men's Prison. Trialing a rehabilitation program for high/maximum security settings across two prison environments during similar time periods provided opportunities to examine the utility of the program across differing physical environments and security settings. In both instances, the prisons involved went to significant efforts to adapt non-ideal prison settings into therapeutic environments conducive to running intensive, long-term group programs. Additionally, prison staff were trained in program principles and use of the DASA to help monitor prisoner risk and therapeutic change. Psychologists providing the individual and group therapy to prisoners were supervised closely during the pilot, and post-program semi-structured interviews were undertaken to complement a quantitative evaluation of program outcomes.

The structure of the HRPP was aligned with the "domain model for personality treatment" developed by John Livesley (2012). This model outlines a framework for an evidence-based approach to conceptualizing personality dysfunction in order to understand interpersonal behavior, tailoring treatment approaches based on these conceptualizations, and selecting appropriate treatment methods to structure therapy based on general principles of therapeutic change. This targeted intervention aims to improve emotional control and behavioral stability, and reduce aggression. Livesley's model takes a phased approach to treatment that assumes personality change occurs in the context of the therapeutic relationship, which needs to be firmly established at the early stages of treatment. The core therapeutic principles underlying this model require the therapist to

- establish and maintain a structure and frame to treatment;
- build and maintain a collaborative relationship;
- maintain consistency;
- promote validation;
- build motivation;
- encourage self-observation and self-reflection.

A review of phase one of the HRPP delivery (Wilson & Kilgour, 2015) used results from exit interviews, DASA results, staff observations, and a comparison of prisoner misconducts and incidents in the 6 months pre-program and subsequent to first contact with the program. Therapy providers were generally rated highly by prisoners in terms of competence, genuineness, and trust. Participants thought that the program had acceptable structure and that they were appropriately challenged by facilitators as to attitudes and behavior. Prison staff appeared to engage well, and participants generally saw them as "fair" in their interactions. Typically, there was at least one prison officer whom they perceived as a good support during the program. The men participating in the HRPP perceived themselves as having changed while on the program, with themes of increased awareness and being less reactive and angry. Official records of misconducts and incidents (events) confirmed the participants' increased self-control, with a 34.4% decrease in the number of events recorded. Of note was the almost 70% reduction in violent events. Violence against staff reduced from 14 assaults (4 assaults and 10 violence threats) during the pre-program phase to no assaults and 2 threats (an 86% reduction) following first contact. The number of weeks when program participants were involved in no recorded events more than doubled from 4 weeks (in the 6 months pre-program) to 10 weeks in the 6 months from initial contact. Similarly, the number of weeks with no violence-related events went from 9 to 21 in the same time frame. Thus, not only was there an overall reduction in events, the number of "event-free days" more than doubled during the program period.

Similar to our experience, an international meta-analysis (French & Gendreau, 2006) also found that increasing the numbers of prisoners involved in prison treatment programs significantly reduced misconduct rates. The more such programs target criminogenic needs, the greater the effect size in relation to misconducts. Educational and vocational programs alone were not found to be effective programs in this regard. In summary, it appears that addressing dynamic needs related to antisocial behavior results in improvements to prisoner behavior and better staff–prisoner relations than results from interventions for non-criminogenic needs (French & Gendreau, 2006).

But are men who engage and complete treatment able to sustain these changes over the longer term? Not all men who complete treatment are successful in avoiding misconduct. We followed a small group of 10 men who remained in prison after attending a high-intensity program for serious offending (Isaacson, Kilgour, & Polaschek, 2012). We were interested in prisoners' ongoing change processes following treatment in a dedicated therapeutic environment, when returned to mainstream prison placement while awaiting parole board decisions. Semi-structured interviews were conducted with these men and the custody staff working with them. Interviewees were intentionally selected because they had either no new misconducts, or conversely, three or more misconducts in the 12 months following treatment. Interview data were then thematically analyzed.

We hypothesized that there would be demographic differences between these two treatment graduate groups and some factors did distinguish between group membership (e.g., criminal history variables, prior prison incidents). Other factors that appeared to distinguish between low and high prison incident groups included the nature of relationships with custodial staff and the presence of situational factors supporting change. Those in the lower incident group, for example, were more likely to be housed in smaller, stable, self-care or minimum security units where men were exposed to more experienced and older custodial staff who were more confident in exercising authority and discretion. In contrast, graduates less successful in reducing prison incidents experienced situational factors that hindered change, including being housed in larger, unpredictable, higher security units where staff were generally younger, rules were applied with less flexibility, and relationships were less personalized and often believed to be characterized by unfair treatment. For both groups, staff were generally supportive of rehabilitation programs and noted that prisoners who had attended treatment had changed, were easier to manage, more polite, and had future goals. Of interest was that all the men perceived themselves to be making prosocial changes, regardless of recent misconduct history.

These findings contribute toward initial understandings of the complex interplay between subjective and situational factors that support, or hinder, change within a post-treatment custodial environment. The literature suggests that over-emphasizing either extremes of care or control can, respectively, result in poor compliance levels or serve to alienate offenders (see Gelsthorpe & Padfield, 2003; Paparozzi & Gendreau, 2005; Skeem & Manchak, 2008). This emphasizes the importance of good custodial relationships when supporting program graduates' efforts to change. Additionally, a graduate's vulnerability to negative peer influences and skill deficits related to poor developmental socialization are factors associated with a slower change process and a greater likelihood of continuing to incur prison incidents post-program. The development of Psychologically Informed Planned Environments (PIPEs) by the UK's National Offender Management Service is an excellent example of a specifically designed environment where prison staff received additional training to address these graduate support issues.

Isaacson and her colleagues (2012) finished with some broad suggestions to improve the management and reintegration of program graduates who remained in prison. These include:

- Better post-treatment support for those program graduates who are at more vulnerable, earlier stages along the continua of change.
- Transitioning program graduates to units that emphasize rehabilitation and easing up on strict compliance while also maintaining good professional boundaries.
- Ongoing support and rehabilitation for prisoners with substance use problems.
- Providing frontline custodial staff with an overview of treatment concepts and strategies and easy-to-access, summarized information pertinent to individualized rehabilitation and risk management.
- Ongoing support for frontline staff to enhance a balance of "care and control" and professional discretion within their duties.

In summary, the change process in response to management initiatives for difficult and disruptive prisoners should be conceptualized as a dynamic, and sometimes cyclical, process or journey that often included lapses.

Conclusions

Is there hope for the management of offenders such as "Simon"? We believe so. Managing difficult and disruptive prisoner behavior is the "hard stuff" of custodial practice. Essentially, we argue for a multidimensional approach to this issue and that psychology has something of real value to bring to this area. For example, there is a need to broaden the management role from a strictly security focus through imposition of punitive power, to one that includes influence through relationship and a focus on rehabilitation. This broadening of role cannot be superficial and needs structural change, training, and ongoing supervision as well as a change in day-to-day tasks that reflect the rehabilitative role. Both environmental factors (e.g., prison design) and individual personality functioning of both prisoners and (sometimes) prison officers need to be considered and understood.

We see the core principles for managing difficult and disruptive prisoners as including:

- Assessment of key personal characteristics (in particular personality).
- Understanding the role of the current environment in maintaining behavior.
- Including the consideration of situational factors (e.g., parole board or court appearance, prison transfer, etc.) related to the prisoner's behavior.
- Using structured and actuarial measures to identify broad and more immediate or acute contributions to risk.
- Recognizing that difficult and dangerous behavior may have different functions depending on the above factors and, therefore, recognizing the importance of a functional analysis of the prisoner's behavior.
- Valuing and engaging the staff working with these prisoners on a day-to-day basis, both in terms of undertaking assessments and in terms of the development and implementation of management plans.
- Designing intensive interventions for difficult and disruptive prisoners using best-practice psychological models that directly address contributions to emotional regulation, personality dysfunction, and other offense-focused needs.
- Monitoring and evaluating program outcomes and adjusting these based on feedback from prison staff and prisoners.

If violence is the key issue for disruptive and difficult prisoners, then there is a need for accurate assessment to understand and know when to be mindful of safety, or when to intervene and to provide dedicated intensive therapy by suitable trained and supported psychologists working alongside prison staff.

Finally, psychology needs to develop closer and more sensitive working relationships with custody staff in order to address the above issues. Neither field has all the answers, but by working together more effectively we can improve outcomes for difficult and disruptive prisoners, such as Simon, reduce serious misconducts including violence, and provide a safer prison environment.

Notes

1   Running a "shop" is a New Zealand prison description of prisoners offering high-value items, often "treat" food, for sale to other prisoners, for either money or trade. Unsanctioned shops often lead to debt and intimidation by the seller for overdue payments.
2   When interviewed, prisoners often reported being told they had to "spar" (i.e., make the motions of boxing without landing heavy blows, usually as a form of training) as part of gang activity, or that they were being assaulted but did not want to be seen as an informer, so they instead described the assault to authorities as "sparring."

Key Readings

Craissati, J., Minoudis, P., Shaw, J., Chuan, S. J., Simons, S., & Joseph, N. (2011). *Working with personality disordered offenders: A practitioners guide.* London, UK: Ministry of Justice National Offender Management Service Retrieved from http://www.forensicnetwork.scot.nhs.uk/wp-content/uploads/NOMS-Working-with-personality-disordered-ofenders-A-practitioners-guide-January-2011.pdf

French, S. A., & Gendreau, P. (2006). Reducing prison misconducts: What works! *Criminal Justice and Behavior*, 33, 185–218.

Konnikova, M. (2015, June 12). The real lesson of the Stanford prison experiment. The New Yorker. Retrieved from https://www.newyorker.com/science/maria-konnikova/the-real-lesson-of-the-stanford-prison-experiment

Liebling, A., Price, D., & Shefer, G. (2011). *The prison officer* (2nd ed.). Abingdon, UK: Willan.

Livesley, W. J. (2012). Integrated treatment: A conceptual framework for an evidence-based approach to the treatment of personality disorder. *Journal of Personality Disorders*, 26, 17–42.

References

Andrews, D. A., Bonta, J., & Wormith, J. S. (2004). *LS/CMI: Level of Service/Case Management Inventory.* Toronto, Canada: Multi-Health Systems.

Antonio, M. E., Young, J. L., & Wingeard, L. M. (2009). Reinforcing positive behavior in a prison: Whose responsibility is it? *Journal of Offender Rehabilitation*, 48, 53–66.

Bonta, J., & Andrews, D. A. (2017). *The psychology of criminal conduct* (6th ed.). London, UK: Routledge.

Boudoukha, A. H., Altintas, E., Rusinek, S., Fantini-Hauwei, C., & Hautekeete, M. (2013). Inmates-to-staff assaults, PTSD and burnout: Profiles of risk and vulnerability. *Journal of Interpersonal Violence*, 28, 2332–2350.

Coid, J. W. (1998). The management of dangerous psychopaths in prison. In T. Millon, E. Simonsen, M. Birket-Smith, & R. Davis (Eds.), *Psychopathy: Antisocial, criminal, and violent behavior* (pp. 431–457). New York, NY: Guilford.

Cooke, D. J. (1998). The development of the Prison Behaviour Rating Scale. *Criminal Justice and Behavior*, 25, 482–506.

Coyle, A. (1987). The management of dangerous and difficult prisoners. *The Howard Journal*, 26, 139–152.

Craissati, J., Minoudis, P., Shaw, J., Chuan, S. J., Simons, S., & Joseph, N. (2011). *Working with personality disordered offenders: A practitioners guide.* London, UK: Ministry of Justice National Offender Management Service Retrieved from http://www.forensicnetwork.scot.nhs.uk/wp-content/uploads/NOMS-Working-with-personality-disordered-ofenders-A-practitioners-guide-January-2011.pdf

Cullen, F. T., Jonson, C. L., & Nagin, D. S. (2011). Prisons do not reduce recidivism: The high cost of ignoring science. *The Prison Journal*, 91, 48–65.

Cunningham, M. D., & Sorensen, J. R. (2010). Improbable predictions at capital sentencing: Contrasting prison violence outcomes. *Journal of the American Academy of Psychiatry and the Law*, 38, 61–72.

DiLulio, J. J. (1987). *Governing prisons: A comparative study of correctional management.* London, UK: Collier Macmillan.

Ditchfield, J. (1990). *Control in prisons: A review of the literature* (Home Office Research Study No.118). London, UK: Her Majesty's Stationary Office.

Edens, J., Buffington-Vollum, J., Keilen, A., Roskamp, P., & Anthony, C. (2005). Predictions of future dangerousness in capital murder trials: Is it time to "disinvent the wheel?". *Law and Human Behavior*, 29, 55–86.

Fox, S. (2010). The role of the prison officer (dangerous and severe personality disorder in the prison system). In N. Murphy, & D. McVey (Eds.), *Treating personality disorder: Creating robust services for people with complex mental health needs* (pp. 220–238). New York, NY: Routledge.

French, S. A., & Gendreau, P. (2006). Reducing prison misconducts: What works! *Criminal Justice and Behavior*, 33, 185–218.

Gadon, L., Johnstone, L., & Cooke, D. J. (2006). Situational variables and institutional violence: A systematic review of the literature. *Clinical Psychology Review*, 26, 515–534.

Gelsthorpe, L., & Padfield, N. (Eds.) (2003). *Exercising discretion: Decision-making in the criminal justice system and beyond.* Cullompton, UK: Willan.

Guy, L. S., Edens, J. F., Anthony, C., & Douglas, K. S. (2005). Does misconduct predict institutional misconduct among adults? A meta-analytic investigation. *Journal of Consulting and Clinical Psychology*, 73, 1056–1064.

Hare, R. D. (1998). Psychopaths and their nature: Implications for the mental health and criminal justice systems. In T. Millon, E. Simonsen, M. Birket-Smith, & R. Davis (Eds.), *Psychopathy: Antisocial, criminal, and violent behavior* (pp. 188–212). New York, NY: Guilford.

Isaacson, A., Kilgour, G., & Polaschek, D. (2012). *STURP Graduates who remain in prison: An exploratory study of the post-treatment prison environment and what contributes to change.* Unpublished research report. Wellington, New Zealand: Department of Corrections.

Johnstone, L., & Cooke, D. J. (2008). *Promoting Risk Intervention by Situational Management: Structured professional guidelines for assessing situational risk factors for violence in institutional settings.* Unpublished manuscript.

Kilgour, G., Paramo, R., & Wilson, N. J. (2013). *Staff assault survey.* Unpublished research report. Office of the Chief Psychologist, Department of Corrections, New Zealand.

Kilgour, G., & Wilson, N. J. (2015). *The Dynamic Appraisal of Situational Aggression (DASA): An updated report on the trial use of the measure.* Unpublished research report. Wellington, New Zealand: Office of Chief Psychologist, Department of Corrections.

King, K., Steiner, B., & Breach, S. R. (2008). Violence in the supermax: A self-fulfilling prophecy. *The Prison Journal*, 88, 144–168.

Konnikova, M. (2015, June 12). The real lesson of the Stanford prison experiment. The New Yorker. Retrieved from https://www.newyorker.com/science/maria-konnikova/the-real-lesson-of-the-stanford-prison-experiment

Liebling, A., & Price, D. (2001). *The prison officer.* Tortworth, UK: Prison Service and Waterside Press.

Liebling, A., Price, D., & Shefer, G. (2011). *The prison officer* (2nd ed.). Abingdon, UK: Willan.

Livesley, W. J. (2012). Integrated treatment: A conceptual framework for an evidence-based approach to the treatment of personality disorder. *Journal of Personality Disorders*, 26, 17–42.

Lykken, D. (1995). *The antisocial personalities.* Hillsdale, NJ: Lawrence Erlbaum.

Monahan, J., Steadman, H. J., Silver, E., Appelbaum, P. S., Robbins, P. C., Mulvey, E. P., … & Banks, S. (2001). *Rethinking risk assessment: The MacArthur study of mental disorder and violence.* Oxford, UK: Oxford University Press.

Ogloff, J. R. P., & Daffern, M. (2006). The Dynamic Appraisal of Situational Aggression: An instrument to assess risk for imminent aggression in psychiatric patients. *Behavioral Sciences & the Law*, 24, 799–813.

Paparozzi, M., & Gendreau, P. (2005). An intensive supervision programme that worked: Service delivery, professional orientation and organisational supportiveness. *The Prison Journal*, 85, 445–466.

Skeem, J. L., & Manchak, S. (2008). Back to the future: From Klockar's model of effective supervision to evidence-based practice in probation. *Journal of Offender Rehabilitation*, 47, 220–247.

Toch, H., Adams, K., & Grant, J. D. (1989). *Coping: Maladaption in prisons.* Oxford, UK: Transaction.

Walters, G. (2003). Predicting institutional adjustment and recidivism with the Psychopathy Checklist factor scores: A meta-analysis. *Law and Human Behaviour*, 27, 541–558.

Webster, C. D., Douglas, K. S., Eaves, D., & Hart, S. D. (1997). *HCR-20: Assessing risk of violence (version 2).* Vancouver, Canada: Mental Health Law & Policy Institute, Simon Fraser University.

Wilson, N. J., & Kilgour, G. (2015). The High Risk Personality Programme—revised: An evaluation report. *Practice: The New Zealand Corrections Journal*, 3, 10–18.

Wilson, N. J., & Tamatea, A. (2010). Beyond punishment: Applying PRISM in a New Zealand maximum security prison. *International Journal of Forensic Mental Health*, 9, 192–204.

Wilson, N. J., & Tamatea, A. (2013). Challenging the "urban myth" of psychopathy untreatability: The High-Risk Personality Programme. *Psychology, Crime & Law*, 19, 493–510.

Zimbardo, P. G. (2004). A situationalist perspective on the psychology of evil: Understanding how good people are transformed into perpetrators. In A. Miller (Ed.), *The social psychology of good and evil: Understanding our capacity for kindness and cruelty* (pp. 21–50). New York, NY: Guilford.

7

Managing Suicide and Self-Harm

Caroline Logan and Jayne L. Taylor
Greater Manchester Mental Health NHS Foundation Trust &
University of Manchester

> One cannot help but feel that [the failure of the State to prevent self-inflicted deaths in custody] is because as a society we value the lives of those in custody less than those at liberty.
>
> (Harris, 2016, p. xii)

Introduction

Suicide and self-harmful behavior present an enormous challenge to those who manage correctional services for men, women, and young people internationally (e.g., Pratt, 2016; Walker & Towl, 2016; World Health Organisation [WHO], 2007). Across multiple jurisdictions, and over at least the past two decades, the prevalence of completed suicide among those detained in correctional services has greatly exceeded that observed in the general population. Specifically, among incarcerated men and adolescent boys in most countries, the rate of completed suicide is between 5 and 10 times higher than that observed in men and boys in the general population (e.g., Fazel, Benning, & Danesh, 2005; Fazel, Grann, Kling, & Hawton, 2011; Fruehwald, Frottier, Eher, Gutierrez, & Ritter, 2000; Kariminia et al., 2007). More worryingly, among women and adolescent girls in prison, the rate of completed suicide is approximately 20 times higher than that observed in the same group in the general population, also across jurisdictions (e.g., Fazel & Benning, 2009; Fazel et al., 2011; Liebling & Ludlow, 2016). Further, the rate of completed suicide in correctional settings appears to be increasing (Pratt, 2016), and elevated risk of suicide appears to extend beyond release (Binswanger et al., 2007; Pratt, Piper, Appleby, Webb, & Shaw, 2006), raising important but as yet unanswered questions about the extent to which risk in this cohort is accounted for by detention as opposed to more general factors related to the reasons why people offend in the first place (King et al., 2015).

The rate of non-fatal self-harmful behavior is also high among those in custody; upwards of 5% of imprisoned men and 20% of imprisoned women and adolescent girls have engaged in self-directed harmful behavior (Hawton, Linsell, Adeniji, Sariaslan, & Fazel, 2014) compared to less than 1% of the general population (Bebbington et al., 2010). Self-harmful behavior is a tragedy in itself. However, the link between self-harm and suicide is well known; around half

The Wiley International Handbook of Correctional Psychology, First Edition. Edited by Devon L. L. Polaschek, Andrew Day, and Clive R. Hollin.
© 2019 John Wiley & Sons Ltd. Published 2019 by John Wiley & Sons Ltd.

of those who complete suicide have a history of self-harm (Blaauw, Kerkhof, & Hayes, 2005; Fruehwald, Matschnig, Koenig, Bauer, & Frottier, 2004; Patterson & Hughes, 2008; Shaw, Baker, Hunt, Moloney, & Appleby, 2004), and those who self-harm are estimated to have a 30 times greater risk of completed suicide compared to the general population (Hawton, Fagg, Platt, & Hawkins, 1993). It is with justification, therefore, that our concern about completed suicide among those detained in correctional settings includes self-harmful behavior also.

Among imprisoned men, women, and young people, serious mental health problems, including substance abuse and dependence, and personality disorders are common (e.g., Fazel & Danesh, 2002; Singleton et al., 1998). As might be expected, therefore, so too are relationship problems, poor educational attainment and employment histories, early and multiple traumas, compromised physical health, and a morass of other co-occurring psychological, social, and biological challenges (e.g., Blaauw et al., 2005). While the number of people imprisoned is increasing in many countries in the world (Walmsley, 2015), financial constraints internationally impact on the availability of a sufficient number of appropriately trained personnel to staff prisons and to safely manage the needs of those troubled individuals trusted to their care (Forrester et al., 2013). In spite of enthusiastic initiatives worldwide to prevent and limit completed suicide and self-harm in prisons, self-destructive behavior persists with the vigor of a pernicious epidemic.

This chapter does not promise a fresh remedy for this intractable problem. Instead, it focuses on the nature of the problems faced by correctional services because of their experience of a complex interplay between large numbers of detained vulnerable people and limited resources with which to simultaneously address that vulnerability and manage risk. This chapter also considers some of the reasons why successive attempts to provide solutions to the high rate of completed suicide and self-harm in prison have been less successful than hoped. However, the chapter begins by outlining the scale and nature of the problem of completed suicide and self-harm currently faced by correctional services; this is because being able to describe the challenge faced is an essential requirement in any discussion about its containment and management. We will then discuss a range of the most relevant risk and protective factors for suicidal and self-harmful behavior in prisons, followed by the current individual, group, and environmental strategies proposed to manage suicide and self-harm in this setting; approaches will be described briefly and their efficacy, where there is information available, is discussed. The chapter will then examine what appear to be the barriers to their effective operation, and conclude with a set of good practice recommendations.

The Scale and Nature of the Problem of Suicide and Self-Harm

The Problem of Nomenclature

The joint and separate literatures on suicide and self-harm are considerable. However, they are both—and together—clear on one important fact (Leitner & Barr, 2011): the use of terms to denote suicidal and self-harmful behavior has not been entirely consistent across studies. Terms commonly used to depict "suicidal behavior," such as suicidal ideation, self-harm and self-injury, attempted suicide, also parasuicide, and completed suicide, may be used differently in different studies; for example, in terms of the amount of suicidal intent the authors assume to be driving behavior (Leitner, Barr, & Hobby, 2008). Also, such terms may be used without any attempt to account for the ways in which each behavior may be linked to another or how or why a person may move from one form of behavior to another (Leitner et al., 2008). This situation is problematic because it creates difficulties in the comparison of studies in order to accumulate enough of the best kind of evidence of the problems being faced by individuals and by the services that care for them, and of the potential effectiveness of interventions with different populations in different locations. This problem is compounded in correctional settings because of how "self-inflicted" deaths may be recorded (e.g., with a coroner's verdict of suicide, but also with an open verdict, or death by misadventure, or as accidental death; Snow & McHugh, 2002), which has a significant impact on research into the problem in these locations (Pratt, 2016; Walker & Towl, 2016).

Therefore, this chapter will reflect what is *generally agreed*—that for behavior to be described as suicide-related, there should be evidence of an intent or desire for that behavior to lead to the end of that person's life (i.e., suicidal intent; e.g., Leitner & Barr, 2011). However, the term *self-harm* will be used to refer to a broader range of behaviors engaged in with deliberation by the individual, which may or may not involve suicidal intent. This latter explanation reflects the reality in clinical practice that motives for self-harmful behavior are not always clear or known to those who engage in it and that correctional services and the practitioners who work within them must engage and work with that lack of clarity on a daily basis.

Overview of the Problem

As indicated in the introduction, suicide and self-harmful behavior are both common problems in correctional settings—more common in prison than in the community, especially among incarcerated women and adolescent girls—and a phenomenon that appears to be on the increase in many jurisdictions (Pratt, 2016). Completed suicide is more of a problem among young prisoners (mid-20s or younger) than those who are older, which is also in contrast to what is observed in the community, especially among men (Liebling & Ludlow, 2016), where it is those who are older who are more at risk. Further, completed suicide appears most common among male prisoners in the Scandinavian countries and least common among those in Australia and New Zealand (Fazel et al., 2011).

Completed suicide is most frequently noted among men, women, and young people who are on remand or imprisoned for short sentences, often for property offenses (e.g., Humber, Webb, Piper, Appleby, & Shaw, 2013; Noonan & Grinder, 2013). Suicides typically occur within 1 month of incarceration, often within the first day or so of detention. However, these associations are not a unanimous finding, with a number of studies reporting an association between self-inflicted death and long sentences (e.g., Fruehwald et al., 2004; Winter, 2003; Wobeser, Datema, Bechard, & Ford, 2002), and completed suicides among those serving sentences for serious violent or sexual offenses, including offenses of intimate partner violence (Dear, Slattery, & Hillan, 2001). Transitions, relocations, and cell changes within sentences are particularly disruptive, especially for vulnerable groups, including women (e.g., McKenzie, Serfaty, & Crawford, 2003). This "early in sentence" trend is evident in self-harmful behavior also, with around one third of all incidents of self-harm being reported within the first 7 days of reception into prison (Shaw et al., 2004). Prisoners with drug and alcohol problems, including withdrawal, psychiatric disorders, especially untreated conditions or those for which inadequate or incomplete treatment has been received, and suicidal thoughts, are considered to be especially at risk (Blaauw et al., 2005; Fruehwald et al., 2004; Shaw et al., 2004).

As has been noted already, suicidal behavior occurs at elevated rates in those who offend, whether they are incarcerated or not (King et al., 2015). What is it about life in prison specifically that contributes to the elevated risks observed? Prison life limits the means by which suicide may be attempted and self-harm achieved. While self-poisoning is common in community samples, it is less frequently observed in correctional settings (Walker & Towl, 2016). This is most likely because people who self-poison in the community often report or are reported for treatment—thus, their behavior is detected and recorded—and because the means to self-poison are readily available. Cutting injuries are believed to be less likely to result in detection in the community. In contrast, prisons record a much higher prevalence of cutting injuries than in the community (Hawton, i Comabella, Haw, & Saunders, 2013), and death and self-injury by self-strangulation and hanging are most common there (e.g., Howard League for Penal Reform, 2003). In correctional settings, self-harmful and suicidal behaviors are prevalent at night more so than in the daytime, and among prisoners in single cells more so than in shared accommodation (Fazel, Cartwright, Norman-Nott, & Hawton, 2008).

A variety of potential explanations have been offered for the problems of completed suicide and self-harmful behavior in correctional settings (Liebling & Ludlow, 2016). In brief, explanations include (a) an increasing prison population, population turnover, and overcrowding in prison buildings that were not built to manage the diverse needs of such a large, varied, growing, and complex population, (b) the vulnerability of offenders entering prison, drawn as they are from high-risk groups in the community (e.g., those who misuse substances, those with mental health problems, and those who experienced disrupted caregiving as children, (c) the impact on such vulnerable offenders of the "pains of imprisonment" (e.g., loss of liberty; Sykes, 1958; see below), and (d) the impact on vulnerable people of problems directly related to prison life and the management of prison environments (e.g., low and declining staffing levels, limited time spent out of cell engaged in purposeful activity). Most likely, the causes of the high level of self-harm and completed suicide in prison are a combination of two or more if not all of these hypotheses. These potential explanations, singly and in combination, will be explored further below in a review of risk factors for suicide and self-harm in correctional settings.

Risk Factors for Suicide and Self-Harm in Correctional Settings

Risk factors for suicide in prison are a combination of individual and situational or environmental factors, very much as they are in individuals who are not in custody. Although they may be differentiated in this way, as internal and external, risk factors of whatever source are closely related, with the impact of one hugely determined by the influence of another. This makes their separation out somewhat artificial, and enhances the role of formulation (see below) as the process by which the range of risk and indeed protective factors are brought together in the form of a tentative explanation for risk in the individual case.

In general, and reflecting the long history of research in the field, key risk factors for suicidal behavior may be broadly divided into four categories (e.g., Hawton & van Heeringen, 2000; Leitner et al., 2008; Logan, 2013): *experience of suicidal behavior and preparation* (e.g., previous attempts at completed suicide; a history of self-harmful behavior; a history of suicidal behavior in the family or close social network; planning for suicide; easy access to means; attitudes and beliefs tolerant of suicidal behavior); *psychological adjustment* (e.g., feelings of hopelessness; problems with stress and coping; impulse control problems; problems with planning, thinking, self-awareness, and mood stabilization; problems with child abuse; experience of acute distress or loss); *social adjustment* (e.g., social isolation; difficulties with rule adherence); and *mental and physical health needs* (e.g., serious mental and/or physical illness with incapacitation; substance use problems; serious mood episode; problems with adherence to treatment or treatment response; recent change in care arrangements).

In considering the risk of suicidal behavior in the context of correctional settings specifically, some qualification of our understanding of these risk factors is required. This is because the context in which imprisonment is both encountered and experienced by the individual is an essential additional consideration: the risk of completed suicide and self-harmful behavior in correctional settings is inseparable from the place where it is both observed and managed (Marzano, Hawton, Rivlin, & Fazel, 2011). Factors that are in addition to those generally acknowledged to be relevant to suicide and self-harm generally, or whose impact is potentially greater for someone who is an incarcerated offender, are now reviewed.

Prison Life

The term "pains of imprisonment" (Sykes, 1958) encapsulates a variety of common features of prison life that make it a challenging environment to endure, especially by individuals already compromised by problems adapting to incarceration or who have pre-existing problems in other areas (e.g., substance dependence, learning difficulties, adverse life experiences, low self-esteem; Liebling, Durie, Stiles, & Tait, 2005). Completed suicides in correctional settings have been linked to the experience of bullying and harassment, to a lack of purposeful activity, to reduced or no contact with families and important social networks and sources of social support on the outside, to untreated mental health problems, to a history of self-harmful behavior, and to volatility or unstable mood and/or mental state (e.g., Blaauw, Kerkhof, Winkel, & Sheridan, 2001; Leese, Thomas, & Snow, 2006; Liebling, 1992; Rojas & Stenberg, 2010). Individuals in prison at risk of suicidal or self-harmful behavior are more likely to need support that is not available at the levels required (Forrester et al., 2013). They may be more vulnerable to threats or attacks from others, have fewer personal skills and resources to manage the complex social demands of prison, and react more impulsively to challenge and therefore with less thought and more negative emotion in need of relief (Ludlow et al., 2015). Hopelessness, intense anguish that may be linked to their offense, fear, and loss of social support and personal dignity are thought to be particularly prominent drivers for suicidal behavior in prison, intensified by what has been described as high likelihood of demeaning and careless treatment in crowded, impersonal custodial settings (Liebling & Ludlow, 2016). Access to means, especially ligature points (e.g., window bars) and the means of tying ligatures (e.g., clothing) during unsupervised periods or when staffing is reduced (e.g., at night or at weekends), compounds the risk (Liebling 2006). Not everyone experiences intense feelings of distress on their imprisonment, but it is a more familiar experience to those who are already vulnerable (Liebling et al., 2005). Identifying and managing risk in this vulnerable population immediately following their reception into prison is critical in the management of their risk in the longer term.

Prisoner Status and Sentence

In many jurisdictions, being a remand prisoner has been found to be associated with particular risks of self-harmful and suicidal behavior (e.g., in England and Wales, Humber et al., 2013). When remanded, especially if young, acutely vulnerable, and separated from important sources

of social support, fears about harassment, loss, dependence on staff for the most basic of privileges, dependence on substances no longer readily available, and an unknown future may be
perceived as overwhelming (Fazel et al., 2008). However, this finding is not noted everywhere
(e.g., Dalton, 1999; Fruehwald et al., 2004; Joukamaa, 1997; Taterelli, Mancinelli, Taggi, &
Polidori, 1999; Winter, 2003), possibly because of variable policies about the identification
and management of acute mental health problems and substance withdrawal on reception
(WHO, 2007).

In terms of risk in already sentenced prisoners, an association has been found between risk
of suicidal behavior and long sentences (Dooley, 1990). For example, Towl and Crighton
(1998) noted an increasing prevalence of completed suicide in longer sentenced prisoners
(5 years plus, including life-sentenced prisoners). However, long sentences are given for more
serious crimes or for repeat offending, and it is unclear whether sentence length as a risk factor
is really about the duration of custody or the reason for that custody (Dear et al., 2001). In
England and Wales, approximately a quarter of individuals who completed suicide were
charged with or already convicted of a violent or sexual offense (Fazel et al., 2008; Shaw et al.,
2004). Serious violent offending, especially in the context of intimate relationships, has been
associated with at least a twofold increase in the risk of completed suicide compared to controls (e.g., Fruehwald et al., 2004; Humber et al., 2013).

Mental Health Problems

Mental health problems are a critical risk factor for completed suicide and self-harmful behavior
regardless of location (Hawton et al., 2013). However, it is generally believed that prisons expose
already vulnerable men, women, and young people to additional risk (e.g., Liebling & Ludlow,
2016); that is, the experience of prison exacerbates risk in those already vulnerable due to poor
mental health. Singleton et al. (1998) noted that psychiatric morbidity is extensive among prisoners, and co-occurring conditions are frequent; one in seven prisoners experience four or more
comorbid psychiatric disorders concurrently. A history of psychotic disorders, depression, drug
misuse, and anxiety disorders, including post-traumatic stress disorder (PTSD), especially if
linked to experience of abuse or neglect (Goff, Rose, Rose, & Purves, 2007), social anxiety, and
panic disorders, are noted frequently in those with suicidal ideation and behavior in custody
(Rivlin, Hawton, Marzano, & Fazel, 2010; Walker, Shaw, Turpin, Reid, & Abel, 2017).

Shaw et al. (2004) examined a sample of 157 men and women who had completed suicide
when in custody in prison. The authors noted that almost one third of the sample had been in
contact with psychiatric services prior to being incarcerated and 12% had been hospitalized
because of mental ill-health. In this sample, the authors noted that a total of 70% had at least
one diagnosis of a psychiatric condition, the most commonly occurring being a variety of
affective disorder (17%) and schizophrenia (6%), which is consistent with other studies of
prison suicide (e.g., Backett, 1987). Twenty-nine percent had more than one psychiatric diagnosis, and almost a third had been transferred to a psychiatric hospital at some point during
their sentence. At the time of their death, a total of 17% of the sample were inpatients in a
prison healthcare facility. Other studies have reported higher rates of prior psychiatric contact
in samples of men and women who have completed suicide in prison; for example, 62% of
33 deaths in prisons in Scotland (Backett, 1987), 76% in 25 deaths in prisons in Texas (He,
Felthous, Holzer, Nathan, & Veasey, 2001). Taterelli et al. (1999) reported similar figures in
Italy. However, these estimates are compromised by how data are recorded in each jurisdiction, with evidence of mental health problems being identified only if psychiatric care is sought,

and with no consideration being given to the motivation of the offender to seek assistance for mental health problems or the quality of the health care eventually provided (Pratt, 2016).

With respect to self-harmful behavior, some small differences have been noted in the mental health problems observed (Fulwiler, Forbes, Santangelo, & Folstein, 1997). For example, mood instability and poor impulse control appear more common in those who self-harm compared to those who attempt or complete suicide, in whom major depressive disorder is a more likely observation (Lohner & Konrad, 2006). It is perhaps not a surprise that this is the case. The general purpose of completed suicide is to end life, while the objective of many incidents of self-harmful behavior is the attempt to adapt: in effect, a form of self-preservation (Gratz, 2003; Pattison & Kahan, 1983). Therefore, while mental health problems are common to those who engage in both activities, and there is a link between the two forms of behavior, the problems experienced vary slightly and progression from self-harmful behavior to completed suicide is not at all inevitable because, sometimes, self-harm does achieve the outcomes sought (Dulit, Fyer, Leon, Brodsky, & Frances, 1994).

Substance misuse

The key issues about substance misuse as a risk factor for suicidal and self-harmful behavior are (a) the influence of substance withdrawal during transitions into and between prisons when the individual may be highly vulnerable for other reasons (Towl & Crighton, 1998), and (b) the reasons why a person may consume substances to abusive levels in the first place, such as to assist coping (Quina & Brown, 2013), often in relation to the experience of early abuse (Driessen, Schroeder, Widmann, von Schonfeld, & Schneider, 2006), self-medication (Brady, 2001), and so on. While substance misuse is a common experience of those in prison (e.g., Singleton et al., 1998), it does appear more prevalent among those who engage in suicidal or self-harmful behavior.

Personality disorder

There is good evidence that personality disorder in general, but more specifically, the disorders characterized by instability and impulsivity (e.g., borderline and antisocial personality disorders), are more common in those who complete suicide compared to this prevalence in the population in general (e.g., Harris & Barraclough, 1997). However, there are at least two problems in trying to establish the specific role of personality dysfunction on self-harmful conduct in prisoner samples. First, personality disorders are common in prison settings (e.g., Fazel & Danesh, 2002), making it problematic to identify their particular contribution to risk, especially when they are rarely diagnosed with any formality and it is unclear whether it is a primary or additional diagnosis. Second, while borderline personality disorder is the diagnosis most often linked to suicidal behavior and self-harm, the diagnosis is confounded with the behavior—self-harm is a symptom of borderline personality disorder, which means that self-harmful behavior cannot be *explained* by this diagnosis. What appears to forge the links between personality problems and suicide and self-harm risk are poor impulse control (common in both the borderline and antisocial presentations) and poor interpersonal skills, including difficulties with conflict resolution and achieving and sustaining meaningful intimacy with another person (also common in the borderline and antisocial presentations, but not exclusively so; Nestor, 2002). In the absence of a large-scale and methodologically sound study of the role of personality disorder in the suicidal behavior of prisoners, the nature of the risk associated with such symptomatology will remain unclear (Pratt, 2016).

A History of Suicidal and Self-Harmful Behavior

In the risk field, it is well established that a history of engaging in the harmful behavior of concern is an important guide to the nature and likelihood of any kind of recurrence (e.g., Monahan et al., 2001). This applies as much to suicidal behavior (Logan, 2013) as it does to violence (Douglas, Hart, Webster, & Belfrage, 2013) and sexual violence (Hart et al., 2003). In the general population, a history of suicidal behavior is associated with a significantly increased risk of completed suicide (e.g., a 30-fold increase, Cooper et al., 2005; Hawton et al., 1993), especially during the year following a self-harmful event (Owens, Horrocks, & House, 2002). In prison samples, while around 5–6% of men and adolescent boys and 20–24% of women and adolescent girls engage in self-harmful or suicidal behavior every year (Hawton et al., 2013), a history of such behavior is common among those who complete suicide (Pratt, 2016). For example, Dooley (1990) observed that almost half of a sample of 296 men and women who had completed suicide in prison had a recorded history of self-harmful behavior, 22% during their current period of detention. Shaw and colleagues (2004) reported a very similar finding in their more recent study of 157 prison suicides, as did Fruehwald et al. (2004) in their Austrian sample and Blaauw et al. (2005) in the Netherlands, and similar if not higher rates have been reported in studies in North America (e.g., Daniel & Fleming, 2006; He et al., 2001; Patterson & Hughes, 2008; Winter 2003). Where mental health problems combine with a history of self-harmful if not suicidal behavior, risk of completed suicide appears particularly elevated (Fazel et al., 2008).

However, there are difficulties in relying on recorded incidents of self-harmful behavior prior to completed suicide as an indicator of suicide risk, because not all self-harmful incidents, even any at all, may have been recorded for any individual man, woman, or young person (Ludlow et al., 2015). Also, among men, fatal first attempts at suicide are significantly more likely (Isomesta & Lonnqvist, 1998). Self-harmful behavior may be seen as an expression of what has been proposed as a "common suicidal process" (Goldney & Burvill, 1980, p. 2); it may be an early and overt symptom of a distress that could in due course lead to a final act of despair (Hawton et al., 2014; Humber et al., 2013). Risk of self-harm and completed suicide may therefore be broadly comparable in terms of both their motivation and their prevention (Liebling & Ludlow, 2016), more often reactive to a transient state than purposive (Dear, Thomson, & Hills, 2000), more frequently impulsive than planned (Liebling, 1992).

Gender

It is generally the case that men are more likely than women to complete suicide, and that risk increases with age among men while it decreases with age among women (Bertolote & Fleischmann, 2002). This difference is for a variety of reasons, including the tendency by men to use more fatal means of taking their life (Värnik et al., 2008) and for men to suffer more from lost or failed relationships compared to women, who often have wider social networks and valued caregiving roles to protect them (Möller-Leimkühler, 2003).

The rate of completed suicide among women and girls in prison is comparable to that observed among men and boys; in the community, the suicide rate for men exceeds that of women by a factor of 2.5 to 1 (Liebling & Ludlow, 2016). Among men in prison, remand and life-sentenced prisoners are thought to be particularly at risk of completed suicide, as well as those with a history of self-harmful behavior who have mental health problems, including serious substance misuse (Backett, 1987; Dooley, 1990; Fazel et al., 2008; Liebling 1992; Shaw et al., 2004). Among women and adolescent girls in prison, non-fatal suicidal and self-harmful behaviors are more common than among incarcerated men and boys (e.g., Borrill et al., 2003;

Hawton et al., 2013; Klonsky, Oltmanns, & Turkheimer, 2003; Liebling & Ludlow, 2016), and the repetition of self-harmful behavior is more the rule than the exception among women (Hawton et al., 2013).

A suggested reason why women are thought to be particularly at risk of non-fatal self-harmful behavior is because many of the imprisoned cohort were vulnerable and disempowered *before* they were imprisoned; it has been proposed that being in custody compounds this vulnerability and disempowers women further (Harris, 2016; McKenzie et al., 2003). On their imprisonment, women are more likely to be separated from those for whom they have a primary caregiving role (e.g., their children), resulting in their dependents being put into care and future contact being jeopardized (e.g., Corston, 2007). Remand status, substance withdrawal, prior incarceration, single cell accommodation, and negative experiences of imprisonment (e.g., bullying) as well as poor social support, recent stressful life events, including loss, and past trauma, especially child abuse, have been found to be particularly relevant risk factors for women (e.g., Marzano et al., 2011). Long-term vulnerabilities are often cited as primary reasons for self-harming, whereas prison-related variables (such as transfers, or fear of bullying or violence) are commonly described as proximal or triggering factors.

There has been comparatively little attention paid to the suicidal and self-harmful behavior of women compared to that of men (Liebling & Ludlow, 2016). This may be because it is assumed that suicidal intent in women is generally low and therefore the real problem of suicide is less severe in this group; these were just acts of self-harm, internalized expressions of distress, that went "wrong," in an environment that offers few safe ways of expressing strong feelings of distress (Liebling, 1994). However, it may also be the case that the behavior of women is regarded as "manipulative" and therefore less worthy of serious study. Whatever explanation is actually correct, there remains much still to be understood about self-harmful behavior in women and girls, both about its causes and about its management.

Concluding Comments

If a person comes to believe that there is little option but to inflict physical injury on themselves or to end their own life, then feelings of entrapment and defeat are likely to predominate, a sense of social and emotional isolation to be strongly felt, one's sense of self distorted or lost, and the belief increasingly realized that there is little if any prospect of relief or rescue (Pratt, 2016). The suicidal and self-harmful behavior of men, women, and young people in custody is a major concern: because of its prevalence, because of the complexity of its many and interrelated causes and correlates, and because it occurs in a restricted environment that enhances risk factors and provides few obvious opportunities for protection and strength. If self-harmful behavior in prison is multifaceted, then the management of its risk needs to be multifaceted also, incorporating a range of coordinated individual, social, and environmental or cultural interventions. Focus on any one area at the expense of another is unlikely to significantly impact on the overall problem (Pratt, 2016). And it is to interventions that we will now turn.

Interventions to Manage Suicide and Self-Harm

The prevention of completed suicide and the prevention or limitation of self-harmful behavior in terms of its frequency and severity is or should be about the promotion of wellbeing, of individuals, of the groups to which they belong, and of the environments within which they reside, whatever their purpose (Liebling & Ludlow, 2016). However, it is unclear exactly what might work for which prisoners at risk of self-inflicted harm and in what circumstances because so few studies of good quality have been carried out into the effects of the interventions available (Perry, Waterman, & House, 2016). In this section, we will consider the main forms of individual, social, and environmental intervention that have been proposed to address the specific problem of self-harmful and suicidal behavior and how and, indeed, if they work.

Individual Interventions

Obvious and first-line individual interventions for prisoners at risk of self-directed harm are, for example, psychological and/or psychopharmacological therapy with a specialist mental health practitioner in relation to a specific problem (e.g., in-reach teams, addressing problems such as psychosis, depression, PTSD, personality disorder), counseling with a more generalist practitioner for less severe problems (e.g., substance misuse, anxiety, low mood), peer support schemes such as those supported by the Samaritans but operated by trained and supported fellow prisoners and intended to help in times of crisis (the "Listener Scheme"; Pratt, 2016), and buddy schemes also run by fellow prisoners and intended to counter social isolation and aid adaptation to prison life (Walker & Towl, 2016). While cognitive behavioral therapy, problem-solving therapy, and interpersonal therapy have been highlighted as promising interventions for suicidal behavior (Brown et al., 2005; Gaynes et al., 2004) compared with treatment as usual, this kind of work is still only at the piloting stage with prisoners (e.g., problem-solving training, Perry et al., 2016; cognitive behavioral suicide prevention therapy, Pratt et al., 2015). Currently, there are few if any evidence-based psychological interventions targeting suicidal behavior routinely available to prisoners, despite recommendations that such interventions be prioritized (Pratt, 2016).

Interventions intended to intensively case manage the risk of self-harmful and suicidal behavior include schemes to contain self-harm once threatened or reported. In prisons in England and Wales, for example, there is a scheme called the Assessment, Care in Custody and Teamwork (ACCT) procedure. This was implemented in 2004 and is intended to be a prisoner-centered, proactive, flexible care-planning arrangement that promotes the intensive case management of high-risk men, women, and young people (HM Prison Service, 2001). The ACCT procedure has been subject to a number of evaluations, both before full implementation across the prison system in the two countries (Humber, Hayes, Senior, Fahy, Shaw, 2011) and since (Harris, 2015; Rickford & Edgar, 2005). In general, the ACCT procedure appears to be a useful way of managing risk of self-harm and suicide. However, the implementation of the ACCT procedure is not thought to be complete in all cases (not everyone at risk is on an ACCT, and the majority of people who complete suicide are not subject to any interventions for at-risk prisoners) or effective enough in some (Marzano et al., 2011; Pratt, 2016; Rickford & Edgar, 2005).

With women and adolescent girls who are at risk of suicidal or self-harmful behavior, trauma-informed care and practice is particularly recommended (Walker & Towl, 2016), although it is clearly a requirement for men also. Such services are intended to ensure that practitioners and also service users understand trauma and its impact across the life span, promote safety, ensure clinical competence and skills, support control, choice, and autonomy, work toward the sharing of power and governance, create pathways of care, and promote the belief that healing happens and there is reason for hope (Stathopoulos, Quadara, Fileborn, & Clark, 2012).

With women and adolescent girls in mind, the WORSHIP project (Women Offenders Repeat Self-Harm Intervention Pilot) was designed as an individual intervention for self-harmful behavior. Involving a combination of four to eight sessions of psychodynamic interpersonal therapy for women and girls with a history of self-harm and recently managed on the ACCT scheme, a treatment group was compared to an active control group in three women's prisons in England (Walker et al., 2017). While women in both groups improved, the women in the active treatment group improved most and for longest, in terms of reduced self-harm and need for intense risk management using ACCT (Walker et al., 2017).

With male prisoners, a trial of cognitive behavioral suicide prevention (CBSP) therapy has shown some promising results (Pratt, 2016). Typically delivered over 4–6 months, clients are provided with 20 one-to-one sessions with a trained and supervised therapist, where each session lasts between 30 and 60 minutes. Sessions commence with a focus on engagement and the assessment of needs, and the person's history of suicidal and self-harmful behaviors. A formulation is prepared that is the basis for the treatment to follow, which involves skills development (e.g., helpful coping strategies, building resilience), wellbeing enhancement, and the development of plans to maintain wellbeing. The application of CBSP in prisoners appears to have some potential; those who received the intervention were less than half as likely to engage in self-harmful behavior compared to a control group sample, and there were significant differences in a range of psychometric measures of depressed mood, hopelessness, and self-esteem (Pratt et al., 2015).

Formulation

A key way in which individual risk is understood with a view to its management is through the clinical process of formulation (Sturmey & McMurran, 2011). Formulation is the preparation of an organizational framework for exposing the underlying mechanism of a person's risk of self-harmful behavior with a view to proposing action to facilitate change (Logan, 2017a). The process of formulation identifies key risk and protective factors relating to self-harm and draws them together into a proposed explanation for why self-harmful behavior has happened previously in the individual and why it might happen again and under what circumstances. The formulation process is intended to identify the most relevant motivational drivers for self-harm and suicide in the individual case. Common drivers for self-directed harm include its role in (a) producing a sense of relief from unwanted or overwhelming emotions (Briere & Gill, 1998; Nock, Prinstein, & Sterba, 2010) including relief from anger or aggression (Snow, 2002), (b) stress management and coping (Miller & Fritzon, 2007), (c) self-punishment in response to feelings of shame (Hillbrand, Young, & Krystal, 1996), and (d) an expression of hopelessness (Dockley, 2001). Sutton (2008) identifies additional motivational drivers for self-harm including (e) achieving a sense of personal control in the midst of chaos, or (f) a sense of calm, (g) self-harm as a crisis intervention, in effect a forceful physical hard-stop to events or feelings that are running away from the individual, (h) as a means of achieving a state of comfortable numbness, (i) an act of cleansing, (j) a means of confirming rather than denying or terminating existence, and (k) a most basic means of communication, often most relevant in a prison setting. However, while formulation is an essential clinical practice, much work remains to be done to demonstrate the effectiveness of formulation as an aid to eventual risk management (Logan, 2017b).

Group Interventions

Group interventions specifically for people at risk of self-harmful behavior are not common, and few have been subject to any kind of rigorous evaluation (Walker & Towl, 2016). In a review of cognitive behavioral therapy (CBT) interventions for suicidal behavior, Tarrier,

Taylor, and Gooding (2008) examined the efficacy of this intervention for self-harmful men and women compared to individual CBT alone or individual CBT combined with a CBT group. While individual and combined group/individual interventions were seen to be effective for participants, group CBT alone was not. Unfortunately, in the main, neither individual nor group CBT approaches to address the risk of suicidal and self-harmful behavior have been extended to working with men and women in prison in any systematic way (Pratt, 2016).

In the women's prisons, there is some evidence for a combination of individual and group (e.g., skills in emotion regulation) interventions providing forensically modified dialectical behavior therapy[1] (DBT) to women with self-harmful behavior and who are at risk of suicide (Gee & Reed, 2013). This intervention found some positive outcomes in terms of a reduction in the time individual women spent on the ACCT risk management scheme, a reduction in the number of adjudications for rule-breaking behavior, an improvement in the symptoms of mental disorder, and a good level of participant satisfaction (Gee & Reed, 2013). However, the findings for the application of forensically modified DBT via individual and group interventions are mixed, and further research on applications to prison samples is required (Walker & Towl, 2016).

Environmental Interventions

Environmental measures to manage the risk of self-harmful behavior in prison may be divided into (a) measures that address risk factors in the physical space, specifically addressing access to the means by which individuals may harm themselves and (b) those that address the management of custodial settings by the people that operate them. With respect to the physical environment, self-harm and suicide in prison is associated with the availability of both items that may be used to self-harm (e.g., the availability of clothing, belts, laces that may be used to tie ligatures, implements with which to cut, substances with which to overdose or alter level of awareness) and the means to use them (e.g., ligature points). Most prisons are required to manage the risks associated with accessible points from which ligatures may be suspended (e.g., window bars, door handles, and accessible edges), including through making available safe ligature cut-down tools, which prison officers are increasingly required to carry on their person at all times when on duty. Isolation, including in single cell accommodation and safer cells including in health care and seclusion, are thought to increase the risk of self-harmful behavior because they provide at-risk prisoners with the opportunity to incubate feelings of distress and despair and to act on them unhindered, especially at night, at weekends, and in the summer months when staffing and activity levels are lower than at other times (Fazel et al., 2008). The use of segregation, strip, and unfurnished cells in the management of suicidal prisoners is not thought to be suitable (Pratt, 2016).

With respect to prison procedures to mitigate risk of harm, Walker and Towl (2016) recommend a suite of measures to manage the many ways in which the prison setting can generate and maximize risk. For example, they recommend that (a) a custodial environment be created in which specialist screening and support is available to new admissions to prison from their often stressful reception into the establishment, (b) prisoners are doubled up or placed in dormitory accommodation to reduce isolation and minimize opportunity to act, (c) they are imprisoned close to home and the potential for meaningful social support, (d) they have available supportive networks such as through the Samaritans, and (e) they have access to adequate, appropriate, and responsive health care (see also WHO, 2007). Further, Walker and Towl (2016) recommended that (f) prisons are adequately staffed by prison officers who work in partnership with healthcare providers, all of whom are comprehensively trained in the core role as well as in assisting self-harmful prisoners, and (g) that they receive long-term supervisory support to do so (Humber et al., 2011; Power, Swanson, Luke, Jackson, & Biggam, 2003; Senior et al., 2007). Suicide prevention should be the responsibility of every member of prison staff and not just mental health professionals, and in a coordinated rather than piecemeal way (Pratt, 2016). Further, offenders themselves should be consulted in what is ideally a collaborative risk assessment, formulation, and management process, both in terms of individuals at risk and the prison's approach to managing risk in individual establishments, such as through the training and support of listeners and mentors (Pratt, 2016; Walker & Towl, 2016).

However, overcrowded, unstable or disorganized, unpredictable, and unsafe prisons, where access to purposeful activity or to general and specialized support services is limited, are thought to reduce the power of these measures to be effective. Understaffing is a major issue in prisons in England and Wales, and elsewhere, meaning that it is very difficult for the trained staff available to provide individual prisoners with the attention they need (Harris, 2016). This can lead the staff that *are* available to feel more helpless and at risk of protecting and distancing themselves from the emotional demands of the task by labeling such behavior as "attention-seeking" or "manipulative." Staff who respond compassionately may also be labeled as "care bears" or other such disrespectful terms (Walker & Towl, 2016). These organizational challenges are thought to exacerbate the risk of self-harmful behavior and completed suicide in prisons (e.g., Leese et al., 2006; Liebling, 1992; Rabe, 2012). Indeed, Liebling and Ludlow (2016), discussing environmental risk factors for the self-harmful behavior of prisoners, highlight "the withdrawal of care and kindness from prison landings" as an important consideration in the too busy, overcrowded, ever-changing prisons in England and Wales that are perceived to be increasingly unsafe (p. 238).

The assessment of the risks posed by environments rather than individuals has been pioneered by Johnstone and Cooke (2008). In their work on *Promoting Risk Intervention by Situational Management* (PRISM) they advocate the assessment and formulation of environmental risks using a structured professional judgment approach. Although the focus of their work is on violence in institutions like prisons and forensic mental health facilities, the same variables are likely to be relevant to the management of risk of self-harmful behavior. The PRISM process involves the evaluation of risk factors in five domains: the *history* of harmful behavior in the institution (e.g., the severity, frequency, and diversity of harmful behavior), *physical and security factors* (i.e., the quality of the physical environment and the availability and accessibility of appropriate resources; whether physical, procedural, and relational security procedures are appropriate to the nature and level of risk), *organizational* factors (e.g., the ethos and priorities of the establishment; the quality and competence of leadership and management in respect of risk; how responsive the establishment is to organizational conflict; the adequacy of policies and procedures on risk management); *staff issues* (e.g., recruitment and retention; adequacy of staffing levels; experience, skill mix, training and support; morale); and *case management* (e.g., population mix; interventions for harm reduction; the availability of individual assessments and interventions, and quality of life experiences). Organizations, such as individual prisons and hospitals, are invited to self-assess using the PRISM guidance, in order to help them highlight shortfalls and prepare situation-specific plans for remediation. While research is limited, early indications are that the PRISM offers a valuable way of highlighting problems and empowering organizations to prepare bespoke plans for meaningful improvement in violence-prone environments (Johnstone & Cooke, 2010), work that could prove hugely important in developing a better understanding of how environments prone to high levels of self-harm and suicide develop and can be managed more effectively.

Other initiatives aimed at widespread improvements in the custodial environment that will have a knock-on effect on risk include the Royal College of Psychiatrists' *Enabling Environments* scheme (Haigh, Harrison, Johnson, Paget, & Williams, 2012; Turley, Payne, & Webster, 2013). This scheme is intended to foster positive relationships between staff and inmates, and among inmates, in order to promote good mental health. The scheme requires organizations, specifically units, prison wings or hospital wards, whole prisons, and whole hospitals, to work toward the demonstration of 10 core principles of an enabling environment (Royal College of Psychiatrists, 2013): belonging, boundaries, communication, development, involvement, safety, structure, empowerment, leadership, and openness. While evaluations of the impact of this scheme in prisons are awaited, the initiative does appear to have good face validity at least.

Concluding Comments

Interventions for men, women, and young people at risk of self-harmful behavior exist but they are few and far between, and research on the effectiveness of those that do exist is very limited. Consequently, the management of people at risk is haphazard and inconsistent across time and place. This is an unfortunate situation, leaving the needs of vulnerable prisoners substantially unaddressed.

Barriers to Implementation

Why are interventions for vulnerable prisoners at risk of self-harmful behavior not better organized, operationalized, and evaluated? Why do repeated calls to address this challenge seemingly go unheard? There are two obvious barriers to the implementation of better systems to support and help vulnerable prisoners.

First, there is a need for a coordinated response to the challenge of self-harmful behavior by vulnerable and at-risk men, women, and young people in prison. A coordinated response means competent staff selection, training, and support procedures, in addition to effective interventions that are responsive to need, in terms of both the nature and the severity of that need, and safe environments that manage the opportunities presented to such prisoners to act harmfully toward themselves. Such a coordinated response, therefore, needs good leadership both overall and within individual establishments (Coyle, 2016). Because there is uncertainty in the research about what works with whom, and because prisons have many competing priorities, staff are stretched across a wide range of tasks rather than able to focus on self-harm and suicide specifically. Therefore, well-intentioned plans to prevent and manage risk of suicide and self-harm are rendered unsustainable or implemented in only a piecemeal way, which severely limits their overall effectiveness.

Second, a coordinated response to vulnerable prisoners requires financial support. Such support, in addition to progressive leadership, is required in order to enable sufficient numbers of staff to receive the training and support they require in order to understand what works for whom and to implement interventions in a sensitive and compassionate way for the time it takes to manage and eventually reduce risk. However, funding is limited and cuts in correctional services are endemic in many jurisdictions. Staff have multiple roles and little time. Also, increasing numbers of men, women, and young people are being sent to prison with significant problems and vulnerabilities that pre-date their incarceration, meaning the demand for support and intervention is increasing just as the capacity of staff to respond appears to be declining (Forrester et al., 2013).

An additional barrier may well be disagreement over what prison is there to achieve: whether to punish and deter or to rehabilitate and possibly even repair, to protect the public or to enhance prisoner welfare and desistance from offending (e.g., Coyle, 2016; McNeill & Schinkel, 2016). Disagreement can be healthy, but it can also be deeply paralyzing when it becomes the subject of political debate and point-scoring, especially when evidence supporting one argument over the other is inconclusive.

Concluding Comments and Good Practice Recommendations

This chapter has provided a brief review of suicide and self-harm in prison settings. The problem is substantial and the challenges are immense, and with rising prison populations and declining resources to manage some of society's most vulnerable men, women, and young people, things are likely to get worse before they get better. This is a desperate situation to be in, given the despair and need of the individuals involved. So, what can services do in the meantime to understand the people in their care and to respond as effectively as they possibly can with the limited resources and opportunities they have which to do so? We propose the following recommendations:

1   That the field move from assessing risk to formulating—or understanding—the risk that individual prisoners pose in terms of their potential to harm themselves. *Formulation-based risk management* is advocated over that based on diagnosis alone (e.g., borderline personality disorder; National Offender Management Service and NHS England, 2015). Formulation-based risk management is believed to encourage staff to be more compassionate about the clients they work with, thus making their responses more sensitive and their working relationships more meaningful and effective in themselves (Logan & Ramsden, 2015).

2   That services focus on *situational risk factors* as much as, if not more so than, on *individual risk factors* for self-harmful behavior. Therefore, if prisons could endeavor to appoint and protect leadership positions for senior staff charged with implementing a local suicide prevention strategy and the time of more junior staff to implement good practice guidelines, this would go some way toward overcoming the problems generated by increasing prison overcrowding and decreasing staff numbers (Coyle, 2016). We recommend specialist staff selection, training, and support to address the needs of vulnerable prisoners—because the numbers of such prisoners will only increase and the rising numbers of self-inflicted injuries and deaths will eventually precipitate such a response. We encourage services to embrace a comprehensive assessment of situational risk in their facility, such as would be structured by the PRISM guidelines discussed above, in order that they have more control over shaping a situation-specific risk management plan (Johnstone & Cooke, 2008).

3   That *prevention* of suicide and self-harm can be considered in three levels: primary (dealing with the problems that lead to risk, such as childhood abuse and neglect, substance misuse, limited education and employment opportunities), secondary (dealing with the impact of these problems, such as through access to health care and educational opportunities in

prison), and tertiary (dealing with the long-term management of these problems, such as through interventions to directly address risk of self-harm and suicide). Much of what has been discussed in this chapter have been efforts at tertiary prevention, that is, ways of managing the long-term effects of the problems that gave rise to risk in the first place. We would like to endorse the existing view that managing the risk of suicide and self-harm in prisons in the long term means more attention to primary and secondary prevention. Therefore, we advocate more support and funding for first night and reception centers in prisons, more comprehensive mental health in-reach services, more education and employment support schemes, and programs that support the kinds of problems that underpin self-harm risk as much as the risk of reoffending, programs such as thinking skills, interpersonal problem-solving, substance misuse programs, and so on. The emphasis on tertiary prevention in prisons is a clear indication that services are responding too late.

Note

1   Forensically modified DBT involves changes to the delivery of therapy, such as changing the reliance on telephone consultation with the therapist, and increasing emphasis on treatment components such as safe personal and interpersonal problem-solving in a prison context where choices about engaging with others are limited.

Key Readings

Humber, N., Webb, R., Piper, M., Appleby, L., & Shaw, J. (2013). A national case-control study of risk factors among prisoners in England and Wales. *Social Psychiatry and Psychiatric Epidemiology*, 48, 1177–1185.
Leitner, M., & Barr, W. (2011). Understanding and managing self-harm in mental health services. In R. Whittington, & C. Logan (Eds.), *Self-harm and violence: Towards best practice in managing risk in mental health services* (pp. 53–78). Chichester, UK: Wiley.
Liebling, A., & Ludlow, A. (2016). Suicide, distress and the quality of prison life. In Y. Jewkes, J. Bennett, & B. Crewe (Eds.), *Handbook on prisons* (2nd ed.) (pp. 224–245). London, UK: Routledge.
Pratt, D. (Ed.) (2016). *The prevention of suicide in prison: Cognitive behavioural approaches*. London, UK: Routledge.
Walker, T., & Towl, G. (2016). *Preventing self-injury and suicide in women's prisons*. Hook, UK: Waterside Press.

References

Backett, S. (1987). Suicide in Scottish prisons. *British Journal of Psychiatry*, 151, 218–221.
Bebbington, P., Minot, S., Cooper, C., Dennis, M., Meltzer, H., Jenkins, R., & Brugha, T. (2010). Suicidal ideation, self-harm and attempted suicide: Results from the British psychiatric morbidity survey 2000. *European Psychiatry*, 25, 427–431.
Bertolote, J., & Fleischmann, A. (2002). A global perspective in the epidemiology of suicide. *Suicidologi*, 7, 6–8.
Binswanger, I., Stern, M., Deyo, R., Heagerty, P., Cheadle, A., Elmore, J., & Koepsell, T. (2007). Release from prison: A high risk of death for former inmates. *New England Journal of Medicine*, 356, 157–165.

Blaauw, E., Kerkhof, A., & Hayes, L. (2005). Demographic, criminal, and psychiatric factors related to inmate suicide. *Suicide and Life-Threatening Behavior*, 35, 63–75.

Blaauw, E., Kerkhof, A., Winkel, F., & Sheridan, L. (2001). Identifying suicide risk in penal institutions in the Netherlands. *British Journal of Forensic Practice*, 3, 22–28.

Borrill, J., Burnett, R., Atkins, R., Miller, S., Briggs, D., Weaver, T., & Maden, A. (2003). Patterns of self-harm and attempted suicide among White and Black/mixed race female prisoners. *Criminal Behaviour and Mental Health*, 13, 229–240.

Brady, K. (2001). Comorbid post-traumatic stress disorder and substance use disorders. *Psychiatric Annals*, 31, 313–319.

Briere, J., & Gill, E. (1998). Self-mutilation in clinical and general population samples: Prevalence, correlates, and functions. *American Journal of Orthopsychiatry*, 68, 609–620.

Brown, G., Ten Have, T., Henriques, G., Xie, S., Hollander, J., & Beck, A. (2005). Cognitive therapy for the prevention of suicide attempts: A randomized controlled trial. *Journal of the American Medical Association*, 294, 563–570.

Cooper, J., Kapur, N., Webb, R., Lawlor, M., Guthrie, E., Mackway-Jones, K., & Appleby, L. (2005). Suicide after deliberate self-harm: A 4-year cohort study. *American Journal of Psychiatry*, 162, 297–303.

Corston, J., (2007). *The Corston report: A report by Baroness Jean Corston of a review of women with particular vulnerabilities in the criminal justice system.* Retrieved from http://webarchive.nationalarchives.gov.uk/+/http://www.homeoffice.gov.uk/documents/corston-report

Coyle, A. (2016). Prisons in context. In Y. Jewkes, J. Bennett, & B. Crewe (Eds.), *Handbook on prisons* (2nd ed., ed.) (pp. 7–23). London, UK: Routledge.

Dalton, V. (1999). Suicide in prison 1980 to 1998: National overview. *Trends and Issues in Crime and Criminal Justice*, 126, 1.

Daniel, A., & Fleming, J. (2006). Suicides in a state correctional system, 1992–2002: A review. *Journal of Correctional Health Care*, 12, 24–35.

Dear, G., Slattery, J., & Hillan, R. (2001). Evaluations of the quality of coping reported by prisoners who have self-harmed and those who have not. *Suicide and Life-threatening Behavior*, 31, 442–450.

Dear, G., Thomson, D., & Hills, A. (2000). Self-harm in prison: Manipulators can also be suicide attempters. *Criminal Justice and Behavior*, 27, 160–175.

Dockley, A. (2001). Suicide and self-harm prevention: Repetitive self-harm among women in prison. *Prison Service Journal*, 138, 27–29.

Dooley, E. (1990). Prison suicide in England and Wales, 1972–87. *British Journal of Psychiatry*, 156, 40–45.

Douglas, K., Hart, S., Webster, C., & Belfrage, H. (2013). *HCR-20: Assessing risk for violence* (3rd ed.). Vancouver, Canada: Mental Health, Law and Policy Institute, Simon Fraser University.

Driessen, M., Schroeder, T., Widmann, B., von Schonfeld, C., & Schneider, F. (2006). Childhood trauma, psychiatric disorders, and criminal behavior in prisoners in Germany: A comparative study in incarcerated women and men. *Journal of Clinical Psychiatry*, 67, 1486–1492.

Dulit, R., Fyer, M., Leon, A., Brodsky, B., & Frances, A. (1994). Clinical correlates of self-mutilation in borderline personality disorder. *American Journal of Psychiatry*, 151, 1305–1311.

Fazel, S., & Benning, R. (2009). Suicides in female prisoners in England and Wales, 1978–2004. *British Journal of Psychiatry*, 194, 183–184.

Fazel, S., Benning, R., & Danesh, J. (2005). Suicides in male prisoners in England and Wales, 1978–2003. *The Lancet*, 366, 1301–1302.

Fazel, S., Cartwright, J., Norman-Nott, A., & Hawton, K. (2008). Suicide in prisoners: A systematic review of risk factors. *Journal of Clinical Psychiatry*, 69, 1721–1731.

Fazel, S., & Danesh, J. (2002). Serious mental disorder in 23,000 prisoners: A systematic review of 62 surveys. *The Lancet*, 359(9306), 545–550.

Fazel, S., Grann, M., Kling, B., & Hawton, K. (2011). Prison suicide in 12 countries: An ecological study of 861 suicides during 2003–2007. *Social Psychiatry and Psychiatric Epidemiology*, 46, 191–195.

Forrester, A., Exworthy, T., Olumoroti, O., Sessay, M., Parrott, J., Spencer, S. J., & Whyte, S. (2013). Variations in prison mental health services in England and Wales. *International Journal of Law and Psychiatry*, 36, 326–332.

Fruehwald, S., Frottier, P., Eher, R., Gutierrez, K., & Ritter, K. (2000). Prison suicides in Austria, 1975–1997. *Suicide and Life-threatening Behavior*, 30, 360–369.

Fruehwald, S., Matschnig, T., Koenig, F., Bauer, P., & Frottier, P. (2004). Suicide in custody. *British Journal of Psychiatry*, 185, 494–498.

Fulwiler, C., Forbes, C., Santangelo, S., & Folstein, M. (1997). Self-mutilation and suicide attempt: Distinguishing features in prisoners. *Journal of the American Academy of Psychiatry and the Law Online*, 25, 69–77.

Gaynes, B., West, S., Ford, C., Frame, P., Klein, J., & Lohr, K. (2004). Screening for suicide risk in adults: A summary of the evidence for the US Preventive Services Task Force. *Annals of Internal Medicine*, 140, 822–835.

Gee, J., & Reed, S. (2013). The HoST programme: A pilot evaluation of modified dialectical behavior therapy with female offenders diagnosed with borderline personality disorder. *European Journal of Psychotherapy and Counseling*, 15, 233–252.

Goff, A., Rose, E., Rose, S., & Purves, D. (2007). Does PTSD occur in sentenced prison populations? A systematic literature review. *Criminal Behaviour and Mental Health*, 17, 152–162.

Goldney, R., & Burvill, P. (1980). Review trends in suicidal behaviour and its management. *Australian and New Zealand Journal of Psychiatry*, 14, 1–15.

Gratz, K. (2003). Risk factors for and functions of deliberate self-harm: An empirical and conceptual review. *Clinical Psychology: Science and Practice*, 10, 192–205.

Haigh, R., Harrison, T., Johnson, R., Paget, S., & Williams, S. (2012). Psychologically informed environments and the "enabling environments" initiative. *Housing, Care and Support*, 15, 34–42.

Harris, E., & Barraclough, B. (1997). Suicide as an outcome for mental disorders: A meta-analysis. *British Journal of Psychiatry*, 170, 205–228.

Harris, T. (2015). *Changing prisons, saving lives: Report of the independent review into self-inflicted deaths in custody of 18–24 year olds*. London, United Kingdom: Her Majesty's Stationery Office. Retrieved from http://dera.ioe.ac.uk/23552/1/moj-harris-review-web-accessible.pdf

Harris, T. (2016). Foreword. In T. Walker, & G. Towl (Eds.), *Preventing self-injury and suicide in women's prisons* (pp. xi–xiv). London, UK Hook, UK: Waterside Press.

Hart, S., Kropp, P., Laws, D., Klaver, J., Logan, C., & Watt, K. (2003). *The Risk for Sexual Violence Protocol: Structured professional guidelines for assessing risk of sexual violence*. Vancouver, Canada: Mental Health, Law and Policy Institute, Simon Fraser University.

Hawton, K., Fagg, J., Platt, S., & Hawkins, M. (1993). Factors associated with suicide after parasuicide in young people. *British Medical Journal*, 306(6893), 1641–1644.

Hawton, K., i Comabella, C., Haw, C., & Saunders, K. (2013). Risk factors for suicide in individuals with depression: A systematic review. *Journal of Affective Disorders*, 147, 17–28.

Hawton, K., Linsell, L., Adeniji, T., Sariaslan, A., & Fazel, S. (2014). Self-harm in prisons in England and Wales: An epidemiological study of prevalence, risk factors, clustering, and subsequent suicide. *The Lancet*, 383(9923), 1147–1154.

Hawton, K., & Van Heeringen, K. (Eds.) (2000). *The international handbook of suicide and attempted suicide*. Chichester, UK: Wiley.

He, X., Felthous, A., Holzer, C., Nathan, P., & Veasey, S. (2001). Factors in prison suicide: One year study in Texas. *Journal of Forensic Science*, 46, 896–901.

Hillbrand, M., Young, J., & Krystal, J. (1996). Recurrent self-injurious behavior in forensic patients. *Psychiatric Quarterly*, 67, 33–45.

HM Prison Service (2001). *Prevention of suicide and self-harm in the prison service*. London, UK: Ministry of Justice.

Howard League for Penal Reform (2003). *Suicide and self-harm prevention: The management of self-injury in prison.* London, UK: Author.

Humber, N., Hayes, A., Senior, J., Fahy, T., & Shaw, J. (2011). Identifying, monitoring and managing prisoners at risk of self-harm/suicide in England and Wales. *Journal of Forensic Psychiatry and Psychology*, 22, 22–51.

Humber, N., Webb, R., Piper, M., Appleby, L., & Shaw, J. (2013). A national case-control study of risk factors among prisoners in England and Wales. *Social Psychiatry and Psychiatric Epidemiology*, 48, 1177–1185.

Isomesta, E., & Lonnqvist, J. (1998). Suicide attempts preceding completed suicide. *British Journal of Psychiatry*, 173, 531–535.

Johnstone, L., & Cooke, D. (2008). *PRISM: Promoting Risk Intervention by Situational Management: Structured professional guidelines for assessing situational risk factors for violence in institutions* (1st ed.). Vancouver, Canada: Mental Health, Law and Policy Institute, Simon Fraser University.

Johnstone, L., & Cooke, D. (2010). PRISM: A promising paradigm for assessing and managing institutional violence: Findings from a multiple case study analysis of five Scottish prisons. *International Journal of Forensic Mental Health*, 9, 180–191.

Joukamaa, M. (1997). Prison suicide in Finland, 1969–1992. *Forensic Science International*, 89, 167–174.

Kariminia, A., Law, M., Butler, T., Levy, M., Corben, S., Kaldor, J., & Grant, L. (2007). Suicide risk among recently released prisoners in New South Wales, Australia. *Medical Journal of Australia*, 187, 387–390.

King, C., Senior, J., Webb, R. T., Millar, T., Piper, M., Pearsall, A., … & Shaw, J. (2015). Suicide by people in a community justice pathway: Population-based nested case–control study. *British Journal of Psychiatry*, 207, 175–176.

Klonsky, E., Oltmanns, T., & Turkheimer, E. (2003). Deliberate self-harm in a nonclinical population: Prevalence and psychological correlates. *American Journal of Psychiatry*, 160, 1501–1508.

Leese, M., Thomas, S., & Snow, L. (2006). An ecological study of factors associated with rates of self-inflicted death in prisons in England and Wales. *International Journal of Law and Psychiatry*, 29, 355–360.

Leitner, M., & Barr, W. (2011). Understanding and managing self-harm in mental health services. In R. Whittington, & C. Logan (Eds.), *Self-harm and violence: Towards best practice in managing risk in mental health services* (pp. 53–78). Chichester, UK: Wiley.

Leitner, M., Barr, W., & Hobby, L. (2008). Effectiveness of interventions to prevent suicide and suicidal behaviour: A systematic review. Scottish Government Social Research, Edinburgh, UK. Retrieved from www.scotland.gov.uk/Resource/Doc/208329/0055247.pdf

Liebling, A. (1992). *Suicides in prison.* London, UK: Routledge.

Liebling, A. (1994). Suicide amongst women prisoners. *Howard Journal of Criminal Justice*, 33, 1–9.

Liebling, A. (2006). The role of the prison environment in prison suicide and prisoner distress. In G. Dear (Ed.), *Preventing suicide and other self-injury in prison.* Basingstoke, UK: Palgrave-McMillan.

Liebling, A., Durie, L., Stiles, A., & Tait, S. (2005). Revisiting prison suicide: The role of fairness and distress. In A. Liebling, & A. Maruna (Eds.), *The effects of imprisonment* (pp. 209–231). London, UK: Routledge.

Liebling, A., & Ludlow, A. (2016). Suicide, distress and the quality of prison life. In Y. Jewkes, J. Bennett, & B. Crewe (Eds.), *Handbook on prisons* (2nd ed., ed.) (pp. 224–245). London, UK: Routledge.

Logan, C. (2013). Suicide and deliberate self-injury. In C. Logan, & L. Johnstone (Eds.), *Managing clinical risk: A guide to effective practice* (pp. 115–141). London, UK: Routledge.

Logan, C. (2017a). Formulation for forensic practitioners. In R. Roesch, & A. Cook (Eds.), *Handbook of forensic mental health services* (pp. 153–178). New York, NY: Routledge.

Logan, C. (2017b). Forensic case formulation of violence and aggression. In P. Sturmey (Ed.), *The Wiley handbook of violence and aggression.* Chichester, UK: Wiley.

128 *Caroline Logan and Jayne L. Taylor*

Logan, C., & Ramsden, J. (2015). Working in partnership: Making it happen for high-risk personality disordered offenders. *Journal of Forensic Practice*, 17, 171–179.

Lohner, J., & Konrad, N. (2006). Deliberate self-harm and suicide attempt in custody: Distinguishing features in male inmates' self-injurious behavior. *International Journal of Law and Psychiatry*, 29, 370–385.

Ludlow, A., Schmidt, B., Akoensi, T., Liebling, A., Giacomantonio, C., & Sutherland, A. (2015). *Self-inflicted deaths in NOMS' custody amongst 18–24 year olds: Staff experience, knowledge and views.* Santa Monica, CA: RAND Corporation.

Marzano, L., Hawton, K., Rivlin, A., & Fazel, S. (2011). Psychosocial influences on prisoner suicide: A case-control study of near-lethal self-harm in women prisoners. *Social Science and Medicine*, 72, 874–883.

McKenzie, K., Serfaty, M., & Crawford, M. (2003). Suicide in ethnic minority groups. *British Journal of Psychiatry*, 183, 100–101.

McNeill, F., & Schinkel, M. (2016). Prisons and desistance. In Y. Jewkes, J. Bennett, & B. Crewe (Eds.), *Handbook on prisons* (2nd ed., ed.) (pp. 607–621). London, UK: Routledge.

Miller, S., & Fritzon, K. (2007). Functional consistency across two behavioural modalities: Fire-setting and self-harm in female special hospital patients. *Criminal Behaviour and Mental Health*, 17, 31–44.

Möller-Leimkühler, A. M. (2003). The gender gap in suicide and premature death or: Why are men so vulnerable? *European Archives of Psychiatry and Clinical Neuroscience*, 253, 1–8.

Monahan, J., Steadman, H. J., Silver, E., Appelbaum, P. S., Robbins, P. C., Mulvey, E. P., ... & Banks (2001). *Rethinking risk assessment: The MacArthur study of mental disorder and violence.* New York, NY: Oxford University Press.

National Offender Management Service and NHS England (2015). *Working with personality disordered offenders* (2nd ed.). London, UK: Author Retrieved from http://www.gov.uk/government/publications/working-with-offenders-with-personality-disorder-a-practitioners-guide

Nestor, P. G. (2002). Mental disorder and violence: Personality dimensions and clinical features. *American Journal of Psychiatry*, 159, 1973–1978.

Nock, M., Prinstein, M., & Sterba, S. (2010). Revealing the form and function of self-injurious thoughts and behaviors: A real-time ecological assessment study among adolescents and young adults. *Journal of Abnormal Psychology*, 118, 816–827.

Noonan, M., & Grinder, S. (2013). *Mortality in local jails and state prisons, 2000–2011: Statistical tables.* US Department of Justice and Bureau of Justice Statistics, August, NCJ 242186. Retrieved from http://www.bjs.gov/content/pub/pdf/mljsp0011.pdf

Owens, D., Horrocks, J., & House, A. (2002). Fatal and non-fatal repetition of self-harm. *British Journal of Psychiatry*, 181, 193–199.

Patterson, R., & Hughes, K. (2008). Review of completed suicides in the California Department of Corrections and Rehabilitation, 1999 to 2004. *Psychiatric Services*, 59, 676–682.

Pattison, E., & Kahan, J. (1983). The deliberate self-harm syndrome. *American Journal of Psychiatry*, 140, 867–872.

Perry, A., Waterman, M., & House, A. (2016). Problem-solving training for suicidal prisoners. In D. Pratt (Ed.), *The prevention of suicide in prison: Cognitive behavioural approaches* (pp. 69–84). London, UK: Routledge.

Power, K., Swanson, V., Luke, R., Jackson, C., & Biggam, F. (2003). Act and care: Evaluation of the revised SPS suicide risk management strategy. Occasional Paper Series, 1.

Pratt, D. (Ed.) (2016). *The prevention of suicide in prison: Cognitive behavioural approaches.* London, UK: Routledge.

Pratt, D., Piper, M., Appleby, L., Webb, R., & Shaw, J. (2006). Suicide in recently released prisoners: A population-based cohort study. *The Lancet*, 368(9530), 119–123.

Pratt, D., Tarrier, N., Dunn, G., Awenat, Y., Shaw, J., Ulph, F., & Gooding, P. (2015). Cognitive-behavioural suicide prevention for male prisoners: A pilot randomized controlled trial. *Psychological Medicine*, 45, 3441–3451.

Quina, K., & Brown, L. (Eds.) (2013). *Trauma and dissociation in convicted offenders: Gender, science and treatment issues.* New York, NY: Routledge.

Rabe, K. (2012). Prison structure, inmate mortality and suicide risk in Europe. *International Journal of Law and Psychiatry, 35,* 222–230.

Rickford, D., & Edgar, K. (2005). *Troubled inside: Responding to the mental health needs of men in prison.* Prison Reform Trust, UK. Retrieved from www.prisonreformtrust.org.uk/Portals/0/Documents/Troubled%20Inside_Men%20report%20corrected.pdf

Rivlin, A., Hawton, K., Marzano, L., & Fazel, S. (2010). Psychiatric disorders in male prisoners who made near-lethal suicide attempts: Case-control study. *British Journal of Psychiatry, 197,* 313–319.

Rojas, Y., & Stenberg, S. (2010). Early life circumstances and male suicide: A 30-year follow-up of a Stockholm cohort born in 1953. *Social Science and Medicine, 70,* 420–427.

Royal College of Psychiatrists (2013). *Enabling environments standards.* London, UK: Author Retrieved from www.rcpsych.ac.uk/pdf/ee%20standards%20-%202013.pdf

Senior, J., Hayes, A., Pratt, D., Thomas, S., Fahy, T., Leese, M., ... & Shaw, J. (2007). The identification and management of suicide risk in local prisons. *Journal of Forensic Psychiatry and Psychology, 18,* 368–380.

Shaw, J., Baker, D., Hunt, I., Moloney, A., & Appleby, L. (2004). Suicide by prisoners: A national clinical survey. *British Journal of Psychiatry, 184,* 263–267.

Singleton, N., Coid, J., Bebbington, P., Jenkins, R., Brugha, T., Lewis, G., & Farrell, M. (1998). *The National Survey of Psychiatric Morbidity among prisoners and the future of prison.* London, UK: The Stationary Office.

Snow, L. (2002). Prisoners' motives for self-injury and attempted suicide. *British Journal of Forensic Practice, 4,* 18–29.

Snow, L., & McHugh, M. (2002). The aftermath of a death in prison custody. In G. J. Towl, L. Snow, & M. McHugh (Eds.), *Suicide in prisons* (pp. 135–155). Oxford, UK: Blackwell.

Stathopoulos, M., Quadara, A., Fileborn, B., & Clark, H. (2012). *Addressing women's victimization histories in custodial settings.* ACSSA Issues 13. Melbourne: Australian Institute of Family Studies. Retrieved from https://aifs.gov.au/publications/addressing-womens-victimisation-histories-custodial-settings

Sturmey, P., & McMurran, M. (Eds.) (2011). *Forensic case formulation.* Chichester, UK: Wiley.

Sutton, J. (2008). *Healing the hurt within: Understand self-injury and self-harm, and heal the emotional wounds.* Oxford, UK: Howtobooks.

Sykes, G. (1958). *The society of captives: A study of a maximum security prison.* Princeton, NJ: Princeton University Press.

Tarrier, N., Taylor, K., & Gooding, P. (2008). Cognitive-behavioral interventions to reduce suicide behavior: A systematic review and meta-analysis. *Behavior Modification, 32,* 77–108.

Taterelli, R., Mancinelli, I., Taggi, F., & Polidori, G. (1999). Suicide in Italian prisons in 1996 and 1997: A descriptive epidemiological study. *International Journal of Offender Therapy and Comparative Criminology, 43,* 438–447.

Towl, G., & Crighton, D. (1998). Suicide in prisons in England and Wales from 1988 to 1995. *Criminal Behaviour and Mental Health, 8,* 184–192.

Turley, C., Payne, C., & Webster, S. (2013). *Enabling features of psychologically informed planned environments.* London, UK: National Offender Management Service.

Värnik, A., Kolves, K., van der Feltz-Cornelis, C. M., Marusic, A., Oskarsson, H., Palmer, A., ... & Giupponi, G. (2008). Suicide methods in Europe: A gender-specific analysis of countries participating in the European Alliance against depression. *Journal of Epidemiology and Community Health, 62,* 545–551.

Walker, T., Shaw, J., Turpin, C., Reid, C., & Abel, K. (2017). The WORSHIP II study: A pilot of psychodynamic interpersonal therapy with women offenders who self-harm. *Journal of Forensic Psychiatry and Psychology, 28,* 158–171.

Walker, T., & Towl, G. (2016). *Preventing self-injury and suicide in women's prisons.* Hook, UK: Waterside Press.

Walmsley, R. (2015). *World prison population list* (11th ed.). London, UK: Kings College London, International Centre for Prison Studies Retrieved from http://www.prisonstudies.org/sites/default/files/resources/downloads/world_prison_population_list_11th_edition_0.pdf

Winter, M. (2003). County jail suicides in a mid-western state: Moving beyond the use of profiles. *Prison Journal*, 83, 130–148.

Wobeser, W., Datema, J., Bechard, B., & Ford, P. (2002). Causes of death among people in custody in Ontario, 1990–1999. *Canadian Medical Association Journal*, 167, 1109–1113.

World Health Organisation (2007). *Preventing suicide in jails and prisons*. Geneva, Switzerland: Author.

8

Solitary Confinement and Punishment: Effects on Misconducts and Recidivism

Paul Gendreau

University of New Brunswick, Canada

Claire Goggin

St. Thomas University, New Brunswick, Canada

In the past several years, the use of solitary confinement (SC) in prisons has dominated debate in the field of penology. In contrast to the daily schedule in regular prisons, SC generally involves restricted environmental stimulation (e.g., auditory, visual, kinesthetic; see Suedfeld, 1980) as inmates are typically locked up for 23 hours per day with limited or no access to recreational and/or program services (Gendreau & Labrecque, 2016). Two viewpoints have characterized the debate regarding the effects of this type of incarceration (Gendreau & Labrecque, 2016). One school of thought contends that SC is a form of "torture" that, with increasing levels of exposure, produces lasting emotional damage, even psychosis (Grassian, 1983; Haney, 2012; Jackson, 2001; Kupers, 2008; Scharff Smith, 2006). The other point of view purports that the effects of brief periods of SC (e.g., 30 days) are much less pronounced and that other factors, such as how inmates are treated or extent of available services, are more likely contributing to SC's putative iatrogenic effects (Clements et al., 2007; Gendreau & Bonta, 1984; Gendreau & Labrecque, 2016; Gendreau & Thériault, 2011; O'Donnell, 2014; O'Keefe et al., 2013; Wormith, 1984). In fact, the latter perspective is supported by the results of two independently conducted meta-analyses of the effects of SC on various behavioral outcomes (Morgan et al., 2016). That said, we nevertheless share the concerns expressed by others regarding the potential negative effects of lengthy exposure to SC.

The purpose of this chapter, however, is to address a quite different question: that is, the opinion that SC may, in fact, have salutary effects. Advocates of this perspective are champions of the "get tough" school in corrections which has, in part, contributed to the proliferation of supermax prisons, particularly in the United States (see Mears, 2013; Stubblefield, 2002).[5] It holds that the punitive conditions of SC serve as a punisher which suppresses inmates' post-SC antisocial behavior, thereby helping to maintain a "law and order" climate in prisons (Mears & Castro, 2006). Moreover, it is argued that the punitive aspects of SC will also reduce post-release recidivism.

The Wiley International Handbook of Correctional Psychology, First Edition. Edited by Devon L. L. Polaschek, Andrew Day, and Clive R. Hollin.

Fortunately, some prisons keep records regarding the use of SC per inmate relative to individual outcomes, such as institutional misconducts and post-release recidivism. These data offer an opportunity to draw general conclusions about the utility of SC as a punisher. Prior to reviewing the available evidence on the effectiveness of SC, however, it is useful to discuss what is known about the impact of prison conditions in general on inmate behavior. Too often SC is considered in isolation when compared with other elements of prison life, and this can foster inaccuracies about SC's general effects (Gendreau & Labrecque, 2016).

In order to address this question, we begin by briefly summarizing the literature on the effects of general and specific conditions of prison life on criminal outcomes. This includes a discussion of two topics that have been overlooked in prison research: the effects of corporal punishment and the effects of the "personality" of prisons (e.g., negative climate) on offender behavior. Subsequently, we provide recent evidence regarding the effects of SC on misconducts and recidivism and follow this with a brief discussion of how theory explains these findings.

Techniques for Punishing Inmates

The Pain of Prison Life: General Conditions

An enduring view in penology has been that the experience of prison is a punishing one for offenders, and works to reduce recidivism through the process of stigmatization, dehumanization, and loss of income (see Gendreau & Goggin, 2014). Briefly, there have been several meta-analyses that have addressed this issue (Gendreau, Goggin, & Cullen, 1999; Jonson, 2010, 2013; Nagin, Cullen, & Jonson, 2009; Smith, Goggin, & Gendreau, 2002; Villettaz, Killias, & Zoder, 2006) and the conclusions from these studies are unequivocal: prison generally increases recidivism by a factor of several percentage points with the worst outcomes typically reported for lower-risk offenders (Gendreau & Goggin, 2014; Gendreau & Smith, 2012; Tanasichuk, Wormith, & Guzzo, 2009). This latter finding is contrary to the prediction of economists who contend that lower-risk inmates (i.e., those who have stronger prosocial bonds) are more amenable to punishment as they have the most to lose both financially and socially (Nagin, 1998; Orsagh & Chen, 1988).

Although the effects of prison on misconducts have been little studied, the evidence to date does suggest that the criminal identity of low-risk inmates actually increases over time (Walters, 2003). This may explain why misconduct rates among low-risk offenders tend to increase over the length of the sentence relative to those of higher-risk peers (Smith, 2006).

Special Conditions of Prison Life

Four aspects of prison life, each of which is generally regarded as a punishing condition, are thought to produce extra hardship for inmates.[6] They include the "harshness" of prison life, prison crowding, the negative environmental climate or "personality" of a prison, and the use of corporal punishment. It is expected that the effect of each of these conditions is a reduction in antisocial behavior (e.g., prison misconducts, recidivism).

"Harshness" of prison life

A general assumption in the penological literature is that living in maximum security environments is more punishing because conditions are necessarily "harsher" than those in lower-security units and that the experience of these conditions will have a direct effect in reducing post-release recidivism. The available research, however, suggests otherwise. For example, after controlling for offender risk level, inmates housed in maximum versus minimum security facilities are more likely to engage in post-release recidivism (Gaes & Camp, 2009; Jonson, 2010). Specifically, Jonson (2010) reported an $r = .16$ (95% CI [.11, .22]) between more versus less harsh conditions and recidivism across 204,926 inmates. Similarly, Gaes and Camp (2009) reported $\varphi = .10$ (95% CI [.03, .17]) between placement in maximum versus minimum security classification units and recidivism across 561 inmates.[7]

At the same time, caution is advised in interpreting these findings; comparisons of outcome among inmate groups living at different classification levels is problematic as researchers typically have knowledge of only a few static factors (e.g., criminal record) with which to assess the equivalence of offender groups. Also, with limited first-hand access to prisons, and no means of looking into the black box of prison life over time, it is virtually impossible to precisely determine the relative "harshness" of life at varying security levels (e.g., reduced privileges, poor medical care and food services, and, crucially, the relationship between inmates and staff).

Effects of Crowding

It is routinely assumed that crowded institutional living conditions necessarily impose undue hardships on inmates which, in turn, contribute to increased levels of antisocial behavior. This is a deceptively complex literature in terms of how crowding, among other things, is defined (Steiner & Wooldredge, 2008, 2009). While more studies are required, the available evidence from three meta-analyses indicates that crowding is only weakly related (i.e., $r_{range} = .02$ to .11) to increases in misconduct rates (Bonta & Gendreau, 1990; Franklin, Franklin, & Pratt, 2006; Gendreau, Goggin, & Law, 1997).

Effects of prison "personality"

The effect of correctional climate (CC), or prison "personality," on offender behavior has received renewed attention in the literature (Clements et al., 2007; Goggin, 2008; Moos, 1968). This is, in part, a consequence of research examining the effect of supermax units on inmate adjustment (see Gibbons & Katzenbach, 2006; Haney, 1997; Useem & Kimball, 1989) as well as claims by "get tough" proponents who maintain that harsher living conditions within prisons (e.g., no services, the lash, etc.) are effective in reducing recidivism (see Gendreau & Smith, 2012).

Employing data from a comprehensive survey of Canadian federal prison inmates ($n = 4,283$), Goggin (2008) evaluated the effects of perceived correctional climate on rates of inmate infractions and post-release recidivism during a 5-year follow-up. The survey sampled from domains key to an evaluation of CC, including (a) facility living conditions, (b) safety, health, and security, and (c) inmate programming, among others. The mean score on the survey was 29%, where higher scores indicated more negative perceptions of prison climate.

Approximately 30% of inmates committed at least one serious misconduct, with 49% committing at least one non-serious infraction. As expected, institutional classification level contributed to more negative CC ratings, with medium and maximum security facilities receiving poorer ratings than minimum security units (maximum: 30%, 95% CI [29%, 31%]; medium: 30%, 95% CI [30%, 31%]; minimum: 23%, 95% CI [23%, 24%]. More negative CC ratings were also associated with higher levels of both serious and non-serious prison misconducts as well as post-release recidivism, particularly among inmates in maximum security units (serious misconducts: $\varphi = .37$, 95% CI [.34, .40]; non-serious misconducts: $\varphi = .36$, 95% CI

[.33, .39]; recidivism: φ = .11, 95% CI [.06, .16]. These results run counter to what "get tough" proponents have predicted regarding the effects of prison. That is, inmates who rated conditions of confinement more negatively engaged in more, not less, antisocial behavior. Results were also examined separately by levels of offender risk[8] and institutional security level. For low- (n = 407) and moderate- (n = 264) risk inmates housed in maximum security facilities, correlations between CC and outcome ranged from .13 to .24 with *recidivism* and .15 to .26 with *recidivism new charge*. By contrast, high-risk inmates (n = 246) housed in maximum security showed minimal effects of CC on outcome (i.e., *recidivism*: r = −.01; *recidivism new charge*: r = .04). Similar results—that low-risk inmates are more adversely affected by more restrictive prison environments than are high-risk inmates—have also been reported by Smith (2006) under different experimental conditions.

The housing of low-risk inmates in maximum security units is an important consideration for prison management practices (see Bonta & Motiuk, 1986) as, in Goggin (2008), higher mean CC ratings were reported for low-risk inmates in maximum versus minimum security settings, with no overlap in respective *CIs*. This result suggests that, for low-risk inmates, it may be the conditions of their confinement that contribute to more negative perceptions of CC and, ultimately, poorer outcomes.

In addition, pre-post assessments of procriminal attitudes in mixed samples of inmates have shown increases in levels of antisocial values among low-risk inmates after only a brief sentence. For example, Walters (2003) used the *Social Identity as a Criminal* scale to examine the degree to which offenders identified with criminal others during a 6-month prison stay. The sample was divided on the basis of their degree of jail/prison experience (i.e., <6 months vs. >5 years). A comparison of pre versus post scores on the SIC indicated that lower-risk offenders (i.e., those with less experience; n = 55) showed a significant increase ($p<.05$) in expressed criminal values (i.e., *I have a lot in common with other criminals; In general, being a criminal is an important part of my self-image*) as compared with higher-risk offenders (i.e., those with more experience; n = 93).

Effects of corporal punishment

Historically, corporal punishment (i.e., caning, the strap, whipping) was used to control inmate behavior (Allan, 1954). While it has been abolished for some time, there are still calls for its use, even in academic circles, where it is regarded as a lesser punishment than incarceration (Moskos, 2011).[9] The first author witnessed the use of corporal punishment in Canadian federal prisons during the early 1960s, at a time when use of the strap was widely endorsed in Canadian corrections (for complete details on the procedure, see Allan, 1954). Between 1957 and 1967, the strap was administered 332 times at the federal level, or an average of 30 times per year (Farrell, 1999). The practice was eventually abolished in 1972 in both Canada and the United States following its discontinuation in the United Kingdom in 1962.

Three empirical studies have examined the effectiveness of corporal punishment on criminal outcomes. Caldwell (1944) examined the effect of the whip on recidivism rates among 320 Delaware inmates sentenced between 1920 and 1939. In this case, whipping was used in conjunction with a period of imprisonment. During a 3-year follow-up, Caldwell reported that 62% of the sample had recidivated. Two additional cohorts of offenders served as comparison groups. In each case, they had received sentences that included whipping but were not whipped. Caldwell reported recidivism rates of 51% over 5 years for offenders sentenced in 1928 (n = 93) and 34% over 2 years for those sentenced in 1940 (n = 120). Overall, based on our calculations using Caldwell's raw data, whipping resulted in higher recidivism rates among both cohorts (i.e., φ_{1928} = .10, 95% CI [.02, .18]; φ_{1940} = .25, 95% CI [.19, .30]).

In a related study, the relationship between caning and future absconding was examined among juveniles in a training center in England (Clarke, 1966). There was a slight suppression effect of caning on absconding when results were examined by age, with 39% of caned juniors (i.e., ≤15 years) recidivating as compared with 61% of those who were not caned. The opposite result was reported for seniors (i.e., aged 15–17 years) where 54% of those caned recidivated as compared with 46% of those who were not caned (Clarke, 1966). While the results from this study are admittedly difficult to interpret, our conclusion is that, overall, there was little effect of caning. It should be noted, however, that in both Caldwell (1944) and Clarke (1966) the authors cautioned that a number of confounding variables could have affected their findings. Of note, offender risk assessment was not a feature of the correctional landscape at the time these studies were conducted but it is highly plausible that the groups studied varied on that dimension.

Finally, Gendreau and Kennedy (1974) reviewed the use of the strap at a provincial prison in Ontario and found that the use of such a sanction did not suppress future misconduct behavior among those who experienced it. Nor did it act as a deterrent for other inmates in the general prison population. Further, the intensity of punishment (i.e., strap frequency) was not related to outcome.[10] Alarmingly, in the opinion of correctional staff who worked in the setting at the time (1948–1956), 60% of inmates who were strapped were not guilty of an offense or were being punished for alleged infractions which were trivial in nature and had not merited such a severe punishment.

Effects of Solitary Confinement

Germane to the present discussion, there is a dearth of studies which have examined the effects of SC on prison misconducts. More commonly, researchers have assessed the impact of SC on post-release recidivism (Labrecque, 2015). As detailed in Table 8.1, the majority of such studies have reported non-significant differences in the recidivism rates of SC versus non-SC offenders. This pattern of results was particularly pronounced among those studies which used propensity matching procedures[11] in establishing the relative correspondence between SC and non-SC groups. Matching was typically based on offender demographics, criminal history, type of crime, and risk level (Butler, Steiner, Makarios, & Travis, 2013; Lovell, Johnson, & Cain, 2007). The only exception to this pattern of results was a study by Mears and Bales (2009) which also used propensity matching but reported slightly higher recidivism rates ($p<.05$) among SC versus non-SC offenders (i.e., 24.2% vs. 20.5%, respectively). Finally, the study by Motiuk and Blanchette (2001) which reported significantly higher recidivism rates among SC inmates did not include a matched comparison group. It should be noted that, in each of the above studies, inmates were not randomly assigned to SC. Rather, SC was used as a sanction in response to institutional misbehavior. Comparison groups were comprised of randomly selected non-SC inmates who were matched on relevant factors with inmates in the SC condition.

There are three studies which have evaluated the effects of SC on inmate misconducts. This is of interest as some contend that SC controls institutional antisocial behaviors once inmates who experience it are returned to the general population. Results to date, however, have been mixed (see Table 8.2).

For example, Briggs, Sundt, and Castellano (2003) used interrupted time series analysis[12] to evaluate the effects of SC on infraction rates before and after implementation of supermax

Table 8.1 Details of Studies Examining the Effects of Solitary Confinement on Recidivism

Study	Matching variables	Follow-up	Outcome	% R (n) SC	No SC
Butler et al. (2013)	Age, race, risk level, index offense, education, marital status, type of sentence, gang member, sex offender	1	rearrest	51% (57)	39%* (57)
	Age, race, risk level, index offense, education, marital status, type of sentence, gang member, sex offender	1	felony rearrest	25% (57)	16%* (57)
	Age, race, risk level, index offense, education, marital status, type of sentence, gang member, sex offender	7	reincarceration	67% (57)	56%* (57)
Lovell et al. (2007)	Criminal history, sex offender, misconduct rate, race, index offense, age of release, mental health status	3	new felony	53% (200)	46%* (200)
Mears and Bales (2009)	Age, race, index offense, criminal history, time served, misconducts	3	any recidivism	58.8% (1,241)	57.6%* (1,241)
	Age, race, index offense, criminal history, time served, misconducts	3	violent recidivism	24.2% (1,241)	20.5%** (1,241)
Motiuk and Blanchette (2001)	Comparison group randomly selected but not matched	< 1	any reincarceration	53.3% (478)	34.2%** (453)
	Comparison group randomly selected but not matched	< 1	reincarceration new offense	17.9% (478)	11.3%** (453)

Source: Based on data from Butler et al. (2013), Lovell et al. (2007), Mears and Bales (2009), Motiuk and Blanchette (2001).
Note. Matching variables = variables upon which treatment and comparison groups were matched; Follow-up = length of follow-up in years; Outcome = type of outcome; % R = percentage of sample who recidivated per prison condition; n = sample size per prison condition; SC = solitary confinement; No SC = no solitary confinement.
* $p > .05$.
** $p < .05$.

units in three US state prison systems, including Arizona, Illinois, and Minnesota. Dependent variables included inmate-on-inmate and inmate-on-staff assaults.[13] With respect to the former outcome, no significant decrease in inmate-on-inmate assaults was reported after implementation of supermax units in each of the prisons studied. Inmate-on-staff assaults, however, varied by prison such that rates in Illinois were reduced while those in Arizona increased significantly ($p < .05$) over the short term and, finally, Minnesota experienced no change in rates of such assaults. Of note, caution is advised in interpreting these results given that they are derived from aggregate data which substantially inflate the magnitude of relationships between variables (i.e., Clark & Avery, 1975; Freedman, Pisani, Purves, & Adhikari, 1991; Gendreau & Smith, 2007).[14]

Table 8.2   Effects of Solitary Confinement on Selected Outcomes ($n = 14{,}311$)

Type of outcome	r CI$_L$	r CI$_U$	z$_r$ CI$_L$	z$_r$ CI$_U$	Cohen's d
SC experience					
any non-violent misconducts	.10		.10		0.20
	[.08, .12]		[.08, .12]		
number of violent misconducts	.03		.03		0.06
	[.01, .05]		[.02, .05]		
number of non-violent misconducts	.09		.09		0.18
	[.07, .11]		[.07, .11]		
Days in SC					
any violent misconducts	.05		.05		0.10
	[.03, .07]		[.03, .07]		
any non-violent misconducts	.10		.10		0.20
	[.08, .12]		[.08, .12]		
number of non-violent misconducts	.09		.09		0.18
	[.07, .11]		[.07, .11]		

Source: Based on data abstracted from Labrecque (2015).
Note. r = Pearson correlation coefficient; z_r = Fisher's r to z transformation; Prevalence = occurrence of misconducts during follow-up; Incidence = number of misconducts occurring during follow-up.

More recently, Morris (2016) compared the responses of inmates who committed a violent misconduct while in prison and, as a result, experienced either a brief period of SC ($n = 917$) or a non-SC sanction ($n = 917$). In order to control for the effects of selected moderators, prior to analysis, the two inmate groups were matched on a number of static variables (i.e., age, ethnicity, education, marital status, criminal history, misconduct history, etc.).[15] During a 1-year follow-up, Morris reported no meaningful differences in either the violent misconduct rates of the two groups ($r = .01$) or the number of days to their first subsequent violent misconduct ($r = .004$). He concluded that, at least for inmates who experience SC as a sanction rather than as administrative segregation, the impact of SC is inconsequential as measured by the frequency and timing of post-SC misconducts.

Lastly, Labrecque (2015) used a pooled time series panel design,[16] a longitudinal strategy, to evaluate the effects of SC, including length of SC, on the misconduct behaviors of 14,311 inmates during a 36-month follow-up. The majority of the sample were male (95.0%) and assessed as low risk (91.0%), based on the Reentry Accountability Plan (RAP), a static risk assessment scale used by the Ohio Department of Rehabilitation and Correction (ODRC). Misconducts were defined as violent, non-violent, or drug incidents following release from SC. Using both bivariate and multivariate analyses, Labrecque reported minimal effects of SC in reducing future misconducts. Similarly, length of time in SC was not related to either violent or non-violent institutional misconducts during follow-up ($r_{range} = .01$ to $.09$).

Why Is SC not an Effective Punisher?

In summary, there is no credible body of evidence that suggests that SC functions as a deterrent in suppressing misconducts or post-release recidivism. And given the size of the samples in the available studies, it would take a considerable number of large-sample studies producing contrary results to overturn these findings (i.e., Gendreau & Smith, 2007; Rosenthal, 1991). Presently, the aforementioned data, along with other evidence being gathered, will be subjected to a meta-analysis to examine potential effect size moderators and to determine the precision of our estimates of the effects of SC on misconducts and recidivism.[17]

Finally, we turn to theory to assess the degree to which it explains the above summary of findings. In our view, the reason that some "get tough" aficionados regard SC as an effective punisher of antisocial behavior is a belief in deterrence theory and a failure to recognize the utility of a functional behavioral approach to the topic.

Deterrence theory maintains that antisocial behavior can be controlled by the presence of fear-invoking punishments or sanctions (i.e., SC). It is the theory of choice for many in the disciplines of economics and criminology, as well as among the general public (see DeJong, 1997; Gendreau et al., 1999; Gendreau & Ross, 1981; Roberts, Crutcher, & Verbrugge, 2007). No doubt some will bridle at our characterization of deterrence theory as a common-sense view of how behavior operates, one that is full of red flags and loaded language which obscures the reality of how behavior is effectively modified. In that vein, if a condition is perceived to be aversive, painful, hurtful, or traumatic it must be so and, by consequence, it must, without exception, suppress behavior. Given these terms of reference, SC would certainly seem to fit the bill. As noted previously, one school of thought depicts it as torture which produces functional disability and psychosis (i.e., Grassian, 1983; Haney, 2012). This "all or nothing" perspective dismisses the fact that a meaningful percentage of inmates in SC are there by choice. They fear for their safety, simply want to do quiet time self-therapy for personal problems, or are trying to manipulate the system due to gang affiliations (R. Morgan, personal communication, February 25, 2016; O'Donnell, 2014; Suedfeld, 1980). And, this view cavalierly ignores the results of hundreds of studies from the sensory deprivation literature which confirm that brief periods of restricted environmental stimulation, essentially the conditions within SC, have few if any negative effects on inmates' mood or perceptual functioning (Suedfeld, 1975).[18]

By contrast, a functional understanding of the utility of punishment as a behavior change mechanism is based on a specific temporal sequence examining behavioral–environmental interactions derived from an extensive, and complex, body of findings from rigorous studies within the experimental learning and behavior modification literatures. For example, "punishers" known to be effective in suppressing behavior (e.g., physically aversive stimuli, response cost, time out, and several others) and the conditional factors requisite for their effectiveness (e.g., punishment is administered immediately, at maximum intensity, very briefly, and at every occurrence of the antisocial behavior with no opportunity of escape) have been comprehensively documented (see Azrin & Holz, 1966; Hineline & Rosales-Ruiz, 2013; Matson & Dilorenzo, 1984). Unfortunately, space does not permit further discussion on this topic as applied to SC. We invite interested readers to review the 14 requisite conditions under which punishment is effective (Matson & DiLorenzo, 1984, pp. 140–143), most of which are impossible to apply in a typical prison environment.

In closing, we wish to assure readers that there is a positive side to this question of the use of SC that goes beyond the parameters of this chapter. Rather than using SC to punish offenders, there are ways to ameliorate the current state of affairs. SC is relied upon far too often and a more strategic use of administrative, assessment, and treatment strategies could effectively reduce the use of SC without jeopardizing the safety of prison staff and inmates (Gendreau & Labrecque, 2016; Gendreau, Listwan, Kuhns, & Exum, 2014; Morgan et al., 2016; Smith, 2016; Wortley, 2002).

Notes

1   At this writing, there are 64 supermax units in the United States, two in Canada, and 27 in western Europe and Australia. It should be noted that most are not entirely composed of SC cells.

2   Throughout this chapter we refer to a punisher or punishment as any stimulus that reduces the probability of a future behavioral response. Its efficacy in doing so is predicated on the immediate delivery of the punishing stimulus (Azrin & Holz, 1966). With regard to the topic at hand, a punisher is any of the prison conditions described, including SC, which is presumed to be the "strongest" punisher. The behavior being punished is prison misconducts and post-release recidivism. In order for punishment to be effective, 14 criteria must be met (i.e., immediacy, brevity, maximum intensity, etc.; see Azrin & Holz, 1966).

3   All offenders in the latter study were assessed as high risk and randomly assigned to either maximum or minimum security units.

4   While unvalidated, construction of the risk scale was consistent with the principles of offender risk assessment established by Bonta and Andrews (2017) and others (Andrews, Bonta, & Wormith, 2006; Gendreau et al., 1997; Gendreau, Little, & Goggin, 1996). It included 16 risk-relevant factors derived from responses to questions in the inmate survey (i.e., demographic, criminal history, index incarceration, and current sentence dimensions).

5   Moskos (2011) qualifies his remarks by suggesting that the lash should be used in place of a sentence of incarceration.

6   A stimulus that inflicts pain, such as a strap or electric shock, can be a punisher, but in these circumstances, it violated 13 of the 14 requisite behavior-change criteria identified by Azrin & Holz (1966).

7   Propensity matching is a statistical procedure which attempts to evaluate the impact of a procedure or intervention while accounting for the factors that are associated with receiving that procedure or intervention (Rosenbaum & Rubin, 1983).

8   Interrupted time series analysis is a statistical technique that allows for multiple observations at regular intervals of a behavior (i.e., misconducts) before and after the introduction of an intervention (i.e., sanction) in order to determine the relationship between the independent and dependent variables (McDowell, McCleary, Meidinger, & Hay, 1980).

9   It should be noted that, even in supermax units, there is sufficient movement of inmates that incidental contact can lead to assaultive infractions.

10 When measuring the association between two conditions (i.e., SC and outcome), it is important that the level of analysis used is consistent. For example, correlations calculated between data gathered at the individual level have much smaller effects than those calculated using data gathered at the aggregate level (Gendreau & Smith, 2007).

11 Static variables are offender characteristics which reflect historical behaviors or experiences that may (i.e., criminal history) or may not (i.e., social class of origin) be predictive of antisocial behavior. Dynamic variables, on the other hand, are changeable offender characteristics that are predictive of antisocial behavior. For a detailed discussion of static and dynamic predictors and their implications for offender treatment and outcome see Bonta and Andrews (2017).

12 A pooled time series panel design is a statistical technique which combines time series and cross-sectional data to provide improved prediction of outcome for the population of interest (Sayrs, 1989).

13 It should be noted that in all of the studies we reviewed, there was no information regarding the nature of the SC environments themselves. As individual differences in the quality of life in these environments may have significant moderating effects on outcomes, it is important that researchers have access to such data.

14 In keeping with Suedfeld (1975), we are referring to SC environments in which inmates are treated humanely and fairly, from both the psychological and the medical standpoints. All bets are off when that is not the case, but, under those circumstances, the problem lies in human relationships, which goes far beyond the effects of the physical conditions within SC (Gendreau & Labrecque, 2016; Gendreau & Thériault, 2011).

Key Readings

Azrin, N. H., & Holz, W. C. (1966). Punishment. In W. K. Honig (Ed.), *Operant behavior: Areas of research and application* (pp. 380–447). Englewood Cliffs, NJ: Prentice Hall.

Bonta, J. L., & Andrews, D. A. (2017). *The psychology of criminal conduct* (6th ed.). London, UK: Routledge.

Bonta, J. L., & Gendreau, P. (1990). Re-examining the cruel and unusual punishment of prison life. *Law and Human Behavior*, 14, 347–372.

Gendreau, P., & Goggin, C. (2014). Practicing psychology in correctional settings. In I. B. Weiner, & R. K. Otto (Eds.), *The handbook of forensic psychology* (4th ed.) (pp. 759–793). Hoboken, NJ: Wiley.

Gendreau, P., & Labrecque, R. M. (2016). The effects of administrative segregation: A lesson in knowledge cumulation. In J. Wooldredge, & P. Smith (Eds.), *The Oxford handbook on prisons and imprisonment* . New York, NY: Oxford Handbooks Online.

Gendreau, P., & Smith, P. (2012). Assessment and treatment strategies for correctional institutions. In J. A. Dvoskin, J. L. Skeem, R. W. Novaco, & K. S. Douglas (Eds.), *Using social science to reduce violent offending* (pp. 157–178). New York, NY: Oxford University Press.

Hineline, P. N., & Rosales-Ruiz, J. (2013). Behavior in relation to aversive events: Punishment and negative reinforcement. In G. J. Madden, W. V. Dube, T. D. Hackenberg, G. P. Hanley, & K. A. Lattal (Eds.), *APA handbook of behavior analysis. Vol. 1: Methods and principles* (pp. 483–512). Washington, DC: American Psychological Association.

Matson, J. L., & Dilorenzo, T. M. (1984). *Punishment and its alternatives*. New York, NY: Springer.

Morgan, R. D., Gendreau, P., Smith, P., Gray, A. L., Labrecque, R. M., MacLean, N., … & Mills, J. F. (2016). Quantitative syntheses of the effects of administrative segregation on inmates' well-being. *Psychology, Public Policy, and the Law*, 22, 439–461.

References

Allan, R. M. (1954). Minutes of evidence for March 23, 1954 from witness Mr. R. M. Allan, Warden, Kingston Penitentiary. Joint Committee of the Senate and House of Commons on Capital and Corporal Punishment and Lotteries, 1953–1955. Retrieved from http://www.corpun.com/cajur2.htm

Andrews, D. A., Bonta, J., & Wormith, S. (2006). Recent past and near future of risk and/or need assessment. *Crime and Delinquency*, 52, 7–27.

Azrin, N. H., & Holz, W. C. (1966). Punishment. In W. K. Honig (Ed.), *Operant behavior: Areas of research and application* (pp. 380–447). Englewood Cliffs, NJ: Prentice Hall.

Bonta, J. L., & Andrews, D. A. (2017). *The psychology of criminal conduct* (6th ed.). London, UK: Routledge.

Bonta, J., & Gendreau, P. (1990). Re-examining the cruel and unusual punishment of prison life. *Law and Human Behavior*, 14, 347–372.

Bonta, J., & Motiuk, L. L. (1986, August). Use of the Level of Supervision Inventory for assessing incarcerates. Paper presented at the annual meeting of the American Psychological Association, Washington, DC.

Briggs, C. S., Sundt, J. L., & Castellano, T. C. (2003). The effect of supermaximum security prisons on aggregate levels of institutional violence. *Criminology*, 41, 1341–1376.

Butler, H. D., Steiner, B., Makarios, M. D., & Travis, L. F. (2013). *Assessing the effects of exposure to different prison environments on offender recidivism*. Presented at the annual meeting of the Academy of Criminal Justice Sciences in Dallas, TX.

Caldwell, R. G. (1944). The deterrent influence of corporal punishment upon prisoners who have been whipped. *American Sociological Review*, 9, 171–177.

Clark, W. A. V., & Avery, K. L. (1975). The effects of data aggregation in statistical analysis. *Geographical Analysis*, 8, 428–438.

Clarke, R. V. G. (1966). Approved school boy absconders and corporal punishment. *British Journal of Criminology*, 6, 364–375.

Clements, C. B., Althouse, R., Ax, R. K., Magaletta, P. R., Fagan, T. J., & Wormith, J. S. (2007). Systemic issues and correctional outcomes: Expanding the scope of correctional psychology. *Criminal Justice and Behavior*, 34, 919–932.

DeJong, C. (1997). Survival analysis and specific deterrence: Integrating theoretical and empirical models of recidivism. *Criminology*, 35, 561–575.

Farrell, C. (1999). The Canadian prison strap. Part 3: The equipment used. Retrieved from http://www.corpun.com/canada3.htm

Franklin, T. W., Franklin, C. A., & Pratt, T. C. (2006). Examining the empirical relationship between prison crowding and inmate misconduct: A meta-analysis of conflicting research results. *Journal of Criminal Justice*, 34, 401–412.

Freedman, D., Pisani, R., Purves, R., & Adhikari, A. (1991). *Statistics* (2nd ed.). New York, NY: Norton.

Gaes, G. G., & Camp, S. D. (2009). Unintended consequences: Experimental evidence for the criminogenic effect of prison security level placement on post-release recidivism. *Journal of Experimental Criminology*, 5, 139–162.

Gendreau, P., & Bonta, J. (1984). Solitary confinement is not cruel and unusual punishment: Sometimes people are! *Canadian Journal of Criminology*, 26, 467–478.

Gendreau, P., & Goggin, C. (2014). Practicing psychology in correctional settings. In I. B. Weiner, & R. K. Otto (Eds.), *The handbook of forensic psychology* (4th ed.) (pp. 759–793). Hoboken, NJ: Wiley.

Gendreau, P., Goggin, C., & Cullen, F. T. (1999). *The effects of prison sentences on recidivism (1999–3)*. Ottawa, Canada: Solicitor General Canada.

Gendreau, P., Goggin, C., & Law, M. (1997). Predicting prison misconducts. *Criminal Justice and Behavior*, 24, 414–431.

Gendreau, P., & Kennedy, S. (1974, June). The effectiveness of corporal punishment on misconducts. Paper presented at the Opinicon Conference, Chaffey's Locks, Ontario, Canada.

Gendreau, P., & Labrecque, R. M. (2016). The effects of administrative segregation: A lesson in knowledge cumulation. In J. Wooldredge, & P. Smith (Eds.), *The Oxford handbook on prisons and imprisonment* (pp. 340–366). New York, NY: Oxford Handbooks Online.

Gendreau, P., Listwan, S. J., Kuhns, J. B., & Exum, L. M. (2014). Making prisoners accountable: The potential of contingency management programs. *Criminal Justice and Behavior*, 41, 1079–1102.

Gendreau, P., Little, T., & Goggin, C. (1996). A meta-analysis of the predictors of adult offender recidivism: What works! *Criminology*, 34, 575–608.

Gendreau, P., & Ross, R. R. (1981). Correctional potency: Treatment and deterrence on trial. In R. Roesch, & R. R. Corrado (Eds.), *Evaluation and criminal justice policy* (pp. 29–57). Beverly Hills, CA: Sage.

Gendreau, P., & Smith, P. (2007). Influencing the "people who count": Some perspectives on the reporting of meta-analytic results for prediction and treatment outcomes with offenders. *Criminal Justice and Behavior*, 34(12), 1536–1559.

Gendreau, P., & Smith, P. (2012). Assessment and treatment strategies for correctional institutions. In J. A. Dvoskin, J. L. Skeem, R. W. Novaco, & K. S. Douglas (Eds.), *Using social science to reduce violent offending* (pp. 157–178). New York, NY: Oxford University Press.

Gendreau, P., & Thériault, Y. (2011). Bibliotherapy for cynics revisited: Commentary on a one year longitudinal study of the psychological effects of administrative segregation. *Corrections and Mental Health: An Update of the National Institute of Corrections*.

Gibbons, J. J., & de Katzenbach, N. B. (2006). Confronting confinement: A report of the commission on safety and abuse in America's prisons. *Washington University Journal of Law and Policy*, 22, 385–562.

Goggin, C. (2008). *Is prison "personality" associated with offender recidivism?* Retrieved from. *Dissertation Abstracts International, B: Sciences and Engineering,* 72(8), 4972.

Grassian, S. (1983). Psychopathological effects of solitary confinement. *American Journal of Psychiatry,* 140, 1450–1454.

Haney, C. (1997). Psychology and the limits to prison pain: Confronting the coming crisis in eighth amendment law. *Psychology, Public Policy, and Law,* 3, 499–588.

Haney, C. (2012). Testimony of professor Craig Haney to the Senate Judiciary Subcommittee on the Constitution, Civil Rights, and Human Rights Hearing on Solitary Confinement (June 19, 2012). Retrieved from http://www.judiciary.senate.gov

Hineline, P. N., & Rosales-Ruiz, J. (2013). Behavior in relation to aversive events: Punishment and negative reinforcement. In G. J. Madden, W. V. Dube, T. D. Hackenberg, G. P. Hanley, & K. A. Lattal (Eds.), *APA handbook of behavior analysis. Vol. 1: Methods and principles* (pp. 483–512). Washington, DC: American Psychological Association.

Jackson, M. (2001). The psychological effects of administrative segregation. *Canadian Journal of Criminology,* 43, 109–116.

Jonson, C. L. (2010). *The impact of imprisonment on reoffending: A meta-analysis* (Order No. 3438930). Available from ProQuest Dissertations & Theses Global. (848937035). Retrieved from https://login. proxy.hil.unb.ca/login?url=http://search.proquest.com/docview/848937035?accountid=14611

Jonson, C. L. (2013). The effects of imprisonment. In F. T. Cullen, & P. Wilcox (Eds.), *The Oxford handbook of criminological theory* (pp. 672–690). New York, NY: Oxford University Press.

Kupers, T. A. (2008). What to do with the survivors? Coping with the long-term effects of isolated confinement. *Criminal Justice and Behavior,* 35, 1005–1016.

Labrecque, R. M. (2015). *The effect of solitary confinement on institutional misconduct: A longitudinal evaluation* (Order No. 3734617). Available from ProQuest Dissertations & Theses Global. (1738093027). Retrieved from https://login.proxy.hil.unb.ca/login?url=http://search.proquest. com/docview/1738093027?accountid=14611

Lovell, D., Johnson, L. C., & Cain, K. C. (2007). Recidivism of supermax prisoners in Washington state. *Crime and Delinquency,* 53(4), 633–656.

Matson, J. L., & Dilorenzo, T. M. (1984). *Punishment and its alternatives.* New York, NY: Springer.

McDowell, D., McCleary, R., Meidinger, E. E., & Hay, R. A. (1980). *Interrupted time series analysis.* Newbury Park, CA: Sage Publications.

Mears, D. P. (2013). Supermax prisons: The policy and the evidence. *Criminology and Public Policy,* 12, 681–719.

Mears, D. P., & Bales, W. D. (2009). Supermax incarceration and recidivism. *Criminology,* 47, 1131–1166.

Mears, D. P., & Castro, J. L. (2006). Wardens' views on the wisdom of supermax prisons. *Crime and Delinquency,* 52, 398–431.

Moos, R. H. (1968). The assessment of social climates of correctional institutions. *Journal of Research in Crime and Delinquency,* 5, 174–188.

Morgan, R. D., Gendreau, P., Smith, P., Gray, A. L., Labrecque, R. M., MacLean, N., … & Mills, J. F. (2016). Quantitative syntheses of the effects of administrative segregation on inmates' well-being. *Psychology, Public Policy, and the Law,* 22, 439–461.

Morris, R. G. (2016). Exploring the effect of exposure to short-term solitary confinement among violent prison inmates. *Journal of Quantitative Criminology,* 32, 1–22.

Moskos, P. (2011, May/June). Bring back the lash: Why flogging is more humane than prison. *Washington Monthly,* 43(5/6), 12–14.

Motiuk, L. L., & Blanchette, K. (2001). Characteristics of administratively segregated offenders in federal corrections. *Canadian Journal of Criminology,* 43(1), 131–143.

Nagin, D. S. (1998). Criminal deterrence research at the outset of the twenty-first century. In M. Tonry (Ed.), *Crime and justice: A review of research* (Vol. 23) (pp. 1–42). Chicago, IL: University of Chicago Press.

Nagin, D. S., Cullen, F. T., & Jonson, C. L. (2009). Imprisonment and reoffending. In M. Tonry (Ed.), *Crime and justice: A review of research* (Vol. 38) (pp. 115–200). Chicago, IL: University of Chicago Press.

O'Donnell, I. (2014). *Prisoners, solitude and time.* Oxford, UK: Oxford University Press.

O'Keefe, M. L., Klebe, K. J., Metzner, J., Dvoskin, J., Fellner, J., & Stucker, A. (2013). A longitudinal study of administrative segregation. *Journal of the American Academy of Psychiatry and the Law*, 41, 49–60.

Orsagh, T., & Chen, J.-R. (1988). The effect of time served on recidivism: An interdisciplinary theory. *Journal of Quantitative Criminology*, 4, 155–171.

Roberts, J. V., Crutcher, N., & Verbrugge, P. (2007). Public attitudes to sentencing in Canada: Exploring recent findings. *Canadian Journal of Criminology and Criminal Justice*, 49, 75–107.

Rosenbaum, P. R., & Rubin, D. B. (1983). The central role of the propensity score in observational studies for causal effects. *Biometrika*, 70, 41–55.

Rosenthal, R. (1991). *Meta-analytic procedures for social research.* Newbury Park, CA: Sage.

Sayrs, L. W. (1989). *Pooled times series analysis.* Newbury Park, CA: Sage.

Scharff Smith, P. (2006). The effects of solitary confinement on prison inmates: A brief history and review of the literature. In M. Tonry (Ed.), *Crime and justice: A review of research* (Vol. 34) (pp. 441–528). Chicago, IL: University of Chicago Press.

Smith, P. (2006). *The effects of incarceration on recidivism: A longitudinal examination of program participation and institutional adjustment in federally sentenced adult male offenders* (Unpublished doctoral dissertation). University of Cincinnati, OH.

Smith, P. (2016). Toward an understanding of "what works" in segregation: Implementing correctional programming and re-entry-focused services in restrictive housing units (NCJ25034). In *Restrictive housing in the US: Challenges and future directions* (pp. 331–366). Washington, DC: Department of Justice, National Institute of Justice.

Smith, P., Goggin, C., & Gendreau, P. (2002). *The effects of prison sentences and intermediate sanctions on recidivism: General effects and individual differences (2002–3).* Ottawa, Canada: Solicitor General Canada.

Steiner, B., & Wooldredge, J. (2008). Inmate versus facility effects on prison rule violations. *Criminal Justice and Behavior*, 35, 438–456.

Steiner, B., & Wooldredge, J. (2009). Re-thinking the link between institutional crowding and inmate misconduct. *The Prison Journal*, 89, 205–233.

Stubblefield, R. (2002). Prisons should not coddle inmates. In R. Espejo (Ed.), *America's prisons: Opposing viewpoints* (pp. 100–104). San Diego, CA: Greenhaven Press.

Suedfeld, P. (1975). The benefits of boredom: Sensory deprivation reconsidered: The effects of monotonous environments are not always negative; sometimes sensory deprivation has high utility. *American Scientist*, 63, 60–69.

Suedfeld, P. (1980). *Restricted environmental stimulation: Research and clinical applications.* New York, NY: Wiley.

Tanasichuk, C. L., Wormith, S. J., & Guzzo, L. (2009). *The predictive validity of the Level of Service Inventory—Ontario Revision (LSI-OR) with Aboriginal offenders.* Unpublished manuscript, Department of Psychology, University of Saskatchewan, Saskatoon, Canada.

Useem, B., & Kimball, P. (1989). *States of siege: US prison riots 1971–1986.* New York, NY: Oxford University Press.

Villettaz, P., Killias, M., & Zoder, I. (2006). *The effects of custodial vs. non-custodial sentences on re-offending: A systematic review of the state of knowledge.* Oslo, Norway: Campbell Collaboration.

Walters, G. D. (2003). Changes in criminal thinking and identity in novice and experienced inmates: Prisonization revisited. *Criminal Justice and Behavior*, 30, 399–421.

Wormith, J. S. (1984). The controversy over the effects of long-term imprisonment. *Canadian Journal of Criminology*, 26, 423–437.

Wortley, R. (2002). *Situational prison control: Crime prevention in correctional institutions.* Cambridge, UK: Cambridge University Press.

9

The Challenge of Managing Aging Prisoners

Ronald H. Aday
Middle Tennessee State University, USA

Tina Maschi
Fordham University Graduate School of Social Service, New York, USA

The growth of an aging prison population is a major concern in nearly every region of the world as prison administrators face the challenges associated with accommodating inmates for whom most facilities were never designed (Aday, 2003; Doron & Love, 2013). Unprecedented patterns of growth in the numbers of older prisoners have been extensively documented throughout Australia (Baidawi & Trotter, 2015), Canada (Shantz & Frigon, 2009), the United Kingdom (Davoren et al., 2015; Mann, 2012; O'Hara et al., 2016), Japan (Maschi, Viola, & Sun, 2013), and the United States (Kerbs & Jolley, 2014). Similar trends have been observed in other regions, creating a global aging prisoner crisis of epic proportion (United Nations Office on Drugs and Crime [UNODC], 2009). With this has come a growing recognition of the need for new policy and practices to meet the needs of aging prisoners.

Health Status

Large-scale surveys conducted on health-related concerns in US prisons have estimated that 45% of offenders ages 50 and older, and 82% of those 65 and older, have chronic health problems (Leigey & Hodge, 2012; Sterns, Lax, Sed, Keohane, & Sterns, 2008). In fact, 46% of inmates over the age of 50 reported having health problems at the time of their entry into prison (Beckett, Peterneli-Taylor, & Johnson, 2003). These include sensory deficits (such as vision and hearing problems), arthritis, back problems, heart diseases, respiratory diseases, diabetes, cognitive disorders, and substance abuse (Aday & Farney, 2014; Fazel, Hope, O'Donnell, Piper, & Jacoby, 2001; Leigey, 2014). Many aging prisoners have an astonishingly low level of health literacy which, when matched with a high level of chronic medical conditions, requires substantial treatment expenditure (Hurley, 2014).

The degenerative effects of chronic conditions are particularly pronounced for older prisoners due to the comorbidities found in approximately 85% of older inmates (Aday & Krabill, 2011; Loeb & AduDagga, 2006). Numerous studies have reported the average

The Wiley International Handbook of Correctional Psychology, First Edition. Edited by Devon L. L. Polaschek, Andrew Day, and Clive R. Hollin.
© 2019 John Wiley & Sons Ltd. Published 2019 by John Wiley & Sons Ltd.

number of chronic medical conditions among older inmates to be three or more (e.g., Aday, 2003; Loeb, Steffensmeier, & Myco, 2007), leading to a greater likelihood of functional impairment. Poor outcomes related to the process of accelerated aging can also result in older prisoners requiring long periods of time to recover from injury or illness (Curtin, 2007).

The poor health status of older inmates can be attributed to previous lifestyle and socioeconomic factors (Glamser & Cabana, 2003). As a result, the gap between chronological and physiological age in prisoners is especially marked (Leigey, 2014). This rapid decline or accelerated biological aging has been attributed, in part, to the negative impact of the prison environment, as listed below (see also Aday, 2003; Anno, Gram, Lawrence, & Shansky, 2004; Mitka, 2004; Vaughn & Collins, 2004):

- Participation in high-risk behaviors (smoking, drugs, alcohol, unhealthy diets).
- Unhealthy lifestyles fostered in prison, including poor diets and general lack of exercise.
- Greater rate of infectious disease in prison than persons of the same age on the outside.
- Harshness and stressors associated with prison life particularly for those housed in maximum security institutions designed for younger inmates.
- Limited access to medical care and inappropriate diagnosis and/or undertreatment of serious medical problems by prison medical personnel.

The quality of penal health care is of primary importance for aging female inmates, who as a general rule place a greater demand on prison medical and psychiatric services than males (Caldwell, Jarvis, & Rosefield, 2001; Gibbons & Katzenbach, 2006). With backgrounds of poverty and unemployment, exposure to violence and victimization, and drug abuse, most have suffered from personal stress, trauma, and fear (Aday & Farney, 2014). Large non-randomized studies have also found that older female prisoners are twice as likely to describe their health in negative terms as older male prisoners (Kratcoski & Babb, 1990). As a result, women seek health care at two and a half times the rate of males, although prisons frequently fail to appropriately adjust staffing ratios to meet the demands for health care among female prisoners (Ammar & Erez, 2000).

Functional Health Status

Studies have reported the prevalence of functional impairments among aging prisoners to be approximately 10% for older men, and slightly higher (16%) for women (Colsher, Wallace, Loeffelholz, & Sales, 1992; Fazel et al., 2001). Table 9.1 provides an interesting comparison of the gender differences in the functional health status of two large samples of older inmates housed in the United States. Such functional impairments create adverse experiences for geriatric inmates as well as become important predictors of healthcare costs (Williams et al., 2006).

Based on a large-scale study of older prisoners in Australia, Baidawi and Trotter (2015) recently reported that 22% of prisoners aged 50 years and older required some assistance in day-to-day tasks, with getting into upper bunks, stairs, and bathroom facilities presenting the greatest challenges. Other activities unique to the prison setting can also be difficult for individuals of an advanced age. For example, over two thirds of older offenders report significant difficulties in completing common prison activities of daily living (PADL), such as standing in line for counts, dropping for alarms, or walking long distances to the dining hall (Williams et al., 2006). It should be pointed out that as prisoners continue to age, health problems become increasing debilitating, thereby elevating the risk of fall or injury, lowering morale,

Table 9.1 Gender Comparisons for Functional Health Status Among Older Inmates

Characteristic	Males = 302	Females = 327
Vision problems	39.3	87.6
Hearing problems	72.9	32.4
Difficulty walking long distances	48.6	57.2
Difficulty standing up to 15 minutes	37.5	59.3
Incapable of ascending/descending stairs	51.4	33.1
Require ground level housing	60.2	49.7
Require a flat, even terrain for walking	52.5	38.6
Require a lower bunk	68.9	84.1

Note. Mean age for males is 65; Mean age for females 56. Based on data from Aday (2003) and Aday and Krabill (2011).

and increasing concerns about personal safety. Any decline in sensory-motor functioning becomes more detrimental in a prison environment where poor lighting and noise can pose significant problems. Taken together, concerns such as the need to walk distances between buildings and to take periodic breaks while engaged in the activities themselves, can place the older prisoner in situations where he or she feels too overwhelmed to fulfill work duties or simply cope with day-to-day prison activities (Aday, 2003; Aday & Krabill, 2011; Harrison, 2006). A variety of medical services, assistive devices such as canes, walkers, and wheelchairs, and environmental accommodations are required to support those inmates experiencing functional impairment (Blowers, Jolley, & Kerbs, 2014).

Social Milieu

Creating an effective social milieu is one of the most crucial, yet most challenging, tasks that prison administrators will likely be presented with when preparing to manage a growing geriatric prison population (Baidawi & Trotter, 2015; Cox & Lawrence, 2010). Coping with the losses associated with incarceration can prove particularly trying for elderly inmates, especially if it is their first time in prison. These include losses of liberty, autonomy, security, products and services, and heterosexual relations. Prison offers a new subculture, a foreign set of rules, and language that can be overwhelming for mentally or physically fragile inmates. In particular, stark living environments evoke a wide range of human emotions in geriatric inmates, including "frustration, anger, fear, sadness, and resentment" (Haney, 2006, p. 169). Older, more frail inmates may also devote a substantial portion of their day-to-day existence to trying to minimize the dangers of imprisonment.

Despite more liberal visiting and correspondence policies in recent times, inmates still must relinquish substantial contact with family and friends on the outside. For example, the Bureau of Justice Statistics (1999) reported that only 43% of inmates housed in US prisons had received a personal visit from at least one child since incarceration (Mumola, 2000). In a large sample of over 500 older offenders, Maschi, Viola, Morgen, and Koskinen (2013) found that over two thirds of their sample had no contact with their marital or life partner or parents and the majority reported no contact with their children or their grandchildren. Aday and Krabill (2011) also reported that one third of a large sample of older females never receive face-to-face family visits, although about 80% do remain in contact with family either by visits, letters, or phone. A number of barriers have been identified that currently serve to reduce inmate–family interactions. These include geographical distance, lodging and travel expenses, and work conflicts (Aday & Krabill, 2011; Arditti & Few, 2006; Christian, 2005). Institutional barriers also exist which include restrictive visitation times and rules (Hoffman, Dickenson, & Dunn, 2007), and lack of access to phones or excessive financial charges associated with long-distance calls has also been identified as an issue (Wahidin, 2004).

Overall, geriatric offenders have much smaller social networks than other segments of the inmate population (Bond, Thompson, & Malloy, 2005). A significant number, for example, are single, separated, or divorced (Aday, 2003; Aday & Krabill, 2011; Kratcoski & Babb, 1990; Maschi et al., 2014). Due to circumstances not always within the offenders' immediate range of personal control, other relationships are also highly fragile, volatile, and vulnerable to deterioration or dissolution without formal intervention and assistance. As a result, older prisoners often develop very close friendships with each other, working together in peer-supported programs (Cox & Lawrence, 2010). In many instances, very close bonds are formed due to circumstances and life events, such as the death of a close friend outside of prison.

Despite the prevalence of loss in correctional settings, prison administrators have been slow to develop and implement structured policies and programming to facilitate the grieving process. Mirroring mainstream society, correctional organizations recognize specific "grieving rules" defining the parameters of acceptable grief reactions (Harner, Hentz, & Evangelista, 2011; Jones & Beck, 2007). For example, grieving rights, in most social contexts (including prisons), are typically reserved exclusively for individuals related to the deceased by blood or marriage. This denies a relatively large circle of survivors (i.e., partners in non-traditional relationships, ex-spouses or lovers, close friends) the opportunity to place closure on relationships (Aday & Krabill, 2016). Social norms may further disenfranchise grievers by identifying which feelings, somatic symptoms, or behavioral reactions can be utilized in coping with stress, preselecting the rituals for survivors, and defining the time frame within which the grieving process is completed (Corr, 1998). Too much emphasis is often placed on "getting over" the loss rather than engaging in the intrapsychic work needed to derive meaning from the experience and restore order to one's social world.

Mental and Emotional Health

The general health condition and background experiences of older prisoners have been linked to a host of mental health disturbances. Studies have reported the prevalence of specific mental conditions to be exceptionally high, occasionally exceeding half of the older prison population (Fazel et al., 2001; James & Glaze, 2006; Sterns et al., 2008). While depression and anxiety are commonly found among older offenders, others may require treatment for issues such as substance abuse, personality disorders, psychological distress, and schizophrenia, while those in advanced age may need support for Alzheimer's and other dementias (Aday & Krabill, 2011; Baidawi & Trotter, 2015; Caverly, 2006, Cox & Lawrence, 2010; Meeks et al., 2008; Regan, Alderson, & Regan, 2002).

While many prisoners may arrive in prison with mental health issues, others will develop such impairments once exposed to prison life. For example, it has been suggested that the harshness of prison creates heightened feelings of anxiety and deprivation (Dhami, Ayton, & Loewenstein, 2007; Maeve, 1999) which can lead to further depression for the most vulnerable inmates who have particular difficulties with prison adjustment. Care is needed to recognize the effect that variables such as gender, race/ethnicity, crime, sentence length, medical

histories, social supports, and individual personality factors also have on psychological adjustment (Aday & Krabill, 2011; Merten, Bishop, & Williams, 2012; Regan et al., 2002).

Prisoners who enter prison with the weight of a lengthy sentence are initially often in a state
of total shock, with denial, depression, and numbness common (Aday & Krabill, 2011). Any
signs of inattentiveness to older inmates who exhibit special physical, cognitive, or social needs
are more likely to adversely affect the marginalized groups, especially those with mental health
issues. Older, frail offenders, in particular, often find the prison environment to be unsafe, with
excessive background noise, crowded conditions, and lack of adequate healthcare delivery
(Aday, 2003; Strupp & Willmott, 2005). Overwhelmed by their situation, some inmates
become so depressed they have difficulty sleeping, refuse to eat, and may require emergency
mental health intervention. With excessive depressive symptoms, it is not uncommon for
incarcerated elders to contemplate suicide (Aday, Dye, & Kaiser, 2014; Dye & Aday, 2013).

Female inmates typically have higher rates of mental health problems than males (James &
Glaze, 2006). Aday and Krabill (2011), for example, reported that in a group of 327 older
women (mean age = 56) only 23% scored within a normal depression range. One third of this
sample was diagnosed with moderate depressive symptoms while a quarter scored in the high
range and one-in-five reported severe levels of depression. Although there were no racial differences found, the authors did find that older incarcerated women with abuse histories were
far more likely to suffer from depression and other mental disorders. These findings support
other studies that have found a significant link with childhood and adult traumatic experiences
and life-event stressors as predictors of comorbid psychiatric conditions including anxiety,
depression, post-traumatic stress disorder (PTSD), and drug and alcohol abuse and associated
health problems (Haugebrook, Zgoba, Kimaschi, Morgen, & Brown, 2010; Messina & Grella,
2006). For inmates entering prison with a low sense of self-esteem and fractured external
support group, the prison environment can also serve as a source of distress leading to a
further decline in mental wellbeing (Aday & Krabill, 2011; Baidawi & Trotter, 2015).

As an increasing number of inmates continue to "age in place," the onset of dementia is
becoming a more common occurrence (Wilson & Barboza, 2010). Complicating the matter is
the strict regimented lifestyle of prison which tends to hinder a detection of mild cognitive
impairment and early-stage dementia (Sterns et al., 2008). In addition, problems associated with
the lack of routine screening for cognitive impairment are compounded by the co-occurring
multiple health conditions that frequently present among those diagnosed with dementia
(Bowers, Jolley, & Kerbs, 2013). It is especially important that correctional staff make accommodations when responding to cognitively impaired prisoners who lack the ability to comprehend and remember (Hodel & Sanchez, 2012). For example, in any given day, surviving and
thriving in the larger prison subculture requires elders to perform tasks such as familiarizing
themselves with, identifying, and adhering to staff commands, presenting themselves for structured activities, avoiding potentially conflict-ridden situations, and following medicals' prescribed
instructions (Harrison, 2006; Roof, 2010). Due to the fact that these prisoners are highly vulnerable to victimization, inmate-driven "peer support" or "social aides" programs have been
introduced as a case management strategy (Harrison, 2006; Hodel & Sanchez, 2012).

Older inmates with multiple health conditions and who are mentally fragile frequently find
themselves engaging in thoughts about dying in prison (Aday, 2006; Deaton, Aday, & Wahidin, 2009). To many inmates, dying in prison is one of the most dreadful things they can
encounter (Byock, 2002), and the notion of dying in a foreign place in a dependent and
undignified state is often very distressing. Inmates also frequently report negative experiences
associated with watching other inmates die in prison and the lack of respect they received

(Deaton et al., 2009). Contributing to this anxiety are thoughts associated with getting sick in prison or having to rely on prison health care in a time of crisis. When medical staff deny care (such as withholding or delaying essential medications; Vaughn & Collins, 2004), inmates become more anxious about end-of-life issues (Aday, 2006). In many cases, healthcare access is "continually thwarted by rules, custodial priorities, poor healthcare management, incompetence, and indifference" (Stroller, 2003, p. 2263).

Contemporary correctional policy in many countries rests on the assumption that older prisoners will be better adjusted, more compliant, and less disruptive than their younger counterparts (Turner & Trotter, 2010). Unfortunately, geriatric mental health problems are not easily diagnosed or treated in a prison setting. Older prisoners are highly unlikely to disclose their problems or symptoms, even when treatment is available (Yorston & Taylor, 2006). Instead, they desire to preserve their image among prison peers—denying or suppressing their true emotions in favor of a more socially desirable appearance (Aday, 2003). Older adults who suffer from depression, for example, may simply reduce their activity level, withdraw, and become invisible (Sterns et al., 2008).

With such a high level of mental health concerns among this population, correctional institutions are prime locations for intervention. An individualized case management approach should be adopted in response to the diverse set of needs identified among older offenders. Provision of care should be informed and influenced by factors such as the older adults' experiences with trauma and victimization (Maschi, Morgen, Zgoba, Courtney, & Ristow, 2011), physical health statuses (Leigey & Hodge, 2012; Merten et al., 2012), general willingness to participate in prison programming (Meeks et al., 2008), treatment preferences (Phillips, Allen, Presnell, Decoster, & Cavanaugh, 2011; Phillips, Allen, Salekin, & Cavanaugh, 2009), spiritual/religious orientations (Aday, Krabill, & Deaton, 2014; Allen et al., 2013; Dye, Aday, Farney, & Raley, 2014), grief/bereavement concerns (Aday & Krabill, 2016; Olsen & McEwen, 2004; Stevenson & McCutchen, 2006), death-related fears (Aday, 2006; Deaton et al., 2009), and community reintegration needs (Blevins & Blowers, 2014; Higgins & Severson, 2009). Work with geriatric offenders who have specific problems (i.e., substance abuse, dementias), moreover, should involve care to ethical concerns related to decision-making (Dawes, 2009; Fazel, McMillan, & O'Donnell, 2002). Improved coordination, without question, should be encouraged between the mental health team, medical services, and community health (Cox & Lawrence, 2010; Roof, 2010). In looking to the future, best-practice models (Hodel & Sanchez, 2012; Kopera-Frye, Harrison, Iribarne, & Harrison, 2013; Wilson & Barboza, 2010) should be identified, evaluated, and utilized by others in service delivery.

Housing Accommodations

There has been an ongoing debate about the advantages and disadvantages of both mainstreaming and segregating older inmates (Aday, 2003; Blowers et al., 2014; Kerbs & Jolley, 2009). Those who call for age-segregation housing argue that placing vulnerable inmates in the general prison population can compromise their safety (Kerbs, Jolley, & Kanaboshi, 2015), citing research that shows that older inmates are frequently threatened, intimidated, and insulted by younger inmates (e.g., Kerbs & Jolley, 2009). Vega and Silverman (1988) have also reported that abrasive relations with other inmates are the most disturbing incidents that elderly prisoners have to cope with. As a consequence, older inmates report feeling unsafe and vulnerable to attack, leading them to prefer being grouped together with people of their own age (Aday, 2003). While fewer incidents of victimization are reported in women's institutions, some harassment, cussing, teasing, pushing around, and other minor incidents are evident (Aday & Krabill, 2011).

Some states have already projected a significant cost saving by grouping their older medically needy inmates together (Blowers et al., 2014). This potentially reduces the health-related costs associated with duplication and fragmentation, especially for poorly equipped facilities (Anno et al., 2004). In addition, grouping inmates with similar programming needs can also be productive in reducing healthcare demands. In such environments, older inmates have the opportunity to engage in the kind of age- and health-specific activities that promote healthy aging practices (Harrison, 2006). Likewise, age-segregation allows well trained medical staff to be assigned to work in a concentrated number of facilities, and this would improve the quality of care that is provided. Other correctional staff who work with this population, but receive limited preparation, would also benefit from this. For example, frontline correctional officers frequently have to make decisions relevant to the health and wellbeing of aging inmates, and the specialized training provided in specialist "nursing-home"-like facilities could improve the overall quality of healthcare delivery (Aday, 2006; Sterns et al., 2008).

Grouping inmates with mental and cognitive impairments has also been suggested to be a sensible response to the rise of dementia cases among older inmates (Harrison, 2006; Wilson & Barboza, 2010). Prisoners with dementia are not always noticed until they are unable to cope with everyday activities. As their symptoms increase, the prisoner will have difficulty following rules, socializing appropriately, or performing simple tasks such as eating, dressing, and bathing. As deterioration progresses, inmates in the general population are also vulnerable to bullying and victimization by other prisoners or alternatively may become aggressive to staff and other prisoners (Dawes, 2009). Older inmates who have not been diagnosed with dementia can run the risk of reprimand or punishment by security staff who may fail to understand symptoms of the disease (Maschi, Kwak, Ko, & Morrissey, 2012; Wilson & Barboza, 2010). Proponents of the age-segregation perspective stress that specialized facilities are needed to create a safe environment with the necessary support levels needed to accommodate this growing subgroup of older inmates (Aday, 2003).

While the overwhelming majority of aging inmates are housed in age-integrated facilities, correctional administrators have had no choice but to build special needs facilities (or secure nursing homes) to accommodate the safety and health needs of frail geriatric inmates. However, due to the significant growth of the older adult population, it is virtually impossible to provide this. In the United States, for example, nearly 300,000 older prisoners currently reside in state and federal prisons, with that number expected to reach 500,000 by 2025 (Human Rights Watch [HRW], 2012). Given the fact that older inmates are a diverse group, those supporting an integrative approach feel housing arrangements should be based on need rather than solely on age (Hill, Williams, Cobe, & Lindquist, 2006). Living in a specialized facility can lead to inactivity, lack of work opportunities or access to prison programming, and in some cases, eventual withdrawal and increased depressive states. Also, being assigned to a special facility may create geographical barriers for inmates to want to remain in close proximity to family and friends (Aday, 2003).

In the United States approximately half of the states now provide geriatric accommodations, ranging from selected clustering or dedicated units to free-standing prisons or dedicated secure nursing home facilities (Abner, 2006; Sterns et al., 2008). Other countries, such as Canada, Australia, Japan, and countries in Western Europe, are now providing special geriatric accommodations emphasizing a quieter, medically oriented living environment (UNODC, 2009). Although prisons differ markedly in terms of the breadth and range of activities being offered specifically to accommodate this special needs group, handrails, lower bunks on main-floor tiers, elevated toilets, and wheelchair accessibility are become more common. Additional amenities in newer facilities include prison-controlled thermostats, fluorescent lighting, strobe-lit fire alarms, non-slippery flooring services, hospital-style beds equipped with extra padding, toilets, sinks, and showers that are handicapped accessible (Anno et al., 2004; Harrison, 2006).

Despite an increase in facility accommodations, older inmates do not typically have access to structured routine activities that provide opportunities for physical, mental, and social engagement suited to their changing capacities and needs (Blowers et al., 2014). Moreover, programming is not currently geared toward practical and age-appropriate activities that assist older inmates to maximize their level of functioning (Aday, 2003; Crowley & Sparks, 2006). One of the most comprehensive best-practice models introduced to date designed and implemented to accommodate the special needs of the geriatric offender is the Structured Senior Living Program (SSLP), known as True Grit, at the Northern Nevada Correctional Center (Harrison, 2006). True Grit was established in 2004 as a response to the unique needs of an increasing number of vulnerable elderly inmates. The primary goals of the program are to make available daily activities that include the encouragement of "personal, mental, emotional, and spiritual growth" among its 160 active participants. The program also requires each inmate to participate in educational activities that directly confront their reason for incarceration (i.e., drug or sex offenses). Since its inception, the program has served 325 men, including 38 who died while in prison and another 102 who were successfully paroled. The prisoners are housed together in a separate unit and given a set of physical, social, and mental activities to perform on a regular basis. One of the most critical components responsible for the success of the program is the highly structured eligibility requirements (Harrison & Benedetti, 2009). Table 9.2 provides a summary of the program rules and diverse activities targeted at both cognitively and physically impaired inmates. The significance of True Grit can't be overstated given the fact that it was built based on sheer creativity and community partnerships. The program uses no state tax dollars and relies on a cadre of inmate and community volunteers.

Harrison and Benedetti (2009) have documented a number of program successes for True Grit, with the majority (81%) of inmates reporting that life in this enhanced environment is much better than when they were in the general inmate population. Diversion therapy activities utilized by the program are considered to be highly effective in enhancing participants' overall quality of life, and some assist in both cognitive and physical therapy (Harrison & Benedetti, 2009; Kopera-Frye et al., 2013). Commonly accepted physical diversion activities are crocheting and knitting, both of which assist in the ease of arthritic pain in the hands and fingers (Harrison, 2006). Cognitive therapies, like puzzles, reading, and writing, help to keep the mind stimulated and sustain personal creativity, lending to the overall quality of life and increase in personal health of elderly persons. Not all members of True Grit engage in all enrichment activities. Some of the oldest-old are unable to participate in vigorous athletics, although a significant number do enjoy wheelchair aerobics and wheelchair fitness.

To assess program effectiveness, Harrison (2015) compared various cognitive and behavioral outcomes of those on an approved wait list for True Grit ($n = 156$) with 153 active program participants. At the time of the study, the average length of membership in the program was 2.75 years, but some of the participants had been members for up to 8 years. The findings demonstrate that when living in an enriched living environment for as little as 6 months, older

Table 9.2 True Grit: Structured Senior Living Program (SSLP) Northern Nevada Correctional Center

Participants: The minimum age limit is 60 years and inmates must be referred by a caseworker, have a positive history of prison adjustment, and be willing to abide by strict rules.

Program rules: Each True Grit participant must sign a contract when entering the program and each participant is required to complete the following activities:

- Initialing the daily program sign-in sheet, and reading the Activity Board for a listing of the daily program activities.
- Maintaining personal hygiene: grooming, showering, and wearing clean clothing.
- Maintaining personal living area including making the bed, ensuring food items are properly stored, cleaning the inmate's personal living area, and adhering to all housing unit and personal living area rules.
- Initialing the daily work assignment sheet and completing the assigned SSLP daily tasks, which normally include cleaning hallways, activity rooms, bathrooms, showers, and other general living areas.
- Maintaining personal SSLP and State-issued clothing ensuring that all clothing items are clean and in good repair.

Program diversity: Diversion therapy activities that are considered to be highly effective in enhancing the participants' overall qualities of life include:

Life skills training. Through guest speakers and the use of current periodicals, the Community Involvement Program helps participants increase interpersonal and social skills important whether they remain in prison or reintegrate into the free world. Such activities and skills include: meal planning on a budget, nutrition, microwave cooking, decision-making, time management, goal setting, victimization awareness (elder abuse, identify theft, and telephone and internet scams), financial planning, and acquiring or reacquiring necessary identification documents.

Music appreciation. With a comprehensive collection of cassette tapes and compact disks (CDs), participants enjoy jazz, big bands, 60s, 70s, and 80s rock & roll, country and western, contemporary, and classical music. Each day a different type of music is featured in the SSLP Activity Rooms.

Music groups. Several music groups provide a variety of activities and opportunities for social engagement. The SSLP Choir—a 20-man ensemble—performs weekly. The SSLP doo-wop group, along with rock, country and spiritual groups, frequently practice and entertain fellow inmates.

Art appreciation. Many SSLP members are talented artists and a successful drawing and painting program is an active component of True Grit. Led by a talented retired art teacher from a nearby college, the program emphasizes drawing with pencils, charcoal, and pastels, and painting with acrylics and oils.

Beading. Beading provides enhanced cognitive function and improved manual dexterity and is a regular activity that provides participants with the opportunity to learn how to create beaded jewelry, wrist- or headbands, decorative beaded art objects, and other unique items.

Puzzles and games. Active participation in puzzles and games provides cognitive therapy, problem-solving, and coping skills training. Many of these activities are designed to stimulate areas of the brain damaged by dementia and Alzheimer's disease, while all offer an opportunity for socialization and fun.

Crafts program. As a means of enhancing and maintaining physical dexterity for those with arthritis, the program provides materials for latch-hooking rugs, crocheting afghans, and creating needlepoint art. Several dozen men work regularly on individual projects in this voluntary diversion therapy activity.

Physical fitness activities. The SSLP's physical fitness program includes an assortment of weekly aerobic exercise opportunities, games, and activities. These include the use of exercise equipment, weight training, stretching, volleyball, tennis, softball, horseshoes, ping-pong, basketball, billiards, and walking. True Grit offers an impressive selection of sporting activities designed with the needs of geriatric offenders in mind. For those confined to wheelchairs, wheelchair softball, basketball, and bowling provide attractive opportunities for involvement.

Pet therapy. With the assistance of the local area Delta Society, every month, two or three dogs make visits to the program, providing the men (many of whom are serving life sentences) companionship and the opportunity to bond with therapy dogs.

Writing groups. This program assists men who will be serving, in effect, life sentences with the opportunity to prepare themselves physically, mentally, spiritually, and emotionally for end-of-life issues.

Note. Adapted from Harrison (2006) and Harrison and Benedetti (2009).

inmates (mean age = 67) produced better cognitive flexibility, memory, intellectual ability, and processing speed, enhanced verbal fluency, and improved problem-solving ability in comparison to those living in the general prison population. In addition to significantly lower rates of depression and lower dependency on psychotropic and psychoactive medications for those currently in True Grit, visuospatial functioning and physical mobility were also more pronounced for those in the experimental group.

Future Directions

As the aging prisoner population becomes more diverse, policy-makers must address how to best accommodate this growing population. Covenants dispatched by the United Nations' *Handbook on Prisoners with Special Needs* (UNODC, 2009) have offered recommendations for accommodating the special needs of aging prisoners (see Maschi, Viola, & Sun, 2013) which include suggestions for courts to scrutinize sentencing policies, including lengthy sentencing practices and age-appropriate correctional policies and practices as well as the development of alternatives to incarceration and diversion programs for older seriously ill and terminally ill offenders. For optimum prison management for older inmates, these recommendations include:

- Management policies and strategies involving the input of a multidisciplinary team of prison specialists working in coordination particularly in the area of medical care.
- The provision of geriatric-specific staff training and encouraging staff to engage with community organizations to best ensure a continuum of care upon reentry.
- The use of individualized assessment, programming, planning, and monitoring as necessary to identify the varied and changing needs of older prisoners.
- The protection of older vulnerable prisoners from victimization utilizing age-segregation when necessary to ensure a safe living environment.
- The standardization of age-appropriate programming, including counseling for end-of-life issues, recreational activities, education, and suitable work opportunities.
- The introduction of health promotional activities such as healthy diets and wellness programming encouraging successful aging and reducing financial healthcare burdens.
- The delivery of activities encouraging maintaining family links, which improves mental wellbeing and prospects of successful resettlement.
- The offering of programs where other prisoners' assistance in helping care for older prisoners after careful screening and assessment can enhance the quality of life for aging prisoners.
- The greater utilization of early conditional and compassionate release of older prisoners, including preparation for release as well as post-release support.

Kerbs and Jolley (2014) suggest the need for evidenced-based research that rigorously evaluates the current outcomes of dedicated geriatric facilities. For several decades now, numerous states have operated special needs facilities without identifying important best-practice models that are based on research outcomes. Questions remain about the quality of mental and physical health care that older inmates receive in today's prison environment, where overcrowded conditions are frequent and healthcare costs are controlled. More primary research is needed to examine the type and quality of care inmates receive (e.g., palliative, preventive, acute, and chronic care) and the utility of such care (diagnosis, assessment, treatment, and follow-up services) as well as the short- and long-term outcomes of the medical care they receive. Since many individuals enter prison with numerous mental and physical health conditions, it is important to know if these conditions have improved once the time to reenter society comes. If not, it can be suggested that the mandated prison healthcare system has failed in its efforts to establish a successful intervention strategy (Clear & Frost, 2014).

Conclusion

In concluding our discussion on the special challenges of the geriatric offender, some degree of attention must be placed on current global sentencing policies. One of the major factors leading to the aging prison crisis is sentencing laws that tie the court's hands in determining an appropriate sentence. For older adults, even terms of 5–10 years can become the equivalent of a life sentence. Given current sentencing policies, it is a given that many inmates will grow old and die in prison. Punitive sentencing policies must be restructured to ensure that men and women are not detained unnecessarily into their later adult years, especially when they are no longer a risk to society (Chiu, 2010; Human Rights Watch, 2012). Newly developed risk assessment inventories specifically designed to measure recidivism risk in older offenders have been suggested to facilitate reentry decisions (Kerbs & Jolley, 2014), but more work in developing these tools is clearly needed. Likewise, parole boards, which often refuse to release long-serving inmates for second-chance opportunities, must revisit their role in "warehousing" such large numbers of elderly inmates. Policy-makers and professionals who provide services to older inmates must, as a consequence, place a greater emphasis on conceptualizing "aging in place" as a positive and worthwhile goal. Going forward, any number of strategies, both inside and outside prison, must be implemented to manage the aging prison population as it expands to unprecedented levels in the coming decades.

Key Readings

Kerbs, J. J., & Jolley, J. M. (2014). *Senior citizens behind bars: Challenges for the criminal justice system.* (pp. 1–19). Boulder, CO: Lynne Rienner.
Maschi, T., Suftin, S., & O'Connell, B. (2012). Aging, mental health, and the criminal justice system: A content analysis of the literature. *Journal of Forensic Social Work*, 2, 62–185.
Trotter, C., & Baidawi, S. (2014). Older prisoners: Challenges for inmates and prison management. *Australian & New Zealand Journal of Criminology*, 48, 200–218.

References

Abner, C. (2006, November/December). Graying prisons. States face challenges of an aging inmate population. *State News*, 49, 8–12.
Aday, R. H. (2003). *Aging prisoners: Crisis in American corrections.* Westport, CT: Praeger.
Aday, R. H. (2006). Aging prisoners' concerns toward dying in prison. *Omega: Journal of Death and Dying*, 52, 199–216.
Aday, R. H., Dye, M., & Kaiser, A. (2014). Examining the traumatic effects of sexual victimization on the health of incarcerated women. *Women & Criminal Justice*, 24, 1–21.

Aday, R. H., & Farney, L. (2014). Malign neglect: Older women's perception of health care in prison. *Journal of Bioethics Inquiry*, 11, 359–372.

Aday, R. H., & Krabill, J. J. (2011). *Women aging in prison: A neglected population in the criminal justice system*. Boulder, CO: Lynne Rienner.

Aday, R. H., & Krabill, J. J. (2016). The silenced emotion: Older women and grief in prison. In D. L. Harris, & T. C. Bordere (Eds.), *Handbook of social justice in loss and grief* (pp. 138–153). New York, NY: Routledge.

Aday, R. H., Krabill, J. J., & Deaton, D. (2014). Religion in the lives of older incarcerated women serving life. *Journal of Women and Aging*, 26, 238–256.

Allen, R. S., Harris, G. M., Crowther, M. R., Oliver, J. S., Cavanaugh, R., & Phillips, L. L. (2013). Does religiousness and spirituality moderate the relations between physical and mental health among aging prisoners. *International Journal of Geriatric Psychiatry*, 28, 710–717.

Ammar, N. H., & Erez, E. (2000). Health care delivery systems in women's prisons: The case of Ohio. *Federal Probation*, 64, 19–27.

Anno, J., Gram, C., Lawrence, J. E., & Shansky, R. (2004). *Correctional health care: Addressing the needs of elderly, chronically ill and terminally ill inmates*. Washington, DC: National Institute of Corrections Retrieved from https://nicic.gov/correctional-health-care-addressing-needs-elderly-chronically-ill-and-terminally-ill-inmates

Arditti, J. A., & Few, A. L. (2006). Mothers' reentry into family life following incarceration. *Criminal Justice Policy Review*, 17, 103–121.

Baidawi, S., & Trotter, C. (2015). Psychological distress among older prisoners: A literature review. *Journal of Social Work*, 5, 234–257.

Beckett, J., Peterneli-Taylor, C. P., & Johnson, R. (2003). Aging matters: Growing old in the correctional system. *Journal of Psychosocial Nursing and Mental Health Services*, 41, 12–18.

Blevins, K. R., & Blowers, A. N. (2014). Community reentry and aging inmates. In J. J. Kerbs, & J. M. Jolley (Eds.), *Senior citizens behind bars* (pp. 201–222). Boulder, CO: Lynne Rienner.

Blowers, A. N., Jolley, J. M., & Kerbs, J. J. (2014). The age-segregation debate. In J. J. Kerbs, & J. M. Jolley (Eds.), *Senior citizens behind bars: Challenges for the criminal justice system* (pp. 133–156). Boulder, CO: Lynne Rienner.

Bond, G. D., Thompson, L. A., & Malloy, D. M. (2005). Lifespan differences in the social network of prison inmates. *International Journal of Aging and Human Development*, 61, 161–178.

Bowers, A. M., Jolley, J. M., & Kerbs, J. J. (2013). The age-segregation debate. In J. J. Kerbs, & J. M. Jolley (Eds.), *Senior citizens behind bars* (pp. 201–221). Boulder, CO: Lynne Rienner.

Byock, I. (2002). Dying well in corrections: Why should we care? *Journal of Correctional Health Care*, 9(2), 102–117.

Bureau of Justice Statistics (1999). *Sourcebook of criminal justice statistics*. Washington, DC: US Government Printing Office.

Caldwell, C., Jarvis, M., & Rosefield, H. (2001). Issues impact today's geriatric female offenders. *Corrections Today*, 65, 110–113.

Caverly, S. J. (2006). Older mentally ill inmates: A descriptive study. *Journal of Correctional Health Care*, 12, 262–268.

Chiu, T. (2010). *It's about time: Aging prisoners, increasing costs, and geriatric release*. New York, NY: Vera Institute of Justice. Retrieved from https://www.vera.org/publications/its-about-time-aging-prisoners-increasing-costs-and-geriatric-release

Christian, J. (2005). Riding the bus: Barriers to prison visitation and family management strategies. *Journal of Contemporary Criminal Justice*, 21, 31–48.

Clear, T. R., & Frost, N. A. (2014). *The punishment imperative*. New York, NY: New York University Press.

Colsher, P. L., Wallace, R. B., Loeffelholz, P. L., & Sales, M. (1992). Health statuses of older male prisoners. *American Journal of Public Health*, 82, 881–884.

Corr, C. A. (1998). Enhancing the concept of disenfranchised grief. *Omega: Journal of Death and Dying*, 38(1), 1–20.

Cox, J. F., & Lawrence, J. E. (2010). Planning services for elderly inmates with mental illness. *Corrections Today*, 74, 74–78.

Crowley, E., & Sparks, R. (2006). Is there life after imprisonment? *Criminology and Criminal Justice*, 6, 63–82.

Curtin, T. (2007). The continuing problem of America's aging prison population and the search for a cost effective socially acceptable means of addressing it. *The Elder Law Journal*, 15, 473–502.

Davoren, M., Fitzpathrick, M., Caddow, F., Caddow, M., O'Neill, C., O'Neill, H., & Kennedy, H. G. (2015). Older men and older women remand prisoners: Mental illness, physical illness, offending patterns and needs. *International Psycogeriatrics*, 27, 747–755.

Dawes, J. (2009). Ageing prisoners: Issues for social work. *Australian Social Work*, 62, 258–271.

Deaton, D., Aday, R. H., & Wahidin, A. (2009). The effect of health and penal harm on aging female prisoners' views of dying in prison. *Omega: Journal of Death & Dying*, 60, 33–50.

Dhami, M. K., Ayton, P., & Loewenstein, G. (2007). Adaptation to imprisonment: Indigenous or imported. *Criminal Justice and Behavior*, 34, 1085–1100.

Doron, I. I., & Love, H. (2013). Aging prisoners: A brief report of key legal and policy dilemmas. *International Journal of Criminology and Sociology*, 2, 322–327.

Dye, M., & Aday, R. H. (2013). "I just wanted to die": Pre-prison and current suicide ideation among women serving life sentences. *Criminal Justice and Behavior*, 40, 832–849.

Dye, M., Aday, R. H., Farney, L., & Raley, J. (2014). The rock I cling to: Religious engagement in the lives of life-sentenced women. *The Prison Journal*, 94, 388–408.

Fazel, S., Hope, T., O'Donnell, I., Piper, M., & Jacoby, R. (2001). Health of elderly male prisoners: Worse than the general population, worse than younger prisoners. *Age and Ageing*, 30, 403–407.

Fazel, S., McMillan, J., & O'Donnell, I. (2002). Dementia in prison: Ethical and legal implications. *Journal of Medical Ethics*, 28, 156–159.

Gibbons, J. J., & Katzenbach, N. B. (2006). Confronting confinement. *Washington University Journal of Law & Policy*, 22, 385–563. Retrieved from https://openscholarship.wustl.edu/cgi/viewcontent.cgi?article=1363&context=law_journal_law_policy

Glamser, F., & Cabana, D. (2003). Dying in a total institution: The case of death in prison. In C. Bryant (Ed.), *Handbook on death and dying* (pp. 495–501). Thousand Oaks, CA: Sage.

Haney, C. (2006). *Reforming punishment: Psychological limits to the pains of imprisonment*. Washington, DC: American Psychological Association.

Harner, H. M., Hentz, P. M., & Evangelista, M. L. (2011). Grief interrupted: The experience of loss among incarcerated women. *Qualitative Health Research*, 21, 454–464.

Harrison, M. T. (2006). True Grit: An innovative program for elderly inmates. *Corrections Today*, 68, 46–49.

Harrison, M. T. (2015). *An enriched structured living environment for older adult male prisoners may help to maintain cognitive abilities*. Ann Arbor, MI: ProQuest LLC.

Harrison, M. T., & Benedetti, J. (2009). Comprehensive geriatric programs in a time of shrinking resources: "True Grit" revisited. *Corrections Today*, 71, 44–47.

Haugebrook, S., Zgoba, K., Kimaschi, T., Morgen, K., & Brown, D. (2010). Trauma, stress, health, and mental health issues among ethnically diverse older adult prisoners. *Journal of Correctional Health Care*, 16(3), 220–229.

Higgins, D., & Severson, M. G. (2009). Community reentry and older adult offenders: Redefining social work roles. *Journal of Gerontological Social Work*, 52, 784–802.

Hill, T., Williams, B., Cobe, G., & Lindquist, K. (2006). *Aging inmates: Challenges for healthcare and custody*. San Francisco, CA: Lumetra.

Hodel, B., & Sanchez, H. G. (2012). The special needs program for inmate-patients with dementia: A psychosocial program provided in the prison system. *Dementia*, 12, 654–660.

Hoffman, H. C., Dickenson, G. E., & Dunn, C. L. (2007). Communication policy changes in state adult correctional facilities from 1971–2005. *Criminal Justice Review*, 32, 47–64.

Human Rights Watch. (2012). *Old behind bars.* New York, NY: Author Retrieved from https://www. hrw.org/sites/default/files/reports/usprisons0112webwcover_0.pdf

Hurley, M. H. (2014). *Aging in prison: The integration of research and practice.* Dunham, NC: Carolina Academic Press.

James, D., & Glaze, L. (2006). *Mental health problems of prisons and jail inmates.* Washington, DC: Bureau of Justice Statistics.

Jones, S. J., & Beck, E. (2007). Disenfranchised grief and nonfinite loss experienced by family of death row inmates. *Omega: Journal of Death and Dying, 54, 281–299.*

Kerbs, J. J., & Jolley, J. M. (2009). A commentary on age segregation for older prisoners: Philosophical and pragmatic considerations for correctional systems. *Criminal Justice Review, 34, 119–139.*

Kerbs, J. J., & Jolley, J. M. (2014). A path to evidence-based policies and practices. In J. J. Kerbs, & J. M. Jolley (Eds.), *Senior citizens behind bars: Challenges for the criminal justice system* (pp. 1–19). Boulder, CO: Lynne Rienner.

Kerbs, J. J., Jolley, J. M., & Kanaboshi, N. (2015). The interplay between law and social science in the age-segregation debate. *Journal of Crime and Justice, 38, 77–95.*

Kopera-Frye, K., Harrison, M. T., Iribarne, J., & Harrison, W. (2013). Veterans aging in place behind bars: A structured living program that works. *Psychological Services, 10, 79–86.*

Kratcoski, P. C., & Babb, S. (1990). Adjustment of older inmates: An analysis of structure and gender. *Journal of Contemporary Criminal Justice, 6, 264–281.*

Leigey, M. E. (2014). Bio-psycho-social needs. In J. J. Kerbs, & J. M. Jolley (Eds.), *Senior citizens behind bars* (pp. 43–68). Boulder, CO: Lynne Rienner.

Leigey, M. E., & Hodge, J. P. (2012). Gray matters: Gender differences in the physical and mental health of older inmates. *Women & Criminal Justice, 22, 289–308.*

Loeb, S. J., & AduDagga, A. (2006). Health-related research on older inmates: An integrative review. *Research in Nursing & Health, 20, 556–565.*

Loeb, S. J., Steffensmeier, D., & Myco, P. M. (2007). In their own words: Older male prisoners' health beliefs and concerns for the future. *Geriatric Nursing, 28, 319–329.*

Maeve, M. K. (1999). Adjudicated health: Incarcerated women and the social construction of health. *Crime, Law & Social Change, 31, 49–71.*

Mann, N. (2012). *Doing harder time? The experiences of an aging male prison population in England and Wales.* Farnham, UK: Ashgate.

Maschi, T., Kwak, J., Ko, E. J., & Morrissey, M. (2012). Forget me not: Dementia in prisons. *The Gerontologist, 52, 441–451.*

Maschi, T., Morgen, K., Zgoba, K., Courtney, D., & Ristow, J. (2011). Trauma, stressful life events, and post-traumatic stress symptoms: Do subjective experiences matter? *Gerontologist, 51, 675–686.*

Maschi, T., Viola, D., Morgen, K., Harrison, K., Harrison, M. T., & Koskien, L. (2014). Bridging community and prison for older adults and their families: Invoking human rights and intergenerational family justice. *Intergenerational Journal of Prisoner Health, 19, 1–19.*

Maschi, T., Viola, D., Morgen, K., & Koskinen, L. (2013). Trauma and stress, grief, loss, and separation among older adults in prison: The protective role of coping resources on physical and mental health. *Journal of Crime and Justice, 38, 113–136.*

Maschi, T., Viola, D., & Sun, F. (2013). The high cost of the international aging prisoner crisis: Well-being as the common denominator for action. *Gerontologist, 53, 543–554.*

Meeks, S., Sublett, R., Kostiwa, I., Rodgers, J. R., & Haddix, D. (2008). Treating depression in the prison nursing home. *Clinical Case Studies, 7, 555–574.*

Merten, M. J., Bishop, A. J., & Williams, A. L. (2012). Prison health and valuation of life, loneliness, and depressed mood. *American Journal of Health Behavior, 36, 275–288.*

Messina, N., & Grella, C. (2006). Childhood trauma and women's health outcomes in a California prison population. *American Journal of Popular Health, 96, 1842–1848.*

Mitka, M. (2004). Aging prisoners stressing health care system. *Journal of the American Medical Association, 292, 423–424.*

Mumola, C. J. (2000). *Incarcerated parents and their children* ( )Bureau of Justice Statistics special report. Washington, DC: US Department of Justice.

O'Hara, K., Forsyth, K., Webb, R., Senior, J., Hayes, A. J., Challis, D. J., … & Shaw, J. (2016). Links between depressive symptoms and unmet health and social needs among older prisoners. *Age and Aging*, 45, 158–163.

Olsen, M. J., & McEwen, M. A. (2004). Grief counseling in a medium security prison. *Journal for Specialists in Group Work*, 29, 225–236.

Phillips, L. L., Allen, R. S., Presnell, A. H., Decoster, J., & Cavanaugh, R. (2011). Aging prisoners' treatment selection: Does prospect theory enhance understanding of end-of-life medical decisions? *Gerontologist*, 51, 663–674.

Phillips, L. L., Allen, R. S., Salekin, K. L., & Cavanaugh, R. (2009). Care alternatives in prison systems: Factors influencing end-of-life treatment selection. *Criminal Justice and Behavior*, 36, 620–634.

Regan, J. J., Alderson, A., & Regan, W. M. (2002). Psychiatric disorders in aging prisoners. *Clinical Gerontologist*, 26, 8–13.

Roof, J. G. (2010). Geriatric offenders. In C. L. Scott (Ed.), *Handbook of correctional mental health* (2nd ed.) (pp. 373–594). Arlington, VA: American Psychiatric Publishing.

Shantz, L. R., & Frigon, L. (2009). Aging women and health: From pains of imprisonment to the pains of reintegration. *International Journal of Prisoner Health*, 5, 3–16.

Sterns, A. A., Lax, G., Sed, S., Keohane, P., & Sterns, R. S. (2008). Growing wave of older prisoners: A national survey of older prisoner health, mental health, and programming. *Corrections Today*, 70, 70–76.

Stevenson, R. G., & McCutchen, R. (2006). When meaning has lost its way: Life and loss behind bars. *Illness, Crisis & Loss*, 14, 103–119.

Stroller, N. (2003). Space, place, and movement as aspects of health care in three women's prisons. *Social Science and Medicine*, 5, 2263–2275.

Strupp, H., & Willmott, D. (2005). *Dignity denied: The price of imprisoning women in California*. San Francisco, CA: Legal Services for Prisoners with Children.

Turner, S., & Trotter, C. (2010). *Growing old in prison? A review of national and international research on ageing offenders*. Melbourne, Australia: Department of Justice.

United Nations Office on Drugs and Crime. (2009). *Handbook on prisoners with special needs*. New York, NY: United Nations Retrieved from https://www.unodc.org/pdf/criminal_justice/Handbook_on_Prisoners_with_Special_Needs.pdf

Vaughn, M. S., & Collins, S. C. (2004). Medical malpractice in correctional facilities: State tort remedies for inappropriate and inadequate health care administered to prisoners. *The Prison Journal*, 84, 505–534.

Vega, W. M., & Silverman, M. (1988). Stress and the elderly convict. *International Journal of Offender Therapy and Comparative Criminology*, 32, 153–162.

Wahidin, A. (2004). *Older women in the criminal justice system: Running out of time*. London, UK: Jessica Kingsley.

Williams, B., Lindquist, K., Sudore, R., Strupp, H., Wilmott, D., & Walter, L. (2006). Being old and doing time: Functional impairment and the adverse experiences of geriatric female offenders. *Journal of the American Geriatrics Society*, 54, 702–707.

Wilson, J., & Barboza, S. (2010). The looming challenge of dementia in corrections. *Correct Care*, 24, 12–14.

Yorston, G. A., & Taylor, P. G. (2006). Commentary: Older offenders—No place to go? *Journal of American Academy of Psychiatry and Law*, 34, 333–337.

10

The Challenge of Managing Offenders With Intellectual and Developmental Disabilities Through Secure and Community Service Pathways

William Lindsay and Danyal Ansari
NHS Greater Glasgow & Clyde, UK

Introduction

Historically, intellectual and developmental disability (IDD) has been closely associated with criminal behavior and, for the first part of the twentieth century at least, community responses were focused on isolation and containment. This might seem extreme, but even a brief review of historical writing shows how entrenched this approach was. For example, John Connolly (1884, reported in Trent, 1994), the Chief Physician to the asylum at Hanwell, England, wrote of the humane management of "idiots" in institutions and of his enthusiasm for institutional care. Kerlin (1858), a very important figure in the field of IDD, published a series of 22 case illustrations where he wrote, for example, of one case, "he was a moral idiot, he recognized no obligation to God nor man and having some appreciation of the value of money and property, nothing that could be appropriated was safe from his reach . . . His honest face covered the most mature dishonesty" (p. 48). Here, there is evidence of how the link between IDD and crime was conceptualized as well as an attribution of cunning and culpability that was to pervade the wider Western culture. In fact, these authors were part of a general movement which increasingly regarded IDD as a menace. Scheerenberger (1983), for example, noted that:

> By the 1880s, mentally retarded persons were no longer viewed as unfortunates or innocents who, with proper training, could fill a positive role in the home and/or community. As a class they had become undesirable, frequently viewed as a great evil of humanity, the social parasite, criminal, prostitute, and pauper (p. 116).

By 1889, Kerlin had developed his theories on the association between IDD and crime to argue that crime, rather than being the work of the devil, was the result of an individual's inability to understand moral sense and also their physical infirmity, both of which were non-remediable and inherited. Kerlin (and others) certainly linked IDD with a range of social vices,

The Wiley International Handbook of Correctional Psychology, First Edition. Edited by Devon L. L. Polaschek, Andrew Day, and Clive R. Hollin.
© 2019 John Wiley & Sons Ltd. Published 2019 by John Wiley & Sons Ltd.

including drunkenness, delinquency, prostitution, and crime, and concerns were voiced around the Western world about the need for containment. Barr (an institution superintendent) addressed the Association of Medical Officers thus:

> One hundred thousand of the feeble minded in the United States alone, consistently increasing by birth and immigration . . . crowd our schools, walk our streets and fill alike jails and positions of trust, reproducing their kind and vitiating the moral atmosphere. Science and experience have searched them out . . ." (cited by Trent, 1994, p. 144).

The development of mental testing was a further innovation and, using these concepts, Goddard (1920) introduced the term "feeble mindedness" to include all forms of intellectual disability. Those with a mental age of 2 years or less were termed "idiots," those with a mental age of 3–7 years "imbeciles," and those with a mental age of 8–12 years "morons." Crucially, the addition of the latter category more than doubled the number of people classified in this way. The subsequent introduction of the categories of "mild intellectual disability" and "borderline intelligence" that followed the development of testing later tripled prevalence rates. Terman (1911), one of the pioneers of psychometric testing, wrote that: "there is no investigator who denies the fearful role of mental deficiency in the production of vice, crime and delinquency … not all criminals are feeble minded but all feeble minded are at least potential criminals" (p. 11).

We have drawn attention to these historical statements to make the point that any modern consideration of the management of offenders with IDD should be aware of a cultural context in which alarmist, and highly prejudicial, recommendations may be put forward about how to manage people with IDD. Prejudice can still be detected, for example, when local services for people with IDD wish to establish a group home in a particular residential area. However, for decades now, no one has seen IDD as a causative factor in crime and it is foolish to over-emphasize IDD in any discussion or treatise on criminology. The aim of this chapter then is to review secure and community forensic IDD services, and to consider the essential treatment requirements for such services. This, we hope, is of relevance to anyone working in a correctional context where access to specialist disability services is often lacking.

Secure Services

Secure services for people with IDD in the United Kingdom tend to be multidisciplinary inpatient services with three levels of security: high, medium, and low, according to assessed risk of the individual. High secure is for offenders assessed to present a "grave and immediate" danger; medium secure services are for those who are assessed to present a "significant" danger, but do not require the highest level of security; and low secure services represent the final stage of a treatment pathway prior to resettlement into the community or for those detained under the Mental Health Act who cannot be treated in open mental health settings. In the United Kingdom there are 48 high secure beds, provided by the National Health Service (NHS), 604 medium secure beds, roughly equally split between the NHS and independent sector, and 1,741 low secure beds, with around three quarters being provided by the independent sector (Royal College of Psychiatrists, 2013). Around 70% of secure forensic beds for people with IDD are low secure, suggesting either that the significant majority do not present a grave or significant danger to the public or that the more dangerous offenders with IDD are in prison. It is, however, in the community that most offenders with IDD are managed, and without adequate community support they will be at increased risk of recidivism and inappropriate imprisonment.

Characteristics of Offenders with IDD Across Settings

Work with mainstream offenders on risk assessment has identified some developmental variables as risk factors for future offending. Harris, Rice, and Quinsey (1993), for example, identified attachment difficulties (parents separated prior to the age of 16), behavioral problems at school, and the early onset of aggression as associated with reoffending in adulthood. Several others have also suggested that insecure attachment in childhood is associated with offending in adulthood (e.g., Fago, 2006; Ward, Hudson, & Marshall 1996). A large-scale follow-up study of over 3,000 mentally disordered offenders by Monahan et al. (2001) also reported that the experience of physical abuse in childhood, parental alcohol abuse, living apart from either parent prior to age of 15, and witnessing parental disputes were associated with future violence.

Research on characteristics and risk factors for offenders with IDD has noted similar trends to those in mainstream research. For example, a study of violent men with IDD by Novaco and Taylor (2008) sought to determine whether earlier exposure to parental anger and aggression was related to assault and violence in a sample of 105 male forensic inpatients. They found that witnessing parental violence in childhood was significantly related to anger and aggression in adulthood. Lindsay, Steptoe, and Haut (2012) later compared the characteristics of 126 violent offenders and 156 sexual offenders, all with IDD, and found that significantly more of the violent offenders had experienced physical abuse in childhood while significantly more of the sexual offenders had experienced sexual abuse in childhood. In addition, poor family relationships have been associated with future offending incidents in people with IDD (Beail & Warden, 1995; Lindsay, Elliot, & Astell, 2004).

Emerson and Halpin (2013) conducted a secondary analysis of the Longitudinal Study of Young People in England data set (Natcen, 2010), comprised of 15,772 young people, 532 of whom were identified as having mild intellectual disability. For the sample as a whole, living with a single parent and four indicators of social, economic, and environmental adversity were identified as significant risk factors for contact with the police and antisocial behavior. Those with intellectual disability were significantly more likely than others to be exposed to all risk factors, including living with a single parent, living in an area of deprivation, living in rented accommodation, living in a workless household, and being eligible for free school meals. Although the group with a mild disability were significantly more likely to have police contact and to report antisocial behavior, when these risk factors were controlled for, intellectual disability itself was significantly associated with lower rates of antisocial behavior. This study suggests that it is deprivation and childhood adversity that are more crucial in the development of antisocial and criminal behavior in people with IDD.

Major mental illness, while no less prevalent in offenders with IDD than in the general population of people with IDD, has not been shown to be consistently associated with crime. Lunsky et al. (2011), for example, compared cohorts of forensic and non-forensic patients with IDD, reporting that the forensic group had lower frequencies of mood disorder, while there were no differences in other mental illnesses. However, the forensic group did have significantly higher rates of personality disorder. Lindsay, Carson, et al. (2012) also found no differences between sexual offenders and violent offenders on the rates of mental illness, although the rates for both groups were consistent with findings from other populations with

IDD at around 35%. A large study by Vinkers (2013) involving data on 12,186 individuals in the Netherlands, who had been subject to pre-trial psychiatric reports, found that those with an IQ of less than 70 had lower rates (non-significant) of psychotic disorder than those with an IQ above 85. However, Raina and Lunsky (2010) reported that in their sample, a small ($n = 39$) forensic sample with IDD had a significantly higher frequency of psychosis diagnosis than a matched sample of non-forensic patients.

Reed, Russell, Xenitidis, and Murphy (2004) compared offenders and non-offenders with IDD who were detained in low secure care. There was no significant difference between the two study groups in terms of age, gender, ethnicity, IQ, period of detention, or type of comorbid psychiatric disorder, although autistic disorder was diagnosed significantly more frequently in the non-offender group ($\chi^2[1,63] = 4.16$, $p = .04$). In contrast, a diagnosis of personality disorder was more common in the offender group, but this difference did not reach statistical significance ($p = .07$). There was also no significant between-group difference in the total rate of challenging behavior, even though the non-offender group was significantly more assaultive to staff and other patients, and used weapons more frequently. In contrast, the offender group had a significantly higher rate of self-injurious behavior.

Personality disorder (PD) has been implicated as a risk factor for criminal behavior in all types of offenders, including those with IDD. Alexander et al. (2010) compared 77 patients with personality disorder against 61 without (all had IDD). They found significantly higher rates of previous violent offending, significantly higher rates of substance abuse, and significantly higher previous detention under "criminal" sections in the PD group. It should be noted, however, that in this study the similarities between the two groups outweighed the differences. Hogue et al. (2006) constructed a regression model for the prediction of secure or community provision in 212 offenders with IDD using a range of offense, diagnostic, and legal detention variables. PD diagnosis and labels indicative of a history of previous antisociality emerged as strong predictors of admission to secure provision. However, these authors did note that clinicians working in maximum secure hospitals were more comfortable in making a diagnosis of personality disorder and this was likely to have influenced their results. This was supported by Lindsay et al. (2017), who compared personality diagnoses from two different sources for the same 212 patients. Offenders with IDD in the community had low levels of PD diagnosis based on case file review, while structured assessments of the same participants revealed significantly higher rates. It was also the case that case file diagnoses of PD had no predictive relationship with violence while the structured assessments had a significant predictive relationship with future violence.

It is apparent that social policy significantly affects patterns of criminal justice contact in offenders with IDD. Lund (1990), for example, found an increase in sexual offenders with IDD appearing in court at that time compared with previous years. He concluded that this increase was likely to be a result of the implementation of psychiatric deinstitutionalization policies which led to more offenders with IDD living in the community. Lindsay, Haut, and Steptoe (2011), in a more recent study of 309 offenders, found that of those referred between 1989 and 1996, 20% were referred from criminal justice services (including courts) while from 2003 to 2008, this proportion had risen to 83%. These differences were thought to reflect significant changes in social policy over this period. Raina, Arenovich, Jones, and Lunsky (2012), in a study of 138 individuals with IDD in crisis, found that police were more likely to arrest someone if the incident involved aggression and he or she was living independently or with family in the community. Once again, this suggests that deinstitutionalization policies and the number of people with IDD living in community are important determinants of criminal justice involvement.

In the Northumbria/Cambridge/Abertay pathways (NCAP) study of 477 offenders with IDD who had been referred to secure and community forensic services, O'Brien et al. (2010) reported that 51% had a mild intellectual disability, 17% were classified as borderline intelligence, 8% moderate intellectual disability, and 7% severe intellectual disability. Level of cognitive ability was not known in 12%, and 5% had an IQ greater than 80. The most common developmental disorder was attention deficit hyperactivity disorder (ADHD; 15%), and rates of autistic spectrum disorder were recorded at 10% (broadly consistent with a population of people with IDD in general). The combined category of anxiety/obsessive-compulsive disorder (OCD) was the most common adult psychiatric disorder (13%), with depression (11%), personality disorder (11%), schizophrenia (9%), other psychotic disorders (9%), and bipolar disorder (6%) also relatively common. A significant number (42%) had a current major physical health problem, including epilepsy (19%), other neurological problems (7%), and 21% had some other physical condition requiring regular medical treatment. In relation to developmental adversity, 24% had suffered some type of severe deprivation in childhood and 55% had documented histories of child abuse and neglect, including non-accidental injury (12%), sexual abuse (11%), and neglect (5%). The offending incidents that led to their referral were subsequently analyzed in terms of their nature and referral destination (Lindsay et al., 2010). Physical aggression and verbal aggression were the most frequent referral reasons (at 49% and 33%, respectively), with a combination of contact and non-contact sexual offenses also relatively common (29%). The next most frequent referral reason was property damage (19%). Substance abuse was implicated in the index behavior in only 6% of cases. Those referred to low/medium secure services were significantly more likely to be referred for aggression, while those referred to community forensic services and maximum secure services were more likely to have a sexual offense as the index behavior. Finally, referrals to low/medium secure services were more likely to involve substance abuse, but substance abuse remained relatively low compared to the rates reported for mainstream offenders (see McMurran, 2012). The average age at first recorded offense increased in line with the decreasing security of the facility; maximum secure (11.7 years), low/medium secure (12.9 years), community forensic (14.5 years), generic community (17.5 years).

When these data were entered into a regression model to predict community or secure provision by Carson et al. (2010), the results suggested a person would be more likely to be referred to a community service and if she or he lived in the community, and had an IQ of less than 50. In contrast, being charged, showing physical aggression, having a greater diversity of problem behaviors, and being referred by a tertiary (secure) healthcare service all increased the likelihood of referral to secure services. This model correctly predicted referral direction of 85.7% of cases. Carson et al. (2014) then constructed a similar regression model just for sex offenders ($n = 131$). Those who had committed a sexual offense were more likely to be referred to the community if they were living in the community and more likely to be referred to secure services if they had a greater diversity of problem behavior in addition to the sexual offense.

Community Management of Offenders

There have been several studies of offenders with IDD who live in community settings. In one of these, Wheeler et al. (2009) conducted a series of analyses of 237 referrals to community forensic IDD services. In terms of reason for referral, physical and verbal aggression (at 52% and 40%, respectively) were the most common. Other index incidents included property damage (24%), inappropriate sexual behavior (18%), fire-setting (1%), substance abuse (3.8%), theft

(5%), and cruelty or neglect of children (11%). These figures are of interest in so far as inappropriate sexual behavior and fire-setting—problems that have been associated with offenders with IDD—are not overly represented. Indeed, fire-setting was recorded at a particularly low rate. In this sample, neglect/cruelty in relation to children was relatively common (11%), although this particular problem has not been identified in other samples of offenders with IDD in secure settings. Those recorded in this category were predominantly female, and this almost certainly reflects the changes in the way in which people with IDD live more ordinary lives in the community following the large deinstitutionalization processes. Wheeler et al. then reviewed factors predicting criminal justice service involvement. In addition to mild IDD, younger age, physical aggression, theft, having no routine activity, not being in a relationship, and previous criminal justice involvement were all predictors of referral to the justice system. All of these factors suggest that those who have the ability to live more independently (i.e., those with mild IDD or borderline intelligence) are less likely to become involved in the justice system.

This study is important for a number of reasons. First, it reviews a range of referrals into forensic IDD services rather than using data from those already in treatment. It also identified physical aggression as the most frequent trigger for a referral, followed by property damage and then inappropriate sexual behavior. Data relevant to neglect and cruelty in relation to children were also collected.

In a series of studies involving community forensic IDD services, Lindsay and colleagues (Lindsay et al., 2004; Lindsay, Whitfield, & Carson, 2007; Lindsay, Holland, et al., 2013) have reported findings related to 309 referrals with mild IDD and borderline intelligence followed up for up to 20 years. In contrast to the Wheeler et al. (2009) study, this data set only included those who had been accepted for assessment and treatment. They split their sample into male sex offenders (n = 156), male non-sexual offenders (predominantly violence, n = 128), and female offenders (n = 27). The sex offenders were significantly older than the male non-sexual offenders (35 vs. 30 years). Across all groups, violence and aggression were the most frequent reasons for referral. However, because of the nature of the sample (only those accepted for treatment), sexual offenses clearly featured prominently and fire-raising featured in only 5% of referrals. In terms of diagnoses, mental illness was recorded in 31% of all male referrals and 71% of female referrals. Anxiety was diagnosed in around 16% of the male referrals and in 38% of females, while alcohol problems were recorded in 24% of the violent offenders, 16% of sex offenders, and 33% of female offenders.

Across these studies, it is noteworthy that violence was the most frequent reason for referral to community forensic IDD services, including criminal justice services. Sexual behavior did feature prominently and this is especially evident in the Wheeler et al. (2009) study since this incorporated all referrals. Fire-setting did not feature prominently in either study, and although mental illness was prominent, any service for this client group should take this into account. The studies also provide support for the suggestion that criminal justice involvement has become much more common in the past decade, reflecting changes in community provision for people with IDD.

The Identification of Risk Factors and Characteristics of Effective Service

Several developmental factors are rated in some contemporary risk assessment tools. For example, the Violence Risk Appraisal Guide (Quinsey, Harris, Rice, & Cormier, 2006) assesses two developmental factors that contribute to the risk of further violence. The first is whether or not the individual has lived with his or her biological parents until the age of 16 (not having lived with parents contributed to risk). The second is behavioral problems at school. As these are static risk factors, it is the dynamic risk factors identified by Andrews and Bonta (2006) that are the focus for intervention by forensic learning disability teams. This generally involves providing treatment that promotes self-regulation (including through substance use treatment) and reduces the strength of antisocial attitudes. It is also a strength of IDD services that they are able to coordinate social, educational, housing, employment, and health services around an individual in a manner that can addresses the various risk factors environmentally. Nonetheless, there are obvious challenges in finding appropriate housing and securing an appropriate service provider. Carson et al. (2014) have suggested that the very identification of service for offenders with IDD may itself constitute a protective factor.

One study that is relevant to the success of community placement was conducted by Lindsay et al. (2004). They reviewed the predictors of sexual offense recidivism in 52 male sex offenders with mild intellectual disability. They identified a number of variables associated with reoffending in this group, including poor response to treatment, poor compliance with management or treatment regimes, low treatment motivation, denial that a crime had taken place, antisocial attitudes, and allowances made by staff. It was concluded that a successful service will provide the following: planning for accommodation, provision of prosocial support, monitoring of prosocial and antisocial influences, planning for occupation or regular activity, planned leisure activity, regular service follow-up, and consistency among staff. Treatment for high levels of anger, substance abuse, low motivation, antisociality, attitudes consistent with offending, and maladaptive social problem-solving should all be available. (see Alexander et al., 2010; Lindsay, Holland, et al., 2013).

Lindsay, Steptoe, Wallace, Haut, and Brewster (2013) conducted a review of treatment for 197 offenders with IDD who had been accepted into a range of forensic IDD services over a 12-month period. They noted a surprising lack of treatment addressing criminogenic need, particularly in community settings, where only 9% of those referred received treatment that was directly related to the reason for referral. They suggested that this gap may occur because generic community services have a wide range of focus and responsibility, with people being referred for family breakdown, mental illness, challenging behavior, relationship difficulties, and so on.

Conclusion

This chapter has described the characteristics of those people with IDD who are referred through with the criminal justice and court system or directly to community and forensic mental health services. It is apparent that relatively little is known about the needs of those in prison and that there is great scope to strengthen treatment responses that address those factors that are associated with future risk of offending. It is important to emphasize that service delivery in this area occurs in the context of social policy that has a powerful influence on service access, as well as the continuing influence of stereotypes about the nature of the association between IDD and criminal behavior.

Key Readings

Andrews, D. A., & Bonta, J. (2006). *The psychology of criminal conduct* (4th ed.). Newark, NJ: Anderson.

Lindsay, W. R., Holland, A. J., Carson, D., Taylor, J. L., O'Brien, G., Steptoe, L., & Wheeler, J. (2013). Responsivity to criminogenic need in forensic intellectual disability services. *Journal of Intellectual Disability Research*, 57, 172–181.

Lindsay, W. R., Steptoe, L., Wallace, L., Haut, F., & Brewster, E. (2013). An evaluation and 20-year follow-up of recidivism in a community intellectual disability service. *Criminal Behaviour and Mental Health*, 23, 138–149.

O'Brien, G., Taylor, J. L., Lindsay, W. R., Holland, A. J., Carson, D., Steptoe, L., … & Wheeler, J. R. (2010). A multi-centre study of adults with learning disabilities referred to services for antisocial or offending behaviour: Demographic, individual, offending and service characteristics. *Journal of Learning Disabilities and Offending Behaviour*, 1(2), 5–15.

Wheeler, J. R., Holland, A. J., Bambrick, M., Lindsay, W. R., Carson, D., Steptoe, L., … & O'Brien, G. (2009). Community services and people with intellectual disabilities who engage in anti-social or offending behaviour: Referral rates, characteristics, and care pathways. *Journal of Forensic Psychiatry & Psychology*, 20, 717–740.

References

Alexander, R. T., Green, E. N., O'Mahoney, B., Guneratna, I., Gangadharan, S., & Hoare, S. (2010). Personality disorders in offenders with intellectual disability: A comparison of clinical, forensic and outcome variables and implications for service provision. *Journal of Intellectual Disability Research*, 54, 650–658.

Andrews, D. A., & Bonta, J. (2006). *The psychology of criminal conduct* (4th ed.). Newark, NJ: Anderson.

Beail, N., & Warden, S. (1995). Sexual abuse of adults with learning disabilities. *Journal of Intellectual Disability Research*, 39, 382–387.

Carson, D., Lindsay, W. R., Holland, A. J., Taylor, J. T., O'Brien, G., Wheeler, J. R., … & Johnston, S. (2014). Sex offenders with intellectual disability referred to levels of community and secure provision: Comparison and prediction of pathway. *Legal and Criminological Psychology*, 19, 373–384.

Carson, D., Lindsay, W. R., O'Brien, G., Holland, A. J., Taylor, J. T., Wheeler, J. R., … & Johnston, S. (2010). Referrals into services for offenders with intellectual disabilities: Variables predicting community or secure provision. *Criminal Behaviour and Mental Health*, 20, 39–50.

Emerson, E., & Halpin, S. (2013). Anti-social behaviour and police contact among 13- to 15-year-old English adolescents with and without mild/moderate intellectual disability. *Journal of Applied Research in Intellectual Disabilities*, 26, 362–369.

Fago, D. P. (2006). Comorbid psychopathology in child, adolescent and adult sexual offenders. In C. Hilarski, & J. Wodarski (Eds.), *Comprehensive mental health practice with sex offenders and their families* (pp. 139–218). Binghamton, NY: Haworth Press.

Goddard, H. H. (1920). *Human efficiency and levels of intelligence*. Princeton, NJ: Princeton University Press.

Harris, G. T., Rice, M. E., & Quinsey, V. L. (1993). Violent recidivism of mentally disordered offenders: The development of a statistical prediction instrument. *Criminal Justice and Behaviour*, 20, 315–335.

Hogue, T. E., Steptoe, L., Taylor, J. L., Lindsay, W. R., Mooney, P., Pinkney, L., … & O'Brien, G. (2006). A comparison of offenders with intellectual disability across three levels of security. *Criminal Behaviour and Mental Health*, 16, 13–28.

Kerlin, N. I. (1858). *A brief history of twenty-two imbecile children*. Philadelphia, PA: Hunt.

Lindsay, W. R., Elliot, S. F., & Astell, A. (2004). Predictors of sexual offence recidivism in offenders with intellectual disabilities. *Journal of Applied Research in Intellectual Disabilities*, 17, 299–305.

Lindsay, W. R., Haut, F., & Steptoe, L. (2011). Changes in referral patterns for offenders with intellectual disability: A 20-year follow-up study. *Journal of Forensic Psychiatry and Psychology.*, 22, 513–517.

Lindsay, W. R., Holland, A. J., Carson, D., Taylor, J. L., O'Brien, G., Steptoe, L., & Wheeler, J. (2013). Responsivity to criminogenic need in forensic intellectual disability services. *Journal of Intellectual Disability Research*, 57, 172–181.

Lindsay, W. R., O'Brien, G., Carson, D. R., Holland, A. J., Taylor, J. L., Wheeler, J. R., ... & Johnston, S. (2010). Pathways into services for offenders with intellectual disabilities: Childhood experiences, diagnostic information, and offence variables. *Criminal Justice and Behaviour*, 37, 678–694.

Lindsay, W. R., Steptoe, L., & Haut, F. (2012). The sexual and physical abuse histories of offenders with intellectual disability. *Journal of Intellectual Disability Research*, 56, 326–331.

Lindsay, W. R., Steptoe, L., Wallace, L., Haut, F., & Brewster, E. (2013). An evaluation and 20-year follow-up of recidivism in a community intellectual disability service. *Criminal Behaviour and Mental Health*, 23, 138–149.

Lindsay, W. R., van Logten, A., Didden, R., Steptoe, L., Taylor, J. L., & Hogue, T. E. (2017). The validity of two diagnostic systems for personality disorder in people with intellectual disabilities: A short report. *Journal of Intellectual Disabilities and Offending Behaviour*, 8(3), 104–110.

Lindsay, W. R., Whitfield, E., & Carson, D. (2007). An assessment for attitudes consistent with sexual offending for use with offenders with intellectual disability. *Legal and Criminological Psychology*, 12, 55–68.

Lund, J. (1990). Mentally retarded criminal offenders in Denmark. *British Journal of Psychiatry*, 156, 726–731.

Lunsky, Y., Gracey, C., Koegl, C., Bradley, E., Durbin, J., & Raina, P. (2011). The clinical profile and service needs of psychiatric inpatients with intellectual disabilities and forensic involvement. *Psychology Crime and Law*, 17, 9–25.

McMurran, M. (2012). *Alcohol-related violence: Prevention and treatment*. Chichester, UK: Wiley-Blackwell.

Monahan, J., Steadman, H., Silver, E., Appelbaum, P., Robbins, T., Mulvey, E., ... & Banks, S. (2001). *Re-thinking risk assessment: The MacArthur study of mental disorder and violence*. New York, NY: Oxford University Press.

Natcen (2010). *LSYPE user guide to the datasets: Wave one to wave five*. London, UK: Department for Children, Schools and Families.

Novaco, R. W., & Taylor, J. L. (2008). Anger and assaultiveness of male forensic patients with developmental disabilities: Links to volatile parents. *Aggressive Behaviour*, 34, 380–393.

O'Brien, G., Taylor, J. L., Lindsay, W. R., Holland, A. J., Carson, D., Steptoe, L., ... & Wheeler, J. R. (2010). A multi-centre study of adults with learning disabilities referred to services for antisocial or offending behaviour: Demographic, individual, offending and service characteristics. *Journal of Learning Disabilities and Offending Behaviour*, 1(2), 5–15.

Quinsey, V. L., Harris, G. T., Rice, M. E., & Cormier, C. A. (2006). *Violent offenders: Appraising and managing risk* (2nd ed.). Washington, DC: American Psychological Association.

Raina, P., Arenovich, T., Jones, J., & Lunsky, Y. (2012). Pathways into the criminal justice system for individuals with intellectual disabilities. *Journal of Applied Research in Intellectual Disabilities*, 26, 404–409.

Raina, P., & Lunsky, Y. (2010). A comparison study of adults with intellectual disability and psychiatric disorder with and without forensic involvement. *Research in Developmental Disabilities*, 31, 218–223.

Reed, S., Russell, A., Xenitidis, K., & Murphy, D. G. M. (2004). People with learning disabilities in a low secure in-patient unit: Comparison of offenders and non-offenders. *The British Journal of Psychiatry*, 185, 499–504.

Royal College of Psychiatrists. (2013, July). People with learning disability and mental health, behavioural or forensic problems: The role of in-patient services. Retrieved from https://www.rcpsych.ac.uk/pdf/FR ID 03 for website.pdf

Scheerenberger, R. C. (1983). *A history of mental retardation*. London, UK: Brooks.

Terman, L. (1911). *The measurement of intelligence*. Boston, MA: Houghton Mifflin.

Trent, J. W. (1994). *Inventing the feeble mind: A history of mental retardation in the United States.* Berkeley, CA: University of California Press.

Vinkers, D. (2013). Pre-trial reported defendants in the Netherlands with intellectual disability, borderline and normal intellectual functioning. *Journal of Applied Research in Intellectual Disabilities*, 26, 357–361.

Ward, T., Hudson, S. M., & Marshall, W. L. (1996). Attachment style in sex offenders: A preliminary study. *Journal of Sex Research*, 33, 17–26.

Wheeler, J. R., Holland, A. J., Bambrick, M., Lindsay, W. R., Carson, D., Steptoe, L., ... & O'Brien, G. (2009). Community services and people with intellectual disabilities who engage in anti-social or offending behaviour: Referral rates, characteristics, and care pathways. *Journal of Forensic Psychiatry & Psychology*, 20, 717–740.

11

Families, Parenting, and Visits in Prison

Clare-Ann Fortune and Karen Salmon
Victoria University of Wellington, New Zealand

Introduction

Incarceration, by its very nature, involves the separation of an individual from their family, friends, and usual networks (Cochran & Mears, 2013). The majority of incarcerated men and women are also parents (Flynn, Naylor, & Arias, 2016; Hairston, 2002a, 2002b). Thus, as international prison populations rise, there are repercussions that stretch far beyond the men and women who are imprisoned; there are unseen members of our communities, including children, who are, figuratively speaking, serving these sentences alongside the incarcerated individual (Celinska & Siegel, 2010; Clopton & East, 2008; Flynn et al., 2016; Hairston, 2002a, 2002b). Although there is some variability, the focus tends to be on the consequences for the incarcerated individual's violation of the law and the potential risk they pose to the community, and there is rarely consideration for their role as caregivers/parents or for their dependent children (Flynn et al., 2016). While recognizing the role of imprisonment as a consequence for an individual's criminal behavior and issues of public protection (Deflem, 2014), the un/under-recognized impact of incarceration on the incarcerated individuals' families needs to be considered. There is evidence to suggest that the majority of families with an incarcerated member are negatively affected in multiple ways (Celinska & Siegel, 2010; Hairston, 2002b; Sharrat, 2014). The lack of attention to children of incarcerated parents is of concern and is also contrary to the United Nations Convention on the Rights of the Child, which sets out what is considered necessary in order to enable children to reach their full potential, and provides guidelines designed to protect the rights of children, particularly those in vulnerable circumstances (Office of the United Nations Commissioner for Human Rights, n.d.).

In the United States, anywhere from 20 to 60% of parents report no contact with their children while they are in state and federal prisons (Clopton & East, 2008), and both children and parents can experience distress as a result (Murray, Farrington, Sekol, & Olsen, 2009). One study based on interviews with 34 children (aged 8–17 years), has suggested that the best way to support children during the period of parental incarceration is to support their parents and caregivers (Nesmith & Ruhland, 2008).

The Wiley International Handbook of Correctional Psychology, First Edition. Edited by Devon L. L. Polaschek, Andrew Day, and Clive R. Hollin.
© 2019 John Wiley & Sons Ltd. Published 2019 by John Wiley & Sons Ltd.

Prison visitations are one way of ameliorating the effects of parental incarceration. However, justice system agencies can fail to recognize the negative impact of incarceration and the positive role that prison visits and other forms of contact can have in supporting incarcerated individuals and their families (Loucks, 2002). Families, including children, may be positive resources and assets for the incarcerated individual (Brooks-Gordon & Bainham, 2004; Celinska & Siegel, 2010; Hairston, 2002b). It is, however, also important to recognize that, in some instances, incarcerated parents, custodial parents/caregivers, or the child may not want contact, or contact would be inappropriate for some reason (e.g., where the incarcerated parent was previously abusive toward the child; Hairston, 2002a).

This chapter starts by looking at the impact incarceration can have on children, caregivers, and the incarcerated parent. We will explore factors influencing whether prison visits occur (barriers) and the potential risks and benefits associated with visits. Practical implications are considered for those whose work brings them into contact with incarcerated parents and children and/or who are part of the process of prison visitations. There are limitations in the amount of research and in the methodological and statistical approaches employed in research into prison visitations (Cochran & Mears, 2013). In this chapter we strive to provide an overview of the most consistent findings but will, finally, discuss some of the limitations and suggest potential avenues for addressing these.

Impact of Incarceration on Families

For some families, imprisonment of a family member may provide some relief from difficult circumstances (e.g., exposure to abuse or domestic violence, or financial pressure due to gambling or drug use). However, for other families, the negative impacts of imprisonment can include stigma and financial difficulties (Murray et al., 2009), emotional responses to the separation, and loss and disruption to intimate adult relationships (Hairston, 2002b). Financial implications include the loss of income that the incarcerated parent contributed to the household (regardless of whether or not this was obtained legally), and the financial demands imposed by legal fees, costs for maintaining the prisoner while they are incarcerated (e.g., money and other items), and costs of maintaining contact (Brooks-Gordon & Bainham, 2004; Hairston, 2002a, 2002b).

Impact on Incarcerated Parents

Most parents who are incarcerated are fathers, but there are increasing numbers of mothers (Celinska & Siegel, 2010; Sabol, Couture, & Harrison, 2007). In a review of the literature on fathers in prison (Hairston, 2002a), it was concluded that incarceration had negative impacts on father–child relationships in situations where the father had been involved in the care/life of the child prior to incarceration. This was compounded by the fact that fathers in prison also tended not to see their children, resulting in little opportunity for them to provide social or emotional support to their children.

A particular difficulty for women who are incarcerated is that they are more likely than men to have been the primary caregiver of their children (Celinska & Siegel, 2010); thus the incarceration of women can be associated with a greater immediate loss for children (Brooks-Gordon & Bainham, 2004). Mothers report finding it particularly difficult to adjust to separation from their children, but, in general, parents of both genders worry about the wellbeing of their children in their absence and whether or not the separation will negatively impact the parent–child relationship long term (Celinska & Siegel, 2010; Hairston, 1991a, 2002b). Most incarcerated parents plan to reunite with their children on their release but fear, with good foundation in some instances, that their children will be taken from them, or they will be replaced in the child's life by someone else (Hairston, 1991a, 2002b). With each prison term the likelihood of the incarcerated caregiver, often the mother, maintaining custody of their children decreases and risk of recidivism increases (Hairston, 1991a). In general, mental health difficulties are common among women in prison (Green, Miranda, Daroowalla, & Siddique, 2005), while separation from children during incarceration has specifically been associated with poor mental health. For example, in a sample of 94 incarcerated mothers, having fewer visits from children was associated with higher levels of depressive symptomatology (Poehlmann, 2005). Although it appears mothers' feelings of distress, depression, or guilt are particularly high in response to the initial separation from children, these do reduce somewhat but still remain present during their period of imprisonment (Poehlmann, 2005).

Although they are unable to be involved on a daily basis, many incarcerated parents want to continue to show care and concern for their children and other family members, and to participate in some decision-making when possible (Hairston, 2002b). Some prisoners struggle, however, to adjust to participating in family processes and events from a distance (Hairston, 2002b).

Impact on Non-incarcerated Partners, Caregivers, and Other Adults

Family responsibilities shift when an involved parent is incarcerated. When the incarcerated individual is a father, caregiving often falls to women, mothers, and other female relatives (Hairston, 2002b). As mentioned above, some family members experience feelings of guilt and relief when another family member is incarcerated, while others might feel resentful for having to assist financially and practically (e.g., providing childcare), particularly if this has occurred before (Brooks-Gordon & Bainham, 2004; Hairston, 2002b).

Those who step in to take over care are often unprepared for the needs of children of incarcerated parents. They can also experience stress due to such factors as loss of income of the imprisoned parent and increased financial pressure in maintaining the household (Brooks-Gordon & Bainham, 2004; Clopton & East, 2008; Hairston, 2002b), balancing childcare with employment responsibilities (some caregivers have to give up employment to provide childcare), providing for the children's health care, interacting with the education system, and coping with the children's emotional and behavioral issues (Clopton & East, 2008; Hairston, 2002b). Caregivers are often ambivalent about ensuring children visit the incarcerated parent, and are unsure about what to tell children about why their parent is absent (Hairston, 2002b). Caregivers may also be concerned about the impact on the child of anticipating and undertaking a prison visit (see below for further discussion; Clopton & East, 2008).

Research suggests some families are able to adjust to accommodate the missing member (Hairston, 2002b). Some families do seek assistance from external organizations, while others perceive this as risky because it leaves the family open to external scrutiny, may result in children being removed from their care, or may leave them vulnerable to experiencing shame or stigma (Hairston, 2002b). Although families may struggle and could do with accessing benefits or other support, many decide it is not worth the risk (Hairston, 2002b).

Impact on Children

There is growing recognition that children are impacted by parental incarceration (Brooks-Gordon & Bainham, 2004). Not surprisingly, parental incarceration primarily affects the children the incarcerated parent was actively supporting—whether financially or in other ways such as providing childcare—while it has little to no direct impact on children with whom the parent had no involvement (Hairston, 2002b).

As part of a wider study of 209 families, involving 424 children, a subgroup of 25 children (aged 3–18 years) with incarcerated fathers were interviewed; 17 were full interviews while 8 were only partial interviews (Boswell, 2002). Children reported on the effects, usually negative, that separation due to parental incarceration had on their lives (Boswell, 2002). They typically experienced a range of changes, including disruption and instability in their living situation, separation from siblings, and changes in school (Clopton & East, 2008; Murray et al., 2009). When fathers are imprisoned, children are most likely to live with their mother. When mothers are imprisoned, children are more likely to live with a relative other than a parent (e.g., grandparent, aunt), with a small percentage living in out-of-home placements such as foster care (Clopton & East, 2008; Hairston, 2002b). Problems finding suitable accommodation for affected children often occur due to the limited time available to make arrangements (e.g., in remand situations) and lack of preparation by parents, who are themselves often negatively impacted by the general chaotic and dysfunctional nature of the family circumstances (Flynn et al., 2016). In Boswell's study, the children described feeling sad and distressed about a range of issues since their fathers were incarcerated (Boswell, 2002). Issues that caused children distress included concern for their incarcerated parent's wellbeing, that their parent may not come home, and that the financial stress the family was under would continue; this contributed to children experiencing both social and emotional difficulties (Boswell, 2002; Hairston, 1991a).

Wakefield and Wilderman (2011a) state that "the average effect of paternal incarceration on children is harmful, not helpful, and consistently in the direction of more mental health and behavioural problems" (p. 791). In the Cambridge Study in Delinquent Development, separation due to parental incarceration in the first 10 years of life was associated with increased risk of antisocial behavior in boys at 8–11 years of age compared to four control groups where separation occurred for other reasons (Murray & Farrington, 2005). Even when controlling for other parental convictions and other childhood risk factors, parental incarceration was still found to predict antisocial outcomes through the life-course (Murray & Farrington, 2005).

Research suggests male and female children may respond differently to parental incarceration. For example, in a subsample of the Fragile Families and Child Wellbeing longitudinal study (born 1998–2000) in the United States (boys, $n = 1,190$, and girls, $n = 1,085$), Wilderman (2010) explored the effect of paternal incarceration on children's physical aggression at age 5 years. A range of variables were controlled for, including (a) parental characteristics (parental age, education, and self-control), (b) parental behaviors and home environment (e.g., number of children in the household, family poverty status, quality of the parental relationship), (c) neighborhood factors (e.g., level of social disorder and collective efficacy), (d) exposure to domestic violence, excessive use of corporal punishment, and harsh or erratic parenting, and (e) child characteristics (e.g., race, nicotine exposure in utero, low birthweight; see Wilderman, 2010, for further details). Wilderman found that paternal incarceration was associated with increased levels of physically aggressive behavior in boys at age 5.

The gender of the incarcerated parent also seems to influence the scale and nature of the impact on children. The relationship between *paternal* incarceration and behavioral problems in children (Wilderman & Turney, 2014) is a relatively robust finding, and does not appear to be mediated by other family factors (e.g., parental age, number of children in the household; Wildermann, 2010). But studies have found mixed results, from negative, to positive, to no effect, of *maternal* incarceration on children (Wilderman & Turney, 2014). In another paper from the Fragile Families and Child Wellbeing study, children with incarcerated mothers had high levels of behavioral problems and faced other disadvantages (e.g., poorer parent–child relationships, higher levels of maternal stress, lower levels of maternal and paternal post-secondary education, higher levels of maternal substance use during pregnancy, high levels of paternal and maternal substance use). But these poorer outcomes for children were often present in the child's life prior to maternal incarceration and were not independently associated with incarceration itself (Wilderman & Turney, 2014).

Maternal incarceration has been associated with higher levels of a range of teacher-reported behavior problems, such as poorer self-control, attention, and concentration, lower levels of cooperation, and higher levels of social and oppositional behavior difficulties (Wilderman & Turney, 2014). For some children poorer grades were evident, though for others there were no effects on test scores (Wilderman & Turney, 2014). Children have also reported having an incarcerated parent impacts their school experience (Boswell, 2002). Children's experiences of telling friends and school staff range from positive (e.g., being supported and having an avenue to talk about and share their emotions) through to negative (bullying, shaming, etc.).

In general, children of incarcerated parents are more likely than children without an incarcerated parent to demonstrate externalizing behavioral problems, and experience mental health difficulties (e.g., anxiety and depression; Murray et al., 2009). However, even though some important covariates have been controlled for in relevant studies (e.g., maternal and paternal age, education and self-control, child's ethnicity, number of siblings, maternal smoking, domestic violence, harsh punishment, etc.; Wilderman, 2010), it is not yet clear from existing research if these difficulties were *caused* by parental incarceration or were a result of the disadvantaged life these children experienced prior to the parental incarceration (Murray et al., 2009). One reason is that some key variables associated with parental imprisonment, such as prior behavioral problems, are not controlled for (Murray et al., 2009). What is clear is that, overall, children of incarcerated parents experience a range of disadvantages, and are at increased risk of psychological and behavioral difficulties (Murray & Farrington, 2005).

Prison Visits

In instances where contact is desired by an incarcerated parent and a child, and appropriate (e.g., the parent is *not* the perpetrator of abuse), obstacles can prevent this occurring or mean the contact is suboptimum when it occurs. For incarcerated parents, obstacles can have short-term (e.g., no contact while imprisoned) as well as longer-term implications for their parental role (e.g., legal termination of their parental role, poor parent–child attachment, rejection by the child). Although the rights of children are protected in the form of local legislation (e.g., national or state) and international agreements (e.g., United Nations Convention on the Rights of the Child; United Nations Children's Fund [UNICEF], 2006) visits often do not occur or do not occur frequently due to a range of barriers (see Table 11.1 for examples).

Some prisoners have no or few visits because they have no contact with their family and/or friends, or because of the challenges families face in visiting (Cochran & Mears, 2013). When faced with barriers to prison visits, caregivers have to decide how to prioritize their resources (Clopton & East, 2008; Loucks, 2002). Other barriers to maintaining parent–child relationships during incarceration can include the father's own social and emotional difficulties, such as their substance use, health and mental health difficulties, frequent incarceration, and poor parenting skills/knowledge (Hairston, 2002a).

The completion of each visit also necessarily results in the child having to leave their incarcerated parent (Siennick, Mears, & Bales, 2013). This process of repeated separation is particularly problematic in women's prisons; indeed, findings show that the main concern of incarcerated women is their children's wellbeing (Brooks-Gordon & Bainham, 2004). In semi-structured interviews with 74 mothers before and during incarceration, the mothers identified some of the difficulties incarceration created, including coping with the separation from their children and having to "mother" from prison (Celinska & Siegel, 2010). The women found that prison impacted their ability to maintain their maternal identity but also being able to actively stay involved in their children's lives and maintain the mother–child relationship.

Some incarcerated parents minimize or avoid contact with their children for a range of reasons (Hairston, 2002b), some of which are summarized in Table 11.1. In other instances, children may not know their parent is incarcerated (Hairston, 1991a, 2002b). External agency policies and practices can also prevent visitations occurring (Hairston, 1991a, 2002b). Finally, lack of contact during incarceration may simply be a reflection of the state of things prior to incarceration where a parent may not have been involved in their lives pre-prison (Hairston, 2002a).

Risks and Benefits of Visits for Children

Prison visits can also have, at least in the short term, negative effects for children. For example, about half of children exhibit behavioral reactions such as high levels of excitability and hyperactivity prior to a visit (Clopton & East, 2008). Findings of a survey of adults accompanying children indicated this is typically short lived, lasting the day of the visit (Clopton & East, 2008); however, accompanying adults can find such behaviors difficult to cope with in light of the other stressors they are coping with in relation to the visit.

Despite short-term negative effects, visits can have a range of positive effects. They reassure children about their parents' wellbeing, reduce negative feelings due to separation, and assist with overcoming some of negative effects associated with the absence of a parent and with family disruption (Clopton & East, 2008; Hairston, 2002b). Visits can also assist with the process of family reunification by supporting the ongoing involvement of and attachment to the incarcerated parent (Clopton & East, 2008; Hairston, 2002b). Contact can reassure children that they are still loved and cared about by their parent, and that their parent is managing their period of incarceration (Hairston, 1991a).

In the study by Boswell (2002), described previously, children's perceptions of visits varied between facilities, but overall, children liked spending time with their parent. In general, they viewed the constraints imposed on the process and arrangements of visits negatively (e.g., being searched, unfriendly correctional staff, seeing their parent's movements restricted, short visits, and long waits) and would have liked to have visits—processes and facilities—that allowed for as normative an interaction with their incarcerated parent as possible (Boswell, 2002). Children reported they appreciated positive aspects in facilities which were suitable for children (e.g., having a crèche), family visits, and friendly staff (Boswell, 2002).

Table 11.1 Barriers to Visits

Barrier	Description
Children dependent on adults	Children are dependent on their caregiver to facilitate a visit and the caregiver may not be willing to facilitate or allow this or could limit contact due to conflict between the key parties (Brooks-Gordon & Bainham, 2004; Clopton & East, 2008; Hairston, 1991a, 2002a, 2002b; Tasca, 2016).
Transport difficulties	Transport difficulties for visitors associated with remote prison locations and individuals being incarcerated considerable distances from their family (Celinska & Siegel, 2010; Hairston, 1991a, 2002a).
Costs	Costs associated with visits include travel costs to the prison, food and accommodation, caregivers or other adults having to take time off work, and finding childcare for other children in order to facilitate the visit (Brooks-Gordon & Bainham, 2004; Celinska & Siegel, 2010; Clopton & East, 2008; Cochran & Mears, 2013; Hairston, 1991a, 2002b; Loucks, 2002).
Rules and regulations	Families may lack understanding about the justice process (Hairston, 2002b) and/or experience difficulties navigating their way through a complex range of rules and regulations (Cochran & Mears, 2013). Correctional services can fail to disseminate information, and families may struggle to access information they need (Hairston, 2002b). Available information may be out of date, policies and rules may change without being adequately promoted (e.g., updated dress codes), and/or there may be variability in the nature and application of various policies across and within institutions (Hairston, 2002b), many of which are not child friendly (Loucks, 2002) and can appear restrictive and arbitrary to visitors (Brooks-Gordon & Bainham, 2004; Celinska & Siegel, 2010; Hairston, 2002a, 2002b). For example, there can be variability in (a) type and nature of visits (e.g., number of visitors, if children are allowed, if physical contact is allowed, and whether extended visits for children occur), (b) booking times, and (c) processes (e.g., required paperwork and acceptable forms of identification, who must accompany a child on visit, limiting the "privilege" of child visits and allowing children to only visit parents who are listed on the birth certificate (Brooks-Gordon & Bainham, 2004; Hairston, 2002a, 2002b).
Visit logistics	Concerns about visit logistics include long waits and relatively short visitations (Brooks-Gordon & Bainham, 2004; Clopton & East, 2008; Hairston, 2002b) resulting in stress and exhaustion (Loucks, 2002) for children as well as caregivers. The process of accessing the prison can be humiliating, intimidating, and frustrating for many, with body frisks, searches, poor treatment from staff, long waits, and dirty, overcrowded, noisy, and hot facilities (Brooks-Gordon & Bainham, 2004; Hairston, 2002a, 2002b). Visits can be canceled due to a prison lockdown at short notice (Brooks-Gordon & Bainham, 2004).
Environment	Concerns raised about prisons being unsuitable places for children, including (a) due to the higher rates of mental health difficulties in prisons than in community populations, (b) the relative standard of health care available in prisons, (c) environments which are not child-centered (e.g., lack of available appropriate food and no suitable activities for children; Hairston, 2002a, 2002b), (d) prisons supporting the development of beliefs which are procriminal in nature, and (e) exposure to violence (Brooks-Gordon & Bainham, 2004; Hairston, 2002a). These concerns are shared by prisoners and their families, and by correctional and social services professionals (Hairston, 2002b).

(Continued)

Table 11.1 (*Continued*)

Barrier	Description
Parents minimize or avoid contact with their children	Incarcerated parents limit contact for a range of reasons, including (a) to facilitate coping with the pressures associated with being imprisoned, (b) to avoid their own feelings of embarrassment, hurt, guilt, and powerless, and (c) to avoid finding out about things occurring outside the prison setting that they are missing out on and can do little or nothing about (Brooks-Gordon & Bainham, 2004; Hairston, 1991a, 2002a; Siennick et al., 2013). The holding of particular beliefs may impact the likelihood of contact occurring with children, such as believing (a) the children do not want contact, (b) the environment and regulations are not conducive to children visiting, and wanting to protect their children from the stress of a visit, particularly when a previous visit had been distressing for the child/ren, (c) visits are unnecessary as they will only be away for a short period of time, (d) there is nothing they can do for their children while incarcerated and they will "make up" for it after their release, and (e) disengaging from their children will allow them to move on with their lives and avoid them experiencing further hurt (Hairston, 1991a, 2002a, 2002b).

Risks and Benefits of Visits for Prisoners

Findings are mixed about whether or not family visits have a positive, negative, or even null effect on in-prison behaviors, depending on a number of factors. For example, visits from children can be associated with positive effects such as promoting mental health through reducing isolation, and supporting relationships and parental role and responsibilities (Cochran & Mears, 2013; De Claire & Dixon, 2015; de Motte, Bailey, & Ward, 2012; Hairston, 1991a). Some studies have concluded visits are associated with modest improvements in in-prison behavior. Other studies have found no effect; yet others have found visits to be associated with negative effects (Cochran & Mears, 2013; Siennick et al., 2013).

What is clear is that the effects of visits on prisoner conduct are complex (De Claire & Dixon, 2015; Siennick et al., 2013). Researchers have explored possible explanations around why this variability in findings might have occurred, though more research is needed to further unravel the influential factors. For example, in their review, Cochran and Mears (2013) found visits from individuals (family and others) with a history of offending can be problematic (e.g., due to bringing in contraband or reinforcing antisocial norms). In a large cohort of 7,000 inmates, Siennick et al. (2013) found visits from children, spouses, and other relatives were associated with decreased in-prison conduct problems leading up to visits, and then increased conduct issues in the week following visitations, which then gradually declined to normal levels. The pattern of visits from family seems to play a role. For example, it has also been found that more frequent visits were associated with a more rapid decline in conduct issues following visits (Siennick et al., 2013). In another study, those who were visited by children were found to be more likely to engage in rule-violating behaviors than those who did not receive visits from children (Benning & Lahm, 2016); though a review found rates of misconduct were higher for those who had visits initially but the visits did not continue (Cochran and Mears, 2013).

Some research implicates cultural background as an important factor. For example, research has found that non-Caucasian (e.g., African American, Hispanic, American Indian, Asian) mothers who received visits from children were more likely to violate rules, while mothers with higher levels of education were less likely to violate rules following visits by their children, compared to those with lower education levels (Benning & Lahm, 2016). Some participants in this research reported that their rule violation was associated with the pain that parents, particularly mothers, experience as a result of visits from their children (Benning & Lahm, 2016). However, the study did not explore the level of rule violation, which likely ranged from minor through to potentially more severe and violent, and also did not account for variables such as the number or regularity of visits, or the relationship between the timing of visits and misconduct (Benning & Lahm, 2016).

Mother and baby units are offered in some jurisdictions, enabling very young children to stay with their mothers (Brooks-Gordon & Bainham, 2004). The provision of these units recognizes the importance of, and supports the development of, an early attachment relationship between mother and child. But there are concerns about the impact separation will have on the child, when it occurs, and the unsuitability of prison environments for supporting child development (e.g., lack of developmentally appropriate stimuli; 11 Million, 2008). Despite efforts in some instances to support the development or maintenance of the mother–child relationship, such facilities are not offered to fathers, even when they may have been the primary caregiver prior to their incarceration (Brooks-Gordon & Bainham, 2004; Flynn et al., 2016).

Maintaining contact can be associated with wider positive outcomes for prisoners, families, the community, and institutions (Hairston, 2002b), including increases in successful reintegration and corresponding reductions in the risk of recidivism (De Claire & Dixon, 2015; Loucks, 2002) as well as the prevention of delinquency in children (Hairston, 2002b). For example, in a sample of almost 4,000 inmates in Florida prisons, visits were associated with small to modest reductions in all forms of recidivism (e.g., violence, property, drug offences) over a 3-year follow-up period, particularly when the visits were from spouses and other significant individuals, and occurred more frequently (Mears, Cochran, Siennick, & Bales 2012). Successful reentry for male prisoners is associated with those who are able to (a) maintain strong links with their families during their period of incarceration, and (b) establish a "responsible" partner (e.g., husband) and parenting role after release (Hairston, 1991b, 2002b). Although much of this research has focused on incarcerated males, family process factors have also been found to be strongly predictive of success for female prisoners (Dowden & Andrews, 1999).

Implications for Prison Visits

Practical Implications

While recognizing the role of incarceration in the justice system, it is also important for those involved (e.g., policy-makers, judges, psychologists, corrections officers, and managers) to consider the impact incarceration will have on children and families (Comfort, Nurse, McKay, & Kramer, 2011). Children of prisoners are a vulnerable group and they potentially experience short- and long-term negative effects due to factors associated with their parent's incarceration. The Cambridge Study found that, relative to children whose parent was not incarcerated, children with an incarcerated parent were at increased risk of poorer outcomes, including poorer mental health, lower levels of education and employment attainment, and increased antisocial behavior (Murray & Farrington, 2005). These social, economic, and wellbeing costs indicate that policy-makers need to take action (Comfort et al., 2011). Until agencies and professionals involved in the justice system start taking children into account, particularly when their primary caregiver is incarcerated, children "will continue to be disadvantaged by a system which considers them only as collateral damage in the exercise of justice" (Flynn et al., 2016, p. 351).

In an exploration of how the adult criminal justice system responds to the needs of arrested parents in Victoria, Australia, Flynn et al. (2016) raised a number of issues that are also relevant to other jurisdictions. For example, they suggest that in the current system there is little coordination between agencies, with no one agency/government department taking responsibility for ensuring the welfare and rights of the children are protected. Professionals must be cognizant of the intended and unintended effects correctional and other policies may have for prisoners and their families, including children, such as implications for family finances, relationships, contact and, in some jurisdictions, even termination of parental rights (Hairston, 2002a). There are benefits for children and parents in nurturing parent–child relationships during incarceration, thus professionals such as psychologists have a responsibility to support the occurrence of visits, while mitigating potential risks: for example, through the provision of suitable visiting environments (Hairston, 2002b).

Although correctional institutions may recognize the part prison visitations play in parent–child relationships (Hairston, 2002a), correctional *policy* also has an important role to play in family visits (Hairston, 2002a). As discussed above, barriers to visits include visitation policies and environments that do not necessarily support parent–child relationships (Celinska & Siegel, 2010; Hairston, 2002a). Visits can be a cost-effective approach (Mears et al., 2012) to assisting with maintaining relationships during a prison sentence while also increasing the likelihood that family will assist prisoners during reentry/reintegration (Cochran & Mears, 2013).

There are some relatively cost-effective ways in which the likelihood and frequency of visits could be increased (Cochran & Mears, 2013). Reducing common barriers to visits such as travel distance and associated factors (e.g., travel costs) could be addressed by housing prisoners closer to home (Cochran & Mears, 2013). Other practical remedies include simplifying complex regulations, effectively communicating changes to rules so that visitors understand them, increasing visitor hours and keeping them consistent, better access to visitor parking and public transport, reducing fees associated with visits, and improving visitor facilities (Cochran & Mears, 2013).

Attending to the physical environment by ensuring it is child/family friendly may maximize the chances of visits occurring (Benning & Lahm, 2016). Increasing the range of services provided as part of prison visitor centers would facilitate an increase in the support families of prisoners receive (Loucks, 2002). Despite an increasing commitment by many prison services to improve visiting conditions, especially for children (Brooks-Gordon & Bainham, 2004), there is still variability in the quality of facilities (e.g., from simple waiting rooms through to fully staffed facilities which provide support, counseling, and advocacy) and nature and length of visits (Brooks-Gordon & Bainham, 2004; Hairston, 2002b; Loucks, 2002).

Policies usually allow for a range of forms of contact (Celinska & Siegel, 2010; Hairston, 2002a). Children like visits overall, but also appreciate other forms of contact such as letters, phone calls, photographs, presents, and cards (Boswell, 2002). For parents, letters can reduce their stress as they allow contact while eliminating parental stress caused by children entering the prison environment (De Claire & Dixon, 2015). Policies that support a range of contact modalities should be actively encouraged as a means to maintain parent–child relationships, if contact is appropriate (it may be inappropriate if, for example, the incarcerated parent is the perpetrator of child sexual abuse).

Formal and informal supports for children and families are important (Boswell, 2002). Where imprisonment does occur, providing formal family and child support services is warranted. These services can facilitate visits, help families and children to cope with shame, guilt, and loss, and assist them in making "positive choices about their own behaviour and responses" (Boswell, 2002, p. 24; Murray & Farrington, 2005). Both during prison and, perhaps more critically, post-release, parenting programs can play a role in helping to optimize the parent–child relationship, increasing family cohesion and teaching parenting skills (e.g., use of appropriate discipline and behavior management strategies; Benning & Lahm, 2016; Eddy et al., 2008; Hoffmann, Byrd, & Kightlinger, 2010). In-prison components of these programs could also address substance use and mental health difficulties, as well as how to parent from prison and manage the reintegration period (Benning & Lahm, 2016; Eddy et al., 2008).

Research Implications

There are also implications for researchers. Although some of the earliest work in the field dates to the 1950s and was pivotal in providing some insights into the effects of prison visits, research in this area is still limited and a more nuanced consideration of visitations is needed (e.g., beyond looking at visits as a binary event: a visit occurred or did not occur; Cochran & Mears, 2013). Much of the research to date has also been qualitative and involved relatively small samples. Only a limited number of studies in the last 10–15 years have employed more robust methodological and statistical approaches (Cochran & Mears, 2013). More research is needed to tease apart some of the factors contributing to the positive and negative effects of visitations on incarcerated parents (e.g., on in-prison behavior and recidivism post-release) and their children, such as the type of visitors (e.g., spouse vs. friend) and/or pattern of visits (frequency and consistency of visits), expectations and perceptions of visits (e.g., motivation to change), ethnicity/race, and so on (Cochran & Mears, 2013), which previous research has not addressed at all or not adequately addressed to date. Cochran and Mears (2013) have suggested a conceptual framework with five dimensions of prison visits (the timing of visits; visitation patterns over time; type of visits; visitation experience; prisoner/inmate characteristics) in order to move theorizing forward and guide research (Cochran & Mears, 2013).

Conclusion

Creating a balance between the justice system achieving its aims and the interests of families, including children, is a complex process (Flynn et al., 2016). However, it is important to recognize the potential impact of parental incarceration on their children (Murray et al., 2009). There is rarely consideration of families, including children, when dealing with adults, many of whom are parents, in the justice system. There are the more direct and obvious costs of imprisonment but also the indirect costs (Wakefield & Wilderman, 2011b). Parental incarceration is associated with a range of negative outcomes for children, including emotional, social, and behavioral difficulties, although the nature of these impacts may vary depending on such factors as the gender of the incarcerated parent. These effects can be short- and longer-term, as not only does incarceration cause disruption to the parenting relationship (where one exists) during the period of confinement, but many parents and children also struggle to resume their relationship on release (Hairston, 2002a), particularly if contact while in prison was disrupted or ceased altogether. Overall, children of prisoners "are a highly vulnerable group with multiple risk factors for adverse outcomes" (Murray & Farrington, 2005, p. 1269).

Communication between the incarcerated person and family members, whether by visits or some other form of contact, is central to maintaining relationships and alleviating some of the negative effects of separation during incarceration for both the incarcerated parent and their child/ren (Hairston, 2002b). Visits also support longer-term benefits such as reductions in all forms of recidivism (De Claire & Dixon, 2015; Loucks, 2002) as well as the prevention of delinquency in children (Cochran & Mears, 2013; Hairston, 2002b). However, policy (e.g., around distance between incarcerated parents and their children) and practical aspects (e.g., process of accessing the prison for a visit, and the physical environment itself) must be child friendly in order to minimize the potential negative effects on children and maximize the potential positive outcomes of visits, including encouraging future visits.

Key Readings

Benning, C. L., & Lahm, K. F. (2016). Effects of parent–child relationships on inmate behavior: A comparison of male and female inmates. *International Journal of Offender Therapy and Comparative Criminology*, 60, 189–207.

Flynn, C., Naylor, B., & Arias, P. F. (2016). Responding to the needs of children of parents arrested in Victoria, Australia: The role of the adult criminal justice system. *Australian & New Zealand Journal of Criminology*, 49, 351–369.

Sharratt, K. (2014). Children's experiences of contact with imprisoned parents: A comparison between four European countries. *European Journal of Criminology*, 11, 760–775.

Tasca, M. (2016). The gatekeepers of contact: Child–caregiver dyads and parental prison visitation. *Criminal Justice and Behavior*, 43(6), 739–758.

Publications from the Fragile Families and Child Wellbeing Study and Cambridge Study in Delinquency Development such as:

Murray, J., Farrington, D. P., Sekol, I., & Olsen, R. F. (2009). Effects of parental imprisonment on child antisocial behaviour and mental health: A systematic review. *Campbell Systematic Reviews*, 4, Retrieved from https://www.campbellcollaboration.org/library/parental-imprisonment-child-antisocial-behaviour-crime-mental-health.html

Wilderman, C. (2010). Paternal incarceration and children's physically aggressive behaviors: Evidence from the Fragile Families and Child Wellbeing Study. *Social Forces*, 89, 285–309.

References

11 Million (2008). *Prison mother and baby units – Do they meet the best interests of the children?* London, UK: 11 Million, Children's Commissioner of England.

Benning, C. L., & Lahm, K. F. (2016). Effects of parent–child relationships on inmate behavior: A comparison of male and female inmates. *International Journal of Offender Therapy and Comparative Criminology*, 60, 189–207.

Boswell, G. (2002). Imprisoned fathers: The children's view. *The Howard Journal*, 41(1), 14–26.

Brooks-Gordon, B., & Bainham, A. (2004). Prisoners' families and the regulation of contact. *Journal of Social Welfare and Family Law*, 26, 263–280.

Celinska, K., & Siegel, J. A. (2010). Mothers in trouble: Coping with actual or pending separation from children due to incarceration. *The Prison Journal*, 90, 447–474.

Clopton, K. L., & East, K. K. (2008). "Are there other kids like me?" Children with a parent in prison. *Early Childhood Education Journal*, 36, 195–198.

Cochran, J. C., & Mears, D. P. (2013). Social isolation and inmate behavior: A conceptual framework for theorizing prison visitation and guiding and assessing research. *Journal of Criminal Justice*, 41, 252–261.

Comfort, M. L., Nurse, A. M., McKay, T., & Kramer, K. (2011). Taking children into account: Addressing the intergenerational effects of parental incarceration. *Criminology & Public Policy*, 10, 839–850.

De Claire, K., & Dixon, L. (2015). The effects of prison visits on prisoners' wellbeing, prison rule-breaking behaviour and recidivism. *Trauma, Violence and Abuse*, 18, 185–199.

de Motte, C., Bailey, D., & Ward, J. (2012). How does prison visiting affect female offenders' mental health? Implications for education and development. *The Journal of Mental Health Training, Education and Practice*, 7, 170–179.

Deflem, M. (2014). Introduction: The prison world. *Punishment and Incarceration: A Global Perspective*, 19, ix–xii.

Dowden, C., & Andrews, D. A. (1999). What works for female offenders: A meta-analytic review. *Crime and Delinquency*, 45, 438–452.

Eddy, J. M., Martinez, C. R., Schiffmann, T., Newton, R., Olin, L., Leve, L., ... & Shortt, J. W. (2008). Development of a multisystemic parent management training intervention for incarcerated parents, their children and families. *Clinical Psychologist*, 12, 86–98.

Flynn, C., Naylor, B., & Arias, P. F. (2016). Responding to the needs of children of parents arrested in Victoria, Australia: The role of the adult criminal justice system. *Australian & New Zealand Journal of Criminology*, 49, 351–369.

Green, B. L., Miranda, J., Daroowalla, A., & Siddique, J. (2005). Trauma exposure, mental health functioning, and program needs of women in jail. *Crime & Delinquency*, 51(1), 133–151.

Hairston, C. F. (1991a). Mothers in jail: Parent-child separation and jail visitation. *Affilia*, 6(2), 9–27.

Hairston, C. F. (1991b). Family ties during imprisonment: Important to whom and for what? *Journal of Sociology & Social Welfare*, 18, 87–104.

Hairston, C. F. (2002a). Fathers in prison: Responsible fatherhood and responsible public policy. *Marriage & Family Review*, 32(3–4), 111–135.

Hairston, C. F. (2002b, January 30–31). *Prisoners and families: Parenting issues during incarceration.* Paper presented at the From Prison to Home: The Effect of Incarceration and Reentry on Children, Families and Communities conference, National Institutes of Health Natcher Conference Center, Bethesda, Maryland.

Hoffmann, H. C., Byrd, A. L., & Kightlinger, A. M. (2010). Prison programs and services for incarcerated parents and their underage children: Results from a national survey of correctional facilities. *The Prison Journal*, 90, 397–416.

Loucks, N. (2002). Just visiting? A review of the role of prison visitors' centres. Retrieved from www.prisonreformtrust.org.uk/Publications/AZ

Mears, D. P., Cochran, J. C., Siennick, S. E., & Bales, W. D. (2012). Prison visitation and recidivism. *Justice Quarterly*, 29, 888–918.

Murray, J., & Farrington, D. P. (2005). Parental imprisonment: Effects on boys' antisocial behaviour and delinquency through the life-course. *Journal of Child Psychology and Psychiatry*, 46, 1269–1278.

Murray, J., Farrington, D. P., Sekol, I., & Olsen, R. F. (2009). Effects of parental imprisonment on child antisocial behaviour and mental health: A systematic review. *Campbell Systematic Reviews*, 4, Retrieved from https://www.campbellcollaboration.org/library/parental-imprisonment-child-antisocial-behaviour-crime-mental-health.html

Nesmith, A., & Ruhland, E. (2008). Children of incarcerated parents: Challenges and resiliency, in their own words. *Children and Youth Services Review*, 30, 1119–1130.

Office of the United Nations Commissioner for Human Rights. (n.d.). Convention on the Rights of the Child. Retrieved from http://www.ohchr.org/Documents/ProfessionalInterest/crc.pdf

Poehlmann, J. (2005). Incarcerated mothers' contact with children, perceived family relationships, and depressive symptoms. *Journal of Family Psychology*, 19, 350–357.

Sabol, W. J., Couture, H., & Harrison, P. M. (2007). *Prisoners in 2006.* (NCJ 219416). Office of Justice Programs, US Department of Justice. Retrieved from http://www.bjs.gov/content/pub/pdf/p06.pdf

Sharratt, K. (2014). Children's experiences of contact with imprisoned parents: A comparison between four European countries. *Europeran Journal of Criminology*, 11, 760–775.

Siennick, S. E., Mears, D. P., & Bales, W. D. (2013). Here and gone: Anticipation and separation effects of prison visits on inmate infractions. *Journal of Research in Crime and Delinquency*, 50, 417–444.

Tasca, M. (2016). The gatekeepers of contact: Child–caregiver dyads and parental prison visitation. *Criminal Justice and Behavior*, 43(6), 739–758.

United Nations Children's Fund (UNICEF). (2006). *Convention on the Rights of the Child*. Retrieved from http://www.unicef.org/crc/index_30229.html

Wakefield, S., & Wilderman, C. (2011a). Executive summary: Mass imprisonment and racial disparities in childhood behavioral problems. *Criminology & Public Policy*, 10, 791–792.

Wakefield, S., & Wilderman, C. (2011b). Mass imprisonment and racial disparities in childhood behavioral problems. *Criminology & Public Policy*, 10, 793–817.

Wilderman, C. (2010). Paternal incarceration and children's physically aggressive behaviors: Evidence from the Fragile Families and Child Wellbeing Study. *Social Forces*, 89, 285–309.

Wilderman, C., & Turney, K. (2014). Positive, negative, or null? The effects of maternal incarceration on children's behavioral problems. *Demography*, 51, 1041–1068.

Part III

Foundational Knowledge of Offending and Offenders

.

12

The Psychology of Violent Offending

Devon L. L. Polaschek
University of Waikato (Te Whare Wānanga o Waikato), New Zealand

Violent offending is a type of criminal behavior: one that varies widely in severity from minor assaults to mass murder and terrorist attacks. Depending on the definition and the jurisdiction, it can include fighting between men, sexual assaults, physical violence with and without weapons causing trivial to lethal injuries, certain accidental killings, kidnapping, robberies, damage to property, and other acts that threaten physical harm. It includes a core of acts widely agreed to comprise violence, such as intentional killing, but also some that may be illegal in one culture or time, but not in another (Tolan, 2007). Crime legislation in recent years has extended the range farther to include acts of stalking, harassment, smacking children, and cyberbullying. Among other criminal offences, violent offences are relatively rare in frequency, and are the most serious; convictions tend to attract the heaviest sentences (Felson, 2014).

Different jurisdictions have distinct definitions. In US (federal) legislation (US Code Title 18 Part I, Chapter 1, Section 16[1] a crime of violence is

1 an offense that has as an element the use, attempted use, or threatened use of physical force against the person or property of another, or
2 any other offense that is a felony and that, by its nature, involves a substantial risk that physical force against the person or property of another may be used in the course of committing the offense.

But in other jurisdictions all forms of minor assault are also included in formal definitions, making it important to be sure exactly which definition is in play when evaluating apparent differences between violent crime rates across countries, even on relatively consistently defined crimes such as homicide (Segessenmann, 2002).

A variety of classification systems has been developed to help to make sense of the diversity of violent offences. For example, the Australian Bureau of Statistics classifies violent offences by considering:

Whether violence is involved. If violence is involved the nature and level of the violence is considered including whether a weapon was used, whether abduction or deprivation of liberty was

The Wiley International Handbook of Correctional Psychology, First Edition. Edited by Devon L. L. Polaschek, Andrew Day, and Clive R. Hollin.

involved, whether the violence was sexual in nature and the outcome of the violence (e.g. whether life was taken, threatened or endangered). (Pink, 2011, p. 6)

Like this one, classifications used in the criminal justice system are mainly concerned with the topographical form of the behavior, its victim(s), what the apparent goal(s) were (e.g., sexual activity, acquiring property), the severity of the force used or injuries inflicted, and some contextual factors such as the presence of co-offenders, the use of weapons, and so on.

Violent offending can also be understood as a type of social behavior; although by definition illegal, violent offences can also be conceptualized on a continuum of aggressive behaviors, many of which are not illegal and may even meet with approval at times. Aggressive behavior has been defined as "any form of behavior directed toward the goal of harming or injuring another living being who is motivated to avoid such treatment" (Baron & Richardson, 1994, p. 7), where harm is defined as causing physical injury or hurt feelings, damaging a person's image, reputation, or social relationships, and stealing or damaging others' valued possessions, or harming other people, or animals owned by the person. The components common to all aggressive behavior are that (a) it is understood and intended by the actor to harm or injure, regardless of whether that intent is realized, and (b) the recipient has not consented to and does not accept the imposition of the harm (Krahé, 2013). This second component excludes medical and dental procedures, boxing and other forms of recreational and professional fighting, and consenting sexual practices.

Understanding Violence

Goal- or Motive-Based Psychological Typologies of Aggression

In addition to the criminal code distinctions between types of violence, psychologists hold onto the typological distinction between expressive (also called affective, reactive, hostile, or dispute-related) aggression and instrumental (proactive or predatory) aggression (Buss, 1961; Felson, 2005). Expressive aggression is described as being driven by anger, with its immediate goal to harm the recipient. It is also viewed as a reaction or retaliation to some form of external trigger, and impulsive, reflecting some loss of self-control capacity (Youngs, Ioannou, & Eagles, 2016). It may be reinforced solely by the reduction in tension that follows from having expressed oneself. People often say after such outbursts that they are satisfied that the other person now knows how they felt as a result.

The second distinct type is instrumental or proactive aggression. It is characterized as premeditated and unprovoked, with a goal beyond immediate victim harm, such as gaining material goods, addressing damage to one's social standing, or dispensing "justice" (i.e., punishing a deserving other). The distinction between these two is important legally, where evidence of premeditation versus provocation may be seen as having probative value (Fontaine, 2008). For instance, violent offenders awaiting trial may tend to de-emphasize the premeditative aspects of their offending, to reduce perceptions of culpability (Laurell, Belfrage, & Hellström, 2014). Although the law has long recognized that self-control should be taken into account in deciding the proportionality of sentencing, law is based on commonsense ideas about human cognition and behavior, such as the concept of "the reasonable man" (Fontaine, 2007), and therefore often does not map onto psychological understandings of human behavior. Yet psychology and law seem to have aligned these two definitions to a reasonable extent (Bushman & Anderson, 2001).

So, although this distinction has commonsense appeal, it does not hold up theoretically or in practice, because a number of the underlying assumptions are overly simplistic. For social cognitive psychologists, the expressive–instrumental distinction confounds types of cognitive processing with types of aggression. First, instrumental aggression actually shares with expressive aggression that it can occur rapidly in response to specific environmental triggers and be driven by automated scripts, especially for experienced aggressors (i.e., without apparent premeditation; Bushman & Anderson, 2001). The concept of *planned impulsivity* (Pithers, 1990) has been used to refer to this behavior, because the perpetrator can claim a lack of premeditation, when in fact the only spontaneous part of the behavior is that it happened in this place at this time. Conversely, both instrumental and reactive aggression can be premeditated, occurring after meaningful decision-making on the part of the offender (Felson, 2014). Second, anger is not uniquely associated with expressive aggression; several distinct roles for anger can be delineated, applying to both forms of aggression (Bushman & Anderson, 2001); for example, becoming angry (a) because the victim transgressed (e.g., partner was late getting dinner on the table) and seeking to punish her or teach her a lesson through the use of force, (b) when a robbery victim resists letting go of the sought-after property, leading to a severe beating of the victim, or (c) because the victim is the last in a long line of daily stressors and cannot defend themselves ("kicking the cat"). Third, the same motives can drive either type of aggression, while the exact same act when observed externally, may be driven by multiple motives (Bushman & Anderson, 2001). Finally, in practice many acts appear to be a blend of both types of aggression, and offenders seldom show evidence of specializing in one or another (Woodworth & Porter, 2002).

Perhaps the most substantial problem lies with arguing that angry aggression is a special type of aggression (Anderson & Bushman, 2002). There are at least two questionable assumptions about angry or hostile aggression that argue against this. One is that behavior can be caused by an emotion. For cognitive behavioral theorists and therapists, what we get angry about is very much determined by how we think. Angry aggression in pure form relies on the circularity of the concept of provocation: that a provoking stimulus is provoking because it provokes. In law, the basic idea of provocation in Commonwealth countries whose legal system is UK-based, was that affronts to a man's social standing, including his ownership of women (i.e., sexual jealousy) and his masculinity (e.g., being approached by another man for sex), justified a comprehensive loss of self-control (heat-of-passion crimes), leading to excessive violence and possibly death for the offending party(ies). But in reality, provocation is very much in the eye of the beholder (i.e., the interpretation of cues, whether accurate or not, is what drives both the anger and the "rightness" of the aggressive behavior), or may be defined by the shared, learned rules of a particular subgroup (e.g., rival gang members). Those most prone to reactive aggression are also those who are most likely to make aggression-supportive interpretations of (i.e., be provoked by) another person's behavior (Dodge & Schwartz, 1997).

The second problematic assumption is that people are static entities, rather than constantly learning and updating their understanding of the way the world works. Consider this example: a child wants to ride another child's tricycle. He thinks "[the rider] has been riding long enough. It is my turn now. He is being unfair and not sharing like he is supposed to." He gets angry and pushes the other child off the tricycle. The child runs off crying to his mother. The aggressor gets the tricycle. This example (adapted from Bushman & Anderson, 2001) is a commonly observed among the most violent members of our society, toddlers (Tremblay, 2003). It illustrates an important point about the distinction between hostile and instrumental aggression. The first time a child does an act like this, maybe it *is* an example of angry aggression. But the child in this scenario learns as a result that this act gets him what he wants: to ride the tricycle (i.e., an instrumental outcome). He may also learn that his anger was just, and that he can dispense his own justice. The next time he does a similar act, is it hostile or instrumental? We can learn early in life that purely affective aggression has other, valued outcomes; that particular acts can achieve particular goals. We learn that anger itself can be expressed strategically, given that being angry will change the behavior of others around us. Arguably we even learn when it is acceptable to lose self-control.

Pushing someone off a wheeled vehicle could be treated as a serious assault had an adult carried it out, but one of the key developmental tasks of becoming a prosocial child and adult is to learn not to do these more overt forms of aggression; many of us are successfully socialized to achieve that standard most of the time (Tremblay, 2003). But in the process we have many opportunities to develop schemas (i.e., cognitive structures that hold diverse information about a concept such as aggression, its properties, and how it relates to other concepts) and scripts (i.e., specific types of schemas that guide how to behave in various scenarios). Scripts serve to shape how we interpret social situations, how they should be played out, and what our roles could or should be (Huesmann, 1988). Scripts are part of a social information processing approach to aggressive behavior, and help to solve the problems underlying the hostile–instrumental dichotomy. In essence, taking a knowledge structure approach, every person has built up schemas about anger and aggression and, in particular, scripts that they use in order to interpret whether, for example, they are justified in getting angry when a person behaves in a particular way, and how they should respond to this transgression in the current context (Allen, Anderson, & Bushman, 2017).

Understanding Motives Through Social Interactionist Theory

The hostile/instrumental distinction also is inconsistent with more recent research on goal setting. The key ideas are that behavior can be underpinned by more than one goal at a time, and it is important to distinguish between proximate, immediate goals ("to harm…") and ultimate goals (…"in order to achieve"…). For example, Felson and Tedeschi (1994) argued that violence can be viewed as part of a wider pattern of socially coercive behavior (i.e., behavior we use to shape others' behavior in desired ways). They argued that there are three main goals or motives for aggression: to control the recipient's behavior, to achieve justice or retributive aims, and to protect or enhance self-image (Felson, 2002). Tedeschi and Felson (1994) suggested that these aims are not ends in themselves, but means to achieving much more meaningful goals or outcomes. Specifically, (a) people use threats of force or actual force to gain the victim's compliance (proximate outcome) so that the perpetrator can acquire particular resources and services, or can ensure their own safety (terminal outcome); and (b) people harm or punish others using physical violence (proximate outcome) in order to right a wrong (i.e., dispense justice for a perceived transgression), increase the perpetrator's social standing ("I am a mean dude who is not to be messed with"), or deter the victim or bystanders from behaving that way again in the future (all three are terminal outcomes).

Tedeschi and Felson's (1994) model is useful for formulating a wide variety of violent offences whether they are thought of as expressive or instrumental. For example, a man is challenged to a fight by another man in a bar, and subsequently assaults him. He is outraged and his immediate aim is to harm him, but by doing so he hopes to make it clear that he is a higher status man than the challenger, who should refrain from challenging him again. Perceived lack of respect is a common instigator of violent offending (Polaschek, 2008), and may be defended against both by men who simply want to be left alone and those who are seeking to increase their status (Polaschek, Calvert, & Gannon, 2009).

In a second scenario, a small-time drug seller discovers that his drug supplier has cheated him. He's angry about being ripped off, but bides his time, contemplating how best to respond. One day he wakes up, discovers he has run out of money again, and decides to act now, to solve two problems at once. He goes around to the dealer's house, assaults him, and steals his drug supply and cash. He acquires resources that deal with his cash flow problem and teaches the man a lesson too, punishing him for cheating him and making it clear to him and others that he should be respected and not ripped off again. In this example, Tedeschi and Felson's (1994) model accommodates the pursuit of more than one terminal goal (Polaschek, 2008).

Finally, a man wakes up one morning and finds that his wife is not in the house. They attended a New Year's party the previous night. He returned early, feeling unwell and leaving his wife in the care of her sister. Now he quickly becomes anxious, and then angry, suspecting her of infidelity after he left her. He rings the party host, and discovers that she was seen leaving with a man. Without further thought, he goes around to the man's house, in an increasingly angry state, finds the two of them in bed, and beats the man to death. This is the classic "crime of passion," implying that the precipitating circumstances are so dramatic as to have temporarily deranged the perpetrator into acting without his usual sense of purpose. Yet the other man no longer threatens his relationship, and he has had the satisfaction of dispensing his own justice, perhaps restoring his threatened social standing with others, and his wife may be deterred from future acts of infidelity (Polaschek, 2008). Can human beings really act this purposefully under such stressful circumstances? Social cognitive theorists would argue that they can, based on having learned scripts for such scenarios early in life.

Theories of Aggressive Behavior

Psychology has produced few theories specifically for criminal violence. One of the most flexible frameworks for accommodating research on causes of violence is the general aggression model (GAM; Anderson & Bushman, 2002), which, as the name suggests, is a model of aggression rather than violence. It includes a fledgling[2] model of how stable person-based aggressiveness develops, based on exposure to violent media. More recently, the authors have acknowledged the potential relevance of biological (attention deficit hyperactivity disorder [ADHD], impairment in executive cognitive functions, imbalances in hormones, and low arousability; Allen et al., 2017), and environment-based (pro-violence cultural norms, problematic family or parenting factors, adverse life conditions, being victimized, living in deprived and violent communities, involvement with violent or antisocial peers, group conflict, diffusion of responsibility, and excessive contact with violent media) factors (Allen et al., 2017). The GAM is described as a framework that integrates the progression of theories going back to the frustration-aggression hypotheses of the 1930s (Dollard, Doob, Miller, Mowrer, & Sears, 1939), including social learning theory (Bandura, 1973) and then progressing to the developing information processing and social cognitive models (Crick & Dodge, 1994; Huesmann, 1988). Alongside the GAM, there are alternative well-conceived integrative frameworks, sometimes combining distal and proximal factors to explain a single aggressive event (e.g., Huesmann, 2017).

The GAM's event-based model is useful in the context of violent offences. It can accommodate a wide range of factors to explain the occurrence of an act of violence, or its avoidance. This part of the GAM begins with inputs from both stable individual differences in aggressiveness and research on key acute risk factors (i.e., situational factors). Relevant individual difference variables include (but are not limited to): unstable high self-esteem and narcissism, aggressive self-image, long-term goals supportive of aggression, high self-efficacy for aggressive behavior, normative acceptance of aggression, positive attitudes toward aggression, hostile attribution biases, aggressive behavioral scripts, moral justification of violence, dehumanization, displacement of responsibility, high trait anger, certain personality disorders, low self-control, high neuroticism, low agreeableness, and low conscientiousness (Allen et al., 2017).

Situational factors that increase the likelihood of aggression and violence are alcohol, physical pain, heat, noxious stimuli, anonymity, provocation, recent exposure to violent media, recent exposure to weapons, or even pictures of weapons, congested driving circumstances, and crowding, social ostracism or rejection, social stress, and exercise (Allen et al., 2017; Anderson, Benjamin, & Bartholow, 1998; Groves & Anderson, 2017).

Together these inputs feed three distinct but often interacting routes—affective, cognitive, or arousal-based—to the final outcome in an event model: aggressive or non-aggressive action. These routes together make up the person's *present internal state*. The affect route is well known: increased hostility and anger facilitates thoughts of aggression. Other forms of negative emotionality may also pose increased risk. The arousal route draws on Zillman's (1988) excitation transfer theory, which postulates that arousal caused by experiences such as physical exercise or hot weather can be misattributed to anger, leading the aroused person to appraise the apparent provocateur as far more provoking than if the appraiser had been calm at the time. The cognitive route stipulates that aggression may be precipitated by cognition, such as expectations that it will achieve the actor's desired goal, or beliefs that violence is normal, or even required, in this context. Research underpinning the GAM reminds us not only that cognition can lead to affect and arousal, but that arousal and affect can alter cognition too, creating complex loops of reciprocal action.

As this internal state develops, it feeds into a cycle of appraisal and decision-making processes that vary in both their speed and quality. Under time pressure, appraisals are rapid and automatic, and may lead quickly to aggression if it looks to the appraiser that it would "work." If there is more time, and the person has more self-regulatory capacity, more effortful, conscious reappraisals may occur. The person may actively search their own memory, or the scene, for alternative views of the situation, which in turn may alter the present internal state. There can be a number of cycles of evaluating alternative inferences and discarding them. At some point, the person will reach a final appraisal and then will act; but the outcome may still be aggressive, and may still be committed in a state of high arousal and emotion, because the reappraisals may revive or maintain high emotion levels.

Several authors have applied or extended the GAM to explaining criminal violence. First, DeWall, Anderson, and Bushman (2011) outlined four applications of the GAM: to intimate partner violence (IPV), group or internecine violence, climate change, and suicide. The application to IPV is unnecessarily restricted in that the authors assumed that when sufficient time is available for thoughtful processing, the perpetrator will choose a non-aggressive option; but as I noted above, this is not a "given" if the person still reaches the conclusion that aggression is useful, justified, or necessary. The application to intergroup violence may have some portability to gang warfare, a pervasive concern for criminal justice systems, though the examples given by DeWall et al. are ethnic or nation-based.

A review by Gilbert and Daffern (2010) supports the relevance of the aggression-related knowledge structures described in the person-based portion of the GAM. Although their review noted the limited body of research on the psychological treatment of violent offenders, it supported the idea that programs for violent offenders need to be more specialized (possibly even individualized) to adequately address the degree of entrenchment, and the range of cognitive factors built into the GAM. The GAM is also applied to the treatment of IPV offenders by Warburton and Anderson (2018).

Theories of Criminal Behavior

Correctional psychology has often viewed violent behavior as a distinct domain of criminal behavior, much in the same way as it has viewed sexual offending. But the argument for distinguishing violence from other crime is not especially strong; viewing violence as belonging not only to the wider domain of aggressive behavior, but also to the wider domain of criminal behavior may enhance psychological understanding of and responses to violence. Whereas aggressive behavior is, for the most part, not illegal, criminal behavior is. So, to the extent that we can argue that criminal violence is an extension of crime, then understanding it requires that we also understand intent to harm in a manner that breaks the law.

In fact, specialization or its absence is one of the most important questions underlying theory development within the domain of criminal behavior. If there is little evidence to support specialization, then there is also no argument for crime-specific theories (Lynam, Piquero, & Moffitt, 2004), and potentially, no argument for crime-specific interventions (e.g., for violence). So, before proceeding to examine theories and models based on criminal behavior, it is useful to review what is known about patterns of violent and non-violent offending and evidence for specialization.

Frequency of self-reported violent crime

Although violent offences can be very serious and even lethal, minor violent acts are fairly common. For example, Archer, Holloway, and McLoughlin (1995) reported that 61% of a male student sample had been in at least one fight in the previous 3 years. Similarly, 75% of men in an unemployed sample reported a fight in the previous 5 years (Archer et al., 1995). Commission of assault, especially by men, is relatively common in longitudinal samples (e.g., 37% of men in the Farrington study reported having committed an assault between 27 and 32 years of age; only 3.3% were convicted; Farrington, 2007). In the Dunedin study,[3] 24.5% of 21-year-old men (Moffitt, Krueger, Caspi, & Fagan, 2000) and 13.5% of 26-year-old men (Moffitt, Caspi, Harrington, & Milne, 2002) reported physically abusing their partner in the past year. Adult women's self-reported past-year estimates of perpetration of moderate violence toward an intimate partner vary between 15.9 and 25.8% (Williams, Ghandour, & Kub, 2008); in the Dunedin study, at 21 years 39.6% of women reported carrying out some form of physical partner abuse in the past 12 months (Moffitt et al., 2000).

Of the student assaults reported to Archer et al. (1995), 15% came to police attention. Among the self-reported assaults in the Cambridge study, just 1 in every 132 led to a conviction (Farrington, 2007; Farrington et al., 2006). On average, about 24% of family violence incidents are reported to New Zealand Police (Ministry of Justice Research and Evaluation Team, 2014). But even though official figures are much lower than the real picture, there is a relationship between self-reported crime and conviction: rates of self-reported offences are often higher in those with convictions: 3 times higher in the Farrington sample.

Distribution of violent offences and specialization

Crime is very unevenly distributed across individuals. Several large studies have shown that about 5–6% of offenders commit about half of all identified crimes (Farrington, Ohlin, & Wilson, 1986, cited in Moffitt, 1993), or sometimes that 5–6% of a cohort (including non-offenders) is similarly disproportionately involved in crime (Moffitt, 1993). It is also the case that this group is disproportionately involved in violent crime, shows an earlier onset of criminality and of violence, preceded by multiple personal and social risk factors and adverse experiences, and may take longer to desist than others (Farrington, 2007). Non-violent offences often outnumber violent by at least 3 to 1 (Farrington, 2007). Similarly, those who commit violent offences are a minority of convicted offenders, often around 10% of a cohort (Brennan, Mednick, & John, 1989). But the more violent offences there are, the more the offender may also be involved in other types of offending (e.g., property, status, or drug offences; Thornberry, Huizinga, & Loeber, 1995).

Within this versatile high-risk pattern, there is some evidence for specialization. For example, Lynam et al. (2004) found no evidence of specialization in official offences, but did find some evidence with self-reported crime. Specialists were defined as those that reported that at most half of their offending was violent, and on predictors of career type, violence specialists and chronic versatile offenders who had somewhat fewer violent offences, by definition, were more similar to each other than to non-violent and non-criminal subgroups. A seminal study conducted using a complete Danish male birth cohort born in the 1940s examined three different definitions of specialization. They found that men with a first conviction for violence were much more likely to have a subsequent violent conviction than those with none, and there were more offenders with multiple violent offences than would be predicted by chance (Brennan et al., 1989). However, they did not argue the other way: that the bulk of violent offences is committed by violence specialists.

Even among types of violence, we may have over-focused on specialization. Most programs for violence perpetrators are for intimate partner violence. But there are likely to be common causal factors underlying violence by men both toward other men and toward women (Fleming, Gruskin, Rojo, & Dworkin, 2015). And different forms of violence are often perpetrated by the same offenders, whether youth, IPV perpetrators (Holzworth-Munroe & Stuart, 1994), or early-onset adult offenders (Moffitt et al., 2002). IPV and general crime perpetration also partly overlap within offenders (Hilton & Eke, 2016; Moffitt et al., 2000), and share some but not all developmental predictors and correlates (Farrington, 1994) as do IPV and other forms of violence. Generally, the pattern of personality correlates for instance is one of lower constraint in the convicted violent offenders compared to offenders with no convictions for violence, and to family violence perpetrators with no violence outside the home (Moffitt et al., 2002). We can speculate then, that temperament or personality may be more important with those who are more frequently and diversely violent.

Linking violent and non-violent offending

At least three distinct arguments can be made for why violent offending and other criminal offending, where they co-occur, should be considered as part of a whole rather than as distinct entities. First, during a criminal event, violent and non-violent elements may co-occur in a seamless manner, with offenders being ultimately charged with both violent and non-violent acts at the same scene. Offenders seldom seem to think of these two types of criminal actions as distinct, especially not when intimidation and threats are included as violent behavior. An offence may begin violently and then extend into other crimes. For example, a man who is assaulting his cousin for being disrespectful to his girlfriend also then steals his iPod because the offender always liked it. And a burglary of a house can easily turn into a violent offence if a member of the household is unexpectedly present, and resistant.

Second, most medium- to high-risk offenders commit both violent and non-violent crimes during their careers. Even for chronic offenders, the most common pattern is one of occasional violence and more frequent arrests for diverse other crimes (Brame, Mulvey, & Piquero, 2001; Weiner, 1989).

Third, risk factors for crime overlap risk factors for violent crime, suggesting common etiology. For example, among already identified violent offenders, scales constructed using potentially changeable risk factors for violence are at least as good at predicting the occurrence of any new crime, including non-violent crime, as they are violence (e.g., Wong & Gordon, 2006), and instruments that are well established as predictive of recidivism in general tend to predict violent recidivism as well (e.g., Level of Service Inventory—Revised [LSI-R], Psychopathy Checklist—Revised [PCL-R]; Gendreau, Little, & Goggin, 1996; Leistico, Salekin, DeCoster, & Rogers, 2008; Yang, Wong, & Coid, 2010). This overlap suggests that among those whose offending includes violence, there are common risk factors for both types of crime, which is also borne out in theory and practice. For example, the Dunedin study found that early socioeconomic and developmental adversity factors predicted violent and non-violent offending in 18-year-old men. Early temperament uniquely predicted violent crime (Henry, Caspi, Moffitt, & Silva, 1996). Relatedly, Felson (2014) notes that to understand criminal violence, we need to understand why people both break the law and harm others. According to this way of thinking, violent offenders are lawbreakers who are also prepared to inflict direct harm on others. Lynam et al. (2004) showed they are also the offenders with the most negative emotionality and lowest constraint, as young adults. And finally, they are also rule-breaking in non-criminal ways.

Taken together, these patterns of overlap between violence, other crime, and their correlates suggests that multivariate frameworks and theories developed for those with high levels of antisocial and criminal propensity will also offer at least partial explanations of violent events and why some people commit many more of them than others.

The Integrated Cognitive Antisocial Potential Theory

The integrated cognitive antisocial potential (ICAP) theory was first proposed by Farrington (1992). The version described here is from Farrington (2003); see Figure 12.1. The context for Farrington's work is an approach known as developmental and life-course criminology, which is explicitly concerned with a developmental approach to understanding offending, including which risk factors apply at each stage of life, and how life events relate to changes in people's antisocial potential through the life span, at the individual level.

ICAP was designed to explain offending in young men of low socioeconomic status, based on research from the Cambridge Study in Delinquent Development. It draws together research findings with ideas from diverse sociological and psychological sources (e.g., strain, attachment, learning, and routine activities theories). The ICAP's key construct is antisocial potential (AP): the "potential to commit antisocial acts" (Farrington, 2003, p. 231). This potential varies both over time and across people. Variations across people in "trait" AP are explained by factors that differ from those that explain short-term variations in antisocial potential. The two interact the most strongly for those who commit violent and other criminal acts. As the top

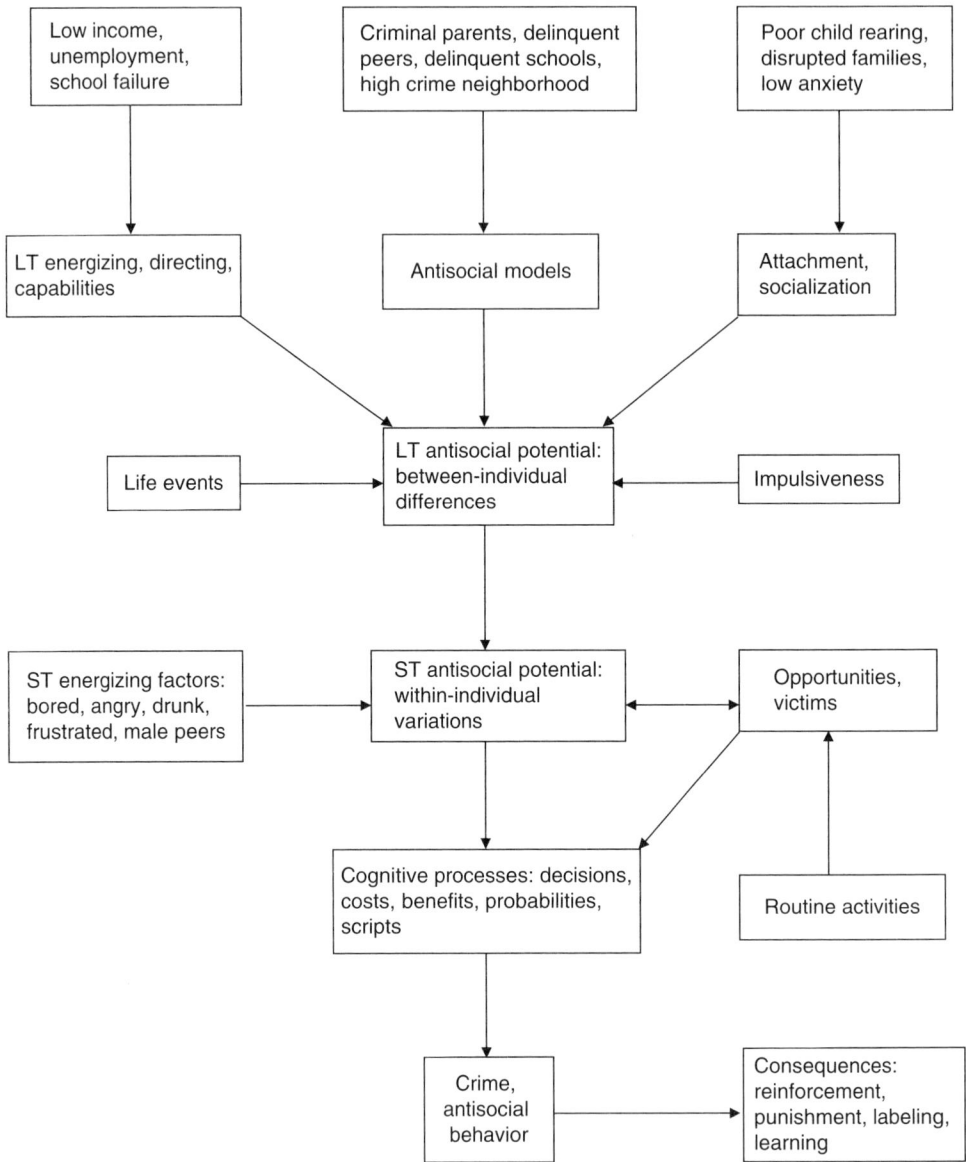

Figure 12.1 The Integrated Cognitive Antisocial Potential (ICAP) Theory. Note: LT = Long-term; ST = Short-term. © American Society of Criminology. Reproduced with permission.

portion of Figure 12.1 shows, childhood and adolescent development of the trait dispositions and vulnerabilities feed into AP in violent offenders. The bottom portion shows the circumstantial or situational factors that can trigger a specific offence, whether violent or otherwise, given individual stable differences in antisocial potential (Figure 12.1). In this regard, the ICAP resembles the GAM's combination of personality and event models; the major difference is in the ICAP's more explicit incorporation of crime-related factors (e.g., attachment to parents, socialization by delinquent peers, low anxious temperament, school failure) and processes (e.g., routine activities), drawing on criminological research on risk factors. The cognitive processes are not unpacked to the same extent as they are in the GAM and there is no explicit pathway to non-offending. Farrington (2003) also noted the minimal attention to genetic, hormonal and biological and protective factors, and desistance. Farrington (2007) proposed that the ICAP applied well to violent offending and described how. In doing so, he did not propose any significant changes to the theory in its general form. Instead he showed how it could accommodate violence-relevant examples (e.g., distinct situational factors such as escalation of a disagreement). Farrington (2007) also noted that longitudinal studies that direct themselves toward the development of violence potential are needed. The ICAP theory notes low anxiety and high impulsivity as the main temperamental factors pertinent to violent and non-violent crime; negative emotionality (found to be relevant specifically to violence in the newer Dunedin longitudinal cohort study; see above) and alienation (i.e., a sense of perceived victimization; Blonigen & Krueger, 2007, also noted in the Dunedin study) are not noted in the ICAP. It has now been subject to a number of empirical investigations in which antisocial potential was operationalized quite simply, using scores over time and in two generations on a brief antisocial beliefs scale (Farrington & McGee, 2017, in press). Farrington and colleagues acknowledge that despite the broad applicability of the model to violent and non-violence crime within a single criminal career, nevertheless situational factors may vary for types of crime; the model may benefit from further refinement in this regard (Farrington & McGee, 2017).

Life-Course Persistent Offenders

Tested initially on similar sources of information (e.g., the Dunedin study) and with a similar orientation toward explaining stable differences in propensity for criminal behavior to that of Farrington, Moffitt's (1993) typology of life-course persistent and adolescence-limited offenders is another durable theory of how some people are convicted of far more crimes, more diverse types of crimes, and more violent crime than most of the remainder of their cohort. According to Moffitt, chronic and high-risk offenders are the small proportion of young people (mainly male) who show very early impairments in neuropsychological functioning, include difficult temperament, delays in motor and language development, clumsiness, irritability, overactivity, and chronic inattention. These challenging infants are often parented by adults who share their characteristics, or are engaged in lifestyles that create adversity for the developing child (Moffitt, 1993).

The Dunedin study showed that children whose measurements as early as 3 and 5 years old showed them to be more stress-reactive, impulsive, aggressive, and prone to giving up easily with higher scores on *lack of control*, "an inability to modulate impulsive expression, impersistence in problem solving, as well as sensitivity to stress and challenge that is expressed in affectively charged negative reactions" (Caspi, Henry, McGee, Moffitt, & Silva, 1995, p. 59) were also more likely to have violent convictions at 18 years (Caspi et al., 1995). The Dunedin study is broader, both in the sample recruited and in the variables measured, than the Cambridge study (e.g., including myriad health variables).

A strength in Moffitt's theory is the proposed mechanisms for how factors interact to funnel people away from adaptive and successful lifestyles as they get older, shutting down escape routes to more successful functioning: cumulative and contemporary continuities. *Cumulative* continuities are those that accumulate over time, as "doors" to possible lifestyles close, or consequences snowball from the initial difficulties. So, a child who is irritable, restless, and aggressive in early schooling will have a gradually deteriorating range of academic and social outcomes that will lead to low-quality relationships and poor employment options in adulthood. *Contemporary* continuity arises when those same initial problems simply transmit themselves across the life-course. Irritable, restless, and aggressive children become similar adults who then have poor work options and unstable close relationships. According to Moffitt (1993), chains of both types of continuities unfold from early in life through to adulthood.

However, even the more positively adjusted adolescence-onset type can become trapped in a criminal lifestyle. A third mechanism that maintains people's criminal propensity after it might otherwise wane is *snares:* consequences of one's actions that make it hard even for motivated persistent offenders to work their way back to a better life. For example, offenders who might otherwise have moved into desistance instead may get caught up in a gang, or become addicted to expensive drugs, or have tattoos that discourage prosocial others from interacting with them.

Moffitt's life-course persistence theory is well supported by subsequent research (Caspi & Moffitt, 1995; Moffitt, 2007; Moffitt et al., 2002; Odgers et al., 2008; Piquero, Farrington, Nagin, & Moffitt, 2010). But its ability to account for development beyond young adulthood has come in for some challenge, with some preferring the term *early-onset stable antisocial behavior* to life-course persistent (Hodgins, 2007). Persistency or desistance well into adulthood are influenced by contemporaneous environmental events (Sivertsson & Carlsson, 2015). Most persistent violent offenders do show improvements in criminal and other outcomes later in life, if more slowly than their peers (Farrington, Piquero, & Jennings, 2013), and the theory is silent on the important question of how desistance and other positive life outcomes occur or develop (Polaschek, 2017). More extensive reviews suggest the differences between different trajectories proposed by Moffitt and others are more in degree than in kind (Jolliffe, Farrington, Piquero, Loeber, & Hill, 2017).

Both social psychological and developmental life-course theories are helpful in pointing up the myriad factors from different sources and at different stages in the process that may influence or at least predict violent behavior. Because these theories are seeking to explain observed patterns in longitudinal data—most relevant to this chapter being that violence is disproportionately committed by the more criminally committed offenders—they don't really explain exactly why these two phenomena go together. What is it about committing more crime that also seems to make it more likely that the person will also do more harmful crime? Is it the co-occurrence of social environmental risk factors and temperament that tips someone who would otherwise be a petty criminal into violence? Is it low constraint that explains both frequency and severity of rule-breaking?

Heterogeneity, Subtyping, and Psychopathy

Relatedly, there may be meaningful heterogeneity among repetitively violent offenders that future theory and research should seek to address. To date, most subtyping of offenders with respect to violence has been simplistically limited to those with and without psychopathy or its equivalents (see Blackburn, 1999, for an exception). For example, Hodgins (2007, citing Frick & Marsee, 2006), has noted that among boys with conduct problems, those without callous-unemotional (CU) traits display emotionally driven aggressive behavior, often in reaction to perceived or actual hostility from others. Conduct disorder is commonly comorbid with attention deficit hyperactivity disorder (ADHD), and in combination predicts adult criminality.

But CU traits may accompany conduct disorder and when they do, there is increased risk of aggression and crime in general. Hodgins (2007) noted that progress in prevention and treatment is hampered by difficulties to date in genetic research and in studies using technology such as magnetic resonance imaging (MRI) to understand expected differences in brain structure and function associated with hypothesized subtypes. To date, the connections between childhood "pre-psychopathy" and adult psychopathy are also not robust. Although there are demonstrations of CU children who go on to be psychopathic teens and young adults, it seems likely there are psychopathic adults who did not develop via that route.

And it is also unlikely that CU children are homogeneous: primary and secondary variants—the latter with significant anxiety symptoms—have been found among high CU adolescents too (Kimonis, Frick, Cauffman, & Goldweber, 2012; Kimonis, Skeem, Cauffman, & Dmitrieva, 2011). Those with anxiety were found to be violent more often over a 2-year period of incarceration than those without, with 92% of secondary variants detected for violence over that period compared to 54% of primary variants. The proportion of acts coded later as instrumental was equivalent across variants, but secondary variants committed more reactive acts.

With adults, one cluster analysis of a large sample of offenders meeting criteria for Antisocial Personality Disorder (AsPD; APA, 1994) yielded four types: primary and secondary psychopathy—the latter characterized by high anxiety and impulsivity—along with a non-psychopathic AsPD group and an unexpected fourth type, fearful psychopathy. Although no differences were found for general recidivism in the year after release from custody, 10% each of the secondary and fearful subtypes recidivated violently, compared to 5% of the primary psychopaths (a non-significant difference; Poythress et al., 2010). A meta-analysis found that the personality trait facets (affective and interpersonal features) were not predictive of violence while the more generic antisocial behavior and lifestyle features were (Yang et al., 2010). Another recent study found the PCL-R did not predict recent serious institutional violence, verbal or physical aggression incidents, and arrest for violence (Camp, Skeem, Barchard, Lilienfeld, & Poythress, 2013). These results and others suggest not only that we should be cautious in how we view relations between psychopathy and violence, but also that relying on psychopathy alone may have limitations as a way of understanding heterogeneity in violent behavior, response to treatment, criminal career progression, and other factors relevant to understanding criminal violence.

Neurobiology

Key biological variables at a number of different levels have been associated with violence; for example: inheritable temperament factors such as low constraint, high negative emotionality, and low resting heart rate; differences in monoamine oxidase A (MAOA) metabolism, less developed pre-frontal cortical structures, and differences in serotonin metabolism. Discussion of these variables has been limited in this chapter because of a tendency to overvalue their explanatory power at this early stage in such research.

The term *biology* in psychology is often used unhelpfully as a kind of shorthand, to signal consideration of a diverse grab bag of correlates of human cognition, affect, and behavior, and sometimes with the implication that their demonstrated presence somehow causes that behavior to be more predetermined than we would otherwise assume. But as Patrick and

Bernat (2009, p. 223) noted, "The brain is the essential common pathway through which heredity and experience operate to shape core psychological processes that determine behavior," meaning that we would *expect* both inherited factors and experience to operate on the brain in ways that are associated with differences in behavior.

For example, why would it surprise us to discover that the brains of high-risk violent offenders show patterns of activation in response to relevant tasks that differ from those of non-offenders? Wouldn't we infer such differences from their behavior? It does not follow that discovering these correlational differences explains the differences in behavior or alters criminal responsibility, any more than the myriad developmental events already discussed that predispose them to be much more likely to behave violently than you or I changes their legal culpability. Grimshaw (2018) recently commented pertinently that "all emotional responses, behaviors and experiences have neural foundations" (p. 15). Neuroscientific explanations, whether correct or not, have been judged more satisfying as explanations by lay people (Weisberg, Keil, Goodstein, Rawson, & Gray, 2008), which means it behooves us to ensure they are actually explaining rather than just describing phenomena.

It is currently unclear the extent to which differences in brain structure identified with psychopathy or criminal history may be beneficial in understanding violence. Simply identifying that "brains are involved" is unlikely to be helpful. For example, it has been asserted recently with regard to psychopathy that

> brain dysfunction in [particular] areas may contribute to the disinhibited, reward-driven, callous–unemotional behavior exhibited by psychopathic individuals. Deepening our understanding of these neural mechanisms and their contribution to psychopathy may inform the development of appropriate interventions, sanctions, and policies for addressing psychopathy in the criminal justice system. (Ling & Raine, 2018, p. 306)

Deepening understanding will result not from the discovery of markers themselves, but from understanding these associations and in particular their contribution to future behavior. Perhaps the most beneficial outcome of future research in these domains, as Ling and Raine (2018) imply, is in its potential to disentangle heterogeneity among violent offenders in a way that has implications for prediction of future violence or response to intervention.

Meanwhile, it is important for applied psychologists to have a clearer understanding of the different types of information yielded by different types of studies of biology. For example, etiological studies may identify proportions of genetic contribution to persistent aggression (i.e., behavioral genetics, e.g., twin studies). Molecular genetic studies are another example. Perhaps the best known is the gene–environment interaction, whereby the functional polymorphism associated with low MAOA activity has been found to interact with maltreatment during childhood, possibly via the mechanism of a failure to protect against neurotransmitter changes associated with abuse in a way that may promote violent behavior in adulthood. In other words, MAOA has an essential role in neurotransmitter regulation (Caspi et al., 2002). This finding is important for its ability to account for significant heterogeneity in responses to abuse, but its relationship to adult aggressive behavior is less consistent; it appears to be related to impulsive reactive aggression, and may increase the risk of this type of violence in adults through effects on social cognition (e.g., increased threat perception; Buckholtz & Meyer-Lindenberg, 2009). In fact, these authors suggest that rather than the sensationalist interpretation that such research has identified the "violence gene" or "warrior gene," this research is helpful mainly in pointing toward the relevant associated neural systems.

Understanding genetic and genetic-environmental interactions is one level of causal biological analysis. A second type of study translates these variables into brain structures and their functions and psychophysiological processes (e.g., using MRI, or dynamically measuring neurochemicals) that lead to violent behavior.

Many studies at this stage are better characterized as "marker studies", useful for suggesting potential areas for etiological research but not yet contributing in their own right to etiology, any more than do some of the psychological (e.g., alcohol use) or social markers (e.g., broken home) unless they are subsequently developed into mechanisms. They answer the much simpler question of whether there are biological differences between people who show different levels of a particular behavior (e.g., violence). Again these studies may use various technology such as MRI, positron emission tomography (PET), and electroencephalogram (EEG), neurotransmitter assays, and so on (Patrick & Bernat, 2009). For example, reduced P300 brainwave activity as detected using EEG technology is found in people with a history of impulsive aggression. It appears that it is itself a marker of inheritable externalizing temperament, which leads to diverse social and personal dysfunction, not just violent behavior. Knowing that a person is high on externalizing temperament, how does knowledge of distinct P300 response shed light on whether it results in behavior with distinct characteristics? These are vital questions to be addressed as investigations of biological markers of violence continue.

Conclusions

Violent offending, particularly under the umbrella of aggressive or coercive behavior, has received the most attention in psychology from theorists and, particularly, experimental researchers. Consequently, much of the empirical base consists of cross-sectional studies with an emphasis on situational influences, or interactions between situational and person-based influences at that point in time. This body of work is particularly strong in elucidating cognitive factors, with much of it being conducted within a social cognitive framework, and it is useful in indicating the circumstances in which violence is more or less likely to occur.

But the individual propensity for violence in various circumstances is not randomly distributed across the population. So in contrast to this knowledge, developmental life-course criminology has proposed and tested violence-prone trajectories of criminal development, alongside less crime- and violence-prone types, to identify who is most likely to be violent across time. Theories such as Moffitt's developmental taxonomy and Farrington's ICAP help to address the key factors that lead to the propensity to be involved in crime and violence across the life-course, and promote the view that these factors are more similar than different over time for each type of crime. Some of this work has also considered protective factors (Pardini, Loeber, Farrington, & Stouthamer-Loeber, 2012), and desistance, or at least long-term adjustment including reductions in reoffending (Jennings, Rocque, Fox, Piquero, & Farrington, 2016).

One area that is missing therefore is longitudinal psychological research specifically focused on criminal violence, and accompanying theory. This approach, by necessity, would recognize overlapping risk factors for different types of outcomes (e.g., other crime, other aggressive behavior), but would intend to make violence its primary focus, rather than secondary to a wider focus on crime or aggression. In the meantime, the best view of the psychological causes of violent behavior combines individual risk factors for crime with situational precipitants, recognizing that it is more than likely that situational precipitants may be distinct for different types of violence and for violent versus non-violent crime. More analyses of temperamental factors from a psychological perspective would be a good addition to this literature, since temperament tentatively has been identified as distinctively involved in violence (Henry et al., 1996). Currently, examinations of temperament or personality in psychology are limited often to correlates or components of psychopathy, with the problem being that psychopathy really needs unpacking into its constituent components to advance this approach further. Similarly, diagnoses of personality disorder more generally are of little help, since the resulting labels pathologize people while conferring little explanatory power. Advances on the personality front would be better conceptualizing the key issues in terms of transdiagnostic mechanisms, rather than diagnostic categories (Clarkin, Cain, & Livesley, 2015; Livesley, 2012).

Research into the roles of biological and genetic factors continues to develop as new technologies develop. However, good theory is needed to ensure that we don't simply mistake markers of mechanisms, that we already see in behavior, for actual causes. Some biological markers, such as low resting heart rate, or chronic hypervigilance due to early trauma exposure, seem more likely to have potential explanatory power in violent career development over time than do cross-sectional studies conducted in adults in a lab environment that show differences in brain functions and structures, but time will tell in this rapidly developing field.

Notes

1   Retrieved from https://www.law.cornell.edu/uscode/text/18/16.
2   The earlier versions used the example of violent media as the main developmental factor (Anderson & Bushman, 2002), and until recently, had limited inclusion of biological and cultural factors as influences on the development of aggressive personality (Allen et al., 2017). The final section of the chapter, on the development of violent offenders, discusses more complete accounts of how a predisposition to violent behavior develops.
3   The Dunedin Multidisciplinary Health and Development Study, known as the Dunedin study, is based in the University of Otago, New Zealand. It is following the lives of 1,037 people born at Dunedin's maternity hospital between April 1, 1972, and March 31, 1973. The sample is largely composed of European New Zealanders.

Key Readings

Anderson, C. A., & Bushman, B. J. (2002). Human aggression. *Annual Review of Psychology*, 53, 27–51.

Farrington, D. P. (2007). Origins of violent behavior over the life span. In D. J. Flannery, A. T. Vazsonyi, & I. D. Waldman (Eds.), *The Cambridge handbook of violent behavior and aggression* (pp. 19–48). Cambridge, UK: Cambridge University Press.

Hodgins, S., Viding, E., & Plodowski, A. (Eds.) (2009). *The neurobiological basis of violence: Science and rehabilitation*. Oxford, UK: Oxford University Press.

Moffitt, T. E., Caspi, A., Harrington, H., & Milne, B. J. (2002). Males on the life-course-persistent and adolescence-limited antisocial pathways: Follow-up at age 26 years. *Development and Psychopathology*, 14, 179–207.

Poythress, N. G., Edens, J. F., Skeem, J. L., Lilienfeld, S. O., Douglas, K. S., Frick, P. J., ... & Wang, T. (2010). Identifying subtypes among offenders with antisocial personality disorder: A cluster-analytic study. *Journal of Abnormal Psychology*, 119, 389–400.

References

Allen, J. J., Anderson, C. A., & Bushman, B. (2017). The general aggression model. *Current Opinion in Psychology*, 19, 75–80.

American Psychiatric Association (1994). *Diagnostic and Statistical Manual of Mental Disorders* (4th ed.). Washington DC: Author.

Anderson, C. A., Benjamin, A. J., & Bartholow, B. D. (1998). Does the gun pull the trigger? Automatic priming effects of weapon pictures and weapon names. *Psychological Science*, 9, 308–314.

Anderson, C. A., & Bushman, B. J. (2002). Human aggression. *Annual Review of Psychology*, 53, 27–51.

Archer, J., Holloway, R., & McLoughlin, K. (1995). Self-reported physical aggression among young men. *Aggressive Behavior*, 21, 325–342.

Bandura, A. (1973). *Aggression: A social learning analysis.* Englewood Cliffs, NJ: Prentice Hall.

Baron, R. A., & Richardson, D. R. (1994). *Human aggression* (2nd ed.). New York, NY: Plenum.

Blackburn, R. (1999). Violence and personality distinguishing among violent offenders. In D. Curran, & W. G. McCarthey (Eds.), *Psychological perspectives on serious criminal risk* (pp. 109–127). Leicester, UK: BPS.

Blonigen, D. M., & Krueger, R. F. (2007). Personality and vioelnce: The unifying role of structrual models of personality. In D. J. Flannery, A. T. Vazsonyi, & I. D. Waldman (Eds.), *The Cambridge handbook of violent behavior and aggression* (pp. 288–305). Cambridge, UK: Cambridge University Press.

Brame, R., Mulvey, E. P., & Piquero, A. R. (2001). On the development of different kinds of criminal activity. *Sociological Methods & Research*, 29, 319–341.

Brennan, P., Mednick, S., & John, R. (1989). Specialization in violence: Evidence of a criminal sub-group. *Criminology*, 27, 437–453.

Buckholtz, J. W., & Meyer-Lindenberg, A. (2009). Gene-brain associations: The example of MAOA. In S. Hodgins, E. Viding, & A. Plodowski (Eds.), *The neurobiological basis of violence: Science and rehabilitation* (pp. 265–285). Oxford, UK: Oxford University Press.

Bushman, B. J., & Anderson, C. A. (2001). Is it time to pull the plug on the hostile vs. instrumental aggression dichotomy? *Psychological Review*, 108, 273–279.

Buss, A. H. (1961). *The psychology of aggression.* New York, NY: Wiley.

Camp, J., Skeem, J. L., Barchard, K., Lilienfeld, S., & Poythress, N. G. (2013). Psychopathic predators? getting specific about the relation between psychopathy/antisociality and violence. *Journal of Consulting and Clinical Psychology*, 81, 467–480.

Caspi, A., Henry, B., McGee, R., Moffitt, T., & Silva, P. (1995). Temperamental origins of child and adolescent behavior problems: From age 3 to age 15. *Child Development*, 66, 55–68.

Caspi, A., McClay, J., Moffitt, T. E., Mill, J., Martin, J., Craig, I. W., … & Poulton, R. (2002). Role of genotype in the cycle of violence in maltreated children. *Science*, 297(5582), 851–854.

Caspi, A., & Moffitt, T. E. (1995). The continuity of maladaptive behavior: From description to understanding in the study of antisocial behavior. In D. Cicchetti, & D. J. Cohen (Eds.), *Developmental psychopathology* (Vol. 2: Risk, disorder and adaptation) (pp. 472–511). Oxford, UK: Wiley.

Clarkin, J. F., Cain, N., & Livesley, W. J. (2015). An integrated approach to treatment of patients with personality disorders. *Journal of Psychotherapy Integration*, 25, 3–12.

Crick, N. R., & Dodge, K. A. (1994). A review and reformulation of social information-processing mechanisms in children's social adjustment. *Psychological Bulletin*, 115, 74–101.

DeWall, C. N., Anderson, C. A., & Bushman, B. J. (2011). The general aggression model: Theoretical extensions to violence. *Psychology of Violence*, 1, 245–258.

Dodge, K. A., & Schwartz, D. (1997). Social information processing mechanisms in aggressive behavior. In D. M. Stoff, J. Breiling, & J. D. Maser (Eds.), *Handbook of antisocial behavior* (pp. 171–180). New York, NY: Wiley.

Dollard, J., Doob, L. W., Miller, N. E., Mowrer, O. H., & Sears, R. R. (1939). *Frustration and aggression.* New Haven, CT: Yale University Press.

Farrington, D. P. (1992). Explaining the beginning, progress, and ending of antisocial behavior from birth to adulthood. In J. McCord (Ed.), *Facts, frameworks and forecasts: Advances in criminological theory* (Vol. 3) (pp. 253–286). New Brunswick, NJ: Transaction.

Farrington, D. P. (1994). Childhood, adolescent, and adult features of violent males. In L. R. Huesmann (Ed.), *Aggressive behavior: Current perspectives* (pp. 215–240). New York, NY: Plenum.

Farrington, D. P. (2003). Developmental and life-course criminology: Key theoretical and empirical issues—the 2002 Sutherland Award address. *Criminology*, 41, 221–255.

Farrington, D. P. (2007). Origins of violent behavior over the life span. In D. J. Flannery, A. T. Vazsonyi, & I. D. Waldman (Eds.), *The Cambridge handbook of violent behavior and aggression* (pp. 19–48). Cambridge, UK: Cambridge University Press.

Farrington, D. P., Coid, J. W., Harnett, L., Jolliffe, D., Soteriou, N., Turner, R., & West, D. J. (2006). *Criminal careers up to the age of 50 and life success up to the age of 48: New findings from the Cambridge Study in Delinquent Development.* London, UK: Home Office.

Farrington, D. P., & McGee, T. R. (in press). The Integrated Cognitive Antisocial Potential (ICAP) theory: New empirical tests. In D. P. Farrington, L. Kazemian, & A. R. Piquero (Eds.), *The Oxford handbook on developmental and life-course criminology.* New York, NY: Oxford University Press.

Farrington, D. P., Piquero, A. R., & Jennings, W. G. (2013). *Offending from childhood to late middle age: Recent results from the Cambridge Study in Delinquent Development.* New York, NY: Springer.

Felson, R. B. (2002). *Violence and gender re-examined.* Washington, DC: American Psychological Association.

Felson, R. B. (2005). Violence as instrumental behavior. In K. Kelloway, J. Barling, & J. Hurrell (Eds.), *Handbook of workplace violence* (pp. 7–28). Thousand Oaks, CA: Sage.

Felson, R. B. (2014). What are violent offenders thinking? In B. LeClerc, & R. Wortley (Eds.), *Cognition and crime: Offender decision making and script analyses* (pp. 12–25). Abingdon, UK: Routledge.

Felson, R. B., & Tedeschi, J. T. (Eds.) (1994). *Aggression and violence: Social interactionist perspectives.* Washington, DC: American Psychological Association.

Fleming, P. J., Gruskin, S., Rojo, F., & Dworkin, S. L. (2015). Men's violence against women and men are inter-related: Recommendations for simultaneous intervention. *Social Science and Medicine*, 146, 249–256.

Fontaine, R. G. (2007). Disentangling the psychology and law of instrumental and reactive subtypes of aggression. *Psychology, Public Policy, and Law*, 13, 143–165.

Fontaine, R. G. (2008). Reactive cognition, reactive emotion: Toward a more psychologically informed understanding of reactive homicide. *Psychology, Public Policy, and Law*, 14, 243–261.

Frick, P. J., & Marsee, M. A. (2006). Psychopathy and developmental pathways to antisocial behavior in youth. In C. J. Patrick (Ed.), *Handbook of psychopathy* (pp. 355–374). New York, NY: Guilford.

Gendreau, P., Little, T., & Goggin, C. (1996). A meta-analysis of the predictors of adult offender recidivism: What works! *Criminology*, 34, 575–607.

Gilbert, F., & Daffern, M. (2010). Intergrating contemporary aggression theory with violent offender treatment: How thoroughly do interventions target violent behavior? *Aggression and Violent Behavior*, 15, 167–180.

Grimshaw, G. M. (2018). Affective neuroscience: A primer with implications for forensic psychology. *Psychology, Crime & Law*, 24, 258–278.

Groves, C. L., & Anderson, C. A. (2017). Aversive events and aggression. In B. J. Bushman (Ed.), *Aggression and violence: A social psychological perspective* (pp. 139–154). New York, NY: Routledge.

Henry, B., Caspi, A., Moffitt, T. E., & Silva, P. A. (1996). Temperamental and familial predictors of violent and nonviolent criminal convictions: Age 3 to age 18. *Developmental Psychology*, 32, 614–623.

Hilton, N. Z., & Eke, A. W. (2016). Non-specialization of criminal careers among intimate partner violence offenders. *Criminal Justice and Behavior*, 43, 1347–1363.

Hodgins, S. (2007). Persistent violent offending: What do we know? *British Journal of Psychiatry*, 190(Suppl. 49), s12–s14.

Holzworth-Munroe, A., & Stuart, G. L. (1994). Typologies of male batterers: Three subtypes and the differences among them. *Psychological Bulletin*, 116, 476–497.

Huesmann, L. R. (1988). An information processing model for the development of aggression. *Aggressive Behavior*, 14, 13–24.

Huesmann, L. R. (2017). Aversive events and aggression. In B. J. Bushman (Ed.), *Aggression and violence: A social psychological perspective* (pp. 3–21). New York, NY: Routledge.

Jennings, W. G., Rocque, M., Fox, B. H., Piquero, A. R., & Farrington, D. P. (2016). Can they recover? An assessment of adult adjustment problems among males in the abstainer, recovery, life-course persistent, and adolescence-limited pathways followed up to age 56 in the Cambridge Study in Delinquent Development. *Development and Psychopathology*, 28, 537–549.

Jolliffe, D., Farrington, D. P., Piquero, A. R., Loeber, R., & Hill, K. G. (2017). Systematic review of early risk factors for life-course-persistent, adolescence-limited, and late-onset offenders in prospective longitudinal studies. *Aggression and Violent Behavior*, 33, 15–23.

Kimonis, E. R., Frick, P. J., Cauffman, E., & Goldweber, A. (2012). Primary and secondary variants of juvenile psychopathy differ in emotional processing. *Law and Human Behavior*, 24, 1091–1103.

Kimonis, E. R., Skeem, J. L., Cauffman, E., & Dmitrieva, J. (2011). Are secondary variants of juvenile psychopathy more reactively violent and less psychosocially mature than primary variants. *Law and Human Behavior*, 35, 381–391.

Krahé, B. (2013). *The social psychology of aggression* (2nd ed.). London, UK: Psychology Press.

Laurell, J., Belfrage, H., & Hellström, Å. (2014). Deceptive behaviour and instrumental violence among psychopathic and non-psychopathic violent forensic psychiatric patients. *Psychology, Crime & Law*, 20, 467–479.

Leistico, A., Salekin, R. T., DeCoster, J., & Rogers, R. (2008). A large-scale meta-analysis relating the Hare measures of psychopathy to antisocial conduct. *Law and Human Behavior*, 32, 28–45.

Livesley, W. J. (2012). Integrated treatment: A conceptual framework for an evidence-based approach to the treatment of personality disorder. *Journal of Personality Disorders*, 26, 17–42.

Ling, S., & Raine, A. (2018). The neuroscience of psychopathy and forensic implications. *Psychology, Crime & Law*, 24, 296–312.

Lynam, D. R., Piquero, A. R., & Moffitt, T. E. (2004). Specialisation and propensity to violence: Support from self-reports but not official records. *Journal of Contemporary Criminal Justice*, 20, 215–228.

Ministry of Justice Research and Evaluation Team. (2014). New Zealand crime and safety survey main findings. Retrieved from http://www.justice.govt.nz/assets/Documents/Publications/NZCASS-201602-Main-Findings-Report-Updated.pdf

Moffitt, T. E. (1993). Adolescence-limited and life-course-persistent antisocial behavior: A developmental taxonomy. *Psychological Review*, 100, 674–701.

Moffitt, T. E. (2007). A review of research on the taxonomy of life-course persistent versus adolescence-limited antisocial behavior. In D. J. Flannery, A. T. Vazsonyi, & I. D. Waldman (Eds.), *The Cambridge handbook of violent behaviour and aggression* (pp. 49–74). Cambridge, UK: Cambridge University Press.

Moffitt, T. E., Caspi, A., Harrington, H., & Milne, B. J. (2002). Males on the life-course-persistent and adolescence-limited antisocial pathways: Follow-up at age 26 years. *Development and Psychopathology*, 14, 179–207.

Moffitt, T. E., Krueger, R. F., Caspi, A., & Fagan, J. (2000). Partner abuse and general crime: How are they the same? How are they different? *Criminology*, 38, 199–232.

Odgers, C. A., Moffitt, T. E., Broadbent, J. M., Dickson, N., Hancox, R. J., Harrington, H., … & Caspi, A. (2008). Female and male antisocial trajectories: From childhood origins to adult outcomes. *Development and Psychopathology*, 20, 673–716.

Pardini, D. A., Loeber, R., Farrington, D. P., & Stouthamer-Loeber, M. (2012). Identifying direct protective factors for nonviolence. *American Journal of Preventive Medicine*, 43(2S1), S28–S40.

Patrick, C. J., & Bernat, E. M. (2009). From markers to mechanisms: Using psychophysiological measures to elucidate basic processes underlying aggressive externalizing behaviour. In S. Hodgins, E. Viding, & A. Plodowski (Eds.), *The neurobiological basis of violence: Science and rehabilitation* (pp. 223–250). Oxford, UK: Oxford University Press.

Pink, B. (2011). *Australian and New Zealand Standard Offence Classification (ANZSOC) Australia.* Canberra, Australia: ABS Retrieved from http://www.ausstats.abs.gov.au/Ausstats/subscriber.nsf/0/5CE97E870F7A29EDCA2578A200143125/$File/12340_2011.pdf

Piquero, A. R., Farrington, D. P., Nagin, D. S., & Moffitt, T. E. (2010). Trajectories of offending and their relation to life failure in late middle age: Findings from the Cambridge Study in Delinquent Development. *Journal of Research in Crime and Delinquency, 47*, 151–173.

Pithers, W. D. (1990). Relapse prevention with sexual aggressors: A method for maintaining therapeutic gain and enhancing external supervision. In W. L. Marshall, D. R. Laws, & H. E. Barbaree (Eds.), *Handbook of sexual assault: Issues, theories, and treatment of the offender* (pp. 343–361). New York, NY: Plenum.

Polaschek, D. L. L. (2008). Violent offenders. In K. Fritzon, & P. Wilson (Eds.), *Forensic and criminal psychology: An Australasian perspective* (pp. 75–85). North Ryde, Australia: McGraw-Hill.

Polaschek, D. L. L. (2017). Prevention of recidivism in violent and aggressive offenders. In P. Sturmey (Ed.), *The Wiley handbook of violence and aggression.* Chichester, UK: Wiley.

Polaschek, D. L. L., Calvert, S. W., & Gannon, T. A. (2009). Linking violent thinking: Implicit theory-based research with violent offenders. *Journal of Interpersonal Violence, 24*, 75–96.

Poythress, N. G., Edens, J. F., Skeem, J. L., Lilienfeld, S. O., Douglas, K. S., Frick, P. J., … & Wang, T. (2010). Identifying subtypes among offenders with antisocial personality disorder: A cluster-analytic study. *Journal of Abnormal Psychology, 119*, 389–400.

Segessenmann, T. (2002). International comparison of recorded violent crime rates for 2000. Wellington. Retrieved from https://www.justice.govt.nz/assets/Documents/Publications/international-comparisons-of-violent-crime.pdf

Sivertsson, F., & Carlsson, C. (2015). Continuity, change, and contradictions: Risk and agency in criminal careers to age 59. *Criminal Justice and Behavior, 42*, 382–411.

Thornberry, T. P., Huizinga, D., & Loeber, R. (1995). The prevention of serious delinquency and violence. Implications from the program of research on the causes and correlates of delinquency. In J. C. Howell, B. Krisberg, J. D. Hawkins, & J. J. Wilson (Eds.), *Serious, violent, and chronic juvenile offenders: A sourcebook* (pp. 213–237). London, UK: Sage.

Tolan, P. H. (2007). Understanding violence). In D. J. Flannery, A. T. Vazsonyi, & I. D. Waldman (Eds.), *The Cambridge handbook of violent behavior and aggression* (pp. 5–18). Cambridge, UK: Cambridge University Press.

Tremblay, R. E. (2003). Why socialization fails: The case of chronic physical aggression. In B. B. Lahey, T. E. Moffitt, & A. Caspi (Eds.), *Causes of conduct disorder and juvenile delinquency* (pp. 182–224). New York, NY: Guilford.

Warburton, W., & Anderson, C. A. (2018). On the clinical applications of the general aggression model to understanding domestic violence. In R. A. Javier, & W. G. Herron (Eds.), *Understanding domestic violence: Theories, challenges, remedies* (pp. 71–106). Lanham, MD: Rowman and Littlefield.

Weiner, N. A. (1989). Violent criminal careers and "violent career criminals": An overview of the research literature. In N. A. Weiner, & M. E. Wolfgang (Eds.), *Violent crime, violent criminals* (pp. 35–138). Newbury Park, CA: Sage.

Weisberg, D. S., Keil, F. C., Goodstein, J., Rawson, E., & Gray, J. R. (2008). The seductive allure of neuroscientific explanations. *Journal of Cognitive Neuroscience, 20*(3), 470–477.

Williams, J. R., Ghandour, R. M., & Kub, J. E. (2008). Female perpetration of violence in heterosexual intimate relationships: Adolescence through adulthood. *Trauma, Violence and Abuse, 9*, 227–249.

Wong, S. C. P., & Gordon, A. (2006). The validity and reliability of the violence risk scale: A treatment-friendly violence risk assessment tool. *Psychology, Public Policy, and Law, 12*, 279–309.

Woodworth, M., & Porter, S. (2002). In cold blood: Characteristics of criminal homicides as a function of psychopathy. *Journal of Abnormal Psychology*, 111, 436–445.

Yang, M., Wong, S. C. P., & Coid, J. W. (2010). The efficacy of violence prediction: A meta-analytic comparison of nine risk assessment tools. *Psychological Bulletin*, 136, 740–767.

Youngs, D., Ioannou, M., & Eagles, J. (2016). Expressive and instrumental offending: Reconciling the paradox of specialisation and versatility. *International Journal of Offender and Comparative Criminology*, 60, 397–422.

Zillman, D. (1988). Cognitive-excitation interdependencies in aggressive behavior. *Aggressive Behavior*, 14, 51–64.

13

The Psychology of Intimate Partner Violence and Abuse

Kate Walker
Coventry University, UK

Erica Bowen
University of Worcester, UK

Definitions of Intimate Partner Violence and Abuse

Controversies exist regarding the definition of intimate partner violence and abuse (IPVA). Legislation has been used to develop statutory definitions of IPVA, and there are a range of societal, legal, and research-based definitions, which tend to vary considerably. Definitions typically vary in relation to two factors: (a) the types of relationships that are included; and (b) the acts that are defined as "violence" and "abuse."

Types of Relationships

Contemporary definitions have moved beyond defining "domestic violence" in terms of marital-type relationships. Indeed, legislative and governmental definitions more typically include family relationships within this terminology. The World Health Organization (WHO, 2012) acknowledges that while "the term 'domestic violence' is used in many countries to refer to partner violence it can also encompass child or elder abuse, or abuse by any member of a household" (p. 1). In the United Kingdom, the cross-government definition of "domestic abuse" has been extended to include "those aged 16 or over who are, or have been, intimate partners or family members regardless of gender or sexuality" (Home Office, 2012), and "partner violence" is defined separately as violence between current or former intimates, reflecting the evidence that men and women can be victims of domestic violence perpetrated by partners and ex-partners. There is compelling evidence that violence against an intimate can be used by men and women and can spill over (for males and females) into the parent–child relationship (Dixon & Graham-Kevan, 2011).

The Wiley International Handbook of Correctional Psychology, First Edition. Edited by Devon L. L. Polaschek, Andrew Day, and Clive R. Hollin.
© 2019 John Wiley & Sons Ltd. Published 2019 by John Wiley & Sons Ltd.

Types of Behaviors

Traditionally, many considered that IPVA constituted only physical and sexual violence (Buzawa, 2013), although it is now understood that partner violence includes psychological/emotional abuse, and controlling behaviors (i.e., economic abuse, coercion as well as physical and sexual abuse), all of which have a severe impact on victims (Jordan, Campbell, & Follingstad, 2010). At the time of writing this chapter, section 76 of the Serious Crime Act of England and Wales stipulates that repeated coercive or controlling behaviors are a criminal offense (Home Office, 2015). In addition, France has already criminalized psychological or mental abuse, where mental violence is defined as repeated acts which could be constituted by words or other mechanisms, to degrade one's quality of life and cause a change to one's mental or physical state; evidence can take the form of slander, testimony, text messages, and e-mails (Erlanger, 2010).

Prevalence of IPVA

General Populations

It is extremely difficult to acquire accurate figures of the prevalence (i.e., proportion of populations) or incidence (number of new cases over time) of IPVA. Measuring IPVA is hampered by several issues, including: absence of a statutory and consistent definition of the problem; lack of uniformity in the behaviors included and measured; reluctance of victims to report abuse; and a lack of consistency and reliability of measures used (e.g., self-report, victim-report, reconviction rates, reoffending rates). Falshaw, Bates, Patel, Corbett, and Friendship (2003) suggested that although reconviction is a standard outcome measure, it is a narrow and proxy measure as it relies on someone being caught and convicted. The use of reconviction data is also reliant on accurate recordings of reconvictions, and consequently official records provide an incomplete and biased view of prevalence (Dobash, Dobash, Cavanagh, & Lewis, 1999). Measuring IPVA reconviction is further complicated by the fact that in many countries there is no specific IPVA criminal act, so the perpetrators' charges will vary (e.g., assault, actual bodily harm, or grievous bodily harm), which makes it difficult to accurately capture data. Population-based victimization surveys that ask victims directly about their experiences of violence are the most reliable source of information for establishing scale and nature of IPVA in general populations (see United Nations Office on Drugs and Crime and United Nations Economic Commission for Europe, 2010).

Female Victimization

The WHO (2013) presented a global systematic review of physical and sexual violence against women by a current or former intimate partner. Almost one third (30%) of all women sampled from 79 countries who had been in a relationship had experienced physical and/or sexual violence by their intimate partner. Prevalence varied considerably by WHO region, with the lowest rates of 23.2% in high-income regions (e.g., Australia, United Kingdom, United States); the highest rate of 37.7% was found in South East Asia (e.g., Bangladesh, Sri Lanka). Similarly, in their review of 243 articles of data from industrialized English-speaking nations, Desmarais, Reeves, Nicholls, Telford, and Fiebert (2012) found a lifetime pooled prevalence rate (i.e., the proportion of females in the population who have ever experienced physical and/or sexual violence in their lifetime) of 23.1% and rates of 18.8% for past-year victimization (i.e., prevalence rates just based on victimization for the previous year). The highest pooled estimate was 36.5% for South Africa. A more recent survey of 42,000 women across 28 European Union member states found that 31% of women had experienced one or more acts of physical violence from a partner since the age of 15, and 43% had experienced psychological violence in their current or previous relationships (European Agency for Fundamental Rights, 2014). Most women who experience several (four or more) forms of psychological violence had also experienced physical and/or sexual violence from their partners.

The most recent findings in the United Kingdom (Office for National Statistics, 2015) show that, overall, 28.3% of women had experienced any IPVA from the age of 16 (equivalent to an estimated 4.6 million female victims), and in the past year, 8.5% of women (equates to approximately 1.2.million female victims) reported experiencing any type of IPVA. For women, non-sexual partner abuse (defined as physical force, emotional or financial abuse, or threats carried out by a current or former partner) was the most commonly experienced type of IPVA since 16 (22.0%), followed by stalking (21.5%), and then sexual assault (19.9%). In the past year, twice as many women as men reported having experienced non-sexual partner abuse (5.9% of women and 2.8% of men) and more women (4.4%) than men (2.5%) reported having experienced stalking.

Male Victimization

Male victimization, although increasingly acknowledged, remains under-researched and there are no large-scale global prevalence reports of its occurrence. Desmarais et al. (2012), in their extensive review of 91 articles that documented the prevalence of physical (only) IPVA victimization in industrialized, English-speaking nations, noted that lifetime victimization was 21.7% averaged across studies and past-year victimization was 19.8% across studies. In the United States, the most recent findings from the National Intimate Partner and Sexual Violence Survey (National Center for Injury Prevention and Control; Black et al., 2011) of 16,507 adults (9,086 women and 7,421 men), found that more than 1 in 4 men (28.5%) had experienced rape, physical violence, and/or stalking by an intimate partner in their lifetime. The most recent findings in the United Kingdom (Office for National Statistics, 2015) show that, overall, 14.7% of men had experienced any domestic abuse since the age of 16 (equivalent to an estimated 2.4 million male victims), and in the past year, 4.4% of men (equivalent to 700,000 male victims) had experienced any type of IPVA. As already identified, a higher percentage of women than men reported having ever experienced any type of IPVA since the age of 16 (28.3%) and in the previous year (8.5%). For men, the most commonly experienced types of abuse were stalking (9.8%), non-sexual (physical force, emotional or financial abuse or threats), and partner abuse (9.6%). Since the age of 16, 3.6% of men had experienced some form of sexual assault, and in the past year, 0.7% of men reported they had experienced sexual assault. Each of the categories of abuse (non-sexual, sexual assault, and stalking) showed significantly higher prevalence levels for women compared with men. The largest difference between the sexes was shown for sexual assault, with 19.9% of women and 3.6% of men having experienced sexual assault (including attempts) since the age of 16.

Corrections Populations

Although there is a relative abundance of prevalence data concerning IPVA in general population samples, considerably less is known about the prevalence of IPVA victimization among corrections populations, despite the fact that many of the risk factors for criminality in general are also risk factors for IPVA victimization and perpetration (Magdol et al., 1997). The relevance of women offenders' IPVA victimization histories to their offending is relatively well documented (e.g., Salisbury & Van Voorhis, 2009), although statistics concerning the prevalence of IPVA experiences among incarcerated populations are not routinely collected. MacDonald (2013) cites European data indicating that 50% of English women inmates had experienced domestic violence and that this rose to nearly 75% of Finnish women inmates. Perhaps unsurprisingly, the prevalence of IPVA victimization among male inmates has received less consideration, possibly through the assumption that men are more often perpetrators, and that victimization experiences may be of less significance and impact to men. However, even though men are more often perpetrators, it is surprising that even the number of IPVA perpetrators within prison is unknown (Day, Richardson, Bowen, & Bernardi, 2014). Obtaining accurate prevalence data from incarcerated populations is complicated by the lack of specific IPVA offenses, which means that conviction data are unhelpful in determining prevalence (Day et al., 2014). Moreover, it is likely that even if conviction data were helpful, the actual prevalence of IPVA perpetrators would be higher than that identified by the offenses for which they are convicted, as many individuals will have histories of unidentified IPVA. In using a self-report methodology, White, Gondolf, Robertson, Goodwin, and Caraveo (2002) found that 1 in 3 (33%) inmates acknowledged *recent* violence against an intimate female partner. Again, the actual prevalence is likely to be higher due to self-report bias and also the restrictive term "recent" which, depending on sentence length, would naturally exclude a proportion of offenders.

IPVA Perpetration and Gender

There is ample evidence that women can and do use violence, but debate remains as to whether the violence used by men and women is qualitatively and quantitatively the same and therefore whether IPVA can be considered as a gender-symmetric phenomenon (Bowen, 2011). The feminist perspective (e.g., Dobash & Dobash, 1979) advocates that patriarchal societal structures and the resulting male dominance and female subordination causes IPVA, and that female use of violence comes solely from them having to respond to their own victimization (i.e., the use of self-defense [Saunders, 1988] or as a pre-emptive strike [Bograd, 1988]). Conversely the family violence perspective advocates that violence is a tactic used by individuals (male and female) to settle interpersonal conflict, and therefore violence within the family is merely an extension of that tactic (Bowen, 2011). It remains the case that there is compelling evidence that violence against an intimate can be used by men and women in a unidirectional or reciprocal manner.

Profiles of IPVA

Typology research arguably attempts to reconcile the feminist and family violence perspective, particularly as evidenced in the work of Johnson and colleagues (e.g., Johnson, 1995, 2006). Within this research distinctions are made among types of violence used; these distinctions are as much about controlling behavior as violence. Johnson distinguished among types of IPVA that are defined by the extent to which the perpetrator and his or her partner use violence in order to attempt to control the relationship. Johnson (2006) suggested that IPVA types should be distinguished based on the extent to which violence reflects one or both members of the dyad's intention to exert power and control over their partner. Therefore, the types that were developed constitute a typology of individual violence that is rooted in information about the couple and defined by the control context within which the violence is embedded. The four main types that have been identified are: intimate terrorism (IT); violent resistance (VR); situational couple violence (SCV); and mutual violent control (MVC). Kelly and Johnson (2008) added a fifth type, which they called separation-instigated violence (SIV).

Researchers have suggested that IT, also referred to as coercive controlling violence (Kelly & Johnson, 2008), is perpetrated mainly by men. For example Johnson (2006) found, based on analysis of the Pittsburg data (interviews with 274 married and formerly married women living in southwestern Pennsylvania in the late 1970s; Frieze & Browne, 1989), that 97% of IT or coercive controlling violence was reported by women to be perpetrated by men. Likewise, in a British sample examined by Graham-Kevan and Archer (2003), 87% of the coercive controlling violence was reported to be perpetrated by men when assessed using a self-report measure of controlling behaviors completed by a diverse sample of male offenders, female shelter residents, and a mixed-sex sample of students. It has been found that this type of violence, although not always frequent and/or severe, tends overall to be more frequent and severe than other types of IPVA (Johnson, 2006). VR was developed from finding that many women resist IT or coercive controlling violence with violence of their own, and so this violence takes place as an immediate reaction to an assault, to protect oneself from (further) injury (Kelly & Johnson, 2008). VR is predominantly used by females in response to male IT. SCV is the most common type of violence found in general populations and is perpetrated by both males and females. It has been suggested that this type of violence is *not* a "minor" version of coercive controlling violence and is *not* embedded in a pattern of power and control within the relationship. Generally, this is physical violence that has escalated from arguments between partners, particularly in couples where one or both have poor ability to manage conflict and/or poor anger control (Johnson, 1995, 2006). Based on large-scale surveys, it has been suggested that SCV is initiated at similar rates by males and females (e.g., Kwong, Bartholomew, & Dutton, 1999). MVC is the scenario where both individuals are violent and controlling so that both partners vie for control over the other. So, typically this violence pattern is gender-symmetrical in heterosexual relationships (Johnson, 2006). However, it has been suggested that this type is very rare (Johnson & Ferraro, 2000). Finally, SIV is seen symmetrically in both men and women, and this violence is described as uncharacteristic and unexpected incidents of violence perpetrated by a partner with a history of civilized and contained behavior (Kelly & Johnson, 2008). This violence is triggered by a traumatic experience such as a traumatic separation (e.g., the home emptied and the children taken when the parent is at work), the discovery of the partner in bed with someone else, being left by the partner, or being shocked by divorce action.

Theories of IPVA

Several theories have been proposed to account for the use of violence in an intimate relationship, although it has been argued that in isolation these fail to encapsulate the complexity of all of the variables associated with IPVA (Bell & Naugle, 2008). There is a range of theories that offer explanatory variables for IPVA at different analytical levels, from sociocultural to interpersonal and intra-individual, and it has been argued that they should not be regarded as mutually exclusive (Woodin & O'Leary, 2009). This ecology of IPVA highlights the interaction between factors that operate at different levels of closeness to individual experience

(Bowen, 2011). The most widely cited ecological model is that by Bronfenbrenner (1979) which has been adapted by Gulliver and Fanslow (2016) to organize empirical research concerning the risk and protective factors for IPVA, and is adopted here as a framework for examining risk factors for IPVA. This framework acknowledges the complex interplay between ecological systems and how the interaction of these different factors within each system ultimately leads to IPVA (Edleson & Tolman, 1992).

Bronfenbrenner (1979) initially identified three social contexts as the *microsystem, macrosystem*, and *exosystem*, and Dutton (1985) added the individual or *ontogenic* system, thereby proposing four levels of risk factors for IPVA specifically. More recently, the Violence Prevention Alliance (2016) named these levels Society, Community, Relationship, and Individual. Heise (2011) has also expanded the key components of the ecological model further within the "Male Partner" and "Relationship" layers in order to conceptualize a life-course pathway in relation to the development of the perpetration of IPVA. Further, the "Relationship" layer was clarified in order to include the interaction between individual and partner, and the situational conflict arena in which IPVA occurs. These systems provide a useful heuristic within which to organize our consideration of risk factors for, and theories of, IPVA. What follows is a selection of the relevant literature, a full appraisal of which is outside the scope of this chapter.

The macrosystem/society level includes cultural values and beliefs or sociocultural influences. Theories located at this level are sociocultural theories: that is, feminist theory (Dobash & Dobash, 1977; Walker, 1984) and power theory (Straus, 1976, 1977), which identify gender roles, gender inequality, power and control, patriarchy, social acceptance of violence, and societal beliefs about IPVA as risk factors (Schechter, 1982). Theories at this level generally view IPVA as behaviors of males against their female partners, caused by societal rules that are supportive of male dominance and female subordination (Dobash & Dobash, 1979; Yllo, 2005). Patriarchy is therefore viewed as a direct cause of male violence against a female intimate (Bell & Naugle, 2008). Within an ecological framework, patriarchy would be viewed as an indirect cause of IPVA. Nevertheless, interventions for IPVA often conceptualize patriarchy as a direct cause (see Bowen & Day, Chapter 33). Although feminist/sociocultural theories have dominated research and policy, it has been argued that such theories are underdeveloped (Hunnicutt, 2009). There is little empirical evidence to support a strong relationship between IPVA and patriarchy (Stith, Smith, Penn, Ward, & Tritt, 2004), and several researchers have found no consistent relationship between patriarchal beliefs, male-dominated families, and IPVA (e.g., Dutton, 1994). Polaschek (2006) suggested that feminist perspectives fail to account for the range and diversity of research findings that are evident in relation to IPVA, and these theories do fail to account for female initiated IPVA (Dutton & Corvo, 2006).

The exosystem/community level includes connections between culture and families; that is, formal and informal social structures of the individual (e.g., friendships, workplace, legal institutions, social institutions) that connect the offender and their family to the larger culture. This system includes sociodemographic factors such as ethnicity within a minority cultural group, immigration status, and socioeconomic disadvantage (Connolly, Friedlander, Pepler, Craig, & Laporte, 2010). Low income has been found to be a male offender risk factor (e.g., Cunradi, Caetano, & Schafer, 2002), although it has been found that, generally, risk factors within this level exert small effect sizes on IPVA as this level is assumed to be distal from the violence (Stith et al., 2004). A negative association between age and IPVA has been reported in two multi-wave prospective longitudinal studies (Johnson, Giordano, Manning, & Longmore, 2015; Kim, Laurent, Capaldi, & Feingold, 2008). Other exosystem risk factors include education (e.g., Cunradi et al., 2002) and employment (e.g., Rankin, Saunders, & Williams,

2000). A study by Cunradi et al. (2002) found that education was a stronger predictor of couples reporting IPVA than employment, but that income was a stronger predictor than education and employment across the main ethnic groups included in their study (Euro American, African American, Hispanic).

Race and ethnicity have also been examined, and it has been found that being a member of a minority group is a risk factor for IPVA (Capaldi, Knoble, Shortt, & Kim, 2012). A consistent finding is the association between being African American and risk of IPVA (Ramisetty-Mikler, Caetano, & McGrath, 2007). Indeed Ramisetty-Mikler et al. (2007) found that IPVA perpetration was twice as frequent in African American men and women based on findings from a longitudinal study that included an analysis of interviews with 406 White, 232 Black, and 387 Hispanic couples. The association between ethnicity and IPVA has also been found in New Zealand (Marie, Fergusson, & Boden, 2008), where Māori were at higher risk of IPVA perpetration and victimization, for both men and women compared to non-Māori individuals. It has been suggested, however, that effects attributed to race may actually reflect other socio-economic variables (e.g., being unmarried, lower income, lower educational attainment, unemployment, and being less financially secure).

The microsystem/relationship level represents the individual level characteristics of the immediate setting where the IPVA is occurring. Family unit and relationship dynamics as well as the antecedents and consequences of IPVA are included within this system. Therefore, in its most simplistic explanation, this system includes the risk factors for IPVA that arise from the characteristics of families and individuals. Stith et al. (2004) suggested that risk factors at the microsystem level are the most important risk markers for IPVA, as these are the factors that are associated with direct interactions or the contexts within which IPVA exists and occurs. Many risk factors at this level have been identified. These include: marital satisfaction (e.g., Shortt, Capaldi, Kim, & Tiberio, 2013); history of using physical violence (e.g., Weisz, Tolman, & Saunders, 2000); emotionally abusing a partner (e.g., Rankin et al., 2000); forcing a partner to have sex (e.g., Rankin et al., 2000), and exposure to IPVA in family of origin (e.g., Levendosky, 2013). A moderate association exists between witnessing parental IPVA and later perpetration and victimization of IPVA by men and women (Capaldi et al., 2012). Social learning theory (Bandura, 1971, 1973) has been widely applied to findings regarding the intergenerational transmission of violence, and in particular, suggests that methods for resolving conflict in relationships are learned during childhood by observing peers and parental relationships (Mihalic & Elliott, 1997). However, this theory does not account for those who have not experienced violence in their families but still perpetrate violence against intimates (Delsol & Margolin, 2004).

The ontogenetic/individual level reflects the individual's developmental history, including offender characteristics associated with their response to the stressors at the microsystem and exosystem levels. Several risk factors have been identified at this level and these include: psychopathology and personality (e.g., Brasfield, 2014); attachment (e.g., Genest & Mathieu, 2014); anger/hostility (e.g., Birkley & Eckhardt, 2015); self-esteem (e.g., Papadakaki, Tzamalouka, Chatzifotiou, & Chliaoutakis, 2009); substance and alcohol abuse (e.g., Salom, Williams, Najman, & Alati, 2015); hostile attributions, attitudes, and beliefs (e.g., McKinney, Caetano, Ramisetty-Mikler, & Nelson, 2009); depression (Simmons, Knight, & Menard, 2015; White & Satyen, 2015); negative emotionality and jealousy (e.g., Rodriguez, DiBello, Øverup, & Neighbors, 2015); communication difficulties (e.g., Messinger, Rickert, Fry, Lessel, & Davidson, 2012), and personal experience of stress (e.g., Probst et al., 2008).

Ehrensaft, Cohen, and Johnson (2006) examined the longitudinal association between IPVA and specific diagnosed disorders as per the *Diagnostic and Statistical Manual of Mental Disorders, Fourth Edition* (DSM-IV), including: (a) Cluster A (paranoid, schizoid, and schizotypal); Cluster B (histrionic, narcissistic, and borderline disorders); and Cluster C (avoidant, dependent, and obsessive-compulsive disorder). They controlled for socioeconomic status, race, sex, age, and other personality disorder symptoms. Cluster A and B symptoms in the early 20s predicted later perpetration of IPVA. From an attachment theory perspective, IPVA has been proposed as being an attempt to establish or maintain a level of personal security within the relationship (Bowlby, 1984). A threat to or disruption of the attachment relationship causes individuals to become alarmed and the resulting anxiety leads to responses, violence for some, designed to preserve the attachment system (Bowlby, 1984). Researchers have established a relationship between insecure attachment and IPVA, finding higher levels of preoccupied and fearful (Dutton, Saunders, Starzomski, & Bartholomew, 1994) or preoccupied and dismissing (Babcock, Jacobson, Gottman, & Yerington, 2000) styles in violent males compared to non-violent males. Likewise, male and female individuals in reciprocally violent relationships report higher levels of preoccupied attachment compared to those in non-violent relationships (Bookwala & Zdaniuk, 1998). These attachment styles are also features of the clinical presentation of many Cluster A and B psychopathologies.

In relation to drugs and alcohol, there is ample evidence to suggest alcohol has a variety of functional roles in relation to IPVA, such as, impairing cognitive functioning, limiting the capacity to comprehend social cues, and increasing the risk of violence for those with aggressive predispositions or deficient social perceptual processes (Clements & Schumacher, 2010). It has also been identified that alcohol may have a spurious link to IPV, in that it may be used as a post hoc excuse or justification (Zhang, Welte, & Wieczorek, 2002) where individuals use forms of "deviance disavowal" (Gelles & Straus, 1979): for example, blaming alcohol post hoc, drinking so that others will excuse their behaviors based on them being drunk, or drinking to embolden them to use IPV.

Personal experience of stress is another factor that has been identified as being related to use of IPVA. Specifically, Neff, Holamon, and Schluter (1995) found that financial stress was associated with IPVA perpetration for both men and women. Probst et al. (2008) suggested that parental stress was a prominent factor that led to intimate partner violence between couples. There is therefore evidence that stress is associated with IPVA, although findings do also suggest that the effects of this variable are likely to be moderated by other factors such as ethnicity (Capaldi et al., 2012). Research regarding the role of personal experience of stress has not received as much attention as some of the other factors discussed and warrants further attention, particularly because these factors are dynamic and can therefore be targeted in interventions.

The large number of risk factors identified in this chapter lends support to the complicated nature of domestic violence. Given the complexity, it is unreasonable to assume that any one variable would account for a large amount of the variance in explaining intimate partner violence. Careful consideration is required regarding how a range of different factors interact and exist in tandem and how these inter-correlations between variables then manifest into violent and abusive behaviors. Based on this observation, intervention providers need to take a case formulation approach so that they can determine how risk factors present and interact in any given case they are working with, so they can effectively treat individuals and meet their needs.

Desistance from IPVA

Some men stop using physical violence in their intimate relationships (Whitaker, Le, & Niolon, 2010), although no one single theory or model has been developed to explain why and how this process occurs (for a review see Walker, Bowen, & Brown, 2013). Although there is evidence that for some, IPVA continues over time after initial onset (e.g., Coker et al., 2008), other studies have established that physical violence can stop *within* relationships (Whitaker et al., 2010) and more so *between* relationships (Fritz & Slep, 2009). Desistance is associated with less severe and frequent violence in relationships (Whitaker et al., 2010). Individual characteristics distinguish desisters from persisters (Walker, Bowen, Brown, & Sleath, 2015). For example, Walker et al. (2015) examined differences in personality pathology between desisters (perpetrators who had not used physical violence for at least 12 months), persisters, and non-violent controls using the Millon Clinical Multiaxial Inventory-III subscales. Cluster A and Cluster B disorders at a diagnostic level were more often reported in men who had used violence against intimates compared to men in the control group. The rates and percentages of clinically meaningful traits and disorders were lower for the desisters than the persisters, with the desisters more like the controls than the persisters. This research, however, was based on cross-sectional data and examined physical violence only, so potential psychopathology differences need to be examined over time, while considering all types of IPVA.

Studies of post-intervention change indicate that change is a complex process that needs to be addressed at several levels and requires both agentic and structural change to happen. Curwood, DeGeer, Hymmen, and Lehmann (2011) found change was required on three levels: (a) individual (e.g., stress and anger management); (b) interpersonal and relational (e.g., improved communication and patience); and (c) external (e.g., employment status or career aspirations). Likewise, Silvergleid and Mankowski (2006) identified several levels of change that were required by men who had completed IPV programs, including: (a) individual (e.g., learning new skills, self-awareness, and decision to change); (b) community (e.g., fear of losing partner, involvement in criminal justice system); (c) organizational (e.g., treatment group facilitators' influence); and (d) group level (e.g., impact of other men attending treatment). Although these studies offer some insights into change processes, it is not known if all of the men in the samples were or were not still using violence as this was not assessed in the majority of the studies.

Walker, Bowen, Brown, and Sleath (2014) developed a conceptual model in order to understand and examine the actual process itself of desistance from physical IPVA. Desistance was operationalized as being 1 year free from using physical violence. The change from persister to desister did not happen as a result of discrete unique incidents, but instead occurred through a number of catalysts or stimulants of change. These catalysts/stimulants were experienced gradually and accumulated over time in number and in type. Individuals experienced negative consequences following their violence (e.g., impact of violence on family, Criminal Justice involvement) and negative emotional responses (e.g., guilt, shame, and fear). This led to an autonomous decision to change that was indicative of cognitive changes or changes in the way that they thought. Desistance was an active process and was not achieved passively. Successful desisters developed a different view of the world; they managed triggers to violence (that previously when present would have resulted in use of physical violence) and being non-violent became conceptualized as the manifestation of the individuals' new ways of being (i.e., they saw themselves as having characteristics associated with non-violent people). It is therefore clear that the path from persistence to desistance is not a straightforward linear journey that is shared by all IPVA offenders, but is complex, dynamic, and idiosyncratic, and men's use of and cessation from violence needs to be understood within the context of *each* individual's life.

A recent study (Giordano, Johnson, Manning, Longmore, & Minter, 2015), drawing on in-depth interviews (*n* = 89) with participants in the fifth wave (2011–2012) of a longitudinal study of adolescent and young adult romantic relationships, examined longer-term desistance from IPVA. On average, all desisters had been violence free for 3.2 years. They found that possibility of arrest, individual's role as a parent, and relationship-based motivations (e.g., change of perspective about violence, change in relationship behaviors, including infidelity and negative communication) were catalysts for making changes. Relationship-based motivations were central features in the narratives of desisters, and context-specific learning experiences within each individual's romantic relationship served as an "important basis for making concrete, forward looking changes" (Giordano et al., 2015, p. 356). Based on this it is clear that agency and attitudinal and behavioral changes as well as specific contextual factors are associated with secondary desistance from IPVA. Overall, it still remains the case that more research is required to fully understand the process of desistance from IPVA; longitudinal studies are required that allow a direct observation of change *while* it is occurring, because prior research has generally been limited to focusing on the products of change (e.g., has the perpetrator stopped using violence?) as opposed to the process of change (e.g., how and why has the perpetrator stopped using violence?). Process of change research needs to include an examination of not only physical violence but also all the different types of behaviors (e.g., non-physical, controlling coercive) now acknowledged as being forms of IPVA.

Summary and Conclusion

It is evident from the literature reviewed in this chapter that IPVA is a significant societal issue that carries with it a substantial burden of disease and mortality. In addition, our understanding and definition of IPVA has improved over time, to now acknowledging the full spectrum of behaviors that might be involved in a relationship characterized by IPVA. Although several theoretical positions have been proposed to account for IPVA, none of these have been developed specifically as a theory of IPVA per se. Moreover, it is clear from the evidence reviewed that many factors at an individual, dyadic, social, and societal level influence the likelihood of IPVA occurring in any given relationship, thereby making it difficult to fully theorize its occurrence. However, what the literature does show is that individual cases need to be appraised in relation to the risk factors that are salient to them. A "one size fits all" explanation of IPVA would fail to account for many violent and abusive relationships. Indeed, if intervention is guided by theory, then the literature indicates that holistic intervention approaches are needed that reflect the whole ecology of risk factors associated with IPVA. This means a range of different approaches may be needed to more appropriately address the IPVA-related risk and individual needs of perpetrators. Evidence shows that some IPVA male perpetrators can fully engage in the process of change assisted by interventions, and that successful desistance arises from offenders developing the recognition that their behavior is wrong and harmful, and increasing their understanding and management of their personal risk factors and risk situations. Understanding risk and protective factors provides a starting point for intervention. Chapter 33 (Bowen and Day) explores how corrections-based treatment for IPVA has evolved over time and discusses clinical issues relevant to working with IPVA perpetrators in a corrections setting.

Key Readings

Bell, K. M., & Naugle, A. E. (2008). Intimate partner violence theoretical considerations: Moving towards a contextual framework. *Clinical Psychology Review*, 28, 1096–1107.

Bowen, E. (2011). *The rehabilitation of partner-violent men*. Chichester, UK: Wiley-Blackwell.

Dixon, L., & Graham-Kevan, N. (2011). Understanding the nature and etiology of intimate partner violence and implications for practice and policy. *Clinical Psychology Review*, 31, 1145–1155.

Johnson, M. P. (2006). Conflict and control: Gender symmetry and asymmetry in domestic violence. *Violence Against Women*, 12, 1003–1018.

Walker, K., Bowen, E., Brown, S., & Sleath, E. (2014). Desistance from intimate partner violence: A conceptual model and framework for practitioners for managing the process of change. *Journal of Interpersonal Violence*, 30, 2726–2750.

References

Babcock, J. C., Jacobson, N. S., Gottman, J. M., & Yerington, T. P. (2000). Attachment, emotional regulation, and the function of marital violence: Differences between secure, preoccupied, and dismissing violent and nonviolent husbands. *Journal of Family Violence*, 15, 391–409.

Bandura, A. (1971). *Psychological modelling*. Chicago, IL: Aldine-Atherton.

Bandura, A. (1973). *Aggression: A social learning analysis*. Englewood Cliffs, NJ: Prentice Hall.

Bell, K. M., & Naugle, A. E. (2008). Intimate partner violence theoretical considerations: Moving towards a contextual framework. *Clinical Psychology Review*, 28, 1096–1107.

Birkley, E. L., & Eckhardt, C. I. (2015). Anger, hostility, internalizing negative emotions, and intimate partner violence perpetration: A meta-analytic review. *Clinical Psychology Review*, 37, 40–56.

Black, M. C., Basile, K. C., Breiding, M. J., Smith, S. G., Walters, M. L., Merrick, M. T., ... & Stevens, M. R. (2011). *The National Intimate Partner and Sexual Violence Survey (NISVS): 2010 summary report*. Atlanta, GA: National Center for Injury Prevention and Control, Centers for Disease Control and Prevention.

Bograd, M. (1988). Feminist perspectives on wife abuse: An introduction. In K. Yllo, & M. Bograd (Eds.), *Feminist perspectives on wife abuse* (pp. 11–27). Thousand Oaks, CA: Sage.

Bookwala, J., & Zdaniuk, B. (1998). Adult attachment styles and aggressive behavior within dating relationships. *Journal of Social and Personal Relationships*, 15, 175–190.

Bowen, E. (2011). *The rehabilitation of partner-violent men*. Chichester, UK: Wiley-Blackwell.

Bowlby, J. (1984). Violence in the family as a disorder of the attachment and caregiving systems. *The American Journal of Psychoanalysis*, 44, 9–27.

Brasfield, R. (2014). The absence of evidence is not the evidence of absence: The abusive personality as a disordered mental state. *Aggression and Violent Behavior*, 19, 515–522.

Bronfenbrenner, U. (1979). Contexts of child rearing: Problems and prospects. *American Psychologist*, 34, 844–850.

Buzawa, E. S. (2013). Victims of domestic violence. In R. C. Davis, A. J. Lurigio, & S. Herman (Eds.), *Victims of crime* (4th ed.) (pp. 36–60). Los Angeles, CA: Sage.

Capaldi, D. M., Knoble, N. B., Shortt, J. W., & Kim, H. K. (2012). A systematic review of risk factors for intimate partner violence. *Partner Abuse*, 3, 231–280.

Clements, K., & Schumacher, J. A. (2010). Perceptual biases in social cognition as potential moderators of the relationship between alcohol and intimate partner violence: A review. *Aggression and Violent Behavior*, 15, 357–368.

Coker, A. L., Flerx, V. C., Smith, P. H., Whitaker, D. J., Fadden, M. K., & Williams, M. (2008). Intimate partner violence incidence and continuation in a primary care screening program. *American Journal of Epidemiology*, 165, 821–827.

Connolly, J., Friedlander, L., Pepler, D., Craig, W., & Laporte, L. (2010). The ecology of adolescent dating aggression: Attitudes, relationships, media use, and socio-demographic risk factors. *Journal of Aggression, Maltreatment & Trauma*, 19, 469–491.

Cunradi, C. B., Caetano, R., & Schafer, J. (2002). Socioeconomic predictors of intimate partner violence among White, Black, and Hispanic couples in the United States. *Journal of Family Violence*, 17, 377–389.

Curwood, S. E., DeGeer, I., Hymmen, P., & Lehmann, P. (2011). Using strength-based approaches to explore pretreatment change in men who abuse their partners. *Journal of Interpersonal Violence*, 26, 2698–2715.

Day, A., Richardson, T., Bowen, E., & Bernardi, J. (2014). Intimate partner violence in prisoners: Toward effective assessment and intervention. *Aggression and Violent Behavior*, 19, 579–583.

Delsol, C., & Margolin, G. (2004). The role of family-of-origin violence in men's marital violence perpetration. *Clinical Psychology Review*, 24, 99–122.

Desmarais, S. L., Reeves, K. A., Nicholls, T. L., Telford, R. P., & Fiebert, M. S. (2012). Prevalence of physical violence in intimate relationships, part 1: Rates of male and female victimization. *Partner Abuse*, 3, 140–169.

Dixon, L., & Graham–Kevan, N. (2011). Understanding the nature and etiology of intimate partner violence and implications for practice and policy. *Clinical Psychology Review*, 31, 1145–1155.

Dobash, R. E., & Dobash, R. P. (1977). Wives: The appropriate victims of marital violence. *Victimology*, 2, 426–442.

Dobash, R. P., & Dobash, R. E. (1979). *Violence against wives: A case against the patriarchy*. New York, NY: Free Press.

Dobash, R. P., Dobash, R. E., Cavanagh, K., & Lewis, R. (1999). *Changing violent men*. London, UK: Sage.

Dutton, D. G. (1985). An ecologically nested theory of male violence toward intimates. *International Journal of Women's Studies*, 8, 404–413.

Dutton, D. G. (1994). Patriarchy and wife assault: The ecological fallacy. *Violence and Victims*, 9, 167–182.

Dutton, D. G., & Corvo, K. (2006). Transforming a flawed policy: A call to revive psychology and science in domestic violence research and practice. *Aggression and Violent Behavior*, 11, 457–483.

Dutton, D. G., Saunders, K., Starzomski, A., & Bartholomew, K. (1994). Intimacy-anger and insecure attachment as precursors of abuse in intimate relationships. *Journal of Applied Social Psychology*, 24, 1367–1386.

Edleson, J. L., & Tolman, R. M. (1992). *Intervention for men who batter: An ecological approach*. Thousand Oaks, CA: Sage.

Ehrensaft, M. K., Cohen, P., & Johnson, J. G. (2006). Development of personality disorder symptoms and the risk for partner violence. *Journal of Abnormal Psychology*, 115, 474–483.

Erlanger, S. (2010, June 29). France make "psychological violence" a crime. *The New York Times*. Retrieved from http://www.nytimes.com/2010/06/30/world/europe/30france.html

European Agency for Fundamental Rights. (2014). Violence against women: An EU-wide survey. Retrieved from http://fra.europa.eu/sites/default/files/fra_uploads/fra-2014-vaw-survey-main-results-apr14_en.pdf

Falshaw, L., Bates, A., Patel, V., Corbett, C., & Friendship, C. (2003). Assessing reconviction, reoffending and recidivism in a sample of UK sexual offenders. *Legal and Criminological Psychology*, 8, 207–215.

Frieze, I. H., & Browne, A. (1989). Violence in marriage. In L. Ohlin, & M. Tonry (Eds.), *Family violence* (pp. 163–218). Chicago, IL: University of Chicago Press.

Fritz, P. A. T., & Slep, A. M. S. (2009). Stability of physical and psychological adolescent dating aggression across time and partners. *Journal of Clinical Child & Adolescent Psychology*, 38, 303–314.

Gelles, R. J., & Straus, M. A. (1979). Determinants of violence in the family: Towards a theoretical integration. In W. I. Burr, R. Hill, F. I. Nye, & I. L. Reiss (Eds.), *Contemporary theories about the family* (pp. 549–581). New York, NY: The Free Press.

Genest, A. A., & Mathieu, C. (2014). Intimate partner violence: The role of attachment on men's anger. *Partner Abuse*, 5, 375–387.

Giordano, P. C., Johnson, W. L., Manning, W. D., Longmore, M. A., & Minter, M. D. (2015). Intimate partner violence in young adulthood: Narratives of persistence and desistance. *Criminology*, 53, 330–365.

Graham-Kevan, N., & Archer, J. (2003). Intimate terrorism and common couple violence: A test of Johnson's predictions in four British samples. *Journal of Interpersonal Violence*, 18, 1247–1270.

Gulliver, P., & Fanslow, J. (2016). *Understanding research on risk and protective factors for intimate partner violence*. Auckland, New Zealand: New Zealand Family Violence Clearinghouse, University of Auckland.

Heise, L. (2011). *What works to prevent partner violence? An evidence overview*. London, UK: London School of Hygiene and Tropical Medicine.

Home Office. (2012). Cross-government definition of domestic violence—A consultation. Summary of responses. Retrieved from https://www.gov.uk/government/uploads/system/uploads/attachment_data/file/157800/domestic-violence-definition.pdf

Home Office. (2015). Coercive or controlling behaviour now a crime. Retrieved from https://www.gov.uk/government/news/coercive-or-controlling-behaviour-now-a-crime

Hunnicutt, G. (2009). Varieties of patriarchy and violence against women: Resurrecting "patriarchy" as a theoretical tool. *Violence Against Women*, 15, 553–573.

Johnson, M. P. (1995). Patriarchal terrorism and common couple violence: Two forms of violence against women. *Journal of Marriage & the Family*, 57, 283–294.

Johnson, M. P. (2006). Conflict and control: Gender symmetry and asymmetry in domestic violence. *Violence Against Women*, 12, 1003–1018.

Johnson, M. P., & Ferraro, K. J. (2000). Research on domestic violence in the 1990s: Making distinctions. *Journal of Marriage and the Family*, 62, 948–963.

Johnson, W. L., Giordano, P. C., Manning, W. D., & Longmore, M. A. (2015). The age–IPV curve: Changes in the perpetration of intimate partner violence during adolescence and young adulthood. *Journal of Youth and Adolescence*, 44, 708–726.

Jordan, C. E., Campbell, R., & Follingstad, D. (2010). Violence and women's mental health: The impact of physical, sexual, and psychological aggression. *Annual Review of Clinical Psychology*, 6, 607–628.

Kelly, J. B., & Johnson, M. P. (2008). Differentiation among types of intimate partner violence: Research update and implications for interventions. *Family Court Review*, 46, 476–499.

Kim, H. K., Laurent, H. K., Capaldi, D. M., & Feingold, A. (2008). Men's aggression toward women: A 10-year panel study. *Journal of Marriage and Family*, 70, 1169–1187.

Kwong, M. J., Bartholomew, K., & Dutton, D. G. (1999). Gender differences in patterns of relationship violence in Alberta. *Canadian Journal of Behavioral Science*, 31, 150–160.

Levendosky, A. A. (2013). Drawing conclusions: An intergenerational transmission of violence perspective. *Psychodynamic Psychiatry*, 41, 351–360.

MacDonald, M. (2013). Women prisoners, mental health, violence and abuse. *International Journal of Law and Psychiatry*, 36, 293–303.

Magdol, L., Moffitt, T. E., Caspi, A., Newman, D. L., Fagan, J., & Silva, P. A. (1997). Gender differences in partner violence in a birth cohort of 21-year-olds: Bridging the gap between clinical and epidemiological approaches. *Journal of Consulting and Clinical Psychology*, 65, 68–78.

Marie, D., Fergusson, D. M., & Boden, J. M. (2008). Ethnic identity and intimate partner violence in a New Zealand birth cohort. *Social Policy Journal of New Zealand*, 33, 126–145.

McKinney, C. M., Caetano, R., Ramisetty-Mikler, S., & Nelson, S. (2009). Childhood family violence and perpetration and victimization of intimate partner violence: Findings from a national population-based study of couples. *Annals of Epidemiology*, 19, 25–32.

Messinger, A. M., Rickert, V. I., Fry, D. A., Lessel, H., & Davidson, L. L. (2012). Revisiting the role of communication in adolescent intimate partner violence. *Journal of Interpersonal Violence*, 27, 2920–2935.

Mihalic, S. W., & Elliott, D. (1997). A social learning theory model of marital violence. *Journal of Family Violence*, 12, 21–47.

Neff, J. A., Holamon, B., & Schluter, T. D. (1995). Spousal violence among Anglos, Blacks, and Mexican Americans: The role of demographic variables, psychosocial predictors, and alcohol consumption. *Journal of Family Violence*, 10, 1–21.

Office for National Statistics. (2015). Violent crime and sexual offences—intimate personal violence and serious sexual assault. Retrieved from http://www.ons.gov.uk/ons/rel/crime-stats/crime-statistics/focus-on-violent-crime-and-sexual-offences--2013-14/rpt-chapter-4.html

Papadakaki, M., Tzamalouka, G. S., Chatzifotiou, S., & Chliaoutakis, J. (2009). Seeking for risk factors of intimate partner violence (IPV) in a Greek national sample: The role of self-esteem. *Journal of Interpersonal Violence*, 24, 732–750.

Polaschek, D. (2006). Violent offender programmes: Concept, theory and practice. In C. R. Hollin, & E. J. Palmer (Eds.), *Offender behavior programmes: Development, controversies and applications* (pp. 113–154). Chichester, UK: Wiley.

Probst, J. C., Wang, J. Y., Martin, A. B., Moore, C. G., Paul, B. M., & Samuels, M. E. (2008). Potentially violent disagreements and parenting stress among American Indian/Alaska native families: Analysis across seven states. *Maternal and Child Health Journal*, 12, S91–S102.

Ramisetty-Mikler, S., Caetano, R., & McGrath, C. (2007). Sexual aggression among White, Black, and Hispanic couples in the US: Alcohol use, physical assault and psychological aggression as its correlates. *The American Journal of Drug and Alcohol Abuse*, 33, 31–43.

Rankin, L. B., Saunders, D. G., & Williams, R. A. (2000). Mediators of attachment style, social support, and sense of belonging in predicting woman abuse by African American men. *Journal of Interpersonal Violence*, 15, 1060–1080.

Rodriguez, L. M., DiBello, A. M., Øverup, C. S., & Neighbors, C. (2015). The price of distrust: Trust, anxious attachment, jealousy, and partner abuse. *Partner Abuse*, 6, 298–319.

Salisbury, E. J., & Van Voorhis, P. (2009). Gendered pathways: A quantitative investigation of women probationers' paths to incarceration. *Criminal Justice and Behavior*, 36, 541–466.

Salom, C. L., Williams, G. M., Najman, J. M., & Alati, R. (2015). Substance use and mental health disorders are linked to different forms of intimate partner violence victimization. *Drug & Alcohol Dependence*, 151, 121–127.

Saunders, D. G. (1988). Wife abuse, husband abuse or mutual combat? A feminist perspective on the empirical findings. In K. Yllo, & M. Bograd (Eds.), *Feminist perspectives on wife abuse* (pp. 90–113). Thousand Oaks, CA: Sage.

Schechter, S. (1982). *Women and male violence: The visions and struggles of the battered women's movement.* Cambridge, MA: South End Press.

Shortt, J. W., Capaldi, D. M., Kim, H. K., & Tiberio, S. S. (2013). The interplay between interpersonal stress and psychological intimate partner violence over time for young at-risk couples. *Journal of Youth and Adolescence*, 42, 619–632.

Silvergleid, C. S., & Mankowski, E. S. (2006). How batterer intervention programs work: Participant and facilitator accounts of processes of change. *Journal of Interpersonal Violence*, 21, 139–159.

Simmons, S. B., Knight, K. E., & Menard, S. (2015). Consequences of intimate partner violence on substance use and depression for women and men. *Journal of Family Violence*, 30, 351–361.

Stith, S. M., Smith, D. B., Penn, C. E., Ward, D. B., & Tritt, D. (2004). Intimate partner physical abuse perpetration and victimization risk factors: A meta-analytic review. *Aggression and Violent Behavior*, 10, 65–98.

Straus, M. A. (1976). Sexual inequality, cultural norms, and wife-beating. *Victimology*, 1, 54–70.

Straus, M. A. (1977). Wife beating: How common and why? *Victimology*, 2, 443–458.

United Nations Office on Drugs and Crime and United Nations Economic Commission for Europe (2010). *Manual on victimization surveys.* Geneva, Switzerland: United Nations.

Violence Prevention Alliance. The ecological framework. (2016). Retrieved from http://www.who.int/violenceprevention/approach/ecology/en

Walker, K., Bowen, E., & Brown, S. (2013). Desistance from intimate partner violence: A critical review. *Aggression and Violent Behavior*, 18, 271–280.

Walker, K., Bowen, E., Brown, S., & Sleath, E. (2014). Desistance from intimate partner violence: A conceptual model and framework for practitioners for managing the process of change. *Journal of Interpersonal Violence*, 30, 2726–2750.

Walker, K., Bowen, E., Brown, S., & Sleath, E. (2015). An examination of psychopathology among men who have suspended the use of violence in their intimate relationships. *Journal of Family Violence*, 30, 539–554.

Walker, L. E. A. (1984). *The battered woman syndrome*. New York, NY: Springer.

Weisz, A. N., Tolman, R. M., & Saunders, D. G. (2000). Assessing the risk of severe domestic violence: The importance of survivors' predictions. *Journal of Interpersonal Violence*, 15, 75–90.

Whitaker, D. J., Le, B., & Niolon, P. H. (2010). Persistence and desistance of the perpetration of physical aggression across relationships. *Journal of Interpersonal Violence*, 25, 591–609.

White, M. E., & Satyen, L. (2015). Cross-cultural differences in intimate partner violence and depression: A systematic review. *Aggression and Violent Behavior*, 24, 120–130.

White, R. J., Gondolf, E. W., Robertson, D. U., Goodwin, B. J., & Caraveo, L. E. (2002). Extent and characteristics of woman batterers among federal inmates. *International Journal of Offender Therapy and Comparative Criminology*, 46, 412–426.

Woodin, E. M., & O'Leary, K. D. (2009). Theoretical approaches to the etiology of partner violence. In D. J. Whittaker, & J. R. Lutzker (Eds.), *Preventing partner violence: Research and evidence-based intervention strategies* (pp. 41–66). Washington, DC: American Psychological Association.

World Health Organization. (2012). Understanding and addressing violence against women: Intimate partner violence. Retrieved from http://apps.who.int/iris/bitstream/10665/77432/1/WHO_RHR_12.36_eng.pdf

World Health Organization. (2013). Global and regional estimates of violence against women: Prevalence and health effects of intimate partner violence and non-partner sexual violence. Retrieved from http://apps.who.int/iris/bitstream/handle/10665/85239/9789241564625_eng.pdf?sequence=1

Yllo, K. A. (2005). Through a feminist lens: Gender, diversity and violence extending the feminist framework. In D. R. Loseke, R. J. Gelles, & M. M. Cavanaugh (Eds.), *Current controversies on family violence* (2nd ed.) (pp. 19–34). Newbury Park, CA: Sage.

Zhang, L., Welte, J. W., & Wieczorek, W. W. (2002). The role of aggression-related alcohol expectancies in explaining the link between alcohol and violent behavior. *Substance Use & Misuse*, 37, 457–471.

14

The Serious and Violent Young Offender: Examining the Multi-Domain Risk Profile, Mental Health, and Treatment Intervention Strategies

Raymond R. Corrado
Simon Fraser University, Canada

Adrienne M. F. Peters
Memorial University of Newfoundland, Canada

Jeff Mathesius
Simon Fraser University, Canada

The Multi-Risk Profile of the Serious and Violent Juvenile Offender

Several individual characteristics and life experiences influence a young person's propensity to commit a serious/violent offense. It has been well established, for example, that the serious and violent juvenile offender (SVO) is more likely to have been exposed to multiple pre/peri-natal risks, to exhibit poor behavioral and emotional regulation in childhood, and to exhibit neurological deficits (see Corrado, Leschied, Lussier, & Whatley, 2015; Farrington, Loeber, Jolliffe, & Pardini, 2008; Moffitt, 1993). At the family level, the risk profile often includes the intergenerational transmission of behavioral problems and delinquency (e.g., Bailey, Hill, Oesterle, & Hawkins, 2009; Loeber & Stouthamer-Loeber, 1986; Tzoumakis, Lussier, & Corrado, 2014), low parental education, and inconsistent parental discipline (Corrado et al., 2015; Corrado, Roesch, Hart, & Gierowski, 2002; Lussier, Corrado, Healey, Tzoumakis, & Deslauriers-Varin, 2011). Environmental contexts are also important. SVOs are more likely to reside in socially disorganized neighborhoods (Sampson & Groves, 1989) where violence is commonplace and where communities have low collective efficacy (Morenoff, Sampson, & Raudenbush, 2001).

These individual characteristics and life experiences inevitably have a profound impact on the mental health of young people and, in this chapter, we identify this as critical to any adequate understanding of the SVO risk profile and to the development of effective interventions. These early social experiences and the biological and psychological factors referred to above

The Wiley International Handbook of Correctional Psychology, First Edition. Edited by Devon L. L. Polaschek, Andrew Day, and Clive R. Hollin.

are likely to be associated with the onset of aggressive and violent behavior which, in turn, further contributes to the development of mental health problems. Relative to community adolescent populations, incarcerated youth display psychosis at 10 times higher rates, attention deficit hyperactivity disorder (ADHD) at between 2 and 4 times higher rates, and conduct disorder (CD) at between 5 and 20 times higher rates (Costello, Egger, & Angold, 2005; Loeber, Burke, Lahey, Winters, & Zera, 2000; Polanczyk, de Lima, Horta, Biederman, & Rohde, 2007).

High rates of comorbidity among youth within the justice system have also been reported. Utilizing a large stratified sample ($n = 1,829$) of incarcerated youth, Abram et al. (2015) found 2 in 3 youth exhibited 1+ mental disorders, while approximately 1 in 4 boys and 1 in 3 girls presented with severe comorbidity (i.e., 3+ mental disorders). Rates of mental illness decreased upon release from prison, but were still high after a 5-year follow-up period, with approximately 50% of boys and girls still exhibiting 1+ mental disorders. Extremely high levels of substance use within serious-violent-chronic and incarcerated youth samples are also particularly common (Baglivio, Jackowski, Greenwald, & Howell, 2014). The Vancouver Longitudinal study of Serious and Violent Young Offenders, for example, found that 65% of incarcerated juveniles used cocaine, 48% used crack cocaine, 45% used methamphetamine, and 18% used heroin (Corrado & McCuish, 2012).

Adolescent mental illness has at least two important implications for the juvenile justice system. First, certain forms of mental illness, particularly those related to externalizing behavioral disorders (e.g., ADHD, CD) and personality disorders, are strongly associated with conduct problems and criminal behavior (e.g., Coid, Yang, Tyrer, Roberts, & Ullrich, 2006; Corrado, DeLisi, Hart, & McCuish, 2015; Schubert, Mulvey, & Glasheen, 2011; Teplin, Welty, Abram, Dulcan, & Washburn, 2012). In contrast, while some descriptive research indicates that certain internalizing disorders are also prevalent in offender samples and associated with higher arrest rates and antisocial activity (e.g., Fazel, Doll, & Langstrom, 2008), these effects disappear when controlling for other risk factors (Schubert et al., 2011). However, when internalizing disorders are *comorbid* with externalizing disorders, this dual presentation appears to delineate those youth who are involved in persistent antisocial behavior (Loeber, Stouthamer-Loeber, & Raskin White, 1999). Not surprisingly, substantial proportions of incarcerated youth present with comorbid internalizing and externalizing disorders (Abram et al., 2015).

Regarding personality disorder, psychopathy is one of the best predictors of violent offending (e.g., Corrado et al., 2015; Douglas, Vincent, & Edens, 2006; Vaughn, Howard, & DeLisi, 2008). Recent work by McCuish, Corrado, Hart, and DeLisi (2015) clearly demonstrates that symptoms of psychopathy are indicative of involvement in chronic general offending from age 12 to 28, even while controlling for key criminogenic covariates. Certain symptoms of psychopathy also are associated with involvement in high levels of violent, as opposed to non-violent, criminal careers.

A second set of challenges arising from this (comorbid) mental health profile relate to the development of appropriate policy and programming responses. Typically, such programs are under-resourced or not consistently available; yet, mental illness and associated symptomatology (e.g., anxiety, anger-irritability) make adjustment to institutional life difficult (Cesaroni & Peterson-Badali, 2005). Not infrequently, the mutual frustration among staff and youth has been associated with increased levels of institutional misconduct, as well as self-harm (Abram et al., 2008). Relatedly, DeLisi et al. (2010) observed that trauma symptoms, a central clinical indicator of post-traumatic stress disorder (PTSD), were associated with higher suicide risk and even sexual misconduct in a large sample ($n = 813$) of serious delinquents detained by the California Youth Authority. Youth with high levels of trauma symptomatology also exhibited the most severe mental health profiles (i.e., more depression, anxiety, somatic complaints, thought disturbances, and substance use). This ever-growing body of research provides critical insight into the necessary risk/needs factors to be targeted for treatment intervention and paints a picture of the necessary complexity involved in attempting to intervene within these vulnerable populations.

Programming in Youth Custodial and Residential Settings

The use of the formal justice system (Petitclerc, Gatti, Vitaro, & Tremblay, 2013), specifically punitive interventions including incarceration and other institutional/residential placements for young offenders without systematic and effective treatment programs, has been determined to be, at best, ineffective (Lipsey & Cullen, 2007) and, at worst, criminogenic (Bales & Piquero, 2012; Sedlak & McPherson, 2010) if used as the primary response to SVOs. A growing body of research, however, provides clear support for the effectiveness of rehabilitative programming for youth involved in the criminal justice system (Koehler, Lösel, Akoensi, & Humphreys, 2013; Mihalic & Elliott, 2015), although an extremely small number of SVOs will require longer, stricter sanctions, including institutional/custodial placement, diverse programming in custody, and, after release, critical "wraparound"[1] services in the community.

A range of evidence-based intervention programs now exist for incarcerated young offenders that address their risk and criminogenic needs. In their Risk-Need-Responsivity (RNR) model of offender rehabilitation, Andrews, Bonta, and Hoge (1990) were among the first researchers to identify several principles that are associated with improved criminal justice outcomes for SVOs. This combined strategy has been shown to represent an effective mode of responding to the risks/needs of young offenders (Dowden & Andrews, 1999; Vieira, Skilling, & Peterson-Badali, 2009) when implemented with high levels of integrity (Vincent, Guy, Gershenson, & McCabe, 2012), and in particular, when rehabilitative interventions/services are matched to youth's risk level (see Brogan, Haney-Caron, NeMoyer, & DeMatteo, 2015).

Effective Institutional Programs

As suggested earlier, institutional placement for young people who have come into contact with the youth justice system should be used restrictively. For minor young offenders, community-based models have been effective; however, for young offenders in institutional settings (e.g., custody), access to appropriate programs that address their educational, mental health, and substance abuse needs have been less evident (Penner, Roesch, & Viljoen, 2011; Sedlak & McPherson, 2010). Youth detention centers nonetheless continue to be the primary location of treatment/intervention for SVOs.

Lipsey and Cullen (2007) identified wide variability in the types of programs delivered, how they were delivered, and their effectiveness. This variability, particularly in terms of the type of programs being delivered, suggests a need for standardization across juvenile justice service settings/institutions. The myriad of programs that have been implemented in youth custodial and residential facilities include those that: focus on one risk domain; target several risk factors together; are individual- or group-based; focus on one sub-population (e.g., minority groups or young women) or target all youth demographics. Each of these program modalities are further differentiated on the basis of their intended outcomes, whether these relate to lowering the risk of recidivism, enhancing school performance and/or life skills, improving psychological functioning, reducing substance use, modifying aggressive behaviors, or improving relationships with others (e.g., family, prosocial peers) and oneself (e.g., improved self-esteem).

There are large variations in the effect sizes of intervention programs for young offenders. This is illustrated in Garrido and Morales' (2007) meta-analytic review of studies that assessed the impact of rehabilitative interventions on serious (i.e., violent or chronic) young offenders (aged 12–21 years) in secure settings. All studies included in their meta-analysis employed an experimental or quasi-experimental design, and the final sample consisted of 6,658 serious young offenders from 17 separate published and unpublished research reports. The programs included in these studies focused on the individual, the group, the family, peers, or were multi-focused and were classified as cognitive behavioral, cognitive, educational, and non-behavioral/cognitive. The analyses revealed that youth who had a lower likelihood of reoffending for general and serious offenses had participated in a program (compared to no intervention) and the programs with the strongest effect sizes had a cognitive component and were multi-focused. Importantly, there were no significant differences in the outcomes for violent and chronic offenders, suggesting that specialized programs are not necessarily required for these two groups.

The above-mentioned review, however, suggests that there is no single intervention model that can be implemented to address every risk or vulnerability factor and prevent the recidivism for select groups of young offenders. Rather, multiple intervention programs that target the child's/youth's unique risk factors must be utilized to provide the specialized treatment that is required by the child/youth. Additionally, evidence that youth who receive longer interventions are more likely to have successful outcomes (Lipsey, 2009) suggests that correctional administrators and service providers in all institutional settings (whether in detention or in the community) should provide serious, violent, chronic young offenders with intensive long-term support based on their identified risk and central needs. For the diverse profiles of SVOs in custody, programs therefore need to address *each* individual risk/need factor in a coordinated manner.

Types of Programs

The remainder of this chapter reviews evidence-based programming interventions offered to youth in correctional and residential settings, as these settings are, in many countries, reserved for only the most serious-/violent-/chronic young offenders, a practice that is gradually being adopted in other traditionally conservative "crime control" nations, including the United Kingdom and parts of the United States. The following sections are delineated based on program type.

Education

The most common youth custody intervention is educational programming. This includes standard school curricula and modified coursework and activities as well as the graduate equivalency diploma (Young, Dembo, & Henderson, 2007). School, or a variation of educational or vocational training, is often required in detention facilities, since education often is mandatory until age 16. Educational programs assist youth in developing relationships with educational supports, enhancing study skills, and improving educational gratification, performance, and overall outcomes. This is typically provided through contracts with local school boards and therefore consists of standard school systems' policies and governance regarding curriculum and practices. Despite the prevalence of these programs, there is no standardized curriculum or guidelines for their delivery (Koyama, 2012). Thus, while the customization of programing is an advantage, it results in considerable variability and the coursework offered can be fundamentally different by facility. Youth in criminal justice facilities also often have special educational needs with pre-existing challenges in school settings, including school failure and poor relationships with teachers, and learning disabilities (see Macomber et al., 2010).

The Florida Department of Juvenile Justice's Avon Park Youth Academy (APYA) custodial program, which includes a voluntary community reentry component STREET[2] Smart program (SS), has demonstrated impressive positive educational and employment outcomes. The APYA/SS provides training to youth aged 16–18 who have encountered struggles in traditional school/employment training programs (National Council on Crime and Delinquency, 2009). Educational and vocational services are provided through individualized, competency-based approaches that are delivered with high intensity. The complementary SS component employs transition specialists for wraparound services for the first 12 months following release from custody to facilitate a positive transition back into the community.

An evaluation of APYA examined the outcomes for 360 moderate-risk youth assigned to the experimental APYA group and 345 youth designated as part of the control group. Despite their designation as moderate risk,[3] many youth had been arrested for a serious and/or violent offense previously and also met the criteria for chronic offending.[4] Regarding educational outcomes, although youth assigned to the control group were significantly more likely to pursue further education following their discharge from justice system involvement, youth in the treatment group were significantly more likely to obtain their high school diploma, either while in secure custody or within 2 years of being released (National Council on Crime and Delinquency, 2009). APYA youth were also more likely to be employed and received higher wages than those who were not assigned to the program. Most importantly, 1 year after completing APYA/SS programming, youth in this experimental group were less likely to recidivate with a serious or property-related offense. With the exception of Hispanic youth, lower rates of recidivism for the APYA youth, however, were not sustained at the three-year follow up time.

A number of reasons for the education-related and initial success of this program have been proposed. First, the APYA/SS program had been operating for several years and had established consistent program implementation and high program fidelity. The young offender sample also comprised youth who had been incarcerated for slightly less than 1 year on average, which allowed for a relatively long intervention period. APYA and SS staff worked collaboratively with youth and external service agencies to build case management and release planning, and assist youth in setting goals in key risk/need domains (e.g., family, education/employment/vocation, housing and independent living). This initially entailed multiple needs assessments completed when youth entered APYA and shortly before their release. A "phased approach" was an additional strength; youth began with a basic program model and expectations, then steadily graduated to the next level. In light of research indicating that a majority (i.e., more than 80%) of serious young offenders achieve a high school diploma (Stouthamer-Loeber, Wei, Loeber, & Masten, 2004), the critical piece in this is the development of human and social capital connecting youth/young adults to employment opportunities. Among the recommendations to enhance the success of the APYA/SS program is the provision of additional evidence-based practices, more specifically, transitional living support between secure custody and community reentry, as well as functional family therapy and cognitive-behavioral therapy. In doing so, the program can begin to address issues that are often associated with reoffending, such as challenges with independent living, family problems, and substance use.

The US Departments of Education and Justice (2014) have proposed five principles for secure/institutional settings that provide high-quality youth education. These (abridged) recommendations included: (a) a safe environment that prioritizes education and learning through the necessary behavioral and social support services; (b) necessary funding to offer educational opportunities comparable to those available to all young people in the community; (c) education from qualified educators who can effectively motivate youth to learn; (d) curricula that matches the standards used in non-custodial academic and career/technical education institutions to prepare youth for later employment; and, (e) services that promote coordination between various youth and family systems and successful community reentry (US Departments of Education and Justice, 2014).

Substance Abuse

Given the earlier discussed link between serious-/violent-/chronic youth offending and drug use, substance abuse programs, primarily drug and alcohol education, are the second most commonly delivered programs in youth custody (Young et al., 2007). Lipsey (2005, as cited in Young et al., 2007) reported that substance programs that targeted the development of youth's interpersonal skills along with individual counseling and behavioral interventions had the greatest impacts on recidivism. While these factors have led to the largest successes generally, treatment programming in institutional settings delivered with a high degree of integrity and length was most beneficial (Lipsey, Howell, Kelly, Chapman, & Carver, 2010).

Motivational Interviewing (MI) in institutional settings can also assist incarcerated youth with substance abuse problems. MI is typically delivered several times a week by a counselor and operates on the assumption that counselors' expressions of understanding and empathy can motivate young offenders to guide their own decision-making regarding future substance use. The counselor describes likely implications of their client's decisions and encourages positive goal setting and the monitoring of the achievement of these goals. A Campbell Review of 59 studies that validly implemented MI concluded that (compared to individuals who did not receive MI or who received minimal intervention, such as assessment and feedback) MI participants had greater reductions in substance use (Smedslund et al., 2011). Conversely, those who received other forms of active substance abuse treatment did not have significantly worse substance use outcomes. The reviewers concluded with the caveat that MI is a short-term practice and, therefore, may not result in sustainable changes to risky substance use behaviors. Still other researchers who have linked substance use problems among incarcerated youth to elevated rates of serious and violent serious recidivism have recommended the use of MI with these samples, to enhance offenders' engagement with correctional programming (van der Put, Creemers, & Hoeve, 2014).

A more intensive intervention, multisystemic therapy—substance abuse (MST-SA), is considered to be a leading substance abuse intervention model that increases prosocial attachments through structured therapy delivered to the individual and the family in both community and correctional environments. MST-SA programs that have undergone rigorous testing have reported reduced substance abuse and recidivism, significantly reducing the incidence of official and self-reported violent crimes (e.g., major and minor assault, and robbery; Henggeler, Clingempeel, Brondino, & Pickrel, 2002).

Physical and Mental Health

Given higher rates of physical illness and disease in high-risk and incarcerated youth (Barnert, Perry, & Morris, 2016; Koegl, 2010), physical and mental health services are commonly offered in correctional settings (Young et al., 2007). More generally, youth who have come into conflict with the law have often been exposed to numerous negative stimuli and events, including very early exposure to toxins as a result of maternal substance use during pregnancy, obstetric complications, and birth defects (Liu, 2011), in addition to health-related problems, substance use issues, and antisocial behaviors of their parents (Tzoumakis et al., 2014). National correctional approaches to mental health typically have been dependent on the prevalence of, and access to, treatment services (see Penner et al., 2011), despite explicit articles of the United Nations' *Convention of the Rights of the Child* (1989) outlining youth's rights to an adequate standard of health and treatment of illness.

The Mendota Juvenile Treatment Center (MJTC) is a promising program for incarcerated youth with mental illness. MJTC focuses on SVOs, as well as those who have psychopathic traits, in a residential setting. It is a "clinical–correctional hybrid" through collaboration between a secure correctional facility and a mental health facility. The ratio of professional staff to youth (1 : 28 for psychiatrists; 1 : 26 for psychologists; 1 : 14 for social workers) is much higher than in traditional secure youth facilities (Caldwell & Van Rybroek, 2005), and while more traditional personnel supervise the custody units, a trained psychiatric nurse is involved with the youth's daily activities. Youth are also housed in smaller units than they would be in traditional correctional settings.

Evaluations of the MJTC model suggest that participation reduced participants' general recidivism even while accounting for time-at-risk,[5] compared to a comparison group that received standard mental health services. This reduction held for serious and violent recidivism (Caldwell, Skeem, Salekin, & Van Rybroek, 2006). Given the extreme vulnerability of so many young offenders in custody (Peters & Corrado, 2013), the negative impact of the traditional model of youth custody and mental health resource programming (i.e., security-based rule enforcement, sanctions/reward incentives, education/leisure programs, and general health resources) is likely insufficient as an approach to treatment and rehabilitation.

Family Integrated Transition (FIT) programs have also been developed to address comorbid problems among incarcerated youth populations. Their primary focus is to assist young people with mental illness, including substance use disorders, who are preparing to return to the community (Trupin, Kerns, Walker, DeRobertis, & Stewart, 2011). This transitional period is particularly challenging for many youth (Underwood & Knight, 2006), and necessitates the provision of consistent care/support (Desai et al., 2006). FIT is an integrated, transitional program that identifies risk areas and protective factors through a programming model that combines multisystemic therapy (MST), dialectical behavior therapy, and motivational enhancement. The program is non-confrontational and aims to improve behaviors and relationships, increase opportunities to engage in educational and vocational activities, manage youth's substance use and mental health issues, and reduce rates of recidivism. Trupin et al. (2011) assessed the reoffending outcomes of 105 youth with co-occurring mental health and substance use disorders who participated in FIT. The experimental group's recidivism rate was compared to that of 169 youth with the same risk profiles who would have been eligible for FIT but were outside the catchment area, and were supervised through traditional parole. Based on the results of a Cox regression, in the 3-year post-custody period there were no significant differences for overall, violent felony/serious, or misdemeanor/non-serious recidivism between FIT and non-FIT youth. However, there was a 30% reduction in felony reoffense for the experimental group compared to the control group.

Trauma

Young offenders entering correctional and other secure facilities have disproportionately experienced multiple traumas in their childhoods, often by witnessing or directly experiencing various forms of violence and abuse. These early traumas can be one of the distinct pathways to delinquency (Steiner et al., 2011), and serious-/violent-/chronic offending (Corrado & Freedman, 2011; Fox, Perez, Cass, Baglivio, & Epps, 2015). Trauma-Focused Cognitive Behavioral Therapy (TF-CBT) attempts to diminish this risk factor by supporting the healthy development of children and young adolescents and, thereby, mitigating the likelihood of this pathway to offending. TF-CBT can be offered to younger adolescents incarcerated in inpatient (or outpatient) settings (i.e., in-custody or in-community). This approach has been shown to significantly improve parenting skills and reduce post-traumatic stress symptomatology and both externalizing and internalizing behaviors (Deblinger, Mannarino, Cohen, & Steer, 2004). However, custodial settings are not commonly viewed as therapeutic environments for addressing trauma because staff frequently view youth primarily as offenders rather than as abuse victims. As a result, TF-CBT programs are not routinely provided outside of health/mental health facilities. The high rates of PTSD among young offenders, especially females, nonetheless suggests that these programs should be situated within custody contexts, particularly when comorbid with substance abuse disorders (often self-medicating onset), as PTSD has been associated with aggressive and violent behaviors (Fox et al., 2015).

Special Programming Considerations

There has been a long-standing policy debate about the inherent advantages of community-based programming/treatment over the use of secure correctional placements. This remains contentious; although it appears that programs have the greatest success when delivered in the community, there is also evidence that there are effective evidence-based rehabilitative residential programs for SVOs. A large meta-analysis by Lipsey (2009) concluded that program setting and/or supervision level (e.g., no official supervision, diversionary practices, probation, or youth custodial facility) did not significantly distinguish effective interventions from less effective ones. Despite the above promising youth custody programs, three key policy concerns remain.

The first challenge is associated with the delivery of necessarily intrusive programs in a more salient or meaningful manner to young offenders while also utilizing constructive techniques to hold youth accountable. A second challenge is ensuring the internal validity of the programs that are delivered (i.e., the robustness and consistency in their execution and follow-up). Conducting systematic interviews with program staff and administrators (e.g., reviewing the delivery of programs or services and documenting specific intervention activities) is often necessary to ensure program fidelity and integrity (see Mowbray, Holter, Teague, & Bybee, 2003). Related to this is the need for systematic data collection that allows for an assessment of whether programs have met youth's identified needs and reduced reoffending. However, measurement of program success also should move away from the traditional emphasis on the simplistic dichotomous recidivism outcome (recidivated/did not recidivate) toward an emphasis on examining whether the criminal *trajectory* of the offender has been significantly reduced (Lussier & Davies, 2011).

A third related challenge arises in efforts to ensure that program "dosage" is matched to the young person's risk level. There is evidence, for example, that lengthier custodial stays reduce positive outcomes (Loughran et al., 2009) and that a moderate intensity or dosage of treatment has the greatest impact on the recidivism for medium- and high-risk offenders, in adults at least (Makarios, Sperber, & Latessa, 2014). Lengthier custody sentences for SVOs associated with "tough on crime" policies do not reduce recidivism. However, in certain national and subnational jurisdictions, youth remanded or sentenced to custody typically received short sentences or were only held for a brief time in response to administrative violations (Alam, 2015).

Among the most challenging policy themes is the transition from custody to community (Koyama, 2012; Young et al., 2007). It is essential to ensure the continuity of custody-based programming and case management planning into the community. To achieve this policy objective, it will likely require specific legislation and policies. Canada's *Youth Criminal Justice Act* (2002), for example, requires that young offenders sentenced to custody serve the first two thirds of their sentence in a youth facility and the final one third supervised in the community.

The research findings on the impact of post-custody programs have been mixed; however, a recent meta-analysis by Weaver and Campbell (2015) showed that treatment effects were more pronounced when aftercare programs were implemented for older youth (i.e., over 16 years of age), and for youth who had committed violent offenses. For younger offenders (i.e., under 16 years), rehabilitative programs were enhanced when families/caregivers were incorporated into the community part of the plan (Latimer, 2001). In effect, there is considerable evidence that age-related risk/needs profiles exist and require commensurate distinctive program resources, especially intensive aggression management interventions to modify the attitudes and behaviors of youth who have already exhibited violent tendencies (Farrington & Welsh, 2006; Lussier et al., 2011).

Conclusion

Youth who have perpetrated serious/violent offenses, especially persistent serious/violent offenses, although typically few in number, constitute a group that are of particular concern to the community. They continue to require theoretical understanding and empirical research to assist policy-makers and practitioners in their efforts to develop custody and custody-to-community programs that prevent serious-/violent long-term criminal trajectories. The economic and social costs resulting from SVOs are dramatic and long-lasting—both for the individual and for the community. Since most SVOs have encountered varied and entrenched challenges from early developmental stages, the need to intervene early and systematically appears essential. Not only do these adverse early experiences contribute to seriously harmful externalizing behaviors, but they can also initiate the onset of substance use/abuse and mental illness, which further perpetuate serious-/violent offending. The RNR rehabilitation framework has emphasized substance abuse as a central area of criminogenic need, with mental illness identified as a key impediment to a young person's treatment responsivity. Additionally, the detrimental effects of incarceration on youth can likely be mitigated by closely supervised and structured settings that incorporate evidenced-based intervention programs. This, paired with integrated detention-to-community programing, provides a unique policy opportunity to mitigate serious long-term offending trajectories.

While the development of and investment in new programming is a central component in understanding and responding to SVOs, there are several existing programs that have demonstrated effectiveness in reducing general and serious recidivism and improving other need outcomes, such as familial relationships, performance in school, and substance use/dependence. The key programs for incarcerated serious-/violent (and chronic) adolescent offenders include a focus on skills development through targeting educational/vocational needs (e.g., following

APYA activities) and on addressing substance abuse issues (e.g., MI, MST-SA, and MST-FIT) and mental illness (e.g., MST-FIT, MJTC, and TF-CBT). More generally, correctional programming that is multi-focused and incorporates the modification of cognitive processes can be effective at reducing general and serious recidivism.

Notes

1   "Wraparound" programs utilize community services spanning multiple sectors (e.g., education, health, mental health) that are designed to target the unique needs of at-risk children and their families to promote positive developmental outcomes.
2   Acronym for: success, transition assistance, reduce recidivism, employment, education, training.
3   Based on youth's most serious index offense. The most serious index offense for 63.1% of the intervention group was a property offense; 15.3% a drug-related offense; 13.3% a person-related offense; 5.0% a public order offense; and 3.3% a weapon only offense (National Council on Crime and Delinquency (2009).
4   The mean number of criminal arrests among the APYA was 5.7 (compared to 5.8 for the control group) and the mean number of previous felony arrests and violent felony arrests were 3.1 and 0.5, respectively, for both groups.
5   Time-at-risk refers to the amount of time a youth is in the community and is "at-risk" to reoffend.

Key Readings

Corrado, R. R., & McCuish, E. C. (2015). The contribution of mental health disorders to antisocial behavior pathways. In J. Morizot, & L. Kazemian (Eds.), *The development of criminal and antisocial behavior: Theory, research and practical applications* (pp. 365–378). Cham, Switzerland: Springer.
Fazel, S., Doll, H., & Langstrom, N. (2008). Mental disorders among adolescents in juvenile detention and correctional facilities: A systematic review and metaregression analysis of 25 surveys. *Journal of the American Academy of Child and Adolescent Psychiatry*, 47(9), 1010–1019.
Sawyer, A. M., & Borduin, C. M. (2011). Effects of multisystemic therapy through midlife: A 21.9-year follow-up to a randomized clinical trial with serious and violent juvenile offenders. *Journal of Consulting and Clinical Psychology*, 79, 643–652.
Schubert, C. A., Mulvey, E., & Glasheen, C. (2011). Influence of mental health and substance use problems and criminogenic risk on outcomes in serious juvenile offenders. *Journal of the American Academy of Child and Adolescent Psychiatry*, 50(9), 925–937.

References

Abram, K. M., Choe, J. Y., Washburn, J. J., Teplin, L. A., King, D. C., & Dulcan, M. K. (2008). Suicidal ideation and behaviors among youths in juvenile detention. *Journal of the American Academy of Child and Adolescent Psychiatry*, 47(3), 291–300.
Abram, K. M., Zwecker, N. A., Welty, L. J., Hershfield, J. A., Dulcan, M. K., & Teplin, L. A. (2015). Comorbidity and continuity of psychiatry disorders in youth after detention: A prospective longitudinal study. *JAMA Psychiatry*, 72, 84–93.
Alam, S. (2015). Youth court statistics in Canada, 2013/2014. Statistics Canada. Retrieved from https://www150.statcan.gc.ca/n1/pub/85-002-x/2015001/article/14224-eng.htm

Andrews, D. A., Bonta, J., & Hoge, R. D. (1990). Classification for effective rehabilitation: Rediscovering psychology. *Criminal Justice and Behavior*, 17, 19–52.

Baglivio, M. T., Jackowski, K., Greenwald, M. A., & Howell, J. C. (2014). Serious, violent, and chronic juvenile offenders. *Criminology & Public Policy*, 13, 83–116.

Bailey, J. A., Hill, K. G., Oesterle, S., & Hawkins, J. D. (2009). Parenting practices and problem behavior across three generations: Monitoring harsh discipline and drug use in the intergenerational transmission of externalizing behavior. *Developmental Psychology*, 45(5), 1214–1226.

Bales, W. D., & Piquero, A. R. (2012). Assessing the impact of imprisonment on recidivism. *Journal of Experimental Criminology*, 8, 71–101.

Barnert, E. S., Perry, R., & Morris, R. E. (2016). Juvenile incarceration and health. *Academic Pediatrics*, 16, 99–109.

Brogan, L., Haney-Caron, E., NeMoyer, A., & DeMatteo, D. (2015). Applying the Risk-Needs-Responsivity (RNR) model to juvenile justice. *Criminal Justice Review*, 40, 277–302.

Caldwell, M., Skeem, J., Salekin, R., & Van Rybroek, G. (2006). Treatment response of adolescent offenders with psychopathy features: A 2-year follow-up. *Criminal Justice and Behavior*, 33(5), 571–596.

Caldwell, M. F., & Van Rybroek, G. J. (2005). Reducing violence in serious juvenile offenders using intensive treatment. *International Journal of Law and Psychiatry*, 28, 622–636.

Cesaroni, C., & Peterson-Badali, M. (2005). Young offenders in custody: Risk and adjustment. *Criminal Justice and Behavior*, 32(3), 251–277.

Coid, J., Yang, M., Tyrer, P., Roberts, A., & Ullrich, S. (2006). Prevalence and correlates of personality disorder in Great Britain. *The British Journal of Psychiatry*, 188(5), 423–431.

Corrado, R. R., DeLisi, M., Hart, S. D., & McCuish, E. C. (2015). Can the causal mechanisms underlying chronic, serious, and violent offending trajectories be elucidated using thepsychopathy construct? *Journal of Criminal Justice*, 43(4), 251–261.

Corrado, R. R., & Freedman, L. (2011). Risk profiles, trajectories, and intervention points for serious and chronic young offenders. *International Journal of Child, Youth and Family Studies*, 2(2.1), 197–232.

Corrado, R. R., Leschied, A., Lussier, P., & Whatley, J. (2015). *Serious and violent young offenders and youth criminal justice: A Canadian perspective.* Burnaby, BC: SFU.

Corrado, R. R., & McCuish, E. C. (2012). *A lifestyles theoretical perspective on patterns of substance use and offending profiles of juvenile offenders.* Paper presented at the American Society of Criminology, Chicago, IL.

Corrado, R. R., Roesch, R., Hart, S. D., & Gierowski, J. K. (2002). *Multi-problem violent youth: A foundation for comparative research on needs, interventions, and outcomes.* Burke, VA: IOS Press.

Costello, E. J., Egger, H., & Angold, A. (2005). 10-year research update review: The epidemiology of child and adolescent psychiatric disorders: I. Methods and public health burden. *Journal of the American Academy of Child and Adolescent Psychiatry*, 44(10), 972–986.

Deblinger, E., Mannarino, A. P., Cohen, J. A., & Steer, R. A. (2004). A follow-up study of a multisite, randomized, controlled trial for children with sexual abuse-related PTSD symptoms. *Journal of the American Academy of Child and Adolescent Psychiatry*, 45, 1474–1484.

DeLisi, M., Drury, A. J., Kosloski, J. W., Caudill, J. W., Conis, P. J., Anderson, C. A., … & Beaver, K. M. (2010). The cycle of violence behind bars: Traumatization and institutional misconduct among juvenile delinquents in confinement. *Youth Violence and Juvenile Justice*, 8, 107–121.

Desai, R. A., Goulet, J. L., Robbins, J., Chapman, J. F., Migdole, S. J., & Hoge, M. A. (2006). Mental health care in juvenile detention facilities: A review. *Journal of the American Academy of Psychiatry and the Law*, 34, 204–214.

Douglas, K. S., Vincent, G. M., & Edens, J. F. (2006). Risk for criminal recidivism: The role of psychopathy. In C. J. Patrick (Ed.), *The handbook of psychopathy*. New York, NY: Guilford Press.

Dowden, C., & Andrews, D. A. (1999). What works in young offender treatment: A meta- analysis. *Forum on Corrections Research*, 11, 21–24.

Farrington, D. P., Loeber, R., Jolliffe, D., & Pardini, D. A. (2008). Promotive and risk processes at different life stages. In R. Loeber, D. P. Farrington, M. Stouthamer-Loeber, & H. Raskin White (Eds.), *Violence and serious theft: Development and prediction from childhood to adulthood* (pp. 169–230). New York, NY: Routledge.

Farrington, D. P., & Welsh, B. C. (2006). *Saving children from a life of crime: Early risk factors and effective interventions.* Oxford, UK: Oxford University Press.

Fazel, S., Doll, H., & Langstrom, N. (2008). Mental disorders among adolescents in juvenile detention and correctional facilities: A systematic review and metaregression analysis of 25 surveys. *Journal of the American Academy of Child and Adolescent Psychiatry*, 47(9), 1010–1019.

Fox, B. H., Perez, N., Cass, E., Baglivio, M. T., & Epps, N. (2015). Trauma changes everything: Examining the relationship between adverse childhood experiences and serious, violent and chronic juvenile offenders. *Child Abuse and Neglect*, 46, 163–173.

Garrido, V., & Morales, L. A. (2007). Serious (violent or chronic) juvenile offenders: A systematic review of treatment effectiveness in secure corrections. *Campbell Systematic Reviews*, 7, Retrieved from https://campbellcollaboration.org/library/serious-juvenile-offenders-treatment-effectiveness.html

Henggeler, S. W., Clingempeel, W. G., Brondino, M. J., & Pickrel, S. G. (2002). Four-year follow-up of multisystemic therapy with substance-abusing and substance-dependent juvenile offenders. *Journal of the American Academy of Child and Adolescent Psychiatry*, 41, 868–874.

Koegl, C. J. (2010). *Calculation of the long-term medical, mental health and criminal justice system costs associated with early childhood conduct disorder in an Ontario sample children: Structured clinical risk assessment through the Early Assessment Risk Lists for Boys and Girls.* Toronto, Canada: Child Development Institute Retrieved from http://www.excellenceforchildandyouth.ca/sites/default/files/gai_attach/GA-272_Final_Outcomes_Report.pdf

Koehler, J. A., Lösel, F., Akoensi, T. D., & Humphreys, D. K. (2013). A systematic review and meta-analysis on the effects of young offender treatment programs in Europe. *Journal of Experimental Criminology*, 9(1), 19–43.

Koyama, P. R. (2012). The status of education in pre-trial juvenile detention. *Journal of Correctional Education*, 63, 35–68.

Latimer, J. (2001). A meta-analytic examination of youth delinquency, family treatment, and recidivism. *Canadian Journal of Criminology*, 43, 237–253.

Lipsey, M. W. (2009). The primary factors that characterize effective interventions with juvenile offenders: A meta-analytic overview. *Victims and Offenders*, 4, 124–147.

Lipsey, M. W., & Cullen, F. T. (2007). The effectiveness of correctional rehabilitation: A review of systematic reviews. *Annual Review of Law and Social Sciences*, 3, 297–320.

Lipsey, M. W., Howell, J. C., Kelly, M. R., Chapman, G., & Carver, D. (2010). *Improving effectiveness of juvenile justice programs: A new perspective on evidence-based practice.* Washington, DC: Georgetown University, Center for Juvenile Justice Reform.

Liu, J. (2011). Early health risk factors for violence: Conceptualization, review of the evidence, and implications. *Aggression and Violent Behavior*, 16, 63–73.

Loeber, R., Burke, J., Lahey, B., Winters, A., & Zera, M. (2000). Oppositional defiant and conduct disorder: A review of the past 10 years, part I. *Journal of the American Academy of Child and Adolescent Psychiatry*, 39, 1484–1486.

Loeber, R., & Stouthamer-Loeber, M. (1986). Family factors as correlates and predictors of juvenile conduct problems and delinquency. *Crime and Justice*, 7, 29–149.

Loeber, R., Stouthamer-Loeber, M., & Raskin White, H. (1999). Developmental aspects of delinquency and internalizing problems and their association with persistent juvenile substance use between ages 7 and 18. *Journal of Clinical Child Psychology*, 28(3), 322–332.

Loughran, T. A., Mulvey, E. P., Schubert, C. A., Fagan, J., Piquero, A. R., & Losoya, S. H. (2009). Estimating a dose-response relationship between length of stay and future recidivism in serious juvenile offenders. *Criminology*, 47, 699–740.

Lussier, P., Corrado, R., Healey, J., Tzoumakis, S., & Deslauriers-Varin, N. (2011). The Cracow instrument for multi-problem violent youth: Examining the postdictive validity with a sample of pre-schoolers. *International Journal of Child, Youth, and Family Studies*, 2(2.1), 294–329.

Lussier, P., & Davies, G. (2011). A person-oriented perspective on sexual offenders, offending trajectories, and risk of recidivism: A new challenge for policymakers, risk assessors, and actuarial prediction? *Psychology, Public Policy, and Law*, 17, 530–561.

Macomber, D., Skiba, T., Blackmon, J., Esposito, E., Hart, L., Mambrino, E., … & Grigorenko, E. L. (2010). Education in juvenile detention facilities in the state of Connecticut: A glance at the system. *Journal of Correctional Education*, 61, 223–261.

Makarios, M., Sperber, K. G., & Latessa, E. J. (2014). Treatment dosage and the risk principle: A refinement and extension. *Journal of Offender Rehabilitation*, 53, 334–350.

McCuish, E. C., Corrado, R. R., Hart, S. D., & DeLisi, M. (2015). The role of symptoms of psychopathy in persistent violence over the criminal career into full adulthood. *Journal of Criminal Justice*, 43(4), 345–356.

Mihalic, S. F., & Elliott, D. S. (2015). Evidence-based programs registry: Blueprints for healthy youth development. *Evaluation and Program Planning*, 48, 124–131.

Moffitt, T. E. (1993). Adolescence-limited and life-course-persistent antisocial behavior: A developmental taxonomy. *Psychological Review*, 100(4), 674–701.

Morenoff, J. D., Sampson, R. J., & Raudenbush, S. W. (2001). Neighborhood inequality, collective efficacy, and the spatial dynamics of urban violence. *Criminology*, 39(3), 517–559.

Mowbray, C. T., Holter, M. C., Teague, G. B., & Bybee, D. (2003). Fidelity criteria: Development, measurement, and validation. *American Journal of Evaluation*, 24(3), 315–340.

National Council on Crime and Delinquency (2009). *In search of evidence-based practice in juvenile corrections: An evaluation of Florida's Avon Park Youth Academy and STREET Smart program.* Madison, WI: Author. Retrieved from https://www.ncjrs.gov/pdffiles1/ojjdp/grants/228804.pdf

Penner, E. K., Roesch, R., & Viljoen, J. L. (2011). Young offenders in custody: An international comparison of mental health services. *International Journal of Forensic Mental Health*, 10, 215–232.

Peters, A. M. F., & Corrado, R. R. (2013). An examination of the early "strains" of imprisonment among young offenders incarcerated for serious crimes. *Journal of Juvenile Justice*, 2(2), 50–68.

Petitclerc, A., Gatti, U., Vitaro, F., & Tremblay, R. E. (2013). Effects of juvenile court exposure on crime in young adulthood. *Journal of Child Psychology and Psychiatry*, 54, 291–297.

Polanczyk, G., de Lima, M. S., Horta, B. L., Biederman, J., & Rohde, L. A. (2007). The worldwide prevalence of ADHD: A systematic review and metaregression analysis. *American Journal of Psychiatry*, 164, 942–948.

van der Put, C. E., Creemers, H. E., & Hoeve, M. (2014). Differences between juvenile offenders with and without substance use problems in the prevalence and impact of risk and protective factors for criminal recidivism. *Drug and Alcohol Dependence*, 134, 267–274.

Sampson, R. J., & Groves, W. B. (1989). Community structure and crime: Testing social-disorganization theory. *American Journal of Sociology*, 94(4), 774–802.

Schubert, C. A., Mulvey, E., & Glasheen, C. (2011). Influence of mental health and substance use problems and criminogenic risk on outcomes in serious juvenile offenders. *Journal of the American Academy of Child and Adolescent Psychiatry*, 50(9), 925–937.

Sedlak, A. J., & McPherson, K. S. (2010). *Youth's needs and services: Findings from the survey of youth in residential placement.* Juvenile Justice Bulletin. Washington, DC: Department of Justice, Office of Justice Programs, Office of Juvenile Justice and Delinquency Prevention.

Smedslund, G., Berg, R. C., Hammerstrøm, K. T., Steiro, A., Leiknes, K. A., Dahl, H. M., & Karlsen, K. (2011). Motivational interviewing for substance abuse. Campbell Systematic Reviews, 6. Retrieved from https://campbellcollaboration.org/library/motivational-interviewing-for-substance-abuse.html

Steiner, H., Silverman, M., Karnik, N. J., Huemer, J., Plattner, B., Clark, C. E., ... & Haapanen, R. (2011). Psychopathology, trauma and delinquency: Subtypes of aggression and their relevance for understanding young offenders. *Child and Adolescent Psychiatry and Mental Health*, 5, 21–32.

Stouthamer-Loeber, M., Wei, E., Loeber, R., & Masten, A. S. (2004). Desistance from persistent serious delinquency in the transition to adulthood. *Development and Psychopathology*, 16, 897–918.

Teplin, L. A., Welty, L. J., Abram, K. M., Dulcan, M. K., & Washburn, J. J. (2012). Prevalence and persistence of psychiatry disorders in youth after detention: A prospective longitudinal study. *Archives of General Psychiatry*, 69(10), 1031–1043.

Trupin, E. J., Kerns, S. E. U., Walker, S. C., DeRobertis, M. T., & Stewart, D. G. (2011). Family integrated transitions: A promising program for juvenile offenders with co-occurring disorders. *Journal of Child and Adolescent Substance Abuse*, 20, 421–436.

Tzoumakis, S., Lussier, P., & Corrado, R. R. (2014). Profiles of maternal parenting practices: Exploring the link with maternal delinquency, offending, mental health, and children's physical aggression. *International Journal of Offender Therapy and Comparative Criminology*, 59(12), 1267–1296.

US Departments of Education and Justice (2014). *Guiding principles for providing high-quality education in juvenile justice secure care settings.* Washington, DC: Author Retrieved from http://www2.ed.gov/policy/gen/guid/correctional-education/guiding-principles.pdf

Underwood, L. A., & Knight, P. (2006). Treatment and post-release rehabilitative programs for juvenile offenders. *Child and Adolescent Psychiatric Clinics of North America*, 15, 539–556.

United Nations. (1989). Convention on the Rights of the Child. UN General Assembly Document, A/RES/44/25. Treaty Series, 1577, 3.

Vaughn, M. G., Howard, M. O., & DeLisi, M. (2008). Psychopathic personality traits and delinquent careers: An empirical examination. *International Journal of Law and Psychiatry*, 31(5), 407–416.

Vieira, T. A., Skilling, T. A., & Peterson-Badali, M. (2009). Matching court-ordered services with treatment needs predicting treatment success with young offenders. *Criminal Justice and Behavior*, 36(4), 385–401.

Vincent, G. M., Guy, L. S., Gershenson, B. G., & McCabe, P. (2012). Does risk assessment make a difference? Results of implementing the SAVRY in juvenile probation. *Behavioral Sciences & the Law*, 30(4), 384–405.

Weaver, R. D., & Campbell, D. (2015). Fresh start: A meta-analysis of aftercare programs for juvenile offenders. *Research on Social Work Practice*, 25(2), 201–212.

Young, D. W., Dembo, R., & Henderson, C. E. (2007). A national survey of substance abuse treatment for juvenile offenders. *Journal of Substance Abuse Treatment*, 32, 255–266.

Youth Criminal Justice Act, S.C. 2002, c. 1.

15

The Psychology of Sexual Offending

Sarah Brown

Coventry University, UK

Introduction

Sex offenses account for a small percentage of all violent crimes, yet they provoke a great deal of concern in practitioners, policy-makers, and the public. This has resulted in them being the subject of more attention than any other type of offense, with more research being conducted on these offenses compared to other types of crime. Similarly, compared to other offense types, for individuals who have committed sexual offenses, there are a greater number of intervention programs, risk assessments, and other practice tools and resources, and a greater variety of criminal justice responses, including mandatory polygraph assessments, registries and community notification, residency restrictions, and civil commitment. Criminal justice, policy, and public responses to individuals who have committed sex offenses are notoriously punitive, yet a great deal of effort and resources have also been invested in rehabilitative programs and, in some areas, in support initiatives (e.g., circles of support).

Although some initiatives targeted at preventing sexual abuse have a long history (e.g., Stop It Now), these approaches have been receiving greater attention more recently and are being adopted more widely, with the introduction of new (and often controversial) approaches, such as the Dunkelfeld project (https://www.dont-offend.org). Most individuals convicted of a sexual offense are managed and supervised in the community at some point, either immediately following sentencing or after a period of incarceration. This presents a number of challenges for those working with these individuals as a result of potentially negative community responses, the types of legislation that apply to them (e.g., community notification), the constantly changing legislation, updated research knowledge and associated recommendations for best practice, updated and changing risk tools/resources, and the harm that could result from reoffending. The aim of this chapter is to provide a brief overview of what we know about sexual offenses and those who commit them and the reasons for this.

The Wiley International Handbook of Correctional Psychology, First Edition. Edited by Devon L. L. Polaschek, Andrew Day, and Clive R. Hollin.

Sexual Offenses

The term *sexual offenses* covers a variety of offenses, including rape, sexual assault, offenses against children, and those related to exploitation, sex working, trafficking, and the possession, generation, and distribution of child sexual exploitation material (CSEM) and other illegal sexual material. In most jurisdictions many of these offenses are clearly labeled as sexual offenses; for example in England and Wales they are covered by the Sexual Offences Act (2003).

Other offenses fall under different types of legislation, where similar crimes can be committed for sexual and non-sexual purposes; for example in England and Wales the trafficking of individuals falls under the Modern Slavery Act (2015), which includes trafficking for sexual exploitation or abuse. Other offenses do not typically include sexual behaviors and/or sexual motivations (e.g., homicide and burglary) but may have sexual behaviors and motivation in some instances.

Hence, it can be difficult to identify all individuals who have committed a sexual offense. Furthermore, although strictly speaking a *legal* definition, the terms *sexual offense* and particularly *sexual offender* are often used more widely to refer to individuals who have engaged in, or whom it is believed have engaged in, behaviors that are illegal, whether or not they have been officially sanctioned for these behaviors.

Types of Sexual Offenses

Due to the wide variety of sexual offenses, a range of terms (including a range of slang and informal terms) have been used to refer to groups of sexual offenses and those who commit them. For example, *rapist* is typically used to refer to individuals who have committed contact offenses against adults, while *child sexual offenders* and *child molesters* refer to those who have committed contact offenses against children. Individuals who have engaged in online CSEM crimes are often referred to as *online offenders*. This range of terms can be confusing, especially as different people mean slightly different things when they use the terms and the terms can be used to over-include individuals inappropriately, often with the terms inducing stereotypes and negative perceptions. For example, in surveys of the public, *sex offender* is commonly associated with a high risk of reoffending and non-amenability to treatment (Katz-Schiavone, Levenson, & Ackerman, 2008; Levenson, Brannon, Fortney, & Baker, 2007).

Moreover, the commonly used terms sex offender and *juvenile sex offender* were associated with increased support for policies including internet disclosure and residency restrictions in a national sample of the public in the United States, compared to "people who have committed crimes of a sexual nature" and "minor youth who have committed crimes of a sexual nature" (Harris & Socia, 2016). For these reasons, there have been attempts by practitioners and academics more recently to avoid labeling people (e.g., rapist and sex offender) and to label instead their behaviors (children who have engaged in harmful sexual behaviors). Even when we do this, differences between legal jurisdictions, lack of clarity around definitions in reports and research studies, use of different definitions, and so on make it difficult to identify which offenses/people are being referred to and to compare the findings across studies and prevalence and incidence rates.

Pedophilia/Pedophile

Pedophile is a term that is often used interchangeably with (child) sex offender (and *child molester*). It is important to note that pedophilia and other paraphilias have distinct clinical definitions and criteria for diagnosis. There is much debate about the inclusion of sex-related diagnoses in mental health manuals such as the *Diagnostic and Statistical Manual of Mental Disorders, Fifth Edition* (DSM-5; American Psychiatric Association, 2013) and the *Classification of Diseases and Related Health Problems*, or ICD-10, (World Health Organization, 1992) that is beyond the scope of this chapter. Paraphilias are defined as intense and persistent sexual interests and require both the presence of paraphilic urges and the existence of distress, dysfunction, and/or acting on the urges. In the DSM-5, eight are specifically identified: voyeuristic, exhibitionistic, frotteuristic, sexual masochism, sexual sadism, pedophilic, fetishistic, and transvestic disorders. Behaviors associated with many of these, especially if non-consensual, are illegal in many jurisdictions.

Pedophilia relates to sexual interests toward pre-pubescent children, yet the term, along with *pedophile*, is used to describe many more people than would meet the DMS-5 criteria. For example, it is often used in relation to crimes that involve pubescent or post-pubescent children. These terms are also commonly used much more broadly as negative terms and insults. Crucially, it is important to note that not all sex offenses (even all those committed against children) are committed by individuals who meet clinical definitions of pedophilia (or other paraphilias). In addition, although often the source of much skepticism and debate, not all people who meet the criteria for pedophilic/paraphilia diagnoses commit sexual offenses.

This is a very important point as it has been shown that public attitudes toward this group are punitive. For example, 14% of a sample surveyed in two German cities and 28% of English speakers surveyed online agreed that people with pedophilia were better off dead even if they never had committed criminal acts (Jahnke, Imhoff, & Hoyer, 2015). Even when compared to "individuals who have sexual interest in (prepubescent) children," punitive attitudes to pedophiles were stronger (Imhoff, 2015). Moreover, punitive attitudes to pedophiles were positively associated with social desirability, indicating that condemning pedophiles is seen as being socially acceptable. The association between pedophilia and sexual offending is also problematic as it encourages assumptions that sexual offenses are generally motivated by sexual interests/arousal and that individuals who commit sexual offenses commit a huge number of offenses and are very likely to reoffend. These assumptions are not correct, as is discussed in more detail later in the chapter.

Prevalence

It is difficult to accurately assess the number of sexual offenses for a number of reasons: societal denial, the secrecy of the offense, the consequences of disclosure for victims, and the lack of a standard definition and methodology. Official recording practices and policy can change over time and incidents that are reported to authorities may not be officially recorded. Thus, estimates of the incidence (estimates of the number of new cases in a given period of time) and prevalence (estimates of the proportion of a population that has been affected by the phenomenon) are unreliable and provide a confused picture. For example, in 1981, Safafino estimated that 336,200 sex offenses were committed against children each year in the United States, which varied considerably from the estimate of 44,700 by the National Centre on Child

Sexual Abuse and Neglect (NCCAN; Goldman & Padayachi, 2000). Rind, Tromovitch and Bauserman (1998, cited in Goldman & Padayachi, 2000) reported that estimates of the prevalence of abuse victimization for males ranged from 3 to 37%, with a mean estimate of 17%; and for females ranged from 8 to 71%, with a mean of 28%. It is clear, then, that a considerable proportion of the population will be the victim of at least one sexual offense during their lifetime.

Estimating the number of individuals who perpetrate these offenses is similarly problematic. Davies (1998) extrapolated that there were 1.1 million individuals who had victimized children in the United Kingdom (which had at the time a total population of approximately 58.8 million).[1] Marshall (1997) revealed that by the time they were 40, 1 in 90 men born in 1953 in England and Wales (at least 165,000 men) had been convicted of a serious sexual offense (e.g., rape, incest, gross indecency) against a child; 1 in 60 had been convicted of a sexual offense, which included less serious offenses. More recently the Ministry of Justice (2016) reported that there were just under 52,500 registered sex offenders in England and Wales, which is 104 people in 100,000 or 1 in every 1,000 persons. It is important to note, however, that not all those who are convicted of sexual offenses are required to register. Moreover, given the large numbers of people being identified and convicted for CSEM offenses in particular, this is still likely to be an underestimate of all those who are actually engaging in illegal sexual behaviors. Chief Constable Simon Bailey, the National Police Chiefs' Council lead for child protection, reported in February 2017 that 400 individuals were being arrested each month in England/Wales for online CSEM offenses. Hence, the level of offending is significant.

Who Commits Sexual Offenses?

Heterogeneity

Studies have shown that there is a myth of homogeneity regarding the sex offending population across the domains of media and public policy (Galeste, Fradella, & Vogel, 2012; Harris, Lobanov-Rostovsky, & Levenson, 2010; Sample & Bray, 2006). It is important to note, however, that individuals who commit sexual offenses vary widely both between and within offense types. Individuals who sexually offend come from all walks of life, varying in terms of basic demographics, socioeconomic level, education and employment, relationship status, health and mental health, prior legal involvement, and other characteristics. While some individuals who commit sexual offenses may share characteristics with non-sexual offenders, the majority do not have extensive criminal histories or criminal lifestyles.

Furthermore, patterns of offending often do not replicate those of other types of crime. For example, although the age–crime curve is an established criminological pattern, individuals who commit sexual offenses vary more widely in age. McKillop, Brown, Smallbone, and Pritchard (2015) found that in a sample of males convicted of sexual offenses in Queensland, Australia, the majority (66%) reported that they were aged between 25 and 49 when they committed their first sexual offense; 25% were aged between 18 and 24; and 8% were aged over 50. In a sample who reported first offending during adolescence, the majority (47%) were aged 13 or 14 when they first offended and 14% were aged under 13 years. Hence there is no typical sex offender.

Moreover, despite media and stereotypical images of lonely, isolated men who offend in this way because they are "evil," "sick," or "mad" and ultimately different in some way from the "normal" members of society, individuals who perpetrate sexual offenses cannot be easily distinguished from those who do not, other than by the commission of these criminal acts. There is no battery of questions or psychometric tests that can be used to distinguish individuals likely to commit sexual offenses from those who are not.

Females

Although it is widely accepted that the majority of sexual offenses are committed by men, we should not underestimate the number of offenses perpetrated by women. Several barriers exist to reporting female-perpetrated abuse, such as the common perception that sexual abuse perpetrated by women is harmless in comparison to male-perpetrated abuse, and traditional stereotypes and sexual scripts that portray females as sexually passive and innocent (Oliver, 2007). When individuals are surveyed about their sexual victimization experiences, the incidence of female-perpetrated sex offenses is higher than indicated by the number of women convicted of sexual offenses. For example, up to 63% of female and 27% of male survivors report sexual victimization by women (Schwartz & Cellini, 1995), yet estimates vary widely. A recent meta-analysis found the prevalence rate of sexual offenses committed by females ranged from 2% for sexual offenses reported to law enforcement to 11.6% reported in victimization surveys (Cortoni, Babchishin, & Rat, 2016). Males were much more likely to self-report victimization by females compared to females.

Stereotypical portrayals suggest that the impact of offenses perpetrated by women is less than that perpetrated by men, yet the empirical evidence highlights that there are more similarities than differences between males and female in terms of the degree of intrusiveness or the use of violence (Allen, 1991; Denov, 2004a; Elliot, 1993; Kaufman, Wallace, Johnson, & Reeder, 1995) and that victims often experience extreme stigma, shame, and isolation (Elliot, 1993; Hislop, 2001; Saradjian, 1997). Despite this, research and attention to this group is still sparse, leading to a lack of tools, resources, and interventions.

Co-offending is a particular characteristic of female sexual offending which differentiates it from male sex offending. For example, Williams and Bierie (2015) found that a co-offender was present in 38.1% of the cases involving females compared to 11.8% involving males (Williams and Bierie (2015). Recent high-profile cases in the United Kingdom have highlighted groups and gangs of men systematically grooming and sexually exploiting children and young people (see Berelowitz, Clifton, Firimin, Gulyurtlu, & Edwards, 2013), and so the numbers of co-offending men may be higher than has previously been recognized.

Denov's (2004b) examination of professional responses identified a propensity among police officers to assume that in co-offending cases, female participation was male coerced. Adshead (2011) explained how techniques are frequently used that reduce women's agency and responsibility for violence compared to their male counterparts, and compared to non-offending women. Similarly, Eldridge and Saradjian (2000) suggested that because violence in the form of sexual abuse by women is such a transgression of our expectations of female behavior, it has been difficult to understand why women behave in this way. The majority of typologies developed to describe sexual abuse by women differentiate single and co-offenders.

Juveniles

The exact prevalence is difficult to establish, but it is clear that a considerable proportion of sexual offenses are perpetrated by children and young people under the age of 18. For example, Finkelhor, Ormrod, and Chaffin (2009) reported that in the United States, one quarter (26%)

of all sex offenders were youths and more than one third (36%) of those who offended did so against youth victims.

Children and young people who commit sexual offenses are often assumed to be at high risk of persistent sexual offending into and throughout their adulthood. This assumption was originally fueled by early clinical studies in which it was reported that adults convicted of sexual offenses typically began sexual offending as adolescents (Abel, Becker, Mittelman, Rouleau, & Murphy, 1987; Groth, Longo, & McFadin, 1982). However, the weight of evidence now indicates instead that most adolescents who commit sexual offenses do not go on to offend sexually as adults (e.g., Lussier & Blokland, 2014; Nisbet, Wilson, & Smallbone, 2004). In fact, they tend to reoffend more frequently with non-sexual crimes than with sexual crimes (Keelan & Fremouw, 2013). Those adolescents who do continue to commit sexual offenses into adulthood tend to desist by their early 30s (Lussier & Blokland, 2014). Further, most adults convicted of sexual offenses did not begin sexually offending in their adolescence (Marshall, Barbaree, & Eccles, 1991; McKillop, Smallbone, Wortley, & Andjic, 2012; Smallbone & Wortley, 2004). This pattern appears to hold for both adult-victim and child-victim sexual offending.

Strangers?

One consequence of the media image of sex offenders is that when thinking about sexual offenses, we tend to imagine the most violent predatory crimes, and a continued emphasis on "stranger-danger" appears to underpin much legislation such as community notification and residency restrictions. However, sexual offending encompasses a wide range of behaviors, including viewing and creating CSEM, trafficking, exposure, and a range of contact offenses, including penetration. These offenses can be enacted using force that varies from subtle coercion through to overt physical violence.

As Cowburn and Dominelli (2001, p. 403) pointed out, there are

> two images—the dangerous beast and the harmless, largely incompetent and misunderstood dirty old man.... In this context, there is no stereotype that relates to the abuser who offends against children for whom he has a responsibility of care.

This is despite the fact that it has long been established that both children and adults are at most risk of being sexually abused and/or murdered by those we know and trust. For example, in our recent study (McKillop, Brown, Smallbone, & Wortley, 2015) of individuals imprisoned for sexual offenses against children in Queensland, Australia, over half of the sample (53%) reported that their first victim was from their family and just under half (47%) from outside the family. Just 6% reported abusing a stranger. The majority (63%) had known their victims for more than 1 year prior to the first abuse incident and one third (33%) had established relationships with the victims for less than 1 year.

The most common familial victims were step-children (25%) or biological children (13%). The most common non-familial victims were children of friends (13%), neighbors (7%), or children met through work (7%). Similar patterns are observed in adult survivors. For example, in a US general population survey asking women about their victimization (Kilpatrick, Resnick, Ruggiero, Conoscenti, & McCauley, 2007), 11% reported forcible rapes were committed by strangers; the remainder were perpetrated by (ex-)husbands (10%), (step-)fathers (11%), boyfriends (14%), other relative (18%), friend (12%), classmate (2%), and other non-relative

(22%). Furthermore, most offenses take place in private locations. Four fifths of the abuse against children reported in our study (McKillop et al., 2015) took place in domestic settings (80%). Of the 20 offenses committed in non-domestic settings, three were in organizational settings and 17 in public settings.

Desistance

The "evil predatory monster" image and media portrayal of sexual offending imply that all those convicted of sexual offenses have an enduring high risk of recidivism. The New York Governor, George Pataki, was cited as saying "… studies have shown that sex offenders are more likely to repeat their crime than any other crime." (reported by Zgoba, Sager, & Witt, 2003, p. 135). The public appear to have similar beliefs. For example, Levenson et al. (2007) found that the average member of the general public believes that 75% of sex offenders will reoffend. In reality, however, and notwithstanding the range of difficulties associated with measuring recidivism (see Przybylski, n.d., for a more detailed discussion), most individuals convicted of a sexual offense, whether adults or juveniles, are never convicted of another sexual crime (Hanson & Morton-Bourgon, 2005). In their large meta-analysis, Hanson and Morton-Bourgon (2005) found that 14% sexually reoffended over a period averaging 5–6 years, with rates increasing the longer the follow-up period, reaching 24% after 15 years. Even studies with long follow-up periods and thorough searches for reoffending rarely calculate recidivism rates in excess of 40% (Hanson & Bussière, 1996).

Contrary to public perceptions, many of those who reoffend do not specialize in one type of sex crime, or even in sexual offenses. This is evidenced by Hanson and Morton-Bourgon's (2005) finding that those convicted of sexual offenses had a 5- to 6-year recidivism rate for sex crimes and non-sexual violent crimes combined of approximately 36%. Moreover, the risk of recidivism for those convicted of sexual offenses is not higher than other groups of offenders. This is clearly demonstrated by the 1-year recidivism data for England and Wales recorded by the Ministry of Justice for adult (n = 473,000) and juvenile offenders (n = 35,000) who were released from custody, received a non-custodial conviction at court, or received a caution in the period July 2014–June 2015 (Ministry of Justice, 2016). One quarter (25%; adults 24%, juveniles 38%) committed a proven reoffense within 1 year. Adult offenders with an index offense of theft had the highest proven reoffending rate of 42.0%; the second highest, 31.7%, was for those with an index offense of robbery. The third lowest rate was for those with sexual index offenses, 13.2%, with the lowest rates for summary motoring and fraud index offenses. In the juvenile cohort, those with an index offense of robbery had the highest proven reoffending rate, at 43.9%, closely followed by those with an index offense of public order, at 43.4%. Those with the lowest rate had a sexual index offense and reoffended at a rate of 15.5%.

Average rates of recidivism, however, mask a great deal of variation between offense types and between individuals with different offense histories and characteristics, with some displaying higher rates of recidivism and many very low rates of recidivism (see Lievore, 2003, for a review). Hanson and Morton-Bourgon (2005) reported 15-year recidivism rates of 13% for incest offenders, 24% for rapists, and 35% for those who had sexually abused boys. Predictors of general recidivism were similar for other types of offenders. The main factors that increased risk of sexual reoffending, however, in both adults and adolescents, were sexual deviancy and antisocial orientation. For the categories of deviant sexual attitudes and intimacy deficits, some variables were related to sexual recidivism, such as emotional identification with children, and conflicts in intimate relationships; but some, such as loneliness, were not. Hanson and Morton-Bourgon (2005) concluded that more research was needed to identify the aspects of attitudes and social functioning most associated with persistent sexual offending.

These findings and many others demonstrate how many of the variables that have been believed to be related to sexual offending have not been supported by research evidence. There has been much debate, for example, about the link between empathy and sexual offending (see Brown, 2017, for more information). Although denial is still often a factor used to exclude offenders from treatment and has long been believed to be a risk factor, the latest research developments suggest that it is a protective factor, particularly given the value of family and community support in desistance (see Blagden, Winder, Gregson, & Thorne, 2014; Ware, Marshall, & Marshall, 2015; for more information about interventions and treatment, see Marshall, Chapter 32).

It is also important to note that much of the research has been conducted on convicted offenders, which might mean that the factors that have been identified in this population do not represent all people who engage in harmful sexual behaviors. Only recently, for example, have individuals been convicted of offenses relating to online CSEM, and these individuals do not feature in recidivism studies with long follow-up periods, as they have not been released for long enough or in many instances have not yet come to the end of their sentences. Although much research has investigated this group of individuals, in particular comparing the characteristics of those convicted of online CSEM with those convicted of contact offenses, there is still much to establish about this group of individuals. The extent of awareness of offending in other contexts—such as in groups and gangs, by individuals offending in organizations, by those in other positions of trust (e.g., sports coaches), and sex trafficking—has been growing in recent years. Although some individuals who abused or exploited people in these contexts will have been convicted and included in studies previously, these types of offenses currently have a very limited evidence-base: meaning that we do not know if individuals who commit these offenses are similar to other contact or online CSEM offenders, or if they have different characteristics and require different theories and explanations.

Theories

A number of theories have been developed to explain sexual offending. Some try to explain sexual offending broadly (i.e., across a range of offense types) and others have been more focused (e.g., by explaining child sexual abuse, or the use of online CSEM). Some theories have been centered on one or a small number of features, often called single-factor theories, and others have included a range of factors, often referred to as multi-factor theories. The majority of theories have been developed to explain offending by adult men, but some have been developed for adult women (see Harris, 2010), juveniles (for a review of theories for juveniles, see Leversee, n.d.), and female juveniles (Frey, 2010). As can be seen from this overview of the array of theories, and given the range of offenses and individuals who commit them, it is very difficult to explain the causes of these behaviors, which are multifaceted and complex. Moreover, despite the number of theories and research studies, our understanding of the causes of offending and the reasons why some desist and others continue offending over long periods of time is limited.

It is beyond the scope of this chapter to review all the theories that have been developed to explain sexual offending. One of the more recently developed theories is the integrated theory

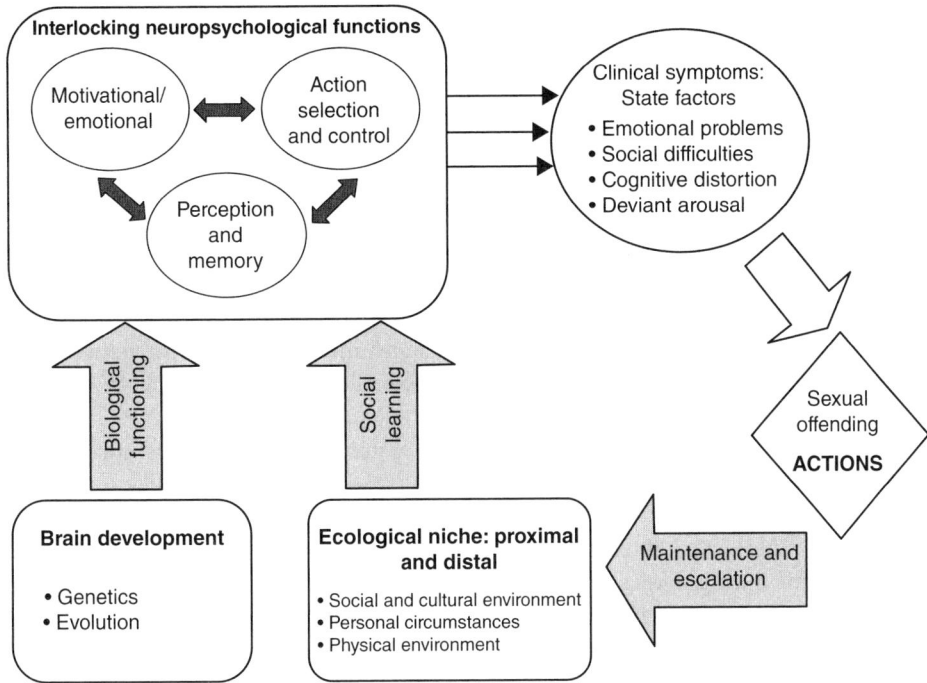

Figure 15.1 Schematic illustration of the ITSO. Source: Ward and Beech (2016). © John Wiley & Sons, Ltd. Reproduced with permission.

of sexual offending—revised (ITSO; Ward & Beech, 2016). This was designed as a broad framework to inform the construction of more specific theories of particular types of sexual offending (e.g., rape, child sexual abuse), and to unify theories (Ward & Beech, 2016). In order to get a good understanding of the ITSO, it is important to read Ward and Beech's (2016) chapter.

In summary, and as shown in Figure 15.1, sexual offending is argued to be a consequence of many casual factors operating at different levels in biological (evolution, genetic variations, and neurobiology influenced by genetic inheritance and brain development), ecological (social and cultural environment, personal circumstances, physical environment, and learning), core neuropsychological systems, and personal agency domains (i.e., reflecting on possible reasons for acting, deciding on a course of action, and then [intentionally] acting in accordance with one's goals). According to this framework, these factors and the relationships between them are constantly changing and dynamic. Genetic predispositions, developmental processes, and social learning influence brain development, which results in three connected neuropsychological systems that can be conceptualized as resulting in desire, belief, and action.

Ward and Beech (2016) argued that these elements combine to generate four sets of clinical problems that have been evidenced in individuals who have committed sexual offenses (Mann, Hanson, & Thornton, 2010). These are deviant arousal, offense-related thoughts and fantasies, negative/positive emotional states, and social difficulties. Personal agency then mediates these factors to increase the likelihood that an individual will sexually offend (Ward & Beech, 2016). The outcomes of these behaviors in turn influence a feedback loop that influences the future likelihood of offending. As can be seen, this is a complex theory that attempts to explain not only the cause of the first sexual offenses, but also why this behavior is continued in some people and not in others. Many previous theories tended to explain only one or other of these two important aspects. This means that different strategies need to be used in general prevention methods to reduce the risk that the first offense is committed, compared to strategies to encourage desistance in those who have already engaged in harmful sexual behaviors. This is a distinction that is not always made in our prevention efforts.

Most of the theories that have been developed to explain sexual offending focus on factors that relate to an individual's history and/or their characteristics, thoughts, and demographics, as is evidenced in the ITSO. Situational theories that have been influential in understanding many non-sexual crimes have often been overlooked in relation to sexual offending. This has meant that the circumstances and interpersonal contexts within which these offenses occur have also been overlooked (Smallbone, Marshall, & Wortley, 2008; Wortley & Smallbone, 2006).

There are a number of reasons, however, why a greater focus on this approach might enhance our understanding of and efforts to prevent sexual offending. Unlike for other types of crimes, as discussed previously, there appear to be two periods that are associated with increased risk of child sexual abuse: adolescence and mid- to late 30s (Hanson, 2002). Harmful sexual behavior during adolescence has been argued to be an extension of existing antisocial or aggressive tendencies, whereby the emergence of sexually aggressive or abusive behavior coincides with the onset of ordinary sexual exploration and peer activities in adolescence (Caldwell, 2002; Finkelhor et al., 2009; Zimring, 2004). Hence, it may be partly explained by the psychological, physiological, and social changes—these factors are all included in the ITSO—occurring during adolescence that generate sexual motivations and present new opportunities for sexual interaction, but at the same time limit adolescents' capacities for responsible decision-making (Haigh, 2009). An immature understanding of sexuality, sexual relationships, and sexual behavior may compound these factors (Rich, 2011). Adolescents are also likely to be subjected to lower levels of supervision and external control than in earlier stages of their development (Calder, 2001).

Although many individual and psychosocial factors have been identified in sexual offending, as per the ITSO (Ward & Beech, 2016), sexual offending that starts during adulthood can also coincide with changes in family, work, and social circumstances (e.g., [step-]fatherhood, child-oriented employment), which enable unsupervised access to children (Hanson, 2002; Laub & Sampson, 2003; Thornberry & Krohn, 2005). Sexual abuse incidents, for the most part, occur in contexts of ordinary social interaction, and situational approaches, such as routine activities theories (Cohen & Felson, 1979; Hindelang, Gottfredson, & Garofalo, 1978) and rational choice theory (Cornish & Clarke, 1986), can be used to understand why crimes take place in particular locations, at particular times. Routine activities theorists view crimes as the "function of the convergence of likely offenders and suitable targets in the absence of capable guardians" (Cohen & Felson, 1979, p. 590). All three of these components are necessary for the crime to occur. Focused on decision-making, rational choice theorists argue that offenders make choices to offend according to the perceived risk and effort involved relative to reward (Cornish & Clarke, 1986, 2003).

There is some empirical support for this approach. For example, Smallbone and Wortley's (2000) research showed that, for the most part, individuals who sexually abused children did not actively seek out opportunities to exploit children sexually, at least not initially. Instead they took advantage of opportunities in the context of their everyday lives, and in particular the context of caregiver duties. Evidence that younger children tend to be at greater risk of familial abuse and older children non-familial abuse (Fischer & McDonald, 1998; Smallbone et al., 2008; Snyder, 2000) is consistent with expected changes in children's routine activities from within the home to outside the home as they grow older. Leclerc, Smallbone, and Wortley (2015) found that situational factors such as the presence of a guardian influenced offenses, for example in terms of the severity and duration of sexual abuse.

Similarly, McKillop et al. (2015) found that individuals' reported first incidents of sexual abuse against children most often occurred in the home, and that older victims were more likely to be sexually abused by someone outside their families and in the later hours of the day compared to younger victims. We concluded that this pattern supported routine activities theories because victims were those to whom individuals had access and offenses occurred in contexts and during times where the perpetrators and victims were most likely to be interacting with each other. In their meta-analysis, Babchishin, Hanson, and VanZuylen (2015) found that contact offenders were more likely to have access to children than offenders who have engaged in CSEM offenses. Thus, more could be understood about the situational dynamics of these incidents in both adolescence and adulthood to establish why individual vulnerabilities lead to sexually abusive behavior at particular times and places. This is particularly relevant to the first sexual abuse incident where motivations to sexually offend might not yet be well established, which means that contextual factors might have a greater influence at this stage. For example, Wortley (2001, 2008) suggested that situations might serve to pressure, prompt, provoke, or permit sexually abusive behavior. This indicates that situations not only provide opportunities for sexual offenses, but they can also induce motivation in a previously unmotivated individual (Wortley, 2001).

Summary and Conclusion

There are many stereotypes and misperceptions around those who perpetrator sexual offenses, which can have an impact on how we treat and engage with these individuals. It is important, therefore, that practitioners have a good and accurate understanding of these offenses and the individuals who engage in harmful sexual behavior. It is clear that a large number of individuals experience sexual violence as either children or adults and that a large number of individuals perpetrate these offenses. Contrary to popular perceptions, however, it is not easy to identify those who perpetrate sexual offenses as there are no clear differences between them and the non-offending population. Individuals who commit sexual offenses come from all walks of life and are not characterized by mental and/or personality disorders. Moreover, harmful sexual behavior is engaged in by children and young people, women, and known and trusted individuals more than is commonly believed. The evidence shows that reoffending rates are not as high as many expect, although rates vary between types of offenses and between individuals who have committed the same offenses. Theories that attempt to explain why individuals commit sexual offenses are complex and include many variables, many of which will not be present in all cases, meaning that an individual assessment is needed for each individual and that a simple model of intervention is unlikely to be effective (see Marshall, Chapter 32). Furthermore, greater consideration of situation and contextual factors, in addition to intra-personal factors, may enable a greater understanding of the causes of sexual abuse and the development of effective prevention strategies.

Note

1   For a discussion of discussion of prevalence and incidence in relation to the United States, please see Wiseman (n.d.).

Key Readings

Bateman, J., & Milner, J. (2014). *Children and young people whose behavior is sexually concerning or harmful. Assessing risk and developing safety plans.* Philadelphia, PA: Jessica Kingsley.
Centre for Sex Offender Management (CSOM). Retrieved from http://csom.org/index.html
Gannon, T. A., & Cortoni, F. (2010). *Female sexual offenders. Theory, assessment and treatment.* London, UK: Wiley-Blackwell.
Gannon, T. A., & Ward, T. (Eds.) *Sexual offending: Cognition, emotion, and motivation.* Oxford, UK: Wiley-Blackwell.
Laws, D. R., & Ward, T. (2010). *Desistance from sex offending: Alternatives to throwing away the keys.* New York, NY: Guilford Press.
Sex Offender Management Assessment and Planning Initiative (SMART). Office of Justice Programs. Retrieved from https://www.smart.gov/SOMAPI/index.html

References

Abel, G. G., Becker, J. V., Mittelman, M. S., Rouleau, J. L., & Murphy, W. (1987). Self-reported sex crime of non-incarcerated paraphiliacs. *Journal of Interpersonal Violence*, 2, 3–25.
Adshead, G. (2011). Same but different: Constructions of female violence in forensic mental health. *International Journal of Feminist Approaches to Bioethics*, 4, 41–68.
Allen, C. M. (1991). *Women and men who sexually abuse children: A comparative analysis.* Orwell, VT: The Safer Society Press.
American Psychiatric Association (2013). *Diagnostic and statistical manual of mental disorders* (5th ed.). Arlington, VA: American Psychiatric.
Babchishin, K. M., Hanson, R. K., & VanZuylen, H. (2015). Online child pornography offenders are different: A meta-analysis of the characteristics of online and offline sex offenders against children. *Archives of Sexual Behavior*, 44(1), 45–66.
Berelowitz, S., Clifton, J., Firimin, C., Gulyurtlu, S., & Edwards, G. (2013). *"If only someone had listened": Office of the Children's Commissioner's inquiry into child sexual exploitation in gangs and groups.* London, UK: The Office of the Children's Commissioner.
Blagden, N., Winder, B., Gregson, M., & Thorne, K. (2014). Making sense of denial in sexual offenders: A qualitative phenomenological and repertory grid analysis. *Journal of Interpersonal Violence*, 29(9), 1698–1731.
Brown, S. J. (2017). Bridging the cognitive–emotion divide: Empathy and sexual offending. In T. A. Gannon, & T. Ward (Eds.), *Sexual offending: Cognition, emotion, and motivation* (pp. 53–70). Oxford, UK: Wiley-Blackwell.
Calder, M. C. (2001). *Juveniles and children who sexually abuse: Frameworks for assessment* (3rd ed.). Lyme Regis, UK: Russell House Publishing.
Caldwell, M. F. (2002). What we do not know about juvenile sexual reoffense risk. *Child Maltreatment*, 7, 291–302.
Cohen, L. E., & Felson, M. (1979). Social change and crime rate trends: A routine activity approach. *American Sociological Review*, 44, 588–608.

Cornish, D. B., & Clarke, R. V. (1986). Introduction. In D. Cornish, & R. Clarke (Eds.), *The reasoning criminal* (pp. 1–16). New York, NY: Springer-Verlag.

Cornish, D. B., & Clarke, R. V. (2003). Opportunities, precipitators and criminal dispositions: A reply to Wortley's critique of situational crime prevention. In M. J. Smith, & D. B. Cornish (Eds.), *Theory for practice in situational crime prevention* (pp. 41–96). Monsey, NJ: Criminal Justice Press.

Cortoni, F., Babchishin, K. M., & Rat, C. (2016). The proportion of sexual offenders who are female is higher than thought: A meta-analysis. *Criminal Justice and Behavior*, 44(2), 145–162.

Cowburn, M., & Dominelli, L. (2001). Masking hegemonic masculinity: Reconstructing the paedophile as the dangerous stranger. *British Journal of Social Work*, 31, 399–415.

Davies, N. (1998, June 2). The epidemic in our midst that went unnoticed. *The Guardian*, pp. 4–5.

Denov, M. S. (2004a). The long-term effects of child sexual abuse by female perpetrators: A qualitative study of male and female victims. *Journal of Interpersonal Violence*, 19, 1137–1156.

Denov, M. S. (2004b). *Perspectives on female sex offending: A culture of denial*. Aldershot, UK: Ashgate.

Eldridge, H. J., & Saradjian, J. (2000). Replacing the function of abusive behaviors for the offender: Remaking relapse prevention in working with women who sexually abuse children. In D. R. Laws, S. M. Hudson, & T. Ward (Eds.), *Remaking relapse prevention with sex offenders: A sourcebook* (pp. 402–426). Thousand Oaks, CA: Sage.

Elliot, M. (1993). *Female sexual abuse of children: The ultimate taboo*. Chichester, UK: Wiley.

Finkelhor, D., Ormrod, R., & Chaffin, M. (2009). Juveniles who commit sex offenses against minors. *Office of Juvenile Justice and Delinquency Prevention Juvenile Justice Bulletin*. Retrieved from https://www.ncjrs.gov/pdffiles1/ojjdp/227763.pdf

Fischer, D. G., & McDonald, W. L. (1998). Characteristics of intrafamilial and extrafamilial child sexual abuse. *Child Abuse and Neglect*, 22(9), 915–929.

Frey, L. L. (2010). The juvenile sex offender: Characteristics, treatment and research. In T. A. Gannon, & F. Cortoni (Eds.), *Female sexual offenders. Theory, assessment and treatment* (pp. 53–72). London, UK: Wiley-Blackwell.

Galeste, M., Fradella, H., & Vogel, B. (2012). Sex offender myths in print media: Separating fact from fiction in US newspapers. *Western Criminology Review*, 13, 4–24.

Goldman, J. D. G., & Padayachi, U. K. (2000). Some methodological problems in estimating incidence and prevalence in child sexual abuse research. *Journal of Sex Research*, 37(4), 305–314.

Groth, A. N., Longo, R. E., & McFadin, J. B. (1982). Undetected recidivism among rapists and child molesters. *Crime and Delinquency*, 28, 450–458.

Haigh, Y. (2009). Desistance from crime: Reflections on the transitional experiences of young people with a history of offending. *Journal of Youth Studies*, 12(3), 307–322.

Hanson, R. K. (2002). Recidivism and age: Follow-up data from 4,673 sexual offenders. *Journal of Interpersonal Violence*, 17, 1046–1062.

Hanson, R. K., & Bussière, M. T. (1996). Predictors of sexual offender recidivism: A meta-analysis. (User Report 96-04). Ottawa, Canada: Department of the Solicitor General of Canada.

Hanson, R. K., & Morton-Bourgon, K. E. (2005). The characteristics of persistent sexual offenders: A meta-analysis of recidivism studies. *Journal of Consulting and Clinical Psychology*, 73(6), 1154–1163.

Harris, A. J., Lobanov-Rostovsky, C., & Levenson, J. S. (2010). Widening the net: The effects of transitioning to the Adam Walsh Act's federally mandated sex offender classification system. *Criminal Justice and Behavior*, 37(5), 503–519.

Harris, A. J., & Socia, K. M. (2016). What's in a name? Evaluating the effects of the "sex offender" label on public opinions and beliefs. *Sexual Abuse: A Journal of Research and Treatment*, 28(7), 660–678.

Harris, D. A. (2010). Theories of female sexual offending. In T. A. Gannon, & F. Cortoni (Eds.), *Female sexual offenders. Theory, assessment and treatment* (pp. 31–52). London, UK: Wiley-Blackwell.

Hindelang, M. J., Gottfredson, M. R., & Garofalo, J. (1978). *Victims of personal crime: An empirical foundation for a theory of personal victimisation*. Cambridge, UK: Ballinger.

Hislop, J. (2001). *Female sex offenders: What therapists, law enforcement and child protective services need to know*. Ravensdale, WA: Issues Press.

Imhoff, R. (2015). Punitive attitudes against pedophiles or persons with sexual interest in children: Does the label matter? *Archives of Sexual Behavior*, 44(1), 35–44.

Jahnke, S., Imhoff, R., & Hoyer, J. (2015). Stigmatization of people with pedophilia: Two comparative surveys. *Archives of Sexual Behavior*, 44(1), 21–34.

Katz-Schiavone, S., Levenson, J. S., & Ackerman, A. R. (2008). Myths and facts about sexual violence: Public perceptions and implications for prevention. *Journal of Criminal Justice and Popular Culture*, 15(3), 291–311.

Kaufman, K., Wallace, A., Johnson, C. F., & Reeder, M. L. (1995). Comparing female and male perpetrators' modus operandi: Victims' reports of sexual abuse. *Journal of Interpersonal Violence*, 10, 322–333.

Keelan, M. C., & Fremouw, W. J. (2013). Child versus peer/adult offenders: A critical review of the juvenile sex offender literature. *Aggression and Violent Behavior*, 18(6), 732–744.

Kilpatrick, D. G., Resnick, H. S., Ruggiero, K. J., Conoscenti, L. M., & McCauley, J. (2007). *Drug-facilitated, incapacitated, and forcible rape: A national study*. Charleston, SC: National Crime Victims Research & Treatment Center Retrieved from https://www.ncjrs.gov/pdffiles1/nij/grants/219181.pdf

Laub, J. H., & Sampson, R. J. (2003). *Shared beginnings, divergent lives: Delinquent boys to age 70*. Cambridge, MA: Harvard University Press.

Leclerc, B., Smallbone, S. W., & Wortley, R. K. (2015). Prevention nearby: The influence of the presence of a potential guardian on the severity of child sexual abuse. *Sexual Abuse: A Journal of Research and Treatment*, 27(2), 189–204.

Levenson, J. S., Brannon, Y. N., Fortney, T., & Baker, J. (2007). Public perceptions about sex offenders and community protection policies. *Analyses of Social Issues and Public Policy*, 7, 137–161.

Leversee, T. (n.d.). Etiology and typologies of juveniles who have committed sexual offenses. *Sex Offender Management Assessment and Planning Initiative (SMART)*. Office of Justice Programs. Retrieved from https://www.smart.gov/SOMAPI/sec2/ch2_etiology.html

Lievore, D. (2003). *Recidivism of sexual assault offenders: Rates, risk factors and treatment efficacy*. A report prepared for the Office of the Status of Women by the Australian Institute of Criminology.

Lussier, P., & Blokland, A. (2014). The adolescence–adulthood transition and Robin's continuity paradox: Criminal career patterns of juvenile and adult sex offenders in a prospective longitudinal birth cohort study. *Journal of Criminal Justice*, 42, 153–163.

Mann, R. E., Hanson, R. K., & Thornton, D. (2010). Assessing risk for sexual recidivism: Some proposals on the nature of psychologically meaningful risk factors. *Sexual Abuse: A Journal of Research and Treatment*, 22, 191–217.

Marshall, P. (1997). *The prevalence of convictions for sexual offending*. Research findings no. 55. London, UK: HMSO.

Marshall, W. L., Barbaree, H. E., & Eccles, A. (1991). Early onset and deviant sexuality in child molesters. *Journal of Interpersonal Violence*, 6, 323–336.

McKillop, N., Brown, S. J., Smallbone, S. W., & Pritchard, K. (2015). Similarities and differences in adolescence-onset and adult-onset sexual abuse offending. *Child Abuse and Neglect*, 46, 37–46.

McKillop, N., Brown, S. J., Smallbone, S. W., & Wortley, R. K. (2015). How victim age affects the context and timing of child sexual abuse: Applying the routine activities approach to the first sexual abuse incident. *Crime Science Special Issue: Child Sexual Abuse*, 4(17), 1–20 Retrieved from http://www.crimesciencejournal.com/content/pdf/s40163-015-0031-8.pdf

McKillop, N., Smallbone, S. W., Wortley, R. K., & Andjic, I. (2012). Offenders' attachment and sexual abuse onset: A test of theoretical propositions. *Sexual Abuse: A Journal of Research and Treatment*, 24(6), 591–610.

Ministry of Justice. (2016). *Multi-agency public protection arrangements annual report 2015/16*. Ministry of Justice Statistics Bulletin. Retrieved from https://www.gov.uk/government/uploads/system/uploads/attachment_data/file/563117/MAPPA_Annual_Report_2015-16.pdf

Modern Slavery Act (2015) c.30. London, UK: The Stationary Office.

Nisbet, I. A., Wilson, P. H., & Smallbone, S. W. (2004). A prospective longitudinal study of sexual recidivism among adolescent sex offenders. *Sexual Abuse: A Journal of Research and Treatment*, 16(3), 223–233.

Oliver, B. E. (2007). Preventing female-perpetrated sexual abuse. *Trauma Violence Abuse*, 8(1), 19–32.

Przybylski, R. (n.d.). Adult sex offender recidivism. *Sex Offender Management Assessment and Planning Initiative (SMART)*. Office of Justice Programs. Retrieved from https://www.smart.gov/SOMAPI/sec1/ch5_recidivism.html

Rich, P. (2011). *Understanding, assessing, and rehabilitating juvenile sex offenders* (2nd ed.). New York, NY: Wiley.

Sample, L. L., & Bray, T. M. (2006). Are sex offenders different? An examination of rearrest patterns. *Criminal Justice Policy Review*, 17, 83–102.

Saradjian, J. (1997). Factors that specifically exacerbate the trauma of victims of childhood sexual abuse by maternal perpetrators. *Journal of Sexual Aggression*, 3, 3–14.

Schwartz, B. K., & Cellini, H. R. (Eds.) (1995). *The sex offender: Corrections, treatment, and legal practice*. Kingston, NJ: Civic Research Institute.

Sexual Offences Act (2003) c.42, London, UK: The Stationary Office.

Smallbone, S. W., & Wortley, R. K. (2000). *Child sexual abuse in Queensland: Offender characteristics and modus operandi*. Brisbane, Australia: Queensland Crime Commission.

Smallbone, S. W., Marshall, W. L., & Wortley, R. K. (2008). *Preventing child sexual abuse: Evidence, policy and practice*. Cullompton, UK: Willan.

Smallbone, S. W., & Wortley, R. K. (2004). Onset, persistence and versatility of offending among adult males convicted of sexual offenses against children. *Sexual Abuse: A Journal of Research and Treatment*, 16, 285–298.

Snyder, H. N. (2000). *Sexual assault of young children as reported to law enforcement: Victim, incident, and offender characteristics*. Washington, DC: US Department of Justice, Bureau of Justice Statistics.

Thornberry, T. P., & Krohn, M. D. (2005). Applying interactional theory in the explanation of continuity and change in antisocial behavior. In *Advances in criminological theory* (Vol. 14) (pp. 183–210). New Brunswick, NJ: Transaction.

Ward, T., & Beech, A. R. (2016). The integrated theory of sexual offending—revised. A multifield perspective. In D. P. Boer (Ed.), *The Wiley handbook on the theories, assessment, and treatment of sexual offending* (pp. 123–137). London, UK: Wiley-Blackwell Retrieved from http://onlinelibrary.wiley.com/doi/10.1002/9781118574003.wattso006/pdf

Ware, J., Marshall, W. L., & Marshall, L. E. (2015). Categorical denial in convicted sex offenders: The concept, its meaning, and its implication for risk and treatment. *Aggression and Violent Behavior*, 25, 215–226.

Williams, K. S., & Bierie, D. M. (2015). An incident-based comparison of female and male sexual offenders. *Sexual Abuse: A Journal of Research & Treatment*, 27(3), 235–257.

Wiseman, J. (n.d.). Incidence and prevalence of sexual offending. *Sex Offender Management Assessment and Planning Initiative (SMART)*. Office of Justice Programs. Retrieved from https://www.smart.gov/SOMAPI/sec1/ch1_incidence.html

World Health Organization (1992). *International statistical classification of diseases and related health problems (International Classification of Diseases—10th revision, ICD-10)*. Geneva, Switzerland: Author.

Wortley, R. K. (2001). A classification of techniques for controlling situational precipitators of crime. *Security Journal*, 14(4), 63–82.

Wortley, R. K. (2008). Situational precipitators of crime. In R. K. Wortley, & L. Mazerolle (Eds.), *Environmental criminology and crime analysis* (pp. 48–66). Cullompton, UK: Willan.

Wortley, R. K., & Smallbone, S. W. (2006). Applying situational principles to sexual offenses against children. In R. K. Wortley, & S. W. Smallbone (Eds.), *Situational prevention of child sexual abuse* (Vol. 19) *Crime prevention studies* (pp. 7–35). Monsey, NY: Criminal Justice Press.

Zgoba, K. M., Sager, W. R., & Witt, P. H. (2003). Evaluation of New Jersey's sex offender treatment program at the Adult Diagnostic and Treatment Center: Preliminary results. *Journal of Psychiatry and Law*, 31(2), 133–164.

Zimring, F. E. (2004). *An American travesty: Legal responses to adolescent sexual offending.* Chicago, IL: University of Chicago Press.

16

Severe Mental Illness: Crime, Antisocial and Aggressive Behavior

Sheilagh Hodgins
Université de Montréal, Canada

Sanja Klein
Justus-Liebig-University, Giessen, Germany

Severe Mental Illness and Crime

The severe mental illnesses, or psychoses, include schizophrenia, schizo-affective disorder, bipolar disorder, and other psychoses. Three types of investigations have been conducted to determine the risk that persons with these disorders present for criminal offending. One, studies of population cohorts compare the criminal records of cohort members who were, and who were not, admitted to hospital with diagnosis of a severe mental illness. These studies all showed that greater proportions of both males and females with, than without, severe mental illness had been convicted of criminal offenses. The differences between persons with, than without, severe mental illness were greater for violent than for non-violent crime, and the associations between severe mental illness and violent and non-violent crime were stronger for females than for males (Fazel & Grann, 2006; Hodgins, 2008; Hodgins, Mednick, Brennan, Schulsinger, & Engberg, 1996). Two, follow-up studies which compared the criminal activities of persons with severe mental illness who were discharged from inpatient psychiatric wards to those of non-disordered persons living in the same community consistently showed that more of those with severe mental illness than their non-ill neighbors were convicted of crimes. As in the population cohort studies, the association between severe mental illness and offending was greatest for violent crimes (Hodgins, 1998). Three, a meta-analysis confirmed higher rates of severe mental illness among convicted offenders than in the general population (Fazel & Seewald, 2012). Subsequent studies of population cohorts (Brennan, Mednick, & Hodgins, 2000; Fazel, Lichtenstein, Grann, Goodwin, & Långström, 2010) confirmed that the association of severe mental illness with criminality, and especially violent criminality, was almost entirely due to schizophrenia.

Schizophrenia[1] and Crime

Robust evidence shows that both males and females with schizophrenia are at elevated risk, as compared to the general population, of conviction for non-violent criminal offenses, at higher risk of conviction for violent criminal offenses, and at even higher risk of conviction for homicide. For example, we examined a birth cohort composed of all the 358,180 persons born in Denmark from 1944 through 1947 followed until they were in their mid-40s. We excluded those who had died or emigrated before the end of the follow-up period. The official criminal records of cohort members who had been admitted to a psychiatric ward at least once with a discharge diagnosis of schizophrenia were compared to those with no psychiatric admissions. The risk of a violent crime was elevated 4.6 (3.8–5.6) times among the men and 23.2 (14.4–37.4) times among the women with schizophrenia as compared to those with no admissions to a psychiatric ward (Brennan et al., 2000). Other studies have reported similar elevations in risk among persons with schizophrenia (Arseneault, Moffitt, Caspi, Taylor, & Silva, 2000; Fazel et al., 2010; Tiihonen, Isohanni, Räsänen, Koiranen, & Moring, 1997; Wallace et al., 2004). Most violent offenses committed by persons with schizophrenia are assaults. Homicides attract much attention from the media, but they are rare. In some countries all persons accused of homicide undergo thorough psychiatric evaluations prior to trial. These evaluations have been used to estimate the proportion of homicides that are committed by individuals with schizophrenia, and estimates vary from 6 to 28% (Erb, Hodgins, Freese, Müller-Isberner, & Jöckel, 2001). Schizophrenia affects just under 1% of the general population, yet a meta-analysis estimated that it affects 6.48% of homicide offenders (Large, Smith, & Nielssen, 2009).

   This association between schizophrenia and violent offending has been observed by different research teams who recruited samples from countries with different cultures and health and justice systems, and who measured the association of schizophrenia and offending using different experimental designs. No evidence indicates that these findings resulted from biases within the criminal justice systems of the various countries where the research was conducted (Hodgins & Janson, 2002). The convictions that are documented in these many studies result from crimes committed in the community and not in hospitals.

Conclusion

Robust evidence shows that individuals with schizophrenia are more likely than those without this disorder to be convicted, or found not guilty because of a mental disorder, of crimes, especially violent crimes. Importantly, individuals with schizophrenia are also more likely to engage in aggressive behavior toward others (Hodgins, Alderton, Cree, Aboud, & Mak, 2007; Swanson et al., 2006). Only some of the incidents of aggressive behavior lead to criminal prosecution. The correlates of violent crime and aggressive behavior are similar.

Crime Prior to a First Episode of Schizophrenia

Most (72%) people with schizophrenia who will commit a criminal offense do so prior to first contact with mental health services (Wallace et al., 2004). This fact is reflected in the results of a recent meta-analysis showing that 35% of individuals who contacted services for a first episode of psychosis had previously committed at least one assault (Large & Nielssen, 2011). Another meta-analysis showed that the risk of homicide is 15.5 times higher in individuals

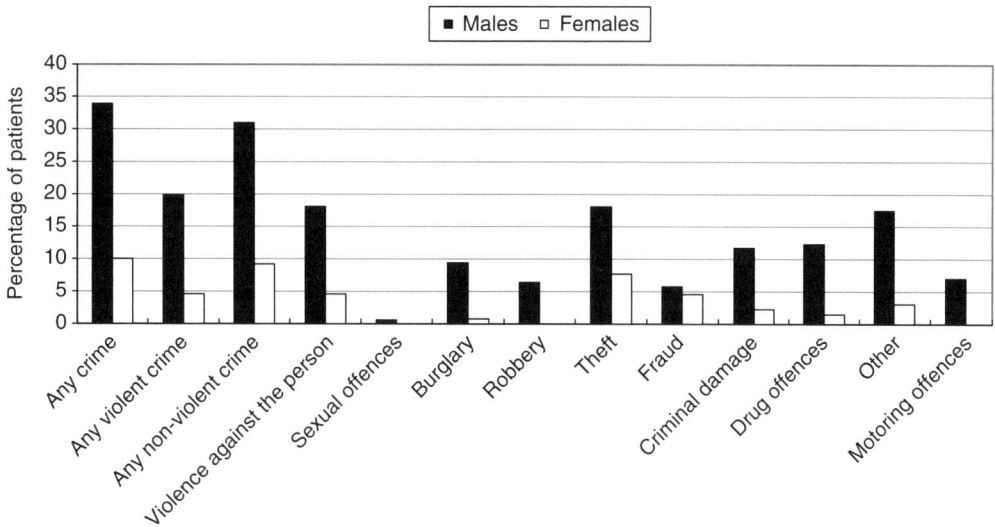

Figure 16.1 Percentages of first-episode patients convicted of crimes prior to illness onset in specific offence categories.

experiencing a first episode of psychosis who were not treated as compared to the general population (Nielssen & Large, 2010).

We conducted another study, in London, of all patients experiencing a first episode of psychosis who sought treatment in one mental health trust (Hodgins et al., 2010). The sample included 168 men and 133 women, on average 30 years old, most of whom presented schizophrenia and the others major affective disorders. Official criminal records were obtained from the Home Office Offenders' Index and the Police National Computer (PNC). We defined convictions to include both convictions and judgments of not guilty by reason of insanity or diminished responsibility. Prior to onset of psychosis, one-third of the men and 10% of the women had been convicted of at least one offense, and 19.9% of the men and 4.6% of the women had been convicted of at least one violent crime. As shown in Figure 16.1, the most common offenses among males were violence against the person, theft, and other offenses, and among women theft, violence against the person, and fraud.

Another recent study, of a large sample of patients recruited from first-episode clinics in England, shows similar results. The patients were categorized according to self-reports of delinquency prior to contact with mental health services: 48.5% low, 28.7% stable moderate, 13.2% stable high, and 9.7% early adolescent-onset high-to-moderate. During the year following initial contact with mental health services, compared with the stable low group, those in the moderate delinquency group were twice as likely to report violence, and the stable high delinquency group was 3.5 times more likely to report violence (Winsper et al., 2013).

Consistent with these findings that show that by first contact with clinical services for psychosis, a significant proportion of patients have a record of assaults, are results of studies conducted among adolescents in the juvenile justice system and adolescents in treatment for substance misuse. A study in Denmark examined all the offenders aged 15–19 in 1992. Of the 780 who were still alive in Denmark in 2001, 3.3% had developed schizophrenia as compared to the expected 0.7%. The odds of developing schizophrenia among those with a history of violent criminal offending (as compared to those with only non-violent offending)

Table 16.1 Comparisons of Diagnoses of Schizophrenia Among Cohorts

	% with Schizophrenia			
	Adolescent substance misuse	*General population*	*Odds ratio*	*95% Confidence interval*
Males				
Cohort 1 (*n* = 1,660) to age 50	5.1% (84)	1.4% (23)	3.79	2.38–6.05
Cohort 2 (*n* = 949) to age 35	4.5% (45)	1.1% (11)	4.24	2.18–8.24
Females				
Cohort 1 (*n* = 332) to age 50	7.2% (24)	0.9% (3)	8.55	2.55–28.66
Cohort 2 (*n* = 566) to age 35	4.8% (27)	0.7% (4)	7.04	2.45–2.25

were 4.59 (1.54–13.74) (Gosden, Kramp, Gabrielsen, Andersen, & Sestoft, 2005). Similarly, among adolescents in treatment for substance misuse there are an elevated number who are developing schizophrenia. Since the mid-1960s there has only been one clinic for adolescents with substance use problems in Stockholm County, Sweden. We examined the 1992 clients treated at this clinic from 1968 through 1971 (Cohort 1) and the 1,576 clients from 1980 through 1984 (Cohort 2). For both Cohort 1 and 2, a random sample of the general population (GP1 and GP2) that included the same number of individuals was matched for sex, birth date, and birth place. Cohort 1 and GP1 were followed to age 50, and Cohort 2 and GP2 to age 35, in order to determine the numbers who developed schizophrenia. As presented in Table 16.1, the proportions of both males and females who did not seek treatment for substance misuse in adolescence who developed schizophrenia by age 50 are approximately 1% consistent with robust evidence of the prevalence of schizophrenia in the population. By contrast, among individuals who sought treatment for substance misuse in adolescence, the proportions who subsequently developed schizophrenia are approximately four times higher among the males and seven times higher among the females (Hodgins, Larm, & Westerman, 2016).

Conclusion

A significant proportion of adolescents and young adults presenting to mental health services in a first episode of psychosis have a record of criminal convictions and/or a history of antisocial and aggressive behavior (AAB), and teenagers engaging in AAB are at increased risk to develop schizophrenia. These findings clearly show that the increased risk of AAB among persons with schizophrenia is present before the first acute episode of psychosis. As soon as positive psychotic symptoms (hallucinations, delusions) onset it is necessary to initiate treatment with antipsychotic medication in order to obtain the best possible reduction in symptoms (Marion-Veyron et al., 2015) and to prevent aggressive behavior (Fazel, Zetterqvist, Larsson, Långström, & Lichtenstein, 2014). Consequently, adolescents and adults who are engaging in AAB, whether in the community, the juvenile or adult justice system, substance misuse clinics, or schools, require screening to determine whether they are developing schizophrenia, and those presenting to mental health services in a first episode of psychosis require assessment to identify previous AAB and/or criminality.

Psychotic Symptoms and Aggressive Behavior

It is generally assumed that positive psychotic symptoms "cause" AAB among persons with schizophrenia. However, evidence does not support this assumption. When levels of positive psychotic symptoms are high, the risk of aggressive behavior is high and is reduced by antipsychotic medication (Fazel et al., 2014). However, among some persons with schizophrenia, even when psychotic symptoms are reduced, AAB remains high and it is associated with other factors such as male sex, young age, a history of conduct problems, previous aggressive behavior, and illicit drug use (Hodgins & Riaz, 2011).

A Typology of Persons with Schizophrenia Who Engage in AAB and/or Crime

As in the general population, offenders and persons who engage in AAB who have, or who are developing schizophrenia, constitute a population that is heterogeneous with respect to age of onset and persistence of AAB. Investigations have identified three distinct types: Type I—display AAB from a young age that remains stable through adulthood undisturbed by the onset of schizophrenia; Type II—no history of conduct problems in childhood and adolescence, with aggressive behavior beginning as schizophrenia onsets; and Type III—a small group with no history of AAB who engage in one act of serious violence in the third or fourth decade of life.

Type I: Schizophrenia Preceded by Conduct Disorder

Conduct disorder (CD), a diagnosis that may be given to children prior to age 15, is an antecedent of schizophrenia. For example, in a prospective investigation that followed a New Zealand birth cohort to age 26, 40% of the cohort members who developed schizophreniform disorders had displayed CD prior to age 15 (Arseneault et al., 2003). In clinical samples of adults with schizophrenia, the prevalence of CD is approximately 20% among both women and men (Hodgins, Côté, & Toupin, 1998), but for example in a UK sample of inpatients with severe mental illness, CD prior to age 15 characterized 42.0% of the men and 22.4% of the women (Hodgins, Cree, Alderton, & Mak, 2008). Among patients with schizophrenia in forensic services the prevalence of CD is even higher, and among those in correctional facilities it is further elevated (Hodgins et al., 1998). The prevalence of CD is higher among people with schizophrenia than in the general population, and among men and women with schizophrenia the prevalence is similar while in the general population the prevalence is much higher among males. Thus, not only is the proportion of offenders greater in the population of persons who develop schizophrenia than in the general population, so is the proportion of offenders who display an early onset and stable pattern of AAB.

We examined a sample of 248 men with schizophrenia, aged on average 39.8 years. We compared the 52 men who had presented CD prior to age 15 with the others who had no childhood/adolescent history of antisocial behavior. Incident Rate Ratios (IRR) were calculated to estimate the association between CD and the number of convictions for violent crimes. A diagnosis of CD prior to age 15 was associated with an increase of 2.29 (1.31–4.03) in the number of convictions for violent crimes after controlling for lifetime diagnoses of alcohol and/or drug abuse and/or dependence. As illustrated in Figure 16.2, each CD

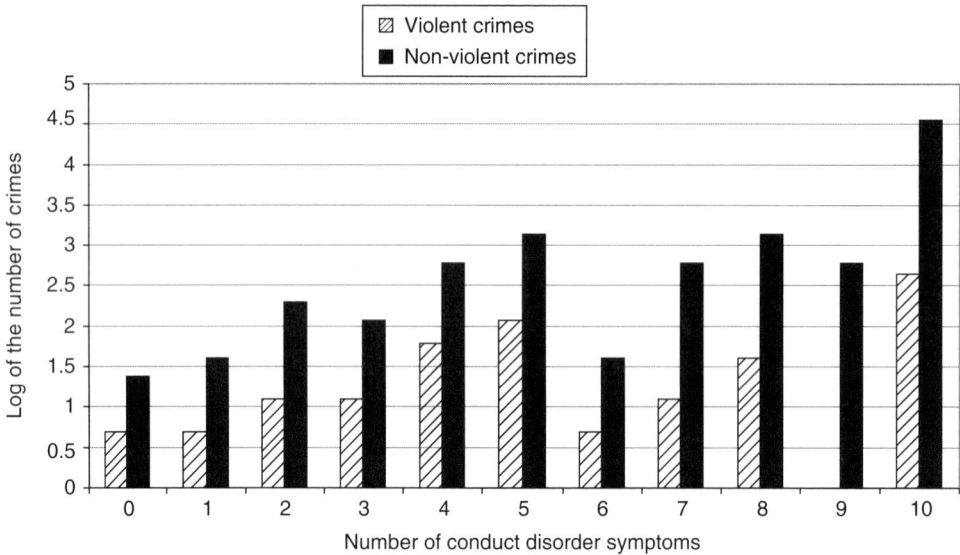

Figure 16.2 Number of non-violent and violent crimes as a function of the number of conduct disorder symptoms among men with schizophrenia.

symptom present before the age of 15 was associated with a 1.15 (1.06–1.25) increase in the number of convictions for violent crimes, again after controlling for diagnoses of substance misuse disorders. A diagnosis of CD and the number of CD symptoms were also associated with the number of convictions for non-violent crimes (Hodgins, Tiihonen, & Ross, 2005).

We have replicated these results in a sample of UK inpatients with severe mental illness (Hodgins et al., 2008). After controlling for sex, age, and current alcohol and drug use, CD prior to age 15 was associated with a twofold increase in the number of convictions for violent crimes. No sex differences in the associations of CD and later offending were detected. The results of these two studies indicate that among individuals who develop schizophrenia, as among those who do not (Hodgins, 2008), CD in childhood is a precursor of criminal offending in adulthood, and concur with results from other studies that used different definitions of childhood conduct problems (Hodgins, Piatosa, & Schiffer, 2014).

Both in the general population (Moffitt & Caspi, 2001) and among people with schizophrenia, CD is not only a precursor of criminal convictions for violent and non-violent crime, but also of aggressive behavior toward others that has not led to criminal prosecution (Hodgins et al., 2008; Swanson et al., 2006). Thus, the accumulated evidence indicates that CD is a precursor of schizophrenia in a minority of cases, that CD is more common among individuals who develop schizophrenia than in the general population, and that among adults with schizophrenia, a diagnosis of CD and the number of CD symptoms present prior to age 15 are associated with criminal convictions for non-violent and for violent crimes and with aggressive behavior toward others. Adult men with schizophrenia and a history of CD show abnormalities of brain structure, some of which are similar to those observed among men with schizophrenia and others that are similar to offenders with no severe mental illness but who presented CD in childhood (Schiffer et al., 2013).

Factors contributing to the development of schizophrenia preceded by conduct disorder

Both schizophrenia (Weinberger, 1987) and CD (Blair, Leibenluft, & Pine, 2014) are disorders of abnormal neurodevelopment. Schizophrenia is highly heritable (Kendler & O'Donovan, 2014) and CD is moderately heritable (Bornovalova, Hicks, Iacono, & McGue, 2010). The effects of the genes conferring vulnerability for either disorder are increased by addition or interaction with environmental stressors such as maltreatment, other stressful life events, poor relationships with parents, and antisocial peers (Byrd & Manuck, 2014; Hicks, South, Dirago, Iacono, & McGue, 2009).

Children who are developing schizophrenia already at age 2 show motor abnormalities such as delays in walking and talking and specific neurological soft signs (Walker, Savoie, & Davis, 1994). In the subsequent years there is further evidence of motor deficiencies, neurological signs, receptive language deficits (Welham et al., 2009), lower than average IQ (Dickson, Laurens, Cullen, & Hodgins, 2012), and, by mid-childhood, psychotic-like experiences (Kelleher & Cannon, 2011; Laurens et al., 2007). In toddlerhood, all children must learn to not engage in aggressive behavior (Broidy et al., 2003). Perhaps, one or several of the impairments characterizing those children developing schizophrenia limits learning not be physically aggressive and to resolve interpersonal conflicts using other strategies, for example, negotiating. Additionally, difficulty in recognizing emotions in the faces of others, and perceiving neutral faces as threatening, may further contribute to the development of CD. Poor recognition of emotions in faces, especially fear and anger (Weiss et al., 2006), is associated with violent behavior among men with (Frommann, Brandt, Schwarze, Schmidbauer, & Wölwer, 2009; Fullam & Dolan, 2006) and without schizophrenia (Frick & Marsee, 2007). Children developing schizophrenia are at increased risk of maltreatment (Fisher et al., 2009) that is known to increase the risk of AAB. In some individuals developing schizophrenia, part of the genetic vulnerability may be genes that interact with heavy cannabis use in early adolescence to increase the risk of schizophrenia onset (Colizzi et al., 2015). Importantly, however, it is those with CD who are developing schizophrenia who are most likely to misuse cannabis in early adolescence (Malcolm et al., 2011).

Conclusion

The largest subgroup of offenders with schizophrenia are those who present a history of CD that emerged in childhood. These individuals are the most persistent offenders and almost all misuse substances. In addition to AAB, they present antisocial attitudes and ways of thinking, and many meet criteria for a diagnosis of antisocial personality disorder, and/or present elevated psychopathy scores. Both in the mental health system and in the criminal justice system, these individuals show poor compliance with treatment for their mental illness and with programs to reduce AAB.

Type II: Offenders With Schizophrenia and no Childhood History of Antisocial Behavior who Begin Offending at Illness Onset

Some offenders with schizophrenia present no history of AAB prior to illness onset. Thereafter, they repeatedly engage in aggressive behavior toward others. The most important study describing this type of offender with schizophrenia was conducted in Denmark using national health and criminal registers (Munkner, Haastrup, Joergensen, & Kramp, 2005). All Danes born after 1963 who acquired a diagnosis of schizophrenia by 1999 were included in the cohort. First, those who died, emigrated from Denmark, disappeared, or were diagnosed before age 15, the legal age for criminal responsibility in Denmark, were excluded, leaving 4,619 persons with schizophrenia. Among them, 422 committed violent offenses and 818 non-violent offenses before first contact with psychiatric services; 241 committed a first non-violent offense and 144 a violent offense after first contact with services but before the diagnosis of schizophrenia. The 3,138 individuals who had not committed crimes by the time they were diagnosed with schizophrenia were, on average, 23.8 years old at diagnosis. Of them, 396 (13%) were convicted of a non-violent crime and 215 of a violent crime during the follow-up period that lasted from 6 months to 20 years with a median of 5.4 years. Being convicted of a crime was associated with a younger age at diagnosis, male sex, and having a substance use disorder.

Conclusion

Little is known about individuals with no history of AAB who begin engaging in aggressive behavior as they develop schizophrenia. We hypothesize that misuse of substances, massive changes in brain structure and functioning associated with illness onset, and the individual's reaction to these changes increase the risk of aggressive behavior.

Type III: Chronic Schizophrenia and Severe Violence

These are usually men in their late 30s with schizophrenia and no history of AAB who kill, or try to kill, someone, often a caregiver. In a sample of 248 men with schizophrenia, we found that scores for the items from the *Psychopathy Checklist—Revised* (Hare, 2003) that assess the affective trait callousness were associated with violent offending and with negative symptoms, but not with CD or substance misuse (Sunak, 2006). Similarly, in a study of persistently aggressive inpatients, three distinct groups were identified, one of which was characterized by a lack of remorse (Nolan et al., 2003). We hypothesize that among older patients, callousness may result from progressive brain changes that underlie schizophrenia and increase the risk for aggressive behavior.

Conclusion

The age of onset and persistence of AAB identifies three distinct types of offenders with schizophrenia. Research indicates that the etiology and treatment needs of each type are distinct.

Treatment

People with schizophrenia who engage in AAB and/or criminal offending require effective treatments for schizophrenia and for AAB that are coordinated by assertive case management (Hodgins & Müller-Isberner, 2004; Hodgins, Müller-Isberner, et al., 2007). Effective treatment for schizophrenia includes antipsychotic medication, psycho-education, cognitive rehabilitation (Moritz et al., 2014), work-related training (Charzyńska, Kucharska, & Mortimer, 2015), and long-term outpatient care (Kane et al., 2015). Those engaging in AAB additionally require treatments targeting AAB. Those with a childhood history of CD are relatively easy to identify from self-reports, reports from parents and older siblings, and from juvenile justice records. The challenge is to adequately treat both the schizophrenia and the life-long pattern of AAB given that antisocial attitudes and ways of thinking, seriously, and negatively, impact compliance (Hodgins et al., 2011; Hodgins et al., 2009; Hodgins, Müller-Isberner, et al., 2007; Marion-Veyron et al., 2015). There are few randomized controlled trials evaluating the effectiveness of cognitive behavioral treatments aimed at reducing AAB among persons with schizophrenia (Cullen et al., 2012a, 2012b; Rees-Jones, Gudjonsson, & Young, 2012; Yip et al., 2013). Forensic assertive case management ensures treatment of schizophrenia and prevention of AAB (Kolla & Hodgins, 2013), while outpatient commitment orders ensure compliance with mental health treatments (Han & Redlich, 2015). The second type of patient, those who only recently began engaging in AAB, is more difficult to detect at first presentation to mental health services for psychosis as their families deny their aggressive behavior. When such an individual is prosecuted, the criminal justice system often fails to identify schizophrenia and to initiate appropriate and adequate treatment. Present evidence suggests the need for treatment with antipsychotic medication and other effective treatments for schizophrenia, plus treatments to prevent substance misuse. The third type of offender with schizophrenia requires continued treatment for the schizophrenia and close monitoring to detect changes in readiness to behave aggressively.

Consequences of treatment on crime rates

All of the available evidence indicates that appropriate treatment of schizophrenia would lower crime rates. Presently, however, most general psychiatric adult services do not provide specific treatments aimed at reducing AAB and/or offending among patients with schizophrenia (Hodgins, Müller-Isberner, et al., 2007) and some prison services do not adequately treat schizophrenia. For example, we studied 205 inpatients with severe mental illness from a UK inner city mental health trust, most of whom suffered from schizophrenia. Official criminal records indicated that 46.7% of the men and 16.5% of the women had at least one conviction for a violent crime, and on average, the violent offenders had each been convicted of more than two crimes. The 82 men with criminal records had committed 1,792 crimes and the 23 female offenders had committed 458 crimes (Hodgins, Alderton, et al., 2007). Two years later, the patients with criminal records had not received any treatments aimed at reducing criminality, or AAB, including none for substance misuse (Hodgins et al., 2009). While patients with schizophrenia within general adult psychiatric services usually do not receive specific treatments aimed at reducing their antisocial and aggressive behavior or criminality, they are prescribed, and encouraged, to take antipsychotic medications. However, within prisons this is not always the case. In a UK study of prisoners convicted for sexual or violent offenses, 94 were found to suffer from schizophrenia, of whom 75 received at least minimal treatment, and 53 continued to receive treatment after discharge. During the 2 years after discharge, violence was reported by 50% of the offenders who received no treatment, 27% of those treated in prison, and 25% of those who received treatment both in prison and after release (Hodgins, 2014). Forensic psychiatric hospitals treat both schizophrenia and AAB. In a study conducted in four countries, we showed that treatment in forensic hospitals improved schizophrenia and prevented recidivism, unlike treatment in general psychiatric hospitals (Hodgins, Müller-Isberner, et al., 2007).

Based on the available evidence, preventing crime by people with schizophrenia would reduce the homicide rate anywhere from 6 to 28%, depending on the country, but also reduce the rate of other forms of violence. In the Danish cohort described above, 2.2% of the men had severe mental illness and they committed 8.4% of the physically aggressive sex offenses, 9.0% of the non-physically aggressive sex offenses, and in all they comprised 8.1% of the sex offenders (Alden, Brennan, Hodgins, & Mednick, 2007). If they had been appropriately treated, more than 8% of all sex offenses in Denmark in this period could have been prevented.

Conclusions

Robust evidence confirms that individuals who are developing, or who already have schizo-phrenia, are at increased risk to engage in AAB. Some incidents of AAB lead to criminal pros-ecution; most do not. When positive psychotic symptoms are high (an acute episode of psychosis), aggressive behavior is common and only associated with symptoms. When these symptoms are lowered by antipsychotic medications, other factors, such as a childhood/adolescent history of AAB, substance misuse, young age, and male sex, predict future AAB and crime. Among persons with schizophrenia who engage in AAB and/or offending, there are at least three types. The most versatile and prolific offenders are those who present a childhood and adolescent history of CD. Another type begins engaging in aggressive behavior as illness onsets. A third, small group includes older patients who engage in violence and show callousness.

Most individuals with schizophrenia who will commit a crime do so prior to their first contact with mental health services for psychosis. Consequently, at first contact with mental health services for an episode of psychosis, all patients require assessments to determine whether, when, and how aggressive behavior occurred. Given the elevated risk of criminality among persons with schizophrenia, offenders require assessment for psychosis. All patients with schizophrenia require antipsychotic medications, psycho-education, and community care. Those with a history of CD additionally require cognitive behavioral treatments targeting their longstanding AAB and strategies to ensure compliance with treatment. Those who begin offending at illness onset require additional treatments for substance misuse. Finally, evidence suggests that adequate and appropriate treatment of schizophrenia as early as possible once psychotic symptoms onset, accompanied by effective treatments for AAB, would contribute to reducing violent crimes rates.

Note

1　The term *schizophrenia* includes also schizo-affective disorder. Schizophrenia is defined as a severe mental illness, or a psychotic illness. Typically, it onsets in late adolescence or early adulthood, somewhat later in females than in males. It includes episodes of acute psychosis characterized by high levels of positive psychotic symptoms such as delusions and hallucinations. Within days of beginning antipsychotic medications these symptoms begin to resolve, but, in most cases, they never entirely go away. Stopping medication leads to an increase in symptoms and another acute episode of psychosis.

Key Readings

Fazel, S., & Seewald, K. (2012). Severe mental illness in 33,588 prisoners worldwide: Systematic review and meta-regression analysis. *British Journal of Psychiatry*, 200, 364–373.

Hodgins, S., Côté, G., & Toupin, J. (1998). Major mental disorders and crime: An etiological hypo-thesis. In D. Cooke, A. Forth, & R. D. Hare (Eds.), *Psychopathy: Theory, research and implications for society* (pp. 231–256). Dordrecht, the Netherlands: Kluwer Academic.

Moffitt, T. E., & Caspi, A. (2001). Childhood predictors differentiate life-course persistent and adoles-cence-limited antisocial pathways among males and females. *Development and Psychopathology*, 13, 355–375.

References

Alden, A., Brennan, P., Hodgins, S., & Mednick, S. (2007). Psychotic disorders and sex offending in a Danish birth cohort. *Archives of General Psychiatry*, 64(11), 1251–1258.

Arseneault, L., Cannon, M., Murray, R., Poulton, R., Caspi, A., & Moffitt, T. E. (2003). Childhood origins of violent behavior in adults with schizophreniform disorder. *British Journal of Psychiatry*, 183, 520–525.

Arseneault, L., Moffitt, T. E., Caspi, A., Taylor, P. J., & Silva, P. A. (2000). Mental disorders and violence in a total birth cohort. *Archives of General Psychiatry*, 57(10), 979–986.

Blair, R. J. R., Leibenluft, E., & Pine, D. S. (2014). Conduct disorder and callous-unemotional traits in youth. *New England Journal of Medicine*, 371(23), 2207–2216.

Bornovalova, M. A., Hicks, B. M., Iacono, W. G., & McGue, M. (2010). Familial transmission and heritability of childhood disruptive disorders. *American Journal of Psychiatry*, 167(9), 1066–1074.

Brennan, P. A., Mednick, S. A., & Hodgins, S. (2000). Major mental disorders and criminal violence in a Danish birth cohort. *Archives of General Psychiatry*, 57(5), 494–500.

Broidy, L. M., Nagin, D. S., Tremblay, R. E., Bates, J. E., Brame, B., Dodge, K. A., ... & Vitaro, F. (2003). Developmental trajectories of childhood disruptive behaviors and adolescent delinquency: A six-site, cross-national study. *Developmental Psychology*, 39(2), 222–245.

Byrd, A. L., & Manuck, S. B. (2014). MAOA, childhood maltreatment, and antisocial behavior: Meta-analysis of a gene-environment interaction. *Biological Psychiatry*, 75(1), 9–17.

Charzyńska, K., Kucharska, K., & Mortimer, A. (2015). Does employment promote the process of recovery from schizophrenia? A review of the existing evidence. *International Journal of Occupational Medicine and Environmental Health*, 28(3), 407–418.

Colizzi, M., Iyegbe, C., Powell, J., Blasi, G., Bertolino, A., Murray, R. M., & Di Forti, M. (2015). Interaction between DRD2 and AKT1 genetic variations on risk of psychosis in cannabis users: A case–control study. *NPJ Schizophrenia*, 1, 15025.

Cullen, A. E., Clarke, A. Y., Kuipers, E., Hodgins, S., Dean, K., & Fahy, T. (2012a). A multi-site randomized controlled trial of a cognitive skills programme for male mentally disordered offenders: Social-cognitive outcomes. *Psychological Medicine*, 42(3), 557–569.

Cullen, A. E., Clarke, A. Y., Kuipers, E., Hodgins, S., Dean, K., & Fahy, T. (2012b). A multisite randomized trial of a cognitive skills program for male mentally disordered offenders: Violence and antisocial behavior outcomes. *Journal of Consulting and Clinical Psychology*, 80(6), 1114–1120.

Dickson, H., Laurens, K. R., Cullen, A. E., & Hodgins, S. (2012). Meta-analyses of cognitive and motor function in youth aged 16 years and younger who subsequently develop schizophrenia. *Psychological Medicine*, 42(4), 743–755.

Erb, M., Hodgins, S., Freese, R., Müller-Isberner, R., & Jöckel, D. (2001). Homicide and schizophrenia: Maybe treatment does have a preventive effect. *Criminal Behavior and Mental Health*, 11(1), 6–26.

Fazel, S., & Grann, M. (2006). The population impact of severe mental illness on violent crime. *American Journal of Psychiatry*, 163(8), 1397–1403.

Fazel, S., Lichtenstein, P., Grann, M., Goodwin, G. M., & Långström, N. (2010). Bipolar disorder and violent crime: New evidence from population-based longitudinal studies and systematic review. *Archives of General Psychiatry*, 67(9), 931–938.

Fazel, S., & Seewald, K. (2012). Severe mental illness in 33,588 prisoners worldwide: Systematic review and meta-regression analysis. *British Journal of Psychiatry*, 200(5), 364–373.

Fazel, S., Zetterqvist, J., Larsson, H., Långström, N., & Lichtenstein, P. (2014). Antipsychotics, mood stabilisers, and risk of violent crime. *The Lancet*, 384(9949), 1206–1214.

Fisher, H., Morgan, C., Dazzan, P., Craig, T. K., Morgan, K., Hutchinson, G., ... & Fearon, P. (2009). Gender differences in the association between childhood abuse and psychosis. *British Journal of Psychiatry*, 194(4), 319–325.

Frick, P. J., & Marsee, M. A. (2007). Psychopathy and developmental pathways to antisocial behavior in youth. In C. J. Patrick (Ed.), *Handbook of psychopathy* (pp. 355–374). New York, NY: Guilford Press.

Frommann, N., Brandt, M., Schwarze, C., Schmidbauer, W., & Wölwer, W. (2009). Affect recognition impairments and violence in schizophrenia: A first application of the Training of Affect Recognition (TAR) to offenders suffering from schizophrenia. *European Archives of Psychiatry and Clinical Neuroscience*, 259(1), 1.

Fullam, R., & Dolan, M. (2006). Emotional information processing in violent patients with schizophrenia: Association with psychopathy and symptomatology. *Psychiatry Research*, 141(1), 29–37.

Gosden, N. P., Kramp, P., Gabrielsen, G., Andersen, T. F., & Sestoft, D. (2005). Violence of young criminals predicts schizophrenia: A 9-year register-based followup of 15- to 19-year-old criminals. *Schizophrenia Bulletin*, 31(3), 759–768.

Han, W., & Redlich, A. D. (2015). The impact of community treatment on recidivism among mental health court participants. *Psychiatric Services*, 67(4), 384–390.

Hare, R. D. (2003). *The Hare Psychopathy Checklist—Revised.* (2nd ed.). Toronto, Canada: Multi-Health Systems.

Hicks, B. M., South, S. C., Dirago, A. C., Iacono, W. G., & McGue, M. (2009). Environmental adversity and increasing genetic risk for externalizing disorders. *Archives of General Psychiatry*, 66(6), 640–648.

Hodgins, S. (1998). Epidemiological investigations of the associations between major mental disorders and crime: Methodological limitations and validity of the conclusions. *Social Psychiatry and Psychiatric Epidemiology*, 33(Suppl. 1), S29–S37.

Hodgins, S. (2008). Violent behavior among people with schizophrenia: A framework for investigations of causes, and effective treatment, and prevention. *Philosophical Transactions of the Royal Society B*, 363(1503), 2505–2518.

Hodgins, S. (2014). Among untreated violent offenders with schizophrenia, persecutory delusions are associated with violent recidivism. *Evidence-Based Mental Health*, 17(3), 75.

Hodgins, S., Alderton, J., Cree, A., Aboud, A., & Mak, T. (2007). Aggressive behavior, victimization and crime among severely mentally ill patients requiring hospitalisation. *British Journal of Psychiatry*, 191, 343–350.

Hodgins, S., Calem, M., Shimel, R., Williams, A., Harleston, D., Morgan, C., … & Murray, R. M. (2010). *Criminal offending and distinguishing features of offenders in a sample of persons experiencing a first episode of psychosis. Report to Department of Health.*

Hodgins, S., Calem, M., Shimel, R., Williams, A., Harleston, D., Morgan, C., … & Jones, P. (2011). Criminal offending and distinguishing features of offenders among persons experiencing a first episode of psychosis. *Early Intervention in Psychiatry*, 5(1), 15–23.

Hodgins, S., Côté, G., & Toupin, J. (1998). Major mental disorders and crime: An etiological hypothesis. In D. Cooke, A. Forth, & R. D. Hare (Eds.), *Psychopathy: Theory, research and implications for society* (pp. 231–256). Dordrecht, the Netherlands: Kluwer Academic.

Hodgins, S., Cree, A., Alderton, J., & Mak, T. (2008). From conduct disorder to severe mental illness: Associations with aggressive behavior, crime and victimization. *Psychological Medicine*, 38(7), 975–987.

Hodgins, S., Cree, A., Khalid, F., Patel, K., Sainz-Fuertes, R., Shortt, M., … & Riaz, M. (2009). Do community mental health teams caring for severely mentally ill patients adjust treatments and services based on patients' antisocial or criminal behaviors? *European Psychiatry*, 24(6), 373–379.

Hodgins, S., & Janson, C.-G. (2002). *Criminality and violence among the mentally disordered: The Stockholm Metropolitan Project. Cambridge studies in criminology.* New York, NY: Cambridge University Press.

Hodgins, S., Mednick, S. A., Brennan, P. A., Schulsinger, F., & Engberg, M. (1996). Mental disorder and crime. Evidence from a Danish birth cohort. *Archives of General Psychiatry*, 53(6), 489–496.

Hodgins, S., & Müller-Isberner, R. (2004). Preventing crime by people with schizophrenic disorders: The role of psychiatric services. *British Journal of Psychiatry*, 185, 245–250.

Hodgins, S., Müller-Isberner, R., Freese, R., Tiihonen, J., Repo-Tiihonen, E., Eronen, M., ... & Kronstrand, R. (2007). A comparison of general adult and forensic patients with schizophrenia living in the community. *International Journal of Forensic Mental Health*, 6(1), 63–75.

Hodgins, S., Piatosa, M. J., & Schiffer, B. (2014). Violence among people with schizophrenia: Phenotypes and neurobiology. *Current Topics in Behavioral Neurosciences*, 17, 329–368.

Hodgins, S., & Riaz, M. (2011). Violence and phases of illness: Differential risk and predictors. *European Psychiatry*, 26(8), 518–524.

Hodgins, S., Tiihonen, J., & Ross, D. (2005). The consequences of conduct disorder for males who develop schizophrenia: Associations with criminality, aggressive behavior, substance use, and psychiatric services. *Schizophrenia Research*, 78(2–3), 323–335.

Hodgins, S., Larm, P., & Westerman, J. (2016). Individuals developing schizophrenia are hidden among adolescent substance misusers. *Psychological Medicine*, 46, 3041–3050.

Kane, J. M., Robinson, D. G., Schooler, N. R., Mueser, K. T., Penn, D. L., Rosenheck, R. A., ... & Heinssen, R. K. (2015). Comprehensive versus usual community care for first-episode psychosis: 2-year outcomes from the NIMH RAISE early treatment program. *American Journal of Psychiatry*, 173(4), 362–372.

Kelleher, I., & Cannon, M. (2011). Psychotic-like experiences in the general population: Characterizing a high-risk group for psychosis. *Psychological Medicine*, 41(1), 1–6.

Kendler, K. S., & O'Donovan, M. C. (2014). A breakthrough in schizophrenia genetics. *JAMA Psychiatry*, 71(12), 1319–1320.

Kolla, N., & Hodgins, S. (2013). Treatment of people with schizophrenia who behave violently towards others: A review of the empirical literature on treatment effectiveness. In L. Craig, L. Dixon, & T. A. Gannon (Eds.), *What works in offender rehabilitation. An evidence-based approach to assessment and treatment* (pp. 319–339). Chichester, UK: Wiley-Blackwell.

Large, M. M., & Nielssen, O. (2011). Violence in first-episode psychosis: A systematic review and meta-analysis. *Schizophrenia Research*, 125(2–3), 209–220.

Large, M. M., Smith, G., & Nielssen, O. (2009). The relationship between the rate of homicide by those with schizophrenia and the overall homicide rate: A systematic review and meta-analysis. *Schizophrenia Research*, 112(1–3), 123–129.

Laurens, K. R., Hodgins, S., Maughan, B., Murray, R. M., Rutter, M. L., & Taylor, E. A. (2007). Community screening for psychotic-like experiences and other putative antecedents of schizophrenia in children aged 9–12 years. *Schizophrenia Research*, 90, 130–146.

Malcolm, C. P., Picchioni, M. M., DiForti, M., Sugranyes, G., Cooke, E., Joseph, C., ... & Hodgins, S. (2011). Pre-morbid conduct disorder symptoms are associated with cannabis use among individuals with a first episode of psychosis. *Schizophrenia Research*, 126(1–3), 81–86.

Marion-Veyron, R., Lambert, M., Cotton, S. M., Schimmelmann, B. G., Gravier, B., McGorry, P. D., & Conus, P. (2015). History of offending behavior in first episode psychosis patients: A marker of specific clinical needs and a call for early detection strategies among young offenders. *Schizophrenia Research*, 161(2–3), 163–168.

Moffitt, T. E., & Caspi, A. (2001). Childhood predictors differentiate life-course persistent and adolescence-limited antisocial pathways among males and females. *Development and Psychopathology*, 13(2), 355–375.

Moritz, S., Veckenstedt, R., Andreou, C., Bohn, F., Hottenrott, B., Leighton, L., ... & Roesch-Ely, D. (2014). Sustained and "sleeper" effects of group metacognitive training for schizophrenia: A randomized clinical trial. *JAMA Psychiatry*, 71(10), 1103–1111.

Munkner, R., Haastrup, S., Joergensen, T., & Kramp, P. (2005). Incipient offending among schizophrenia patients after first contact to the psychiatric hospital system. *European Psychiatry*, 20(4), 321–326.

Nielssen, O., & Large, M. M. (2010). Rates of homicide during the first episode of psychosis and after treatment: A systematic review and meta-analysis. *Schizophrenia Bulletin*, 36(4), 702–712.

Nolan, K. A., Czobor, P., Roy, B. B., Platt, M. M., Shope, C. B., Citrome, L. L., & Volavka, J. (2003). Characteristics of assaultive behavior among psychiatric inpatients. *Psychiatric Services*, 54(7), 1012–1016.

Rees-Jones, A., Gudjonsson, G., & Young, S. (2012). A multi-site controlled trial of a cognitive skills program for mentally disordered offenders. *BMC Psychiatry*, 12, 44. doi:org/10.1186/1471-244X-1

Schiffer, B., Leygraf, N., Müller, B. W., Scherbaum, N., Forsting, M., Wiltfang, J., … & Hodgins, S. (2013). Structural brain alterations associated with schizophrenia preceded by conduct disorder: A common and distinct subtype of schizophrenia? *Schizophrenia Bulletin*, 39(5), 1115–1128.

Sunak, S. (2006). Deficient effective experience and violence in schizophrenia (Unpublished master's thesis). King's College, London, UK.

Swanson, J. W., Swartz, M. S., van Dorn, R. A., Elbogen, E. B., Wagner, H. R., Rosenheck, R. A., … & Lieberman, J. A. (2006). A national study of violent behavior in persons with schizophrenia. *Archives of General Psychiatry*, 63(5), 490–499.

Tiihonen, J., Isohanni, M., Räsänen, P., Koiranen, M., & Moring, J. (1997). Specific major mental disorders and criminality: A 26-year prospective study of the 1966 northern Finland birth cohort. *American Journal of Psychiatry*, 154(6), 840–845.

Walker, E. F., Savoie, T., & Davis, D. (1994). Neuromotor precursors of schizophrenia. *Schizophrenia Bulletin*, 20(3), 441–451.

Wallace, C., Mullen, P. E., & Burgess, P. (2004). Criminal offending in schizophrenia over a 25-year period marked by deinstitutionalization and increasing prevalence of comorbid substance use disorders. *American Journal of Psychiatry*, 161(4), 716–727.

Weinberger, D. R. (1987). Implications of normal brain development for the pathogenesis of schizophrenia. *Archives of General Psychiatry*, 44(7), 660–669.

Weiss, E. M., Kohler, C. G., Nolan, K. A., Czobor, P., Volavka, J., Platt, M. M., … & Gur, R. C. (2006). The relationship between history of violent and criminal behavior and recognition of facial expression of emotions in men with schizophrenia and schizoaffective disorder. *Aggressive Behavior*, 32(3), 187–194.

Welham, J., Isohanni, M., Jones, P., McGrath, J., Welham, J., Isohanni, M., … & McGrath, J. (2009). The antecedents of schizophrenia: A review of birth cohort studies. *Schizophrenia Bulletin*, 35(3), 603–623.

Winsper, C., Singh, S. P., Marwaha, S., Amos, T., Lester, H., Everard, L., … & Birchwood, M. (2013). Pathways to violent behavior during first-episode psychosis: A report from the UK national EDEN study. *JAMA Psychiatry*, 70(12), 1287–1293.

Yip, V. C.-Y., Gudjonsson, G. H., Perkins, D., Doidge, A., Hopkin, G., & Young, S. (2013). A non-randomised controlled trial of the R&R2MHP cognitive skills program in high risk male offenders with severe mental illness. *BMC Psychiatry*, 13, 267. doi:org/10.1186/1471-244X-13-267

17

Personality Disorders and Offending

Mary McMurran and Richard C. Howard

University of Nottingham, UK

Introduction

Personality disorders are typified by relatively enduring, inflexible, and pervasive disturbances in how individuals experience and interpret themselves, others, and the world around them. These are reflected in maladaptive patterns of cognition, emotion, and behavior, usually evident in childhood and adolescence, which result in significant problems in psychosocial functioning, particularly in interpersonal relationships.

People diagnosed with personality disorder are, in many respects, a severely disadvantaged group. They suffer more general health problems, use healthcare services more, and have significantly increased rates of premature mortality (Fok et al., 2012; Powers & Oltmanns, 2012). They are also more likely to have financial difficulties and problems maintaining jobs (Noren et al., 2007), experience marital dissatisfaction (South, Turkheimer, & Oltmanns, 2008), and have a poor quality of life (Soeteman, Verheul, & Busschbach, 2008). Most pertinent to this chapter, however, is the association between personality disorder and antisocial behavior and offending, particularly violence. For instance, a systematic review by Yu, Geddes, and Fazel (2012) reported that all personality disorders were associated with a significantly increased risk of violence (odds ratio [OR] = 3.0, 95% confidence interval [CI] – 2.6, 3.5), rising to an OR of 12.8 (95% CI – 7.9, 20.7) for those with antisocial personality disorder. Similarly, the British Prisoner Cohort Study, a prospective follow-up of 1,685 offenders, found that the severity of personality disorder was associated with an increased risk of violent offending within 2 years of being released (Coid, Hickey, Kahtan, Zhang, & Yang, 2007). Furthermore, prisoners with antisocial personality disorder have higher rates of mood disorders, substance use, and psychotic disorders, score lower on social functioning and quality of life measures, and are at a higher risk of committing suicide (Black, Gunter, Loveless, Allen, & Sieleni, 2010).

The significance of these problems to society is magnified when the prevalence of personality disorder is taken into account. Studies variously estimate the prevalence in the general population to be between 4 and 13% (Coid, Yang, Tyrer, Roberts, & Ullrich, 2006; Lenzenweger, Lane, Loranger, & Kessler, 2007; Torgerson, Kringlen, & Kramer, 2001). This exceeds that for other major mental disorders, such as schizophrenia (0.87%), bipolar disorder (0.24%), and major

The Wiley International Handbook of Correctional Psychology, First Edition. Edited by Devon L. L. Polaschek, Andrew Day, and Clive R. Hollin.

depressive disorder (0.35%) (Perälä et al., 2007). There is a particularly high prevalence of personality disorders in criminal justice settings. A review of 28 prison surveys worldwide identified 65% of men diagnosable with any personality disorder and 47% with antisocial personality disorder, with the figures for women being 42 and 21%, respectively (Fazel & Danesh, 2002).

In summary, personality disorders are highly prevalent and the associated problems are severe, including antisocial behavior. There is, therefore, a strong rationale for understanding and treating people with personality disorder, both offenders and non-offenders.

Understanding Personality Disorder

The field of personality disorders is currently in a state of flux, with the recent transition from the fourth to the fifth edition of the American Psychiatric Association's (APA's) *Diagnostic and Statistical Manual, Fifth Edition* (DSM-5: APA, 2013) and the arrival of the 11th edition of the World Health Organization's *International Classification of Diseases* (ICD-11; World Health Organization, 2018). Both DSM-5 and ICD-11 represent a shift away from viewing personality disorders as discrete clinical entities toward seeing them as constellations of maladaptive personality traits that impair everyday functioning, particularly in the realm of interpersonal behavior.

DSM-5

The validity of the DSM-IV categorization of personality disorder had fallen into disrepute on account of a lack of definitional specificity, an inadequate representation of personality disorder severity, arbitrary thresholds for diagnosis, the excessive co-occurrence of personality disorders with each other, the limited validity of some types, the heterogeneity of people diagnosed with any disorder owing to the way only some of the criteria need to be met, and the lack of stability over time of personality disorder diagnoses (Skodol, 2012). After lengthy deliberations, those revising the DSM finally balked at radical change, preferring to retain the diagnostic categories of its predecessor (summarized in Table 17.1) while presenting a new adjunct hybrid model

Table 17.1 DSM-IV and DSM-5 Personality Disorders

Cluster A—Odd or eccentric
Paranoid—Distrust; suspiciousness
Schizoid—Socially and emotionally detached
Schizotypal—Social and interpersonal deficits; cognitive or perceptual distortions

Cluster B—Dramatic, emotional, and erratic
Antisocial—Violation of the rights of others
Borderline—Instability of relationships, self-image, and mood
Histrionic—Excessive emotionality and attention-seeking
Narcissistic—Grandiose; lack of empathy; need for admiration

Cluster C—Anxious and fearful
Avoidant—Socially inhibited; feelings of inadequacy;
Dependent—Clinging; submissive
Obsessive-compulsive—Perfectionist; inflexible

---

which requires assessment of the level of impairment in relation to six specific personality disorder types (antisocial, avoidant, borderline, narcissistic, obsessive-compulsive, and schizo-typal) and the option for a diagnosis that is trait specified (Skodol, 2011). Dysfunctional traits are organized under the five broad domains of negative affectivity, detachment, psychoticism, antagonism, and disinhibition. These broadly reflect the negative (maladaptive) poles of the personality dimensions represented in the five factor model (FFM) of normal personality (Costa & McCrae, 1992), namely neuroticism, extraversion, openness, agreeableness, and conscientiousness. At a descriptive trait level, the FFM of personality helps us to understand more about why specific personality disorders and combinations of personality disorders lead to intra- and inter-personal problems.

ICD-11

ICD-11 also sees personality disorder as essentially reflecting disturbed interpersonal behavior, but takes a more radical departure by jettisoning personality disorder categories altogether in favor of a completely dimensional system of classification where assessment of the severity of personality disorder is paramount. Severity ranges from mild (not associated with substantial harm to self or others) to severe (associated with a past history and future expectation of severe harm to self or others that has caused long-term damage or has endangered life) (Tyrer, Reed, & Crawford, 2015). ICD-11 proposes assessment of dysfunctional personality traits in five trait domains: negative affectivity, disinhibition, detachment, dissociality, and anankastia (i.e, obsessive-compulsive).

Personality disorder severity has been conceptualized in the literature in a number of different ways, including the degree of impairment in social functioning and the number of personality disorders a person has: the greater the degree of impairment and the more personality disorder diagnoses, the greater the severity of personality disorder. Recent research suggests that severity of personality disorder that is defined by the extent of co-occurrence is associated with greater severity of violence perpetrated by personality-disordered offenders (Howard, Khalifa, & Duggan, 2014). That is to say, those diagnosable with more personality disorder types are also those who are most likely to be at high risk of serious violence. The ICD-11 approach is consistent with research findings that support the idea of a general severity factor that transcends diagnostic boundaries and pervades all DSM categories of personality disorder (Conway, Hammen, & Brennan, 2015; Sharp et al., 2015).

Co-Occurrence or "Comorbidity"

The co-occurrence of personality disorders (commonly referred to as comorbidity) is the rule rather than the exception. In forensic samples, it is not uncommon for people diagnosed with personality disorder to have in excess of three different personality disorder diagnoses (Howard et al., 2014). One important co-occurrence in forensic samples is that of antisocial personality disorder with borderline personality disorder, which likely reflects genetic risk factors that are shared by both (Torgersen et al., 2008). As illustrated in Table 17.2, the prevalence of antisocial/borderline comorbidity increases as one ascends the "security ladder," from community to high security. In comparison with offenders who lack these features, those with both antisocial and borderline personality disorders are more likely to reoffend (Tikkanen, Holi, Lindberg, Tiihonen, & Virkkunen, 2009), and to reoffend more quickly (Howard, McCarthy, Huband, & Duggan, 2013), following their release from custody into the

Table 17.2   Rates of Antisocial and Borderline Personality Disorder Co-Occurrence in Forensic and Non-Forensic Samples

	Study	*Sample*	*Percentage co-occurring antisocial and borderline*
	Coid, Yang et al. (2007) (UK)	Male prisoners meeting criteria for "dangerous & severe personality disorder" (n = 212)	62%
	Howard et al. (2014) (UK)	Male offenders with personality disorder detained in medium and high security (n = 100)	44%
	Tikkanen et al. (2009) (Finland)	Male violent alcoholic offenders (n = 167)	28%
	Black et al. (2010) (USA)	Men (n = 264) and women (n = 56) admitted to a low-security correctional facility for assessment	24% women 16% men
	Wetterborg et al. (2015) (Sweden)	Male offenders on probation or parole (n = 108)	18%
Adult community	Howard et al. (2008) (UK)	Male and female community patients seeking treatment for personality disorder (n = 224)	9%
	Coid Coid et al. (2006) (UK)	Community-dwelling men and women in the general population (n = 626)	0.3%

community. They are also more likely to have been seriously violent in their criminal careers (Howard et al., 2014). Finally, they are more likely to have a history of *severe* childhood conduct disorder (Howard, Huband, & Duggan, 2012). For these reasons, individuals showing this particular constellation of maladaptive personality traits represent a class of severely disordered offenders that not only should be of particular concern to correctional practitioners, but also represent a severe challenge to treatment efforts aimed at reducing their risk of violence. To some extent these individuals overlap with "psychopaths," as defined by the *Hare Psychopathy Checklist—Revised* (PCL-R: Hare, 2003), although they show a combination of maladaptive externalizing and internalizing personality traits, and correspond more closely to what is termed *secondary psychopathy* than to primary psychopathy.

Psychopathy

Psychopathy, which has particular relevance to correctional psychology, lacks specific status as a personality disorder in DSM or ICD. However, a recent study by Wygant et al. (2016) suggests that the DSM-5 operationalization of antisocial personality disorder in terms of traits of manipulativeness, deceitfulness, callousness, hostility, irresponsibility, impulsivity, and risk taking has, relative to its categorical representation in DSM-5, moved the antisocial personality disorder construct closer to the traditional construct of psychopathy. These traits, together with grandiosity and restricted affect, were more strongly correlated with several measures of psychopathy, including the PCL-R, than with the categorical classification of antisocial personality disorder.

Research into psychopathy has most commonly used Hare's (2003) PCL-R assessment tool, which considers both traits (grandiosity, selfishness, and callousness) and behaviors (antisocial, irresponsible, and parasitic lifestyle). Compared with lower scorers, those who meet the cutoff for psychopathy begin their criminal careers earlier, commit more types of offenses, offend at a higher frequency, and are more likely to reoffend (Hare, Clark, Grann, & Thornton, 2000).

One criticism of the PCL-R is that it contains items relating to criminal behavior, hence it is unsurprising that it is closely associated with criminality. In fact, this may be an unhelpful mix of the behaviors that we are trying to explain (crime and violence) and the explanatory variables (traits). Skeem and Cooke (2010) have argued that the core features of psychopathy may be an arrogant and deceitful interpersonal style, deficient affective experience, and an impulsive and irresponsible behavioral style and that it is these features that explain crime and violence. However, a recent statistical examination of PCL-R data globally from men and women, offenders and non-offenders, supports the contrary notion that overt antisociality is an essential ingredient of psychopathy along with three other factors: interpersonal (manipulative and insincere), affective (callous and shallow), and lifestyle (impulsive and irresponsible) (Neumann, Hare, & Pardini, 2015). The relationship of psychopathy to violence remains unclear, but a recent review suggested that those aspects of psychopathy that are related to a general predisposition of externalizing, such as emotional impulsiveness, are linked to violent offending (Howard, 2015).

Many researchers have differentiated primary and secondary psychopaths (e.g., Blackburn, 1975; Skeem, Johansson, Andershed, Kerr, & Louden, 2007). While behaviorally alike, the underlying features of the two types differ. In primary psychopathy, the profile is lower trait anxiety, poor ability to form interpersonal attachments, a lack of empathy, and a lack of conscience. In secondary psychopathy, the profile is higher trait anxiety, poor interpersonal functioning, and low empathy, possibly consequent on early traumatic experiences of physical or sexual abuse or other maltreatment. The primary versus secondary distinction overlaps to some extent with the distinction between those scoring high on interpersonal and affective facets of psychopathy (PCL-R Factor 1) whose externalizing behaviors are typified by a combination of lack of empathy and social dominance which are likely driven by a lack of internalizing traits such as anxiety and negative affect (Patrick, Fowles, & Krueger, 2009), and those scoring high on PCL-R Factor 2 whose externalizing behaviors, such as drug and alcohol use and emotionally impulsive acting out, derive principally from a combination of low effortful control and high negative emotionality (DeLisi & Vaughn, 2014). However, recent evidence suggests that PCL-R Factor 2 overlaps strongly with borderline personality disorder in terms of genetic and non-shared environmental risk factors that are common to both (Hunt, Bornovalova, & Patrick, 2015). Therefore one should be wary of dichotomizing primary and secondary psychopathy as reflecting, respectively, inherited and acquired affective deficits. Both likely reflect a combination of genetic and environmental factors (Auty, Farrington, & Coid, 2015).

The two-factor model of the PCL-R has dominated research on psychopathy. However, other models and measures are emerging and these take a broader view of traits that may present a risk for antisocial behavior. Patrick et al. (2009) have recently proposed a triarchic model of psychopathy conceptualized on three separate dimensions: disinhibition (i.e., impulsiveness and emotion regulation difficulties), meanness (i.e., lack of empathy and exploitativeness), and boldness (i.e., social dominance and emotional resilience). They propose that inherent characteristics can produce these behavioral phenotypes, but so too can socialization experiences. Empirical support for this model is accruing (Patrick & Drislane, 2015).

Cooke and Logan (2015) have developed the Comprehensive Assessment of Psychopathic Personality (CAPP), which addresses six domains, each with several symptom areas. The six domains are: attachment, behavioral, cognitive, dominance, emotional, and self. Data so far show the CAPP's construct, concurrent, and predictive validity to be comparable to the PCL-R, but the CAPP may have more clinical utility in terms of understanding and formulating an individual's offending.

Personality Disorder and Violence: What Is the Link?

While the literature clearly indicates that personality disorders overall are associated with an increased risk of violence of three times that of the general population (Yu et al., 2012), it should not be assumed that all personality disorders are linked to violence to an equal degree. The strongest risk in Yu et al.'s meta-analytic review was for antisocial personality disorder. Cluster C personality disorders appear to confer no risk of violence (Johnson et al., 2000) and schizoid personality disorder has been shown to be inversely associated with violence in adult offenders (Howard et al., 2014).

An answer to the question, "what is the link?" is obscured by several factors. First, any link between personality disorders and violence needs to be seen in the context of the link between mental disorder in general and violence. Yu et al.'s (2012) meta-analytic review indicated that people with any personality disorder are three times as likely to have committed an act of violence as people in the general community. However, violence is linked to a range of mental disorders, including schizophrenia, bipolar disorder, and depression. Second, considerable uncertainty exists over how personality disorders should best be conceptualized and assessed, and this is exacerbated by the high degree to which these disorders co-occur. Third, confusion exists over how best to classify violence, given its heterogeneity both as regards the context in which it occurs and its motivation. Lastly, finding an association between personality disorder and violence does not necessarily imply a causal connection between them. Establishing causality requires that the following criteria be met. First, personality disorder must emerge prior to the emergence of violent offending. Second, alternative explanations for the relationship must be excluded, for example, abuse of alcohol and other psychotropic drugs as precipitants of violence. Third, and most importantly, a causal mechanism linking personality disorder with violence must be specified to account for *how* personality disorder causes violence.

Howard (2015) reviewed evidence supporting the view that externalizing tendencies, operating in concert with delusional thinking and proximal contextual factors such as excessive alcohol use and interpersonal stress, increase the likelihood of violence. It was suggested that appetitively motivated violence, driven either by a desire for excitement or by greed and social dominance, was more likely to be associated with externalizing tendencies. In contrast, aversively motivated violence, driven by a desire to protect oneself from a directly perceived interpersonal threat or by a desire for vengeance, was more likely to be associated with delusional thinking. Those in whom externalizing and internalizing tendencies co-occur, such as those showing co-occurring antisocial and borderline personality disorders, would be characterized by a concatenation of maladaptive personality traits that predispose them to both appetitively and aversively motivated violence.

Developmental Pathways to Adult Violence

There is a need to specify developmental trajectories from childhood through adolescence to adult violence. Howard, Hepburn, and Khalifa (2015) reported that severe violence in forensic psychiatric patients was predicted by high scores on two transdiagnostic dimensions of personality disorder: acting out (equivalent to psychopathy) and anxious-inhibited (equivalent to neurotic introversion). However, while acting out independently predicted severe violence, the effect of anxious-inhibited traits on violence appeared to be mediated by delusional ideation. The authors interpreted these findings as suggesting the existence of separate pathways linking externalizing and internalizing personality disorder features with violence. First, an internalizing pathway linked to violence would operate via delusional thinking and general psychopathology, resulting from extremely high and/or inflexible levels of negative emotionality, empathy, and rumination experienced in the context of intense and/or chronic interpersonal stress during adolescence, particularly in young women (Martel, 2013). Second, an externalizing pathway linked to violence would lead from severe conduct disorder in childhood via excessive alcohol use in adolescence to adult antisocial personality, particularly in males when this occurs together with callous-unemotional traits (Frick & Ray, 2014). These pathways would both be expected to operate conjunctively in those with an end-point of severe personality disorder (e.g., those with co-occurring antisocial and borderline personality disorder).

Treatment

Targets of Treatment

Fundamental to the treatment of personality-disordered offenders is clarity about what it is we are aiming to treat. Is it the personality disorder, the socially deviant behavior, or both? This question immediately raises ethical issues relating to the dual role of psychologists working with offenders. On the one hand, there is a need to act in the best interests of the individual offender, and on the other to act in the best interests of a safer society, and these two different sets of demands can be difficult to reconcile (Candilis & Neal, 2014; Ward, 2013). Furthermore, there are different emphases placed on these two roles in forensic mental health systems and criminal justice and correctional systems.

Pickard (2015) is of the opinion that it is ethically justifiable to commit offenders with personality disorder to hospital only if they are then provided with effective treatment. In terms of treatment targets, Blackburn (2002) believed that because the mental disorder is the reason for contact with mental health services, the target should be the alleviation of the disorder—although reduced recidivism may be one indication of successful treatment outcome. The emphasis on violence as a valid clinical outcome may change with the introduction of ICD-11, which includes harm to others as an indicator of severity of personality disorder. The ethical position in criminal justice settings is arguably clearer in that offenders with personality disorder are often referred to rehabilitation programs, where the primary aim is to reduce risk of reoffending. That is, strictly speaking, they are not being treated for any mental disorder.

Professional ethics also dictates that offenders (as any client) should be offered effective interventions. It is likely that programs for personality-disordered offenders would be most effective in reducing reoffending when they target issues relating to the personality disorder. Of course, as previously explained, there are concerns relating to the questionable validity of personality disorder diagnoses and a lack of clarity about the nature of the causal link between personality disorder and offending which makes it essential to evaluate the clinical and criminological outcomes of treatment for personality-disordered offenders and to examine the processes by which treatment has an impact.

In practice, both mental health and criminal justice psychologists offer treatments that aim to ameliorate the symptoms of personality disorder and reduce the risk of offending. Treatments typically target a range of emotional, cognitive, and interpersonal areas of dysfunction that mediate between basic traits (e.g., negative emotionality; impulsiveness) and behavioral outcomes (e.g., self-harm; aggression). These psychosocially developed core areas of dysfunction include emotional dysregulation, maladaptive core beliefs and schemas, attachment difficulties, dysfunctional interpersonal styles, and substance misuse. Identifying which targets are relevant to any one person requires an individual case formulation. This approach mitigates to a considerable degree concerns about the validity of personality disorder diagnoses and the link between personality disorder and offending.

Case formulation is an integration of evidence that explains the origins and maintenance of an individual's offending and offense-related behaviors, elucidates the underlying mechanisms that connect and therefore explain those problems, and points to interventions that will ameliorate those problems (Hart, Sturmey, Logan, & McMurran, 2011). After specifying the client's problem or problems, information relating to personality traits, psychosocial development, and current environmental variables should be integrated within a theoretical framework to identify the antecedents to the problem and the factors that maintain it. The formulation points to targets for intervention, and treatment may be seen as a test of the formulation. (See Sturmey, McMurran, and Daffern, Chapter 29, for a more thorough account of case formulation.)

Many psychologists are uncomfortable with using personality disorder diagnoses, preferring to avoid labeling individuals with what can be seen as a pejorative label. Nonetheless, a classification of personality disorder can be an indicator of dysfunction in a way that trait assessment is not, since extreme traits do not necessarily indicate distress or dysfunction (British Psychological Society, 2006). Furthermore, assessment of personality disorder can be essential in accessing specialist services, particularly where the treatments on offer have been evidenced as effective for a particular disorder. Assessment must be rigorous, and the use of structured assessment instruments is important. The most commonly used are the International Personality Disorder Examination (IPDE; Loranger, 1999) and the Structured Clinical Interview for Axis II disorders (SCID-II; First, Gibbon, Spitzer, Williams, & Benjamin, 1997).

Treatments for Personality Disorder

Attempts to summarize the effectiveness of treatments for personality disorder are hindered by the wide variety of outcomes measured in studies. These include personality disorders, personality traits, maladaptive cognitions, distressing emotions, and problematic behaviors. This array of outcomes prevents the provision of a simple answer to the question, "what works?" Instead, we must address the question, "what works with whom to produce what outcomes?"

Recently, McMurran and Crawford (2016) examined the effectiveness of psychological therapies for personality disorder. There are several promising therapies for people diagnosed with borderline personality disorder. Reduced borderline symptomatology, suicidal behavior, and self-injury have been shown with dialectical behavior therapy (Kliem, Kröger, & Kosfelder, 2010), mentalization-based therapy (Bateman & Fonagy, 2008), cognitive behavioral therapy (CBT) (Davidson et al., 2006), schema-focused therapy (Farrell, Shaw, & Webber, 2009; Giesen-Bloo et al., 2006), systems training for emotional predictability and problem-solving (Blum et al., 2008), cognitive analytic therapy (Chanen et al., 2008), and acceptance-based emotion regulation (Gratz, Tull, & Levy, 2014). CBT also shows promise for improving social functioning in Cluster B personality disorders (Evans et al., 1999), however, CBT may not be effective for men with antisocial personality disorder (Davidson & Tyrer, 1996). Dual focus schema therapy (i.e., focusing on substance misuse and schemas together) shows promise in reducing substance use in dependent personality disorder patients (Ball, Maccarelli, LaPaglia, & Ostrowski, 2011).

Treatments for Offenders with Personality Disorder

Outcome studies of treatments specifically for personality disorder in offender populations are scarce, and few randomized controlled trials (RCTs) have been conducted (Barnao & Ward, 2015). However, some treatments show promise, at least in reducing symptoms associated with personality disorder, although with unknown effects on reoffending.

Dialectical behavior therapy

A 12-month dialectical behavior therapy (DBT) program has been implemented in the Netherlands with men and women diagnosed with borderline personality disorder who were referred to outpatient forensic services (van den Bosch, Hysaj, & Jacobs, 2012). Comparison with a non-forensic sample in treatment revealed few differences in sociodemographic and clinical profiles, and 75% of the forensic sample completed the full program. This is evidence of the feasibility of applying DBT with forensic outpatients, although this study provides no information on effectiveness. Nee and Farman (2005) studied three women in British prisons who were in a DBT program. Measures of self-harm were taken monthly from a pre-treatment baseline, throughout treatment (12 months duration), and during a 6-month follow-up phase. Incidents of self-harm were said to reduce for all three cases, but data were not analyzed. Psychometric tests of borderline symptoms, anger, locus of control, and coping beliefs were said to improve, but no calculations for reliability of change or clinical significance were presented.

Schema-focused therapy

Doyle, Tarrier, Shaw, Dunn, and Dolan (2016) conducted a feasibility study for an RCT of schema-focused therapy with offender-patients diagnosed with personality disorder in a high-security hospital in England. The researchers randomized 63 patients to receive either 18 months of weekly 1-hr schema-focused therapy sessions plus usual treatment ($n = 29$) or usual treatment only ($n = 34$). Data on impulsiveness, anger, interpersonal style, and schemas were collected at baseline and at intervals up to 36 months. Full data were available for 25 (86%) in the schema treatment group and 24 (71%) in the usual treatment group. At final follow-up, intention-to-treat analyses showed no statistically significant between-group differences on impulsiveness, anger, or interpersonal style and a statistically significant difference on only one of the 15 schemas—defectiveness/shame. Scores on this schema were *greater* in the treatment group, which the authors of the study interpreted as possibly reflecting an increase in self- and other awareness in patients with psychopathic traits. However, multiple comparisons may have produced a type 1 error, which means detecting an effect that is not really present.

Mentalization-based therapy

Bateman, Fonagy, and colleagues have developed mentalization-based therapy (MBT) for use in the treatment of antisocial personality disorder (MBT-ASPD) (Bateman et al., n.d.). In the MBT model, antisocial behavior or violence occurs when an understanding of others' mental states is compromised by perceived threats to self-esteem, such as interpersonal rejection or disrespect. MBT-ASPD targets mentalizing problems through a program of group and individual psychotherapy. A pilot study of MBT-ASPD delivered over 18 months to 23 men diagnosed with ASPD in forensic outpatient settings showed significant improvements on self-reported aggression. Bateman and colleagues have now begun to work on a multi-site RCT of MBT-ASPD in probation services in England and Wales.

Systems training for emotional predictability and problem solving

Systems training for emotional predictability and problem-solving (STEPPS) has been evaluated with prisoners diagnosed with borderline personality disorder. In uncontrolled studies with women and men who undertook 20×2-hour weekly sessions of STEPPS, pre- to post-treatment improvements were seen in borderline symptoms, mood, and negative affectivity (Black, Blum, McCormick, & Allen, 2013). These positive findings were greater in magnitude for those with co-occurring antisocial personality disorder, indicating that the presence of antisocial traits should not exclude people from treatment (Black, Simsek-Duran, Blum, McCormick, & Allen, 2015).

Reasoning and rehabilitation

Young et al. (2012) conducted research in a hospital personality disorder service for dangerous offenders, comparing 16 men who received 15×90-minute sessions of a behavioral program called Reasoning and Rehabilitation for Attention Deficit Hyperactivity Disorder (R&R ADHD) with 15 waitlist controls. Participants were assessed on measures of social problem-solving, attitudes to violence, anger, and ADHD symptoms before and after the treatment. Intention-to-treat analyses showed significant improvements for the treatment group over the comparison group on 7 of 13 scales (less impulsive and avoidant problem-solving styles; less machismo; less anger arousal and fewer angry behaviors; fewer ADHD symptoms, and improved emotion control). However, a small sample size, a waitlist comparison group, multiple comparisons, and follow-up immediately post-treatment raise doubts about the validity of these findings.

Treatments for Psychopathy

Although psychopathy does not feature as a personality disorder in its own right in the classification systems of DSM and ICD, knowledge about the treatment of people with psychopathic traits is crucial for correctional psychologists. Reidy, Kearns and DeGue (2013) reviewed treatments for psychopathic violence. There were few evaluations (just 17 over a span of almost 25 years) and, unsurprisingly given the heterogeneity of research design, interventions, and participants, results were inconsistent across studies: some reduced violence, some had no effect, and others increased violence. The state of the evidence permits no conclusions either way about the efficacy or otherwise of treatment for this group. Interventions need to be developed and evaluated, and in the process of this attention should be given to avoid harm. Individually tailored, intensive, cognitive behavioral treatments focusing on dynamic criminogenic needs and based on a broad understanding of psychopathy will likely lead to the most productive outcomes.

Concerns About the Outcome Research

There are some concerns with regard to evaluations of personality disorder treatment outcomes. First, some of the studies use small samples, meaning that the validity of the results is questionable. A systematic review of psychological treatments for personality disorder by

Duggan, Huband, Smailagic, Ferriter, and Adams (2007) included 27 outcome studies, with participant numbers ranging from 22 to 202 (median = 50). In their meta-analysis of DBT outcomes, Kliem et al. (2010) included eight RCTs with samples of between 23 and 180 (median = 43). Sample size will differ for each study, but detecting a modest effect on any outcome requires a sample size larger than these medians. Second, there is a question about how long the effects of treatment last. Follow-up times vary across studies, from immediately post-treatment to up to 2 years, but rarely beyond. To illustrate the importance of follow-up times, Kliem et al. (2010) concluded from their meta-analysis that DBT has a moderate positive effect compared with treatment as usual, but that these positive effects decay over time, suggesting that more attention needs to be paid to the transfer of DBT skills to daily life. Finally, treatments do have their champions, and many of the studies of particular treatments come from the same group of researchers. Positive effects deriving from allegiance to a specific therapy and expertise in its application need to be balanced by evaluations conducted by independent groups. Nonetheless, we may conclude that therapies for people with personality disorder appear to be promising for improving some of the important problems experienced by this disparate client group, but that there is at present insufficient evidence to support the efficacy of personality disorder treatments for offenders specifically. This is not to say that treatment for offenders does not work—a lack of evidence for effectiveness does not mean that treatments are ineffective—but rather that more evaluations of good quality are needed.

Guidelines for the Treatment of People With Personality Disorder

Guidelines have been produced for the treatment of people with borderline personality disorder (e.g., American Psychiatric Association, 2001, updated by Oldham, 2005; National Health and Medical Research Council, 2012; National Institute for Health and Clinical Excellence, 2009a). These place considerable emphasis on general management, including building a trusting therapeutic relationship, actively involving people in treatment decisions, being explicit about what patients can expect from treatment, building a relevant and realistic treatment plan with short- and longer-term goals, assessing risk of self-harm, having contingency and crisis plans, and taking care to provide advance information about treatment endings and avoiding sudden breaks or termination of treatment. Psychological treatments are accepted in these guidelines as the core intervention for people with personality disorder, and short-term treatments of less than 3 months duration should be avoided.

Reflecting the relative paucity of research on other specific personality disorders, there are few other guidelines. One exception is a guideline for antisocial personality disorder by the National Institute for Health Clinical Excellence (2009b). This recommends that adults with antisocial personality disorder who have a history of offending behavior should be offered group-based cognitive and behavioral interventions that focus on reducing offending behavior. This conclusion is based upon evidence of what works with offenders, namely that structured cognitive behavioral programs addressing criminogenic needs are the most effective in reducing reoffending (Andrews & Bonta, 2006). That the evidence comes largely from the correctional contexts indicates, as Polaschek (2010) says, "that the attempt to draw people engaged in chronic rule-violation into the health system by making their behavior the primary evidence for a specific mental disorder called ASPD [antisocial personality disorder] has not yet been successful" (p. 23). Indeed, Polaschek argues convincingly that antisocial individuals are best treated in correctional settings where a range of risk factors, including personality traits, may be assessed and formulated to inform treatment planning.

Current Issues and Future Directions

A better understanding of the relationship between personality disorder and crime is clearly required if effective prevention and treatment programs are to be developed. Evaluations of interventions specifically with personality-disordered offenders in correctional and forensic mental health contexts are also sorely needed. Given that most of the existing research has been conducted with people with borderline personality disorder, there is a pressing need for better evidence about whether psychological treatment can help people with other types of personality disorder, including antisocial personality disorder, and multiple co-occurring personality disorders. The broad range of personality disorders has not been addressed in evaluations, although psychopathy is receiving increasing attention (Polaschek, 2014).

Most psychological treatments for personality disorder are of long duration, meaning that services are expensive and available to relatively small numbers of those who might benefit. Ways of increasing access to psychological treatments for people with personality disorder are needed, but care must be taken that new services are not only efficient but also effective. Attention to potential harms is essential so that these can be avoided (Welsh & Roque, 2014).

Aspects of delivery should also be addressed. Treatment non-completion by people in personality disorder treatment programs is a significant problem (McMurran, Huband, & Overton, 2010), and treatment non-completers have significantly higher hospitalization rates (Webb & McMurran, 2009) and offender-patient non-completers commit more offenses (McCarthy & Duggan, 2010). While it may be that those who do not complete treatment are the high-risk cases who would likely have poor outcomes even if they did complete treatment, it is nonetheless possible that creating the conditions that drive people out of treatment may contribute to treatment failure. It is, therefore, important to attend to issues of engagement through improving services, training staff adequately, designing interventions informed by gender and ethnicity needs, and preparing service users for treatment (McMurran, 2012).

Finally, in some studies specific treatment has been shown to be no more effective in reducing symptoms than good clinical care (Bateman & Fonagy, 2009; Chanen et al., 2008). A considered and coordinated approach to sentence planning, community integration, monitoring, and crisis resolution is likely to be the bedrock for managing offenders with personality disorder.

Conclusion

In conclusion, personality disorder is an important issue in correctional psychology, yet there is much work to be done to improve our understanding of personality disorder and crime, how to manage and treat personality-disordered offenders effectively, and how to configure services to best effect. In practice, correctional psychologists need to understand the range of traits and symptoms that are associated with personality disorder, particularly antisocial personality disorder; these need to be assessed and incorporated into an individual case formulation that will drive a treatment plan; intensive psychological treatments focusing on dynamic criminogenic needs (including personality traits and personality disorder symptoms) are likely to be most effective; attention needs to be paid to engaging the offender in the treatment process and managing the offender through the treatment pathway.

Key Readings

Livesley, J. (2012). Integrated treatment: A conceptual framework for an evidence-based approach to the treatment of personality disorder. *Journal of Personality Disorders, 26,* 17–42.

McMurran, M., & Howard, R. (Eds.) (2009). *Personality, personality disorder and violence.* Chichester, UK: Wiley.

Widiger, T. A. (Ed.) (2012). *The Oxford handbook of personality disorders.* Oxford, UK: University of Oxford Press.

References

American Psychiatric Association (2013). *Diagnostic and statistical manual of mental disorders* (5th ed.). Washington, DC: Author.

Andrews, D. A., & Bonta, J. (2006). *The psychology of criminal conduct* (4th ed.). Cincinnati, OH: Anderson.

Auty, K. M., Farrington, D. P., & Coid, J. W. (2015). Intergenerational transmission of psychopathy and mediation via psychosocial risk factors. *British Journal of Psychiatry, 206,* 26–31.

Ball, S. A., Maccarelli, L. M., LaPaglia, D. M., & Ostrowski, M. J. (2011). Randomized trial of dual-focused vs. single focused individual therapy for personality disorders and substance dependence. *Journal of Nervous and Mental Disease, 199,* 319–328.

Barnao, M., & Ward, T. (2015). Sailing uncharted seas without a compass: A review of interventions in forensic mental health. *Aggression and Violent Behavior, 22,* 77–86.

Bateman, A., & Fonagy, P. (2008). 8-year follow-up of patients treated for borderline personality disorder: Mentalization-based treatment versus treatment as usual. *American Journal of Psychiatry, 165,* 631–638.

Bateman, A., & Fonagy, P. (2009). Randomized controlled trial of outpatient mentalization-based treatment versus structured clinical management for borderline personality disorder. *American Journal of Psychiatry, 166,* 1355–1364.

Bateman, A., Yakeley, J., McGauley, G., Lorenzini, N., O'Connell, J., & Fonagy, P. (n.d.). *A programme of studies to establish the feasibility of a randomised controlled trial for mentalization-based treatment for antisocial personality disorder.* Unpublished report, University College London, UK.

Black, D. W., Blum, N., McCormick, B., & Allen, J. (2013). Systems training for emotional predictability and problem solving (STEPPS) group treatment for offenders with borderline personality disorder. *Journal of Nervous and Mental Disease, 201,* 124–129.

Black, D. W., Gunter, T., Loveless, P., Allen, J., & Sieleni, P. (2010). Antisocial personality disorder in incarcerated offenders: Psychiatric comorbidity and quality of life. *Annals of Clinical Psychiatry, 22,* 113–120.

Black, D. W., Simsek-Duran, F., Blum, N., McCormick, B., & Allen, J. (2015). Do people with borderline personality disorder complicated by antisocial personality disorder benefit from the STEPPS treatment program? *Personality and Mental Health,* online publication. doi:/10.1002/pmh.1326

Blackburn, R. (1975). An empirical classification of psychopathic personality. *British Journal of Psychiatry, 127,* 456–460.

Blackburn, R. (2002). Ethical issues in motivating offenders to change. In M. McMurran (Ed.), *Motivating offenders to change: A guide to enhancing engagement in therapy* (pp. 139–155). Chichester, UK: Wiley.

Blum, N., St. John, D., Pfohl, B., Stuart, S., McCormick, B., Allen, J., … & Black, D. W. (2008). Systems training for emotional predictability and problem solving (STEPPS) for outpatients with borderline personality disorder: A randomized controlled trial and 1-year follow-up. *American Journal of Psychiatry, 165,* 468–478.

British Psychological Society (2006). *Understanding personality disorder*. Leicester, UK: The British Psychological Society.

Candilis, P. J., & Neal, T. M. S. (2014). Not just welfare over justice: Ethics in forensic consultation. *Legal and Criminological Psychology*, 19, 19–21.

Chanen, A. M., Jackson, H. J., McCutcheon, L. K., Jovev, M., Dudgeon, P., Yuen, H. P., … & McGorry, P. D. (2008). Early intervention for adolescents with borderline personality disorder using cognitive analytic therapy: Randomised controlled trial. *British Journal of Psychiatry*, 193, 477–484.

Coid, J., Hickey, N., Kahtan, N., Zhang, T., & Yang, M. (2007). Patients discharged from medium secure forensic psychiatry services: Reconvictions and risk factors. *British Journal of Psychiatry*, 190, 223–229.

Coid, J., Yang, M., Tyrer, P., Roberts, A., & Ullrich, S. (2006). Prevalence and correlates of personality disorder in Great Britain. *British Journal of Psychiatry*, 188, 423–431.

Coid, J., Yang, M., Ullrich, S., Zhang, T., Roberts, A., Roberts, C., … & Farrington, D. (2007). Predicting and understanding risk of re-offending: The Prisoner Cohort Study. Ministry of Justice, Research Summary. Retrieved from http://nomsintranet.org.uk/roh/official-documents/Prediciting%20and%20understanding%20risk%20of%20reoffendng%20Coid%20et%20al.pdf

Conway, C. C., Hammen, C., & Brennan, P. A. (2015). Optimizing prediction of psychosocial and clinical outcomes with a transdiagnostic model of personality disorder. *Journal of Personality Disorders*, 29, 1–22.

Cooke, D. J., & Logan, C. (2015). Capturing clinical complexity: Towards a personality-oriented measure of psychopathy. *Journal of Criminal Justice*, 43, 262–273.

Costa, P. T., & McCrae, R. R. (1992). *Revised NEO personality inventory and the NEO-five factor inventory (NEO-FFI) professional manual*. Odessa, FL: Psychological Assessment Resources.

Davidson, K. M., Norrie, J., Tyrer, P., Gumley, A., Tata, P., Murray, H., & Palmer, S. (2006). The effectiveness of cognitive behaviour therapy for borderline personality disorder: Results from the borderline personality disorder study of cognitive therapy (BOSCOT) trial. *Journal of Personality Disorders*, 20, 450–465.

Davidson, K. M., & Tyrer, P. (1996). Cognitive therapy for antisocial and borderline personality disorders: Single case study series. *British Journal of Clinical Psychology*, 35, 413–429.

DeLisi, M., & Vaughn, M. G. (2014). Foundation for a temperament-based theory of antisocial behaviour and criminal justice system involvement. *Journal of Criminal Justice*, 43, 290–294.

Doyle, M., Tarrier, N., Shaw, J., Dunn, G., & Dolan, M. (2016). Exploratory trial of schema-focussed therapy in a forensic personality disordered population. *Journal of Forensic Psychiatry and Psychology*, 27, 232–247.

Duggan, C., Huband, N., Smailagic, N., Ferriter, M., & Adams, C. (2007). The use of psychological treatments for people with personality disorder: A systematic review of randomized controlled trials. *Personality and Mental Health*, 1, 95–125.

Evans, K., Tyrer, P., Catalan, J., Schmidt, U., Davidson, K., Dent, J., … & Thompson, S. (1999). Manual-assisted cognitive-behaviour therapy (MACT): A randomized controlled trial of a brief intervention with bibliotherapy in the treatment of recurrent deliberate self-harm. *Psychological Medicine*, 29, 19–25.

Farrell, J. M., Shaw, I. A., & Webber, M. A. (2009). A schema-focused approach to group psychotherapy for outpatients with borderline personality disorder: A randomized controlled trial. *Journal of Behavior Therapy and Experimental Psychiatry*, 40, 317–328.

Fazel, S., & Danesh, J. (2002). Serious mental disorder in 23 000 prisoners: A systematic review of 62 surveys. *The Lancet*, 359, 545–550.

First, M. B., Gibbon, M., Spitzer, R. L., Williams, J. B. W., & Benjamin, L. S. (1997). *Structured clinical interview for DSM-IV Axis II personality disorders*. Arlington, VA: American Psychiatric Publishing.

Fok, M., Hayes, R., Chang, C.-K., Stewart, R., Callard, F., & Moran, P. (2012). Life expectancy at birth and all-cause mortality among people with personality disorder. *Journal of Psychosomatic Research*, 73, 104–107.

Frick, P. J., & Ray, J. V. (2014). Evaluating callous-unemotional traits as a personality construct. *Journal of Personality*, 83, 710–722.

Giesen-Bloo, J., van Dyck, R., Spinhoven, P., van Tilburg, W., Dirksen, C., van Asselt, T., ... & Arntz, A. (2006). Outpatient psychotherapy for borderline personality disorder: Randomized trial of schema-focused therapy vs transference-focused therapy. *Archives of General Psychiatry*, 63, 649–659.

Gratz, K. L., Tull, M. T., & Levy, R. (2014). Randomized controlled trial and uncontrolled 9-month follow-up of an adjunctive emotion regulation group therapy for deliberate self-harm among women with borderline personality disorder. *Psychological Medicine*, 44, 2099–2112.

Hare, R. D. (2003). *The Hare Psychopathy Checklist—Revised* (2nd ed.). North Tonawanda, NY: Multi-Health Systems.

Hare, R. D., Clark, D., Grann, M., & Thornton, D. (2000). Psychopathy and the predictive validity of the PCL-R: An international perspective. *Behavioral Sciences & the Law*, 18, 623–645.

Hart, S., Sturmey, P., Logan, C., & McMurran, M. (2011). Forensic case formulation. *International Journal of Forensic Mental Health*, 10, 118–126.

Howard, R. C. (2015). Personality disorders and violence: What is the link? *Borderline Personality Disorder and Emotion Dysregulation*, 2, 12. doi:/10.1186/s40479-015-0033-x

Howard, R. C., Hepburn, E., & Khalifa, N. (2015). Is delusional ideation a critical link in the nexus between personality disorder and violent offending? *Journal of Forensic Psychiatry and Psychology*, 26, 368–382.

Howard, R. C., Huband, N., & Duggan, C. (2012). Adult antisocial syndrome with co-morbid borderline pathology: Association with severe childhood conduct disorder. *Annals of Clinical Psychiatry*, 24, 127–134.

Howard, R. C., Huband, N., Mannion, A., & Duggan, C. (2008). Exploring the link between personality disorder and criminality in a community sample. *Journal of Personality Disorders*, 22, 589–603.

Howard, R. C., Khalifa, N., & Duggan, C. (2014). Antisocial personality disorder comorbid with borderline pathology and psychopathy is associated with severe violence in a forensic sample. *Journal of Forensic Psychiatry and Psychology*, 25, 658–672.

Howard, R. C., McCarthy, L., Huband, N., & Duggan, C. (2013). Re-offending in forensic patients released from secure care: The role of antisocial/borderline co-morbidity, substance dependence, and severe childhood conduct disorder. *Criminal Behaviour and Mental Health*, 23, 191–202.

Hunt, E., Bornovalova, M. A., & Patrick, C. J. (2015). Genetic and environmental overlap between borderline personality disorder traits and psychopathy: Evidence for promotive effects of Factor 2 and protective effects of Factor 1. *Psychological Medicine*, 45, 1471–1481.

Johnson, J. G., Cohen, P., Smailes, E., Kasen, S., Oldham, J. M., Skodol, A. E., & Brooks, J. S. (2000). Adolescent personality disorders associated with violence and criminal behavior during adolescence and early adulthood. *American Journal of Psychiatry*, 157, 1406–1412.

Kliem, S., Kröger, C., & Kosfelder, J. (2010). Dialectical behaviour therapy for borderline personality disorder: A meta-analysis using mixed-effects modelling. *Journal of Consulting and Clinical Psychology*, 78, 936–951.

Lenzenweger, M. F., Lane, M. C., Loranger, A. W., & Kessler, R. C. (2007). DSM-IV personality disorders in the National Comorbidity Survey Replication. *Biological Psychiatry*, 62, 533–564.

Loranger, A. W. (1999). *International Personality Disorder Examination (IPDE)*. Odessa, FL: Psychological Assessment Resources.

Martel, M. M. (2013). Sexual selection and sex differences in the prevalence of childhood externalizing and adolescent internalizing disorders. *Psychological Bulletin*, 139, 1221–1259.

McCarthy, L., & Duggan, C. (2010). Engagement in a medium secure personality disorder service: A comparative study of psychological functioning and offending outcomes. *Criminal Behaviour and Mental Health*, 20, 112–128.

McMurran, M. (2012). Readiness to engage in treatments for personality disorder. *International Journal of Forensic Mental Health*, 11, 289–298.

McMurran, M., & Crawford, M. (2016). Personality disorders. In A. M. Nezu, & C. M. Nezu (Eds.), *The Oxford handbook of cognitive and behavioral therapies* (pp. 438–461). New York, NY: Oxford University Press.

McMurran, M., Huband, N., & Overton, E. (2010). Non-completion of personality disorder treatments: A systematic review of correlates, consequences, and interventions. *Clinical Psychology Review*, 30, 277–287.

National Health and Medical Research Council (2012). *Clinical practice guideline for the management of borderline personality disorder.* Canberra, Australia: Australian Government Retrieved from https://www.nhmrc.gov.au/guidelines-publications/mh25

National Institute for Health and Clinical Excellence (2009a). *Borderline personality disorder: Recognition and management.* London, UK: Author Retrieved from https://www.nice.org.uk/guidance/cg78

National Institute for Health and Clinical Excellence (2009b). *Antisocial personality disorder: Prevention and management.* London, UK: Author Retrieved from www.nice.org.uk/Guidance/CG77

Nee, C., & Farman, S. (2005). Female prisoners with borderline personality disorder: Some promising treatment developments. *Criminal Behaviour and Mental Health*, 15, 2–16.

Neumann, C. S., Hare, R. D., & Pardini, D. A. (2015). Antisociality and the construct of psychopathy: Data from across the globe. *Journal of Personality*, 83, 678–692.

Noren, K., Lindgren, A., Haellstom, T., Thormaehlen, B., Vinnars, B., Wennberg, P., ... & Barber, J. P. (2007). Psychological distress and functional impairment in patients with personality disorders. *Nordic Journal of Psychiatry*, 61, 260–270.

Oldham, J. M. (2005). *Guideline watch: Practice guideline for the treatment of patients with borderline personality disorder.* Arlington, VA: American Psychiatric Association.

Patrick, C. J., & Drislane, L. E. (2015). Triarchic model of psychopathy: Origins, operationalizations, and observed linkages with personality and general psychopathology. *Journal of Personality*, 83, 627–643.

Patrick, C. J., Fowles, D. C., & Krueger, R. F. (2009). Triarchic conceptualization of psychopathy: Developmental origins of disinhibition, boldness, and meanness. *Development and Psychopathology*, 21, 913–938.

Perälä, J., Suvisaari, J., Saarni, S. I., Kuoppasalmi, K., Isometsä, E., Pirkola, S., ... & Lönnqvist, J. (2007). Lifetime prevalence of psychotic and bipolar I disorders in a general population. *Archives of General Psychiatry*, 64, 19–28.

Pickard, H. (2015). Choice, deliberation, violence: Mental capacity and criminal responsibility in personality disorder. *International Journal of Law and Psychiatry*, 40, 15–24.

Polaschek, D. L. L. (2010). What do mental health services offer to people with antisocial personality disorder? A commentary on the NICE Clinical Guideline. *Personality and Mental Health*, 4, 20–29.

Polaschek, D. L. L. (2014). Adult criminals with psychopathy: Common beliefs about treatability and change have little empirical support. *Current Directions in Psychological Science*, 23, 296–301.

Powers, A. D., & Oltmanns, T. F. (2012). Personality disorders and physical health: A longitudinal examination of physical functioning, healthcare utilization, and health-related behaviors in middle-aged adults. *Journal of Personality Disorders*, 26, 524–538.

Reidy, D., Kearns, M. C., & DeGue, S. (2013). Reducing psychopathic violence: A review of the treatment literature. *Aggression and Violent Behaviour*, 18, 527–538.

Sharp, C., Wright, A. G. C., Fowler, J. C., Frueh, B. C., Allen, J. G., Oldham, J., & Clark, L. A. (2015). The structure of personality pathology: Both general ('g') and specific ('s') factors? *Journal of Abnormal Psychology*, 124, 387–398.

Skeem, J., & Cooke, D. J. (2010). Is criminal behaviour a central component of psychopathy? Conceptual directions for resolving the debate. *Psychological Assessment*, 22, 433–435.

Skeem, J., Johansson, P., Andershed, H., Kerr, M., & Louden, J. E. (2007). Two subtypes of psychopathic violent offenders that parallel primary and secondary variants. *Journal of Abnormal Psychology*, 116, 395–409.

Skodol, A. E. (2011). Scientific issues in the revision of personality disorders for DSM-5. *Personality and Mental Health*, 5, 97–111.

Skodol, A. E. (2012). Diagnosis and DSM-5: Work in progress. In T. E. Widiger (Ed.), *The Oxford handbook of personality disorders* (pp. 35–57). New York, NY: Oxford University Press.

Soetemann, D. I., Verheul, R., & Busschbach, J. J. V. (2008). The burden of disease in personality disorders: Diagnosis-specific quality of life. *Journal of Personality Disorders*, 22, 259–268.

South, S. C., Turkheimer, E., & Oltmanns, T. F. (2008). Personality disorder symptoms and marital functioning. *Journal of Consulting and Clinical Psychology*, 76, 769–780.

Tikkanen, R., Holi, M., Lindberg, N., Tiihonen, J., & Virkkunen, M. (2009). Recidivistic offending and mortality in alcoholic violent offenders: A prospective follow-up study. *Psychiatry Research*, 168, 18–25.

Torgersen, S., Czajkowski, N., Jacobson, K., Reichborn-Kjennerud, T., Røysamb, E., Neale, M. C., & Kendler, K. C. (2008). Dimensional representations of DSM-IV Cluster B personality disorders in a population-based sample of Norwegian twins: A multivariate study. *Psychological Medicine*, 38, 1617–1625.

Torgerson, S., Kringlen, E., & Kramer, V. (2001). The prevalence of personality disorders in a community sample. *Archives of General Psychiatry*, 58, 590–596.

Tyrer, P., Reed, G. M., & Crawford, M. J. (2015). Classification, assessment, prevalence, and effect of personality disorder. *Lancet*, 385, 717–726.

van den Bosch, L. M., Hysaj, M., & Jacobs, P. (2012). DBT in an outpatient forensic setting. *International Journal of Law and Psychiatry*, 35, 311–316.

Ward, T. (2013). Addressing the dual relationship problem in forensic and correctional practice. *Aggression and Violent Behavior*, 18, 92–100.

Webb, D. J., & McMurran, M. (2009). A comparison of women who continue and discontinue treatment for borderline personality disorder. *Personality and Mental Health*, 3, 142–149.

Welsh, B. C., & Roque, M. (2014). When crime prevention harms: A review of systematic reviews. *Journal of Experimental Criminology*, 10, 245–266.

Wetterborg, D., Långström, N., Andersson, G., & Enebrink, P. (2015). Borderline personality disorder: Prevalence and psychiatric comorbidity among male offenders on probation in Sweden. *Comprehensive Psychiatry*, 62, 63–70.

World Health Organization (2018). *11th revision of the International Classification of Diseases (ICD-11)*. Geneva, Switzerland: WHO.

Wygant, D. B., Sellbom, M., Sleep, C. E., Wall, T. D., Applegate, K. C., Krueger, R. F., & Patrick, C. J. (2016). Examining the DSM-5 alternative personality disorder model operationalization of antisocial personality disorder and psychopathy in a male correctional sample. *Personality Disorders: Theory, Research and Treatment*, 7, 229–239.

Young, S., Hopkin, G., Perkins, D., Farr, C., Doidge, A., & Gudjonsson, G. (2012). A controlled trial of a cognitive skills program for personality-disordered offenders. *Journal of Attention Disorders*, 17, 598–607.

Yu, R., Geddes, J. R., & Fazel, S. (2012). Personality disorders, violence, and antisocial behaviour: A systematic review and meta-regression analysis. *Journal of Personality Disorders*, 26, 775–792.

18

Indigenous Offenders: Issues and Challenges for Correctional Psychologists

Armon J. Tamatea
University of Waikato, New Zealand

Andrew Day
James Cook University and University of Melbourne, Australia

The overrepresentation of First Nations peoples in post-colonial criminal justice systems is an ongoing critical public policy issue. (Lockwood, Hart, & Stewart, 2015, p. 769)

There are many challenges faced by Indigenous communities that are not experienced by other groups. These relate to political (e.g., colonization, historic and contemporary conflict), moral (e.g., acknowledged status as citizens, or even as persons), and socioeconomic (e.g., land confiscation and resource displacement) issues. To understand Indigenous offenders then, one clearly needs to appreciate the context of Indigenous peoples more broadly. The aim of this chapter, however, is not to provide an overview of this context or to present a comprehensive account of the diversity of Indigenous peoples and offenders. Rather, our intention is to introduce some of the practice issues that are relevant for those who work directly with Indigenous and Aboriginal offenders. Suffice it to say, however, that the context for many Indigenous peoples includes: (a) disproportionate representation in criminal justice environments; (b) discrepancies in sociopolitical autonomy and power; (c) recognition of diversity within communities; (d) marginalization and low participation in correctional psychology practices; and (e) the distortion of cultural values in the justification of offending. An understanding and appreciation of local knowledge, perceptions, and practices is, in our view, a prerequisite for developing correctional interventions that are relevant and sustainable for the offender and their community. Furthermore, there is a case to be made for inviting members of the community to participate collaboratively in the development and application of all assessment tools and rehabilitation practices, if not least to create a joint understanding of the implications and social consequences of these practices for the individual, their families, and even the community.

From the outset we note that other groups defined in a non-dominant context are not the focus of this chapter. However, practitioners who work with other minority groups or

The Wiley International Handbook of Correctional Psychology, First Edition. Edited by Devon L. L. Polaschek, Andrew Day, and Clive R. Hollin.

communities most readily identified by ethnicity (e.g., migrants, refugees) or lifestyle (e.g., lesbian, gay, bisexual, transgender, and intersex [LGBTI], religion) may find some resonance with the issues raised here. This may include large minority groups who also experience discrimination, such as African Americans or those in the United States from Hispanic cultural backgrounds. We also note that the term *Indigenous* is ambiguous and not widely agreed upon, so for the sake of convenience, in this chapter we refer to Indigenous peoples[1] as those who are typically a non-dominant group which has an acknowledged claim to be the original inhabitants of a given land.[2] In some jurisdictions this distinction is quite clear, such as with the Aboriginal and Torres Strait Island peoples of Australia, the various iwi[3] that comprise the Māori of New Zealand, and the Maya of Guatemala. In other regions this is somewhat contested (e.g., Africa, the Middle East) as a result of nomadic migration and dislocation. Peoples who are regarded as Indigenous typically claim the right to define themselves and often reject the notion that outsiders can do so. Self-identification is seen as a basic human right, but not one that is always honored in the correctional setting.

Indigenous Peoples are Over-Represented in Criminal Justice Settings

Perhaps the most tragic feature, common to all Indigenous peoples in the developed world, is their conspicuous over-representation in their respective criminal justice systems. As can be seen in Table 18.1, Indigenous peoples in Canada, Australia, and New Zealand are grossly over-represented in terms of rates of imprisonment and community sentences when their relative presence in the general population is taken into consideration. For instance, although Aboriginal and Torres Strait Island people in Australia comprise only 3% of the general Australian adult population, they represent 27% of the total full-time prisoner population (as at March 2015; Australian Bureau of Statistics, 2015).

Table 18.1   General Comparison of Imprisonment and Community Sentenced Rates of Indigenous Peoples in Australia, Canada, and New Zealand (ca. 2015)

	Imprisoned		Community Sentence/order		General population	
Country	Total	Indigenous	Total	Indigenous	Total	Indigenous
Australia[a]	36,122	9,885 (27.4%)	59,992	11,780 (19.6%)	21,507,717	669,900 (3.1%)
Canada	15,327[b]	3,542 (23.1%)	7,827[b]	1,318 (16.8%)	32,852,325[c]	1,836,035 (5.6%)
New Zealand	8,641[d]	4,389[f] (50.8%)	36,451[d]	15,859[f] (43.4%)	4,242,048[e]	598,605 (14.1%)

[a] Australian Bureau of Statistics, 2014, 2015, 2016.
[b] Public Safety Canada, 2015.
[c] Statistics Canada, 2016.
[d] Department of Corrections (New Zealand), n.d.-a, n.d.-b.
[e] Statistics New Zealand, 2016;
[f] approx.

It is also the case that Indigenous communities are heavily impacted by crime. Although high crime rates characterize many communities irrespective of cultural heritage, Lloyd et al. (2015) argue that *hyper-incarceration* can mean that prison is perceived by those communities as being "accepted, expected and normalized" (p. 2). They add that the cascading risk of growing up in regular contact with the criminal justice system, and in communities where many members are, or have been, incarcerated, can result in the distortion of social norms so that prison can become a social institution that reflects a normative pattern of expectations and behaviors: an anticipated life event. Furthermore, normal everyday processes of interacting with family (siblings, cousins, parents, and friends) are lost, making it increasingly difficult to establish and maintain meaningful relationships with those outside of the prison system, depriving people of the opportunity to live a fulfilling life. The influence of this social context on personal responsibility for behavior is recognized in some parts of the law, and yet it is rarely considered in psychological assessments or interventions. For example, in Australia, although the same sentencing principles are applied in every case, courts are also bound to take into account all material facts, including those which exist only by reason of the offender's membership of an ethnic or other group (*Neal v. R*, 1982; *R v. Fuller-Cust*, 2002). The "material facts" that have been found to be relevant in sentencing Indigenous offenders include the severe social and economic disadvantage, accompanied by endemic alcohol abuse (which exists in some Indigenous communities). Anthony (2010) describes this in relation to the *R v. Fernando* (1992) case law where Justice Wood held that:

> … the equal treatment of Indigenous offenders required, where relevant, consideration of their subjective circumstances, including their Indigenous background where it threw "light on the particular offence and the circumstances of the offender" (p. 62).

The judge added that where alcohol abuse was indicative of the socioeconomic circumstances and environment in which the offender had grown up, that it should be taken into account as a mitigating factor, and that there was a need to consider rehabilitation orders. This was, in his view, because recognition of the relationship between alcohol abuse and violence in Indigenous communities required more carefully considered approaches than imprisonment. In *Police v. Abdulla* (1999), the South Australian Supreme Court held that the Fernando principles should receive "broad application" beyond "Aborigines living in the more remote communities," and the Court of Criminal Appeal has further noted that these principles are "not restricted to traditional Aboriginals" (*R v. Smith*, 2003). This legal acknowledgement of how cultural issues can mitigate personal responsibility for offending requires recognition by those who are seeking to assess risk and delivering offender rehabilitation.

Indigeneity and Power

In a broad sense, indigeneity raises issues of power, historic conflict, contemporary struggles for sociopolitical autonomy, and differential notions of knowledge, meaning, and praxis. The impact of an individual's cultural heritage and sociopolitical legacy can, in important ways, inform the perpetration (and victimization) of violence among specific communities. For instance, Ellerby (1994) described Aboriginal sex offenders in Canada as being more likely than non-Aboriginal sex offenders to exhibit issues associated with: displacement, abandonment, and racism; personal identity confusion; a history of maltreatment; poverty; death due to illness, suicide, and violence; deficits in education, employment skills, financial position, and social supports; and histories of more aggressive sexual behaviors. This suggests that a range of pervasive stressors that have the potential to impact on attitudes toward others and interpersonal behavior may be manifest across a population.

Wohl and Aponte (1995) have further argued that Indigenous peoples have historically been under-served by social services, with societal forces continuing to put these groups at risk. To put this another way, the lack of essential services available for Indigenous people after release from prison may be a significant contributing factor to higher recidivism rates (Lloyd et al., 2015). Without access to comprehensive health care and social support, Indigenous people simply return to the same environments that led to their incarceration.

Correctional services are typically regarded as a government agency, meaning that any services they provide are inextricably linked with those social institutions (such as law enforcement and criminal justice) that have been responsible for historical abuse and the disproportionate exercise of power. This aversive relationship between offenders, their communities, and social institutions—perceived or actual—may adversely influence the level of trust that exists between the offender and the service provider. Homel, Lincoln, and Herd (1999), for example, comment that practitioners cannot understand matters relating to risk without understanding the impact of traumatic experiences such as forced removals and institutionalized racism, as well as the ongoing protection afforded by strong social bonds to family and other factors relevant to cultural resilience, personal control, and family control. Day et al. (2008) have further reported that Indigenous prisoners (in Australia) are more likely to experience symptoms of trauma, have greater difficulty identifying and describing feelings, and perceive higher levels of discrimination than non-Indigenous prisoners.

Indigenous Peoples Are Diverse

Although Indigenous peoples may share common histories or experiences, it should be noted that these communities are not homogeneous, either across peoples or within communities. LaPrairie (2002) has, for example, challenged the then-conventional wisdom about the presumed homogeneity of aboriginal (Canadian) offenders, noting age-group, socioeconomic, risk-need, and Aboriginal status differences, as well as regional variations. In Australia, McCausland and Vivian (2010) also describe considerable variation in rates of Indigenous offending from one area to another, even in those areas that have comparable Indigenous populations to each other. They argue that local factors are critical to any understanding of risk and protective factors in Aboriginal communities. For example, their conversations with key representatives from one Indigenous community indicated that high alcohol consumption, lack of meaningful employment and activity, poverty, and inequality, as well as environmental disruptions (e.g., drought), contributed directly to higher crime rates. In addition, grief and mental health problems, an "acceptance" of crime, a lack of understanding of the criminal justice process (irrespective of regular contact), disjointed, inappropriate, or remote service delivery (as well as poorly evaluated programs), and community dynamics were all identified as attributes of a community in which crime was high. Alternatively, better employment opportunities, a good working relationship with police, a collective sense of a positive future, school–community relationships, strong women leaders, and local solutions to local problems (and perceived lack of government interference) were seen as positive attributes of a community in which crime was low. The take-home message of this type of community research is that the challenges and needs of communities will vary, and practitioners are thus advised to develop an understanding of the communities from which their clients come. However, it is also the case that community-level variables are poorly understood; they have been little investigated or absorbed into mainstream correctional psychology practice.

Marginalization

Indigenous peoples have also been susceptible to social disempowerment resulting from colonization,[4] economic dislocation, and the imposition of alien legal, educational, and religious systems (Lee, 1995). On an everyday level, Indigenous peoples are subject to multiple prejudices in relation to: (a) criminal histories and associations (e.g., gangs); (b) lower socioeconomic status and poverty; and (c) ethnicity. Marginalization involves the tacit or active side-lining of a community, usually as a result of low political influence or consideration. The impact can include reduced subsidization of resources that are necessary for community health. For instance, Nielsen (2004) described Canadian and North American examples of *legal* processes that have forbidden Indigenous peoples from holding religious ceremonies, *educational* processes that have restricted many Indigenous children to poorly resourced schools (thus making them marginally unemployable), *political* processes that have forbidden Indigenous peoples from voting or forming political lobby groups, and *economic* processes that have made it illegal for Indigenous peoples to work off their reservation, reserve, or mission without giving up their Indigenous status. Any attempt to resist or challenge these processes was defined as criminal behavior.

The challenging relationships that can exist between Indigenous peoples and social services can harm efforts to establish the extent of offending in a community. For instance, Day, Jones, Nakata, and McDermott (2012) observed that the extent of violence in some Aboriginal (Australia) communities can be difficult to determine due to under-reporting, a lack of appropriate screening by service providers, and incomplete identification of Indigenous status in data sets. Furthermore, the recognition of marginality in the course of encountering indigeneity and one's role in perpetuating that marginality—tacitly or otherwise—by virtue of representing a state institution can also be aversive to psychologists. The experience of collective guilt and white privilege can be problematic in practice because guilt is an unpleasant emotion that can prompt unhelpful coping responses (such as avoidance or denial), and even threaten social identity through the promotion of shame (Gunn & Wilson, 2011).

Cultural Distortions

Misapplication of customary values and rules is another area that practitioners need to consider when engaging with Indigenous offenders. Offenders may misapply, exaggerate, and/or distort traditional cultural principles or rules to justify their own behavior, thereby setting double standards of behavior (Memmott, 2010). For instance, the reluctance to report the crimes of a family member, particularly in relation to child sexual abuse, can be exacerbated in small populations where everyone in the community is likely to be related to a greater or lesser degree. Greer (in Gordon, 2013), commenting on remote Indigenous Australian communities, noted that the connection with land, family, and where one comes from is foundational to the identity of an Aboriginal person, so anything which may lead to rejection by the community is avoided. As such, reporting sexual assault or even admitting that it happens is seen as striking out against the community, and any victim who speaks out is likely to risk rejection.

Another culturally informed barrier that enables the perpetuation of violence or sexual abuse can involve offenders taking advantage of their special community status to exploit vulnerable persons. For instance, Metge (1995) observed that whanau[5] and community depended on strong leadership from koroua[6] and kuia,[7] and that if a leading kaumātua[8] committed sexual offenses, especially if he had high mana[9] as a repository of esoteric knowledge, community members found it difficult to challenge him openly.

Correctional Psychology and Indigenous Practice

The general focus of effort in correctional psychology has been with achieving two primary outcomes: (a) developing and implementing offense risk measures; and (b) providing effective rehabilitation. In both of these areas the literature has been largely uninformed by cultural differences, an observation made over 20 years ago now by Bonta, Lipinski, and Martin (1992). Indeed, the contemporary scholarly literature prioritizes particular practices, such as the development and validation of actuarial risk assessment tools utilizing methodologies that are atheoretical, objective, and "culture-neutral." Given the inherent bias in this approach toward assuming that experiences are universal (and can be measured through common, standardized metrics), it is not hard to see why such research is often negatively perceived by Indigenous people (Trimble & Fisher, 2006). Furthermore, governments' sporadic interest in indigenous research has contributed to a marginal history of shaping justice projects and influencing policy decision-making (LaPrairie, 1999; van de Vijver & Leung, 2000). This, combined with a bias against the development of Indigenous-led research (especially if engaging alternative forms of knowledge generation), further reflects a selective reinforcement of scientific principles that is often reflected in poor research opportunities for Indigenous-led research (Sue, 1999). The major concern here, however, is that any understanding of the offender quickly becomes decontextualized and thus loses validity. It follows that a primary challenge facing any correctional psychologist is to *understand individuals in their context* and that appreciating the perspective of Indigenous peoples will often involve attempts to understand an alternative and collective worldview that does not superimpose neatly, if at all, on Western notions of knowledge in general or offending behavior in particular. To put this in different, and perhaps more practical, terms, it becomes important for the assessing psychologist to understand the extent to which Indigenous offenders experience unique life events which create offense pathways that are dissimilar to those of dominant cultural groups.

Risk Assessment

In September 2015, the Federal Court of Canada released a decision[10] allowing an action against Correctional Services Canada (CSC) for an unjustified violation of the plaintiff's section 7 right to life, liberty, and security of the person under the *Canadian Charter of Rights and Freedoms*. The plaintiff, Jeffrey Ewert, was a 53-year-old Métis prisoner who was serving two life sentences for second degree murder and attempted murder, and was sentenced to 15 months' imprisonment, to be served concurrently, for an escape from lawful custody conviction. At the time of the decision, he had spent 30 years in various federal correctional facilities. Ewert alleged that the psychological risk assessment tools used by CSC were not culturally appropriate for use with Aboriginal prisoners. Of interest was the debate between a number of expert witnesses about the veracity of the psychological assessment tests used in the case. The expert witness for Ewert provided evidence to demonstrate that the assessment tools were susceptible to various forms of cultural bias and that scores should not be used to inform legal decision-making because of the cultural differences between Aboriginal and non-Aboriginal groups. Based on the weight of the evidence, the Court determined that Ewert had been successful in proving that the assessment tests were unreliable due their susceptibility of cultural bias. Furthermore, the Court found that the results of the tests had a negative impact on Ewert by increasing his security classification and reducing his desire to apply for parole. Although the decision was subsequently overturned on appeal, a recent decision by the Supreme Court of Canada recognized the critical role played by Correctional Service Canada, particularly the use of risk assessment and classification processes, that may be unjustly prolonging the incarceration of Indigenous prisoners disproportionately to their non-Indigenous prisoners. This case highlights one of the unique challenges faced by correctional psychologists who encounter offenders who are not only culturally different from them, but also have a special political status, namely, the applicability of psychological science to Indigenous peoples and the impact that psychological approaches, especially risk assessment, may have for peoples who do not see benefits for them or their communities.

It is certainly the case that most current risk screening and classification tools have been validated with data from dominant culture (male) samples, and the ability of these tools to accurately predict recidivism in other cultural groups remains largely unexamined. This issue has been raised with the Static-99 (Hanson & Morton-Bourgon, 2009), the most commonly used and the most widely researched measure to assess risk of sexual reoffending, used internationally. The Static-99 has been consistently shown to have a moderate level of predictive accuracy for sexual reoffending.

However, differences have also been noted within subsets of the sex offender samples that have been studied. Långström (2004), for example, found that the Static-99 predicted recidivism among Nordic and non-Nordic Europeans, but failed to significantly predict recidivism among the African/Asian offenders in a Swedish national sample. Allan, Dawson, and Allan (2006) also reported poorer predictive validity (area under the ROC [receiver operating characteristic] curve of .65) for Australian Indigenous offenders assessed using another actuarial tool, the Rapid Risk Assessment for Sexual Offense Recidivism (RRASOR), than for non-Indigenous sexual offenders (AUC of .74), although the latter figure is similar to that reported in the original Canadian validation data.

A more recent Australian study by Smallbone and Rallings (2013) also reported that the predictive accuracy of the Static-99 was lower for Indigenous than for non-Indigenous offenders for sexual (AUC = .76 vs. .82), non-sexual violent (AUC = .59 vs. .64), and any violent recidivism (AUC = .67 vs. .77). Although the authors of this study concluded that the Static-99 is no less accurate for Indigenous Australian offenders than it is for many other sexual offender populations, another study of the Static-99-R and Static-2002-R involving five independent Canadian samples has reported a number of significant differences between Aboriginal and non-Aboriginal sexual offenders (Babchishin, Blais, & Helmus, 2012). Aboriginal sexual offenders scored significantly higher than non-Aboriginal sexual offenders on total scores and items related to general criminality, while scoring lower on items related to sexual deviancy. Canadian Aboriginal sexual offenders were found to be significantly younger and to have lengthier criminal histories than non-Aboriginal sexual offenders; they were also found to have lower educational achievement, higher rates of unemployment, and more extensive histories of substance abuse. For risk factors specific to sexual offending, they were less likely to have sexually deviant interests and paraphilias, and less likely to have male victims. In terms of predictive validity for sexual reoffending, the risk factors for general criminality were less predictive for Aboriginal sexual offenders, despite their higher average scores on these factors (risk factors associated with sexual self-regulation, social influences, and relationship stability had similar predictive validity for Aboriginal and non-Aboriginal sexual offenders). The predictive accuracy of the Static-99-R was similar for both groups of offenders, but the Static-2002-R had significantly lower predictive accuracy for Aboriginal sexual offenders.

This study provides additional grounds to suspect that some instruments are less accurate when used with Aboriginal and other ethnic groups that have not been part of the normative samples for those measures, and, indeed, the need for local validation with sub-populations of offenders is now increasingly widely recognized (e.g., Craig & Beech, 2009). This is clearly a position that has some traction in the wider justice system. Maurutto and Hannah-Moffat (2007) have reported concerns from judges, prosecutors, and defense lawyers in Canada about the appropriateness of using actuarial risk assessments instruments and risk-based sentencing for Aboriginal young people, suggesting that risk assessments "introduce speculation and morally laden subjective assessments that reflect white, Western middle-class judgments … [that] could result in more intrusive and punitive dispositions for marginalized youth" (p. 467). The important point here is that the way in which the causes of offending in Indigenous communities are conceptualized has some significant implications for the way in which risk is assessed in a context in which the over- or under-assessment of a particular need may result in the delivery of an inappropriate level of intervention, or lead to an inaccurate overall risk classification rating. In short, it has been suggested that the "Indigenization" of existing measures approach is so subject to misinterpretation and cultural bias that the approach should be completely abandoned (Drew, Adams, & Walker, 2010).

Allard's (2010) review identifies a number of culture-specific risk factors in Australian Indigenous offenders, while noting that the risk factors for Indigenous offending in Australia are largely similar to those for the wider population (and that the higher incidence of these risk factors in Indigenous populations may help to explain higher rates of offending). For example, Allard discusses suggestions that forced removals, dependence on government, and racism (Homel et al., 1999) all contribute to risk of reoffending. In Australia, 8% of the Indigenous adult population was taken away from their family and one third had a relative removed, with strong correlations between having a family member taken and subsequent arrest and incarceration (Dodson & Hunter, 2006). Zubrick et al. (2004) also found that Aboriginal carers who had been forcibly separated from their natural family were almost twice as likely to have been arrested and charged with an offense at some time.

These findings are somewhat consistent with those of a New Zealand longitudinal study of more than 1,000 people born in Christchurch in 1977 (see Department of Corrections, 2007). This reported that although Māori were involved in violent offending at two to three times the rate of non-Māori, ethnicity did not predict offending once controls were introduced for family circumstances (including parental alcohol abuse and offending) and parenting behaviors (use of punishment and level of care). There is also some evidence to suggest that an insecure cultural identity is associated with risk of reoffending. A New Zealand study by Marie, Fergusson, and Boden (2009) reported that those with a Māori and another ethnic identity had higher offending rates than both what they referred to as "sole-Māori" and non-Māori. So, whilst some areas of need (e.g., finance, accommodation, education, employment, substance use; see Bonta & Wormith, 2013) are clearly relevant to offenders from all cultural groups, the case can be made that individualized assessment and specialist service provision is required to understand and address what might be described as "culturally-specific" needs.

It might be assumed that the obvious solution here is to simply commission a series of studies around the world that validate each risk assessment tool with additional data collected from Indigenous offender populations. This would then establish which tools could be used with which groups and lead to the development of a range of new specialized assessment protocols in circumstances where predictive validity cannot be established. The problem, in essence, can be viewed as simply a short-term one, and, in the interim, psychologists have to make some "best guesses" about what to do when asked to assess individuals from groups for whom limited validation data are available. However, reservations about the routine use of risk assessment tools with Indigenous offenders go beyond those associated with concerns about a lack of local validation data to include the possibility that current tools overlook important causes of offending in Indigenous communities and, by doing so, fail to discern the interactions between key drivers of crime such as identity, cultural connectedness, mental illness, and substance abuse (see Day, 2003; Hsu, Caputi, & Byrne, 2009). This is critical to the overarching purpose of most correctional assessments: to inform the delivery of interventions that can meaningfully reduce the chances of further offending taking place. For some, such as Case (2006), there is a need to replace the "risk factor approach," which emphasizes aggregate correlates of crime, with a more holistic and sensitive methodology that considers the underlying causes of their over-representation, including social and economic marginalization grounded in historical processes. This implies that more meaningful, and ultimately more effective, interventions can then emerge.

In concluding this section on assessment, it would be wrong to conclude that critiques of current risk assessment practices are the views of a few radicals. Similar arguments have been presented to support the development of gender-specific assessment practices (see Van Voorhis, Wright, Salisbury, & Bauman, 2010), and concerns have been widely voiced about the historical use of psychometric testing for racial discrimination purposes and the problems associated with the idea of a pan-Indigenous concept of culture that does not reflect between-community differences (it has been estimated that there are more than 600 distinctive Aboriginal cultural groups in Australia alone; Gillies, 2013). The alternative is to develop methods of psychological assessment from the ground up, operationalizing Indigenous theoretical constructs and Indigenous ways of thinking and conceptualizing, and adopting Indigenous knowledge protocols to guide the work. Indigenous consultation methods of this type have been recommended by the United Nations, and yet although measures developed in this manner could also subsequently be subject to statistical validation, the approach has not been widely embraced (or endorsed) by the psychology profession.

Offender Rehabilitation

Offender rehabilitation and reintegration efforts are greatly informed by observing those cultural processes that serve to promote a fair process as well as to develop opportunities for constructive dialogue. Poor sensitivity to cultural encounters (i.e., the misattribution of the causes of behavior) can result in poorly informed assessments, inappropriate interventions, and poor outcomes. This may take the form, for example, of overestimating deviancy and criminality across a given group, overlooking potentially powerful social supports, and undermining the individual's existing coping style. In addition, offenders may be cautious about engaging with the correctional practitioner and concerned that any information provided in treatment will be misused to increase their experience of stigmatization (Korbin, 2002; Patel & Lord, 2001). As with risk assessments, offender rehabilitation processes typically occur in coercive contexts, and although an offender has the right to withdraw consent, the consequences for doing so may be costly (e.g., declined parole) and may also be interpreted as resistance. In the next section, we discuss some opportunities for exploring and understanding the context and realities of Indigenous offenders and some departure points for developing culturally responsive practices that can improve engagement in any effort to change offending behavior.

Understand the Issues for Indigenous Offenders and Their Communities

As discussed throughout this chapter, we advocate that an understanding of offending begins with an understanding of the offender and their context, or what McDermott (2008) refers to as being "clued in," adding that reciprocity, or the *sharing* of information, is central to establishing rapport. A working knowledge of the community from which every offender originates is valuable information for a clinical and cultural formulation. Indigenous peoples (and refugees) are likely to have a history of dislocation and migration that can inform an understanding of any individual's offending behavior. For instance, separation from place and community is inherently stressful, and can incur loss of meaningful role identity, introduction of downward social mobility (e.g., unemployment), and the erosion of family structures and community sanctions and attitudes.

To understand diversity also requires an understanding of systems and injunctions that inform the individual's role(s) within their given community and codes of conduct. So identifying behavior that is considered normative and acceptable within the community and that which is considered abnormal and prohibited (as well as the mechanisms for managing behavior in the interests of the community, such as ostracism, physical punishment, imprisonment) is always going to be important. Ultimately, the challenge for the correctional practitioner is to understand the *meaning* of specific behavior (i.e., offending) under these conditions. Some challenging rehabilitation issues include: (a) language (i.e., determining whether a translator is required) as well as mode of language: intervention efforts that are not well matched to the individual's learning style (i.e., the responsivity principle) may also be less effective if written homework tasks are required from offenders whose primary modality for learning and communication is oral; (b) attitudes toward victims: attending to how victims (e.g., women, children) are located within a community and a family offers insights into how offenders may invoke cultural justifications for their offending; (c) disclosures—describing and discussing offenses, especially sexual assaults—can be confronting for offenders whose culture prohibits open discussion of sexual behavior more broadly; and, (d) shame: those who are interdependent tend to be more concerned about negative evaluations from others than those who are independent. Cull and Wehner (1998), for example, describe shame as being deeply experienced by many Indigenous Australian men who have sexually offended. In addition, deviant behavior may result in loss of face or threat of loss of one's social integrity (Hall, Sue, Narang, & Lilly, 2000).

Cultural biases among practitioners are often inadvertent, denied, and typically beyond immediate awareness (Dana, 2005). To practice in a culturally responsive way involves the development of specific and nuanced understandings of cultural expectations and boundaries.

An important prerequisite to working effectively with Indigenous clients, especially in Australia and New Zealand, is to be accepted as a person who is able to demonstrate appropriate respect to other community members according to cultural protocols. In an Australian Aboriginal context, for instance, unless the wider community supports the treatment that is being offered, there is little likelihood of people participating. Jones, Masters, Griffiths, and Moulday (2002) have suggested a range of additional strategies that can help practitioners engage with the communities and establish their credentials. These include regular, ongoing cultural awareness training; cultural oversight and advice from Indigenous Reference Groups, Elders Councils, or other Indigenous bodies; and regular cultural supervision from cultural experts to assist with matters of everyday practice.

Formative preparation practices and supervision that includes cultural experience and an appreciation of cultural diversity are recommended to promote practitioner self-development. This can also cue dialogue about the role of cultural constructs in correctional practice. Suggested approaches include: (a) developing agency capacity for brokering sound cultural supervision provision from individuals who have good standing in their particular community, as well as institutional or industry knowledge of the field of risk assessment and offender management. Educating practitioners on the histories, beliefs, and practices of their people as well as supporting new assessment practices can also be of immeasurable value in developing sensitivity in practice; and (b) conducting case conference meetings with cultural advisors can enrich cultural knowledge and enhance practitioner confidence. Such meetings may involve highlighting and discussing a critical incident (e.g., non-disclosure), failure to engage, or how to work with the offender's support in an efficacious way—especially if there is distrust of or animosity toward practitioners.

Preparation for any assessment and intervention in the correctional setting will involve the tripartite challenge described by Ridley, Li, and Hill (1998) of: (a) identifying cultural data; (b) interpreting that information; and (c) incorporating findings into a conceptualization that is accurate and comprehensive in communicating risk and risk management issues in ways that are meaningful to the offender. Critical in-session processes and skills that have the potential to enhance effectiveness include: (a) establishing credibility; (b) openness to the offender's explanatory model (cognitive distortions notwithstanding); and (c) being cognizant of etiquette: such as the use of native language with correct pronunciation, knowing proper terms to use regarding traditional cultural beliefs, attitudes, and practices, knowing what subjects may be considered inappropriate to discuss with strangers, use of correct greetings, significance of eye contact and physical touch, customs regarding the sharing of food, and understanding the importance of spending time to get to know each other and create a trusting working alliance before formal procedures are started. Learning to tolerate ambiguity is an important attribute when working with individuals whose model of the world and how they interact with it may be distinct or somewhat at odds with the practitioner's own cultural outlook and values.

Conclusion

In this chapter we have argued that cultural issues arise routinely in any clinical engagement in any correctional setting. It is a grim reality that many Indigenous and minority groups are over-represented in prisons generally, and so the likelihood is great that the practitioner will encounter offenders from other ethnic groups and cultural backgrounds. Adopting an attitude that cultural difference is normative and to be expected implies an openness to diversity that represents a precondition for intercultural communication. The responsibility for strengthening practice in this area lies fully with the correctional profession.

Notes

1   For the sake of brevity, the focus of this chapter will be on Canada, Australia, and New Zealand as these are countries that have a recent history of colonization, share a similar philosophy of offender management, and have the presence of recognized Indigenous populations who are over-represented in their respective criminal justice systems yet are also a minority in their own countries.
2   Some other names for this distinctive status are Aboriginal (Australia and Canada), First Peoples (North America, Canada), or First Nations (Canada).
3   A term which means, loosely, major tribal grouping.
4   Colonization is an historical practice of assuming sovereignty via force or diplomacy.
5   Māori: Family and extended kin relationships.
6   Māoori: Venerated elder male.
7   Māoori: Venerated elder female.
8   Māoori: Elder.
9   Māoori: Prestige or status.
10 Ewert v. Canada, 2015 FC 1093 (CanLII).

Key Readings

Cunneen, C. (1999). Criminology, genocide and forced removal of Indigenous children from their families. *Australian & New Zealand Journal of Criminology*, 32(2), 124–138.

La Prairie, C. (2002). Aboriginal over-representation in the criminal justice system: A tale of nine cities. *Revue Canadienne De Criminologie*, 44(2), 181–208.

Lloyd, J., Delaney-Thiele, D., Abbott, P., Baldry, E., McEntyre, E., Reath, J., ... & Harris, M. (2015). The role of primary health care services to better meet the needs of Aboriginal Australians transitioning from prison to the community. *BMC Family Practice*, 16(1), 1–10.

Martel, J., Brassard, R., & Jaccoud, M. (2011). When two worlds collide: Aboriginal risk management in Canadian corrections. *British Journal of Criminology*, 51, 235–255.

References

Allan, A., Dawson, D., & Allan, M. M. (2006). Prediction of the risk of male sexual reoffending in Australia. *Australian Psychologist*, 41, 60–68.

Allard, T. (2010). *Understanding and preventing Indigenous offending. Research Brief 9.* Canberra, Australia: Indigenous Justice Clearinghouse.

Anthony, T. (2010). *Sentencing Indigenous offenders. Brief 7.* Canberra, Australia: Indigenous Justice Clearinghouse Retrieved from https://www.indigenousjustice.gov.au/wp-content/uploads/mp/files/publications/files/brief007.pdf

Australian Bureau of Statistics. (2014). *Estimates and projections, Aboriginal and Torres Strait Islander Australians, 2001 to 2026.* Retrieved from http://www.abs.gov.au/ausstats/abs@.nsf/Products/C19A0C6E4794A3FACA257CC900143A3D?opendocument

Australian Bureau of Statistics. (2015). *Prisoners in Australia, 2015.* Retrieved from www.abs.gov.au/ ausstats/abs@.nsf/Lookup/by%20Subject/4517.0~2015~Main%20Features~Aboriginal%20 and%20Torres%20Strait%20Islander%20prisoner%20characteristics~7

Australian Bureau of Statistics. (2016). *Summary of findings: Persons in corrective services.* Retrieved from http://www.abs.gov.au/ausstats/abs@.nsf/MediaRealesesByCatalogue/01A3C2BE96FA6185C A2568A90013631C?OpenDocument

Babchishin, K. M., Blais, J., & Helmus, L. (2012). Do static risk factors predict differently for Aboriginal sex offenders? A multi-site comparison using the original and revised Static-99 and Static-2002 scales. *Canadian Journal of Criminology and Criminal Justice*, 54, 1–43.

Bonta, J., Lipinski, S., & Martin, M. (1992). The characteristics of aboriginal recidivists. *Revue Canadienne de Criminologie*, 34, 517–521.

Bonta, J., & Wormith, J. S. (2013). Applying the Risk-Need-Responsivity principles to offender assessment. In L. A. Craig, T. A. Gannon, & L. Dixon (Eds.), *What Works in Offender Rehabilitation: An Evidence-Based Approach to Assessment and Treatment* (pp. 69–93). Oxford, UK: Wiley-Blackwell.

Case, S. P. (2006). Young people "at risk" of what? Challenging risk-focused early intervention as crime prevention. *Youth Justice*, 6(3), 171–179.

Craig, L. A., & Beech, A. R. (2009). Best practice in conducting actuarial risk assessments with adult sexual offenders. *Journal of Sexual Aggression*, 15, 193–210.

Cull, D. M., & Wehner, D. M. (1998). Australian Aborigines: Cultural factors pertaining to the assessment and treatment of Australian Aboriginal sexual offenders. In W. L. Marshall (Ed.), *Sourcebook of treatment programs for sexual offenders* (pp. 431–453). New York, NY: Plenum Press.

Dana, R. H. (2005). *Multicultural assessment: Principles, applications, and examples.* Mahwah, NJ: Lawrence Erlbaum.

Day, A. (2003). Reducing the risk of re-offending among Australian Indigenous offenders: What works for whom? *Journal of Offender Rehabilitation*, 37(2), 1–16.

Day, A., Davey, L., Wanganeen, R., Casey, S., Howells, K., & Nakata, M. (2008). Symptoms of trauma, perceptions of discrimination, and anger: A comparison between Australian Indigenous and nonindigenous prisoners. *Journal of Interpersonal Violence*, 23(2), 245–258.

Day, A., Jones, R., Nakata, M., & McDermott, D. (2012). Indigenous family violence: An attempt to understand the problems and inform appropriate and effective responses to criminal justice system intervention. *Psychiatry, Psychology and Law*, 19(1), 104–117.

Department of Corrections (2007). *Over-representation of Maori in the criminal justice system.* Wellington, NZ: Author Retrieved from https://www.corrections.govt.nz/resources/research_and_statistics/ over-representation-of-maori-in-the-criminal-justice-system.html

Department of Corrections. (n.d.-a). *Community sentences and orders statistics—December 2014.* Retrieved from https://www.corrections.govt.nz/resources/research_and_statistics/community_ sentences_and_orders/CP_Dec_2014.html

Department of Corrections. (n.d.-b). *Prison facts and statistics—December 2014.* http://www. corrections.govt.nz/resources/research_and_statistics/quarterly_prison_statistics/CP_December_ 2014.html

Dodson, M., & Hunter, B. H. (2006). Selected crime and justice issues for Indigenous families. *Family Matters*, 75, 34–41.

Drew, N., Adams, Y., & Walker, R. (2010). Issues in mental health assessment with indigenous Australians. In N. Purdie, P. Dudgeon, & R. Walker (Eds.), *Working together: Aboriginal and Torres Strait Islander mental health and wellbeing principles and practice* (pp. 191–209). Canberra, Australia: Department of Health and Ageing.

Ellerby, L. (1994). Community-based treatment of Aboriginal sex offenders: Facing realities and exploring possibilities. *Forum on Corrections Research*, 6(3), 23–25.

Gillies, C. (2013). Establishing the United Nations' Declaration on the Rights of Indigenous Peoples as the minimum standard for all forensic practice with Australian Indigenous peoples. *Australian Psychologist*, 48, 14–27.

Gordon, Y. (2013, January 19). The evil within. The Sydney Morning Herald. Retrieved from https://www.smh.com.au/national/nsw/the-evil-within-20130118-2cym9.html

Gunn, G. R., & Wilson, A. E. (2011). Acknowledging the skeletons in our closet: The effect of group affirmation on collective guilt, collective shame, and reparatory attitudes. *Personality and Social Psychology Bulletin, 37*(11), 1474–1487.

Hall, G. C. N., Sue, S., Narang, D. S., & Lilly, R. S. (2000). Culture-specific models of men's sexual aggression: Intra- and interpersonal determinants. *Cultural Diversity & Ethnic Minority Psychology, 6*(3), 252–267.

Hanson, R. K., & Morton-Bourgon, K. E. (2009). The accuracy of recidivism risk assessments for sexual offenders: A meta-analysis of 118 prediction studies. *Psychological Assessment, 21*, 1–21.

Homel, R., Lincoln, R., & Herd, B. (1999). Risk and resilience: Crime and violence prevention in Aboriginal communities. *Australian & New Zealand Journal of Criminology, 32*(2), 182–196.

Hsu, C., Caputi, P., & Byrne, M. K. (2009). The Level of Service Inventory—Revised (LSI-R): A useful risk assessment measure for Australian offenders? *Criminal Justice and Behavior, 36*, 728–740.

Jones, R. L., Masters, M., Griffiths, A., & Moulday, N. (2002). Culturally relevant assessment of Indigenous offenders: A literature review. *Australian Psychologist, 37*(3), 187–197.

Korbin, J. E. (2002). Culture and child maltreatment: Cultural competence and beyond. *Child Abuse & Neglect, 26*(6–7), 637–644.

Långström, N. (2004). Accuracy of actuarial procedures for assessment of sexual offender recidivism risk may vary across ethnicity. *Sexual Abuse: A Journal of Research and Treatment, 16*, 107–120.

LaPrairie, C. (1999). The impact of aboriginal justice research on policy: A marginal past and an even more uncertain future. *Canadian Journal of Criminology, 41*(2), 249–260.

La Prairie, C. (2002). Aboriginal over-representation in the criminal justice system: A tale of nine cities. *Revue Canadienne De Criminologie, 44*(2), 181–208.

Lee, N. (1995). Culture conflict and crime in Alaskan native villages. *Journal of Criminal Justice, 23*(2), 177–189.

Lloyd, J., Delaney-Thiele, D., Abbott, P., Baldry, E., McEntyre, E., Reath, J., … & Harris, M. (2015). The role of primary health care services to better meet the needs of Aboriginal Australians transitioning from prison to the community. *BMC Family Practice, 16*(1), 1–10.

Lockwood, K., Hart, T. C., & Stewart, A. (2015). First Nations peoples and judicial sentencing: Main effects and the impact of contextual variability. *British Journal of Criminology, 55*, 769–789.

Marie, D., Fergusson, D. M., & Boden, J. M. (2009). Ethnic identity and exposure to maltreatment in childhood: Evidence from a New Zealand birth cohort. *Social Policy Journal of New Zealand, 36*, 154–171.

Maurutto, P., & Hannah-Moffat, K. (2007). Understanding risk in the context of the Youth Criminal Justice Act. *Canadian Journal of Criminology, 49*(4), 465–491.

McCausland, R., & Vivian, A. (2010). Why do some aboriginal communities have lower crime rates than others? A pilot study. *Australian & New Zealand Journal of Criminology, 43*(2), 301–332.

McDermott, D. (2008, September). *Deep listening: Working with Indigenous mental distress*. Workshop on Social and Cultural Transitions, Northern Territory, Australia.

Memmott, P. (2010). On regional and cultural approaches to Australian Indigenous violence. *Australian & New Zealand Journal of Criminology, 43*(2), 333–355.

Metge, J. (1995). *New growth from old: The whanau in the modern world*. Wellington, New Zealand: Victoria University Press.

Neal v. R, 149 CLR 305 (1982).

Nielsen, M. O. (2004). A comparison of the community roles of Indigenous-operated criminal justice organizations in Canada, the United States, and Australia. *American Indian Culture and Research Journal, 28*(3), 57–75.

Patel, K., & Lord, A. (2001). Ethnic minority sex offenders' experiences of treatment. *Journal of Sexual Aggression, 7*(1), 40–50.

Police v. Abdulla, 74 SASR 337 (1999).

Public Safety Canada. (2015). *Corrections and conditional release statistical overview: 2014 annual report.* Retrieved from https://s3.amazonaws.com/s3.documentcloud.org/documents/2110762/ps-sp-1483284-v1-corrections-and-conditional.pdf

R v. Fernando, 76 A Crim R 58 (NSW) (1992).

R v. Fuller-Cust, 6 VR 496 (2002).

R v. Smith, SASC 263 (2003).

Ridley, C. R., Li, L. C., & Hill, C. L. (1998). Multicultural assessment: Re-examination, reconceptualization, and practical application. *The Counseling Psychologist*, 26(6), 827–910.

Smallbone, S., & Rallings, M. (2013). Short-term predictive validity of the Static-99 and Static-99-R for Indigenous and nonindigenous Australian sexual offenders. *Sexual Abuse*, 25(3), 302–316.

Statistics Canada. (2016). *Census program.* Retrieved from http://www12.statcan.gc.ca

Statistics New Zealand. (2016). *2013 Census.* Retrieved from www.stats.govt.nz/Census

Sue, S. (1999). Science, ethnicity, and bias: Where have we gone wrong? *American Psychologist*, 54, 1070–1077.

Trimble, J. E., & Fisher, C. B. (2006). Introduction: Our shared journey: Lessons from the past to protect the future. In J. E. Trimble, & C. B. Fisher (Eds.), *Handbook of ethical research with ethnocultural populations and communities* (pp. xv–xxix). Thousand Oaks, CA: Sage.

Van de Vijver, F. J. R., & Leung, K. (2000). Methodological issues in psychological research on culture. *Journal of Cross-Cultural Psychology*, 21, 33–51.

Van Voorhis, P., Wright, E. M., Salisbury, E. J., & Bauman, A. (2010). Women's risk factors and their contributions to existing risk/needs assessment: The current status of a gender-responsive supplement. *Criminal Justice and Behavior*, 37, 261–288.

Wohl, J., & Aponte, J. F. (1995). Common themes and future prospects. In J. F. Aponte, R. Young Rivers, & J. Wohl (Eds.), *Psychological interventions and cultural diversity* (pp. 301–316). Boston, MA: Allyn & Bacon.

Zubrick, S., Lawrence, D., Silburn, S., Blair, E., Milroy, H., Wilke, T., & Li, J. (2004). The Western Australian Aboriginal child health survey: The health of Aboriginal children and young people. Perth, Australia: Telethon Institute for Child Health Research. Available at http://aboriginal.childhealthresearch.org.au

19

Female Offenders: Trends, Effective Practices, and Ongoing Debates

Terri Scott, Shelley L. Brown, and Kayla A. Wanamaker

Carleton University, Canada

Girls and women in conflict with the law are slowly garnering serious attention from mainstream correctional scholars. This has not always been the case. Historically, scholars as well as correctional agencies have explicitly or implicitly ignored female offenders. Further, early scholarly writings were inherently sexist—females committed crime because they were less evolved than males (Lombroso & Ferrero, 2004), or motivated by faulty biology or sexual desires (Freud, 1933; Pollack, 1950; Thomas, 1923). In contrast, subsequent theories devoted to understanding male criminal conduct underscored external environmental causes such as lower social class origins (Merton, 1957) or association with criminal peers (Sutherland, 1947; Sutherland & Cressey, 1970).

Contemporary mainstream correctional scholars started conducting female-centered research in the 1990s. However, this literature has been slow to recognize a small but increasingly informative body of work known as the gender-responsive (Van Voorhis, 2012; Van Voorhis & Bauman, 2015) or gender-informed literature (Blanchette & Brown, 2006; Gobeil, Blanchette, & Stewart, 2016). Collectively, mainstream and gender-responsive scholars have made significant strides in understanding, preventing, and treating female criminal conduct.

Consequently, the goal of this chapter is to highlight major advancements, existing challenges, and debates in the field of female offender corrections. First, the nature and prevalence of female-perpetrated crime is briefly described, followed by a review of prominent theories to explain female criminal conduct. Next, recent developments and remaining debates regarding female offender risk assessment and intervention are reviewed. Throughout the chapter, we actively attempt to consider consensual facts, identify existing knowledge gaps, recognize ongoing debates, and highlight points of reconciliation. We use the term *female offender* to encapsulate both girls and women simultaneously. In contrast, the terms *girls* and *women* are reserved for commentary specific to adolescent female offenders and adult female offenders, respectively.

The Wiley International Handbook of Correctional Psychology, First Edition. Edited by Devon L. L. Polaschek, Andrew Day, and Clive R. Hollin.
© 2019 John Wiley & Sons Ltd. Published 2019 by John Wiley & Sons Ltd.

Female Criminal Conduct: Prevalence and Trends

Irrespective of country or methodological approach, the evidence clearly indicates that girls and women commit considerably less crime than boys and men: particularly, less violent crime (Bryant & Cussen, 2015; Office for National Statistics, 2016; United States Department of Justice, n.d.). For example, the Uniform Crime Reports published annually in the United States illustrated that females accounted for 27% of all arrests but only 11.5% of all homicide-related arrests in 2014. Interestingly, this gender gap persisted in virtually all remaining crime categories, albeit to a lesser extent for non-violent crimes such as fraud and property crimes (39% of arrests were females). Noteworthy, however, was that female offenders were just as likely as their male counterparts to be arrested for embezzlement (50% female), and were actually two times more likely to be arrested for prostitution (66.3% females; United States Department of Justice, n.d.).

Although males commit more crime than females, some official statistics suggest that arrest rates for females have increased substantially over the past two decades, whilst the corresponding male rates have either remained constant or declined (Kong & AuCoin, 2008; Snyder, 2011). However, thoughtful analyses conducted within the United States comparing official arrest data with victimization survey results indicate the females are not actually becoming more criminal or violent. Rather, changes in policy and police practice (e.g., zero-tolerance policies) have disproportionately impacted females such that they are now more likely to be charged and convicted for crimes than historically (e.g., relational crimes against family members of a minor nature, crimes occurring on school grounds; Chesney-Lind & Pasko, 2013; Kerig & Schindler, 2013; Schwartz & Steffensmeier, 2012). Thus, whilst girls and women are seemingly accounting for more officially reported crime, it is unlikely that official arrest data reflect an actual surge in female-perpetrated crime (Sickmund & Puzzanchera, 2014). Nonetheless, girls and women are increasingly coming to the attention of the correctional system, and consequently require our focused attention.

Contemporary Theories of Female Criminal Conduct

To fully understand the context of female offending, it is useful to review explanations advanced by different disciplines. As will be demonstrated, the theories of crime that seek to explain female offending have emerged primarily from outside the field of psychology, chiefly from the disciplines of sociology and criminology. Arguably, these theories of female crime fall into one of three broad categories. The first is gender-neutral, developed by males for males, and is accompanied by an explicit or implicit assumption that the theory operates the same for both genders in every respect. The second is female-specific, that is, developed explicitly for female offenders, typically by female scholars with an explicit or implicit assumption that women and girls are different. Female-specific scholars challenge traditional mainstream theories of criminal behavior for assuming generalizability across gender without empirical verification (Belknap, 2015; Blanchette & Brown, 2006; Covington & Bloom, 2006). Finally, the third category is considered a hybrid or pro-feminist perspective (Belknap, 2015; Blanchette & Brown, 2006). Pro-feminist/hybrid theories incorporate aspects from the female-specific and the traditional mainstream (i.e., gender-neutral) perspectives and have been proposed for male and female offenders. One prominent theory within each of these three categories is now described.

A Gender-Neutral Theory of Female Criminal Conduct: Social Learning Theory

Social learning theory (SLT; Akers, 1992) is a social criminological theory that aims to describe how and why both males and females engage in offending behavior. SLT posits that criminal behavior is learned through "definitions" that are supportive or not supportive of crime (Burgess & Akers, 1966; Sutherland, 1947), and through classical and operant conditioning processes. Akers (1998) defined three types of definitions: positive (portrays behavior as acceptable), neutral (portrays behavior as justified), and negative (portrays behavior as unacceptable). An individual is more likely to commit a crime if they associate with others involved in criminal behavior (i.e., differential association), if the end reward of the crime outweighs the cost (i.e., differential reinforcement), if an individual is surrounded by more criminal than prosocial behavior, and finally, if they have attitudes favorable toward crime. Thus, the two core constructs inherent in SLT developed from the influential theories of Bandura (1973) and Sutherland (1947) are associates and attitudes.

There is extensive evidence supporting SLT as a plausible explanation of male criminal behavior (Akers, 1998; Akers & Jensen, 2003; Andrews et al., 2012; Brown & Motiuk, 2005; Green, 2006; Pratt & Cullen, 2000). Meta-analytic reviews conducted specifically using female offender samples have also found a correlational relationship between SLT constructs, such as associates and attitudes, and criminal conduct (Hubbard & Pratt, 2002; Simourd & Andrews, 1994). Similarly, Green's (2006) meta-analytic review illustrated that criminal attitudes and associates predict recidivism among adolescent female offenders, albeit the number of effect sizes was limited relative to the male comparison group. Further, mainstream scholars (e.g., Akers, 1998) as well as some feminist criminological scholars (e.g., Belknap, 2015; Day, Zahn, & Tichavsky, 2015) have used SLT as a framework for understanding why males are more likely to engage in crime in the first place (e.g., males are simply more likely to associate with antisocial peers than females, because boys have greater access outside the home, providing more exposure to negative peers, whereas girls have less access due to more supervision and control in the home). However, other feminist criminological scholars (e.g., Morash, 1999) remain skeptical and emphasize the importance of gender structure and context, and the mechanisms of their influence, which are not sufficiently accounted for in a social learning context. Whilst there has been a vast amount of research supporting the applicability of SLT in explaining offending behavior for males, more research is needed to explore whether SLT can explain the behavior of females. Namely, do the constructs for associates and attitudes predict to the same degree for females as they do for males? Are there differences in the types of associates that predict recidivism for males and females (e.g., peers vs. romantic partners)? Or, are there other variables altogether that need to be considered for females (i.e., female-salient factors)?

A Female-Specific Theory of Female Criminal Conduct: Pathways Theory

Developed from research in the disciplines of psychology (Salisbury & Van Voorhis, 2009), criminology (Bloom, Owen, & Covington, 2005; Covington & Bloom, 2006), and sociology (Ritchie, 1996), pathways theory (PT) posits that women and girls enter into crime because of negative life events such as childhood maltreatment (e.g., abuse and neglect), economic marginalization, and dysfunctional relationships with caregivers or intimate partners (Belknap, 2015; Chesney-Lind, 1997; Finkelhor & Baron, 1986; Simkins & Katz, 2002). It could be argued that these factors are not unique to females; however, there is some evidence to suggest that the experience of these factors is unique for females (Artz, Hoffman-Wanderer, & Moult, 2012). PT further posits that females cope with these negative life events by running away from home and/or abusing drugs. In turn, these coping mechanisms lead to survivalist crimes such as prostitution, dealing drugs, or robbery (Blanchette & Brown, 2006; Chesney-Lind, 1997), bringing females to the attention of the criminal justice system (Chesney-Lind, 1997). Emerging primarily from in-depth interviews to capture the voice and complex situations unique to women and girls, PT is said to be female-specific as the starting point, and focuses on the unique psychological and sociological experiences of females (Belknap, 2001, 2015). As it currently stands, whilst these factors are prevalent for female offenders, the importance of these factors in the prediction of antisocial behavior (i.e., predictive validity and/or causality) is still debatable.

In recent years, there has been a growing body of literature in support of PT. Qualitative studies such as those conducted by Daly (1992), Dehart (2008), Gilfus (1992), Ritchie (1996), and Simpson, Yahner, and Dugan (2008) have found that various forms of victimization (including sexual, emotional, and physical abuse, neglect, and witnessed violence), substance abuse, and economic marginalization are key themes in the lives of women and girls who have committed crime. Further quantitative testing of these findings will allow for more definitive statements regarding causality and provide important empirical evidence in support of this theory, which is beginning to emerge (Brennan, Breitenbach, Dieterich, Salisbury, & Van Voorhis, 2012; Holtfreter & Morash, 2003; Jones, Brown, Wanamaker, & Greiner, 2014; Salisbury & Van Voorhis, 2009). Overall, these studies have reported that childhood maltreatment, substance use, mental health issues, dysfunctional relationships, and economic marginalization are highly prevalent among women and girls who commit crime. Notably, more research using longitudinal multi-wave designs is needed to differentiate correlates from predictors and predictors from causal factors, and move away from the focus on prevalence. Further, as Belknap (2015) notes, much of the existing research has failed to incorporate nuanced questions related to the nature and context of victimization (e.g., sexual abuse by a trusted adult over a prolonged period of time vs. witnessing violence perpetrated between strangers).

A Hybrid/Pro-Feminist Theory of Female Crime: General Strain Theory

General strain theory (GST; Agnew, 1985, 1992; Broidy & Agnew, 1997), although including various etiological factors, does not lend itself to being a true etiological theory of criminal behavior. Specifically, GST is generally event-based and posits that strain or stressful events can produce negative feelings, such as anger and frustration, resulting in aggression and crime in the absence of strong prosocial coping resources. The strains experienced do not lead to criminal behavior directly; rather, GST researchers argue that whether crime will occur or not depends upon a host of variables ranging from personality and self-esteem to the nature of one's peer group (Agnew, 1985, 1992). Importantly, GST explicitly acknowledges that the nature of one's goals, strains, and responses to strains may vary as a function of race, class, and gender. GST identifies three sources of strain: (a) the presence of negative stimuli, (b) the inability to achieve positive goals, and (c) the loss of positively valued stimuli. The individual's response to these strains can result in the onset of antisocial or criminal behavior.

According to Broidy and Agnew (1997), GST can help explain gender differences by examining how individual strains and subsequent coping responses may vary as a function of gender.

They also suggest that the strain of patriarchal oppression may result in coping mechanisms that are criminal in nature. Notably, this aspect of GST dovetails seamlessly with PT, which posits that females use negative coping strategies (e.g., criminalized survival strategies such as drug use and prostitution) in response to a range of negative life events including systemic oppression (Belknap, 2001).

Cernkovich, Lanctôt, and Giordano (2008) have criticized empirical tests of GST for focusing on male samples, or not disaggregating the data by gender even when both genders have been included. Further, strains thought to be female-salient such as childhood abuse, which is not only experienced more often by females, but also often results in adverse coping strategies, are generally excluded from studies (Capowich, Mazerolle, & Piquero, 2001; Cheung & Cheung, 2010). Nonetheless, direct tests of GST and the role of gender are emerging. To date, some research has illustrated that strains such as stressful life events (i.e., divorce, death or illness of a family member, change in school) and being the victim of a crime, either violent or non-violent, are significantly correlated with crime for both genders (Broidy & Agnew, 1997; Hay, 2003; Hoffman & Cerbone, 1999; Kaufman, 2009). However, notable gender differences are surfacing. Negative peer relationships, problems with peers, and educational difficulties appear to be prevalent strains for males (Broidy & Agnew, 1997; Puhrmann, 2015), whereas sexual abuse, excessive family demands, negative relationships with adults, and financial strains emerge as prevalent strains for females (Baron, 2007; Broidy & Agnew, 1997; Mazerolle, 1998; Puhrmann, 2015). In addition to differences in the types of strains experienced, males and females appear to display different emotional responses to strains. For example, Mazerolle (1998) found that men were more likely to externalize their responses to strain (e.g., show anger, act violently) and females were more likely to internalize their responses to strain (e.g., anxiety and depression).

In sum, tests of the complete theory of GST and gender differences are noticeably absent. More research is needed that seeks to identify hypothesized female-specific types of strain (e.g., sexual abuse) as well as male-specific types of strain (e.g., peer conflict). Importantly, the extent to which gender-specific strains emerge as correlates, predictors, or causal factors of criminal conduct requires rigorous investigation. Lastly, more research is needed in terms of how gender may moderate the nature of emotional responses to strain and how gendered emotional responses may or may not translate into different pathways to the criminal justice system.

Risk Assessment and Female Offenders

Risk assessment is the foundation of effective corrections. Being able to reliably and fairly identify which offenders are likely to reoffend versus those who are not has significant implications for security classification, resource planning, and public safety. Risk assessment practices can and should readily accomplish these goals. Historically, risk assessment methods developed and validated on male offenders have been applied to female offenders with little thought or opposition. However, feminist-inspired scholars have frequently challenged this practice (e.g., Hannah-Moffat, 2009; Van Voorhis, 2012), resulting in a growing body of research examining the validity of using male-based tools with females (Smith, Cullen, & Latessa, 2009) as well as the benefits of using risk assessment tools developed specifically for female offenders (e.g., Van Voorhis, Bauman, & Brushett, 2013).

Risk Assessment: Through the Lens of Mainstream Correctional Scholars

Risk assessment begins with the identification of risk factors. Traditionally, a risk factor has been defined as a condition or variable that increases the probability of a negative or undesirable outcome (Bender & Lösel, 1997). In the context of criminal offending, risk factors are associated with an increased likelihood of antisocial or criminal behavior (Cottle, Lee, & Heilbrun, 2001). In mainstream correctional psychology, emphasis is placed on both static and dynamic risk factors. Static risk factors do not change (or change only in one direction) and are not amenable to treatment (Bonta, 2002). In contrast, dynamic factors can change either through intervention or with the passage of time (Serin et al., 2011), resulting in a change to risk ratings (Douglas & Skeem, 2005). Notably, the terms *criminogenic needs* (Bonta & Andrews, 2017) and *dynamic risk factors* can be used interchangeably. Further, criminogenic needs are best conceptualized as a subset of risk factors, as it is argued that when targeted for change, the risk of reengaging in antisocial activity will be reduced (Blanchette & Brown, 2006).

The Risk-Need-Responsivity (RNR) model (Bonta & Andrews, 2017) is one of the most widely accepted and empirically validated paradigms of offender rehabilitation. In brief, the risk principle states that intervention should be matched to risk level; thus, higher risk offenders should receive more intervention in terms of type and dosage than their lower-risk counterparts. The need principle states that intervention strategies should prioritize dynamic risk factors to reduce recidivism, and place less emphasis on non-criminogenic needs as targeting these can lead to increased recidivism (Bonta & Andrews, 2017). In addition, targeting multiple dynamic risks leads to greater effect sizes overall, as offenders typically have more than one factor that needs to be addressed to reduce their risk to reoffend (Gendreau, French, & Taylor, 2002). Lastly, the responsivity principle states that intervention methods should match a typical offender's learning style (e.g., concrete, skills-based) but also be responsive to individual characteristics of the offender (e.g., gender, culture, strengths). Specifically, the principle of general responsivity prescribes that interventions should be cognitive behavioral in nature, whereas specific responsivity focuses on the need to match interventions to an offender's circumstances (e.g., motivation, intelligence, and language, in addition to gender, culture, and age; Brown et al., 2017). Empirical evidence has demonstrated the effectiveness of the RNR model in practice, reducing recidivism when all principles are adhered to (Smith, Gendreau, & Swartz, 2009). There is some documented evidence on the use of the RNR model with women. Dowden and Andrews (1999) found that interventions that target higher risk offenders, focus on criminogenic needs, and use behavioral-social learning with women offenders have been effective. Others, such as Van Voorhis (2012), caution some limitations of the RNR model, particularly among women. For example, Van Voorhis notes that there is a duty to provide services to lower-risk women where feasible, as they can benefit from support in the areas of strengths. She also argues that there is a need to pay attention to the qualitative differences between women and men.

Based on an extensive number of quantitative studies and meta-analytic reviews, Bonta and Andrews (2017) have identified eight global risk factors associated with criminal conduct irrespective of age, gender, or race. These factors, coined the *Central Eight*, are divided into two subsets. The first subset—known as the *Big Four*—are deemed the strongest predictors of criminal conduct. The *Big Four* include one static risk factor: history of antisocial behavior, and three dynamic risk factors: antisocial personality pattern, antisocial cognition, and antisocial associates. Bonta and Andrews (2017) classify the second subset of risk factors as moderate predictors. These include: family/marital problems, education/employment deficits, poor use of leisure time, and substance abuse. Lastly, Andrews and Bonta identify another set of factors designated as the least important risk factors. This subset includes factors such as socioeconomic class of origin and personal distress (e.g., feeling powerless or anxious). Importantly, mainstream correctional psychology scholars argue that targeting dynamic risk factors or criminogenic needs will lower an individual's propensity for further engagement in criminal behavior (Bonta & Andrews, 2017). Thus, the mainstream correctional paradigm advocates that risk assessment tools encompass the *Central Eight*.

Risk Assessment: Through the Lens of Gender-Responsive Scholars

In contrast, feminist-inspired correctional researchers tend to underscore the importance of Andrews and Bonta's mild and moderate level risk factors whilst remaining relatively silent or dismissive of the *Big Four*. Increasingly, research is suggesting that Andrews and Bonta's original *Central Eight* may not function the same way for female offenders, particularly in terms of which risk factors should be prioritized. Arguably, factors that have emerged from PT, such as substance abuse, trauma/victimization, poor mental health (e.g., depression, anxiety, self-injurious behavior), and unhealthy relationships, could be classified as the *Gender-Responsive-Big Four* (*GR-Big Four*), whilst the *Gender-Responsive-Moderate Five* (*GR-Moderate Five*) would hypothetically include low self-worth (self-efficacy/self-esteem/absence of empowerment), economic marginalization/poverty, parental stress, unsafe living situations, and female-specific physical health needs (Blanchette & Brown, 2006; Bloom et al., 2005; Gobeil et al., 2016; Salisbury & Van Voorhis, 2009; Van Voorhis, 2012). Though these factors have emerged from the pathways perspective that highlights the unique experiences of women and girls, the *GR-Big Four* and *GR-Moderate Five* identified above need further empirical work to quantifiably demonstrate their relationship with the onset of criminal behavior and further reoffending.

Importantly, it could be stated that the vast majority of feminist-inspired researchers are not particularly concerned with determining whether certain variables should be classified as risk, criminogenic, or responsivity factors. Rather, the interest is one of making changes to improve individual skills and overall wellbeing (Jones, Brown, Robinson, & Frey, 2015) and less on risk classification per se. From the feminist pathways perspective, they argue that women and girls can be over-classified as high risk if they have multiple needs and/or if they are assessed with risk factors that do not consider the female experience (Robinson, 2015). Overall, a more holistic paradigm is preferred that seeks to ultimately understand how "risk," "need," and "responsivity" factors interact and how these factors can and should be addressed simultaneously. It is argued that this holistic approach will promote not only reductions in recidivism but stronger and healthier connections with family as well as enhanced wellbeing and empowerment (Hannah-Moffat, 2009; Van Voorhis, 2012). Empirical research to test the ability of this model to reduce recidivism and improve the lives of women and girls holistically is warranted.

Preliminary meta-analytic evidence does support Andrews and Bonta's *Central Eight* among female offenders (Green, 2006; Hubbard & Pratt, 2002), albeit that existing predictive meta-analyses with female offenders are based predominately on adolescent samples and include a relatively small number of effect sizes. There is also some evidence that has emerged that suggests that risk factors do not manifest themselves in the same way for males and females.

For example, Andrews et al. (2012) concluded that substance abuse may be more important for female offenders and thus elevated substance abuse to be part of a *Central Five* for female offenders. Similarly, there is increasing evidence that criminal romantic partners are more problematic for female offenders than for males (Benda, 2005; Kerig & Schindler, 2013). There is also some empirical evidence that any form of childhood abuse is a stronger predictor of criminal behavior for females than for males (Green, 2006). Additionally, Belknap (2015) argues that negative outcomes associated with abuse impact females differently than their male counterparts. In particular, females may cope with abuse in more self-destructive ways than their male counterparts, including using substances, running away from home, and engaging in criminal acts (Belknap, 2015; Chesney-Lind, 1997). Lastly, other hypothesized female-specific risk factors are garnering empirical support. For example, Van Voorhis, Wright, Salisbury, and Bauman (2010) found that low self-efficacy and low self-esteem predicted criminal recidivism in a sample of women offenders. In sum, the extent to which certain female-specific needs (e.g., parental stress) should be prioritized as direct treatment targets versus ancillary treatment barriers remains debated.

Gender-Neutral Risk Assessment and Female Offenders: The Evidence

The Level of Service/Case Management Inventory (LS/CMI; Andrews, Bonta, & Wormith, 2004) and the Youth Level of Service/Case Management Inventory (YLS/CMI 2.0; Hoge & Andrews, 2011) are two commonly used (gender-neutral) risk assessment tools designed for use with adult and adolescent offenders, respectively. The LS/CMI and YLS/CMI 2.0 assess the following domains: offense history, family circumstances/parenting, education/employment, peer relationships, substance abuse, leisure/recreation, personality, and treatment responsivity issues.

The psychometric properties of the LSI/CMI, the YLS/CMI 2.0, and their corresponding predecessors are well documented for male offenders (Gendreau, Goggin, & Smith, 2002; Olver, Stockdale, & Wormith, 2014). Importantly, the accumulation of female-focused LSI research has resulted in three different meta-analyses comparing the predictive validity of the YLS/LSI tools in samples of female and male offenders (Olver et al., 2014; Schwalbe, 2008; Smith, Cullen, et al., 2009). In sum, these meta-analytic reviews have essentially demonstrated that overall, the family of LSI-based instruments predicts recidivism equally well for both genders, irrespective of age. Moreover, when Olver et al. conducted a more in-depth analysis of gender, two noteworthy findings emerged. First, adolescent female offenders score higher in the YLS domains of education/employment, family/marital, financial, accommodations, and personal/emotional relative to their male counterparts. Second, the substance abuse and the personal/emotional domains were stronger predictors of general recidivism for the adolescent female offenders compared to their male counterparts. Noteworthy, there was no indication that the women in these studies were "higher risk," suggesting that multiple needs in these areas might be overclassifying these women as higher risk than warranted, a common criticism of the use of these tools with females, to be discussed next.

Criticisms Levied Against Gender-Neutral Risk Assessment Tools

Gender-responsive correctional scholars have levied various criticisms against gender-neutral risk assessments: they unnecessarily over-classify female offenders by either omitting or insufficiently emphasizing key female-specific need factors, failing to account for the unique context of, or pathways to, female criminal conduct, and operating from a deficit- as opposed to strength-based perspective (Blanchette & Brown, 2006; Bloom et al., 2005; Hannah-Moffat, 2009; Hannah-Moffat & Shaw, 2001; Van Voorhis, 2012).

There is no debate that males commit most crime, particularly the most violent and serious forms of crime (Schwartz & Steffensmeier, 2012). Female offenders are less likely to reoffend generally and violently (Kong & AuCoin, 2008). Hannah-Moffat (2009) argues that the trend reported by Kong and AuCoin demonstrates that a "high-risk" female is not the same as a "high-risk" male; that is, their likelihood of reconviction, or the severity of offense should reconviction occur, are not equal. Echoing this sentiment, a symposium of international women offender experts that recently convened in Scotland concluded that most women in the criminal justice system are more "at risk" than "risky" (Brown, 2015). Stated another way, this means that women and girls with greater needs run the risk of further marginalization or being penalized (i.e., "at risk") if gender considerations are not taken into consideration during risk assessment because having more needs could be translated as being a greater risk (i.e., "risky"; Blanchette & Brown, 2006; Hannah-Moffat, 2009; Shaw & Hannah-Moffat, 2000). Further, this conclusion should serve as a reminder that just because a woman has "high needs" (i.e., criminogenic or dynamic needs), this does not mean that she is necessarily "high risk" (Robinson, 2015). However, perhaps what is needed to advance the field is a determination of (a) which hypothesized female needs do in fact elevate recidivism likelihood versus those that do not, and (b) subsequently a determination of how female needs (those that do elevate risk versus those that do not) should be integrated into risk assessment and treatment planning. Whilst research is growing (Brown & Motiuk, 2005; Van Voorhis, 2012) more is needed. In particular, it is possible that certain hypothesized female needs (e.g., self-efficacy) could best be conceptualized as strengths.

Within the literature, there are a myriad of ways to describe strengths. More specifically, strengths have been conceptualized as constructs that might exist to decrease or mitigate risk, which include protective and promotive factors, terms which are often (mis)used interchangeably (Jones et al., 2015). Briefly, protective factors are said to buffer or reduce the effect of a risk factor, such that the probability of a negative outcome is reduced (Jones et al., 2015), particularly among moderate- or higher-risk cases, but not among lower-risk cases (Fougere & Daffern, 2011; Jessor, Van Den Bos, Vanderryn, Costa, & Turbin, 1995; Jones et al., 2015; Lodewijks, de Ruiter, & Doreleijers, 2010). Alternatively, a promotive factor shows a negative correlation with recidivism (i.e., as the promotive factor increases, the risk decreases), across all levels of risk (Farrington, 2013). Not surprisingly, feminist-inspired work has long recognized the importance of strength-based models in offender rehabilitation (Blanchette & Brown, 2006). More empirical work is needed to determine how strengths are expressed by women and girls, and how this differs from their male counterparts, as well as how strengths can be incorporated into assessments of risk to ensure a reliable and valid approach that is reflective of females' unique experiences. Thus, the integration of a strengths-based paradigm into risk assessment is an indisputable point of reconciliation between gender-responsive and gender-neutral scholars.

Gender-Responsive Risk Assessment Tools

The field appears to be moving toward the development of tools built from the ground up specifically for women or girls. Two recent and notable examples include the Women's Risk Need Assessment (WRNA; Van Voorhis et al., 2013) and the Service Planning Instrument for

Women (SPIn-W; Orbis Partners, 2007). The WRNA measures gender-informed risk, need, and strength factors. Shorter versions of the tool have also been developed for use in pre-trial settings (Gehring & Van Voorhis, 2014). To date, the results are promising. The WRNA predicts prison misconducts and criminal recidivism (e.g., area under the curve [AUC] averaging .70). Importantly, the WRNA improves the predictive accuracy of the gender-neutral LS/CMI among women offenders (Van Voorhis et al., 2013).

The SPIn-W is comprised of theoretically and empirically derived risk, needs, and strength factors to be used for case planning and management for offenders in community or custodial settings (Orbis Partners, 2007). The SPIn-W includes a number of hypothesized gender-responsive items such as child custody and parenting, domestic victimization, relationships and interpersonal skills, mental health, social support, and community living. Notably, many of these gender-responsive items apply equally to men and women (e.g., need for solid social support); however, the manifestation of these items as they pertain to women has been taken into consideration. Items in the general domains of attitudes, aggression, and interpersonal/cognitive skills have been tailored to address how they manifest in female populations. Different cutoff scores for overall risk level have been established for women offenders (Orbis Partners, 2007). Lastly, a recent evaluation involving 274 women offenders revealed that the SPIn-W predicted rearrests during a 12-month follow-up period with a high degree of predictive accuracy (AUC = .73; Robinson, Van Dieten, & Millson, 2012). As a comparison, Olver et al. (2014) found that across a set of the Level of Service (LS) scales, the LS total scores predicted general recidivism across female samples (r_w = .35), which, according to Rice and Harris (2005), would correspond to an AUC of approximately .70. The findings reported for the gender-responsive tools discussed above are demonstrating a high degree of predictive accuracy. An important next step would be a rigorous evaluation of the predictive value that gender-informed assessment tools add above and beyond the gender-neutral approaches. That is, do gender-informed assessments predict better for women and girls than do gender-neutral assessments, a conclusion which cannot be reached by simply comparing AUC values (Howard, 2017).

Effective Intervention With Female Offenders

There is general consensus within correctional psychology that RNR-based programs yield the greatest reductions in recidivism, at least among male offenders (Bonta & Andrews, 2017). Additionally, there is some meta-analytic support that RNR-based programs work equally well with female offenders (see Dowden & Andrews, 1999). However, all aspects of the RNR model have not been universally accepted among gender-responsive scholars.

Van Voorhis (2012) accepts that there is sufficient evidence to support the risk principle; treatment intensity should match level of risk. However, she underscores that there is also a duty to provide services to lower-risk women where feasible, since they too can benefit by augmenting existing strength domains such as the presence of prosocial influences, an important component of gender-responsive models, as discussed. Though there has been increased attention in the literature focusing on the importance of strength factors in offender assessment, more empirical work is needed to validate the importance of these factors in the gender-responsive model and how these factors are different (if at all) from their male counterparts. Van Voorhis further believes that the RNR's classification system erroneously categorizes a number of important female-specific need factors as responsivity factors. Specifically, she contends that a failure to classify factors such as parental stress as "needs" is disconcerting because it blocks the treatment of criminogenic needs, a sentiment also echoed by Hannah-Moffat (2009). For example, if parental stress is left unaddressed, then progress will not occur in other criminogenic domains such as antisocial thinking. Simply put, if lower-level basic needs are not met (e.g., food, shelter, childcare), it is not possible for an individual to focus on addressing some of those higher-level (criminogenic) needs, congruent with Maslow's hierarchy of needs; you must address lower-level needs in the hierarchy prior to being able to successfully achieve resolution of needs at the higher level (Maslow, 1943). In sum, Van Voorhis (2012) asserts that "it is not enough to address old treatment targets with a focus that might be more amenable to women … serious attention and priority must be given to a modified list of risk factors" (p. 132). Without a doubt, female centered research examining the extent to which female-specific needs (e.g., maltreatment histories, parental stress, access to safe living environments) elevate risk to reoffend or interact with traditional criminogenic needs such as antisocial thinking (thus serving as barriers to treatment), in our opinion, should be a priority focus among gender-informed scholars for the next decade.

Defining "Gender-Responsive" in Practice

Exciting advancements have been made in formulating gender-responsive (inherently female) programming principles since Canada's seminal creation and adoption of five women-centered guidelines: empowerment, meaningful and responsible choices, respect and dignity, supportive environment, and shared responsibility (Task Force on Federally Sentenced Women, 1990). First, Blanchette and Brown (2006) reformulated Andrews and Bonta's (2003) original responsivity principle, in essence making it truly gender-informed:

> A gender-informed responsivity principle states that in general, optimal treatment response will be achieved when treatment providers deliver structured behavioral interventions [grounded in feminist philosophies as well as social learning theory] in an emphatic and empowering manner [strength-based model] while simultaneously adopting a firm but fair approach (p. 126).

Similarly, Bloom et al. (2005, also see Covington & Bloom, 2006) have produced one of the most influential sets of gender-responsive principles for correctional settings. Grounded in pathways theory (Belknap, 2015), relational theory (Miller, 1976), and trauma and addictions-based theories (Lewis, 2015), Bloom et al. state that a gender (female) responsive philosophy necessitates the recognition that women's pathways to crime as well as the context of women's lives *are* different than men. Further, a gender-responsive model actively incorporates social and cultural factors, prioritizes mental health, addictions, and trauma-related targets, adopts a strength-based model, and emphasizes the promotion of self-efficacy/empowerment.

Not only have Bloom et al.'s principles been echoed in the context of substance abuse programming for women (Grella, 2008), they are also increasingly being implemented in spirit around the world. In December 2010, the United Nations unanimously voted in favor of 70 rules designed to reduce female incarceration whilst meeting the specific needs of incarcerated women (Penal Reform International, 2013). These rules—known as the UN Bangkok Rules—acknowledge that incarcerated women have unique needs relative to their male counterparts (e.g., require access to gender-specific health care) and that women prisoners should be treated humanely and with dignity (e.g., neither restrained during childbirth, placed in solitary confinement whilst breast feeding, nor subject to strip searches by male staff).

Importantly, the UN Bangkok Rules emphasize the need to maintain family connections between incarcerated women and their children (Penal Reform International, 2013).

Not surprisingly, the acceptance of gender-responsive principles has translated into the development and evaluation of correctional programs designed specifically for female offenders. Some notable examples include America's *Beyond Violence* (Covington, 2013), Canada's *Moving On* (Van Dieten & MacKenna, 2001), and England's *Together Women Project* (Granville, 2012). Whilst these programs are classified as gender-responsive, it is important to emphasize that many gender-responsive programs actively incorporate elements long supported within mainstream correctional circles. For example, *Moving On* combines cognitive behaviorism (a commonly accepted mainstream correctional approach) with relational and empowering elements (a decidedly gender-responsive approach). Notably, *Moving On* has been evaluated and has shown promising reductions in recidivism (Gehring, Van Voorhis, & Bell, 2009).

The proliferation of gender-responsive correctional interventions coupled with accompanying evaluations have recently allowed Gobeil et al. (2016) to conduct a seminal meta-analysis of female offender programming. The authors examined 37 treatment outcome studies involving 22,000 women offenders. In sum, the meta-analysis revealed that the odds of not reoffending were 22–35% higher for women who participated in correctional interventions versus those who did not. Interestingly, programs classified as gender-responsive were just as effective as gender-neutral interventions. However, curiously, gender-responsive interventions were significantly more likely to be associated with reductions in recidivism when analyses were restricted to methodologically rigorous studies. Further, a number of the programs that were classified as gender-responsive often (a) targeted substance abuse—a need factor routinely prioritized by both gender-neutral and gender-responsive scholars—and (b) incorporated elements of cognitive behaviorism—a traditional mainstream correctional approach. Thus, the results of this meta-analysis provide clear support for an integrated approach.

Recently, it has been found that gender-responsive treatment was more effective for women who had experienced prior trauma, depression and anxiety, anger/irritability, alcohol/drug abuse, and somatic complaints (Day et al., 2015; Saxena, Messina, & Grella, 2014). These results are promising, but importantly they remind us that women are not a homogeneous group. Within-group differences must also be considered, and as such gender-responsive approaches may not work for all women and girls alike. More research is needed to tease out these differences.

Conclusion

Our field has made considerable advancements. Theoretically, disciplinary divides are slowly eroding as evidenced by Belknap's (2015) conciliatory recognition that a number of mainstream theories are actually pro-feminist and consequently merit serious consideration in understanding female criminal conduct. In the applied realm, feminist-inspired researchers are making significant gains in the development and evaluation of risk assessment tools developed from the ground up for females (Orbis Partners, 2007; Van Voorhis et al., 2013). Salient in these tools is the inclusion of strengths—a recognized gender-responsive trademark. Gender-responsive treatment programs are also being developed (e.g., *Creating Regulation and Resiliency*, Orbis Partners & Core Associates, 2015) and evaluated rigorously (Gobeil et al., 2016). Whilst significant debates remain (e.g., do female offenders have different criminogenic need factors than their male counterparts?), correctional agencies continue to adopt female-specific initiatives grounded in the extant gender-informed literature. Importantly, real-world correctional responses to female offenders appear to be less concerned with discerning whether or not something should be classified as a "criminogenic factor" or a "responsivity factor." Rather, correctional organizations are adopting a holistic approach that views traditional criminogenic needs (e.g., addictions) and female-specific needs (e.g., parental stress) as equally important targets that must be addressed simultaneously to effect recidivism reductions (e.g., Prison Reform Trust, 2014). Lastly, though female offenders are not the frontrunners in the commission of crime, they most definitely are no longer "correctional afterthoughts."

Key Readings

Belknap, J. (2015). *The invisible woman: Gender, crime and justice* (4th ed.). Stamford, CT: Cengage Learning.

Chesney-Lind, M., & Pasko, L. (2013). *The female offender: Girls, women, and crime* (3rd ed.). Thousand Oaks, CA: Sage.

Day, J. C., Zahn, M. A., & Tichavsky, L. P. (2015). What works and for whom? The effects of gender responsive programming on girls and boys in secure detention. *Journal of Research in Crime and Delinquency*, 52(1), 93–129.

Gobeil, R., Blanchette, K., & Stewart, L. (2016). A meta-analytic review of correctional interventions for women offenders: Gender-neutral versus gender-informed approaches. *Criminal Justice and Behavior*, 43, 301–322.

Van Voorhis, P. (2012). On behalf of women offenders: Women's place in the science of evidence-based practice. *Criminology & Public Policy*, 11, 111–145.

References

Agnew, R. (1985). A revised strain theory of delinquency. *Social Forces*, 64, 151–167.

Agnew, R. (1992). Foundation for a general strain theory of crime and delinquency. *Criminology*, 30, 47–87.

Akers, R. L. (1992). Linking sociology and its specialties: The case of criminology. *Social Forces*, 71, 1–16.

Akers, R. L. (1998). *Social learning and social structure: A general theory of crime and deviance.* New Brunswick, NJ: Transaction.

Akers, R. L., & Jensen, G. F. (2003). *Advances in criminological theory: Social learning theory and the explanation of crime: A guide for the new century.* New Brunswick, NJ: Transaction.

Andrews, D. A., & Bonta, J. (2003). *The psychology of criminal conduct* (3rd ed.). Cincinnati, OH: Anderson.

Andrews, D. A., Bonta, J., & Wormith, J. S. (2004). *The Level of Service/Case Management Inventory (LS/CMI): User's manual.* Toronto, Canada: Multi-Health Systems.

Andrews, D. A., Guzzo, L., Raynor, P., Rowe, R. C., Rettinger, L. J., Brews, A., & Wormith, J. S. (2012). Are the major risk/need factors predictors of both female and male reoffending? A test with the eight domains of the Level of Service/Case Management Inventory. *International Journal of Offender Therapy and Comparative Criminology*, 56, 113–133.

Artz, L., Hoffman-Wanderer, Y., & Moult, K. (2012) *Women, crime and incarceration: Exploring pathways of women in conflict with the law.* Research paper. Retrieved from http://policyresearch. limpopo.gov.za/bitstream/handle/123456789/762/Women%2C%20Crime%20and%20 Incarceration-%20Exploring%20Pathways%20of%20Women%20in%20Conflict%20with%20Law. pdf?sequence=1

Bandura, A. (1973). *Aggression: A social learning analysis.* Englewood Cliffs, NJ: Prentice Hall.

Baron, S. W. (2007). Street youth, gender, financial strain, and crime: Exploring Broidy and Agnew's extension to general strain theory. *Sociological Abstracts*, 28, 273–302.

Belknap, J. (2001). *The invisible woman: Gender, crime and justice* (2nd ed.). Belmont, CA: Thomson Wadsworth.

Belknap, J. (2015). *The invisible woman: Gender, crime and justice* (4th ed.). Stamford, CT: Cengage Learning.

Benda, B. B. (2005). Gender differences in life course theory of recidivism: A survival analysis. *International Journal of Offender Therapy and Comparative Criminology.*, 493, 325–342.

Bender, D., & Lösel, F. (1997). Protective and risk effects of peer relations and social support on antisocial behavior in adolescents from multi-problem milieus. *Journal of Adolescence*, 20, 661–678.

Blanchette, K. D., & Brown, S. L. (2006). *The assessment and treatment of women offenders: An integrative perspective* Wiley Series in Forensic Clinical Psychology. Chichester, UK: Wiley.

Bloom, B. E., Owen, B., & Covington, S. S. (2005). *Gender-responsive strategies for women offenders. A summary of research, practice, and guiding principles for women offenders.* Washington, DC: National Institute of Corrections, US Department of Justice. Retrieved from https://www.centerforgenderandjustice.org/assets/files/bloomowensummaryofrpg.pdf

Bonta, J. (2002). Offender risk assessment: Guidelines for selection and use. *Criminal Justice and Behavior*, 29, 355–379.

Bonta, J., & Andrews, D. A. (2017). *The psychology of criminal conduct* (6th ed.). London, UK: Routledge.

Brennan, T., Breitenbach, M., Dieterich, W., Salisbury, E. J., & Van Voorhis, P. (2012). Women's pathways to serious and habitual crime: A person-centered analysis incorporating gender-responsive factors. *Criminal Justice and Behavior*, 39, 1481–1508.

Broidy, L., & Agnew, R. (1997). Gender and crime: A general strain theory perspective. *Journal of Research in Crime and Delinquency*, 34, 275–306.

Brown, S. L. (2015, May). *The Canadian story of women offenders: Success, lessons learned, persistent challenges.* Invited plenary at From Vision to Reality—Transforming Scotland's Care of Women in Custody International Symposium; Edinburgh, Scotland.

Brown, S. L., & Motiuk, L. L. (2005). *The Dynamic Factors Identification and Analysis (DFIA) component of the Offender Intake Assessment (OIA) process: A meta-analytic, psychometric and consultative review.* Report R-164. Correctional Service Canada.

Brown, S. L., Serin, R., Forth, A., Nunes, K., Bennell, C., & Pozzulo, J. (2017). *Psychology of criminal behavior: A Canadian perspective* (2nd ed.). Toronto, Canada: Pearson Canada.

Bryant, W., & Cussen, T. (2015). *Homicide in Australia: 2010–11 to 2011–12: National Homicide Monitoring Program report (ISSN 1836–2095).* Australia Institute of Criminology. Retrieved from https://aic.gov.au/file/5676/download?token=rNaUCxW1

Burgess, R. L., & Akers, R. L. (1966). A differential association reinforcement theory of criminal behavior. *Social Problems*, 14, 128–147.

Capowich, G. E., Mazerolle, P., & Piquero, A. (2001). General strain theory, situational anger, and social networks: An assessment of conditioning influences. *Journal of Criminal Justice*, 29, 445–461.

Cernkovich, S. A., Lanctôt, N., & Giordano, P. C. (2008). Predicting adolescent and adult antisocial behavior among adjudicated delinquent females. *Criminology & Penology*, 54, 3–33.

Chesney-Lind, M. (1997). *The female offender: Girls, women and crime.* Thousand Oaks, CA: Sage.

Chesney-Lind, M., & Pasko, L. (2013). *The female offender: Girls, women, and crime* (3rd ed.). Thousand Oaks, CA: Sage.

Cheung, N. W. T., & Cheung, Y. W. (2010). Strain, self-control, and gender differences in delinquency among Chinese adolescents: Extending general strain theory. *Sociological Perspectives*, 53, 321–345.

Cottle, C. C., Lee, R. J., & Heilbrun, K. (2001). The prediction of criminal recidivism in juveniles: A meta-analysis. *Criminal Justice and Behavior*, 28, 367–394.

Covington, S. S. (2013). *Beyond violence: A prevention program for criminal justice-involved women*. Hoboken, NJ: Wiley.

Covington, S. S., & Bloom, B. E. (2006). Gender-responsive treatment and services in correctional settings. In E. Leeder (Ed.), *Inside and out: Women, prison, and therapy* (pp. 9–34). Binghamton, NY: Haworth Press.

Daly, K. (1992). Women's pathways to felony court: Feminist theories of lawbreaking and problems of representation. *Review of Law and Women's Studies*, 2(11), 11–52.

Day, J. C., Zahn, M. A., & Tichavsky, L. P. (2015). What works and for whom? The effects of gender-responsive programming on girls and boys in secure detention. *Journal of Research in Crime and Delinquency*, 52, 93–129.

Dehart, D. D. (2008). Pathways to prison: Impact of victimization in the lives of incarcerated women. *Violence Against Women*, 14, 1362–1381.

Douglas, K. S., & Skeem, J. L. (2005). Violence risk assessment: Getting specific about being dynamic. *Psychology, Public Policy, and Law*, 11, 347–383.

Dowden, C., & Andrews, D. A. (1999). What works for female offenders: A meta-analytic review. *Crime & Delinquency*, 45, 438–452.

Farrington, D. (2013). *Protective factors and resilience*. Ottawa, Canada: National Crime Prevention Centre.

Finkelhor, D., & Baron, L. (1986). High-risk children. In D. Finkelhor (Ed.), *A sourcebook on child sexual abuse* (pp. 60–88). Beverly Hills, CA: Sage.

Fougere, A., & Daffern, M. (2011). Resilience in young offenders. *International Journal of Forensic Mental Health*, 10, 244–253.

Freud, S. (1933). *New introduction lectures on psychoanalysis*. New York, NY: Norton.

Gehring, K. S., & Van Voorhis, P. (2014). Needs and pretrial failure: Additional risk factors for female and male pretrial defendants. *Criminal Justice and Behavior*, 41, 943–970.

Gehring, K. S., Van Voorhis, P., & Bell, V. R. (2009). *"What Works" for female probationers? An evaluation of the Moving On program*. Retrieved from http://www.uc.edu/content/dam/uc/womenoffenders/docs/MOVING%20ON.pdf

Gendreau, P., French, S., & Taylor, A. (2002). *What works, what doesn't work*. Invited submission to the International Community Corrections Association Monograph Series Project, Ottawa, Canada.

Gendreau, P., Goggin, C., & Smith, P. (2002). Is the PCL-R really the "unparalleled" measure of offender risk? *Criminal Justice and Behavior*, 29, 397–426.

Gilfus, M. E. (1992). From victims to survivors to offenders: Women's routes of entry and immersion into street crime. *Women & Criminal Justice*, 4, 63–90.

Gobeil, R., Blanchette, K., & Stewart, L. (2016). A meta-analytic review of correctional interventions for women offenders: Gender-neutral versus gender-informed approaches. *Criminal Justice and Behavior*, 43, 301–322.

Granville, G. (2012). *The Together Women Centre for Vulnerable Women: Independent evaluation report: Second stage: Project impact and outcomes*. Retrieved from www.salfordfoundation.org.uk/downloads/twpevaluationreportfinaljanuary2012-110633.pdf

Green, L. (2006). *Gender influences and methodological considerations in adolescent risk-need assessment: A meta-analysis* (Unpublished master's thesis). University of New Brunswick, Canada.

Grella, C. E. (2008). From generic to gender-responsive treatment: Changes in social policies, treatment services, and outcomes of women in substance abuse treatment. *Journal of Psychoactive Drugs, SARC Supplement*, 5, 327–343.

Hannah-Moffat, K. (2009). Gridlock or mutability: Reconsidering gender and risk assessment. *Criminology & Public Policy*, 8, 209–219.

Hannah-Moffat, K., & Shaw, M. (2001). Risk assessment in Canadian corrections: Some diverse and gendered issues. *Women, Girls, & Criminal Justice*, 2, 4–45.

Hay, C. (2003). Family strain, gender, and delinquency. *Sociological Perspectives*, 46, 107–135.

Hoffman, J. P., & Cerbone, F. G. (1999). Stressful life events and delinquency escalation in early adolescence. *Criminology*, 37, 343–374.

Hoge, R. D., & Andrews, D. A. (2011). *Youth Level of Service/Case Management Inventory* (2nd ed.). YLS/CMI 2.0 Interview guide). Toronto, Canada: Multi-Health Systems.

Holtfreter, K., & Morash, M. (2003). The needs of women offenders: Implications for corrections programming. *Women and Criminal Justice*, 14, 137–160.

Howard, P. D. (2017). The effect of sample heterogeneity and risk categorization on area under the curve predictive validity metrics. *Criminal Justice and Behavior*, 44(1), 103–120.

Hubbard, D. J., & Pratt, T. C. (2002). A meta-analysis of the predictors of delinquency among girls. *Journal of Offender Rehabilitation*, 34, 1–13.

Jessor, R., Van Den Bos, J., Vanderryn, J., Costa, F. M., & Turbin, M. S. (1995). Protective factors in adolescent problem behavior: Moderator effects and developmental change. *Developmental Psychology*, 31(6), 923–933.

Jones, N. J., Brown, S. L., Robinson, D., & Frey, D. (2015). Incorporating strengths into quantitative assessments of criminal risk for adult offenders: The Service Planning Instrument. *Criminal Justice and Behavior*, 42, 321–338.

Jones, N. J., Brown, S. L., Wanamaker, K. A., & Greiner, L. (2014). A quantitative exploration of gendered pathways to crime in a sample of male and female juvenile offenders. *Feminist Criminology*, 9, 113–136.

Kaufman, J. M. (2009). Gendered responses to serious strain: The argument for a general strain theory of deviance. *Justice Quarterly*, 26, 410–444.

Kerig, P. K., & Schindler, S. R. (2013). Engendering the evidence base: A critical review of the conceptual and empirical foundations of gender-responsive interventions for girls' delinquency. *Laws*, 2, 244–282.

Kong, R., & AuCoin, K. (2008). Female offenders in Canada. *Juristat*, 28, 1–23.

Lewis, M. (2015). *The biology of desire: Why addiction is not a disease*. New York, NY: Doubleday.

Lodewijks, H. P. B., de Ruiter, C., & Doreleijers, T. A. H. (2010). The impact of protective factors in desistance from violent offending: A study in three samples of adolescent offenders. *Journal of Interpersonal Violence*, 25, 568–587.

Lombroso, C., & Ferrero, G. (2004). *Criminal woman, the prostitute, and the normal woman*. (N. H. Rafter and M. Gibson, Trans. Durham and London, UK: Duke University Press Original work published 1893.

Maslow, A. H. (1943). A theory of human motivation. *Psychological Review*, 50, 370–396.

Mazerolle, P. (1998). Gender, general strain, and delinquency: An empirical examination. *Justice Quarterly*, 15, 65–91.

Merton, R. K. (1957). *Social theory and social structure*. New York, NY: Free Press.

Miller, J. B. (1976). *Towards a new psychology of women*. Boston, MA: Beacon Press.

Morash, M. (1999). A consideration of gender in relation to social learning and social structure: A general theory of crime and deviance. *Theoretical Criminology*, 3, 451–462.

Office for National Statistics. (2016). *Profile of offenders involved in violent crime*. Retrieved from https://www.ons.gov.uk/peoplepopulationandcommunity/crimeandjustice/compendium/focusonviolentcrimeandsexualoffences/yearendingmarch2015/chapter1overviewofviolentcrimeandsexualoffences#profile-of-offenders-involved-in-violent-crimes

Olver, M. E., Stockdale, K. C., & Wormith, J. S. (2014). Thirty years of research on the level of service scales: A meta-analytic examination of predictive accuracy and sources of variability. *Psychological Assessment*, 26, 156–176.

Orbis Partners (2007). *Service Planning Instrument for Women (SPIn-W)*. Ottawa, Canada: Author.

Orbis Partners & Core Associates, LLC. (2015). *Creating Regulation and Resilience (CR/2)*. Retrieved from http://orbispartners.com/programs/cr2

Penal Reform International (2013). *The UN Bangkok rules on women offenders and prisoners: A short guide*. Retrieved from http://www.penalreform.org/resource/united-nations-bangkok-rules-women-offenders-prisoners-short

Pollack, O. (1950). *The criminality of women*. Philadelphia, PA: University of Philadelphia Press.

Pratt, T. C., & Cullen, F. T. (2000). The empirical status of Gottfredson and Hirschi's general theory of crime: A meta-analysis. *Criminology*, 38, 931–960.

Prison Reform Trust (2014). *Brighter futures: Working together to reduce women's reoffending*. Retrieved from www.prisonreformtrust.org.uk/Portals/0/Documents/Brighter%20Futures%2025314web.pdf

Puhrmann, A. (2015). *Gender and general strain theory: An examination of the role of gendered strains and negative emotions on crime* (Unpublished doctoral thesis). University of Miami, FL.

Rice, M. E., & Harris, G. T. (2005). Comparing effect sizes in follow-up studies: ROC area, Cohen's *d*, and *r*. *Law and Human Behavior*, 29(5), 615–620.

Ritchie, B. E. (1996). *Compelled to crime: The gender entrapment of Black battered women*. New York, NY: Routledge.

Robinson, D., Van Dieten, M., & Millson, W. (2012). The women offender case management model in the state of Connecticut. *Journal of Community Corrections*, 21, 7–24.

Robinson, G. (May, 2015). *From vision to reality: Transforming Scotland's care of women in custody*. Symposium presented at the International Symposium to Consider the Future Direction of Custody for Women in Scotland, Edinburgh, Scotland.

Salisbury, E. J., & Van Voorhis, P. (2009). Gendered pathways: A quantitative investigation of women probationers' paths to incarceration. *Criminal Justice and Behavior*, 36, 541–566.

Saxena, P., Messina, N. P., & Grella, C. E. (2014). Who benefits from gender-responsive treatment? Accounting for abuse history on longitudinal outcomes for women in prison. *Criminal Justice and Behavior*, 41, 417–432.

Schwalbe, C. S. (2008). A meta-analysis of juvenile justice risk assessment instruments: Predictive validity by gender. *Criminal Justice and Behavior*, 35, 1367–1381.

Schwartz, J., & Steffensmeier, D. (2012). Stability and change in girls' delinquency and the gender gap: Trends in violence and alcohol offending across multiple sources of evidence. In S. Miller, L. D. Leve, & P. Kerig (Eds.), *Delinquent girls: Contexts, relationships, and adaptation* (pp. 3–23). Cham, Switzerland: Springer.

Serin, R., Forth, A., Brown, S., Nunes, K., Bennell, C., & Pozzulo, J. (2011). *Psychology of criminal behavior*. Toronto, Canada: Pearson Canada.

Shaw, M., & Hannah-Moffat, K. (2000). Gender, diversity and risk assessment in Canadian corrections. *Probation Journal*, 47(3), 163–172.

Sickmund, M., & Puzzanchera, C. (2014). *Juvenile offenders and victims: 2014 National Report*. Pittsburgh, PA: National Center for Juvenile Justice.

Simkins, S., & Katz, S. (2002). Criminalizing abused girls. *Violence Against Women*, 8, 1474–1499.

Simourd, L., & Andrews, D. A. (1994). Correlates of delinquency: A look at gender differences. *Forum on Corrections Research*, 6, 26–31.

Simpson, S. S., Yahner, J. L., & Dugan, L. (2008). Understanding women's pathways to jail: Analysing the lives of incarcerated women. *Australian & New Zealand Journal of Criminology*, 41, 84–108.

Smith, P., Cullen, F. T., & Latessa, E. J. (2009). Can 14,737 women be wrong? A meta-analysis of the LSI-R and recidivism for female offenders. *Criminology and Public Policy*, 8, 183–208.

Smith, P., Gendreau, P., & Swartz, K. (2009). Validating the principles of effective intervention: A systematic review of the contributions of meta-analysis in the field of corrections. *Victims and Offenders*, 4, 148–169.

Snyder, H. N. (2011). *Patterns and trends: Arrests in the United States, 1980–2009*. US Department of Justice, Office of Justice Programs, Bureau of Justice Statistics. Retrieved from https://www.bjs.gov/content/pub/pdf/aus8009.pdf

Sutherland, E. H. (1947). *Principles of criminology* (4th ed.). Philadelphia, PA: J. B. Lippincott.

Sutherland, E. H., & Cressey, D. R. (1970). *Principles of criminology* (6th ed.). New York, NY: Lippincott.

Task Force on Federally Sentenced Women. (1990). *Creating choices: Report of the Task Force on Federally Sentenced Women*. Ottawa, Canada: Correctional Services of Canada. Retrieved from www.csc-scc.gc.ca/women/toce-eng.shtml

Thomas, W. I. (1923). *The unadjusted girl*. Boston, MA: Little, Brown and Company.

United States Department of Justice, Federal Bureau of Investigation, Criminal Justice Information Services Division. (n.d.). 2014 Crime in the United States. Uniform Crime Reports. Retrieved from https://www.fbi.gov/about-us/cjis/ucr/crime-in-the-u.s/2014/crime-in-the-u.s.-2014/tables/table-42

Van Dieten, M., & MacKenna, P. (2001). *Moving on facilitator's guide*. Toronto, Canada: Orbis Partners.

Van Voorhis, P. (2012). On behalf of women offenders: Women's place in the science of evidence-based practice. *Criminology & Public Policy*, 11(2), 111–145.

Van Voorhis, P., & Bauman, A. (2015, October). *Monitoring the quality of gender-responsive programs*. Symposium presented at the Adult and Juvenile Female Offenders (AJFO) Conference, Hartford, CT.

Van Voorhis, P., Bauman, A., & Brushett, R. (2013). *Revalidation of the women's risk needs assessment: Probation results final report January 2013*. Retrieved from https://www.researchgate.net/publication/308727342_Revalidation_of_the_Women's_Risk_Needs_Assessment_Institutional_Results_-_Final_Report

Van Voorhis, P., Wright, E. M., Salisbury, E., & Bauman, A. (2010). Women's risk factors and their contributions to existing risk/needs assessment. *Criminal Justice and Behavior*, 37, 261–288.

20

The Psychology of Desistance

Devon L. L. Polaschek

University of Waikato (Te Whare Wānanga o Waikato), New Zealand

Desistance refers to the process of moving away from criminal behavior: how it is people "give up" crime. It also refers to the related outcome: attaining a period of crime-free living. Desistance is often talked about in a manner similar to alcohol addiction: as if people are either active criminals (heavy daily drinkers) or law-abiding citizens (teatotalers), and as if turning away from the underlying habit is the process of turning over a new leaf: once made, a decision to quit is followed by immediate and longstanding cessation. But people rarely move away from ingrained lifestyles and habits overnight, whatever the nature of the problem. For myriad reasons the process is typically more complex and prolonged, unless the person's foray into crime was a transient departure from a relatively established prosocial lifestyle.

The phenomenon of desistance has long been noted in the criminological literature. But the psychological and social processes that accompany it have received limited attention until the past 30 years or so. This chapter first reviews definitions of desistance before examining the light shed by criminal career research on who desists and when. Next we move on to theories and research on these social and psychological processes involved in desistance, and relationships between efforts to rehabilitate and reintegrate offenders, which are arguably efforts to stimulate or enhance desistance. The chapter concludes with a brief section on women offenders.

What Is Desistance?

Defining desistance is somewhat challenging (Bushway, Piquero, Mazerolle, Broidy, & Cauffman, 2001). First, the ultimate outcome, being crime-free, needs to be defined. In reality, many people who think of themselves as law-abiding and have never given a moment's thought to desisting from crime do not themselves meet an absolute crime-free standard, and even people who describe themselves as having given up crime, often still do minor, low-level offenses (Leibrich, 1993).

Much of what is known about desistance relies on official records to tell us about people's "crime-free" status, such as arrest or reconviction. This is obviously a very indirect indicator, given what we know of relationships between actual crime and these official indices.[1] Even in the research defining desistance in terms of an absence of convictions or arrests, still there is little consistency within such definitions (Kazemian, 2007). For some, decreases in the rate, diversity, and seriousness of offending may qualify for the label of desistance, especially from a process perspective (e.g., Loeber & LeBlanc, 1990; see also Laub & Sampson, 2001). Although actual crime and convictions are related, it is likely that the processes and timing of self-reported desistance and official desistance are different (Farrington, Ttofi, Crago, & Coid, 2014). For instance, there may be a period of more successfully avoiding detection before actual desistance occurs. The accuracy of the picture can be further complicated by short follow-up times, and a limited understanding of the causes of intermittency, or "gaps" in official offending careers, which together can lead to the attribution of career termination to someone who is merely pausing during a criminal career (see below).

Studies using official indicators often also are lacking information about the current role of the people themselves in their apparent absence of offending (Bushway et al., 2001). A useful distinction has been made between identifying desistance for policy purposes, and understanding it theoretically (Bersani & Doherty, 2018). It may be possible to use longitudinal predictors to identify, for instance, which of a cohort of currently offending youths will have officially achieved desistance within the next 5 years without formal intervention: a useful finding for policy purposes.

However, a theoretical understanding of desistance has much more potential to be used to support or enhance the process for those who do not achieve desistance easily. A theoretical understanding of the process usually is built on a definition that includes information about the extent to which the person is making an effort to desist, successfully or otherwise. Even high-risk offenders have periods lasting weeks to months where it appears—at least officially—that they are largely offense-free. But is this pause due to any kind of commitment to, or engagement in, behavioral change? A definition that distinguishes between potentially incidental career pauses and more enduring cessation is Maruna and Farrall's (2004) distinction between primary desistance—any respite from criminal activity without any self-awareness or intent—and secondary desistance—a (probably longer) period of non-offending that is accompanied by self-awareness, and even identity change in the offender. Recognizing how far apart these two types or stages may be for some offenders, Maruna and Farrall (2004) proposed a third, intermediate stage. *Proto-secondary desistance* refers to a conscious cessation of criminal activity for several years that is followed by resumption of criminal behavior.

Others have also developed stringent definitions that require evidence of a commitment made by the offender not just to cease criminal activity, but also to show positive psychological and social change: "desistance is not obtained in the early stages of transition even as an offender begins to be crime-free. Desistance has not occurred until prosocial habits, legitimate employment and self-regulation have taken hold …" (Serin & Lloyd, 2009, p. 359). Similarly, Laub and Sampson (2001) considered desistance to be the causal process that sustains having stopped offending: beginning before the final part of the offending career and continuing beyond the last offense.

For psychology, the main interest is arguably in the process of desisting rather than the outcome. This process is inherently a change process, and thus psychology—especially those parts that focus on changing habitual behavior—should have something to offer to its understanding. Both criminal behavior and the associated psychological and social factors are important to defining this process. However, before we examine psychological factors involved in achieving and sustaining desistance, we review a sizeable literature that largely omits an examination of the offender's role in desistance.

Identifying and Describing Criminal Career Paths

A preliminary step in understanding desistance requires that we understand its backdrop or context, which includes both the causes of crime and individual patterns of criminal behavior over time (Laub & Sampson, 2001). Age is one of the most robust predictors of criminal involvement. The age-crime curve, which has been formally recognized since the nineteenth century (Laws & Ward, 2011), suggests that most crime is committed by adolescents and young adults, with a steady drop-off in the number of crimes per capita from about the mid-20s, reaching near-zero by the late 40s.

The age-crime curve is usually displayed as the rate of offenses by the age of those who were detected for committing them. So it is not possible from these aggregated figures to determine individual offenders' career patterns, but there is some agreement that a substantial proportion of the rapid increase and decrease in crime volume through later adolescence and early adulthood is driven by people with relatively brief offending careers (McVie, 2005; Moffitt, 1993). Although often spoken of as though it were invariant, this classic bell-curve shape actually varies by crime type (e.g., violence has a later onset; Rosenfeld, White, & Esbensen, 2012), gender (Loeber et al., 2015), and location (Farrington & Wikström, 1994), and various other contextual factors (DeLisi & Piquero, 2011).

The phenomenon of desistance gained increased recognition with the development of group-based trajectory modeling and growth curve modeling, which, from the 1990s, enhanced the analysis of criminal career data from longitudinal studies (Nagin, 2016) by enabling researchers to break down the age-crime pattern into various semi-distinct trajectories based on grouping individuals' patterns over time. Using a variety of different databases, researchers have generally identified between four and six distinct curves (Piquero, 2008).[2] These curves, trajectories, or paths distinguish subgroups of offenders on three main variables: onset and length of offending engagement, rate of offending at different periods over that length, and therefore, periods when offending rates are increasing and decreasing.

For example, Sampson and Laub (2003), based on the Gluecks' sample (Glueck & Glueck, 1950) derived five within-individual trajectories spanning ages 7–70. The one most closely resembling a classic desister pathway (bell-shaped and peaking at about 15 years old at a rate of fewer than 1 offense per year) represented 20% of the sample. There were two low-rate chronic curves; one peaked in the teens below a rate of 0.5 and desisted at around 40 years (24%), and the second didn't peak until the mid-30s at a rate a little over 0.5 (8%) and desisted about 20 years later. Neither was bell-shaped due to the low peak rate. Moderate-rate desisters (26%) peaked at a rate between 1 and 1.5 in the late teens and were near zero at 40 years. Moderate-rate chronics (18%) didn't peak until around 24 years, at a rate of almost 1.5, and were still at about .1 at 70. Just 3% were high-rate chronic, already at a rate of .5 at 7 years old, peaking at more than 2.5 and then not until around 38 years, and not desisting until they were in their 60s on average. Therefore, the key points of difference are the age at desistance, the mean rate of offending, and the rate of change in offending over time. All groups were close to complete desistance by the age of 60, regardless of rate and length of career. Surprisingly, Sampson and Laub found little evidence that pathway membership was related to early risk factors such as temperament, or parental behavior during offenders' childhoods.

A second approach is based on longitudinal studies that have followed people into at least late middle age. Here, predetermined definitions rather than the statistical techniques themselves have been used to create groups. Then, the researchers examine whether different careers have distinct etiological pathways and, potentially, distinct desistance pathways

(Piquero, Farrington, Nagin, & Moffitt, 2010). For example, Farrington, Ttofi, and Coid (2009) divided their sample into *adolescence-limited* (first convicted between 10 and 20 and not after 20), *late-onset* (convictions started between 21 and 50), *persistent* (convictions in both age bands), and *non-offenders*. They then examined childhood and adolescent predictors of group membership, identifying which factors best predicted persistence after 21 years. They also examined key adaptive living achievements at 48 years. By that time, the adolescence-limited group were almost indistinguishable from non-offenders in life success. Persistent offenders were the least successful, with all groups showing improvements with age across various indices (e.g., accommodation, employment, cohabitation, alcohol and drug use, fighting, self-reported offending; Farrington et al., 2009).

Similarly, although Moffitt (1993) theorized two types of offending careers: adolescence-limited (AL) and life-course persistent (LCP), examination with the men in the Dunedin longitudinal sample[3] identified a *recovery* group (8%), who were extremely antisocial as children but not extreme in adolescence, an *abstainer* group with no antisocial behavior between 5 and 18 years (5%), and an *unclassified* group, who were essentially representative of the mean scores for the whole sample on measures of antisociality between 5 and 18 (51% of the sample). AL and LCP groups represented 26% and 10% of the sample, respectively. They went on to examine similarities and differences across the five groups in childhood temperament and family factors, adolescent behavior, mental disorders, and current functioning at age 26 years (Moffitt et al., 2002).

Regardless of the different number and shape of trajectories, it is still the case that from an official point of view, most people either never really get started with offending, or if they do, they desist by early adulthood. Even though those with adolescent onset may be as involved in crime in parts or all of their adolescence as early-onset offenders (Stouthamer-Loeber, Wei, Loeber, & Masten, 2004), still most do not persist. For that reason, although research has identified early predictors and contemporaneous correlates of those who desist early, these approaches are still simply descriptive. For example, using Pittsburgh Youth Study data, boys' predictors of desistance in early adulthood measured at age 13–16 included being accountable, believing one will get caught, positive peer relationships, little peer substance use, and limited experience of parental physical punishment (Stouthamer-Loeber et al., 2004). But even though these are longitudinal results they shed no real light on the process by which these variables lead to desistance.

The other important criminal career concept for understanding desistance is intermittency. In longitudinal quantitative research, intermittency is often defined simply based on the time between known offenses. But again, this definition explains little, because everyone has gaps between offenses: one cannot be engaged in crime all day, every day, and much of most criminals' lives may be spent in other routine activities of living. Intermittency is of psychological relevance when such gaps or changes in offending rate are explored to better understand the relevant influences. For example, drug career research shows patterns of acquisitive property offending linked to level of heroin dependence, with post-treatment periods where heroin use and crime commission were lower (Anglin & Speckart, 1988). Periods in custody often lead to gaps in official offending; periods in full-time work or a protective relationship, or periods of illness or parenting may have a similar effect, and so on.

Little research has been conducted on the gaps between offenses. Analysis using the 1958 Philadelphia Birth Cohort showed that these gaps do increase with age, in support of a "gradual slowing down" model of career termination (Baker, Metcalfe, & Piquero, 2015) rather than the leaf-turning model described early in this chapter. A qualitative analysis of Swedish men born between 1943 and 1951 (Carlsson, 2012) showed that those most involved in offending early in life, and interviewed in their 60s, described two different types of intermittency. The first was taking a kind of "time out" from offending, perhaps during a period of interesting employment, or immediately after release from prison, or during a particularly affluent period, or when feeling "burnt out" with regard to crime, but with no overt intent to desist over a longer period. In fact, interviewees described a sense of "not being done yet" with crime (p. 924). So this type is characterized by an awareness of being oriented away from criminal activity, but with no particular focus in desistance.

The second type described in Carlsson (2012) may follow several episodes of the first for the most persistent and chronic offenders, but may also be typical of those involved in a non-trivial level of crime as an adolescent who transition away from it into adulthood (Shapland & Bottoms, 2011). Carlsson labeled this type as *intermittency as attempted change* (p. 924), in which offenders refer explicitly to trying to "go straight." When these men reengaged in crime, the process was more like one of abstinence violation, as described in the addictions literature. In other words, reinvolvement was experienced as failure rather than a matter for indifference.

Giordano's (2014) most recent follow-up of her marginalized Ohio sample (see below) at age 39 shows a similar picture to this second type. Some people initially labeled as desisters in the first follow-up had reengaged with crime at a later follow-up. The long-term perspective on these lapses suggested a lack of access to what these researchers have referred to as a "respectability package" (a combination of a good marriage and employment options; Giordano, Cernkovich, & Rudolph, 2002).

Theoretical Accounts of Desistance

Even when not limited to official indices, desistance in the career criminal research literature has sometimes still been described in a theoretically empty way (e.g., as "the voluntary termination of serious criminal participation"; Shover, 1996, p. 121), or sometimes as a result of aging and maturation (Carlsson, 2012), which is equally uninformative given its lack of specificity about which parts of these processes are relevant. Theoretical accounts of desistance focus more on the processes by which people reduce and cease their criminal involvement. Theoretical accounts of desistance vary in how they see the balance between individual person factors and environmental factors (e.g., the social environment). Both of these types of factors can be relatively more changeable or not, and social factors from a wide range of sources can be influential (e.g., media, school, peers).

Sampson and Laub's Theory of Age-Graded Informal Social Control

Sampson and Laub's theoretical position is at one end of this continuum, in that they emphasize the influence of social institutions in creating turning points that can lead to desistance. Their work is based on an extraordinary reconstruction of the data set originally collected by Glueck and Glueck when the boys were 14, 25, and 32, on 1,000 male delinquents and non-delinquents, case-matched on age, ethnicity (all were white), and IQ, and on low-income home location. The Gluecks began in 1940 with Boston boys born between 1924 and 1932. No further data were collected after the age of 32 until Sampson and Laub relocated almost all of the 500 delinquent boys, when they were around 70. They collected new data from them, including narrative accounts from a small subsample, between 1987 and 1993 (Laub & Sampson, 2003; Sampson & Laub, 1993).

Sampson and Laub's (1993) central thesis is that social connectedness over the life-course comes from a variety of sources—starting with parents, peers, and school, then marriage, military service, and employment as we get older—but at a higher level, these influences all share that they provide a fairly constant source of social control through the resulting social bonds. They argue that continuity of behavior over time can be understood through the influences of childhood factors and individual factors such as child temperament, but key experiences in teenage and early adult years can alter that trajectory, for better or for worse. Major life events that alter the path are referred to as *turning points*. The key events they identified— marriage, military service, reform school, work, and changing where people lived—share that they forced the man into a fresh start away from previous risk factors, provided a new structure for routine activities, provided opportunities to develop prosocially with good support and oversight, and supported him to transform his identity (Sampson & Laub, 2005). They revised their original theory (Sampson & Laub, 1993) somewhat in Laub and Sampson (2003) by according additional causal roles to routine activities, and to human agency: both in ongoing continuity and in desistance. They recognized, at least cursorily, that an individual's ability to exercise choice is an underlying cause, along with features of the immediate situation (Laub, Sampson, & Sweeten, 2006). They made no specific claims about how agency contributes to desistance but noted that such a variable is crucial if we are to explain the loss of predictive value in later life of data based on the early years of life.

Interestingly, they noted that some of those they followed up after more than 30 years were not able to provide any conscious insights into how they desisted (Laub & Sampson, 2003), raising the likelihood that conscious intention may not be needed to permanently desist from crime, and that narrative identity accounts which emphasize awareness (e.g., Maruna, 2001) may be a function of later cohorts of more psychologically aware desisters. An alternative explanation may be that the very highly retrospective nature of this study made it hard for the men to remember what happened at the time (perhaps 20 or 30 years previous).

Giordano and colleagues (Giordano, Schroeder, & Cernkovich, 2007) critiqued aspects of Sampson and Laub's age-graded theory of social control. First, they noted the importance of marriage to the theory, and in particular the role of the spouse's behavior in regulating the former offender. But there is no explanation of why this sometimes fails: some offenders keep offending through the marriage, or even leave it to continue. In other words, the theory lacks a mechanism for why the offender allows his wife to influence his lifestyle for the better. Giordano et al. similarly thought the theory to be restricted by its failure to embrace social learning, which makes it difficult to accommodate the situation of an offender who has a strong bond to an antisocial spouse. In a way, Laub and Sampson's theory parallels some of the limitations of behaviorism in psychology; it represents a relatively rigid view of the importance of external factors and their behavior-changing abilities, and gives internal psychological factors no causal role. This rigidity makes it very difficult to explain why turning points only sometimes turn people.

Giordano's Cognitive Transformation Theory

Giordano's cognitive transformation theory is a more person-based account of desistance than Sampson and Laub's and proposes that cognitive factors drive changes that initiate and support desistance, somewhat independently of social structural events and institutions (Giordano et al., 2002).

Like Sampson and Laub's (1993), and like Maruna's (below), this theory is developed from the data, in this case a longitudinal sample of women and men, first recruited as adolescent offenders. The women's sample of 127 juvenile delinquents was recruited first from the only women's facility in Ohio at that time, and was paired with a similar sample of male delinquents from various Ohio institutions, recruited and interviewed in 1982. In 1995, 109 women and 101 men were tracked and re-interviewed. Giordano's sample is particularly important for being 35–40 years younger than the Glueck sample used by Sampson and Laub, and for its focus on women. It also includes a wider ethnic mix than the Gluecks' all-white sample.

From the 1995 follow-up, Giordano et al. (2002) identified four steps in cognitive transformations associated with desistance: (a) openness to change, a precondition signaling the possibility of transformation; (b) recognition of the positive possibilities that a hook for change offers (e.g., an opportunity to engage in some form of bond or activity that will shield the offender from her personal and environmental risk factors); (c) being able to imagine oneself as a transformed person (i.e., a new identity); and (d) transformation of how the (former) offender views her previous lifestyle and activities (i.e., as no longer valued or relevant). They suggested that these factors are most relevant when offenders find themselves in situations that are neither replete with opportunities to reform, nor so impoverished that agency makes no difference.

Because the cohort is much younger than the Glueck sample, Giordano et al. suggest it may therefore also be the case that changes in the way social institutions function in more recent years account for some of the differences found. For example, neither marriage nor employment offer the strong, stable influence they did in past eras, when often a man didn't marry until he had saved enough money to support a family, and might stay in the same job for decades. Although this "respectability package" (Giordano et al., 2002) of marriage and full-time employment was common in the affluent period in which the Glueck men were maturing (by 31 years, 66% of them were married), it was rare in the Ohio sample: by 31 years, 27% of women and 24% of men were married; only 17% had achieved both marriage and employment and few African American women had achieved either (Giordano, 2014). These lower figures may explain why Giordano and colleagues found that participants' ratings of attachment to partners and job stability did not show statistically significant links to desistance (Giordano et al., 2002). Put simply, they argued that "(a) there is more to life than transition events and (b) there is more to transition events than is reflected in their social control potential" (Giordano et al., 2007, p. 1648). Interestingly, Moffitt and colleagues have made a similar comment: while good marriages and employment may support desistance, their work on the Dunedin sample suggests there are few signs that LCP men can get onto the "on ramp" with respect to these opportunities as they get older (Moffitt, Caspi, Harrington, & Milne, 2002).

A significant part of the debate between theorists like Giordano (taking a relatively subjective position on how change happens) and those like Laub and Sampson (stronger emphasis on social structural factors) is that it unpacks some of the possibilities for what structural variables like marriage and employment represent. In the example above, being able to save enough money for marriage might itself be a function of greater impulse control or better problem-solving. It might also be that working toward a goal such as saving for marriage creates greater commitment to conformity, or leads to more social approval, and so on. Ultimately it seems clear from qualitative data that both personal and social are important, but subjective theorists would argue that the complex dynamic interactions between people and their social worlds that strengthen engagement in desistance are driven more by people (i.e., agency, self-regulation capacity, self-efficacy) than by the environment alone (Giordano, 2014), and there is some tentative quantitative evidence to support this contention (LeBel, Burnett, Maruna, & Bushway, 2008).

Cognitive transformation theory has undergone further development in the past decade (Giordano, 2014; Giordano et al., 2007), in response to the second follow-up wave, completed when research participants were 39 years old. The Giordano et al. (2007) revision of their theory gives more emphasis to the role of emotions in persistence and desistance. In essence, Giordano et al. posit, first, that the negative emotions (e.g., anger) that may have originated in an adverse childhood and fed the motivation for crime weaken as the emerging adult has the opportunity to take on new, more socially diverse roles (e.g., a person comes to accept the deficiencies of their dysfunctional parent). Second, they suggest that the positive emotions associated with crime (e.g., the thrill, social status, positive criminal identity) weaken. Third, emotional regulation improves as the individual matures, making it a bit easier to pursue long-term goals prosocially.

The most recent round of interviews uncovered some previous desisters who had lapsed, largely due to environmental adversity (Giordano, 2014). At 39, desisters pointed to the influence of a variety of external influences in helping them to desist (e.g., religion, having children, psychological treatment), but it is equally clear that for other offenders, these same factors were not hooks for change (e.g., having children did not alter the criminal commitment of some). Effective hooks for change (e.g., completing a treatment program) provided more detail for the change blueprint, were positive in orientation and directed the person toward the future, with options for the new self that were satisfying and conventional, and led to support from prosocial others (Giordano, 2014). Although Giordano's theory is described in symbolic interactionist terms, in which trying on new roles is a fundamental component of the stimulus for change, it is readily conceptualized as describing change as an interaction between internal cognitive and emotional factors and social environmental stimuli. Most notably, the role-playing component could be viewed as a form of behavioral experiment—where an intentional attempt at new behavior is used to elicit feedback from the world that changes cognition (Bennett-Levy et al., 2004)—which allows the theory to accommodate the potentially powerful reciprocal influences between cognition and behavior. Interestingly, this potential flexibility in Giordano's approach has been a source of criticism from others (Bushway & Paternoster, 2014).

Maruna's Narrative Identity Theory

Maruna's work is often suggested to offer a critique of desistance from the extreme person-variable perspective; his innovative thinking on desistance derives in large part from his Liverpool desistance study: a series of interviews with two samples, chosen to "maximize the likelihood of identifying individuals at the two extremes of a long process of change" (Maruna, 2001, p. 45). Persisters were people who indicated that their offending was ongoing and they felt powerless to "go straight" (Maruna, 2001), even if they professed that they wanted to. In fact, the passivity and defeatism of his persisters is striking.

The desisters, in stark contrast, were quietly confident that their last offense had occurred 2–3 years previously: a substantial achievement in a career criminal. Desisters' interview narratives were based on the idea that their redemption from crime led to a current lifestyle dedicated to being true to themselves, pursuing a significant life purpose, with control over their destinies and a desire to give something constructive back to their communities ("making good"; Maruna, 2001, p. 9). Maruna's main mechanism is one of cognitive transformation, and his work gives a very strong role to human agency and the ability to construct a new self-identity: to "re-envision their past self" (Bersani & Doherty, 2018, p. 315). In contrast to some other theories, Maruna's desisters do not view their past as positive, but have reconfigured it in the desisting present to make a more coherent story in which it was essential to the person they have become.

Bushway and Paternoster's Identity Theory of Desistance

More recently, another identity-based integrative theoretical framework has been proposed by Paternoster and Bushway (2009; see also Bushway & Paternoster, 2014). They draw on aspects of social psychology to contrast the offender's current working self with positive and negative future selves. According to their view, desistance begins when offenders' views of the negative, unsatisfying, and disappointing aspects of their criminal lifestyle crystallize to the point where they realize that the future is bleak without change. The initial impetus then comes from a desire to avoid becoming that future "feared self" (Bushway & Paternoster, 2014, p. 67). A key component of their theory is that identity change toward a desisting self needs to begin before the individual moves toward more prosocial people, roles, and institutions. Although the decision to change identity is portrayed largely as rational, it is triggered by an emotion: a sense of dissatisfaction and fear. They describe their position theoretically as much more "cognitive, internal, and individualist, at least initially" (2014, p. 67) than other theories.

Paternoster and colleagues have tested aspects of identity theory in recent quantitative research. Two studies used the Rutgers Health and Human Development Project data (Paternoster, Bachman, Kerrison, M'Connell, & Smith, 2016; Rocque, Posick, & Paternoster, 2016). One found, using growth-curve modeling with data collected between the ages of 12 and 30, that prosocial identity increased with age, and that after controlling for adult social bond strength, sex, race, socioeconomic status, poor grades, peer delinquency, parental attachment, marital status, and children, it was a significant predictor of reduced criminal involvement over time (Rocque et al., 2016). The second study showed that released prisoners who sought help for drug use problems and took other practical steps showed improvements in identity over time and in rates of arrest and drug use (Na, Paternoster, & Bachman, 2015). This line of research is preliminary, with measures of identity that vary in quality, and designs that do not necessarily elucidate the order of change, but it suggests, unsurprisingly, that identity is related to desistance.

Moffitt's Maturation Theory of Adolescence-Limited Offending

Embedded in Moffitt's (1993) taxonomy is a theory of how desistance occurs for the quite numerous individuals who become somewhat involved in offending as adolescents but do not continue much beyond that age. According to Moffitt, these AL teenagers differ from the LCP type by virtue of the inconsistency of their antisocial behavior across domains. The implication is that they are sensitive to the contingencies for antisocial and prosocial behavior in a way that LCP offenders are not, both across situations within the same temporal period, and across time. Just as the gap between biological and social maturity motivates ALs' mimicry of LCP offenders, according to Moffitt, so the closing of that gap causes the attractions of a criminal identity and of crime itself to wane much more rapidly than for entrenched LCP offenders. It is much easier for AL offenders to shed the trappings of criminality in early adulthood because they are likely to have both more social capital and more personal capabilities than LCP offenders, due to the direct and snowball effects of having fewer early risk factors and more early-onset protective factors. They have more functional cognitive skills, better resumes, and nicer personality styles. Furthermore, the theory assumes that their offending behavior is largely a social or peer group phenomenon that does not result in the lasting development of criminogenic needs (e.g., pro-offending attitudes) the way it appears to for LCP offenders (Moffitt et al., 2002). One study that supports this view showed that would-be desisters at 20 reported conformist lifestyle aspirations and law-abiding values. Criminal acts occurred despite these dissonant values and ambitions, largely due to habitual responses and temptation by peers. Desistance was more successful with the use of family support, and deliberate efforts to avoid peers and other sources of temptation (Shapland & Bottoms, 2011).

This process of realigning lifestyle with conventional aspirations and values can be thwarted for AL offenders who have become ensnared in the consequences of their forays into criminality. For example, it may be harder to exit from crime if they have a criminal record that prevents employment, or children who depend on them for a level of income they can't earn legitimately, or drug addiction. Although Moffitt's theory has more generally stimulated considerable research, there has been little on desistance for either pathway.

The research support for all of these theories is largely qualitative, rich, and interesting, but flawed by its retrospective nature, because people are inaccurate in recalling key characteristics of their lives over even several years, and some of these studies rely on much longer periods. A second weakness is in not recognizing that all people actively reconstruct their pasts to support and justify the present, consistent with cognitive dissonance theory.

Further, some of the theories would predict that desistance will be a fundamentally different process for the offender who is deeply embedded in a criminal lifestyle compared to those whose engagement with crime has been more flirtatious. This individual difference, along with cohort effects, and differences in the external resources available to offenders who want to desist, all need taking into account, because they have implications for the explanatory depth required of a more complete desistance theory. There is a need for replication and for prospective prediction of desistance, which probably means that longitudinal studies of at-risk individuals may need to build in more desistance-theory relevant variables. Relatedly, studies that currently measure "subjective" variables (i.e., individual psychological variables) typically do not include the sorts of factors that are targeted for change in offender rehabilitation (e.g., improved problem-solving and ability to relate to people). Including both criminogenic needs and improvements in the skills used to undermine them, or conversely, measurement of strength-based rehabilitation variables, would help to bridge the obvious gap at present between rehabilitation and desistance fields. Perhaps the biggest problem with all of these theories is the difficulty in identifying what it is that actually "turns" a person: why then and why that? If we understood this better, it would open up the possibility of focusing interventions more specifically on simulating the conditions in which turning points could be made to occur.

Offender Rehabilitation, Reintegration, and Desistance

Trajectory research and theories of desistance suggest that some people reach an enduring desisting state much earlier in life than do others. Those who get caught up in the consequences of their offending (i.e., snares) and those whose difficulties are both broader and more long-standing may be among those who stop offending more slowly, or later in life. There are substantial benefits for them and for a society if they "go straight" earlier, but how might that happen?

A number of research projects suggest that the state of affairs for many chronic offenders is one of wavering between persistence and desistance (Burnett, 2004; Healy, 2010; Leibrich, 1993), something that is very hard to detect from quantitative criminal career research. Burnett even argued that it was a misrepresentation of reality to categorize people as persisters and desisters: it "misrepresents the switching, vacillating nature of desistance from offending." She also questioned whether turning points really were derived from key events or experiences. Rather, she suggested that "(i)nstead of crossroads and junctions, a more apt analogy is that of a multi-lane motorway, the middle lane representing the individual's ambivalence and the lanes either side representing persistence and desistence" (Burnett, 2000, p. 6). What perpetuates this ambivalence?

Post-Custodial Desistance Research

As Carlsson's (2012) research suggested, offenders reported some criminal career gaps were due to periods of intentional desistance from crime that ultimately failed. Similarly, Giordano (2014) found that some of the desisters in an earlier period of her study had subsequently been reconvicted again, due at least in part to a lack of resources for success. These findings suggest that at any time a number of offenders may be making active attempts to desist that ultimately fail, referred to as *proto-secondary desistance* (see above, What Is Desistance?) by Maruna and Farrall (2004). These findings also suggest that the research literatures on offender rehabilitation and on reintegration (resettlement, reentry) are relevant to understanding all forms of desistance.

Imprisonment is, among other things, intended to create a pause in offending, and often is reported as a period of self-reflection and renewed commitment to desistance. In a New Zealand sample of very high-risk male parolees (the New Zealand Parole Project data set; NZPP) interviewed just before they left prison, about 45% reported they had already been trying to go straight prior to the offenses leading to their current imprisonment; of these about half had been trying as hard as they could to desist (rated 6 on a 6-point Likert scale). During these interviews, ratings were also made for a number of questions pertaining to their imminent release on parole. Prisoners' ratings of how committed to desistance they were just prior to this imminent release correlated significantly with all five recidivism outcomes over the first year after release (parole violation, reconviction with and without parole violations included, reconviction for violence, reimprisonment). Confidence in their ability to desist was not a significant predictor, and nor was simply wanting to desist (cf. Shapland & Bottoms, 2011). All of these ratings were high (mean scores ranged 4.9–5.2 on a 1–6 scale) regardless of outcome. The best combination of predictors was commitment to desistance and how much net change they thought they had made during this prison sentence (both positive and negative change were rated, and perceptions of negative change were particularly important in predicting recidivism; Polaschek & Yesberg, 2015). The findings are consistent with another study that found that those who said they were definitely going to desist, later reported significantly lower reoffending (Farrall, Bottoms, & Shapland, 2010).

This research needs replicating, but suggests (a) that a desire to "go straight" may pre-date career termination, possibly even by years; (b) self-report ratings are valid predictors of recidivism, and (c) perceptions of the amount and type of change, especially negative change, made in prison may also be important.

The NZPP sample is mostly non-European, with a mean age in the early 30s and upward of 40 previous convictions. Almost all of those in the sample also had multiple violent convictions. By contrast, Burnett's research with the Oxford Recidivism Study (Burnett, 1992) followed 130 men with previous convictions for property offending through three waves of interviews: just prior to release from prison, 4–6 months after release (n = 99), and 7–20 months after release (n = 67 men). This sample were mostly in their 20s and were property offenders with between 3 and 14 previous convictions; 86% were Anglo-European in ethnic origin.

As for the NZPP data set, the majority (80%) of participants wanted to "go straight" prior to release. But almost two thirds subsequently self-reported new offending (Burnett, 2000). Fitting with Giordano's research, a key finding was that a crime-free life was regarded as a "best-case scenario," requiring that certain social and personal conditions be in place (e.g. sufficient income, able to avoid alcohol or drug use). Without these requirements, the men recognized they were vulnerable to their admitted "Plan B," returning to crime (Burnett, 2000). In other words, they lacked confidence or self-efficacy with regard to desistance, potentially because of practical obstacles associated with reentry. Persisters were expecting to find life in the community more challenging than were desisters, and when followed up, reported greater actual social and practical difficulties (employment, accommodation, relationships, drug abuse, etc.). Unfortunately, the small sample size prevented these findings from being analyzed statistically.

A later study with the same data set related its findings to a 10-year recidivism follow-up (LeBel et al., 2008). This study is important because it attempted to investigate the optimal temporal ordering of personal ("subjective/agency") versus social factors measured prior to release and soon after in predicting conviction-defined desistance. Again, although there were interesting findings, they ran into challenges with sample size that limited the questions that could be answered. For example, they could not examine the important question of whether pre-release subjective factors were mediated by social factors in the community.

Analyses suggested that greater hope and less internalized stigma just prior to release each predicted desistance a decade later, but ratings of regret (p = .06), shame, and identity as a family man did not. Ratings of reentry problems 4–6 months after release were also predictive. For reimprisonment, only reentry problems were significant ($p < .05$), with hope, identity as a family man, and low stigma all close to significance (.05 < ps ≤ .10). But when combined with reentry problems, none of the subjective variables except internalized stigma were independently predictive of recidivism. This study, then, was a glimpse into the world of potential interactions between subjective and social factors in desistance, suggesting that practical reentry issues may have been more important for this sample than the psychological variables measured. However, the range of psychological variables was limited and omitted those typically associated with effective rehabilitation, for instance.

Increasing Success in Official Desistance Through Rehabilitation

The career pathway research reviewed early in this chapter suggests that the "natural history" of criminal careers can make the pathway to desistance very long indeed. Criminal justice policy-makers and practitioners have been searching for ways to enhance desistance—at least as defined officially, as reconviction—for just as long. The development of offender rehabilitation programs that reduce the proportion of reconvicted individuals is one major approach, though the effectiveness of these programs has rarely been investigated through the lens of actual desistance rather than rearrest or reconviction, and little is known about how programs assist in effecting desistance after release.

Effective rehabilitation programs focus on changing dynamic risk factors, with the presumption that doing so will make desistance easier. Examples of dynamic risk factors include: criminal attitudes, values, and identity; criminal peers; a restless, impulsive, aggressive temperament; poor emotional regulation; problematic alcohol and drug use; lack of engagement with schooling or employment; a lack of supportive prosocial family; and unstructured use of leisure time (Bonta & Andrews, 2017). Many of these issues come straight out of the early development of LCP offenders.

Reductions in risk of criminal behavior are associated with (a) supporting offenders to re-evaluate the criminal influences in their lives (e.g., deprecating attitudes to "going straight," gang identities, peers who encourage crime, believing the world owes one a living or that violence is justified). If these types of re-evaluations occur they can engender or renew motivation to desist, and then (b) teaching skills that are envisioned to make desistance easier through providing smoother access to prosocial alternatives or making them more satisfying. For example, teaching time-out, meditation, mindfulness, relaxation, problem-solving, communication, and basic parenting skills may reduce the assessed presence of most of the criminogenic needs above.

These are usually called "RNR programs" (Polaschek, 2012), meaning that they are cognitive behavioral programs that conform to the Risk-Need-Responsivity (RNR) model (Bonta & Andrews, 2017). The explicit policy focus of the RNR model is on reducing reconviction, a central goal for many correctional agencies. Is this goal incompatible with the process of offender desistance? RNR programs should have wide-ranging effects not just in avoiding offending, but in creating substitute prosocial lifestyles, if run well. There is tentative evidence that their effects are not simply risk-preventing, and that participants use program content to improve other aspects of their lives (Coupland, 2015), bearing in mind that these effects are rarely considered in evaluating programs. In fact, giving people a wider range of options for living without crime is one of the most important achievements of these programs. Left to themselves, offenders tend to approach the practical side of desistance with behavioral avoidance (Shapland & Bottoms, 2011; Wilson, 2003), which can lead to unsustainably impoverished lifestyles.

The development of psychology-based programs that reduce reconviction has occurred largely independently of research into the desistance process. This hypothetical bifurcation has been enhanced unhelpfully in recent years by theorists and commentators characterizing programs under the RNR umbrella as "risk-management-oriented,"[4] and creating an artificially bright contrast with "strength-based" interventions—most notably those associated with the Good Lives Model (GLM)—that focus more overtly on reorienting offenders to choosing and building their post-desistance life processes without direct reference to risky ways of thinking and behaving (McNeill, 2012). According to this way of thinking, a focus on changing criminogenic needs, as seen in RNR programs, is a weak and indirect method of promoting desistance, through time spent on relapse prevention/risk management strategies that translate during and after treatment into the pursuit of avoidance goals (Laws & Ward, 2011; McNeill, Farrall, Lightowler, & Maruna, 2012). A more effective approach is to instead support offenders in developing or freeing their sense of personal agency in the authentic pursuit of primary goods (e.g. relatedness, excellence in work; Ward & Gannon, 2006), indirectly causing risk factors to become irrelevant (Laws & Ward, 2011). Despite the confidence expressed in the inherent effectiveness of these newer approaches, more than a decade later there remain no published outcome evaluations of GLM programs. Very few studies have even examined the GLM in a treatment context, so it is difficult to evaluate or compare claims made about the model in relation to desistance.

Meanwhile, it is easy to understand why the RNR model may not appear to critics to be attuned to psychological desistance processes (Laws & Ward, 2011), given that at best its overall policy goal of reducing reoffending sounds avoidance-focused. But effective programs under this framework must look to life after offending, if they are to engage each offender and support change. And the limited evidence examining the effects of such programs suggests that they are helpful for desistance. For example, in the NZPP ($n \approx 300$), half of the sample had completed an intensive psychological treatment program of 8–12 months' duration prior to parole, while the other half (the comparison sample) had taken part in few or no effective interventions. Polaschek (2016, pp. 183–184) reported that:

> the pattern of relationships between desistance and dynamic risk variables (i.e., criminogenic needs, measured at release) was found to be equivalent in treated and comparison participants. But the treatment sample had significantly more positive scores on all variables (i.e. lower risk and higher protective factors, greater engagement with desistance processes and better quality of life in the community) than those who did not attend the program and, in turn significantly lower rates of reconviction. Treated offenders also independently rated themselves as having greater agency for desistance and were rated by therapists and researchers as being significantly more engaged in behavior changes consistent with desistance. These results come from a series of routinely delivered programs that identify themselves as being consistent with RNR principles; demonstrating that programs with the policy goal of reducing reoffending by tackling dynamic risk, in turn can build protective skills and life circumstances, and support agency and identity changes during the highest risk phase of transition into the community.

Consistent with cognitive dissonance theory, prisoners on longer sentences typically report that they have changed in important ways during their time in prison, when interviewed just prior to release. Their beliefs about how much change they have made do not necessarily tally with external observations of their behavior, and unless they have been in a treatment program, the type of change often contemplating new behavior rather than trying it. Polaschek and Yesberg (2015) found that while treated and comparison prisoners were equivalent on ratings of wanting to desist and confidence in their ability to desist, treatment graduates were significantly more committed to desisting. In later analyses, avoiding reconviction in the first 12 months after release was independently predicted by both pre-release dynamic risk and desistance commitment; but when current stage of change was added in, desistance commitment was no longer a significant predictor. On average, treated men were already showing early signs of behavioral change at release, whereas comparison men were in contemplation. Commitment to desistance was rated more highly by men who were already showing more externally observable behavioral change, and the latter was more likely if they had been through the treatment program during their imprisonment sentence (Polaschek, 2016).

Reintegration and Desistance

Writing and research on reintegrating offenders after criminal sanctions has also developed quite separately from RNR-based interventions. Much of it has been driven by concerns about rapid growth in prison musters, high levels of parole violation that lead to reincarceration, initiatives that increase imprisonment of low-risk offenders (e.g., the War on Drugs), and perceptions of increased obstacles to re-establishing community life post-release (Polaschek, Yesberg, & Chauhan, 2018).

According to the most commonly described reintegration perspective, desistance fails not because people still like living in prison, nor because they continued to be at risk of crime due to poor emotional regulation, ongoing drug use, criminal attitudes, criminal peers, low resistance to temptations, and so on. Rather, if they fail, it is because they were returned to the community in circumstances that might be unsustainable for anyone: without the basic resources to succeed (Visher & Travis, 2011), such as adequate housing, health care, financial support, employment, and social support (Burnett, 2009; Griffiths, Dandurand, & Murdoch, 2007). The exact mechanisms underlying this perspective are not usually clearly outlined, but the implication is that offenders may fall back into criminal behavior because they can't "make it" alone.

With an imprisonment rate well above most other nations, the United States is particularly likely to be dealing with the reentry of people who formerly had little criminal history but now find themselves with little social capital and forced to live in a relatively narrow range of deprived and crime-infested urban neighborhoods (Travis & Western, 2014; Visher & Travis, 2011). Changes in laws and regulations for offenders (e.g., offender registration, residential and employment restrictions) have further served to increase barriers to establishing oneself in the community, making return to prison a rational choice (Braga, Piehl, & Hureau, 2009). From this perspective, preparing and planning for release coupled with post-release assistance in accessing necessities will enhance conviction-free survival (Duwe, 2013; Graffam & Shinkfield, 2012; Mears & Cochran, 2015; Veysey, Ostermann, & Lanterman, 2014). Anecdotal accounts are plentiful of prisoners entering the community ill-prepared. But comprehensive reentry programs—pre-release, post-release, or both—have been subject to evaluation with mixed results (Braga et al., 2009; Duwe, 2012; Garland & Hass, 2015; Lattimore & Visher, 2013; Roman, Brooks, Lagerson, Chalfin, & Tereschenko, 2007; Taylor, 2013; Wilson & Davis, 2006; Zhang, Roberts, & Callanan, 2006).

As with all intervention evaluations, especially when the evidence for their effectiveness is equivocal, it is important to establish whether the purported mechanism is supported too (see Chapters 24 and 25): in this case whether actual improvement in preparation and resources *is* associated with desistance. Research into whether the quality of preparation or readiness for release affects survival has been investigated (Visher & Lattimore, 2007; Wolff, Shi, & Schumann, 2012). New Zealand research using samples of high-risk violent offenders released with or without intensive custodial treatment has produced several relevant findings. Less feasible release plans predicted reconviction in high-risk treated prisoners, even when static risk of reconviction was already taken into account (Polaschek, Kilgour, & Wilson, 2018). A series of studies that measured the quality of release plans (e.g., rated accommodation, employment, social support) found that higher-quality plans predicted who avoided reconviction (Dickson, Polaschek, & Casey, 2013, with high-risk violent offenders; Willis & Grace, 2008, 2009, with child-sex offenders), and worked via the mechanism of improved quality of basic life conditions in the community (Dickson, Polaschek, & Wilson, 2017). The treatment programs attended by many of the men in these studies also include an explicit release planning component (Polaschek & Kilgour, 2013). NZPP data compares treated men with untreated, and shows that treated men have better quality release plans and are living in better circumstances in the first few months after release—with better social capital—than are those who have not attended these programs. But the basic relationships between plan quality, release circumstances, and recidivism hold with both samples.

Desistance and Women Offenders

Longitudinal research cohorts vary in whether they include girls and women (e.g., Dunedin) or only men (e.g., Cambridge). Evidence to date suggests that the LCP pathway is very rare in women (Moffitt et al., 2002), and most women don't begin offending in earnest until adolescence at the earliest. However, for those women who were on the LCP pathway, adult outcomes, including likelihood of violence perpetration, were poorer than for AL women, just as they were for men. Like men, at age 32, LCP women showed poorer outcomes across a range of non-criminal indices of success and wellbeing, including mental and physical health (Odgers et al., 2008).

In a recent review that integrated findings from both quantitative and qualitative desistance studies of women, Rodermond, Kruttschnitt, Slotboom, and Bijleveld (2016) concluded that both a reduction in the rate of criminal behavior and complete cessation were related to economic independence, education, employment, mental health, and motherhood. Although they found that the stress of motherhood could cause a relapse into offending, in general, parenting appeared to provide a strong incentive to maintain a crime-free lifestyle: more so than for men. Women's desistance was also more affected by access to a high-quality positive intimate relationship and strong friendship and family bonds than was men's. Women's desistance was less influenced by employment, possibly because they were more likely to be in low-paying jobs that did not alleviate financial stress (Rodermond et al., 2016). Rodermond et al. concluded that current theories of desistance appear relevant to women, and that the research literature on women is fairly small, and limited mainly to the United States.

Conclusions and Future Directions

People who commit more than one or two offenses vary widely in when they start offending, how often they offend, the size of the gaps between offenses or even active offending periods, and even when they stop offending. Given all of this natural variation, it is challenging to define desistance consistently, especially in studies where information is not available about offenders' contributions to observed patterns, including current goals with respect to offending or not.

Current theories on the process of desistance vary in the balance they accord to social structural and person-based factors, but research suggests both may be important. These theories, though they are almost all built on qualitative interview studies of desisters, for the most part concentrate on the process as if it were only important to explain desistance in association with successful career *termination*. Several studies hint at desistance as a much more fluid and extended process, bearing a resemblance to any other habit-based disorder that people are trying to stop, but in which lapses occur periodically on the route to enduring cessation. Longitudinal research that tracks people through these phases over a longer period, and measures desistance-relevant psychological and social factors, would be valuable in building such theories.

System-based efforts to increase successful post-custodial survival are relevant to desistance because they are at least deliberate attempts to increase intermittency, or proto-secondary desistance. Understanding more about how reintegration and treatment programs interact with these same variables would inform intervention design, and ultimately the question of how social and personal elements interact for success. Research on how and why such intervention effects seem to "wear off" over time would also be informative.

Turning back to the Dunedin study, both early-onset men and early-onset women had significantly poorer mental and physical health and economic outcomes at 32 years (Odgers et al., 2008). Relatedly, the long-term follow-up for the Cambridge male cohort shows substantial continued improvement on basic indices of life success between 32 and 48 years for persisters (convicted before and after their 21st birthday), but at 48 years, this group still fell well behind those who had never been convicted. Overall, two thirds were living successfully and had not been reconvicted in the previous 5 years, compared to almost all desisters, late-onset offenders, and unconvicted offenders (Farrington et al., 2006). Taken together, these findings remind us that successful desistance may require a much bigger commitment for some offenders than others, and, even after giving up crime, life may still be marginal, even in middle age. They also offer up the possibility that desistance from crime for these individuals may be easier to support if a range of services is offered, including health care.

Notes

1   For example, in the Cambridge Study in Delinquent Development, 30 crimes were self-reported by their perpetrators for every one resulting in conviction (Farrington, Ttofi, Crago, & Coid, 2014). A study of rape attrition in five countries showed about 4% resulted in convition (Daly & Bouhours, 2010). In New Zealand, an estimated 76 and 87% of family violence events go unreported to police (Fanslow & Robinson, 2010; Ministry of Justice Research and Evaluation Team, 2014).
2   Trajectory modeling techniques are intended to create subgroups or subtypes, meaning that the resulting number of categories is influenced by the modeling method used (Bushway, Sweeten, & Nieuwbeerta, 2009) and decisions made by the researchers about the preferred solution; division between subtypes can be arbitrary (Walters, 2012).
3   The Dunedin Multidisciplinary Health and Development Study, known as the Dunedin study, is based in the University of Otago, New Zealand. It is following the lives of 1,037 people born at Dunedin's maternity hospital between April 1, 1972, and March 31, 1973. The sample is composed predominantly of European New Zealanders.
4   In the RNR tradition, "risk management" refers to the use of information about acute risk factors to manage imminent offending (e.g., relapse prevention strategies; Laws, 1995). By contrast, treatment programs spend most of their energy on risk reduction, making this term, used by proponents of the Good Lives Model (GLM; e.g., Ward & Gannon, 2006), a confusing mischaracterization. It is most likely that this misunderstanding occurred because the GLM arose from the sex offender treatment domain, where, instead of an RNR focus, over time these programs became punitive and narrowly focused on avoidance of risk through relapse prevention (e.g. Laws, 1995).

Key Readings

Farrington, D. P., Coid, J. W., Harnett, L., Jolliffe, D., Soteriou, N., Turner, R., & West, D. J. (2006). *Criminal careers up to the age of 50 and life success up to the age of 48: New findings from the Cambridge Study in Delinquent Development.* London, UK: Home Office.

Laub, J. H., & Sampson, R. J. (2003). *Shared beginnings, divergent lives: Delinquent boys to age 70.* Cambridge, MA: Harvard University Press.

Maruna, S. (2001). *Making good: How ex-convicts reform and rebuild their lives.* Washington, DC: American Psychological Association.

Polaschek, D. L. L. (2016). Desistance and dynamic risk factors belong together. *Psychology, Crime & Law*, 22, 171–189.

Rodermond, E., Kruttschnitt, C., Slotboom, A., & Bijleveld, C. C. J. H. (2016). Female desistance: A review of the literature. *European Journal of Criminology*, 13, 3–28.

References

Anglin, M. D., & Speckart, G. (1988). Narcotics use and crime: A multisample-multimethod analysis. *Criminology*, 26, 197–233.

Baker, T. B., Metcalfe, C. F., & Piquero, A. R. (2015). Measuring the intermittency of criminal careers. *Crime & Delinquency*, 61, 1078–1103.

Bennett-Levy, J., Westbrook, D., Fennell, M., Cooper, M., Rouf, K., & Hackmann, A. (2004). Behavioural experiments: Historical and conceptual underpinnings. In J. Bennett-Levy, G. Butler, M. Fennell, A. Hackman, M. Mueller, & D. Westbrook (Eds.), *Oxford guide to behavioural experiments in cognitive therapy* (pp. 1–20). Oxford, UK: Oxford University Press.

Bersani, B. E., & Doherty, E. E. (2018). Desistance from offending in the twenty-first century. *Annual Review of Criminology*, 1, 311–334.

Bonta, J., & Andrews, D. A. (2017). *The psychology of criminal conduct* (6th ed.). London, UK: Routledge.

Braga, A. A., Piehl, A. M., & Hureau, D. (2009). Controlling violent offenders released to the community: An evaluation of the Boston Reentry Initiative. *Journal of Research in Crime and Delinquency*, 46, 411–436.

Burnett, R. (1992). *The dynamics of recidivism*. Oxford, UK: University of Oxford Centre for Criminological Research.

Burnett, R. (2000). Understanding criminal careers through a series of in-depth interviews. *Offender Program Report*, 4(1), 1–15.

Burnett, R. (2004). To reoffend or not to reoffend? The ambivalence of convicted property offenders. In S. Maruna, & R. Immarigeon (Eds.), *After crime and punishment: Pathways to offender reintegration* (pp. 152–180). Cullumpton, UK: Willan.

Burnett, R. (2009). Post-corrections reintegration: Prisoner resettlement and desistance from crime. In J. R. Adler, & J. M. Gray (Eds.), *Forensic psychology: Concepts, debates, and practice* (2nd ed.) (pp. 508–528). Cullumpton, UK: Willan.

Bushway, S. D., Piquero, A. R., Mazerolle, P., Broidy, L., & Cauffman, E. (2001). A developmental framework for empirical research on desistance. *Criminology*, 39, 491–515.

Bushway, S. D., & Paternoster, R. (2014). Identity and desistance from crime. In J. A. Humphrey, & P. Cordella (Eds.), *Effective interventions in the lives of criminal offenders* (pp. 63–92). New York, NY: Springer.

Bushway, S. D., Sweeten, G., & Nieuwbeerta, P. (2009). Measuring long term individual trajectories of offending using multiple methods. *Journal of Quantitative Criminology*, 25, 259–286.

Carlsson, C. (2012). Processes of intermittency in criminal careers: Notes from a Swedish study on life courses and crime. *International Journal of Offender Therapy and Comparative Criminology*, 57, 913–938.

Coupland, R. B. A. (2015). *An examination of dynamic risk, protective factors, and treatment-related change in violent offenders* (Unpublished doctoral dissertation). University of Saskatchewan. Sasakatoon, Canada.

Daly, K., & Bouhours, B. (2010). Rape and attrition in the legal process: A comparative analysis of five countries. *Crime and Justice*, 39, 565–650.

DeLisi, M., & Piquero, A. R. (2011). New frontiers in criminal careers research, 2000–2011: A state-of-the-art review. *Journal of Criminal Justice*, 39, 289–301.

Dickson, S. R., Polaschek, D. L. L., & Casey, A. R. (2013). Can the quality of high-risk violent prisoners' release plans predict recidivism following intensive rehabilitation? A comparison with risk assessment instruments. *Psychology, Crime & Law*, 19, 371–389.

Dickson, S. R., Polaschek, D. L. L., & Wilson, M. J. (2017). How do plans enhance desistance? Translating release plans into parole experiences for high risk parolees. Manuscript under review.

Duwe, G. (2012). Evaluating the Minnesota Comprehensive Offender Reentry Plan (MCORP): Results from a randomized experiment. *Justice Quarterly*, 29, 347–383.

Duwe, G. (2013). *An evaluation of the Minnesota Comprehensive Offender Reentry Plan (MCORP) Pilot project: Final report*. St. Paul, MN: Minnesota Department of Corrections.

Fanslow, J. L., & Robinson, E. M. (2010). Help-seeking reported by a representative sample of women victims of intimate partner violence in New Zealand. *Journal of Interpersonal Violence*, 25, 929–951.

Farrall, S., Bottoms, A., & Shapland, J. (2010). Social structures and desistance from crime. *European Journal of Criminology*, 7, 546–570.

Farrington, D. P., Coid, J. W., Harnett, L., Jolliffe, D., Soteriou, N., Turner, R., & West, D. J. (2006). *Criminal careers up to the age of 50 and life success up to the age of 48: New findings from the Cambridge Study in Delinquent Development*. London, UK: Home Office.

Farrington, D. P., Ttofi, M. M., & Coid, J. W. (2009). Development of adolescence-limited, late-onset, and persistent offenders from age 8 to age 48. *Aggressive Behavior*, 35, 150–163.

Farrington, D. P., Ttofi, M. M., Crago, R. V., & Coid, J. W. (2014). Prevalence, frequency, onset, desistance and criminal career duration in self-reports compared with official records. *Criminal Behaviour and Mental Health*, 24, 241–253.

Farrington, D. P., & Wikström, P. H. (1994). Criminal careers in London and Stockholm: A cross-national comparative study. In E. G. M. Weitekamp, & H.-J. Kerner (Eds.), *Cross-national longitudinal research on human development and criminal behaviour* (pp. 65–89). Dordrecht, the Netherlands: Kluwer.

Garland, B. E., & Hass, A. Y. (2015). An outcome evaluation of a midwestern prisoner reentry initiative. *Criminal Justice Policy Review*, 2015, 293–314.

Giordano, P. C. (2014). Gender, crime, and desistance: Toward a theory of cognitive transformation. In J. A. Humphrey, & P. Cordella (Eds.), *Effective interventions in the lives of criminal offenders* (pp. 41–62). New York, NY: Springer.

Giordano, P. C., Cernkovich, S. A., & Rudolph, J. L. (2002). Gender, crime, and desistance: Toward a theory of cognitive transformation. *American Journal of Sociology*, 107, 990–1064.

Giordano, P. C., Schroeder, R. D., & Cernkovich, S. A. (2007). Emotions and crime over the life course: A neo-Meadian perspective on criminal continuity and change. *American Journal of Sociology*, 112, 1603–1661.

Glueck, S., & Glueck, E. (1950). *Unraveling juvenile delinquency*. New York, NY: Commonwealth Fund.

Graffam, J., & Shinkfield, A. (2012). The life conditions of Australian ex-prisoners: An analysis of inter-personal, subsistence, and support conditions. *International Journal of Offender Therapy and Comparative Criminology*, 56, 897–916.

Griffiths, C. T., Dandurand, Y., & Murdoch, D. (2007). *The social reintegration of offenders and crime prevention*. Research Report: 2007-2. Ottawa, Canada: Public Safety Canada. Retrieved from https://www.publicsafety.gc.ca/cnt/rsrcs/pblctns/scl-rntgrtn/scl-rntgrtn-eng.pdf

Healy, D. (2010). *The dynamics of desistance: Charting pathways through change*. Abingdon, UK: Routledge.

Kazemian, L. (2007). Desistance from crime: Theoretical, empirical, methodological, and policy considerations. *Journal of Contemporary Criminal Justice*, 23, 5–27.

Lattimore, P. K., & Visher, C. A. (2013). The impact of prison reentry services on short-term outcomes: Evidence from a multisite evaluation. *Evaluation Review*, 37, 274–313.

Laub, J. H., & Sampson, R. J. (2001). Understanding desistance from crime. *Crime and Justice*, 28, 1–69.

Laub, J. H., & Sampson, R. J. (2003). *Shared beginnings, divergent lives: Delinquent boys to age 70.* Cambridge, MA: Harvard University Press.

Laub, J. H., Sampson, R. J., & Sweeten, G. A. (2006). Assessing Sampson and Laub's life-course theory of crime. In F. T. Cullen, J. P. Wright, & K. R. Blevins (Eds.), *Taking stock: The status of criminological theory* (pp. 313–333). New Brunswick, NJ: Transaction.

Laws, D. R. (1995). A theory of relapse prevention. In W. O'Donohue, & L. Krasner (Eds.), *Theories of behavior therapy: Exploring behavior change* (pp. 445–473). Washington, DC: American Psychological Association.

Laws, D. R., & Ward, T. (2011). *Desistance from sex offending: Alternatives to throwing away the keys.* New York, NY: Guilford.

LeBel, T. P., Burnett, R., Maruna, S., & Bushway, S. D. (2008). The "chicken and egg" of subjective and social factors in desistance from crime. *European Journal of Criminology*, 5, 131–159.

Leibrich, J. (1993). *Straight to the point: Angles on giving up crime.* Dunedin, New Zealand: University of Otago/Department of Justice.

Loeber, R., Farrington, D. P., Hipwell, A. E., Stepp, S. D., Pardini, D., & Ahonen, L. (2015). Constancy and change in the prevalence and frequency of offending when based on longitudinal self-reports or official records: Comparisons by gender, race, and crime type. *Journal of Developmental and Life-Course Criminology*, 1, 150–168.

Loeber, R., & LeBlanc, M. (1990). Toward a developmental criminology. In M. Tonry, & N. Morris (Eds.), *Crime and justice: A review of research* (Vol. 12) (pp. 375–473). Chicago, IL: University of Chicago Press.

Maruna, S. (2001). *Making good: How ex-convicts reform and rebuild their lives.* Washington, DC: American Psychological Association.

Maruna, S., & Farrall, S. (2004). Desistance from crime: A theoretical reformulation. *Kölner Zeitschrift für Soziologie und Sozialpsychologie*, 42, 1–24.

McNeill, F. (2012). Four forms of "offender" rehabilitation: Towards an interdisciplinary perspective. *Legal and Criminological Psychology*, 17, 18–36.

McNeill, F., Farrall, S., Lightowler, C., & Maruna, S. (2012). Reexamining evidence-based practice in community corrections: Beyond "a confined view" of what works. *Justice Research and Policy*, 14, 35–60.

McVie, S. (2005). *Patterns of deviance underlying the age-crime curve: The long-term evidence.* Retrieved from http://www.britsoccrim.org/volume7/007.pdf

Mears, D. P., & Cochran, J. C. (2015). *Prisoner reentry in the era of mass incarceration.* Thousand Oaks, CA: Sage.

Ministry of Justice Research and Evaluation Team. (2014). *New Zealand crime and safety survey main findings.* Wellington, New Zealand: Ministry of Justice. Retrieved from http://www.justice.govt.nz/assets/Documents/Publications/NZCASS-201602-Main-Findings-Report-Updated.pdf

Moffitt, T. E. (1993). Adolescence-limited and life-course-persistent antisocial behavior: A developmental taxonomy. *Psychological Review*, 100, 674–701.

Moffitt, T. E., Caspi, A., Harrington, H., & Milne, B. J. (2002). Males on the life-course-persistent and adolescence-limited antisocial pathways: Follow-up at age 26 years. *Development and Psychopathology*, 14, 179–207.

Na, C., Paternoster, R., & Bachman, R. (2015). Within-individual change in arrests in a sample of serious offenders: The role of identity. *Journal of Developmental and Life-Course Criminology*, 1, 385–410.

Nagin, D. S. (2016). Group-based trajectory modeling and criminal career research. *Journal of Research in Crime and Delinquency*, 53, 356–371.

Odgers, C. A., Moffitt, T. E., Broadbent, J. M., Dickson, N., Hancox, R. J., Harrington, H., … & Caspi, A. (2008). Female and male antisocial trajectories: From childhood origins to adult outcomes. *Development and Psychopathology*, 20, 673–716.

Paternoster, R., Bachman, R., Kerrison, E., M'Connell, D., & Smith, L. (2016). Desistance from crime and identity: An empirical test with survival time. *Criminal Justice and Behavior*, 43, 1204–1224.

Paternoster, R., & Bushway, S. D. (2009). Desistance and the "feared self": Toward an identity theory of criminal desistance. *The Journal of Criminal Law and Criminology*, 99, 1103–1156.

Piquero, A. R. (2008). Taking stock of developmental trajectories of criminal activity over the life course. In A. M. Liberman (Ed.), *The long view of crime: A synthesis of longitudinal research* (pp. 23–78). New York, NY: Springer.

Piquero, A. R., Farrington, D. P., Nagin, D. S., & Moffitt, T. E. (2010). Trajectories of offending and their relation to life failure in late middle age: Findings from the Cambridge Study in Delinquent Development. *Journal of Research in Crime and Delinquency*, 47, 151–173.

Polaschek, D. L. L. (2012). An appraisal of the Risk-Need-Responsivity model of offender rehabilitation and its application in correctional treatment. *Legal and Criminological Psychology*, 17, 1–17.

Polaschek, D. L. L. (2016). Desistance and dynamic risk factors belong together. *Psychology, Crime & Law*, 22, 171–189.

Polaschek, D. L. L., & Kilgour, T. G. (2013). New Zealand's special treatment units: The development and implementation of intensive treatment for high-risk male prisoners. *Psychology, Crime & Law*, 11, 511–526.

Polaschek, D. L. L., Kilgour, T. G., & Wilson, N. J. (2018). Pre-release measurement of release plan feasibility: Scale development and predictive validity with high-risk prisoners. Unpublished manuscript.

Polaschek, D. L. L., & Yesberg, J. A. (2015). Desistance in high-risk prisoners: Pre-release self-reported desistance commitment and perceptions of change predict 12-month survival. *Practice: The New Zealand Corrections Journal*, 3(1), 24–29.

Polaschek, D. L. L., Yesberg, J. A., & Chauhan, P. (2018). A year without a conviction: An integrated examination of potential mechanisms for successful re-entry in high-risk violent prisoners. *Criminal Justice and Behavior*, 45, 425–446.

Rocque, M., Posick, C., & Paternoster, R. (2016). Identities through time: An exploration of identity change as a cause of desistance. *Justice Quarterly*, 33, 45–72.

Rodermond, E., Kruttschnitt, C., Slotboom, A., & Bijleveld, C. C. J. H. (2016). Female desistance: A review of the literature. *European Journal of Criminology*, 13, 3–28.

Roman, J., Brooks, L., Lagerson, E., Chalfin, A., & Tereschenko, B. (2007). *Impact and cost-benefit analysis of the Maryland Reentry Partnership Initiative*. Washington, DC: Urban Institute, Justice Policy Center. Retrieved from https://www.prisonlegalnews.org/media/publications/urban%20institute,%20impact%20of%20maryland%20reentry%20partnership%20initiative,%202007.pdf

Rosenfeld, R., White, H. R., & Esbensen, F. (2012). Special categories of serious and violent offenders: Drug dealers, gang members, homicide offenders, and sex offenders. In R. Loeber, & D. P. Farrington (Eds.), *From juvenile delinquency to adult crime: Criminal careers, justice policy, and prevention* (pp. 118–149). New York, NY: Oxford University Press.

Sampson, R. J., & Laub, J. H. (1993). *Crime in the making: Pathways and turning points through life*. Cambridge, MA: Harvard University Press.

Sampson, R. J., & Laub, J. H. (2003). Life-course desisters? Trajectories of crime among delinquent boys followed to age 70. *Criminology*, 41, 555–592.

Sampson, R. J., & Laub, J. H. (2005). A life-course view of the development of crime. *The Annals of the American Academy of Political and Social Science*, 602, 12–45.

Serin, R. C., & Lloyd, C. D. (2009). Examining the process of offender change: The transition to crime desistance. *Psychology, Crime & Law*, 15(4), 347–364.

Shapland, J., & Bottoms, A. (2011). Reflections on social values, offending and desistance among young adult recidivists. *Punishment & Society*, 13, 256–282.

Shover, N. (1996). *Great pretenders: Pursuits and careers of persistent thieves*. New York, NY: Westview Press.

Stouthamer-Loeber, M., Wei, E., Loeber, R., & Masten, A. S. (2004). Desistance from persistent serious delinquency in the transition to adulthood. *Development and Psychopathology*, 16, 897–918.

Taylor, C. J. (2013). Tolerance of minor setbacks in a challenging reentry experience: An evaluation of a federal reentry court. *Criminal Justice Policy Review*, 24, 49–70.

Travis, J., & Western, B. (Eds.) (2014). *The growth of incarceration in the United States: Exploring causes and consequences*. Washington, DC: National Academies Press.

Veysey, B. M., Ostermann, M., & Lanterman, J. L. (2014). The effectiveness of enhanced parole supervision and community services: New Jersey's serious and violent offender reentry initiative. *The Prison Journal*, 94, 435–453.

Visher, C. A., & Lattimore, P. K. (2007). Major study examines prisoners and their reentry needs. *NIJ Journal*, 258, 30–33.

Visher, C. A., & Travis, J. (2011). Life on the outside: Returning home after incarceration. *The Prison Journal*, 91(Suppl. 3), 102S–119S.

Walters, G. D. (2012). Developmental trajectories of delinquent behavior: One pattern or several. *Criminal Justice and Behavior*, 39, 1192–1203.

Ward, T., & Gannon, T. A. (2006). Rehabilitation, etiology, and self-regulation: The comprehensive Good Lives Model of treatment for sexual offenders. *Aggression and Violent Behavior*, 11, 77–94.

Willis, G. M., & Grace, R. C. (2008). The quality of community reintegration planning for child molesters: Effects on sexual recidivism. *Sexual Abuse: A Journal of Research and Treatment*, 20, 218–240.

Willis, G. M., & Grace, R. C. (2009). Assessment of community reintegration planning for sex offenders: Poor planning predicts recidivism. *Criminal Justice and Behavior*, 36(5), 494–512.

Wilson, J. A., & Davis, R. C. (2006). Good intentions meet hard realities: An evaluation of the Project Greenlight reentry program. *Criminology & Public Policy*, 5, 303–338.

Wilson, N. J. (2003). *The utility of the Psychopathy Checklist-Screening Version for predicting serious violent recidivism for a New Zealand offender sample* (Unpublished doctoral dissertatin). University of Waikato, New Zealand.

Wolff, N., Shi, J., & Schumann, B. E. (2012). Reentry preparedness among soon-to-be-released inmates and the role of time served. *Journal of Criminal Justice*, 40, 379–385.

Zhang, S. X., Roberts, R. E. L., & Callanan, V. J. (2006). Preventing parolees from returning to prison through community-based reintegration. *Crime & Delinquency*, 52, 551–571.

Part IV

Intervention: Theory, Design, Implementation, and Evaluation

21

Psychologically Relevant Theories of Crime and Offender Rehabilitation

Sharon Casey
Deakin University, Australia

As with any other behavior, crime is shaped by multiple internal and external factors which have the potential to impact at any point over the life-course. This is illustrated in the work of Haas and Cusson (2015), who attempted to identify the best theoretical approach upon which to base violence prevention programs. They asked a large sample of 20-year-old Swiss males (N = 21,312) to complete a series of questionnaires designed to test the link between those risk factors identified by the different theories and self-reported violence. Despite each theory[1] making some contribution, none predicted more than 30% of violent incidents. What did show greatest promise was a combination of items derived from different theoretical perspectives (i.e., psychopathology items in the survey as well as those that assessed rational choice, childhood trauma, and victimization). This clearly demonstrates the importance of considering a range of theoretical perspectives when designing interventions. In this chapter, some of the main theoretical perspectives on criminal behavior are reviewed.

General Strain Theory

Whereas earlier views of strain theory cited economic disparities (Merton, 1938) or subcultural values (Cloward & Ohlin, 1960; Cohen, 1955) as causal agents to offending, Agnew's (1992, 1995, 2001a, 2001b, 2006), general strain theory (GST) adopted a social-psychological approach, conceptualizing strain as a general phenomenon that could be either objective or subjective. In this theory, *objective strain evaluation* refers to the experience of an event or condition usually disliked by all members of an individual's group (e.g., physical assault), although evaluation varies as a function of group characteristics (e.g., age, gender). *Subjective strain evaluation* applies to events or conditions disliked by the individual who is (or has) experienced them. As subjective evaluations can differ, objective strain evaluations may be influenced by individual traits (e.g., irritability), personal and social resources (e.g., self-efficacy, social support), goals/values/identities, and other life circumstances. Closely linked

The Wiley International Handbook of Correctional Psychology, First Edition. Edited by Devon L. L. Polaschek, Andrew Day, and Clive R. Hollin.
© 2019 John Wiley & Sons Ltd. Published 2019 by John Wiley & Sons Ltd.

to subjective strain is the individual's *emotional response*. While two individuals may have the same subjective evaluation (e.g., dislike), their emotional response to strain may differ markedly (e.g., mild anger vs. outrage or anger vs. emotional distress).

Agnew (2001a; see also Agnew & Brezina, 1997; Broidy & Agnew, 1997) has identified three major categories of strain that are relevant to understanding criminal behavior: *failure to achieve positively valued goals* (e.g., autonomy, employment); *removal (or threatened removal) of positive stimuli* (e.g., loss of a romantic partner, theft of valued possessions); and *presentation (or threat of) negative or noxious stimuli* (e.g., victimization).[2] Moreover, Agnew's (2002) research suggests that strain can be categorized beyond *experienced* strain (i.e., physical victimization) to include *vicarious strain* (i.e., victimization experienced by those close to the individual) and *anticipated strain* (i.e., expectations of a current strain continuing or new strains being experienced). Some strains are also said to be more conducive to crime than others, particularly those of a higher magnitude: those which are severe, frequent, of long duration, recent, expected to continue into the future, and involving core goals, needs, values, identities, and/or activities. Associated with low social control, these strains result in a degree of pressure for criminal coping, given perceptions that they are unjust and involve the voluntary and intentional violation of relevant justice norms. Agnew (2013) has noted that strains of this nature are not only more easily resolved through crime but also expose the individual to anti-social models who reinforce criminal behavior and/or belief systems.

Irrespective of type, strain is said to result in *negative affect*, which, depending on whether blame is attributed to the self or others, may be inwardly (e.g., depression, anxiety, guilt) or outwardly directed (e.g., anger, hostility, frustration). It is suggested that criminal behavior develops when negative affect creates pressure to engage in some form of *corrective action*, with crime being one method of coping (Agnew, 1992, 1995). Although immediate relief can occur, this may only be temporary, thus increasing the risk of greater long-term negative consequences (Turanovic & Pratt, 2009). For example, crime might be used to reduce or escape from strains (e.g., theft to obtain money; see Rebellon, Leeper Piquero, Piquero, & Thaxton, 2009), to gain revenge against either the source of strain or its related targets (e.g., assaulting abusive peers; see Ousey, Wilcox, & Schreck, 2015), or to alleviate negative emotions (e.g., substance use to feel better; see Zweig, Yhaner, Visher, & Lattimore, 2015). Crime may also occur when strain leads to a reduction in social control (e.g., abuse during childhood resulting in a loss of attachment), promoting the social learning of crime (e.g., association with delinquent peers), and the development of crime-related traits (e.g., harsh discipline resulting in negative affect that is an antecedent for offending).

What GST offers the correctional psychologist is an explanation of: (a) causes and correlates of crime that lie in the offender's immediate social environment; and (b) how individual and environmental factors influence emotional reactions to subjective strain (e.g., not being treated how one would like to be treated; Agnew, 2001a). Strain has been shown to result in substance use (Agnew, & Raskin White, 1992; Zweig et al., 2015), antisocial behavior (e.g., Mazerolle, Burton, Cullen, Evans, & Payne, 2000; Ousey et al., 2015), a lack of achievement in education/employment (e.g., Baron, 2008), and association with antisocial peers (e.g., Agnew & Brezina, 1997). All are recognized as important risk factors for offending and, therefore, targets for intervention. GST also highlights the mediating[3] role of anger in aggressive behavior (e.g., Brezina, 2010) and both acquisitive (e.g., Baron, 2008; Rebellon et al., 2009) and violent (Baron, 2008) crime. GST can thus be used to articulate relevant theoretical elements of a rehabilitation program's rationale and how these might be addressed in treatment.

Developmental and Life-Course Theories of Offending

Dynamic in approach, developmental and life-course (DLC) theories are concerned with three main issues: the development of offending and antisocial behavior; risk and protective factors at different ages; and the effects of life events on the course of development. In this way, risk is conceptualized less in terms of static traits and more in relation to a developmental process. DLC theories are thus primarily concerned with understanding transactions between individual characteristics (e.g., cognitive abilities, temperament) and age-graded developmental contexts such as social factors (e.g., family and peer relations, school, employment) that serve to mediate both pro- and antisocial pathways, and thereby explain the continuity and stability of offending across the life span. Accordingly, DLC theorists (e.g., Catalano & Hawkins, 1996; Farrington, 2005, 2007; Moffitt, 1990, 1993, 1997; Sampson & Laub, 2005) have argued that their findings not only illustrate the heterogeneity of criminal behavior, but also demonstrate how crime data serve to contradict claims of an invariant age-crime relationship across groups, societies, and life stages.

Moffitt's (1990, 1993, 1997; Moffitt & Caspi, 2001) *developmental taxonomy of antisocial behavior* identifies two discrete categories of offenders, the adolescence-limited and the life-course persistent—each with its own distinctive pathway. Adolescent-limited offenders represent the majority of people who do not engage in delinquent or criminal behavior prior to or post the adolescent period. Lacking notable conduct problems in childhood, they display relatively little continuity or consistency in antisocial behavior over time and across situations. Moffit has argued this group is not maladjusted, but exhibits social mimicry of their early-onset peers that is motivated by a desire to demonstrate maturity and personal independence. The adolescence-limited offender eventually experiences a lack of motivation for delinquent or criminal acts as his or her biological and social ages converge (i.e., they exit the "maturity gap").

In contrast, a smaller group (around 5%) of life-course persistent offenders exhibit antisocial behavior at a much earlier age, with persistent problem behavior beginning in childhood and continuing into adulthood. Moffitt (1997) cites individual vulnerabilities and difficulties coupled with adverse child-rearing practices as responsible for their life-course persistent patterns of antisocial behavior. Difficult temperaments in childhood stem from what Moffitt describes as neuropsychological deficits (genetic and/or prenatal[4]) that impact on verbal intelligence (i.e., reading ability, receptive listening, problem-solving skill, memory, speech articulation, and writing) and executive function (manifested as inattention, hyperactivity, and impulsivity; Henry, Caspi, Moffit, & Silva, 1996; Moffit, 1993, 1997). According to Moffitt, these neuropsychological deficits make children restless, fidgety, destructive, non-compliant, and prone to violent outbursts; these children also lack the necessary parental support that might ameliorate any negative behavioral effects. Problem behaviors thus become increasingly entrenched and persist into adulthood (Moffitt, Lynam, & Silva, 1994).

Another DLC approach is Catalano and Hawkins' (1996) *social development model* (SDM), which specifies how risk and protective factors interact to encourage either prosocial or antisocial development (see Hawkins et al., 2007). Key to the SDM is the process of forming bonds with agents of socialization (e.g., parents, peers, school, and the wider community). Bonds form when socialization processes are consistent, that is, when reinforcement (reward) is consistent with that received for previous, similar involvements with a social unit.[5] In this sense, bonds serve as informal social controls that influence future behavior (Catalano et al., 2011).

Bond preservation requires continued conformity; non-conforming behavior will jeopardize the bond whereas conformity is rewarded with its preservation.

SDM theory suggests that an individual's strength of attachment to a social unit will be determined by the perceived level of reinforcement received in response to group involvement, with rewards determined by the skills and ability to facilitate engagement with the socializing unit. It is a sequence that characterizes both prosocial and antisocial developmental pathways; those on a prosocial trajectory will have opportunities to develop prosocial associations. If skilled, the individual will be reinforced during interactions (e.g., praised, accepted by peers), form bonds to prosocial others, come to believe in the conventional moral order, and engage in conventional conduct. Conversely, if antisocial opportunities for interaction are positively reinforced, the result may be close social bonds with deviant others, the internalization of antisocial values, and subsequent antisocial behavior. The *skill to successfully interact* thus plays an integral role in this theory as it suggests that simply being exposed to prosocial influences will not be sufficient to ensure healthy social development—those who lack effective social and/or emotional skills risk rejection and failure which, in turn, might lead them to seek out antisocial peers. Three "exogenous" factors are said to propel the individual along the pro- or the antisocial pathway: (a) his or her position in the social structure that provides differential opportunity; (b) external constraints (i.e., access to prosocial constraints); and (c) individual constitutional factors (e.g., hyperactivity, difficult temperament) (Hawkins et al., 2007).

Sampson and Laub's (1993, 1997, 2003, 2005) *age-graded theory of informal social control and cumulative disadvantage* also highlights the importance of informal social controls (e.g., involvement in family, work, school), suggesting that crime is more likely when social bonds are weakened or broken. Informal social controls, which stem from the social relations between individuals and institutions at each stage of the life-course, are characterized as a form of social investment or social capital, or what Hagan (1998) describes as the "knowledge and sense of obligations, expectations, trustworthiness, information channels, norms, and sanctions that these relations engender" (p. 503). Bonds to society create social capital and build interdependent systems of obligations that make crime too costly to commit (Sampson & Laub, 1993). Individuals accumulate variable amounts of social capital via these informal social control networks.

In terms of explaining the continuity of antisocial behavior across various life stages, those low in social capital (and with past criminal involvement) are said to experience cumulative disadvantage. This highlights one of the distinguishing features of Sampson and Laub's theoretical position—that criminal careers are characterized by change and dynamism. Prosocial adult social bonds, irrespective of the offender's age, serve to "right" previously deviant pathways and thereby place the individual on a trajectory toward more successful outcomes (Laub, Nagin, & Sampson, 1998; Sampson & Laub, 1993). A second key feature of the theory is the importance of human agency—the capacity to exercise control over one's life—as a determinant of criminal trajectories (Laub & Sampson, 2003). The individual as agent is viewed as having the capacity to construct his or her own life as a consequence of the choices made and actions taken with the opportunities that arise.

The key construct in Farrington's (2005) *integrated cognitive antisocial potential* (ICAP) theory is antisocial potential (AP). According to Farrington, the *potential* to commit antisocial acts is dependent upon particular cognitive processes (thinking and decision-making) around opportunities and victims. Characterized as both a long- and short-term phenomenon (Farrington, 2003), long-term AP is related to the development of stable, between-individual differences (e.g., impulsivity, strain, modeling, failure to develop prosocial attachments, life events), whereas short-term AP provides the opportunity or incentive to offend (e.g., anger, boredom, frustration, intoxication). In terms of type and trajectory, versatile rather than specialized offending is proposed, with AP levels peaking in the adolescent years due to the effects of maturational factors that directly influence crime rates (e.g., an increase in peer influence and a decrease in family influence). While risk factors have been hypothesized for long-term AP (e.g., desire for material goods, status among intimates, excitement, sexual satisfaction), these are said to result in high AP only when the individual habitually chooses antisocial methods. Offending is, therefore, the recourse of those who find it difficult to satisfy their needs legitimately, although the particular antisocial method used is said to be dependent upon physical capabilities and behavioral skills. One important point that emerges from the ICAP theory is the atypical nature of offending; even those labeled high risk are unlikely to spend all their time engaged in criminal activities (e.g., Horney, Osgood, & Marshall, 1995). Whether a crime is committed (for any level of AP) is dependent upon several factors, including: (a) cognitive processes (e.g., cost–benefit analysis); and (b) stored behavioral repertoire or scripts based on past experience. Furthermore, learning processes may lead to changes in long-term AP and future cognitive decision-making processes. The likelihood of this is greater when the consequences are either reinforcing (e.g., gaining material goods or peer approval) or punishing (e.g., legal sanctions; parental disapproval). Where the consequences involve labeling or stigmatizing the individual there is an increased likelihood that AP will be increased.

In summary, DLC theorists highlight a broad range of risk factors which contribute to crime and delinquency. These relate to individual children and young people (e.g., poor problem-solving skills; poor social skills; hyperactivity/disruptive behavior; impulsivity), their families (substance abuse; criminality; antisocial models; family violence and disharmony; abuse), schooling (school failure; deviant peer group; normative beliefs about aggression), and the wider communities in which they live (socioeconomic disadvantage; neighborhood violence and crime; cultural norms concerning violence as acceptable response to frustration; lack of support services). The key for the correctional psychologist is to match what the DLC approaches have to offer in terms of identifying risk factors with what is now known about effective interventions based on an evidence-based practice approach. For example, there is meta-analytic evidence (e.g., Lipsey & Wilson, 1998, 2001) to show reductions in reoffending of between 10 and 40% (depending on the quality of the intervention) when social development skills (e.g., interpersonal relations, self-control, school achievement, and specific job skills) are targeted. These skills are evident in all of the theories described above. As such, practitioners can use one or more theories to develop a conceptual framework to help understand the causal mechanisms of an individual's criminal behavior. Moreover, the focus on developmental patterns of continuity and change (e.g., Catalano & Hawkins, 1996; Sampson & Laub, 1997) with respect to transitions in social roles (e.g., first employment; development of agency) also provides an opportunity to identify individual and environmental factors that shape persistence and/or changes in behavior.

Rational Choice Theory

According to rational choice theory (RCT), we all behave in an instrumental, outcome-oriented way. That is, an individual will commit a crime if the *expected utility* exceeds its *expected costs* (i.e., instrumental rationality; Becker, 1968). Rather than being a passive victim of social conditions or driven by psychological traits (e.g., low self-control), the offender is thus perceived as someone who commits crime in an effort to "maximize physical well-being or social advantages while trying to minimize adverse effects such as sanctions" (Kroneberg, Heintze, & Mehlkop, 2010, p. 260). Two propositions underpin RCT: (a) that the individual weighs the costs or consequences of crime against the benefit of crime prior to engaging in criminal behavior; and (b) that he or she chooses criminal behavior when the rewards outweigh the costs.

Cornish and Clarke (1986) also make a distinction between two types of decision-making. *Criminal involvement* decisions are those which involve general decisions to engage in crime as opposed to satisfying needs and wants with non-criminal alternatives; this is said to be a multistage process that unfolds over a long period of time. The *criminal event* involves decision-making about the particular crime in terms of how, when, and where it will be carried out. In other words, the decision has been made by the individual that s/he is ready to engage in crime, but a range of situational factors still need to be considered before a choice is made to follow through on that decision (e.g., the risk of apprehension, the seriousness of the expected punishment, the value of the criminal enterprise, and his or her immediate need for criminal gain or, alternatively, the economic benefits are no longer available, the risk of apprehension is too great).

Rational choice theorists view crime as both *offense-specific* and *offender-specific*, suggesting that separate theoretical models are necessary for particular types of crime (Bouffard, 2002; Cornish & Clarke, 1987). The decision process leading to the use of illicit drugs (Che & Benson, 2014), for example, is thought to be different to the decision process for burglary (see Nee, 2015). Separate models are also required to explain *initial involvement*, the *criminal event*, and the decision to *persist in* or *desist from* criminal activity. In the crime of burglary, for example, the offense-specific thought processes might include: an evaluation of the target yield; the probability of security devices at the premises; police patrol effectiveness; availability of a getaway car; ease of selling the stolen merchandize; presence of occupants; presence of guard dogs; points of entry and exit (Nee & Meenaghan, 2006). The idea of offender-specific crime highlights that individuals do not engage in random acts of antisocial behavior. Rather, prior to committing a crime a decision is made by the individual about whether they have the capabilities necessary to commit the crime. This might include an evaluation of whether s/he possesses the skills necessary to commit the crime; whether s/he needs money or other valuables; whether legitimate financial alternatives to crime exist; his/her fear of expected punishment; his/her physical dexterity; and his/her health and strength. This is illustrated in the research of Nee (2004), who examined the motivation and decision-making of burglars and found a consistently high degree of planning in their decisions about which residential properties were targeted.

Although RCT has been criticized for being more applicable to financial market decisions than criminal behavior (other than simple instrumental crimes), Loughram, Paternoster, Chalfin, and Wilson (2016) offer a strong counter-argument. Rather than narrowly conceptualized formal sanctions (i.e., severity of punishment if detected) and expected utility (i.e., financial remunerations when apprehension is avoided), they highlight the non-financial gains that can influence decision-making. These can include perceived intrinsic or social benefits, such as increased social standing, pleasure and/or enjoyment derived from breaking social rules (Katz, 1990), or simply the thrill or kick associated with perpetrating the crime (Nagin & Paternoster, 1993). This is particularly relevant in the rehabilitation context where "cost–benefit analysis" is often a component of treatment programs that utilize cognitive behavioral approaches. Moreover, Bouffard (2007) has shown that when individuals are asked to generate their own consequences, the weight accorded to formal or informal sanctions is a product of individual difference factors. A cost–benefit analysis that simply attempts to change perceptions about the certainty and severity of formal sanctions is, therefore, unlikely to have the intended impact, particularly if the offender fails to see the relevance of that particular consequence. More beneficial would be an approach that is sufficiently flexible to ensure that the relevant consequences of crime for the offender are one factor that informs the change process.

General Theory of Crime

The most frequently cited, and perhaps most important, of the criminological theories (see Armstrong, 2005; Buker, 2011; Piquero, Jennings, & Farrington, 2010; Piquero, Jennings, Farrington, Diamond, & Reingle Gonzalez, 2016) is Gottfredson and Hirschi's (1990) *general theory of crime*, which is more commonly referred to as *self-control theory*. Conceptualized as a relatively stable individual characteristic, it is hypothesized that self-control is acquired through a process of early childhood socialization when the ability to defer gratification is learned. Low self-control is comprised of six interrelated characteristics: (a) impulsivity and the inability to delay gratification; (b) a lack of persistence, tenacity, or diligence; (c) risk-seeking; (d) a preference for physical activity over mental, verbal, or knowledge-based activity; (e) self-centeredness and indifference to others; and (f) a volatile temper. Gottfredson and Hirschi argued that, once established, individual differences tend to remain stable across the life-course. Low self-control is used to explain antisocial, delinquent, and criminal behavior: Behavior is based on the perceived short-term positive consequences of actions without any consideration of the long-term negative consequences that might result from those actions. This is said to explain why a high proportion of offenders tend to exhibit versatile rather than specialist offending patterns (Chapple & Hope, 2003; DeLisi, 2001; McGloin, Sullivan, & Piquero, 2009).

Based on their examination of several crime types, Gottfredson and Hirschi (1990) concluded that crimes: (a) are stimulating, dangerous, or thrilling; (b) require little skill or planning; (c) result in pain or discomfort for victim; (d) provide immediate, easy, and simple satisfaction of desires; and (e) supply few or insufficient long-term benefits. Moreover, an individual's criminal propensity (as defined by self-control) can be linked to other deviant behaviors—termed "analogous acts"—which also offer immediate benefit and gratification (e.g., smoking, excessive drug and alcohol use, risky sexual behavior) and may be related to crime. At a broader level, low self-control has also been associated with deficits in engagement with conventional social institutions (such as education, the workplace, marriage and the family) as success in these realms requires planning, commitment, and the ability to delay gratification.

According to Hirschi and Gottfredson (2001), whereas self-control is malleable up until late childhood (age 10–12 years), any improvement after this point occurs via socialization. Consequently, within-individual levels of self-control may increase over the life-course but between-individual rankings remain constant. Despite this supposition, there have been challenges to the notion of absolute stability in within-individual levels of self-control (e.g., Turner & Piquero, 2002; Winfree, Taylor, He, & Esbensen, 2006), with the most compelling evidence coming from Piquero et al. (2010), whose meta-analysis showed that changes in both self-control and delinquency in late childhood and adolescence followed earlier intervention (effect sizes ranging from a moderate, $d = .28$, to a substantial, $d = .61$). Effects were generally found to hold across different moderator variables and groupings as well as by outcome source (parent, teacher, direct observer, self-, and clinical report). A subsequent systematic review by Buker (2011) not only supported these findings but also concluded that the formation of self-control is much more complex than Gottfredson and Hirschi (1990) proposed. Buker identified several biological (e.g., genetic, neuropsychological, psychopathological) and social structural factors (e.g., family structure, neighborhood conditions, religious involvement) which, he proposed, affect the generation of self-control. Importantly, Buker's review supports the contention that self-control can be developed through direct and indirect intervention strategies.

Despite the polemic that has emerged following recent reviews, there is, nonetheless, utility in the fundamental premise of an association between low social control and antisocial, delinquent, and criminal behavior. Empirical evidence is available to support the relationship across different offense types, including property crime (Shekarkhar & Gibson, 2011), violent crime (e.g., Piquero, MacDonald, Dobrin, Daigle, & Cullen, 2005; Shekarkhar & Gibson, 2011), and substance use (e.g., Jones, Lynam, & Piquero, 2011), although this relationship appears to be more pronounced for males. Gottfredson and Hirschi's (1990) original theory also has merit in terms of identifying what an offender sees as the benefits and/or pleasurable outcomes of antisocial behavior. This can be useful when developing a cost–benefit analysis of an offender's behavior, including an explanation of the short-term positive gains associated with antisocial and/or risky behavior. Of particular importance is recent research which indicates that low self-control can be modified, highlighting the relevance of targeting constructs such as impulsivity and risk taking in offender rehabilitation programs.

Social Cognitive Theory

Social cognitive theory (SCT) is Bandura's (1999, 2001) attempt to integrate cognitive and behavioral models of human self-development, adaptation, and change from an agentic perspective. Human functioning is explained in terms of triadic reciprocal causation (Bandura, 1986) whereby internal personal factors (cognitive, affective, biological), behavioral patterns, and environmental influences function as interacting determinants that have multiple, bidirectional influences on one another. Consequently, cause and effect can move in a variety of ways: environment can affect behavior (classic behaviorism); characteristics within the person can influence behavior (trait approaches); and behavior can cause changes in the environment. Thus, while Bandura maintains the behaviorist notion that response consequences mediate behavior, he argues that behavior is strongly regulated via antecedent cognitive processes. Response consequences are also used to form expectations of behavioral outcomes, with the capacity to form these expectations enabling predictions about behavioral outcomes before behavior is performed. In other words, what and how the individual thinks affects behavior while, at the same time, how that person behaves will affect how they think.

According to SCT, two cognitive factors are central to understanding offending behavior: *perceived self-efficacy* and *outcome expectancies*. Perceived self-efficacy is concerned with an individual's beliefs in his or her capability to exercise control over his or her own functioning and challenging environmental demands (Bandura, 1997, 2001). From an SCT perspective, efficacy beliefs are the foundation of human agency: irrespective of what other factors might serve as guides or motivators, these are rooted in the individual's core belief in his or her power to influence his or her own actions. Whereas self-efficacy refers to control or agency, outcome expectancies relate to the perceptions of possible behavioral consequences. The construction of outcome expectations results from observations regarding the conditional relationships between environmental events in the individual and occur via two sources: (a) the immediate experience of certain behavior; or (b) the observation of others' experiences of the behavior in question. Bandura (2001) has argued that it is the ability to engage in the anticipatory evaluation of expected outcomes of current behaviors that promotes forethought-fulness, reflectiveness, and self-regulation.

Finally, Bandura's (1986, 2002) theory of moral disengagement provides a framework within which to understand how moral self-sanctions can be disengaged from inhumane con-duct (Bandura, 1986). SCT stipulates that moral reasoning is linked to moral action through "affective self-regulatory mechanisms by which moral agency is exercised" (Bandura, 2002, p. 101). Disengagement occurs progressively, initially with mildly harmful acts that through repetition lead to diminished self-reproof to a point where a lack of self-censure enables seriously harmful acts to be performed (i.e., routinized inhumane practices). According to Bandura, Barbaranelli, Caprara, and Pastorelli (1996), there are four major points in the self-regulatory system at which internal moral control can be separated from detrimental conduct. Thus an individual can disengage from self-sanctions by: (a1) re-construing the conduct (e.g., moral justification, euphemistic labeling, advantageous comparison); (b) obscuring personal causal agency (e.g., displacement or diffusion of responsibility); (c) misrepresenting or disre-garding the negative consequences of the action (e.g., minimizing, ignoring, or misconstruing consequences); and (d) vilifying the victims by maltreating, blaming, and/or devaluing them (e.g., dehumanization, misattributions of blame).

The utility of SCT with respect to understanding offending behavior is its foundation in human agency. Characterized by a set of core features that include intentionality and fore-thought, self-regulation by self-reactive influence, and self-reflectiveness about individual capabilities, quality of functioning, and the meaning and purpose of life pursuits, it demon-strates how individuals are both the producers and the products of agentic transactions within the broad network of social systems they inhabit. Bandura's (1986, 2002) theory of moral disengagement is particularly useful in terms of illustrating the manner in which people can choose to not activate self-regulatory mechanisms that govern moral conduct and thereby jus-tify their offending behavior: both to themselves and to others. And given the centrality of substance abuse to offending behavior, the hypothesized role of low self-regulatory efficacy and the pleasurable outcome expectations around illicit (and licit) substances offer some insight into the motivators for use and, by extension, the drug–crime nexus. Thus SCT high-lights the importance of increasing self-efficacy, particularly given the central role of efficacy in the self-regulation of motivation through goal challenges and outcome expectations, both of which are important in terms of maintaining commitment to change when faced with obstacles or the potential for failure (Bandura, 2001).

Integrated Theories

There have been a number of attempts to integrate competing theories in ways that can more directly inform assessment and intervention strategies. These apply for specific types of behavior, such as aggression and violence, and to offending behavior more generally. For example, five different theories underpin the *general aggression model* (GAM; see Anderson

1997; Anderson & Bushman, 2002), which tries to integrate existing "mini-theories of aggression into a unified whole" (Anderson & Bushman, 2002, p. 33). In so doing, its proponents suggest the framework has four main advantages over previously developed theories of aggression: (a) greater parsimony; (b) better explanations of aggressive acts based on multiple motives (e.g., both instrumental and affect-based aggression; (c) it can assist in the development of more comprehensive interventions to treat chronically aggressive individuals whose treatment attempts have previously failed due to the focus on single types of aggression or the use of single mini-theoretical approaches to treatment; and (d) its broader insights into child rearing and development issues.

An alternative approach, and one adopted by a number of criminologists (e.g., Thornberry, 1987; Thornberry & Krohn, 2001, 2005), is to integrate different theories, whereby the concepts and central propositions of pre-existing theories are combined into a new single set of integrated concepts and propositions. This method informs Andrews and Bonta's (2003, 2006, 2010) *personal, interpersonal and community-reinforcement theory (PIC-R)*, which is presented as a general personality and social cognitive approach to understanding criminal conduct that incorporates theoretical elements from behaviorism, social learning, motivational, control, social cognitive, and personality theories. People are seen as exercising agency over their behavior (consistent with SCT) and are, therefore, considered to be active, conscious, willful, and goal-oriented (Andrews & Dowden, 2007). Crime is viewed as the outcome when the rewards are perceived to outweigh costs, with various proximal and distal factors influencing this balance. These risk factors are categorized along four dimensions: *situational* (e.g., opportunities, stressors, facilitators, inhibitors); *personal* (e.g., antisocial cognitions, history of antisocial behavior, antisocial personality, biological factors); *interpersonal* (e.g., antisocial associates, antisocial family); and community (e.g., neighborhood, community justice influences). While the categories differ as a function of temporal proximity to the immediate situation, each has the propensity to influence the individual to commit crime.

Conclusion

Theories of crime and criminal behavior help the correctional psychologists to understand how the presence of risk factors leads to criminal behavior. This type of understanding is critical to both psychological assessment and intervention (Ward & Fortune, 2016). Because it is unlikely that any offense will be explained from a single theoretical perspective, it is important that practitioners have a broad understanding of those theories that are relevant to the offense and offender with whom they are dealing.

Notes

1 Theories tested included social conflict and reaction theories; differential association theory; rational choice and lifestyle theories; control theory; childhood trauma theory; and a psychopathology model.
2 Psychologists typically understand these constructs in terms of positive and negative reinforcement.
3 Mediating and moderating variables are examples of third variables. A mediating variable (mediator) can explain the relationship between the independent/predictor variable and the dependent/criterion variable. Mediation *for design* can be used in interventions designed specifically to change the mediating variable; mediation *for explanation* is used after the effect of X (the independent

variable) on Y (the dependent variable) has been shown to explain the mediating process of the third variable (see MacKinnon, 2011). Mediating for design is commonly used with interventions designed to affect behavior. Interventions based on theory hypothesize expected changes in the mediating variable and, if correct, show how changes to the mediating variable lead to changes in the outcome variable (i.e., there is a causal relationship between the mediator and the outcome variable). If the causal mediating variable (s) theory is correct, an intervention that changes the outcome will change the mediator. If it is hypothesized that anger (the mediating variable) is causally related to aggressive and violent behavior (outcome variable), an intervention designed to reduce the incidence of aggression and violence should result in a reduced anger. In contrast, a moderator is a qualitative (e.g., sex, ethnicity, socioeconomic status) or quantitative (e.g., treatment dosage) variable that affects the direction and/or strength of the relationship between an independent/predictor variable and a dependent/criterion variable. In an analysis of variance model, it can result in interaction effects (see Baron & Kenny, 1986). Moderation analysis is used to test, for example, whether an intervention has similar effects across groups (e.g., males and females); to identify iatrogenic effects in subgroups; and for specificity of effects (i.e., those for whom an intervention was successful and those for whom it did not work).

4 Prenatal conditions include poor nutrition, inadequate health care, and alcohol or drug use during pregnancy.

5 Members of a social unit generally share a common set of norms, beliefs, and values, thus an individual's bond will determine not only attachments to others within that unit but the level of commitment or investment the individual has in terms of adhering to or supporting the norms and values of that unit.

Key Readings

Andrews, D. A., & Bonta, J. (2010). *The psychology of criminal conduct* (5th ed.). New Providence, NJ: Matthew Bender.

Bandura, A. (2001). Social cognitive theory: An agentic perspective. *Annual Review of Psychology*, 52, 1–26.

Gottfredson, M. R., & Hirschi, T. (1990). *A general theory of crime*. Stanford, CA: Stanford University Press.

Moffitt, T. E., & Caspi, A. (2001). Childhood predictors differentiate life-course persistent and adolescence-limited antisocial pathways among males and females. *Development and Psychopathology*, 13, 355–375.

References

Agnew, R. (1992). Foundation for a general strain theory of crime and delinquency. *Criminology*, 30, 47–87.

Agnew, R. (1995). Testing the leading crime theories: An alternative strategy focusing on motivational process. *Journal of Research in Crime and Delinquency*, 32, 363–398.

Agnew, R. (2001a). Building on the foundation of general strain theory: Specifying the types of strain most likely to lead to crime and delinquency. *Journal of Research in Crime and Delinquency*, 38, 319–352.

Agnew, R. (2001b). An overview of general strain theory. In R. Paternoster, & R. Bachman (Eds.), *Explaining criminals and crime* (pp. 161–174). Los Angeles, CA: Roxbury.

Agnew, R. (2002). Experienced, vicarious, and anticipated strain: An exploratory study on physical victimization and delinquency. *Justice Quarterly*, 19, 603–632.

Agnew, R. (2006). *Pressured into crime: An overview of general strain theory.* Los Angeles, CA: Roxbury.

Agnew, R. (2013). When criminal coping is likely: An extension of general strain theory. *Deviant Behavior,* 34, 653–670.

Agnew, R., & Brezina, T. (1997). Relational problems with peers, gender and delinquency. *Youth and Society,* 29, 84–111.

Agnew, R., & Raskin White, H. (1992). An empirical test of general strain theory. *Criminology,* 30, 475–500.

Anderson, C. A. (1997). Effects of violent movies and trait hostility on hostile feelings and aggressive thoughts. *Aggressive Behavior,* 23, 161–178.

Anderson, C. A., & Bushman, B. J. (2002). Human aggression. *Annual Review of Psychology,* 53, 27–51.

Andrews, D. A., & Bonta, J. (2003). *The psychology of criminal conduct* (3rd ed.). Cincinnatti, OH: Anderson.

Andrews, D. A., & Bonta, J. (2006). *The psychology of criminal conduct* (4th ed.). Albany, NY: Anderson.

Andrews, D. A., & Bonta, J. (2010). *The psychology of criminal conduct* (5th ed.). New Providence, NJ: Matthew Bender.

Andrews, D. A., & Dowden, C. (2007). The risk-need-responsivity model of assessment and human service in prevention and corrections: Crime-prevention jurisprudence. *Canadian Journal of Criminology and Criminal Justice,* 49, 439–464.

Armstrong, T. A. (2005). Evaluating the competing assumptions of Gottfredson and Hirschi's (1990) *A general theory of crime* and psychological explanations of aggression. *Western Criminology Review,* 6, 12–21 Retrieved from http://www.westerncriminology.org/documents/WCR/v06n1/article_pdfs/armstrong.pdf

Bandura, A. (1986). *Social foundations of thought and action: A social cognitive theory.* Englewood Cliffs, NJ: Prentice Hall.

Bandura, A. (1997). *Self-efficacy: The exercise of control.* New York, NY: Freeman.

Bandura, A. (1999). Social cognitive theory: An agentic perspective. *Asian Journal of Social Psychology,* 2, 21–41.

Bandura, A. (2001). Social cognitive theory: An agentic perspective. *Annual Review of Psychology,* 52, 1–26.

Bandura, A. (2002). Selective moral disengagement in the exercise of moral agency. *Journal of Moral Education,* 31, 101–119.

Bandura, A., Barbaranelli, C., Caprara, G. V., & Pastorelli, C. (1996). Mechanisms of moral disengagement in the exercise of moral agency. *Journal of Personality & Social Psychology,* 71, 364–374.

Baron, S. W. (2008). Street youth, unemployment, and crime: Is it that simple? Using general strain theory to untangle the relationship. *Canadian Journal of Criminology & Criminal Justice,* 50, 399–434.

Baron, R. M., & Kenny, D. A. (1986). The moderator-mediator variable distinction in social psychological research: Conceptual, strategic, and statistical considerations. *Journal of Personality and Social Psychology,* 51, 1173–1182.

Becker, G. (1968). Crime and punishment: An economic approach. *The Journal of Political Economy,* 76, 169–217.

Bouffard, J. A. (2002). The influence of emotion on rational decision making in sexual aggression. *Journal of Criminal Justice,* 30, 121–134.

Bouffard, J. A. (2007). Predicting differences in the perceived relevance of crime's costs and benefits in a test of rational choice theory. *International Journal of Offender Therapy and Comparative Criminology,* 51, 461–485.

Brezina, T. (2010). Anger, attitudes, and aggressive behavior: Exploring the affective and cognitive foundations of angry aggression. *Journal of Contemporary Criminal Justice,* 26, 186–203.

Broidy, L., & Agnew, R. (1997). Gender and crime: A general strain theory perspective. *Journal of Research in Crime and Delinquency,* 34, 275–306.

Buker, H. (2011). Formation of self-control: Gottfredson and Hirschi's general theory of crime and beyond. *Aggression and Violent Behavior*, 16, 265–276.

Catalano, R. F., & Hawkins, J. D. (1996). The social development model: A theory of antisocial behavior. In J. D. Hawkins (Ed.), *Delinquency and crime: Current theories* (pp. 149–197). New York, NY: Cambridge University Press.

Catalano, R. F., Park, J., Harachi, T. W., Haggerty, K. P., Abbott, R. D., & Hawkins, J. D. (2011). Mediating effects of poverty, gender, individual characteristics, and external constraints on antisocial behavior: A test of the social development model and implications for developmental life-course theory. In D. P. Farrington (Ed.), *Integrated developmental and life-course theories of offending (Vol. 14): Advances in criminological theory* (pp. 93–124). New Brunswick, NJ: Transaction.

Chapple, C. L., & Hope, T. L. (2003). An analysis of the self-control and criminal versatility of gang and dating violence offenders. *Violence and Victims*, 18, 671–690.

Che, Y., & Benson, B. L. (2014). Drug trafficking wars: Enforcement versus smugglers and smugglers versus smugglers. *Journal of Drug Issues*, 44, 150–179.

Cloward, R., & Ohlin, L. (1960). *Delinquency and opportunity: A theory of delinquent gangs*. New York, NY: The Free Press.

Cohen, A. (1955). *Delinquent boys*. New York, NY: Free Press.

Cornish, D. B., & Clarke, R. V. (1986). Introduction. In D. B. Cornish, & R. V. Clarke (Eds.), *The reasoning criminal: Rational choice perspectives on offending*. New York, NY: Springer-Verlag.

Cornish, D. B., & Clarke, R. V. (1987). Understanding crime displacement: An application of rational choice theory. *Criminology*, 25, 933–947.

DeLisi, M. (2001). It's all in the record: Assessing self-control theory with an offender sample. *Criminal Justice Review*, 26, 1–16.

Farrington, D. P. (2003). Key results from the first 40 years of the Cambridge Study in Delinquent Development. In T. P. Thornberry, & M. D. Krohn (Eds.), *Taking stock of delinquency: An overview of findings from contemporary longitudinal studies* (pp. 137–183). New York, NY: Kluwer-Plenum.

Farrington, D. P. (2005). Childhood origins of antisocial behavior. *Clinical Psychology and Psychotherapy*, 12, 177–190.

Farrington, D. P. (2007). Advancing knowledge about desistance. *Journal of Contemporary Criminal Justice*, 23(1), 125–134.

Gottfredson, M. R., & Hirschi, T. (1990). *A general theory of crime*. Stanford, CA: Stanford University Press.

Haas, H., & Cusson, M. (2015). Comparing theories' performance in predicting violence. *International Journal of Law and Psychiatry*, 38, 75–83.

Hagan, J. (1998). Youth development as a capitalization process. In R. Jessor (Ed.), *New perspectives on adolescent risk behavior* (pp. 499–517). New York, NY: Cambridge University Press.

Hawkins, J. D., Smith, B. H., Hill, K. G., Kosterman, R., Catalano, R. F., & Abbott, R. D. (2007). Promoting social development and preventing health and behavior problems during the early elementary grades: Results from the Seattle Social Development Project. *Victims and Offenders*, 2, 161–181.

Henry, B., Caspi, A., Moffit, T. E., & Silva, P. A. (1996). Temperamental and familial predictors of violent and non-violent criminal convictions: Age 3 to age 18. *Developmental Psychology*, 32, 614–623.

Hirschi, T., & Gottfredson, M. G. (2001). Self-control theory. In R. Paternoster, & R. Bachman (Eds.), *Explaining criminals and crime* (pp. 81–96). Los Angeles, CA: Roxbury Press.

Horney, J. D., Osgood, W., & Marshall, I. H. (1995). Criminal careers in the short-term: Intra-individual variability in crime and its relation to local life circumstances. *American Sociological Review*, 60, 655–673 Retrieved from http://www.jstor.org/stable/2096316?seq=1#page_scan_tab_contents

Jones, S., Lynam, D. R., & Piquero, A. R. (2011). Substance use, personality, and inhibitors: Testing predictions about the reconceptualization of self-control. *Crime and Delinquency*, 61, 538–558.

Katz, J. (1990). *Seductions of crime: Moral and sensual attractions of doing evil.* New York, NY: Basic Books.

Kroneberg, C., Heintze, I., & Mehlkop, G. (2010). The interplay of moral norms and instrumental incentives in crime causation. *Criminology,* 48, 259–294.

Laub, J. H., Nagin, D. S., & Sampson, R. J. (1998). Trajectories of change in criminal offending: Good marriages and the desistance process. *American Sociological Review,* 63, 225–238 Retrieved from http://scholar.harvard.edu/sampson/files/1998_asr_trajectories.pdf

Laub, J. H., & Sampson, R. J. (2003). *Shared beginnings, divergent lives: Delinquent boys to age 70.* Cambridge, MA: Harvard University Press.

Lipsey, M. W., & Wilson, D. B. (1998). Effective interventions for serious juvenile offenders: A synthesis of research. In R. Loeber, & D. Farrington (Eds.), *Serious and violent juvenile offenders: Risk factors and successful interventions* (pp. 314–345). Thousand Oaks, CA: Sage.

Lipsey, M. W., & Wilson, D. B. (2001). *Practical meta-analysis.* Thousand Oaks, CA: Sage.

Loughram, T. A., Paternoster, R., Chalfin, A., & Wilson, T. (2016). Can rational choice be considered a general theory of crime? Evidence from individual-level panel data. *Criminology,* 54, 86–112.

MacKinnon, D. P. (2011). Integrating mediators and moderators in research design. *Research on Social Work Practice,* 21, 675–681.

Mazerolle, P., Burton, V. S., Cullen, F. T., Evans, T. D., & Payne, G. L. (2000). Strain, anger, and delinquent adaptations: Specifying general strain theory. *Journal of Criminal Justice,* 28, 89–101.

McGloin, J. M., Sullivan, C. J., & Piquero, A. R. (2009). Aggregating to versatility? Transitions among offender types in the short term. *British Journal of Criminology,* 49, 243–264.

Merton, R. K. (1938). Social structure and anomie. *American Sociological Review,* 3, 672–682 Retrieved from http://www.d.umn.edu/cla/faculty/jhamlin/4111/Readings/MertonAnomie.pdf

Moffitt, T. E. (1990). The neuropsychology of juvenile delinquency: A critical review. In M. Tonry, & N. Morris (Eds.), *Crime and Justice* (Vol. 2) (pp. 99–169). Chicago, IL: University of Chicago Press.

Moffitt, T. E. (1993). Adolescence-limited and life-course persistent antisocial behaviour: A developmental taxonomy. *Psychological Review,* 100(4), 674–701.

Moffitt, T. E. (1997). Adolescent-limited and life-course persistent offending: A complementary pair of developmental taxonomies. In T. P. Thornberry (Ed.), *Advances in criminological theory (Vol. 7): Developmental theories of crime and delinquency* (pp. 11–54). New Brunswick, NJ: Transaction.

Moffitt, T. E., & Caspi, A. (2001). Childhood predictors differentiate life-course persistent and adolescence-limited antisocial pathways among males and females. *Development and Psychopathology,* 13, 355–375.

Moffitt, T. E., Lynam, D. R., & Silva, P. A. (1994). Neuropsychological tests predicting persistent male delinquency. *Criminology,* 32, 277–300.

Nagin, D. S., & Paternoster, R. (1993). Enduring individual differences and rational choice theories of crime. *Law & Society Review,* 27, 467–496.

Nee, C. (2004). The offender's perspective on crime: Methods and principles in data collection. In A. Needs, & G. J. Towl (Eds.), *Applying psychology to forensic practice* (pp. 3–17). London, UK: Blackwell.

Nee, C. (2015). Understanding expertise in burglars: From pre-conscious scanning to action and beyond. *Aggression and Violent Behavior,* 20, 53–61.

Nee, C., & Meenaghan, A. (2006). Expert decision-making in burglars. *British Journal of Criminology,* 46, 935–949.

Ousey, G. C., Wilcox, P., & Schreck, C. J. (2015). Violent victimization, confluence of risks and the nature of criminal behavior: Testing main and interactive effects from Agnew's extension of general strain theory. *Journal of Criminal Justice,* 43, 164–173.

Piquero, A. R., Jennings, W. G., & Farrington, D. P. (2010). On the malleability of self-control: Theoretical and policy implications regarding a general theory of crime. *Justice Quarterly,* 27, 803–834.

Piquero, A. R., Jennings, W. G., Farrington, D. P., Diamond, B., & Reingle Gonzalez, J. (2016). A meta-analysis update on the effectiveness of early self-control improvement programs to improve self-control and reduce delinquency. *Journal of Experimental Criminology*, 12(2), 249–264.

Piquero, A. R., MacDonald, J., Dobrin, A., Daigle, L. E., & Cullen, F. T. (2005). Self-control, violent offending, and homicide victimization: Assessing the general theory of crime. *Journal of Quantitative Criminology*, 21, 55–71.

Rebellon, C. J., Leeper Piquero, N., Piquero, A. R., & Thaxton, S. (2009). Do frustrated economic expectations and objective economic inequity promote crime? A randomized experiment testing Agnew's general strain theory. *European Journal of Criminology*, 6, 47–71.

Sampson, R. J., & Laub, J. H. (1993). *Crime in the making: Pathways and turning points through life*. Cambridge, MA: Harvard University Press.

Sampson, R. J., & Laub, J. H. (1997). A life-course theory of cumulative disadvantage and stability of delinquency. In T. P. Thornberry (Ed.), *Advances in criminological theory (Vol. 7): Developmental theories of crime and delinquency* (pp. 133–162). New Brunswick, NJ: Transaction.

Sampson, R. J., & Laub, J. H. (2003). Life-course desisters? Trajectories of crime among delinquent boys followed to age 70. *Criminology*, 41, 301–339.

Sampson, R. J., & Laub, J. H. (2005). A life-course view of the development of crime. *The Annals of the American Academy of Political and Social Science*, 602(1), 12–45.

Shekarkhar, Z., & Gibson, C. L. (2011). Gender, self-control, and offending behaviors among Latino youth. *Journal of Contemporary Criminal Justice*, 27, 63–80.

Thornberry, T. P. (1987). Toward an interactional theory of delinquency. *Criminology*, 25, 863–891.

Thornberry, T. P., & Krohn, M. D. (2001). The development of delinquency: An interactional perspective. In S. O. White (Ed.), *Handbook of youth and justice* (pp. 289–305). New York, NY: Plenum.

Thornberry, T. P., & Krohn, M. D. (2005). Applying interactional theory to the explanation of continuity and change in antisocial behavior. In D. P. Farrington (Ed.), *Integrated developmental and life-course theories of offending (Vol. 14): Advances in criminological theory* (pp. 183–210). New Brunswick, NJ: Transaction.

Turanovic, J. J., & Pratt, T. C. (2009). The consequences of maladaptive coping: Integrating general strain and self-control theories to specify a causal pathway between victimization and offending. *Journal of Quantitative Criminology*, 29, 321–345.

Turner, M. G., & Piquero, A. R. (2002). The stability of self-control. *Journal of Criminal Justice*, 30, 457–471.

Ward, T., & Fortune, C. (2016). The role of dynamic risk factors in the explanation of offending. *Aggression and Violent Behavior*, 29, 79–88.

Winfree, L. T., Taylor, T. J., He, N., & Esbensen, F.-A. (2006). Self-control and variability over time: Multivariate results using a 5-year, multisite panel of youths. *Crime & Delinquency*, 52, 253–286.

Zweig, J. M., Yhaner, J., Visher, C. A., & Lattimore, P. K. (2015). Using general strain theory to explore the effects of prison victimization experiences on later offending and substance use. *The Prison Journal*, 95, 84–113.

22

Offender Rehabilitation and Theories of Behavior Change

Sharon Casey
Deakin University, Australia

While explanatory theories of crime (e.g., strain theory, Agnew, 1995; general theory of crime, Gottfredson & Hirschi, 1990) as outlined in Chapter 21 are helpful in identifying those factors that contribute most strongly to crime and deviancy (e.g., the role of deviant peers; lack of parental supervision; poor self-regulation; positive reinforcement of antisocial behavior), they offer little guidance on how behavioral change might be achieved. Models of offender rehabilitation (e.g., risk-need-responsivity, Andrews & Bonta, 2010; Good Lives Model, Ward & Maruna, 2007) can help with this task by providing frameworks from which offender needs can be understood and specifying targets for intervention, but they say little about the causal mechanisms through which behavior change actually occurs. The aim of this chapter, therefore, is to review prominent theories of behavior change and to explore how these can assist the development of more effective interventions to address offending behavior. While most interventions designed to change offending behavior typically describe the *therapeutic modality* (most notably group-based cognitive behavioral therapy), they fail to articulate the theoretical underpinnings that explain why targeted behaviors are expected to change (see Michie, Johnston, Francis, Hardeman, & Eccles, 2008). These elements should appear in both program and theory manuals and in program logic models and are illustrated in Table 22.1 to show how they might apply to the delivery of rehabilitation. Specific theories are then discussed.

The Theoretical Domains Framework (Michie et al., 2005) categorizes behavior change theories in relation to three key theoretical domains: motivation, action, and organizational. Of these, motivation and action theories are probably most relevant to the work of the correctional psychologist.

Motivation Theories

Social Cognitive Theory

As illustrated in Table 22.1, social cognitive theory (SCT) is both a motivation theory and an action theory. In other words, it can be used to explain behavior both in those who are unmotivated and in those who are motivated to change. Informed by a triadic reciprocity between

The Wiley International Handbook of Correctional Psychology, First Edition. Edited by Devon L. L. Polaschek, Andrew Day, and Clive R. Hollin.

Table 22.1   Behavior Change Techniques and Illustrative Theoretical Frameworks

Technique (Theoretical framework)	*Definition*
Provide information about the link between risk behavior and offending link (IMB)	General information about behavioral risk, for example, the increased susceptibility for aggressive and violent behavior associated with heavy alcohol use
Provide information on consequences (TRA, TPB, SCT, IMB)	Information about the costs and benefits of action or inaction, focusing on what will happen if the person does or does not perform the targeted behavior
Provide information about the approval of others (TRA, TPB, IMB)	Information about what others think about the person's offending behavior and whether others will approve or disapprove of any proposed behavior change
Prompt intention formation (TRA, TPB, SCT, IMB)	Encouraging the person to decide to act or set a general goal, for example, to make a behavioral resolution such as "I will not drink for the next week"
Prompt barrier identification (SCT)	Identify barriers to performing the behavior and plan ways of overcoming them
Provide general encouragement (SCT)	Praising or rewarding effort or performance without this being contingent on specified behaviors or standards of performance
Set graded tasks (SCT)	Set easy tasks, and increase difficulty until target behavior is performed.
Provide instruction (SCT)	Telling the person how to perform a behavior and/or preparatory behaviors
Model or demonstrate the behavior (SCT)	An expert shows the person how to correctly perform a behavior, for example, in group or on video
Prompt specific goal setting (CT/SRT)	Involves detailed planning of what the person will do, including a definition of the behavior specifying frequency, intensity, or duration and specification of at least one context, that is, where, when, how, or with whom
Prompt review of behavioral goals (SRT)	Review and/or reconsideration of previously set goals or intentions
Prompt self-monitoring of behavior (CT/SRT)	The person is asked to keep a record of specified behavior(s) (e.g., in a diary)
Provide feedback on performance (SRT)	Providing data about recorded behavior or evaluating performance in relation to a set standard or performance by other (i.e., individual receives feedback on their behavior).
Provide contingent rewards (OC)	Praise, encouragement, or material rewards that are explicitly linked to the achievement of specified behaviors
Provide opportunities for social comparison (SCompT)	Facilitate observation of non-expert others' performance (e.g., in group role-play; through a video; or using case study)
Plan social support or social change (social support theories)	Prompting consideration of how others could change individual's behavior to offer help or (instrumental) social support (e.g., "buddy" systems and/or provision of social support)

(Continued)

Table 22.1   (*Continued*)

Technique (Theoretical framework)	Definition
Prompt self-talk	Encourage use of self-instruction and self-encouragement (aloud or silently) to support action
Stress management (stress theories)	May involve a variety of specific techniques (e.g., progressive relaxation; mindfulness) that do not target the behavior but seek to reduce anxiety and stress
Relapse prevention (relapse prevention therapy)	Following initial change, help identify situations likely to result in readopting risk behaviors or failure to maintain new behaviors and help the person plan to avoid or manage these situations
Motivational interviewing	Prompting the person to provide self-motivating statements and evaluations of their own behavior to minimize resistance to change

Note. CT = control theory; IMB = information-motivation-behavioral skills model; TRA = theory of reasoned action; TPB = theory of planned behavior; SCT = social cognitive theory; SCompT = social comparison theory; SRT = self-regulation theory; OC = operant conditioning. © American Psychological Association. Reproduced from Abraham and Michie (2008, p. 382).

behavior, personal factors, and environment (Bandura, 1997), the utility of SCT as both a motivation theory and an action theory lies in its theoretical explanation of how and why people act as they do together with specifications for how to change behavior (via increased self-efficacy) using specific techniques (i.e., mastery experiences, modeling or vicarious experience, persuasion, or physiologically compatible experiences).

The primary constructs of SCT are applicable to behavior change in an offending context, with several identified as key constructs in Andrews and Bonta's (2010) General Personality and Cognitive Social Learning (GPCSL) perspective of criminal conduct; namely, self-efficacy and self-regulation in the immediate psychology of action, and modeling as a principle of antecedent control (i.e., when a change in the stimulus condition alters the probability of the behavior occurring). A prerequisite for change, *knowledge* identifies offending-associated risks and the benefits of a non-offending lifestyle. *Self-efficacy*, the foundation of human motivation and a core element of self-regulated action, provides the core belief that an individual's actions are sufficiently powerful to bring about the desired change. *Outcome expectations* specify the costs and benefits of offending and non-offending behavior and are core elements in most offender change programs (e.g., physical outcomes associated with drug use). *Proximal and distal goals* set the course for behavior change; broader social goals valued by the individual are likely to facilitate motivation whereas personal goals based on individual value systems provide self-incentives. Finally, *perceived facilitators and impediments* are the personal/situational factors which, in conjunction with the broader criminal justice system, have the potential to determine behavior. For the individual, self-efficacy is measured against successful goal attainment (i.e., having fewer impediments makes it easier to perform a behavior), while meeting proximal and distal goals can be impeded by the social and economic structure of the criminal justice system (e.g., availability of staff, resources, or commitment to a rehabilitative ideal).

According to Bandura (2004), self-efficacy is the focal determinant of behavior change. Whether guided or unguided, it involves the performance of tasks and/or activities that influence beliefs about the ability to undertake similar behaviors in the future based on past performance outcomes. Success provides a sense of mastery and serves to increase efficacy beliefs; with repeated success, the effects of occasional failures are more likely to be ameliorated. Although direct experience appears to have the greatest influence on self-efficacy, Bandura (1986) notes that behavior change can also occur simply through observation. The observer learns the modeled behavior, its consequences, and the verbal cues and instructions of the model. Behaviors likely to be the subject of modeling include: emotional responses, the extinction of fearful and avoidant behavior, altruistic behavior, and social and vocational skills. While reinforcement is important, four sub-processes also determine the extent to which observed behavior is modeled: attention (to ensure learning is not impeded); retention (to store necessary information for later retrieval); motor reproduction (practice to improve skills); and motivation (to imitate the modeled behavior).

In the context of offender rehabilitation programs, role-playing and behavioral rehearsal are frequently used to teach new, unfamiliar, and under-utilized social and interpersonal behaviors. A good example of this is cognitive skills training (e.g., *Thinking for Change*, Bush, Glick, & Taymans, 1997, 1998; *Cognitive Skills Training Program*, Porporino, Fabiano, & Robinson, 1991; *Reasoning and Rehabilitation*, Ross & Fabiano, 1985, Ross, Fabiano, & Ewles, 1988). In these programs, offenders are taught to stop and think before acting, how to generate new alternative solutions, consequential thinking, and decision-making about appropriate behavior. Role-playing or the practicing of real situations is typically used to consolidate newly learned coping strategies for situations that tend to prompt maladaptive habits and aggressive or criminal behavior (Lipsey, Landenberger, & Wilson, 2007). Other examples are *Aggression Replacement Training* (ART; Goldstein & Glick, 1987, 1994) and assertiveness training (Alberti & Emmons, 1974, 1975). One component of ART (the "skill-streaming" module) teaches prosocial behaviors through modeling and role-playing, while in assertiveness training, modeling is used by the therapist to help individuals to distinguish between desirable and undesirable behaviors (i.e., discrimination learning), with training typically centered around actual situations in which clients need to be more assertive. Observation is followed by behavioral rehearsal (i.e., imitating and practicing the modeled behaviors), which is accompanied by feedback from the therapist (e.g., suggestions for improvement; social reinforcement).

The use of feedback is important. As Bandura (1977, 1982) has noted, self-efficacy can be increased through verbal persuasion (i.e., telling someone they can perform a particular behavior increases the likelihood of it being attempted and self-efficacy increased). Individuals not skilled in making accurate self-appraisals often depend on others to provide evaluative feedback and judgments about the performance of new behaviors. Important here are the discussions that occur in group programs; motivational discussions can be used to persuade people that they have the ability to perform certain actions. Of course, in these situations the individual's response plays a role in determining his or her level of self-efficacy. How the individual feels about their abilities can be impacted by factors such as mood, emotional states, physical reactions, or stress, in particular how they interpret these reactions rather than their intensity (Bandura, 1994).

Self-Determination Theory

Self-determination theory (SDT; Deci & Ryan, 1985, 2000, 2008; Ryan & Deci, 2008a, 2008b) emphasizes the importance of inner resources for behavioral self-control and personality development. The individual is perceived as having a strong, innate, intrinsic motivational tendency which, optimally, results in the individual being agentic and inspired, striving to learn and master new skills and to apply his or her talents responsibly (Ryan & Deci, 2000). Unlike other theories, however, the focus is not on motivation but on those processes that elicit or sustain motivation (and those that subdue or diminish it). That said, SDT does recognize that people can experience a sense of alienation and may be passive or feel disaffected (Deci & Ryan, 2008), and SDT accounts for these variations by differentiating between the types and quality of motivation. So rather than simply considering total motivation levels, SDT makes a fundamental distinction between *autonomous* and *controlled* motivation. Autonomous motivation includes intrinsic motivation and extrinsic motivation whereas controlled motivation includes external and introjected regulation. Conceived on a relative autonomy continuum, *amotivation* (no intention to act) is at one extreme and *intrinsic* motivation (i.e., the tendency to seek out novelty and challenges, to explore, to learn due to the inherent satisfaction) at the other.

Four levels of external motivation sit between these two and vary in the extent to which regulation is autonomous. The least autonomous of the extrinsically motivated behaviors, labeled *externally regulated*, are performed to satisfy external demands or those governed by reward contingencies. *Introjected regulation* is next, referring to a regulation taken on but not fully accepted or experienced as part of the self (e.g., to avoid feelings of guilt or anxiety) and therefore remaining highly controlled. *Identification and regulation* is more autonomous extrinsic motivation that involves the conscious valuing of behavioral goals and an acceptance for regulating that behavior; the greater the personal relevance the more internalized the regulation and the greater the sense of autonomy. *Integrated regulation* is the most autonomous and occurs when behavioral regulations are evaluated and assimilated (i.e., a regulation is congruent with individual values and needs).

Another important element of SDT is that it does not suggest that behavior change moves in a stage-like fashion, in this case from external regulation toward greater autonomy (Ryan et al., 2011). Moreover, at any one point an individual may have multiple motives each with different levels of autonomy—each subject to change as a function of therapeutic climate or variations in social context or values—that will impact on their overall feeling of autonomy (Ryan et al., 2011).

Based on an extensive body of empirical research, several sub-theories have been postulated which seek to explain the different facets of self-determination theory. These are described in Table 22.2.

According to SDT, for behavior change to occur, the individual needs to internalize and integrate values and skills for change, which is achieved in treatment through the enhancement of autonomy, competence, and relatedness, which increase the likelihood that newly acquired behavioral regulations will be internalized and thus be maintained (Williams, Deci, & Ryan, 1998). The question then for the offender rehabilitation provider is how autonomy, competence, and relatedness can best be met. If autonomy is self-endorsed actions that are volitional rather than controlled, *autonomy support* involves the encouragement of voice, initiative, and choice while minimizing motivators such as control, contingency, and authority. In developing program content then, autonomy can be supported by offering a rationale for engaging in behavior that is meaningful; by providing clients with opportunities for participation and for choice; and rather than external controls (e.g., contingent rewards and punishments are minimized), a preference for actions based on personal reasons and values (e.g., Lynch, Vansteenkiste, Deci, & Ryan, 2011; Reeve & Jang, 2006). The argument is that the more an individual "owns" their reasons for change,

Table 22.2 SDT Sub-Theory Descriptions and Components

Sub-theory	Description	Components
Cognitive evaluation theory (CET; e.g., Deci, 1975; Deci & Moller, 2005)	Concerned with intrinsic motivation variability, particularly its capacity to be enhanced/reduced by external events. Intrinsic motivation only enhanced when competence accompanied by autonomy (i.e., behavior/action experienced as self-determined); if perceived as controlling, autonomy is undermined	*Autonomy:* Acting in according with one's own interests or values (i.e., behavior perceived as self-congruent and volitional) *Competence:* Propensity toward mastery and effectance (i.e., perception that environment can be influenced in desirable ways) *Relatedness:* Sense of connectedness or belongingness with others (i.e., feeling of meaningful closeness with others)
Organismic integration theory (OIT; e.g., Deci & Ryan, 1985, 2000; Ryan, 1995)	Forms of extrinsic motivation/ contextual factors (properties, determinants, consequences) that promote/hinder internalization and integration of regulation for behaviors	*Amotivation:* No intention to act *External regulation:* Actions performed to satisfy external demands or governed by reward contingencies *Introjected regulation:* Taken on (e.g., to avoid feelings of guilt or anxiety) but not fully accepted or experienced as part of the self; remains highly controlled *Identified regulation:* Conscious valuing of behavioral goal or regulation has been accepted; more autonomous or self-determined *Integrated regulation:* Evaluation and assimilation of behavioral regulations (i.e., regulation congruent with individual's values and needs); shares qualities with intrinsic motivation but still external as behaviors not performed for inherent satisfaction *Intrinsic motivation:* Undertaking an activity for its inherent satisfaction
Causality orientations theory (COT; Deci & Ryan, 2008)	Individual differences in how individuals orient to the environment based on information about initiation and regulation of behavior which is reflected in levels of self-determination across situations and domains	*Autonomous orientation:* Acting out of interest in and valuing of what is occurring; strong when psychological needs of autonomy, competence, and relatedness are satisfied *Controlled orientation:* Focus is rewards, gains, and approval; strong when some satisfaction of competence and relatedness needs but autonomy need thwarted *Impersonal orientation:* None of the three psychological needs are met

(Continued)

Table 22.2 (*Continued*)

Sub-theory	Description	Components
Basic psychological needs theory (BPNT; Deci & Ryan, 2008)	Elaboration of the relationship between autonomy, competence, and relatedness and psychological health and wellbeing. BPNT posits each need exerts independent effects on wellness; and that impact of any behavior/event on wellbeing direct response of relation with need satisfaction	*Autonomy* *Competence* *Relatedness*
Goal contents theory (GCT; Deci & Ryan, 2008)	Focuses on long-term goals/aspirations individuals use to guide their activities. Greater emphasis on extrinsic aspirations tends to be associated with more controlled orientation; intrinsic aspirations tend be associated with a more autonomous orientation	*Extrinsic goals:* Focus on external indicators of worth (e.g., wealth, fame, attractiveness) *Intrinsic goals:* More directly linked to satisfaction of basic psychological needs for autonomy, competence, and relatedness (e.g., affiliation, generativity, personal development)
Relationships motivation theory (RMT; Deci and Ryan 2014)	Concerned with development and maintenance of close personal relationships and the role of these in terms of adjustment and wellbeing (as satisfaction of need for relatedness alone not sufficient to ensure high-quality relationships)	*Decreased defensiveness and ego-involvement*

the more autonomous they are and thus the more likely to succeed. However, internalization also requires a sense of effectiveness and mastery, that is, a feeling of competence to change. Practitioners can support competence by assisting clients to develop clear and realistic expectations about what behavior change means for the individual, helping to formulate realistic and achievable goals, encouraging clients in the belief that a behavior is within their capabilities, and providing positive feedback when progress is made (Markland, Ryan, Tobin, & Rollnick, 2005). A key element of SDT is that gaining competence is facilitated by autonomy: Volitional engagement coupled with high willingness to act increases the likelihood of learning and the application of new strategies and competencies. Finally, relatedness is critical to ensuring a strong therapeutic alliance by ensuring the individual feels both significant and safe. Relatedness support comes via such factors as therapist warmth, genuine involvement in the therapeutic endeavor (Ryan & Deci, 2008a), unconditional positive regard (Roth, Assor, Niemiec, Ryan, & Deci, 2009), and involvement (Markland et al., 2005). Importantly, positive regard and involvement must be perceived as authentic; being respected, understood, and cared for are essential to the process of internalization (Ryan, 1995).

Action Theories

Cognitive Behavioral Theories

Rather than a singular approach, the term cognitive behavior therapy (CBT) has been used as an umbrella term for a diverse set of problem-specific interventions which have behavioral and cognitive models of psychological disorders as their common base (Roth & Pilling, 2008). Despite the underlying diversity, these therapies share three fundamental propositions: (a) cognitive activity affects behavior, (b) cognitive activity can be monitored and altered, and (c) behavior change in a desired direction can be effected through cognitive change (Dobson & Dozois, 2010). A meditational position is adopted whereby cognition mediates behavior change, and changes in cognition lead to modifications in behavior and mood (i.e., change is effected when idiosyncratic, dysfunctional modes of thinking are altered). The two critical elements at the core of behavior change from a cognitive behavioral perspective are cognitive structures (i.e., schemas and automatic thoughts) and cognitive mechanisms (i.e., cognitive distortions that require modification) (see Abel, Becker, & Cunningham-Rathner, 1984; Abel et al., 1989; Beck, 1967, 1972; Dozois & Beck, 2008).

The first of these, *schemas*, are acquired early (during infancy and childhood) and used to organize and process incoming information. Once developed, the processes of *assimilation* (incorporation of new information into a pre-existing schema) and *accommodation* (changing or altering a schema based on new information) enable them to be maintained, elaborated upon, or consolidated (Rosen, 1989). As schemas facilitate automatic/heuristic processing, there is a tendency to attend to and encode schema-consistent information while misinterpreting any ambiguous social stimuli in a schema-consistent manner (Fiske & Taylor, 2013). Consequently, there is the risk of early maladaptive schemas becoming established procedural memories, tacit beliefs, or representations of the self or the world. Instead of realistic appraisals being made by a well-adjusted individual, the result would be faulty schemas produce distorted perceptions, faulty problem-solving, and psychological disorders (Beck, 1967; Dozois & Beck, 2008). Researchers in the field of sexual offending (e.g., Mann & Hollin, 2010; Polaschek & Gannon, 2004; Ward, 2000; Ward & Keenan, 1999) have used the term *implicit theories* to describe the schemas (i.e., networks of beliefs and concepts) held by offenders about themselves, their environment, and their victims, that lead to interpretations of the world in offense-supportive ways.

Cognitive distortion, the second element, refers to the maladaptive processing of information and was originally used by Beck (1967) to describe "idiosyncratic thought content indicative of distorted or unrealistic conceptualizations" (p. 324). However, in the offender rehabilitation arena, it more commonly refers to various beliefs, attitudes, perceptions (Maruna & Mann, 2006), justifications, and rationalizations (Abel et al., 1984, 1989) that enable an offender to engage in sexually abusive behavior without experiencing the sense of guilt or anxiety that would usually accompany such a contravention of social norms. According to Ward, Keown, and Gannon (2007), because cognitive distortions reflect belief-based, value-based, and action-based evaluations, they are not driven solely by beliefs, a perspective which fits with the general assumption that cognitive distortions reflect offense-supportive beliefs (Gannon & Polaschek, 2005).

Second-Wave Approaches

The most commonly used CBT methods to date can be described as "second-wave" therapies. These typically fall into one of three classes: coping skills therapies, the focus of which is developing skills to assist in coping within a variety of stressful situations (e.g., the cognitive behavioral coping skills therapy developed for Project MATCH; see Kadden et al., 2003); problem-solving therapies which combine cognitive restructuring techniques and coping skills training procedures (e.g., D'Zurilla & Nezu, 2007; McGuire, 2005); and cognitive restructuring methods which examine and challenge maladaptive thought patterns in order to establish more adaptive thought patterns (e.g., Beck, 1970). In addition to the shared assumption that cognitive activity mediates the environment and, to some degree, the individual's adjustment or maladjustment, Kendall and Kriss (1983) have identified five further dimensions which characterize CBTs: the theoretical orientation of the therapeutic approach and theoretical target of change; aspects of the client–therapist relationship; the cognitive target for change; the type of evidence used for cognitive assessment; and the degree of emphasis which is placed on the client's capacity for self-control. Other (non-theoretical) similarities include that interventions are typically time limited, problem-focused, and either explicitly or implicitly educative in nature (Dobson & Dozois, 2010). Where the therapies differ is in the degree of orientation toward cognitive versus behavioral change.

Perhaps the most well-known of the second-wave approaches, *cognitive therapy* rests on the assumption of a reciprocal relationship between affect and cognition (i.e., one reinforcing the other) to the extent that the manner in which an individual structures reality will determine his or her affective state (Beck, 1971). Beck's (1970) typology of cognitive distortions was developed to describe systematic thinking and include concepts such as arbitrary inference, selective abstraction, over-generalization, magnification, and minimization. Although Beck developed his model to treat depression, it has been applied to a diverse range of disorders. The treatment goal is to supplant distorted appraisals with more realistic and adaptive ones, achieved via a collaborative, psycho-educational approach. Unlike other CBT modalities, a high degree of uniformity exists in terms of the principles and methodologies of cognitive therapy which involves the client engaging in specific learning experiences that are designed to teach them to (a) monitor automatic thoughts; (b) recognize the relationship between cognition, affect, and behavior; (c) test the validity of automatic thoughts; (d) substitute more realistic cognitions for distorted thoughts; and (e) identify and alter underlying beliefs, assumptions, or schemas that predispose the individual to engage in faulty thinking patterns (Kendall & Bemis, 1983).

In the offender rehabilitation field, despite the primary orientation of interventions being labeled cognitive behavioral, there is a heavy emphasis on the cognitive element. This has been particularly so in the field of sex offender-specific treatment for adults (see Jennings & Deming, 2013). Empirical evidence (e.g., Hall, 1996; Marshall, Anderson, & Fernandez, 1999) supports the use of cognitive therapy to change the cognitive distortions and maladaptive beliefs reported by sex offenders. Techniques found to be effective in reducing recidivism include: completion of daily thought records to identify distortions contributing to deviant sexual behaviors, labeling of maladaptive thoughts, and the generation of more adaptive thoughts in a group setting (Murphy, 1990). For non-sexual offenders, the underlying assumption that correcting cognitive distortions leads to improvements in behavior has seen cognitive restructuring used to improve offenders' cognitive skills (e.g., McGuire, 2005) and develop more adaptive reasoning patterns. The argument here is that interventions targeting cognitive distortions not only lead to an improvement in cognitions and behavior but also reductions in recidivism (Lipsey, Wilson, &

Cothern, 2000; Wormith et al., 2007). Two specific cognitive therapy programs, the Juvenile Cognitive Intervention Program (McGlynn, Hahn, & Hagan, 2013) and Responsible Adult Culture (RAC) program (Delvin & Gibbs, 2010), have reported that decreased cognitive distortions are associated with positive outcomes. In the juvenile study, fewer cognitive distortions were associated with reductions in conduct-disordered behavior, while in the adult study decreases were related to lowered recidivism rates and longer recidivism latency.

Third-Wave Approaches

The difference between second- and third-wave therapies (e.g., acceptance and commitment therapy [ACT], Hayes, 2004; Hayes, Strosahl, & Wilson, 1999); dialectical behavior therapy [DBT], Linehan, 1993; mindfulness-based cognitive therapy [MBCT], Segal, Williams, & Teasdale, 2001) is the shift in focus from first-order change strategies that examine the accuracy of perceptions to second-order change strategies that examine the functional utility of different ways of thinking or behaving through techniques such as mindfulness and acceptance. While there are obvious similarities between the two, given the focus on thinking and behavior, third-wave approaches differ in that attention is paid to "metacognitive" processes (e.g., distress about depression), which serves to facilitate awareness (a "mindfulness") of the appraisal process. This highlights another point of difference in some third-wave models in that cognitions and/or behaviors associated with emotional distress or other problems are not corrected but, rather, the "change" is a recognition of faulty metacognitive processes.

Schema-focused therapy (Kellogg & Young, 2006; Young, 1999) was initially developed to treat borderline personality disorder (BPD) and long-standing or relapsing conditions (e.g., chronic depression). According to Young (1999), the failure to meet the developmental needs in a child's relationships with significant others results in early maladaptive schemas which, in turn, determine an individual's level of vulnerability in interpersonal relationships and their (interpersonal) coping behaviors. Early maladaptive schemas are self-perpetuating (Kellogg & Young, 2006) and reinforced by subsequent adverse relationships that serve to foster maladaptive coping styles. When perceived as problematic, painful, or distressing, early maladaptive schemas are dealt with through *schema avoidance* to ensure the problematic schemas are activated, *schema surrender* (i.e., conforming to the schema by changing perceptions and behavior), and *schema neutralization/overcompensation* (acting to neutralize a schema by behaving in a manner opposite to that predicted by the schema). *Schema mode* describes a natural grouping of early maladaptive schemas, distinct mood states, and coping styles and is said to represent that part of the self which develops early in life, when basic needs were not met and were not fully integrated with other facets of the self into an integrated self-system.

DBT (Linehan, 1993), initially developed for chronically parasuicidal women diagnosed with BPD, has subsequently been adapted for the treatment of, for example, comorbid BPD and substance use disorder (see Hunter, Ronsenthal, Lynch, & Linehan, 2016; McMain, Sayrs, Dimeff, & Linehan, 2007), perpetrators (Fruzzetti & Levensky, 2000) and victims (Iverson, Shenk, & Fruzzetti, 2009) of domestic violence, forensic inpatients (Evershed et al., 2003; McCann, Ball, & Ivanoff, 2000), and aggressive/violent offenders (Rosenfeld et al., 2007; Shelton, Keston, Zhang & Trestman, 2011). According to Linehan, BPD occurs as the response to a reciprocal transaction between *emotional vulnerability* (i.e., heightened sensitivity and reactivity and a delayed return to baseline following emotional arousal), an *invalidating environment* (characterized by punishing, ignoring, or trivializing an individual's thoughts, emotions, or self-initiated behavior; can include sexual, physical, and emotional abuse), and *emotional dysregulation* (the multidimensional construct that underlies BPD criterion behaviors). Given the assumption that problem behaviors are the product of dysregulated emotions or maladaptive ways of changing emotional experiences, treatment focuses on reducing ineffective responses linked to dysregulated emotions (Lynch, Chapman, Rosenthal, Kuo, & Linehan, 2006).

Self-Regulation Theory

Self-regulation has been described by Baumeister and Vohs (2007) as the "self's capacity for altering its behaviors" (p. 115). Characterized by a broad range of volitional factors (e.g., goal setting, self-monitoring, activation and the use of self-evaluation, self-efficacy; see Karoly, 1993) that allow for increased flexibility and adaptability, self-regulation enables the individual to adjust to a broad range of social and situational demands. At its core is developing the capacity to override and/or alter responses in ways that allow the individual to constrain unwanted urges and thereby gain control over undesirable responses (Polivy, 1998). According to the strength model (Baumeister, Heatherton, & Tice, 1994; Baumeister & Vohs, 2007; Baumeister, Vohs, & Tice, 2007), self-regulation is said to be comprised of four main processes: standards, monitoring, self-regulatory strength, and, most recently, motivation. The model identifies two types of self-regulation failure: under-regulation (i.e., a failure to exert control over the self) and mis-regulation (i.e., exerting control in misguided or counter-productive ways which then fail to produce the desired result). Failure of any one of the basic features of self-regulation can lead to either type of regulation failure.

A more detailed account of the four components of the strength model is as follows. First, *standards* (e.g., ideals, norms, goals, rules, guidelines) provide the endpoint of the self-regulatory chain and therefore need to be clear, well-defined, and moderate; if standards are too low, there may be a failure to motivate, and standards that are too high may be demotivating. *Monitoring* relies heavily on attention and self-awareness, with attention particularly important to comparisons between the self (or aspects of the self) and standards. When comparisons fall short, self-regulation serves to initiate change-specific operations (e.g., overriding impulses) that elevate the self to the relevant standard. One difficulty with monitoring is its focus on the present (Vohs & Schmeichel, 2003), which increases vulnerability to immediate urges and impulses and makes long-term goals appear less of an imperative. *Self-regulatory strength* (or willpower) is best described as the overall level of self-regulatory ability an individual has available in their pursuit of a given goal (Baumeister et al., 2007; Muraven & Baumeister, 2000). Individual differences have been noted, however, in self-regulatory strengths (and deficits) across a variety of domains (e.g., delay of gratification; see Baumeister & Heatherton, 1996). Self-regulating also appears to be resource limited even for those high in self-regulatory strength, resulting in the temporary failure of self-control when dealing with simultaneous demands (e.g., Muraven & Baumeister, 2000; Vohs & Heatherton, 2000). Finally, *motivation* is considered one of the four necessary "ingredients" for effective self-regulation. Clear standards, effective monitoring, and abundant resources will not be sufficient to enable self-regulation if the individual does not care about reaching his or her goal. That said, it is possible to compensate where one of the four ingredients (i.e., standards, monitoring, self-regulatory strength, motivation) is insufficient. For example, motivation to achieve a standard can help to ameliorate problems associated with low levels of self-regulatory strength. But there are limits on the extent to which motivation can be used to avoid self-regulation failure. While it may be a highly effective substitute for self-regulatory strength, in the absence of a clear standard it may be less so (i.e., the desire to self-regulate would be present but there would be no knowledge about a desirable response).

The connection between self-regulation and emotion regulation occurs by virtue of potentially emotion-arousing situations that might be encountered on a regular basis (Bauer & Baumeister, 2011). In much the same way as a current and desired state are compared in terms of goal attainment, one's current emotional state is compared to a desired emotional state and steps then taken to bring that current state in line with the desired emotional state. Emotion regulation processes are hierarchical in nature (Carver & Scheier, 1982). While concrete behaviors are employed to target lower-order goals (e.g., "Take a deep breath and count to 10"), more abstract principles underpin higher-order goals (e.g., "I want to be in control of my emotions"). Emotion regulation can be used to obtain a range of outcomes, including reductions in subjective distress and the frequency of unacceptable emotion-related behaviors (Kanfer & Kantrowitz, 2002). And like other self-regulatory actions, emotion regulation is subject to a limited pool of resources, with depletion a function of the type of regulatory response used.

Behavior Enactment: Transtheoretical Model of Change

Self-regulation models that describe volitional (or self-determined) processes involved in the initiation and maintenance of actions used to achieve particular goals are known as behavior enactment models. Focusing on the mechanisms that enable the goal setting and goal striving central to behavior change (de Ridder & de Wit, 2006), they are underpinned by two important assumptions: first, that behavior change processes pass through distinct stages, with various factors influencing stage transition; and second, that behavior in each stage is qualitatively different, which requires that interventions targeting change be varied from stage to stage (Weinstein, Rothman, & Sutton, 1998). The transtheoretical model (TTM) of change (Prochaska & DiClemente, 1984, 1986) is perhaps the most influential of the behavior enactment models, particularly in the treatment of addictive/problem behaviors (see Brown, Melchior, Panter, Slaughter, & Huba, 2000; Davidson, Rollnick, & MacEwan, 1991) as well as partner/domestic violence (Begun, Shelley, Strodthoff, & Short, 2001; Easton, Swan, & Sinha, 2000) and general offender rehabilitation (Hemphill & Howell, 2000; McMurran et al., 1998; Williamson, Day, Howells, Bubner, & Jauncey, 2003).

According to the TTM, individuals attempting to change problem behaviors progress through an invariant sequence of change stages, each characterized by different attitudes, thoughts, beliefs, and values toward the change process and accompanied by specific behavioral and change strategies (Begun et al., 2001). Change is not seen as sudden but, more typically, as a prescribed chain involving growing problem awareness, formulating a decision to act differently, developing change strategies during a transitional phase, and strategy implementation (Tucker, Donovan, & Marlatt, 1999). Table 22.3 outlines the identifiable stages and provides examples of potential change strategies. The stages are recursive in nature (Begun et al., 2001) and an individual may undergo several change "cycles" before achieving long-term maintenance (Prochaska, DiClemente, & Norcross, 1992). And while there is periodic spiraling back to previous stages followed by forward progress, these relapses are seen as a predictable pattern in the change process rather than failure. Relapses are reframed, viewed as learning opportunities, and refined as future change opportunities and maintenance.

Although it is the stages of change component that receives greatest attention, the TTM is informed by three key variables: processes of change, decisional balance, and self-efficacy

Table 22.3 Stages of Change Model and Potential Change Strategies

Concept	Definition	Application
Precontemplation	No wish to change/no recognition of a problem	Increase awareness of need for change; personalize information about risks and benefits
Contemplation	Intention to change problem behavior within the next 6 months	Motivate; encourage making specific plans
Preparation	Intention to take immediate action, usually measured as within the next month	Assist with developing and implementing concrete action plans; help set gradual goals
Action	Characterized by specific, overt modifications within the past 6 months	Assist with feedback, problem solving, social support, and reinforcement
Maintenance	Relapse prevention	Assist with coping, reminders, finding alternatives, avoiding slips/relapses (as applicable)
Termination	Change process is complete/no further need to prevent relapse	

(Prochaska & DiClemente, 1986). Conceptually, stages of change explain *when* change is likely to take place; processes of change explains *how* change occurs; decisional balance is an assessment of the *benefits (pros) and costs (cons)* of changing a specific behavior, and self-efficacy (i.e., confidence and temptations) is the individual's *perceived ability* on a given task. The 10 processes of change describe what the individual does to bring about change in affect, behavior, cognitions, or relationships (see DiClemente & Prochaska, 1985; Prochaska & DiClemente, 1986). Five are experiential (consciousness raising/getting the facts; dramatic relief/paying attention to feelings; environmental re-evaluation/noticing one's effect on others; self-re-evaluation/creating a new self-image; and social liberation/noticing public support) and five are behavioral (self-liberation/making a commitment; counter-conditioning/using substitutes; helping relationships/getting support; reinforcement management/using rewards; and stimulus control/managing one's environment). Decisional balance is the mechanism by which an evaluation can be made of an individual's assessment of the benefits (pros) and losses (cons) of behavior change. Five decision-making styles (see Janis & Mann, 1977) are used in making decisions about behavior change: unconflicted adherence (i.e., a decision not to change or lack of belief that there is a "best" option); unconflicted change (i.e., little conflict that behavior change is the best option to pursue); defensive avoidance (i.e., the "least worst" solution from a range of poor options, made with little appraisal of all available options); hypervigilance (i.e., a combination of high anxiety regarding the decision and limited appraisal of the pros and cons of adopting a particular course of action), and vigilance (i.e., an unbiased search for relevant information; careful evaluation of alternatives). Self-efficacy, perhaps the most important construct when assessing intermediate outcomes and predicting future success, is comprised of two components. *Confidence* refers to judgments about the ability to deal with high-risk situations without engaging in specific problem behavior (Prochaska, Redding, & Evers, 1997). Situation-specific, confidence has been shown to linearly increase across the stages of change. *Temptation*, the strength of an individual's desire to engage in specific problem behavior despite high-risk situations, generally decreases across the stages, most obviously between preparation and maintenance (Prochaska & DiClemente, 1984). Finally, the TTM describes five *levels of change* that represents where psychological problems are located within an individual. In ascending order of complexity these are: (a) symptom/situational problems; (b) maladaptive cognitions; (c) current interpersonal conflicts; (d) family/systems conflicts; and, (e) intrapersonal conflicts. While problem behavior can be influenced by multiple conflicts at different levels, this attribution may not be made by the individual concerned, with treatment also limited to one or two levels (Grimley, Prochaska, Velicer, Blais, & DiClemente, 1994). However, just as problems at one level are not experienced in isolation, change on one level is also said to bring about change on others.

The application of the TTM in an offending context has primarily focused on the stages of change component, in particular the recommendation that it be used prior to allocation to treatment programs. This approach would appear to be more effective when done in conjunction with the use of treatment readiness measures (see Day, Casey, Ward, Howells, & Vess, 2010). The rationale is twofold: On the one hand, it serves to optimize treatment outcomes for program participants, while on the other, it helps to ensure that limited resources are put to effective use.

Conclusion

The purpose of this chapter has been to highlight the utility of adopting a theory-based approach to offender rehabilitation and to outline some best-known theories of change. While the past decade or so has seen considerable attention paid to developing the therapeutic modality for program delivery, the underlying theories of behavior change are rarely articulated. A program's change theory is the theory of action as it guides the development of an intervention and serves as the basis for evaluation. Change theories are particularly important in terms of making explicit assumptions about how an intervention will work.

Key Readings

Bandura, A. (1997). *Self-efficacy: The exercise of control*. New York, NY: Freeman.

Baumeister, R. F., & Vohs, K. D. (2007). Self-regulation, ego depletion, and motivation. *Social and Personality Psychology Compass*, 1, 115–128.

Linehan, M. M. (1993). *Cognitive-behavioral treatment of borderline personality disorder*. New York, NY: Guilford Press.

Ryan, R. M., Lynch, M. F., Vansteenkiste, M., & Deci, E. L. (2011). Motivation and autonomy in counseling, psychotherapy, and behavior change: A look at theory and practice. *The Counseling Psychologist*, 39, 193–260.

References

Abel, G. G., Becker, J. V., & Cunningham-Rathner, J. (1984). Complications, consent, and cognitions in sex between children and adults. *International Journal of Law and Psychiatry*, 7, 89–103.

Abel, G. G., Gore, D. K., Holland, C. L., Camp, N., Becker, J. V., & Rathner, B. A. (1989). The measurement of the cognitive distortions of child molesters. *Annals of Sex Research*, 2, 135–153.

Abraham, C., & Michie, S. (2008). A taxonomy of behavior change techniques used in interventions. *Health Psychology, 27*, 379–387.

Agnew, R. (1995). Testing the leading crime theories: An alternative strategy focusing on motivational process. *Journal of Research in Crime and Delinquency, 32*, 363–398.

Alberti, R., & Emmons, M. (1974). *Your perfect right: A guide to assertive behavior.* San Luis Obispo, CA: Impact.

Alberti, R., & Emmons, M. (1975). *Stand up, speak out, talk back.* New York, NY: Pocket Books.

Andrews, D. A., & Bonta, J. (2010). *The psychology of criminal conduct* (5th ed.). New Providence, NJ: Matthew Bender.

Bandura, A. (1977). *Social learning theory.* Englewood Cliffs, NJ: Prentice Hall.

Bandura, A. (1982). Self-efficacy mechanism in human agency. *American Psychologist, 37*, 122–147.

Bandura, A. (1986). *Social foundations of thought and action: A social cognitive theory.* Englewood Cliffs, NJ: Prentice Hall.

Bandura, A. (1994). Regulative function of perceived self-efficacy. In M. G. Rumsey, C. B. Walker, & J. H. Harris (Eds.), *Personal selection and classification* (pp. 261–271). Hillsdale, NJ: Lawrence Erlbaum.

Bandura, A. (1997). *Self-efficacy: The exercise of control.* New York, NY: Freeman.

Bandura, A. (2004). Health promotion by social cognitive means. *Health Education & Behavior, 31*, 143–164.

Bauer, I. M., & Baumeister, R. F. (2011). Self-regulatory strength. In K. D. Vohs, & R. F. Baumeister (Eds.), *Handbook of self-regulation: Research, theory, and applications* (2nd ed.) (pp. 64–82). New York, NY: Guilford Press.

Baumeister, R. F., & Heatherton, T. F. (1996). Self-regulation failure: An overview. *Psychological Inquiry, 7*, 1–15.

Baumeister, R. F., Heatherton, T. F., & Tice, D. M. (1994). *Losing control: How and why people fail at self-regulation.* San Diego, CA: Academic Press.

Baumeister, R. F., & Vohs, K. D. (2007). Self-regulation, ego depletion, and motivation. *Social and Personality Psychology Compass, 1*, 115–128.

Baumeister, R. F., Vohs, K. D., & Tice, D. M. (2007). The strength model of self-control. *Current Directions in Psychological Science, 16*, 351–355.

Beck, A. T. (1967). *Depression: Causes and treatment.* Philadelphia, PA: University of Pennsylvania Press.

Beck, A. T. (1970). Cognitive therapy: Nature and relation to behavior therapy. *Behavior Therapy, 1*, 184–200.

Beck, A. T. (1971). Cognition, affect, and psychopathology. *Archives of General Psychiatry, 24*, 495–500.

Beck, A. T. (1972). The phenomena of depression: A synthesis. In D. Offer, & D. X. Freeman (Eds.), *Modern psychiatry and clinical research* (pp. 136–158). New York, NY: Basic Books.

Beck, A. T. (1976). *Cognitive therapy and the emotional disorders.* New York, NY: International Universities Press.

Begun, A. L., Shelley, G., Strodthoff, T., & Short, L. (2001). Adopting a stages of change approach for individuals who are violent with their intimate partners. *Journal of Aggression, Maltreatment & Trauma, 5*(2), 105–127.

Brown, V. B., Melchior, L. A., Panter, A. T., Slaughter, R., & Huba, G. J. (2000). Women's steps of change and entry into drug abuse treatment. A multidimensional stages of change model. *Journal of Substance Abuse Treatment, 18*, 231–240.

Bush, J., Glick, B., & Taymans, J. (1997, revised 1998). *Thinking for a Change: Integrated cognitive behavior change program.* Washington, DC: National Institute of Corrections, US Department of Justice. Retrieved from http://trainercounselor.com/wp-content/uploads/2011/11/016672-Curriculum.pdf

Carver, C. S., & Scheier, M. F. (1982). Control theory: A useful conceptual framework for personality-social, clinical, and health psychology. *Psychological Bulletin, 92*, 111–135.

Davidson, R., Rollnick, S., & MacEwan, I. (1991). *Counselling problem drinkers.* London, UK: Routledge.

Day, A., Casey, S., Ward, T., Howells, K., & Vess, J. (2010). *Transitions to better lives: Offender readiness and rehabilitation.* Cullompton, UK: Willan.

de Ridder, D. T. D., & de Wit, J. B. F. (2006). Self-regulation in health behavior: Concepts, theories, and central issues. In D. T. D. de Ridder, & J. B. F. de Wit (Eds.), *Self-regulation in health behavior* (pp. 1–23). Chichester, UK: Wiley.

Deci, E. L. (1975). *Intrinsic motivation.* New York, NY: Plenum Press.

Deci, E. L., & Moller, A. C. (2005). The concept of competence: A starting place for understanding intrinsic motivation and self-determined extrinsic motivation. In A. J. Elliot, & C. J. Dweck (Eds.), *Handbook of competence and motivation* (pp. 579–597). New York, NY: Guilford Press.

Deci, E. L., & Ryan, R. M. (1985). *Intrinsic motivation and self-determination in human behavior.* New York, NY: Plenum.

Deci, E. L., & Ryan, R. M. (2000). The "what" and "why" of goal pursuits: Human needs and the self-determination of behavior. *Psychological Inquiry*, 11, 227–268.

Deci, E. L., & Ryan, R. M. (2008). Facilitating optimal motivation and psychological well-being across life's domains. *Canadian Psychology*, 49, 14–23.

Deci, E. L., & Ryan, R. M. (2014). The importance of universal psychological needs for understanding motivation in the workplace. In M. Gagne (Ed.), *The Oxford handbook of work engagement, motivation, and self-determination theory* (pp. 13–32). New York, NY: Oxford University Press.

Delvin, R., & Gibbs, J. (2010). Responsible Adult Culture (ROC) cognitive and behavioral changes at a community-based correctional facility. *Journal of Research in Character Education*, 8, 1–20.

DiClemente, C. C., & Prochaska, J. O. (1985). Processes and stages of self-change: Coping and competence in smoking behavior change. In S. Shiffman, & T. A. Wills (Eds.), *Coping and substance abuse* (pp. 319–343). New York, NY: Academic Press.

Dobson, K. S., & Dozois, D. J. A. (2010). Historical and philosophical bases of the cognitive-behavioral therapies. In K. S. Dobson (Ed.), *Handbook of cognitive behavioral therapies* (pp. 3–38). New York, NY: Guildford Press.

Dozois, D. J. A., & Beck, A. T. (2008). Cognitive schemas, beliefs and assumptions. In K. S. Dobson, & D. J. A. Dozois (Eds.), *Risk factors in depression* (pp. 121–143). Oxford, UK: Elsevier/Academic Press.

D'Zurilla, T. J., & Nezu, A. M. (2007). *Problem-solving therapy: A positive approach to clinical intervention* (3rd ed.). New York, NY: Springer.

Easton, C., Swan, S., & Sinha, R. (2000). Motivation to change substance use among offenders of domestic violence. *Journal of Substance Abuse Treatment*, 19, 1–5.

Evershed, S., Tennant, A., Boomer, D., Rees, A., Barkham, M., & Watson, A. (2003). Practice-based outcomes of dialectical behaviour therapy (DBT) targeting anger and violence, with male forensic patients: A pragmatic and non-contemporaneous comparison. *Criminal Behaviour and Mental Health*, 13, 198–213.

Fiske, S. T., & Taylor, S. E. (2013). *Social cognition: From brains to culture* (2nd ed.). Thousand Oaks, CA: Sage.

Fruzzetti, A. E., & Levensky, E. R. (2000). Dialectical behavior therapy for domestic violence: Rationale and procedures. *Cognitive and Behavioral Practice*, 7, 435–447.

Gannon, T., & Polaschek, D. L. L. (2005). Do child molesters deliberately fake good on cognitive distortion questionnaires? An information processing-based investigation. *Sexual Abuse: A Journal of Research and Treatment*, 17, 183–200.

Goldstein, A. P., & Glick, B. (1987). *Aggression Replacement Training: A comprehensive intervention for aggressive youth.* Champaign, IL: Research Press.

Goldstein, A. P., & Glick, B. (1994). *The prosocial gang: Implementing Aggression Replacement Training.* Thousand Oaks, CA: Sage.

Gottfredson, M. R., & Hirschi, T. (1990). *A general theory of crime*. Stanford, CA: Stanford University Press.

Grimley, D., Prochaska, J. O., Velicer, W. F., Blais, L. M., & DiClemente, C. C. (1994). The transtheoretical model of change. In T. M. Brinthaupt, & R. P. Lipka (Eds.), *Changing the self: Philosophies, techniques, and experiences* (pp. 201–228). Albany, NY: State University of New York Press.

Hall, G. C. (1996). *Theory-based assessment, treatment, and prevention of sexual aggression*. New York, NY: Oxford University Press.

Hayes, S. C. (2004). Acceptance and commitment therapy and the new behavior therapies: Mindfulness, acceptance, and relationship. In S. C. Hayes, V. M. Follette, & M. M. Linehan (Eds.), *Mindfulness and acceptance: Expanding the cognitive-behavioral tradition* (pp. 1–29). New York, NY: Guilford Press.

Hayes, S. C., Strosahl, K., & Wilson, K. G. (1999). *Acceptance and commitment therapy: An experiential approach to behavior change*. New York, NY: Guildford Press.

Hemphill, J. F., & Howell, A. J. (2000). Adolescent offenders and stages of change. *Psychological Assessment*, 12, 371–381.

Hunter, D., Ronsenthal, M. Z., Lynch, T. R., & Linehan, M. M. (2016). Dialectical behavior therapy for individuals with borderline personality disorder and substance use disorders. In A. H. Mack, K. T. Brady, S. I. Miller, & R. J. Frances (Eds.), *Clinical textbook of addictive disorders* (4th ed.) (pp. 648–667). New York, NY: Guilford Press.

Iverson, K. M., Shenk, C., & Fruzzetti, A. E. (2009). Dialectical behavior therapy for women victims of domestic abuse: A pilot study. *Professional Psychology: Research and Practice*, 40, 242–248.

Janis, I. L., & Mann, L. (1977). *Decision making: A psychological analysis of conflict, choice and commitment*. New York, NY: Free Press.

Jennings, J. L., & Deming, A. (2013). Effectively utilizing the "behavioral" in cognitive-behavioral group therapy of sex offenders. *International Journal of Behavioral Consultation and Therapy*, 8, 7–13.

Kadden, R., Carroll, K., Donovan, D., Cooney, N., Monti, P., Abrams, D., ... & Hester, R. (2003). *Cognitive-behavioral coping skills therapy manual: A clinical research guide for therapists treating individuals with alcohol abuse and dependence*. Rockville, MD: National Institute on Alcohol Abuse and Alcoholism Retrieved from http://pubs.niaaa.nih.gov/publications/ProjectMatch/match03.pdf

Kanfer, R., & Kantrowitz, T. M. (2002). Emotion regulation: Command and control of emotion in work life. In R. Lord, R. Klimoski, & R. Kanfer (Eds.), *Emotions in the workplace: Understanding the structure and role of emotions in organizational behavior* (pp. 433–472). San Francisco, CA: Jossey-Bass.

Karoly, P. (1993). Mechanisms of self-regulation: A systems view. *Annual Review of Psychology*, 44, 23–52.

Kellogg, S. H., & Young, J. E. (2006). Schema therapy for borderline personality disorder. *Journal of Clinical Psychology*, 62, 445–458.

Kendall, P. C., & Bemis, K. M. (1983). Thought and action in psychotherapy: The cognitive-behavioral approaches. In M. Hersen, A. E. Kazdin, & A. S. Bellack (Eds.), *The clinical psychology handbook* (pp. 565–592). New York, NY: Pergamon.

Kendall, P. C., & Kriss, M. R. (1983). Cognitive-behavioral interventions. In C. E. Walker (Ed.), *The handbook of clinical psychology: Theory, research, and practice* (pp. 770–819). Homewood, IL: Dow Jones-Irwin.

Linehan, M. M. (1993). *Cognitive-behavioral treatment of borderline personality disorder*. New York, NY: Guilford Press.

Lipsey, M. W., Landenberger, N. A., & Wilson, S. J. (2007). Effects of cognitive-behavioral programs for criminal offenders. *Campbell Systematic Reviews*, 6, 1–27.

Lipsey, M. W., Wilson, D. B., & Cothern, L. (2000). *Effective intervention for serious juvenile offenders* (Juvenile Justice Bulletin). Washington, DC: US Department of Justice, Office of Juvenile Justice and Delinquency Prevention Retrieved from https://www.ncjrs.gov/pdffiles1/ojjdp/181201.pdf

Lynch, T. R., Chapman, A. L., Rosenthal, M. Z., Kuo, J. R., & Linehan, M. M. (2006). Mechanisms of change in dialectical behavior therapy: Theoretical and empirical observations. *Journal of Clinical Psychology*, 62, 459–480.

Lynch, M. F., Vansteenkiste, M., Deci, E. L., & Ryan, R. M. (2011). Autonomy as process and outcome: Revisiting cultural and practical issues in motivation for counseling. *The Counseling Psychologist*, 39, 286–302.

Mann, R., & Hollin, C. (2010). Self-reported schemas in sexual offenders. *Journal of Forensic Psychiatry & Psychology*, 21, 834–851.

Markland, D., Ryan, R. M., Tobin, V. J., & Rollnick, S. (2005). Motivational interviewing and self-determination theory. *Journal of Social and Clinical Psychology*, 24, 811–831.

Marshall, W. L., Anderson, D., & Fernandez, Y. (1999). *Cognitive behavioural treatment of sexual offenders*. Chichester, UK: Wiley.

Maruna, S., & Mann, R. (2006). Fundamental attribution errors? Re-thinking cognitive distortions. *Legal and Criminological Psychology*, 11, 155–177.

McCann, R. A., Ball, E. M., & Ivanoff, A. (2000). DBT with an inpatient forensic population: The CMHIP forensic model. *Cognitive and Behavioral Practice*, 7, 447–456.

McGlynn, A. H., Hahn, P., & Hagan, M. P. (2013). The effect of a cognitive treatment program for male and female juvenile offenders. *International Journal of Offender Therapy and Comparative Criminology*, 57, 1107–1119.

McGuire, J. (2005). The Think First programme. In M. McMurran, & J. McGuire (Eds.), *Social problem solving and offending: Evidence, evaluation and evolution* (pp. 183–206). Chichester, UK: Wiley.

McMain, S., Sayrs, J., Dimeff, L. A., & Linehan, M. M. (2007). Dialectical behavior therapy for individuals with borderline personality disorder and substance dependence. In L. A. Dimeff, & K. Koerner (Eds.), *Dialectical behavior therapy in clinical practice: Applications across disorders and settings* (pp. 145–173). New York, NY: Guildford Press.

McMurran, M., Tyler, P., Hogue, T., Cooper, K., Dunseath, W., & McDaid, D. (1998). Measuring motivation to change in offenders. *Psychology, Crime & Law*, 4, 43–50.

Michie, S., Johnston, M., Abraham, C., Lawton, R., Parker, D., & Walker, A. (2005). Making psychological theory useful for implementing evidence based practice: A consensus approach. *Quality and Safety in Health Care*, 14, 26–33.

Michie, S., Johnston, M., Francis, J., Hardeman, W., & Eccles, M. (2008). From theory to intervention: Mapping theoretically derived behavioural determinants to behaviour change techniques. *Applied Psychology: An International Review*, 57, 660–680.

Muraven, M. R., & Baumeister, R. F. (2000). Self-regulation and depletion of limited resources: Does self-control resemble a muscle? *Psychological Bulletin*, 126, 247–259.

Murphy, W. D. (1990). Assessment and modification of cognitive distortions in sex offenders. In W. L. Marshall, D. R. Laws, & H. E. Barbaree (Eds.), *Handbook of sexual assault: Issues, theories, and treatment of the offender* (pp. 331–342). New York, NY: Plenum.

Polaschek, D. L. L., & Gannon, T. A. (2004). The implicit theories of rapists: What convicted offenders tell us. *Sexual Abuse: A Journal of Research and Treatment*, 16, 299–314.

Polivy, J. (1998). The effects of behavioral inhibition: Integrating internal cues, cognitive behavior, and affect. *Psychological Inquiry*, 9, 181–203.

Porporino, F. J., Fabiano, E. A., & Robinson, D. (1991). *Focusing on successful reintegration: Cognitive skills training for offenders* (Research Rep. No. 19). Ottawa, Canada: Correctional Service of Canada Retrieved from http://www.csc-scc.gc.ca/research/092/r19e_e.pdf

Prochaska, J. O., & DiClemente, C. C. (1984). *The transtheoretical approach: Crossing the traditional boundaries of change*. Homewood, IL: Irwin.

Prochaska, J. O., & DiClemente, C. C. (1986). Toward a comprehensive model of change. In W. R. Miller, & N. Heather (Eds.), *Treating addictive behaviors: Process of change* (pp. 3–27). New York, NY: Plenum Press.

Prochaska, J. O., DiClemente, C. C., & Norcross, J. C. (1992). In search of how people change: Applications to addictive behaviors. *American Psychologist, 47*, 1102–1114.

Prochaska, J. O., Redding, C. A., & Evers, K. E. (1997). The transtheoretical model of change. In K. Glanz, F. M. Lewis, & B. K. Rimer (Eds.), *Health education: Theory, research, and practice* (pp. 60–84). San Francisco, CA: Jossey-Bass.

Reeve, J., & Jang, H. (2006). What teachers say and do to support students' autonomy during a learning activity. *Journal of Educational Psychology, 98*, 209–218.

Rosen, H. (1989). Piagentian theory and cognitive theory. In A. Freeman, K. M. Simon, L. Beutler, & H. Arkowitz (Eds.), *Comprehensive handbook of cognitive therapy* (pp. 189–212). New York, NY: Plenum Press.

Rosenfeld, B., Galietta, M., Ivanoff, A., Garcia-Mansilla, A., Martinez, R., Fava, J., ... & Green, D. (2007). Dialectical behavior therapy for the treatment of stalking offenders. *International Journal of Forensic Mental Health, 6*, 95–103.

Ross, R. R., & Fabiano, E. A. (1985). *Time to think: A cognitive model of delinquency prevention and offender rehabilitation.* Johnson City, TN: Institute of Social Sciences and Arts.

Ross, R. R., Fabiano, E. A., & Ewles, C. D. (1988). Reasoning and rehabilitation. *International Journal of Offender Therapy and Comparative Criminology, 32*, 29–35.

Roth, A. D., & Pilling, S. (2008). Using an evidence-based methodology to identify the competencies required to deliver effective cognitive and behavioral treatment for depression and anxiety disorders. *Behavior and Cognitive Psychology, 36*, 129–147.

Roth, G., Assor, A., Niemiec, C. P., Ryan, R. M., & Deci, E. L. (2009). The emotional and academic consequences of parental conditional regard: Comparing conditional positive regard, conditional negative regard, and autonomy support as parenting practices. *Developmental Psychology, 45*, 1119–1142.

Ryan, R. M. (1995). Psychological needs and the facilitation of integrative processes. *Journal of Personality, 63*, 397–427.

Ryan, R. M., & Deci, E. L. (2000). Self-determination theory and the facilitation of intrinsic motivation, social development, and well-being. *American Psychologist, 55*, 68–78.

Ryan, R. M., & Deci, E. L. (2008a). A self-determination theory approach to psychotherapy: The motivational basis for effective change. *Canadian Psychology, 49*(3), 186–193.

Ryan, R. M., & Deci, E. L. (2008b). Self-determination theory and the role of basic psychological needs in personality and the organization of behavior. In O. P. John, R. W. Robins, & L. A. Pervin (Eds.), *Handbook of personality psychology: Theory and research* (pp. 654–678). New York, NY: Guilford Press.

Ryan, R. M., Lynch, M. F., Vansteenkiste, M., & Deci, E. L. (2011). Motivation and autonomy in counseling, psychotherapy, and behavior change: A look at theory and practice. *The Counseling Psychologist, 39*(2), 193–260.

Segal, Z. V., Williams, J. M. G., & Teasdale, J. T. (2001). *Mindfulness-based cognitive therapy for depression: A new approach to preventing relapse.* New York, NY: Guilford Press.

Shelton, D., Keston, D., Zhang, W., & Trestman, R. (2011). Impact of a dialectic behavior therapy—corrections modified (DBT-CM) upon behaviorally challenged incarcerated male adolescents. *Journal of Child and Adolescent Psychiatric Nursing, 24*, 105–113.

Tucker, J. A., Donovan, D. M., & Marlatt, G. A. (1999). *Changing addictive behavior: Bridging clinical and public health strategies.* New York, NY: Guilford Press.

Vohs, K. D., & Heatherton, T. F. (2000). Self-regulatory failure: A resource-depletion approach. *Psychological Science, 11*, 249–254.

Vohs, K. D., & Schmeichel, B. J. (2003). Self-regulation and the extended now: Controlling the self alters the subjective experience of time. *Journal of Personality and Social Psychology, 85*, 217–230.

Ward, T. (2000). Sexual offenders' cognitive distortions as implicit theories. *Aggression and Violent Behavior, 5*, 491–507.

Ward, T., & Keenan, T. (1999). Child molesters' implicit theories. *Journal of Interpersonal Violence, 14*, 821–838.

Ward, T., Keown, K., & Gannon, T. A. (2007). Child sexual abuse-related cognition: Current research. In T. A. Gannon, T. Ward, A. R. Beech, & D. Fisher (Eds.), *Aggressive offenders' cognition: Theory, research and practice* (pp. 71–91). Chichester, UK: Wiley.

Ward, T., & Maruna, S. (2007). *Rehabilitation: Beyond the risk paradigm.* London, UK: Routledge.

Weinstein, N. D., Rothman, A. J., & Sutton, S. R. (1998). Stage theories of health behavior: Conceptual and methodological issues. *Health Psychology, 17,* 290–299.

Williams, G. C., Deci, E. L., & Ryan, R. M. (1998). Building health-care partnerships by supporting autonomy: Promoting maintained behavior change and positive health outcomes. In P. Hinton-Walker, A. L. Suchman, & R. Botelho (Eds.), *Partnerships, power and process: Transforming health-care delivery* (pp. 67–88). Rochester, NY: University of Rochester Press.

Williamson, P., Day, A., Howells, K., Bubner, S., & Jauncey, S. (2003). Assessing offender readiness to change problems with anger. *Psychology, Crime & Law, 9,* 295–307.

Wormith, J. S., Althouse, R., Simpson, M., Reitzel, L., Fagan, T. J., & Morgan, R. D. (2007). The rehabilitation and reintegration of offenders: The current landscape and some future directions for correctional psychology. *Criminal Justice and Behavior, 34,* 879–892.

Young, J. E. (1999). *Cognitive therapy for personality disorders: A schema-focused approach* (3rd ed.). Sarasota, FL: Professional Resource Press.

23

Program Integrity: A Network Issue

Rob Paramo

Department of Corrections, New Zealand

Introduction

Delivering offending behavior programs with integrity and quality is crucial for effectiveness. It is, however, a difficult task with many different influencing variables to take into account. Most are challenging to identify and mitigate. This chapter aims to revisit important key ideas around program integrity and reknit these in the context of a more recent perspective on program delivery. There has been a range of important principles and concepts identified in relation to program integrity, intervention quality, and outcome (Cullen & Gendreau, 2000; Gendreau, 1996; Gendreau, Goggin, & Smith, 1999, 2001; Hollin, 1995, 2001; Hanson, Bourgon, Helmus, & Hodgson, 2009; Lösel & Schmucker, 2005), but in the past decade, relatively little has been published on the issue. Have we reached an age where high program integrity is a universal feature, easily and consistently measured and clearly linked to positive outcomes? Probably not. Managing the delivery of high-quality, high-integrity, criminogenically focused treatment programs remains a challenge in forensic environments.

The world in which criminogenic programs are designed, delivered, and evaluated is constantly changing in relation to the organizational and sociopolitical forces that envelop offender rehabilitation efforts. This chapter will explore the interdependencies and roles of the different aspects of program development, delivery, and management in an increasingly diverse set of offending behavior program delivery contexts. I argue that in a rapidly changing organizational and societal environment the challenges to delivering interventions do not lessen; they increase, and often in unseen ways for those working in intensive interventions. Our ability to meet those challenges can be hampered by our failure to take a higher-level "whole-of-program" view.

The Wiley International Handbook of Correctional Psychology, First Edition. Edited by Devon L. L. Polaschek, Andrew Day, and Clive R. Hollin.

Program Integrity

The term *program* has likely changed in its meaning over recent years. This would traditionally conjure the picture of a group therapy intervention run by one or more therapists. More recently in correctional style offending behavior programs it has broadened out to be inclusive of standardized individual one-on-one therapies, motivational interventions, and traditional group interventions utilizing one or more therapeutic paradigms. Some programs have also broadened out beyond the group room and are inclusive of a "whole environment" intervention where the program effectively runs 24/7: "Therapeutic Community," "Enabling Environment," and "Community of Change" supported programs among others (Newberry, 2010; Polaschek & Kilgour, 2013; Turley, Payne, & Webster, 2013). For the purposes of this chapter, program refers to standardized or semi-standardized interventions inclusive of individualized and group therapies delivered to offender populations.

What is program integrity in relation to offending behavior programs? Hollin (1995) regarded it as present when a program is "characterized by sound management, tight design and skilled practitioners." He also stated "… the program is conducted in practice as intended in theory and design." Cullen and Gendreau (2000) and Gendreau et al. (1999, 2001) spoke of integrity in program implementation terms. They highlighted four guiding principles: organizational factors, program factors, change agent, and staffing activities. All of these were considered influencers in the successful implementation of a program. They said that without due attention to application, "effectiveness of any state of the art assessment and treatment protocol is diminished" (Gendreau et al., 1999, p. 180). Gendreau and colleagues further highlighted the importance of high program integrity for our understanding of the intended program outcomes. Without high integrity, it is simply not possible to understand poor outcomes: whether they resulted from poor delivery, design, or indeed a combination. These ideas remain relevant and useful in understanding issues of program delivery and management and how these can influence the nature of interventions outcomes.

For the purpose of this chapter I would like to propose an integration and development of Hollin and Gendreau's contributions. I aim to combine ideas of intervention design and program implementation and suggest that these can be influential on program integrity over time and repeated delivery. Additionally, I will incorporate contextual factors that influence (positively and negatively) the style, method, and quality of delivery. I argue all of these factors are central to achieving program integrity; more so where environment is considered part of the treatment program. This combined notion of program integrity is represented in Figure 23.1.

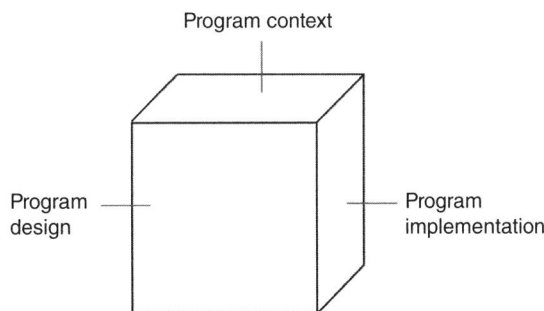

Figure 23.1 Integrated model of program integrity.

I argue that for program integrity to occur in a manner that can be expected to lead toward program effectiveness, an interaction of a number of characteristics is required to certain qualities and quantities. These characteristics could be regarded as the "conditions for success" in terms of enabling a program to have high integrity.

Program Design

In its purest sense, program integrity can be taken as the act of delivering the program as designed. It is possible however that a program lacking in the right quality or best practice design be delivered with high integrity. This program might not though be expected to achieve its desired outcomes (i.e., a program with poor design but well delivered is unlikely to result in a positive treatment effect). Of course, not many programs start as the finished product, and the process of program development is in itself iterative, leading to evaluation, revision, and redelivery. Program integrity is therefore extremely important to the function of program design, and without it program developers are unable to determine what in the program is working. Hollin (1995) highlighted the importance of program integrity in our interpretation of research evidence for interventions, and the risks of concluding design failure incorrectly when integrity was at fault.

It could be argued that design and program integrity are separate issues, certainly in stand-alone programs that receive little in the way of review, revision, and update. However, it is argued that for a program to be effective the standards should be high across design, delivery, and evaluation, and that these aspects become interconnected from the design phase on, leading to a model of continuous improvement. In this review, a program with poor design but delivered with high integrity can be evaluated and revisions be made to improve design. McGuire et al. forged the path with the "what works" literature which formed the basis of accreditation criteria used by the Correctional Services Accreditation Panel (CSAP) (McGuire, Grubin, Losel, & Raynor, 2010; McGuire & Priestley, 1995).

More broadly, effective programs can include a range of therapeutic design features, including cognitive and behavioral methods for behavior change, skills building strategies, and criminogenic within-treatment focus (Bonta & Andrews, 2017; Hanson et al., 2009; Lösel & Schmucker, 2005), and they need to follow a set of principles whereby the right people get the right program at the right time and in the right fashion (Risk-Need-Responsivity [RNR]; Bonta & Andrews, 2017). In many examples of offender programs the design is captured and communicated in treatment manuals, which can detail the relevant theory as well as the plan and content for session delivery.

Program Implementation

The delivery of the program, or program implementation, has typically been a primary focus of integrity and the area of interest in efforts of measurement. Program implementation is made up of two aspects: the first is adherence to design (Hollin, 1995), delivering the program as designed and intended; the second part relates to quality of delivery. The two aspects equate to separating and understanding program content versus therapeutic process. Goggin and Gendreau (2006) explored successful implementation and cited the Andrews et al. (1990) definition of treatment quality as displaying an approach consistent with RNR, displaying interpersonal sensitivity, using clinically well-trained and supervised staff, and following through with relapse prevention and through care. It is therefore not just how well the therapist can stick to the manual, it is also whether they can attend to the individual in the session. If a manual leaves no room for the more dynamic situational therapeutic processing, therapists can be tempted to depart from the program as designed. Program implementation is therefore a balance between adhering to the program and addressing individual and group needs in an effective and dynamic therapeutic manner.

Adherence and quality can be at odds with one another. Hollin (2009) illustrated this conflict with reference to the debate of Marshall and Mann on the use of manuals in group treatment. In this discussion, Hollin highlights apparently diametrically opposed views relating to the benefits of manuals in providing theoretical and practical anchoring, which, in turn, enables consistent delivery over a national-scale program. On the other hand, he highlights the restriction imposed by a manual that does not allow for the discretionary use of therapist skill, so that the therapist is given room to achieve the goals of the program designers, but yet also attend to presenting problems without being completely constrained by a list of prewritten tasks. Hollin correctly draws out key underlying issues relating to the skill and competency of those delivering treatment and to the importance of supervision that supports treatment. These seemingly contradictory viewpoints can and should co-exist. It is possible to have a manual and clinical responsivity, but there is also a range of other factors that contribute to integrity and effectiveness and these have inherent connections. I'll talk about these issues more later in the chapter and suggest how shortfalls in key areas such as staff competency, training or experience, and skill can result in designers attempting to compensate by, for example, designing overly prescriptive and clinically unresponsive manuals.

Program Context

Program context is a core feature of program integrity; that is, without the correct environmental conditions, program integrity will be compromised. Hollin (1995) introduced the notion of *organizational resistance*: the idea that the hosting organization actually presents barriers and difficulties, which can impact on the ability to deliver high-quality and effective programs. He stated "if the organization is not committed to program integrity, even the most highly trained, highly skilled practitioners will have little impact" (p. 205).

Program context is dependent on the scale of the program delivery, and also captures the local environmental settings in which it is delivered, and the wider organization delivering it. Programs can be delivered in secure or community settings, leading to variation in challenges faced. They also might be delivered by a correctional organization, a charity, or a private company. It could be a single program, a standardized program delivered across a region or country. The context will therefore include staff (in and outside of the program), the training, the immediate local delivery environment, and the wider organizational political and policy environment. The program context can be one of the key "influencers" and whether the conditions for success are present for program integrity.

The Brave New World

Many public sector organizations across the world have undergone both financial and bureaucratic change programs, and whether a program sits inside or outside of these organizations, factors impacting on the delivery of programs have been affected. There are now many permutations of program design and delivery, and all of these bring about different challenges to establishing and maintaining program integrity.

For example, in the early 2000s, Her Majesty's Prison Service in the United Kingdom had relatively few service models for design and delivery (i.e., with regard to who developed the program, who delivered it, who supported it, and who evaluated it). The principal model was that a centrally based program development team would write and pilot a program that was then evaluated by program evaluators working alongside developers, before program revision and roll-out of delivery to program teams across multiple delivery sites nationally. There were also programs bought from other jurisdictions and implemented and supported in a similar fashion.

With the greater prevalence of correctional privatization in the United Kingdom we have seen models of contestability and competition change processes of design and delivery of programs. This has increased the variety in the numbers of programs, and the scale at which they are delivered. These changes have in turn led to changes to the roles and relationships between program developers, delivery teams, and evaluators.

Most notably, these different models can produce separation between these three parties, especially when programs may be procured from overseas and/or where third-party delivery teams are commissioned to provide program delivery. Separation can lead to challenges with the process of *technology transfer*.

Technology Transfer

An important feature of ensuring that programs can be delivered as designed is a sense of connection between the design and delivery stages. *Technology transfer* relates to the process of implementing a newly developed program from the design phase to implementation and delivery, at first establishing and then maintaining the integrity of the intervention in question. Gendreau and colleagues (Gendreau, 1996; Gendreau et al., 1999, 2001) have discussed extensively the importance of *technology transfer*, and identified the general tendency of the literature to ignore this element.

In any focus on program integrity there needs to be attention to implementation more broadly: both the initial implementation of a new program, and the ongoing development and support of routine delivery. *Technology transfer* is an important concept for program integrity; it is often achieved well when program developers operate a program support function beyond the initial implementation, as part of the business-as-usual running of the intervention. Additionally, the program support function can be well placed to monitor and provide expert advice to delivery teams. In program support roles there is a need for sufficient separation from delivery teams and for organizational influence and ability to effect change where it is in the interests of the program. An example of where this would be positioned is where a program development and support team are based in a national or regional office. Program support staff need to be sufficiently high in the hierarchy to influence the other parts of the organization that impact directly and indirectly on program delivery and integrity.

Gendreau et al. (2001) argued that it is within a system that is moderately decentralized that effective program implementation takes place, and therefore, presumably, that a *technology transfer* can function well. This notion, of course, makes some level of assumption that the various functions are within a common organization. When programs are procured elsewhere or delivered by third parties (such as a private company, charity, or non-government organization [NGO]) external to the hosting organization the connections enabling program support and *technology transfer* may not be in place, unless special effort is taken.

Third-Party Delivered Programs

In many jurisdictions now, external providers are responsible for program delivery, and program quality, and are accountable for outcomes, such as measured reduced reoffending rates. In some jurisdictions and sectors "payment by results" is used to incentivize performance, enhance third-party accountability, and increase value for the tax dollar. This form of incentive poses a challenge for some small providers of programs whose immediate financial survival may depend on meeting volumetric targets potentially at the expense of quality of delivery.

In wider social investment circles there is a notion of intelligent purchasing in the context of public services provided by third-party organizations. Intelligent purchasing occurs when the purchasing organization has detailed knowledge of what they are buying: they understand the supply, the demand, and the market. Where intelligent purchasing is used in program commissioning, it involves establishment of systems that can measure quality and volume of delivery and outcome. In such cases there tends to be strong level of connection and alignment between the purchasing and hosting organization and the third-party provider.

Velasco-Garrido, Borrowitz, Ovretveit, and Busse (2005) discussed purchasing of high-quality care in contracted health services, and highlighted that fragmentation is a key threat to integrity and quality of service in such scenarios. In fragmented cases, a purchaser's understanding of quality is integral to the correct contractual expectations being placed on providers. Often it is important for the contracting and procurement teams in an organization to use program experts to inform tendering and contracting of program providers. This approach is known as "intelligent purchasing." This becomes key to enable consistency in delivery, expectations, and measurement. Truly embedding the service within the organization becomes the next key challenge; again, the organization's ability to support the program integrity processes and functions will dictate the success or failure of a third-party provider in their attempts to deliver a program with integrity. The payment by results approach appears intentionally hands-off and risks both isolating the program and also unreasonably expecting delivery teams to be responsible for process evaluations of their own program integrity: in essence, requiring them to be both "poacher and gamekeeper" in relation to objectively measuring and improving their own program integrity.

Organizational Resistance

The key concept of *organizational resistance* was introduced by Hollin (1995) in relation to barriers or obstacles that may come up in program delivery, be it in an institution or a community setting. Issues faced over management and decision-making can impact on the establishment and maintenance of program integrity. This can result in issues of control, influence, and management of factors such as staff, training resource, offender availability, finance, and so on. The notion of *organizational resistance* can occur on the ground (at the program level) and at varying stages in the management and oversight of the program (i.e., regionally and/or nationally). The presence of *organizational resistance* can be overt or more subtly present. This could be demonstrated by a clear and expressed low opinion of programs and their attempts at rehabilitation in favor of custodial management and containment. Alternatively, it could also be demonstrated by a prioritization of custodial and deterrence functions above rehabilitative efforts (Day, Casey, Ward, Howells, & Vess, 2013).

Contextual Challenges and Barriers

There is a range of significant factors that contribute to the wider environment when considering the issues in and around developing and maintaining program integrity. Political policy, departmental/organizational values, and individual influences affect an organization's capacity to enable and support, or inhibit, the process of program integrity. The wider factors influencing the environment where programs are delivered need to be considered both situationally and across time. Governmental policy is likely to have a significant direct and indirect impact on the organizational supportiveness or resistance when considering the more immediate and proximal environmental influences on program deliverers. Policy can dictate agendas such as "tough on crime" that have significant ramifications for the resource and priority that can be given for rehabilitation efforts and the surrounding services. A highly deterrent-focused, punitive, or restrictive operational environment can then find itself at odds with the efforts of rehabilitation program providers.

Local Delivery Environments—The Delivery Context

Prison environments can be socially toxic and psychologically harmful. Traditionally, there has been less focus on environmental factors in program evaluation (Harding, 2014). More recently there has been a range of efforts to examine forensic mental health and prison environments and this can be seen in work on therapeutic communities, interventions with personality-disordered prisoner populations, and wider research on social climate (Day, Casey, Vess, & Huisy, 2011; Newberry, 2010). However, prisons can be by their very nature punitive, coercive, and criminogenic environments, often based on a power and control dynamic between custodians and prisoners, and again between subgroups of prisoners. An argument can be made that the simple act of imprisonment is not likely to reduce recidivism and that there is at least some evidence to suggest imprisonment is actually criminogenic for some (Cullen, Jonson, & Nagin, 2011). The logical step may therefore be to assume that for those who have been imprisoned a range of environmental factors needs to be addressed if there is to be a better outcome after this release. Interventions and programs are one avenue for addressing criminogenic needs, but they often occupy only a small percentage of the day and their impact can be diluted or reduced if delivered in inhospitable environments. In the practice experience of the author delivering programs in prisons, participants have provided accounts of their experience of completing therapy in a challenging prison environment. They have spoken of their frustration and concern at completing therapy which promotes the skills of disclosure and prosocial coping which were incongruous, indeed dangerous, for their more immediate survival in a prison environment. Some individuals have likened it to having to take off "armor" and then having to remember to put it back on to remain invulnerable when they step back out on to the prison wing. Thus there seems an imperative to improve and modify the treatment delivery environment for program integrity and ethical reasons. This anecdotal view is supported by evidence that those who experience negative environmental factors such as fear or disempowerment can struggle to make progress in rehabilitation programs (Davis, 2004 cited in Day et al., 2011). Conversely, research by Newberry (2010) found that staff and prisoners perceived social climate at Grendon Therapeutic Community (TC) Prison more positively than other similar security classification prisons and that prisoners experienced lower rates of anxiety, depression, and ultimately reconviction than prisoners at other establishments.

In the United Kingdom, there has been an increase in discussion about therapeutic communities and enhanced or modified prison environments such as the Psychologically Informed Planned Environments (PIPEs), growing from the Personality Disorder Pathways strategy (formerly known as the Dangerous and Severe Personality Disorder services) within the United Kingdom's National Offender Management Service (NOMS; Turley et al., 2013). This work shows an increased recognition of and interest in the importance of deliberately modifying prison environments to create positive "enabling" atmospheres or climates. These physically and psychologically supportive environments help offenders first learn about, and then practice, change by way of (primarily) cognitive behavioral therapy (CBT) programs. These programs in turn have then been used as part of a system that can nurture, support, and facilitate more effective transition through the prison system and then through release into the community.

There have been increased efforts in understanding the impact of environment on psychiatric and correctional populations and the resultant relationship to program attendance and success. This has been put in the context of better understanding responsivity in relation to either toxic or therapeutic climates (Day et al., 2013). Gendreau and Goggin (Chapter 8) speak of the environmental climate of a prison in personality terms and of its impact on offender behavior. Efforts have been made to better explain and measure environmental factors in relation to social climate and impact. An example of this has been the extension of the Essen Climate Evaluation Schema (EssenCES) tool from the hospital settings for which it was designed to trials in prison settings (Day et al., 2011). In this study the authors had prisoners and staff complete the measure, comparing one mainstream prison with rehabilitation programs against a rehabilitation-oriented prison. Support was found for the hypothesis that the rehabilitation prison offered a more therapeutically aligned environment than the mainstream prison. More recently it was concluded that the EssenCES could be a tool that would be useful in assessing environmental factors during periods of organizational change or when initiatives were seeking to improve treatment engagement (Day et al., 2013). Increased efforts to apply and validate this and other environmental and climate measures in prison environments will provide greater opportunity to make the intangible tangible, and present more opportunities to improve program environments. Indeed, the more treatment programs include a broader environmental focus to treatment, the more this becomes relevant for program integrity.

From a practitioner's point of view, the impact of environment on the ability to practically deliver program integrity and quality cannot be underestimated. Problems occur when different operating models fail to accommodate one another sufficiently (custodial vs. therapeutic). The therapy model thereby can struggle when not actively supported. This is where the notion of organizational resistance is illustrated.

Mainstream prison environments tend to focus solely on maintaining safety and security within the prison setting. Arguably, safety and security are a key bottom line for any secure environment; indeed, rehabilitation cannot stand any chance of success without it. However, if there is no capacity to extend beyond this focus (i.e., inability to unlock prisoners for rehabilitation activities) then program integrity can be impacted. Custodial teams may be uninformed about rehabilitation programs and their methods and will see this work as non-essential or unimportant to the day-to-day running of the unit or prison. This can prevent the obvious potential benefit that an effective program can have on improving prisoner compliance, safety, and security in a prison. Where an inflexible focus on safety and security is juxtaposed with a program that requires some environmental changes in order to be implemented with integrity, tensions can arise, leading to *organizational resistance.*

However toxic or anti-therapeutic prison environments can be, they are just one potential symptom of *organizational resistance. Organizational resistance* can occur on multiple levels: directly and indirectly at a local program delivery level, and in the levels of management and influence above it. Mechanisms are required to help identify and mitigate examples of *organizational resistance.* Those mechanisms may take the form of program development teams or program managers at levels where they can make key decisions or influence parts of the organization to support the program implementation. Gendreau et al. (2001) spoke of the need for the program (including its development and management functions) to be moderately decentralized, and Hollin (1995), in relation to *organizational resistance,* to having sufficient policy and practice influence in relation to factors impacting on program functioning.

The Program-Supporting Organization

What would a program integrity-supportive organization look like? Therapeutic communities provide a reference point for modified prison environments where training around staff knowledge and practice focuses on creating a wider pro-therapy environment, which includes custodial staff and local management (Newberry, 2010). More recently within the United Kingdom, NOMS' broader work on interventions and approaches with dangerous and severe personality-disordered (DSPD) prison populations (Atkinson and Tew, 2012; Turley et al., 2013) has led to the PIPEs initiative. Similar to TCs, PIPEs propose that modifying prison environments is a necessary precursor to motivating offenders, and should extend to supporting their treatment change and then providing a pathway for them to maintain therapeutic gains beyond the end of the various offending behavior programs attended. This modification encapsulates the physical but also psychological and social environment in which the interventions are delivered. Staff are selected and trained to make key contributions to the creation of the psychologically safe and enabling environment. Custodial officers are considered central to this and are also specially selected, trained, and supported to be psychologically and relationally minded, in contrast to the traditional custodial role. This increased attention to environment and relational working acts to provide a more pro-therapeutic and supportive environment for the participants of programs. It is also more aligned to the program delivery by capitalizing on similar principles and practices. The work done on modifying and adapting secure environments provides some insight into the efforts and work required to address the ground level of *organizational resistance.* The DSPD work has achieved further success in dealing with higher levels of challenge or *organizational resistance* by virtue of the commitment to common values being supported all the way up to legislative, parliamentary level. The efforts taken with PIPEs and the Personality Disorder Pathways work in NOMS to ensure efforts are endorsed at the highest level give some indication of the lengths to which we may need to go to ensure full adoption of rehabilitative principles and values in large organizations.

Program Features, Mechanisms, and Program Integrity Supporting Functions

Program development and design are key foundations for program integrity. Any sound program needs to be based on empirically supported theoretical and practical methodologies that are linked to criminogenic factors. Effective correctional programs have been shown to include cognitive behavioral orientation, skills practice, and criminogenic focus (Hanson et al., 2009; Lösel & Schmucker, 2005). They need to follow a set of principles whereby the right people get the right program at the right time and in the right fashion (RNR; Bonta & Andrews, 2017). The design of the program is required to remain up to date and responsive to changes in the evidence base (both its own and that from the wider research). If the program fails to maintain itself by way of updates, it can be prone to behaviors such as *program drift*, *program reversal*, and *program non-compliance*, as first illustrated by Hollin (1995). Hollin explained these phenomenal thus: *program drift* occurs where there is a gradual shift over time from the original aims of the program. *Program reversal* occurs when therapy staff work to actively reverse and undermine the approaches used. This could involve alternate theoretical approaches which seek to engage clients in the opposite behaviors to those detailed in the program. *Program non-compliance* is where the therapist elects for their own reasons to change, add to, or omit sections of the program as it was written (Hollin, 1995, p. 197).

The design phase should also build in an evaluation strategy, to include examination of piloting, process evaluation, and outcome evaluation. These data can then be used as part of the program update process.

Selection, training, and support of staff is another feature integral to the wider program and its ability to maintain both integrity and effectiveness. Program design focuses on who the intended recipient of the intervention is, but it should also focus on who the intended deliverer is. This in turn influences the choice of content, modality (group or individual), the therapy methods, and the training and support requirements. Across correctional programs and jurisdictions, a very diverse set of staff types and disciplines can be seen delivering programs. This can include psychologists (qualified and trainee), social workers, probation officers, prison officers, and program facilitators: depending on jurisdiction, there can be a very diverse staff group, with diverse qualifications and prior experience in therapy interventions. A range of considerations needs to underpin the staffing of a program. This includes agreeing a set of staff requirements (maintaining competency) to perform as a provider of programs. Increased volume of program delivery and/or budgetary pressures within public sector organizations can limit the extent professional groups such as qualified therapists (e.g., counselors and psychologists) can feature in more complex psychological programs. A lack of access to highly skilled staff can lead to compensatory measures being taken, such as the use of trainees and non-therapy staff. This can require further adaptation of programs in both manual and training terms and can see some staff groups adopting dual roles (e.g., probation and prison officers, who also adopt roles as sentence administrators and therapists), which may impact on the ability of a facilitator to deliver a program with integrity.

Supervision is a core function of any therapy program. Supervision across a range of health and social service professions can serve a variety of purposes, including exploration of interpersonal reactions, professional development, and learning therapy content and skills. In a manualized program, supervision will invariably explore the dynamic application of documented program content with the client or clients. Ideally, the supervision applied across the program should be cognizant of the issues and processes at play in the program in relation to establishing and preserving program integrity. Supervision offers the opportunity to apply, review, and test application of content, improving the application of skills with a range of clients, situations, and therapy dynamics. Where the structure of supervision can be informed by the program theory, development, and support then it can work as a first level of quality assurance for promotion of program integrity. As with supervision in general, there are risks that can limit the impact of supervision. These include situations where the focus and content of supervision bear little relevance to program content, where there are threats to integrity, and/or when the supervisor lacks adequate knowledge or expertise with the intervention. When used well, supervision can form an important first line of quality and integrity work for a program.

Higher-level "whole of program" integrity monitoring processes are an important part of ensuring a program is being delivered in the manner and with the methods intended. Hollin (1995) highlighted the need for objective review (such as supervision) of programs and advocated for expert observation of the program to form part of a scientist-practitioner approach. This type of review can take a number of different styles and formats, ranging from highly structured quantitative audits against key baselines (e.g., ensuring therapy rooms contain the correct furniture and adhere to specified criteria, program sessions being observed and rated against adherence to manual) to relatively unstructured and more qualitative observational approaches (e.g., observer follows program for period of time and interviews all involved). The methodology for measuring program integrity is important and should be a key consideration during the program design phase. Examples of structured measures vary; one key tool is the Correctional Program Assessment Inventory (CPAI; Goggin & Gendreau, 2006; Lowenkamp & Latessa, 2004; Nesovic, 2003). Integrity checklists are also often used in lesser and more structured formats. Wider system processes can be seen to sit around integrity monitoring, as seen in the United Kingdom with the CSAP and accreditation (McGuire et al., 2010). The method is invariably important and needs to be responsive to the complex and changing correctional environment.

The aim of a higher-level integrity monitoring process would be to establish whether the program concerned is meeting an acceptable level of integrity and to address any shortfalls as they are identified. The point of such processes is emphasized by Henggeler, Melton, Brondino, Scherer, and Hanley (1997), whose evaluation of multi-systemic therapy for violent youth showed that intervention adherence was an important predictor of outcome. Their reflection on the issues of "laboratory effect" and enabling effective technology transfer from university to community delivery settings endorsed the need for clinical and administrative support processes. Integrity monitoring is an important tool in addressing problematic behaviors that take program delivery away from design, such as *program drift*, *reversal*, and *noncompliance* (Hollin, 1995), and can and should act as a second line of quality assurance above supervision. These types of processes ideally should sit above the program delivery and involve staff with sufficient experience and expertise who also have the required distance and objectivity. Integrity monitoring as a function often sits with teams that link with program development, support, and evaluation, and this enables a more coherent approach to technology transfer and ongoing program updating.

External review is a common feature for larger program delivery organizations and an example can be seen with CSAP. CSAP are a panel of international experts, independent of the correctional organizations they review. Their role has been as both a professional and a clinical support, providing expert advice and a process of accreditation, with the goals of establishing and maintaining gold standard programs (McGuire et al., 2010). The CSAP model began life as a highly influential expert panel, but policy shifts eroded it to the status of an advisory panel. The influence it had was useful both for clinicians who were designing and delivering programs and also for the organization that commissioned and provided the delivery environment. The presence of an external expert panel became a useful mechanism to work productively with aspects of organizational resistance. The CSAP had opportunity to engage directly with the program development teams and provide guidance, feedback, and review of program design and delivery. It was also able to engage with and provide an external expert perspective to operational managers and policy-makers from outside of the organization. This at least presented the opportunity to provide clarity on "what works" with programs and identify and mediate internal friction between program developers, deliverers, and operational arms of the organization.

Alternative models are often used where expert peer review (by individuals or specified groups of experts) may be commissioned as part of a process evaluation, or through periodic review of program processes or manuals. Of course, there are dangers in not using external review, such as loss of objectivity, along with the risk that the methods and processes adopted within the program are not validated practices or have become dated.

Program support (the function that performs technology transfer) tends to be a feature of large-scale programs. Correctional organizations that have the capacity and capability to write their own programs often have clinicians in roles that can provide operational and clinical advice and support to the delivery teams. This can help with maintaining a central view of the program and with enabling the delivery teams to maintain the intent and integrity of the program design. On the flip side, it can assist with the quality and integrity monitoring and check for and mitigate the issues of *drift*, *reversal*, and *non-compliance* (as highlighted by Hollin, 1995). Smaller programs face a challenge when considering this function, and the higher-level program support may be limited to the program supervisor. Likewise, third-party designed or delivered programs face a challenge where there may no longer be a relationship between program designer and the deliverers (as the program may be procured and there is no one to provide the program support function beyond the supervisor). Program support may again be limited to the lower-level supervision function. Challenge then exists with issues of enabling technology transfer and of maintaining an objective view of functioning and clinical and operational decisions. The process of monitoring *drift*, *reversal*, and *non-compliance* is considerably harder from within the program than from outside of it.

Where there are shortfalls in certain key program integrity-enabling functions we often may see the introduction of compensatory strategies that are intended to increase assurance that the program can be delivered well, and in a manner that adheres to what was designed. Several examples of these compensatory behaviors are described below.

Many programs are delivered by staff whose pre-employment training has not given them the skills and knowledge to allow them to provide a high-quality rehabilitation program without a highly prescriptive manual. There are likely many reasons for this situation, but some of the most obvious relate to the limited numbers of those staff and the relative high cost of having them deliver programs. As a consequence, program providers may opt for more accessible staff groups to run programs. Alternative staff groups may include psychology graduates, program facilitators, or prison officers. Focus on staff selection then may turn to key interpersonal competencies and attributes, and steps can be taken to better support those staff in their delivery of therapy. Those steps may include bespoke program training, high levels of supervision, and then a more highly detailed and prescriptive manual. Where therapeutic programs are delivered by staff from different backgrounds (such as program facilitators, probation officers, and prison officers) programs may increase measures to support quality of therapeutic delivery, program integrity, and capacity to work responsively. With such programs, it could be suggested that there is increased risk of poor quality delivery, and therefore increased need for monitoring and training support. In some cases (as with probation and prison officers) the issue of dual roles (that of custodian or sentence administrator and case manager) can present added issues and demands that may be challenging to program quality in terms of working with a therapeutic alliance and effective boundaries.

Conversely, where there is a strong pool of highly skilled and qualified staff (e.g., a program that utilizes qualified psychologists as therapists), there are sometimes instances where we see less emphasis placed on program-specific training or program integrity monitoring. This over-reliance on one factor of integrity (having well-experienced and well-trained staff) can see actu-alization of fragility in other areas of program functioning that weaken the ability to deliver a program well. For example, a program could drift away from focusing on criminogenic factors.

Many functions of program integrity can be less explicitly linked together, and major changes to services, such as expenditure reviews, cuts and cost-savings exercises, and organizational restructuring, can erode these relationships unless the organization remains well informed on program integrity and program functions. There are key functions that depend on one another, and if they are not explicitly linked they can become separated or damaged. Because the rela-tionship between cause (separation of functions) and effect (program outcomes) can often be separated in time, it is often difficult organizationally to understand the relationships between functions. The process of restructuring these functions can therefore act as a part of the pro-cess of *organizational resistance*. This can be further compounded if there is an absence of program evaluation, or if the program evaluation is too distal from the program itself (i.e., in cases where organizations only examine reconviction as an outcome and do not explore this fully in relation to program integrity, process evaluation, and functioning). As was mentioned previously, if program integrity is not achieved, then outcome evaluation cannot be under-stood. If program integrity cannot be achieved because the organization is unsupportive and the delivery environment is toxic, then efforts should be made to address these issues before a program can be deemed a failure.

The process of quality and integrity monitoring also can be prone to iatrogenic effects as a result of compensatory behaviors. A program with a strong focus on quality assurance and a process for monitoring program integrity can create high pressure for compliance (e.g., with manuals and processes such as identifying and assessing program participants). Some correc-tional organizations may take audit approaches to integrity monitoring, and as a consequence have key performance indicators (KPI) and targets associated with program volumes (numbers of offenders going through programs) and program integrity (assessed adherence to program protocols). Where a rigid focus is adopted, unintended consequences can follow. These can include the creation of an adversarial relationship between program monitors and deliverers (i.e., poacher vs. gamekeeper), limitations in clinical focus (where program deliverers prioritize targets above clients), and inaccurate measurement of program integrity (where monitoring baselines are incorrect or out of date).

These issues can be a risk in large operational organizations where many other parts of the business are measured and their quality assessed, and programs sit alongside other measurement or audit functions. Such processes can inadvertently become self-limiting (where the measure actually becomes the goal). Clinical governance frameworks used most frequently within health settings set an expectation of clinical excellence by means of continuous improvement. This implies movement and not status quo. An overly operational and rigid focus on audit baselines can mean the measure becoming the target for programs, particularly in pressured delivery environments. The focus for the operational and delivery teams will then stretch no further than meeting the standards for audit, as opposed to a more principle-based striving for clinical excellence. We might expect a high-integrity program to be an effective program, but this is not always the case. To enable a program to work toward being effective, it would need to be reviewed and updated based on research (in general, and on the program in question). This research should also be applied to the methods of measuring quality and integrity. Consideration should be given to who would do this, when, and how. For large-scale programs with dedicated program development teams, the answer may be relatively simple. For small or single delivery programs, "whole of program" integrity monitoring may be more difficult to plan and achieve as part of the implementation. Ideally, the initial design of a program should plan forward and consider the piloting, review and updating, and ongoing monitoring and revision, if it is to be delivered as an ongoing intervention.

Effective planning and ongoing review can assist in managing the risk associated with delivery teams becoming good at being monitored, as opposed to being good at effective treatment and focusing on the target of clinical excellence. Strong professional relationships and clear, targeted, clinically meaningful feedback assist with maintaining a principle-based focus.

In systems that use numerical scoring for quality there is inevitably a top score. Whilst it may be possible to achieve a top score, clinically speaking it is not necessarily possible to achieve perfection. With high operational expectations to perform, it is possible for delivery teams to become practiced and expert at gaining scores in integrity monitoring or audit, rather than maintaining their focus on delivering the best possible treatment. Likewise, where integrity monitoring follows more of an audit style it can become somewhat adversarial. This can see a shift of roles from program developers/monitors and deliverer seeking to deliver best practice to a more "poacher and gamekeeper" dynamic. That is to say, the focus becomes more about measurement. There is a risk that the monitor becomes focused on catching bad practice, and the deliverer seeks to attain the best audit rating. In the case of service buyers and third-party program deliverers, the "poacher and gamekeeper" dynamic could become more pronounced when their funding can be positively or negatively impacted based on performance on audit baselines. With the contract negotiation of third-party program providers, if the concept of "intelligent purchasing" is not adequately adopted as part of the contract design and negotiation, third-party providers may be compelled to adopt the dual role of program deliverer and program monitor. They could then be obliged to be "poacher and gamekeeper," which places them in the difficult position of being contracted to objectively assess and improve their own performance, including identifying their own delivery blind spots. With added pressures around funding and outcomes, this can be an unenviable position in which to place program deliverers. There is also the case of becoming a victim of success. Where smaller programs demonstrate good outcomes there can be a risk of overexpansion. This happens when delivery volumes are increased without full attention to expanding the program supports first. In such cases the existing supporting mechanisms become insufficient to support the weight of delivery.

The Program Integrity Network

Large bureaucratic organizations often have to react to the many external forces of policy, public perception, and government. Through organizational change (including public sector modernization programs, budget cut initiatives, restructuring) parts of the program can inadvertently be carved off, altered, or separated without consideration for the impact on other aspects of program functioning or the wellbeing of the program as a whole. Indeed, some organizations may forget that some parts of the program network have any relationship with program quality or integrity. This can be particularly the case where there is fragmentation between program developers and delivery teams, or where there this more than moderate decentralization of program functions: essentially where program developers lack the required organizational influence.

Organizational resistance can be expressed indirectly by way of lack of understanding of the primary program components. These can include program development and support, staff (selection of, training, and ongoing competency), research evaluation, and integrity monitoring processes. It can also be expressed by a lack of impact and influence of other organizational functions on the program or its varying components. Organizational change initiatives (including budget cut programs and organizational restructures) can be significant destabilizers for an offending behavior program unless program structures are adequately embedded, and the managerial hierarchy is adequately informed or influenced by programs specialists. Danger exists where parts of the program are disparate and links between components are not explicitly understood or maintained. An example of this danger may be seen when the recruitment and initial training of therapists becomes the sole domain of a large correctional organization's human resources department, rather than that of the program delivery department. This could mean that the criteria for selection and recruitment may change over time in line with human resources policy, and could drift away from the interests and needs of the program and its developers. If these needs are not understood, then a wider supportive organizational context may not be established for integrity to be a systemic and achievable feature. Figure 23.2 illustrates core components of a network of features that can provide the backdrop and conditions for success.

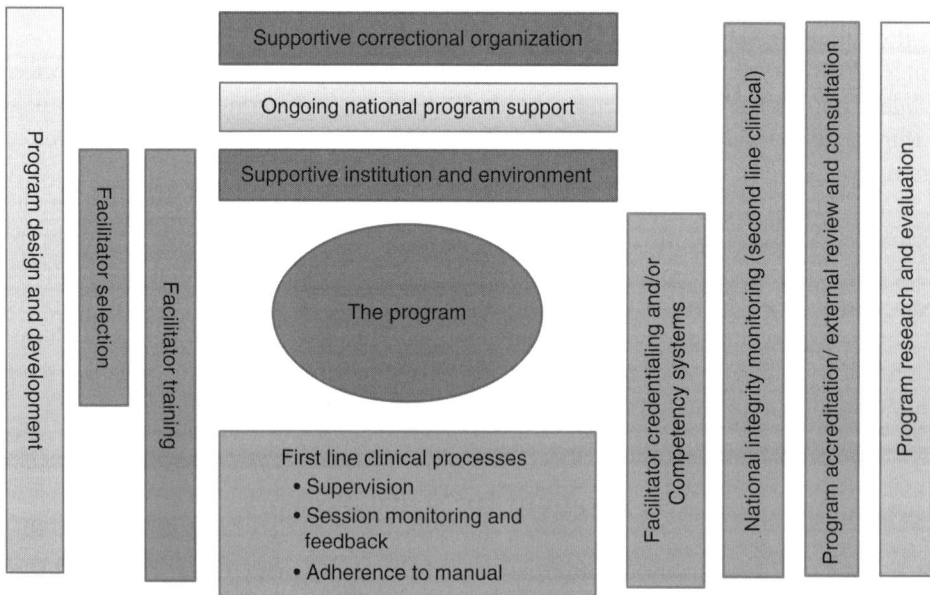

Figure 23.2 The program integrity network.

There is a challenge for any program on its own (and its respective managerial hierarchy—which could be within or outside of the organization) to maintain all potential aspects of the network (and who is to say that Figure 23.2 indeed represents all aspects of what's important to program integrity?). An important question for both program providers and the hosting organizations to ask is "what integrity functions are present around the program and how are they connected to one another"? This question is equally valid for small-scale programs and for those delivered through third-party contracts, or procured "off the shelf." The mapping of integrity functions and processes is important. This can help us understand and mitigate mindfully the effects of the unintended shortfalls in program integrity functions or over-reliance on others. A less mindful or broader view of the program shortcomings can see potential for uniformed design drift by way of compensatory behaviors (i.e., having overly prescriptive manuals to offset use of non-therapeutic staff delivering programs or lack of adequate facilitator training) for problems or issues that might be better addressed by alternate measures.

All of the integrity functions should be considered within the wider context of the program and its impact on the wider network. For example, the end-to-end process of program design, operational support, and outcome research evaluation is linked and should in turn contribute to revision of program methods and content. The initial design should begin with adequate research and evidence base to provide a program designed to meet the needs and intended outcomes (contributing to the goal of it becoming an effective program). Part of this design should focus on a plan and broader strategy for evaluation of short- and longer-term outcomes (Friendship, Falshaw, & Beech, 2003). The data collected by this work will impact on the decisions to revise, update, or change the program. Program integrity remains a key precursor to effective evaluation and revision of design, and the two are interconnected elements required to assist a program in being effective. This information, along with expertise in the practice modalities, is a fundamental part of the function of supporting the clinical delivery of programs on a day-to-day basis. The supporting function is therefore best served at a centralized point by senior clinicians who have a close connection to both the design and evaluation functions for the program. Where the program design does not include a strategy for evaluation, key questions arise around how and when updates can take place and how outcomes are tested. Where there is no relationship between evaluation teams and program developers, questions must be asked about the evaluation framework and its relevance to understanding the functioning of the program and its level of effectiveness. Indeed, if no link (by way of program expertise) exists between evaluators and program developers, then how will short- and longer-term outcomes be related to program behaviors? Again, linked to the assertion of Gendreau et al. (2001) that without program integrity it is not possible to know if the program works or not, without an effective evaluation strategy that links with program development and practice the same problem arises in determining what it is about a program that works or not.

The program must therefore remain central to decision-making around any factors that have an impact on integrity. This is of course only possible where the links in functions are explicitly understood to have a bearing on the program. Figure 23.3 illustrates the program integrity network with the program at the center. Figure 23.3 might be helpful for some programs in reviewing program integrity functions and their connectivity as part of the evaluation and review cycle. Some key questions might include: How are the respective functions connected to or separated from the program and its intended design? Are any key functions missing? Are non-program-related departments responsible for key functions (e.g., in a situation where a

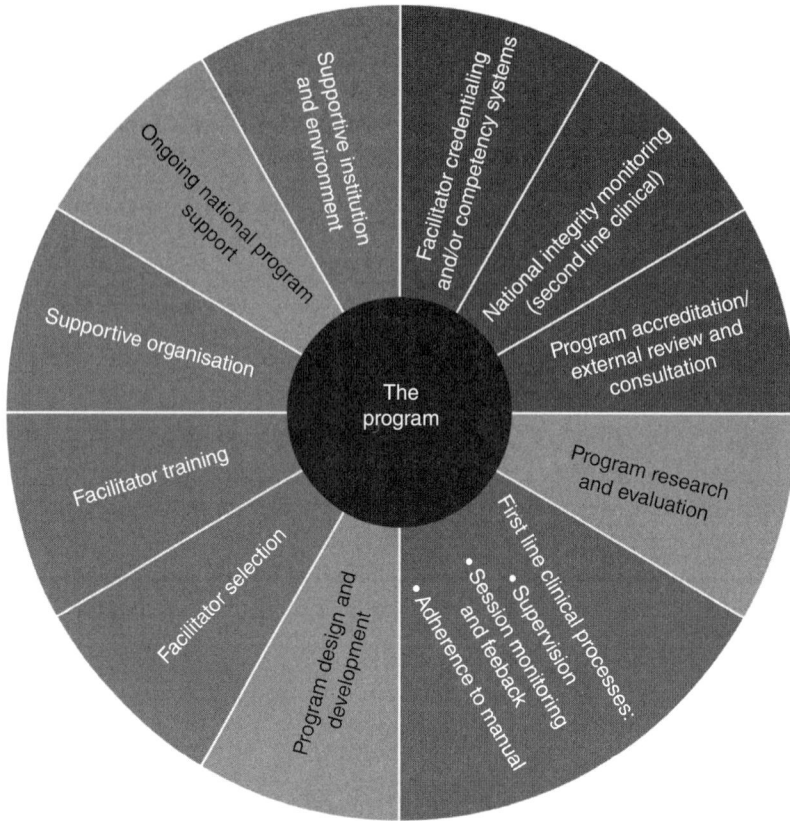

Figure 23.3 Program as a nucleus.

human resources department has written therapist competencies to ensure parity with other roles in the organization)?. Another example might be where integrity monitoring and program evaluation do not consider the impact of environmental factors. Using a visual depiction of integrity functions can assist the process of anchoring and focusing attention on what might be missing.

Conclusions and Discussion

The notion of *organizational resistance* continues to have significance in the world of offending behavior program integrity. Whilst we have clarity around the conditions required within programs to work toward better outcomes, the context outside of programs remains highly influential in setting the conditions for success. With more programs adopting a whole-of-environment approach, and greater understanding of the importance of social climate in rehabilitation, this is ever more important.

Higher-level monitoring processes remain an integral quality assurance measurement, although there is less published on the optimal methodology for these. Challenge exists in ensuring that the measure remains an accurate gauge, and does not inadvertently become the goal. Review and update is required of the monitoring methodology to ensure its clinical sensitivity and relevance.

It is difficult to achieve an optimum balance between clinical and managerial worlds with treatment integrity processes, as Hollin (1995) noted. It is important to continue educating the operational organization about factors important to program integrity, and about treating integrity as a vital precursor to improved effectiveness, and ultimately, outcomes. It should be understood in the context of good design and revision of programs delivered over time. More research is required to develop systems where measurable integrity characteristics (e.g., through the monitoring and evaluation of sessions) can be examined in relation to improved or decreased performance on outcomes. Gendreau et al. (2001) have provided an insight into this world with their work on the CPAI. Having a stronger understanding of the links between the specific components of program integrity and their impact on outcome would be a welcome next stage in the evolution of program integrity.

The model utilized originally with the correctional services accreditation panel at its first inception represents an interesting and unique model for supporting organizations, through provision of independent expert advice. This can address both clinical program issues and wider organizational and environment issues. The process of consultation and external objective review of programs and their systems remains a vital feature for ensuring objectivity for best practice in large-scale interventions. Expert entities like the CSAP can provide real support to both clinical and managerial teams, and can help navigate problems with *organizational resistance*.

The increasing use of private, NGO, and other third-party providers brings a host of new considerations for, and challenges to, ensuring program integrity. Their use emphasizes the need for program integrity experts to assist and inform financial and contract management. The commissioning of external providers and writing of contracts needs to be mindful of the conditions of success for programs, and the "buying" organization needs to be a creative and intelligent purchaser, building links with these services and the hosting organizational systems to give a third-party provider a chance of being successful. Ultimately, these programs need the same connection to integrity functions as those run by the purchasing organization (see Figure 23.3). The notion of technology transfer needs consideration in the procurement, delivery, and support for such services. It is simply not viable for a purchasing organization to adopt a "buy and fly" approach for such services and for them to operate in silos. There needs to be a more involved and reciprocal relationship, and, to stand a chance of success, the external program deliverer needs to be, at least in part, integrated into the host organization.

Rapidly changing social and political climates have a direct impact on the organizational context and the immediate environmental context of program delivery. A real risk in the shifting sands of correctional organizations and in the variable operating models for offending behavior programs is that there is a need to adapt to ensure program integrity remains a sufficiently high priority. Without careful attention the factors that influence program integrity can easily be eroded or worse, lost. Likewise, the program integrity network can be broken up and scattered, leading to a significant loss in program delivery capability.

The challenge for program deliverers, wherever they may be and whether they operate large-scale, small-scale, contracted, or in-house services, is to conceptualize and map program integrity and its supporting functions in their own delivery context. We need to continually work at maintaining the connections of the network and ensure that the organization in which we work understands the wider program picture. Hollin's (1995) notion of *organizational resistance* is no less relevant today, although what might impact positively and negatively on programs may have changed, and may continue to do so.

Maintaining as broad a network as possible and attending to key shortfalls can assist in balancing and preventing the negative characteristics of compensatory behaviors. Maintaining a broad system-wide approach requires a keen eye and constant effort in order to address the risks of organizational resistance. The efforts of assessing and understanding social climate in prisons (as highlighted by Day et al., 2011) indicate promising progress in quantifying the issues of milieu and organizational efforts with rehabilitation. With this increased insight, program providers can continue with their efforts to provide interventions that can help change offenders' lives and reduce reoffending.

Key Readings

Bonta, J., & Andrews, D. A. (2017). *The psychology of criminal conduct* (6th ed.). London, UK: Routledge.

Cullen, F. T., Jonson, C. L., & Nagin, D. S. (2011). Prisons do not reduce recidivism: The high cost of ignoring science. *The Prison Journal*, 91, 48–65.

Gendreau, P. (1996). Offender rehabilitation: What we know and what needs to be done. *Criminal Justice and Behavior*, 23, 144–161.

Gendreau, P., Goggin, C., & Smith, P. (1999). The forgotten issue in effective correctional treatment: Program implementation. *International Journal of Offender Therapy and Comparative Criminology*, 43, 180–187.

Harding, R. (2014). Rehabilitation and prison social climate: Do "what works" rehabilitation programs work better in prisons that have a positive social climate? *Australian & New Zealand Journal of Criminology*,, 47, 163–175.

Hollin, C. R. (1995). The meaning and implications of "programme integrity". In J. McGuire (Ed.), *What works: Reducing reoffending: Guidelines from research and practice* (pp. 195–208). Chichester, UK: Wiley.

McGuire, M., Grubin, D., Losel, F., & Raynor, P. (2010). "What works" and the correctional services accreditation panel: Taking stock from an inside perspective. *Criminology & Criminal Justice*, 10, 37–58.

References

Andrews, D. A., Zinger, I., Hoge, R. D., Bonta, J., Gendreau, P., & Cullen, F. T. (1990). Does correctional treatment work? A clinically relevant and psychologically informed meta-analysis. *Criminology*, 28, 369–404.

Atkinson, R., & Tew, J. (2012). Working with psychopathic offenders: Lessons from the Chromis program. *International Journal of Forensic Mental Health*, 11, 299–311.

Bonta, J., & Andrews, D. A. (2017). *The psychology of criminal conduct* (6th ed.). London, UK: Routledge.

Cullen, F. T., & Gendreau, P. (2000). Assessing correctional rehabilitation: Policy, practice and prospects. In J. Horney (Ed.), *National Institute of Justice Criminal Justice 2000: Changes in decision making and discretion in the criminal justice system* (Vol. 1) (pp. 109–175). Washington, DC: Department of Justice, National Institute of Justice.

Cullen, F. T., Jonson, C. L., & Nagin, D. S. (2011). Prisons do not reduce recidivism: The high cost of ignoring science. *The Prison Journal*, 91, 48–65.

Day, A., Casey, S., Vess, J., & Huisy, G. (2011). *Assessing the social climate of prisons*. Canberra, Australia: Criminology Research Council.

Day, A., Casey, S., Ward, A., Howells, K., & Vess, J. (2013). *Transitions to better lives: Offender readiness and rehabilitation*. Cullompton, UK: Willan.

Friendship, C., Falshaw, L., & Beech, A. R. (2003). Measuring the real impact of accredited offending behaviour programs. *Legal and Criminological Psychology*, 8, 115–127.

Gendreau, P. (1996). Offender rehabilitation: What we know and what needs to be done. *Criminal Justice and Behavior*, 23, 144–161.

Gendreau, P., Goggin, C., & Smith, P. (1999). The forgotten issue in effective correctional treatment: Program implementation. *International Journal of Offender Therapy and Comparative Criminology*, 43, 180–187.

Gendreau, P., Goggin, C., & Smith, P. (2001). Implementation guidelines for correctional programs in the "real world". In G. A. Bernfeld, D. P. Farrington, & A. W. Leschied (Eds.), *Offender rehabilitation in practice* (pp. 228–268). Chichester, UK: Wiley.

Goggin, C., & Gendreau, P. (2006). The implementation and maintenance of quality services in offender rehabilitation programmes. In C. R. Hollin, & E. J. Palmer (Eds.), *Offending behaviour programmes: Development, application and controversies* (pp. 209–245). Chichester, UK: Wiley.

Hanson, R. K., Bourgon, G., Helmus, L., & Hodgson, S. (2009). *A meta-analysis of the effectiveness of treatment for sexual offenders: Risk, need and responsivity*. Ottawa, Canada: Public Safety Canada.

Harding, R. (2014). Rehabilitation and prison social climate: Do "what works" rehabilitation programs work better in prisons that have a positive social climate? *Australian & New Zealand Journal of Criminology*, 47, 163–175.

Henggeler, S. W., Melton, G. B., Brondino, M. J., Scherer, D. G., & Hanley, J. H. (1997). Multisystemic therapy with violent and chronic juvenile offenders and their families: The role of treatment fidelity in successful dissemination. *Journal of Consulting and Clinical Psychology*, 65, 821–833.

Hollin, C. R. (1995). *The meaning and implications of "programme integrity."*. In J. McGuire (Ed.), *What works: Reducing reoffending—Guidelines from research and practice* (pp. 195–208). Chichester, UK: Wiley.

Hollin, C. R. (2001). The role of the consultant in developing effective correctional programs. In G. A. Bernfeld, D. P. Farrington, & A. W. Leschied (Eds.), *Offender rehabilitation in practice* (pp. 269–281). Chichester, UK: Wiley.

Hollin, C. R. (2009). Treatment manuals: The good, the bad and the useful. *Journal of Sexual Aggression*, 15, 133–137.

Lösel, F., & Schmucker, M. (2005). The effectiveness of treatment for sexual offenders: A comprehensive meta-analysis. *Journal of Experimental Criminology*, 1, 1–29.

Lowenkamp, C. T., & Latessa, E. J. (2004). Investigating the relationship between program integrity and correctional program effectiveness. *The Ohio Corrections Research Compendium*, 2, 208–213.

McGuire, J., & Priestley, P. (1995). *Reviewing "what works": Past, present, and future*. In J. McGuire (Ed.), *What works: Reducing reoffending* (pp. 3–34). Chichester, UK: Wiley.

McGuire, M., Grubin, D., Losel, F., & Raynor, P. (2010). "What works" and the correctional services accreditation panel: Taking stock from an inside perspective. *Criminology & Criminal Justice*, 10, 37–58.

Nesovic, A. (2003). *Psychometric evaluation of the Correctional Program Assessment Inventory (CPAI)* (Unpublished doctoral dissertation). Carlton University, Ontario, Canada.

Newberry, M. (2010). A synthesis of outcome research at Grendon Therapeutic Community Prison. *Therapeutic Communities*, 31, 356–371.

Polaschek, D. L. L., & Kilgour, T. G. (2013). New Zealand's special treatment units: The development and implementation of intensive treatment for high-risk male prisoners. *Psychology, Crime & Law*, 19, 511–526.

Turley, C., Payne, C., & Webster, S. (2013). *Enabling features of psychologically informed planned environments.*. Ministry of Justice Analytical Series. London, UK: Ministry of Justice. Retrieved from https://assets.publishing.service.gov.uk/government/uploads/system/uploads/attachment_data/file/211730/enabling-pipe-research-report.pdf

Velasco-Garrido, M., Borowitz, M., Ovretveit, J., & Busse, R. (2005). Purchasing for quality of care. In J. Figueras, M. McKee, E. Mossialos, & R. E. Saltman (Eds.), *Purchasing to improve health systems performance.* European Observatory on Health Systems and Policies Series (pp. 215–235). Maidenhead, UK: Open University Press.

24

Measuring the Intermediate Effects of Offense-Focused Intervention on Offenders

Michael Daffern, Gabrielle Klepfisz, and Tamara Sweller
Swinburne University of Technology, Australia

Andrew Day
James Cook University and University of Melbourne, Australia

The Effect of Programs on Reoffending

Rigorous program evaluation within correctional settings is difficult and ideally incorporated into the design of the program before it is implemented (Polaschek & Collie, 2004). Many potentially effective programs are never adequately evaluated, while others are subject to evaluations using weak designs, often without an appropriate comparison group, reducing our ability to determine whether any treatment has had a particular impact. Further, many program evaluations use recidivism as the primary or sole outcome measure of treatment effectiveness. This approach has several limitations. Most notably, although using officially documented recidivism (e.g., convictions) is helpful in that those people who have a subsequent criminal conviction can truly be said to have not changed, the same cannot be said for those people who do not have a subsequent conviction; many criminal acts go unreported, so relying only on official records may indicate that some people have improved when in fact they have not been caught, charged, and/or convicted. Furthermore, since recidivism is a distal outcome, measured at a time following treatment, numerous extraneous factors (e.g., employment, social support, housing) can influence recidivism rates and the successful reintegration of an offender into the community (Jung & Gulayets, 2011; Serin, Lloyd, Helmus, Derkzen, & Luong, 2013). To address these problems, some authors argue that the assessment of individual performance during treatment (not just post-treatment) and the level of change achieved deserve greater attention (Nunes, Babchishin, & Cortoni, 2011). This is the focus of this chapter.

Before turning to a review of methods for calculating within-treatment change, it is helpful to establish whether contemporary programs have an impact on participants generally. We now turn to a brief overview of treatment outcomes for sexual and non-sexual violent offenders.

In relation to non-sexual violent offenders, there is a surprisingly limited evidence base from which to draw any firm conclusions about the effectiveness of psychological treatment (McGuire, 2008). In what is still the only published meta-analysis of violent offender treatment programs, Polaschek and Collie (2004) identified only nine program evaluations that included a comparison group (matched or randomly allocated) and reported subsequent recidivism rates (although only four studies reported violent recidivism rates). Of these, two were classi-fied as primarily cognitive programs (cognitive skills training and cognitive self-change), three as anger management programs, and three as "multimodal" programs. Polaschek and Collie concluded that although most of the programs they reviewed showed some level of efficacy, it was difficult to draw any firm conclusions about effectiveness given the small number of studies, the weaknesses inherent in some evaluation designs, and variation in other features such as length, setting, staffing, and the lack of basic information about offender characteris-tics such as age and level of risk. In addition, some studies omitted to report important details such as program content and delivery and participant and setting characteristics, and little information was provided about the theoretical basis of programs.

In a systematic review of violent offender treatment conducted for the Ministry of Justice (UK), Jolliffe and Farrington (2007) were able to identify only 11 outcome studies that met the required methodological criteria. They cautiously concluded that "interventions with violent offenders were effective both at reducing general and violent re-offending, with a difference in percentage of participants reconvicted of about eight to eleven per cent for general re-offending measures and seven to eight per cent for violent re-offending measures" (p. iv). They did note, however, that effectiveness varied considerably according to factors such as the content of the intervention, the delivery of the intervention, and the methodology of the study. Collectively, these rather inconsistent findings suggest that much can be done to improve the ways in which violent offender treatment is both conceptualized and delivered, as well as to identify the need for more rigorously designed and controlled evaluation research to be conducted.

Since this review was published, a number of other evaluations have been reported. Serin, Gobeil, and Preston (2009) reported outcomes of an evaluation of a persistently violent offender treatment program offered to Canadian offenders. They compared program com-pleters to two control groups (those who completed an alternative program and those who failed to complete), but identified few differences between the groups on a range of measures (including change on measures of treatment targets, institutional misconduct, and post-release returns to custody). Serin et al. (2009) suggested that this might mean that either the program was effective with only certain groups of violent offenders, or that it did not meet some of the criteria that are usually associated with the more effective programs (e.g., program integrity and intensity). One other Canadian evaluation has, however, produced more prom-ising results. Cortoni, Nunes, and Latendresse (2006) found that completion of a Canadian Correctional Services Violence Prevention Program led to reductions in institutional miscon-duct charges in the 6-month and 1-year periods following program completion, and that those offenders who had completed the program had lower rates of recidivism than non-treated offenders. Finally, Berry (2003) assessed the efficacy of a cognitive behavioral, community-based, residential program in New Zealand in terms of severity of reoffense. Treatment completers registered 35.3% fewer violent convictions than matched controls ($p < .01$, $\phi = .30$) and, although non-significant, the mean severity score of completers' post-treatment convictions (measured as the average days of imprisonment for that offense) was 49% less than the mean severity score for controls. Treated offenders were slower to be reconvicted for violence than control participants. So, while not all studies provide such encouraging results, collectively, there is evidence that despite methodological differences in treatment modality, intensity, participants, content, follow-up, and outcome, violence intervention programs typically exhibit some, albeit modest, level of efficacy in reducing any and/ or violent recidivism. Furthermore, it appears that cognitive behavioral programs that conform to Risk-Need-Responsivity (RNR) principles often achieve higher-than-average effects (Polaschek, 2011).

Various meta-analytic studies have investigated the outcome of sexual offender treatment (e.g., Hanson, Bourgon, Helmus, & Hodgson, 2009; Schmucker & Lösel, 2015). Lösel and Schmucker's (2005) meta-analysis (including both general and sexual offender specific treatment), for example, found that programs designed specifically for sexual offenders had a significant positive effect, with an overall treatment effectiveness of 37% reduction in sexual recidivism. Of note is that this meta-analysis included studies in which both psychological and surgical modes of treatment were administered, which presents additional variables that impact on behavioral change (surgical methods had a larger impact). Lösel and Schmucker (2005) also found that treatment effectiveness was greater for community-based treatment programs than for those delivered in custodial settings. A more recent meta-analysis by Schmucker and Lösel (2015) reported a somewhat lower mean effect size (3.6 percentage points; 10.1% for treated offenders compared to 13.7% for untreated offenders) suggesting greater caution in making claims about the effectiveness of treatment programs.

Hanson et al. (2009) reported that sexual and general recidivism rates for treated sexual offenders were lower than those observed for comparison groups. However, they asserted that the weak research designs of the majority of studies should decrease confidence in the findings, in particular because the effects tended to be stronger in the studies with weak research designs. As a result, they suggested that it is reasonable to conclude that there is no evidence that sexual offender treatment reduces recidivism. Despite this, studies in which the treatment programs adhered to the RNR model consistently demonstrated greater treatment effectiveness than those reporting on treatment programs that did not adhere to these three principles.

Less positive conclusions have, however, emerged from more recent research syntheses. In one systematic review of randomized controlled trials, the main finding was that there was no evidence that active intervention reduced sexual recidivism (Dennis et al., 2012). Dennis et al. (2012) argued that without further randomized controlled trials there could be continued use of ineffective or harmful interventions for sexual offenders, in addition to the misconception that an individual is at reduced risk of reoffending following treatment. As Levenson and Prescott (2013) suggest, purely providing treatment to sexual offenders is not sufficient, and clinicians must work to support clients in their efforts to develop an emotional understanding of the material. Additionally, sexual offender treatment effectiveness studies have generally focused on the *absolute* measure of recidivism rates, thus ignoring *relative* measures of client improvement (e.g., delayed recidivism, decreased severity, or decreased frequency).

In a systematic review of interventions for adults who sexually offended against children, Langstrom et al. (2013) concluded that the evidence is currently insufficient to determine if cognitive behavioral therapy with relapse prevention reduces sexual offending. This review identified little research of acceptable quality relating to the individual-level prevention of child sexual abuse. However, a recent meta-analysis that used a sample of 29 well-controlled comparisons concluded that treatment can effectively reduce recidivism in sexual offenders (Schmucker & Lösel, 2015).

The lack of high-quality studies and the aforementioned results indicate, in our view, that it is still not possible to unambiguously demonstrate treatment effectiveness for either violent or sexually violent offenders and that it cannot be assumed that treatment completion guarantees that the changes required to positively influence recidivism have occurred (Olver & Wong, 2013). Furthermore, although evaluating group-level changes and their relation to recidivism is useful in determining the efficacy of treatment as a whole, evaluating treatment completers as a single cohort may attenuate or mask significant effects among those who do, or do not, receive benefit from treatment (Beggs, 2010).

The importance of focusing on within-treatment change is highlighted in research from the general clinical psychology and psychiatry literature, where distal outcomes are typically not the primary outcome measure; rather, the most common indices of evidence-based practice are more immediate (e.g., no longer meeting criteria for a psychiatric diagnosis). Thus, the detailed examination of within-treatment change may be a useful index of treatment success that can be used as an adjunct or alternative to measuring the recidivism rates of treatment completers versus non-completers.

Risk Factors and Within-Treatment Change

There are two categories of risk factors that are generally considered when determining risk of recidivism: static and dynamic (Andrews et al., 1990). Static factors are those that are unchangeable and, as such, represent unsuitable treatment targets (Mann, Hanson, & Thornton, 2010) and, further, cannot be used to determine whether an offender has improved (or not). Dynamic risk factors are changeable, with their modification or elimination representing the mechanism that underlies a decrease in offending behavior (Serin & Lloyd, 2009). As Douglas and Skeem (2005) outline, a dynamic risk factor must: (a) be an antecedent to, and increase the propensity for, violence; (b) be changeable; and (c) predict changes in violent reoffending as a result of treatment. Although limited research has examined whether individual-level changes in dynamic risk factors are actually associated with reoffending, it seems logical that if offenders complete treatment with fewer dynamic risk factors present then such changes should be associated with reduced recidivism.

Pre-post change scores

One common method to evaluate within-treatment change is to assess whether there is evidence of significant changes on intermediary treatment targets, or proximal offense-related dynamic risk factors (Friendship, Falshaw, & Beech, 2003). These 'criminogenic needs' are functionally related to offending behavior and thus, when used as clinical targets, offer more immediate indicators of treatment success. To this end, individuals may complete psychometric tests measuring dynamic risk factors pre- and post-treatment and raw pre-post difference scores can be used to provide an estimate of treatment change (e.g., Hudson, Wales, Bakker, & Ward, 2002). It is important to note, however, that when using raw pre-post change scores, the magnitude of change on one measure cannot be compared to another measure since such scores are unstandardized and scale-specific (Olver, Beggs Christofferson, & Wong, 2015).

Furthermore, raw pre-post score comparisons make no adjustment for measurement error. Every psychological test encompasses a degree of error, and when estimating change, a limitation is posed by the presence of ceiling and/or floor effects (Hammond & O'Rourke, 2007). For example, those individuals deemed most "deviant" or "high-risk" at pre-treatment have greater scope for improvement. As an attempt to control for this, standardized residual change (RCZ) scores can be calculated by regressing raw change scores onto the pre-treatment scores for each psychometric variable (Beggs & Grace, 2011). The unique variance accounted for by pre-treatment scores can be calculated from these regressions (i.e., obtained change score – predicted change score) and then standardized for each variable (Beggs & Grace, 2011). Thus, while simple change scores reflect the actual amount of change between pre- and post-treatment, without controlling for pre-treatment differences, residualized change scores "seek to determine what the observed change would have been if everyone had started out equal" (Rogosa, Brandt, & Zimowski, 1982, p. 741; Woessner & Schwedler, 2014).

Another issue when using self-report psychological tests to determine change in dynamic risk factors is that these tests may be vulnerable to lying, manipulation, and self-presentation biases. Triangulating self-report data with clinician and observer-rated measures as well as other data pertaining to progress could be used to counter these concerns and validate self-report psychological test data. It should not be assumed that simply because somebody has a history of antisocial conduct that their responses to psychological tests are invalid; offender self-report questionnaires can be both accurate and valid (Mills, Loza, & Kroner, 2003).

The reliable change index

Researchers examining the efficacy of offender rehabilitation programs have recently become interested in using the reliable change index (RCI) to measure individual change. The RCI is a standardized measure of within-treatment change, which adjusts for test reliability and calculates whether change is statistically reliable ($p < .05$) and not simply caused by chance or measurement error (Barnett, Wakeling, Mandeville-Norden, & Rakestrow, 2013). The RCI is calculated using an offender's scores on a predetermined measure and the formula proposed by Christensen and Mendoza (1986, p. 305):

$$RCI = \frac{X_2 - X_1}{S_{diff}}$$

This formula takes into account inherent measurement error, where X_2 represents a subject's post-test score, X_1 represents that same subject's pre-test score, and S_{diff} represents the standard error of the difference between X_2 and X_1:

$$S_{diff} = SD\sqrt{2(SE)^2}$$

The standard error of measurement (SE) is computed with the formula:

$$SE = SD\sqrt{(1 - r_{xx})}$$

SD refers to the pre-treatment standard deviation for the offender group for each measure and r_{xx} refers to the test–retest reliability of that measure. Jacobson and Truax (1991) suggest that an RCI of 1.96 or above reflects real (reliable) change for a two-tailed test with a 95% confidence interval.

The RCI can be used with small sample sizes, which is a common problem in forensic program evaluation. Furthermore, it is capable of providing information that is unattainable through group-level analyses. For example, the RCI can be used to systematically classify and compare individuals based on whether or not they have reliably changed in treatment. Thus, although the RCI cannot replace statistics based on group means, when research examining treatment response is more idiographic, the RCI permits examination of individual progress over time. Ostensibly, knowing whether someone has changed during treatment is central to decisions regarding an offender's conditional release, custodial placement, and further supervision and/or treatment need.

A worked example

Suppose two individuals completed a violent offender treatment program that aimed to reduce anger. Scores for trait anger (T-Ang) were scored at pre- and post-treatment. Person 1 recorded a pre-treatment score of 16 and a post-treatment score of 40. To calculate their RCI, the following steps need to be taken:

$$RCI = \frac{X_2 - X_1}{S_{diff}}$$

$$\text{Therefore, } RCI \frac{40 - 16}{S_{diff}}$$

Let's say that the pre-treatment standard deviation for the offender group on T-Ang is 4.82 and the 14-day test–retest reliability for T-Ang is 0.70.

$$\text{Given that}: S_{diff} = SD\sqrt{2(SE)^2} \text{ and } SE = SD\sqrt{(1 - r_{xx})}$$

$$\text{Therefore, } SE = 4.82\sqrt{(1 - 0.70)} \therefore SE = 2.64$$

$$\text{Therefore, } S_{diff}f = \sqrt{2(2.64)^2} \therefore S_{diff}f = 3.73$$

Now, returning to the original equation:

$$RCI = \frac{40 - 16}{3.73} \therefore RCI = 6.43$$

Note that person 1's level of trait anger *increased* following treatment; since the absolute value of their RCI is greater than 1.96, person 1 has achieved reliably significant change on this measure, despite the change occurring in an undesired direction.

Let's consider another individual. Person 2 recorded a pre-treatment score of 23 and a post-treatment score of 16 on the same measure. From the calculations above, we now know that $S_{diff} = 3.73$. Therefore, to calculate reliable change:

$$RCI = \frac{16 - 23}{3.73} \therefore RCI = 1.88$$

Although this individual seems to have improved in treatment and their trait anger score has *decreased*, since the absolute value of their RCI does not exceed 1.96, person 2 has not reliably changed on this measure during treatment.

Clinically significant change

Some authors argue that it is not merely the magnitude of change that is important, but whether offenders can be classified as functioning at a "normal" level following treatment (Jacobson, Follette, & Revenstorf, 1986). By calculating clinically significant change (CSC), researchers can determine not only whether offenders have reliably changed, but also whether they have achieved a "treated" profile, and are thus psychometrically indistinguishable from a sample of non-offenders (Barnett et al., 2013).

To ascertain whether an individual has achieved CSC, a cutoff point needs to be determined; that is, the point that the subject must cross at the time of post-treatment assessment in order to be deemed changed to a clinically significant degree or to within a functional range. This can be done using the following formula (Jacobson & Truax, 1991, p. 13):

$$c = \frac{s_0 M_1 + s_1 M_0}{s_0 + s_1}$$

Here, s_0 and M_0 represent the standard deviation and mean for the normative population, respectively, whereas s_1 and M_1 represent the standard deviation and mean for the offender population, respectively. By combining post-treatment scores and the amount of change achieved (reliable versus no reliable change), researchers have created descriptive subgroups to differentiate and communicate an individual's response to treatment (see Table 24.1).

Using the CSC method, significant differences between "treated" and "untreated" offenders can be elucidated and more reliably attributed to treatment without the influence of confounding variables (e.g., environmental or motivational factors) (Friendship et al., 2003). Notably, however, the calculation of CSC requires valid and contemporary non-offender norms, and these are often unavailable for forensic-specific measures. Furthermore, the CSC approach depends on the quality of the psychometric measures used.

Table 24.1   CSC Outcome Categories

Category	Description
Recovered	An individual who demonstrated reliable change and who moved from the dysfunctional to the functional range post-treatment
Improved	An individual who demonstrated reliable change but who was not within the functional range post-treatment
Already okay	An individual in the functional range both pre- and post-treatment, irrespective of the amount of change made in treatment
Unchanged	An individual who did not demonstrate reliable change. The individual's score may still move from dysfunctional to functional (or vice versa), yet this change is not reliable
Deteriorated	An individual who demonstrated reliable change in the undesired direction, and who was in the dysfunctional range post-treatment

Note. Adapted from Wakeling, Beech, and Freemantle (2013).

A worked example

Suppose the following descriptive statistics are used for the calculation of the CSC cutoff:

	Normative sample M (SD)	*Offender sample M (SD)*
Trait anger	18.40 (5.42)	23.11 (6.40)

To calculate the cutoff for clinically significant change:

$$c = \frac{s_0 M_1 + s_1 M_0}{s_0 + s_1}$$

$$\therefore c = \frac{(5.42 \times 23.11) + (6.40 \times 18.40)}{5.42 + 6.40} \quad \therefore c = \frac{243.0162}{11.82} = 20.56$$

Accordingly, a score of 20.56 on trait anger represents the point at which an individual moves from the dysfunctional to the functional range on this measure.

Considering the information from the preceding example, person 1 achieved reliably significant change, and moved from the functional (T-Ang = 16) to the dysfunctional (T-Ang = 40) range following treatment. Note that a T-Ang score of 40 is considered "dysfunctional" since it is above the clinically significant change cutoff of 20.56. Based on this information and the CSC categories listed above, person 1 would be classified as having "Deteriorated" following treatment. Conversely, person 2 moved from the dysfunctional (T-Ang = 23) to the functional (T-Ang = 16) range following treatment. However, they did not achieve reliably significant change on trait anger since the absolute value of their RCI did not exceed 1.96. Therefore, person 2 would be classified as "Unchanged" despite moving from the dysfunctional to the functional range. Individuals who remain in a dysfunctional range at post-treatment but who improve over the course of treatment, continue to have outstanding treatment needs. It is likely that these individuals begin the process of change in custody and this process can continue into the community (Olver, Beggs Christofferson, & Wong, 2015). As a result, the measurement of change does not necessarily end once custody-based treatment processes are completed.

Linking Within-Treatment Change and Recidivism

In order to draw conclusions about the meaningfulness of treatment change, Bowen (2012) argues that within-treatment changes must be associated with behavioral change in the expected direction. Few studies have investigated this area and, as yet, there is a lack of reliable and consistent evidence to link within-treatment change in violent and sexual offenders to decreased recidivism. Results of extant research suggest CSC is unrelated to recidivism (Klepfisz, O'Brien, & Daffern, 2014), or its effects are non-significant once risk status is taken into account (e.g., Barnett et al., 2013; Wakeling, Beech, & Freemantle, 2013); for example, Wakeling et al. (2013) found CSC was a modest predictor of recidivism on a number of psychometric tests measuring sexual obsessions, empathy, perspective-taking, rumination, self-esteem, and impulsivity; however, it did not make a significant incremental contribution above risk level.

These findings raise concerns about the validity of reliable and clinically significant change measurements using standardized psychological tests when assessing treatment progress (for discussion see Olver et al., 2015, and Wakeling et al., 2013, who note that the CSC method depends upon the quality of the psychological tests used and the availability of appropriate norms-calculation of CSC relies upon non-offender normative data). Olver et al. (2015) note that many studies have used measures that are unrelated to recidivism. Some psychological tests contain indices of criminogenic needs which have the potential to capture changes in risk; however, most of these lack sufficiently structured guidelines for measuring change or assessing the level of risk reduction that results from the change (Olver, Nicholaichuk, Kingston, & Wong, 2014). Additionally, one of the reasons why studies exploring RCI and CSC with narrowly focused psychological tests that were not designed for forensic purposes reveal non-significant findings is that criminal behavior is complex and multiply determined. Offending is typically the consequence of the interaction and activity of numerous dynamic risk factors. Change in any one dynamic risk factor is unlikely to be sufficient when there are other risk factors present. As such, any assessment strategy requires consideration of various risk and protective factors.

One approach to ensuring breadth in the assessment of dynamic risk and protective factors for change assessment purposes is to assess the offender prior to and after treatment using multi-item structured risk and protective assessment instruments; it is critical these instruments contain dynamic factors. In this approach, change in the total criminogenic need (dynamic items total score) or protective factors is determined through comparison of pre- and post-test scores. Five studies have shown that positive change on the Violence Risk Scale-Sexual Offender Version (VRS-SO, Wong, Olver, Nicholaichuk, & Gordon, 2003) is associated with lower rates of recidivism in sexual offenders, and recent work exploring change scores using dynamic items from the Violence Risk Scale (VRS, Wong & Gordon, 2003) has also provided support for the use of change scores derived from pre and post assessments on the dynamic items on the VRS to predict recidivism. For example, Lewis, Olver, and Wong (2013) found that following completion of the Aggressive Behavior Control program, psychopathic violent offenders' VRS dynamic change scores were significantly negatively correlated with violent recidivism. However, there is limited research into this change assessment methodology and some inconsistent results exist. For example, Klepfisz, O'Brien, and Daffern (2014) assessed change in the VRS, and although offenders typically made positive changes in terms of reducing violence potential, dynamic risk item change scores on the VRS were unrelated to violent recidivism.

Other structured risk assessment instruments incorporating dynamic risk factors, such as the Historical-Clinical-Risk Management-20 (HCR-20v^3) may also be used to measure change, as may measures incorporating protective factors. For example, de Vries Robbé, de Vogel, Douglas, and Nijman (2015) studied 108 (44 violent and 64 sexually violent) discharged forensic psychiatric patients and explored pre- and post-treatment assessments of risk (HCR-20v^3) and protective factors using the Structured Assessment of Protective Factors for Violence Risk (SAPROF; de Vogel, de Ruiter, Bouman, & de Vries Robbé, 2012). Total scores were composed for the HCR-20v^3, the SAPROF, and their subscales. In addition, a total risk minus total protection score was calculated, an HCR-SAPROF index. Results showed that improvements on risk and protective factors during treatment showed good predictive validity for abstention from violence for short- (1 year) as well as long-term (11 years) follow-up.

In terms of the application of CSC measurement to multi-item risk assessment instruments Olver et al. (2015) recently proposed a novel method; they identified individuals who had a score of 17 or lower on the VRS-SO, which equates with an average of 1 point per item for the 17 dynamic items, which indicates than none of the dynamic risk factors should be considered a criminogenic need (see Olver et al., 2015, pp. 99–100 for elaboration). Results revealed CSC-group differences in 5-year rates of sexual and violent recidivism, but when controlling for pre-treatment risk level, the post-treatment CSC category was less important than the risk level in terms of predicting recidivism. In summary, these findings suggest that assessment of change is best approached using multi-item structured risk assessment measures containing dynamic risk items. Change can be reliably assessed using these instruments, but care must be taken to remain mindful of pre-treatment risk level. At the end of treatment, many people will continue to present with some level of risk and some persistent criminogenic needs (ongoing active dynamic risk factors), and some protective factors may be weak or absent. Intervention (treatment and management) should be focused on the remaining risk and protective factors and to a level of intensity that matches the strength of these issues.

Protective Factors

Recently, increased attention has been paid to the risk prevention potential of dynamic protective factors. *Protective factors* are defined as any characteristic of a person or their environment or situation that reduces the risk for future violence (de Vries Robbé, de Vogel, & Stam, 2012). Dynamic protective factors can refer to internal personal characteristics, such as empathy, coping, and self-control; internal motivational factors, such as work, leisure activities, motivation for treatment, and life goals; and external support factors, including social network, professional care, and living circumstances (de Vogel et al., 2012).

Rather than focusing only on risk factors in the form of negative behavior, the development and measurement of positive behavior through intervention is also thought to be important when determining an offender's risk level (see Rogers, 2000). Mooney and Daffern (2013) demonstrated that prosocial skills observed in prison were of greater predictive value for violent recidivism than observed negative behavior. As a result, both prosocial and risk-related behavior must be monitored. This finding is consistent with the assertion that offenders' ability to change might be most effective when they concentrate on building daily prosocial habits, particularly when sequences of behavior occur that parallel offense chains that previously culminated in offending behavior (see discussion of Offense Paralleling Behavior in Daffern, Jones, & Shine, 2010).

Initial studies assessing protective factors using the SAPROF (de Vogel et al., 2012) have provided promising results. In a sample of 108 forensic psychiatric adult male inpatients at the Van der Hoeven Clinic in Utrecht, the Netherlands, de Vries Robbé, de Vogel, Douglas, and Nijman (2015) found that SAPROF change scores were predictive of violent recidivism for 1-year follow-up as well as for long-term follow-up. These findings exemplify that treatment changes can have positive effects on abstention from violence, and that this might be in the form of an increase in protective factors and/or a decrease in risk factors for violence. Coupland's (2015) dissertation was the first to examine the SAPROF in a non-psychiatric forensic sample. Participants included 178 federally incarcerated adult male offenders who participated in the Aggressive Behavior Control treatment program at the Regional Psychiatric Centre in Saskatoon, Canada. In this sample, total SAPROF change scores from pre-treatment to release significantly predicted non-sexual violent recidivism (all convictions and charges) after controlling for pre-treatment protection. Accordingly, offenders who scored low on the SAPROF protection factors had higher and faster rates of violent failure in the community than those with low to moderate scores.

Complications in Assessing the Manifestations of
Dynamic Risk Factors in Correctional Settings

A key challenge in the assessment of dynamic risk and protective factors is determining whether they are present when the environment is designed to prevent risk factors from manifesting. As such, assessors need to consider how dynamic risk factors manifest in the custodial setting (their form may be altered or muted as a consequence of environmental contingencies) and how the absence of a dynamic risk factor in the secure environment may not mean that the risk factor is no longer present (e.g., many sexual offenders will not engage in sexually deviant behavior and they may deny ongoing sexually deviant interests or these interests may not be aroused because of the lack of stimuli). Whether a dynamic risk factor is observable in the prison setting will depend on its strength and whether the environment provides triggers or contains features that suppress the risk factor. In one of the few studies that has investigated this, Sweller, Warren, and Daffern (2016) asked mental health professionals with experience working with sexual offenders in secure settings how they determine whether dynamic risk factors for sexual offending manifest in prison (the examples of risk factors were drawn from two sexual offender risk assessment tools: the Risk of Sexual Violence Protocol (RSVP) and the Violence Risk Scale: Sexual Offender version (VRS:SO). For each risk factor, participants were asked to provide examples of behaviors they might expect if the dynamic risk factors were present and active, and also, to provide examples of behaviors they might observe if these risk factors were no longer active and had been replaced with more prosocial behavior. Results revealed a wide variety of manifest risk-related and positive behaviors. However, in general, participants' responses for risk-related behaviors were more descriptive and they reported more risk-related behaviors than positive behaviors. Participants often stated that the positive behaviors were simply the absence of risk-related behaviors.

This research also identified the difficulty clinicians have in identifying behavior indicative of positive change. This might reflect a range of issues, such as: psychologists being trained in the use of risk assessment tools, which focus on risk-related factors (de Vries Robbé, de Vogel, & de Spa, 2011; Miller, 2006; Rogers, 2000; Sheldrick, 1999); the culture of a custodial environment being based on punishment or consequences for antisocial behavior; and the focus being on observed difficulties or problematic behavior when clinicians discuss clients with custodial staff. These observations are also consistent with previous research on the Offense Analogue and Offense Reduction Behavior Guide for the Violence Risk Scale, which has shown that staff rarely document prosocial behavior (Mooney & Daffern, 2013).

Sweller and colleagues (2016) also noted considerable variation in participants' ease in identifying manifestations of dynamic risk factors. For some risk factors, participants reported many behavioral manifestations (e.g., interpersonal aggression), but for other dynamic risk factors, participants reported very few behavioral manifestations (e.g., sexual deviance). Additional research is clearly required to better understand how dynamic risk factors manifest in prison, and further, why some risk factors may persist but not manifest, and the way in which environmental factors may stimulate or suppress these propensities. Finally, Sweller et al. (2016) noted that some behavioral manifestations identified by participants were uncommon and appeared unrelated to the risk factor in question. This may suggest that some assessors are uncertain about the behaviors that offenders exhibit when a particular dynamic risk factor is manifest; alternatively, there may be idiosyncratic manifestations of these risk factors. Ultimately, this suggests that careful scrutiny of the behavior is required before determining that it is relevant to the person's offending. Sweller and colleagues reported that those risk factors that are more internal to the offender (i.e., related to thoughts and attitudes) produced more uncommon and seemingly irrelevant responses, suggesting that when clinicians cannot directly observe the relevant behavior they are more likely to consider a range of behaviors as relevant to the dynamic risk factor. To help counter these problems, assessors need to understand "normal" responses to incarceration as well as the "typical" manifestations of dynamic risk factors in the custodial environment.

Conclusions

The coherence of current conceptualizations of risk, and therefore change assessments that are based on measurement of risk, has recently been questioned (see Ward & Beech, 2014). However, in this chapter we have suggested that the most valid method currently available to assess the impact of treatment and change over time involves the repeat assessment of dynamic risk and protective factors using clinician-rated multi-item structured risk assessment instruments containing dynamic risk factors instruments with established predictive validity. There are now several studies which show significant relationships between change scores and recidivism for the VRS:SO, VRS, and HCR-20v³. Tools such as the SAPROF, which measures dynamic protective factors, also hold some promise in helping treatment facilitators, release decision-makers, and program evaluators to determine whether meaningful change in violent and sexual offenders has actually occurred.

Key Readings

Beggs, S. (2010). Within-treatment outcome among sexual offenders: A review. *Aggression and Violent Behavior*, 15, 369–379.

Bowen, E. (2012). Within-treatment change: Finding the individual in group outcomes. In E. Bowen, & S. Brown (Eds.), *Perspectives on evaluating criminal justice and corrections* (pp. 145–171). Bingley, UK: Emerald Group.

Ward, T., & Beech, A. (2014). Dynamic risk factors: A theoretical dead-end? *Psychology, Crime & Law*, 21, 1–14.

References

Andrews, D. A., Zinger, I., Hoge, R., Bonta, J., Gendreau, P., & Cullen, F. (1990). Does correctional treatment work? A clinically relevant and psychologically informed meta-analysis. *Criminology*, 28, 369–404.

Barnett, G. D., Wakeling, H., Mandeville-Norden, R., & Rakestrow, J. (2013). Does change in psychometric test scores tell us anything about risk of reconviction in sexual offenders? *Psychology, Crime & Law*, 19, 85–110.

Beggs, S. (2010). Within-treatment outcome among sexual offenders: A review. *Aggression and Violent Behavior*, 15(5), 369–379.

Beggs, S., & Grace, R. (2011). Treatment gain for sexual offenders against children predicts reduced recidivism: A comparative validity study. *Journal of Consulting and Clinical Psychology*, 79(2), 182–192.

Berry, S. (2003). Stopping violent offending in New Zealand: Is treatment an option? *New Zealand Journal of Psychology*, 32(2), 92–100.

Bowen, E. (2012). Within-treatment change: Finding the individual in group outcomes. In E. Bowen, & S. Brown (Eds.), *Perspectives on evaluating criminal justice and corrections* (pp. 145–171). Bingley, UK: Emerald Group.

Christensen, L., & Mendoza, J. I. (1986). A method of addressing change in a single subject: An alteration of the RC index. *Behavior Therapy*, 17, 305–308.

Cortoni, F., Nunes, K. L., & Latendresse, M. (2006). *An examination of the effectiveness of the Violence Prevention Program* (Research report R-178). Ottowa, Canada: Correctional Service of Canada. Retrieved from http://www.csc-scc.gc.ca/research/092/r178_e.pdf

Coupland, R. B. A. (2015). *An examination of dynamic risk, protective factors, and treatment-related change in violent offenders* (Unpublished doctoral dissertation). University of Saskatchewan, Saskatoon, Canada.

Daffern, M., Jones, L., & Shine, J. (2010). *Offence Paralleling Behaviour: A case formulation approach to offender assessment and treatment.* Chichester, UK: Wiley.

de Vogel, V., de Ruiter, C., Bouman, Y., & de Vries Robbé, M. (2012). *SAPROF. Guidelines for the assessment of protective factors for violence risk.* English version. Utrecht, the Netherlands: Forum Educatief.

de Vries Robbé, M., de Vogel, V., & de Spa, E. (2011). Protective factors for violence risk in forensic psychiatric patients: A retrospective validation study of the SAPROF. *International Journal of Forensic Mental Health*, 10(3), 178–186.

de Vries Robbé, M., de Vogel, V., Douglas, K. S., & Nijman, H. L. I. (2015). Changes in dynamic risk and protective factors for violence during inpatient forensic psychiatric treatment: Predicting reductions in post-discharge community recidivism. *Law and Human Behavior*, 39, 53–61.

de Vries Robbé, M., de Vogel, V., & Stam, J. (2012). Protective factors for violence risk: The value for clinical practice. *Psychology*, 3, 1259–1263.

Dennis, J., Khan, O., Ferriter, M., Huband, N., Powney, M., & Duggan, C. (2012). Psychological interventions for adults who have sexually offended or are at risk of offending (Review). *The Cochrane Collaboration*, 2012(12), 1–95.

Douglas, K. S., & Skeem, J. L. (2005). Violence risk assessment: Getting specific about being dynamic. *Psychology, Public Policy, and Law*, 11, 347–383.

Friendship, C., Falshaw, L., & Beech, A. R. (2003). Measuring the real impact of accredited offending behaviour programmes. *Legal and Criminological Psychology*, 8, 115–127.

Hammond, S., & O'Rourke, M. (2007). The measurement of individual change: A didactic account of an idiographic approach. *Psychology, Crime & Law*, 13, 81–95.

Hanson, R., Bourgon, G., Helmus, L., & Hodgson, S. (2009). The principles of effective correctional treatment also apply to sexual offenders: A meta-analysis. *Criminal Justice and Behavior*, 36(9), 865–891.

Hudson, S., Wales, D., Bakker, L., & Ward, T. (2002). Dynamic risk factors: The Kia Marama evaluation. *Sexual Abuse: A Journal of Research and Treatment*, 14, 101–117.

Jacobson, N. S., Follette, W. C., & Revenstorf, D. (1986). Toward a standard definition of clinically significant change. *Behavior Therapy*, 17, 308–311.

Jacobson, N. S., & Truax, P. (1991). Clinical significance: A statistical approach to defining meaningful change in psychotherapy research. *Journal of Consulting and Clinical Psychology*, 51(1), 12–19.

Jolliffe, D., & Farrington, D. P. (2007, December). A systematic review of the national and international evidence on the effectiveness of interventions with violent offenders. *Ministry of Justice Research Series* 16/07. London, UK: Ministry of Justice.

Jung, S., & Gulayets, M. (2011). Using clinical variables to evaluate treatment effectiveness in programmes for sexual offenders. *Journal of Sexual Aggression*, 17(2), 166–180.

Klepfisz, G., O'Brien, K., & Daffern, M. (2014). Violent offenders' within-treatment change in anger, criminal attitudes, and violence risk: Associations with violent recidivism. *International Journal of Forensic Mental Health*, 13(4), 348–362.

Langstrom, N., Enebrink, P., Lauren, E.-M., Lindblom, J., Werko, S., & Hanson, R. (2013). Preventing sexual abusers of children from reoffending: Systematic review of medical and psychological interventions. *British Medical Journal*, 9(347;f4630), 1–11.

Levenson, J., & Prescott, D. (2013). Deja vu: From Furby to Langstrom and the evaluation of sex offender treatment effectiveness. *Journal of Sexual Aggression*, 20(3), 257–266.

Lewis, K., Olver, M. E., & Wong, S. C. P. (2013). The Violence Risk Scale: Predictive validity and linking changes in risk with violent recidivism in a sample of high-risk offenders with psychopathic traits. *Assessment*, 20, 150–164. https://doi.org/10.1177/1073191112441242

Lösel, F., & Schmucker, M. (2005). The effectiveness of treatment for sexual offenders: A comprehensive meta-analysis. *Journal of Experimental Criminology*, 1, 117–146.

Mann, R., Hanson, R., & Thornton, D. (2010). Assessing risk for sexual recidivism: Some proposals on the nature of psychologically meaningful risk factors. *Sexual Abuse: A Journal of Research and Treatment*, 22(2), 191–217.

McGuire, J. (2008). A review of effective interventions for reducing aggression and violence. *Philosophical Transactions of The Royal Society B*, 363(1503), 2577–2597.

Miller, H. (2006). A dynamic assessment of offender risk, needs, and strengths in a sample of pre-release general offenders. *Behavioral Sciences & the Law*, 24(6), 767–782.

Mills, J. F., Loza, W., & Kroner, D. J. (2003). Predictive validity despite social desirability: Evidence for the robustness of self-report among offenders. *Criminal Behaviour and Mental Health*, 13, 140–150.

Mooney, J., & Daffern, M. (2013). The Offence Analogue and Offence Reduction Behaviour Rating Guide as a supplement to violence risk assessment in incarcerated offenders. *International Journal of Forensic Mental Health*, 12(4), 255–264.

Nunes, K. L., Babchishin, K. M., & Cortoni, F. (2011). Measuring treatment change in sex offenders: Clinical and statistical significance. *Criminal Justice and Behavior*, 38(2), 157–173.

Olver, M. E., Beggs Christofferson, S., & Wong, S. C. P. (2015). Evaluation and applications of the clinically significant change method with the Violence Risk Scale-Sexual Offender version: Implications for risk-change communication. *Behavioral Sciences & the Law*, 33(1), 92–110.

Olver, M. E., Nicholaichuk, T., Kingston, D., & Wong, S. C. P. (2014). A multisite examination of sexual violence risk and therapeutic change. *Journal of Consulting and Clinical Psychology*, 82(2), 312–324.

Olver, M. E., & Wong, S. C. P. (2013). Treatment programs for high risk sexual offenders: Program and offender characteristics, attrition, treatment change and recidivism. *Aggression and Violent Behavior*, 18(5), 579–591.

Polaschek, D. L. L. (2011). Many sizes fit all: A preliminary framework for conceptualizing the development and provision of cognitive-behavioral rehabilitation programs for offenders. *Aggression and Violent Behavior*, 16(1), 20–35.

Polaschek, D. L. L., & Collie, R. M. (2004). Rehabilitating serious violent adult offenders: An empirical and theoretical stocktake. *Psychology, Crime & Law*, 10(3), 321–334.

Rogers, R. (2000). The uncritical acceptance of risk assessment in forensic practice. *Law and Human Behavior*, 24(5), 595–605.

Rogosa, D., Brandt, D., & Zimowski, M. (1982). A growth curve approach to the measurement of change. *Psychological Bulletin*, 92, 726–748.

Schmucker, M., & Lösel, F. (2015). The effects of sexual offender treatment on recidivism: An international meta-analysis of sound quality evaluations. *Journal of Experimental Criminology*, 11(4), 597–630.

Serin, R. C., & Lloyd, C. (2009). Examining the process of offender change: The transition to crime desistance. *Psychology, Crime & Law*, 15(4), 347–364.

Serin, R. C., Gobeil, R., & Preston, D. L. (2009). Evaluation of the persistently violent offender treatment program. *International Journal of Offender Therapy and Comparative Criminology*, 53, 57–73.

Serin, R. C., Lloyd, C. D., Helmus, L., Derkzen, D. M., & Luong, D. (2013). Does intra-individual change predict offender recidivism? Searching for the Holy Grail in assessing offender change. *Aggression and Violent Behavior*, 18(1), 32–53.

Sheldrick, C. (1999). Practitioner review: The assessment and management of risk in adolescents. *Journal of Child Psychology and Psychiatry*, 40(4), 507–518.

Sweller, T., Warren, N., & Daffern, M. (2016). Challenges in Determining How Dynamic Risk Factors Manifest in Incarcerated Sexual Offenders. *Psychiatry, Psychology and Law*, 23(5), 765–781.

Wakeling, H., Beech, A. R., & Freemantle, N. (2013). Investigating treatment change and its relationship to recidivism in a sample of 3773 sex offenders in the UK. *Psychology, Crime & Law*, 19, 233–252.

Ward, T., & Beech, A. R. (2014). Dynamic risk factors: A theoretical dead-end? *Psychology, Crime & Law*, 21(2), 1–14.

Woessner, G., & Schwedler, A. (2014). Correctional treatment of sexual and violent offenders: Therapeutic change, prison climate, and recidivism. *Criminal Justice and Behavior*, 41(7), 862–879.

Wong, S. C. P., Olver, M. E., Nicholaichuk, T., & Gordon, A. (2003). *The Violence Risk Scale: Sexual Offender version (VRS-SO)*. Saskatoon, Canada: Regional Psychiatric Centre and University of Saskatchewan.

Wong, S. C. P., & Gordon, A. (2003). *Violence Risk Scale manual*. Saskatoon, Canada: Department of Psychology, University of Saskatchewan.

25

Treatment Outcome Evaluations: How Do We Know What Works?

Devon L. L. Polaschek

University of Waikato (Te Whare Wānanga o Waikato), New Zealand

Evaluating the effects of treatment programs is an essential part of evidence-based practice. In many domains, determining whether an intervention is effective may be as simple as examining whether there was a change in the treatment target following the treatment, compared to when there was no treatment. For example, is depression reduced following cognitive behavioral treatment (Lynch, Laws, & McKenna, 2010). In other areas, the logic model is more complex, with the in-program change measuring a variable that is assumed to be the mechanism for long-term change. For example, surgery to remove lymph nodes after breast cancer diagnosis may prolong life by reducing the likelihood of metastases (Giuliano et al., 2011). But either way, the most common design for establishing whether treatment has an absolute effect on outcome (i.e., compared to no treatment) matches a treatment sample with an untreated sample, using an approach that gives an acceptable degree of confidence that difference in outcome can reasonably be attributed to the treatment itself.

Information about which interventions work[3] is particularly important to those who commission programs for purchase, policy-makers and other government officials, and politicians. It can also be useful for program designers, but to a lesser extent.

Interventions for offenders that lead to a reduced risk of recidivism have been an important proof of concept in a political context where punitive responses, despite robust evidence of their ineffectiveness, are often presented as the preferred options. But in practice, most interventions are never evaluated for their effects on recidivism. Instead their effectiveness is assumed, based on their purported similarity to successful interventions in previous research. On average, when evaluations are done, the quality of evaluation design is weak. Consequently, compared to the volume of research on risk assessment, the research base on what works has increased since the 1980s but remains quite small, especially when more rigorous quality criteria are applied (e.g., eight prospective studies of sex offender programs; Långström, Laurén, Lindblom, Werkö, & Hanson, 2013; 21 studies of youth justice interventions: Evans-Chase & Zhou, 2014).

The Wiley International Handbook of Correctional Psychology, First Edition. Edited by Devon L. L. Polaschek, Andrew Day, and Clive R. Hollin.

Evaluating Evaluation Designs for Recidivism Outcome Studies

There are a number of different standards in use that help consumers of research to make decisions about the quality of the design. The most common is the University of Maryland Scientific Methods Scale (Sherman et al., 1998), developed to assist the US congress with crime prevention initiatives. There are five levels, starting with the least rigorous: (a) cross-sectional correlation between intervention and crime or crime risk factors (i.e., at a single time point); (b) criminal outcome is measured before and after the program; there is no comparison group, or there is a comparison group, but no demonstration that the second group is comparable to the program group; (c) two-group design in which one group is exposed to the program, other factors are controlled, or there are pre-test measures; (d) multiple samples (groups) are included, at least one undertook the program, and the outcome is examined after controlling for other potential differences between groups, or pre-test measures have been taken, and (e) random assignment and data analysis for comparable program and comparison groups.

The main principle involved is the extent to which the design can be used to rule out alternative explanations for any observed differences (i.e., effectiveness of amelioration of threats to internal validity). In Level 1 and 2 designs very little can be deduced. If there is no comparison group, it is not possible to establish, if the outcome has changed, whether that is due to the intervention. Where there are two or more groups, differences between them may be due to pre-existing differences on characteristics related to the outcome (selection biases, e.g., one group is higher in expected recidivism than the other at the outset). This is perhaps the most challenging issue. Meta-analyses quite commonly include studies where there is demonstration that the comparison group is similar enough to the treatment group to rule out confounding explanations for outcomes (MacKenzie & Farrington, 2015). Random assignment is clearly the best method to ensure that the treatment and comparison sample are as similar as possible, including equivalence on factors that make a difference to program outcome but that we neither know about yet, nor can or do measure, but randomization does not miraculously lead to good design. But when it comes to interpreting individual studies, the minimum interpretable design is Level 3 on the Maryland Scale, which means relatively sophisticated, carefully conducted quasi-experimental designs and well conducted randomized controlled trials (RCTs).

Randomized Controlled Trials

RCTs are a type of experiment and therefore differ from many evaluations, not only because participants are randomly allocated to conditions, but because the study is prospectively designed to manipulate intervention type, in common with all "true" scientific experiments. To be really successful, participants and treatment providers must be blind to treatment allocation, to limit expectancy effects for both parties. RCTs represent a small proportion of studies of intervention effects in correctional settings (MacKenzie & Farrington, 2015).

RCTs are most successfully used in medicine in circumstances where it is possible to define reasonably clearly what the treatment is (e.g., a drug) and to develop a credible but biologically inert placebo. Even in medicine though, they are not as suitable for "complex interventions" which can be characterized by: treatment and control conditions that are not easily described, lack of double-blinding or any blinding in the procedure, and challenges to treatment integrity (Hollin, 2008). Some interventions, such as surgery, any treatment where the active treatment is easily detected (e.g., by side effects), or combinations of treatment components, cannot be evaluated this simply, so an RCT may instead compare two existing interventions (MacKenzie & Farrington, 2015). Sometimes the comparison is known as "TAU" for "treatment as usual," which strictly does not mean no treatment, but rather, the pre-existing or routine response. Thus, TAU may itself have some effect above no baseline, but this effect will not necessarily be known. Using an alternative intervention helps to deal with both the ethical concern of not providing any treatment, and the problem of comparison groups knowing they are not getting the treatment because no convincing placebo can be devised. RCTs also cannot be done ethically in some circumstances; for example, where the effects of "no treatment" are known to be harmful (e.g., denying anti-biotics to patients with infections). However, people often describe the situation where randomized participants are denied a treatment of unknown but plausible effectiveness as unethical, when in fact it is equally unethical to send people through a program with an unknown effect, especially where community safety may be affected by the outcome (e.g., sex offenders; Schmucker & Lösel, 2015).

If implemented well, RCTs provide the best design for ascribing effects to the intervention itself, and so if the intervention is associated with better outcomes, we can have confidence that it "works," even though in reality this is probably only true with some members of this sample in this context with this staffing and so on. RCTs are very often referred to as the "gold standard" for intervention evaluation design (Bothwell, Greene, Podolsky, & Jones, 2016), and have acquired something approaching cult status, particularly in social service purchasing models where RCTs have been viewed as the *only* type of design that can provide adequate information about which programs and services to fund. Consequently, even researchers often view them as the crowning achievement of treatment research. But not all RCTs are equal; this enthusiasm and confidence is surprising given how often and easily they can go wrong, the limited range of questions they answer, and how readily threats to internal validity are introduced when they deviate from double-blind designs, as they will in social service contexts.

Before an RCT can commence, it requires careful specification of who will be eligible for referral, exactly what the treatment will be, and when the treatment and the trial will end. The design can fail for a range of reasons. In criminal justice settings, perhaps the most common are (a) refusal or failure of the referring agent to adhere to the randomization requirement (e.g., a judge continues to use their discretion to determine assignments; Gondolf, 2001); and (b) high rates of attrition from at least one of the conditions. High rates of attrition are a long-standing concern with regard to offender interventions (Olver, Stockdale, & Wormith, 2011). In correctional and other RCTs significant proportions of participants may be lost from the trial before it even begins, especially from the comparison group when recruited participants decide to opt out of their allocated (no-) treatment option. It is conservatively suggested therefore that recruitment goals should be not more than 50% of those eligible; but that means those who sign up are not likely to be a random sample of the eligible either (Nichol, Bailey, & Cooper, 2010). The possibility of design collapse due to one or both of these factors is often sufficiently high that it has been recommended that alternative data be collected at the same time, to enable useful research outcomes to be salvaged from the investment (Farrington & Jolliffe, 2002).

The Importance of Blinding

RCTs should be conducted with both the deliverer of the intervention and its recipient blind to the treatment condition. As we noted above, high rates of attrition can occur when participants recognize they are being offered a non-preferred option. RCTs are offered up as the solution to quasi-experimental designs (see below) where there may be a priori differences in motivation to change, for instance, because participants are considered to have allocated themselves to treatment. But the inherent superiority of an RCT when blinding is not possible is likely to be rather overstated. For example, motivation to change is not a static, trait-like factor. Being allocated to a shiny new intervention where the therapists are excited about its potential is very likely to contribute to the participant's engagement and, ultimately, the effectiveness of the program. Both participants and treatment deliverers may have clear a priori expectations about which treatment is effective; although not much researched in correctional settings, such expectations have been found elsewhere to predict therapy outcomes (Lambert, 1992; Rutherford, Wager, & Roose, 2010), and are one example of a variable that cannot easily be matched across treatments (Lewis & Warlow, 2004; Nichol et al., 2010). Thus an RCT may randomly allocate people to treatment, but the treatment itself is hopelessly confounded by its distinctiveness. Many policy-makers and purchasers of programs seem unaware that non-blinding substantially dilutes the differences between RCTs and quasi-experimental evaluations, especially when combined with the atypicality of the programs within RCTs, and the likely atypicality of the participants who agree to take part (as noted above).

RCT as Proof of Concept

RCTs are designed simultaneously with treatment implementation, making issues of treatment integrity a high priority, and making the roll-out a kind of demonstration program; the intervention that is evaluated may bear little resemblance to what can be achieved in a "business-as-usual" environment. It may serve as a proof-of-concept, demonstrating that a particular program *can* work, or can work with a particularly restricted clientele in some cases, but the findings may be of little utility in guiding actual service decisions, where what is possible may be substantially more heterogeneous and less rigorous. In that sense, an RCT prioritizes avoiding threats to internal validity over external or ecological validity, a longstanding challenge in psychological research (Anderson & Bushman, 1997). This issue doesn't just affect programs subject to RCTs but any program that is delivered under unusually rigorous and careful conditions, such as pilot programs (Bonta & Andrews, 2017). Proofs of concept are important but are a very preliminary step in establishing services that can be used widely.

Other Specific Problems with RCTs

Another common problem is that with smaller trials such as those often used in corrections, even with randomization the groups may end up non-equivalent on factors related to outcome (see SOTEP, below, for an example). One solution to this is stratification, where allocations are randomized within subgroups separately, for example, by static risk band. In fact, this approach has been recommended for trials with fewer than 200 cases in each condition (Lewis & Warlow, 2004).

RCTs may also lead to the abandonment of programs that may work for subgroups of offenders, because of the preferred analytical method of dealing with selective attrition. It is very unlikely that those who did not undertake or complete the program are statistically equivalent to those who did. Treatment effects are evaluated using an Intent to Treat (ITT) analysis—also called a "treatment as assigned" analysis: the treatment sample is assumed to be the entire sample referred and allocated to the treatment, whether they were treated or not. In these analyses, it may be that the majority of participants in the treatment group took part in little or none of the intervention. Although this approach protects against possible attrition bias as noted above, it also dilutes any potential treatment effect because of the proportion of untreated people in the treatment sample.

A well-known example of an RCT in correctional psychology that illustrates some of the design issues is the Atascadero, California-based Sex Offender Treatment and Evaluation Project (SOTEP; Marques, Day, Nelson, & West, 1994; Marques, Wiederanders, Day, Nelson, & van Ommeren, 2005). Here, 21% of those allocated to the treatment condition withdrew before they had even been transferred to hospital, and another 18% didn't complete the program, even after staff made efforts to retain as many as possible (Marques et al., 2005). Consequently, in an ITT analysis of outcome, one fifth of those counted as treated had not experienced a single hour of treatment.

There is also no guarantee, even when the groups later examined are the groups as they were originally allocated (rather than at final composition, allowing for attrition), that randomization will have resulted in group equivalence on pre-treatment characteristics related to outcome. This was a problem in SOTEP as well, where the treatment sample was a higher-risk sample overall than the comparisons (Marques et al., 2005), despite the randomized design matching pairs of volunteers for treatment on a number of risk-relevant characteristics before allocating them to treatment versus not (Marques et al., 2005).

RCTs are often assumed to be robustly generalizable because of their rigor. One of the most well-known randomized field experiments in criminology is the Minneapolis study of mandatory arrest for domestic violence, in which police officers dealing with simple domestic assaults randomly allocated suspects to one of three conditions: mandatory arrest, some form of advice, or a 24-hour separation period (Sherman & Berk, 1984). Ironically, their original aims did not claim to be generating universal knowledge (p. 262): "we report here a study of the impact of punishment in a particular setting, for a particular offense, and for particular kinds of individuals." Yet the results were widely adopted soon after the first experiment was disseminated.

The original data have been subject to various forms of reanalysis, and the study has been replicated multiple times. The bottom line appears to be that a determination of whether arrest will work to reduce family harm requires a knowledge of the context in which it is enacted. In particular, reanalysis showed that at least in some sites, married and employed suspects responded better to arrest than others. In short, "in the face of substantial interaction effects it is nonsense to talk about 'what works' on average for a particular site" (Berk, Campbell, Klap, & Western, 1992, p. 705). Nor can the results be generalized readily to other sites. These experiments have been criticized on a variety of other grounds too, such as failure to control for arrest history, insufficiently long follow-up periods, and inadequate factoring in of other interventions following arrest (Dutton, 2006; Hilton, Harris, & Rice, 2007). However, the most important point remains that randomizing does not guarantee generalizability because, no matter how clearly the intervention is designed, how carefully people are allocated to it or not, and how rigorously it is implemented, there will always be contextual factors around it that turn out to be part of the effect. For example, when evaluating a program for partner-violent men, other factors that may contribute to outcome include: police and prosecution practices, swiftness of court proceedings, consequences of dropping out of the program, type and range of responses for victims, and the other types of assistance that may be made available to perpetrators (Gondolf, 2002).

RCTs have also suffered from the problems the wider research publication community, with a bias toward publishing positive results, and in medicine at least, a failure to disclose financial conflicts of interest. RCTs have been important in improving medical knowledge, but after some initial overclaiming about what they could do for medicine, there has been somewhat of a shift in recent years back to viewing them as one tool among others, complemented by observational studies and a raft of approaches that answer different but equally important questions (Bothwell et al., 2016). Ironically, at the same time, new fields are beginning to adopt them with a similar sort of overconfidence about what they can achieve: "development economists have placed RCTs at the center of a new experimental approach, proclaiming their potential to revolutionize social policy during the 21st century, just as randomized trials revolutionized medicine during the 20th" (World Bank, cited in Bothwell et al., 2016, pp. 731–732). But did they?

A number of interventions in medicine will never be validly evaluated by RCTs (e.g., any circumstance where the treatment would be determined based on a nuanced assessment of the client's clinical presentation; Faraoni & Schaefer, 2016). In short, "even though RCTs were developed to produce generalizable, universal biomedical knowledge, they have remained deeply entangled in local social conditions, economics, and politics" (Bothwell et al., 2016, p. 2178). Bothwell goes on to note that new drug RCTs have become so mired in bureaucracy and private corporate agendas that they may cost as much as $30 million, which is also causing them to fall from favor as a mandatory step in approval for use.

Alternative Quasi-Experimental Designs

One of the key issues leading to a favoring of RCTs is a variety of internal validity threats with respect to alternative designs (e.g., observational designs; Nichol et al., 2010). As I have suggested, deciding on an RCT does not make those issues disappear, but in theory the key issue of unobserved but potentially relevant differences associated with opting into treatment, such as the level of participants' motivation to undertake treatment or personal change, may be evenly distributed across conditions at the point of allocation.

In many areas of criminal justice research, RCTs remain relatively rare, reflecting a lack of "up front" investment in intervention evaluation. Without alternative designs, there would be little to say at all about some types of programs. Furthermore, in meta-analyses, quite often there is no significant difference in the overall result when RCTs are compared with quasi-experimental designs (e.g., Babcock, Green, & Robie, 2004; Schmucker & Lösel, 2015), although this pattern should not be seen to support complacency, given that numbers of RCTs may be too small to provide sufficient statistical power for the comparison (MacKenzie & Farrington, 2015).

Quasi-experimental designs are the main alternative. Studies using these designs can be prospective examinations of new or model programs. But often they are conducted retrospectively; some time after the treatment is completed researchers compile the treatment sample from file records, and cast around for a comparison—a far cry from the expected rigor of any prospective study, whether RCT or quasi-experimental. How well matched the participants are then is dependent on what information was collected initially as part of the routine program. The potential to select adequate control groups can be enhanced in systems where systematic assessments of offender characteristics (e.g., criminal risk, dynamic risk factors, responsivity issues) are routinely conducted at reception into the institution or sentence, and are available to researchers. Further, if there are insufficient places in a treatment program, it may be possible to build a comparison group that is composed of people who may have wanted to undertake the treatment and would have been suitable had there been more places, so reducing potential bias in allocation to treatment.

Selection and Matching of Comparison Groups

Earlier evaluations often compared treatment completers with dropouts. But attrition is unlikely to be randomly allocated. Based on pre-treatment characteristics, non-completers are often, though not always, higher-risk cases (Olver et al., 2011; Polaschek, 2010), so such comparisons will tend to inflate the apparent effectiveness of treatment since the treatment group would then be expected to have lower recidivism even without treatment (Hanson & Bussiere, 1998).

Therefore, it is preferable to select a comparison group that is less likely to be biased toward greater untreatability (e.g., did not engage with program, were more impulsive or disruptive), as may be the case with dropouts. A variety of options are used here, but the aim is to match the two samples as closely as possible, especially on variables that are related to recidivism. Sometimes equivalence is argued simply on the basis that the mean scores on relevant variables for the whole sample are statistically similar. A more rigorous approach is for treatment cases to be matched on individual variables (e.g., age, ethnicity, static estimate of criminal risk), but in practice a very large sample of comparisons is often needed to get close matches for each treatment case on more than two or three variables. The result may be a discarding of the majority of treatment or comparison participants or both (e.g., Wong, Gordon, Gu, Lewis, & Olver, 2012), so introducing another source of potential bias.

More recently, propensity scoring methods have been adopted in this field, and are particularly indicated when the pre-treatment data—for both treatment and comparison samples—contain a relatively detailed set of variables from which to model. Propensity scoring involves the estimation for each case of a probability that it would have been allocated to the comparison or treatment condition based on a regression equation built using variables that potentially differ between the two samples and may be correlated with the outcome. There are two main ways in which this probability can be used. First, each comparison case can then be matched with a treatment case, using the closest acceptable match within pre-established tolerances (e.g., Vito, Higgins, & Tewksbury, 2017), a kind of yoked design typical of how the individual variable matching designs above were conducted. Even using propensity matching does not necessarily solve the problem of finding a suitable match for extreme cases, which therefore may need to be dropped, but it can allow much better retention of cases in the analyses, which usefully boosts statistical power (D'Agostino, 1998). Examining stratification of the sample is useful too, if the whole sample is stratified into quintiles and within each quintile one can then examine whether key variables in the regression show similar distributions. When they do, the data are considered to be balanced, and represent a closer approximation of the expected distribution with a randomized design (Jones, D'Agostino, Gondolf, & Heckert, 2004).

Second, the probability can simply be entered as a statistical control into any regression equation that is looking to test for a treatment effect on outcome (D'Agostino, 1998). In this application, a large comparison sample may be available to boost statistical power. However, in this instance, the design is unbalanced by uneven sample sizes, and the resulting analyses require a weighting variable to compensate for these uneven numbers (Moore, 2012).

With the widespread implementation of interventions based on the "what works" research literature in recent decades, it is difficult in some jurisdictions to obtain any comparison group that has not had some form of intervention. The problem with this scenario is that if the intervention provided to the comparison group also has some effect, there may be no difference between comparison and treatment groups (for an example of this scenario, see Serin, Gobeil, & Preston, 2009). At best, the effectiveness of the superior program is going to be diluted because it is not being compared with some more neutral baseline. But then what is a neutral baseline? Often we treat as the baseline a typical prison regime with little in the way of effective social service support, but even these regimes can vary in a way that can affect whether the treatment program appears to be effective. Tougher TAU regimes that have poorer outcomes can boost the apparent effectiveness of the treatment program condition (Lösel, 2001), another local difference that may affect generalization.

Once some form of matching is complete, it becomes possible to examine relationships between group membership and outcome indicators, usually the first instance of some type of recidivism. It has been recommended that using several different recidivism outcomes is preferable over using only one (Lösel, 2001). Knowing local sentencing policies can be important for determining which indices to use. For example, if minor technical violations of parole lead to rapid reimprisonment, as they do in some jurisdictions, then recidivism indices that do not include parole violation will tend to only be possible for those not already recalled to prison—possibly a lower-risk sample than in a jurisdiction where parole violation is treated less severely. Recidivism base rates can also guide selection. For example, a number of treatment evaluations for sex offenders have used very long follow-up periods to boost the base rate of recidivism (Lösel & Schmucker, 2005), implying that the treatment might be expected to exert an effect for a long period, whereas some very high-risk samples achieve optimum base rates for recidivism—around 50%—for some indices within a year of release (Polaschek, Yesberg, Bell, Casey, & Dickson, 2016).

Dealing with Treatment Participant Attrition

Even when participants are allocated according to current system practices, rather than research design needs, treatment attrition occurs. On average it tends to be around a quarter to a third of those who begin treatment (Olver et al., 2011). Some attrition is desirable. Too little attrition suggests the program may be indiscriminately retaining people who are disruptive or make no progress. Too much suggests the program may not be optimally responsive (Polaschek, 2010). There are a number of reasons for attrition. Some may be relatively benign with respect to biasing the remaining sample: a family crisis leads the person to want to change institution to be nearer to home, or a historical relationship difficulty with another prisoner currently in the program is the basis of a request to leave, for instance. But others, such as disruptive behavior, probably are not. We recently found just this pattern: those who dropped out of their own accord were most like those who also completed treatment in regard to key pre-treatment characteristics. Those who were removed by program staff had poorer prognostic indicators (Daly, Fletcher, & Polaschek, 2017).

If a comparison group was selected prospectively, then possibly dropouts in that group will be similar to those in the treatment group, which may mitigate uneven selection bias. But if the comparison group was constructed retrospectively, or there is no way to meaningfully drop out of the control group (i.e., how does one leave "treatment as usual"?), it may not be possible to avoid this issue. The preferred solution, intention-to-treat analyses, as with RCTs, is conservative. The approach dichotomizes dosage into "treated" or "not treated" when a proportion of the treatment group may have received little treatment.

But rather than just reporting intention-to-treat analyses, additional analyses can also be included. When conducting a retrospective quasi-experimental evaluation with an untreated or treatment-as-usual comparison group, there is a second option for dealing transparently with the possible attrition bias problem. Here, the researcher retrospectively matches all treatment cases to not-referred-to-treatment comparisons on chosen matching variables (e.g., propensity matching) while blind to whether or not the treatment case completed treatment. Then, later, it is possible to examine whether any significant effect for the treatment completers compared to their controls is offset by a correspondingly poorer result for those who did not complete. For example, Table 25.1 shows some results from a study of the effectiveness of a program for high-risk violent prisoners that promoted itself as targeting violent offending rather than all offending. The upper part of the table shows the intent-to-treat analysis and the lower portion, the analysis broken down into treatment completers and their controls, and treatment non-completers and their controls (Polaschek, 2011). Although in this case the overall results are similar, the second type of analysis provides more detail about the recidivism picture with non-completers.

One important advantage of breaking down the findings by completers versus non-completers is that it may help to avoid incorrectly attributing non-completers' later recidivism to the effects of leaving the program. One of the complexities of treatment attrition is that it may be a result of a potentially criminogenic reaction to being referred to or starting the program.

Table 25.1 Comparison of Intention-to-Treat Analysis with Breakdown for Treatment Completers and Non-Completers: Percentage Reconvicted for Three Recidivism Outcomes

	Program starters n = 112		Untreated controls n = 112	
	% reconvicted			ϕ
Any reconviction	86		93	.11
Reconviction for violence	65		73	.08
Reimprisonment for violence	45		42	−.04

	TC	TCC		TNC	TNCC	
	% reconvicted		ϕ	% reconvicted		ϕ
Any reconviction	83	95	.19*	93	89	−.06
Reconviction for violence	62	72	.11	71	75	.04
Reimprisonment for violence	43	38	−.05	50	50	0.0

Source: Based on data from Polaschek (2011).
TC = treatment completer, TCC = treatment completer control, TNC = treatment non-completer, TNCC = treatment non-completer control.
* This is the only paired comparison that was statistically significant: $\chi^2(1) = 4.25$, $p = .04$.

When non-completers are higher-risk cases, based on information available prior to allocation to treatment (e.g., static risk assessment results), we would expect them to have higher rates of recidivism afterwards regardless, unless the program was actually more effective with higher-risk than lower-risk cases. If an untreated comparison sample is not matched one-to-one to the relevant treatment sample members as it was in the Polaschek study, the overall comparison sample recidivism may well be lower than for the treatment non-completers, because even had treatment not occurred, they may be from the higher-risk end of the treatment sample. This pattern, when observed, has led to the conclusion that treatment harms non-completers. For example, in a meta-analysis, McMurran and Theodosi (2007) observed that non-completers were more likely to be reconvicted than untreated controls, and concluded that "those who do not complete treatment are actually made worse" (p. 341). But this claim cannot be made unequivocally from the data in this study.

Of course, premature treatment departure may indeed be risk-increasing, but breaking down the results is a necessary first step in clarifying whether poorer results are due to pre-existing characteristics, or suggest more recent changes.

Other Key Issues in Treatment Outcome Evaluation

Recidivism analyses will always be important for accountability for social service and government agencies. However, much of the research on program effects is drawn into the endeavor of demonstrating that the program is linked to lower proportions of people recidivating (at all). Despite progress in accepting that there is a scientific evidence base that robustly establishes which interventions can work, there is still an ongoing need to justify continued expenditure, and it is still commonplace to come across people—sometimes influential people—who believe that nothing works.

However, for those who are designing and providing treatment for offenders, whether the program reduces recidivism is the least interesting question for research. Despite many calls to move beyond this step to investigations of other more informative issues, such as who responds to programs best, how change is effected, what changes, which parts of an intervention are most important, which outcomes are affected, the most effective settings, and so on, progress remains limited. I argued recently (Polaschek, 2017) that one of the more concerning effects of the lack of this research occurs when it is coupled with an overly rigid interpretation of the RNR model (Bonta & Andrews, 2017): as prescribing cognitive behavioral programs, instead of the rather more flexible imprecation to provide interventions that "employ behavioral, social learning, and cognitive behavioral influence and skill building strategies" (p. 176). If we treat evidence-based practice as an entity rather than an ongoing process (Gondolf, 2012), and if poor implementation of cognitive behavioral programs, or insufficient dosage, or poor selection of participants, or any of the myriad threats to program effectiveness results in enough poor outcomes for these programs, we have no wider evolving evidence base on which to fall back. The result may be an increase in the ever-present pressure to discard the whole approach as old-fashioned and ineffective in favor of a new form of correctional quackery (Gendreau, Smith, & Thériault, 2009), or existing approaches based on changing factors not related to reducing recidivism, such as treatment of mental health problems (Bonta, Blais, & Wilson, 2014). The final section of this chapter reviews some general issues in program outcome evaluation research that need consideration in order to expand the evidence base on "what works" and make it more useful.

What is a Program and When is it Completed?

In much of the treatment evaluation literature, a group program is the focus of the evaluation, and if the program also has a fixed length, then the design usually imposes some structure on the totality (e.g., starting with introductions and group building, fixed sequencing of components with some kind of summarizing and future planning at the end). Definitions of treatment completion therefore may define non-completion as departing from the first week through to almost the last. However, programs with rolling admissions are not predicated on the idea of a linear coherent whole with a fixed place to start and finish. Typically, nor is individual treatment, or involvement in therapeutic communities, and so for these interventions, dosage-based analyses which treat treatment exposure as a continuous variable may give a clearer view of treatment effects (Lösel, 2001), as they have in some other literatures (Stark, 1992).

   More challenging is the need to recognize that many programs using recidivism outcomes as their basis presuppose that the program effect is the only relevant influence on recidivism risk, even though the follow-up period may be several years, during which myriad other influences may have washed it away, or interacted in complex ways to enhance change in treatment. For example, following a custody-based treatment program, some offenders may undertake a second program prior to release, while others go on into employment, are given housing assistance, and may undertake a community-based intervention later (e.g., for substance use). Any or all of these subsequent responses may have additive or interactive effects with the treatment the evaluation is focused on. Considered more negatively, prisoners released into supportive environments may do better than those released under poorly planned circumstances with little social capital. These environments may have an additive effect, or perhaps treated offenders are more cooperative with leave planning arrangements, or can develop more social capital due to their improved demeanor and communication skills. This might be an interactive effect of treatment and reintegration planning. And so on.

   Puzzlingly, the possible influence of post-program interventions has seldom been considered in correctional program evaluations, although they are sometimes included in the program definition itself (e.g., Marques et al., 2005). We recently began to investigate post-program effects when we incorporated length of parole into a recidivism evaluation design for a treatment program. About 300 prisoners, half of whom had completed an intensive cognitive behavioral program for high-risk offenders toward the end of their time in custody, were recruited immediately prior to parole. We found a 12 percentage-point difference in 1-year reconviction rates for treatment completers (54%) versus their comparison sample (66%, $\Phi = .12$, 95% CI for $\Phi = [-.03, .27]$ $p = .057$). When the effects of reduced dynamic risk level and release readiness—both measured immediately prior to release—were taken into account, only parole length was a significant factor in predicting recidivism. There were insufficient data to investigate which components of parole were responsible, but it would seem that in this study, parole was reducing risk of recidivism, regardless of treatment in prison (Polaschek, Yesberg, & Chauhan, 2018).

   It is not surprising that we often don't consider the potential influence of other parts of the system, because until recently, often the only apparently therapeutic part of the system was a program or rehabilitative intervention, which often was time limited and delivered to well-defined cohorts. But in the past few years we have seen more development of post-program change-supportive environments (e.g., Psychologically Informed Planned Environments [PIPEs], reintegration units), effective reintegrative interventions that begin in prison and extend into the community, and regular prison and probation staff have been trained in core correctional practices (e.g., relationship-building skills, effective use of problem-solving skills, effective use of approval; Dowden & Andrews, 2004). This is the case in New Zealand, where the use of a structured tool for assessing and remediating risk-related issues on parole, combined with a compliance and support orientation, may have led to more effective parole oversight, in the research above (the Polaschek et al., 2018 study).

In other fields, efforts have been made for some time to investigate system response effects, rather than simply effects on one component of the system, in recognition that it is difficult to do the latter in any meaningful sense. A well-known, well-designed, and large-scale naturalistic study of the effects of perpetrator interventions on partner violence found very few differences in subsequent partner reports of reassault across four distinct intervention systems in four different cities, even though the programs themselves differed in length from 3 to 9 months (Gondolf, 1999). At each of the four sites, there were differences in the range and length of additional services for perpetrators and victims, and one program was pre-trial while the other three were post-conviction. These results led Gondolf to conclude

> It may be that each intervention system is defined more by the composite of its components and experience than by its individual components. Rather than as part of a continuum of systems, each system may be a unique adaptation to a peculiar set of resources, leadership and staffing, court procedures and community expectations. (Gondolf, 1999, p. 58)

Treatment Outcome

The field uses recidivism to determine outcome, and if a program is associated with reduced recidivism then that is positive news. In other fields, treatment success is often measured using a combination of outcomes, of which some will be related to intermediate measures, or mechanisms associated with a longer-term outcome. For example, an intervention for depression in referred suicidal clients might measure depression before, during, and after treatment, and perhaps again at 6 or 12 months. If this hypothetical study then discovered that 5 years after treatment there was no difference in the completed suicide rate for the treatment versus untreated group, would it be concluded that the treatment was completely ineffective? Probably not. But if this was a program designed to reduce recidivism, and 5 years later there was no recidivism effect, it would be.

There are several points of difference. First, most measures of intermediate changes in psychological interventions—that is, changes on variables that are expected to be remediated by the treatment and are linked to any longer-term outcomes (e.g., suicide)—rely on self-report. There is considerably more mistrust in correctional domains about the validity of self-report when offenders have incentives to lie, and self-report is, in any case, a less convincing measure of behavior change than observing the change itself. But perhaps a more important problem is that such measurements seldom continue beyond the end of the program in corrections, so there is no evidence that the treatment change, if there was any, survived the difficult post-treatment period and generalized into the next setting. Even on one of the best measures of treatment change for offenders, the Violence Risk Scale (VRS/VRS-Sex Offender Version), which is a multi-item measure that emphasizes observed behavior change and has been linked to changes in recidivism risk (Lewis, Olver, & Wong, 2013; Olver & Wong, 2013; see also Chapter 24), we know of only one study that examined the pattern of VRS scores after treatment was completed. This proof-of-concept study showed no particular relationship between the pattern of change in treatment, and that in the 6–12 months following the program, for offenders who were still in prison (Yesberg & Polaschek, 2014). One implication is that we judge our programs by whether they are *still* working some time after the end of the program, when we have no idea how long program-related changes may last, even if the program succeeds in effecting change, because we don't measure change beyond the end of the intervention. We also therefore are missing out on important information about what conditions or experiences interact with the program effects to enhance or erode change.

A related issue is whether recidivism is legitimately the only outcome we should pay attention to. This issue has also come up elsewhere too, in medical research trials where "there is an increasing recognition that there are more important things from a patient and societal point of view rather than just being dead or alive" (Nichol et al., 2010, p. S21). Recidivism is a poor indicator of actual crime (Farrington et al., 2006), and dichotomous indices (person X recidivated or did not) fail to capture the reality of how offenders desist (see Chapter 20). Further, it is possible that other indices of change may also be personally and socially important, such as reductions in alcohol and drug use, increased use of problem-solving skills, fewer interpersonal conflicts, better parenting, and so on. A raft of other socially valued changes have been demonstrated following intervention for partner-assaultive men (Kelly & Westmarland, 2015), and in investigating the effects of protective factors on positive community outcomes in prisoners (Coupland, 2015). Corrections rehabilitation programs almost never look at positive outcomes, or actually at any type of behavioral outcome directly, and would assist in understanding how they work.

Finally, longitudinal cohort studies show that the highest-risk offenders have poorer prognostic indices in not only offending, but also health and economic productivity domains as well (Odgers, 2009). This wider pattern of negative outcomes suggests that people with these issues will be a significant burden to multiple government systems over time. So, if containing costs for government is a major focus, more consideration of how these different indicators are connected to each other etiologically, and whether correctional programs or any other intervention alter outcomes in a more holistic manner, may be warranted.

Conclusions

The most informative types of treatment evaluation reveal clues as to who responds best to what. In the words of Schmucker and Lösel (2015, p. 598) "there is a clear need of more differentiated process and outcome evaluations that address the questions of what works with whom, in what contexts, under what conditions, with regard to what outcomes, and also why." Correctional program outcome research has a longstanding history of inadequate funding investment in a number of countries. Those same countries now find themselves even more pressed for resources, relying on rapid evidence reviews and meta-analyses, both of which are limited by a lack of investment in the primary research needed for these reviews. Calls by policy-makers for more RCTs are likely based on the idea that a very small number of RCTs could provide widely generalizable results, but as I suggested earlier in this chapter, this is something of a utopian vision. In fact, it can be argued that the adaptations required to undertake an RCT in the context of offender intervention are severe enough to compromise the design to the point where it is little different from the best designed quasi-experimental study.

There will likely be no substitute for the need to undertake a greater volume of better designed quasi-experimental studies *and* RCTs, and also to give better descriptions of their design details, and conduct more moderator-based analyses, to help identify some of the parameters that affect effectiveness. Where possible then, multiple sites and populations should be used; but in "real life" applications, whole-of-system approaches should be considered, and implementation should also be monitored in order to establish what the intervention actually comprised for each individual. A rarely discussed issue would be to test specific program theories during these evaluations. In correctional programs, instead of just calling something an "RNR" program, describing the particular program theory and theory of change would help with the development of the next generation of effective responses to offending and offenders.

Note

1 Throughout this chapter the term "what works" will refer to treatments or interventions that show an improvement in the relevant outcome variable (e.g., recidivism).

Key Readings

Bothwell, L. E., Greene, J. A., Podolsky, S. H., & Jones, D. S. (2016). Assessing the gold standard: Lessons from the history of RCTs. *New England Journal of Medicine*, 374, 2175–2181.

Gondolf, E. W. (1999). A comparison of four batterer intervention systems: Do court referral, program length, and services matter? *Journal of Interpersonal Violence*, 14, 41–61.

Gondolf, E. W. (2001). Limitations of experimental evaluation of batterer programs. *Trauma, Violence, & Abuse*, 2, 79–88.

Hollin, C. R. (2008). Evaluating offending behaviour programmes: Does only randomization glister? *Criminology and Criminal Justice*, 8, 89–106.

Lösel, F. (2001). Evaluating the effectiveness of correctional programs: Bridging the gap between research and practice. In G. A. Bernfeld, D. P. Farrington, & A. W. Leschied (Eds.), *Offender rehabilitation in practice* (pp. 67–92). Chichester, UK: Wiley.

Polaschek, D. L. L., Yesberg, J. A., & Chauhan, P. (2018). A year without a conviction: An integrated examination of potential mechanisms for successful re-entry in high-risk violent prisoners. *Criminal Justice and Behavior*, 45, 425–446.

References

Anderson, C. A., & Bushman, B. J. (1997). External validity of "trivial" experiments: The case of laboratory aggression. *Review of General Psychology*, 1, 19–41.

Babcock, J. C., Green, C. E., & Robie, C. (2004). Does batterers' treatment work? A meta-analytic review of domestic violence treatment. *Clinical Psychology Review*, 23, 1023–1053.

Berk, R. A., Campbell, A., Klap, R., & Western, B. (1992). The deterrent effect of arrest in incidents of domestic violence: A Bayesian analysis of four field experiments. *American Sociological Review*, 57, 698–708.

Bonta, J., & Andrews, D. A. (2017). *The psychology of criminal conduct* (6th ed.). London, UK: Routledge.

Bonta, J., Blais, J., & Wilson, H. A. (2014). A theoretically informed meta-analysis of the risk for general and violent recidivism for mentally disordered offenders. *Aggression and Violent Behavior*, 19, 278–287.

Bothwell, L. E., Greene, J. A., Podolsky, S. H., & Jones, D. S. (2016). Assessing the gold standard: Lessons from the history of RCTs. *New England Journal of Medicine*, 374, 2175–2181.

Coupland, R. B. A. (2015). *An examination of dynamic risk, protective factors, and treatment-related change in violent offenders* (Unpublished doctoral dissertation). University of Saskatchewan, Sasakatoon, Canada.

D'Agostino, R. B. (1998). Tutorial in biostatistics: Propensity score methods for bias reduction in the comparisons of a treatment to a non-randomized control group. *Statistics in Medicine*, 17, 2265–2281.

Daly, T. E., Fletcher, G. J. O., & Polaschek, D. L. L. (2017). *PCL-psychopathy factors and facets predict involuntary but not voluntary non-completion of treatment in high-risk violent prisoners.* Paper under review.

Dowden, C., & Andrews, D. A. (2004). The importance of staff practice in delivering effective correctional treatment: A meta-analytic review of core correctional practice. *International Journal of Offender Therapy and Comparative Criminology*, 48, 203–214.

Dutton, D. (2006). *Rethinking domestic violence*. Vancouver, Canada: University of British Columbia Press.

Evans-Chase, M., & Zhou, H. (2014). A systematic review of the juvenile justice intervention literature: What it can (and cannot) tell us about what works with delinquent youth. *Crime & Delinquency*, 60, 451–470.

Faraoni, D., & Schaefer, S. T. (2016). Randomized controlled trials vs. observational studies: Why not just live together? *BMC Anaesthesiology*, 16(1102), 1–4.

Farrington, D. P., Coid, J. W., Harnett, L., Jolliffe, D., Soteriou, N., Turner, R., & West, D. J. (2006). *Criminal careers up to the age of 50 and life success up to the age of 48: New findings from the Cambridge Study in Delinquent Development*. London, UK: Home Office.

Farrington, D. P., & Jolliffe, D. (2002). *A feasibility study into using a randomised controlled trial to evaluate treatment pilots in HMP Whitemoor*. Online report 14/02. London, UK: Home Office. Retrieved from http://citeseerx.ist.psu.edu/viewdoc/download?doi=10.1.1.629.3353&rep=rep1&type=pdf

Gendreau, P., Smith, P., & Thériault, Y. L. (2009). Chaos theory and correctional treatment: Common sense, correctional quackery, and the law of fartcatchers. *Journal of Contemporary Criminal Justice*, 25, 384–396.

Giuliano, A. E., Hunt, K. K., Ballman, K. V., Beitsch, P. D., Whitworth, P. W., Blumencranz, P. W., … & Morrow, M. (2011). Axillary dissection vs. no axillary dissection in women with invasive breast cancer and sentinel node metastasis: A randomized clinical trial. *Journal of the American Medical Association*, 305, 569–575.

Gondolf, E. W. (1999). A comparison of four batterer intervention systems: Do court referral, program length, and services matter? *Journal of Interpersonal Violence*, 14, 41–61.

Gondolf, E. W. (2001). Limitations of experimental evaluation of batterer programs. *Trauma, Violence, & Abuse*, 2, 79–88.

Gondolf, E. W. (2002). *Batterer intervention systems: Issues, outcomes, and recommendations*. Thousand Oaks, CA: Sage.

Gondolf, E. W. (2012). *The future of batterer programs: Reassessing evidence-based practice*. Lebanon, NH: Northeastern University.

Hanson, R. K., & Bussiere, M. T. (1998). Predicting relapse: A meta-analysis of sexual offender recidivism studies. *Journal of Consulting and Clinical Psychology*, 66, 348–362.

Hilton, N. Z., Harris, G. T., & Rice, M. E. (2007). The effects of arrest on wife assault recidivism: Controlling for pre-arrest risk. *Criminal Justice and Behavior*, 2006, 1334–1344.

Hollin, C. R. (2008). Evaluating offending behaviour programmes: Does only randomization glister? *Criminology and Criminal Justice*, 8, 89–106.

Jones, A. S., D'Agostino, R. B., Gondolf, E. W., & Heckert, A. (2004). Assessing the effect of batterer program completion on reassault using propensity scores. *Journal of Interpersonal Violence*, 19, 1002–1020.

Kelly, L., & Westmarland, L. (2015). *Domestic violence perpetrator programmes: Steps towards change. Project Mirabal final report.* London and Durham, UK: London Metropolitan University and Durham University.

Lambert, M. J. (1992). Psychotherapy outcome research: Implications for integrative and eclectical therapists. In J. C. Norcross, & M. R. Goldfried (Eds.), *Handbook of psychotherapy integration* (pp. 94–129). New York, NY: Basic Books.

Långström, N., Laurén, E., Lindblom, J., Werkö, S., & Hanson, R. K. (2013). Preventing sexual abusers of children from reoffending: Systematic review of medical and psychological interventions. *British Medical Journal*, 347, f4630.

Lewis, K., Olver, M. E., & Wong, S. C. P. (2013). The violence risk scale: Predictive validity and linking treatment changes with recidivism in a sample of high-risk and personality disordered offenders. *Assessment*, 20, 150–164.

Lewis, S. C., & Warlow, C. P. (2004). How to spot bias and other potential problems in randomised controlled trials. *Journal of Neurology, Neursurgery and Psychiatry*, 75, 181–187.

Lösel, F. (2001). Evaluating the effectiveness of correctional programs: Bridging the gap between research and practice. In G. A. Bernfeld, D. P. Farrington, & A. W. Leschied (Eds.), *Offender rehabilitation in practice* (pp. 67–92). Chichester, UK: Wiley.

Lösel, F., & Schmucker, M. (2005). The effectiveness of treatment for sexual offenders: A comprehensive meta-analysis. *Journal of Experimental Criminology*, 1, 117–146.

Lynch, D., Laws, K. R., & McKenna, P. J. (2010). Cognitive behavioural therapy for major psychiatric disorder: Does it really work? A meta-analytical review of well-controlled trials. *Psychological Medicine*, 40, 9–24.

MacKenzie, D. L., & Farrington, D. P. (2015). Preventing future offending of delinquents and offenders: What have we learned from experiments and meta-analyses? *Journal of Experimental Criminology*, 11, 565–595.

Marques, J. K., Day, D. M., Nelson, C., & West, M. A. (1994). Effects of cognitive-behavioral treatment on sex offender recidivism: Preliminary results of a longitudinal study. *Criminal Justice and Behavior*, 21, 28–54.

Marques, J. K., Wiederanders, M., Day, D. M., Nelson, C., & van Ommeren, A. (2005). Effects of a relapse prevention program on sexual recidivism: Final results from California's Sex Offender Treatment and Evaluation Project (SOTEP). *Sexual Abuse: A Journal of Research and Treatment*, 17, 79–107.

McMurran, M., & Theodosi, E. (2007). Is treatment non-completion associated with increased reconviction over no treatment? *Psychology, Crime & Law*, 13, 333–343.

Moore, L. (2012). *A comparison of offence history and post-release outcomes for sexual offenders against children who attended or did not attend the Kia Marama special treatment unit* (Unpublished master's thesis). University of Canterbury, Christchurch, New Zealand.

Nichol, A. D., Bailey, M., & Cooper, D. J. (2010). Challenging issues in randomised controlled trials. *Injury*, 415, S20–S23.

Odgers, C. L. (2009). The life-course persistent pathway of antisocial behaviour: Risks for violence and poor physical health. In S. Hodgins, E. Viding, & A. Plodowski (Eds.), *The neurobiological basis of violence: Science and rehabilitation* (pp. 23–41). Oxford, UK: Oxford University Press.

Olver, M. E., Stockdale, K. C., & Wormith, J. S. (2011). A meta-analysis of predictors of offender treatment attrition and its relationship to recidivism. *Journal Consulting and Clinical Psychology*, 79, 6–21.

Olver, M. E., & Wong, S. C. P. (2013). Treatment programs for high risk sexual offenders: Program and offender characteristics, attrition, treatment change and recidivism. *Aggression and Violent Behavior*, 18, 579–591.

Polaschek, D. L. L. (2010). Treatment non-completion in high-risk violent offenders: Looking beyond criminal risk and criminogenic needs. *Psychology, Crime & Law*, 16, 525–540.

Polaschek, D. L. L. (2011). High-intensity rehabilitation for violent offenders in New Zealand: Reconviction outcomes for high- and medium-risk prisoners. *Journal of Interpersonal Violence*, 26, 664–682.

Polaschek, D. L. L. (2017, August). *Twenty-five years into the Correctional Rehabilitation Revolution: Keeping the science and art of psychology relevant. Hunter Award Address.* Paper presented at the New Zealand Psychological Society Annual Conference, Christchurch, New Zealand.

Polaschek, D. L. L., Yesberg, J. A., Bell, R. K., Casey, A. R., & Dickson, S. R. (2016). Intensive psychological treatment of high-risk violent offenders: Outcomes and pre-release mechanisms. *Psychology, Crime & Law*, 22, 344–365.

Polaschek, D. L. L., Yesberg, J. A., & Chauhan, P. (2018). A year without a conviction: An integrated examination of potential mechanisms for successful re-entry in high-risk violent prisoners. *Criminal Justice and Behavior*, 45, 425–446.

Rutherford, B. R., Wager, T. D., & Roose, S. P. (2010). Expectancy and the treatment of depression: A review of experimental methodology and effects on patient outcome. *Current Psychiatry Reviews*, 6, 1–10.

Schmucker, M., & Lösel, F. (2015). The effects of sexual offender treatment on recidivism: An international meta-analysis of sound quality evaluations. *Journal of Experimental Criminology*, 11, 597–630.

Serin, R. C., Gobeil, R., & Preston, D. L. (2009). Evaluation of the persistently violent offender treatment program. *Journal of Offender Therapy and Comparative Criminology*, 53, 57–73.

Sherman, L. W., & Berk, R. A. (1984). The specific deterrent effects of arrest for domestic assault. *American Sociological Review*, 49, 261–272.

Sherman, L. W., Gottfredson, D. C., Mackenzie, D. L., Eck, J., Reuter, P., & Bushway, S. D. (1998). *Preventing crime: What works, what doesn't, what's promising.* Washington, DC: National Institute of Justice.

Stark, M. J. (1992). Dropping out of substance abuse treatment: A clinically oriented review. *Clinical Psychology Review*, 12, 93–116.

Vito, G. F., Higgins, G. E., & Tewksbury, R. (2017). The effectiveness of parole supervision: Use of propensity score matching to analyze reincarceration rates in Kentucky. *Criminal Justice Policy Review*, 28, 627–640.

Wong, S. C. P., Gordon, A., Gu, D., Lewis, K., & Olver, M. E. (2012). The effectiveness of violence reduction treatment for psychopathic offenders: Empirical evidence and a treatment model. *International Journal of Forensic Mental Health*, 11, 336–349.

Yesberg, J. A., & Polaschek, D. L. L. (2014). Using information from the violence risk scale to understand different patterns of treatment response: Implications for the management of intensively treated life-sentenced prisoners. *Journal of Interpersonal Violence*, 29, 2991–3013.

Part V
Assessment

26

Evaluating and Managing Risk for Violence Using Structured Professional Judgment

Kevin S. Douglas
Simon Fraser University, Canada

Structured Professional Judgment

Structured Professional Judgment (SPJ) is one of two main options for evaluating the risk of violence posed by offenders, forensic psychiatric patients, and civil psychiatric patients. It is often used either at the entry to a system or institution, in planning for potential release from an institution, or for community monitoring. The SPJ approach is intended to be a comprehensive approach to identifying risk factors, risk level, motivations for violence, and appropriate risk management plans. There are many specific risk assessment instruments that have been developed within the SPJ framework (see Table 26.1). The conceptual underpinnings of each are largely the same. Instruments from the SPJ model have been adopted in roughly 40 countries, and translated into roughly 20 languages. Singh et al. (2014), in a survey of 2,135 clinicians across 44 different countries, reported that the HCR-20 (Historical-Clinical-Risk Management-20; Webster, Eaves, Douglas, & Wintrup, 1995, for Version 1; Webster, Douglas, Eaves, & Hart, 1997, for Version 2; Douglas, Hart, Webster, & Belfrage, 2013, for Version 3) was the most commonly used violence risk assessment instrument. In the next section, the defining features of the SPJ model, and how it differs from actuarial prediction, are discussed.

Comparing and Contrasting the SPJ and Actuarial Approaches

The SPJ approach to violence risk assessment and management was developed in the mid-1990s in part as a response to perceived problems with both a purely unstructured approach to risk assessment and problems with actuarial prediction methods. The unstructured approach, as the name suggests, by definition provides no formal guidance or rules for decision-making (Grove & Meehl, 1996; Meehl, 1954). It is completely reliant upon the discretion of the evaluator: for better or worse.

For this reason, the actuarial approach tries to minimize the role of human decision-making in the estimation of future likelihood of violence. Indeed, as the authors of one such actuarial

The Wiley International Handbook of Correctional Psychology, First Edition. Edited by Devon L. L. Polaschek, Andrew Day, and Clive R. Hollin.

Table 26.1 Select SPJ Violence Risk Assessment Instruments

Instrument	Intended application	Number of items
HCR-20 Version 3 (Douglas, Hart, Webster, & Belfrage, 2013)	Violence among adult males or females	20
SARA (Spousal Assault Risk Assessment Guide; Kropp, Hart, Webster, & Eaves, 1999)	Violence against a current or former intimate partner by a man or a woman	20
START (Short-Term Assessment of Risk and Treatability; Webster et al., 2009)	Short-term violence by adult psychiatric inpatients	20
SVR-20 (Sexual Violence Risk-20; Boer, Hart, Kropp, & Webster, 1997)	Sexual violence among male adults with histories of sexual violence	20
RSVP (Risk for Sexual Violence Protocol; Hart et al., 2003)	Sexual violence among male adults with histories of sexual violence	22
SAVRY (Structured Assessment of Violence Risk in Youth; Borum, Bartel, & Forth, 2006)	Violence among adolescents	30
EARL-20B, Version 2 (Early Assessment Risk List for Boys, EARL-20B, Version 2; Augimeri, Koegl, Webster, & Levene, 2001)	Antisocial and violent behavior in boys under 12	22
SAPROF (SAPROF. Guidelines for the assessment of protective factors for violence risk, 2nd Edition; de Vogel, de Ruiter, Bouman, & de Vries Robbé, 2012)	Violence among adults; to be used in conjunction with HCR-20 or SVR-20	17

instrument wrote: "What we are advising is not the addition of actuarial methods to existing practice, but rather the complete replacement of existing practice with actuarial methods" (Quinsey, Harris, Rice, & Cormier, 1998, p. 171; see also Quinsey, Harris, Rice, & Cormier, 2006, p. 182). The core, defining feature of the actuarial approach is that it "uses an equation, a formula, a graph, or an actuarial table to arrive at a probability, or expected value, of some outcome" (Grove & Meehl, 1996, p. 294). That is, it uses a mechanistic approach to combining risk factors to provide numeric estimates of future likelihood of violence, typically tied to a derivation sample.

It is clear that actuarial methods provide more consistent and valid decisions than unstructured decision-making at the sample level (Grove, Zald, Lebow, Snitz, & Nelson, 2000). Nonetheless, critics of the actuarial approach, the current author included, have noted several potential weaknesses to this approach. Discussed in detail elsewhere (Guy, Douglas, & Hart, 2015), these criticisms include the following concerns: (a) the putatively precise numeric estimates tend to vary across samples, casting doubt on their robustness (see, for example, Mills, Jones, & Kroner, 2005); (b) validity estimates from calibration samples—sometimes used to develop actuarial instruments in the absence of cross-validation—become attenuated upon cross-validation (see, for example, meta-analysis by Blair, Marcus, & Boccaccini, 2008); (c) important risk factors are often excluded from actuarial instruments if they were not predictive in the calibration sample, despite being associated with violence in numerous other samples; (d) risk factors that are not contained on a risk assessment instrument should not be included in the risk assessment, even if they are predictive in other samples and appear to be important in a given case; (e) many actuarial instruments exclude dynamic risk factors, lowering their utility within risk management; and (f) actuarial instruments that weight their risk factors, which many do, presume that these weights are equally relevant to all persons who have them, when in fact the same risk factor can have differential relevance across persons.

The purpose of this chapter is not to re-litigate these debates of decades past, but rather to explain the historical context in which both the actuarial and SPJ approaches to violence risk assessment were developed. As mentioned above, the SPJ approach was developed in response to the perceived weaknesses of both the unstructured approach and the actuarial approach. Although it is not a combination of these two approaches, it does attempt to minimize the weaknesses of each approach, and preserve the strengths of each approach. In the following section, the common features of the SPJ approach—and the instruments developed within this model—are highlighted.

Common Features of SPJ Instruments

Selection of Risk Factors

Risk factors are selected for inclusion on SPJ instruments based on their association with violence (in general, or for specific forms of violence, depending on the instrument) in the broad litera-ture on violence, rather than based on a single sample, as is common with the development of actuarial approaches. The advantage of this approach is that it fosters high content validity and comprehensive coverage of the violence domain while at the same time minimizing the chance that important risk factors will be excluded from the risk assessment instrument. In other words, this approach—sometimes called logical or rational item selection—reduces sample-dependency problems. SPJ instruments typically contain 20–30 risk factors, as shown in Table 26.1. A listing of risk factors contained in the most commonly used SPJ instrument is shown in Table 26.2.

Narrative Categorical Risk Communication

As mentioned above, most actuarial measures rely upon numeric risk communication based on algorithms such as score cutoffs or formulae involving weighted combinations of risk factors (i.e., 25% probability of violence in the coming year, or 10 years, as the case may be). Because such estimates can be highly unstable, are sample-dependent, and have an unclear interpreta-tion at the individual case level, SPJ measures simply do not use them. Rather, SPJ measures adopt a principled, narrative risk estimation and communication method where risk is simply defined as low, moderate, or high. Of course, generally, the more risk factors that a person has, the higher risk she or he will be. Yet, in some instances, a person with few risk factors may pose a high risk, or vice versa. The SPJ approach allows for this, whereas most actuarial approaches do not. The definitions of these risk levels, the principles used to distinguish them, and the research indicating that their predictive validity equals or exceeds actuarial estimates are reviewed later in this chapter.

Risk Factors Are Neither Weighted Algorithmically nor Presumed to Have Equal Importance for All People

The presence of risk factors on an SPJ instrument means that, in general, at the sample or population level, the factor elevates risk for violence. However, the SPJ model does not presume that all risk factors have equal weight for all people. For instance, on the revised (actuarial)

Table 26.2 Risk Factors on the HCR-20 Version 3

Historical Scale (History of Problems with...)

H1. Violence
  a As a Child (12 and Under)
  b As an Adolescent (13–17)
  c As an Adult (18 and Over)

H2. Other Antisocial Behavior
  a As a Child (12 and Under)
  b As an Adolescent (13–17)
  c As an Adult (18 and Over)

H3. Relationships
  a Intimate
  b Non-Intimate

H4. Employment

H5. Substance Use

H6. Major Mental Disorder
  a Psychotic Disorder
  b Major Mood Disorder
  c Other Major Mental Disorders

H7. Personality Disorder
  a Antisocial, Psychopathic, and Dissocial
  b Other Personality Disorders

H8. Traumatic Experiences
  a Victimization / Trauma
  b Adverse Childrearing Experiences

H9. Violent Attitudes

H10. Treatment or Supervision Response

Clinical Scale (Recent Problems with ...)

C1. Insight
  a Mental Disorder
  b Violence Risk
  c Need for Treatment

C2. Violent Ideation or Intent

C3. Symptoms of Major Mental Disorder
  a Psychotic Disorder
  b Major Mood Disorder
  c Other Major Mental Disorders

C4. Instability
  a Affective
  b Behavioral
  c Cognitive

C5. Treatment or Supervision Response
  a Compliance
  b Responsiveness

Table 26.2   (*Continued*)

Risk Management Scale (Future Problems with ...)

R1.   Professional Services and Plans

R2.   Living Situation

R3.   Personal Support

R4.   Treatment or Supervision Response
     a   Compliance
     b   Responsiveness

R5.   Stress or Coping

Violence Risk Appraisal Guide (VRAG-R; Rice, Harris, & Lang, 2013), having had maladjustment during elementary school is weighted more heavily than substance use problems, meaning that, for all persons being evaluated, regardless of the role of substance use problems in contributing to their violence, it *must* be given less weight than maladjustment during elementary school in the risk estimate. In the SPJ model, risk factors indicate *potential* areas of concern for a person. The evaluator must then determine the significance or weight to be given to that particular risk factor for the specific person being evaluated. For instance, psychosis (or substance use, or relationship problems, etc.) might be extremely relevant in understanding one person's risk for violence, but relatively inconsequential to another's. Why presume it has equal meaning for all people, or that its relative ranking of importance vis-à-vis other risk factors must always be the same? The SPJ method of rating or coding risk factors, therefore, while being grounded in empirical findings, is much more responsive to individual differences in the importance of risk factors across people. This method of coding risk factors also represents a bridge between science and practice, or between the nomothetic and idiographic levels of analysis.

SPJ Instruments Are Intended to Inform Treatment and Risk Management Decisions

In the SPJ model, risk assessment is intended not only to provide estimates of level of risk but also to inform necessary risk management efforts. Even if the evaluator will not be providing those management efforts directly, it makes sense to specify the management strategies—based on the risk factors of most relevance and a formulation of risk—that stand the best chance of reducing the risk of violence in the future. Indeed, the risk management strategies that will be implemented in the future are of direct relevance to understanding risk level, and hence are logically linked to the assessment itself. For these reasons, all SPJ instruments include risk factors that are *dynamic* (potentially changeable, and linked to violence), and that may act as causal agents with respect to an individual's violence. Recently developed SPJ instruments also include procedures that facilitate good decisions about risk management, such as formulation and scenario planning. These topics will be discussed later in the chapter.

How Do Evaluators Use the SPJ Model in Practice?

The SPJ model is intended to be both grounded in science *and* useful in practice. Indeed, in the first version of the HCR-20, the authors wrote that "[t]he great challenge in what remains of the 1990s is to integrate the almost separate worlds of research on the prediction of violence and the clinical practice of assessment. At present the two domains scarcely intersect" (Webster et al., 1995, p. v). Since that time, SPJ scholars have attempted to bridge that gap.

Most recent SPJ instruments adopt a similar set of steps in terms of facilitating decisions about violence risk and its management. In essence, SPJ instruments help professionals answer the following questions: What risk factors are present, and, of those, which are most relevant to understanding why a person has been violent? How do these risk factors influence a person's decisions to act violently? What is a coherent formulation of violence risk for this person? What types of violence, under what circumstances, might a person engage in in the future? What management strategies would be best suited to mitigate risk? What risk level is this person?

To illustrate how to use SPJ instruments in practice, the administration steps from the HCR-20 Version 3 (Douglas et al., 2013) are reviewed next. Version 3 embodies and exemplifies contemporary thinking on the SPJ model of violence risk assessment and management. Table 26.3 provides an outline of the core tasks involved.

Step 1: Case Information

There are multiple potential sources of information from which evaluators can draw, including files (police, health and mental health, correctional, employment, nursing, and so on); interviews (with the evaluee, and in some cases other professionals, family members, or victims); and testing information. Much of the information required to complete the rating of the HCR-20 Version 3 is the same as information that would be gathered in any psychosocial history, spanning domains of health, development, education, relationships, employment, criminality, and substance use. In addition, careful and detailed questioning or review of a person's history of violence and violent ideation is recommended. Such an analysis should focus on multiple dimensions of violence (nature, frequency, trajectory, motivations, victims, weapon use). Moreover, evaluators should gather information about a person's future plans, in terms of any programming or management in which they will be engaged, nature of stressors and coping, support networks, living situation, employment, and recreational activities.

Step 2: Presence of Risk Factors

SPJ measures typically employ a simple coding procedure of Yes, Possibly/Partially, No, or Omit with respect to the presence of risk factors. Manuals contain definitions and detailed coding notes. In some of the earlier SPJ instruments, risk factors are coded 0 (No), 1 (Possibly/Partially), Yes (2), or Omit. The meaning of the numeric and non-numeric coding systems is the same. Evaluators also need to determine how often the dynamic risk factors should be re-coded to capture any change that might have occurred. The manuals provide instructions on how to determine this. Table 26.2 presents the HCR-20 Version 3 risk factors as an illustration of the types and organization of risk factors contained within SPJ instruments. Evaluators, in addition to rating these standard risk factors, can include case-specific risk factors if there is case-level evidence that a risk factor that is not included among the 20 standard risk factors played a material role in a person's past violence. In practice, most often the 20 standard risk factors are able to capture all of the risk factors that are present. Evaluators should consider a risk factor that is present to be a potential area of concern with respect to elevating a person's risk: that is, its presence should be considered a hypothesis that the risk factor is relevant to understanding the person's violence risk. Relevance is then considered in Step 3.

Table 26.3   Steps in the SPJ Decision-Making Process as Embodied by the HCR-20 Version 3

Step	Tasks
1	Case Information • Gather information from multiple sources that is sufficient to complete ratings • Include a focus on past acts of violence and violent ideation • Determine credibility of information
2	Presence of Risk Factors • Determine whether risk factors are present, partially or possibly present, or absent • Consider whether there are case-specific risk factors present • Omit risk factors if insufficient information
3	Relevance of Risk Factors • Of the risk factors that are present, determine which are most relevant to understanding why a person has acted violently • Determine whether risk factors have a causal connection, at the individual level, to a person's violence • Consider whether risk factors motivate, disinhibit, or destabilize a person's decision-making
4	Risk Formulation • Integrate risk factors into a meaningful explanation of violence risk • Provide a coherent narrative explaining why a person acts violently
5	Risk Scenarios • Specify the type and nature of future violent acts that is of concern • Outline the conditions under which violence might occur • Consider who the targets of violence might be, the methods of violence, the motivations for violence, and the severity of violence
6	Management Strategies • Specify the level and nature of violence risk management strategies that take into account relevant risk factors, risk formulation, and risk scenarios • Take into consideration monitoring, supervision, treatment, and victim safety strategies
7	Conclusory Opinions • Provide summary risk rating regarding concern about level of risk and case priority (low, moderate, high) • Provide summary risk rating regarding life-threatening violence • Provide summary risk rating regarding imminent violence • Set a date for further case review

Step 3: Relevance of Risk Factors

As described earlier, not all risk factors are equally important to all people. In considering the relevance of risk factors, evaluators must consider the role that they might have played in a person's past violence, or whether they are critical to manage going forward. Most basically, a risk factor is considered relevant at the idiographic level if, based on the case facts, it made a material contribution to a person's violence; it influenced a person's decision to act violently; it impaired a person's decision-making about violence (by, say, destabilizing it); or it is critical to manage because its presence perpetuates risk or allows other risk factors to continue to exist or operate.

One of the functions of determining the relevance of risk factors is to begin to simplify the assessment by honing in on the most important areas of risk. The determination of relevance assists the evaluator in addressing *why* a person has been violent, rather than simply providing a list of risk factors. It forms the basis of the next step in the process: case formulation.

Step 4: Risk Formulation

Formulation is the process of simplifying and integrating information to produce a coherent explanation of a person's violence. Formulation, or case conceptualization, is commonly used within mental health and other professional fields. As it is in other fields, formulation in the violence risk field is guided by theoretical and practical organizing principles to produce an individual theory of violence (Hart & Logan, 2011). Ultimately, its purpose is to answer the question: Why has this person acted violently? The SPJ model draws from situational action theory (Wikström & Treiber, 2009), or decision theory more broadly, to guide consideration of factors that influence a person's decisions to act violently. For instance, some factors might increase the perceived benefits of violence (motivators), others may decrease the perceived cost (disinhibitors), and others may interfere with careful decision-making (destabilizers). Evaluators may choose to draw from other well-established theories of violence as well. The SPJ model can also help evaluators identify root causes, and to form conceptually meaningful clusters of risk factors. This step is intended to be quite flexible in terms of the method by which evaluators formulate a case, allowing for differing areas of professional expertise to be exercised.

Step 5: Risk Scenarios

The scenario planning stage of the assessment is forward-looking, and asks evaluators to specify what they are concerned the evaluee might do in the future. Scenario planning has been used for over a hundred years in the military, and more recently in fields such finance and health care (Hart & Logan, 2011). Its primary purpose is to help plan under conditions of uncertainty. Evaluators are encouraged to derive—based on the preceding steps—a small number of scenarios that describe how future violence might unfold. What would the circumstances be? What might motivate this violence? Are there any identifiable victims? How serious might the harm be? Importantly, what would the warning signs be? This step encourages a proactive consideration of possible types of future violence so that those responsible for risk management might have early notice if a risky situation or process is beginning to unfold.

Step 6: Management Strategies

Based on the scenarios of concern, and the preceding formulation (which in turn integrates relevant risk factors), the next step is to specify what risk management strategies would best mitigate risk. Two simple principles are shared with the Risk-Need-Responsivity (RNR) model of case management (Andrews & Bonta, 2006): that higher-risk cases require more intensive intervention, and that dynamic risk factors (or criminogenic needs) must be targeted. The difference between the RNR approach and the SPJ approach at this step is that the SPJ approach also includes formulation and scenario planning to assist the evaluator in being very specific with recommendations. Under the SPJ approach, risk management includes at least four types of strategies: supervision (i.e., restrictions on freedoms, such as imposition of a curfew); monitoring (i.e., frequency of observation; observation for warning signs); treatment/intervention (i.e., violence reduction treatments that are evidence-based and target dynamic risk factors); and, when appropriate, victim safety planning (i.e., strategies to educate or provide coping mechanisms to known potential victims).

Step 7: Conclusory Opinions

The final step involves making a summary risk rating that communicates the evaluator's level of concern about the likelihood of future violence, and hence the priority level of the case for management resources. As described above, the SPJ approach uses summary risk ratings of low, moderate, and high risk. In general, high-risk cases have more risk factors than moderate or low-risk cases. However, numeric cut-points are not used, as these can be arbitrary, and because it is possible that a small number of risk factors can greatly elevate risk. For this reason, evaluators are asked to consider the degree of intervention or management that would be required to mitigate risk, and their level of concern that the person will be violent in, say, the coming 6–12 months. These summary risk ratings are intended to capture the concerns identified in the previous six steps, and to compel action. Although very simple, these ratings are intended to be structured and principled, and also more responsive to individual cases relative to an actuarial approach.

In the remainder of this chapter, the evidence base for the SPJ approach is discussed. There are several hundred studies on the SPJ approach. Hence, the review will first discuss meta-analyses, and then consider two specific areas of particular interest: summary risk ratings, and dynamic risk.

Research Evaluation

Meta-Analytic Evaluations

In a meta-analysis of 88 studies (1980–2006), Campbell, French, and Gendreau (2009) focused mainly on general recidivism among adults, although some studies included violent recidivism. Depending on the number of studies, they evaluated specific measures (HCR-20, *Hare Psychopathy Checklist—Revised* [PCL-R]; Statistical Information on Recidivism [SIR; Nuffield, 1982], VRAG, Level of Service instruments [*Level of Supervision Inventory*, or LSI, Andrews, 1982, LSI-R, *Level of Service/Case Management Inventory*, or LS/CMI, Andrews, Bonta, & Wormith, 2004]). No single instrument was consistently more strongly related to outcomes than the others. Effect sizes (Zr) for institutional violence ranged from .08 to .28, and for community violent recidivism, they ranged from .22 to .32. Instruments that contained dynamic risk factors produced larger effect sizes than those without.

Hanson and Morton-Bourgon's (2009) meta-analysis of 118 sex offender studies concluded that actuarial assessments were more accurate than unstructured clinical prediction, and that SPJ measures were found to be intermediate. There were only six SPJ studies included. One of these, the Sexual Violence Risk-20 (SVR-20), produced the largest effect sizes, but there were only three studies on this instrument. For this reason, while this meta-analysis provided support for the actuarial method, there were too few studies to draw any conclusions about the SPJ model.

Olver, Stockdale, and Wormith (2009) focused on youth risk assessment in their meta-analysis of 44 studies. They evaluated the *Hare Psychopathy Checklist—Revised: Youth Version* (PCL:YV; Forth, Kosson, & Hare, 2003), the Structured Assessment of Violence Risk in Youth (SAVRY; an SPJ measure), and the *Youth Level of Service/Case Management Inventory* (YLS/CMI; Hoge & Andrews, 2002), an actuarial measure that uses numeric cut-points. As in other meta-analyses, the instruments performed comparably to one another. Effect sizes for the SAVRY ranged from .30 to .38; for the YLS/CMI, from .26 to .32; and for the PCL:YV, from .16 to .28. Viljoen, Mordell, and Beneteau (2012) similarly reported no meaningful differences between SPJ and actuarial instruments in their meta-analysis of youth sex offender risk assessment.

Yang, Wong, and Coid's (2010) meta-analysis was particularly interesting because it compared a number of commonly used risk assessment instruments against the PCL-R as a benchmark. That is, it evaluated whether any measures improve statistically on the PCL-R. They analyzed nine instruments across 28 studies (1999–2008). Across a number of statistical models with different assumptions, there were few differences between instruments. Only two added incrementally to the PCL-R—the HCR-20 (based on 16 samples) and the Offender Group Reconviction Scale (OGRS; Copas & Marshall, 1998; based on two samples).

Another meta-analysis specifically compared just the HCR-20 (Version 2) and the PCL-R (Guy, Douglas, & Hendry, 2010) based on samples ($k = 34$) that contained both instruments. This type of meta-analysis provides the most direct comparison, because the sample character- istics are equal across instruments. Based simply on comparing univariate effect sizes, the two instruments performed comparably (areas under the curve, or AUCs = .69 for both). The authors had access to seven raw data files that comprised part of the 34 studies, and hence were able to conduct meta-analytic logistic regression using these raw data sets. After removing the psychopathy item from the HCR-20 to provide the cleanest comparison between instruments, the authors reported that the HCR-20 added unique, incremental validity to the PCL-R, but the PCL-R did not add incrementally to the HCR-20. Based on odds ratios derived from the logistic regression analyses, when both the HCR-20 and PCL-R were in the regression model, for every one-step increase on the HCR-20, there was a 23% increase in the odds of observing violence, whereas there was a 1% decrease in the odds of violence for every one-step increase on the PCL-R. In addition, the HCR-20's predictive validity was not diminished when its psychopathy item was removed (AUC = .71).

Singh, Grann, and Fazel's (2011) meta-analysis was able to become more specific than earlier meta-analysis. Based on 88 samples that evaluated nine instruments, they used a "binning" strategy to allow for the SPJ low, moderate, high method of risk estimation to be captured. They also "binned" actuarial instruments. Hence, although they focused on the SPJ model's categorical system, they also created categorical indices that are not necessarily used in practice for actuarial measures. And those that were created for SPJ measures also do not map entirely onto their intended use (for instance, combining low and moderate, or moderate and high, into a single category). Further, for five of the 27 SPJ studies included, the cate- gories were based on numeric cut-points, rather than the traditional non-numeric categorical estimate. Instrument-specific analyses were typically based on fewer than 10 studies, and the maximum was 12. Despite this, the authors did report some differences between assessment measures, in that the SAVRY produced the largest effect size. The smallest effect sizes were produced by the PCL and LS measures. Interestingly, instruments designed to evaluate risk for more specific outcomes (that is, violence as opposed to general criminality) had higher effect sizes. Fazel, Singh, Doll, and Grann (2012) reported similar findings based on a meta-analysis of a largely overlapping set of studies.

Most published meta-analyses have not adequately captured the research base on the SPJ model's categorical risk ratings. One as-yet unpublished meta-analysis by Guy (2008) focused on 113 SPJ disseminations, many of which also included actuarial instruments. Guy's findings included the following: summary risk ratings of low, moderate, or high risk were more strongly associated with violence than the total scores that can be produced for research purposes from SPJ measures; across all effect sizes coded, SPJ summary risk ratings of low, moderate, or high risk produced significantly larger effect sizes (AUC = .68; 95% confidence interval [CI_w] = .65–.70) than actuarial instruments (AUC = .62; 95% CI_w = .61–.63); based on a single effect size per study, actuarial instruments and SPJ summary risk ratings were comparably associated with violence (AUCs = .67 and .69, respectively).

Based on meta-analytic findings, it is fair to conclude that SPJ instruments, including their summary risk ratings, are at least as strongly predictive of future violence compared to actuarial instruments or the PCL-R, if not more so. In the next sections, additional findings on the SPJ categorical risk ratings are presented, followed by research on dynamic risk.

Focus on Summary Risk Ratings

As described above, one of the distinctive features of the SPJ approach is that it relies on a non-numeric, categorical risk communication method. There have been at least 45 published studies that have tested whether these judgments are related to future violence.[1] In most of these studies (39, or 87%), the summary risk rating (coded 0, 1, 2 for research purposes) was significantly predictive of future violence. In 18 of these studies, researchers tested the incremental validity of these ratings against the numeric use of the instruments (totaling the risk factors, producing a score) in multivariate analyses. Incremental validity was observed in 16 of the 18 studies (89%).

Dynamic Risk and Risk Reduction

All SPJ instruments contain dynamic risk factors in order to support the model's focus on risk management and risk reduction. The SPJ model assumes that when such risk factors change, violence risk changes. That is, if these risk factors are ameliorated, risk and future violence decreases, and when they are exacerbated, risk and future violence increases. These assumptions of the SPJ model are critical to test.

Early studies focused on testing whether the dynamic items of certain SPJ instruments, such as the HCR-20, changed over the course of hospitalization. For instance, Belfrage and Douglas (2002) showed that several of the HCR-20 C and R items, in addition to the sums of C and R factors, decreased over the course of forensic treatment among 150 forensic inpatients. Douglas and Belfrage (2001) reported similar findings between admission to and discharge from a psychiatric hospital. More recent research has confirmed earlier findings (Ribeiro, Tully, & Fotiadou, 2015).

More recent studies have tested whether changes in dynamic risk factors between two or more time points are associated with subsequent changes in violence. For instance, de Vries Robbé et al. (2015), in a sample of 108 forensic patients released to the community, found that decreases in risk factors (on the HCR-20) and increases in protective factors (on the SAPROF) during forensic treatment were predictive of lower rates of post-discharge violence.

Michel et al. (2013) followed 248 civil and forensic patients in the community across six time points, 4 months apart. Using generalized estimating equations (GEE), they observed that 6 of the 10 HCR-20 C and R items (the aspects of the HCR-20 intended to be most dynamic) changed across time, and that this change was associated with changes in violence in the subsequent time frames. When these risk factors increased, higher rates of violence followed, and when they decreased, lower rates of violence were observed.

Two studies have evaluated the dynamic predictive validity of the recently published third version of the HCR-20. Penney, Marshall, and Simpson (2016) reported that changes in the C and R scales of the HCR-20 Version 3 added incremental predictive validity to the H scale from that instrument in terms of post-discharge violence among forensic patients. In another study, Hogan and Olver (2016) reported that changes in both the presence and the relevance ratings of the HCR-20 Version 3 C and R scales added incremental predictive validity over and above baseline H, C, and R scale scores among forensic patients while in the institution.

Summary and Conclusions

The following conclusions can be drawn about the SPJ model: (a) risk factors and summary risk ratings on SPJ instruments have consistent support in the research; (b) SPJ measures and summary risk ratings are as strongly predictive of violence as the actuarial approach; (c) SPJ measures can index change in risk factors across time; (d) when dynamic risk factors on SPJ instruments change over time, subsequent changes in violence also are observed; (e) there is emerging support that specifically reducing dynamic risk factors through intervention lowers future violence. However, further research on risk reduction is necessary, as is research on the formulation and scenario planning steps of the SPJ model.

Note

1   Arbach-Lucioni, Andres-Pueyo, Pomarol-Clotet, and Gomar-Sones (2011), Belfrage et al. (2012), Braithwaite, Charette, Crocker, and Reyes (2010), Catchpole and Gretton (2003), de Vogel and de Ruiter (2005, 2006), de Vogel, de Ruiter, Hildebrand, Bos, and van de Ven (2004), de Vogel, de Ruiter, van Beek, and Mead (2004), de Vries Robbé, de Vogel, and de Spa (2011), de Vries Robbé, de Vogel, Koster, and Bogaerts (2014), de Vries Robbé, de Vogel, Douglas, and Nijman (2015), de Vries Robbé, de Vogel, Wever, Douglas, and Nijman (2016), Desmarais, Nicholls, Wilson, and Brink (2012), Dolan and Rennie (2008), Douglas, Ogloff, and Hart (2003), Douglas, Yeomans, and Boer (2005), Enebrink, Långström, and Gumpert (2006), Folino (2015), Gammelgård, Koivisto, Eronen, and Kaltiala-Heino (2008), Ho et al. (2015), Hogan and Olver (2016), Jovanović, Toševski, Ivković, Damjanović, and Gašić (2009), Kropp and Hart (2000), Langton, Hogue, Daffern, Mannion, and Howells (2009), Lodewijks, de Ruiter, and Doreleijers (2008), Lodewijks, Doreleijers, and Ruiter (2008), Lodewijks, Doreleijers, Ruiter, and Borum (2008), Meyers and Schmidt (2008), Neal, Miller, and Shealy (2015), Neves, Goncalves, and Palma-Oliveira (2011), O'Shea, Picchioni, Mason, Sugarman, and Dickens (2014), O'Shea et al. (2016), Nonstad et al. (2010), Pedersen, Rasmussen, and Elsass (2010), Penney, Lee, and Moretti (2010), Rajlic and Gretton (2010), Sada et al. (2016), Schaap, Lammers, and de Vogel (2009), Schmidt, Campbell, and Houlding (2011), Sjöstedt and Långström (2002), Strub, Douglas, and Nicholls, (2014), van den Brink, Hooijschuur, van Os, Savenije, and Wiersma (2010), Verbrugge, Goodman-Delahunty, and Frize (2011), Viljoen et al. (2008), Viljoen et al. (2016), Vincent, Chapman, and Cook (2011).

Key Readings

Douglas, K. S., Hart, S. D., Groscup, J. L., & Litwack, T. R. (2014). Assessing violence risk. In I. Weiner, & R. K. Otto (Eds.), *The handbook of forensic psychology* (4th ed.) (pp. 385–441). Hoboken, NJ: Wiley.

Douglas, K. S., Hart, S. D., Webster, C. D., Belfrage, H., Guy, L. S., & Wilson, C. (2014). *Historical-Clinical-Risk Management-20, Version 3 (HCR-20^{V3})*: Development and overview. *International Journal of Forensic Mental Health*, 13, 93–108.

Heilbrun, K., Brooks Holliday, S., & King, C. (2012). Evaluation of violence risk in adults. In R. Roesch, & P. A. Zapf (Eds.), *Forensic assessments in criminal and civil law: A handbook for lawyers* (pp. 74–87). New York, NY: Oxford University Press.

Monahan, J. (2013). Violence risk assessment. In R. K. Otto, & I. B. Weiner (Eds.), *Handbook of psychology: Forensic psychology* (pp. 541–555). Hoboken, NJ: Wiley.

References

Andrews, D. A. (1982). *The Level of Supervision Inventory (LSI): The first follow-up*. Toronto, Canada: Ontario Ministry of Correctional Services.

Andrews, D. A., & Bonta, J. (2006). *The psychology of criminal conduct* (4th ed.). Cincinnati, OH: Anderson.

Andrews, D. A., Bonta, J., & Wormith, S. J. (2004). *The Level of Service/Case Management Inventory (LS/CMI)*. Toronto, Canada: Multi-Health Systems.

Arbach-Lucioni, K., Andres-Pueyo, A., Pomarol-Clotet, E., & Gomar-Sones, J. (2011). Predicting violence in psychiatric inpatients: A prospective study with the HCR-20 violence risk assessment scheme. *Journal of Forensic Psychiatry & Psychology*, 22, 203–222.

Augimeri, L. K., Koegl, C. J., Webster, C. D., & Levene, K. S. (2001). *Early assessment risk list for boys: Version 2*. Toronto, Canada: Earlscourt Child and Family Centre.

Belfrage, H., & Douglas, K. S. (2002). Treatment effects on forensic psychiatric patients measured with the HCR-20 violence risk assessment scheme. *International Journal of Forensic Mental Health*, 1, 25–36.

Belfrage, H., Strand, S., Storey, J. E., Gibas, A., Kropp, P. R., & Hart, S. D. (2012). Assessment and management of risk for intimate partner violence by police officers using the Spousal Assault Risk Assessment Guide. *Law and Human Behavior*, 36, 60–67.

Blair, P. R., Marcus, D. K., & Boccaccini, M. T. (2008). Is there an allegiance effect for assessment instruments? Actuarial risk assessment as an exemplar. *Clinical Psychology: Science and Practice*, 15, 346–360.

Boer, D. P., Hart, S. D., Kropp, P. R., & Webster, C. D. (1997). *Manual for the Sexual Violence Risk–20: Professional guidelines for assessing risk of sexual violence*. Vancouver, Canada: British Columbia Institute on Family Violence and Mental Health, Law, and Policy Institute, Simon Fraser University.

Borum, R., Bartel, P., & Forth, A. (2006). *Manual for the Structured Assessment of Violence Risk in Youth (SAVRY)*. Odessa, FL: Psychological Assessment Resources.

Braithwaite, E., Charette, Y., Crocker, A. G., & Reyes, A. (2010). The predictive validity of clinical ratings of the *Short-Term Assessment of Risk and Treatability* (START). *International Journal of Forensic Mental Health*, 9, 271–281.

Campbell, M. A., French, S., & Gendreau, P. (2009). The prediction of violence in adult offenders: A meta-analytic comparison of instruments and methods of assessment. *Criminal Justice and Behavior*, 36, 567–590.

Catchpole, R. E. H., & Gretton, H. M. (2003). The predictive validity of risk assessment with violent young offenders: A 1-year examination of criminal outcome. *Criminal Justice and Behavior*, 30, 688–708.

Copas, J., & Marshall, P. (1998). The Offender Group Reconviction Scale: The statistical reconviction score for use by probation officers. *Journal of the Royal Statistical Society*, 47C, 159–171.

de Vogel, V., de Ruiter, C., Bouman, Y., & de Vries Robbé, M. (2012). *SAPROF. Guidelines for the assessment of protective factors for violence risk* (2nd ed.). Utrecht, the Netherlands: Forum Educatief.

de Vogel, V., & de Ruiter, C. (2005). The HCR-20 in personality disordered female offenders: A comparison with a matched sample of males. *Clinical Psychology & Psychotherapy*, 12, 226–240.

de Vogel, V., & de Ruiter, C. (2006). Structured professional judgment of violence risk in forensic clinical practice: A prospective study into the predictive validity of the Dutch HCR-20. *Psychology, Crime & Law*, 12, 321–336.

de Vogel, V., de Ruiter, C., Hildebrand, M., Bos, B., & van de Ven, P. (2004). Type of discharge and risk of recidivism measured by the HCR-20: A retrospective study in a Dutch sample of treated forensic psychiatric patients. *International Journal of Forensic Mental Health*, 3, 149–165.

de Vogel, V., de Ruiter, C., van Beek, D., & Mead, G. (2004). Predictive validity of the SVR-20 and Static 99 in a Dutch sample of treated sex offenders. *Law and Human Behavior*, 28, 235–251.

de Vries Robbé, M., de Vogel, V., & de Spa, E. (2011). Protective factors for violence risk in forensic psychiatric patients: A retrospective validation study of the SAPROF. *International Journal of Forensic Mental Health*, 10, 178–186.

de Vries Robbé, M., de Vogel, V., Douglas, K. S., & Nijman, H. L. I. (2015). Changes in dynamic risk and protective factors for violence during inpatient forensic psychiatric treatment: Predicting reductions in postdischarge community recidivism. *Law and Human Behavior*, 39, 53–61.

de Vries Robbé, M., de Vogel, V., Koster, K., & Bogaerts, S. (2014). Assessing protective factors for sexually violent offending with the SAPROF. *Sexual Abuse: A Journal of Research and Treatment*, 27, 51–70.

de Vries Robbé, M., de Vogel, V., Wever, E. C., Douglas, K. S., & Nijman, H. L. I. (2016). Risk and protective factors for inpatient aggression. *Criminal Justice and Behavior*, 43, 1364–1385.

Desmarais, S. L., Nicholls, T., Wilson, C. M., & Brink, J. (2012). Reliability and validity of the *Short-Term Assessment of Risk and Treatability* (START) in assessing risk for inpatient aggression. *Psychological Assessment*, 24, 685–700.

Dolan, M. C., & Rennie, C. E. (2008). The *Structured Assessment of Violence Risk in Youth* as a predictor of recidivism in a United Kingdom cohort of adolescent offenders with conduct disorder. *Psychological Assessment*, 20, 35–46.

Douglas, K. S., & Belfrage, H. (2001). Use of the HCR-20 in violence risk management: Implementation and clinical practice. In K. S. Douglas, C. D. Webster, S. D. Hart, D. Eaves, & J. R. P. Ogloff (Eds.), *HCR-20: Violence risk management companion guide* (pp. 41–58). Burnaby, Canada: Mental Health, Law, and Policy Institute.

Douglas, K. S., Hart, S. D., Webster, C. D., & Belfrage, H. (2013). *HCR-20 (Version 3): Assessing Risk for Violence–user guide*. Burnaby, Canada: Mental Health, Law, and Policy Institute, Simon Fraser University.

Douglas, K. S., Ogloff, J. R. P., & Hart, S. D. (2003). Evaluation of a model of violence risk assessment among forensic psychiatric patients. *Psychiatric Services*, 54, 1372–1379.

Douglas, K. S., Yeomans, M., & Boer, D. P. (2005). Comparative validity analysis of multiple measures of violence risk in a sample of criminal offenders. *Criminal Justice and Behavior*, 32, 479–510.

Enebrink, P., Långström, N., & Gumpert, C. H. (2006). Predicting aggressive and disruptive behavior in referred 6- to 12-year-old boys: Predictive validation of the EARL-20B risk/needs checklist. *Assessment*, 13, 356–367.

Fazel, S., Singh, J. P., Doll, H., & Grann, M. (2012). Use of risk assessment instruments to predict violence and antisocial behaviour in 73 samples involving 24 827 people: Systematic review and meta-analysis. *British Medical Journal*, 345, e4692.

Folino, J. O. (2015). Predictive efficacy of violence risk assessment instruments in Latin-America. *The European Journal of Psychology Applied to Legal Context*, 7(2), 51–58.

Forth, A. E., Kosson, D. S., & Hare, R. D. (2003). *Hare Psychopathy Checklist: Youth Version*. Toronto: Multi-Health Systems.

Gammelgård, M., Koivisto, A., Eronen, M., & Kaltiala-Heino, R. (2008). The predictive validity of the *Structured Assessment of Violence Risk in Youth* (SAVRY) among institutionalised adolescents. *Journal of Forensic Psychiatry & Psychology*, 19, 352–370.

Grove, W. M., & Meehl, P. E. (1996). Comparative efficiency of informal (subjective, impressionistic) and formal (mechanical, algorithmic) prediction procedures: The clinical–statistical controversy. *Psychology, Public Policy, and Law*, 2, 293–323.

Grove, W. M., Zald, D. H., Lebow, B. S., Snitz, B. E., & Nelson, C. (2000). Clinical versus mechanical prediction: A meta-analysis. *Psychological Assessment*, 12, 19–30.

Guy, L. S. (2008). *Performance indicators of the structured professional judgement approach for assessing risk for violence to others: A meta-analytic survey* (Unpublished doctoral dissertation). Simon Fraser University, Burnaby, British Columbia, Canada. Retrieved from http://summit.sfu.ca/system/files/iritems1/9247/etd4194.pdf

Guy, L. S., Douglas, K. S., & Hart, S. D. (2015). Risk assessment and communication. In B. Cutler, & P. Zapf (Eds.), *APA handbook of forensic psychology* (Vol. 1) (pp. 35–86). Washington, DC: American Psychological Association.

Guy, L. S., Douglas, K. S., & Hendry, M. (2010). The role of psychopathic personality disorder in violence risk assessments using the HCR-20. *Journal of Personality Disorders*, 24, 551–580.

Hanson, R. K., & Morton-Bourgon, K. E. (2009). The accuracy of recidivism risk assessments for sexual offenders: A meta-analysis of 118 prediction studies. *Psychological Assessment*, 21, 1–21.

Hart, S. D., Kropp, P. R., Laws, D. R., Klaver, J., Logan, C., & Watt, K. A. (2003). *The Risk for Sexual Violence Protocol (RSVP): Structured professional guidelines for assessing risk of sexual violence*. Burnaby, Canada: Mental Health, Law, and Policy Institute, Simon Fraser University.

Hart, S. D., & Logan, C. (2011). Formulation of violence risk using evidence-based assessments: The Structured Professional Judgment approach. In P. Sturmey, & M. McMurran (Eds.), *Forensic case formulation* (pp. 83–106). Chichester, UK: Wiley-Blackwell.

Ho, R. M., Cheung, H. H., Lai, T. T., Tam, V. F., Yan, C. K., Chan, W. L., & Yuen, K. K. (2015). Use of the Historical, Clinical, Risk Management-20 to assess the risk of violence by discharged psychiatric patients. *Hong Kong Medical Journal*, 21, 45–47.

Hogan, N. R., & Olver, M. E. (2016). Assessing risk for aggression in forensic psychiatric inpatients: An examination of five measures. *Law and Human Behavior*, 40, 233–243.

Hoge, R. D., & Andrews, D. A. (2002). *Youth Level of Service/Case Management Inventory: User's manual*. Toronto, Canada: Multi-Health Systems.

Jovanović, A. A., Toševski, D. L., Ivković, M., Damjanović, A., & Gašić, M. J. (2009). Predicting violence in veterans with posttraumatic stress disorder. *Vojnosanitetski Pregled: Military Medical & Pharmaceutical Journal of Serbia & Montenegro*, 66, 13–21.

Kropp, P. R., & Hart, S. D. (2000). The Spousal Assault Risk Assessment (SARA) Guide: Reliability and validity in adult male offenders. *Law and Human Behavior*, 24, 101–118.

Kropp, P. R., Hart, S. D., Webster, C. D., & Eaves, D. (1999). *Spousal Assault Risk Assessment Guide user's manual*. Toronto, Canada: Multi-Health Systems/British Columbia Institute on Family Violence.

Langton, C. M., Hogue, T. E., Daffern, M., Mannion, A., & Howells, K. (2009). Prediction of institutional aggression among personality disordered forensic patients using actuarial and structured clinical risk assessment tools: Prospective evaluation of the HCR-20, VRS, Static-99, and Risk Matrix 2000. *Psychology, Crime & Law*, 15, 635–659.

Lodewijks, H. P. B., de Ruiter, C., & Doreleijers, T. A. H. (2008). Gender differences in violent outcome and risk assessment in adolescent offenders after residential treatment. *International Journal of Forensic Mental Health*, 7, 133–146.

Lodewijks, H. P. B., Doreleijers, T. A. H., & de Ruiter, C. (2008). SAVRY risk assessment in relation to sentencing and subsequent recidivism in a Dutch sample of violent juvenile offenders. *Criminal Justice and Behavior*, 35, 696–709.

Lodewijks, H. P. B., Doreleijers, T. A. H., de Ruiter, C., & Borum, R. (2008). Predictive validity of the *Structured Assessment of Violence in Youth* (SAVRY) during residential treatment. *International Journal of Law and Psychiatry*, 31, 263–271.

Meehl, P. E. (1954). *Clinical versus statistical prediction: A theoretical analysis and a review of the evidence.* Minneapolis, MN: University of Minnesota Press.

Meyers, J. R., & Schmidt, F. (2008). Predictive validity of the Structured Assessment for Violence Risk in Youth (SAVRY) with juvenile offenders. *Criminal Justice and Behavior*, 35, 344–355.

Michel, S. F., Riaz, M., Webster, C., Hart, S. D., Levander, S., Müller-Isberner, R., … & Hodgins, S. (2013). Using the HCR-20 to predict aggressive behavior among men with schizophrenia living in the community: Accuracy of prediction, general and forensic settings, and dynamic risk factors. *International Journal of Forensic Mental Health*, 12, 1–13.

Mills, J. F., Jones, M. N., & Kroner, D. G. (2005). An examination of the generalizability of the LSI-R and VRAG probability bins. *Criminal Justice and Behavior*, 32, 565–585.

Neal, T. M., Miller, S. L., & Shealy, R. C. (2015). A field study of a comprehensive violence risk assessment battery. *Criminal Justice and Behavior*, 42(9), 952–968.

Neves, A. C., Goncalves, R. A., & Palma-Oliveira, J. M. (2011). Assessing risk for violent and general recidivism: A study of the HCR-20 and the PCL-R with a non-clinical sample of Portuguese offenders. *International Journal of Forensic Mental Health*, 10, 137–149.

Nonstad, K., Nesset, M. B., Kroppan, E., Pedersen, T. W., Nöttestad, J. A., Almvik, R., & Palmstierna, T. (2010). Predictive validity and other psychometric properties of the *Short-Term Assessment of Risk and Treatability* (START) in a Norwegian high secure hospital. *International Journal of Forensic Mental Health*, 9, 294–299.

Nuffield, J. (1982). *Parole decision-making in Canada.* Ottawa, Canada: Communication Division, Solicitor General of Canada.

Olver, M. E., Stockdale, K. C., & Wormith, J. S. (2009). Risk assessment with young offenders: A meta-analysis of three assessment measures. *Criminal Justice and Behavior*, 36, 329–353.

O'Shea, L. E., Picchioni, M. M., Mason, F. L., Sugarman, P. A., & Dickens, G. L. (2014). Differential predictive validity of the Historical, Clinical and Risk Management Scales (HCR–20) for inpatient aggression. *Psychiatry Research*, 220, 669–678.

O'Shea, L. E., Thaker, D., Picchioni, M. M., Mason, F. L., Knight, C., & Dickens, G. L. (2016). Predictive validity of the HCR-20 for violent and non-violent sexual behaviour in a secure mental health service. *Criminal Behaviour and Mental Health*, 26, 366–379.

Pedersen, L., Rasmussen, K., & Elsass, P. (2010). Risk assessment: The value of structured professional judgments. *International Journal of Forensic Mental Health*, 9, 74–81.

Penney, S. R., Lee, Z., & Moretti, M. M. (2010). Gender differences in risk factors for violence: An examination of the predictive validity of the Structured Assessment of Violence Risk in Youth. *Aggressive Behavior*, 36, 390–404.

Penney, S. R., Marshall, L. A., & Simpson, A. I. F. (2016). The assessment of dynamic risk among forensic psychiatric patients transitioning to the community. *Law and Human Behavior*, 40, 374–386.

Quinsey, V. L., Harris, G. T., Rice, M. E., & Cormier, C. A. (1998). *Violent offenders: Appraising and managing risk.* Washington, DC: American Psychological Association.

Quinsey, V. L., Harris, G. T., Rice, M. E., & Cormier, C. (2006). *Violent offenders: Appraising and managing risk* (2nd ed.). Washington, DC: American Psychological Association.

Rajlic, G., & Gretton, H. (2010). An examination of two sexual recidivism risk measures in adolescent offenders. *Criminal Justice and Behavior*, 37, 1066–1085.

Ribeiro, R. B., Tully, J., & Fotiadou, M. (2015). Clinical characteristics and outcomes on discharge of women admitted to a medium secure unit over a 4-year period. *International Journal of Law and Psychiatry*, 39, 83–89.

Rice, M. E., Harris, G. T., & Lang, C. (2013). Validation of and revision to the VRAG and SORAG: The Violence Risk Appraisal Guide—Revised (VRAG-R). *Psychological Assessment*, 25, 951–965.

Evaluating and Managing Risk for Violence Using Structured Professional Judgment   445

Sada, A., Robles-García, R., Martínez-López, N., Hernández-Ramírez, R., Tovilla-Zarate, C. A., López-Munguía, F., ... & Fresán, A. (2016). Assessing the reliability, predictive and construct validity of Historical, Clinical and Risk Management-20 (HCR-20) in Mexican psychiatric inpatients. *Nordic Journal of Psychiatry*, 70, 1–6.

Schaap, G., Lammers, S., & de Vogel, V. (2009). Risk assessment in female forensic psychiatric patients: A quasi-prospective study into the validity of the HCR-20 and PCL-R. *The Journal of Forensic Psychiatry & Psychology*, 20, 354–365.

Schmidt, F., Campbell, M. A., & Houlding, C. (2011). Comparative analyses of the YLS/CMI, SAVRY, and PCL:YV in adolescent offenders: A 10-year follow-up into adulthood. *Youth Violence and Juvenile Justice*, 9, 23–42.

Singh, J. P., Grann, M., & Fazel, S. (2011). A comparative study of violence risk assessment tools: A systematic review and metaregression analysis of 68 studies involving 25,980 participants. *Clinical Psychology Review*, 31(3), 499–513.

Singh, J. P., Desmarais, S. L., Hurducas, C., Arbach-Lucioni, K., Condemarin, C., Dean, K., ... & Otto, R. K. (2014). International perspectives on the practical application of violence risk assessment: A global survey of 44 countries. *International Journal of Forensic Mental Health*, 13, 193–206.

Sjöstedt, G., & Långström, N. (2002). Assessment of risk for criminal recidivism among rapists: A comparison of four different measures. *Psychology, Crime & Law*, 8, 25–40.

Strub, D. S., Douglas, K. S., & Nicholls, T. L. (2014). The validity of Version 3 of the HCR-20 violence risk assessment scheme amongst offenders and civil psychiatric patients. *International Journal of Forensic Mental Health*, 13(2), 148–159.

van den Brink, R. H. S., Hooijschuur, A., van Os, T. W. D. P., Savenije, W., & Wiersma, D. (2010). Routine violence risk assessment in community forensic mental healthcare. *Behavioral Sciences & the Law*, 28, 396–410.

Verbrugge, H. M., Goodman-Delahunty, J., & Frize, M. C. J. (2011). Risk assessment in intellectually disabled offenders: Validation of the suggested ID supplement to the HCR-20. *International Journal of Forensic Mental Health*, 10, 83–91.

Viljoen, J. L., Scalora, M., Cuadra, L., Bader, S., Chávez, V., Ullman, D., & Lawrence, L. (2008). Assessing risk for violence in adolescents who have sexually offended: A comparison of the J-SOAP-II, J-SORRAT-II, and SAVRY. *Criminal Justice and Behavior*, 35, 5–23.

Viljoen, S., Nicholls, T. L., Roesch, R., Gagnon, N., Douglas, K., & Brink, J. (2016). Exploring gender differences in the utility of strength-based risk assessment measures. *International Journal of Forensic Mental Health*, 15, 1–15.

Viljoen, J. L., Mordell, S., & Beneteau, J. L. (2012). Prediction of adolescent sexual reoffending: A meta-analysis of the J-SOAP-II, ERASOR, J-SORRAT-II, and Static-99. *Law and Human Behavior*, 36, 423–438.

Vincent, G. M., Chapman, J., & Cook, N. (2011). Predictive validity of the SAVRY, racial differences, and the contribution of needs factors. *Criminal Justice and Behavior*, 38, 42–62.

Webster, C. D., Douglas, K. S., Eaves, D., & Hart, S. D. (1997). *HCR-20: Assessing Risk for Violence (Version 2)*. Burnaby, Canada: Mental Health, Law, and Policy Institute, Simon Fraser University.

Webster, C. D., Eaves, D., Douglas, K. S., & Wintrup, A. (1995). *The HCR-20 scheme: The assessment of dangerousness and risk*. Burnaby, Canada: Mental Health, Law, and Policy Institute, and Forensic Psychiatric Services Commission of British Columbia.

Webster, C. D., Martin, M. L., Brink, J., Nicholls, T. L., & Desmarais, S. L. (2009). *Manual for the Short-Term Assessment of Risk and Treatability (START) (Version 1.1)*. Coquitlam, Canada: British Columbia Mental Health & Addiction Services.

Wikström, P.-O. H., & Treiber, K. H. (2009). Violence as situational action. *International Journal of Conflict and Violence*, 3, 75–96.

Yang, M., Wong, S. C. P., & Coid, J. (2010). The efficacy of violence prediction: A meta-analytic comparison of nine risk assessment tools. *Psychological Bulletin*, 136, 740–767.

27

The Roles of the Risk Estimate and Clinical Information in Risk Assessments

Daryl G. Kroner

Southern Illinois University Carbondale, USA

This chapter begins by providing an overview of actuarial and clinical information in the context of risk assessments. The area of clinical information is categorized into active and passive types of information. Within the active type of information, perceived risk and self-prediction are highlighted. How clinical information can be included in the three components of risk assessment (risk estimate, risk management, and the explanatory story) is discussed. More specifically, the chapter reviews how clinical information can be integrated into a risk assessment, with a focus on overrides.

The Nature of Actuarial and Clinical Information

The risk assessments described in this chapter are routine risk assessments conducted on criminal justice clients. As discussed below, there will be situations where the routine risk assessment guidelines will not apply (e.g., threat assessment). In these situations, it is usually clinical information that is the focal point. Representing data via actuarial measures or with clinical information are two distinct, mutually exclusive ways to combine data (Grove & Lloyd, 2006). Actuarial information is the use of a mechanistic system that combines variables to derive a probability. Clinical information refers to the use of human judgment to measure person-based information not captured by the instrument used to produce the risk estimate. Associated with clinical information is a saturation of meaning.

For our purposes in distinguishing between actuarial measures and clinical information, it is not the nature of the items that makes the instrument actuarial, but the mechanical nature of how the items are put together. With this definition, the HCR-20 (H "historical" items, C "clinical" items, and R "risk management"; Webster, Douglas, Eaves, & Hart, 1997) could be scored as an actuarial instrument.

Clinical information can include broad content areas and take on many forms. Some types of clinical information are beyond the scope of the current chapter or not considered salient for risk assessments. Information about the risk context can be important and predictive

The Wiley International Handbook of Correctional Psychology, First Edition. Edited by Devon L. L. Polaschek, Andrew Day, and Clive R. Hollin.

(Kroner, Gray, & Goodrich, 2013), but is not considered to be clinical information. Clinical information that is strongly tied to therapeutic processes would not be considered. Some of these processes, such as working through denial and justifications of past patterns, have not been shown to be predictive of recidivism (Hanson & Morton-Bourgon, 2005). In addition, clinical information can be of an observed or client-involved format. Observed clinical information typically includes psychiatric symptoms, personality features, interpersonal style, violence-specific information, threats, and so on.

Passive and Active Clinical Information

Client involvement can be placed into two categories: passive and active. Passive self-report information covers content areas that may contribute to a criminal justice outcome. These content areas typically are not covered on standardized risk assessment instruments, but can overlap with rated content areas (i.e., self-report substance abuse vs. rated substance abuse). The client provides this information via self-report, and the assessor then integrates this information into the risk assessment. The client is not having an active role in the formulation of the risk estimate or risk management strategies. This passive information is used by the assessor to formulate risk management strategies and to develop the explanatory story.

The second type of client involvement is active. In this category, content areas are the assessment of an area or task, but there is the additional component of the client being active in the process of the risk assessment. The client engages in the actual formulation of the risk estimate or risk management strategies. Not only is the client's view of the problems captured (Shlonsky & Wagner, 2005), but the client's information on what the risk estimate level is or on potential intervention areas is integrated into the risk assessment.

Thus, this user information is used to directly inform the risk assessment. The risk-related information generated by the client will overlap with the assessor's efforts. But the risk-related information is not passively generated. There is an active contribution to the risk assessment process.

The gathering of "active" information has additional benefits over the use of passive information. First, it is a small step ("I will have a problem in [this] area upon release" vs. a rated substance abuse problem) toward having the client more involved in transitioning through the criminal justice system. Psychological research has provided evidence that multiple small steps make a large commitment easier (Diclemente, Marinilli, Singh, & Bellino, 2001). Second, a greater commitment to a client's own progress will occur if there is a strong sense of engagement and responsibility (Janis, 1984). Third, the selection of future interventions can be refined with client involvement (Rutter, Manley, Weaver, Crawford, & Fulop, 2004).

This active participation in generating information can be integrated into the task of formulating the risk estimate and risk management strategies. Two areas of gathering active information are (a) the client's perceived risk levels, and (b) client self-prediction of crime-related difficulties.

Perceived Risk

Having clients generate their perceived risk level has previously been suggested to be an integral part of conducting a risk assessment (Kumar & Simpson, 2005). As a state or transient variable, perceived risk has been shown to be a part of the decision-making process to commit crime (van Gelder & de Vries, 2012). For example, perceived risk mediated the relationship between conscientiousness and the decision to participate in crime. In a study with high-risk inpatients, two rated measures and a perceived risk measure were used to predict violence within 2 months of discharge (Skeem, Manchak, Lidz, & Mulvey, 2013). The perceived risk measure had the strongest risk estimate. In addition, the perceived risk measure added incremental validity among the rated predictive measures. Different to measuring actual risk estimates (e.g., 35% chance), perceived risk can be measured through comparisons (i.e., "My chances of doing crime are lower compared to other people with similar childhoods"). Using such a method, perceived risk was able to separate the middle risk range of an actuarial scale (Kroner, 2015). An opposite effect of perceived risk was found in a Canadian study with sexual offenders. This study found that the perception of no risk contributed to an increased risk of sexual recidivism (Hanson & Harris, 2000). Thus, there is a strong rationale for including perceived risk, with supporting evidence of its predictive efficacy. But just how perceived risk relates to a rated predictive measure of risk will require further attention and research. It is possible that the role of perceived risk is different at various risk levels. For example, at the lower levels of rated risk, having a higher perceived risk level may indicate risk factors not captured by the rated instrument. At the higher levels of rated risk, a lower perceived risk may counter some of the false positives that typically occur.

Self-Prediction

The rationale for using self-prediction information is twofold. First, the client has sufficient and adequate self-knowledge to indicate the likelihood of future attitudes and actions. This unique access to internal states suggests an advantage to self-predictions. Some have taken a strong position and claimed that the self is the best expert in predicting outcome behaviors (Vazire & Mehl, 2008). Second, motivating clients who experience some level of coercion can be facilitated through the use of self-prediction. In predicting their own intervention needs, clients can have a legitimate say in how risk is managed and reduced. Self-determination theory, with its emphasis on empirically informed guidelines and principles for motivating clients, can provide some of the rationale for using self-prediction as a motivator for change (Ryan & Deci, 2008).

In a recent study with young offenders from Spain, Hilterman, Nicholls, and van Nieuwen-huizen (2014) developed a self-prediction item covering a period of 6 months. The item asked the participants to rate their risk of committing an offense along a visual analogue scale with six boxes, marked from 0% to 100%. This self-prediction variable was predictive of both general ($r = .25$) and violent recidivism ($r = .21$). But for the multiple regression analyses with rated predictive measures (Structured Assessment of Violence Risk in Youth; Youth Level of Service/Case Management Inventory; Psychopathy Checklist: Youth Version), the self-prediction variable did not enter the model. In a Netherlands study, the Client Self-Appraisal reformulated the Short-Term Assessment of Risk and Treatability (START) items, asking the clients to indicate how an item "can put you at risk …" (van den Brink et al., 2015, p. 2) for a negative outcome. Both the Client Self-Appraisal and START instruments were used to predict violent or criminal behavior. Both the client self-prediction of risk factors (area under the curve = .62) and the case management risk estimate (AUC = .62) added to the prediction of violent and criminal behavior outcomes. Using a US Midwest community sample, probationers were asked to self-predict areas of difficulty with the Transition Inventory (Kroner & Mills, 2015). These areas of difficulty were rated 1 month later by researchers, who were blind to the client's self-predictions.

The strongest correspondence between self-predictions and assessor-rated difficulties was for substance misuse ($r = .65$) and behavioral impulsivity ($r = .55$; Kroner, 2012).

Benefits and Shortcomings of Actuarial and Clinical Information

Both areas of information, actuarial and clinical, have benefits and shortcomings in conducting risk assessments. Understanding the limits of these areas not only keeps our potential over-confidence reined in, but also prompts us to seek knowledge in these areas (Grisso & Vincent, 2005).

Benefits of Actuarial Information

1   The use of an actuarial tool, over time, on average, results in stronger prediction estimates than solely clinical or even structured clinical predictions (Singh, Grann, & Fazel, 2011). This is true for prediction in general (Grove, Zald, Lebow, Snitz, & Nelson, 2000) and for risk assessment instruments (Mossman, 1994).
2   Contributing to stronger prediction is the increased reliability of the risk estimate; that is, the actuarial approach consistently arrives at the same risk estimate from the same information. In making actuarial risk-related decisions, potential cognitive biases in deriving the risk estimate are reduced.

Shortcomings of Actuarial Information

1   Much of the research evaluating an actuarial approach assumes a linear relationship between instrument scores and the criminal justice outcome. This assumption frequently does not hold for low or high instrument scores.
2   Good prediction is determined by a consistent outcome variable. Often the defined outcome is irregular (e.g., situational structures and influences) and potentially unreliable (e.g., varying police arrest thresholds; Goldberg, 1970).
3   Instrument-related base rates that are close to the client's characteristics are needed. The client's characteristics, as reflected by increased scores, need to correspond to changes in outcome base rates. This may not be the case when applying an instrument to a new sample.

Benefits of Clinical Information

1   Clinical information is a major contributor to the causal explanation component of the explanatory story. An explanatory story refers to the use of a literal storyline to make an argument. The reporting of the risk estimate occurs in a report, which explains the meaning and context of the risk estimate.
2   Clinical information generates hypotheses and content that can be used for future research. Westen and Weinberger (2004) make the point that virtually all current psychopathy research presupposed the clinical work of Cleckley. Many of the most mechanical, statistical risk assessment instruments (i.e., the Violence Risk Appraisal Guide [VRAG]) used clinical files—which assume a theoretical orientation—for the pool of items.
3   Most actuarial measures are too limited to provide an adequate causal explanation, and therefore require clinical information to complete the explanatory story. Even authors of

actuarial instruments desire explanation in instruments (see Brouillette-Alarie, Babchishin, Hanson, & Helmus, 2016)!

Shortcomings of Clinical Information

1 Clinical information can be a poor statistical predictor of criminal justice outcomes (Holland, Holt, & Beckett, 1982). One potential reason for clinical information not being statistically equivalent to actuarial measures is the process of attempting to distinguish which variables may or may not be useful for risk estimates (Dawes, Faust, & Meehl, 1989). Although clinical information is a poor predictor of outcomes, a meta-analysis on the predictive accuracy of clinical information indicates a weak but robust predictor (Douglas, Guy, & Hart, 2009). Specific to mental health variables, the use of single variables as predictors may be improved if an interaction term between two variables is used (Beal, Kroner, & Weekes, 2003), or two clinical variables are added together, as defined by comorbidity or co-occurrence (Guebert & Olver, 2014).
2 When clinical information is added to an actuarial measure it typically does not add to the predictive validity of the actuarial tool (Hilterman et al., 2014).
3 One problem in using clinical information is that raters do not *systematically* evaluate whether a clinical predictor increases the client's risk levels (Skeem, Mulvey, & Lidz, 2000).
4 There are low levels of reliability among assessors (Goldberg, 1970; Quinsey & Ambtman, 1979).

Essentials of a Risk Assessment

There are three essential components of a risk assessment: (a) providing a risk estimate, (b) giving guidance on how to reduce and manage the risk, and (c) providing an explanatory story of the events centered on the referral question. The overall purpose is to add information of value on a client's potential for transition in levels of supervision, intervention, or security.

Risk Estimate

Presenting a likelihood or probability statement is the foremost goal in conducting a risk assessment. Some may hold that using any number associated with a risk assessment instrument (percentile, percentages, etc.) represents a risk estimate. But a risk estimate should be reserved for an actuarial probability that is produced by the risk assessment instrument.

Accuracy of the Risk Estimate

A couple of comments on the risk estimate accuracy are provided before moving on to cover more fully the nature of the risk estimate. In terms of public safety, the best measure of accuracy is accomplished though determining a measure's overall accuracy at a group level. The better the group accuracy, the better potential for greater accuracy in formulating the individual risk estimates.

There are other components of risk outcomes, in addition to a risk estimate. Risk assessment outcomes can indicate severity and imminence of the outcome. Depending on the nature of the normative data set used to derive the risk estimate, typically only broad areas of risk can be estimated, such as sexual offending, violent offending, and general offending. There is now sufficient data for some instruments to indicate time till offending (e.g., Static-99; Hanson, Harris, Helmus, & Thornton, 2014).

In addition to the development of better risk estimate accuracy, there are alternative ways to indicate overall accuracy that will assist in giving the risk estimate more applied meaning. One of these ways could be accomplished by using the H-measure to indicate the overall accuracy of the risk estimate. The AUC and similar classification measures treat classification errors (e.g., false positives: we say this person will become violent, when that does not occur vs. false negatives: we say this person will not become violent, when violence does occur) equally. The H-measure does not treat classification errors equally, requiring researcher input on how to weight classification errors (Hand, 2012; Verbraken, Verbeke, & Baesens, 2013). This statistic explicitly balances out the applied expectations of how much weight to give each type of error (Dejaeger, Verbraken, & Baesens, 2013). The researcher chooses a ratio to be applied. In most criminal justice outcomes, the classification error of the smaller class (i.e., predicting that no violence will occur and violence does occur) is of greater concern. Knowing that this is of greater concern, the applied weighted ratio can be, for example, ×2, rather than having equally weighted classification errors.

Group Data to Individual Decisions (G2i)

A contentious issue with the use of a risk estimate is that of applying the risk estimate based on research with others to an individual. Arguments have been put forward that the application of a risk estimate to an individual is not an accurate representation of that individual's risk level, usually indicating the inappropriateness of the application of inferential sample statistics to individuals as opposed to populations (Hart, Michie, & Cooke, 2007). In conducting routine risk assessments, once group-derived probabilities are available, a risk estimate can be applied to an individual (Faigman, Monahan, & Slobogin, 2014). But there may be specific situations where this may not be warranted, which are addressed below in the section on overrides.

The risk estimate is a number for the probability of an event (Mossman, 2015). This risk estimate is based upon the client having similar characteristics to others in the risk category. The development of the risk categories may not describe a fixed, underlying risk group. The category can be developed arbitrarily, with probability of the outcome determining member-ship in the specific categories (Imrey & Dawid, 2015). A client's risk estimate can be derived by using the reference group, which calibrates the offender characteristics captured by the scale that produces the risk estimate. The way this risk estimate (e.g., 20%) is described and reported, though, is important. This risk estimate should be reported as coming from a group of offenders who share similar characteristics (Amenta, Guy, & Edens, 2003). A similar conclusion regarding group to individual issues has been made by others (Dawes et al., 1989; Monahan & Skeem, 2015).

Two points of caution are noted here. First, presenting a statistical risk estimate is not the end point of a risk assessment. This statistical risk estimate requires a context, at both statistical and explanatory levels. Second, the risk estimate, by itself, does not represent causality or explanation. With either atheoretical item content or totally dynamic items, the risk estimate *will not* indicate causality (see Shmueli, 2010 for an overview on the differences between prediction and explanation). The constructs associated with the instrument may help with constructing a causal explanation, but by itself the instrument is not causal. An example of an actuarial instrument "acquiring" more meaning is the recent factor analytic research conducted with the Static 99R (Brouillette-Alarie et al., 2016).

Risk Management

Risk management will cover risk reduction strategies, transition issues (e.g., access to services), and engagement/supervision. Clinical information is essential in the application of risk management strategies. In terms of ordering, the presenting of the risk estimate will generally occur first, followed by risk management strategies (Scurich & John, 2012). Past overviews on risk management have paid minimal attention to client transition issues and, thus, these will receive some attention here.

Key in assisting a client through system transitions is providing the mechanisms and the "how tos" of transitions to both the client and those responsible for the transitioning. Clients with psychiatric symptoms will have difficulties in participating in transitions. In a cohort study, offenders with mental illness were more likely to have previous incarcerations than those without a mental illness (Baillargeon, Binswanger, Penn, Williams, & Murray, 2009). More specifically, the preconditions necessary for transitions (access to, range of, and communication of services) are impeded by psychiatric symptoms (Sweeney et al., 2012). Clients with psychiatric symptoms will need additional assistance just to engage in the providing of services for transition. Only one half of offenders with mental illness will participate in mental health services (Hartwell & Orr, 1999). Among a group of HIV-infected released offenders, 95% had referrals for mental health services, yet only less than half made their appointments (Rich et al., 2001). Most notably, clients with both a serious mental illness and a history of serious violence (~one third of offenders with mental illness) will have further difficulties in transitioning to the community (Wolff, 2005).

The Explanatory Story

Much of the effort in producing risk assessments is focused on the development of risk estimate and risk management strategies, often to the exclusion of the explanatory component. This over-focusing on deriving the risk estimate can undermine much of the risk assessment's usefulness. The risk estimate and risk management strategies need to be placed in a context. A story needs to be told. The storyline is intended to enhance the presentation of the risk estimate and risk management strategies and not to fill in the gaps in the poor application of instruments or the inappropriate use of risk management strategies. The explanatory component of a risk assessment develops and describes the "hows and whys" that contribute to the criminal justice event, risk estimate, and risk management strategies. The better the story, the greater the likelihood that the risk estimate will be used by decision-makers (Schwalbe, 2004). Essential to a "good" story, as argued by Dawes (1999), is the development of a coherent storyline. In the context of conducting risk assessments, the explanatory story integrates the risk estimate and risk management strategies with a coherent storyline to add valuable information to answering the referral question. For example, a report would include how developmental delays and poor decision-making contributed to risk and subsequent criminal activity. This provides the framework for how risk can be best managed.

Research on the plausibility of criminal justice events has found that scenarios with structured sequence of events are rated as more believable (Canter, Grieve, Nicol, & Benneworth, 2003). In addition to the structured sequence of events, the reporting of commonly held beliefs (e.g., alcohol causes crime) about a subject's criminality reduced the plausibility of the scenarios. From a storytelling perspective, it appears that reduced effort in explaining a crime will result in a less believable story. These researchers also found small changes in content and sequence could move perception of the scenario from belief to skepticism. Thus, using a story structure and addressing causation in the specific case with sufficient detail is essential to effective explanation.

Many risk instruments do have a theoretical orientation, but the level of detail necessary to tell a strong story often is not available to construct a story solely from the risk assessment instrument. At a minimum, the information used to score the risk assessment instrument should be woven into the story in sufficient detail for an independent person to "re-score" the instrument. In addition to some detailed content, the mechanics of how risk estimates are derived should be covered. These would include defining low base rates, normative group comparisons, and estimated recidivism rates (Varela, Boccaccini, Cuervo, Murrie, & Clark, 2014). For an effective explanatory story more structure and content is required than solely the information to re-score the instrument, base rates, normative group comparisons, or estimated recidivism rates. A main source for telling a strong story will be clinical information embedded within a theoretical framework (Dawes et al., 1989).

It should be recognized that a single theoretical framework may lack in the coverage of information sufficient to explain the criminal justice behavior. Some theories may be too narrow in scope (e.g., psychopathy) to provide the framework for an explanatory story. Multiple theoretical perspectives may be needed. Matching patterns or prototypes may prove helpful in contributing to an explanatory story (Schwalbe, 2004). Developing an explanatory story that "meshes with case worker experience" (Shlonsky & Wagner, 2005, p. 421) may be a valuable contributor to the coverage of information necessary for an explanatory story.

Many decision-makers appreciate the use of clinical information. Others have made a stronger argument, that decision-makers can favor clinical information over the use of risk instruments (Hilton & Simmons, 2001; Schwalbe, 2004). Having clinical information as an integral part of the explanatory story reduces the emphasis of using risk estimates to the exclusion of clinical information. For consumers and stakeholders who value clinical information, this integration may increase the overall usage and utility of the report.

A purpose of an explanatory story is to provide additional value to the reporting of risk. Additional value can be expressed in two forms. First, the potential benefits of the risk estimate and risk management strategies may need to be articulated (Carson, 2008). For example, stating how the application of the risk estimate can balance restrictive measures and the client's liberties may be of benefit. In the United States, the *Sell v. United States* (2002) decision explicitly requires that this balance be taken into consideration (Hunter, Ritchie, & Spaulding, 2005). Second, value can be added in relation to other information before the decision-making body. If there are other types of assessments being conducted on the client or much information is available to answer the referral question, then addressing how this assessment adds value will be an important component of the report.

A word of caution in using clinical information in an explanatory story: The clinical information needs to be internally consistent and relatively free of logical errors. In an interesting study of psychological forensic reports in Italy, errors were placed into epistemological, inferential, and attributional categories (Iudici, Salvini, Faccio, & Castelnuovo, 2015). Among epistemological errors, confusing judgments of value and data of fact was the most common error. Among inferential errors, the two errors of availability heuristic (It is "well known today that separations are very common") and ad hominem ("At least according to what she says") had the strongest relationship ($r = .30$). Among attribution errors, the two errors of norm of internality (a person is deemed responsible regardless of their condition) and confirmation bias (hypothesis is confirmed regardless of contra-indication) had the strongest relationship ($r = .50$). Given how influential these errors are on related errors, attention to these types of errors in integrating clinical information into the explanatory story would be well advised.

A practical comment on constructing the explanatory story: Using artificial section headings is distracting in telling a story. For example, risk assessment reports typically have a separate section for the reporting and interpreting of self-report instruments. Self-report instruments are just another source of information that should be integrated into the report where the content is covered. Thus, a self-report substance abuse scale would be interpreted in discussing offense patterns and, a second time, in the area addressing supervision strategies. This approach will make the report easier to read, given that most stakeholders and consumers of the report have not been trained in integrating test scores with other information (Mills, Kroner, & Morgan, 2011).

A numeric presentation of a risk estimate from a sufficiently validated instrument (Kroner, Mills, Gray, & Talbert, 2011) and suggestions on how to reduce and manage risk is considered to be best practice. Without a strong explanatory story, solely covering a risk estimate and risk management recommendations is *insufficient* for reporting and communicating risk. A strong explanatory story will not only increase the report's value, but is necessary for adequately presenting the risk estimate. Thus, the use of clinical information is not just a judgment of which clinical factors are of salience to a current client, and may not apply in a subsequent client, but it provides the bedrock for developing an explanatory story.

Solely reporting the risk estimate in research is also *insufficient*. Research on the risk estimate needs to integrate risk context factors into the criteria for determining optimal prediction. This may involve the use of priors (Bayesian-type statistics) or, as previously mentioned, the H-measure. This approach is not just adding another "clinical variable" to the prediction model to determine if greater variance can be accounted for, but it is including contextual parameters, which may be clinical information, into the analyses.

Integrating Clinical Information into the Risk Estimate

Same Instrument Approach

The optimal method of integrating actuarial and clinical risk information is the dynamic actuarial approach (Mills et al., 2011). In this approach, the items used for calculating the risk estimate are of a dynamic and clinical nature. Many recently developed instruments have these intentions. But there is a difference between prediction and explanatory causality (Hanson, 2009, p. 177; Shmueli, 2010). What causes a crime event may not be the central issue to reduce the likelihood of future crime. Even if a risk assessment instrument was dynamic, clinical, and predictive, or met the guidelines for being a causal risk scale (see Monahan & Skeem, 2015), there would still *not be* sufficient causality built into the instrument to adequately present an explanatory story (Shlonsky & Wagner, 2005).

Adding/Choosing Information Approach

This approach uses a guide to gather risk information and then examines each client individually to make a determination of what risk information applies to the current client (DeMatteo, Batastini, Foster, & Hunt, 2010). This may involve discounting risk information or adding what is perceived as risk information.

Anchored Approach

This approach has the assessor calculate the risk estimate and then allows for an alteration to the risk estimate. This is similar to the use of overrides. Optimally, the factors considered should have a robust empirical association with the recidivism risk.

Causal Hypothesis Approach

In this approach, the risk estimate has limited application or may have no role in how the assessor reports or communicates risk. The assessor decides the risk factors that are used and how important they are.

Moving further away from the risk estimate in communicating risk, as indicated by the last three approaches, allows for other influences in the reporting and communicating of risk (additional risk factors, e.g., bed space, place of release, jurisprudence role). These influences, in terms of risk estimates, will systematically decrease the accuracy of an objective risk estimate (Einhorn, 1986).

Overrides

The use of overrides refers to using clinical information to replace or alter the risk estimate. The argument for overrides is that a risk assessment instrument cannot include all of the important information necessary for a complete risk assessment. Such information may include a unique clinical factor, changing environments, protective factors, maturation differences among youth, and physical limitations. Thus, if unique information in this particular case is present, relying solely on the risk estimate will be insufficient. Typically, this unique information is of a clinical nature. Overrides can involve making a risk estimate more conservative or more relaxed. Some authors have suggested that overrides be used only when the probability of recidivism is near zero (Gambrill & Shlonsky, 2000). Others have suggested that the risk estimate score be increased or decreased by no more than 10% of the scale range (Webster, Harris, Rice, Cormier, & Quinsey, 1994). In completing risk assessments, a unique clinical feature may prompt an assessor to integrate, or at least account for, this information in determining the risk estimate. But changing the risk estimate in a non-mechanistic way will reduce the overall predictive accuracy (Mills et al., 2011).

The use of overrides in routine risk assessment will tend to change the purpose of the assessment. A routine assessment provides comments on what is likely to occur, in terms of broad categories (i.e., violent offending, general offending, sexual offending) over a period of time. With significant clinical information (e.g., specific threat against a specific target in a relatively specific time frame), the application of this knowledge changes the purpose of the routine assessment. The purpose of the assessment determines which instrument is chosen, and de facto, which outcomes can be addressed.

Research examining overrides has not provided support for their use. With two Canadian young offender samples (sexual, non-sexual), the use of overrides with the Youth Level of Service/ Case Management Inventory (YLS/CMI; Andrews, Bonta, & Wormith, 2004) was compared to the summed scores without overrides (Schmidt, Sinclair, & Thomasdóttir, 2016). Overrides were used 74% of the time with sexual offenders and 42% of the time with non-sexual offenders. In both samples, the summed YLS/CMI scores adequately predicted violent, non-violent, and sexual outcomes. In both samples, overrides decreased the predictive validity to chance across the three outcomes. Similarly, with Canadian adult sexual and non-sexual offenders (sentenced to less than 2 years in prison), the LS/CMI overrides were compared with the summed scores (Wormith, Hogg, & Guzzo, 2012). Overrides were used 35% of the time with sexual offenders and 15% of the time with non-sexual offenders. As in the Schmidt study, the summed scores adequately predicted violent, non-violent, and sexual offending, whereas the overrides substantively decreased the predictive validity (from above $r = .31$ to lower than $r = .11$). In a meta-analysis of sexual offending recidivism, comparisons were made between a risk estimate score and an override score (Hanson & Morton-Bourgon, 2009). The use of an override decreased the predictive validity. Clearly, the use of overrides introduces unwanted error variance in predicting outcomes.

But there will be times when the clinical information is such that it cannot be ignored. Meehl (1954) describes this situation as the "broken-leg case," referring to routinely predicting when someone will go to the movies, but with a broken leg (person cannot fit in the movie theater chair) the chance of going to the movies is near zero. Meehl argued that these situations are rare. In addition to the logical exclusion of using a risk estimate, there may be powerful clinical information present to exclude a risk estimate. A legal ruling may help in applying this clinical information guideline (*Smith v. Jones*, 1999). In this case, the ruling indicated that if clinical information has a chilling intensity and graphic detail that would leave a reasonable bystander would be convinced, then action needs to be seriously considered. This assessment should prompt the use of the *Tarasoff* criteria (or the equivalent criteria in a specific jurisdiction). The specific threat, which usually includes information on the nature and credibility of the threat and the means available to carry out the threat, will assist in determining if there is a duty to warn/protect. In this situation, the task of the assessment is not to formulate a risk estimate, but to prompt immediate action. Ideally, two assessments would be completed. One would be a routine risk estimate, and the other would address the immediate danger.

Conclusion

Although the best estimate of risk is derived from an instrument that yields actuarial probabilities of recidivism risk, the use of clinical information is necessary to effectively communicate the risk estimate and risk management strategies. Clinical information is essential to risk management and developing the explanatory story. Promising clinical variables are active information involving clients' perceived risk and self-prediction.

Key Readings

Hanson, R. K. (2009). The psychological assessment of risk for crime and violence. *Canadian Psychology*, 50, 172–182.

Harris, G. T., & Rice, M. E. (2015). Progress in violence risk assessment and communication: Hypothesis versus evidence. *Behavioral Sciences & the Law*, 33, 128–145.

Heilbrun, K., Newsham, R., & Pietruszka, V. (2016). Risk communication: An international update. In J. P. Singh, S. Bjorkly, & S. Fazel (Eds.), *International perspectives on violence risk assessment* (pp. 150–165). New York, NY: Oxford University Press.

Mills, J. F. (2017). Violence risk assessment: A brief review, current issues, and future directions. *Canadian Psychology*, 58, 40–49.

Walters, G. D. (2006). Risk-appraisal versus self-report in the prediction of criminal justice outcomes: A meta-analysis. *Criminal Justice and Behavior*, 33, 279–304.

References

Amenta, A. E., Guy, L. S., & Edens, J. F. (2003). Sex offender risk assessment: A cautionary note regarding measures attempting to quantify violence risk. *Journal of Forensic Psychology Practice*, 3, 39–50.

Andrews, D. A., Bonta, J., & Wormith, J. S. (2004). *Level of Service/Case Management Inventory (LS/CMI): An offender assessment system: User's guide*. Toronto, Canada: Multi-Health Systems.

Baillargeon, J., Binswanger, I., Penn, J., Williams, B., & Murray, O. (2009). Psychiatric disorders and repeat incarcerations: The revolving prison door. *American Journal of Psychiatry*, 166, 103–109.

Beal, C. A., Kroner, D. G., & Weekes, J. R. (2003). Persecutory ideation and depression in mild violence among incarcerated adult males. *International Journal of Offender Therapy and Comparative Criminology*, 47, 159–170.

Brouillette-Alarie, S., Babchishin, K. M., Hanson, R. K., & Helmus, L.-M. (2016). Latent constructs of the Static-99R and Static-2002R: A three-factor solution. *Assessment*, 23, 96–111.

Canter, D. V., Grieve, N., Nicol, C., & Benneworth, K. (2003). Narrative plausibility: The impact of sequence and anchoring. *Behavioral Sciences & the Law*, 21, 251–267.

Carson, D. (2008). Justifying risk decisions. *Criminal Behaviour and Mental Health*, 18, 139–144.

Dawes, R. M. (1999). A message from psychologists to economists: Mere predictability doesn't matter like it should (without a good story appended to it). *Journal of Economic Behavior & Organization*, 39, 29–40.

Dawes, R. M., Faust, D., & Meehl, P. E. (1989). Clinical versus actuarial judgment. *Science*, 243, 1668–1674.

Dejaeger, K., Verbraken, T., & Baesens, B. (2013). Toward comprehensible software fault prediction models using Bayesian network classifiers. *IEEE Transactions on Software Engineering*, 39, 237–257.

DeMatteo, D., Batastini, A., Foster, E., & Hunt, E. (2010). Individualizing risk assessment: Balancing idiographic and nomothetic data. *Journal of Forensic Psychology Practice*, 10, 360–371.

Diclemente, C. C., Marinilli, A. S., Singh, M., & Bellino, E. (2001). The role of feedback in the process of health behavior change. *American Journal of Health Behavior*, 25(3), 217–227.

Douglas, K. S., Guy, L. S., & Hart, S. D. (2009). Psychosis as a risk factor for violence to others: A meta-analysis. *Psychological Bulletin*, 135, 679–706.

Einhorn, H. J. (1986). Accepting error to make less error. *Journal of Personality Assessment*, 50, 387–395.

Faigman, D. L., Monahan, J., & Slobogin, C. (2014). Group to individual (G2i) inference in scientific expert testimony. *University of Chicago Law Review*, 81, 417–480.

Gambrill, E., & Shlonsky, A. (2000). Risk assessment in context. *Children and Youth Services Review*, 22, 813–837.

Goldberg, L. R. (1970). Man versus model of man: A rationale, plus some evidence, for a method of improving on clinical inferences. *Psychological Bulletin*, 73, 422–432.

Grisso, T., & Vincent, G. M. (2005). The empirical limits of forensic mental health assessment. *Law and Human Behavior*, 29, 1–5.

Grove, W. M., & Lloyd, M. (2006). Meehl's contribution to clinical versus statistical prediction. *Journal of Abnormal Psychology*, 115, 192–194.

Grove, W. M., Zald, D. H., Lebow, B. S., Snitz, B. E., & Nelson, C. (2000). Clinical versus mechanical prediction: A meta-analysis. *Psychological Assessment*, 12, 19–30.

Guebert, A. F., & Olver, M. E. (2014). An examination of criminogenic needs, mental health concerns, and recidivism in a sample of violent young offenders: Implications for risk, need, and responsivity. *International Journal of Forensic Mental Health*, 13, 295–310.

Hand, D. J. (2012). Assessing the performance of classification methods. *International Statistical Review*, 80, 400–414.

Hanson, R. K. (2009). The psychological assessment of risk for crime and violence. *Canadian Psychology*, 50, 172–182.

Hanson, R. K., & Harris, A. J. R. (2000). Where should we intervene? Dynamic predictors of sexual offense recidivism. *Criminal Justice and Behavior*, 27, 6–35.

Hanson, R. K., Harris, A. J. R., Helmus, L., & Thornton, D. (2014). High-risk sex offenders may not be high risk forever. *Journal of Interpersonal Violence*, 29, 2792–2813.

Hanson, R. K., & Morton-Bourgon, K. E. (2005). The characteristics of persistent sexual offenders: A meta-analysis of recidivism studies. *Journal of Consulting and Clinical Psychology*, 73, 1154–1163.

Hanson, R. K., & Morton-Bourgon, K. E. (2009). The accuracy of recidivism risk assessments for sexual offenders: A meta-analysis of 118 prediction studies. *Psychological Assessment*, 21, 1–21.

Hart, S. D., Michie, C., & Cooke, D. J. (2007). Precision of actuarial risk assessment instruments. *The British Journal of Psychiatry*, 190, s60–s65.

Hartwell, S. W., & Orr, K. (1999). The Massachusetts forensic transition program for mentally ill offenders re-entering the community. *Psychiatric Services*, 50, 1220–1223.

Hilterman, E. L. B., Nicholls, T. L., & Nieuwenhuizen, C. v. (2014). Predictive validity of risk assessments in juvenile offenders comparing the SAVRY, PCL:YV, and YLS/CMI with unstructured clinical assessments. *Assessment*, 21, 324–339.

Hilton, N. Z., & Simmons, J. L. (2001). The influence of actuarial risk assessment in clinical judgments and tribunal decisions about mentally disordered offenders in maximum security. *Law and Human Behavior*, 25, 393–408.

Holland, T. R., Holt, N., & Beckett, G. E. (1982). Prediction of violent versus nonviolent recidivism from prior violent and nonviolent criminality. *Journal of Abnormal Psychology*, 91, 178–182.

Hunter, R. H., Ritchie, A. J., & Spaulding, W. D. (2005). The Sell decision: Implications for psychological assessment and treatment. *Professional Psychology: Research and Practice*, 36, 467–475.

Imrey, P. B., & Dawid, A. P. (2015). A commentary on statistical assessment of violence recidivism risk. *Statistics and Public Policy*, 2, 1–18.

Iudici, A., Salvini, A., Faccio, E., & Castelnuovo, G. (2015). The clinical assessment in the legal field: An empirical study of bias and limitations in forensic expertise. *Frontiers in Psychology*, 6. doi:10.3389/fpsyg.2015.01831

Janis, I. L. (1984). The patient as decision maker. In W. D. Gentry (Ed.), *Handbook of behavioral medicine* (pp. 326–368). New York, NY: Guilford Press.

Kroner, D. G. (2012). Service user involvement in risk assessment and management: The Transition Inventory. *Criminal Behaviour and Mental Health*, 22, 136–147.

Kroner, D. G. (2015, June). Client's risk perception: Contribution to risk prediction. Third North American Correctional and Criminal Justice Psychology Conference, Toronto, Ontario, Canada.

Kroner, D. G., Gray, A. L., & Goodrich, B. (2013). Integrating risk context into risk assessments: The Risk Context Scale. *Assessment*, 20, 135–149.

Kroner, D. G., & Mills, J. F. (2015). *The Transition Inventory: User guide*. Carbondale, IL: Authors.

Kroner, D. G., Mills, J. F., Gray, A., & Talbert, K. O. N. (2011). Clinical assessment in correctional settings. In T. J. Fagan, & R. K. Ax (Eds.), *Correctional mental health: From theory to best practice* (pp. 79–102). Thousand Oaks, CA: Sage.

Kumar, S., & Simpson, A. I. F. (2005). Application of risk assessment for violence methods to general adult psychiatry: A selective literature review. *Australian and New Zealand Journal of Psychiatry*, 39, 328–335.

Meehl, P. E. (1954). *Clinical versus statistical prediction: A theoretical analysis and a review of the evidence.* Minneapolis, MN: University of Minnesota Press.

Mills, J. F., Kroner, D. G., & Morgan, R. D. (2011). *Clinician's guide to violence risk assessment.* New York, NY: Guilford Press.

Monahan, J., & Skeem, J. L. (2015). *Risk assessment in criminal sentencing* (SSRN Scholarly Paper No. ID 2662082). Rochester, NY: Social Science Research Network. Retrieved from http://papers.ssrn.com/abstract=2662082

Mossman, D. (1994). Further comments on portraying the accuracy of violence predictions. *Law and Human Behavior*, 18(5), 587–593.

Mossman, D. (2015). From group data to useful probabilities: The relevance of actuarial risk assessment in individual instances. *Journal of the American Academy of Psychiatry and the Law Online*, 43, 93–102.

Quinsey, V. L., & Ambtman, R. (1979). Variables affecting psychiatrists' and teachers' assessments of the dangerousness of mentally ill offenders. *Journal of Consulting and Clinical Psychology*, 47(2), 353–362.

Rich, J. D., Holmes, L., Salas, C., Macalino, G., Davis, D., Ryczek, J., & Flanigan, T. (2001). Successful linkage of medical care and community services for HIV-positive offenders being released from prison. *Journal of Urban Health*, 78, 279–289.

Rutter, D., Manley, C., Weaver, T., Crawford, M. J., & Fulop, N. (2004). Patients or partners? Case studies of user involvement in the planning and delivery of adult mental health services in London. *Social Science & Medicine*, 58, 1973–1984.

Ryan, R. M., & Deci, E. L. (2008). A self-determination theory approach to psychotherapy: The motivational basis for effective change. *Canadian Psychology*, 49, 186–193.

Schmidt, F., Sinclair, S. M., & Thomasdóttir, S. (2016). Predictive validity of the Youth Level of Service/Case Management Inventory with youth who have committed sexual and non-sexual offenses: The utility of professional override. *Criminal Justice and Behavior*, 43(3), 413–430.

Schwalbe, C. (2004). Re-visioning risk assessment for human service decision making. *Children and Youth Services Review*, 26, 561–576.

Scurich, N., & John, R. S. (2012). Prescriptive approaches to communicating the risk of violence in actuarial risk assessment. *Psychology, Public Policy, and Law*, 18, 50–78.

Sell v. United States, 539 US 166 (Supreme Court 2003).

Shlonsky, A., & Wagner, D. (2005). The next step: Integrating actuarial risk assessment and clinical judgment into an evidence-based practice framework in CPS case management. *Children and Youth Services Review*, 27, 409–427.

Shmueli, G. (2010). To explain or to predict? *Statistical Science*, 25(3), 289–310.

Singh, J. P., Grann, M., & Fazel, S. (2011). A comparative study of violence risk assessment tools: A systematic review and metaregression analysis of 68 studies involving 25,980 participants. *Clinical Psychology Review*, 31, 499–513.

Skeem, J. L., Manchak, S. M., Lidz, C. W., & Mulvey, E. P. (2013). The utility of patients' self-perceptions of violence risk: Consider asking the person who may know best. *Psychiatric Services*, 64, 410–415.

Skeem, J. L., Mulvey, E. P., & Lidz, C. W. (2000). Building mental health professionals' decisional models into tests of predictive validity: The accuracy of contextualized predictions of violence. *Law and Human Behavior*, 24, 607–628.

Smith v. Jones, No. 455 (S.C.R. March 25, 1999).

Sweeney, A., Rose, D., Clement, S., Jichi, F., Jones, I. R., Burns, T., … & Wykes, T. (2012). Understanding service user-defined continuity of care and its relationship to health and social measures: A cross-sectional study. *BMC Health Services Research*, 12, 145.

van den Brink, R. H. S., Troquete, N. A. C., Beintema, H., Mulder, T., van Os, T. W. D. P., Schoevers, R. A., & Wiersma, D. (2015). Risk assessment by client and case manager for shared decision making in outpatient forensic psychiatry. *BMC Psychiatry*, 15, 120.

van Gelder, J.-L., & de Vries, R. E. (2012). Traits and states: Integrating personality and affect into a model of criminal decision making. *Criminology*, 50, 637–671.

Varela, J. G., Boccaccini, M. T., Cuervo, V. A., Murrie, D. C., & Clark, J. W. (2014). Same score, different message: Perceptions of offender risk depend on Static-99R risk communication format. *Law and Human Behavior*, 38, 418–427.

Vazire, S., & Mehl, M. R. (2008). Knowing me, knowing you: The accuracy and unique predictive validity of self-ratings and other-ratings of daily behavior. *Journal of Personality and Social Psychology*, 95, 1202–1216.

Verbraken, T., Verbeke, W., & Baesens, B. (2013). A novel profit maximizing metric for measuring classification performance of customer churn prediction models. *IEEE Transactions on Knowledge and Data Engineering*, 25, 961–973.

Webster, C. D., Douglas, K. S., Eaves, D., & Hart, S. D. (1997). *HCR-20: Assessing risk for violence (version 2)*. Burnaby, Canada: Mental Health, Law, and Policy Institute, Simon Fraser University.

Webster, C. D., Harris, G. T., Rice, M. E., Cormier, C., & Quinsey, V. L. (1994). *The violence prediction scheme: Assessing dangerousness in high risk men* (Vol. xii). Toronto, Canada: University of Toronto Centre of Criminology.

Westen, D., & Weinberger, J. (2004). When clinical description becomes statistical prediction. *American Psychologist*, 59(7), 595–613.

Wolff, N. (2005). Community reintegration of prisoners with mental illness: A social investment perspective. *International Journal of Law and Psychiatry*, 28, 43–58.

Wormith, J. S., Hogg, S., & Guzzo, L. (2012). The predictive validity of a general risk/needs assessment inventory on sexual offender recidivism and an exploration of the professional override. *Criminal Justice and Behavior*, 39, 1511–1538.

28

Offender Risk and Need Assessment: Theory, Research, and Applications

Mark E. Olver
University of Saskatchewan, Canada

Stephen C. P. Wong
University of Saskatchewan, Canada and Swinburne University of Technology, Australia

Risk-Need-Responsivity Model: A Brief Overview

Bonta and Andrews' (2010, 2017) Risk-Need-Responsivity (RNR) model set forth in *The Psychology of Criminal Conduct* (now in its fifth edition) has been highly influential in the assessment, explanation, and intervention of criminal behavior (McGuire, 2008). Briefly, the risk principle posits that service intensity should match offenders' risk level, such that higher-risk offenders receive a higher level of service than lower-risk offenders. Dynamic variables or criminogenic needs linked to the causation and prediction of criminal behavior should be prioritized for service delivery—the need principle. Finally, the responsivity principle suggests that services should be adapted to the unique characteristics of correctional clientele; *general responsivity* maintains that cognitive behavioral approaches delivered with close attention to maintaining therapeutic alliance should be used to promote positive prosocial behaviors, while *specific responsivity* suggests that interventions should be adapted to unique client features such as motivation, learning style, cognitive capability, personality, cultural heritage, and so forth. In the context of this chapter, risk denotes assessments of recidivism probability and/or severity to inform service intensity, while need denotes identifying areas for intervention which, if successful, will reduce risk.

Context of Offender Risk/Need Assessment

Risk and need assessments are conducted in a number of different forensic contexts at all stages of criminal justice proceedings (Hoge, 1999, 2002). Pre-trial assessments, for example, are used to inform bail and remand decisions, with individuals deemed high risk and need (and thus at high flight or recidivism risk pre-trial) more likely to be remanded into custody. Risk assessments can also inform sentence options (e.g., incarceration vs. probation), sentence length (e.g., determinate vs. indeterminate), or the imposition of special provisions (e.g., Dangerous Offender or Sex Offender Civil Commitment). A third forensic application of risk and need assessments is at the

The Wiley International Handbook of Correctional Psychology, First Edition. Edited by Devon L. L. Polaschek, Andrew Day, and Clive R. Hollin.
© 2019 John Wiley & Sons Ltd. Published 2019 by John Wiley & Sons Ltd.

pre-intervention stage to inform the intensity and duration of intervention programs (e.g., a moderate vs. high-intensity program), the type of program (e.g., sex offender vs. domestic violence), and the prioritization of criminogenic needs for treatment. Finally, in the context of post-program or pre-release, risk/need assessments can inform risk changes and identify outstanding needs for further intervention and for release decision-making, including residence, community restrictions, supervision intensity, follow-up programming, support services, and the like. In short, the practice of risk/need assessment is ubiquitous in forensic evaluation and rehabilitation.

Generations of Risk Assessment

Bonta (1996) arranged or differentiated risk assessment approaches into four generations. Rather than suggesting a difference in the sophistication of tools allocated to the different generations, this provides a useful heuristic.

First Generation: Unstructured Clinical Judgment

The first generation uses unstructured clinical judgment to appraise risk and predict recidivism, relying on intuition and the subjective integration of data. This approach has been shown to be less reliable and accurate than other evidence-based approaches (Grove, Zald, Lebow, Snitz, & Nelson, 2000; Hanson & Morton-Bourgon, 2009; Meehl, 1954), and is rarely recommended for general use.

Second Generation: Empirical Actuarial Measures

Second generation instruments use purely statistical approaches to select predictors of recidivism, whether this is defined broadly (e.g., any recidivism), such as in the Offender Group Reconviction Scale (Copas & Marshall, 1998), or specifically (e.g., sexual recidivism), such as in the Static-99R (Babchishin, Blais, & Helmus, 2012). The selection of the predictors and the validation of the tool are entirely empirical and atheoretical in nature, and the validation process is predicated on maximizing the tool's predictive accuracy. The predictors are typically static or historical variables such as criminal history and demographic characteristics. Items may then be differentially weighted to improve prediction based on the magnitude of their univariate relationship with the criterion. An actuarial tool is one in which the aggregation of the ratings of the predictors, be they static or dynamic, is used to predict the outcome, in this case, recidivism. While second generation tools have much better predictive efficacy than unstructured clinical judgment (Bonta, Law, & Hanson, 1998; Hanson & Morton-Bourgon, 2009), their capacity to inform treatment and assess change in risk is limited by the static or historical nature of the predictors.

Third Generation: Structured Professional Judgment and Conventional Risk/Need Measures

The third generation of assessment tools bridges the gap between assessment and intervention through the identification of criminogenic needs for treatment. For example, the items of the Level of Service Inventory—Revised (LSI-R; Andrews & Bonta, 1995), a third generation tool, are rated numerically and summed to yield risk scores linked to recidivism. Structured Professional Judgment (SPJ) approaches (e.g., Sexual Violence Risk-20 [SVR-20]; Boer, Hart, Kropp, & Webster, 1997) are also considered third generation. Items of SPJ tools are not summed to generate numeric scores, but the profile configuration or pattern of risk factors is examined to arrive at risk determinations.

Fourth Generation: Specialized Dynamic Measures

The fourth generation tools feature specialized dynamic approaches. For example, the Level of Service/Case Management Inventory (LS-CMI; Andrews, Bonta, & Wormith, 2006) informs service delivery from intake to case closure. Fourth generation tools not only assess static and dynamic risk factors informed by theory and research, but also link assessment to treatment and explicitly inform risk management efforts. A range of general and specific tools arguably fall under the fourth generation, including the LS-CMI, the Historical-Clinical-Risk Management-20, Version 3 (HCR-20^{V3}) (Douglas, Hart, Webster, & Belfrage, 2011), the Violence Risk Scale (VRS; Wong & Gordon, 1999–2003), and its Sexual Offense version (VRS-SO; Wong, Olver, Nicholaichuk, & Gordon 2003, 2017). Fourth generation instruments can be SPJ (e.g., HCR-20^{V3}) or use actuarial procedures to link numeric scores and recidivism estimates (e.g., LS/CMI; VRS).

Considerations in Selecting a Tool for Risk/Need Assessment

The selection of a risk/need tool depends not only on the properties of the tool, but also on the nature and context of the assessment as well as pragmatic, logistical, and evidentiary considerations. An important consideration, however, is whether or not the instrument has demonstrated good predictive accuracy for its targeted criterion. Rice and Harris (2005) advance a rubric aligning point biserial correlation, area under the curve (AUC), and standardized mean difference (d) values corresponding to the original rubric of Cohen (1988) for effect size magnitudes. In their framework, a small/low predictive effect size would correspond to $r = .10$, $d = .20$, and AUC $= .56$, while a medium/moderate effect size would be $r = .24$, $d = .50$, and AUC $= .64$, and high/large $r = .37+$, $d = .80+$, and AUC $= .71+$.

A multilevel meta-analysis of nine commonly used risk assessment tools (including several of the aforementioned measures) for the prediction of violence across 28 studies by Yang, Wong, and Coid (2010) concluded that all of the tools significantly predicted violent recidivism at comparable magnitudes (AUC $= .65–.71$); observed differences in predictive accuracy were attributable to sample and setting characteristics. The lone exception was Psychopathy Checklist—Revised (PCL-R) Factor 1 (interpersonal and affective characteristics of psychopathy), which did not significantly predict violence. Other meta-analyses of violence prediction tools have generated similar findings (Campbell, Gendreau, & French, 2009), as have meta-analyses of young offender (Olver, Stockdale, & Wormith, 2009), and sex offender (Hanson & Morton-Bourgon, 2009) risk assessment instruments. Since many tools have similar predictive efficacy, at least for violence and sexual offending, the choice of which tool to use should be more a matter of what other functions the tool offers. The following sections introduce some of the most important areas to consider when deciding which tool or approach to adopt.

Gender Considerations

"Gender neutral" proponents (e.g., Andrews & Bonta, 2010) assert that criminogenic needs such as antisocial attitudes and negative peers transcend gender and predict recidivism at comparable magnitudes, while advocates for "gender informed" approaches (e.g., Bloom, Owen, & Covington, 2003) argue that female offenders have unique criminogenic needs (e.g., substance abuse, past abuse/trauma, parenting, mental health, financial, stress) that require specialized assessment. There is supporting evidence for both positions. General risk-need approaches have been shown to predict both general and violent recidivism for males and females in adult (Olver, Stockdale, & Wormith, 2014) and youth samples (Olver et al., 2009; Schwalbe, 2008). There is also evidence that some gender-specific needs demonstrate higher predictive accuracy in female offenders (e.g., Holtfreter, Reisig, & Morash, 2004; Van Voorhis, Wright, Salisbury, & Bauman, 2010), although studies have not found substantive differences (e.g., Rettinger & Andrews, 2010). More research is needed.

Cultural Considerations

Similar debate exists with regard to the use of risk assessment tools with culturally and linguistically diverse populations, such as Indigenous, Black, Hispanic or other individuals of racial/ethnic minority status (see Tamatea & Day, Chapter 18). Several risk assessment tools have been shown to have significant predictive accuracy with racial/ethnic minority groups, and Canadian Indigenous peoples in particular. These include the LSI scales (Olver et al., 2009; Olver, Stockdale, et al., 2014; Wilson & Gutierrez, 2014), Static-99R (Babchishin et al., 2012), VRS-SO (Olver et al., 2016), and PCL-R (Olver, Neumann, Wong, & Hare, 2013). There is, however, ongoing debate about whether predictive accuracy is slightly lower for many of these tools among cultural/racial minorities, underscoring the importance of sentencing guidelines that speak to important social, contextual, and cultural considerations that may impact risk, response to services, and reintegration. In Canada, for example, the Gladue provision (R. v. Gladue, 1999) is a sentencing tool intended to increase the fairness of sentencing of Indigenous peoples, taking into account unique circumstances that may have brought the individual into contact with the justice system.

Static Versus Dynamic Instruments

Static and dynamic tools perform similar but also different functions. If the goal is no more than to predict recidivism at a single time point, static actuarial tools perform very well. However, if the goal is to inform service intensity, identify criminogenic needs, or assess risk change, dynamic tools are better suited. Importantly, there is robust evidence that both static and dynamic tools uniquely and incrementally predict recidivism. For instance, several sex offender measures assessing dynamic risk factors have incremental validity beyond the Static-99R (see Hanson, Harris, Scott, & Helmus, 2007; Olver, Beggs Christofferson, Grace, & Wong, 2014).

Capacity to Inform Risk Management

The SPJ approach has the advantage of being flexible in its application; however, critics contend that the approach lacks transparency in terms of how a configuration or profile of item ratings is translated into an overall estimate of "low," "medium," or "high" risk (see Hanson, 2009), as well as the exact meaning of these three descriptors of risk. SPJ proponents assert that rather than risk prediction, the ultimate purpose of risk assessment is to manage risk and this can be achieved by attending to SPJ items with high ratings (Douglas & Kropp, 2002). Assessments using an actuarial approach with either static or dynamic predictors can also identify individuals deemed high risk for high-intensity services, although, arguably, such tools are more limited in their ability to inform risk management if the predictors are historical or static in nature. In contrast, actuarial tools that incorporate dynamic factors can identify high-risk individuals as well as inform risk management.

Specialized Versus General Instruments

General and specialized instruments are designed to predict broad or specific reoffending outcomes, respectively. Specialized sex offender tools have good predictive accuracy for sexual recidivism (Hanson & Morton-Bourgon, 2009), whereas general recidivism prediction tools, such as the LSI, tend to do a better job of predicting any recidivism (although the LSI is also used to predict violent recidivism). Common to general and specific tools is a general criminality or generic risk/need dimension sometimes referred to as antisocial orientation (Hanson & Morton-Bourgon, 2005), which corresponds highly to the *Central Eight* risk/need domains discussed below. Sex offender specific tools, understandably, also assess sexual deviance, a psychologically meaningful risk factor that assesses unusual or illegal sexual interests and behaviors. Tools specific to the assessment of violence or domestic violence have violence- or domestic violence-specific risk factors in addition to the general criminality domain.

Capacity to Assess Change

The third and fourth generation instruments, SPJ and actuarial, contain putatively dynamic or changeable risk factors that, in theory, could assess risk changes and the probability of subsequent recidivism. Most dynamic risk factor research measures these variables at only one time point without demonstrating their capacity to change or that such changes are risk relevant (Douglas & Skeem, 2005). The family of LSI measures, HCR-20^{V2} and HCR-20^{V3}, VRS, VRS-SO, Stable 2007, SVR-20, and Spousal Assault Risk Assessment (SARA), to name a few, all contain putatively dynamic items. Evidence exists to varying degrees to support the idea that positive risk changes on some of these tools is associated with reductions in recidivism (de Vries Robbé, de Vogel, Douglas, & Nijman, 2015; Hogan & Olver, 2016; Lewis, Olver, & Wong, 2013; Olver, Beggs Christofferson, et al., 2014; Vose, Lowenkamp, Smith, & Cullen, 2009). Some tools, such as the VRS and VRS-SO, contain a rating rubric for assessing risk changes on the dynamic items based on a modified application of the transtheoretical model of change (Prochaska, DiClemente, & Norcross, 1992). The other tools assess change by re-rating the same item through subjectively appraising and reweighting change information which is incorporated into the re-rating. Research is needed to identify the preferred alternative (see Daffern et al., Chapter 24).

Guidelines for Risk/Need Assessment

The following guidelines apply to both general and specific offender populations, including violent offender, sexual offender, and domestically violent offenders. The manuals for SPJ tools (e.g., SVR-20; Boer et al., 1997; SARA; Kropp, Hart, Webster, & Eaves, 1995) have distilled a number of core tenets of effective and evidence-informed principles of assessment, and readers are also encouraged to consult these sources (see also Day, Chapter 30). Several of the points presented below overlap with or are informed by these sources.

Use of Multiple Information Sources

The clinical interview and collateral information from official documents are often the corner-stone of assessment information sources; many instruments referred to in this chapter provide semi-structured interview schedules. Offenders' self-report should never be the sole source of information unless under special circumstances. Whenever possible, one information source needs to be corroborated by others. Lichtenberger, Mather, Kaufman, and Kaufman (2004) have offered a heuristic that two pieces of supporting information are required for every conclusion or interpretive statement made. In addition to interviews, results from psycho-metric testing, institutional files, work records, parole officer reports, police reports (or official synopsis of offense information), treatment progress reports (if available), official criminal records, any decision-making documents on record, and interviews with collateral sources (e.g., correctional workers, nurses, parole officers, other mental health staff, family) should all be used. Such information, in turn, will maximize the comprehensiveness and breadth of information sources available for scoring and interpreting any risk instruments.

Evaluating the Credibility of Information Sources

The credibility of information obtained for forensic assessments needs to be critically scruti-nized, especially that obtained from offender self-report or from those who might have a conflict of interest, such as family members or loved ones. In the case of domestic violence assessments, it is important to recognize that information might be provided under threat of the perpetrator. A forensic lens is needed to filter, interpret, and critically evaluate any information obtained.

The same applies to psychometric testing. Tests of personality and psychopathology, such as the Minnesota Multiphasic Personality Inventory-2 (Butcher et al., 2001), often contain validity indices to assess possible impression management and faking. Measures of cognitive ability can be impacted by lack of effort or motivation. As discussed above, corroborated information can increase reliability. At times, misinformation can also be perpetuated in successive reports. There is no absolute certainty of the veracity of any information obtained, but this does not render information useless. Information presented should be corrobo-rated and the source of the information cited to increase transparency. The psychologist should be forthright about any limitation of the information to ensure that the conclusions drawn are defensible.

Assessment Across Multiple Domains of Functioning

There are many psychological variables and personal and interpersonal needs that pertain to risk and need. Important candidates within the realm of risk/need assessment include rela-tionships and social/interpersonal functioning, sexual functioning and history, vocational and academic functioning (past and any current), personality and psychopathology, impres-sion management and malingering, mental health and emotional functioning (e.g., such as prior diagnoses or current and active symptoms), treatment behavior and response to inter-ventions, cognitive and neuropsychological functioning, acatdemic achievement, vocational interests, activities of daily living and functioning within the community, and attitudes and cognitions. Evaluators, however, may prioritize the domains assessed that are most pertinent to the referral question.

Use of Multiple Assessment Methods

As evidence shows that static and dynamic instruments each have incremental predictive validity with overlapping but different intended purposes (e.g., assessment of baseline risk such as with the Static-99R versus informing treatment planning and evaluating change such as with the VRS-SO), it is important to use the relevant tools. Tools should always be selected on the basis of their intended purpose. For example, a broad risk/need instrument such as the LSI is designed for use across multiple assessment contexts and with most offender populations. More specific assessments should be buttressed by purposely designed instruments (e.g., Static-99R and Stable 2007). Again, assessors should look for converging themes in the data and avoid the mechanical scoring of a risk instrument (or two) and uncritical reporting of the estimated risk of recidivism. Assessments together with an informed case formulation provide not only useful information about level of risk (and thus service intensity), and targeted needs, but also valuable responsivity indicators by which to engage the client and to individualize service delivery.

Assessment of Key Domains

Assessing both static and dynamic risk factors will make the assessment more comprehensive and informative. Most standardized risk assessments will be comprised of either static risk factors (e.g., Offender Group Reconviction Scale [OGRS], Static-99R), dynamic risk factors (e.g., Stable 2007), or both (e.g., LS/CMI, HCR-20^{V3}, VRS, SARA). Particularly germane to this are the *Big Four* covariates of criminal conduct (criminal history, antisocial attitudes, antisocial associates, and antisocial personality) and what have been termed the *Central Eight* (with employment/education, family/marital, leisure recreation, and substance abuse included) (Andrews & Bonta, 2010). Several risk and need tools with dynamic factors will either explicitly assess the central eight domains, or incorporate myriad static and dynamic risk factors that encompass these domains. Details of the *Big Four* and the *Central Eight* are discussed in Tables 28.1 and 28.2, respectively.

In addition to these general risk/need domains, it is important to assess specific predictive factors relevant for specific outcomes. For sexual offenders, sexual deviance (e.g., deviant sexual interests, sexual preoccupation) has been identified as a psychologically meaningful risk factor with robust links to sexual violence (Mann, Hanson, & Thornton, 2010). All sexual offender risk instruments include assessments of deviant sexual interests, although other sources of information, including phallometric testing, other sexual preference testing, or specialized paper and pencil measures of sexual functioning, are also useful. For non-sexually violent and domestically violent offenders, it is relevant to consider specific counterparts to the general risk/need domains, such as attitudes supportive of violence, weapon use, aggressive interpersonal behavior, violence-prone lifestyle, and problems with anger and emotional control.

Assessment of Strengths and Protective and Other Risk Mitigating Factors

Most offenders have some strengths or resiliencies that may not be immediately obvious. The Good Lives Model (Ward, Melzer, & Yates, 2007) speaks at length about the importance of common goods in offender rehabilitation and reintegration, and the expanded RNR model advises evaluators to take note of strengths, as these purportedly mitigate risk, reduce the

Table 28.1 The *Big Four* Domains and their Characteristics

Domain	*Description*
Criminal history	That the best predictor of future behavior (recidivism) is past behavior (criminal history) has abundant support from meta-analyses with general offender populations (Gendreau, Little, & Goggin, 1996), young offenders (Cottle, Lee, & Heilbrun, 2001), mentally disordered offenders (Bonta et al., 1998), and sexual offenders (Hanson & Bussière, 1998). Criminal history is an exceptionally strong predictor of a range of criminal recidivism outcomes. All instruments containing static factors usually measure this domain directly. Interrogating the person's criminal history can reveal offending attitudes and feelings that suggest the presence of important psychological factors that may have important bearing on risk and need, such as sensation seeking, impulsivity, and sexual deviance.
Antisocial attitudes	The general personality and cognitive social learning (GPSL) model of criminal behavior (see Andrews & Bonta, 2010) underscores the contribution of cognitive factors to criminal behavior. Essentially, attitudes refer to a stable conglomerate of thoughts (beliefs), feelings, and behavioral intentions on different dimensions of judgment, such as attitudes on crime, sex with children, climate change, abortion, etc. Meta-analytic results support the predictive efficacy of antisocial attitudes for general and violent recidivism (Olver, Stockdale, et al., 2014) as well as attitudes supportive of sexual offending for sexual recidivism (Helmus, Hanson, Babchishin, & Mann, 2013). Most risk instruments will have item(s) to assess criminal attitudes; self-report measures of criminal attitudes and thinking abound (e.g., Psychological Inventory of Criminal Thinking Styles; Walters, 1995), and can have value in risk/need assessments.
Antisocial associates	This domain, closely linked to antisocial attitudes, is also a key part of the General Personality and Cognitive Social Learning (GPCSL) framework. Antisocial values and attitudes often are imparted by important social learning influences, such as through delinquent friends and family members who role model and reinforce such attitudes and values. The importance of antisocial peers in predicting recidivism is well supported (Bonta et al., 1998; Cottle et al., 2001; Gendreau et al., 1996; Olver, Stockdale, et al., 2014). Many general and specific risk instruments assess antisocial peers, and inquiring about one's social network is an important aspect of risk/need assessments.
Antisocial personality disorder	Personality disorders (PDs) are persistent patterns of maladaptive interpersonal and emotional functioning that tend to be enduring over time and stable across contexts. Antisocial PDs, and psychopathy in particular, have been linked to most if not all recidivism outcomes (e.g., Bonta et al., 1998; Gendreau et al., 1996; Hanson & Bussière, 1998; Hanson & Morton-Bourgon, 2005). The available literature, however, has shown that antisocial personality and psychopathy tend to be stronger predictors of broader base general offending (e.g., general and violent recidivism), but somewhat weaker (but still significant) in the prediction of specific offending (e.g., sexual recidivism). A recent meta-analysis by Hawes, Boccaccini, and Murrie (2013) demonstrated that psychopathy coupled with sexual deviance was associated with a threefold increase in the odds of sexual recidivism.

Table 28.2   The *Central Eight* Domains and their Characteristics

Domain	*Description*
Employment/education	Although this domain falls outside the *Big Four*, it is one of the *Central Eight*. Meta-analytic research has demonstrated that the education/employment domain was the third strongest predictor of the criminogenic needs for general (random effects r = .24, k = 55, n = 97,509) and violent (random effects r = .20, k = 19, n = 55,417) recidivism (Olver, Stockdale, et al., 2014). It stands to reason that poor employment record, work ethic, vocational skills, and educational preparation (perhaps linked to a learning disability) will disadvantage an individual whether on conditional release or at the end of a custodial sentence.
Family/marital	Closely tied to one's peer network are the social and emotional supports within one's immediate or extended family or intimate relationships. Positive familial and marital relationships can provide vital succor and incentive to change antisocial tendencies. At times, they can also serve as significant risk factors if the relationships are antisocial, emotionally volatile/unstable, or enabling. Family/marital functioning predicts general recidivism (Olver, Stockdale, et al., 2014; Gutierrez, Wilson, Rugge, & Bonta, 2013) while intimacy deficits predict sexual recidivism (Hanson & Morton-Bourgon, 2005). Family-related factors are important avenues of inquiry in risk and needs assessments; absent, empty, or non-reinforcing family/martial ties are a concerning indicator for release prospects.
Substance abuse	Drug and alcohol abuse are linked to myriad negative social outcomes of which criminal behavior is only one. These relationships are complex and often reciprocal. Drug/alcohol abuse serves as a disinhibitor for antisocial behavior while much criminal behavior is perpetrated to support a drug dependency or, in the case of trafficking, to be conducted for financial gains. Substance use can also exacerbate mental health symptoms making erratic, impulsive, and volatile behavior more likely. Several meta-analyses demonstrate the predictive associations between substance abuse and recidivism (Bonta et al., 1998; Gendreau et al., 1996; Olver, Stockdale, et al., 2014), and most dynamic risk instruments will include items to assess this domain.
Leisure/recreation	Of the *Central Eight*, the lack of prosocial recreational or leisure interests and poor use of unstructured/leisure time can be easily overlooked. Problems in this area have links to recidivism, though with somewhat smaller magnitude (r = .16 and .12 for general and violent recidivism, respectively; Olver, Stockdale, et al., 2014).

likelihood of recidivism, and increase the likelihood of positive outcomes. The assessment of strengths is often not explicitly incorporated into risk/need assessment tools.

Protective factors that have received some empirical support include intelligence, social support, positive use of leisure time, religion, positive attitude toward intervention, accommodation or housing, and prosocial problem-solving (Lodewijks, de Ruiter, & Dorelei-jers, 2010; Rennie & Dolan, 2010; Ullrich & Coid, 2011). The Structured Assessment of Protective Factors (SAPROF; de Vogel, de Ruiter, Bouman, & de Vries Robbé, 2009) is a clinical rating scale that provides a structured assessment of those protective factors known to be associated with decreased risk for recidivism. Preliminary research results suggest that higher SAPROF scores are associated with decreased violent and general community recidi-vism in Dutch forensic inpatients (de Vries Robbé et al., 2015; Lodewijks et al., 2010) and treated violent Canadian adult male offenders (Coupland, 2015). Coupland (2015) further found that the SAPROF, as well as a collection of protective factors assembled from the extant literature, was also associated with increased positive outcomes, such as obtaining employment, housing, stable relationships, and prosocial activities.

Special Considerations in Offender Risk/Need Assessment

There are a number of special considerations that are identified in most risk/need assessment tool manuals and they are applicable across offender populations and assessment contexts.

To Sum or Not to Sum Items?

The SPJ approach suggests that summing items to inform an overall risk classification is ill-advised. Proponents assert that the SPJ categories have incremental value beyond numeric scores—which has been demonstrated in some studies (Desmarais, Nicholls, Wilson, & Brink, 2012) and not in others (Worling, Bookalam, & Litteljohn, 2012)—and that endorsement of a single item can signal a high level of risk. Adherents of an actuarial approach assert, however, that risk estimates based on numeric scores provide objective evidence of risk and should not be tampered with (see Hanson, 2009), with some evidence that use of the professional over-ride (in tools such as the LS/CMI) erodes predictive accuracy (Wormith, Hogg, & Guzzo, 2012). A separate, but related, issue is the use of item weight to improve predictive accuracy. Although the available dynamic tools (SPJ or actuarial-based) do not use this practice explic-itly, similar results may be achieved by using multiple items to tap key domains, such as using multiple items in a sex offender assessment to assess sexual deviance, an important domain.

Use of Multiple Tools

The use of multiple tools overlaps with the notion of using multiple assessment methods described above, but is specific to the use of risk/need measures. Arguably, multiple tools can increase predictive accuracy and broaden the range of static and dynamic risk factors assessed. This potentially strengthens the information available to prioritize needs for treatment planning and risk management. In addition, the use of a specialized and a general risk/need tools can inform a judgment about different aspects of risk and help to tailor services accordingly. For instance, an individual may be assessed at "moderate" risk for sexual violence but at "high" risk for any recidivism; the intensity of services and supervision can then be tailored to reflect the level of risk for these different outcomes. Sometimes, however, risk tools developed for a common purpose (such as assessing sexual violence risk) can yield contradictory risk estimates (Barbaree, Langton, & Peacock, 2006). Evaluators need to reconcile such disparities through further investigations or appropriate professional judgment. The benefits of using multiple tools must also be balanced against the extra time and effort required.

Assessment of Change

Offender rehabilitation and risk reassessments are all predicated on the dynamic nature of risk. A growing literature has shown that some risk instruments can provide valid appraisals of risk changes that are linked to recidivism changes (see above). The use of multiple time point assessments to capture the contemporary condition of the offender tends to be more accurate than assessment at a single time point (Hanson et al., 2007). The challenge remains, however, about how to systematically incorporate change information across multiple time points into risk appraisals.

One approach is to simply sum re-rated items to generate a new risk total for each reassessment using the instrument. However, re-rating items to capture treatment changes is not straightforward as rating descriptions often cannot reflect treatment- and change-related behaviors such as increased treatment engagement or the building of a new repertoire of prosocial behaviors. As well, most tools do not provide guidance on how to incorporate change information into the re-rating of items. A structured rubric to assess and quantify change, such as the stages of change (SOC) model, has been used in some tools, such as the VRS and VRS-SO. One can then subtract a change score computed using the SOC from the previous assessment total while taking into account the baseline risk level. Olver, Beggs Christofferson, et al. (2014), for instance, illustrate the use of logistic regression modeling over fixed follow-ups to generate a recidivism estimate for a specific baseline risk score and change value. Recidivism rates approximate a logistic function (Hanson, Helmus, & Thornton, 2010), and this approach is systematic and can minimize bias by generating estimates as a function of test scores and the recidivism base rate of the normative sample. The end goal is to systematically use change information and to avoid making careless professional override-type adjustments.

Communication of Risk and Need

A final issue discussed here is the critical practice of communicating risk and need information. Some recent writing (e.g., Hilton, Scurich, & Helmus, 2015) has addressed this issue in detail. For this reason, the present entry will be a very brief overview on a selected topic: the use of arbitrary versus non-arbitrary metrics.

The categories of "low," "medium," and "high" can have different meanings in different risk tools and to different people. Although higher numeric scores in actuarial tools or a greater number or severity of risk factors in SPJ tools reflects a greater probability of recidivism, there is a certain arbitrariness in creating and/or interpreting these categories. For instance, the term "high risk" may be interpreted as 100% likelihood of recidivism, when the reality is often much different. For the LSI-R, "high risk/needs" amounts to 76% of individuals being reincarcerated within 1 year post-release. For the Static-99R, "high risk" (a score of 6; the lowest score for this band) translates into about 12.7% of individuals being charged or convicted for a new sexual offense in the next 5 years (or 28% when the reference group is a high-risk/need sample). On the other hand, "low risk" may be mistakenly interpreted as "no risk," when, in fact, some low-risk offenders will reoffend for various reasons.

   Descriptive labels, such as "high," "medium," and "low," can be buttressed by absolute risk estimates such as the estimated rate of a specific type of recidivism over a fixed time period (e.g., sexual convictions over 1, 5, and 10 years), as indicated above for the LSI-R and the Static-99R. Actual recidivism rates using fixed follow-ups or logistic regression modeling can be used to provide recidivism estimates as a function of specific scores. Another non-arbitrary metric is the *relative risk* or the comparison of an offender's risk level to other offenders, such as the use of percentile ranks. For instance, a score of 47 on the LSI-R places an offender in the high-risk band and the 99th percentile; that is the score is higher than 99% of the normative sample. The use of non-arbitrary metrics such as measures of absolute and relative risk can contextualize descriptive labels such as high, medium, and low and thus facilitates the communication of risk for decision-makers.

Summary and Conclusions

Risk assessment has moved from mere risk prediction to risk management and reduction. For this reason, we recommend using at least one risk tool with dynamic factors and established psychometric properties to assess both risk and need. If the assessment of risk change is required, use tools with validated metrics to assess and track change. We also recommend using tools only for their intended purpose and population. The use of one tool over another is often a matter of personal preference and likely means little when it comes down to just risk prediction. The choice of tools should match the purpose of the assessment. Evaluators are advised to contextualize risk communication, as risk and need are invariably conditional on personal and situational factors.

Key Readings

Andrews, D. A., & Bonta, J. (2010). *The psychology of criminal conduct* (5th ed.). New Providence, NJ: LexisNexis.

Hanson, R. K., & Morton-Bourgon, K. (2009). The accuracy of recidivism risk assessments for sexual offenders: A meta-analysis of 118 prediction studies. *Psychological Assessment*, 21, 1–21.

Yang, M., Wong, S. C. P., & Coid, J. (2010). The efficacy of violence prediction: A meta-analytic comparison of nine risk assessment tools. *Psychological Bulletin*, 136, 740–767.

References

Andrews, D. A., & Bonta, J. (1995). *The Level of Service Inventory—Revised*. Toronto, Canada: Multi-Health Systems.

Andrews, D. A., Bonta, J., & Wormith, J. S. (2006). The recent past and near future of risk and/or needs assessment. *Crime and Delinquency*, 52, 7–27.

Babchishin, K. M., Blais, J., & Helmus, L. (2012). Do static risk factors predict differently for Aboriginal sex offenders? A multi-site comparison using the original and revised Static-99 and Static-2002 scales. *Canadian Journal of Criminology and Criminal Justice*, 1–43.

Barbaree, H. E., Langton, C. M., & Peacock, E. J. (2006). Different actuarial risk measures produce different risk rankings for sexual offenders. *Sexual Abuse: A Journal of Research and Treatment*, 18, 423–440.

Bloom, B., Owen, B., & Covington, S. (2003). *Gender responsive strategies: Research, practice and guiding principles for women offenders*. Washington, DC: National Research Council.

Boer, D. P., Hart, S. D., Kropp, P. R., & Webster, C. D. (1997). *Manual for the Sexual Violence Risk-20: Professional guidelines for assessing risk of sexual violence*. Vancouver, Canada: Institute against Family Violence and the Mental Health, Law, and Policy Institute, Simon Fraser University.

Bonta, J. (1996). Risk needs assessment and treatment. In A. T. Hartland (Ed.), *Choosing correctional options that work: Defining the demand and evaluating the supply* (pp. 18–32). Thousand Oaks, CA: Sage.

Bonta, J., Law, M., & Hanson, R. K. (1998). The prediction of criminal and violent recidivism among mentally disordered offenders: A meta-analysis. *Psychological Bulletin*, 123, 123–142.

Bonta, J., & Andrews, D. A. (2017). *The psychology of criminal conduct* (6th ed.). New York, NY: Routledge.

Butcher, J., Graham, J., Ben-Porath, Y., Tellegen, A., Grant Dahlstrom, W. G., & Kaemmer, B. (2001). *Minnesota Multiphasic Personality Inventory-2*. Minneapolis, MN: University of Minnesota Press.

Campbell, M. A., French, S., & Gendreau, P. (2009). The prediction of violence in adult offenders: A meta-analytic comparison of instruments and methods of assessment. *Criminal Justice and Behavior*, 36, 567–590.

Cohen, J. (1988). *Statistical power analysis for the behavioral sciences* (2nd ed.). Hillsdale, NJ: Lawrence Erlbaum.

Copas, J., & Marshall, P. (1998). The Offender Group Reconviction Scale: The statistical reconviction score for use by probation officers. *Journal of the Royal Statistical Society, Series C*, 47, 159–171.

Cottle, C. C., Lee, R. J., & Heilbrun, K. (2001). The prediction of criminal recidivism in juveniles: A meta-analysis. *Criminal Justice and Behavior*, 28, 367–394.

Coupland, R. B. A. (2015). An examination of dynamic risk, protective factors, and treatment-related change in violent offenders (Unpublished doctoral dissertation). University of Saskatchewan, Saskatoon, Canada.

de Vogel, V., de Ruiter, C., Bouman, Y. H. A., & de Vries Robbé, M. (2009). *SAPROF: guidelines for the assessment of protective factors for violence risk*. Utrecht, The Netherlands: Forum Educatief.

de Vries Robbé, M., de Vogel, V., Douglas, K. S., & Nijman, H. L. I. (2015). Changes in dynamic risk and protective factors for violence during inpatient forensic psychiatric treatment: Predicting reductions in postdischarge community recidivism. *Law and Human Behavior*, 39, 53–61.

Desmarais, S. L., Nicholls, T. L., Wilson, C. M., & Brink, J. (2012). Using dynamic risk and protective factors to predict inpatient aggression: Reliability and validity of the START assessments. *Psychological Assessment*, 24, 685–700.

Douglas, K. S., & Skeem, J. (2005). Violence risk assessment: Getting specific about being dynamic. *Psychology, Public Policy, and Law*, 11, 347–383.

Douglas, K. S., Hart, S. D., Webster, C. D., & Belfrage, H. (2011). *Historical Clinical Risk Management (Version 3): Professional guidelines for evaluating risk of violence [draft 2.1]*. Vancouver, Canada: Mental Health, Law, and Policy Institute, Simon Fraser University.

Douglas, K. S., & Kropp, P. R. (2002). A prevention-based paradigm for violence risk assessment: Clinical and research applications. *Criminal Justice and Behavior*, 29, 617–658.

Gendreau, P., Little, T., & Goggin, C. (1996). A meta-analysis of the predictors of adult offender recidivism: What works! *Criminology*, 34, 575–595.

Grove, W. M., Zald, D. H., Lebow, B. S., Snitz, B. E., & Nelson, C. (2000). Clinical versus mechanical prediction: A meta-analysis. *Psychological Assessment*, 12, 19–30.

Gutierrez, L., Wilson, H., Rugge, T., & Bonta, J. (2013). The prediction of recidivism with Aboriginal offenders: A theoretically informed meta-analysis. *Canadian Journal of Criminology and Criminal Justice*, 55, 55–99.

Hanson, R. K. (2009). The psychological assessment of risk for crime and violence. *Canadian Psychology*, 50, 172–182.

Hanson, R. K., & Bussière, M. T. (1998). Predicting relapse: A meta-analysis of sexual offender recidivism studies. *Journal of Consulting and Clinical Psychology*, 66, 348–362.

Hanson, R. K., Harris, A. J. R., Scott, T., & Helmus, L. (2007). *Assessing the risk of sex offenders on community supervision.* (User Report No. 2007-05). Ottawa, Canada: Public Safety and Emergency Preparedness Canada.

Hanson, R. K., Helmus, L., & Thornton, D. (2010). Predicting recidivism among sexual offenders: A multi-site study of Static-2002. *Law and Human Behavior*, 34, 198–211.

Hanson, R. K., & Morton-Bourgon, K. (2005). The characteristics of persistent sexual offenders: A meta-analysis of recidivism studies. *Journal of Consulting and Clinical Psychology*, 73, 1154–1163.

Hanson, R. K., & Morton-Bourgon, K. (2009). The accuracy of recidivism risk assessments for sexual offenders: A meta-analysis of 118 prediction studies. *Psychological Assessment*, 21, 1–21.

Hawes, S. W., Boccaccini, M. T., & Murrie, D. C. (2013). Psychopathy and the combination of psychopathy and sexual deviance as predictors of sexual recidivism: Meta-analytic findings using the Psychopathy Checklist—Revised. *Psychological Assessment*, 25, 233–243.

Helmus, L., Hanson, R. K., Babchishin, K. M., & Mann, R. E. (2013). Attitudes supportive of sexual offending predict recidivism: A meta-analysis. *Trauma, Violence, & Abuse*, 14, 34–53.

Hilton, N. Z., Scurich, N., & Helmus, L. M. (2015). Communicating the risk of violent and offending behavior: Review and introduction to this special issue. *Behavioral Sciences and the Law*, 33, 1–18.

Hogan, N. R., & Olver, M. E. (2016). Assessing risk for aggression in forensic psychiatric inpatients: An examination of five measures. *Law and Human Behavior*, 40, 233–243.

Hoge, R. D. (1999). An expanded role for psychological assessments in juvenile justice systems. *Criminal Justice and Behavior*, 26, 251–266.

Hoge, R. D. (2002). Standardized assessments for assessing risk and need in youthful offenders. *Criminal Justice and Behavior*, 29, 380–396.

Holtfreter, K., Reisig, M. D., & Morash, M. (2004). Poverty, state capital, and recidivism among women offenders. *Criminology & Public Policy*, 3, 185–208.

Kropp, P. R., Hart, S. D., Webster, C. W., & Eaves, D. (1995). *Manual for the Spousal Assault Risk Assessment Guide* (2nd ed.). Vancouver, Canada: British Columbia Institute on Family Violence.

Lewis, K., Olver, M. E., & Wong, S. C. P. (2013). The Violence Risk Scale: Predictive validity and linking treatment changes with recidivism in a sample of high-risk offenders with psychopathic traits. *Assessment*, 20, 150–164.

Lichtenberger, E. O., Mather, N., Kaufman, N. L., & Kaufman, A. S. (2004). *Essentials of assessment report writing.* New York, NY: Wiley.

Lodewijks, H. P. B., de Ruiter, C., & Doreleijers, T. (2010). The impact of protective factors in desistance from violent reoffending: A study in three samples of adolescent offenders. *Journal of Interpersonal Violence*, 25, 568–587.

Mann, R. E., Hanson, R. K., & Thornton, D. (2010). Assessing risk for sexual recidivism: Some proposals on the nature of psychologically meaningful risk factors. *Sexual Abuse: A Journal of Research and Treatment*, 22, 191–217.

McGuire, J. (2008). A review of effective interventions for reducing aggression and violence. *Philosophical Transactions of The Royal Society*, 363(1503), 2483–2622.

Meehl, P. E. (1954). *Clinical vs. statistical prediction.* Minneapolis, MN: University of Minnesota Press.

Olver, M. E., Beggs Christofferson, S. M., Grace, R. C., & Wong, S. C. P. (2014). Incorporating change information into sexual offender risk assessments using the Violence Risk Scale-Sexual Offender version. *Sexual Abuse: A Journal of Research and Treatment*, 26, 472–499.

Olver, M. E., Neumann, C. S., Wong, S. C. P., & Hare, R. D. (2013). The structural and predictive properties of the PCL-R in Canadian Aboriginal and non-Aboriginal offenders. *Psychological Assessment*, 25, 167–179.

Olver, M. E., Sowden, J. N., Kingston, D. A., Nicholaichuk, T. P., Gordon, A., Beggs Christofferson, S. M., & Wong, S. C. P. (2016, May 18). Predictive accuracy of VRS-SO risk and change scores in treated Canadian Aboriginal and non-Aboriginal sexual offenders. *Sexual Abuse: A Journal of Research and Treatment*, 30, 254–275. doi:10.1177/1079063216649594

Olver, M. E., Stockdale, K. C., & Wormith, J. S. (2009). Risk assessment with young offenders: A meta-analysis of three assessment measures. *Criminal Justice and Behavior*, 36, 329–353.

Olver, M. E., Stockdale, K. C., & Wormith, J. S. (2014). Thirty years of research on the Level of Service scales: A meta-analytic examination of predictive accuracy and sources of variability. *Psychological Assessment*, 26, 156–176.

Prochaska, J. O., DiClemente, C. C., & Norcross, J. C. (1992). In search of how people change: Applications to the addictive behaviors. *American Psychologist*, 47, 1102–1114.

R. v. Gladue. (1999). 1 S.C.R. 688.

Rennie, C., & Dolan, M. (2010). The significance of protective factors in the assessment of risk. *Criminal Behaviour and Mental Health*, 20, 8–22.

Rettinger, L. J., & Andrews, D. A. (2010). General risk and need, gender specificity, and the recidivism of female offenders. *Criminal Justice and Behavior*, 37, 29–46.

Rice, M. E., & Harris, G. T. (2005). Comparing effect sizes in follow-up studies: ROC area, Cohen's d, and r. *Law and Human Behavior*, 29, 615–620.

Schwalbe, C. S. (2008). A meta-analysis of juvenile justice risk assessment instruments: Predictive validity by gender. *Criminal Justice and Behavior*, 35, 1367–1381.

Ullrich, S., & Coid, J. (2011). Protective factors for violence among released prisoners: Effects over time and interactions with static risk. *Journal of Consulting and Clinical Psychology*, 79, 381–390.

Van Voorhis, P., Wright, E. M., Salisbury, E., & Bauman, A. (2010). Women's risk factors and their contributions to existing risk/needs assessment: The current status of a gender responsive supplement. *Criminal Justice and Behavior*, 37, 261–288.

Vose, B., Lowenkamp, C. T., Smith, P., & Cullen, F. T. (2009). Gender and the predictive validity of the LSI-R: A study of parolees and probationers. *Journal of Contemporary Criminal Justice*, 25, 459–471.

Walters, G. D. (1995). The Psychological Inventory of Criminal Thinking Styles: Reliability and preliminary validity. *Criminal Justice and Behavior*, 22, 307–325.

Ward, T., Melzer, J., & Yates, P. (2007). Reconstructing the Risk-Need-Responsivity model: A theoretical elaboration and evaluation. *Aggression and Violent Behavior*, 12, 208–228.

Wilson, H. A., & Gutierrez, L. (2014). Does one size fit all? A meta-analysis examining the predictive ability of the Level of Service Inventory with Aboriginal offenders. *Criminal Justice and Behavior*, 41, 196–219.

Wong, S. C. P., Olver, M. E., Nicholaichuk, T. P., & Gordon, A. (2003, 2017). *The Violence Risk Scale: Sexual Offense version (VRS-SO)*. Regional Psychiatric Centre and University of Saskatchewan, Saskatoon, Canada.

Wong, S. C. P., & Gordon, A. (1999–2003). *Violence Risk Scale*. Regional Psychiatric Centre and the University of Saskatchewan, Saskatoon, Canada: Author.

Worling, J. R., Bookalam, D., & Litteljohn, A. (2012). Prospective validity of the Estimate of Risk of Adolescent Sexual Offense Recidivism (ERASOR). *Sexual Abuse: A Journal of Research and Treatment*, 24, 203–223.

Wormith, J. S., Hogg, S., & Guzzo, L. (2012). The predictive validity of a general risk/needs assessment inventory on sexual offender recidivism and an exploration of the professional override. *Criminal Justice and Behavior*, 39, 1511–1538.

Yang, M., Wong, S. C. P., & Coid, J. (2010). The efficacy of violence prediction: A meta-analytic comparison of nine risk assessment tools. *Psychological Bulletin*, 136, 740–767.

29

Case Formulation and Treatment Planning

Peter Sturmey
Queens College, City University of New York, USA

Mary McMurran
University of Nottingham, UK

Michael Daffern
Swinburne University of Technology, Australia

Case Formulation

Case formulation is the organization of information about the client to help explain the origins and maintenance of problems and identify what treatments are likely to be effective, ineffective, or even harmful (Eells, 2007; Johnstone & Dallos, 2006; Sturmey & McMurran, 2011). A case formulation differs from a specific problem formulation in that it addresses the whole person. It seeks to articulate the central mechanisms that cause and maintain the individual's main problems and explain how they are related (Persons & Tomkins, 2007). This individualized (idiographic) approach contrasts with general or standardized (nomothetic) approaches to offender assessment, such as those based on the results of actuarial risk-needs tools (e.g., a high-risk violent offender may be referred for treatment whereas a low-risk violent offender may not), or classifications (e.g., a history of violent offending may result in a classification as a "violent offender" and lead to referral to a standardized violent offender treatment program), or diagnosis (e.g., a person may be diagnosed as "personality disordered" and referred to specialist services).

Constructing a Case Formulation

One widely used approach to constructing a case formulation is to assess and integrate information relating to a range of domains, including biological, psychological, familial, social, and cultural (Weerasekera, 1996). The acronym "5 Ps" is used to structure the process as follows: (a) *Problem*, which refers to a definition of the problem or the constellation of problems and identification of a desired alternative, which will be the therapy end-point; (b) *Precipitating factors*, which are the proximal internal and external factors that trigger the problem(s); (c) *Perpetuating factors*, which are those internal and external factors that maintain the problem(s); (d) *Predisposing factors*, which are the distal internal and external factors that increase the person's vulnerability to the problem(s); and (e) *Protective factors*, which are those internal and external factors that help the person cope with or recover from the problem(s) or prevent relapse. Information about these 5 Ps does not in itself make a case formulation. Rather, case formulation involves integrating the information collected by describing the developmental processes and the functions that the problem behaviors have for the individual, with the ultimate aim being to create an understanding of the individual as she or he is now. The product of the case formulation process depends inter alia on the quality of the information available, the underpinning theory chosen to explain the individual's development, and whether the individual has been invited to discuss the personal meaning of events and processes and become a co-producer of the formulation (British Psychological Society, 2011). These issues will be discussed with specific reference to forensic case formulation.

Forensic Case Formulation

In forensic psychology, the primary purpose of working with offenders is to reduce the propensity or risk for further criminal behavior, and this is preferably done with concurrent attention being paid to the personal needs of the individual offender (Ward, 2013). However, interweaving risk reduction and the amelioration of an individual's problems presents a conceptual problem in case formulation. Some authors say that case formulations do not have to be true, they just have to be useful (Butler, 1998), while others view formulations as hypotheses that, when tested through evaluation of formulation-based predictions and formulation-based interventions, reveal the validity—or otherwise—of the formulation. There are different requirements for general clinical utility and maximally effective risk assessment and reduction.

In risk assessment and management, it is of great importance that formulations are of high validity so that interventions can be selected appropriately to reduce risk and to avoid implementing interventions that might actually lead to greater harm (i.e., increased risk) than not intervening at all. Nonetheless, the principles of case formulation are the same in both clinical and risk scenarios, although the outcomes may concern the public more in risk assessment cases. These principles are detailed below.

Quality of Information

The validity of the forensic case formulation will depend upon the quality of the evidence upon which it is based. Some important considerations include the fact that offending behavior is usually not observable and that violence or problematic sexual behavior is often low frequency, context-specific, and cannot be elicited for ethical reasons (Hart, Sturmey, Logan, & McMurran, 2011). The focus, therefore, is usually on assessing variables related to risk, such as risky beliefs (e.g., endorsement of violence), risky emotions (e.g., anger), and risky behaviors (e.g., drinking alcohol). These may be only indirectly related to the offending behavior and care must be taken to select those variables for which there is robust evidence of a relationship to offending. Furthermore, formulations often draw upon Offense Paralleling Behavior (OPB; Daffern et al., 2007), which is discussed below.

The validity of collateral sources of information also requires consideration. Records may be incomplete or contain misinformation based on the self-report of an offender who was responding to an interview situation in which his or her responses may have had legal consequences. Frequent retelling of an untruthful account may also affect the individual's memory for what really happened (and consolidate distortions) so that even current interview information may also be inaccurate. Similarly, offenders may fake good on psychometric assessments. One approach to overcoming these threats to validity is to seek accounts from victims and from others who have knowledge of the offense (e.g., family members, police officers, probation officers; Gresswell & Kruppa, 1994) or to use measures designed to assess socially desirable responding (Paulhus, 1991).

Underpinning Theory

While case formulation can be based upon any theory of human behavior, in offender work cognitive and behavioral theories prevail. There is considerable evidence about what works in offender treatment based upon the personality and cognitive social learning theory of criminal conduct (Andrews & Bonta, 2006). This points to a focus in case formulation on the eight major dynamic risk factors for reoffending, namely, a history of antisocial behavior, an antisocial personality pattern, antisocial cognition, antisocial associates, poor quality relationships, low levels of school or work performance, lack of prosocial leisure activities, and substance abuse. Including known risk factors for specific offense types (e.g., violence, sexual crimes) in the case formulation is an important part of the process of structured professional judgment (Hart & Logan, 2011).

The Good Lives Model (GLM; Ward, 2002) of offender rehabilitation contains the proposal that reoffending can also be prevented by equipping offenders with the capabilities required to meet their needs in socially acceptable and personally meaningful ways. In many ways, this idea is consistent with the 5 Ps approach, with the focus on identifying protective factors. In our own research, we interviewed convicted adult male prisoners, finding that they understood that to stop offending they needed to develop positive life areas, including work, relationships, accommodation, health, and leisure activities (McMurran, Theodosi, Sweeney, & Sellen, 2008). It is important to assess positive aspects for inclusion in strength-based case formulations.

While case formulations driven by different theories may be equally valid and useful, they can lead to treatments that conflict. For example, a psychopharmacological treatment may lead to an illness belief, whereas a cognitive behavioral treatment may need a strong belief in personal agency. Issues about how to integrate different approaches are usually avoided by simply including different factors without integrating different theoretical approaches (British Psychological Society, 2011). Thus, biological, psychological, social, and cultural factors can be included within a cognitive and behavioral psychology framework. Of course, case formulations often need to be shared with and agreed by the individual's treatment team members, who will have different theoretical perspectives (e.g., psychological, medical, social). Case formulations may be produced jointly by these teams to facilitate the production of coherent treatment plans and prevent conflicting treatments (Johnstone, 2014).

Co-Production

Given concerns about veracity, it may be that offenders' input to the case formulation is sought more for some purposes than others. Where risk assessments are concerned, it may be that professionals' judgment is given more emphasis. Where treatment planning is concerned, co-production of the case formulation is an important means to engage the offender in the treatment process.

Quality of Case Formulation

Hart et al. (2011) have described the features of a good-quality case formulation. They argued that the case formulation should be a coherent and understandable narrative account. It should be based on sufficient good-quality and relevant factual information that is interpreted using a generally accepted theory, and yield detailed and testable predictions about which strategies will be most effective in treatment and management. They also suggest that the case formulation is usually produced with the person to whom it refers.

These features were used to construct a 10-item case formulation quality checklist (CFQC) (McMurran, Logan, & Hart, 2012), which was designed to rate the quality of case formulations on a Likert scale. The CFQC showed good inter-rater reliability (intraclass correlation [ICC] = .63–.75), excellent test–retest reliability (ICC = .85–.99), and excellent internal consistency (Cronbach's alpha = .92) (Minoudis et al., 2013). However, feedback from raters was that the checklist could be improved, and so the opinions of professionals who had used the CFQC were sought and used as a basis for its revision (McMurran & Bruford, 2016). The revised items relate to the following descriptors: *Narrative*, in that the formulation is presented in everyday language that tells a coherent, ordered, and meaningful story; *Theory*, in that the formulation is consistent with an empirically supported theory; *Coherent factual foundation*, in that the formulation is based on an adequate amount of good-quality, relevant information about the past and the present time that is tied together to show relationships; and *Predictive*, in that the formulation goes beyond simple description to make detailed and testable predictions about which strategies will be most effective in treating and managing harmful behavior. The crucial question, of course, is whether a good-quality formulation adds value to offender management and treatment.

Case Formulation: Does it Work?

In order to show that case formulation "works," researchers must demonstrate several things. First, they must reliably make case formulations; that is, the persons making formulations must agree on the essential features. Second, they must also agree on the implications of the formulation for indicated and contra-indicated treatments. Third, when evidence-based practices already exist, formulation-based treatment must improve treatment outcomes in some manner beyond that which routine treatment would have achieved. This latter outcome might be difficult to achieve in cases where there are already highly effective, classification-based treatments. In the forensic context there are, however, few examples of highly effective (in terms of reducing criminal recidivism) classification-based (offense type, e.g., violent or sexual offender) treatments—most treatments have at best a modest impact. Forensic case formulation-driven interventions must therefore improve risk reduction beyond typical procedures (treatments and management) that would have been used anyway to reduce risk. Before reviewing evidence pertaining to outcomes of forensic formulation-based interventions we shall describe outcomes for general clinical interventions that are formulation based.

Ghaderi (2006) has published a well-designed randomized controlled trial that provided some evidence of how case formulation can improve treatment outcomes for bulimia beyond established, evidence-based diagnosis-based treatment. Fifty patients with bulimia were randomized to one of two treatments; one group participated in evidence-based manualized cognitive behavioral therapy (CBT) and the other received various individualized modifications to the standard manual based on the formulation (e.g., greater use of interventions based on rule-governed behavior). Although both treatments were effective, only 69% of participants in the standard treatment, but 92% of those in individualized treatment, were classified as responders. Additionally, 80% of the non-responders were in the standardized CBT group. These outcomes are impressive because the comparison treatment was one that had extensive research supporting its use as an evidence-based practice.

In a similar but more recent study, Johansson et al. (2012) compared the outcomes of standardized online CBT for depression with those of individualized CBT and an active treatment control that participated in weekly discussions. They randomized 121 participants to each condition, the majority of whom had acute depression and comorbid conditions such as stress, anxiety, and sleep disorders. Most were taking or had taken psychotropic medication. Both CBT groups received online training for depression that had previously been shown to be effective. The individualized group also received a personalized treatment plan developed by the research team based on the available diagnostic and self-report data from the participants. Although the outcomes generally favored individualized treatments, these differences were seen most clearly in individuals with more severe depression where individualization of treatment resulted in much better outcomes than standardized treatment on measures of depression and quality of life.

In contrast to these preceding studies, not all evaluations of case formulation have reported positive results. A most intriguing study comes from Schulte, Kunzel, Pepping, and Schulte-Bahrenberg (1992), who assigned individuals with various phobias to standardized exposure treatment not based on a case formulation, treatment based on a case formulation, and a control group that received treatment based on the individualized plan drawn up for a person in the second treatment group. There was no evidence that formulation helped. All groups improved, but the standardized treatment group improved most quickly and all three groups were equivalent at 6-month follow-up. The key negative finding was that there was no difference between the formulation-based treatment group and the yoked control.

There is also evidence of the negative effects of case formulation. Chadwick, Williams, and Mackenzie (2003) developed collaborative case formulations with individuals with psychotic disorders. They found that the formulations had little impact on either the therapeutic relationship or psychotic beliefs. They also noted that some participants reported that they found collaborating in their own case formulation to be a negative experience, for example, because it highlighted the lifelong nature of their problems.

Based on this non-systematic review of outcomes studies we can only conclude that, in some circumstances, case formulation may produce treatment outcomes that are sometimes similar to and sometimes better than standard evidence-based treatment, although there is little evidence at this time for the validity of forensic case formulation. At this time, because of the lack of studies, there is little evidence that collaborative case formulation is effective, but practitioners should also be aware of the possible negative effects for some participants. An important issue for future research to address is to reliably distinguish between individualization of treatment that is based clearly on the formulation versus individualization of treatment based on non-formulation factors such as client preferences for treatment and ease of implementation.

Does Forensic Case Formulation Work?

The previous section reported contradictory outcomes from studies attempting to evaluate case formulation. Despite the increasing popularity of some forms of forensic case formulation, such as OPB (Daffern et al., 2007) and the development of some quality measures that can be applied to formulating forensic cases (McMurran & Bruford, 2016), there are currently no data that establish whether forensic case formulation improves offender treatment outcomes. This may, in part, reflect some of the limitations of case formulation generally, as well as the specific challenges associated with forensic case formulation.

Why these Ambiguous Outcomes?

It is perplexing that a clinical skill that has often been identified as a core clinical competency for many different clinicians does not clearly and robustly result in superior client outcomes than standard treatment. Why is this? Despite recent elucidation of the key components of case formulation (in the forensic field, see Hart et al., 2011), the field has yet to agree on what an adequate formulation is. The results of a systematic review of the reliability of case formulations by Flinn, Braham, and das Nair (2015) support this idea. These authors systematically searched the literature and identified 18 studies in which formulations were used. Most used cognitive, psychodynamic, and integrative models. The reliability data were disappointing: one third of the 18 studies reported little better than chance agreement and only one reported substantive reliability. Only one study reported any test–retest reliability.

Why are formulations—even in research studies—so often unreliable? There may be several reasons. Some have pointed out the similarity with other forms of unstructured judgments, suggesting that unreliability may come from the unconstrained behavior of clinicians in the absence of clear criteria for what constitutes a formulation. Another possibility is the lack of adequate training required to develop a formulation. Although formulators may attend courses, there is little evidence that these provide the extensive practice and feedback required to acquire such a complex skill and apply it to novel problems that vary topographically and functionally from the training examples.

A key consideration when developing an adequate formulation is validity. One critical aspect for this—and perhaps the key function of case formulation—is to predict the best treatment for the particular person being assessed and to avoid harmful treatments. Making an accurate and reliable formulation is, of course, of little use if practitioners fail to translate it reliably and validly to an effective treatment plan. This crucial aspect of case formulation does not appear to have been studied.

Formulation-based intervention might fail at any of at least four steps. First, the practitioner may not have made any formulation. For example, although some studies mention the individualization of treatment, the mechanism by which this occurs is not made explicit. Thus, treatment individualization that occurs in the context of an existing treatment package might involve dropping or adding treatment components when such individualization may not map explicitly onto the case formulation. Second, a formulation may be made, but the formulation may not be adequately competent. This could arise out of lack of clarity about what constitutes an adequate formulation and lack of effective practitioner training. Third, formulation-based treatment might fail because the practitioner does not translate a sufficiently competent formulation into a treatment plan that truly reflects the formulation. Finally, both the formulation and the treatment plan might be adequate, but the plan may not be implemented with sufficient fidelity to ensure client progress.

Perhaps part of the problem in implementing formulation-based treatment lies in the reluctance to explicitly embrace a specific theoretical framework. Rather, current approaches seek to accommodate a wide range of practitioner preferences and perhaps to appear reasonable by attempting to integrate different theoretical formulations. For example, Weerasekera's

(1996) popular 5 Ps approach uses categories of variables that can be adapted to many different theoretical approaches. In response to "Perpetuating factors" a formulator might write: (a) "The core schema that s/he is stupid and unworthy has perpetuated the client's depression"; (b) "Loss of positive reinforcement for adaptive, healthy behavior resulted in response allocation to depressed behavior"; or (c) "The family history of depression indicates a high genetic load for depression." Are any or all of these clinician responses an adequate response to the question? If the definition of an adequate case formulation is theory-specific then, depending on which theory is chosen, only some of the answers are correct. If the formulation requires integration from different theories, then no single answer is adequate.

The failure to specify explicitly what constitutes an adequate formulation is a significant block to progress in this area. One practical solution might be to select one of the most commonly used frameworks—either CBT or integrated formulations—and develop criteria for adequate formulations and multiple models (perhaps good and bad) along with reliable measures of the adequacy of the formulations for use in training (e.g., McMurran & Bruford's CFQC). There are two approaches to measuring the adequacy of formulations—global ratings of formulation adequacy and specific therapist responses. In the former approach, experts use Likert scales to rate overall impressions of dimensions, such as "high/low integration of history and presenting problem," and "treatment linked to formulation." In the latter, one might specify specific formulator responses, such as "states a link between history and presenting problem such as 'because Jamil did not learn problem-solving skills as a child he now uses violence to remove unpleasant interactions with authority figures'." Both approaches have strengths and may have different uses in terms of training formulators and identifying formulations that are deemed adequate.

Forensic Case Formulation: The Case of Ms. Elizabeth Brown

In this section we present a typical complex forensic case. We then illustrate the application of case formulation to this particular case using OPB as the theoretical framework.

Case Study

Ms. Elizabeth Brown is serving a 14-year prison sentence for murder. She killed a female acquaintance when she thought this person was taunting her.

Ms. Brown experienced a disadvantaged and deprived childhood. She is an only child who did not meet her biological father; her stepfather was alcohol dependent and repeatedly violent toward Ms. Brown and her mother; if she misbehaved, even mildly, then her stepfather ruthlessly beat her. Additionally, he publicly taunted her, particularly when he was intoxicated and in the presence of other men.

As Ms. Brown's stepfather was an infantryman in the Australian army, the family moved regularly and Ms. Brown attended many schools. She struggled to make friends and was teased by her peers due to her small stature and timidity. Sometimes she hit other children who teased her. Typically, her reactions to teasing were excessive, and on occasions she hit other children with whatever makeshift weapon she could readily grab. In early adolescence Ms. Brown's attendance at school and her academic achievements worsened. She gravitated toward other alienated youth and avoided teachers and peers. She started using drugs and alcohol, truanted, and began breaking into houses, often on her own, to obtain property to sell, which she used to purchase drugs.

When Ms. Brown was 15 her mother was diagnosed with cancer. She separated from her partner and returned to live with her own mother, where she could be closer to specialist healthcare providers. Ms. Brown was forced to remain with her stepfather. None of her other relatives could or would look after her.

Ms. Brown's stepfather began making sexual advances toward her. She ran away from home, only to be returned by the police. She did not tell anybody of the sexual advances. Ms. Brown's stepfather continued to attempt sexual abuse, and after she threatened to tell the police about his behavior her stepfather complained to human services that she was unmanageable and that he did not want to look after her. Ms. Brown was placed in secure care. She remembers returning home one day and being "forced" into a car by a social worker.

She was moved from secure care to live with a foster family, where she was physically and sexually abused. One night after she was sexually abused, Ms. Brown waited until her foster father was asleep; she then struck him with a golf club. Ms. Brown was convicted and spent 2 years in youth detention. On release she moved to live with her mother, who by this time had found her own home. She obtained employment in a local factory but gave most of her wages to her mother, upon her demand, which Ms. Brown resented. Her drug use increased and she started dealing drugs to support her dependence. Her mother chastised her for her criminal and "degenerate" ways and demanded she leave the house. Ms. Brown stole a car and drove to outback Australia, where she met a young woman she had previously been incarcerated with. After drinking heavily one night her acquaintance began taunting her for being a "dirty loser." She killed this acquaintance by clubbing her to death with a tree branch.

In prison, Ms. Brown reacted angrily and aggressively when staff directed her toward any activity; she became isolative, eventually refusing to leave her cell. Ms. Brown then assaulted staff and fellow prisoners who approached her in her cell. Eventually she was segregated.

OPB-Informed Formulation

Assessment for treatment eligibility and needs analysis in many correctional services typically involves the administration of a structured measure comprising static and dynamic risk factors. Such assessment would indicate the presence of various dynamic risk factors that would become the focus of treatment. In standardized programming where service provision assumes common causes and functions of violence for all offenders ("one size fits all" programming), Ms. Brown would be referred to a standardized multi-module violence intervention program. Some aspects of this type of treatment would clearly be relevant (e.g., substance use, attitudes regarding the legitimacy of violence, social problem-solving); however, an individual OPB-informed case formulation may indicate other important vulnerabilities and tendencies (e.g., tying together her history of neglect, rejection, and abuse with her perceived need to aggress against others who she perceives to be threatening and punitive). The case formulation would provide opportunity to establish a cohesive narrative that provides meaning for her criminal and related behavior so that treatment providers and possibly correctional staff can be specific in their interactions and responses to Ms. Brown's behavior can be tailored and coherent with the formulation.

Space does not permit the presentation of an elaborate case formulation, and the limited details provided (above) limit nuance. However, key features of a formulation focusing upon Ms. Brown's repeated assaults upon others would include acknowledgement of the proximal role of rejection and mistreatment, particularly by older females, and the likely influence of early and repeated mistreatment and neglect on the development of sensitivity to perceived rejection and potential mistreatment. Early abuse and trauma would likely have sensitized

Ms. Brown to the development of schema relevant to rejection; neglect would have contributed to poor coping, and early exposure to violence appears to have resulted in her learning violence-supportive beliefs (that violence is reasonable in some situations) and behaviors that make violence likely (the development of "self-defense" skills and facility with weapons). Ultimately, her history of mistreatment resulted in episodes of acute interpersonal discomfort and problems articulating her distress; her avoidance in prison likely helped her manage or reduce intense hostile cognition and angry feelings. In prison, Ms. Brown has learned to use violence to create distance from others and protect herself from impending harm. In the prison setting, her aggression can be seen as OPB in that it often followed rejection and intimidation.

Critical to the use of the OPB approach is the idea that interventions should draw upon and be responsive to behaviors that emerge within the prisoner's environment that are similar to (parallel) the client's offending. This is of course dependent upon a reference formulation, which focuses upon the development of the person's previous offending; subsequent behaviors are then compared to determine whether they are similar (parallel) to the reference formulation. The key task for treatment providers is to identify OPBs and incorporate these into treatment. Informed by case formulation, Ms. Brown's institutional behavior is interpreted in relation to the reference formulation. For example, consider the following behavior, which was observed whilst she was in custody:

Early during her incarceration Ms. Brown was chastised by her Custodial Case Manager (a middle aged woman) who believed Ms. Brown's work performance was poor and her cell was untidy. Later that day, Ms. Brown's cell-mate told her to shower because her body odor was intolerable. Ms. Brown then his assaulted her cell-mate with a kettle located in their cell.

Such events provide information that can confirm (or refute) earlier formulations (e.g., if the reference formulation was that Ms. Brown's violence was preceded (proximally) by feeling rejected then this in-custody assault may indicate this formulation was valid) and indicate current treatment needs (e.g., a sensitivity to taunting and rejection and a belief that attacking others in this context is acceptable). Accordingly, treatment may include learning to cope with taunting and rejection through the development of assertive behavior, self-control of mood, and engaging in alternative behaviors that induce positive mood. Treatment would also focus on Ms. Brown's beliefs that violence is acceptable. Within custody, treatment may include a review with Ms. Brown of in-custody incidents, drawing links to her previous offending behaviors. Collaboratively, therapists and Ms. Brown would identify possible future events where Ms. Brown's feelings of rejection may be activated; these would become opportunities for her to practice new behaviors that are specifically relevant to her treatment needs (e.g., assertive behavior, self-control of mood, and engaging in alternative behaviors that induce positive mood).

Within custodial settings, similar (paralleling) behaviors are sometimes readily observable; however, sometimes OPB does not arise or is difficult to see. In such cases, consideration needs to be given to the strength of the underlying propensities (e.g., in Ms. Brown's case, how strong her sensitivity to rejection is) that are relevant to offending and OPB, whether these are triggered within the institution (e.g., a child sex offender may not become aroused when there are few young people in the vicinity or, in Ms. Brown's case, assaults against peers may only occur after rejection by an older adult female—a "mother" figure), and whether environmental constraints (e.g., regular supervision) inhibit the manifestation of these propensities (Mann, Thornton, Wakama, Dyson, & Atkinson, 2010).

Returning to Ms. Brown's case, an early barrier to progress was her unwillingness to speak about emotional issues and her tendency to avoid challenging situations. One reason was her unwillingness to speak directly about her feelings, particularly when she was feeling vulnerable and rejected. She refused to speak with staff and other prisoners and she tended to isolate herself, particularly when she felt others were judging her negatively. In this context, she became frightened and angry and rehearsed violent scripts. This prototypical response had preceded earlier violent incidents. Since avoidance of talking about emotions was a primary barrier to progress, it was therefore decided to begin to address this issue first. In Ms. Brown's case, it was recommended that individual psychotherapy be offered prior to group-based violent offender treatment. Group treatment was not immediately appropriate. Individual psychological treatment began first with a focus on the therapeutic relationship, then moved on to mood and thought monitoring to sensitize Ms. Brown to her own thoughts and feelings, a necessary task before she attempted to share these with her peers and custodial staff. Ms. Brown was initially unwilling to acknowledge and discuss negative emotional experiences like sadness and anger—understandably, since anger had been met with violence when she was young. Whenever events occurred in the prison setting, for example, if she yelled at another person, then these behaviors became the focus of discussion. These behaviors were considered end points in an OPB sequence (commencing with behavior of other people who did something Ms. Brown perceived to be a sign of rejection, followed by fear, anger, and thoughts about the need to act violently). Given her tendency to not confide in others when she felt vulnerable and angry, it was important to monitor these events, encourage discussion, and facilitate rehearsal of alternative, more prosocial and adaptive ways of responding to these perceived provocations. Staff were encouraged to support and reinforce Ms. Brown when she tried to express herself and solve problems adaptively. When she was eventually capable of sitting with others and expressing herself, she also participated in offense-focused group treatment. These OPB and the positive changes she made in relation to expressing herself and interacting with others, along with her mood and thought diaries, were monitored to gauge progress. Although acts of violence may ordinarily be discussed within violent offender treatment programs, the OPB approach encourages the generation of a reference formulation based on the client's past offending behavior and then monitoring of OPB so relevant issues can be introduced to treatment and considered in progress reviews. The OPB approach should assist staff to understand the purpose of their interactions and how their behavior is relevant to each client's treatment goals beyond simple modeling of prosocial behavior. For other case studies using the OPB approach, see Gresswell and Dawson (2010).

Although OPB is relatively novel, the notion of working with manifestations of persistent pathology within therapeutic settings is not. Similar concepts are used within functional analytic psychotherapy (Kohlenberg & Tsai, 1994) and some forms of cognitive therapy (Birchwood, 1994). A common theme in these approaches is that more adaptive behavior may be shaped by the contingent responding of therapists to the clients' problems and improved behaviors when they occur in the therapeutic environment (in therapeutic groups, one-to-one sessions, and the treatment milieu). Critical to this type of work is the identification of these proxy behaviors. Skinner (1953) also used this notion when he proposed that the job of the therapist was to teach the client to discriminate behavior–environment relationships through the use of self-recording and to teach themselves, with the minimum help necessary from the therapist, to engage in self-control outside of the therapy sessions. The use of in-custody behavior to inform forensic treatment (Wong & Gordon, 2003) and release decision-making (Clark, Fisher, & McDougall, 1994) is also not new.

Formulation Summary

Case formulation is the identification and integration of information from individuals into a coherent whole that predicts effective and ineffective treatments. This approach has the potential to improve client outcomes beyond standardized, diagnostic-based treatments packages, at least in some circumstances. Forensic case formulation has special challenges, and research into the application of case formulation in forensic contexts is in its early stages. In future, research should focus on developing definitions of adequate case formulations, reliable and valid measures of case formulation, and explicit, competency-based approaches to training practitioners. One promising approach to validating formulations in forensic contexts focuses on Offense Paralleling Behavior.

Key Readings

Daffern, M., Jones, L., & Shine, J. (Eds.) (2010). *Offence Paralleling Behaviour: An individualized approach to offender assessment and treatment.* Chichester, UK: Wiley.
Sturmey, P. (2008). *Behavioral case formulation and intervention. A functional analytic approach.* Chichester, UK: Wiley-Blackwell.
Sturmey, P., & McMurran, M. (Eds.) (2011). *Forensic case formulation.* Chichester, UK: Wiley-Blackwell.

References

Andrews, D. A., & Bonta, J. (2006). *The psychology of criminal conduct* (4th ed.). Cincinnati, OH: Anderson.
Birchwood, M. (1994). Cognitive early intervention. In G. Haddock, & P. Slade (Eds.), *Cognitive behavioural approaches to schizophrenia.* London, UK: Routledge.
British Psychological Society (2011). *Good practice guidelines on the use of psychological formulation.* Leicester, UK: Author.
Butler, G. (1998). Clinical formulation. In A. S. Bellack, & M. Hersen (Eds.), *Comprehensive clinical psychology.* Oxford, UK: Pergamon.
Chadwick, P., Williams, C., & Mackenzie, J. (2003). Impact of case formulation in cognitive behaviour therapy for psychosis. *Behaviour Research and Therapy, 41,* 671–680.
Clark, D., Fisher, M. J., & McDougall, C. (1994). A new methodology for assessing the level of risk in incarcerated offenders. *British Journal of Criminology, 33,* 436–448.
Daffern, M., Jones, L., Howells, K., Shine, J., Mikton, C., & Tunbridge, V. C. (2007). Refining the definition of Offence Paralleling Behaviour. *Criminal Behaviour and Mental Health, 17,* 265–273.
Eells, T. D. (Ed.) (2007). *Handbook of psychotherapy case formulation* (2nd ed.). New York, NY: Guilford Press.
Flinn, L., Braham, L., & das Nair, R. (2015). How reliable are case formulations? A systematic literature review. *British Journal of Clinical Psychology, 54,* 266–290.
Ghaderi, A. (2006). Does individualization matter? A randomized trial of standardized (focused) versus individualized (broad) cognitive behaviour therapy for bulimia nervosa. *Behaviour Research and Therapy, 44,* 273–288.
Gresswell, D. M., & Dawson, D. L. (2010). Offence Paralleling Behaviour and multiple sequential functional analysis. In M. Daffern, L. Jones, & J. Shine (Eds.), *Offence Paralleling Behaviour: A case formulation approach to offender assessment and treatment* (pp. 121–135). Chichester, UK: Wiley.

Gresswell, D. M., & Kruppa, I. (1994). Special demands of assessment in a secure setting. In M. McMurran, & J. E. Hodge (Eds.), *The assessment of criminal behaviours of clients in secure settings* (pp. 35–52). London, UK: Jessica Kingsley.

Hart, S., & Logan, C. (2011). Formulation of violence risk using evidence-based assessments: The structured professional judgment approach. In M. McMurran, & P. Sturmey (Eds.), *Forensic case formulation* (pp. 83–106). Chichester, UK: Wiley.

Hart, S., Sturmey, P., Logan, C., & McMurran, M. (2011). Forensic case formulation. *International Journal of Forensic Mental Health*, 10, 118–126.

Johansson, R., Sjöberg, E., Sjögren, M., Johnsson, E., Carlbring, P., Andersson, T., … & Andersson, G. (2012). Tailored vs. standardized internet-based cognitive behavior therapy for depression and comorbid symptoms: A randomized controlled trial. *PLoS One*, 7(5), e36905.

Johnstone, L. (2014). Using formulation in teams. In L. Johnstone, & R. Dallos (Eds.), *Formulation in psychology and psychotherapy: Making sense of people's problems* (2nd ed.) (pp. 216–242). Hove, UK: Routledge.

Johnstone, L., & Dallos, R. (2006). *Formulation in psychology and psychotherapy: Making sense of people's problems*. Hove, UK: Routledge.

Kohlenberg, R. J., & Tsai, M. (1994). Functional analytic psychotherapy: A radical behavioral approach to treatment and integration. *Journal of Psychotherapy Integration*, 4, 175–201.

Mann, R., Thornton, D., Wakama, S., Dyson, M., & Atkinson, D. (2010). Applying the concept of Offence Paralleling Behaviour to sex offender assessment in secure settings. In M. Daffern, L. Jones, & J. Shine (Eds.), *Offence paralleling behaviour: A case formulation approach to offender assessment and treatment* (pp. 121–135). Chichester, UK: Wiley.

McMurran, M., & Bruford, S. (2016). Case formulation quality checklist: A revision based upon clinicians' views. *Journal of Forensic Practice*, 18, 31–38.

McMurran, M., Logan, C., & Hart, S. (2012). *Case formulation quality checklist*. University of Nottingham, UK. Unpublished checklist.

McMurran, M., Theodosi, E., Sweeney, A., & Sellen, J. (2008). What do prisoners want? Current concerns of adult male prisoners. *Psychology, Crime & Law*, 14, 267–274.

Minoudis, P., Craissati, J., Shaw, J., McMurran, M., Freestone, M., Chuan, S. J., & Leonard, A. (2013). An evaluation of case formulation training and consultation with probation officers. *Criminal Behaviour and Mental Health*, 23, 252–262.

Paulhus, D. L. (1991). Measurement and control of response bias. In J. P. Robinson, P. R. Shaver, & L. S. Wrightsman (Eds.), *Measures of personality and social psychological attitudes* (pp. 17–59). San Diego, CA: Academic Press.

Persons, J. B., & Tomkins, M. A. (2007). Cognitive-behavioral case formulation. In T. D. Eells (Ed.), *Handbook of psychotherapy case formulation* (2nd ed.) (pp. 290–316). New York, NY: Guilford Press.

Schulte, D., Kunzel, R., Pepping, G., & Schulte-Bahrenberg, T. (1992). Tailor-made versus standardized therapy for phobic patients. *Advances in Behaviour, Research and Therapy*, 14, 67–92.

Skinner, B. F. (1953). *Science and human behavior*. New York, NY: Macmillan.

Sturmey, P., & McMurran, M. (Eds.) (2011). *Forensic case formulation*. Chichester, UK: Wiley-Blackwell.

Ward, T. (2002). Good lives and the rehabilitation of offenders: Promises and problems. *Aggression and Violent Behaviour*, 7, 513–528.

Ward, T. (2013). Addressing the dual relationship problem in forensic and correctional practice. *Aggression and Violent Behavior*, 18, 92–100.

Weerasekera, P. (1996). *Multiperspective case formulation: A step towards treatment integration*. Malabar, FL: Krieger.

Wong, S., & Gordon, A. (2003). *Violence Risk Scale manual*. Saskatoon, Canada: Department of Psychology, University of Saskatchewan.

30

Psychological Assessment in the Correctional Setting

Andrew Day

James Cook University and University of Melbourne, Australia

Introduction

Although psychological assessment is clearly a core area of practice for all correctional psychologists, any attempt to describe a typical approach to assessment is by no means as straightforward as might be assumed. This may, in part, be because every psychologist is different and has developed his or her own style, preferences, and approach, but also because of the many different reasons why a psychologist might be asked to assess an offender[1] and the need to tailor the specific approach that is adopted to the question being asked. Hunsley and Mash (2008) identify seven quite distinctive purposes of psychological assessments in mental health settings: (a) diagnosis; (b) screening; (c) prognosis and other predictions; (d) case conceptualization/formulation; (e) treatment design and planning; (f) treatment monitoring; and (g) treatment evaluation. These different purposes also arise in the correctional setting where the psychologist might, for example, be asked to assess whether an offender is depressed and at risk of self-harm (diagnosis and screening), whether he or she will present a significant risk to others following release from custody (prognosis), how risk might be managed most effectively in the community (case conceptualization and treatment planning), or whether attending a rehabilitation program is being, or has been, effective in reducing risk (monitoring and evaluation).

Many of the chapters in the Handbook provide useful information about how the correctional assessment might proceed. For example, David Cooke discusses the assessment of risk of violence (Chapter 5), Caroline Logan and Jayne Taylor similarly discuss risk for suicide and self-harm (Chapter 7), Kevin Douglas (Chapter 26) and Daryl Kroner (Chapter 27) consider the assessment of risk of reoffending, and Peter Sturmey and colleagues consider different approaches to case formulation (Chapter 29). Michael Daffern and colleagues (Chapter 24) review different approaches to how change in treatment might best be assessed, and various other chapters consider assessment issues that are specific to working with particular groups, such as violent and sexual offenders (see Chapters 12–15). So, what might we reasonably conclude from all of these contributions? Well, we can start with the observation that for all of these authors, psychological assessment is the initial stage of a *systematic* process of collecting and integrating *relevant* information about an individual's presenting problems. We can also

The Wiley International Handbook of Correctional Psychology, First Edition. Edited by Devon L. L. Polaschek, Andrew Day, and Clive R. Hollin.

observe that, in the correctional setting, an individual's problems are often understood first and foremost in relation to the offenses that he or she has been convicted of (or charged with). The italicized words are deliberate and intended to emphasize that psychological assessment should be *systematic* in so far as all enquiries which are desirable and appropriate should be made before any opinion is presented. This is because the results of any assessment can have a profound impact on a person's life and it is therefore an ethical responsibility to provide evidence that supports any opinions or recommendations that are offered. Questions about the *relevance* of the data highlight the central role that professional judgment plays in psychological assessment. Simply reporting how an offender responded to a standardized interview proforma or scored on a psychometric test (or for that matter communicating a standardized computer-generated test report) does not constitute professional psychological practice. Rather it is the responsibility of the correctional psychologist to establish how the different types of information collected in the course of an assessment should inform the opinion. In this respect, the assessor's role is akin to solving a complex jigsaw puzzle—the process begins with determining the critical pieces of the puzzle which are then put together in a logical manner to present a more complete picture.

Self-Report

The jigsaw pieces will invariably include information from a variety of sources: client history; psychometric testing; relevant legal criteria; and any collateral information that is available, such as that which is sometimes available in sentencing remarks or police statements. However, the starting point in many assessments is the personal history. It is this that provides the context and allows the psychologist to develop an individualized understanding of the problem and interpret the significance of other sources of data. White, Day, Hackett, and Dalby (2015) suggest that potentially relevant information here will include "family" history (e.g., the individual's relationship with parents/siblings/grandparents), as well as a history of relationships, schooling, and employment. From a psychological perspective, it will nearly always be important to understand physical and mental health, childhood behavioral problems (and any exposure to separation, trauma, or abuse), and peer and family groupings, as well as the role of substance use. Significant life events might include: family trauma (the death of a spouse, child, parent, or friend); relationship changes (divorce, partner separation); family changes (marriage, pregnancy, birth); education (school achievement and failure, school changes, bullying); employment issues (workload excesses, conflict, dismissal, retirement); health and mental health issues (injury or illness, exposure to physical, sexual, or emotional abuse); exposure to trauma (e.g., personal injury, flood, fire disasters, victim of crime, motor vehicle accident); financial issues (e.g., loss of housing, foreclosure on a loan, financial debts relating to drugs, gambling, legal costs); substance usage (excessive alcohol and drugs issues); and legal issues (e.g., court trial, incarceration). The way in which the person being assessed has responded to different stressors is often of particular interest as this can help to inform judgments about how he or she might react in the future. Finally, a correctional psychology assessment would nearly always involve the collection of detailed information about the offending history (especially convictions and sentences), as well as previous attendance and the completion of any offending behavior or rehabilitation programs. This component of the assessment will often also consider the offender's motivation to not offend, his or her willingness to attend treatment and engage with supervision, and the level of support that is available from family, friends, and professionals to achieve this.

While the clinical interview is often the main source of information in an assessment, it is important to be aware of the limitations of the approach. For example, some offenders will have little insight into the causes of their behavior. Others may have only a limited capacity to accurately self-report, due to poor attention and concentration, or perhaps memory problems. Others may actively seek to create a certain impression—and offenders generally have been shown to display a tendency to minimize behavior linked to their crimes (see Henning & Holdford, 2006; Mills & Kroner, 2005, 2006; Tan & Grace, 2008). Nesca and Dalby (2013) go so far as to recommend that "all forensic interviews must begin with the assumption that the interviewee is motivated to lie or distort information and, as a result, cannot be completely trusted" (p. 40).

So how might the psychologist tell the truth from a lie, a misrepresentation, or an exaggeration of essentially truthful facts? One increasingly important approach is to administer psychometric tools that try to assess response bias. In their simplest form these measures determine an individual's tendency to seeing him or herself in a more positive light than reality would indicate (or, on occasion, presenting more negatively than is actually the case). Commonly used psychometric tests that incorporate response bias measures include the Personality Assessment Inventory (Negative Impression Management; Positive Impression Management scales and others; Morey, 2007), the Minnesota Multiphasic Personality Inventory, second edition, Lie, Infrequency, and Correction scales (see Otto, 2002; Pope, Butcher, & Seelen, 1993), and the Millon Clinical Multiaxial Inventory-III Disclosure, Desirability, Debasement, Validity, and Inconsistency scales (see McCann, 2002). Other structured assessment tools have been specifically developed to assess "malingering," which has been defined as the purposeful production of false or grossly exaggerated symptoms with the goal of receiving a reward or benefit. For example, the Structured Interview of Reported Symptoms (SIRS; SIRS-2; Rogers, Bagby, & Dickens, 1992) was originally developed to detect malingering of mental illness and is made up of eight primary scales (assessing rare symptoms, improbable and absurd symptoms, symptom combinations, blatant symptoms, subtle symptoms, symptom severity, symptom selectivity, and reported versus observed symptoms). In addition, various neuropsychological measures of malingering are available that identify responses that are well outside the expected normative performance range. Tests such as the Test of Memory Malingering (Tombaugh, 1996) involve memory tasks in which the subject is instructed that the task is relatively difficult, when in fact, normative data shows it to be relatively easy. Those without severe and obvious memory impairments who perform poorly on such tests are suspected of faking pathology. Of course, it should go without saying that the best way to ensure the veracity of self-report is to make every effort to corroborate interview data with other sources of information, such as behavioral observations from correctional staff members or family, police or court reports, and even school or employer records.

Psychometric Assessment

It is often useful to be able to compare information about how the person sees himself or herself relative to others, according to defined criteria. Psychological tests can be used to determine the offender's capacity to perform particular tasks, whether they be cognitive or perceptual, tasks of learning, behavior, or motor skills. In each of these situations, "performance" can be compared with statistical norms and thus scores indicate an individual's ability relative to comparative sample groups. This is essential, for example, when determining whether an offender has a particular disability, although some of the most useful psychometrics investigate constructs that are directly associated with criminal behavior. These include the Psychological Inventory of Criminal Thinking Style (see Walters, 2002; Chapter 40), which assesses a range of beliefs and attitudes relevant to offending.

Selecting the appropriate test to use in an assessment is an important skill that can mean the difference between an opinion that is empirically supported and one that is poorly justified. For example, providing an opinion about a person's intellectual functioning will always have more weight when it is based on the results of a standardized assessment than when it is based on clinical judgment alone. Evidence-based assessment protocols have been developed that can help with this task, identifying specific criteria to evaluate some of the assessment tools that are commonly used in practice. Hunsley and Mash (2007, 2008) have argued that psychologists should opt for instruments that are psychometrically strong. In addition to evidence of reliability, validity, and clinical utility, measures should also have appropriate norms for norm-referenced interpretation and/or replicated supporting evidence regarding the accuracy (i.e., sensitivity, specificity, predictive power, etc.) of cutoff scores used for criterion-referenced interpretation. This extends to individual characteristics, with a need for psychometric tests to be sensitive to an individual's age, gender, race, and ethnicity, as well as specific cultural factors. At the same time, and as Casey, Day, Ward, and Vess (2012) have pointed out, it is important to remember that not all psychometric properties apply to all assessment purposes—while group validity statistics (e.g., sensitivity, specificity, positive and negative predictive power) are relevant to diagnosis and prognosis, they are much less relevant when the assessment relates to treatment monitoring or evaluation aims. Thus, what is considered to be a "good" test will relate to the specific purpose for which it is being used.

The Assessment of Risk and Needs

One of the most important types of assessment in the correctional setting is the assessment of risk of reoffending (see Olver & Wong, Chapter 28). Judgments about the offender's probability of reoffending can be used to guide both management and rehabilitation options, as well as to classify risk in a way that directly informs both treatment and case management (Bonta & Wormith, 2014). Risk/need assessment tools generally serve both of these purposes by classifying offenders and identifying which should be referred for treatment (see Gordon, Kelty, & Julian, 2015). The use of structured, standardized, and formal measures of risk can also help to ensure that the wide range of factors that are known to be associated with future offending are properly considered in the assessment, as well as helping to eliminate the possible biases of individual practitioners.

Implicit in any attempt to quantify risk of reoffending is the belief that some individuals will be less at risk of offending than others and so risk assessments seek to identify the presence of those characteristics of the individual and their circumstances that impact systematically on the offending behavior: by either increasing or decreasing its likelihood. Professional approaches to risk assessment have typically relied on one of three main approaches, which are sometimes referred to as the "clinical," the "actuarial," or as "structured professional judgment," although multi-method approaches to assessment are increasingly common particularly when assessing higher-risk offenders. In brief, clinical predictions of risk involve professional judgments about an individual's likelihood of reoffending based upon the assessor's knowledge of that individual. The actuarial approach involves assessing risk on the basis of the presence of offense and offender characteristics that have an empirically established relationship with the criminal behavior. Structured professional judgment approaches rely on the application of a structured approach that considers these characteristics, but, as the name suggests, also draw on professional judgment to determine a final risk rating (see Chapter 26). This method places more emphasis on how to best manage the risk that an offender presents with (rather than classifying levels of risk), despite being described by Bonta and Wormith (2014) as representing a "step backwards."

Psychologists who use risk-needs tools must know, and be able to convey to those who use their reports, the accuracy of the assessment method they use—especially in terms of predictive validity (or predictive accuracy) in relation to risk classification. This typically refers to the proportion of correct classifications or outcome predictions that an instrument is capable of making—for a particular population for a particular outcome. This can be reported in relation to the rate of true positives (e.g., when an offender is predicted to reoffend and does so) and the rate of true negatives (e.g., when an offender is predicted not to reoffend and does not reoffend). It is particularly important to be clear about the empirical basis of classifications such as "high" risk, particularly when these terms are used in jurisdictions where validation data has not been published, or when risk tools are used with minority groups (see Chapter 18). For example, the predictive validity of one of the most widely used risk/needs tools, the Level of Service Inventory—Revised (LSI-R; Andrews & Bonta, 1995), is higher for general recidivism than it is for violent recidivism, with a systematic review and meta-regression analysis by Singh, Grann, and Fazel (2011) concluding that the predictive validity for the LSI-R was the lowest of the nine different tools commonly used to predict violent recidivism. It is, of course, quite possible that the more recently developed Level of Service/Case Management Inventory (LS/CMI; Andrews, Bonta, & Wormith, 2004) performs better; Olver, Stockdale, and Wormith's (2014) review reported a medium-to-large effect size for general offending for this tool and a small, but statistically significant, effect size for violent recidivism, but more validation studies are clearly needed. The key point here, though, is that the selection of any tool will always need to be informed by the data available relevant to the particular goal of the assessment.

Assessing the presence and intensity of dynamic risk factors (or those that are amenable to change) is of particular importance when the aim is to develop a treatment or management plan that aims to reduce the risk of reoffending (see Klepfisz, Daffern, & Day, 2016). Of the LSI-R (Andrews & Bonta, 1995; see Chapter 28), of those subscales assessing those risk/need factors that have received strong support for their ability to predict future offending (*Central Eight*), seven assess dynamic risk. Listed in order of influence, these are antisocial personality pattern, antisocial cognitions, antisocial associates, family/marital, school/work, leisure/recreation, and substance abuse (for a full discussion, see Andrews & Bonta, 2010; Andrews et al., 2011). These would all appear relevant to any assessment of change over time, although it is also important to note that dynamic risk factors may also be specific to the type of offending being considered (e.g., there are particular risk factors for family violence that do not apply to other types of offending; see Chapter 34). Dynamic risk factors are also difficult constructs to reliably assess. Girard and Wormith (2004), for example, have reported poor internal consistency for some LSI-R subscales (alpha = .32 for the family/marital section), and the evidence that change in these area is directly associated with reductions in subsequent offending is often lacking (see Klepfisz et al., 2016). In addition, dynamic risk factors often represent heterogeneous and overlapping symptoms that co-vary in numerous ways. This means that known offenders with the same risk profile can often present in markedly different ways (Ward & Fortune, 2016). This is clearly an area where our current assessment approaches need to improve.

Finally, it is always important to consider issues relevant to imminent risk in any psychological assessment, including the risk to others (see Chapter 5) or of self-harm or suicide (see Chapter 7). Here it is important to note that there is no evidence that asking about suicidal thoughts will prompt suicidal behavior in someone who had not previously considered the possibility of suicide. When there is reason to believe that an offender is significantly depressed, is experiencing suicidal thoughts, has made plans, and has access to the means to self-harm, urgent psychiatric consultation should be considered as communication about these concerns should occur with institutional staff. It may also be useful to refer to clinical practice guidelines developed for the general management of self-harm (National Institute for Clinical Excellence, 2004).

Case Formulation

At the beginning of this chapter it was suggested that the routine administration of tests or the completion of a standardized interview proforma does not, by itself, constitute professional psychological practice. To put this another way, the goal of an assessment should not simply be to complete an interview, list areas of need that are identified, and then present a laundry list of what might need to happen if these needs are to be addressed. A correctional psychologist who completes an assessment that identifies that an offender has needs in the areas of substance use and employment training, for example, should not simply recommend referral to a drug and alcohol and vocational training program. Rather, psychological assessment is inherently a decision-making task in which the assessor has to formulate and test hypotheses, often relying on incomplete or inconsistent data. She or he then has to arrive at a conceptualization of the case that can be used to meaningfully guide service delivery. And it is this that is the hallmark of professional practice.

The case formulation (see Chapter 29) should be used to inform an opinion about the most appropriate intervention and management strategies. This will typically involve an in-depth analysis of events and situations both before and after the offending, with the goal of developing an accurate and complete account of those behavioral and environmental factors that contribute to ongoing risk. The key point here is that risk will always be contingent upon situational or contextual factors, and it is through the case formulation that the psychologist considers these. Casey et al. (2012) have explained this in the following way: "even high-risk cases will not be at imminent risk at all times, but will vary in their likelihood of re-offending, depending on such factors as access to victims, current degree of alcohol or drug use, access to and compliance with treatment and supervision services, the nature of interpersonal relationships and support systems, and current mood states" (p. 93). Even those with a similar profile in terms of risk assessment scores will require different risk management plans. It is also worth noting here that effective offender management should never focus exclusively on individual characteristics and pathology, but also take account of the social context in which behavior takes place. Here the potentially transformative experiences of employment, social support, education, intimate relationships, changes in identity, and opportunities to meet human needs in ways that do not involve offending become directly relevant (see Laws & Ward, 2010).

In the correctional setting, the most widely used approach to case formulation has been derived from a method of psychological assessment known as functional analysis. Originally developed as part of the assessment process for entry into behavior modification programs, the aim of functional analysis is to establish the purpose of an action or behavior and to specify the variables that maintain that behavior, as well as to identify other more prosocial behaviors that satisfy a similar purpose (see Daffern, Jones, & Shine, 2010). This type of assessment thus focuses on the current presentation of the problem, which is then contextualized through exploration with the client of earlier formative events and experiences, and how these have shaped subsequent beliefs, emotions, and, importantly, behavior. There is, however, no consensus about what should be included in a good case formulation, even among psychologists, and a range of different approaches are used. Sturmey (2010) has nonetheless suggested that most case formulations share a number of common features. For example, they identify key aspects of a presenting problem, account for both the onset and the maintenance of the problem, and inform the development of a treatment plan that is tailored to meet the needs of the individual. Sturmey argues, however, that they differ in relation to which variables are considered to be important, the emphasis placed on historical antecedents to behavior, the extent to which the formulation identifies opportunities for intervention, and the role of the therapeutic relationship in the formulation process. While some see these differences as relatively unimportant, "others see them as fundamental and irreconcilable" (Sturmey, 2010, p. 27).

A Collaborative Approach to Assessment

For almost any assessment to produce a meaningful outcome, the psychologist will need to develop a relationship (or "alliance") with the person being assessed, as well as with other relevant stakeholders such as staff members (and, on occasion, family members or even victims of crime). There is a need for social, cultural, and gender sensitivity here, as when the method of assessment is inappropriate or insensitive, offenders may simply not participate fully or not gain any benefit. A number of general communication skills are required, including those that show regard and concern through the use of appropriate verbal and non-verbal behavior (e.g., sitting attentively and facilitating responses, expressing empathy and listening actively, allowing and encouraging the offender to express his or her feelings, and handling embarrassing or disturbing topics directly and sensitively).

Offenders understandably often report a desire to be well informed about how the correctional system will manage them and what it expects of them. The psychologist can be a key source of information about these matters, especially regarding the rehabilitation opportunities that may exist. It is important to deliver information in plain language English, explain difficult terms, and avoid the use of psychological jargon. It is helpful to assess the offender's level of understanding before providing additional information and this might involve actively encouraging the offender to ask questions, making use of simple diagrams and pictures, and/or repeating and summarizing important information or writing it down. Finally, when relevant, carefully explain the treatment options that are available (including no treatment) and ask how much detail he or she would like to know about each option. This should include a discussion of what might change as a result of treatment, as well as acknowledging uncertainty that any treatment will be successful.

Barber's (1991) discussion of case work with involuntary clients from a social work perspective is particularly useful here. He made the observation that:

> work with involuntary clients must begin with the recognition that the interaction between the worker and client is based on *conflict* rather than co-operation, that social work with involuntary clients is a *political*, not a therapeutic, process involving the socially sanctioned use of power. The political nature of this activity becomes obvious when one calls to mind what it means to be an involuntary client in the first place (p. 45).

Barber went on to note that the "ultimate beneficiary of the work done will be those who in some way suffered from the client's aberrant behavior in the first place" (p. 45). Thus, for Barber, the role of the worker is to negotiate a settlement between the client and society at large, and it is important the offender is aware of this from the very outset of any intervention.

Barber then proposed a model of what he terms "negotiated casework" that describes the nature of the relationship between the involuntary client and the service provider. Applying this to the psychological assessment of offenders would suggest that any assessment should begin by "clearing the air" and directing attention to the circumstances that led to the assessment. This should be followed by identifying legitimate offender interests and attending to any objections that the offender might have to participating. Then any non-negotiable aspects of the assessment can be discussed, including reporting requirements, as well as what is negotiable.

Conclusions

Psychological assessment in the correctional setting is clearly a complex task, with the choice of approach determined primarily by the nature of the referral question. Nonetheless, it is possible to identify a number of common elements in any assessment process, such as the use of the clinical interview, standardized or psychometrically valid tools, and the case formulation. In this chapter, it has been suggested that all three are typically required if a robust professional opinion is to be offered: the clinical interview can personalize the assessment and identify key psychological and environmental factors relevant to the problem under consideration; psychometric assessment can help the assessor interpret the type and severity of the issue by placing the offender's responses in the context of what is normal in other populations; and finally, the case formulation can draw different sources of information together to explain why the psychologist has arrived at a particular opinion and to present the rationale underlying any recommendations. There is nonetheless clearly much work to be done to improve the quality of the assessments that are routinely conducted in the correctional setting, including the development of more psychometrically robust and evidence-based assessment methods and consistent approaches to case formulation and reporting.

Note

1   The term *offender* is used in this chapter for simplicity, but it is important to note that some correctional clients will not have been found guilty of any offenses or are awaiting trial.

Key Readings

Ackerman, M. J. (2010). *Essentials of forensic psychological assessment.* New York, NY: Wiley.

Casey, S., Day, A., Ward, T., & Vess, J. (2012). *Foundations of offender rehabilitation.* Oxford, UK: Routledge.

Craig, L. A., Dixon, L., & Gannon, T. A. (Eds.) *What works in offender rehabilitation: An evidence-based approach to assessment and treatment.* New York, NY: Wiley-Blackwell.

References

Andrews, D. A., & Bonta, J. (1995). *The Level of Service Inventory—Revised*. Toronto, Canada: Multi-Health Systems.

Andrews, D. A., & Bonta, J. (2010). *The psychology of criminal conduct* (5th ed.). New Providence, NJ: Anderson.

Andrews, D. A., Bonta, J., & Wormith, J. S. (2004). *The Level of Service/Case Management Inventory (LS/CMI): User's manual*. Toronto, Canada: Multi-Health Systems.

Andrews, D. A., Guzzo, L., Raynor, P., Rowe, R. C., Rettinger, L. J., Brews, A., & Wormith, J. S. (2011). Are the major risk/need factors predictive of both female and male reoffending? A test with the eight domains of the Level of Service/Case Management Inventory. *International Journal of Offender Therapy and Comparative Criminology*, 56, 113–133.

Barber, J. G. (1991). *Beyond casework*. Basingstoke, UK: MacMillan.

Bonta, J., & Wormith, J. S. (2014). Applying the Risk-Need-Responsivity principles to offender assessment. In L. A. Craig, L. Dixon, & T. A. Gannon (Eds.), *What works in offender rehabilitation: An evidence-based approach to assessment and treatment* (pp. 72–93). New York, NY: Wiley-Blackwell.

Casey, S., Day, A., Ward, T., & Vess, J. (2012). *Foundations of offender rehabilitation*. Oxford, UK: Routledge.

Daffern, M., Jones, L., & Shine, J. (Eds.) (2010). *Offence Paralleling Behaviour: A case formulation approach to offender assessment and intervention*. Chichester, UK: Wiley.

Girard, L., & Wormith, J. S. (2004). The predictive validity of the Level of Service Inventory—Ontario Revision on general and violent recidivism among various offender groups. *Criminal Justice and Behavior*, 31, 150–181.

Gordon, H., Kelty, S. F., & Julian, R. (2015). Psychometric evaluation of the Level of Service/Case Management Inventory among Australian offenders completing community-based sentences. *Criminal Justice and Behavior*, 42, 1089–1109.

Henning, K., & Holdford, R. (2006). Minimization, denial, and victim blaming by batterers: How much does the truth matter? *Criminal Justice and Behavior*, 33, 110–130.

Hunsley, J., & Mash, E. J. (2007). Evidence-based assessment. *Annual Review of Clinical Psychology*, 3, 57–79.

Hunsley, J., & Mash, E. J. (2008). Developing criteria for evidence-based assessment: An introduction to assessments that work. In J. Hunsley, & E. J. Mash (Eds.), *A guide to assessments that work* (pp. 3–14). New York, NY: Oxford University Press.

Klepfisz, G., Daffern, M., & Day, A. (2016). Understanding dynamic risk factors for violence. *Psychology, Crime & Law*, 22, 124–137.

Laws, D. R., & Ward, T. (2010). *Desistance from sex offending: Alternatives to throwing away the keys*. New York, NY: Guilford Press.

McCann, J. T. (2002). Guidelines for forensic application of the MCMI-III. *Journal of Forensic Psychology Practice*, 2, 55–69.

Mills, J. F., & Kroner, D. G. (2005). An investigation into the relationship between socially desirable responding and offender self-report. *Psychological Services*, 2, 70–80.

Mills, J. F., & Kroner, D. G. (2006). Impression management and self-report among violent offenders. *Journal of Interpersonal Violence*, 21, 178–192.

Morey, L. C. (2007). *Personality Assessment Inventory manual*. Odessa, FL: Psychological Assessment Resources.

National Institute for Clinical Excellence (2004). *Self-harm: The short-term physical and psychological management and secondary prevention of self-harm in primary and secondary care*. NICE Clinical Guidelines, No. 16. Leicester, UK: British Psychological Society.

Nesca, M., & Dalby, J. T. (2013). *Forensic interviewing in criminal court matters*. Springfield, IL: C.C. Thomas.

Olver, M. E., Stockdale, K. C., & Wormith, J. S. (2014). Thirty years of research on the level of service scales: A meta-analytic examination of predictive accuracy and sources of variability. *Psychological Assessment*, 26, 156–176.

Otto, R. K. (2002). Use of the MMPI-2 in forensic settings. *Journal of Forensic Psychology Practice*, 2, 71–91.

Pope, K., Butcher, J. N., & Seelen, J. (1993). *The MMPI, MMPI-2 & MMPI-A in court*. Washington, DC: American Psychological Association.

Rogers, R., Bagby, R. M., & Dickens, S. E. (1992). *Structured Interview of Reported Symptoms (SIRS) professional manual*. Odessa, FL: Psychological Assessment Resources.

Singh, J. P., Grann, M., & Fazel, S. (2011). A comparative study of violence risk assessment tools: A systematic review and meta-regression analysis of 68 studies involving 25,980 participants. *Clinical Psychology Review*, 31, 499–513.

Sturmey, P. (2010). Case formulation in forensic psychology. In M. Daffern, L. Jones, & J. Shine (Eds.), *Offence Paralleling Behaviour: A case formulation approach to offender assessment and intervention* (pp. 25–52). Chichester, UK: Wiley.

Tan, L., & Grace, R. C. (2008). Social desirability and sexual offenders: A review. *Sexual Abuse: A Journal of Research and Treatment*, 20, 61–87.

Tombaugh, T. N. (1996). *Test of Memory Malingering (TOMM)*. New York, NY: Multi-Health Systems.

Walters, G. D. (2002). The Psychological Inventory of Criminal Thinking Styles (PICTS): A review and meta-analysis. *Assessment*, 9, 278–291.

Ward, T., & Fortune, C.-A. (2016). From dynamic risk factors to causal processes: A methodological framework. *Psychology, Crime & Law*, 22, 190–202.

White, J., Day, A., Hackett, L., & Dalby, J. T. (2015). *Writing reports for court: An international guide for psychologists who work in the criminal jurisdiction*. Melbourne, Australia: Australian Academic Press.

Part VI
Treatment: Specific Populations and Problems

31

Interventions to Reduce Recidivism in Adult Violent Offenders

Devon L. L. Polaschek
University of Waikato (Te Whare Wānanga o Waikato), New Zealand

In correctional populations, violence is disproportionately attributable to a relatively small group of mainly men who are versatile criminals. This cohort, called "early-onset" or "life-course persistent" offenders (Hodgins, 2007), can be distinguished from their peers from an early age by a wide range of family factors (e.g., poor parenting, abuse, neglect, poverty) and difficult temperament, including subtle neuropsychological deficits. The official onset of violent offending is usually a little later than for other crime, and violent crime is typically only a small proportion of the overall offending pattern. As they mature, cohort members begin to be known to a wide range of government services, not only as a result of antisocial behavior, but also because of disadvantage and inadequate care and oversight. Alongside their repeated contact with law enforcement, they also have a number of other difficulties and health issues compared to less criminal members of the community. In adulthood, they are slower to desist from crime, and are delayed in other developmental adult milestones, such as maintaining stable relationships, employment, and accommodation (e.g., Farrington et al., 2006; Odgers, 2009; Reising, Ttofi, Farrington, & Piquero, in press).

It is something of a misnomer to talk of actual violence—rather than convictions for violent crime—as having a later onset. In reality, violent behavior is most prevalent in toddlers, but most grow up to be primarily prosocial (Seguin, Sylvers, & Lilienfeld, 2007). So, it is probably more accurate to assume that early-onset offenders are those who did not reduce their use of childhood violence, and were not arrested until after other types of offending had brought them to the attention of law enforcement.

The case for violence being a problem that is distinct from other antisocial conduct is weak. For example, there is little evidence that there are distinct neuropsychological drivers of violence (Seguin et al., 2007). Genetics research has found no compelling evidence of violence specificity (Vassos, Collier, & Fazel, 2014). And there is little in the way of evidence of effective pharmacological approaches for persistent violence that would suggest the presence of distinct neurobiological mechanisms (Citrome & Volavka, 2014). There is also little evidence that repetitive violence is associated with unique psychological characteristics, based on the presence or intensity of dynamic or static risk factors. Risk assessment tools designed to predict the likelihood of further violence are at least as accurate in predicting who will commit a

The Wiley International Handbook of Correctional Psychology, First Edition. Edited by Devon L. L. Polaschek, Andrew Day, and Clive R. Hollin.
© 2019 John Wiley & Sons Ltd. Published 2019 by John Wiley & Sons Ltd.

non-violent offense (e.g., Violence Risk Scale [VRS] with correctional clients; Wong & Gordon, 2006), and this observation appears to be true even with measures designed and used primarily with psychiatric patients (see Brookstein, Daffern, & Ogloff, 2016; Shepherd, Campbell, & Ogloff, 2017). Taken together, these findings suggest that interventions to reduce violence should not focus only on those risk factors that seem intuitively relevant to violence. Even though we may not fully understand mechanisms that connect violence to less obvious risk factors such as criminal peers, or attitudes to rule violation, their ability to predict both violence and antisocial behavior more generally suggests that interventions will have more impact if they focus broadly. With this in mind, this chapter is mainly about the treatment of a violence-prone segment of the correctional population, rather than more broadly about the treatment of violence itself.

A Brief 50-Year History of Violent Offender Treatment

Psychologically based correctional treatment for violent offenders in the early part of the behavioral and cognitive behavioral eras was heavily influenced by developing models of clinical treatment for a variety of disorders (e.g., depression, anxiety disorders). Consequently, when it came to violent behavior, the focus was on managing problematic anger. Applications of Novaco and colleagues' anger management approach (Novaco, 1979), which was itself an adaptation of Meichenbaum's stress inoculation work (Meichenbaum, 1975), became widespread during the late 1980s and 1990s, but few were evaluated for effectiveness in reducing risk for violence, and there was little evidence that they worked in this regard (Polaschek & Collie, 2004).[1] Subsequent evaluations suggested that most were too brief to be effective, based on the number of hours of provision we now associate with effective programs (Heseltine, Howells, & Day, 2010). These programs were also not designed to address the high levels of trait anger that are characteristic of violent offenders. High trait anger is theorized to readily activate aggressive behavioral scripts (Gilbert, Daffern, Talevski, & Ogloff, 2013) which are then difficult to regulate through effortful self-control: the main approach taught in brief anger management programs. Later research also suggested that a focus on anger as a problematic emotion with respect to crime and violence was too narrow. Rather, it appears that it is negative emotionality more generally that is associated with antisocial and violent behavior (Patrick & Zempolich, 1997; Roberton, Daffern, & Bucks, 2015). In short, high-risk violent offenders likely needed more specialized and substantial assistance than these early brief anger management programs could provide.

Around the same time, the meta-analytic literature on intervention-relevant correlates of reduced recidivism was also indicating that a more complete or intensive approach was needed. A crucial development here was in more effective risk assessment instruments and the development of scales that incorporated dynamic risk factors (Craig, Beech, & Cortoni, 2013). These made it theoretically possible to select more risk-homogeneous groups of offenders and to link risk assessment to treatment change. Over time, more intensive programs with a greater number of components and more diverse learning methods began to emerge.

Application in hindsight of the guidance of the Risk-Need-Responsivity (RNR) model to the treatment of violent offenders indicates that programs should be multimodal, focus on a preponderance of dynamic risk factors, put resources mainly into higher risk cases, use change-inducing staff practices, and so on (Bonta & Andrews, 2017). At best, we can speculate that using low-intensity interventions targeting a small range of needs with higher-risk cases was ineffective: at worst, it may even have had an iatrogenic effect (Gondolf & Russell, 1986). We turn next to the empirical evidence on the effectiveness of these early efforts, and of later, more RNR-consistent, programs.

What Works in the Treatment of Violent Offenders?

Recidivism outcome evaluations remain rare for treatment of adult violent offenders (Polaschek & Collie, 2004). Jolliffe and Farrington's (2007) meta-analysis of program evaluations, for example, identified only 11 relevant studies. Two were rated as low in quality and one was a randomized design; the remainder were quasi-experimental designs. They reported an overall absolute reduction of 8–11% in reconviction of any type, and 7–8% in violent recidivism. Although the level of detail available in the studies was limited, they coded the following moderators: anger control ($n=8$), cognitive behavioral skills training ($n=9$), moral training ($n=4$), life skills training (e.g., basic education, literacy; $n=6$), use of role-playing to teach skills ($n=7$), empathy training ($n=4$), planning for relapse ($n=5$), and homework (e.g., skills practice outside of the session; $n=4$). Effects on reconviction were higher for programs that targeted cognitive and emotional regulation skills, and those that included role-plays, relapse prevention, and homework. Electronic monitoring and a brief alcohol intervention were not associated with improvements in recidivism, and the inclusion of empathy training and of educational components also was associated with a significantly smaller effect on recidivism. Evaluations using treatment completers only, rather than intention-to-treat analyses (see Chapter 25), yielded higher effect sizes overall. The tentative conclusions were that programs *could* be effective but that the paucity of research limited investigation.

Around the same time, McGuire (2008) conducted a detailed qualitative review of meta-analyses of intervention effects that were relevant to the question of whether aggressive or violent behavior can be treated effectively. McGuire's comprehensive list of meta-analyses included those for youth offenders, partner violence, sexual offending, and psychopathy. He concluded that at least some interventions can reduce violent behavior.

A more recent review of cognitive behavioral therapy (CBT)-based interventions for adult male violent offenders included 14 studies with comparison groups and recidivism data, both general and violence-related (Henwood, Chou, & Browne, 2015). Of the 14, most were prison-based, five were described as typical anger management approaches, while five others that were focused more intensively on violence reduction in higher-risk offenders were also described as "anger management."[2] They found a relative reduction of 23% in the proportion reconvicted for any offense, but there was significant heterogeneity across studies. Only six studies reported violent reconviction rates, and they showed a 28% relative risk reduction for men in treatment samples. The overall effect size was smaller for higher-risk offenders in intensive correctional programs than for offenders completing less intensive anger-focused programs. However, the latter tended not to report the risk levels of attendees, and recidivism base rates for those in the less intensive program comparison groups were generally at the lower end, suggesting that a lower-risk cohort was being treated. The authors concluded that, in contrast to the Jolliffe and Farrington meta-analysis, their results show anger management to be more effective than more intensive multimodal correctional programs They did acknowledge, however, that this conclusion was based largely on a single moderate-intensity program with an effect size that included in the treatment sample only those who had completed treatment (Dowden, Blanchette, & Serin, 1999). The failure to take into account non-completers in this study may mean the positive treatment result was due to selective attrition rather than the treatment itself (i.e., non-completers' performances were so poor that the treatment effect may be based solely on better pre-existing prognostic characteristics of those who completed).

Taken together, the two meta-analyses suggest that recidivism in violent offenders and violent recidivism in offenders may be reduced in association with participation in an intervention that is based on cognitive and behavioral components directed at changing attributes that are likely to be linked to offending. But we are some distance away from understanding why some programs appear to be effective while others are not.

Since these analyses were conducted, several additional relevant studies have been published. A large evaluation of the Enhanced Thinking Skills program (ETS; Travers, Mann, & Hollin, 2014) compared UK male prisoners' estimated risk of reconviction—based on a tool built from static factors—with their actual outcomes over 2 years. ETS is a cognitive behavioral program delivered in groups over 20 two-hour session, and includes training in problem-solving, empathy and perspective-taking, impulse control, and reasoning critically. It is intended for medium- to high-risk offenders with assessed thinking deficits in these areas. The sample included over 6,000 offenders with an index violent offense and another 3,000 who were imprisoned for robbery. The design was within-group rather than a comparison with untreated offenders; treated participants were compared to their estimated reconviction rate based on an adequately validated risk assessment scale. As I noted above, reconviction rates were examined by risk band, and showed absolute differences of around 10% in all bands compared to estimated outcomes, except in the "very high" and "very low" bands. Those with violent offenses tended to show improvements in subsequent offending compared to predictions, but robbery offenders, if anything, did more poorly on recidivism than expected after ETS treatment completion (Travers et al., 2014).

A quasi-experimental study in New Zealand compared men who had completed the intensive prison-based program for high-risk and violent offenders with men who were eligible for, but not referred to, the program. Based on four recidivism indices in the first 12 months after release, effect sizes (phi) between .15 and .24 were reported (Polaschek, Yesberg, Bell, Casey, & Dickson, 2016). The authors argued that they had protected somewhat against a selection bias resulting from the omission of non-completers in this study: the completers were well matched on a variety of indices to the less-treated comparison sample, but unobserved biases not due to treatment may still have accounted for these results. An earlier quasi-experimental evaluation of the first of these programs, but based on a design that included non-completers and matched untreated comparisons, found smaller but similar trends in recidivism reduction (Polaschek, 2011).

A contrasting result comes from a quasi-experimental evaluation of a Zurich-based male offender sample that was mandated to treatment by the sentencing court and provided with individualized formulation-based interventions based on identification of the "underlying psychological mechanism that caused the offence" (p. 86) and on the "RNR principle" (Seewald et al., 2018, p. 86). Treatment was provided in individual or group format depending on this formulation, by certified therapists who were well trained and supervised, and the interventions themselves were routinely audited for quality. The follow-up period was almost 8 years. A comparison group of offenders had similar index offenses and at least 10 months of sentence, but did not receive treatment. This group had significantly higher scores on the Psychopathy Checklist—Revised (PCL-R) and the Violence Risk Appraisal Guide (VRAG), suggesting they may have been at higher risk of criminal and violent recidivism than the treatment group, and were significantly younger at follow-up, all factors that could contribute to better outcomes for the treatment group in the absence of a treatment effect. During follow-up, 11.7% of the treatment group and 15.8% of the comparison group were charged with a serious violent or sexual offense, a low base rate for such a long period. Consequently, even without controlling for the pre-existing differences in the groups, there was no significant difference in regard to the odds of recidivating. The methodology of the study was statistically rigorous. Another factor that may have influenced the failure to detect a sample difference may be the relatively constructive and positive nature of the baseline correctional system in which the comparison group was embedded, one that emphasizes case management and rehabilitation, psychiatric care, and interventions based on level of risk (Seewald et al., 2018).

As useful as program evaluations can be in justifying ongoing funding and extended provision of services, they are of little additional use. Currently there is a trend toward defining randomized controlled trials (RCTs), for example, as if they were the sine qua non of operationally relevant research. But RCTs are premised on a clear understanding of what it is about the trial intervention that is responsible for its effectiveness (i.e., the mechanisms). Without this knowledge, a favorable result from an RCT does not necessarily lead to effectiveness in subsequent replications in new settings by different treatment providers to varying treatment recipients, because, simply put, we don't know which variations matter. What if the setting was an unmeasured contributor to the effectiveness of the original RCT, for instance?

Mechanisms Underlying Effective Treatment

Identifying the mechanisms by which correctional treatment affects behavior is very difficult, given the complexity of factors that are likely to be associated with effects. Researchers are limited in their ability to exert the level of design control needed to allow strong causal statements to be made. Often the best we can do is to undertake longitudinal correlational studies (e.g., based on measures taken before or during a program, and then at some interval after) and then infer the underlying mechanisms. Even then, as Ward and colleagues remind us, the variables that we think are involved may still be acting as proxy for the *real* causal mechanisms (Ward & Beech, 2015).

A range of plausible risk factors for violent offending have been included in these studies: procriminal and antisocial attitudes and beliefs, aggression- and violence-supportive beliefs, problem-solving, components of anger expression and control, provocation, hostility, impulsivity, and empathy. Notably, there is more often an emphasis on aspects of cognition and affect—especially anger—and a number of other factors that are likely to be associated with violence do not usually feature in these studies: criminal peers, alcohol or drug use, or history of aggressive or violent behavior in the institution or community. Only rarely have personality traits been measured pre- and post-treatment (e.g., Woessner & Schwedler, 2014). Other potentially relevant desistance-related factors, such as positive social support and stable accommodation, have largely been overlooked, perhaps because they are seen as being outside the realm of traditional psychological treatment foci.

Nevertheless, according to dynamic risk factor theory, and the RNR model in particular, change in dynamic risk factors during treatment should be a major source of change in recidivism risk. Therefore, a logical first step to identifying mechanisms is to measure in-treatment change (see Chapter 24) on some of the variables listed above, and investigate whether it is related to recidivism.

Some of the research on these putative risk factors has relied on self-report measures from offenders. Interestingly, self-report measures have been shown to have good predictive validity for recidivism in a number of studies with offenders (Kroner & Loza, 2001; Loza, Loza-Fanous, & Heseltine, 2007; Mills, Loza, & Kroner, 2003), especially if the measures are relevant to constructs related to recidivism (Walters, 2006). These results suggest simplistic notions about the invalidity of offender self-report based on a desire to lie, deceive, or manipulate are not necessarily well founded. But self-report measures of *change* in the treatment of violent offenders have not yet turned out to be as informative.

Offender self-rated positive change has been reported, based on measures taken before and after treatment: with youth (e.g., Guerra & Slaby, 1990) and with adult violent offenders (Hughes, 1993; Klepfisz, O'Brien, & Daffern, 2014; Polaschek, 2009; Polaschek, Bell, Calvert, & Takarangi, 2010; Tew, Dixon, Harkins, & Bennett, 2012; Woessner & Schwedler, 2014). But although a small number of studies have reported both in-treatment change *and* recidivism outcomes for violence, there is almost no research analyzing whether the two are linked, a required step in order to establish claims about mechanisms (Serin, Lloyd, Helmus, Derkzen, & Luong, 2013).

Research supporting the role of change in dynamic risk factors in reducing violence risk, measured using methods other than self-report, is even more limited. In the United Kingdom, a specific violence prediction scale (the OASys Violence Predictor [OVP]) has been developed for use with the Offender Assessment System (OASys), which is the dominant risk/needs assessment tool for offender management (Howard & Dixon, 2012). The OVP includes the dynamic risk factors of failing to recognize impact of offending on victim/society/community, accommodation, employability, alcohol misuse, current psychiatric treatment, temper control, and antisocial attitudes, which together constitute 40 points of the 100-point scale, the remainder being static violence-risk items. Howard and Dixon (2013) conducted a multiple-wave study of the OVP items collected in routine operational use, often by trained probation officers and sometimes by less trained staff (i.e., this was not a treatment study, and there were multiple repeated measures of the items available for analysis). On a very large sample of UK offenders, most OVP items measured more recently in time were demonstrated to add incrementally to the prediction of violent recidivism over those same factors measured earlier in time. Notably, recognition of the impact of offending was changeable, but the changes were not related to recidivism, and psychiatric treatment, while predictive, was rare and changed infrequently. Thus, five of the items met the standard of a dynamic risk factor for violence.

Lewis, Olver, and Wong (2013) demonstrated that VRS (Wong & Gordon, 1998–2003, 2006) change scores could predict violent recidivism when pre-treatment risk was controlled for in a sample of Canadian federal offenders taking part in this type of treatment (see also Olver, Lewis, & Wong, 2013; Wong, Gordon, Gu, Lewis, & Olver, 2012; but also, Klepfisz et al., 2014; and Chapter 24). Studies like these may be more suited to investigating whether change on risk factors is associated with recidivism because they tend to consider items in bundles rather than individually, which may increase the range of change scores and so the ability to detect practically meaningful changes in risk compared to studies investigating change in a single factor. Relatedly, it is conceptually unlikely that changes in a single construct (e.g., trait anger) will materially affect risk in higher-risk offenders, who by definition are likely to have a number of dynamic risk factors. This research suggests that the overall mechanism of change in dynamic risk factors has some support. But again, because factors are aggregated, these scales do not specifically indicate whether any particular risk factor is related to change in risk, nor do they answer the more challenging question of the potentially complex interactions that may exist between factors in the change process.

Indirect Mechanisms of Change

Along with dynamic risk factor change, a number of factors may be important in supporting change less directly. Further research on many of these is needed. An example is the overall climate of the unit or setting in which the intervention is conducted (Day & Doyle, 2010). It is intuitively appealing that change-supportive environments enhance the amount of change made, and may enhance maintenance, but the topic is rarely studied. Prison climate factors were positively correlated with the amount of change on dynamic risk in one study, but risk change did not predict outcomes, and the authors noted that since both were measured using offender self-report, correlations could be simply a function of a common response bias (Woessner & Schwedler, 2014).

Another factor that may be indirectly related to outcome is treatment group composition. A single study showed that groups composed of higher-risk participants or a greater range of participant risk were associated with attenuated individual treatment outcomes, through an interaction with individual participants' change capacity, a concept similar to treatment readiness and responsivity, and defined as "a desire to learn, attend to, and engage with the program content" (Lloyd, Hanby, & Serin, 2014, p. 299). The magnitude of the variance accounted for by group composition—up to 40% in this study—suggests that it warrants further examination. Also uninvestigated is whether individual treatment is effective versus group treatment or some combination.

The therapeutic alliance and therapist factors are also expected to be important determinants of effective treatment, through indirect effects on offenders' engagement with change (i.e., alliance influences on outcomes are mediated by engagement). There has been little research on therapeutic alliance with violent offenders other than with partner violence (Taft & Murphy, 2007). Further research is needed to establish whether it is the alliance per se or change in how it develops over time that is most relevant in determining program gains for general violent offenders (Polaschek & Ross, 2010).

Intervention Design

Although generally useful, guidelines about the trends associated with improved outcomes still leave program designers with plenty of decisions to make about the overall principles and components of treatment design for violent offenders. The review above shows that many factors that are important for program design have limited evidence either way, a situation that is similar to the sex offender field (Biere & Mann, 2017). Nevertheless, interventions to reduce violence continue to be needed, developed, and offered (King, 2012; Klepfisz et al., 2014; Polaschek & Kilgour, 2013; Ware, Cieplucha, & Matsuo, 2011; Wong & Gordon, 2013). All of these programs are designed to comply with the RNR model (Bonta & Andrews, 2017). They use cognitive and behavioral methods to support change directed toward multiple criminogenic needs. Group treatment is the most common format; some adjunct individual sessions may be provided. In most, therapy staff are highly trained and qualified, and custody staff primarily retain a security role, although they may also model positive interactions with offenders and gather behavioral observations on behalf of therapy staff. Treatment is relatively time-occupying (10–30 hours per week, over months rather than years), and typically a pair of program staff work with a single group of offenders throughout the course of treatment.

Conceptually, intensive violent offender treatments can be organized into three phases. During the first phase, the focus is on motivation and engagement: socializing offenders to the treatment process. Motivational interviewing techniques are used to ready offenders for further treatment by helping them identify treatment needs that are meaningful to them, and the personal benefits of participation. Typically, this phase enhances the alliance and group cohesion, and familiarizes the participants with needed skills for an effective group culture (e.g., listening and feedback skills, managing social anxiety and mistrust, talking in front of group). The second phase more explicitly focuses on prosocial skill acquisition. The skills taught enhance self-efficacy for desistance (e.g., prosocial thinking, problem-solving, managing volatile affect and substance use, prosocial relationships, communication, and conflict resolution) while simultaneously providing rewarding alternatives to criminogenic skills and solutions. Finally, the third phase consolidates new skills, and plans are made for life after treatment (e.g., moving to another unit, work release, parole; Polaschek & Kilgour, 2013; Wong & Gordon, 2013).

Future Directions

When participants engage well with these programs—and they have the capacity to engage with offenders with low readiness for change, high capacity for reoffending, and an array of changeable risk factors that are well entrenched—9–12 months of program will lead to the early stages of behavioral change (Perkins, Farr, Romero, Kirkpatrick, & Ebrahimjee, 2015; Polaschek et al., 2016; Wong et al., 2012). But some risk factors will remain untouched, and new behavior is still often effortful and inconsistent, as offenders enter new, often more challenging environments.

Other forms of assistance and intervention may help both with increasing the durability of change and with creating environments in which there are fewer "tests" or challenges to new behavior. The overall effect size of treatment interventions may thus be boosted by adding other services after treatment, in custody, and later in the community. Consequently, program managers and service providers have looked for ways to augment treatment effects with aftercare: preparation for release and support after release.

In fact, reentry support alone can be effective. For example, in the Boston Reentry Initiative (BRI; Braga, Piehl, & Hureau, 2009), propensity-matched BRI-released prisoners were compared with an earlier treatment-as-usual sample of equally high-risk, violent offenders. BRI prisoners had individual case management and release plans, mentors, and comprehensive service planning and engagement prior to and following release. Braga et al. (2009) found significant reductions in any new arrests and in violent rearrests. Similarly, the Minnesota Comprehensive Reentry Plan (MCORP) pilot provided continuity of case management for offenders from prison through reentry, leading to enhanced access to employment, accommodation, social support, and other services. Randomly assigned MCORP releases showed 20–25% reductions in rates of recidivism on four of five measures compared to business-as-usual releases (Duwe, 2014).

Even simple release plans may make a difference. We rated the quality of release plans on such factors as employment, accommodation, prosocial support, and plans for avoiding antisocial associates and other risks in the release environment. Higher-quality plans at the point of release were associated with lower likelihood of reimprisonment (but not reconviction) even when controlling for static and dynamic risk scores (including the Psychopathy Checklist: Screening Version [PCL:SV] and the VRS; Dickson, Polaschek, & Casey, 2013).

Recent evidence also shows that how probation officers perform their roles can contribute to reductions in recidivism (Bonta, Rugge, Scott, Bourgon, & Yessine, 2008), over and above criminal risk levels (Polaschek, 2016), and even with offenders with mental disorders (Skeem, Eno Louden, Polaschek, & Camp, 2007). A small-sample UK investigation of dangerous and severe personality disorder (DSPD) offenders undergoing outpatient treatment found that the addition of supported housing reduced reconviction (Bruce, Crowley, Jeffcote, & Coulston, 2014). These pointers to elements and services that may help later on suggest that systematically combining treatment with follow-on interventions such as individual case management, release planning, and post-release support may: (a) offer the easiest way to enhance treatment effects by supporting generalization, and (b) increase confidence in the highest-risk offenders' anticipated post-release safety levels to the point where release can be considered at all (Maden, Williams, Wong, & Leis, 2004).

Our research has also demonstrated that high-risk violent offenders on longer parole were less likely to be reconvicted in the first year after release than those with just 6 months of post-release supervision, suggesting that parole supervision itself may be a successful intervention (Polaschek, Yesberg, & Chauhan, 2018). It was also found that, regardless of whether parolees had attended intensive prison-based treatment or not, those with better release plans prior to parole had better relationships with their probation officers 2 months after release, leading to better life circumstances at 3 months, which in turn predicted recidivism or its absence at 1 year. The intensively treated men had more positive scores on every changeable follow-up variable, leading more of them to survive the first year after release without convictions (Polaschek, 2015). Such longitudinal research could serve as a model for planning and evaluating release pathways and for unpacking the mechanisms of change and desistance; clearly these are areas for future investigation, especially with violent offender programs.

Conclusions

Violence among youth is seen as a "pervasive public health problem" (Matjasko et al., 2012, p. 540). Perhaps this explains why it was already possible a decade ago to conduct a meta-review based on 37 meta-analyses and 15 systematic reviews with young people (Matjasko et al., 2012). The body of similar research on offenders who are only a few years older is so small as to imply that we have largely lost interest in researching what works by that age. In an era of "evidence-based practice" there is still little funding set aside for research to enhance the generally paltry foundations on which to draw, most treatment efforts are never seriously evaluated, and there is no systematic effort across the research community to provide fundamental knowledge needed for program design and implementation, and for understanding and measuring program change. There is no question that this is a challenging area of practice, and a very difficult one in which to conduct research. If evidence-based practice is important in the treatment of violent offenders, joint commitments between funders, program providers, and researchers are needed. Alternatively, if a strong case can be made that violent offenders are simply high-risk offenders, perhaps we would be better off simply consolidating resources and efforts on that population.

Notes

1   When we conducted the Polaschek and Collie (2004) review, we reported the Dowden, Blanchette, and Serin (1999) results for the Anger and Other Emotions Management Program (AOEMP) as "a rare convincing demonstration that AM can reduce violent recidivism in high-risk mainstream offenders with a history of violence, and in just 50 hours of intervention" (p. 324). Unfortunately, we were not aware at that time of the results for non-completers of AOEMP, showing a much higher rate of recidivism for this group than for the untreated group (reported in Dowden & Serin, 2001). Taking both results together, as would be done in an intention-to-treat design (see Chapter 25), it is likely that referral to this program was not associated with a reduction in recidivism.
2   Categorizing violence reduction programs uniformly as "anger management" may obscure crucial variations in components addressing communication skills, relationship skills, problem-solving, and distorted cognition. Although bearing similar labels, there are variations in the content of these components based on whether the main aim is simply reducing anger expression, or reducing the use of violence as an entrenched short cut for prosocial behavior in the face of anger triggers.

Key Readings

Braga, A. A., Piehl, A. M., & Hureau, D. (2009). Controlling violent offenders released to the community: An evaluation of the Boston Reentry Initiative. *Journal of Research in Crime and Delinquency*, 46(4), 411–436.

Lewis, K., Olver, M. E., & Wong, S. C. P. (2013). The Violence Risk Scale: Predictive validity and linking treatment changes with recidivism in a sample of high-risk and personality disordered offenders. *Assessment*, 20, 150–164.

Polaschek, D. L. L., & Collie, R. M. (2004). Rehabilitating serious violent adult offenders: An empirical and theoretical stocktake. *Psychology, Crime & Law*, 10, 321–334.

Polaschek, D. L. L., Yesberg, J. A., Bell, R. K., Casey, A. R., & Dickson, S. R. (2016). Intensive psychological treatment of high-risk violent offenders: Outcomes and pre-release mechanisms. *Psychology, Crime & Law*, 22, 344–365.

Serin, R. C., Lloyd, C. D., Helmus, L., Derkzen, D. M., & Luong, D. (2013). Does intra-individual change predict offender recidivism? Searching for the Holy Grail in assessing offender change. *Aggression and Violent Behavior*, 18, 32–53.

References

Biere, D. M., & Mann, R. E. (2017). The history and future of prison psychology. *Psychology, Public Policy, and Law*, 23, 478–489.

Bonta, J., & Andrews, D. A. (2017). *The psychology of criminal conduct* (6th ed.). London, UK: Routledge.

Bonta, J., Rugge, T., Scott, T., Bourgon, G., & Yessine, A. (2008). Exploring the black box of community supervision. *Journal of Offender Rehabilitation*, 47, 248–270.

Braga, A. A., Piehl, A. M., & Hureau, D. (2009). Controlling violent offenders released to the community: An evaluation of the Boston Reentry Initiative. *Journal of Research in Crime and Delinquency*, 46(4), 411–436.

Brookstein, D., Daffern, M., & Ogloff, J. (2016). For better or worse: The predictive validity of the HCR-20 V3 and the VRAG-R in community settings. Paper presented at the International Association of Forensic Mental Health Services Conference, New York.

Bruce, M., Crowley, S., Jeffcote, N., & Coulston, B. (2014). Community DSPD pilot services in South London: Rates of reconviction and impact of supported housing on reducing recidivism. *Criminal Behaviour and Mental Health*, 24, 129–140.

Citrome, L., & Volavka, J. (2014). The psychopharmacology of violence: Making sensible decisions. *CNS Spectrums*, 19, 411–418.

Craig, L. A., Beech, A. R., & Cortoni, F. (2013). What works in assessing risk in sexual and violent offenders. In L. A. Craig, L. Dixon, & T. A. Gannon (Eds.), *What works in offender rehabilitation: An evidence-based approach to assessment and treatment* (pp. 94–114). Chichester, UK: Wiley.

Day, A., & Doyle, P. (2010). Violent offender rehabilitation and the therapeutic community model of treatment: Towards integrated service provision? *Aggression and Violent Behavior*, 15, 380–387.

Dickson, S. R., Polaschek, D. L. L., & Casey, A. R. (2013). Can the quality of high-risk violent prisoners' release plans predict recidivism following intensive rehabilitation? A comparison with risk assessment instruments. *Psychology, Crime & Law*, 19, 371–389.

Dowden, C., Blanchette, K., & Serin, R. (1999). *Anger management programming for federal male inmates: An effective intervention. Research report R-82*. Ottawa, Canada: Correctional Service of Canada.

Dowden, C., & Serin, R. (2001). *Anger management programming for offenders: The impact of program performance measures. Research report R-106*. Ottawa, Canada: Correctional Service of Canada.

Duwe, G. (2014). A randomized experiment of a prisoner reentry programe: Updated results from an evaluation of the Minnesota Comprehensive Reentry Plan (MCORP). *Criminal Justice Studies*, 27, 172–190.

Farrington, D. P., Coid, J. W., Harnett, L., Jolliffe, D., Soteriou, N., Turner, R., & West, D. J. (2006). *Criminal careers up to the age of 50 and life success up to the age of 48: New findings from the Cambridge Study in Delinquent Development*. London, UK: Home Office.

Gilbert, F., Daffern, M., Talevski, D., & Ogloff, J. R. P. (2013). The role of aggression-related cognition in the aggressive behavior of offenders: A general aggression model perspective. *Criminal Justice and Behavior*, 40, 119–138.

Gondolf, E. W., & Russell, D. (1986). The case against anger control treatment programs for batterers. *Response*, 9(3), 2–5.

Guerra, N. G., & Slaby, R. G. (1990). Cognitive mediators of aggression in adolescent offenders: 2. Intervention. *Developmental Psychology*, 26, 269–277.

Henwood, K. S., Chou, S., & Browne, K. D. (2015). A systematic review and meta-analysis on the effectiveness of CBT informed anger management. *Aggression and Violent Behavior*, 25, 280–292.

Heseltine, K., Howells, K., & Day, A. (2010). Brief anger interventions with offenders may be ineffective: A replication and extension. *Behaviour Research and Therapy*, 48, 246–250.

Hodgins, S. (2007). Persistent violent offending: What do we know? *British Journal of Psychiatry*, 190(Suppl. 49), s12–s14.

Howard, P. D., & Dixon, L. (2012). The construction and validation of the OASys violence predictor: Advancing violence risk assessment in the English and Welsh correctional services. *Criminal Justice and Behavior*, 39, 287–307.

Howard, P. D., & Dixon, L. (2013). Identifying change in the likelihood of violent recidivism: Causal dynamic risk factors in the OASys violence predictor. *Law and Human Behavior*, 37, 163–174.

Hughes, G. (1993). Anger management program outcomes. *Forum on Corrections Research*, 5, 5–9.

Jolliffe, D., & Farrington, D. P. (2007). *A systematic review of the national and international evidence of interventions with violent offenders* ()Ministry of Justice Research Series 16/07. London, UK: Ministry of Justice.

King, L. L. (2012). Tai Aroha—the first two years: A formative evaluation of a residential community-based programme for offenders. Wellington, New Zealand: Wellington Psychological Services, Department of Corrections. Retrieved from https://www.corrections.govt.nz/__data/assets/pdf_file/0006/674475/COR_Tai_Aroha_WEB.pdf

Klepfisz, G., O'Brien, K., & Daffern, M. (2014). Violent offenders' within-treatment change in anger, criminal attitudes, and violence risk: Associations with violent recidivism. *International Journal of Forensic Mental Health*, 13, 348–362.

Kroner, D. G., & Loza, W. (2001). Evidence for the efficacy of self-report in predicting nonviolent and violent recidivism. *Journal of Interpersonal Violence*, 16, 168–177.

Lewis, K., Olver, M. E., & Wong, S. C. P. (2013). The Violence Risk Scale: Predictive validity and linking treatment changes with recidivism in a sample of high-risk and personality disordered offenders. *Assessment*, 20, 150–164.

Lloyd, C. D., Hanby, L. J., & Serin, R. C. (2014). Rehabilitation group coparticipants' risk levels are associated with offenders' treatment performance, treatment change, and recidivism. *Journal of Consulting & Clinical Psychology*, 82, 298–411.

Loza, W., Loza-Fanous, A., & Heseltine, K. (2007). The myth of offenders' deception on self-report measure predicting recidivism: Example from the Self-Appraisal Questionnaire. *Journal of Interpersonal Violence*, 23, 671–683.

Maden, A., Williams, J., Wong, S. C. P., & Leis, T. A. (2004). Treating dangerous and severe personality disorder in high security: Lessons from the Regional Psychiatric Centre, Saskatoon, Canada. *Journal of Forensic Psychiatry and Psychology*, 15, 375–390.

Matjasko, J. L., Vivolo-Kantor, A. M., Massetti, G. M., Hollaind, K. M., Holt, M., & Cruz, J. D. (2012). A systematic meta-review of evaluations of youth violence prevention programs: Common and divergent findings from 25 years of meta-analyses and systematic reviews. *Aggression and Violent Behavior*, 17, 540–552.

McGuire, J. (2008). A review of effective interventions for reducing aggression and violence. *Philosophical Transactions of the Royal Society B*, 363, 2577–2497.

Meichenbaum, D. H. (1975). *Stress inoculation training*. New York, NY: Pergamon.

Mills, J. F., Loza, W., & Kroner, D. G. (2003). Predictive validity despite social desirability: Evidence for the robustness of self-report among offenders. *Criminal Behaviour and Mental Health*, 13, 140–150.

Novaco, R. W. (1979). The cognitive regulation of anger and stress. In P. C. Kendall, & S. D. Hollon (Eds.), *Cognitive behavioral interventions: Theory, research, and procedures* (pp. 241–285). New York, NY: Academic Press.

Odgers, C. L. (2009). The life-course persistent pathway of antisocial behaviour: Risks for violence and poor physical health. In S. Hodgins, E. Viding, & A. Plodowski (Eds.), *The neurobiological basis of violence: Science and rehabilitation* (pp. 23–41). Oxford, UK: Oxford University Press.

Olver, M. E., Lewis, K., & Wong, S. C. P. (2013). Risk reduction treatment of high-risk psychopathic offenders: The relationship of psychopathy and treatment change to violent recidivism. *Personality Disorders: Theory, Research, and Treatment*, 4, 160–167.

Patrick, C. J., & Zempolich, K. A. (1997). Emotionality and violent behavior in psychopaths: A biosocial analysis. In A. Raine, P. A. Brennan, D. P. Farrington, & S. A. Mednick (Eds.), *Biosocial bases of violence* (pp. 145–161). New York, NY: Plenum.

Perkins, D., Farr, C., Romero, J., Kirkpatrick, T., & Ebrahimjee, A. (2015). DSPD ten years on at Broadmoor. *The Prison Service Journal*, 128(March, 2015), 10–16.

Polaschek, D. L. L. (2009). Te Whare Manaakitanga/Rimutaka Violence Prevention Unit Evaluation Report VI. Evaluating the predictive validity of psychometric assessment measures: Treatment completion and recidivism outcomes (prospective evaluation sample). Wellington, New Zealand: Unpublished report for the New Zealand Department of Corrections.

Polaschek, D. L. L. (2011). High-intensity rehabilitation for violent offenders in New Zealand: Reconviction outcomes for high- and medium-risk prisoners. *Journal of Interpersonal Violence*, 26, 664–682.

Polaschek, D. L. L. (2015, June). *Reintegration, rehabilitation, or both? Unpacking factors that contribute to community outcomes for high risk violent offenders*. Paper presented at the Keynote address at the Third North American Corrections and Criminal Justice Psychology Conference, Ottawa, Canada.

Polaschek, D. L. L. (2016). Do relationships matter? Examining the quality of probation officers' interactions with parolees in preventing recidivism. *Practice: The New Zealand Corrections Journal*, 4(1), 5–9.

Polaschek, D. L. L., Bell, R. K., Calvert, S. W., & Takarangi, M. K. T. (2010). Cognitive-behavioural rehabilitation of high-risk violent offenders: Investigating treatment change with explicit and implicit measures. *Applied Cognitive Psychology*, 24, 437–449.

Polaschek, D. L. L., & Collie, R. M. (2004). Rehabilitating serious violent adult offenders: An empirical and theoretical stocktake. *Psychology, Crime & Law*, 10, 321–334.

Polaschek, D. L. L., & Kilgour, T. G. (2013). New Zealand's special treatment units: The development and implementation of intensive treatment for high-risk male prisoners. *Psychology, Crime & Law*, 11, 511–526.

Polaschek, D. L. L., & Ross, E. C. (2010). Do early therapeutic alliance, motivation, and stages of change predict therapy change for high-risk, psychopathic violent prisoners? *Criminal Behaviour and Mental Health*, 20, 100–111.

Polaschek, D. L. L., Yesberg, J. A., Bell, R. K., Casey, A. R., & Dickson, S. R. (2016). Intensive psychological treatment of high-risk violent offenders: Outcomes and pre-release mechanisms. *Psychology, Crime & Law*, 22, 344–365.

Polaschek, D. L. L., Yesberg, J. A., & Chauhan, P. (2018). A year without a conviction: An integrated examination of potential mechanisms for successful reentry in high-risk violent prisoners. *Criminal Justice and Behavior*, 45, 425–446.

Reising, K., Ttofi, M. M., Farrington, D. P., & Piquero, A. R. (in press). Depression and anxiety outcomes of offending trajectories: A systematic review of prospective longitudinal studies. *Journal of Criminal Justice*.

Roberton, T., Daffern, M., & Bucks, R. S. (2015). Beyond anger control: Difficulty attending to emotions also predicts aggression in offenders. *Psychology of Violence*, 5, 74–83.

Seewald, K., Rossegger, A., Gerth, J., Urbaniok, F., Phillips, G., & Endrass, J. (2018). Effectiveness of a risk–need–responsivity-based treatment program for violent and sexual offenders: Results of a retrospective, quasi-experimental study. *Legal and Criminological Psychology*, 23, 85–99.

Seguin, J. R., Sylvers, P., & Lilienfeld, S. O. (2007). The neuropsychology of violence. In D. J. Flannery, A. T. Vazsonyi, & I. D. Waldman (Eds.), *The Cambridge handbook of violent behavior and aggression* (pp. 187–214). Cambridge, UK: Cambridge University Press.

Serin, R. C., Lloyd, C. D., Helmus, L., Derkzen, D. M., & Luong, D. (2013). Does intra-individual change predict offender recidivism? Searching for the Holy Grail in assessing offender change. *Aggression and Violent Behavior*, 18, 32–53.

Shepherd, S. M., Campbell, R. E., & Ogloff, J. R. P. (2017). The Utility of the HCR–20 in an Australian sample of forensic psychiatric patients. *Psychiatry, Psychology and Law*, 25, 273–282.

Skeem, J. L., Eno Louden, J., Polaschek, D. L. L., & Camp, J. (2007). Assessing relationship quality in mandated community treatment: Blending care with control. *Psychological Assessment*, 19, 397–410.

Taft, C. T., & Murphy, C. M. (2007). The working alliance in intervention for partner violence perpetrators: Recent research and theory. *Journal of Family Violence*, 22, 11–18.

Tew, J., Dixon, L., Harkins, L., & Bennett, A. L. (2012). Investigating changes in anger and aggression in offenders with high levels of psychopathic traits attending the Chromis violence reduction programme. *Criminal Behaviour and Mental Health*, 22, 191–201.

Travers, R., Mann, R. E., & Hollin, C. R. (2014). Who benefits from cognitive skills programs? Differential impact by risk and offense type. *Criminal Justice and Behavior*, 41, 1103–1129.

Vassos, E., Collier, D. A., & Fazel, S. (2014). Systematic meta-analyses and field synopsis of genetic association studies of violence and aggression. *Molecular Psychiatry*, 19, 471–477.

Walters, G. D. (2006). Risk-appraisal versus self-report in the prediction of criminal justice outcomes. *Criminal Justice and Behavior*, 33, 279–304.

Ward, T., & Beech, A. R. (2015). Dynamic risk factors: A theoretical dead-end? *Psychology, Crime & Law*, 29, 100–113.

Ware, J., Cieplucha, C., & Matsuo, D. (2011). The Violent Offenders Therapeutic Programme (VOTP)— Rationale and effectiveness. *Australasian Journal of Correctional Staff Development*, 6, 1–12.

Woessner, G., & Schwedler, A. (2014). Correctional treatment of sexual and violent offenders: Therapeutic change, prison climate, and recidivism. *Criminal Justice and Behavior*, 41, 862–879.

Wong, S. C. P., & Gordon, A. (1998–2003). Violence Risk Scale. Unpublished manuscript, Saskatoon, Saskatchewan, Canada.

Wong, S. C. P., & Gordon, A. (2006). The validity and reliability of the Violence Risk Scale: A treatment-friendly violence risk assessment tool. *Psychology, Public Policy, and Law*, 12, 279–309.

Wong, S. C. P., & Gordon, A. (2013). The Violence Reduction Program: A treatment program for violence-prone forensic clients. *Psychology, Crime & Law*, 11, 461–475.

Wong, S. C. P., Gordon, A., Gu, D., Lewis, K., & Olver, M. E. (2012). The effectiveness of violence reduction treatment for psychopathic offenders: Empirical evidence and a treatment model. *International Journal of Forensic Mental Health*, 11, 336–349.

32

Effective Sex Offender Treatment in Correctional Settings: A Strengths-Based Approach

Liam E. Marshall

Rockwood Psychotherapy & Consulting and Waypoint Centre for Mental Health Care, Canada

Seligman (Seligman & Csikszentmihalyi, 2000; Seligman & Peterson, 2003) has claimed that, since the end of World War II, the psychological treatment of all disorders has primarily been concerned with clients' deficits. He called for a shift in focus such that equal attention is paid to clients' strengths. As a result, recent years have seen a proliferation of so-called Strength-Based Approaches (SBAs) as part of the more general positive psychology movement (Linley & Joseph, 2004; Snyder & Lopez, 2005). This has, more recently, also been apparent in the treatment of sex offenders, although the literature on the value of SBAs is still quite limited, especially as it relates to its use with sexual offenders in correctional settings.

In order to clarify my view of an SBA I will begin by discussing what an SBA is not. Using an SBA approach does not, for example, require therapists to be "soft" on sex offenders or to not challenge problematic attitudes and cognitions. An SBA treatment program does not take the responsibility for change away from the sex offender. Ideally, an SBA aims to instill a sense of self-efficacy and hope for an offense-free future, with responsibility for change remaining in the hands of the sexual offender. An SBA is also not inherently inconsistent with the enhancement of empathy toward the victims of the offender's crimes. That is, an SBA is the collaborative seeking out of those components of empathy which the offender demonstrates, using this strength to build further empathic capacity. Furthermore, an SBA does not require treatment providers to ignore (and, in fact, encourages attention to) the Risk-Need-Responsivity (RNR) principles (Andrews & Bonta, 2006) that will be described later in this chapter. An SBA treatment program is also not any more costly to operate than other approaches and in all likelihood will reduce overall costs to the correctional system and society through less treatment refusal and attrition (and therefore lower recidivism), and lower rates of turnover among treatment staff and higher morale. Finally, like any psychological treatment, an SBA is not a cure. Rather, treatment should be seen as the launching point for the rest of the sex offender's life. The techniques and skills learned in treatment will need to be continually improved and monitored as will the strengths and deficits identified.

The Wiley International Handbook of Correctional Psychology, First Edition. Edited by Devon L. L. Polaschek, Andrew Day, and Clive R. Hollin.

An SBA is a positive, motivational, and optimistic approach to treatment grounded in engaging the sex offender in change. The SBA for sex offenders described in this chapter is, however, not a pure SBA approach, such as that described by Padesky and Mooney (2012) for use in clinical cognitive behavioral therapy (CBT) for anxiety and depression. For these authors, using an SBA involves no examination of deficits. Rather, the SBA described in this chapter takes an integrated approach in which deficits are addressed, but identifying and building the client's strengths is also emphasized.

There are essentially three empirically informed theoretical models that are integrated into our SBA approach that serve to guide the design and implementation of treatment: the RNR model (Andrews & Bonta, 2006); the Good Lives Model (Ward, 2002); and the recent movement in clinical work described as positive psychology (Carr, 2011; Peterson, 2006; Seligman & Csikszentmihalyi, 2000). Each is briefly outlined below.

The Risk-Need-Responsivity Model

The RNR model was created by Andrews and his colleagues from the results of a series of meta-analyses of offender treatment outcome studies (Andrews et al., 1990; Dowden & Andrews, 2004; Dowden, Antonowicz, & Andrews, 2003). These authors demonstrated that programs which targeted high-risk offenders, addressed criminogenic needs, and delivered treatment in an appropriate way, were more effective in reducing recidivism than those that did not pay attention to these principles. It appears that each component of the RNR model adds to reductions in recidivism and that there is an additive effect. For example, programs that adhered to two of the RNR principles were also shown to be effective but less so than those that addressed all three, while those that adhered to just one had little impact, and those that adhered to none of the three principles had either no effect or, in some cases, marginally increased recidivism. A recent replication of the utility of the RNR model applied to the treatment of sexual offenders, by Hanson, Bourgon, Helmus, and Hodgson (2009), confirmed the RNR principles to apply equally well to sexual offender treatment. As with Dowden and colleagues' replication (Dowden & Andrews, 2004; Dowden et al., 2003), Hanson et al. found that the risk principle had quite a small effect (as it also did in Andrews' studies), and therefore they suggested it was best viewed as an administrative guide for allocating resources rather than a basis for designing and implementing treatment. In all of these studies on the RNR model, it was the need and responsivity principles that exerted the greatest influence on the effectiveness of treatment.

The need principle demonstrates that treatment must address those features of offenders that have been shown to predict recidivism. Andrews and Bonta (2006) showed that when treatment programs properly adhere to the need principle it accounts for a substantial amount of change (effect size = .19). The stable dynamic risk features (i.e., criminogenic factors) that have so far been empirically identified in sexual offenders include: attitudes supportive of sexual offending (tolerance of offending, adversarial sexual beliefs, hostility toward women, emotional congruence with children); deficits in perspective-taking; poor coping skills; intimacy deficits and emotional loneliness; deviant sexual interests; sexual pre-occupation; sexual entitlement; and behavioral, sexual, and emotional self-regulation problems. Programs that address all of these needs are thus likely to be maximally effective, whereas, those that do not are likely to be less effective, proportional to the number they do not address. Of note, however, is that Andrews and his colleagues also identified that some non-criminogenic factors may be usefully addressed in treatment, but only if they serve to enhance offender motivation (e.g., raising self-esteem) or if they are directly related to criminogenic factors (e.g., poor empathic skills are characteristic of people who lack intimacy). However, the evidence indicates that addressing too many non-criminogenic factors reduces treatment effectiveness (Andrews & Bonta, 2006).

The responsivity principle is concerned with the way treatment is delivered. It has two components, general and specific responsivity. Specific responsivity refers to the need to adjust treatment delivery to the unique characteristics of each individual treatment participant (e.g., learning style and capacity, social and cultural characteristics, and day-to-day fluctuations in mood and motivation). For example, many treatment centers have created special programs for offenders with restricted cognitive capacities. We have also adjusted the delivery of our program to accommodate the unique features of those clients who score in the psychopathic range on the Psychopathy Checklist—Revised (PCL-R; Hare, 1991).

The general component of responsivity has often been believed to be satisfied by employing a CBT approach. Hanson et al. (2009) counted all CBT programs included in their meta-analysis as adhering to the general responsivity principle, even though they vary considerably in almost all aspects (see surveys by Burton & Smith-Darden, 2001; McGrath, Cumming, & Burchard, 2003; McGrath, Cumming, Burchard, Zeoli, & Ellerby, 2010). As Andrews and Bonta (2006) clearly demonstrated, the crucial features of the general responsivity principle are not necessarily met by adopting CBT but rather are captured by what they call the Core Correctional Practices (CCPs), which define the appropriate delivery of treatment. Therapists need, for example, to be empathic, warm, supportive, respectful, and motivational, and to reward the expression of prosocial attitudes and behaviors. Consistent with the notion of CCPs, W. L. Marshall, and colleagues (Marshall et al., 2002, 2003) have shown that therapists working with sexual offenders who are characteristically empathic and warm, who are rewarding and somewhat directive, are significantly more likely to instill beneficial changes among sexual offenders, whereas those who display an aggressively confrontational style are less effective. Further, Beech and colleagues (Beech & Fordham, 1997; Beech & Hamilton-Giachritsis, 2005) have shown that when therapists created groups that were cohesive and expressive, sexual offenders were more likely to make significant treatment gains.

In summary, programs which adhere to the RNR principles, whether they are CBT or not, are very likely to be most effective, whereas those that fail to incorporate these principles (and in particular the need and responsivity principles) are almost certain to fail to generate significant benefits. In most applications of RNR, however, criminogenic needs are described in terms of deficits, and offender strengths tend to be overlooked. A therapist seeking to implement an SBA thus needs to look for those strengths or find elements of strength within criminogenic domains of need.

Positive Psychology

Seligman (2002) pointed out that clinical psychology post-World War II has been based on a deficit model where the focus in treatment has been on the client's failings and dysfunctions. Such an exclusive focus on deficits and difficulties, Seligman suggests, is demotivating. Positive psychology, on the other hand, equips clients with the skills necessary to fulfill their potential while at the same time not neglecting efforts to ameliorate problems and difficulties. Positive psychology does so by assisting clients to identify their strengths and use these as the basis upon which to build. This encourages effective engagement in treatment.

Ward and Stewart (2003) have pointed out that building sex offender's strengths, if directed appropriately, can reciprocally inhibit current difficulties. Indeed, in some ways, many current treatment programs for sexual offenders have strength-based elements. For example, building the skills, self-confidence, and attitudes essential to functioning effectively in relationships necessarily allows the sexual offender to overcome deficiencies in intimacy and thereby reduce loneliness—both of which are criminogenic factors (Mann, Hanson, & Thornton, 2010). In this sense, the advantage of a positive psychology approach is the emphasis on building skills and a focus on the client's potential for this, and this offers a more hopeful view of the future. Instilling hope for the future in clients with various disorders has been shown to generate benefits from treatment and to reduce relapses (Snyder, 1994). Elsewhere, we have also described a positive motivational preparatory program (Marshall, Marshall, Fernandez, Malcolm, & Moulden, 2008), which was found to significantly increase hope in sexual offenders, enhance subsequent engagement in treatment, and reduce recidivism.

Another of the advantages of a positive psychology approach is that it explicitly states that clients should continue the development of their strengths after completing treatment. While relapse prevention (RP) programs also insist on continuing the processes addressed in treatment, the focus is deficit-oriented; RP clients are required to identify various circumstances, persons, and thoughts that they must continue to avoid because, it is assumed, they still have deviant propensities. Such a negative focus is not motivating and does not instill hope for an offense-free and satisfying future.

The Good Lives Model

Perhaps the approach to sex offender treatment that most closely matches a positive psychology or strengths-based approach is the Good Lives Model (GLM). The GLM was created by Ward (2002) from a large body of research on the human need for self-fulfillment. This demonstrates that all people, whether they are aware of it or not, seek to achieve success in several domains of functioning. Ward originally identified nine such domains: (a) optimal mental, physical, and sexual health; (b) knowledge; (c) mastery in work and play; (d) autonomy; (e) inner peace; (f) relatedness; (g) creativity; (h) spirituality; and (i) happiness. The GLM offers an approach to treatment which aims to provide sexual offenders with the skills and attitudes necessary to develop a more satisfying life through addressing unmet needs in these areas.

Ward (2002) suggested that, in their deviant acts, sexual offenders are seeking to fulfill the same needs that others pursue in prosocial ways because they lack the skills and attitudes to meet these needs in appropriate ways. Providing sexual offenders with sensible approach goals (i.e., the issues involved in the nine domains identified above) and the skills and attitudes necessary to meet these goals in prosocial ways, will, therefore, result in reductions in reoffending. Interestingly, in their examination of sexual offenders who refused treatment, Mann and Webster (2002) found that one of the most common reasons sexual offenders gave for not entering treatment was that they believed it would not be aimed at helping them to meet their needs. Treatment refusers said that they wanted treatment to provide them with the capacity to develop a better, more satisfying life. They believed treatment would simply focus on their offenses, with the purpose being to stamp out their propensity to reoffend, whereas they expressed a desire to participate in treatment that was both non-offense focused and could improve their functioning. Therefore, offenders appeared to want what Ward's GLM offers, and this seems likely to result in less refusal of treatment and greater commitment to the goals of treatment.

Ward, Collie, and Bourke (2009) have subsequently argued that the criminogenic needs identified in Andrews and Bonta's (2006) RNR model simply reflect the absence of the skills necessary to achieve success in the domains the GLM identifies. Therefore, Ward and colleagues claim that providing sexual offenders with an appropriate set of skills will necessarily overcome the deficits inherent in the criminogenic needs and thus result in more effective treatment. However, although the GLM is not inconsistent with, and is likely facilitative of, an SBA, it does not necessarily result in an SBA. Rather, it is important for therapists to balance the observed lack of skills and attitudes in sexual offenders with the development of strengths.

Challenges to Rehabilitation in the Correctional Setting

Prior to describing our SBA program in greater detail, we will now consider some of the challenges to implementing sex offender treatment programs in correctional settings. As clinicians in correctional settings are well aware, many challenges arise when trying to provide treatment in a correctional setting. For example, treatment staff are often expected to be delivering programming 5 days per week, leaving little time for other important activities, such as reading literature or receiving supervision. The system may inadvertently undermine the ability for the treatment program to get and keep participants, for example by having the group room in a high-profile location where other offenders can identify participants as sex offenders simply by going to that location. Also, some correctional staff may not be in favor of providing treatment to sex offenders because "they don't deserve it," or because they think that psychological treatment for sex offenders is ineffective.

More generally, Dr. Ruth Mann (Mann, 2015), of Her Majesty's Prison System in England and Wales, has described the features of making prisons rehabilitative and placed them in a hierarchy of rehabilitation needs. Mann describes the challenges that arise when trying to ensure a correctional setting is rehabilitative in order of priority. That is, unless the conditions of the earliest of the priority order are met, the latter stages of the priority order are unlikely to result in successful rehabilitation. The priorities in order are the need for: (a) a physical and social environment that is safe and decent so as to be supportive of rehabilitation; (b) non-treatment staff to be rehabilitative in their interactions with offenders; (c) prioritizing treatments on those issues that are known to reduce reoffending by focusing on known criminogenic factors; and (d) helping offenders with reintegration back into the general community. Each of these features of rehabilitation in a correctional setting relies on the satisfaction of the previous condition. For example, when incarcerated sex offenders are concerned for their personal safety, they are unlikely to participate in a treatment program where attending could identify them as a sex offender. Further, if the sex offender is practicing prosocial behaviors in the treatment program but is exposed to antisocial behaviors by non-treatment staff with whom they spend a greater amount of time, this may reduce his or her ability and commitment to practice the gains made in the treatment program. Finally, if the sex offender is released to the community without the supports, knowledge, and skills necessary to be successful, this is likely to undermine any gains made in treatment while incarcerated. Consequently, it is important for treatment providers to consider and meet the challenges to successful implementation of sex offender treatment in correctional settings. We have attempted to overcome these challenges by working collaboratively in a non-hierarchical way with non-treatment staff and management in our correctional settings and with supervisors and decision-makers in the community.

Therapeutic Process

Group or individual treatment

It appears that the current evidence, limited though as it is, indicates there may be no strong differences between providing sex offender treatment in an individual or group format. Whether therapists choose to run group therapy, individual therapy, or a combination of the two, seems to rely more on therapists' preference and concerns about efficiency. For example, Sawyer (2002) points out that group treatment is far more resource efficient than individual therapy; that is, group treatment can deal with far more clients within any time period and it is cost-effective. Sex offenders also sometimes appear to be able to better understand their own behavior by hearing about the experiences of other group members. Further, when group members challenge or ask questions of each other, it allows the therapist to gauge the amount of insight and learning that group member has gained through the quality and depth of the challenges and questions. Neither of these would occur in individual therapy. We also have noticed that when treatment is run as a combination of group and individual sessions, particants appear less likely to participate in-depth in the group sessions, preferring to discuss personal matters in the individual sessions, presumably over fear of embarrassment or social anxiety. However, there are a number of circumstances in which individual therapy may be necessary or preferred, for example in settings where there are very few sex offenders.

Closed or rolling groups

If therapists decide to employ group therapy over individual therapy, then the next step is to decide whether to run "closed" or "open" (often called "rolling") groups. Closed groups are those where all participants start and finish at the same time and the topics, or exercises, are completed at the same time by each group member. In open groups, there is a continuous intake of clients and the target or exercise each group member is working on is dependent on their stage in treatment. When one client has completed all targets of therapy and is discharged, a new client can immediately takes up the place. This can be highly efficient for therapists who are faced with limited resources and time, and beneficial to the differing functioning level of each client. According to Ware, Mann, and Wakeling (2009), each group member can proceed at his own pace without having to keep up with, or wait for, other participants. This is particularly useful for group members with impaired cognitive capacity.

Ware and Bright (2008) compared the open and closed group approaches, finding that offenders preferred the dynamics of an open group approach the most. Apparently this was also more appealing to the correctional service due to open spaces always being filled with new group members. The closed group, on the other hand, only had half of available treatment places filled. Equally importantly, Ware and Bright (2008) found that the attrition rate dropped dramatically when the closed groups were switched to an open-ended format. Another important point was that therapists felt more effective and expressed more positive attitudes toward the open-ended groups; they felt more at ease and less pressured to achieve changes at any point in the program. They noted that in closed groups they always felt pressured to get clients to the same point for each target, particularly when there was a disparity between clients in their capacity to grasp the essentials of the program component.

Number per week and duration of sessions

When considering the number of sessions per week, and the duration of each session, there is little empirical data to draw upon when it comes to developing SBA approaches. Yet, basic research in human and animal learning (Eysenck, 1959; Kazdin, 1978; Ullman & Krasner, 1965) can inform decisions about the optimal frequency and duration of training sessions. In this research a comparison is made between what is called "massed practice" and "distributed practice" (Cepeda, Pashler, Vul, Wixted, & Rohrer, 2006). In massed practice, a topic is studied as a whole and in long sessions. An example of massed practice for sex offenders would be three to five, or more, 1-hour sessions, 5 days per week. In distributed practice, the treatment is broken up into smaller segments and studied for a shorter duration, with larger gaps between each study segment (Dellarosa & Bourne, 1985; Dempster, 1988; Underwood, 1961). An example of a distributed practice treatment schedule would be 1–3 hour long sessions 2–3 days per week. Results of this research consistently show an advantage for distributed practice in terms of long-term retention of the material (Moss, 1995). Research on human learning ought to serve as guidelines for deciding the frequency and duration of treatment sessions. Unfortunately, this literature does not seem to be familiar to most CBT therapists working within correctional settings.

Based on these observations, we suggest that therapists limit the number of SBA sessions to a maximum of three per week, each no more than 3 hours in duration with a short break near the middle of each session. Our experience has been that under these conditions both the therapists' and the offenders' enthusiasm for the materials in the program is maintained. Also, clients can be given work to complete in between sessions. This work, in our opinion, is crucial to the generalization of learning beyond the treatment room. In an open-ended group, clients can take as much time as they need to assimilate ideas and learn the necessary skills. In closed groups, clients are required to complete each module at the same rate as do the other group members. In this case, the open-ended group format appears to us to be more advantageous to maximizing the benefits of distributed practice.

Therapist features

Psychotherapists from a broad range of therapeutic orientations have accepted the crucial role the therapist plays in successfully treating clients (Luborsky, Crits-Christoph, Mintz, & Auerbach, 1988). The quality of the therapist–client relationship accounts for a significant proportion of the variance accounted for in treatment effectiveness (Morgan, Luborsky, Crits-Christoph, Curtis, & Solomon, 1982). In fact, Norcross (2002) showed that the therapeutic alliance explained up to 30% of treatment-induced changes, whereas the application of specific techniques accounted for only 15% of this variance. Successful therapeutic outcomes depend therefore both on the therapist's interpersonal skills and on specific techniques, but clearly the relationship features are the strongest factors in generating treatment benefits.

W. L. Marshall and colleagues (Marshall et al., 2002, 2003) evaluated the influence of these therapist features on indices of behavior change in sex offender treatment. Correlational analyses between the ratings of the therapists and behavior change scores revealed significant relationships on measures of a variety of coping skills, various indices of perspective-taking ability, several measures of cognitive distortions, and aspects of relationship skills. Similar to the CCPs described earlier, the four most important therapist features of sex offender therapists, according to this research, were warmth, empathy, rewardingness, and directiveness. Most importantly, confrontation by therapists was found to be negatively correlated ($r = -.31$) with various indices of behavior change. The combination of empathy, warmth, rewardingness, and directiveness accounted for between 30 and 60% of the changes observed in the positive benefits of treatment as measured by the various indices of change. This is considerably more than the effects of therapist features in the general literature, which typically range from 20 to 30%. Apparently therapist characteristics are more influential with sex offender clients than with other clients. No doubt this is due both to lack of trust among sex offenders about the intentions of professionals and to their understandable reluctance to disclose anything about themselves for fear it will cause them even more problems.

The Rockwood Strength-Based Sex Offender Treatment Program

The main correctional program for sex offenders, and other variations of that program (such as the motivational preparatory program and a program for categorical deniers), that we have provided in correctional settings has been described in detail in a recent book commissioned by the American Psychological Association (Marshall, Marshall, Serran, & O'Brien, 2011). This SBA incorporates all of the features of the RNR model, is framed around the GLM and positive psychology, and is designed to be motivational. It is built around three treatment phases.

Phase 1: Engagement

The goal of Phase 1 is to introduce the program, and engage and motivate the participants. In this phase of treatment, the goal is not necessarily to make progress on criminogenic issues. Rather, the goal is to successfully engage the sex offender in the change process. This involves helping the clients to identify their individual strengths, and to begin working with their strengths. We make it clear, and we repeat this throughout treatment, that our aim is to prepare them sufficiently to have a better life in the future that is inconsistent with sexual offending.

The main components of Phase 1 include the revealing of background and proximal criminogenic factors, the enhancement of self-esteem, improved coping and mood management, and the enhancement of empathy. However, the targets of Phase 1 include any other issues that help the offender engage in the treatment process. The background criminogenic factors are those that are evident in the life history of our clients from which the therapist and the clients can collaboratively infer difficulties that need to be addressed as well as client strengths. Difficulties might include unresolved issues to do with their parents or other relationships, unresolved losses, other emotional issues, educational deficits, relationship difficulties (e.g., intimacy, emotional loneliness, jealousy, limited or inappropriate friendships), or employment problems. The identification of strengths involves looking for times and circumstances in the sex offender's life where he managed well and/or was, at least, offending-free. These issues are best revealed by having the offender write an autobiography limited to no more than six to eight pages.

From the autobiography or timeline, we (i.e., client and therapist) deduce the relevant strengths of the client as well as the problems that need to be addressed if she or he is to function effectively. For the proximal factors, we have the client present a disclosure of the lead-up to the events that reasonably immediately preceded the offense. Our requirements for disclosure differ from those typically requested in most CBT programs. Indeed, almost every program we have observed or read about requires each client to divulge in his disclosure every detail of the behaviors that occurred during the offense, with the additional demand that these details match the official record (usually either the victim's report or the police report of the crime). There is, however, no evidence that accepting full responsibility for offending is related to a reduction in risk. In fact, Maruna (2001) has demonstrated that those offenders who casually acknowledge their guilt are more likely to reoffend than are those who offer excuses or evade responsibility. Consistent with this observation, large-scale meta-analyses involving thousands of offenders have demonstrated that those offenders who deny having committed an offense are no more likely to reoffend than are those who fully admit (Hanson & Bussière, 1998; Hanson & Morton-Bourgon, 2005).

What we ask clients to do is to tell us in their disclosure what happened in their lives during the 3–6 months prior to their offense and what events and experiences occurred on the days immediately prior to the offense. We explicitly point out that we do not want them to tell us what they did during the offense and that we will not ask them for these details at any time during treatment. Most offenders are pleasantly surprised by this and it appears to alleviate their anxiety about this exercise and puts them in a positive frame of mind regarding treatment. From this account, in conjunction with their autobiography, we can collaboratively infer both stable dynamic risk factors and acute dynamic risk factors that are unique to the individual, thus providing a basis for the emergence of an individualized case formulation.

Once we have progressed through the above exercises and are confident that the client is at least somewhat engaged in the therapy process, we can now turn our attention to addressing those issues described as being criminogenic.

Phase 2: Criminogenic Targets

Before we focus on the specific targets of Phase 2, we need to note that those issues we addressed in Phase 1 are not necessarily seen as completed. Throughout treatment we seize on naturally occurring opportunities to continue the enhancement of self-esteem, the reduction of shame, the increase in empathy, and the promotion of coping skills and mood management. We also frequently refer back to the client's autobiography and offense precursors, when targeting other issues. Thus our program is not modularized but is an ongoing comprehensive psychotherapeutic process that takes advantage of every opportunity for learning, and our case formulation is constantly evolving.

The targets specifically introduced in Phase 2 are those that have been shown to predict recidivism in sexual offenders. We address attitudes and cognitions, self-regulation (including emotional self-regulation), and relationship issues. The selection of these criminogenic factors rests on a series of meta-analyses (e.g., Craig, Browne, & Stringer, 2003; Hanson & Bussière, 1998; Hanson & Morton-Bourgon, 2005) as well as other research reports (e.g., Thornton, 2002; Thornton & Beech, 2002). The results of these studies have been summarized by several authors (e.g., Cortoni, 2009; Craig, Beech, & Harkins, 2009; Craig, Browne, & Beech, 2008; Hanson, 2006; Mann et al., 2010) and the reader is referred to those sources for more detailed considerations.

Phase 3: Self-Management

This final phase of the program aims at integrating what has been learned so far into plans for release and for the continued development of a more fulfilling life. The first step involves identifying the goals, and plans to achieve these goals. Next, we have the participants generate a self-management plan that can assist them not only to avoid risk-related circumstances, but more importantly, to generate positive approach-goal focused strategies that are exclusive of offending. Included in this self-management plan is a list of warning signs that are related to previous maladaptive self-regulation and approach strategies that are exclusive of opportunities for offending. A warning sign and approach-goal list is generated by the group participant to enhance their awareness of personal risk factors and activities they can engage in which keep them away from opportunities to offend. The client also generates a similar list for his/her supports in the community, as a lack of community social supports has been shown to predict reoffending (Hanson & Harris, 2000) and is unlikely to help the offender achieve a "good life." Generating this self-management plan allows us to examine the depth and breadth of the offender's understanding of risk factors, ability to take feedback from others, and awareness of prosocial activities. Finally, we have the participants generate a concrete plan for the future including: where they will live and why that is the best place for them to reside; who they will live with and who their community supports will be; what they will do for an income; and finally, what they will do with leisure time.

Treatment Outcome

There are at least two possible ways to evaluate the effectiveness of treatments for incarcerated sex offenders (see Chapters 24 and 25). One involves evaluations measuring changes in the targets of treatment both pre- and post-participation in a sex offender treatment program. In the case of programs focused on criminogenic factors, these measures should evaluate changes on these features. Assessments of avoidance strategies would be added when relapse prevention components are included. Evaluations of this type would ideally be a requirement of all programs in order to show that the interventions do what they claim to do (i.e., produce changes in criminogenic and other features). Unfortunately, there have been very few reports of such outcome assessments.

The second type of possible outcome evaluations is usually thought to be crucial and often demanded by funders and other stakeholders, that is, the long-term effects of the treatment program on rates of recidivism. Demonstrating reductions in the number of treatment participants reoffending is the goal of all sex offender treatment programs. However, such evaluations cannot be completed until the program has processed substantial numbers of clients who have been released into society for at least 3–5 years. These requirements have limited the number of programs that have been appropriately evaluated in this way. There are also many challenges when conducting these types of studies, such as: the need to have an adequate database from which to draw information on reoffending; determining the minimum time at risk adequate to say whether the intervention was effective (a minimum of 3 years, 1 year, 1 month, 1 day?); how to handle treatment dropouts, or participants who are deported, or completers who did not achieve the targets of treatment; adequacy of the matching of the comparison group(s).

Except for a series of reports of the first type of outcome assessment by W. L. Marshall and his colleagues of Rockwood's SBA, there are no other detailed studies of change in criminogenic features derived from an SBA sex offender treatment program. Marshall's studies showed that the Rockwood's program enhanced the clients' self-esteem (Marshall, Champagne, Sturgeon, & Bryce, 1997), significantly improved relationship skills (Marshall, Bryce, Hudson, Ward, & Moth, 1996), increased victim empathy (Marshall, O'Sullivan, & Fernandez, 1996), reduced denial and minimizations (Marshall, 1994), and normalized sexual interests (Marshall, 1997). While these reports offer encouragement, not all the targets addressed in these studies reflect currently established criminogenic features and none examined any GLM-like factors.

Perhaps the most thorough currently available of the second type of evaluation of an SBA described above, is embodied in a report by Olver, Marshall, Marshall, and Nicholaichuck (2019). These researchers examined the long-term (8.5 years) rates of reoffending among three groups of Canadian federally incarcerated sex offenders. Olver et al. compared sexual recidivism rates of a group of 107 untreated sex offenders with 625 treated by Correctional Service of Canada's (CSC) standard program, and with 579 clients treated in the Rockwood SBA program.

The outcome from Olver et al.'s long-term evaluation revealed significant advantages for Rockwood's program. The reoffense rates over the 8-year follow-up were: untreated offenders = 20.2%; CSC's program = 10.7%; Rockwood's program = 4.2%. It is important to note that all differences in recidivism rates are statistically significant, so that even with a some-what greater deficit focus, CSC's program nevertheless markedly reduced reoffending. Specific examination of the results with high-risk offenders offers even greater encouragement for Rockwood's SBA approach: Re-offense rates over the 8-year follow-up for only high-risk offenders were: Rockwood = 10.3%; CSC = 19.6%; untreated offenders = 45%. In addition, both refusal rates at the initial offer of treatment and attrition rates for Rockwood have been shown to be very low (3.8 and 4.2%, respectively).

These results offer support for the recent move away from a deficit-focused approach to a more strengths-based program. While the Rockwood program has some elements of the GLM, it does not meet the full requirements of such a program as outlined by Willis, Prescott, and Yates (2016). There is no attempt in the Rockwood SBA, for example, to add a compre-hensive treatment segment aimed at training clients in the skills needed to achieve satisfaction in all areas identified in the GLM. Indeed, the low reoffense rate derived from the Rockwood evaluation suggests that doing so would be very unlikely to produce further reductions in reoffending. In fact to do so would border on over-treating the clients, which may diminish rather than enhance the benefits of treatment (see Lovins, Lowenkamp, & Latessa, 2009).

Summary and Conclusions

This chapter has described Strengths-Based Approaches to the treatment of sexual offenders. We outlined some key features of an SBA and the theoretical underpinnings of such a program, before describing the challenges that sex offender treatment providers face in making any treatment program successful in a correctional setting. Finally, we presented our SBA group treatment program and summarized the available outcome data, which appear to support the utility of such an approach. Although, our SBA treatment program was not 100% effective (and no treatment program has ever been or is likely to be), it does appear to have positively impacted both refusal and attrition rates and to have reduced recidivism. This effect was even stronger when applied to high-risk sex offenders. These data along with the unexamined potential benefits for treatment providers, such as lower stress and greater satisfaction with providing treatment, all suggest that further exploration and implementation of SBAs for incarcerated sexual offenders is warranted.

Key Readings

Hanson, R. K., Bourgon, G., Helmus, L., & Hodgson, S. (2009). The principles of effective correctional treatment also apply to sexual offenders: A meta-analysis. *Criminal Justice and Behavior, 36*, 865–891.

Mann, R. E., Hanson, R. K., & Thornton, D. (2010). Assessing risk for sexual recidivism: Some pro-posals on the nature of psychologically meaningful risk factors. *Sexual Abuse: A Journal of Research and Treatment, 22*, 191–217.

Marshall, W. L., Marshall, L. E., Serran, G. A., & O'Brien, M. D. (2011). *Rehabilitating sexual offenders: A strength-based approach.* Washington, DC: American Psychological Association.

Ward, T. (2002). Good lives and the rehabilitation of offenders: Promises and problems. *Aggression and Violent Behavior, 7,* 513–528.

References

Andrews, D. A., & Bonta, J. (2006). *The psychology of criminal conduct* (4th ed.). Cincinnati, OH: Anderson.

Andrews, D. A., Zinger, I., Hoge, R. D., Bonta, J., Gendreau, P., & Cullen, F. T. (1990). Does correctional treatment work? A clinically relevant and psychologically informed meta-analysis. *Criminology, 28,* 369–404.

Beech, A. R., & Fordham, A. S. (1997). Therapeutic climate of sexual offender treatment programs. *Sexual Abuse: A Journal of Research and Treatment, 9,* 219–237.

Beech, A. R., & Hamilton-Giachritsis, C. E. (2005). Relationship between therapeutic climate and treatment outcome in group-based sexual offender treatment programs. *Sexual Abuse: A Journal of Research and Treatment, 17,* 127–140.

Burton, D. L., & Smith-Darden, J. (2001). *North American survey of sexual abuser treatment and models: Summary data 2000.* Brandon, VT: Safer Society Press.

Carr, A. (2011). *Positive psychology: The science of happiness and human strengths.* London, UK: Routledge.

Cepeda, N. J., Pashler, H., Vul, E., Wixted, J. T., & Rohrer, D. (2006). Distributed practice in verbal recall tasks: A review and quantitative synthesis. *Psychological Bulletin, 132,* 354–380.

Cortoni, F. (2009). Factors associated with sexual recidivism. In A. R. Beech, L. A. Craig, & K. D. Browne (Eds.), *Assessment and treatment of sex offenders: A handbook* (pp. 39–52). Chichester, UK: Wiley.

Craig, L. A., Beech, A. R., & Harkins, L. (2009). The predictive accuracy of risk factors and frameworks. In A. R. Beech, L. A. Craig, & K. Browne (Eds.), *Assessment and treatment of sex offenders: A handbook* (pp. 53–74). Chichester, UK: Wiley.

Craig, L. A., Browne, K. D., & Beech, A. R. (2008). *Assessing risk in sex offenders: A practitioner's guide.* West Sussex, UK: Wiley.

Craig, L. A., Browne, K. D., & Stringer, I. (2003). Risk scales and factors predictive of sexual offence recidivism. *Trauma, Violence, & Abuse, 4,* 45–69.

Dellarosa, D., & Bourne, L. E. (1985). Surface form and the spacing effect. *Memory & Cognition, 13*(6), 529–537.

Dempster, F. N. (1988). The spacing effect: A case study in the failure to apply the results of psychological research. *American Psychologist, 43*(8), 627–634.

Dowden, C., & Andrews, D. A. (2004). The importance of staff practice in delivering effective correctional treatment: A meta-analytic review of core correctional practice. *International Journal of Offender Therapy and Comparative Criminology, 48,* 203–214.

Dowden, C., Antonowicz, D., & Andrews, D. A. (2003). The effectiveness of relapse prevention with offenders: A meta-analysis. *International Journal of Offender Therapy and Comparative Criminology, 47,* 516–528.

Eysenck, H. J. (1959). *Manual of the Maudsley personality inventory.* London, UK: University of London Press.

Hanson, R. K. (2006). Does Static-99 predict recidivism among older sexual offenders? *Sexual abuse: A journal of research and treatment, 18,* 343–355.

Hanson, R. K., Bourgon, G., Helmus, L., & Hodgson, S. (2009). The principles of effective correctional treatment also apply to sexual offenders: A meta-analysis. *Criminal Justice and Behavior, 36,* 865–891.

Hanson, R. K., & Bussière, M. T. (1998). Predicting relapse: A meta-analysis of sexual offender recidivism studies. *Journal of Consulting and Clinical Psychology, 66,* 348–362.

Hanson, R. K., & Harris, A. J. R. (2000). Where should we intervene? Dynamic predictors of sex offense recidivism. *Criminal Justice and Behavior*, 27, 6–35.

Hanson, R. K., & Morton-Bourgon, K. (2005). The characteristics of persistent sexual offenders: A meta-analysis of recidivism studies. *Journal of Consulting and Clinical Psychology*, 73, 1154–1163.

Hare, R. D. (1991). *Manual for the Revised Psychopathy Checklist.* Toronto, Canada: Multi-Health Systems.

Kazdin, A. E. (1978). *History of behavior modification: Experimental foundations of contemporary research.* Baltimore, MD: University Park Press.

Linley, P. A., & Joseph, S. (Eds.) (2004). *Positive psychology in practice.* Hoboken, NJ: Wiley.

Lovins, B., Lowenkamp, C. T., & Latessa, E. J. (2009). Applying the risk principle to sex offenders: Can treatment make some sex offenders worse? *The Prison Journal*, 89, 344–357.

Luborsky, L., Crits-Christoph, P., Mintz, J., & Auerbach, A. (1988). *Who will benefit from psychotherapy? Predicting therapeutic outcomes.* New York, NY: Basic Books.

Mann, R. E. (April, 2015). *How can prisons reduce reoffending?* Paper presented at the 9th annual St. Joseph's Healthcare Hamilton's Forensic Psychiatry Program and Mental Health & Addiction Program, and McMaster University, Risk & Recovery conference, Hamilton, Canada.

Mann, R. E., Hanson, R. K., & Thornton, D. (2010). Assessing risk for sexual recidivism: Some proposals on the nature of psychologically meaningful risk factors. *Sexual Abuse: A Journal of Research and Treatment*, 22(2), 191–217.

Mann, R. E., & Webster, S. D. (2002, October). *Understanding resistance and denial.* Paper presented at the 21st Annual Research and Treatment Conference of the Association for the Treatment of Sexual Abusers, Montreal, Canada.

Marshall, L. E., Marshall, W. L., Fernandez, Y. M., Malcolm, P. B., & Moulden, H. M. (2008). The Rockwood preparatory program for sexual offenders: Description and preliminary appraisal. *Sexual Abuse: A Journal of Research and Treatment*, 20, 25–42.

Marshall, W. L. (1994). Treatment effects on denial and minimization in incarcerated sex offenders. *Behavior Research and Therapy*, 32, 559–564.

Marshall, W. L. (1997). The relationship between self-esteem and deviant sexual arousal in nonfamilial child molesters. *Behavior Modification*, 21, 86–96.

Marshall, W. L., Bryce, P., Hudson, S. M., Ward, T., & Moth, B. (1996). The enhancement of intimacy and the reduction of loneliness among child molesters. *Journal of Family Violence*, 11, 219–235.

Marshall, W. L., Champagne, F., Sturgeon, C., & Bryce, P. (1997). Increasing the self-esteem of child molesters. *Sexual Abuse: A Journal of Research and Treatment*, 9, 321–333.

Marshall, W. L., Marshall, L. E., Serran, G. A., & O'Brien, M. D. (2011). *Rehabilitating sexual offenders: A strength-based approach.* Washington, DC: American Psychological Association.

Marshall, W. L., O'Sullivan, C., & Fernandez, Y. M. (1996). The enhancement of victim empathy among incarcerated child molesters. *Legal and Criminological Psychology*, 1, 95–102.

Marshall, W. L., Serran, G., Moulden, H., Mulloy, R., Fernandez, Y. M., Mann, R., & Thornton, D. (2002). Therapist features in sexual offender treatment: Their reliable identification and influence on behaviour change. *Clinical Psychology & Psychotherapy*, 9, 395–405.

Marshall, W. L., Serran, G. A., Fernandez, Y. M., Mulloy, R., Mann, R. E., & Thornton, D. (2003). Therapist characteristics in the treatment of sexual offenders: Tentative data on their relationship with indices of behaviour change. *Journal of Sexual Aggression*, 9, 25–30.

Maruna, S. (2001). *Making good: How ex-convicts reform and rebuild their lives.* Washington DC: American Psychological Association.

McGrath, R. J., Cumming, G. R., & Burchard, B. L. (2003). *Current practices and trends in sexual abuser management: Safer Society 2002 nationwide survey.* Brandon, VT: Safer Society Press.

McGrath, R. J., Cumming, G. R., Burchard, B. L., Zeoli, S., & Ellerby, L. (2010). *Current practices and emerging trends in sexual abuser management.* Brandon, VT: Safer Society Press.

Morgan, R., Luborsky, L., Crits-Christoph, P., Curtis, H., & Solomon, J. (1982). Predicting the outcomes of psychotherapy by the Penn Helping Alliance Rating Method. *Archives of General Psychiatry*, 39(4), 397–402.

Moss, V. D. (1995). *The efficacy of massed versus distributed practice as a function of desired learning outcomes and grade level of the student* (Doctoral dissertation). Utah State University. Retrieved from https://digitalcommons.usu.edu/cgi/viewcontent.cgi?article=4569&context=etd.

Norcross, J. C. (2002). *Psychotherapy relationships that work: Therapist contributions and responsiveness to patients.* New York, NY: Oxford University Press.

Olver, M. E., Marshall, L. E., Marshall, W. L., & Nicholaichuck, T. P. (2019). A long-term outcome assessment of the effects on subsequent reoffense rates of a strength-based treatment program for sex offenders. Sexual Abuse.

Padesky, C. A., & Mooney, K. A. (2012). Strengths-based cognitive-behavioural therapy: A four-step model to build resilience. *Clinical Psychology and Psychotherapy*, 19, 283–290.

Peterson, C. (2006). *A primer in positive psychology.* New York, NY: Oxford University Press.

Sawyer, S. (2002). Group therapy with adult sex offenders. In B. K. Schwartz, & H. Cellini (Eds.), *The sex offender: Current treatment modalities and systems issues* (Vol. 4) (pp. 14.1–14.15). Kingston, NJ: Civic Research Institute.

Seligman, M. E. P. (2002). *Authentic happiness: Using the new positive psychology to realize your potential for lasting fulfillment.* New York, NY: Free Press.

Seligman, M. E. P., & Csikszentmihalyi, M. (2000). Positive psychology: An introduction. *American Psychologist*, 55, 5–14.

Seligman, M. E. P., & Peterson, C. (2003). Positive clinical psychology. In L. G. Aspinwall, & U. M. Staudinger (Eds.), *A psychology of human strengths: Fundamental questions and future directions for a positive psychology* (pp. 305–317). Washington, DC: American Psychological Association.

Snyder, C. R. (1994). *The psychology of hope: You can get there from here.* New York, NY: Free Press.

Snyder, C. R., & Lopez, S. J. (Eds.) (2005). *Handbook of positive psychology.* New York, NY: Oxford University Press.

Thornton, D. (2002). Constructing and testing a framework for dynamic risk assessment. *Sexual Abuse: A Journal of Research and Treatment*, 14, 139–153.

Thornton, D., & Beech, A. R. (2002, October). *Integrating statistical and psychological factors through the structured risk assessment model.* Paper presented at the 21st Annual Research and Treatment Conference of the Association for the Treatment of Sexual Abusers, Montreal, Ontario, Canada.

Ullman, L. P., & Krasner, L. (Eds.) (1965). *Research in behavior modification: New developments in implications.* New York, NY: Holt Rinehart and Winston.

Underwood, B. J. (1961). Ten years of massed practice on distributed practice. *Psychological Review*, 68, 229–247.

Ward, T. (2002). Good lives and the rehabilitation of offenders: Promises and problems. *Aggression and Violent Behavior*, 7, 513–528.

Ward, T., Collie, R. M., & Bourke, P. (2009). Models of offender rehabilitation: The Good Lives Model and the Risk-Need-Responsivity model. In A. R. Beech, L. A. Craig, & K. D. Browne (Eds.), *Assessment and treatment of sex offenders: A handbook* (pp. 293–310). Chichester, UK: Wiley.

Ward, T., & Stewart, C. A. (2003). The treatment of sex offenders: Risk management and good lives. *Professional Psychology: Research and Practice*, 34, 353–360.

Ware, J., & Bright, D. A. (2008). Evolution of a treatment programme for sex offenders: Changes to the NSW Custody-Based Intensive Treatment (CUBIT). *Psychiatry, Psychology and Law*, 15, 340–349.

Ware, J., Mann, R. E., & Wakeling, H. C. (2009). Group versus individual treatment: What is the best modality for treating sexual offenders? *Sexual Abuse in Australia and New Zealand*, 1, 70–78.

Willis, G. M., Prescott, D. S., & Yates, P. M. (2016). Application of an integrated good lives approach to sex offender treatment. In D. Boer (Ed.), (Series Ed.) *The Wiley handbook on the theories, assessment, and treatment of sexual offending* (Vol. 3, Treatment, L. E. Marshall & W. L. Marshall [Vol. Eds.],) (pp. 1355–1368). Chichester, UK: Wiley.

33

Treating Intimate Partner Violence and Abuse

Erica Bowen
University of Worcester, UK

Andrew Day
James Cook University and University of Melbourne, Australia

Introduction

Despite numerous attempts to demonstrate that treatment does actually change perpetrator behavior, the available data, to date, on standard group interventions for batterers have been described as "underwhelming" (Banks, Kini, & Babcock, 2014, p. 169), with the only published meta-analytic review of evaluations of programs offered to mandated clients concluding that "the mean effect for victim reported outcomes was zero" (Feder & Wilson, 2005, p. 239). However, even small effects can be socially significant. For example, Babcock, Green, and Robie's (2004) meta-analysis of treatment outcomes for court mandated and self-referred clients identified that treatment led to a 5% decrease in violence. This was calculated to equate in the United States to 42,000 fewer women being victimized. Consequently, the rationale for intervening with known perpetrators is reasonably well established, especially in a context in which the alternatives (e.g., imprisonment alone) are unlikely to work (e.g., Trevena & Poynton, 2016); Ventura and Davis (2005), for example, reported that length of incarceration was not linked to the likelihood of recidivism in a sample of over 500 convicted intimate partner violence offenders who served periods of jail time ranging from 5 to 180 days. The aim of this chapter then is to describe some of the most widely used approaches to treatment and articulate some of the challenges that arise in trying to treat intimate partner violence and abuse (IPVA) perpetrators in a correctional setting. We use the term IPVA in this chapter to refer to physical violence, sexual violence, stalking, and psychological aggression (including coercive acts) by a current or former intimate partner (see Breiding, Basile, Smith, Black, & Mahendra, 2015). We suggest that progress in this area has, in part, been hampered by an inadequate understanding of the differences that exist within the perpetrator population. In our view, this lack of understanding has undermined the likelihood of treatment being generally effective.

Our focus in this chapter, and in nearly all of the available empirical studies that we draw upon, is on violence that is perpetrated by men on women. This is because, even though some types of IPVA are perpetrated about equally by women and men (Kimmel, 2002), the violence experienced by women is likely to be more physically harmful than that experienced by men. This is not to suggest that violence perpetrated by women, or that which occurs in same-sex

The Wiley International Handbook of Correctional Psychology, First Edition. Edited by Devon L. L. Polaschek, Andrew Day, and Clive R. Hollin.

relationships, is uncommon, or that it should be regarded as trivial. Rather, it suggests that different approaches to treatment may be needed for these groups, based on a careful assessment of relevant risk factors and precipitating situations.

Intervention Paradigms

The 1980s and 1990s saw the proliferation of counseling services for male IPV perpetrators across the United States, although specialized services were slower to emerge in other parts of the world. Adams (1989) has suggested that the early approaches to intervention with male IPV perpetrators can be characterized as drawing on five main therapeutic models, which we briefly describe below because features of each remain present in contemporary programs. Each model reflects the underlying theoretical or ideological position adopted by practitioners to explain IPVA, and consequently they vary in their ability to adequately account for IPVA and respond to the needs of IPVA perpetrators.

The Insight Model

The insight model reflects an individual psychodynamic approach to treatment which focuses on understanding underlying psychological causes of violence. These causes may include (but are not limited to) poor impulse control, fear of intimacy, dependency, fear of abandonment, depression, and the long-lasting effects of childhood trauma. In this model, violence is viewed as occurring in response to real or perceived threats, with underlying emotional deficits understood as a consequence of earlier negative childhood experiences. Consequently, the overarching aim of treatment is to help perpetrators achieve insight into how their current behavior has been influenced by past experience, with a view to then learning more appropriate methods of responding to conflict in current relationships. It is further expected that violent men will develop a more positive self-image as a result of improved insight, which then also contributes to behavioral change (Adams, 1989).

The insight model has, however, been criticized for ignoring the functional nature of IPVA and minimizing its criminal nature (Pence & Paymar, 1993). There is also evidence that the causes of IPVA can only be attributed to psychopathology in a minority of cases (e.g., Tiff, 1993). Moreover, many of the "symptoms" (e.g., depression, low self-esteem) targeted by this approach have been dismissed as consequences rather than causes of IPVA (Hamberger & Hasting, 1993), although the empirical research delineating the causal direction of these associations remains limited.

The Ventilation Model

The ventilation model conceptualizes IPVA as an artifact of suppressed anger and emotional repression. Popular during the 1960s, this idea was ensconced within Gestalt therapy—among other approaches—and the model advocates the open expression of anger in order to overcome emotional repression and facilitate more functional communication (Rubin, 1970, cited in Adams, 1989). Influenced by Freud's theorizing regarding the therapeutic benefits of emotional catharsis (Bushman, 2002) this model's advocates see the suppression of anger as leading to uncontrollable outbursts, or to internalization that presents as other physical symptoms (such as depression). Treatment models based on this approach often promote the inclusion of couples as the target for intervention, with both members of a couple encouraged to participate in activities that are designed to expel frustration and anger (Adams, 1989). However, the model remains controversial in light of evidence that directly challenges the efficacy of ventilation as a method of reducing aggressive urges (Franzoi, 1996), and empirical evidence that rumination increases rather than decreases aggressive responses (Bushman, 2002).

The Interaction Model

Based on systems theory, the interaction model views IPVA as arising out of interactions between two or more people within a family with deficient communication patterns (Neidig, 1984). The overarching goal of therapy is to enable partners to identify their role in those communications that result in violence at points and, from this perspective, both partners are equally culpable for the use of violence and share responsibility for stopping it (Deschner, 1984). Consequently, treatment is offered for couples together, although this approach has been widely criticized for not adequately addressing issues of responsibility for violence and implicitly holding both individuals responsible for abusive behaviors. Moreover, some have argued that it actively jeopardizes the safety and independence of female victims (Robertson, 1999).

Cognitive Behavioral Therapy

Cognitive behavioral approaches to working with perpetrators typically locate the causes of violence within the individual, explaining it in terms of various socio-cognitive deficits that significantly impair not only the capacity to reason, but also how the individual sees and understands the self, other people, and the world (e.g., Ross & Fabiano, 1985). Perpetrators are also seen as lacking the social problem-solving skills necessary to identify and deal with the problems that are often associated with everyday living (McMurran, Fyffe, McCarthy, Duggan, & Latham, 2001). It follows that the focus of intervention is often on changing maladaptive cognitions, or what are commonly referred to as cognitive distortions,[1] and that individual differences in relation to the levels of self-control that individuals are able to exert over their emotions, their behavior, their personal skills, and their personal standards are all important treatment targets. Violence is understood as a learned behavior that serves particular functions, but can be un-learned through a process of re-training (Babcock et al., 2004). The main criticism leveled at cognitive behavioral therapy (CBT) approaches concern their failure to incorporate any substantial analysis of gender power (Adams, 1989), although contemporary models do consider this (e.g., Pence & Paymar, 1993). Other criticisms concern the skills training approach, which is viewed as having the potential to be misused by perpetrators who are motivated to manipulate and control their partners (Robertson, 1999). There is, however, little empirical data to actually support the idea that such misuse actually occurs.

Duluth Psycho-Educational Model

The most widely adopted treatment approach is the "Duluth" psycho-education model. The underlying program theory asserts that the primary cause of IPVA is patriarchal ideology and the implicit or explicit societal sanctioning of men's power and control over women (Babcock et al., 2004). The "Power and Control Wheel" (Pence & Paymar, 1993) is used as a teaching tool to illustrate the range of controlling tactics that are routinely adopted by perpetrators. The basic aims of intervention are to educate men about their use of these

tactics (e.g., financial control, intimidation, minimization and denial, male privilege, isolation) in order to improve motivation to adopt behavior that is characteristic of egalitarian
relationships (e.g., negotiation, trust). The Duluth program combines a psycho-educational
men's program with a strong multi-agency approach to risk management, whereby intervention is closely linked to the judicial system. The ongoing safety of victims is given paramount
importance, and particular account is paid to research demonstrating that women may continue in relationships with abusive partners because of a lack of economic resources, social
support networks, and low self-efficacy, among other factors (Chronister, 2007). The focus
of the Duluth model is thus much broader than just intervention with perpetrators. It is a
system response to domestic violence, involving a multi-agency approach with formal protocols and responsibilities that are not centered or reliant on individual change. Although
often viewed as distinctive from the models described above, there is often considerable
overlap between psycho-educational "Duluth" interventions and CBT interventions (Babcock et al., 2004), both of which more often combine an analysis of gender with skills
training. Indeed, Bowen (2011a) directly compared the content of Duluth and alternative
models used in the United Kingdom and found considerable overlap in theoretical and technique description: the main difference being the use of the Power and Control Wheel to
inform the structure of the Duluth-based model.

The Duluth approach, although widely favored, is also not without its critics. Dutton and
Corvo (2007), for example, have argued that the underlying program theory is fundamentally
flawed as a consequence of a simplistic analysis of IPVA as arising from one causal variable:
patriarchy. They cite studies which show that women self-report higher rates of physical violence toward male partners than males report toward female partners as evidence that IPVA
perpetration is not exclusively a male characteristic.

More Recent Developments

Despite there being no definitive empirical evidence to support the adoption of one approach
over another (see Babcock et al., 2004; Feder & Wilson, 2005) and growing evidence supporting the absence of a significant effect for existing treatment models, many organizations and
service providers have felt the need to develop standards and protocols to guide the development
and delivery of programs. The most recently published survey of standards in 45 US states,
conducted by Maiuro and Eberle (2008), nonetheless concluded that considerable variation
existed in relation to recommended treatment length (from 12 to more than 52 weeks), with
the majority of standards requiring a minimum of 24–26 weeks. The vast majority (98%) specified group therapy as the preferred modality of intervention, with Georgia and Maine explicitly
prohibiting the use of individual therapy, and the majority (68%) prohibiting any form of couple
therapy. Maiuro and Eberle further note that in two thirds of the standards, although the theoretical preamble focuses on the role of power, control, and patriarchal social systems in IPVA,
the actual intervention content focuses on improving emotion regulation, victim empathy,
communication and negotiation, and anger management. One State specifically prohibited the
inclusion of any analysis of anger and associated skills training,[2] although the majority of the
standards recognize that IPVA is determined by multiple risk factors and that, as a consequence,
multiple areas need to be targeted.

Group work with perpetrators remains the dominant mode of delivery. However, in light of
the evidence of very small treatment effects for these models (Feder & Wilson, 2005),

researchers and practitioners have sought new methods of working. Central to these innovations is an acknowledgement of the importance of the therapeutic or working alliance to offender engagement in group processes (Holdsworth, Bowen, Brown, & Howat, 2014) and, more fundamentally, the process of reducing IPVA is increasingly characterized as a therapeutic endeavor, even when the setting for intervention is the criminal justice system. Consequently, two new approaches have recently emerged within the IPVA treatment literature: solution-focused brief therapy (SFBT) and motivational interviewing (MI): only MI will be examined here due to the dearth of rigorous evidence concerning SFBT approaches (readers are referred to Lee, Sebold, & Uken, 2003, for a description of SFBT with IPVA perpetrators).

IPVA differs from many other types of violent offending in so far as it typically occurs behind closed doors, where the only witnesses are victims. As a result, the facts of the offending are often difficult to establish, and male perpetrators are likely to dispute the evidence that is presented to the police and/or the courts in relation to the frequency and intensity of their violence. They may also question the reliability of the victim statements and, on a basic level, challenge the idea that they were personally responsible for the violence, seeing themselves as victims of circumstances (Thomas, 2003). In our experience, many men arrive in treatment expressing a sense of injustice because they feel that their partner was equally responsible for the circumstances that led to the requirement to attend the program. They regularly cite mitigation or provocation that led to their violence, and see the response from courts as an over-reaction; as they see it, the violence is, at best, "a joint problem" and, at worst, "her responsibility."

Given these justifications it is unsurprising that program facilitators commonly report encountering hostility, resistance, and non-compliance from their clients, especially in the early stages of treatment. Not only are they often reluctant participants who have low levels of problem awareness and poor motivation to attend, but they are often unclear about what is expected of them. Some claim no understanding of the legal process, whereas for others the length of time between offending and entry into treatment is important evidence that treatment is unwarranted. In interviews we conducted with perpetrators at the start of treatment, the majority stated that they had primarily resolved the issues that led to their referral to the program (Day, O'Leary, Chung, & Justo, 2009). Although generally resigned to having to attend the program, they did not, however, completely dismiss the potential for benefits to arise. In our view, focusing on how treatment can help perpetrators to achieve personally meaningful goals in non-violent ways (whether these be about relationships, children, or mental health issues) can only help to improve the quality of therapeutic engagement required for behavior change to occur.

MI (see Miller & Rollnick, 1991; Chapter 38) was designed to help individuals move through a series of stages of change in the course of resolving problematic behavior. It has been suggested that MI may be a useful model for addressing denial in IPVA because an initial goal of MI is to confront clients with the discrepancy between what they believe/want and how they behave. In MI, denial is not addressed by direct confrontation; instead the client is invited to make the arguments for change him or herself. The therapist serves to provide the direction (e.g., through the use of open-ended questions that invite "change talk") and the atmosphere (i.e., one of unconditional positive regard) to facilitate the development of such arguments. MI has been evaluated as an adjunct to more typical IPVA intervention approaches, although a small randomized controlled trial of a pure MI versus no intervention model found that IPVA offenders who were assigned to the MI condition (MI completed before court mandated treatment) made significantly better progress in relation to the stages of change and responsibility-taking for violent behavior than those in the control group

(Kistenmacher & Weiss, 2008). Musser, Semiatin, Taft, and Murphy (2008) also noted that although a two-session MI pre-intervention module led to improved in-session behaviors, compliance, engagement, help-seeking, and readiness to change, there was a marginally non-significant effect on partner-reported experience of abuse in a 6-month follow-up when compared to those who had no pre-intervention MI sessions. It is clear that a broader program of evaluation work is required that enables direct comparison of treatment modalities and pre-treatment motivation enhancement approaches in order to determine the most effective method of IPVA treatment.

Correctional Programs

Although it has been noted that the prison setting provides an important treatment opportunity (Pascual-Leone, Bierman, Arnold, & Stasiak, 2011), relatively little is known about the features of effective intervention when it is offered in prison settings. This may be because programs specifically aimed at IPVA are relatively uncommon given the practical and legal constraints that exist in these settings; for example, we know that many perpetrators receive custodial sentences that do not provide sufficient time for them to complete a custodial program (for example, an offense under the California Penal Code 243(e)(1) carries a maximum jail sentence of 1 year; more serious offenses may be prosecuted as misdemeanors or felonies). Even more challenging is the fact that offenses against intimate partners may not be specifically coded (for example in England and Wales, Australia, and New Zealand), making it difficult to identify those who might require treatment. Some brief descriptions of some of the correctional programs that have been developed are provided below to illustrate what is currently available. These programs typically draw heavily on the cognitive behavioral and psychoeducational approaches outlined above.

The Canadian Prison Service Program

Correctional Service Canada offers a moderate- and a high-intensity program for IPVA offenders (Stewart, Gabora, Kropp, & Lee, 2014). The moderate program is 25 sessions long, whilst the high-intensity program is 78 sessions. Both are predicated on an ecological analysis of risk factors (see Heise, 1998; Chapter 13), and aim to address risk factors at each ecological level. The first session gives the offender time to evaluate his goals for change and assess the possibilities for change. Initial modules are designed to increase engagement and motivation to change and also to educate offenders about the nature of IPVA (e.g., the range of behaviors that are involved and the factors that can lead someone to perpetrating IPVA). Modules then progress to incorporate cognitive skills training and the restructuring of beliefs and attitudes that support IPVA, and the development of skills to aid emotion management, specifically with reference to jealousy, anger, and fear of relationship loss. In addition, participants are trained in communication and negotiation skills. Later modules focus on relapse prevention and include identifying coping strategies to avoid or manage high-risk situations, the identification of people who contribute to high-risk situations, and also the identification of a support network to draw upon should high-risk situations arise, people who will also support the maintenance of a commitment to healthy relationships. The high-intensity program contains a greater emphasis on personal autobiographies and understanding the ontogenic determinants of IPVA, as well as placing a greater emphasis on parenting.

Stewart et al. (2014) examined the impact of this program on criminogenic needs ($n = 572$) as well as post-release behavior ($n = 246$, average time at risk 1 year). It was found that those who completed treatment reported significantly lower levels of jealousy, fewer negative attitudes about relationships, better recognition and application of relapse prevention skills, greater respect for their partners, increased treatment readiness and responsivity, and more engagement in positive behaviors and attitudes. For the high-intensity group there was also a significant difference between treated and untreated offenders for both spousal and any violence. Four percent of the treated and 14% of untreated offenders committed a further domestic violence offense, which represented a 71% decrease in spousal violence recidivism. In addition, 11% of the treated high-intensity and 26% of the untreated high-intensity group committed a new violent offense, which represented a 60% reduction in recidivism. For the moderate-intensity group, however, the differences observed were not statistically significant.

Building Better Relationships: National Offender Management Service of England and Wales

Drawing upon an extensive review of the literature (Bowen, 2011b), the National Offender Management Service in England and Wales has developed a group-based intervention for convicted IPVA perpetrators named Building Better Relationships (BBR). This program is due to replace the existing Duluth-informed Integrated Domestic Abuse Program (IDAP) in the community and the prison-based Healthy Relationship Program that was based on the Canadian Corrections model previously described. BBR is based on the General Aggression Model (De Wall, Anderson, & Bushman, 2011), which is a socio-cognitive model of aggression that emphasizes the role of: person and situation inputs, present internal states, and outcomes of appraisal and decision-making processes. BBR comprises 28 sessions, four of which are one-to-one (two at the start, and then two in between group-based modules); the remaining 24 are group based. The group-based sessions form three modules of eight sessions that focus on "my thinking," "my emotions," and "my relationship" (Ministry of Justice, n.d.). The actual therapeutic techniques used reflect a range of styles, including CBT, dialectical behavior therapy, and mindfulness training, and a self-directed goal orientation is included. No evaluation data are currently available for this model.

A small number of other prison program evaluations have been conducted. These include an early uncontrolled study by Wolfus and Bierman (1996) which reported promising short-term effectiveness, although prisoners in this study were not followed up after release. An unpublished dissertation by Ley (2005), in which a 26-week CBT group treatment was evaluated, reported a reduction in the rate of recidivism at 1 year post-release for the treatment group. Pascual-Leone et al. (2012) also reported that prisoners who attended an experiential and emotion-focused group treatment program abstained from violent offenses for longer than those who did not. Finally, Yorke, Friedman, and Hurt (2010) reported positive cognitive change in maximum security prisoners who attended a 22-session psycho-educational and cognitive behavioral program in California as part of a therapeutic community approach to treating substance use.

Community Corrections Programs

Two Australian programs are described here to illustrate the type of intervention that is often made available to IPVA offenders serving community-based orders, including those who have been released from prison under supervision. The first of these, the Domestic Abuse Program

(DAP), is based on the UK's Duluth-informed IDAP program. It is a 10-week, 20-session (40–50-hour) group program (Blatch, O'Sullivan, Delaney, van Doorn, & Sweller, 2016) that combines several theoretical approaches, including the Risk-Need-Responsivity (RNR) principles (Andrews & Bonta, 2010) and principles of CBT (Polaschek, 2011; Thakker & Gannon, 2010). The program itself comprises five modules (Miller, 2010). The first focuses on identifying abuse and uses psycho-educational material to develop offenders' knowledge and understanding of abuse, and CBT techniques to modify antisocial and pro-violent cognitions. The second module focuses on managing emotions, beliefs, and attitudes, and is designed to challenge participants' cognitions, feelings, and behaviors associated with the promotion, or maintenance, of violent behaviors. The third module, offense mapping, enables participants to analyze the antecedents, warning signs, and high-risk situations through behavior chain analysis. The fourth module focuses on victim impact, and introduces psycho-educational and Duluth-style material to increase victim empathy and address impact issues. The last module introduces sexual respect, relationship skills and safety strategies, conflict management, communication skills, and dispute resolution techniques. In contrast to the first four sessions of each module, the final session is relatively unstructured to promote therapeutic engagement and address group process issues.

Blatch et al. (2016) recently compared recidivism outcomes of the treatment group with those of a propensity score-matched control group. Program enrolment was shown to be associated with significant improvement in the odds of time to first general reconviction (15%) and first violent reconviction (by 27%) compared to controls. Reconviction rates were significantly lower (by 15%) for attendees who completed the program (62% of those who started it); for those who did not complete the program, no significant treatment effect was found.

The Gold Coast Domestic Violence Offender Education and Intervention Program for Male Perpetrators (Australia; Moore, 2009) is a 26-session program with a rolling enrolment format, delivered in a community corrections setting with a maximum of 12 group participants at any one time. There are eight modules in the program, each lasting approximately three sessions, and each of which is based on the segments of the Duluth Power and Control Wheel that reflect women's experiences of financial, sexual, emotional, mental, and physical abuse. Videos are used to demonstrate common domestic violence situations and illustrate the various obvious and subtle tactics that perpetrators use to exert power and control. In order to ensure that victims' perspectives are represented, one of the videos contains discussions generated by a group of women (previous victims) who speak about what they felt when their partners used a particular type of controlling or abusive behavior. No outcome evaluation data are currently available for this model.

Characteristics of Perpetrators

There is some debate concerning the extent to which males who perpetrate IPVA are specialists, that is, use violence only toward female intimate partners, or generalists who engage in violent offending toward non-intimates as well as in other types of offending (Bouffard, Wright, Muftić, & Bouffard, 2008). This is clearly a key issue which will have a significant bearing on the type of intervention that is likely to be effective. The available empirical evidence, however, does not provide a definitive answer to this question, although early research did suggest that the overlap between partner violence and crime exceeds that which would be expected by chance (e.g., Marvell & Moody, 1999). Based on an analysis of data from a longitudinal community cohort sample of 849 non-offenders, Moffitt, Kreuger, Caspi, and

Fagan (2000) concluded that general crime and partner violence were conceptually distinct, although they were correlated. In addition, although both were associated with negative emotionality, partner violence was not associated with low self-control, whereas general crime was.

Most recently, Herrero, Torres, Fernández-Suárez, and Rodríguez-Díaz (2016) found, in a sample of 110 Spanish prisoners convicted of violence against a female partner, that generalists (with a varied criminal history, 75% of the sample) in contrast to specialists (intimate partner-violent criminal histories, 25% of the sample) had an earlier onset of criminality, and higher psychopathology indicative of antisocial and borderline personality disorder characteristics, greater substance abuse and hostile sexism, and were less likely to report that their family of origin was characterized by open expressions of anger.

There are several available reviews of the multitude of risk factors for IPVA (e.g., Bowen, 2011b; Stith, Smith, Penn, Ward, & Tritt, 2004; and see Chapter 13). However, when examining individual studies there is considerable variation in the extent of empirical support for each individual risk factor. Although methodological differences can account for some of this variation, it is likely that the presence of multiple IPVA perpetrator "types" within samples contaminates the results. Indeed, there is reason to suspect that IPVA perpetrators are heterogeneous in relation to both the extent to which they "specialize" in IPVA behaviors and also the risk factors that contribute to these different presentations. Typology research brings together patterns of risk factors and suggests theoretically that there are broadly two underlying dimensions of psychopathology that fuel IPVA behaviors: antisocial and borderline personality traits.

In their seminal theoretical typology of IPVA perpetrators, Holtzworth-Munroe and Stuart (1994) proposed that there are three broad categories of IPVA perpetrator that vary in terms of the severity and generality of IPVA and violence used, and psychopathology (see Table 33.1).

Within this typology, the Family Only (FO) perpetrator is characterized as a specialist offender who is only violent toward intimate partners, has low levels of psychopathology, and has attitudes that do not endorse the use of violence and which are favorable toward women. Conflict is theorized to occur in response to poor communication and conflict resolution strategies: often as a "last resort." The violence is suggested to be low frequency, and low severity. Holtzworth-Munroe and Stuart (1994) suggested that this profile is most likely to be identified in samples of IPVA perpetrators who self-refer for treatment in the community, and is less likely to be present within corrections samples. In Herrero et al.'s (2016) study, a small proportion of their specialists had been incarcerated after murdering their intimate partner. In addition, they were likely to have been imprisoned for violation of non-contact orders. Perpetrators with this profile are most likely to desist over time (Holtzworth-Munroe, Meehan, Herron, Rehman, & Stuart, 2003).

The Dysphoric/Borderline (DB) group, in contrast, evidence considerable psychopathology in the form of borderline personality disorder traits; their violence is explosive and characterized as cyclical in nature. Fundamental to the violence of these individuals is an insecure attachment profile developed through a childhood history of considerable trauma, typically as primary victims of abuse and secondary victims of inter-parental violence. Their preoccupied attachment style means that they are likely to have a fundamental need to be in an intimate relationship in order to fulfill their attachment needs, but are also hypervigilant to perceived threat to those relationships. As a consequence, violence arises as a response to perceived or threatened loss, initiated as a way of regaining proximity to the attachment figure: in this case, the partner. Also referred to by Dutton (2006) as the "Abusive Personality," this type is regarded as more likely than the other two categories to abuse their own children (Herron & Holtzworth-Munroe, 2002).

Table 33.1 Core Characteristics of the Three IPVA Perpetrator Subtypes Described by Holtzworth-Munroe and Stuart (1994)

Risk factor	Family Only (FO)	Dysphoric/ Borderline (DB)	Generally Violent/ Antisocial (GVA)
Genetic influences	Low	Moderate	High
Parental violence	Low-moderate	Moderate	Moderate-high
Childhood abuse/rejection	Low-moderate	Moderate	Moderate-high
Association with deviant peers	Low	Low-moderate	High
Attachment style	Secure or preoccupied	Preoccupied	Dismissing
Interpersonal dependency	Moderate	High	Low
Empathy	Moderate	Low-moderate	Low
Marital social skills	Low-moderate	Low	Low
Non-marital social skills	Moderate-high	Moderate	Low
Hostile attitudes toward women	No	Moderate-high	High
Pro-violence attitudes	Low	moderate	High

Note. © American Psychological Association. Adapted from Holtzworth-Munroe and Stuart (1994).

Finally, the Generally Violent/Antisocial (GVA) group would be characterized as criminal generalists: engaging in a wide range of criminal behaviors including violence, and violence generalized to victims outside of intimate relationships. Unlike the other two groups, genetic factors linked to impulsivity are expected to play a role in the behaviors exhibited by GVA offenders. In addition, although they are also likely to have witnessed inter-parental violence and experienced childhood abuse, they are more likely to have developed a dismissive rather than a preoccupied attachment style. This style is central to their antisocial personality trait presentation. Consequently, these offenders do not invest in or value relationships to the same extent as the other types, and instead view individuals in fairly utilitarian terms, as pawns to be commanded and controlled. This group has very hostile attitudes toward women and attitudes that endorse the use of violence. Day and Bowen (2015) theorized that this group is likely to engage in high levels of coercive control, and use high levels of coercive physical violence, including sexual coercion and threatened forced sexual activity.

Although this typology seems to provide a neat way of characterizing different subgroups of IPVA perpetrator, concern remains regarding the development, use, and clinical relevance of typologies in general. Capaldi and Kim (2007), for example, raise important concerns regarding whether the previously identified subtypes truly reflect "different" groups, or reflect a continuum of risk (low, medium, high) characterized by the intersection of violence severity and psychopathology. Indeed, evidence from studies conducted to validate Holtzworth-Munroe and Stuart's (1994) typology suggest that this might be the case. For example, Holtzworth-Munroe, Meehan, Herron, Rehman, and Stuart (2000) attempted to validate the typology on a community sample of 102 men who had been physically aggressive to their wives. The results of their analysis yielded four, rather than three, subgroups. The expected groups of FO, GVA, and DB offenders were confirmed, and in addition, a "Low-Level Antisocial" group was identified. This group was characterized by moderate scores on antisociality, marital violence, and general violence, and was positioned as intermediate to the FO and GVA groups.

Risk-Needs Assessment

Given the ubiquity of generic risk-needs assessment tools to determine the need for intervention in most Western correctional systems (see Chapters 28 and 30), it is important to make some observations about their suitability for use in predicting IPVA. Day, Richardson, Bowen, and Bernardi (2014) have argued that these tools are often not violence-specific and it is relatively common for prisoners to be assessed as at "moderate" or "low" risk of recidivism, even when there are grounds for considerable concern about IPVA (e.g., when an offender plans to return to live with his victims or makes specific threats to a partner). In fact, risk-needs tools of this type are not victim-specific, and detailed information about the history of IPVA and the circumstances in which it occurred is not routinely considered, despite the fact that, unlike almost any other offense, it is often possible to predict who an offender's next victim will be and where the offense will occur. Accordingly, it is usually recommended that general risk-needs assessments are augmented with those that specifically assess IPVA risk factors such as attempted strangulation, imminent or recent separation, and/or victim beliefs regarding the threat of serious violence (Bowen, 2011b). It is also acknowledged by the authors of several major reviews of this area (e.g., Bowen, 2011b; Messing & Thaller, 2013) that risk assessment tools have not been validated in all of the jurisdictions in which they are used, including instruments for screening risk of violence, for categorizing perpetrators, and for assessing lethality or the level of harm associated with the behavior being predicted. Although past research has shown that general violence risk instruments are equally as good as IPVA-specific risk assessment tools at predicting IPVA recidivism (Hanson, Helmus, & Bourgon, 2007), there is a need to ensure that the appropriate range of risk and criminogenic need factors identified in IPVA-specific tools are assessed in order to develop effective risk management strategies.

Conclusions

The material reviewed in this chapter clearly suggests that correctional populations are suitable for IPVA treatment and that more systematic efforts are needed to identify and address IPVA risk in this population. However, for this to happen we need to develop a better understanding of the nature and prevalence of IPVA-related risk and need, and to develop treatment approaches that are more sensitive to the heterogeneity that exists within the offender population. In our view, this will inevitably involve the greater use of therapeutic methods to maximize motivation and reduce defensiveness.

Notes

1 This is a term which has become widely used to refer to particular beliefs that are considered to be important causal antecedents to offending (i.e., criminogenic; see Walters, Chapter 40).
2 This despite empirical evidence resoundingly characterizing IPVA perpetrators as having high trait anger, regardless of how this is assessed and the setting (see Norlander & Eckhardt, 2005).

Key Readings

Bowen, E. (2011a). *The rehabilitation of partner-violent men*. Chichester, UK: Wiley-Blackwell.
Babcock, J. C., Green, C. E., & Robie, C. (2004). Does batterers' treatment work? A meta-analytic review of domestic violence treatment. *Clinical Psychology Review*, 23, 1023–1053.

Day, A., Richardson, T., Bowen, E., & Bernardi, J. (2014). Intimate partner violence in prisoners: Towards effective assessment and intervention. *Aggression and Violent Behavior*, 19, 579–583.

Stewart, L. A., Gabora, N., Kropp, P. R., & Lee, Z. (2014). The effectiveness of Risk-Needs-Responsivity-based family violence programmes with male offenders. *Journal of Family Violence*, 29, 151–164.

References

Adams, D. (1989). Feminist-based interventions for battering men. In P. L. Caesar, & L. K. Hamberger (Eds.), *Treating men who batter: Theory, practice, and programs* (pp. 3–23). New York, NY: Springer.

Andrews, D., & Bonta, J. (2010). *The psychology of criminal conduct* (5th ed.). Cincinnati, OH: Anderson.

Babcock, J. C., Green, C. E., & Robie, C. (2004). Does batterers' treatment work? A meta-analytic review of domestic violence treatment. *Clinical Psychology Review*, 23, 1023–1053.

Banks, J., Kini, S., & Babcock, J. (2014). Interventions that work to stop intimate partner violence. In L. A. Craig, L. Dixon, & T. A. Gannon (Eds.), *What works in offender rehabilitation: An evidence-based approach to assessment and treatment* (pp. 159–172). Chichester, UK: Wiley-Blackwell.

Blatch, C., O'Sullivan, K., Delaney, J. J., van Doorn, G., & Sweller, T. (2016). Evaluation of an Australian domestic abuse program for offending males. *Journal of Aggression, Conflict and Peace Research*, 8, 4–20.

Bouffard, L. A., Wright, K. A., Muftić, L. R., & Bouffard, J. A. (2008). Gender differences in specialization in intimate partner violence: Comparing the gender symmetry and violent resistance perspectives. *Justice Quarterly*, 25, 570–594.

Bowen, E. (2011a). *The rehabilitation of partner-violent men*. Chichester, UK: Wiley-Blackwell.

Bowen, E. (2011b). An overview of partner violence risk assessment and the potential role of female victim risk appraisals. *Aggression and Violent Behaviour*, 16, 214–226.

Breiding, M. J., Basile, K. C., Smith, S. G., Black, M. C., & Mahendra, R. R. (2015). *Intimate partner violence surveillance: Uniform definitions and recommended data elements, version 2.0*. Atlanta, GA: National Center for Injury Prevention and Control, Centers for Disease Control and Prevention.

Bushman, B. J. (2002). Does venting anger feed or extinguish the flame? Catharsis, rumination, distraction, anger and aggressive responding. *Personality and Social Psychology Bulletin*, 28, 724–731.

Capaldi, D. M., & Kim, H. K. (2007). Typological approaches to violence in couples: A critique and alternative conceptual approach. *Clinical Psychology Review*, 27, 253–265.

Chronister, K. M. (2007). Contextualizing women domestic violence survivors' economic and emotional dependencies. *The American Psychologist*, 62(7), 706–708.

Day, A., & Bowen, E. (2015). Offending competency and coercive control in intimate partner violence. *Aggression and Violent Behavior*, 20, 62–71.

Day, A., O'Leary, P., Chung, D., & Justo, D. (2009). *Integrated responses to domestic violence: Research and practice experiences in working with men*. Annandale, Australia: The Federation Press.

Day, A., Richardson, T., Bowen, E., & Bernardi, J. (2014). Intimate partner violence in prisoners: Towards effective assessment and intervention. *Aggression and Violent Behavior*, 19, 579–583.

De Wall, C. N., Anderson, C. A., & Bushman, B. J. (2011). The general-aggression model: Theoretical extensions to violence. *Psychology of Violence*, 1, 245–258.

Deschner, J. P. (1984). *The hitting habit: Anger control for battering couples*. New York, NY: Free Press.

Dutton, D. G. (2006). *The abusive personality: Violence and control in intimate relationships*. New York, NY: Guilford Press.

Dutton, D. G., & Corvo, K. (2007). The Duluth model: A data-impervious paradigm and a failed strategy. *Aggression and Violent Behavior*, 12, 658–667.

Feder, L., & Wilson, D. B. (2005). A meta-analytic review of court-mandated batterer intervention programs: Can courts affect abusers' behavior? *Journal of Experimental Criminology*, 1, 239–262.

Franzoi, S. L. (1996). *Social psychology*. Madison, WI: Wm. C. Brown.

Hamberger, L. K., & Hastings, J. E. (1993). Court-mandated treatment of men who assault their partner: Issues, controversies, and outcomes. In N. Z. Hilton (Ed.), *Legal responses to wife assault* (pp. 188–229). Newbury Park, CA: Sage.

Hanson, R. K., Helmus, L., & Bourgon, G. (2007). *The validity of risk assessments for intimate partner violence: A meta-analysis. Report 2007–07.* Ottawa, Canada: Public Safety Canada.

Heise, L. L. (1998). Violence against women: An integrated, ecological framework. *Violence Against Women*, 4, 262–290.

Herrero, J., Torres, A., Fernández-Suárez, A., & Rodríguez-Díaz, F. J. (2016). Generalists versus specialists: Toward a typology of batterers in prison. *The European Journal of Psychology Applied to Legal Context*, 8, 19–26.

Herron, K., & Holtzworth-Munroe, A. (2002). Child abuse potential: A comparison of subtypes of maritally violent men and nonviolent men. *Journal of Family Violence*, 17(1), 1–21.

Holdsworth, E., Bowen, E., Brown, S., & Howat, D. (2014). Offender engagement in group programs and associations with offender characteristics and treatment factors: A review. *Aggression and Violent Behavior*, 19, 102–121.

Holtzworth-Munroe, A., Meehan, J. C., Herron, K., Rehman, U., & Stuart, G. L. (2000). Testing the Holtzworth-Munroe and Stuart (1994) batterer typology. *Journal of Consulting and Clinical Psychology*, 68(6), 1000–1008.

Holtzworth-Munroe, A., Meehan, J. C., Herron, K., Rehman, U., & Stuart, G. L. (2003). Do subtypes of maritally violent men continue to differ over time? *Journal of Consulting and Clinical Psychology*, 71, 728–740.

Holtzworth-Munroe, A., & Stuart, G. L. (1994). Typologies of male batterers: Three subtypes and the differences among them. *Psychological Bulletin*, 116, 476–497.

Kimmel, M. S. (2002). "Gender symmetry" in domestic violence: A substantive and methodological research review. *Violence Against Women*, 8, 1332–1363.

Kistenmacher, B. R., & Weiss, R. L. (2008). Motivational interviewing as a mechanism for change in men who batter: A randomised controlled trial. *Violence and Victims*, 23, 558–570.

Lee, M. Y., Sebold, J., & Uken, A. (2003). *Solution-focused treatment of domestic violence offenders: Accountability for change.* Oxford, UK: Oxford University Press.

Ley, L. F. (2005). *A study of domestic violence recidivism following treatment among incarcerated men who batter* (Unpublished doctoral dissertation). University of Miami, FL.

Maiuro, R. D., & Eberle, J. A. (2008). State standards for domestic violence perpetrator treatment: Current status, trends and recommendations. *Violence and Victims*, 23, 133–155.

Marvell, T. B., & Moody, C. E. (1999). Female and male homicide victimization rates: Comparing trends and regressors. *Criminology*, 37, 879–900.

McMurran, M., Fyffe, S., McCarthy, L., Duggan, C., & Latham, A. (2001). "Stop & Think!": social problem-solving therapy with personality-disorderd offenders. *Criminal Behaviour and Mental Health*, 11(4), 273–285.

Messing, J. T., & Thaller, J. (2013). The average predictive validity of intimate partner violence risk. *Journal of Interpersonal Violence*, 28, 1537–1558.

Miller, S. (2010). Discussing the Duluth curriculum: Creating a process of change for men who batter. *Violence Against Women*, 16(9), 1007–1021.

Miller, W. R., & Rollnick, S. (1991). *Motivational interviewing: Preparing people to change addictive behavior.* New York, NY: Guilford Press.

Ministry of Justice. (n.d.). Building Better Relationships (BBR) information for sentencers. Retrieved from www.devon.gov.uk/building-better-relationships-information-for-sentencers.pdf

Moffitt, T. E., Kreuger, R. F., Caspi, A., & Fagan, J. (2000). Partner abuse and general crime: Are they the same? How are they different? *Criminology*, 38, 199–232.

Moore, S. (2009). The Gold Coast Domestic Violence Male Offender Education and Intervention Program for male perpetrators. In A. Day, P. O'Leary, D. Chung, & D. Justo (Eds.), *Integrated responses to domestic violence: Research and practice experiences in working with men* (pp. 95–107). Annandale, Australia: The Federation Press.

Musser, P. H., Semiatin, J. N., Taft, C. T., & Murphy, C. M. (2008). Motivational interviewing as a pregroup intervention for partner-violent men. *Violence and Victims*, 23(5), 539–557.

Neidig, P. H. (1984). Women's shelters, men's collectives and other issues in the field of spouse abuse. *Victimology*, 9, 464–476.

Norlander, B., & Eckhardt, C. I. (2005). Anger, hostility and male perpetrators of intimate partner violence: A meta-analytic review. *Clinical Psychology Review*, 25, 119–152.

Pascual-Leone, A., Bierman, R., Arnold, R., & Stasiak, E. (2011). Emotion-focused therapy for incarcerated offenders of intimate partner violence: A 3-year outcome using a new whole-sample matching method. *Psychotherapy Research*, 21(3), 331–347.

Pence, E., & Paymar, M. (1993). *Education groups for men who batter: The Duluth model*. New York, NY: Springer.

Polaschek, D. L. (2011). Many sizes fit all: A preliminary framework for conceptualizing the development and provision of cognitive–behavioral rehabilitation programs for offenders. *Aggression and Violent Behavior*, 16(1), 20–35.

Robertson, N. (1999). Stopping violence programmes: Enhancing the safety of battered women or producing better-educated batterers? *New Zealand Journal of Psychology*, 28, 68–78.

Ross, R., & Fabiano, E. A. (1985). *Time to think. A cognitive model of delinquency prevention and offender rehabilitation*. Johnson City, TN: Institute of Social Sciences and Arts.

Stewart, L. A., Gabora, N., Kropp, P. R., & Lee, Z. (2014). The effectiveness of Risk-Needs-Responsivity-based family violence programmes with male offenders. *Journal of Family Violence*, 29, 151–164.

Stith, S. M., Smith, D. B., Penn, C. E., Ward, D. B., & Tritt, D. (2004). Intimate partner physical abuse perpetration and victimization risk factors: A meta-analytic review. *Aggression and Violent Behavior*, 10, 65–98.

Thakker, J., & Gannon, T. A. (2010). Rape treatment: An overview of current knowledge. *Behaviour Change*, 27, 227–250.

Thomas, S. P. (2003). Men's anger: A phenomenological exploration of its meaning in a middle-class sample of American men. *Psychology of Men and Masculinity*, 4, 163–175.

Tiff, L. L. (1993). *Battering of women: The failure of intervention and the case for prevention*. Boulder, CO: Westview Press.

Trevena, J., & Poynton, S. (2016). Does a prison sentence affect future domestic violence reoffending? *Contemporary Issues in Crime and Justice*, 190, 1–11.

Ventura, L. A., & Davis, G. (2005). Intimate partner violence: Court case conviction and recidivism. *Violence Against Women*, 11, 255–277.

Wolfus, B., & Bierman, R. (1996). An evaluation of a group treatment program for incarcerated male batterers. *International Journal of Offender Therapy and Comparative Criminology*, 40(4), 318–333.

Yorke, N. J., Friedman, B. D., & Hurt, P. (2010). Implementing a batterer's intervention program in a correctional setting: A tertiary prevention model. *Journal of Offender Rehabilitation*, 49(7), 456–478.

34

Interventions to Reduce Alcohol-Related Offending*

James McGuire
University of Liverpool, UK

Crime is a problem of considerable public concern and citizens look to criminal justice agencies to control and reduce it. Alcohol, while a legalized substance used by many citizens in a problem-free manner, is also associated with higher levels of harm than any other substance, at least in the United Kingdom (Nutt, King, & Phillips, 2010). In addition to its damage to health, alcohol is associated with the occurrence of numerous accidental injuries and deaths. It is also believed to be a factor in many types of crime, giving rise to particular alarm with respect to its association with personal violence. The mechanisms that underpin those connections are complex and not fully explained, and it is likely that there are several pathways operating. One focus of research in this area has been on finding methods or interventions that can reduce levels and/or severity of alcohol-related offending. Information relating to this would potentially be of immense value to correctional psychologists, who regularly encounter the problem of alcohol-related offending in their professional work. To engage effectively in that work, as elsewhere, psychologists seek to draw on relevant research findings. The objective of this chapter therefore is to present a review of the available outcome research on that question. Before doing that, however, we first consider some of the evidence showing linkages between alcohol and crime.

Alcohol–Crime Connections

The use of alcohol appears to have been a regular and almost ubiquitous feature of human societies since the earliest times. Some anthropologists have even suggested that the Neolithic revolution, in which humans gradually shifted from a nomadic life to one centered on agriculture, had its origins in the urge to cultivate plants not for making bread but for brewing beer (Braidwood et al., 1953). Suggestions that other species, such as the African elephant, use

*This chapter is in part based on a Rapid Evidence Assessment initially prepared for the Correctional Services Advisory and Accreditation Panel, Commissioning Strategies Group (CSG) in the Ministry of Justice, London, and has been revised and updated since originally prepared. The author thanks the CSG for agreement to reproduce portions of the material in this form.

The Wiley International Handbook of Correctional Psychology, First Edition. Edited by Devon L. L. Polaschek, Andrew Day, and Clive R. Hollin.
© 2019 John Wiley & Sons Ltd. Published 2019 by John Wiley & Sons Ltd.

decaying vegetation to become inebriated have, however, not been supported (Morris, Humphreys, & Reynolds, 2006). Alcohol use seems to be a uniquely human activity.

Although in the majority of societies alcohol is a legalized drug, there are laws governing access to it. Under some circumstances offenses can arise in direct violation of those laws (e.g., sales to under-age persons, public drunkenness, drunken driving). The broader concern in criminal justice, however, is often with the extent to which alcohol affects numerous other kinds of antisocial conduct, including both acquisitive and violent offenses.

There is a consensus that alcohol use is a factor that contributes to involvement in criminal activity, and alongside use of illegal drugs it remains one of the *Central Eight* risk-need factors identified by Bonta and Andrews (2017). Given some differences in how they are linked to offending, alcohol and other substance misuse should be assessed separately. For example, there are indications that alcohol may be more closely linked to violence than to other types of offense, although findings on this are not entirely consistent. But such an association is particularly worrying, and many violent acts are attributed to drinking. Findings relevant to this include the following.

- Arrest records from several countries suggest that a large proportion of violent offenses (with a range of 40–66%) are committed when perpetrators are under the influence of alcohol (Graham, Parkes, McAuley, & Doi, 2012).
- A large proportion of victims participating in the Crime Survey for England and Wales (47% in 2014–2015) believed offenders to be under the influence of alcohol at the time of a violent incident (Office for National Statistics, 2016).
- Surveys show sizeable proportions of convicted adults in prison or on probation have alcohol-related problems. For example, a UK survey found 63% of male and 39% of female sentenced prisoners had engaged in "hazardous drinking" in the year before being imprisoned (Singleton, Meltzer, Gatward, Coid, & Deasy, 1998).
- A rapid evidence review of studies on levels of alcohol use disorders in criminal justice populations found very high prevalence rates as compared to the general population; this emerged from studies in police custody suites, courts, probation, and prisons (Newbury-Birch et al., 2015).
- Interview studies with persistent offenders reveal a temporal relationship between life stresses, alcohol consumption, and criminal recidivism (Zamble & Quinsey, 1997).
- Self-report diary studies show specific temporal associations between drinking and assaults on intimate partners (e.g., Fals-Stewart, 2003), and a Swedish study with remand prisoners also found alcohol to be a significant trigger of interpersonal violence (Lundholm, Haggård, Möller, Hallqvist, & Thiblin, 2013).
- Reviews of research on links between alcohol and sexual assault suggest that while alcohol may not play a direct causal role in sexual aggression, the timing of its use may be a precipitating factor (Abbey, 2011; Kraanen & Emmelkamp, 2011; Lorenz & Ullman, 2016).
- In a secure mental health unit in Sweden, alcohol was found to be associated with a higher risk of aggression within a 24-hour period of ingestion than other types of drugs (Haggard-Grann, Hallqvist, Langström, & Möller, 2006).
- Laboratory and experimental studies show that alcohol has various deleterious effects on reasoning, emotional control, and decision-making (Exum, 2006; Field, Wiers, Christiansen, Fillmore, & Verster, 2010).

Additional evidence comes from a 30-year follow-up of a New Zealand birth cohort ($n = 1,265$), showing that when other factors are taken into account, alcohol has particular links with two kinds of offense: impulsive violent assaults; and property damage, vandalism, and arson (Boden, Fergusson & Horwood, 2012). Similar results emerged from a study of offense patterns among a large representative sample of American prisoners (n = 18,016). Homicide, physical assault, sexual assault, robbery, and other "confrontational" offenses were more likely to be committed by an intoxicated offender than were other types of crime (Felson & Staff, 2010).

Notwithstanding this sizeable body of research, the mechanisms that mediate the alcohol-crime connection are not fully understood. Ethanol, the active ingredient in alcoholic drinks, has a pharmacological effect largely as a central nervous system (CNS) depressant. It does not itself directly induce violent or other criminal behavior (Boles & Miotto, 2003), though it is thought it might do so in conjunction with a pre-existing propensity to aggressiveness (Giancola, 2006). However, it appears more likely to contribute to violence via one or more of the following mediating processes.

- Disinhibition: a reduced capacity for exercising deliberate, conscious, or "executive" control over impulses. One proposal is that this is due to the "depletion of cognitive resources" caused by intoxication (Hirsch, Galinksy, & Zhong, 2011); although the extent of this is a function of the level of consumption, and the effects may be very specific (Montgomery, Fisk, Murphy, Ryland, & Hilton, 2012).
- Outcome expectancies: individuals' beliefs about alcohol, and what they anticipate will be its effects, will influence their pattern of drinking, alongside their prior likelihood of being aggressive (McMurran, 2007). Decisions to drink may be a function of these factors (Zhang, Welte, & Wieczorek, 2002).
- Narrowing of selective attention, focusing on a limited range of information (e.g., perceived threats) within a shortened time-span, an effect that has been called "alcoholic myopia" (Giancola, Josephs, Parrott, & Duke, 2010; Steele & Josephs, 1990).
- Anxiolytic effect: some individuals drink in order to gain social confidence, and may experience a temporary lift in self-esteem from drinking. They may then remain vulnerable to interpersonal risks and threats and thereby prone to aggression (McMurran, 2011).
- A range of other individual factors influence the strength of the alcohol-crime relationship. It may be modulated by personality, attitudes, and possibly by specific constellations of factors such as a hyper-masculine or "macho" orientation that also fosters high alcohol consumption (Graham & West, 2001). This may be particularly manifest in a subgroup of the young adult male population (McMurran, Hoyte, & Jinks, 2012), at least in Western economies.

In all likelihood, there is also a range of sociocultural, temporal, and situational factors operating when people drink alcohol, deriving from the places or events where that occurs, the purposes it serves, and the contexts in which individuals have learned to consume it (Moore, 2001). The latter are associated in many societies not only with reward and pleasure, but with social ease and enjoyment, high excitement, and "letting go." Problems of antisocial, criminal, and violent behavior are most likely to arise in the context of prolonged or habitual heavy drinking, or of binge-drinking—especially where that involves "pre-loading," drinking more cheaply at home prior to visiting costly night-time venues (Hughes, Anderson, Morleo, & Bellis, 2008).

To summarize, there is a voluminous literature across several disciplines on the effects and the uses of alcohol, and on possible reasons why it may contribute to criminal offending generally and to violent behavior more specifically. Our focus here is on evidence that some aspects of the harmful effects of alcohol, in this case its links with criminal offending, can be altered and what the strength is of any results indicating this. In assessment of individual offenders, and in planning treatment regimes, evidence pertaining to this should provide invaluable guidance in appraising levels of risk and criminogenic needs, thereby informing the design and delivery of effective rehabilitation services.

Research Review

There are numerous reviews with varying degrees of relevance to the area of interest here, for example on the effectiveness of alcohol or other substance abuse treatment from a health perspective, or on the reduction of violent offending from a criminal justice stance. Some reviews focused predominantly on substances other than alcohol, and on substance-related as opposed to criminal justice outcomes (e.g., Holloway, Bennett, & Farrington, 2005). Others included pharmacological interventions and legal sanctions but found few studies of psychosocial treatments (e.g., Roberts, Hayes, Carlisle, & Shaw, 2007). McMurran (2012, 2013; McMurran, Riemsma, Manning, Misso, & Kleijnen, 2011) integrated results of a small number of studies with findings that were promising but not conclusive. Separately, there are reviews of the effects of policing initiatives in reducing alcohol-related violence in Australia (Liu, Ferris, Higginson, & Lynham, 2016), and of large-scale, population-level interventions (Martineau, Tyner, Lorenc, Petticrew, & Lock, 2013), both of which are beyond the scope of the present chapter.

Search Strategy

The remainder of this chapter draws on an evidence review involving search of a series of 14 electronic databases or websites. They were: PsycINFO, Scopus, MEDLINE, CINAHL, Web of Knowledge, Cochrane Collaboration and Campbell Collaboration libraries, the National Institute of Health and Clinical Excellence (NICE), Criminal Justice Abstracts (US National Criminal Justice Reference Service), the Home Office Research, Development and Statistics Directorate, the Netherlands Institute for the Study of Criminality and Law Enforcement, Swedish National Council for Crime Prevention, Public Safety Canada, and the Australian Institute of Criminology. Searches were conducted with various permutations of the following terms: alcohol*, violen*, offend*, crim*, intervention, treatment, program*, prison, probation. Initial searches covered the 15-year period 1997–2012, subsequently extended backwards to 1992 and updated to 2017 on a more limited set of databases.

The search was confined to studies of psychosocial interventions with adults. Degree dissertations and documents not published in English were excluded. Studies of sexual offending and studies entirely or primarily focused on offenders diagnosed with mental disorders, if treated in hospital settings, were also excluded. It was considered that several other risk-need and contextual factors applied in those instances and that they should be the focus of separate reviews.

From an initial total of 3,770 documents located via these searches, after screening and application of selection criteria, a set of 294 documents was downloaded for more detailed scrutiny. Following further exclusions, a smaller group of 47 studies was retained for full review. Among this final set, 25 studies were carried out in the United States, 17 in England and Wales, and one each in Australia, Canada, New Zealand, Spain, and Sweden.

These studies were subjected to quality appraisal using the Maryland *Scientific Methods Scale* (SMS: Farrington, Gottfredson, Sherman, & Welsh, 2002). This entails assigning scores from

1 to 5 according to each study's level of methodological rigor. Scores of 4 and 5 are allotted to high-quality quasi-experimental studies (QEs) and to randomized controlled trials (RCTs), respectively.

Key Findings

The objective in what follows is not to provide full details of the review just outlined, but to summarize what emerged from it with regard to interventions with positive outcomes. Unsurprisingly, given the formidable nature of the problems, some interventions had little or no effect. There was also wide variation in the quality of research designs, and due to weaknesses in this respect, there were reports from which no firm conclusions could be drawn. For example, some studies had high rates of attrition, while in others there were uncertainties over the comparability of experimental and comparison samples, and follow-up periods were often fairly short. By contrast, several methods of working secured more positive outcomes, though sometimes based on a single study only. What follows is centered on studies that had stronger evaluation designs.

In terms of structure, procedure, and content, the methods that emerged as yielding benefits are quite diverse. Table 34.1 illustrates this diversity focusing on the studies that achieved levels 4 and 5 on the Maryland SMS. Note that this includes only those studies where positive effects were found on reoffending as an outcome variable, as opposed to substance-related or other outcomes.

Alcohol and related substance abuse treatment, sometimes provided in prison or on parole, or alternatively in clinic settings, has demonstrated benefits in terms of lowered alcohol consumption. Of the five studies that were found in which these programs were evaluated, four found some evidence of an impact on reoffending rates. One was a large-scale, multi-site study in England and Wales (Gossop, Trakada, Stewart, & Witton, 2005), but this was a longitudinal single cohort study with no untreated comparison sample. However, another was a quasi-experimental study of early parole release to alcohol treatment which found evidence of significant reductions in recidivism (Zanis et al., 2003).

Alcohol-Related Partner Violence

The largest single batch of studies that was found is in the area of combined interventions for intimate partner violence (IPV) and alcohol or substance abuse problems. The most extensively tested approach to this, initially known as behavioral marital therapy but subsequently renamed *behavioral couples therapy* (BCT), was developed by staff of the Harvard Families and Addictions Program (O'Farrell & Murphy, 1995). There are numerous studies reported by this group, some dealing with verbal aggression only (O'Farrell, Murphy, Neavins, & Van Hutton, 2000), but others reporting partner violence over a 2-year follow-up (O'Farrell, Murphy, Stephan, Fals-Stewart, & Murphy, 2004). Methods utilized in BCT are illustrated by O'Farrell and Schein (2011). While some of the studies have only modest sample sizes, others are far larger and, although not randomized trials, they mostly meet the standards endorsed for high-quality quasi-experiments (Des Jarlais, Lyles, Crepaz, & TREND Group, 2004).

Although these studies were not conducted in a criminal justice setting, the severity of the combined problems of alcohol use and partner violence could potentially inform the design of interventions in community-based correctional settings, for example in work with offenders on probation or parole. The overall effectiveness of BCT was evaluated in a

Table 34.1 Summary of Positive Outcomes (Reductions in Reoffending) in Higher-Quality Studies

Target problem or group	Intervention	Evidence
SMS = 5: Random assignment to experimental and comparison groups		
Alcohol-related domestic violence / Spousal abuse	Substance Abuse Domestic Violence (SADV) program	Easton et al. (2007)
Alcohol-related domestic violence / Spousal abuse	Motivational interventions	Schumacher et al. (2011)
Prisoners	Motivational interventions	Forsberg et al. (2011) Stein et al. (2010)
Probationers	Brief interventions	Newbury-Birch et al. (2014)
Prisoners with histories of violence and alcohol abuse	Reentry modified therapeutic community	Sacks et al. (2004, 2008, 2012) Sullivan et al. (2007)
Drink-driving recidivism	Electronic monitoring: short-term effects only	Lapham et al. (2007)
Prisoners	Control of Violence for Angry Impulsive Drinkers (COVAID) program	Bowes et al. (2014)
SMS = 4: Comparison between equivalent groups, one with, one without the intervention		
Alcohol-related domestic violence / Spousal abuse	Behavioral Couples Therapy	McCrady et al. (2016) O'Farrell et al. (1999) O'Farrell et al. (2004) Rotunda et al. (2008) Ruff et al. (2010) Schumm et al. (2009)
Alcohol-related violent offending	Multiple Offender Alcoholism Project (MOAP): community reinforcement model	Funderburk et al. (1993)
Driving while intoxicated	Turning Point program	Pratt et al. (2000)
Prisoners allocated to parole	Community-based substance abuse treatment	Zanis et al. (2003)
Prisoners	SMART recovery program	Blatch et al. (2016)

SMS = Maryland Scientific Methods Score.

meta-analysis by Powers, Vedel, and Emmelkamp (2008), who found a mean effect size for combined substance abuse and relationship outcomes of 0.54; however, these authors did not focus on offending as such. An independent review of the studies was reported by McCrady et al. (2016).

Tentative results in a similar direction have come from studies by other research groups working in a similar area, most notably from the *Substance Abuse Domestic Violence* (SADV) program developed by a group at Yale University (Scott & Easton, 2010; Stuart et al., 2003). These results came from randomized controlled trials, and participants were court-mandated to attend the SADV program. In a study of an otherwise unsuccessful intervention designed to reduce IPV, Gondolf (1999) found that men who were accessing alcohol or other drug treatment had a lower rate of assault than those not doing so, and for severe assaults, a rate of reoffending which was half that of men not accessing such services (thought this fell just short of statistical significance).

We might anticipate that the presence of alcohol would compound the already sizeable challenges of addressing the problem of IPV and would compromise treatment effectiveness.

On the contrary, the effects reported in the above studies are more favorable and more consistent than those obtained in the IPV field in general. This might suggest that alcohol contributed a large part of the problem in these relationships. Where relationship violence in the absence of alcohol is traceable to more fundamental sources (e.g., gender attitudes) it may be less amenable to intervention.

Therapeutic Communities

Therapeutic communities (TCs) in the penal system, like their counterparts elsewhere, are customarily focused on treatment of alcohol or other substance abuse problems. In UK prisons (though less often in other jurisdictions), they are also generally associated with the management of prisoners with histories of violent offending, proportions of whom are diagnosed with personality disorders. Overall results from these studies are encouraging, although available reports do not always provide sufficient detail on study samples, and leave some problems of interpretation due to uncertain comparability of cohorts. The most impressive results of relevance to our purposes here have come from three inter-linked RCTs reporting evaluation of a 12-month modified TC operated by the Department of Corrections in Colorado. Participation began in prisons but was followed by an after-care program that also took the form of a therapeutic community (Sacks, Banks, McKendrick, & Sacks, 2008; Sacks, Chaple, Sacks, McKendrick, & Cleland, 2012; Sacks, Sacks, McKendrick, Banks, & Stommel, 2004; Sullivan, McKendrick, Sacks, & Banks, 2007).

Participants reported an average age of first alcohol use of 13.5 years (Sacks et al., 2004) and were identified as having multiple problems of alcohol and other substance use. Among the sample studied by Sacks et al. (2004), one third were alcohol-dependent, and 60% were under the influence of alcohol or drugs at the time of their offense. At the point of intervention, they had already served a number of years in prison. The after-care component appeared to be a pivotal element of the positive effects observed for this intervention, as the prison TC condition alone did not always differ from the comparison condition. While data suggest a high proportion of the TC participants had histories of violent offending including weapon use, it is unclear what fraction of this may have been alcohol-related, and there is no breakdown of subsequent recidivism by offense category. Outcomes were, however, very positive: the 12-month reincarceration rates for TC participants as compared to "treatment as usual" were 19 and 38%, respectively. Corresponding figures for overall criminal activity were 38 versus 62%, and for alcohol or drug offenses 37 versus 58%.

Thus, while this TC appears to be supported by relatively strong evidence, it remains difficult to draw specific conclusions as to its value for addressing alcohol-related violence, given that for large proportions of samples there was comorbid other substance abuse. Striking results were obtained from a therapeutic community in Asturias, Spain, but this has a weaker design consisting of a comparison between those who completed treatment in the TC and those who did not; there is a large difference in outcomes between the two groups but there may also be differences in prior characteristics (Fernández-Hermida, Secades-Villa, Fernández-Ludeña, & Marina-González, 2002). While no studies were found reporting on TCs designed exclusively for alcohol treatment (concomitant alcohol and other substance misuse is more common), the effects observed in these studies surpass those found for TCs in relation to other substance abuse alone (Smith, Gates, & Foxcroft, 2006) and they are also larger than those described in earlier reviews of the use of therapeutic communities in criminal justice settings (Lipton, Pearson, Cleland, & Yee, 2002).

Driving Under the Influence/While Intoxicated (DUI/DWI) Interventions

Some positive findings emerge from studies that were located on drink-driving offenses. Numerous approaches have been applied to this widespread problem. Some studies in this area have very large samples (e.g., over 35,000 in the study by Voas, Marques, Tippetts, & Beirness, 1999, of the *Alberta Interlock* program). The weight of evidence suggests that the system-wide, judicial, or sentencing innovations are often less successful than expected (Lapham & Todd, 2012). The take-up of the interlock program was so low (8.9%) as to virtually minimize its chances of success, and the effects even for those who participated were short-lived. Other fundamentally punitive or deterrence-based approaches to such high-frequency offenses also appear to have negligible effects (Lapham, C'de Baca, Lapidus, & McMillan, 2007; Taxman & Piquero, 1998), and one intervention entailing victim impact statements had a counter-productive effect (C'de Baca, Lapham, Liang, & Skipper, 2001).

In complete contrast, several studies have obtained more positive effects, including those of DUI courts when they are followed by a treatment program (Ronan, Collins, & Rosky, 2009). An example is the *Turning Point* program which was supported by several early evaluations and by a 10-year follow-up (Pratt, Holsinger, & Latessa, 2000); another is an intensive cognitive skills program entailing court-mandated attendance (Moore, Harrison, Young, & Ochshorn, 2008). Unfortunately, not all of these studies had untreated comparison samples and none was a randomized trial.

A systematic review of 42 studies of interventions in this area located some modestly encouraging results (Miller, Curtis, Sønderland, Day, & Droste, 2015). That was, however, in a context in which most evaluation designs were weak, with only three meeting criteria for a score of 5 on the Maryland Scale and eight meriting a score of 4. The most promising findings were from evaluations of Intensive Supervision Programs with multimodal components, entailing education, substance abuse treatment, and electronic or other forms of monitoring. These "consistently reported significant reductions in DUI recidivism" (Miller et al., 2015, p. 27).

Motivational Interventions

Studies of motivational interventions (MIs) or enhancement are typically based on relatively small samples. Drawing on a model of "brief, opportunistic" attempts at engagement, they are fairly short-term exercises but their flexibility has led them to be used in a wide range of settings. They have been used in the context of arrest referral schemes (Sharp & Atherton, 2006), in probation (Harper & Hardy, 2000), and also in prisons (Forsberg, Ernst, Sundqvist, & Farbring, 2011; Stein, Caviness, Anderson, Herbert, & Clarke, 2010). Effects are almost uniformly positive but they do not always outperform parallel treatments (i.e. between-group differences are non-significant), and there are suggestions from other reviews that they may be more effective when not manual-guided (Hettema, Steele, & Miller, 2005). The research here points toward two general findings: one that MI can be effective as a method of engagement, the other that its effects may attenuate between 3 and 12 months, and the latter suggests that it may be optimistic to expect more than this given the minimal nature of the contact. However, these points have not been demonstrated specifically among correctional populations, and a review by Newbury-Birch et al. (2015) of the use of brief interventions in criminal justice in the United Kingdom found a dearth of follow-up data and in many instances even of alcohol screening information. Thus no conclusions could be drawn about intervention effects.

A potentially valuable departure may be to conjoin use of these brief interventions to an ensuing, more intensive type of activity, given that MI is associated with higher retention, for example after leaving prison (Davis, Baer, Saxon, & Kivlahan, 2003). Adopting a variation of brief interventions with a partly "motivational" component, some impressive results were obtained from the *Screening and Brief Intervention for Offenders in the Probation Setting* study (SIPS; Newbury-Birch et al., 2014). Offender managers were trained in a specific set of interactional techniques. Probationers given brief advice or lifestyle counselling related to drinking had 12-month reconviction rates of 36 and 38% as compared to 50% for a control group given an alcohol information leaflet only.

Structured Programs

Given that structured or "manualized" programs have become a familiar feature of offender rehabilitation services, only a small number were identified in this review. No support was found for the use of coerced or court-mandated alcohol treatment. In England and Wales, the 2003 Criminal Justice Act introduced a series of "additional requirements" to probation, one of them an Alcohol Treatment Requirement (ATR) imposed as an adjunct to probation supervision. Ashby, Horrocks, and Kelly (2010) reported promising preliminary findings from evaluation of this in one area. Subsequently, however, employing survival analysis with larger samples, McSweeney (2015) found no impact on rates of reconviction.

Other probation-based programs designed to reduce offending associated with alcohol or other substances have produced mixed results. Hollis (2007) combined data on two substance misuse programs, *Drink-Impaired Drivers* (DIDS) and *Addressing Substance-Related Offending* (ASRO), comparing actual reconviction rates with those predicted by a risk assessment instrument, the Offender Group Reconviction Scale (OGRS-2). In a total sample of 5,081 adults on probation, a significant reduction was found in actual as compared to predicted 2-year reconviction rates. However, when Palmer et al. (2011, 2012) evaluated the same programs separately using comparison samples, group differences were non-significant.

Several studies evaluated a program directly addressing alcohol-related violence, *Control of Violence for Angry Impulsive Drinkers* (COVAID). Three studies found an impact on mediating variables associated with violence risk (Bowes, McMurran, Williams, David, & Zammit, 2012; McCulloch & McMurran, 2008; McMurran and Cusens, 2003). A fourth study reported a small quantity of outcome information (Maguire & Nettleton, 2003). At a later stage, Bowes et al. (2014) reported a pilot RCT of the program. At an average of 17-months follow-up, the rates of reconviction of the COVAID group were 13 and 20% lower than that of the controls for violent and any offending, respectively.

Some programs have adopted a more behavioral orientation. The *Multiple Offender Alcoholism Project* (MOAP) employed a "community reinforcement" model incorporating contingency management methods of catalyzing and sustaining change. An evaluation showed preliminary evidence of effectiveness in reducing both alcohol consumption and violent reoffending (Funderburk, MacKenzie, DeHaven, Stefan, & Allen, 1993). However, the evaluation study, designed to answer questions regarding implementation, is not completely rigorous, and the presentation of the results departs somewhat from a conventional format. Nevertheless, the study could provide useful information for project development. In an RCT employing a similar approach, collaborative behavioral management, with prison parolees across six sites, Friedmann et al. (2011) found positive effects on rates of marijuana and alcohol misuse.

However, rates of self-reported reoffending and recorded rearrest were generally low and group differences fell just short of significance.

In a study of 3,962 Australian prisoners (male and female) with alcohol and other substance abuse problems, Blatch, O'Sullivan, Delaney and Rathbone (2016) compared outcomes for those who attended specially devised programs *Getting SMART* and *SMART Recovery*, or the two combined, with a propensity score-matched control group comprising 2,882 prisoners who had participated in any other program during the period 2007–2011. The total time at risk post-release was just over 3 years. Using survival analysis, those who attended the first program or the combined programs had significantly lower rates of reconviction than controls: respectively 19 and 22% lower for general recidivism, and 30 and 42% lower for violent recidivism. There was an association between attending more program sessions and a longer time to reconviction. Attendance at literacy and vocational programs while in prison was also associated with sizeable reductions in general and violent recidivism (30 and 41%, respectively).

Conclusions

This chapter has assembled a wide range of research on whether it is possible to reduce alcohol-related offending. Given the variety of interventions found to have encouraging results, it is not easy to extract more specific conclusions about which attributes they have in common. What appears to be important, based on examining the methods with more promising outcomes, is a combination of factors that include the acquisition of new skills for communicating and for managing interpersonal conflicts, the establishment of new patterns of cognition, and development of self-control of negative emotions. Collectively, the work summarized here demonstrates the possibility of successfully addressing the problem of alcohol-related offending, one often seen as particularly challenging.

With reference to reducing reoffending in correctional populations, the overall status of the evidence can perhaps suitably be described as better than just promising, but not yet sufficient to be convincing. To make it so, clearly more research is needed. The studies and results to date tentatively offer directions for further progress in both practice and research. Given the frequency with which alcohol is associated with serious offenses, and the ways in which it can complicate other issues to be addressed in correctional settings, it is important for psychologists to be aware of these connections. In work with individual clients, in supervision of others, and in advice to agencies, the use of careful assessment to understand the nature of such links is an essential step to take before embarking on interventions; and in doing the latter, it is vital to be equipped with sound evidence concerning approaches that are more likely to work.

Key Readings

Graham, L., Parkes, T., McAuley, A., & Doi, L. (2012). *Alcohol problems in the criminal justice system: An opportunity for intervention.* Copenhagen, Denmark: World Health Organization Regional Office for Europe.

Lewis, M. (2015). *The biology of desire: Why addiction is not a disease.* New York, NY: Public Affairs.

McMurran, M. (Ed.) (2013). *Alcohol-related violence: Prevention and treatment.* Chichester, UK: Wiley-Blackwell.

References

Abbey, A. (2011). Alcohol's role in sexual violence perpetration: Theoretical explanations, existing evidence and future directions. *Drug and Alcohol Review*, 30, 481–489.

Ashby, J., Horrocks, C., & Kelly, N. (2010). Delivering the Alcohol Treatment Requirement: Assessing the outcomes and impact of coercive treatment for alcohol misuse. *Probation Journal*, 58, 52–67.

Blatch, C., O'Sullivan, K., Delaney, J. J., & Rathbone, D. (2016). Getting SMART, SMART Recovery© programs and reoffending. *Journal of Forensic Practice*, 18, 3–16.

Boden, J. M., Fergusson, D. M., & Horwood, L. J. (2012). Alcohol misuse and violent behavior: Findings from a 30-year longitudinal study. *Drug and Alcohol Dependence*, 122, 135–141.

Boles, S. M., & Miotto, K. (2003). Substance abuse and violence: A review of the literature. *Aggression and Violent Behavior*, 8, 155–174.

Bonta, J., & Andrews, D. A. (2017). *The psychology of criminal conduct*. London, UK: Routledge.

Bowes, N., McMurran, M., Evans, C., Oatley, G., Williams, B., & David, S. (2014). Treating alcohol-related violence: A feasibility study of a randomised controlled trial in prisons. *Journal of Forensic Psychiatry and Psychology*, 25, 152–163.

Bowes, N., McMurran, M., Williams, B., David, S., & Zammit, I. (2012). Treating alcohol-related violence: Intermediate outcomes in a feasibility study for a randomized controlled trial in prisons. *Criminal Justice and Behavior*, 398, 333–344.

Braidwood, R. J., Sauer, J. D., Helbaek, H., Mangelsdorf, P. C., Cutler, H. C., Coon, C. S., ... & Oppenheim, A. L. (1953). Symposium: Did man once live by beer alone? *American Anthropologist*, 55, 515–526.

C'de Baca, J., Lapham, S. C., Liang, H. C., & Skipper, B. J. (2001). Victim impact panels: Do they impact drunk drivers? A follow-up of female and male, first-time and repeat offenders. *Journal of Studies on Alcohol*, 62, 615–620.

Davis, T. M., Baer, J. S., Saxon, A. J., & Kivlahan, D. R. (2003). Brief motivational feedback improves post-incarceration treatment contact among veterans with substance use disorders. *Drug and Alcohol Dependence*, 69, 197–203.

Des Jarlais, D. C., Lyles, C., Crepaz, N., & TREND Group (2004). Improving the reporting quality of nonrandomized evaluations of behavioral and public health interventions: The TREND statement. *American Journal of Public Health*, 94, 361–366.

Easton, C. J., Mandel, D. L., Hunkele, K. A., Nich, C., Rounsaville, B. J., & Carroll, K. M. (2007). A cognitive behavioral therapy for alcohol-dependent domestic violence offenders: An integrated Substance Abuse-Domestic Violence treatment approach (SADV). *American Journal on Addictions*, 16, 24–31.

Exum, M. L. (2006). Alcohol and aggression: An integration of findings from experimental studies. *Journal of Criminal Justice*, 34, 131–145.

Fals-Stewart, W. (2003). The occurrence of partner physical aggression on days of alcohol consumption: A longitudinal diary study. *Journal of Consulting and Clinical Psychology*, 71, 41–52.

Farrington, D. P., Gottfredson, D. C., Sherman, L. W., & Welsh, B. C. (2002). The Maryland Scientific Methods Scale. In L. W. Sherman, D. P. Farrington, B. C. Welsh, & D. L. MacKenzie (Eds.), *Evidence-based crime prevention* (pp. 13–21). London, UK: Routledge.

Felson, R. B., & Staff, J. (2010). The effects of alcohol intoxication on violent versus other offending. *Criminal Justice and Behavior*, 37, 1343–1360.

Fernández-Hermida, J.-R., Secades-Villa, R., Fernández-Ludeña, J.-J., & Marina-González, P.-A. (2002). Effectiveness of a therapeutic community treatment in Spain: A long-term follow-up study. *European Addiction Research*, 8, 22–29.

Field, M., Wiers, R. W., Christiansen, P., Fillmore, M. T., & Verster, J. C. (2010). Acute alcohol effects on inhibitory control and implicit cognition: Implications for loss of control over drinking. *Alcoholism: Clinical and Experimental Research*, 34, 1346–1352.

Forsberg, L. G., Ernst, D., Sundqvist, K., & Farbring, C. Å. (2011). Motivational interviewing delivered by existing prison staff: A randomized controlled study of effectiveness on substance abuse after release. *Substance Use and Misuse*, 46, 1477–1485.

Friedmann, P. D., Green, T. C., Taxman, F. S., Harrington, M., Rhodes, A. G., Katz, E., … & Fletcher, B. W. (2011). Collaborative behavioral management among parolees: Drug use, crime and re-arrest in the Step'n'Out randomized trial. *Addiction*, 107, 1099–1108.

Funderburk, F., MacKenzie, A., DeHaven, G. P., Stefan, R., & Allen, R. P. (1993). Evaluation of the Multiple Offender Alcoholism Project: Quasiexperimental evaluation strategy with a focus on individual change and quality of life. *Evaluation and Program Planning*, 16, 181–191.

Giancola, P. R. (2006). Influence of subjective intoxication, breath alcohol concentration, and expectancies on the alcohol-aggression relationship. *Alcoholism: Clinical and Experimental Research*, 30, 844–850.

Giancola, P. R., Josephs, R. A., Parrott, D. J., & Duke, A. A. (2010). Alcohol myopia revisited: Clarifying aggression and other acts of disinhibition through a distorted lens. *Perspectives on Psychological Science*, 5, 265–278.

Gondolf, E. W. (1999). A comparison of four batterer intervention systems: Do court referral, program length, and services matter? *Journal of Interpersonal Violence*, 14, 41–61.

Gossop, M., Trakada, K., Stewart, D., & Witton, J. (2005). Reduction in criminal convictions after addiction treatment: 5-year follow-up. *Drug and Alcohol Dependence*, 79, 295–302.

Graham, K., & West, P. (2001). Alcohol and crime: Examining the link. In N. Heather, T. J. Peters, & T. Stockwell (Eds.), *International handbook of alcohol dependence and problems* (pp. 439–470). Chichester, UK: Wiley.

Graham, L., Parkes, T., McAuley, A., & Doi, L. (2012). *Alcohol problems in the criminal justice system: An opportunity for intervention.* Copenhagen, Denmark: World Health Organization Regional Office for Europe.

Haggard-Grann, U., Hallqvist, J., Langström, N., & Möller, J. (2006). The role of alcohol and drugs in triggering criminal violence: A case cross-over study. *Addiction*, 101, 100–108.

Harper, R., & Hardy, S. (2000). An evaluation of motivational interviewing as a method of intervention with clients in a probation setting. *British Journal of Social Work*, 30, 393–400.

Hettema, J., Steele, J., & Miller, W. R. (2005). Motivational interviewing. *Annual Review of Clinical Psychology*, 1, 91–111.

Hirsch, J. B., Galinksy, A. D., & Zhong, C.-B. (2011). Drunk, powerful, and in the dark: How general processes of disinhibition produce both prosocial and antisocial behavior. *Perspectives on Psychological Science*, 6, 415–427.

Hollis, V. (2007). *Reconviction analysis of Interim Accredited Programmes Software (IAPS) data.* London, UK: Research Development Statistics, National Offender Management Service.

Holloway, K., Bennett, T., & Farrington, D. (2005). *The effectiveness of criminal justice and treatment programmes in reducing drug related crime: A systematic review.* Home Office Online report 26/05. London, UK: Home Office.

Hughes, K., Anderson, Z., Morleo, M., & Bellis, M. A. (2008). Alcohol, nightlife and violence: The relative contributions of drinking before and during nights out to negative health and criminal justice outcomes. *Addiction*, 103, 60–65.

Kraanen, F. L., & Emmelkamp, P. M. G. (2011). Substance misuse and substance use disorders in sex offenders: A review. *Clinical Psychology Review*, 31, 478–489.

Lapham, S. C., C'de Baca, J., Lapidus, J., & McMillan, G. P. (2007). Randomized sanctions to reduce re-offense among repeat impaired-driving offenders. *Addiction*, 102, 1618–1625.

Lapham, S. C., & Todd, M. (2012). Do deterrence and social-control theories predict driving after drinking 15 years after a DWI conviction? *Accident Analysis and Prevention*, 45, 142–151.

Lipton, D. S., Pearson, F. S., Cleland, C. M., & Yee, D. (2002). The effects of therapeutic communities and milieu therapy on recidivism. In J. McGuire (Ed.), *Offender rehabilitation and treatment: Effective programmes and policies to reduce re-offending* (pp. 39–77). Chichester, UK: Wiley.

Liu, T., Ferris, J., Higginson, A., & Lynham, A. (2016). Systematic review of Australian policing interventions to reduce alcohol-related violence: A maxillofacial perspective. *Addictive Behaviors Reports*, 4, 1–12.

Lorenz, K., & Ullman, S. E. (2016). Alcohol and sexual assault victimization: Research findings and future direction. *Aggression and Violent Behavior*, 31, 82–94.

Lundholm, L., Haggård, U., Möller, J., Hallqvist, J., & Thiblin, I. (2013). The triggering effect of alcohol and illicit drugs on violent crime in a remand prison population: A case crossover study. *Drug and Alcohol Dependence*, 129, 110–115.

Maguire, M., & Nettleton, H. (2003). *Reducing alcohol-related violence and disorder: An evaluation of the "TASC" project.* Home Office Research Study 265. London, UK: Home Office Research, Development and Statistics Directorate.

Martineau, F., Tyner, E., Lorenc, T., Petticrew, M., & Lock, K. (2013). Population-level interventions to reduce alcohol-level harm: An overview of systematic reviews. *Preventive Medicine*, 57, 278–296.

McCrady, B. S., Wilson, A. D., Muñoz, R. E., Fink, B. C., Fokas, K., & Borders, A. (2016). Alcohol-focused behavioral couple therapy. *Family Process*, 55, 443–459.

McCulloch, A., & McMurran, M. (2008). Evaluation of a treatment programme for alcohol-related aggression. *Criminal Behaviour and Mental Health*, 18, 224–231.

McMurran, M. (2007). The relationships between alcohol-aggression proneness, general alcohol expectancies, hazardous drinking, and alcohol-related violence in adult male prisoners. *Psychology, Crime & Law*, 13, 275–284.

McMurran, M. (2011). Anxiety, alcohol intoxication, and aggression. *Legal and Criminological Psychology*, 16, 357–371.

McMurran, M. (2012). Individual-level interventions for alcohol-related violence: A rapid evidence assessment. *Criminal Behaviour and Mental Health*, 22, 14–28.

McMurran, M. (2013). Treatments for offenders in prisons and the community. In M. McMurran (Ed.), *Alcohol-related violence: Prevention and treatment* (pp. 205–225). Chichester, UK: Wiley-Blackwell.

McMurran, M., & Cusens, B. (2003). Controlling alcohol-related violence: A treatment programme. *Criminal Behaviour and Mental Health*, 13, 59–76.

McMurran, M., Hoyte, H., & Jinks, M. (2012). Triggers for alcohol-related violence in young male offenders. *Legal and Criminological Psychology*, 17, 307–321.

McMurran, M., Riemsma, R., Manning, N., Misso, K., & Kleijnen, J. (2011). Interventions for alcohol-related offending by women: A systematic review. *Clinical Psychology Review*, 31, 909–922.

McSweeney, T. (2015). Calling time on "alcohol-related" crime? Examining the impact of court-mandated alcohol treatment on offending using propensity score matching. *Criminology and Criminal Justice*, 15, 464–483.

Miller, P. G., Curtis, A., Sønderland, A., Day, A., & Droste, N. (2015). Effectiveness of interventions for convicted DUI offenders in reducing recidivism: A systematic review of the peer-reviewed scientific literature. *The American Journal of Drug and Alcohol Abuse*, 41, 16–29.

Montgomery, C., Fisk, J. E., Murphy, P. N., Ryland, I., & Hilton, J. (2012). The effects of heavy social drinking on executive function: A systematic review and meta-analytic study of existing literature and new empirical findings. *Human Psychopharmacology: Clinical and Experimental*, 27, 187–199.

Moore, D. (2001). The anthropology of drinking. In N. Heather, T. J. Peters, & T. Stockwell (Eds.), *International handbook of alcohol dependence and problems* (pp. 471–487). Chichester, UK: Wiley.

Moore, K. A., Harrison, M., Young, M. S., & Ochshorn, E. (2008). A cognitive therapy program for repeat DUI offenders. *Journal of Criminal Justice*, 36, 539–545.

Morris, S., Humphreys, D., & Reynolds, D. (2006). Myth, marula, and elephant: An assessment of voluntary alcohol intoxication of the African elephant (*Loxodonta africana*) following feeding on the fruit of the marula tree (*Sclerocarya birrea*). *Physiological and Biochemical Zoology*, 79, 363–369.

Newbury-Birch, D., Coulton, S., Bland, M., Cassidy, P., Dale, V., Deluca, P., … & Drummond, C. (2014). Alcohol screening and brief interventions for offenders in the probation setting (SIPS trial): A pragmatic multicentre cluster randomised controlled trial. *Alcohol and Alcoholism*, 49, 540–548.

Newbury-Birch, D., McGovern, R., Birch, J., O'Neill, G., Kaner, H., Sondhi, A., & Lynch, K. (2015). A rapid systematic review of what we know about alcohol use disorders and brief interventions in the criminal justice system. *International Journal of Prisoner Health*, 12, 57–70.

Nutt, D., King, L. A., & Phillips, L. D. (2010). Drug harms in the UK: A multicriteria decision analysis. *Lancet*, 376, 1558–1565.

O'Farrell, T. J., & Murphy, C. M. (1995). Marital violence before and after alcoholism treatment. *Journal of Consulting and Clinical Psychology*, 65, 256–262.

O'Farrell, T. J., Murphy, C. M., Neavins, T. M., & Van Hutton, V. (2000). Verbal aggression among male alcoholic patients and their wives in the year before and two years after alcoholism treatment. *Journal of Family Violence*, 15, 295–310.

O'Farrell, T. J., Murphy, C. M., Stephan, S. H., Fals-Stewart, W., & Murphy, M. (2004). Partner violence before and after couples-based alcoholism treatment for male alcoholic patients: The role of treatment involvement and abstinence. *Journal of Consulting and Clinical Psychology*, 72, 202–217.

O'Farrell, T. J., & Schein, A. Z. (2011). Behavioral couples therapy for alcoholism and drug abuse. *Journal of Family Psychotherapy*, 22, 193–215.

O'Farrell, T. J., Van Hutton, V., & Murphy, C. M. (1999). Domestic violence before and after alcoholism treatment: A two-year longitudinal study. *Journal of Studies on Alcohol*, 60, 317–321.

Office for National Statistics (2016). *Focus on violent crime and sexual offences: Year ending March 2015*. London, UK: Author.

Palmer, E. J., Hatcher, R. M., McGuire, J., Bilby, C., Ayres, L., Ayres, T. C., & Hollin, C. T. (2012). Evaluation of the Addressing Substance-Related Offending (ASRO) program for substance-abusing offenders in the community: A reconviction analysis. *Substance Use and Misuse*, 46, 1072–1080.

Palmer, E. J., Hatcher, R. M., McGuire, J., Bilby, C., Ayres, L., & Hollin, C. R. (2011). The effect on reconviction of an intervention for drink-driving offenders in the community. *International Journal of Offender Therapy and Comparative Criminology*, 56, 525–538.

Powers, M. B., Vedel, E., & Emmelkamp, P. M. G. (2008). Behavioral couples therapy (BCT) for alcohol and drug use disorders: A meta-analysis. *Clinical Psychology Review*, 28, 952–962.

Pratt, T. C., Holsinger, A. M., & Latessa, E. J. (2000). Treating the chronic DUI offender: "Turning Point" ten years later. *Journal of Criminal Justice*, 28, 271–281.

Roberts, A. J., Hayes, A. J., Carlisle, J., & Shaw, J. (2007). *Review of drug and alcohol treatments in prison and community settings: A systematic review conducted on behalf of the Prison Health Research Network*. University of Manchester. Retrieved from http://www.ohrn.nhs.uk/resource/Research/SMreview.pdf

Ronan, S. M., Collins, P. A., & Rosky, J. W. (2009). The effectiveness of Idaho DUI and misdemeanor/DUI courts: Outcome evaluation. *Journal of Offender Rehabilitation*, 48, 154–165.

Rotunda, R. J., O'Farrell, T. J., Murphy, M., & Babey, S. A. (2008). Behavioral couples therapy for comorbid substance use disorders and combat-related posttraumatic stress disorder among male veterans: An initial evaluation. *Addictive Behaviors*, 33, 180–187.

Ruff, S., McComb, J. L., Coker, C. J., & Sprenkle, D. H. (2010). Behavioral couples therapy for the treatment of substance abuse: A substantive and methodological review of O'Farrell, Fals-Stewart, and colleagues' program of research. *Family Process*, 49, 439–456.

Sacks, S., Banks, S., McKendrick, K., & Sacks, J. Y. (2008). Modified therapeutic community for co-occurring disorders: A summary of four studies. *Journal of Substance Abuse Treatment*, 34, 112–122.

Sacks, S., Chaple, M., Sacks, J. Y., McKendrick, K., & Cleland, C. M. (2012). Randomized trial of a re-entry modified therapeutic community for offenders with co-occurring disorders: Crime outcomes. *Journal of Substance Abuse Treatment*, 42, 247–259.

Sacks, S., Sacks, J. Y., McKendrick, K., Banks, S., & Stommel, J. (2004). Modified TC for MICA offenders: Crime outcomes. *Behavioral Sciences & the Law*, 22, 477–501.

Schumacher, J. A., Coffey, S. F., Stasiewicz, P. R., Murphy, C. M., Leonard, K. E., & Fals-Stewart, W. (2011). Development of a brief motivational enhancement intervention for intimate partner violence in alcohol treatment settings. *Journal of Aggression, Maltreatment & Trauma*, 20, 103–127.

Schumm, J. A., O'Farrell, T. J., Murphy, C. M., & Fals-Stewart, W. (2009). Partner violence before and after couples-based alcoholism treatment for female alcoholic patients. *Journal of Consulting and Clinical Psychology*, 77, 1136–1146.

Scott, M. C., & Easton, C. J. (2010). Racial differences in treatment effect among men in a substance abuse and domestic violence program. *American Journal of Drug and Alcohol Abuse*, 36, 357–362.

Sharp, D., & Atherton, S. R. (2006). Out on the town: An evaluation of brief motivational interventions to address the risk associated with problematic alcohol use. *International Journal of Offender Therapy and Comparative Criminology*, 50, 540–558.

Singleton, N., Meltzer, H., Gatward, R., Coid, J., & Deasy, D. (1998). *Psychiatric morbidity among prisoners: Summary report*. London, UK: Office for National Statistics.

Smith, L. A., Gates, S., & Foxcroft, D. (2006). Therapeutic communities for substance related disorder. *Cochrane Database of Systematic Reviews*, (1), Art. No.: CD005338. doi:10.1002/14651858. CD005338.pub2

Steele, C. M., & Josephs, R. A. (1990). Alcoholic myopia: Its prized and dangerous effects. *American Psychologist*, 45, 921–933.

Stein, M. D., Caviness, C. M., Anderson, B. J., Herbert, M., & Clarke, J. G. (2010). A brief alcohol intervention for hazardously drinking incarcerated women. *Addiction*, 105, 466–475.

Stuart, G. L., Ramsey, S. E., Moore, T. M., Kahler, C. W., Farrell, L. E., Recupero, P. R., & Brown, R. A. (2003). Reductions in marital violence following treatment for alcohol dependence. *Journal of Interpersonal Violence*, 18, 1113–1131.

Sullivan, C. J., McKendrick, K., Sacks, S., & Banks, S. (2007). Modified therapeutic community treatment for offenders with MICA disorders: Substance abuse outcomes. *American Journal of Drug and Alcohol Abuse*, 33, 823–832.

Taxman, F. S., & Piquero, A. (1998). On preventing drunk driving recidivism: An examination of rehabilitation and punishment approaches. *Journal of Criminal Justice*, 26, 129–143.

Voas, R. B., Marques, P. R., Tippetts, A. S., & Beirness, D. J. (1999). The Alberta Interlock program: The evaluation of a province-wide program on DUI recidivism. *Addiction*, 94, 1849–1859.

Zamble, E., & Quinsey, V. (1997). *The criminal recidivism process*. Cambridge, UK: Cambridge University Press.

Zanis, D. A., Mulvaney, F., Coviello, D., Alterman, A. I., Savitz, B., & Thompson, W. (2003). The effectiveness of early parole to substance abuse treatment facilities on 24-month criminal recidivism. *Journal of Drug Issues*, 3, 223–226.

Zhang, L., Welte, J. W., & Wieczorek, W. W. (2002). The role of aggression-related alcohol expectancies in explaining the link between alcohol and violent behavior. *Substance Use and Misuse*, 37, 457–471.

35

Prison Substance Misuse Interventions and Offending

Sharon Casey
Deakin University, Australia

Andrew Day
James Cook University and University of Melbourne, Australia

There is now substantial evidence to demonstrate a close association between substance misuse and offending. One meta-analysis of research in this area by Bennett, Holloway, and Farrington (2008), for example, concluded that the odds of offending are between 2.8 and 3.8 times greater for drug users than non-drug users, and are particularly high for specific types of drug use, such as crack and heroin. As a result of statistics such as these, substance misuse has been identified as one of the "Central Eight" risk factors for reoffending (Andrews & Bonta, 2010) and is widely identified as a key target of correctional rehabilitation. However, service delivery in this area is impacted by a number of issues. These include the financial burden associated with providing treatment to the large number of offenders who present with substance use problems, the general complexity of substance misuse disorders, and the particular challenges associated with successfully reintegrating this particular group of offenders back into the community (Visher, La Vigne, & Travis, 2004).

From the outset, it is important to note that the use of illicit substances can constitute an offense in its own right, as well as lead to other types of drug offense (e.g., trafficking). In addition, substance use can be a consequence rather than a cause of offending—some offenders use drugs and/or alcohol to "celebrate" the successful commission of a crime (Menard & Mihalic, 2001). It is often the case, however, that the impaired judgment associated with intoxication results in impulsive and/or criminal behavior (see Haggård-Grann, Hallqvist, Långström, & Möller, 2006; Howells, Day, & Thomas-Peter, 2004). Furthermore, because substance use cannot usually be supported through legitimate means, it is common for offenders to engage in acquisitive crime in order to finance ongoing use.

An important consideration for any psychologist who is interested in understanding the role that substance misuse plays in offending is the extent to which the association is a product of one or more shared variables, such as poor impulse control, a generally deviant lifestyle, or close association with criminal peers (see Bennett & Holloway, 2005; McSweeney & Hough, 2005, for reviews). It may be that efforts to reduce the risk of further offending are better directed at these factors, and making decisions about the focus of any intervention are far from

---

The Wiley International Handbook of Correctional Psychology, First Edition. Edited by Devon L. L. Polaschek, Andrew Day, and Clive R. Hollin.

straightforward, given that many of the known risk factors for offending are the same as those for substance misuse (e.g., poor social support systems, difficulty in school, deviant peer group membership). It is also quite possible that the two behaviors are functionally independent from one other (i.e., substance misuse has no direct association with offending). In this circumstance, substance misuse treatment cannot be expected to reduce reoffending.

Prison Substance Misuse Programs

A number of different types of treatment program have been delivered in correctional settings. These include harm minimization programs that aim to enhance awareness of the physiological effects of substance use and high-risk behaviors (e.g., overdose, blood-borne infection and other disease transmission), and pharmacological programs (e.g., opioid substitution treatment). Psycho-educational programs are also offered to improve the individual's understanding and awareness of the link between substance misuse and offending and enhance motivation to enter more intensive treatment. Group programs, which are generally of a higher intensity, and prison-based therapeutic communities represent the most intensive types of prison intervention.

In a relatively recent update of their systematic review examining the effectiveness of interventions for incarcerated offenders, Mitchell, Wilson, and MacKenzie (2012) reported that whereas some of these interventions were modestly effective in reducing recidivism (e.g., therapeutic communities), others were associated with reductions in recidivism but not drug use (e.g., counseling programs), reduced substance use but had little impact on recidivism (e.g., narcotic maintenance programs), or had little effect on either recidivism or drug use (i.e., boot camps). Given that the focus of this chapter is on the impact of drug treatment program outcomes on criminal behavior, it is also worth noting that vast majority of reviews undertaken over the past two decades (e.g., Bahr, Masters, & Taylor, 2012; Marsch, 1998; Mitchell, Wilson, & MacKenzie, 2006; Mitchell et al., 2012; Pearson & Lipton, 1999; Prendergast, Podus, Chang, & Urada, 2002) have involved studies undertaken in the United States. This is important given that the thresholds for incarceration differ between jurisdictions and, as a consequence, it cannot be assumed that the population of offenders who are identified as requiring substance misuse treatment in one country will be comparable with those in another. Another limitation to keep in mind when interpreting outcomes of these studies is the effect of selection bias in light of evidence that differences in pre-treatment characteristics (e.g., motivation, previous criminal history, drug dependence) can not only produce lower drug use in treatment groups but also reflect on the severity of crime committed post-treatment (see Huebner & Cobbina, 2007). Notwithstanding these issues, it is the US research that provides the strongest available evidence for what works in reducing recidivism for offenders with substance use problems.

Group-Based Treatment Programs

The most frequently adopted interventions for "moderate-" to "high-" risk offenders are group-based cognitive and behavioral skills training programs in which substance abuse, offending behavior, and other issues (e.g., problem-solving, life skills, communication skills, relapse prevention) are addressed. A good example of this type of program is from Canada, where corrections offer a range of moderate National Substance Abuse Program

(NSAP-Moderate) and high-intensity (NSAP-High) substance abuse programs that target both mainstream and Aboriginal offenders. The high-intensity programs are described as cognitive behavioral in orientation and augmented by motivational interviewing (Miller & Rollnick, 1991), rational emotive behavior therapy (Ellis, McInerney, DiGiuseppe, & Yeager, 1988), problem-solving (D'Zurilla, Nezu, & Maydeu-Olivares, 1999), and relapse prevention (Marlatt & Gordon, 1985; Parks & Marlatt, 1999), with adaptations for Aboriginal participants informed by their spiritual, emotional, mental, and physical needs. Evaluations (e.g., Grant, Kunic, MacPerson, McKeown, & Hanson, 2003; Nafekh, Allegri, Stys, & Jense, 2009) have shown that those participants who successfully complete the high-intensity program have lower rates of recidivism than matched controls, and a greater likelihood (4.5 times for non-Aboriginal and 7.2 times for Aboriginal) of discretionary release. Non-Aboriginal offenders who did reoffend were also significantly less likely to be returned to prison (and if they were, the odds of the offense being violent were extremely low). While similar findings were noted for non-Aboriginal participants who participated in the moderate-intensity program, the odds for discretionary release (1.4), while significant, were much lower than for the high-intensity group. This finding also applied to the likelihood of return to prison and the odds of being sentenced for a violent offense. No significant difference was found between Aboriginal offenders in the treatment and matched control groups.

The Rehabilitation for Addicted Prisoners Trust (RAPt) provides intensive prison-based drug treatment in the United Kingdom (England and Wales prison system), addressing both substance dependence and criminal behavior using a model that integrates several complementary theoretical approaches: motivational enhancement therapy and cognitive behavioral therapy (e.g., Bahr et al., 2012; Brown et al., 2006; McMurran, 2007) at treatment outset, followed by a 12-step Narcotics Anonymous (NA) treatment plan (e.g., Gossop, Stewart, & Marsden, 2007). A recent evaluation of RAPt conducted by Kopak, Dean, Procto, Millerm, and Hoffmann (2015) compared recidivism rates for male prisoners who completed the program with two groups: those who failed to complete; and a comparison group who undertook an alternative in-prison drug treatment program. Program completers were less likely to reoffend than both the comparison group and those who failed to complete the program. And consistent with findings reported by Bennett et al. (2008), this study also revealed a relationship between drug type and increased recidivism—with those using heroin or cocaine (crack or powder) more likely to reoffend. Similarly, offense type was identified as a key consideration, with participants convicted of property offenses (including acquisitive crimes) having a greater likelihood of reoffending within 12 months of release.

Despite the high proportion of women who commit crime either under the influence of drugs or as a means to support drug use (e.g., Adams, Luekefeld, & Peden, 2008; Chesney-Lind & Pasko, 2013; Johnson, 2004, 2006; Roll, Prendergast, Richardson, Burdon, & Ramirez, 2005), and the greater proportion of female prisoners who meet the criteria for current substance use problems, there is little evidence about the impact of prison-based treatment for women. The Women Offender Substance Abuse Program (WOSAP), conducted by the Correctional Service of Canada, is a gender-specific substance abuse program delivered to women assessed as moderate to high need for substance abuse intervention. Its design is unique, offering a continuum of interventions and services (admission to prison to warrant expiry) which are matched to each woman's specific needs (and includes peer support and activities designed to foster a positive culture). Treatment is comprised of three institutional treatment modules, Engagement and Education (E&E), Intensive Therapeutic Treatment (ITT), and Relapse Prevention and Maintenance (RPM); Community Relapse Prevention and

Maintenance (CRPM) is offered to women under community supervision. An evaluation conducted by Matheson, Doherty, and Grant (2009) compared return to custody rates after 1 year for women (N = 560) who had participated in ITT-WOSAP, and women who had participated in E&E and/or RPM only, to those of women who had participated in the previous treatment program. The evaluation also examined whether women who participated in any aspect of WOSAP and received the CRPM component were less likely to return to custody than women who did not engage in maintenance post-release. Overall, 41% of the total sample was returned to custody within 1 year of leaving prison, with the lowest rate of return for the ITT-WOSAP (39%) group, followed by those who participated in E&E and/or RPM (43%). The highest return rate was among women who completed the treatment program prior to WOSAP being implemented (47%). These findings suggest that intensive substance abuse programming (i.e., ITT-WOSAP) is more beneficial in reducing the return to custody rate, especially when post-release programming (CRPM) is offered. Of the women who completed CRPM, only 5% were returned to custody, which was significantly lower than those who did not undertake the program (38%). Such outcomes offer support for the recent claim by Swopes, Davis, and Scholl (2017) that women in prison require substance use treatment that is broader than that conceptualized for males and should include, among other things, modules dealing with family or domestic violence and trauma.

Therapeutic Communities

The evidence base supporting the delivery of group-based treatment is limited when compared to that which documents the effects of prison-based therapeutic communities (e.g., Lipton, Pearson, Cleland, & Yee, 2002). While the content of both types of program is similar—addressing issues such as understanding substance use and offending, developing mechanisms to cope with cravings and withdrawal, developing alternative behaviors, managing emotions, enhancing problem-solving and communication, and developing relapse prevention plans—the therapeutic community (TC) approach differs markedly from group-based programs. For example, TC participants are (usually) separated from the mainstream prison culture and immersed in a dedicated treatment environment.

Although there are different types of TC (see Chapter 37), it is the "concept-based" models that generally provide specialist substance misuse treatment. In these programs, drug-using individuals are seen as experiencing relational problems (Malinowski, 2003), as being immature, and as being unable to delay gratification (Wexler, 1997). This is counteracted by the setting of therapeutic goals that promote social adjustment. Programs are typically based on an abstinence-based model of care, and their primary goal is to promote independence and self-responsibility, making the individual the active agent in his or her recovery. The confrontation of negative behavior is also seen as a key therapeutic component (Kooyman, 2001), and those who have been in the community for longer are expected to serve as positive role models for newer members. The model thus utilizes the prison community as a place to learn, model, and embed new adaptive patterns of behavior.

Initial evaluations have revealed statistically significant reductions in recidivism rates for those who complete therapeutic community treatment when compared with an untreated or "treatment as usual" group, particularly for higher-risk offenders (e.g., Wexler, De Leon, Thomas, Kressel, & Peters, 1999; Wexler, Melnick, & Cao, 2004). Longer-term evaluations have, however, seen some revisions made to these initial findings (see Holloway, Bennett, & Farrington, 2006; Welsh, 2007). For example, Zhang, Roberts, and McCollister (2011) examined 5-year outcomes (return to prison rates) for a sample drawn from the Substance Abuse Treatment Facility, a Californian State prison-based therapeutic community program. A comparison of outcomes between the treatment group (25% of whom had received aftercare) and an untreated case-matched group revealed only a small non-significant difference in the return to prison rate between those who received aftercare (47.5%) and those who did not (57.1%). At 1-year follow-up, the return to prison rate for the combined therapeutic community group (54.7%) was marginally higher than that of the comparison group (51.9%), and by 5 years the rate was almost identical. Given that participants returned to prison at the same rate and were arrested at the same rate for similar offenses, the authors concluded that their findings failed to support the efficacy of therapeutic communities, at least as implemented in this Californian prison. These findings are consistent with another 5-year evaluation (Prendergast, Hall, Wexler, Melnick, & Cao, 2004), which examined post-release data for the Amity TC program, an in-prison program offered in San Diego, California (see Wexler et al., 1999). Whereas 1- and 2-year evaluations revealed reduced recidivism for the treatment group as compared to the no treatment group, by 5-year follow-up no significant differences were noted in terms of recidivism rates for TC completers and TC dropouts; nor did recidivism rates for these groups differ for offenders who had entered but not completed a 6–12-month community residential treatment facility post-release. The most successful at post-release were older offenders who completed the post-release treatment program, both in terms of delayed (or no) return to prison and in terms of an increased likelihood of remaining drug free.

While evaluations of modified therapeutic communities for incarcerated female offenders with substance abuse problems have been undertaken, these have not been subject to the same longitudinal analysis as those involving male cohorts and thus care needs to be taken when interpreting their findings. Nonetheless, Hall, Prendergast, Wellisch, Patten, and Cao (2004) evaluated outcomes for the Forever Free program, an intensive 6-month (4 hours per day/5 days per week) program delivered near the end of the women's sentence. At 1-year follow-up, significantly fewer Forever Free clients (50%) reported being arrested than the comparison group (75%), although the difference in terms of reincarceration was non-significant (50% vs. 62%). The CREST Outreach Center is a therapeutic community which links prison and community-based treatment through a graduated compulsory work release in the US State of Delaware. Over the 6-month program, participants spend the first 3 months engaged in full-time substance abuse treatment followed by 3 months involved in a work-release program. An outcome evaluation conducted by Robbins, Martin, and Surratt (2009) compared CREST completers, non-completers, and a comparison group (who did not receive treatment) over an 18-month follow-up period. Women who completed CREST were significantly (Odds Ratio = 2.3) more likely than those not receiving treatment (the comparison group) to remain arrest-free; no significant difference was noted in terms of recidivism between CREST non-completers and the comparison group with regard to the likelihood of rearrest. CREST completers were also more likely to remain drug-free and use drugs less extensively during their first 18 months out of prison than non-completers and women in the comparison group.

Psychopharmacology

Finally, it is important that correctional psychologists are aware of the evidence to support the use of other forms of treatment, including pharmacotherapy. While the use of this type of treatment differs across jurisdictions, the primary forms of maintenance medications used within correctional environments are methadone and buprenorphine. Both have been reported to be effective in reducing opiate and cocaine use in a series of randomized clinical trials (e.g., Marsch et al., 2005; Montoya et al., 2004). More recently, naltrexone, which occupies opioid receptors rather than having agonist effects (by preventing or reversing the effects produced by opioid agonists) has provided another option (e.g., Cornish et al., 1997), although until recently compliance issues have presented problems (see Lobmaier, Kunøe, Gossop, Katevoll, & Waal, 2010). However, the introduction of sustained-release naltrexone as a depot or implant formulation does offer a viable alternative to methadone and buprenorphine (Comer, Sullivan, & Hulse, 2007; Sullivan et al., 2007).

The impact that pharmacotherapy has on offending is, however, not easily established. For example, the updated systematic review conducted by Mitchell et al. (2012) reported no association between narcotic maintenance programs and a statistically significant reduction in recidivism. However, Egli, Pina, Skovbo Christensen, Aebi, and Killias (2009), whose systematic review focused entirely on whether substitution therapy impacted on reoffending (including comparisons of competing treatments, and restricted to studies meeting level 4 on the Maryland scale [Sherman et al., 1997]), produced slightly different results. In their study, no significant reduction in crime was noted with methadone maintenance treatment (MMT), with the exception that some studies showed decreasing criminality during the treatment period. And while the effect of buprenorphine was also non-significant in reducing offending, there was a tendency for the effects to be more positive as compared to MMT (or placebos). The other two substitution therapies considered were heroin and naltrexone. Interestingly, a comparison of heroin and methadone maintenance found a significant decrease in criminality measures for heroin substitution over MMT. Finally, while naltrexone is not a substitution treatment (but an inhibiting substance), comparisons with two alternative treatments (counseling and behavior therapy) were made. Although the sample was too small to draw definitive conclusions, the findings suggested that naltrexone reduced criminality significantly more than either of the psychological interventions.

Factors Impacting on Assessment and Treatment

Perhaps one of the greatest difficulties faced by correctional psychologists who work with offenders who present with substance misuse problems is decision-making about assessment and treatment referral. A number of factors, some of which are interrelated, would appear to be at play here. First, unlike violent or sexual offending, there are no established offense-specific risk/need measures, making it necessary for practitioners to rely on generalist tools (e.g., the Level of Service/Case Management Inventory [LS/CMI], Andrews, Bonta, & Wormith, 2004. Heterogeneity of presentation (discussed below) also means that while substance use may be identified as a criminogenic need, certain responsivity issues (e.g., female offenders, level of addiction) can make it difficult to focus on the specific treatment needs of the individual (McMurran, 2007). Of the various generalist tools available, the Level of Service Inventory—Revised (LSI-R; Andrews & Bonta, 1995) has been used in one of the few specific validations for drug-involved offenders. Conducted by Kelly and Welsh (2008) with a group of participants who undertook a 12-month in-prison substance abuse treatment program, this study examined the predictive validity of both total LSI-R scores and the Drug and Alcohol Problems subscale scores. As expected, at 15 months post-release, offenders with higher total LSI-R scores had greater odds of reincarceration, as did those with higher scores on the Drug and Alcohol Problems subscale.

In terms of substance misuse, the assessment tools that are typically used are the same as those used in non-correctional environments and can be grouped as being relevant to: (a) screening and diagnosis; (b) case conceptualization and treatment planning; and (c) treatment monitoring and treatment evaluation (Hunsley & Mash, 2008). Screening tools are usually brief, quick-to-administer measures that identify people who may be in need of further evaluation or assistance and, while diagnosis is often conducted without a formal structured set of questions, when a formal system is needed the Structured Clinical Interview for DSM-5 Clinical Version (SCID; First, Williams, Karg, & Spitzer, 2015) is often used. Commonly used screening tools include the Drug Abuse Screening Test (DAST-20; Skinner, 1982, 2001) and the Substance Abuse Subtle Screening Inventory-2 (SASSI-2; Miller, 1985/1999). While the Addiction Severity Index (ASI; McLellan, Alterman, Cacciola, Metzger, & O'Brien, 1992) provides measures of severity across several domains (e.g., mental health, legal status, family) and the Texas Christian University Drug Screen V (Institute of Behavioral Research, 2014) provides information on different aspects of the individual's life, both miss important details regarding the individual's pathway into both substance use and offending. These are important considerations as, like violent and sexual offenders, there is a high degree of heterogeneity among the substance using offender population (see Bennett et al., 2008; Bennett & Holloway, 2009; Nurco, 1998). This impacts not only on assessment but also on identifying the most appropriate treatment options; it also illustrates why individual assessment of both risk and need is warranted.

Jolley and Kerbs (2010) offer some guidance on assessment approaches by describing a method to establish the extent to which substance misuse is part of a broader antisocial pattern of behavior. Their model, designed for in-prison substance abuse treatment programming, is informed by the principles of effective intervention and framed within a model of service delivery based on an enhanced risk-need-responsivity (RNR) perspective (i.e., tracking an individual's pathway through an organizational context that has implemented the RNR principles into routine practice). The offender moves from an initial (standardized) risk assessment that examines propensity for future relapse and recidivism which serves to place offenders into programs at an appropriate level of service intensity (i.e., service structure, dosage, duration, services). Following the administration of the risk assessment, offenders are then assessed for specific criminogenic needs and, once need is identified, provided with responsive services. General responsivity programs reflect behavioral, social learning, and cognitive behavioral strategies and are driven by organizational demands and tracked through indicators of program integrity that express the degree to which interventions are implemented as intended. Overall treatment outcomes are assessed via both proximal and distal measures (e.g., changes over treatment, relapse, recidivism), and, given the importance of context, organizational factors (e.g., culture, climate, resources, and funding) are also measured to determine how these influence the implementation of everything from risk assessments to outcome evaluations. The value in this approach, according to Jolley and Kerbs, is that it enables treatment to take on a "far more nuanced and expanded meaning" (p. 285) that includes matching evidence-based interventions to the unique modifiable characteristics of each offender. This, it is argued, increases the likelihood of success (i.e., reduced recidivism).

A second relevant factor here is the relationship between drug use and offending. As noted, the strength of the drug–crime relationship can vary as a function of the substance involved (Bennett et al., 2008) and crime type (Bennett & Holloway, 2009; Bennett et al., 2008; Casavant & Collin, 2001), with addiction status also being influential (Best et al., 2008; Nurco, 1998; Van Roeyen, Anderson, Vanderplasschen, Colman, & Vander Laenen, 2017). The diversity of offenses associated with substance use is particularly broad and includes, for example, prostitution (e.g., as a source of funds or as a coping mechanism to deal with working conditions; see Bennett & Holloway, 2009); economically compulsive crimes (e.g., shoplifting, theft, robbery, and burglary) which may be repeated in quick succession to build a temporary "financial surplus" and thereby reduce the period between offenses (Hochstetler, 2002); and violent crimes (e.g., the pharmacological effects or drug disputes settled through violent retaliation; Van Roeyen et al., 2017).

The importance of substance type, offense pattern, and addiction status were highlighted by Nurco (1998), who, based on three decades of research, distinguished between two types of drug-using offender: "primary drug users" whose offending was shown to escalate during periods of addiction, and "primary offenders" where involvement in crime preceded drug use. From a community safety perspective, one of the major findings from the body of research undertaken by Nurco and his colleagues (e.g., Ball, Schaffer, & Nurco, 1983; Nurco, Cisin, & Balter, 1981a, 1981b, 1981c) was that while those involved in crime pre-addiction constituted less than half the sample examined, they committed significantly more crime (e.g., 91% of drug dealing as reported in Ball et al., 1983). What is also of interest is that during non-addiction periods, primary drug users (i.e., low-crime offenders) engaged in criminal activity at a much lower rate, and committed crimes of a lesser severity, than primary offenders (i.e., high-crime offenders), who continued to offend at a relatively high rate and committed crimes of a higher severity. In terms of substance use patterns, although primary offenders showed a greater propensity for narcotic drugs during periods of addiction, their overall heroin use was significantly less than that of primary drug users. The generally high rates of heroin and cocaine use during addiction periods displayed by primary drug users, coupled with the sharp increase in crime during these periods, were interpreted as consistent with an economic explanation for criminal activity rather than based on criminal predisposition.

More recently, Raftery, Casey, and Day (2017) adopted a grounded theory approach to define the specific offending behavior characteristics of a group of prisoners undergoing mandated substance use treatment. Analysis of the function of the offense (i.e., why it was committed) and how it linked with their substance use revealed two groups similar to those identified by Nurco and colleagues: Substance Related Offenders (SROs) who reported initial substance use preceded any involvement in criminal activity and that current offenses were economically motivated (i.e., they lacked a legitimate means to finance their dependence); and Substance Coincidental Offenders (SCOs) who reported that criminal behavior commenced prior to, or concurrent with, regular substance misuse and reported more extensive criminal histories which commenced at a much younger age. What this research indicates is the need for correctional psychologists to be aware that, like other offense categories and offender types, the etiological pathways or trajectories for offenders with substance misuse problems are highly heterogeneous. It is important for correctional psychologists to be aware of the underlying functions of substance use, the motivations for continued use, the relationship between use and criminal behavior, and the level of readiness and motivation for change. This requires a well-developed case formulation that provides an etiological framework for understanding the process by which each individual offends (see Chapter 29).

One final factor that requires consideration is legal coercion (i.e., compulsory or mandated treatment) and its role in the delivery of treatment. While the use of the criminal justice system to mandate offenders to receive psychological treatment is one of the most controversial aspects of service provision, it is, nonetheless, the practice of many jurisdictions across the world. Moreover, Israelsson and Gerdner's (2011) comparison of data from three time points (1986, 1999, and 2009) has revealed, whereas the use of compulsory *civil* commitments decreased in the 104 countries surveyed, there was both a steady increase in compulsory care within *criminal justice legislation* and a substantial increase in the *maximum period* of mandated care. A key component of drug control policy in the United States, United Kingdom, Europe, and Australia over several decades (see Bright & Martire, 2012; Seddon, 2007; Stevens et al., 2005; Rengifo & Stemen, 2009), coerced treatment can occur at various stages of the legal process (e.g., arrest, pre-trial, pre-sentence, post-conviction, pre-release, post-release) and, depending on the jurisdiction, the focus may be abstinence or harm reduction. Across jurisdictions there may also be differences in terms of who is directed to treatment and the process by which entry occurs. For example, in some cases the offender is given to the option to enter treatment or serve another form of punishment (typically prison), while in others treatment is ordered, without the offender's consent, as part of the sentence (Stevens et al., 2005). In terms of the type of offender directed to treatment, orders frequently come via dedicated drug courts where the focus tends to be on those charged with drug-related offenses, persistent offenders whose crimes are drug-related, or offenders who are assessed as being drug-dependent (see Birgden & Grant, 2010; Sevigny, Fuleihan, & Ferdik, 2014; Turner et al., 2002).

Debate around coerced treatment has raised ethical and moral questions relating to issues of justice and human rights (see Seddon, 2007). These issues are pertinent to correctional psychologists. While policy-makers have argued in favor of coerced treatment on the grounds of benevolence and crime prevention, the alternative position put by Seddon (2007) is that individuals who live in liberal societies have no obligation to act in a manner that is "good for them." The right to refuse treatment falls under Article 8 of the European Convention on Human Rights (Council of Europe, 2010). That said, Caplan (2006) has argued that addiction diminishes autonomy and, therefore, compulsory treatment for a finite period may be justifiable in order to restore autonomy. It is, however, an argument that carries little weight in the current political climate when one considers the changing positions regarding the length of mandatory sentences in some countries (see Israelsson & Gerdner, 2011) and the inconsistent use of pharmacotherapies (Robertson & Swartz, 2018). In some jurisdictions, most notably the United States, where the criminalization of substance-using offenders has been responsible for the highest rate of imprisonment in the Western world, ideological objections to the use of pharmacotherapies has seen a preference for medication-free treatment. This can be attributed to a lack of knowledge about the benefits of a medical approach and an over-reliance on non-medical models of addiction; alternatively, it reflects the persistent misuse and diversion of substitution therapies by addicted offenders.

The second point, that legal coercion is necessary for crime prevention, lacks gravitas. Just as past debates have pointed out that the role of imprisonment as rehabilitation is incompatible with justice (e.g., Morris, 1974), the same ethical principle applies when treating the individual as a means not as an end. For correctional practitioners, the belief that individuals have intrinsic value is contrary to the argument that their rights should be sacrificed on crime prevention grounds (i.e., for the protection of others). This debate becomes even more polemical when treatment is simply a euphemism for punishment with addiction control the primary, less than transparent, goal (Fischer, 2003). Thus, the more pertinent issue faced by the correctional psychologist is whether the individual who is given the choice of entering treatment can provide informed consent. Obtaining informed consent from a vulnerable individual is ethically problematic even when that offer is framed as a choice and the individual views it as an opportunity (Seddon, 2007). Research seems to suggest that motivation and treatment readiness are defining factors in determining outcomes irrespective of whether entry is coerced or voluntary (e.g., Hiller, Knight, Leukefeld, & Simpson, 2002), nor can the perceived coercion be directly inferred from a referral source (e.g., Young, 2002; Young & Belenko, 2002). Again, the importance of individual case formulation comes into play with the correctional psychologist using this to assess motivation for treatment and treatment readiness as well as examine the offender's level of problem recognition and desire for help.

Conclusion

In their recent review, we identified two key implications of this body of work for correctional practice (Casey & Day, 2014). The first was that substance misuse treatment can have positive effects on reducing reoffending and, given the high prevalence of substance misuse in correctional populations, should be considered to be a core component of any rehabilitation strategy. Second, despite some inconsistencies, prison-based therapeutic community models of substance misuse treatment should be considered the treatment of choice. There remains, however, a need for the further development of group-delivered cognitive behavioral programs and pharmacological treatments. They go on to argue that the most significant reductions in reoffending are likely to occur under the following conditions (p. 366):

- when efforts are made to establish the nature of the relationship between the misuse of licit and/or illicit substances and criminal behavior, and this information is used to guide program content;
- when risk of reoffending is formally assessed and programs are targeted toward higher-risk offenders;
- when pharmacological (substitution) treatment is offered as an adjunctive treatment and substance misuse treatment is followed up by intensive post- release support and supervision services; and
- when program content takes account of how the strength of the drugs–crime connection varies by the type of drug(s) used.

While these suggestions would appear reasonably straightforward, the treatment of offenders with substance misuse problems has been hampered by a lack of research in the area, despite the extraordinary high number of offenders who enter prison each year. From the outset, the correctional psychologist makes decisions about risk and need based on generalist rather than offense-specific tools. Treatment options can be influenced by fiscal constraints, government policy, and public sentiment (Rengifo & Stemen, 2009), and despite an abundance of research the evidence-base remains equivocal in terms how best to approach treatment. What does seem evident is that offenders differ in their pathway to drug use and crime. The benefit of psychology is the capacity to identify those pathways and develop individualized treatment options.

Key Readings

Bennett, T., Holloway, K., & Farrington, D. (2008). The statistical association between drug misuse and crime: A meta-analysis. *Aggression and Violent Behavior*, 13, 107–118.

Best, D., Day, E., Homayoun, S., Lenton, H., Moverley, R., & Openshaw, M. (2008). Treatment retention in the drug intervention programme: Do primary drug users fare better than primary offenders? *Drugs: Education, Prevention and Policy*, 15, 201–209.

Seddon, T. (2007). Coerced drug treatment in the criminal justice system. *Criminology and Criminal Justice*, 7(3), 269–286.

Zhang, S. X., Roberts, R. E. L., & McCollister, K. E. (2011). Therapeutic community in a Californian prison: Treatment outcomes after 5 years. *Crime and Delinquency*, 57, 82–101.

References

Adams, S., Luekefeld, C. G., & Peden, A. R. (2008). Substance abuse treatment for women offenders: A research review. *Journal of Addictions Nursing*, 19, 61–75.

Andrews, D. A., & Bonta, J. (1995). *The Level of Service Inventory—Revised*. Toronto, Canada: Multi-Health Systems.

Andrews, D. A., & Bonta, J. (2010). *The psychology of criminal conduct* (5th ed.). New Providence, NJ: Matthew Bender.

Andrews, D. A., Bonta, J., & Wormith, S. (2004). *The Level of Service/Case Management Inventory user's manual*. North Tonawanda, NY: Multi-Health Systems.

Bahr, S. J., Masters, A. L., & Taylor, B. M. (2012). What works in substance abuse treatment programs for offenders? *The Prison Journal*, 92, 155–174.

Ball, J. C., Shaffer, J. W., & Nurco, D. N. (1983). The day-to-day criminality of heroin addicts in Baltimore: A study in the continuity of offence rates. *Drug and Alcohol Dependence*, 12, 119–142.

Bennett, T., & Holloway, K. (2005). *Understanding drugs, alcohol and crime*. Maidenhead, UK: Open University Press.

Bennett, T., & Holloway, K. (2009). The causal connections between drug misuse and crime. *British Journal of Criminology*, 49, 513–531.

Bennett, T., Holloway, K., & Farrington, D. (2008). The statistical association between drug misuse and crime: A meta-analysis. *Aggression and Violent Behavior*, 13, 107–118.

Best, D., Day, E., Homayoun, S., Lenton, H., Moverley, R., & Openshaw, M. (2008). Treatment retention in the drug intervention programme: Do primary drug users fare better than primary offenders? *Drugs: Education, Prevention and Policy*, 15, 201–209.

Birgden, A., & Grant, L. (2010). Establishing a compulsory drug treatment prison: Therapeutic policy, principles, and practices in addressing offender rights and rehabilitation. *International Journal of Law and Psychiatry*, 33, 341–349.

Bright, D. A., & Martire, K. A. (2012). Does coerced treatment of substance-using offenders lead to improvements in substance use and recidivism? A review of the treatment efficacy literature. *Australian Psychologist*, 48, 69–81.

Brown, S. A., Glasner-Edwards, S. V., Tate, S. R., McQuaid, J. R., Chalekian, J., & Granholm, E. (2006). Integrated cognitive behavioural therapy versus twelve-step facilitation therapy for substance-dependent adults with depressive disorders. *Journal of Psychoactive Drugs*, 38, 449–460.

Caplan, A. L. (2006). Ethical issues surrounding forced, mandated, or coerced treatment. *Journal of Substance Abuse Treatment*, 31, 117–120.

Casavant, L., & Collin, C. (2001). *Illegal drug use and crime: A complex relationship*. Parliament of Canada, Senate Special Committee on Illegal drugs. Retrieved from http://www.parl.gc.ca/content/sen/committee/371/ille/library/collin-e.htm

Casey, S., & Day, A. (2014). Prison substance misuse programs and offender rehabilitation. *Psychology, Crime & Law*, 21, 360–369.

Chesney-Lind, M., & Pasko, L. (2013). *The female offender: Girls, women, and crime* (3rd ed.). Thousand Oaks, CA: Sage.

Comer, S. D., Sullivan, M. A., & Hulse, G. K. (2007). Sustained-release naltrexone: Novel treatment for opioid dependence. *Expert Opinion on Investigational Drugs*, 16, 1285–1294.

Cornish, J. W., Metzger, D., Woody, G. E., Wilson, D., McLellan, A. T., Vandergrift, B., & O'Brien, C. P. (1997). Naltrexone pharmacotherapy for opioid dependent federal probationers. *Journal of Substance Abuse Treatment*, 14, 529–534.

Council of Europe. (2010). *European Convention on Human Rights*. Retrieved from http://www.echr.coe.int/Documents/Convention_ENG.pdf

D'Zurilla, T. J., Nezu, A. M., & Maydeu-Olivares, A. (1999). *Manual for the Social Problem-Solving Inventory–Revised*. North Tonawanda, NY: Multi-Health Systems.

Egli, N., Pina, M., Skovbo Christensen, P., Aebi, M. F., & Killias, M. (2009). Effects of drug substitution programs on offending among drug-addicts. *Campbell Systematic Reviews*, 5, Retrieved from https://www.campbellcollaboration.org/library/drug-substitution-programmes-offending-drug-addicts.html

Ellis, A., McInerney, J. F., DiGiuseppe, R., & Yeager, R. J. (1988). *Rational emotive therapy with alcoholics and substance abusers*. Toronto, Canada: Allyn & Bacon.

First, M. B., Williams, J. B. W., Karg, R. S., & Spitzer, R. L. (2015). *Structured Clinical Interview for DSM-5 Disorders, Clinician Version (SCID-5-CV)*. Arlington, VA: American Psychiatric Association.

Fischer, B. (2003). Doing good with a vengeance: A critical assessment of the practices, effects and implications of drug treatment courts in North America. *Criminal Justice*, 3(3), 227–248.

Gossop, M., Stewart, D., & Marsden, J. (2007). Attendance at Narcotics Anonymous and Alcoholics Anonymous meetings, frequency of attendance, and substance use outcomes after residential treatment for drug dependence: A 5-year follow-up study. *Addiction*, 103, 119–125.

Grant, B., Kunic, D., MacPerson, P., McKeown, C., & Hanson, E. (2003). *The High Intensity Substance Abuse Program (HI-SAP): Results from the pilot programs*. Research Report No. R-140. Ottawa, Canada: Research Branch, Correctional Service of Canada. Retrieved from http://www.csc-scc.gc.ca/research/092/r140_e.pdf

Haggård-Grann, U., Hallqvist, J., Långström, N., & Möller, J. (2006). The role of alcohol and drugs in triggering criminal violence: A case-crossover study. *Addiction*, 100, 100–108.

Hall, E. A., Prendergast, M. L., Wellisch, J., Patten, M., & Cao, Y. (2004). Treating drug-abusing women prisoners: An outcome evaluation of the Forever Free program. *The Prison Journal*, 84, 81–105.

Hiller, M. L., Knight, K., Leukefeld, C., & Simpson, D. D. (2002). Motivation as a predictor of therapeutic engagement in mandated residential substance abuse treatment. *Criminal Justice and Behavior*, 29, 56–75.

Hochstetler, A. (2002). Sprees and runs: The construction of opportunity in criminal episodes. *Deviant Behavior*, 23, 45–74.

Holloway, K. R., Bennett, T. H., & Farrington, D. P. (2006). The effectiveness of drug treatment programs in reducing criminal behavior: A meta-analysis. *Psicothema*, 18, 620–629 Retrieved from http://www.psicothema.com/pdf/3262.pdf

Howells, K., Day, A., & Thomas-Peter, B. (2004). Changing violent behaviour: Criminological and psychiatric models compared. *Journal of Forensic Psychiatry and Psychology*, 15, 391–406.

Huebner, B. M., & Cobbina, J. (2007). The effect of drug use, drug treatment participation, and treatment completion on probationer recidivism. *Journal of Drug Issues*, 37, 619–641.

Hunsley, J., & Mash, E. J. (2008). Developing criteria for evidence-based assessment: An introduction to assessments that work. In J. Hunsley, & E. J. Mash (Eds.), *A guide to assessments that work* (pp. 3–14). New York, NY: Oxford University Press.

Institute of Behavioral Research (2014). *Texas Christian University Drug Screen V*. Fort Worth, TX: Texas Christian University, Institute of Behavioral Research Retrieved from http://ibr.tcu.edu

Israelsson, M., & Gerdner, A. (2011). Compulsory commitment to care of substance misusers: International trends during 25 years. *European Addiction Research*, 18, 302–321.

Johnson, H. (2004). Key findings from the drug use careers of female offenders study. *Trends & Issues in Crime & Criminal Justice*, 289, 1–6 Retrieved from https://aic.gov.au/publications/tandi/tandi289

Johnson, H. (2006). Drug use by incarcerated women offenders. *Drug & Alcohol Review*, 25, 433–437.

Jolley, J. M., & Kerbs, J. J. (2010). Risk, need, and responsivity: Unrealized potential for the international delivery of substance abuse treatment in prison. *International Criminal Justice Review*, 20, 280–301.

Kelly, C. E., & Welsh, W. N. (2008). The predictive validity of the Level of Service Inventory—Revised for drug-involved offenders. *Criminal Justice and Behavior*, 35, 819–831.

Kooyman, M. (2001). The history of therapeutic communities: A view from Europe. In B. Rawlings, & R. Yates (Eds.), *Therapeutic communities for the treatment of drug users* (pp. 59–79). London, UK: Jessica Kingsley.

Kopak, A. M., Dean, L. V., Procto, S. L., Millerm, L., & Hoffmann, N. G. (2015). Effectiveness of the Rehabilitation for Addicted Prisoners Trust (RAPt) programme. *Journal of Substance Use*, 20, 254–261.

Lipton, D. S., Pearson, F. S., Cleland, C. M., & Yee, D. (2002). The effectiveness of cognitive-behavioural treatment methods on recidivism. In J. McGuire (Ed.), *Offender rehabilitation and treatment: Effective programmes and policies to reduce re-offending* (pp. 79–112). Chichester, UK: Wiley.

Lobmaier, P. P., Kunøe, M., Gossop, N., Katevoll, T., & Waal, H. (2010). Naltrexone implants compared to methadone: Outcomes six months after prison release. *European Addiction Research*, 16, 139–145.

Malinowski, A. (2003). What works with substance users in prison? *Journal of Substance Use*, 8, 223–233.

Marlatt, G. A., & Gordon, J. R. (Eds.) (1985). *Relapse prevention: Maintenance strategies in the treatment of addictive behaviors*. New York, NY: Guilford Press.

Marsch, L. A. (1998). The efficacy of methadone maintenance interventions in reducing illicit opiate use, HIV risk behavior and criminality: A meta-analysis. *Addiction*, 93, 515–532.

Marsch, L. A., Stephens, M. A., Mudric, T., Strain, E. C., Bigelow, G. E., & Johnson, R. E. (2005). Predictors of outcome in LAAM, buprenorphine, and methadone treatment for opioid dependence. *Experimental and Clinical Psychopharmacology*, 13, 293–302.

Matheson, F. I., Doherty, S., & Grant, B. A. (2009). *Women offender substance abuse programming & community reintegration*. Research Report No R-202. Addictions Research Centre, Research Branch, Correctional Service Canada. Retrieved from http://www.csc-scc.gc.ca/research/092/r202-eng.pdf

McLellan, A. T., Alterman, A. I., Cacciola, J., Metzger, D., & O'Brien, C. P. (1992). A new measure of substance abuse treatment: Initial studies of the treatment services review. *Journal of Nervous and Mental Disease*, 180, 101–110.

McMurran, M. (2007). What works in substance misuse treatments for offenders? *Criminal Behaviour and Mental Health*, 17, 225–233.

McSweeney, T., & Hough, M. (2005). *Drugs and alcohol*. Cullompton, UK: Willan.

Menard, S., & Mihalic, S. (2001). The tripartite conceptual framework in adolescence and adulthood: Evidence from a national sample. *Journal of Drug Issues*, 31, 905–940.

Miller, G. A. (1985/1999). *The Substance Abuse Subtle Screening Inventory (SASSI) manual* (2nd ed.). Springville, IN: The SASSI Institute.

Miller, W. R., & Rollnick, S. (Eds.) (1991). *Motivational interviewing: Preparing people to change addictive behavior*. New York, NY: Guilford Press.

Mitchell, O., Wilson, D. B., & MacKenzie, D. L. (2006). *The effectiveness of incarceration-based drug treatment on criminal behavior*. Campbell Systematic Reviews. Retrieved from https://campbellcollaboration.org/library/download/215_28088b2227e2742a8415b2ff52d0cd8c.html

Mitchell, O., Wilson, D. B., & MacKenzie, D. L. (2012). The effectiveness of incarceration-based drug treatment on criminal behavior: A systematic review. *Campbell Systematic Reviews*, 8, Retrieved from https://www.campbellcollaboration.org/library/effectiveness-of-incarceration-based-drug-treatment.html

Montoya, I. D., Gorelick, D. A., Preston, K. L., Schroeder, J. R., Umbricht, A., Cheskin, L. J., & Fudala, P. J. (2004). Randomized trial of buprenorphine for treatment of concurrent opiate and cocaine dependence. *Clinical Pharmacology and Therapeutics*, 75, 34–48.

Morris, N. (1974). *The future of imprisonment*. Chicago, IL: University of Chicago Press.

Nafekh, M., Allegri, N., Stys, Y., & Jense, T. (2009). *Correctional Service Canada's correctional program evaluation*. Retrieved from http://www.csc-scc.gc.ca/text/pa/cop-prog/cp-eval-eng.shtml#sec1_3_3

Nurco, D. N., Cisin, I. H., & Balter, M. B. (1981a). Addict careers I: A new typology. *The International Journal of the Addictions*, 16(8), 1305–1325.

Nurco, D. N., Cisin, I. H., & Balter, M. B. (1981b). Addict careers II: The first ten years. *The International Journal of the Addictions*, 16(8), 1327–1356.

Nurco, D. N., Cisin, I. H., & Balter, M. B. (1981c). Addict careers III: Trends across time. *The International Journal of the Addictions*, 16(8), 1357–1372.

Nurco, D. N. (1998). A long-term program of research on drug use and crime. *Substance Use & Misuse*, 33, 1817–1837.

Parks, G. A., & Marlatt, G. A. (1999). Keeping "what works" working: Cognitive behavioral relapse prevention with substance abusing offenders. In E. J. Latessa (Ed.), *Strategic solutions: The International Community Corrections Association examines substance abuse* (pp. 161–233). Lanham, MD: American Correctional Association.

Pearson, F., & Lipton, D. (1999). A meta-analytic review of the effectiveness of corrections-based treatments for drug abuse. *The Prison Journal*, 79, 384–410.

Prendergast, M. L., Podus, D., Chang, E., & Urada, D. (2002). The effectiveness of drug abuse treatment: A meta-analysis of comparison group studies. *Drug and Alcohol Dependence*, 67, 53–72.

Prendergast, M. L., Hall, E. A., Wexler, H. K., Melnick, G., & Cao, Y. (2004). Amity prison-based therapeutic community: 5-year outcomes. *The Prison Journal*, 84, 36–60.

Raftery, S., Casey, S., & Day, A. (2017). *Understanding the ways in which drug use provides a pathway into criminal behaviour.* University of South Australia, Adelaide, Australia. Unpublished

Rengifo, A. F., & Stemen, D. (2009). The impact of drug treatment on recidivism: Do mandatory programs make a difference? Evidence from Kansas's Senate Bill 123. *Crime & Delinquency*, 59, 930–950.

Robbins, D. A., Martin, S. S., & Surratt, H. L. (2009). Substance abuse treatment, anticipated maternal roles, and reentry success of drug-involved women prisoners. *Crime & Delinquency*, 55, 388–411.

Robertson, A. G., & Swartz, M. S. (2018). Extended-release naltrexone and drug treatment courts: Policy and evidence for implementing an evidence-based treatment. *Journal of Substance Abuse Treatment*, 85, 101–104.

Roll, J. M., Prendergast, M., Richardson, K., Burdon, W., & Ramirez, A. (2005). Identifying predictors of treatment outcome in a drug court program. *American Journal of Drug and Alcohol Abuse*, 31, 641–657.

Seddon, T. (2007). Coerced drug treatment in the criminal justice system. *Criminology and Criminal Justice*, 7, 269–286.

Sevigny, E. L., Fuleihan, B. K., & Ferdik, F. V. (2014). Do drug courts reduce the use of incarceration? A meta-analysis. *Journal of Criminal Justice*, 41, 416–425.

Sherman, L. W., Gottfredson, D., Mackenzie, D., Eck, J., Reuter, P., & Bushway, S. (1997). *Preventing crime: What works, what doesn't, what's promising?.* A report to the United States Congress. University of Maryland, Department of Criminology and Criminal Justice. Retrieved from https://www.ncjrs.gov/pdffiles/171676.PDF

Skinner, H. A. (1982). The drug abuse screening test. *Addictive Behavior*, 7, 363–371.

Skinner, H. A. (2001). Assessment of substance abuse. Drug abuse screening test. In R. Carson-Dewitt (Ed.), *Encylopedia of drugs, alcohol & addictive behaviour* (2nd ed.) (pp. 147–148). Durham, NC: Macmillan.

Stevens, A., Berto, D., Heckmann, W., Kerschl, V., Oeuvray, K., Ooyen, M., … & Uchtenhagen, A. (2005). Quasi-compulsory treatment of drug dependent offenders: An international literature review. *Substance Use & Misuse*, 40, 269–283.

Sullivan, M. A., Garawi, F., Bisaga, A., Comer, S. D., Carpenter, K., Raby, W. N., … & Nunes, E. V. (2007). Management of relapse in naltrexone maintenance for heroin dependence. *Drug & Alcohol Dependence*, 91, 289–292.

Swopes, R. M., Davis, J. L., & Scholl, J. A. (2017). Treating substance abuse and trauma symptoms in incarcerated women: An effectiveness study. *Journal of Interpersonal Violence*, 32, 1143–1165.

Turner, S., Longshore, D., Wenzel, S., Deschenes, E., Greenwood, P., Fain, T., ... & McBride, D. (2002). A decade of drug treatment court research. *Substance Use & Misuse*, 37(12–13), 1489–1527.

Van Roeyen, S., Anderson, S., Vanderplasschen, W., Colman, C., & Vander Laenen, F. (2017). Desistance in drug-using offenders: A narrative review. *European Journal of Criminology*, 14, 606–625.

Visher, C., La Vigne, N. G., & Travis, J. (2004). *Returning home: Understanding the challenges of prisoner re-entry*. Washington, DC: Urban Institute Retrieved from http://www.urban.org/url. cfm?ID=410974

Welsh, W. N. (2007). A multisite evaluation of prison-based therapeutic community drug treatment. *Criminal Justice and Behavior*, 34, 1481–1498.

Wexler, H. K. (1997). Therapeutic communities in American prisons. In E. Cullen, L. Jones, & R. Woodward (Eds.), *Therapeutic communities for offenders* (pp. 161–179). Chichester, UK: Wiley.

Wexler, H. K., De Leon, G., Thomas, G., Kressel, D., & Peters, J. (1999). The Amity prison TC evaluation: Reincarceration outcomes. *Criminal Justice and Behavior*, 26, 147–167.

Wexler, H. K., Melnick, G., & Cao, Y. (2004). Risk and prison substance abuse treatment outcomes: A replication and challenge. *The Prison Journal*, 84, 106–120.

Young, D. (2002). Impacts of perceived legal pressure on retention in drug treatment. *Criminal Justice and Behavior*, 29, 27–55.

Young, D., & Belenko, S. (2002). Program retention and perceived coercion in three models of mandatory drug treatment. *Journal of Drug Issues*, 32, 297–328.

Zhang, S. X., Roberts, R. E. L., & McCollister, K. E. (2011). Therapeutic community in a Californian prison: Treatment outcomes after 5 years. *Crime and Delinquency*, 57, 82–101.

Part VII
Treatment: Modalities and Approaches

36

An Examination of Individual Versus Group Treatment in Correctional Settings

Jason Davies
Swansea University and Abertawe Bro Morgannwg University Health Board, UK

Foundations

The Impact of Psychological Treatment

Psychological therapies have become a key element in the quest to manage risk and reduce reoffending (McGuire, 2013). The past 25 years have seen the rapid expansion of treatment programs designed to directly address specific types of offending (e.g., sexual or violent offending) and address broader criminogenic factors (e.g., ineffective social problem-solving and substance misuse). Broadly speaking, most of these interventions are guided by the "human service" principles of risk (high risk = higher dose/priority), need (targeting criminogenic risk factors), and responsivity (matching the style and mode of the treatment to the client) (Andrews & Bonta, 2010). Increasingly, offender strengths and possible protective factors are targeted to help clients develop ways to meet their needs through means that are prosocial rather than harmful in nature (Ward & Maruna, 2007).

McGuire (2013) recently reviewed 100 systematic or meta-analytic studies that have examined the impact of an array of interventions for offenders (including violent, sexual, and domestic abuse offenses). He concluded that overall, treatment of offenders is associated with small to moderate effect sizes, usually in relation to recidivism—measured in a variety of study-specific ways. However, even where small effects are reported, this can mean a difference of several percentage points in reconviction rates between those in the treated and those in the non-treated groups. Taking the evidence as a whole, it seems reasonable to conclude "something works"; a shift from the view that "nothing works" (see Martinson, 1974) prevalent in the 1970s. However, as shown in McGuire (2013), not everything works, treatments may work for some but not others, and interventions can have iatrogenic effects (see also Lilienfeld, 2007, for a wider discussion). Importantly, the quality of outcome studies has been questioned (e.g., Babcock, Green, & Robie, 2004; Hanson, Bourgon, Helmus, & Hodgson, 2009), with Hanson and colleagues commenting that for sexual offender treatment, "reviewers

The Wiley International Handbook of Correctional Psychology, First Edition. Edited by Devon L. L. Polaschek, Andrew Day, and Clive R. Hollin.

restricting themselves to the better-quality, published studies … could reasonably conclude that there is no evidence that treatment reduces sexual recidivism" (p. 881). Thus, the evidence highlights the wide scope for improvements to be made; services should use these small effect sizes to argue to "improve their services by adding components or tailoring their treatments" (Babcock et al., 2004, p. 1048).

What is Good Therapy Made of?

The large variability in outcomes across studies has led practitioners and researchers to examine factors which might contribute to successful outcomes. Researchers have consistently concluded that interventions for offenders that contain the principles of risk, need, and responsivity (Andrews & Bonta, 2010) lead to better outcomes (e.g., McGuire, 2013). However, within the wider psychotherapy literature, evidence that where treatment works there is often a nonsignificant difference between active psychological treatments (Luborsky et al., 2002) has led to investigations of the impact on outcome of common factors (i.e. "those dimensions of the treatment setting (therapist, therapy, client) that are not specific to any particular technique" (Lambert, 2005, p. 856). Some have argued that these might be more important than studying "specific therapy ingredients" (Messer & Wampold, 2002, p. 21) and that perhaps therapists should focus on empirically supported principles of change (ESP) rather than specific therapies (Rosen & Davison, 2003). The therapeutic alliance is one such factor that has been linked to effective therapy in numerous studies (e.g., Luborsky, McLellan, & Diguer, 1997; Marshall, Fernandez, & Serran, 2003; Marshall et al., 2002; McGuire, 2013).

The growing attention being paid to the impact of client, treatment, and therapist characteristics on outcome is in stark contrast to the extremely limited research considering the modality through which the treatment is delivered in forensic settings (e.g., O'Brien, Sullivan, & Daffern, 2016). This chapter will therefore draw on the more extensive literature within general psychotherapy research to examine individual and group treatment delivery. Where available, this will be augmented by research from areas of forensic practice.

The Case for Individual Therapy

Individual therapy provides a one-to-one context within which psychological treatment can take place. It offers the opportunity to provide highly personalized interventions based on an idiographic case formulation (see Chapter 29). It also enables the pace, content, and timing of the intervention to be tailored to best fit the requirements (and responsivity needs) of the client. Individual treatment can focus on changes in readiness and on rupture resolution (between therapist and client) in ways that may not be possible in the context of a group.

Many arguments for forensic services providing treatment in an individual forum have been put forward. Within the sexual offender treatment arena, Mann and Fernandez (2006) note that individual therapy provides greater opportunities to explore an individual's offense cycle, and affords the client and the therapist increased flexibility to tailor the therapy to specific needs. Individual treatment can provide higher levels of confidentiality for clients than is possible in group-delivered treatments (Gannon, 2015; McGuire, 2013). This may be important in circumstances such as those where the offense, or elements of the offense, are highly unusual. There are several factors that may signal the need for individual treatment. Those with complex mental health problems may only be able to participate in individually delivered treatment (Abracen & Looman, 2016), while factors such as anxiety and disruptive behavior (where these are not the core focus of the treatment) may be more readily addressed in individual treatment (Mann & Fernandez, 2006).

There are also practical reasons why an individual approach to intervention might be selected within a forensic context. First, there may not be sufficient people to make a group viable (Gannon, 2015). This issue is not uncommon in many forensic settings, either because of a lack of common treatment needs or because of small numbers of clients. Delaying treatment to wait for sufficient participants raises ethical, professional, and practical concerns, although an open-ended or rolling treatment program format could address this (Ware, Mann, & Wakeling, 2009). Second, there may be individuals who are unwilling to attend groups (Ware et al., 2009). This may be for a multitude of reasons. While there is little research examining preference within the forensic literature, and some debate about facilitating choice, in a study of treatment for panic and agoraphobia, participants stated a strong preference for individual rather than group treatment (Sharp, Power, & Swanson, 2004). However, almost all of a small (and possibly select) sample of participants who had received a group-based sexual offender therapy program reported their group experience as fairly or extremely positive (Garrett, Oliver, Wilcox, & Middleton, 2003). This suggests that although some individuals may state a preference for individual therapy, a group program may be acceptable once undertaken. Third, for some clients it will be known from the pre-treatment assessment that any standard intervention will require significant modification in order to address key needs or responsivity issues. These might include the inability to function in a group setting (e.g., social impairments, disruptiveness; Ware et al., 2009), anticipation by treatment providers that the individual might decompensate during treatment (Looman & Abracen, 2014), or other specific impairments. In such circumstances individual treatment is likely to be the most practical solution, enabling each client to receive personal attention and a tailored intervention (Tucker & Oei, 2007).

Overall, individual therapy can be seen to provide a "highly flexible platform" (Gannon, 2015, p. 100) which can be responsive to unique criminogenic or responsivity factors, including learning style and literacy (Hollin & Palmer, 2006). However, flexibility may come at a price (e.g., for treatment focus and integrity) unless it is judiciously managed. Individual therapy can also allow more stringent assessment of each clients' progress (O'Shea, Spence, & Donovan, 2014), especially when robust practice-based evidence designs are adopted (e.g., Davies, Howells, & Jones, 2007; Davies & Sheldon, 2012).

Arguments for Group Delivery

Group treatment typically involves two or more therapists or facilitators providing treatment to three or more (typically 6–12) participants, although much larger groups (20+) have been reported (Day, personal communication). Although there is little information and no evidence about how content varies with group size, it is likely that larger groups will contain more (psycho)educational content and be supplemented by individual sessions to support personalization of material. Within forensic services, providing psychological interventions in a group format is commonplace (Ware et al., 2009), and this appears to be especially true where treatments are designed and delivered to address criminogenic factors. Whilst many of the arguments for group delivery are based on the counterpoint to individual therapy (e.g., the ability to meet the common needs of several people in one session), there are also a number of specific advantages associated with group treatment that have been described in the literature.

There are many possible therapeutic and service-level advantages of providing treatment in a group format, most of which are a result of the presence of multiple participants in the sessions. Mann and Fernandez (2006) note that the group process itself (e.g., interpersonal dynamics) can form an invaluable element of the intervention. This may be through adding new perspectives to an individuals' viewpoint or interpretation, and through harnessing mutual support. Opportunities for interpersonal learning, imitation, and finding common experience have been described (Tucker & Oei, 2007). Within a group setting, the support and cohesion experienced by the participants has been related to outcome and this is likely to be, at least partly, influenced by therapist characteristics (Marshall et al., 2003). Group interventions may offer a sense of shared problems (Abracen & Looman, 2016) and allow individuals to challenge one another's views (Hollin & Palmer, 2006). Such challenges may be particularly important when specific insights are available to peers which may not be readily evident to the therapist(s) (Ware et al., 2009). Indeed, comments made by other group members may be more powerful than those given by the therapist (Abracen & Looman, 2016). Group treatment can also enable vicarious learning (Ware et al., 2009), that is, learning knowledge and skills by watching and listening to others. For many who have committed offenses, a group format will also provide a forum in which secrecy associated with their offending can be tackled (Ware et al., 2009). Perhaps it is for the reasons above that a group forum is commonly adopted in self-help/peer-led interventions (e.g., Alcoholics Anonymous).

From a service perspective, group-based interventions provide a level of consistency of treatment across participants (Hollin & Palmer, 2006). Obviously, each participant may take different things from the same content, and might experience the group differently; however, it can be demonstrated that each person will have been exposed to the same treatment at the same time. This can make evaluation and attempts at generalization more straightforward. Group therapy may be more cost-effective in relation to staffing and resources. Developing manualized group interventions makes it possible to train a broad range of staff to deliver treatments (Hollin & Palmer, 2006). However, as argued by Day, Kozar, and Davey (2013), effective therapy—individual or group—is likely to be the result of "deep learning" facilitated through the flexible delivery of a program. This is likely to require specialist post-graduate training and supervision (Day et al., 2013). Thus, manualized group treatment, with appropriately trained staff, could meet the needs of a large number of people in a "routine" way if these principles can be achieved.

A few specific potential disadvantages that are not present in individual treatment are experienced in group-delivered treatment. It has been suggested that group treatment could have a negative impact on those who participate because of what they are exposed to from others within the group. It is possible that hearing offense accounts and others' experiences in a group could lead either to vicarious traumatization or to vicarious arousal. However, while these are theoretically possible, there is little empirical evidence to support such concerns (Ware et al., 2009). It is important to recognize that those providing the treatment (regardless of modality) also face such a potential hazard—support and supervision are likely to help in combatting this (Davies, 2015). It is also possible that members might collude to support problematic thinking or behaviors during the intervention, and that group process could hinder treatment and negatively impact on participants. For example, confrontation of an individual by other group members, dominance of discussions within the group by a small number of members, and a reluctance to discuss (difficult) material in a "public" forum can all be problematic (Tucker & Oei, 2007). There may also be variation in levels of understanding and differing degrees/rates of change (Tucker & Oei, 2007), which could have negative influences on individuals and the group as a whole. Such issues might lead to subsequent failure to attend or to individuals dropping out of treatment. Skillful facilitation by experienced facilitators can often mitigate such problems; however, this will require additional high-level knowledge of and skills in group process.

Group or Individual: Which Is Best?

Having considered some of the reasons why group or individual delivery might be used, research examining the impact of each modality will be examined from three perspectives: the impact of modality on outcomes; the impact of modality on dropout and treatment completion; and the cost-effectiveness of each modality. However, it must be emphasized that the available evidence is typically drawn from non-forensic settings; limited to cognitive behavioral therapy (CBT)-based interventions; based on studies that are limited in terms of design and sample size; where comparing group and individual modalities is a secondary aim; where participants in each modality differ; and without directly reporting impact metrics such as effect size.

The Impact of Modality on Treatment Outcomes

According to Ware and colleagues (2009) "the consensus from the general psychotherapy literature is that the two modalities of treatment are equally effective for most mental disorders" (p. 73). Equivalence has also been reported in interpersonal psychotherapy for adolescents with depression (O'Shea et al., 2014), binge eating disorder (Ricca et al., 2010), panic and agoraphobia (Sharp et al., 2004), and anxiety disorders in young people (Wergeland et al., 2014); in the treatment of anger with individuals with a learning disability (Rose, O'Brien, & Rose, 2009); for high-risk sexual offenders (Abracen & Looman, 2016); and for substance misuse (Sobell, Sobell, & Agrawal, 2009). Conversely, studies from the general psychotherapy literature also show that individual treatment may be superior to group-based interventions. These include an advantage of individual delivery for (a) somatizing patients (when measures of health-related quality of life are used as outcomes; Gili et al., 2014); (b) possibly for those with depression (when CBT is the treatment approach used in both modalities; McRoberts & Burlingame, 1998); (c) social phobia (Mörtberg, Clark, & Bejerot, 2011; Mörtberg, Clark, Sundin, & Åberg Wistedt, 2007); and (d) substance misuse (Marques & Formigoni, 2001).

Scrutiny of this apparent equivalence, or the superiority of one modality over another, hides a much more complex picture. For example, although treatment equivalence was found with women receiving treatment for severe psychological difficulties consequent on childhood sexual abuse (Ryan, Nitsun, Gilbert, & Mason, 2010), their selection into modality was based on participant preference rather than random or convenience allocation. It is not known what impact preference has on participation and outcome, although, as noted by (Black, 1996), treatments that require active participation may be affected by the client's beliefs and preferences. In addition, differences of time in treatment (dose) and/or the time over which treatment is delivered (intensity) are often found. In the Mörtberg et al. (2007) study, the number of sessions for each modality was the same (16); however, the intensity was markedly different (16 weeks for individual and 3 weeks for group). Others have shown that group treatment provides more therapy time (e.g., Looman & Abracen, 2014—sexual offender treatment: group participants spent approximately three times as much time in treatment; Rose et al., 2009—anger treatment, learning disability: group spent approximately twice as much time in treatment), although examples of matched treatment do exist (e.g., Marques & Formigoni, 2001—substance misuse). Again, what is not known is whether more time is needed in one modality to provide an equivalent dose to the other; however, the notion of a minimum dose might be important regardless of modality. Abracen, Gallo, Looman, and Goodwill (2016) found that for high-risk groups, a moderate treatment dose (19 hours or less) led to improvements; however, high doses (20 or more hours) led to further significant gains (7.7 vs. 11.6 times less likely to recidivate). Such data both reinforce and offer some specificity for operationalizing the "risk principle" regardless of modality. The source of the outcome data might also be important. With alcohol-dependent patients, Marques and Formigoni (2001) found significant self-reported changes for group and individually delivered treatment, although a higher percentage of the individually treated clients reported shifts to abstinent/moderate drinking at follow-up (66 vs. 47%). Although collateral information from informants (typically spouses) showed agreement with the self-rating in 70% of cases, their reports showed the group format slightly outperformed the individual treatment. Thus, when change is viewed from multiple perspectives/using multiple indices, findings may differ or be directionally opposing. Modality differences might also show themselves in other ways. In a study of treatment for obsessive-compulsive disorder (OCD), Jónsson, Hougaard, and Bennedsen (2010) found broadly equivalent outcomes (with maybe a little to favor individually delivered treatment). However, they suggest that the individually delivered treatment may have resulted in quicker gains among participants. Conversely, group treatment for depression may have advantages over individual when short-duration intervention is used (i.e., 10 or fewer sessions; McRoberts & Burlingame, 1998). These "process" differences are important areas for further research as time restrictions or "time critical delivery" of treatment is often present in forensic settings; for instance, when a client has a short sentence.

While outcome equivalence across modality may be true for many, there may be specific groups for whom individual treatment is indicated. In a study of a preventative intervention for preadolescent aggressive children, Lochman, Dishion, and Powell (2015) found that a subset of children (those with low levels of inhibitory control pre-intervention) responded poorly in a group when compared to the individual modality of the treatment. In addition, Abracen and Looman (2016) showed no significant difference in recidivism rates between combined individual and group sex offender treatment and individually delivered treatment. However, the authors suggest that it may have been the ability to address individual complex mental health needs (e.g., a history of head injury, major mental illness, or intellectual impairment) that accounts for the equivalence.

Relating all these findings to forensic settings allows a few conclusions to be drawn. First, individual and group treatment are likely to be *at least* equivalent for many needs; second, choice in offender treatment has rarely been considered but may impact on outcome; third, risk, need, and responsivity factors need to be embedded in treatment regardless of modality; forth, the speed and process of changes may differ between modalities; and fifth, gathering collateral information is an important adjunct to self-report information. However, while there are views expressed, there is little clear evidence about who benefits most when treatment is offered through a group or individual format.

Dropout and Completion

Treatment completion is receiving increasing attention because of the links between attrition and treatment outcomes. There is growing evidence that starting treatment then dropping out before the end may be associated with higher levels of recidivism (e.g., Marshall et al., 2003;

Olver, Stockdale, & Wormith, 2011). Broadly, treatment non-completion can take place at two points—before treatment begins (i.e. failure to start treatment) and at some point during the intervention (e.g., leaving, failing to attend, or being excluded). A range of factors are beginning to be identified that might be associated with dropout (for example see McMurran, Huband, & Duggan, 2010; Olver et al., 2011); however, these and their impact may differ for individual and group treatment. As one example, emerging evidence indicates that poor alliance might increase treatment dropout among sexual offenders (Marshall et al., 2003), although for anxiety or depression treatment, alliance between therapist and client was linked to an increased rate of treatment completion for individual but not group therapy (McEvoy, Burgess, & Nathan, 2014). Treatment non-completion raises a series of interrelated questions: Do people take up group or individual treatment at different rates? Do more people drop out of group or individual therapy? Do more people get excluded from group or individual therapy? How might completion of treatment (group or individual) be maximized? What impact might personal choice have? What effect does mandated versus voluntary (self-referred) attendance in treatment have? How does completion of individual or group treatment impact on outcomes? There is also a more subtle form of dropout whereby the individual attends but doesn't engage with treatment—something that could be termed *psychological dropout*.

Research shows that high numbers of participants drop out during treatment (Hollin & Palmer, 2006), with a third or more not completing correctional[1] treatment programs (Olver et al., 2011). Treatment programs for domestically violent offending appear to have the highest dropout rates (over 50% when both pre-program non-completion and dropout after starting are combined; Olver et al., 2011). Perhaps unsurprisingly, programs delivered in custodial settings appear to have lower overall dropout than those in the community (Olver et al., 2011), with some evidence that delays in starting treatment may reduce uptake. As already noted, dropout rates in group versus individual therapy have been found to be similar when the participants have had choice over the modality of treatment (Ryan et al., 2010); however, much higher dropout has been found for group CBT treatment (vs. individual) for panic disorder and agoraphobia in a community setting (47 and 16%, respectively; Sharp et al., 2004). It may be that simple prompts may help address potential non-attendance and dropout. Sobell et al. (2009) reported no differences in dropout between modalities for drug and alcohol treatment; however, group (but not individual) participants were telephoned to remind them of their therapy the day before each session.

Attrition is clearly a huge concern because of the cost, practical, and outcome implications associated with it. This means practitioners and researchers need to focus attention on facilitating entry into treatment and, once in, helping people stay. Again, there is insufficient evidence to confidently draw conclusions about the differing effects of the modality on dropout or on strategies that might work to mitigate possible attrition. Further, the question of whether reminders and/or individual intervention in high dropout areas (e.g., community-based domestic abuse programs) would reduce this problem remains to be investigated.

Cost-Effectiveness

One central argument for the delivery of group treatment is the apparent cost-effectiveness achieved by providing treatment to a larger number of people at the same time. Although such cost saving appears to be both an intuitive conclusion and a simple argument to evidence, in reality this is not necessarily the case. In considering treatment cost, it is worth noting that indirect forms of treatment such as bibliotherapy and computer-mediated interventions potentially carry with them the highest of all resource savings. However, these are generally used as part of a stepped care model (for the "mildest" end of treatment needs and lowest risk) with those able to use self-directed treatment, and thus likely to have a limited role in correctional settings.

An attempt to directly assess the cost-effectiveness of CBT revealed a wide range of approaches being used by researchers seeking to tackle this question (Tucker & Oei, 2007). In order to produce a cost-effectiveness calculation a two-step process is required. Step one requires an understanding of the relative impact (clinical effectiveness) of each treatment form, that is, the overall effect of the treatment, the equivalence of/degree to which one modality outperforms the other, and any differences between who enters one treatment modality or the other. Step two demands that a robust approach to determining cost be used. Researchers vary widely in their approach to costings and specifying what is and isn't included in their calculations. For offending risk, this might include the costs (economic and emotional) of future offenses and the "savings" made if harms are reduced or removed. A number of approaches to calculating costs have been described, such as the management, accountant, and economist perspectives (see Wolff, Helminiak, & Tebes, 1997, for a discussion).

Tucker and Oei (2007) found that group and individual treatment outcomes (for a range of problems including substance misuse) were typically reported as equivalent or with individual interventions showing a slightly greater effect (step one, above). They also found that group therapy was generally reported to be cheaper (step two, above). Combining these, it could be concluded that group approaches were more cost-effective. However, as they note, most cost calculations were based solely on therapist delivery time. Sobell et al. (2009) also found group delivery of drug and alcohol treatment to be cheaper—again, only therapist time to deliver the intervention was included. Obviously, these findings don't take account of the fact that group or individual treatment may be the most cost-effective approach for some clients or needs and not others (Tucker & Oei, 2007). Although the cost of delivering the treatment (i.e., cost of therapist time) is widely used, accurate cost comparison is only possible when all costs are included and the financial implications of factors such as dropout (and associated recidivism) are made. McCrone, Weeramanthri, and Knapp (2005) estimate that providing therapy accounts for less than half of the overall group or individual treatment costs. Additional costs will include training and ongoing therapist supervision, which may differ significantly between modalities. For example, Jónsson et al. (2010) found that therapists viewed group-based treatment as more demanding (e.g., requiring more preparation time). Thus, a wide range of "hidden costs" need to be considered.

Developing a standardized approach and a metric such as a "cost per unit gain" would be a way of making meaningful comparisons between treatments and modalities in the way that effect size reporting has aided research into comparative effectiveness. As with research to understand dropout and non-completion of individual and group-delivered therapy, cost-effectiveness research is underdeveloped in the forensic field and thus we are again left unable to determine, with any certainty, the relative cost-effectiveness of each modality, either generally or for specific client groups.

Building the Evidence Base

Can Differences Be Detected?

Modality equivalence would appear to be good news and suggest that, in most situations, group or individual approaches could be used interchangeably, depending on factors such as the availability of resources. However, if we review the evidence base it is clear that small samples plague attempts to compare individual and group interventions. This, and reliance on different forms and sources of data, may explain equivalence and the occasions where one modality has outperformed the other. Sample size is critical to the question of "which modality is best" as small samples mean that the difference between the two forms of intervention must be large in order for them *not* to be seen as equivalent (Tucker & Oei, 2007). In other words, many of the studies comparing individual and group treatment lack power (McRoberts & Burlingame, 1998), thus apparent modality equivalence may simply be an artifact of this.

Is There an Equal Playing Field?

If we wish to investigate if individual and group modalities produce equivalent outcomes or if one outperforms the other, we need to ensure that they are matched on key criteria (McRoberts & Burlingame, 1998). This includes being in the same setting, having participants with similar "presentations," and delivering equivalent treatment. This requires attention to treatment length and intensity as well as consideration of the impact of personal preferences or being directed to one modality or the other. As already discussed, individuals may be placed in a modality for specific reasons although this appears unidirectional as only examples for selection into individual treatment (instead of group) could be found.

Do Researchers Influence Outcome?

An important and perhaps unexpected observation of modality and outcome research concerns the possible effect of investigator allegiance or expectation. McRoberts and Burlingame (1998) found that where group-delivered treatment was expected to be superior, findings favored group treatment, whilst in studies where investigators expected group and individual modality equivalence, individual treatment tended to be superior. In their research they also found that the period in which the study was conducted also had an effect on which modality was the most effective. Early research (pre-1981) favored groups, whilst those most recent to the research census date (1987–1997) favored individual treatment. Thus, the impact of belief and choice on outcome may be true for study findings as well as for individual gains.

Building a Solid Evidence Base

In order to build a solid evidence base for treatment in general and for when to use individual or group-delivered treatment, it is clear that any large sample research needs to be of good quality with sufficient participants to provide adequate power. However, statistical difference at the level of the group may not be enough. For example, Rose et al. (2009) found that although statistically significant changes were demonstrated, a much smaller set of participants met their criteria for reliable and meaningful change (see Chapter 24). This leads us to consider a more sophisticated set of questions. Given that all studies show a large number of people who remain untreated, we need to know—are the same individuals demonstrating change (positive or negative) in each modality of treatment and "Who will only benefit from treatment if it is completed individually rather than within a group" (Ware et al., 2009, p. 75) or vice versa? This is likely to require a move away from a simplistic view of "which is best at the group average level" and toward attempts to determine "what worked best for whom." Use of methods such as single case designs (e.g., Davies & Sheldon, 2012), along with practitioners routinely collecting and sharing outcome evidence, should be encouraged and perhaps expected. In addition, there are a number of points researchers (and practitioners) should hold in mind to aid interpretation and application of their study findings by others. First, researchers should report effect size in order to provide uniformity when describing the degree of change observed; second (and related to the first), researchers should adopt a common metric—a cost per unit gain—that allows cost-effectiveness of treatments to be compared; third, researchers need to attend directly to the question of modality equivalence when designing treatment studies; and finally, implementing rigorous practice-based evidence approaches (Barkham, Hardy, & Mellor-Clark, 2010) should be expected.

Individual and Group: A Best of Both Worlds?

Although this chapter has focused on using individual or group approaches to treatment, modalities may be complimentary and suited to different aspects of need (e.g., Friedman, 2013; O'Brien et al., 2016). This may mean that individual and group treatment could be offered successively (for example initially engaging in individual treatment with a view to joining a group intervention) or concurrently (to deliver different treatment components). There are now a number of treatment approaches that combine modalities and concurrently deliver some components of the intervention in a group format and others in an individual context. Examples of this combined approach include dialectical behaviour therapy (Linehan, 1993), a treatment program for anger (Jones & Hollin, 2004), and a schema therapy intervention (Dickhaut & Arntz, 2014). In each of these interventions, the authors distinguish the functions of each modality (e.g., group for skills learning and group process; individual for personalization and promoting engagement). However, evidence that supports using group and individual delivery in this way (rather than delivering all the treatment in a group or individually) still needs to be collected (Nagi & Davies, 2017).

Conclusions

Individual or Group: A Decision Guide

As we have seen, the evidence concerning modality choice in forensic settings is limited, although opinion and various "customs and practice" have been documented. If we accept that group and individual modalities are *at least* equivalent for many areas of need, and that both are better than no treatment, it is possible to identify principles to guide modality choice. Figure 36.1 provides a modality selection guide; however, it is hoped that the findings of future research will enable this flowchart to be evidenced and/or revised.

Individual or Group: The Next Steps

Determining the most appropriate treatment modality raises a lot of unanswered questions. Practitioners and researchers should work together to help understand who each treatment modality might be best suited to and whether combining modalities might be indicated. This may be determined by client factors but also may depend on what is being provided or the

Step 1: Examine the evidence

Is there any evidence that rules out using either individual or group delivery of the intervention planned (from a similar setting and with clients with similar presentations) i.e., has one modality been shown to be superior in high-quality studies?

Yes → Follow the evidence

Step 2: Consider practicalities

Are there sufficient clients requiring the same or a similar intervention with which to form a group AND could a group be facilitated? (e.g., room, appropriately trained facilitators)

No → Individual treatment

Step 3: Level of need

Is there a high level of need within the setting for the type of treatment proposed?

No → Individual treatment

Provide group treatment as standard with individual treatment for those with specific needs or preferences. Continue to step 4.

Step 4: Client factors

Are there reasons to exclude the client from a group because of responsivity issues, additional treatment needs, need for increased confidentiality/security or likely impact of/on a group?

Yes → Individual treatment

Step 5: Client preferences

Has the client refused to enter one modality or other OR has the client expressed a strong preference for one or other?

Yes → Provide selected modality unless there are other over-riding issues

Step 6: Treatment/offence characteristics

Are there unique features of the offence (or treatment target) that would require significant adaptation/tailoring of a group treatment OR is there need to develop an idiographic case formulation and provide individualized treatment based on this?

Yes → Individual treatment

Step 7: Group program

Does the client meet the criteria for entry into the group AND does the client broadly fit the case conceptualization that the group is based upon?

Yes → Group treatment

No → Individual treatment

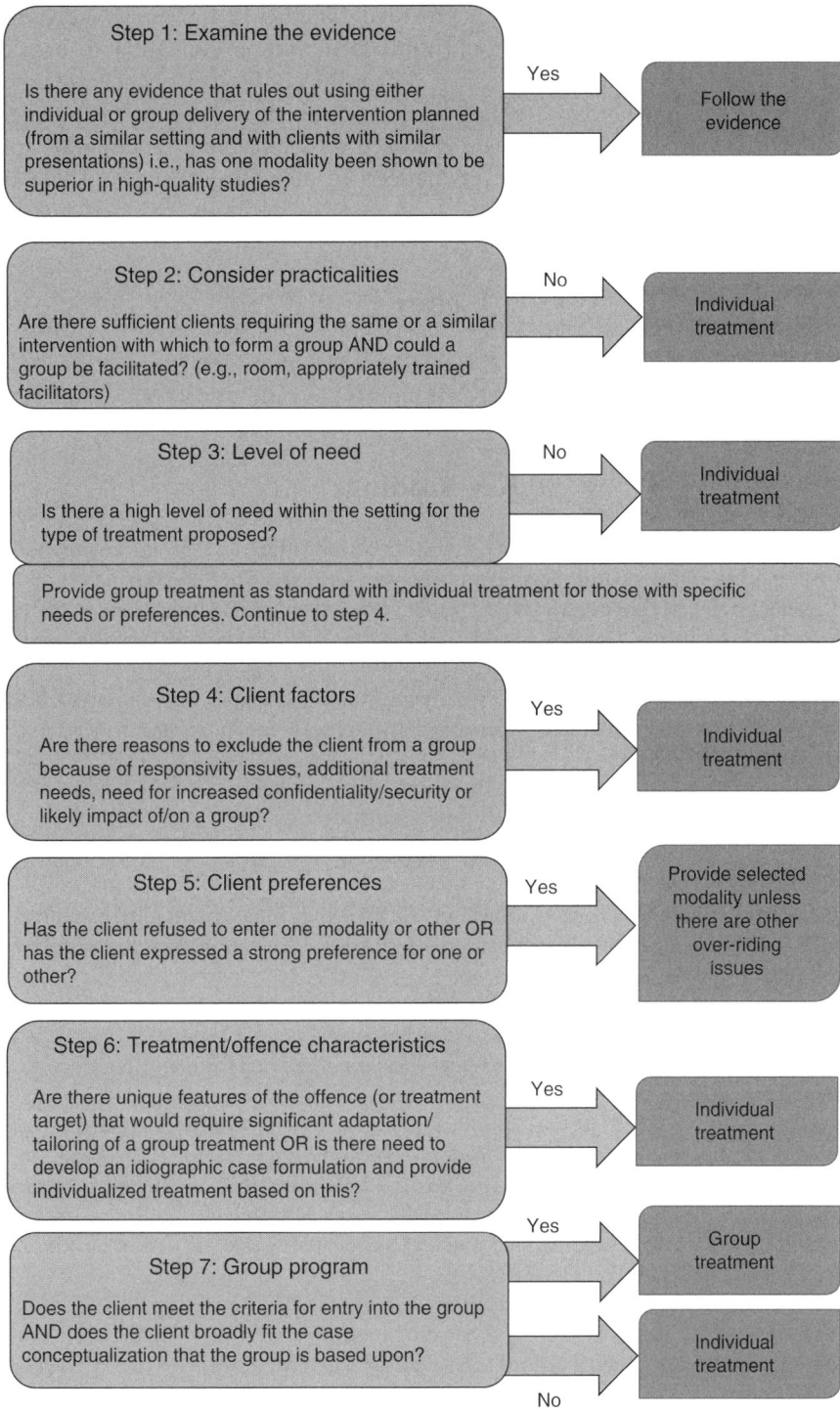

Figure 36.1 Steps to determining group or individual treatment delivery in correctional settings.

needs being addressed. Where treatment is provided (whether in a group or individually or a combination of these), practitioners should undertake routine evaluation to provide local knowledge of what works and to what extent. Regardless of the treatment modality, quality training and supervision are necessary; however, much needs to be done to understand the impact of these on outcome. Finally, there is a need to complement randomized controlled trials and group research with detailed evaluations of individual change to help build an evidence base in this area.

Note

1   In this chapter, "correctional" refers to all settings in which those who have offended may receive treatment. This includes prison, community and inpatient forensic mental health settings.

Key Readings

Marques, A., & Formigoni, M. (2001). Comparison of individual and group cognitive-behavioral therapy for alcohol and/or drug-dependent patients. *Addiction*, 96, 835–846.

O'Brien, K., Sullivan, D., & Daffern, M. (2016). Integrating individual and group-based offence-focused psychological treatments: Towards a model for best practice. *Psychiatry, Psychology and Law*, 23, 746–764.

Rosen, G. M., & Davison, G. C. (2003). Psychology should list empirically supported principles of change (ESPs) and not credential trademarked therapies or other treatment packages. *Behavior Modification*, 27, 300–312.

References

Abracen, J., Gallo, A., Looman, J., & Goodwill, A. (2016). Individual community-based treatment of offenders with mental illness: Relationship to recidivism. *Journal of Interpersonal Violence*, 31, 1842–1858.

Abracen, J., & Looman, J. (2016). Social skills and individual therapy. In *Treatment of high-risk sexual offenders* (pp. 126–153). Chichester, UK: Wiley Blackwell.

Andrews, D. A., & Bonta, J. (2010). *The psychology of criminal conduct* (5th ed.). New Providence, NJ: LexisNexis.

Babcock, J. C., Green, C. E., & Robie, C. (2004). Does batterers' treatment work? A meta-analytic review of domestic violence treatment. *Clinical Psychology Review*, 23(8), 1023–1053.

Barkham, M., Hardy, G. E., & Mellor-Clark, J. (Eds.) (2010). *Developing and delivering practice-based evidence: A guide for the psychological therapies*. Chichester. UK: Wiley.

Black, N. (1996). Why we need observational studies to evaluate the effectiveness of health care. *British Medical Journal*, 312(7040), 1215–1218.

Davies, J. (2015). *Supervision for forensic practitioners*. London, UK: Routledge.

Davies, J., Howells, K., & Jones, L. (2007). Evaluating innovative treatments in forensic mental health: A role for single case methodology? *Journal of Forensic Psychiatry & Psychology*, 18(3), 353–367.

Davies, J., & Sheldon, K. (2012). Single case methodologies. In K. Sheldon, J. Davies, & K. Howells (Eds.), *Research in practice for forensic professionals* (pp. 161–188). London, UK: Routledge.

Day, A., Kozar, C., & Davey, L. (2013). Treatment approaches and offending behavior programs: Some critical issues. *Aggression and Violent Behavior*, 18, 630–635.

Dickhaut, V., & Arntz, A. (2014). Combined group and individual schema therapy for borderline personality disorder: A pilot study. *Journal of Behavior Therapy and Experimental Psychiatry*, 45, 242–251.

Friedman, R. (2013). Individual or group therapy? Indications for optimal therapy. *Group Analysis*, 46, 164–170.

Gannon, T. A. (2015). Treatment of men who have sexually abused adults. In D. T. Wilcox, T. Garrett, & L. Harkins (Eds.), *Sex offender treatment: A case study approach to issues and interventions* (pp. 85–104). Chichester, UK: Wiley-Blackwell.

Garrett, T., Oliver, C., Wilcox, D. T., & Middleton, D. (2003). Who cares? The views of sexual offenders about the group treatment they receive. *Sexual Abuse: A Journal of Research and Treatment*, 15(4), 323–338.

Gili, M., Magallón, R., López-Navarro, E., Roca, M., Moreno, S., Bauzá, N., & García-Cammpayo, J. (2014). Health related quality of life changes in somatising patients after individual versus group cognitive behavioural therapy: A randomized clinical trial. *Journal of Psychosomatic Research*, 76(2), 89–93.

Hanson, R. K., Bourgon, G., Helmus, L., & Hodgson, S. (2009). The principles of effective correctional treatment also apply to sexual offenders: A meta-analysis. *Criminal Justice and Behavior*, 36(9), 865–891.

Hollin, C. R., & Palmer, E. J. (2006). Offending behaviour programmes: Controversies and resolutions. In C. R. Holling, & E. J. Palmer (Eds.), *Offending Behaviour Programmes: Development, Application and Controversies* (pp. 247–278). Chichester, UK: Wiley.

Jones, D., & Hollin, C. R. (2004). Managing problematic anger: The development of a treatment program for personality disordered patients in high security. *International Journal of Forensic Mental Health*, 3(2), 197–210.

Jónsson, H., Hougaard, E., & Bennedsen, B. E. (2010). Randomized comparative study of group versus individual cognitive behavioural therapy for obsessive compulsive disorder. *Acta Psychiatrica Scandinavica*, 123(5), 387–397.

Lambert, M. J. (2005). Early response in psychotherapy: Further evidence for the importance of common factors rather than "placebo effects". *Journal of Clinical Psychology*, 61(7), 855–869.

Lilienfeld, S. O. (2007). Psychological treatments that cause harm. *Perspectives on Psychological Science*, 2(1), 53–70.

Linehan, M. (1993). *Cognitive-behavioral treatment of borderline personality disorder*. New York, NY: Guilford Press.

Lochman, J. E., Dishion, T. J., & Powell, N. P. (2015). Evidence-based preventive intervention for preadolescent aggressive children: One-year outcomes following randomization to group versus individual delivery. *Journal of Consulting and Clinical Psychology*, 83(4), 728–735.

Looman, J., & Abracen, J. (2014). Efficacy of group versus individual treatment of sex offenders. *Sexual Abuse in Australia and New Zealand*, 6(1), 48–56.

Luborsky, L., McLellan, A. T., & Diguer, L. (1997). The psychotherapist matters: Comparison of outcomes across twenty-two therapists and seven patient samples. *Clinical Psychology: Science and Practice*, 4(1), 53–65.

Luborsky, L., Rosenthal, R., Diguer, L., Andrusyna, T., Berman, J., Levitt, J., ... & Krause, E. D. (2002). The dodo bird verdict is alive and well—mostly. *Clinical Psychology: Science and Practice*, 9, 2–12.

Mann, R. E., & Fernandez, Y. M. (2006). Sex offender programmes: Concept, theory and practice. In C. R. Holling, & E. J. Palmer (Eds.), *Offending Behaviour Programmes: Development, Application and Controversies* (pp. 155–177). Chichester, UK: Wiley.

Marques, A., & Formigoni, M. (2001). Comparison of individual and group cognitive-behavioral therapy for alcohol and/or drug-dependent patients. *Addiction*, 96, 835–846.

Marshall, W. L., Fernandez, Y. M., & Serran, G. A. (2003). Process variables in the treatment of sexual offenders: A review of the relevant literature. *Aggression and Violent Behavior*, 8, 205–234.

Marshall, W. L., Serran, G., Moulden, H., Mulloy, R., Fernandez, Y. M., Mann, R., & Thornton, D. (2002). Therapist features in sexual offender treatment: Their reliable identification and influence on behaviour change. *Clinical Psychology & Psychotherapy*, 9(6), 395–405.

Martinson, R. (1974). What works? Questions and answers about prison reform. *The Public Interest*, 35, 22–54.

McCrone, P., Weeramanthri, T., & Knapp, M. (2005). Cost-effectiveness of individual versus group psychotherapy for sexually abused girls. *Child and Adolescent Mental Health*, 10(1), 26–31.

McEvoy, P. M., Burgess, M. M., & Nathan, P. (2014). The relationship between interpersonal problems, therapeutic alliance, and outcomes following group and individual cognitive behaviour therapy. *Journal of Affective Disorders*, 157(C), 25–32.

McGuire, J. (2013). "What Works" to reduce re-offending: 18 years on. In L. A. Craig, L. Dixon, & T. A. Gannon (Eds.), *What works in offender rehabilitation: An evidence-based approach to assessment and treatment* (pp. 20–49). Chichester, UK: Wiley Blackwell.

McMurran, M., Huband, N., & Duggan, C. (2010). A comparison of treatment completers and non-completers of an in-patient treatment programme for male personality-disordered offenders. *Psychology and Psychotherapy: Theory, Research and Practice*, 81(2), 193–198.

McRoberts, C., & Burlingame, G. M. (1998). Comparative efficacy of individual and group psychotherapy: A meta-analytic perspective. *Group Dynamics: Theory, Research and Practice*, 2(2), 101–117.

Messer, S., & Wampold, B. (2002). Let's face facts: Common factors are more potent than specific therapy ingredients. *Clinical Psychology: Science and Practice*, 9, 21–25.

Mörtberg, E., Clark, D. M., & Bejerot, S. (2011). Intensive group cognitive therapy and individual cognitive therapy for social phobia: Sustained improvement at 5-year follow-up. *Journal of Anxiety Disorders*, 25(8), 994–1000.

Mörtberg, E., Clark, D. M., Sundin, Ö., & Åberg Wistedt, A. (2007). Intensive group cognitive treatment and individual cognitive therapy vs. treatment as usual in social phobia: A randomized controlled trial. *Acta Psychiatrica Scandinavica*, 115(2), 142–154.

Nagi, C., & Davies, J. (2017). Chapter 12: Individual Psychological Therapy with Associated Groupwork. In Jason Davies & Claire Nagi (Eds). Individual Psychological Therapies in Forensic Settings: Research and Practice. Abingdon: Routledge.

O'Shea, G., Spence, S. H., & Donovan, C. L. (2014). Group versus individual interpersonal Psychotherapy for depressed adolescents. *Behavioural and Cognitive Psychotherapy*, 43(01), 1–19.

O'Brien, K., Sullivan, D., & Daffern, M. (2016). *Integrating individual and group-based offence-focussed psychological treatments: Towards a model for best practice* (Vol. 23). (pp. 746–764) Psychiatry, Psychology and Law.

Olver, M. E., Stockdale, K. C., & Wormith, J. S. (2011). A meta-analysis of predictors of offender treatment attrition and its relationship to recidivism. *Journal of Consulting and Clinical Psychology*, 79(1), 6–21.

Ricca, V., Castellini, G., Mannucci, E., Sauro Lo, C., Ravaldi, C., Rotella, C. M., & Faravelli, C. (2010). Comparison of individual and group cognitive behavioral therapy for binge eating disorder. A randomized, three-year follow-up study. *Appetite*, 55(3), 656–665.

Rose, J., O'Brien, A., & Rose, D. (2009). Group and individual cognitive behavioural interventions for anger. *Advances in Mental Health and Learning Disabilities*, 3(4), 45–49.

Rosen, G. M., & Davison, G. C. (2003). Psychology should list empirically supported principles of change (ESPs) and not credential trademarked therapies or other treatment packages. *Behavior Modification*, 27(3), 300–312.

Ryan, M., Nitsun, M., Gilbert, L., & Mason, H. (2010). A prospective study of the effectiveness of group and individual psychotherapy for women CSA survivors. *Psychology and Psychotherapy: Theory, Research and Practice*, 78(4), 465–480.

Sharp, D. M., Power, K. G., & Swanson, V. (2004). A comparison of the efficacy and acceptability of group versus individual cognitive behaviour therapy in the treatment of panic disorder and agoraphobia in primary care. *Clinical Psychology & Psychotherapy*, 11(2), 73–82.

Sobell, L. C., Sobell, M. B., & Agrawal, S. (2009). Randomized controlled trial of a cognitive-behavioral motivational intervention in a group versus individual format for substance use disorders. *Psychology of Addictive Behaviors*, 23(4), 672–683.

Tucker, M., & Oei, T. P. S. (2007). Is group more cost effective than individual cognitive behaviour therapy? The evidence is not solid yet. *Behavioural and Cognitive Psychotherapy*, 35(01), 77–91.

Ward, T., & Maruna, S. (2007). *Rehabilitation*. Abingdon, UK: Routledge.

Ware, J., Mann, R. E., & Wakeling, H. C. (2009). Group versus individual treatment: What is the best modality for treating sexual offenders? *Sexual Abuse in Australia and New Zealand*, 1(2), 70–78.

Wergeland, G. J. H., Fjermestad, K. W., Marin, C. E., Haugland, B. S.-M., Bjaastad, J. F., Oeding, K., ... & Heiervang, E. R. (2014). An effectiveness study of individual vs. group cognitive behavioral therapy for anxiety disorders in youth. *Behaviour Research and Therapy*, 57(C), 1–12.

Wolff, N., Helminiak, T. W., & Tebes, J. K. (1997). Getting the cost right in cost-effectiveness analyses. *American Journal of Psychiatry*, 154(6), 736–743.

37

Communal Living
as the Agent of Change

Geraldine Akerman

HMP Grendon, UK

The origins of the therapeutic community (TC) movement can be attributed to William Tuke (a renowned Quaker philanthropist) and the moral treatment movement, which emphasized the importance of work, a healthy environment, and warm interpersonal relationships (Campling, 2001; Kennard, 2000). The model evolved as specialist treatment units were set up for men returning from World War II who presented with acute symptoms of distress or combat fatigue,[1] were demonstrating problematic behavior, and were known to be troublemakers. Rather than using a traditional medical model in which service veterans were treated as patients, pioneers of the TC approach (Maxwell Jones, Wilfred Bion, Siegmund Foulkes, John Rickman, Tom Main, and Stuart Whitely, to name a few) provided a setting in which residents could explore their presenting problems and etiology. *Residents*—the term used to refer to those living in a TC—were given responsibility for change rather than being viewed as passive patients, and it was soon apparent that they were able to build on their service experience and form a mutually supportive community.

Maxwell Jones wrote extensively about his work at Mill Hill (1946; 1952; 1953; 1956; 1968), earning him the title of "father" of the TC model (Manning, 1976). Robert Rapoport (1960), who led independent research over 4 years at the Henderson Hospital, was also an influential figure. Rapoport coined the phrase "community as doctor" to describe how the social environment was the agent of change, rather than any single intervention used within it. He wrote about the importance of all members, including staff, participating equally in decision-making ("democratization") and sharing responsibility for problem-solving, decision-making, and domestic arrangements. "Communalism," which involves each individual offering a unique contribution and perspective to the community, and "Permissiveness," or the need to tolerate each other's thoughts, words, and actions within boundaries and to have a shared responsibility, were also identified as key principles of treatment success. A fourth principle, "Reality Confrontation," involves residents providing feedback to others about the impact of unacceptable behavior on others. Accordingly, all interactions that occur in the TC are explored through a "culture of enquiry" so as to better understand their meaning and purpose.

The Wiley International Handbook of Correctional Psychology, First Edition. Edited by Devon L. L. Polaschek, Andrew Day, and Clive R. Hollin.

A TC Program

The TC model is now used throughout the world. The Consortium for Therapeutic Communities (TCTC), the organization which unites those working in all aspects of health and social care which use the TC model, lists members throughout Europe, Scandinavia, Australasia, and the United States. De Boer-van Schaik and Derks (2010), for example, have described the application of the model, based on the Maxwell Jones model, in a forensic psychiatric hospital in the Netherlands.

Although TCs vary in the way in which they are implemented,[2] a TC typically strives to be a facsimile of everyday living, providing countless therapeutic opportunities for the resident to acquire the skills that are needed to live in the outside world. Each individual has a therapy plan, which is reviewed at regular intervals, addressing those treatment needs that are identified at the initial assessment. Each day is comprised of therapy sessions, association time, and attention to the living quarters. Community meetings enable the administration of community living, examining aspects of interactions, and assigning tasks, as well as allowing therapeutic discussion examining everyday behavior and its effects on self and others. Small therapy groups provide the opportunity for more in-depth exploration of aspects of the residents' histories related to the current problems, often tracing back from presenting behavior, through previous enactments, to the basis of and beliefs underpinning and leading to such acts. The work of the small group is fed back to the community by residents and staff to encourage them to process the dynamics at play. In addition, a range of creative therapies, such as art therapy, psychodrama, music therapy, and drama therapy are utilized in order to use alternative ways of accessing underlying emotions, some of which may be pre-verbal and so not as responsive to talking therapy. All other aspects of the day, for instance education, recreation, preparing and serving meals, cleaning, and maintaining the living environment, serve as opportunities to develop social and life skills. Shuker (2018) describes how the relationships in TCs enable the therapy to be effective. Throughout therapy a focus remains on future plans and so residents are encouraged to develop links with the wider community to which they will be returning. As they move through their therapy journey and leave the TC, many maintain contact with the community through letters, phone calls, and visits. Strength-based approaches are emphasized, so that work is collaborative rather than imposed, thus helping residents to develop personal responsibility. Working alongside a diverse staff team, including nurses, prison officers, therapists, psychologists, and offender managers, provides the resident with opportunities to undermine previous barriers to engaging with treatment providers, and to explore unresolved antiauthority views. Parker (2007) describes the extent to which those working in such a setting rely on the residents for dynamic security, being close enough to residents so as to be able to assess day-to-day risk but detached enough to be objective.

Types of Therapeutic Community

There are two main types of TC: the democratic TC (DTC), in which the hierarchy is flattened and decision-making is shared among residents and staff; and the concept TC, (CTC), which is generally used to combat addiction by working through a hierarchy including the use of rewards. Both the DTC and CTC models have been applied in correctional settings where the primary goal of treatment is to address offending behavior. Adler (1982) highlighted how a locked environment can provide a useful additional layer of containment in which to undertake therapy, providing what Winnecot (1960) had described as a "holding space": a safe space in which residents can mature emotionally and explore their own development. In both models, consideration is given to all aspects of day-to-day running of the unit in which the TC is housed, and tasks such as cleaning, cooking, and washing are shared. The two models are reviewed next, including their application in various settings and evidence relating to their effectiveness.

Democratic Therapeutic Communities

The majority of those who volunteer for treatment in a DTC have suffered neglect, physical or sexual abuse, and disrupted attachment. Logan-Greene and Jones (2015) suggest that neglect is the most common form of maltreatment of children and contributes to the prediction of aggression and delinquency in adolescents (particularly males) even after controlling for other forms of maltreatment. Psychoanalytic principles were subsequently adapted for use in TCs: Terms such as *transference* (when a person attributes characteristics which belong to previous persons they related to), *counter transference* (the emotions evoked in the recipient of transference), and *defense mechanisms* (unconscious psychological mechanism to reduce anxiety raised by external stimuli) became widely adopted to help residents (and staff) understand how their interactions are affected by past relationships. In line with Bowlby's (1988) attachment theory, the therapist and the TC aim to provide a safe place from which to explore and examine past experiences, and allow the revisiting of painful and shameful experiences and fantasies. The adoption of familiar stereotypes, such as "staff don't care" and "females are more caring than males" are also carefully examined so as to prevent conflict in the community (e.g., "splitting" where one group is seen as "good" and another as "bad"). Other psychodynamic concepts are considered, such as Winnecot (1960)'s theory of "holding," whereby the therapeutic environment created and perpetuated by the therapists replaces the damaged role the primary caregiver gives to the developing child resulting in them feeling safe and cared for. The therapists help the resident process painful emotions and act in a containing role as they make sense of such painful and unresolved emotions.

Members of a multidisciplinary team thus help residents to carefully consider the meaning of their actions, emotional expression, and responses. Residents are encouraged to use examples of their own behavior to help other group members understand and acknowledge their actions and possible options available to them. This way of living has been described as a "living-learning experience" (Jones, 1968, p. 106) in which mistakes can be made and alternative ways of functioning can be developed, under what Genders and Player (1995) described as microscopic precision. The underlying logic here is that the intense and rich environment of a TC provides a corrective emotional experience that helps to repair previous damage to the developing ego.

The DTC model of change, often found in forensic settings in the United Kingdom, uses psychodynamic therapy to explore personal development and to understand underlying motivations—including those that are unconscious—which developed in formative years. The DTC model thus uses psychodynamic formulation to understand the origin of the problematic behavior and explicitly works across four domains to facilitate insight and change: self-management (coping, problem-solving); relationship skills; beliefs (including antisocial values and attitudes); and emotional management and functioning.

Haigh (2013) described the embodiment of a therapeutic environment based on his extensive experience of working with the DTC model. He described the five experiences necessary for health "primary emotional development": attachments, containment, communication, inclusion, and agency. He viewed these as progressive steps from nakedness and vulnerability, through containment and communication into inclusion (likening this to adolescence), and finally being able to achieve independence with a sense of agency. This is similar to the model proposed by Genders and Player (1995), who stated that residents go through entry, attachment, community-mindedness, individuation, and detachment as they complete treatment. Accordingly, DTCs place much emphasis on understanding the therapeutic issues that arise when joining and leaving.

In the United Kingdom a number of custodial establishments house CTCs and DTCs. Her Majesty's Prison (HMP)[3] Grendon, which opened in September 1962 as an experimental psychiatric prison, is unique in that the whole institution is a dedicated DTC. It has been documented extensively (Brookes, 2010; Genders & Player, 1995; Shine & Morris, 1999; Shuker, 2010; Shuker & Sullivan, 2010; Stevens, 2010). Elsewhere (HMPs Gartree, Dovegate, see Cullen & Mackenzie, 2011, and Warren Hill) TCs house adult male offenders in units within a prison, and HMP Send houses adult women in a unit within a women's prison. Evidence provided from interacting on a day-to-day basis allows exploration of Offense Paralleling Behavior which may emerge. This is a pattern of behavior which replicates that which led to offending in the past (Daffern, Jones, & Shine, 2010) and helps to assess the risk of repeating inappropriate behavior.

More recently, specific DTCs have been designed and implemented for those with learning difficulties (TC+), in secure hospitals and custodial settings (Taylor, 2013; Taylor, Morissey, Trout, & Bennett, 2012). The TC+ program is more structured and uses a range of treatment modalities (e.g., creative therapies, action role-play), and there is a higher staff-to-resident ratio. To be eligible, the participant has to have a diagnosis of personality disorder, not be actively psychotic or on the autistic spectrum, and be considered able to particulate in therapy for a minimum of 2 years. The first cohort described by Taylor et al. (2012) included those with mild to borderline intellectual disability.

Concept Therapeutic Communities

CTCs are said to have started in 1958 at Synanon, in Santa Monica, California, when a group of ex-addicts set up a self-supporting community (Vanderplasschen et al., 2013). They are based on the 12-step program and there are a variety of examples currently running, including Stay'n Out (see Varma & Williams, 2008), Phoenix House, and Project Return. George DeLeon has been highly influential in the development of the CTC model in correctional settings. While DTCs use psychodynamic therapy to help understand underlying motivation, CTCs concentrate more on managing drug abuse and helping addicted people to tolerate frustration or delay gratification. Much like DTCs, the aim of CTCs is to develop personal identity, attitudes supportive of abstinence, and behavior conducive to positive social values (e.g., a good work ethic, communal responsibility). CTCs place more emphasis on the role of staff as guides or mentors. They use encounter groups (originally called "the game"), to examine their behavior and reflect on that which needs to change. Positive persuasion, confrontation by peers, and the prosocial environment are the primary agents of change, with progress reinforced with positive affirmation. Loss of status or privilege is used as a consequence of rule-breaking. Residents work through phases of treatment from induction to leaving (Brookes, 2010; Day & Doyle, 2010; De Leon, 2000; Fortune, Ward, & Polaschek, 2014; Lipton, 2010; Rawlings, 1998; Woodward, 1999). The four principles on which a concept-based TC functions are: community as the agent of change, residents taking on more responsibility and leadership of the TC as they progress through treatment, the confrontation of inappropriate behavior, and individuals taking responsibility for their own change.

The *concepts* explain the nature of addiction, rather than more general difficulties in functioning. One example is the "community wheel." It describes the community as a spinning wheel with new residents on the outside and consequently vulnerable to lapsing to substance misuse. By becoming more involved in the working of the community they become more central and thus more secure.

There are three phases of treatment: introduction/orientation, working and living in the community, and finally, reentry into the wider community, during which phase residents may go out to work and return in the evening. New residents are encouraged to act "as if" they accept the basic CTC rules, until these become internalized. They are not expected to take responsibility for others until later in treatment when those who have progressed are often employed in a mentor role. CTCs offer additional services, such as family therapy, educational and psycho-educational programs, health services, and vocational support.

Finally, great emphasis is placed on aftercare since lapses are deemed common. Vanderplasschen et al. (2013) opined "addiction is increasingly regarded as a chronic lapsing disorder where recovery is possible, but often the one that requires intensive and even multiple treatment episodes and/or strong community resources" (p. 1).

Comparing DTCs and CTCs

One of the key differences between DTCs and CTCs is that a CTC tends to focus on changing problematic behavior, generally substance misuse, whereas DTCs would also seek to develop social maturation and more profound personality change (Jones, 1984).

Lipton (2010) suggests that the CTC model sees substance misuse and offending as symptoms of disorder of the whole person (not unlike personality disorder), that prosocial values need to be developed, and that abstinence is a prerequisite for recovery. This is similar to the ideals of a DTC, particularly those which are prison-based and so house those who have breached society's rules. DTCs, however, focus more on the development of insight (understanding the development of the problematic beliefs, emotions, and behavior), use professional staff, do not necessarily expect abstinence as a prerequisite of change, and encourage community rather than individual responsibility. The CTC model requires abstinence, tends to employ both ex-addicts and professional staff, and places less emphasis on the initial development of problematic behavior and more on the individual than the community. The CTC model also emphasizes the importance of aftercare once the resident moves on. In more recent years, the implementation of Psychologically Informed Planned Environments (PIPEs[4]) has helped to support those leaving intensive treatment (see Akerman, Needs, & Bainbridge, 2018; Turley, Payne, & Webster, 2013).

Efficacy of the TCs

The TC model has evolved over many years and been found to be effective with those with mental health difficulties (Kennard, 2000, 2008), personality disorder (Kennard, 2000; Shuker & Sullivan, 2010), for female offenders (McDonald, 2009; Stewart & Parker, 2007), in the community (Tucker, 2000), and for disturbed children (Diamond, 2013). Effectiveness is measured in various ways, for instance reduced reoffending, improved wellbeing, abstaining from substance misuse, and so forth. Early correctional research (Gunn, Robertson, Dell, & Way, 1978; Newton, 1971) found that those who spent time at HMP Grendon showed little improvement in likelihood of reconviction when compared to those matched by offense-type, age, and risk levels. Later (Marshall, 1997; Taylor, 2000) found that those who participated for 9 months had a higher risk of reconviction, compared to those who had applied to transfer to HMP Grendon but had not done so (the waiting list), again raising concern. However, they also reported that those who remained for over 18 months fared better than those who remained on the waiting list. Over time it has been difficult to repeat this research, largely due to the lack of a suitable control group to compare treatment group data and the complex needs of those participating. More recently, De Boer-van Schaik and Derks (2010) reported a reduction in recidivism following treatment as well as a reduction in absconding and escaping.

De Leon (2010) highlights the disparity in the TCs he evaluated: for instance the range of personality profiles (offending, substance misuse, personality disorders); the treatment setting (residential, non-residential, secure), urban or rural settings, and the presence or not of aftercare, all of which can impact on the outcome and efficacy. Vanderplasschen, Vande-velde, and Broekaert (2015) highlighted that because of the variance in those who seek treatment in a TC, there is a need to establish who benefits from a TC and at what point it is most effective.

DTCs deal with a much wider range of issues than CTCs, for instance personality disorder, offending, and mental health difficulties, as well as substance misuse. This makes it more difficult to assess their efficacy. Indeed, Lipton (2010) noted that the complexity of the needs of men in prison-based DTC (high levels of psychopathic traits, psychological distress, and history of abuse and suicide ideation) meant it would be unlikely that they would be accepted in an American prison CTC and so would not be included in such research in the United States. For instance, the Stay'n Out program tends to take first-time offenders who are younger than average inmates and not those who have committed sexual offenses or arson, or those with a history of violence (Varma & Williams, 2008). In addition to reoffending, there are a number of other ways through which success can be evaluated (for instance, reduced drug use, remaining employed, lower costs to healthcare providers, etc.), and some of these will now be considered.

De Leon (2010) completed a review of research into TCs and found "the weight of evidence for all sources is compelling in supporting the hypothesis that the TC is effective and cost effective treatment for certain sub-types of substance abusers" (p. 104). DeLeon reported a reduction in drug use and criminality and an increase in employment, all of which were modified by the time in treatment.

Pitts and Yates (2010) detailed a cost–benefit analysis of an Australasian-based TC, taking into consideration direct medical costs, financial costs for law enforcement and judicial ser-vices, and loss of earnings for the resident. It did not include costs to victims and families and the wider society (e.g., through insurance claims, fear of crime). The authors acknowledged that it was a small-scale study but found that simply allowing for savings in the costs listed while the residents were in treatment, without any potential long-term costs after they left, made the TC cost-effective. Should the resident then go on to remain drug- and crime-free and be a prosocial member of society, the balance is repaid. Likewise, Berg and Anderson (1999) found that those who completed their Norwegian TC would have repaid the cost of it through tax revenues in a relatively short time.

De Leon (2010) provided evidence from controlled studies, including Mitchell, Wilson, and Mackenzie (2007), who concluded that TCs have a high level of empirical support for treatment aimed at this population (i.e., incarcerated prisoners). Similarly, Pearson and Lipton's (1999) meta-analysis of seven prison-based TCs showed six of the seven evaluations reported reduced recidivism over comparison groups. Conversely, Smith, Gates, and Foxcroft (2006) stated they found little evidence that TCs produced better results than other residential treatment. They concluded that a prison TC may be better than prison alone or mental health-based programs. DeLeon also commented on the cost–benefit analysis of TC treatment in terms of reduction in further reoffending, gains in employment, and reduced costs to clinical provision for those suffering with mental illness.

Given the problems highlighted in evaluating such complex interventions, in addition to a reliance on reconviction as an outcome measure, many other outcomes of treatment are considered. There is evidence, for example, that both models create a prison setting characterized by less violence, misbehavior, and drug use (Miller & Brown, 2010; Wexler & Prendergast, 2010). This in itself is a positive outcome. Newton (2010), reports on the reduction in prison offending while the men were residing in a prison-based TC. This group of men were found to have seven times the average of governor reports prior to transfer to HMP Grendon and showed improved behavior which continued once they moved through their sentence. The reduction remained significant for men serving both determinate and indeterminate sentences and was not mirrored in the comparison group. The UK's National Offender Management Service (NOMS) has commissioned evaluation research into the effects of TCs, the results of which should be available in 2019.

TCs have also been found to create a more positive climate than regular units. Day, Casey, Vess, and Huisy (2012) reported that staff and residents described them more positively, and as more supportive of rehabilitation. The biannual review of the quality of UK prison life initiative, Measuring the Quality of Prison Life (MQPL, 2014), uses data collected by independent researchers in the form of questionnaires, prisoner discussion groups, and staff views. The data consistently shows that residents score the way they are treated at HMP Grendon on the indices (decency, wellbeing, order, drug culture, safety, etc.) more favorably than at other establishments.

As this is a group who can be prone to impulsive and self-harming behavior, consideration is also given to the impact of treatment in a TC on such actions. Rivlin (2010) described the reduction in self-injurious acts, in a population with a high base rate of such behavior, and while undergoing deep exploratory work which would generally evoke powerful emotions. Rivlin's research highlighted the significance of relationships with staff and other residents as important factors in the reduction of self-harm.

Clinical and Practice Issues

Impact on Staff

Those working in a TC need a great deal of resilience as they find themselves working through a range of emotional states on a daily basis, constantly working out which are their own and which are being projected and introjected from residents. There is often a fine line between evoking powerful emotions and helping residents to manage them such that they are not acted on. Specialist training is given to help staff to recognize the difference in their role from that within offending behavior programs (OBPs) in other custodial settings. OBPs are often highly manualized, staff training being specific to the manual. The work in DTCs is less structured, in so far as members of a group will bring the material they wish to discuss into any given session; training needs to equip staff with the flexibility needed for this approach.

Constant consideration is given to how each member of the community is faring in the emotional turmoil of a TC. Kennard (2000) explained the basic "dos and don'ts for beginners," including the importance of interacting with residents, and viewing the time in the TC as an opportunity to learn more about oneself. He counseled that one should be authentic and not afraid to make mistakes, and resist offering clever interpretations among other suggestions. Consideration is given to relationships between residents, between staff, and between the two groups. Given the intensity of the work for staff, time is spent considering how the work is impacting on them and ensuring that vicarious trauma (i.e., the therapist being negatively affected by the material disclosed), parallel process (relationships within the staff team, within the resident group, and between the two groups), and the risk of collective disturbance highlighted in trauma theory (the community being disturbed by the material discussed in therapy) are considered as a matter of course.

The DTC program includes time for staff to reflect together on the impact of the intensity of the work and how individual residents or particular work in therapy is impacting on them. A small body of research has explored several aspects of the impact of treatment on staff members, for instance coping with suicidal thoughts, and expressions of anger, not being able to discuss therapy work with family, the therapist holding dual roles, for instance prison officer and therapist (McManus, 2010), and developing a therapeutic alliance with those who have committed violent acts (Akerman, 2010). The flattened hierarchy in a DTC can feel threatening to a prison officer who is used to giving orders. In fact, all grades of staff describe feeling de-skilled when they join a TC. Called variously Sensitivity, Staff Support, or Staff Reflective groups, they provide a safe space for staff to explore dynamics they are experiencing. Individual and/or group supervision is provided, and in many settings external staff support agencies are provided in cases of personal crisis.

Akerman (2010) and Polaschek and Gannon (2004) describe the particular difficulties encountered while developing a therapeutic relationship with a person who has committed a sexual offense. Polaschek and Gannon highlight that the attitudes the participants in treatment hold toward females (e.g., viewing females as there to meet their sexual needs or as inferior to males) may impact on their relationship. The staff support group gives the opportunity to explore the impact of being the object of powerful emotions residents have developed and repressed over many years. The staff team recognizes the potential for splitting and helps to process emotions and give them back to the resident, much as early caregivers would do, rather than punish and reject them. A healthy staff team recognizes when it is leaning toward being too punitive or too lenient, just as caring parents would, and seeks to maintain a healthy balance. The importance of transparent decision-making is emphasized such that when requests by residents are not granted, the reasons why are explained, so as to help them to develop an understanding and tolerance of not getting all wishes met and tolerating uncertainty.

Impact on Residents

Being in a DTC requires residents to commit themselves to intensive therapy; it requires a robust character who is psychologically minded and generally one who is experiencing some degree of personal distress which drives them to seek the intervention. Akerman and Geraghty

(2016) report the content of a focus group comprised of two therapists and 10 residents. They found a similar impact on group members (i.e., that they too had to challenge long-held beliefs, and learn to tolerate and manage their own long-repressed emotions as well as those of others) as has been found with research on practitioners (Deutsch, 1984; Worthington, 2012). Participants found discussion of some subjects difficult (e.g., sexual feelings, masturbation, violent fantasies), describing therapy as the longest relationship they had ever had, and outlining the turmoil and conflict they learned to manage without leaving. Other themes included learning to bear their own shame, guilt, horror, repulsion, and remorse, which had helped them empathize with others and tolerate their material. Akerman and Geraghty concluded that group members process transference and counter-transference in much the same way that staff do. Akerman and Geraghty's (2016) study highlighted why a DTC is not suitable for all prisoners or staff, in that all those involved need to be willing to participate in the process, which is not usually the case in a mainstream prison.

Conclusion

This chapter has described the evolution of community and prison/hospital-based concept and democratic therapeutic communities, how they developed, and their similarities and differences. The two models described have much in common, in that they work holistically, with a person-centered approach, to help address the difficulties caused by drug and alcohol addiction and personality disorder. In terms of future research there is ongoing need to be creative in designing robust evaluations to test effectiveness. Research has indicated that TCs can be effective in a number of areas of functioning, such as improved custodial behavior and less self-harm, while studies into effects on reduction in reoffending continue. TCs can provide residents with a unique opportunity to explore their life in detail and practice new ways of relating to others while challenging their own attitudes and behavior in a safe setting. While this level of introspection is not suitable for all, it can be highly prized by those who go through the journey as staff or resident.

Acknowledgments

Thanks are given to residents C.A., H.G., D.M., & F.S. for collaborating on this chapter, experts by experience.

Notes

1   The needs of ex-armed service personnel in custody are still considered at HMP Grendon (Bonnett, Akerman, & M.T., 2014).
2   Although there is variance between units and how they apply the TC principles, in the United Kingdom, accreditation by the Prison Service ensures that there is little program drift, and peer review by members of TCTC (a professional body which is part of the Royal College of Psychiatrists Centre for Quality Improvement) ensures that TC standards are adhered to. The document developed for accreditation of the TC at HMP Grendon, describing the complexity and intensity of working with residents with diverse risk and needs, was aptly named "Regulating Anarchy" (Shine & Morris, 1999).

3   HMP Grendon was opened in response to a Home Office report (1932) highlighting the need for help to counter persistent offending related to "abnormal mental factors."

4   PIPEs were developed with guidance provided by the Royal College of Psychiatrists' "Enabling Environments" (Johnson & Haigh, 2011).

Key Readings

De Leon, G. (2010). Is the therapeutic community an evidence-based treatment? What the evidence says. *Therapeutic Communities*, 31, 104–128.

Miller, S., & Brown, J. (2010). HMP Dovegate's therapeutic community: An analysis of reconviction data. *Therapeutic Communities Journal*, 31, 62–75.

Shuker, R., & Sullivan, E. (Eds.) *Grendon and the emergence of forensic therapeutic communities: Developments in research and practice*. Chichester, UK: Wiley.

Stevens, A. (2013). *Offender rehabilitation and therapeutic communities: Enabling change the TC way*. Oxford, UK: Routledge.

References

Adler, G. (1982). Recent psychoanalytic contributions to the understanding and treatment of criminal behavior. *International Journal of Offender Therapy and Comparative Criminology*, 26, 281–287.

Akerman, G. (2010). Undertaking therapy at HMP Grendon with men who have committed sexual offences. In R. Shuker, & E. Sullivan (Eds.), *Grendon and the emergence of forensic therapeutic communities: Developments in research and practice* (pp. 171–182). Chichester, UK: Wiley.

Akerman, G., & Geraghty, K. A. (2016). An exploration of clients' experiences of group therapy. *Therapeutic Communities: The International Journal of Therapeutic Communities*, 37, 101–108.

Akerman, G., Needs, A., & Bainbridge, C. (Eds.) (2018). *Transforming environments and offender rehabilitation: Understanding and harnessing contextual factors in the rehabilitation of offenders*. Abingdon, UK: Taylor & Francis.

Berg, J., & Anderson, S. (1999). Drug addiction rehabilitation: A burden on society. *International Journal of Rehabilitation Research*, 15, 301–309.

Bonnett, S., Akerman, G., & M.T. (2014). One intervention for ex-service personnel in custody: The veterans group at HMP Grendon. *Forensic Update*, 115, 34–39.

Bowlby, J. (1988). *A secure base: Clinical applications of attachment theory*. London, UK: Routledge.

Brookes, M. (2010). Putting principles into practice: The therapeutic community regime at HMP Grendon and its relationship with the "Good Lives" model. In R. Shuker, & E. Sullivan (Eds.), *Grendon and the emergence of forensic therapeutic communities: Developments in research and practice* (pp. 99–113). Chichester, UK: Wiley.

Campling, P. (2001). Therapeutic communities. *Advances in Psychiatric Treatment*, 7, 365–372.

Cullen, E., & Mackenzie, J. (2011). *Dovegate: A therapeutic community in a private prison and developments in therapeutic work with personality disordered offenders*. Hook, UK: Waterside Press.

Daffern, M., Jones, L., & Shine, J. (Eds.) (2010). *Offence Paralleling Behaviour*. Chichester, UK: Wiley.

Day, A., Casey, S., Vess, J., & Huisy, G. (2012). Assessing the therapeutic climate of prisons. *Criminal Justice and Behavior*, 39, 156–168.

Day, A., & Doyle, P. (2010). Violent offender rehabilitation and the therapeutic community model of treatment: Towards integrated service provision. *Aggression and Violent Behavior*, 15, 380–386.

De Boer-van Schaik, J., & Derks, F. (2010). The Van der Hoeven Clinic: A flexible and innovative forensic psychiatric hospital based on therapeutic communities principles. In R. Shuker, & E. Sullivan (Eds.), *Grendon and the emergence of forensic therapeutic communities: Developments in research and practice* (pp. 46–60). Chichester, UK: Wiley.

De Leon, G. (2000). *The therapeutic community: Theory, model, and method.* New York, NY: Springer.

De Leon, G. (2010). Is the therapeutic community an evidence-based treatment? What the evidence says. *Therapeutic Communities*, 31, 104–128.

Deutsch, C. J. (1984). Self-reported sources of stress among psychotherapists. *Professional Psychology: Research and Practice*, 15, 833–845.

Diamond, J. (2013). Guest editorial: Current therapeutic community work with children and young people. *Therapeutic Communities: The International Journal of Therapeutic Communities*, 36, 89–102.

Fortune, C. A., Ward, T., & Polaschek, D. L. L. (2014). The Good Lives Model and therapeutic environments in forensic settings. *Therapeutic Communities: The International Journal of Therapeutic Communities*, 3, 95–104.

Genders, E., & Player, E. (1995). *Grendon: A study of a therapeutic prison.* Oxford, UK: Oxford University Press.

Gunn, J., Robertson, G., Dell, S., & Way, C. (1978). *Psychiatric aspects of imprisonment.* London, UK: Academic Press.

Haigh, R. (2013). The quintessence of a therapeutic environment. *Therapeutic Communities: The International Journal of Therapeutic Communities*, 34, 6–15.

Home Office. (1932). *Report of the Departmental Committee on Persistant Offenders*, Cmnd 4090. London, UK: Stationery Office.

Johnson, R., & Haigh, R. (2011). Social psychiatry and social policy for the 21st century: New concepts for new needs—the "Enabling Environments" initiative. *Mental Health and Social Inclusion*, 15, 17–23.

Jones, M. (1946). Rehabilitation of forces neurosis patients to civilian life. *British Medical Journal*, 1, 533–535.

Jones, M. (1952). *Social psychiatry: A study of therapeutic communities.* London, UK: Tavistock.

Jones, M. (1953). *The therapeutic community: A new treatment method in psychiatry.* New York, NY: Basis Books.

Jones, M. (1956). The concept of a therapeutic community. *American Journal of Psychiatry*, 112, 647–650.

Jones, M. (1968). *Social psychiatry in practice: The idea of the therapeutic community.* Harmondsworth, UK: Penguin.

Jones, M. (1984). *Why two therapeutic communities? Journal of Psychoactive Drugs*, 16, 23–26.

Kennard, D. (2000). *An introduction to therapeutic communities. Therapeutic communities* (Vol. 1). London, UK: Jessica Kingsley.

Kennard, D. (2008). A view of the evolution of therapeutic communities. In J. Gale, A. Realpe, & E. Pedrial (Eds.), *Therapeutic communities for psychosis: Philosophy, history and clinical practice* (pp. 4–15). Abingdon, UK: Routledge.

Lipton, D. S. (2010). A therapeutic community with a difference: Comparing American concept-based therapeutic communities and British democratic communities for prison inmates. In R. Shuker, & E. Sullivan (Eds.), *Grendon and the emergence of forensic therapeutic communities: Developments in research and practice* (pp. 61–77). Chichester, UK: Wiley.

Logan-Greene, P., & Jones, A. S. (2015). Chronic neglect and aggression/delinquency: A longitudinal examination. *Child Abuse & Neglect*, 45, 9–20.

Manning, N. P. (1976). Innovation in social policy. The case for the therapeutic community. *Journal of Social Policy*, 3, 265–279.

Marshall, P. (1997). *A reconviction study of HMP Grendon therapeutic community.* Home Office Research and Statistics: Research Findings Number 53. London, UK: Home Office Research Development and Statistics Directorate.

McDonald, D. (2009). Empowering female inmates: An exploratory study of a prison therapeutic community for substance abuse and its impact on the coping skills of substance-abusing women. *Therapeutic Communities*, 3, 71–88.

McManus, J. (2010). The experiences of officers in a therapeutic prison: An interpretative phenomenological analysis. In R. Shuker, & E. Sullivan (Eds.), *Grendon and the emergence of forensic therapeutic communities: Developments in research and practice* (pp. 217–232). Chichester, UK: Wiley.

Measuring the Quality of Prison Life. (2014). Survey carried out at HMP Grendon 13th to 16th October 2014. Communities/Audit and Corporate Assurance/Measuring the Quality of Prison Life.

Miller, S., & Brown, J. (2010). HMP Dovegate's therapeutic community: An analysis of reconviction data. *Therapeutic Communities Journal*, 31, 62–75.

Mitchell, O., Wilson, D. B., & MacKenzie, D. L. (2007). Does incarceration-based drug treatment reduce recidivism? A meta-analytic synthesis of the research. *Journal of Experimental Criminology*, 3, 353–375.

Newton, M. (1971). Reconviction after Grendon. Chief Psychologist Report series B, 1. Prison Department, Home Office. Abridged version in J. Shine (Ed.). (2000). *A compilation of Grendon research*. Tortworth, UK: Leyhill Press. Available from HMP Grendon, Grendon Underwood, Aylesbury, Bucks, HP18OTL.

Newton, M. (2010). Changes in prison reoffending among residents in a prison-based therapeutic community. In R. Shuker, & E. Sullivan (Eds.), *Grendon and the emergence of forensic therapeutic communities: Developments in research and practice* (pp. 281–293). Chichester, UK: Wiley.

Parker, M. (2007). *Dynamic security. The therapeutic community in prison*. London, UK: Jessica Kingsley.

Pearson, F. S., & Lipton, D. S. (1999). A meta-analytic review of the effectiveness of correction-based treatment for drug abuse. *Prison Journal*, 78, 384–410.

Pitts, J., & Yates, R. (2010). Cost benefits of therapeutic community programming: Results of a self-funded survey. *Therapeutic Communities*, 31, 129–144.

Polaschek, D. L. L., & Gannon, T. A. (2004). The implicit theories of rapists: What convicted offenders tell us. *Sexual Abuse: A Journal of Research and Treatment*, 16, 299–314.

Rapoport, R. (1960). *Community as doctor: New perspectives on a therapeutic community*. London, UK: Tavistock.

Rawlings, B. (1998). The therapeutic community in the prison: Problems in maintaining therapeutic integrity. *Therapeutic Communities*, 19, 281–294.

Rivlin, A. (2010). Suicide and self-injurious behaviour at HMP Grendon. In R. Shuker, & E. Sullivan (Eds.), *Grendon and the emergence of forensic therapeutic communities: Developments in research and practice* (pp. 265–281). Chichester, UK: Wiley.

Shine, J., & Morris, M. (1999). Regulating anarchy. The Grendon programme. Tortworth, UK: Leyhill Press. Available from HMP Grendon, Grendon Underwood, Aylesbury, Bucks, HP18OTL.

Shuker, R. (2010). Forensic therapeutic communities: A critique of treatment models and evidence base. *The Howard Journal*, 5, 463–477.

Shuker, R. (2018). Relationships and social contexts. In G. Akerman, A. Needs, & C. Bainbridge (Eds.), *Transforming environments and offender rehabilitation: Understanding and harnessing contextual factors in the rehabilitation of offenders* (pp. 213–226). Abingdon, UK: Taylor & Francis.

Shuker, R., & Sullivan, E. (Eds.) (2010). *Grendon and the emergence of forensic therapeutic communities: Developments in research and practice*. Chichester, UK: Wiley.

Smith, L. A., Gates, S., & Foxcroft, D. (2006). Therapeutic communities for substance-related disorder. *Cochrane Database of Systematic Reviews*, 1, CD005338.

Stevens, A. (2010). Introducing forensic democratic therapeutic communities. In R. Shuker, & E. Sullivan (Eds.), *Grendon and the emergence of forensic therapeutic communities: Developments in research and practice* (pp. 7–24). Chichester, UK: Wiley.

Stewart, C., & Parker, M. (2007). Send: The women's therapeutic community in prison. In M. Parker (Ed.), *Dynamic security. The therapeutic community in prison* (pp. 69–82). London, UK: Jessica Kingsley.

Taylor, J. (2013). The evolution of a therapeutic community for offenders with a learning difficulty and personality disorder: Part two—increasing responsivity. *Therapeutic Communities: The International Journal of Therapeutic Communities*, 34, 29–40.

Taylor, J., Morissey, C., Trout, S., & Bennett, C. (2012). The evolution of a therapeutic community for offenders with a learning difficulty and personality disorder: Part one—clinical characteristics. *Therapeutic Communities: The International Journal of Therapeutic Communities*, 33, 144–154.

Taylor, R. (2000). *Seven-year reconviction study of HMP Grendon therapeutic community*. London, UK: Home Office, Policing and Reducing Crime Research Unit Research, Development and Statistics Directorate.

Tucker, S. (2000). *A therapeutic community approach to care in the community: Dialogue and dwelling*. Therapeutic communities (Vol. 3). London, UK: Jessica Kingsley.

Turley, C., Payne, C. D., & Webster, S. (2013). Enabling features of Psychologically Informed Planned Environments. *National Prisoner Management Service & Ministry of Justice analytic series*. London, UK: Ministry of Justice National Offender Management Service.

Vanderplasschen, W., Colpaert, C., Autrique, M., Rapp, R. C., Pearce, S., Broekaert, E., & Vandevelde, S. (2013). Therapeutic communities for addictions: A review of their effectiveness from a recovery-oriented perspective. *The Scientific World Journal*, 2013 Article ID 427817, 1–23.

Vanderplasschen, W., Vandevelde, S., & Broekaert, E. (2015). Core characteristics, treatment process and retention in therapeutic communities for addictions: A summary of four studies. *Therapeutic Communities: The International Journal for Therapeutic and Supportive Organizations*, 36, 89–102.

Varma, S., & Williams, R. (2008). Stay'n Out:The evolution of a prison-based therapeutic community over 30 years. *Therapeutic Communities*, 29, 89–95.

Wexler, H. K., & Prendergast, M. L. (2010). Therapeutic communities in United States' prisons: Effectiveness and challenges. *Therapeutic communities*, 31, 157–175.

Winnecot, D. W. (1960). The theory of the parent-infant relationship. *International Journal of Psychonalysis*, 41, 585–595.

Woodward, R. (1999). The prison communities. Therapy within a custodial setting. In P. Campling, & R. Haigh (Eds.), *Therapeutic communities, past, present and future* (pp. 162–173). London, UK: Jessica Kingsley.

Worthington, R. (2012). Prison organisational climate: Exploring the impact of climate on emotional wellbeing. *The British Journal of Forensic Practice*, 14, 192–203.

38

Integrating Motivational Interviewing with Risk-Need-Responsivity-Based Practice in Community Corrections: Collaboratively Focusing on What Matters Most

Raymond Chip Tafrate, Tom Hogan, and Damon Mitchell

Central Connecticut State University, USA

Increasingly, correctional agencies around the world are being asked to do more than temporarily control or sanction the population under their authority; they are expected to positively influence the behavioral trajectories of their clients. In the United States, budget woes and social justice concerns have curbed the nation's appetite for "mass incarceration" in favor of treatment and the increased use of community supervision. But decades of experience clearly demonstrate that transforming what actually occurs during supervision takes more than good intentions (Bonta, Rugge, Scott, Bourgon, & Yessine, 2008; Bonta, Bourgon, Rugge, Gress, & Gutierrez, 2013).

Community corrections officers (CCOs) entered the 1990s with high caseloads and a growing emphasis on surveillance, drug testing, and "accountability": a supervision model some dubbed "tail 'em, nail 'em, jail 'em." It quickly became evident that punishing hundreds of thousands of seemingly defiant supervision violators only added to the prison population explosion. Soon, intermediate sanctions and "response-to-non-compliance" protocols were thrown in the mix with the hope of diverting violators away from incarceration ("tail 'em, nail 'em, but *don't* jail 'em"). By the end of the decade, the seemingly disparate goals of improving public safety and controlling prison spending merged into the singular policy goal of "reducing recidivism." As the new millennium began, new practices were finding their way into community corrections and increasing numbers of probation and parole officers were being trained in motivational interviewing (MI).

Credible behavioral research has emerged showing that reducing recidivism can be achieved, and in some cases dramatically (Andrews et al., 1990; Landenberger & Lipsey, 2005;

The Wiley International Handbook of Correctional Psychology, First Edition. Edited by Devon L. L. Polaschek, Andrew Day, and Clive R. Hollin.

Lipsey, Chapman, & Landenberger, 2001). More importantly, the specific practices that produce these beneficial effects are better understood, although efforts to introduce these methods into effective, and ultimately routine, correctional practices have led to an identity crisis of sorts for CCOs. This crisis centers around two fundamental questions. First, *what is the role of CCOs?* Is it primarily to monitor adherence to the mandates of probation or is it to facilitate behavior change in clients? Second, *what foundational skills should CCOs possess?* Are they primarily administrative or clinical? We begin with the premise that CCOs can, and should, play an active role in supporting behavior change among justice-involved clients. This chapter will therefore focus on the nature of the second question, as the trend over the past decade has been one of mounting expectations for CCOs to utilize therapeutic techniques in their supervision sessions. Psychologists increasingly play critical roles in the development, implementation, and evaluation of such training initiatives with CCOs (for an example see Rugge & Bonta, 2014). In order to be valuable consultants and trainers to criminal justice agencies, psychologists must become familiar with the therapeutic skills and models best suited for community corrections agencies and how they can be adapted to the roles and responsibilities that are a part of the daily routines of CCOs (Tafrate, Mitchell, & Simourd, 2018).

Overview of the MI Model

There is often a strong temptation for correctional practitioners to jump straight into identifying solutions and offering suggestions intended to help their clients solve problems. In community supervision, this well-intended temptation is magnified by a CCO–client power differential that can lead to CCOs telling clients what they should, and should not, do. The consequence of such an interaction style is to inadvertently elicit from clients a host of reasons why the CCO's supervision plans are untenable or unnecessary.

The main objectives in using MI in forensic practice are to promote engagement in the supervision process, and to elicit and explore the client's own motivations regarding change goals related to relevant criminal risk factors and life areas. In this way of working, CCOs and clients collaboratively discuss reasons *why* change would be important as well as *how* clients might go about it. The tone or *spirit* of MI conversations is non-judgmental, non-confrontational, respectful, inquisitive, supportive, and collaborative, with an emphasis on client autonomy and self-direction.

MI is built on a platform of four core counseling skills (known as OARS; open questions, affirmations, reflections, summarizations) that are used across four broad and dynamic processes: engaging, focusing, evoking intrinsic motivation, and change planning (Miller & Rollnick, 2013). The four processes of MI provide a practical structure for moving forward with justice-involved clients who almost always feel coerced into supervision, programming, or treatment. Productive conversations emerge by listening to clients' perspectives (engaging), exploring what clients see as most important in terms of changing risk-relevant life areas (focusing), eliciting clients' reasons for making changes (evoking), and collaboratively gathering ideas for how change might happen (planning). The amount of time spent in each process will vary across clients, and the processes are best thought of as fluid and overlapping, rather than as discrete stages. For more detailed discussions of the four processes see Miller and Rollnick (2013) and Schumacher and Madson (2015).

OARS Skills

The OARS skills are not unique to MI and are common across many models of counseling. However, within an MI context, the skills are used with a level of precision and fluency not typically found in other models. As discussed below, MI training provides a critical platform of core skills often missing in CCO's repertoires.

Open Questions

Open questions encourage clients to be active participants in supervision sessions and to do most of the talking. An emphasis on open questions tends to promote insightful responses and broaden the conversation because the client has the latitude to reveal what is most important. Most CCOs easily grasp the difference between open and closed questions; closed questions can be answered with minimal information, while open questions require more elaboration. Yet emphasizing open questions in real-world supervision sessions can be more challenging than it seems. Fluency with this skill can be fostered through observation or review of recorded work samples. Box 38.1 provides some examples of typical open questions that are framed around relevant criminal risk factors.

Affirmations

Justice-involved clients receive a constant stream of communication from others about what they are doing wrong. Effective CCOs quickly demonstrate that they grasp the critical risk areas for a particular client, but also show that they recognize existing competencies, strengths, and things that are going well. Keying into positive aspects of a client's life reduces defensiveness, enhances engagement, and provides opportunities to selectively reinforce prosocial behaviors.

Affirmations are statements of appreciation for the client's accomplishments or strengths and are formulated according to a specific structure. Guidelines are offered by Miller and

---

Box 38.1 Sample Open Questions About Criminal Risk Factors

"What happened with the incident that led to your arrest?—Walk me through it."
"How did you first get involved with the criminal justice system?"
"What are your biggest concerns about staying in the gang?"
"If you decided to make new friends, how would you go about it?"
"What are the most important reasons to stay involved with your son?"
"How are your family relationships going right now?—Tell me about each one."
"What have been your biggest successes and challenges regarding work?"
"If you were to stay in school, how might your life be different?"
"How do you spend your time during a typical day?—Give me an overview."
"How do drugs fit in with your history of arrests?"
"How have your drinking patterns changed over the past 5 years?"
"What are you likely to lose if you end up back in prison?"
"In terms of changing something, what seems most urgent for you now?" "Why?"

Rollnick (2013) and Rosengren (2018) and include: (a) organizing the statement around the word "you" and resisting the temptation to start with the word "I," (b) affirming specific behaviors and descriptions of those behaviors, (c) attending to strengths rather that deficits, (d) and being genuine by identifying legitimate strengths and avoiding compliments that might seem superficial or insincere. Examples of affirmations constructed around criminal risk factors are provided in Box 38.2.

Reflections

The key skill in MI is reflective listening. Thoughtful use of reflections helps clarify the meaning of what clients are communicating, reduces defensiveness, and invites continued exploration. Skillful reflections involve more than parroting back what the client said. A reflection is a reasonable guess—delivered in the form of a statement—that emphasizes the meaning behind what a client has communicated (Miller & Rollnick, 2013). For most CCOs, forming reflections can feel unnatural at first. Developing proficiency in reflecting will take time, practice, and feedback. One of the best ways to improve is to pay attention to clients' reactions after reflections are delivered. Reflections that are on target produce continued talking, nodding, and sometimes enthusiastic agreement (e.g., "*Yes, you definitely understand what I am saying*"). When reflections miss the mark, the reaction may be a facial expression of non-agreement, or the client may correct the statement and possibly provide additional information (e.g., "*No, I only smoke pot when I'm hanging out with Brad*"). Once CCOs know what to look for, they will have a source of feedback to improve their reflecting skills.

Reflecting becomes incredibly valuable once a level of fluency is reached, allowing CCOs to constructively respond to all sorts of challenging statements. While there are many ways to launch into reflections, we recommend starting with the following sentence stems: *It sounds like …, You're feeling …, It seems …, So, you …, So…,* and *You….* For discussions about using more complex reflections see Rosengren (2018), and for video demonstrations see Miller, Moyers, and Rollnick (2013). A segment from a brief conversation about a justice-involved client's struggle with substance use provides an example of using reflections to enhance motivation for treatment.

Box 38.2   Sample Affirmations Related to Criminal Risk Factors

"It has taken a lot of courage for you to step back and take a serious look at the last few years of your life."
"You have worked hard to avoid the people who have negatively influenced you in the past and you've been successful in making new friends."
"It is obvious that you want to be a good father."
"For someone who has faced so much adversity in finding full-time employment, you continue to get part-time work and resist the temptation to go back to selling drugs."
"You really have taken steps to move away from hanging around at the places that have created problems for you in the past."
"You have done a good job in slowing down your drinking."

CCO: *"Liz, I see on your court order that the judge ordered drug treatment and testing."*

CLIENT: *"Yeah, I think she's tired of seeing me in court all the time."* (laughing nervously)

CCO: *"She wants things to go better for you…"*

CLIENT: *"I guess … I don't know. I mean she's always treated me OK. She's a nice person … Maybe she's too nice … I don't know. I mean she does her job. I know she'll lock me up if I don't get it together. But she doesn't put me down just because I'm an addict."*

CCO: *"She sees more than your rap sheet …"*

CLIENT: (crying) *"I know I keep messing up. But I hate being like that. I know I can do better. I have to. This might be my last chance. But sometimes it's just so hard."*

CCO: *"It can be a struggle and at the same time you keep telling yourself, 'Keep on trying, I can do this …'"*

CLIENT: *"I've been clean before. I had almost two year's clean time … And I've been doing good for almost a month now. But for me it's not just drugs. I don't want to get into everything but that's why I wanted to get back into the Women's Program. It's the only thing that works for me. I'm lucky they took me back and I'm going to do whatever it takes to make it work."*

Summarizations

Reflecting conveys a moment-by-moment understanding of what the client means. In contrast, summarizing reaches back further and captures larger amounts of information, helping clients organize their experiences. The most common place to put a summary is at the end of an interaction, although summaries may be strategically inserted at various points in a conversation. Common phrases for launching into summaries include: *"Let's pull together what we have been talking about …,"* *"Let me see if I understand what you have told me so far …,"* or *"We're running down on time so let's pull together what is most important …"* Developing effective summaries largely hinges on brevity and selectivity: highlighting three or four important issues is usually sufficient (Rosengren, 2018). We routinely encourage CCOs to get in the habit of ending their supervision sessions with a summary. In the example below, the summary highlights several criminal risk areas: criminal companions, employment, and family relationships.

CCO: *"John, let's pull together what is most important before we wrap up for today. You've told me a couple of things about your parole that really stood out. You mentioned how it's easier for you to avoid your old friends when you know exactly what to say when you run into them, like we just practiced. And keeping the job is key for you, it keeps you busy and you look forward to going. And calling your aunt every afternoon really helps you to stay positive and connected to your family."*

Evoking Change Talk Around Relevant Criminal Risk Areas

Evoking, in community corrections, is the process of supporting and encouraging justice-involved clients in voicing their own motivations for changing the risk-relevant areas of their lives. Evoking rests on the premise that what clients hear themselves say during interactions is more important than what CCOs say to them (Malcom Berg-Smith, 2010). Therefore, the process of evoking change language lies at the strategic heart of the MI approach.

Two technical terms are relevant for understanding verbalizations related to change: *sustain talk* and *change talk*. Sustain talk is client speech that favors not changing or that favors maintaining the status quo (Miller & Rollnick, 2013). With justice-involved clients, sustain talk often takes the form of justifications or minimizations related to risky, self-defeating, or criminal behaviors. Below are some examples of sustain talk.

"*You need to understand, where I live people are like, 'Do it to him or he'll do it to you.' You have to fight to survive.*"

"*Whenever we took a car, it's not like we kept it forever. They get their ride back and they get insurance on top of that.*"

"*All that happened was she came at me and I defended myself. What am I supposed to do, stand there and just take it 'cause I'm the guy? I just pushed her, so I don't see why this is such a big deal.*"

"*These crackheads are going to buy it from someone. So I sold a couple of rocks. I never hurt anyone.*"

Change talk, on the other hand, is any client speech that favors movement toward, and commitment to, change (Miller & Rollnick, 2013). Change talk sounds more like: "*I used to be so slick. Like the easy money would last forever. Like I was smarter than everyone. But in and out three times, doing 8 years … My family won't even talk to me anymore. I can't live like this any longer. I have to get my act together.*" It is important to keep in mind that change talk can also be subtle and does not necessarily involve a 100% commitment to suddenly change (e.g., "*Anyone who drinks is gonna have problems; and I know a lot of people that are more messed up than I am.*"). In this example, the first part of the sentence is change talk, while the second is sustain talk.

In general, as people begin to think about changing behaviors it is quite normal for them to have voices on both sides of the change equation (for and against change). Losing weight might produce a number of health and lifestyle benefits but it might also mean forgoing some favorite junk foods. Quitting smoking can reduce the risk of cancer and heart disease, but in the short-term, it can also cause irritability. Although it might seem as though stopping criminal conduct *should* be different from changing other behaviors, the process seems to be similar. For example, an illicit drug user can long for the benefits of sobriety while also dreading the discomfort of going through withdrawal. Again, in MI parlance, the spoken rationale for continuing the old behavior is called "sustain talk," while statements in favor of changing the behavior are known as "change talk." A cynical CCO might dismiss these kinds of statements as "excuses" and examples of clients "*telling us what they think we want to hear,*" but there is more to it than manipulation.

In terms of key research findings, the ratio of change talk to sustain talk during practitioner–client interactions is an important marker for subsequent change and is associated with treatment outcomes. In other words, what clients say *is* related to what they actually do. Specifically, a predominance of change talk predicts actual behavior change, whereas a higher proportion of sustain talk (or equal levels of sustain talk and change talk) are predictive of not changing (Moyers, Martin, Houck, Christopher, & Tonigan, 2009). More importantly, levels of client change talk and sustain talk can be influenced by the way in which the practitioner responds (Glynn & Moyers, 2010). With training and practice, CCOs can learn how to draw out a client's own reasons for making changes in relevant criminal risk areas. One goal, and benefit, of using MI in community corrections is to increase client change talk during supervision sessions.

Change Talk Subtypes

Change talk is organized across two levels and seven specific verbalization subtypes. The first level is known as *preparatory change talk* and consists of four change talk subtypes that can be remembered using the acronym DARN (*desire, ability, reasons,* and *need*). Preparatory change talk signals energy in favor of change. Examples include:

Desire: "*I want to live a sober life, not worrying all the time that I might drop a dirty urine.*"

Ability: "*If I run into an old friend, I can just point to the ankle bracelet and tell them I already have one foot in jail—I think they'll leave me alone.*"

Reasons: "*If I made better decisions I'll be like a real father—not just seeing my kids on visiting day.*"

Need: "*I need to get my act together—I don't think my girlfriend will be there for me if I mess up again.*"

The second level of change talk is known as *mobilizing change talk*. It consists of three change talk subtypes that can be remembered by the acronym CAT (*commitment, activation,* and *taking steps*). Mobilizing change talk indicates the person may be farther along in terms of making a specific change. *Commitment* is when clients verbalize a concrete and specific next step about an action they will take ("*I'll have my resume done by the end of the week*"). *Activation* is signaled when clients discuss things they are considering doing or getting ready to do ("*I'm thinking about joining the NA softball team with my sponsor tomorrow night*"). *Taking steps* refers to clients reporting specific things they have done that move them in the direction of change ("*I got a new cell phone number. Anyone who knows the old number, I don't want to talk to anymore*").

Responding to Naturally Occurring Change Talk

One of the benefits of becoming more familiar with change talk is that CCOs will notice much more motivation emerging in client conversations than they had previously detected. Since many clients are ambivalent about the consequences of their criminal conduct, change talk will often bubble up naturally. How CCOs respond, as change talk emerges, will influence whether more change talk occurs. The OARS skills mentioned earlier can be used to evoke more change talk.

For example, imagine that a client tells his CCO: "*I know my record is bad but I really want to do things on the up-and-up from now on. Hanging around at the bar all day is not taking me anywhere.*" An MI-skilled CCO might respond in the following ways:

"*Sounds like this is a turning point for you.*" (Reflection)

"*Why it is so important for you to make this change now?*" (Open question)

"*You have really thought about your life and it's great that you recognize you want to find better ways to spend your time.*" (Affirmation)

As the interaction nears the end, the CCO can incorporate any change talk that emerged into a closing summary:

> *Let's pull together what we've talked about. You've been looking back at the last few years and you're thinking all you have to show for it is a broken hand, a series of superficial sex partners, and a bill from your lawyer. When you think about it now, going to the bar every night was like you were stuck being an 18-year-old: for the last 10 years. A lot of your buddies have started families and you don't want to be the last barfly. And your new girlfriend doesn't drink and you'd rather spend time with her and her folks.*

Actively Eliciting Change Talk

Justice-involve clients *might* make spontaneous change talk statements, but they might not. Also, any naturally occurring change talk *might* be about key risk-relevant issues, but might not. CCOs *might* notice and effectively respond to spontaneous change talk, but again, they might not. Because CCOs are often attending to multiple work tasks during supervision contacts, it is not unusual for change talk to go unnoticed or unexplored.

Because the stakes are so high (e.g., loss of freedom, harm to others), we believe that reducing a client's risk of recidivism is too important to be left entirely to the client. Deliberately introducing key topics allows CCOs to strategically focus on relevant criminal risk areas and engage clients in the change process. This is especially critical when working with high-risk clients in the early stages of supervision. One way of establishing a focus is to invite change talk around risk-relevant life areas using open questions constructed to elicit such verbalizations. These are sometimes known as "change talk questions" because the answers invite DARN-CAT verbalizations (Malcom Berg-Smith, 2010). Table 38.1 provides sample change talk

Table 38.1 Questions Likely to Evoke Change Talk

Change talk subtype	Change talk questions
Desire	"*Why would you like to work on making better decisions?* "*What do you want to get out of this period of supervision?*"
Ability	"*What gives you confidence that you can avoid your old friends?*" "*What strengths do you have that will help you to re-invent your future?*"
Reasons	"*What are the two most important reasons for you to stay out of jail?*" "*How would _ _ _ _* benefit you?*" (* keeping this job, attending this program, spending time with positive friends, reducing your drug use, etc.)
Need	"*How important is it for you to change course now?*" "*What is at stake if you do not get a handle on your impulsive decision-making?*"
Commitment	"*What are your plans for going to the employment program?*" "*How will you handle the negative influence from your brother?*"
Activation	"*What might you do to treat your girlfriend better?*" "*Think about a situation that might pop up over the next day or two that will be risky for you. What would be the best way for you to deal with it?*"
Taking Steps	"*What have you taken from this whole experience that is already helping you make better decisions?*" "*What are some things you are doing now that are helping you to maintain your sobriety?*"

questions related to criminal risk factors and life areas. CCOs can try these out or develop their own questions that fit the characteristics of a specific case. While many CCOs can become quite adept at asking strategic open questions "on the fly," it is often helpful to have a few ready in advance.

There will be times when attending to change talk will infuse supervision sessions with a negative and heavy tone because the content will be about regrets, losses, and reasons to avoid bad outcomes associated with risk-relevant life areas. CCOs can be caught off guard by these kinds of dramatic revelations and should be prepared for them. At other times, attending to change talk will result in conversations that are more uplifting and optimistic: hopes and aspirations for a better life, more inner peace, and increased happiness. Both types of conversations are acceptable. A common progression is to move from a focus on the negative consequences linked to risky patterns to more positive anticipated outcomes of making changes.

Responding to, and Avoiding, Sustain Talk

During interactions with their clients, CCOs will also encounter naturally occurring sustain talk. Sustain talk is normal. Simply because it occurs with justice-involved clients does not mean it is indicative of pathological traits (e.g., antisociality). Smoking cessation counselors hear it. So do hospital dieticians. Because of court-mandated conditions and programming, with their implicit loss of personal choice, and the pervasive threat of punishment inherent in community supervision, levels of sustain talk may be particularly high during CCO–client interactions. CCOs may automatically believe that a lack of buy-in from the client is indicative of a resistant or defiant temperament. However, CCOs who understand the nature of sustain talk, and how to respond to it, will be more effective in working through it.

With successful engagement, less sustain talk may occur from the start. When sustain talk does emerge, responding with reprimands or threats of punishment will likely cause the client to become more guarded or argumentative. Even when clients acquiesce to official authority, they are often rendered passive and not invested in making changes in the risk-relevant areas of their lives. Motivation to change cannot be applied *to* a client like spray paint on an assembly line. Grasping the client's perspective is critical, which means acknowledging sustain talk when it occurs.

Imagine a CCO hears the client say: "*I don't see why I should have to go to a program. I haven't used anything for over 2 weeks.*" A CCO might respond:

> "*It seems really unfair to you—like your efforts to stay clean aren't being taken seriously.*" (Reflection)

> "*The way you see it, it's almost like we're using the program as a kind of punishment.*" (Reflection)

Although somewhat counter-intuitive, when a CCO avoids the impulse to instantly confront or challenge the sustain talk, change talk will often naturally emerge. CCOs may be rightly concerned that reflections like these might come across as agreeing with antisocial justifications. Adding the phrase, "*The way you see it …*" more clearly emphasizes that the reflection conveys the CCO's understanding of the client's perspective, not the CCO's endorsement of it.

During a single supervision session, change talk and sustain talk will naturally rise and fall. Even when clients have voiced strong arguments in favor of change, sustain talk will inevitably surface. MI-skilled CCOs will carefully listen for, and differentially reinforce, change talk (over sustain talk) throughout the supervision process.

Because CCOs are attempting to increase change talk, caution is warranted about asking questions likely to evoke sustain talk. Unfortunately, such questions are common in community corrections settings. Here are some examples of questions to generally avoid.

"Why are you still hanging out with your old friends?"

"Why haven't you taken steps to control your drug use?"

"Don't you want to get along better with your parents?"

"Why haven't you found a job yet?"

"What are the pros and cons of smoking pot?" (Known as a decisional balance)

Such questions are ill advised because they will inadvertently increase levels of sustain talk during supervision sessions. There will certainly be times when such questions are useful in understanding a client's perspective and exploring potential roadblocks to change. However, as a general guideline, if the response to a specific question is likely to produce sustain talk, the CCO should have a good rationale for asking it (Miller & Rollnick, 2013). The decisional balance technique, exploring the pros and cons of a specific risky behavior, is very common. This maneuver provides both sides (change talk and sustain talk) but does not always guarantee a higher ratio of change talk (Miller & Rose, 2015).

There are many things to pay attention to in supervision sessions with justice-involved clients. In cognitive behavioral therapy (CBT), practitioners are taught to pay attention to specific types of client verbalizations suggestive of cognitive distortions, irrational beliefs, and dysfunctional schemas because these cognitive constructs are believed to be central to various forms of psychopathology. MI, in contrast, emphasizes a constellation of language constructs related to motivation and subsequent change, and for practitioners accustomed to CBT interventions, learning MI is like adding a new set of headphones to listen to client verbalizations. Not surprisingly, it often takes time to learn to identify, respond to, and elicit this form of client language. We have found that with effort and practice, CCOs can achieve high levels of competency with this skill.

Why Use MI in Community Corrections?

MI provides CCOs with foundational skills

MI provides a platform of clinical skills for CCOs who often enter the field with a narrow range of competencies for interacting with justice-involved clients. MI can be immediately and practically useful in community corrections because it moves CCOs away from confrontation, advice-giving, and referrals to interventions for which the client is not yet ready. In the absence of MI skills, the default option for many CCOs becomes an authoritarian or adversarial stance (Tafrate & Luther, 2014). Even among CCOs who want healthy change for their clients, confrontational communication styles persist because alternative styles of relating to clients have not been adequately developed. We see the acquisition of MI skills as a critical foundation that aids CCOs in establishing rapport, conducting assessments, identifying collaborative goals, and guiding conversations in productive directions (Tafrate et al., 2018).

MI enhances client motivation

In traditional mental health treatment, clients often seek help voluntarily, are able to identify and acknowledge their symptoms, and want those symptoms reduced or removed with the hope of improved functioning and wellbeing. The symptoms *are* the focus of intervention. In contrast, justice-involved clients are often mandated to treatment for their offending behavior, can be relatively unaware of their risky patterns, and are quite naturally uninterested in changing some of them. For many justice-involved clients who enter supervision, there is a tendency to minimize the role of their antisocial lifestyles (e.g., routines, relationships, and destructive habits) in contributing to their criminal justice problems.

Unfortunately, a recent meta-analysis reached the stark conclusion that there is no consistent evidence that mandated offender treatment is effective, whereas voluntary treatment in both institutional and community forensic settings is associated with positive effects (Parhar, Wormith, Derkzen, & Beauregard, 2008). One implication of this finding is that in order for mandated treatment to be effective, clients must develop an interest in change akin to that of their voluntary counterparts. In essence, we should strive to create an environment where clients, who tell us they are "*forced to be here*," come to say they "*want to make changes anyway*" (Tafrate, Mitchell, & Novaco, 2014, p. 474).

It is for this reason that MI conversations can be extremely valuable to CCOs because they can build awareness of the connections between the client's lifestyle choices and subsequent losses (e.g., damaged relationships, ruined career paths, financial problems, and incarcerations) and build motivation around changing relevant criminal risk areas. Effective practice involves taking the time to establish positive working relationships, eliciting from clients their motivations for making changes, exploring the impact of criminal patterns on clients' life trajectories, identifying potential strengths, and delving into what clients value most. In short, MI can move justice-involved clients toward greater engagement and collaboration (Anstiss, Polaschek, & Wilson, 2011; Austin, Williams, & Kilgour, 2011; McMurran, 2009).

MI Can be Integrated with Risk-Based Models of Rehabilitation

MI is meant to be a brief approach to help resolve ambivalence about behavior or lifestyle changes. It is not meant to be a stand-alone intervention or the only modality used by CCOs. In more traditional clinical settings, Miller and Rollnick (2009) note that "it would make little sense, however, to have a practice that offers only MI" (p. 136). When working with forensic clients to alter entrenched criminal thinking and risky behavior patterns, MI conversations will not be enough.

As discussed in Chapters 26–28, a literature has emerged around the identification of risk factors specifically linked with continued criminal behavior (we have been referring to them in this chapter as criminal risk factors). These risk factors have been dubbed the *Central Eight*: criminal history, antisocial personality, criminogenic thinking, antisocial companions, family/marital dysfunction, poor attitude toward and/or achievement in work/school, aimless use of leisure time, and substance abuse (Andrews & Bonta, 2010; Bonta & Andrews, 2017). One of the pivotal findings over the past decade is that interventions (Smith, Gendreau, & Swartz, 2009) and community supervision (Bonta et al., 2011; see Chapter 44) focused on criminal risk factors produce larger reductions in reoffending than efforts focused on other factors.

At first glance, the Risk-Need-Responsivity model (RNR; Andrews, Bonta, & Hoge, 1990) and its companion listing of the *Central Eight* risk domains for criminal behavior may seem somewhat incompatible with the inherently optimistic view of human nature embodied in MI. For several reasons, we believe the process of targeting criminal risk factors in supervision actually provides an ideal opportunity to seamlessly blend MI and RNR principles.

First, since the majority of the risk factors are changeable (the exception is criminal history) the model is optimistic about justice-involved clients' potential for change. Second, the risk model has a preventative goal: reduce the client's risk profile before further justice involvement and losses occur. Third, risk reduction conceptualizations involve tailoring interventions to the unique life circumstances of a particular client. Fourth, there is often a complex interrelationship between risk factors. For example, consider a probationer who is unemployed and spends the better part of his free time with friends who drink heavily and use drugs. His friends reinforce his unproductive beliefs about work, his drug use diminishes the likelihood of passing pre-employment drug screens, and his substance use and criminal companions distance him from prosocial family members. Thus, the various risk factors influence each other in an interrelated destructive system. Conversely, a *positive* change in one of these areas will facilitate *positive* changes in the others. For example, full-time employment would result in less time with the antisocial friends, less time to engage in substance use, and exposure to new peers who express prosocial thoughts and who model more productive lifestyles. Therefore, in many cases, CCOs will not have to focus their efforts on changing all the relevant criminal risk factors related to a particular case. Instead, a strategic focus on one or two can create a positive ripple effect (Mitchell, Tafrate, & Freeman, 2015; Mitchell, Wormith, & Tafrate, 2016; Tafrate et al., 2018).

The RNR model points to the right targets for CCOs to focus on in supervision, while MI provides the interaction style to make supervision effective! It is our view that in community corrections, MI conversations should be focused on the risk-relevant factors most associated with future criminality. The rest of this chapter highlights the integration of MI and RNR using two case examples to demonstrate how MI conversations can be focused on criminal risk factors. You may have also noticed the focus on criminal risk factors in the earlier examples demonstrating the use of OARS skills. It is the active and persistent focus on criminogenic factors that makes the application of MI in community corrections different than its use in other treatment settings (Owens & Tafrate, 2016; Tafrate & Luther, 2014; Tafrate, Mitchell, & Simourd, 2018).

Integrating MI in the Initial Client Contact: A Case Example

We strongly believe that what happens during the first interaction, indeed what happens in the first moments of the first interaction, is critical and sets the stage for what follows. During trainings with CCOs, we sometimes play video or audio clips of actual first contacts done by prior trainees so that CCOs can get a sense of how it sounds when MI skills are integrated into the initial CCO-client meeting. A common response from trainees is that we must have cherry-picked a talkative or unusually cooperative client for the sample recording. While this is not the case (we have collected countless superb work samples), it seems that many CCOs are not used to seeing clients who are open, cooperative, and eager to change the risk-relevant areas of their lives. We are not suggesting that it takes only a few minutes to radically alter justice-involved clients' long-standing patterns. However, we do believe a few well-spent minutes can get the process headed in the best possible direction. Below is a sample of how we incorporate MI in the initial CCO-client session. Box 38.3 describes some background information.

Box 38.3 Behind the Scenes: Prior to the First Session

Jen has been a probation officer for 3 years. This morning her workday began badly when Greg, her supervisor, called her into his office. "*Jen, you need to get over to court to testify. There is a violation hearing on someone you did the court intake on last year. He didn't sign the conditions form. C'mon, Jen, you should have known better … You know when you first meet with someone the most important thing is to go over the conditions.*" When Jen finally gets back from court, she has a new client (Tony) waiting for her. Jen feels stressed.

Tony is 24 years old. He was arrested 4 months ago after a physical altercation with his girlfriend. At the time of his arrest, the police officer told him, "*Look, our department policy is on any domestic someone gets locked up. Tonight it's your turn.*" The day he was sentenced, his lawyer said to him, "*We got a great offer on this. No jail!—2 years' probation. You plead guilty today and it will be all over.*" Yesterday, Tony's older brother, a parolee, gave him some advice about being on probation, "*When you're talking to your probation officer always remember it's just like talking to a cop. Don't ever admit to doing anything wrong. They'll act all buddy-buddy then wham! All they want to do is lock you up.*" While Tony waits for Jen to return from court, another client in the waiting room tells him, "*Man, you're going to get hosed. That Jen gets all the domestic cases. She makes all the dudes report in every week! And now they make you go to these stupid classes for six months! And they even expect you to pay for it! Yeah, they just want to mess with you 24-7. I'm glad she's not my P.O.*"

Strategy for the Initial Approach

Let's assume for the moment that Tony is assessed as moderate to high risk of reoffending. Because of what Tony experienced behind the scenes, prior to meeting his CCO, he is likely to begin supervision with a range of undesirable thoughts and beliefs about the supervision process. Since he is likely to view the supervision process through a negative lens, what should Jen do when she first meets with Tony?

Jen is one of the new breed of probation officers. As she brings Tony to her office, she tries to put the morning's chaos behind her. She has been trained in MI, RNR, and CBT and knows how to blend these models when she meets with her clients. She has conducted supervision in the traditional manner long enough to know this new way is more efficient and works better. She has also received enough ongoing coaching with these new approaches to have achieved a level of proficiency. When she meets with Tony, every word out of her mouth, every pause will be intentional. She will sound confident, non-judgmental, and purposeful.

Jen will start the session with a brief focusing statement; letting Tony know what's going to happen will help reduce his anxiety and it subtly allows Jen to take the lead. CBT is directive, and setting the agenda is critical. And Jen has learned that helping Tony to change is too important to him, to his girlfriend, and to the community to be left to chance. In the first moments, Jen will also describe her complex role. She has legal authority and responsibilities, something Tony already knows. Being up front about this helps to develop trust and establish professional boundaries. But Jen will also let Tony know that she wants him to do well and complete probation successfully. She's noticed this is something her clients *don't* expect to hear. It is disarming and helps to reduce their defensiveness. This is also one reason why Jen reviews court mandates later in the session, when her clients are more at ease. In her opening statement, Jen also describes supervision as a process of personal change related to those risk areas most relevant to Tony's life (RNR). This subtly lets Tony know that he is expected to play an active role; passive "compliance" will not be enough. This establishes a forward-looking and hopeful narrative. "Framing" supervision as beneficial prompts clients to devote more effort, and it "primes" Jen's clients to follow her lead. Her CBT and RNR skills are applied in a way that is both subtly directive and collaborative. It is done *with* her clients, not *to* them. Finally, she'll ask Tony what he wants to get out of being on probation. This will reinforce the positive frame and will prompt Tony to become an active partner in his probation early in the session. It is here that Jen's MI training has prepared her to make the most of whatever Tony's responses might be. In the first few moments of the first interaction, Jen will begin to integrate the three models (RNR, CBT, & MI). Here's how it went:

CCO:	*"Hi Tony, I'm Jen _ _ _ _, I'm your probation officer. Thank you for waiting this morning. I was called to court unexpectedly ..."*
CLIENT:	*"That's all right. It happens."*
CCO:	*"Thank you. I'll do my best to avoid keeping you waiting in the future. Today I want to let you know a little about what to expect when we meet. Part of my job is to uphold the expectations of the court and another part is to provide support and information about community resources and to help you gain skills and knowledge to complete your probation successfully and keep you from returning to the court in the future. We'll work together to identify some of your strengths and some of the things you've struggled with that could put you most at risk for having future problems. But I'd like to hear from you first ... How can being on probation be helpful to you?"*
CLIENT:	*(silence)*
CCO:	*(silence)*
CLIENT:	*"I don't know."*
CCO:	*(silence)*
CLIENT:	*"Well, I guess it's probably good for me to have someone to kind of keep an eye on me. I mean ... that can keep me on my toes ... So I don't do stupid stuff."*
CCO:	*"Like a guardrail that stops you from going off the road?"*
CLIENT:	*"Yeah, I mean sometimes I'm my own worst enemy, you know?"*
CCO:	*"You sometimes make decisions and then you're kicking yourself, thinking 'Hey, why'd I do that?'"*
CLIENT:	*"Exactly! And I have some good things going for me. I don't want to mess things up. I mean, you probably hear this all the time but I mean it. I don't want to end up in jail. I don't want to lose my girlfriend. She's the best thing that's ever happened to me. ... So maybe that's something I can do better at, not messing things up."*
CCO:	*"Making better decisions."*
CLIENT:	*"Yeah, I could probably do better with that. I mean, no one's perfect."*
CCO:	*"So that's something we'll spend some time on when we meet; we'll work on your thinking and decision-making. We'll also talk about your relationship with your girlfriend. How else can being on probation help you?"*

[The conversation continues for about 15 minutes with Tony identifying the risk-relevant areas he thinks are most important to work on.]

Integrating MI to Establish a Supervision Focus on Criminal Risk Factors: A Case Example

For CCOs and clients alike, the monitoring/information gathering focus of traditional supervision contacts can seem repetitive and superficial, even when the client is agreeable. Such interactions do little to get into the fabric of clients' lives and alter the risk areas that are most relevant. Here's an example of a typical "check-in" style contact:

CCO: *"How's it going?"*
CLIENT: *"Not bad. Pretty good, actually."*
CCO: *"Are you at the same address?"*
CLIENT: *"Yeah, no changes."*
CCO: *"You working?"*
CLIENT: *"Not yet. I've been looking, it's tough these days."*
CCO: *"You still going to the program?"*
CLIENT: *"Yeah, I think I have three classes left, it's going OK. It's not so bad."*
CCO: *"Make sure they send me a completion letter so you get credit for going."*
CLIENT: *"I will."*

Gus sees himself as an "old-school" probation officer. In the past, he has conducted many sessions like the one shown above. But he's just attended MI training and he actually thinks it has value. It feels different and he notices that clients are responding better. He's surprised at how talkative some of his clients can be. With a non-judgmental manner, a strategic open question, and some skillful silence, he can often unleash a flood of client verbalizations. Here he first meets with Ray, a 19-year-old with a weapons conviction.

CCO: *"Ray, tell me a little about how you ended up here."*
CLIENT: *"Well ... I heard this gang was going to mess with my brother."*
CCO: (silence)
CLIENT: *"He's only 15 and I look out for him since my father was killed... And I don't really want to make trouble 'cause my girl's about to have a baby, but, I'm hanging with my crew, and I'll be honest, we all were a little high and being stupid ... and someone says we should go say something to those dudes. So we go up there and all of a sudden there's cops everywhere and they know me already ... And this one cop says I dropped a gun in the bushes ... And the court put me in this Day Reporting place but I guess I missed some sessions ... so they gave me probation instead."*

In short order, Ray has put a number of significant issues on the table. He's also made several potential change talk statements. *Any* reflective response at this point will probably preserve the collaborative tone of the interaction and prompt the client to say more. So what should Gus say next? Consider how each of these reflective statements will influence the direction of the conversation with Ray:

CCO: *"It seems like you have a lot of things going on right now ..."*
CCO: *"It sounds like you care about your brother ..."*
CCO: *"The police have their eye on you ..."*
CCO: *"When you've been referred to programs it hasn't gone well ..."*
CCO: *"When you get high you're more likely to do things you regret later ..."*

> CCO: *"With your baby on the way, you're more concerned about getting into trouble now ..."*
>
> CCO: *"It seemed like the best way to deal with the other gang was to grab a gun and confront them with your own crew ..."*

CCOs sometimes remark that MI allows them to "get lots of good information" from clients. But getting clients to reveal a lot is a byproduct of MI, not its strategic purpose. CCOs have also said that MI "helps to build rapport" and "allows clients to be heard." True, the absence of conflict that officers expect to encounter does make it seem like something fundamentally different is occurring. And, in a field that may be overly reliant on coercion and punishment, this is progress. But MI was not developed to make alcohol counselors likeable. It emerged as a more effective means of helping problem drinkers reduce their consumption of alcohol. Implicit in all of the MI effectiveness studies (substance abuse, health care, reoffending, etc.) is that both the practitioners and the researchers had a clearly defined target behavior to treat and measure. In the same way, moving from "niceness" to effectiveness in community corrections means CCOs must have a clear, well-informed sense of what behaviors (or criminal risk factors) they specifically want the client to attend to. As described earlier, in MI jargon, this is known as a focus.

We believe CCOs face a bigger challenge than needle exchange workers, hospital social workers, or alcohol counselors. Not because their clients are tougher (they're often the same people). It's because the behavioral focus of these other helping professionals is often defined by the sign over the program door. But "criminal behavior" can take many forms. This means that CCOs themselves must have a clear sense of the most important life areas to focus on with a particular client. Without such a focus, supervision sessions can seem circular or aimless. Let's assume Gus has learned MI but that he has not yet been trained in RNR concepts. The interaction might sound something like this:

> CCO: *"It seems like you have a lot of things going on right now."*
>
> CLIENT: *"That's not even the half of it. My girl's freaking out because her uncle went in the hospital. He has diabetes. And my little brother started skipping school."*
>
> CCO: *"So you're stressed out, your family is struggling, and now you're on probation. What do you think will help you to avoid getting into trouble in the future?"*
>
> CLIENT: *"To be honest with you? These cops need to ease up ... Like everybody I know is either in jail or on probation. And there's nothing you can do. It's like when your time comes you're 'gonna get locked up too. It's all a set-up."*

Although, in this interaction, Ray has "opened up," he is attributing his fate to others, namely the police. Not only is this strengthening a risky thinking pattern, it is also undermining his self-efficacy. How can anyone change a problem that is beyond their control? It is hard to be powerless and motivated at the same time.

But what if Gus also had a good understanding of the criminal risk factors most associated with future criminality (e.g., the effects of antisocial companions, risky thinking patterns)? Such an understanding would influence Gus's decision about how he would respond to the client. What if Gus had responded this way?

> CCO: *"It seemed like the best way to deal with the other gang was to grab a gun and confront them with your own crew."*
>
> CLIENT: *"We were just going there to let them know to leave my brother alone. I just needed to be careful in case they got crazy, you know?"*

CCO:	*"You were telling yourself the gun protects you and at the same time it's having the gun that led to your arrest."*
CLIENT:	*"Like I said, we were high, it makes me stupid. It's not like I'm a dope fiend or anything but I know it's going to have to stop now 'cause I'm on probation."*
CCO:	*"It sounds like you're trying to go in a different direction now."*
CLIENT:	*"I have to. I'm going to be a father. I owe 4 years on this case."*
CCO:	*"Help me understand that better."*
CLIENT:	*"'Cause if I catch a new case or I get violated I'll get locked up. I want to be there for my girl. And I want to be like a real father, not just a name on the birth certificate."*
CCO:	(silence)
CLIENT:	*"I mean the other dudes, they don't get it, you know? They tell me the baby is for the girl to take care of. They say I should be like a man."*
CCO:	*"They don't get it."*
CLIENT:	*"No!"*
CCO:	*"Ray, you have a really good sense of where things are at in your life. You want to be there for your family, you want to stay out of trouble. Let's take a step back for a moment and think about how to make it happen. You've mentioned a couple of things that can trip you up: you talked about the pot use and how it affects your judgment, you talked about who you spend time with, and you've mentioned that you sometimes make risky decisions without thinking them through. Which one seems like the top priority for you to think about for the next couple of days?"*
CLIENT:	*"I don't know. I mean… I guess probably not being around the other dudes … I probably need to lay low for a while."*
CCO:	*"So let's focus on that right now. Let's talk about how you can avoid them."*

[The conversation continues for about 15 minutes. Gus guides Ray in identifying steps he can take to distance himself from antisocial companions.]

During this interaction, Gus allowed Ray to speak, but he did so skillfully and strategically. He remained non-judgmental, but he was not neutral. Gus has a legitimate perspective. His official role requires it. And Ray needs his CCO to be more than just a good listener—he needs direction from someone who understands how certain risk factors jeopardize his goals and freedom. Gus intentionally guided the exchange to highlight key themes that will be touched on again and again during the course of supervision. Gus also helped Ray to feel at ease discussing his views about being a good father. The session ended with a focus on a significant risk factor (e.g., antisocial companions). But Gus also helped Ray to develop a short-term action plan. Gus left with a clear sense about a next step—not just a good feeling.

The exchange also shows how clients may not spontaneously self-identify all of the relevant criminal risk factors that influence their own propensity for reoffending. The lack of disclosure may not be solely the result of defensiveness. It may reflect clients' genuine belief that their arrest(s) are caused by historical events or current factors beyond their control—the police, the "system," a difficult life history, a felony record, their significant other, etc. While these issues can have real consequence, they may not be as important as other risk factors. Some clients like Ray *will* also see their substance use as a problem. But was Ray's offense really *caused* by his use of marijuana? What about his antisocial companions? Or, was it his distorted thinking about needing a weapon?

A CCO trained in MI, with little appreciation for the range of criminal risk factors, would most likely have heard Ray's change talk about his drug use and made cannabis the primary focus of supervision, ignoring the influence of companions and criminogenic thinking. Gus heard Ray's change talk about marijuana use too. But luckily for Ray, Ray's family, and the community, Gus heard more than that.

Final Thoughts

As the above examples illustrate, highly skilled CCOs can move clients toward change in the most criminally relevant life areas with surprising efficiency. We have found that community corrections agencies do better when they view MI as one of several skill sets that CCOs will use with their clients, and thoughtfully consider how best to integrate MI with other risk reduction strategies. Also, since MI is a complex communication style that requires training, repetition, and ongoing coaching to become proficient (Schumacher & Madson, 2015), a long-term view of developing CCOs' skills is essential. Developing agency capacity to run booster sessions, conduct coding, and provide constructive feedback on recorded work samples is necessary for CCOs to transfer MI skills to real-world practice.

In some ways, this chapter ends where it began. The cultural legacy of the "Get Tough" era in criminal justice continues to influence community corrections. Much has been said about the changing community corrections "paradigm," but what actually occurs during CCO–client interactions continues to revolve around referrals to programs, drug testing, and monitoring compliance with various mandates. Even when sessions are non-confrontational they tend to be used for gathering and disseminating information. MI training introduces a way of thinking about justice-involved clients that can be hard to square with CCOs' own beliefs, previous experiences, and their required work tasks. CCOs can assume their clients are cunning and potentially dangerous adversaries who need to be outwitted and controlled, which invariably leads to an authoritarian/aggressive/gotcha approach. Or they can view their clients as people who have within them both the desire and the ability to change, and who deserve the chance to do so. Unless CCOs see themselves as agents of change, they will see little value in continuing to use MI (or RNR and CBT). What has become clear is that being an effective CCO is a much more complicated job than previously assumed. CCOs of the future will need to have a sophisticated knowledge base and be proficient in an assortment of high-level skills. MI is certainly one of those skills sets! However, by itself, MI will not be enough. It is the integration of MI with other empirically supported models for reducing criminal behavior that holds the greatest promise for achieving successful outcomes in community corrections.

Key Readings

Miller, W. R., Moyers, T. B., & Rollnick, S. (2013). *Motivational interviewing* [Professional training DVDs]. Carson City, NV: The Change Companies.

Miller, W. R., & Rollnick, S. (2013). *Motivational interviewing: Helping people change* (3rd ed.). New York, NY: Guilford Press.

Tafrate, R. C., & Luther, J. D. (2014). Integrating motivational interviewing with forensic CBT: Promoting treatment engagement and behavior change with justice-involved clients. In R. Tafrate, & D. Mitchell (Eds.), *Forensic CBT: A handbook for clinical practice* (pp. 411–435). Chichester, UK: Wiley.

Tafrate, R. C., Mitchell, D., & Simourd, D. J. (2018). *CBT with justice-involved clients: Interventions for antisocial and self-destructive behaviors.* New York, NY: Guilford Press.

References

Andrews, D. A., & Bonta, J. (2010). Rehabilitating criminal justice policy and practice. *Psychology, Public Policy, and Law*, 16, 39–55.

Andrews, D. A., Bonta, J., & Hoge, R. D. (1990). Classification for effective rehabilitation: Rediscovering psychology. *Criminal Justice and Behavior*, 17, 19–52.

Andrews, D. A., Zinger, I., Hoge, R. D., Bonta, J., Gendreau, P., & Cullen, F. T. (1990). Does correctional treatment work? A clinically relevant and psychologically informed meta-analysis. *Criminology*, 28, 369–404.

Anstiss, B., Polaschek, D. L. L., & Wilson, M. (2011). A brief motivational interviewing intervention with prisoners: When you lead a horse to water, can it drink for itself? *Psychology, Crime, & Law*, 17, 689–710.

Austin, K., Williams, M. W., & Kilgour, G. (2011). The effectiveness of motivational interviewing with offenders: An outcome evaluation. *New Zealand Journal of Psychology*, 40, 55–67.

Bonta, J., & Andrews, D. A. (2017). *The psychology of criminal conduct* (6th ed.). London, UK: Routledge.

Bonta, J., Bourgon, G., Rugge, T., Gress, C., & Gutierrez, L. (2013). Taking the leap: From demonstration project to real world implementation. *Justice Research and Policy*, 15, 1–19.

Bonta, J., Bourgon, G., Rugge, T., Scott, T.-L., Yessine, A., Gutierrez, L., & Li, J. (2011). An experimental demonstration of training probation officers in evidence-based community supervision. *Criminal Justice and Behavior*, 38, 1127–1148.

Bonta, J., Rugge, T., Scott, T.-L., Bourgon, G., & Yessine, A. (2008). Exploring the black box of community supervision. *Journal of Offender Rehabilitation*, 47, 248–270.

Glynn, L. H., & Moyers, T. B. (2010). Chasing change talk: The clinician's role in evoking client language about change. *Journal of Substance Abuse Treatment*, 39, 65–70.

Landenberger, N. A., & Lipsey, M. W. (2005). The positive effects of cognitive behavioral programs for offenders: A meta-analysis of factors associated with effective treatment. *Journal of Experimental Criminology*, 1, 451–476.

Lipsey, M. W., Chapman, G. L., & Landenberger, N. A. (2001). Cognitive-behavioral programs for offenders. *Annals of the American Academy of Political and Social Science*, 578, 144–147.

Malcom Berg-Smith, S. (2010). *Guiding the learning of motivational interviewing: A resource for trainers* [Professional training DVDs]. Available from http://www.berg-smithtraining.com/dvd.html

McMurran, M. (2009). Motivational interviewing with offenders: A systematic review. *Legal and Criminological Psychology*, 14, 83–100.

Miller, W. R., Moyers, T. B., & Rollnick, S. (2013). *Motivational interviewing* [Professional training DVDs]. Carson City, NV: The Change Companies.

Miller, W. R., & Rollnick, S. (2009). Ten things that motivational interviewing is not. *Behavioural and Cognitive Psychotherapy*, 37, 129–140.

Miller, W. R., & Rollnick, S. (2013). *Motivational interviewing: Helping people change* (3rd ed.). New York, NY: Guilford Press.

Miller, W. R., & Rose, G. S. (2015). Motivational interviewing and decisional balance: Contrasting responses to client ambivalence. *Behavioral and Cognitive Psychotherapy*, 43, 129–141.

Mitchell, D., Tafrate, R., & Freeman, A. (2015). Antisocial personality disorder. In A. Beck, D. Davis, & A. Freeman (Eds.), *Cognitive therapy of personality disorders* (3rd ed.) (pp. 346–365). New York, NY: Guilford Press.

Mitchell, D., Wormith, J. S., & Tafrate, R. C. (2016). Implications of Risk-Need-Responsivity principles for forensic CBT. *The Behavior Therapist*, 39, 147–153.

Moyers, T. B., Martin, T., Houck, J. M., Christopher, P. J., & Tonigan, J. S. (2009). From in-session behaviors to drinking outcomes: A causal chain for motivational interviewing. *Journal of Consulting and Clinical Psychology*, 77, 1113–1124.

Owens, M. D., & Tafrate, R. C. (2016). Finding the niche for motivational interviewing in forensic practice. *The Behavior Therapist*, 39, 178–180.

Parhar, K. K., Wormith, S., Derkzen, D. M., & Beauregard, A. M. (2008). Offender coercion in treatment: A meta-analysis of effectiveness. *Criminal Justice and Behavior*, 35, 1109–1135.

Rosengren, D. B. (2018). *Building motivational interviewing skills: A practitioner workbook*. New York, NY: Guilford Press.

Rugge, T., & Bonta, J. (2014). Training community corrections officers on cognitive-behavioral intervention strategies. In R. C. Tafrate, & D. Mitchell (Eds.), *Forensic CBT: A handbook for clinical practice* (pp. 122–136). Chichester, UK: Wiley.

Schumacher, J. A., & Madson, M. B. (2015). *Fundamentals of motivational interviewing: Tips and strategies for addressing common clinical challenges*. New York, NY: Oxford University Press.

Smith, P., Gendreau, P., & Swartz, K. (2009). Validating the principles of effective intervention: A systematic review of the contributions of meta-analysis in the field of corrections. *Victims and Offenders*, 4, 148–169.

Tafrate, R. C., & Luther, J. D. (2014). Integrating motivational interviewing with forensic CBT: Promoting treatment engagement and behavior change with justice-involved clients. In R. Tafrate, & D. Mitchell (Eds.), *Forensic CBT: A handbook for clinical practice* (pp. 411–435). Chichester, UK: Wiley.

Tafrate, R., Mitchell, D., & Novaco, R. (2014). Forensic CBT: Five recommendations for clinical practice and five topics in need of more attention. In R. Tafrate, & D. Mitchell (Eds.), *Forensic CBT: A handbook for clinical practice* (pp. 473–486). Chichester, UK: Wiley.

Tafrate, R. C., Mitchell, D., & Simourd, D. J. (2018). *CBT with justice-involved clients: Interventions for antisocial and self-destructive behaviors*. New York, NY: Guilford Press.

39

What is Cognitive Behavioral Therapy (CBT) With Offenders?

Clive R. Hollin
University of Leicester, UK

Punish or Cure?

It is widely accepted that a criminal act, once detected and proven, will lead to punishment in order that the offender is seen to be penalized for what they have done. One school of thought maintains that the association between crime and punishment is purely on the basis of what Honderich (1976) called "orthodox retributivism" (p. 156). The punishment is forthcoming, as Honderich stated, simply because the offender has broken the law. No other justifications are needed, or outcomes claimed for the administration of punishment. In contrast, utilitarian approaches argue that the punishment should have one or more additional aims alongside retribution, such as specifically deterring the offender from crime, or deterring other members of society generally, or protecting the public, or rehabilitating the offender back into society (Walker, 1991).

The notion of rehabilitating rather than simply punishing offenders dates back to the turn of the nineteenth century and the liberal reforms of the penal system. A variety of rehabilitative techniques—educating offenders, employment skills training, and various therapeutic techniques including cognitive behavioral therapy—have been used since that time in an attempt to bring about positive changes in the offender's life. It is not, however, always clear exactly what outcome these changes aim to achieve; is it to make the offender a better educated person, or more employable in the job market, or better adjusted psychologically, or less likely to commit more crimes?

The use of psychological therapies with offenders has been a topic of sometimes acrimonious debate (Andrews & Wormith, 1989). The arguments have swung between the position that therapies are ineffective and nothing works (Martinson, 1974) and compilations of evidence to the contrary (Gendreau & Ross, 1979). In part, the debate is confounded by the outcome variable under discussion: there is no doubt that psychological techniques can be effective in changing behavior, including that of offenders; the question is whether those changes bring about a reduction in offending. This point is exemplified by the use of social

The Wiley International Handbook of Correctional Psychology, First Edition. Edited by Devon L. L. Polaschek, Andrew Day, and Clive R. Hollin.
© 2019 John Wiley & Sons Ltd. Published 2019 by John Wiley & Sons Ltd.

skills training with offenders: it is clear that social skills training can improve the social competence of offenders (Henderson & Hollin, 1983), although it is moot as to whether the final product of such endeavor is socially skilled offenders rather than non-recidivists (Hollin & Henderson, 1984).

The point regarding outcome raises the critical distinction between *criminogenic* and *non-criminogenic* needs. The former are those aspects of an offender's functioning, such as their drug use or uncontrollable temper, that can be demonstrably linked to their criminal behavior; the latter are features of an offender's behavior, such as needing dental care or having panic attacks, that may be problematic for the individual but which are not related to their offending. This is not to say that non-criminogenic needs are unimportant, rather that understanding the distinction between criminogenic and non-criminogenic needs points at what outcome may be expected from an intervention directed at either type of need.

Cognitive Behavioral Therapy: Theory and Techniques

Cognitive behavioral therapy (CBT) is concerned with the interactions between an individual and their (mainly social) environment (see Chapter 1). In a particular situation, how does the person think, feel and act? How do they perceive the effect of their actions on other people? As discussed below, these various facets of social functioning can be used to help understand antisocial behavior.

"Thinking"

The "thinking" aspect of social functioning may be divided into *social perception* and *social cognition*.

Social perception

The ability to recognize, understand, and interpret interpersonal cues is central to competent social functioning (Argyle, 1983). Several studies have found that delinquents, including aggressive offenders, may have difficulties in selecting appropriate social cues for attention during social interactions and in understanding their meaning (Akhtar & Bradley, 1991; Lipton, McDonel, & McFall, 1987). The misperception of social cues may lead to misattribution of intent so that others are mistakenly seen as hostile or threatening (Crick & Dodge, 1996).

Social cognition

As with social perception, social cognition has a demonstrable association with antisocial and criminal behavior (McMurran & McGuire, 2008). Thus, depending upon their perception and understanding of the situation, the individual will select the response they judge to be appropriate to events as they see them. The process of response selection requires the cognitive skills to create feasible courses of action and to consider alternatives and their probable consequences with regard to achieving the desired outcome. Several studies have suggested that offenders, male and female, may experience difficulties with certain social situations such that they may use a limited range of alternatives to solve interpersonal problems and have a greater reliance upon verbal and physical aggression (Palmer & Hollin, 1996; Ward & McFall, 1986).

Moral values

As we are socialized, so we develop standards and values, or *morals*, for our own behavior and that of others. Kohlberg (1964) argued that moral reasoning develops in a sequential manner through three levels. At the lower levels, moral reasoning is concrete in orientation, focused on pleasing oneself and avoiding punishment. At higher levels, reasoning becomes more abstract, incorporating abstract concepts such as justice and rights.

Kohlberg (1964) explained antisocial behavior in terms of a developmental delay in moral reasoning: when the opportunity for offending arises, the absence of internal controls over behavior leads to hedonistic, self-centered moral decisions and so to offending. The evidence is supportive of Kolhberg's position that delinquents typically show lower levels of moral reasoning than non-delinquents (Nelson, Smith, & Dodd, 1990). However, these lower levels of reasoning may be specific to areas related to offending, may not be the same for males and females (Palmer & Hollin, 1997), and are also related to other aspects of psychological functioning (Palmer & Hollin, 2001).

Gibbs (1993) made the point that moral reasoning is associated with other aspects of social cognition. Gibbs suggested that a connection between moral development and social information processing is evident in the form of *cognitive distortions*. A cognitive distortion is an attitude or belief the individual holds which they use in defense of their antisocial behavior. A *primary cognitive distortion* based upon self-centered moral reasoning is, for example, "If I want it, I take it." *Distorted secondary cognitions* may result from the primary distortion and serve to rationalize or mislabel the behavior. Thus, the primary cognitive distortion "I want it, I take it" may be rationalized by using a secondary cognitive distortion such as blaming others for the offense: if a car owner leaves their vehicle unlocked then they are asking to have it stolen and therefore deserve the loss when it happens; the car theft is then explained away as "just a laugh" or "not really serious." The same processes are evident in aggressive people when the actions of other people are seen in an inaccurate manner, typically as their having hostile intent, so that "they were asking for it" (primary distortion) with the supportive secondary distortions that the victim "could have had it worse" and "they were not too badly hurt so no real damage was done" (Gibbs, 1996). When expressed verbally these cognitive distortions may be reinforced by the offender's peer group.

Emotions

Anger is the emotion most often associated with crime, particularly acts of violence (Zamble & Quinsey, 1997). However, anger in itself is not criminogenic; it is the *dysfunctional* expression of anger which may have negative consequences. Novaco's approach to the relationship between dysfunctional anger and violent behavior, in sympathy with cognitive behavioral theory, views anger as a subjective emotional state, incorporating physiological and cognitive activity, and related to the physical and social aspects of the environmental circumstances (Novaco, 1975, 1994).

Novaco suggested that anger, in the form of idiosyncratic patterns of cognitive and physiological arousal, is triggered by an environmental event. The trigger for anger may be the words and actions of another person as perceived, accurately or not, by the individual concerned. Physiological arousal is evident in increased autonomic nervous system activity, a rise in body temperature, perspiration, muscular tension, and increased cardiovascular activity. The cognitive processes are an interplay between information-processing biases, such as *attentional cueing*, a tendency to see other people as hostile and provoking, and *anchoring of effects* whereby once the individual makes an initial value judgment this position is maintained regardless of any evidence to the contrary.

Once aroused, the individual may label their internal state as "angry"; this labelling is a function of the individual's schemas based on their previous experience. As their experience is influenced by their information-processing biases so the likelihood of anger increases given similar triggers. The escalation from anger to violence is associated with disinhibition of internal control from increasing levels of physiological arousal and the use of drugs or alcohol.

Social performance

With respect to social performance, the third aspect of social functioning, offenders may display less competent social skills than non-offenders (Spence, 1981), although obviously this is not the case for all offenders (Veneziano & Veneziano, 1988). Nor, as noted above, is it invariably a cause of offending.

CBT With Offenders: Cognitive Behavioral Methods of Change

Operant theory, behavior modification, and behavior therapy (Martin & Pear, 1999) formed the platform from which CBT grew, incorporating concepts from social learning theory (Bandura, 1977), so behavioral approaches became *cognitive* behavioral with the advent of cognitive behavior modification and cognitive behavioral therapy (Meichenbaum, 1977). The later development of social skills training added to the therapeutic repertoire, incorporating cognitive and behavioral techniques (Hollin & Trower, 1986a, 1986b).

There are various therapeutic methods grouped under the rubric of cognitive behavioral; these range from residential and community programs for groups of offenders to work with individual offenders (Hollin, 1990; Kirigin, Braukmann, Atwater, & Worl, 1982; Latessa, 2006). In CBT the focus is on changing patterns of thinking and their associated beliefs, attitudes, and values. With offenders the emphasis will be upon the aspects of cognitive functioning associated with criminal behavior. The aim may be that the offender learns to recognize the thinking patterns associated with their offending and develops new ways of thinking, such as using problem-solving skills, to change thinking and behavior. The goal may be to develop empathy for others, including those who suffer because of criminal acts, or to learn to manage emotional arousal. Several techniques are associated with cognitive behavioral practice: including modeling, skills training, self-instructional training, thought stopping, emotional control training, and problem-solving training.

Thus, CBT aims to engender change in internal states, sometimes both psychological and physiological, so that covert change will precipitate overt, behavioral change. These changes in behavior will elicit new patterns of social reinforcement thereby maintaining the new behaviors.

As CBT typically uses a range of techniques, sometimes addressed at several different targets for change, *multimodal programs* became increasingly widely used. Thus, for example, Aggression Replacement Training (ART; Goldstein & Glick, 1987; Goldstein, Nensén, Daleflod, & Kalt, 2004) is comprised of three modules aimed at bring about change in cognition (moral values), emotional control (anger management), and behavior (skills streaming). The methods used within ART are traditional cognitive behavioral methods, based on anger control, problem-solving skills training, and social skills training. The development of multimodal programs proved to be the forerunner of offending behavior programs, which emerged from a searching examination of the outcome literature.

Does CBT Work With Offenders?

A wide range of therapeutic techniques associated with psychological theory and research has been used with offenders (see Chapter 1). While eschewing the notion of a silver bullet that will cure offending, is it possible that some therapeutic techniques are better suited for offender populations than others? While much debated, the efficacy of psychologically based interventions with offenders is an empirical question. The emergence in the 1980s of the now widely used statistical technique of meta-analysis provided a means by which to determine the reliable and consistent findings from a large number of primary studies.

Meta-Analysis

The advantages of meta-analysis, particularly as compared to a narrative review, lie in both its openness to replication and its procedural transparency. In the offender treatment literature coding systems for meta-analysis have been developed to take into account variations in type of offender, type of offense, treatment setting, type of outcome, and duration of follow-up period (e.g., Lipsey, 1992). Of course, the findings of any meta-analysis are dependent upon the quality of the primary research studies. Since the first reported meta-analysis (Garrett, 1985), there have been over 50 meta-analytic studies of offender treatment, incorporating hundreds of primary research studies (for reviews, see McGuire, 2002, 2008). A large number of meta-analyses have focused on primary studies conducted with male young offenders, but other meta-analyses have included women offenders, sexual offenders, and violent offenders (see Hollin & Palmer, 2006a).

The findings of these analyses are in broad agreement that crime reduction through treatment is best achieved through use of a *constructional* approach with interventions, directed at criminogenic needs, which are multimodal in orientation (i.e., take cognizance of thoughts, emotions, and behavior). *Eliminative* interventions solely based on deterrence or punishment have a negative effect on reducing crime. The meta-analyses strongly indicate that effective interventions are cognitive behavioral in nature, may take the form of structured programs with specific aims and objectives, and focus on offenders with a high risk of reoffending. The meta-analyses were also informative with regard to organization of treatment delivery: the high-effect interventions had good levels of treatment integrity (see Hollin, 1995), were delivered by trained staff with high levels of organizational support, and were monitored and evaluated.

These empirical findings became known collectively as "*What Works*" (McGuire, 1995a) and were gathered by Andrews (Andrews, 1995; Andrews, Bonta, & Hoge, 1990) to form the three key principles of effective practice with offenders: (a) the *risk principle*, such that interventions are most effective with medium- to high-risk offenders; (b) the *needs principle*, which maintains that treatment should be directed at an offender's criminogenic needs; (c) the *responsivity principle*, which holds that treatment should be matched with the offenders' characteristics such as gender, ethnicity, and level of intelligence. In order to put these principles into practice, practitioners and researchers combined to develop Offending Behavior Programs (OBP).

Offending Behavior Programs

The importance of a structured approach for effective interventions with offenders was in sympathy with the arguments for the use of manualized treatment programs in mainstream clinical services generally (Wilson, 1996). The first fully manualized OBP to be widely used with offenders was a Canadian program called *Reasoning and Rehabilitation* (R&R; Ross, Fabiano, & Ewles, 1988; Ross, Fabiano, & Ross, 1989).

Reasoning and Rehabilitation

The aim of R&R is to enable the offender to learn new, prosocial ways of thinking to increase the likelihood of reductions in criminal behavior. R&R incorporates cognitive behavioral techniques, including role-playing, modeling, and reinforcement, to assist the offender's development of reflective, rather than reactive, styles of thinking. This change in thinking style leads to greater self-control, improved social problem-solving skills, and changes in the attitudes and beliefs that justify criminal behavior. R&R is intended to be used by appropriately trained and supported staff, not just professional therapists. The delivery of R&R includes the use of video monitoring of sessions to facilitate feedback to treatment staff and, importantly, to monitor treatment integrity (Andrews & Dowden, 2005). R&R has been used in many countries within both institutional and community settings. The evaluations show that R&R achieves positive results with significantly lower rates of reconviction for male adults who complete the program (Tong & Farrington, 2006).

Straight Thinking on Probation

Mid-Glamorgan Probation Service introduced an adaption of R&R called Straight Thinking on Probation (STOP; Knott, 1995; McGuire, 1995b; Raynor & Vanstone, 1996). An evaluation of STOP found that the actual and the predicted reconviction rates at 12-months follow-up were the same for the treatment and comparison groups (Raynor & Vanstone, 1997). However, for those offenders who did not drop out of the program there was a significantly lower reconviction rate than predicted. The positive results after 1 year were not maintained at a 2-year follow-up.

Enhanced Thinking Skills

Enhanced Thinking Skills (ETS) is a cognitive skills program, similar to R&R, developed for use in the English and Welsh Prison and Probation Services (Clark, 2000). As with R&R, evaluations have shown ETS to be effective in institutional settings with adult male offenders, particularly when offenders complete the program (Blud, Travers, Nugent, & Thornton, 2003; Falshaw, Friendship, Travers, & Nugent, 2004). There are also positive outcomes when ETS is completed in the community (Hollin et al., 2008; McGuire et al., 2008).

Think First

Think First is a general cognitive skills program developed in England for use in prisons and community probation services (McGuire, 2005). Think First is similar to R&R and ETS but with a greater emphasis on criminal behavior. Think First introduced pre-group sessions to prepare and engage offenders and post-group sessions to develop relapse prevention strategies. The evaluations of Think First have shown significant decreases in reconviction among male offenders who complete the program (McGuire et al., 2008; Roberts, 2004).

Alongside the more general cognitive skills OBPs, specialist programs for different types of offender have emerged. The specialist programs are designed for violent offenders (Polaschek, 2006), sexually violent offenders (Marshall & Hollin, 2015), and offenders with drug and alcohol problems (McMurran, 2006). While OBPs have been assimilated into mainstream practice in offender rehabilitation, there have been several professional and practical developments.

Developing Programs

Women offenders

While OBPs are generally designed for male offenders, it cannot be assumed that women offenders have the same criminogenic needs as men or that women will necessarily respond to the same style of program (Dowden & Andrews, 1999; Hollin & Palmer, 2006b). This point necessarily means that attention should be turned to the specific criminogenic needs of female offenders. Where criminogenic needs are not gender specific it cannot be assumed that their etiology is the same for men and women, nor that specific individual needs carry the same weight for men and women. In addition, from a delivery perspective, it cannot be assumed that program responsivity is the same for men and women offenders: the same material may need to be tailored differently to engage male and female offenders.

The issues pertinent to gender equally apply to other specific offender characteristics, such as intellectual level, literacy, and race (Bourgon & Bonta, 2014).

Manuals

Most OBPs are manual-based so that the many practical aspects of the intervention—such as the session content and sequencing, and methods of delivery—are written in detail and collated in the form of a manual. The use of manuals in correctional practice facilitates the use of non-specialist staff, such as prison officers, to be trained to deliver interventions to large numbers of offenders. Manuals are not peculiar to OBPs and have been widely used in clinical practice generally (Duncan, Nicol, & Ager, 2004; Najavits, Weiss, Shaw, & Dierberger, 2000; Wilson, 1996, 1997).

McCulloch and McMurran (2007) conducted a survey of experts in the field of offender treatment for their views on the components of a good treatment manual. The experts placed value on theoretical clarity, explicit aims and objectives, detailed information regarding delivery, and the use of plain language and a clear format. The debate on the use of manuals continues to engage practitioners, particularly regarding the trade-off between the large quantity of offenders that can be engaged by manualized OBPs versus the quality of interventions delivered by staff who are not trained therapists (Hollin, 2009; Mann, 2009; Marshall, 2009).

Does CBT in the Form of OBPs Work?

As OBPs aim to reduce offending, so this outcome is the natural outcome for evaluations. In discussing program evaluation, Gondolf (2004) noted that: "[Evaluation] is a difficult and complex task that complicates the interpretation of the evaluation results" (p. 607). The difficulties begin with the choice of research design (see Chapter 25). It is generally taken that an experimental design in the form of a randomized controlled trial (RCT) is the strongest design for treatment evaluation. However, Farrington, Gottfredson, Sherman, and Welsh (2002) made the point that, "While randomized experiments in principle have the highest interval validity, in practice they are uncommon in criminology and also often have implementation problems" (p. 17). In addition, there are questions over the assumed "gold standard" of randomized experiments in the context of the evaluation of OBPs (Hollin, 2008, 2010). Thus, quasi-experimental designs are often the design of choice for OBP evaluations, despite their mistaken dismissal in some quarters as unsatisfactory (e.g., Debidin & Lovbakke, 2005).

A quasi-experimental evaluation considers the outcome for the treatment group with a comparison group not considered for treatment. There are two main strategies by which to assure the comparability of treatment and comparison groups. The first is to match control and experimental groups on key variables, such as age and type of offense, related to outcome (i.e., reoffending). Friendship, Blud, Erikson, Travers, and Thornton (2003) used this type of matching in an evaluation of a cognitive skills program for prisoners. However, Friendship el al. said that they had the not uncommon practical problem of finding an exact match for every offender in the treatment group. The second approach lies in using statistical control, typically using multivariate statistics, of key variables. Palmer et al. (2007) evaluated OBPs within the Probation Service in England and Wales using a comparison group of offenders who had served a period on probation but had not participated in an OBP. The treatment and comparison groups were broadly similar on a range of variables and a reasonable match to the national profile of offenders serving probation orders. The comparison of the reconviction rates for the two groups involved statistical control of age, risk of reconviction, and offense type and history. An issue with non-randomized studies lies in the possibility that an uncontrolled variable introduces a systematic variation between groups which may influence the findings.

An alternative strategy to case matching, particularly with a high rate of dropout, is to use propensity scores (D'Agostino, 1998). In this type of analysis, a propensity to drop out of treatment using established predictors is calculated for each offender. The sample is then subdivided into quintiles, from high to low propensity, and an outcome analysis is calculated for each quintile. This strategy has been used in the evaluation of OBPs (Jones, D'Agostino, Gondolf, & Heckert, 2004; McGuire et al., 2008).

There will be dropouts from most interventions, and those offenders who fail to complete an OBP have been the focus of a debate. Two studies of attrition found that reconviction rates are higher for dropouts compared to offenders who complete treatment (McMurran & Theodosi, 2007; Olver, Stockdale, & Wormith, 2011). Knowledge of which offenders are most likely to drop out allows for the development of strategies to counter non-completion. In addition, Olver et al. note the possibility of an iatrogenic effect associated with dropout as seen in an increase in antiauthority attitudes, emotional distress, and neglect of problematic personal issues.

Comparisons of program completers and dropouts have shown that completers are more likely to have had full-time employment and some educational attainment, while dropouts are younger, more likely to have a history of violence, to have dropped out of school, and to have a higher risk of reoffending (Van Voorhis, Spruance, Ritchey, Listwan, & Seabrook, 2004; Wormith & Olver, 2002). Can dropout be explained just in terms of the static variables of age, history of violence, and so on? Casey, Day, Howells, and Ward (2007) introduce a dynamic element in suggesting that some may be ready to change and to try to stop offending. For such offenders, program completion and later non-offending is a product of both their readiness to change *and* the effects of the program. This view is in accord with the finding reported by Clarke, Simmonds, and Wydall (2004) that non-offending program completers said that their readiness to change was critical in their completing and benefiting from a program.

As well as the characteristics of the offenders, there are organizational reasons why once having started a program offenders do not go on to complete. Van Voorhis et al. (2004) recorded a completion rate of 60% for the R&R program across 23 programs conducted in 16 parole districts. However, the completion rates varied from a low of 42% completion to a high of 80%, indicating considerable variation in organizational performance in managing offenders through to completion. In line with this view, Palmer et al. (2008, 2009) reported high rates of misallocation to programs such that offenders assessed as either too low- or too high-risk according the program admission criteria were nonetheless participating in programs (a state of affairs which poses considerable problems for evaluating outcome).

Wormith and Olver (2002) noted that some offenders opt out of treatment while others are removed by program administrators. McMurran and McCulloch (2007) interviewed non-completers and recorded several reasons for their dropout: (a) administrative procedures such as early release from prison; (b) being expelled from the group for disciplinary reasons; (c) offender ill-health; (d) dislike of group treatment; (e) not engaging with the program because it was seen as irrelevant; (f) some dropouts said that the program was too slow and patronizing and others that it was over-demanding. There are other organizational factors such as not managing varying levels of offender literacy such that those with literacy problems are more likely to drop out of programs (Briggs, Gray, & Stephens, 2003). Also, long delays between acceptance for and starting a program may have a negative effect on an offender eventually choosing to start a program (Clarke et al., 2004).

In all, evaluations of OBPs have found associations between rates of program completion, program dropout, and effectiveness in terms of reduced offending. These associations are the product of complex interactions between the individual offender, program characteristics, and organizational functioning.

Conclusion

The use of cognitive behavioral methods in correctional practice has moved through a number of phases following the rise of a rehabilitative philosophy in the criminal justice system. The first applications of a cognitive behavioral approach were on a relatively small scale with individual offenders or small groups of delinquents in residential settings. The accrual over time of evidence evaluating the effect of smaller-scale cognitive behavioral interventions culminated in the meta-analyses. The findings from the meta-analyses of these studies gave rise to the notion of "what works" and the formulation of the principles of effective practice aimed at reducing offending.

In some criminal justice systems there has been a substantial investment, in both prison and the community, in initiatives based on "what works" evidence, which crystallized in the form of offending behavior programs. In the United Kingdom, the development and application of OBPs, based primarily on cognitive behavioral principles, has been evident on a previously unimagined scale. The evaluation of OBPs has shown that they can be of benefit in bringing about reductions in crime. For the future, those concerned with correctional practice may learn from the implementation and running of OBPs; researchers can profit by refining methodologies and developing theory.

Key Readings

Hollin, C. R. (1999). Treatment programmes for offenders: Meta-analysis, "what works," and beyond. *International Journal of Psychiatry and Law, 22*, 361–372.

Hollin, C. R., & Palmer, E. J. (Eds.) (2016). *Offending behaviour programmes: Development, application, and controversies.* Chichester, UK: Wiley.

Lipsey, M. W. (1992). Juvenile delinquency treatment: A meta-analytic inquiry into the variability of effects. In T. Cook, D. Cooper, H. Corday, H. Hartman, L. Hedges, R. Light, et al. (Eds.), *Meta-analysis for explanation: A casebook* (pp. 83–127). New York, NY: Russell Sage Foundation.

McGuire, J. (Ed.) (1995). *What works: Reducing reoffending.* Chichester, UK: Wiley.

References

Akhtar, N., & Bradley, E. J. (1991). Social information processing deficits of aggressive children: Present findings and implication for social skills training. *Clinical Psychology Review*, 11, 621–644.

Andrews, D. A. (1995). The psychology of criminal conduct and effective treatment. In J. McGuire (Ed.), *What works: Reducing reoffending—guidelines for research and practice* (pp. 35–62). Chichester, UK: Wiley.

Andrews, D. A., Bonta, J., & Hoge, R. D. (1990). Classification for effective rehabilitation: Rediscovering psychology. *Criminal Justice and Behavior*, 17, 19–52.

Andrews, D. A., & Dowden, C. (2005). Managing correctional treatment for reduced recidivism: A meta-analytic review of programme integrity. *Legal and Criminological Psychology*, 10, 173–187.

Andrews, D. A., & Wormith, J. S. (1989). Personality and crime: Knowledge destruction and construction in criminology. *Justice Quarterly*, 6, 289–309.

Argyle, M. (1983). *The psychology of interpersonal behaviour* (4th ed.). Harmondsworth, UK: Penguin Books.

Bandura, A. (1977). *Social learning theory.* Englewood Cliffs, NJ: Prentice Hall.

Blud, L., Travers, R., Nugent, F., & Thornton, D. M. (2003). Accreditation of offending behaviour programmes in HM Prison Service: "What works" in practice. *Legal and Criminological Psychology*, 8, 69–81.

Bourgon, G., & Bonta, J. (2014). Reconsidering the responsivity principle: A way to move forward. *Federal Probation*, 78, 3–10.

Briggs, S., Gray, B., & Stephens, K. (2003). *Offender literacy and attrition from the enhanced thinking skills programme.* West Yorkshire, UK: National Probation Service.

Casey, S., Day, A., Howells, K., & Ward, T. (2007). Assessing suitability for offender rehabilitation: Development and validation of the treatment readiness questionnaire. *Criminal Justice and Behavior*, 34, 1427–1440.

Clark, D. A. (2000). *Theory manual for enhanced thinking skills.* Prepared for the Joint Prison Probation Accreditation Panel. Home Office: London.

Clarke, A., Simmonds, R., & Wydall, S. (2004). *Delivering cognitive skills programmes in prison: A qualitative study.* Home Office Online Report 27/04. London: Home Office.

Crick, N. R., & Dodge, K. A. (1996). Social information-processing mechanisms in reactive and proactive aggression. *Child Development*, 67, 993–1002.

D'Agostino, R. B. (1998). Propensity score methods for bias reduction in the comparison of a treatment to a non-randomized control group. *Statistics in Medicine*, 17, 2265–2281.

Debidin, M., & Lovbakke, J. (2005). Offending behaviour programmes in prison and probation. In G. Harper, & C. Chitty (Eds.), *The impact of corrections on re-offending: A review of "what works"* (2nd ed.) (pp. 31–55). Home Office Research Study 291). London, UK: Home Office.

Dowden, C., & Andrews, D. A. (1999). What works for female offenders: A meta-analytic review. *Crime & Delinquency*, 45, 438–452.

Duncan, E. A. S., Nicol, M. M., & Ager, A. (2004). Factors that constitute a good cognitive behavioural treatment manual: A Delphi study. *Behavioural and Cognitive Psychotherapy*, 32, 99–213.

Falshaw, L., Friendship, C., Travers, L., & Nugent, F. (2004). Searching for "what works": HM Prison Service accredited cognitive skills programmes. *British Journal of Forensic Practice*, 6, 3–13.

Farrington, D. P., Gottfredson, D. C., Sherman, L. W., & Welsh, B. C. (2002). The Maryland scientific methods scale. In L. W. Sherman, D. P. Farrington, B. C. Welsh, & D. L. MacKenzie (Eds.), *Evidence-based crime prevention* (pp. 13–21). London, UK: Routledge.

Friendship, C., Blud, L., Erikson, M., Travers, L., & Thornton, D. M. (2003). Cognitive-behavioural treatment for imprisoned offenders: An evaluation of HM Prison Service's cognitive skills programmes. *Legal and Criminological Psychology*, 8, 103–114.

Garrett, C. G. (1985). Effects of residential treatment on adjudicated delinquents: A meta-analysis. *Journal of Research in Crime and Delinquency*, 22, 287–308.

Gendreau, P., & Ross, B. (1979). Effective correctional treatment: Bibliotherapy for cynics. *Crime & Delinquency*, 25, 463–489.

Gibbs, J. C. (1993). Moral-cognitive interventions. In A. P. Goldstein, & C. R. Huff (Eds.), *The gang intervention handbook* (pp. 159–185). Champaign, IL: Research Press.

Gibbs, J. C. (1996). Sociomoral group treatment for young offenders. In C. R. Hollin, & K. Howells (Eds.), *Clinical approaches to working with young offenders* (pp. 129–149). Chichester, UK: Wiley.

Goldstein, A. P., & Glick, B. (1987). *Aggression replacement training: A comprehensive intervention for adolescent youth.* Champaign, IL: Research Press.

Goldstein, A. P., Nensén, R., Daleflod, B., & Kalt, M. (Eds.) (2004). *New perspectives on aggression replacement training.* Chichester, UK: Wiley.

Gondolf, E. W. (2004). Evaluating batterer counselling programs: A difficult task showing some effects and implications. *Aggression and Violent Behaviour*, 9, 605–631.

Henderson, M., & Hollin, C. (1983). A critical review of social skills training with young offenders. *Criminal Justice and Behavior*, 10, 316–341.

Hollin, C. R. (1990). *Cognitive-behavioral interventions with young offenders.* Elmsford, NY: Pergamon Press.

Hollin, C. R. (1995). The meaning and implications of "programme integrity". In J. McGuire (Ed.), *What works: Effective methods to reduce reoffending* (pp. 195–208). Chichester, UK: Wiley.

Hollin, C. R. (2008). Evaluating offending behaviour programmes: Does only randomisation glister? *Criminology & Criminal Justice*, 8, 89–106.

Hollin, C. R. (2009). Treatment manuals: The good, the bad and the useful. *Journal of Sexual Aggression*, 15, 133–137.

Hollin, C. R. (2010). Randomised control trials. In J. Brown, & E. Campbell (Eds.), *The Cambridge handbook of forensic psychology* (pp. 837–842). Cambridge, UK: Cambridge University Press.

Hollin, C. R., & Henderson, M. (1984). Social skills training with young offenders: False expectations and the "failure" of treatment. *Behavioural Psychotherapy*, 12, 331–341.

Hollin, C. R., McGuire, J., Hounsome, J. C., Hatcher, R. M., Bilby, C. A. L., & Palmer, E. J. (2008). Cognitive skills offending behavior programs in the community: A reconviction analysis. *Criminal Justice and Behavior*, 35, 269–283.

Hollin, C. R., & Palmer, E. J. (2006a). Offending behaviour programmes: History and development. In C. R. Hollin, & E. J. Palmer (Eds.), *Offending behaviour programmes: Development, application, and controversies* (pp. 1–32). Chichester, UK: Wiley.

Hollin, C. R., & Palmer, E. J. (2006b). Criminogenic need and women offenders: A critique of the literature. *Legal and Criminological Psychology*, 11, 179–195.

Hollin, C. R., & Trower, P. (Eds.) (1986a). *Handbook of social skills training, volume 1: Applications across the life span.* Oxford, UK: Pergamon Press.

Hollin, C. R., & Trower, P. (Eds.) (1986b). *Handbook of social skills training, volume 2: Clinical applications and new directions.* Oxford, UK: Pergamon Press.

Honderich, T. (1976). *Punishment: The supposed justifications* (Rev. ed.). Harmondsworth, UK: Penguin Books.

Jones, A. S., D'Agostino, R. B., Gondolf, E. W., & Heckert, A. (2004). Assessing the effect of batterer program completion on reassault using propensity scores. *Journal of Interpersonal Violence*, 19, 1002–1020.

Kirigin, K. A., Braukmann, C. J., Atwater, J. D., & Worl, M. M. (1982). An evaluation of Teaching-Family (Achievement Place) group homes for juvenile offenders. *Journal of Applied Behavior Analysis*, 15, 1–16.

Knott, C. (1995). The STOP programme: Reasoning and Rehabilitation in a British setting. In J. McGuire (Ed.), *What works: Reducing reoffending* (pp. 115–126). Chichester, UK: Wiley.

Kohlberg, L. (1964). Development of moral character and moral ideology. In M. Hoffman, & L. Hoffman (Eds.), *Review of child development research* (Vol. 1) (pp. 383–431). New York, NY: Russell Sage Foundation.

Latessa, E. (2006). Effectiveness of cognitive behavioral interventions for youthful offenders: Review of the research. In B. Glick (Ed.), *Cognitive behavioral interventions with at-risk youth* (pp. 1–17). Kingston, NJ: Civic Research Institute.

Lipsey, M. W. (1992). Juvenile delinquency treatment: A meta-analytic inquiry into the variability of effects. In T. D. Cook, H. Cooper, D. S. Cordray, H. Hartmann, L. V. Hedges, R. J. Light, et al. (Eds.), *Meta-analysis for explanation: A casebook* (pp. 83–127). New York, NY: Russell Sage Foundation.

Lipton, D. N., McDonel, E. C., & McFall, R. M. (1987). Heterosocial perception in rapists. *Journal of Consulting and Clinical Psychology*, 55, 17–21.

Mann, R. E. (2009). Sex offender treatment: The case for manualization. *Journal of Sexual Aggression*, 15, 121–131.

Marshall, W. L. (2009). Manualization: A blessing or a curse? *Journal of Sexual Aggression*, 15, 109–120.

Marshall, W. L., & Hollin, C. (2015). Historical developments in sex offender treatment. *Journal of Sexual Aggression*, 21, 125–135.

Martin, G., & Pear, J. (1999). *Behavior modification: What it is and how to do it* (6th ed.). Upper Saddle River, NJ: Prentice Hall.

Martinson, R. (1974). What works? Questions and answers about prison reform. *The Public Interest*, 35, 22–54.

McCulloch, A., & McMurran, M. (2007). The features of a good offender treatment programme manual: A Delphi survey of experts. *Psychology, Crime & Law*, 13, 265–274.

McGuire, J. (Ed.) (1995a). *What works: Effective methods to reduce reoffending*. Chichester, UK: Wiley.

McGuire, J. (1995b). Reasoning and Rehabilitation programs in the UK. In R. R. Ross, & B. Ross (Eds.), *Thinking straight: The Reasoning and Rehabilitation program for delinquency prevention and offender rehabilitation* (pp. 261–282). Ottawa, Canada: Air Training and Publications.

McGuire, J. (2002). Integrating findings from research reviews. In J. McGuire (Ed.), *Offender rehabilitation and treatment: Effective programmes and policies to reduce re-offending* (pp. 3–38). Chichester, UK: Wiley.

McGuire, J. (2005). The *Think First* programme. In M. McMurran, & J. McGuire (Eds.), *Social problem solving and offending: Evidence, evaluation and evolution* (pp. 183–206). Chichester, UK: Wiley.

McGuire, J. (2008). A review of effective interventions for reducing aggression and violence. *Philosophical Transactions of the Royal Society B*, 363, 2577–2597.

McGuire, J., Bilby, C. A. L., Hatcher, R. M., Hollin, C. R., Hounsome, J., & Palmer, E. J. (2008). Evaluation of structured cognitive-behavioural treatment programmes in reducing criminal recidivism. *Journal of Experimental Criminology*, 4, 21–40.

McMurran, M. (2006). Drug and alcohol programmes: Concept, theory, and practice. In C. R. Hollin, & E. J. Palmer (Eds.), *Offending behaviour programmes: Development, application, and controversies* (pp. 179–207). Chichester, UK: Wiley.

McMurran, M., & McCulloch, A. (2007). Why don't offenders complete treatment? Prisoners' reasons for non-completion of a cognitive skills programme. *Psychology, Crime & Law*, 13, 345–354.

McMurran, M., & McGuire, J. (Eds.) (2008). *Social problem solving and offending: Evidence, evaluation and evolution*. Chichester, UK: Wiley.

McMurran, M., & Theodosi, E. (2007). Is treatment non-completion associated with increased reconviction over no treatment? *Psychology, Crime & Law*, 13, 333–343.

Meichenbaum, D. M. (1977). *Cognitive behavior modification*. New York, NY: Plenum Press.

Najavits, L. M., Weiss, R. D., Shaw, S. R., & Dierberger, A. E. (2000). Psychotherapists' views of treatment manuals. *Professional Psychology: Research and Practice*, 31, 404–408.

Nelson, J. R., Smith, D. J., & Dodd, J. (1990). The moral reasoning of juvenile delinquents: A meta-analysis. *Journal of Abnormal Child Psychology*, 18, 709–727.

Novaco, R. W. (1975). *Anger control: The development and evaluation of an experimental treatment.* Lexington, MA: D. C. Heath.

Novaco, R. W. (1994). Anger as a risk factor for violence among the mentally disordered. In J. Monahan, & H. Steadman (Eds.), *Violence and mental disorder: Developments in risk assessment* (pp. 21–59). Chicago, IL: University of Chicago Press.

Olver, M. E., Stockdale, K. C., & Wormith, J. S. (2011). A meta-analysis of predictors of offender treatment attrition and its relationship to recidivism. *Journal of Consulting and Clinical Psychology*, 79, 6–21.

Palmer, E. J., & Hollin, C. R. (1996). Assessing adolescent problems: An overview of the Adolescent Problem Inventory. *Journal of Adolescence*, 19, 347–354.

Palmer, E. J., & Hollin, C. R. (1997). The influence of perceptions of own parenting on sociomoral reasoning, attributions for criminal behaviour, and self-reported delinquency. *Personality and Individual Differences*, 23, 193–197.

Palmer, E. J., & Hollin, C. R. (2001). Sociomoral reasoning, perceptions of parenting and self-reported delinquency in adolescents. *Applied Cognitive Psychology*, 15, 85–100.

Palmer, E. J., McGuire, J., Hatcher, R. M., Hounsome, J. C., Bilby, C. A. L., & Hollin, C. R. (2008). The importance of appropriate allocation to offending behavior programs. *International Journal of Offender Therapy and Comparative Criminology*, 52, 206–221.

Palmer, E. J., McGuire, J., Hatcher, R. M., Hounsome, J. C., Bilby, C. A. L., & Hollin, C. R. (2009). Allocation to offending behaviour programmes in the English and Welsh Probation Service. *Criminal Justice and Behavior*, 36, 909–922.

Palmer, E. J., McGuire, J., Hounsome, J. C., Hatcher, R. M., Bilby, C. A., & Hollin, C. R. (2007). Offending behaviour programmes in the community: The effects on reconviction of three programmes with adult male offenders. *Legal and Criminological Psychology*, 12, 251–264.

Polaschek, D. L. L. (2006). Violent offender programmes: Concept, theory, and practice. In C. R. Hollin, & E. J. Palmer (Eds.), *Offending behaviour programmes: Development, application, and controversies* (pp. 113–154). Chichester, UK: Wiley.

Raynor, P., & Vanstone, M. (1996). Reasoning and Rehabilitation in Britain: The results of the Straight Thinking on Probation (STOP) program. *International Journal of Offender Therapy and Comparative Criminology*, 40, 272–284.

Raynor, P., & Vanstone, M. (1997). *Straight Thinking on Probation (STOP): The Mid-Glamorgan experiment.* Oxford, UK: University of Oxford, Centre for Criminological Research, Probation Studies Unit No. 4.

Roberts, C. (2004). Offending behaviour programmes: Emerging evidence and implications for practice. In R. Burnett, & C. Roberts (Eds.), *What works in probation and youth justice: Developing evidence-based practice* (pp. 134–158). Cullompton, UK: Willan.

Ross, R. R., Fabiano, E. A., & Ewles, C. D. (1988). Reasoning and Rehabilitation. *International Journal of Offender Therapy and Comparative Criminology*, 32, 29–35.

Ross, R. R., Fabiano, E. A., & Ross, B. (1989). *Reasoning and Rehabilitation: A handbook for teaching cognitive skills.* Ottawa, Canada: The Cognitive Centre.

Spence, S. H. (1981). Differences in social skills performance between institutionalized juvenile male offenders and a comparable group of boys without offence records. *British Journal of Clinical Psychology*, 20, 163–171.

Tong, L. S. J., & Farrington, D. P. (2006). How effective is the "Reasoning and Rehabilitation" programme in reducing re-offending? A meta-analysis of evaluations in four countries. *Psychology, Crime & Law*, 12, 3–24.

Van Voorhis, P., Spruance, L. M., Ritchey, P. N., Listwan, S. J., & Seabrook, R. (2004). The Georgia cognitive skills experiment: A replication of Reasoning and Rehabilitation. *Criminal Justice and Behavior*, 31, 282–305.

Veneziano, C., & Veneziano, L. (1988). Knowledge of social skills among institutionalized juvenile delinquents: An assessment. *Criminal Justice and Behavior*, 15, 152–171.

Walker, N. (1991). *Why punish?*. Oxford, UK: Oxford University Press.

Ward, C. I., & McFall, R. M. (1986). Further validation of the problem inventory for adolescent girls: Comparing caucasian and Black delinquents and nondelinquents. *Journal of Consulting and Clinical Psychology*, 54, 732–733.

Wilson, G. T. (1996). Manual-based treatments: The clinical application of research findings. *Behaviour Research and Therapy*, 34, 295–314.

Wilson, G. T. (1997). Treatment manuals in clinical practice. *Behaviour Research and Therapy*, 35, 205–210.

Wormith, J. S., & Olver, M. E. (2002). Offender treatment attrition and its relationship with risk, responsivity, and recidivism. *Criminal Justice and Behavior*, 29, 447–471.

Zamble, E., & Quinsey, V. L. (1997). *The criminal recidivism process*. Cambridge, UK: Cambridge University Press.

40

Criminal Thinking: Theory and Practice

Glenn D. Walters

Kutztown University, USA

As one of the "Big Four" predictors of recidivism (Andrews & Bonta, 2010) one would expect criminal thinking to assume a prominent position in criminology and criminal justice. The fact that it does not suggests that the field is either biased against psychologically based theories of crime (Walsh & Ellis, 2007) or is not sufficiently cognizant of the benefits of such an approach for the field. In an informal review of criminology and criminal justice textbooks, I discovered that criminal thinking was rarely mentioned, and when it was, it was relegated to a brief paragraph that typically overlooked the subtleties and complexities of the criminal thinking construct. This, however, may have as much to do with psychologists' failure to articulate the potential contributions of a psychological perspective on crime as it is does with criminologists' hesitance to take psychological theories of crime seriously. The purpose of this chapter, then, was to illustrate the relevance of criminal thinking to criminological theory and the applicability of lifestyle assessment and intervention to criminal justice practice.

What is Criminal Thinking?

Before discussing the relevance of criminal thinking to criminological theory and criminal justice practice I would like to offer a simple definition of criminal thinking. For the purposes of this chapter I define criminal thinking as a set of attitudes or beliefs connected to criminal behavior that support and maintain a criminal lifestyle. Research indicates that: (a) criminal thinking follows rather than precedes criminal behavior, developmentally (Walters, 2015a), (b) criminal thinking differs in degree rather than in kind (Walters & McCoy, 2007), and (c) criminal thinking promotes future crime by mediating other important criminological variables and influences (Walters, 2015b). Many criminological processes are linked in chain-like fashion through the mediating effect of criminal thinking. Understanding this mediating effect is a key to understanding criminal behavior.

Criminal thinking encompasses *what* an offender thinks as well as *how* an offender thinks. The former is referred to as criminal thought content (e.g., "I don't like cops") and the latter as criminal thought process (e.g., "I've been locked up for 10 years, society owes me").

The Wiley International Handbook of Correctional Psychology, First Edition. Edited by Devon L. L. Polaschek, Andrew Day, and Clive R. Hollin.

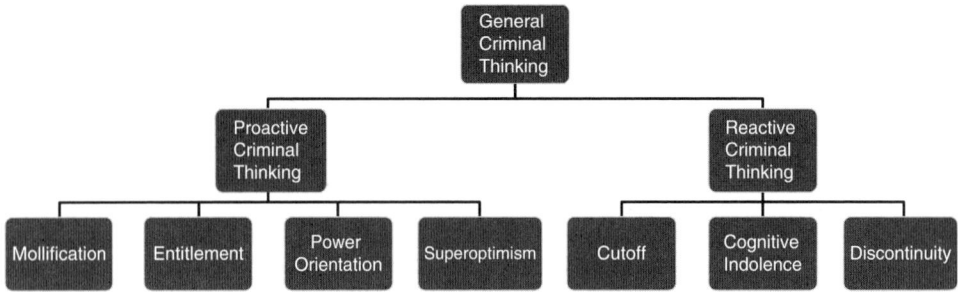

Figure 40.1   Hierarchical structure of the PICTS.

Assessing both criminal thought content and criminal thought process is important in gaining an appreciation of criminal thinking and its relationship to criminal behavior. Although most instruments used to assess criminal thinking target both criminal thought content and criminal thought process, some instruments are designed more for one than the other. Instruments like the Criminal Sentiments Scale-Modified (CSS-M; Simourd, 1997) and Measures of Criminal Attitudes and Associates (MCAA; Mills, Kroner, & Forth, 2002) are designed primarily for criminal thought content. The Psychological Inventory of Criminal Thinking Styles (PICTS: Walters, 1995), on the other hand, is designed primarily for criminal thought process.

The PICTS is an 80-item self-report inventory designed to assess eight thinking styles orig-inally believed to support a criminal lifestyle (Walters, 1990): Mollification (Mo), Cutoff (Co), Entitlement (En), Power Orientation (Po), Sentimentality (Sn), Superoptimism (So), Cognitive Indolence (Ci), and Discontinuity (Ds). Each item is rated on a 4-point Likert-type scale (1 = disagree, 2 = uncertain, 3 = agree, 4 = strongly agree). Analyses based on item response theory (IRT) have shown that the PICTS has a hierarchical latent structure with seven of the eight thinking styles at the bottom of the hierarchy (Sn excluded), two higher-order factors (Proactive Criminal Thinking, Reactive Criminal Thinking) in the middle, and a superordinate factor (General Criminal Thinking) at the top (Walters, Hagman, & Cohn, 2011: see Figure 40.1). The General Criminal Thinking (GCT) score is calculated by sum-ming the raw scores for Mo, Co, En, Po, So, Ci, and Ds, Proactive Criminal Thinking (P) is calculated by summing the raw scores for Mo, En, Po, and So, and Reactive Criminal Thinking (R) is calculated by summing the raw scores for Co, Ci, and Ds. Table 40.1 briefly describes each of the thinking styles.

Theory

The most theoretically fertile components of criminal thinking are proactive and reactive criminal thinking. As such, they will serve as the centerpiece for this discussion on theory. Proactive and reactive criminal thinking are conceptualized as overlapping dimensions (see Figure 40.2) based on research showing dimensional latent structure (Walters, 2009b) and inter-correlations in the moderate to high range (.50–.75: Walters, 2012a). This level of inter-correlation suggests that proactive and reactive criminal thinking share anywhere from a quarter to half of their variance. There is no definitive answer as to why these dimensions correlate so highly, although several explanations are possible. First, they may derive from some of the same antecedent conditions. Second, they may co-occur because they support the

Table 40.1 Superordinate, Higher-Order, and Lower-Level Thinking Styles that Form
the Hierarchical Model of Criminal Thinking

Superordinate thinking style	
General Criminal Thinking	General tendency to think in self-serving and impulsive ways conducive to the commission of criminal behavior.
Higher-order thinking styles	
Proactive Criminal Thinking	Goal-directed criminal thinking that is planned, organized, and designed to achieve a particular end.
Reactive Criminal Thinking	Emotion-driven criminal thinking that is impulsive, irresponsible, and seeks immediate gratification.
Lower-level thinking styles	
Mollification	Blaming one's prior criminality on external circumstances and events or making excuses for one's antisocial behavior.
Entitlement	Sense of privilege, ownership, or uniqueness sometimes expressed as a misidentification of wants as needs.
Power Orientation	Desire to exercise control over the external environment, often by exerting power over other people.
Superoptimism	Belief that one can indefinitely engage in antisocial behavior and not suffer the negative consequences.
Cutoff	Rapid elimination of various deterrents to crime with the aid of a drug, musical theme, or phrase (e.g., "fuck it").
Cognitive Indolence	Failure to critically evaluate one's plans and ideas, resulting in impulsive decision-making and pursuit of immediate gratification.
Discontinuity	Easy distractibility in the face of a constantly changing environment, leading to a lack of consistency and direction.

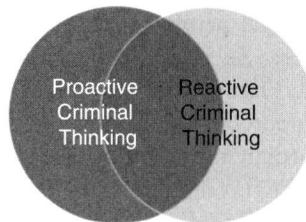

Figure 40.2 Venn diagram of the overlap between proactive and reactive criminal thinking.

same behavior (crime). Third, they may influence, shape, and feed off one another. Despite the overlap, the emphasis here will be on the differences between the two dimensions. These points of differentiation are also points of integration with biological, psychological, and sociological theories of crime.

Definition

Proactive criminal thinking is defined as goal-directed cognition designed to accomplish a criminal objective or antisocial aim. It is considered instrumental in the sense that it is designed to achieve an objective beyond the behavior. Reactive criminal thinking, by comparison, is emotions-centered cognition often stimulated by environmentally based change or challenge.

Robbery is normally considered an instrumental offense because the objective is the item being stolen, not the robbery itself, whereas assault is generally classified as a reactive offense to the extent that physical assault is the objective. Interviews conducted with convicted robbers, however, note that most robberies are unplanned (Feeney, 1986; Morrison & O'Donnell, 1996) and driven by both reactive (e.g., excitement or desperation: Bureau of Justice Statistics, 1994) and proactive factors. Assault, on the other hand, may be driven as much by instrumental motives, like the desire to intimidate or assert power and control over others (Chambers, Ward, Eccleston, & Brown, 2009), as it is by reactive intentions. This illustrates the fact that most crimes are driven by a combination of proactive and reactive causes and that the two dimensions have a great deal in common.

Besides providing points of differentiation between proactive and reactive criminal thinking, these definitional issues also highlight points of integration between criminal thinking and existing criminological theories. Notions of proactive and reactive criminal thought have their genesis in earlier models of proactive and reactive childhood aggression (Dodge & Coie, 1987). Like proactive criminal thinking, proactive childhood aggression is planned, goal-directed, and instrumental, and like reactive criminal thinking, reactive childhood aggression is emotional, impulsive, and usually in response to a real or imagined threat. Similar to proactive and reactive criminal thinking, proactive and reactive childhood aggression are best conceptualized as overlapping dimensions (Poulin & Boivin, 2000). Lifestyle theory proposes that proactive and reactive criminal thinking derive directly from the two dimensions of childhood aggression.

Criminal Pattern

Crimes with a strong proactive component are often planned, predatory, and cold-blooded, whereas crimes with a strong reactive component are often impulsive, reckless, and hot-blooded. Although these two criminal patterns often co-occur, it is their role as points of differentiation that concerns us here. As a point of integration, the proactive component of criminal thinking is consistent with Hare's (1996) views on psychopathy, with both reflecting the predatory nature of crime (Woodworth & Porter, 2002). In fact, it has been shown that proactive criminal thinking may mediate the relationship between the callous and selfish facets of psychopathy and violent offending (Walters & DeLisi, 2015). The reactive component of criminal thinking, by contrast, is consistent with Gottfredson and Hirschi's (1990) general theory of crime. The essence of Gottfredson and Hirschi's theory, low self-control, may, in fact, serve as a behavioral antecedent to reactive criminal thinking, and reactive criminal thinking may mediate the relationship between low self-control and crime. In a recent study on this topic, Walters (2015a) determined that low self-control predicted reactive criminal thinking and reactive criminal thinking mediated the relationship between low self-control and delinquency, whereas low self-control did not mediate the relationship between reactive criminal thinking and delinquency.

Temperament

Temperament can be defined as an individual's innate tendency to respond to the environment in a specific way. This innate tendency is never exclusively biological, except at conception, because even in the womb it is being shaped by the organism's interactions with the environment (Kagan, 2010). Several different temperament dimensions have been proposed (e.g., activity level, regularity, approach-withdrawal, adaptability: Chess & Thomas, 1977), but two in particular are vital in differentiating between proactive and reactive criminal thinking. The two dimensions that distinguish between proactive and reactive criminal thinking are fearlessness and disinhibition. Fearlessness derives from Lykken's (1957) low-fear hypothesis, which holds that primary psychopathy is a function of weak electrodermal reactivity and diminished fear conditioning. Disinhibition derives from research on the externalizing spectrum (Krueger, Markon, Patrick, Benning, & Kramer, 2007). The point of differentiation is that where fearlessness involves a deficit in avoiding punishment, disinhibition involves a deficit in approaching reward. A key point of integration is research supporting DeLisi and Vaughn's (2014) temperament model of criminology in which early temperament has been found to be linked to later externalizing/low self-control behavior (Walters, 2014a, 2015a).

Biological Antecedents

There are currently no studies on the biological antecedents of criminal thinking, although there is one study on the biological correlates of fearlessness and disinhibition. Walters and Kiehl (2015) recently correlated Psychopathy Checklist proxies for fearlessness and disinhibition with gray matter volumes in the limbic systems of delinquent adolescent males. As predicted, scores on the fearlessness dimension correlated negatively with gray matter volumes in the amygdala and scores on the disinhibition dimension correlated negatively with gray matter volumes in the hippocampus. Given research showing that the amygdala plays a major role in fear conditioning (Shechner, Hong, Britton, Pine, & Fox, 2014) and the hippocampus plays a leading role in behavior inhibition (Cherbuin et al., 2008), these results suggest that temperament dimensions held to be important in the development of crime and delinquency may have a biological basis. Further research is required to determine what effect, if any, these biological antecedents have on proactive and reactive criminal thinking and whether these antecedents actually predict proactive and reactive criminal thinking rather than simply serving as markers of criminal thought or behavior.

Sociological Antecedents

Two of the more popular theories of criminology, Sutherland's (1947) differential association theory and Gottfredson and Hirschi's (1990) general theory of crime, interpret the well-documented relationship between peer delinquency and participant delinquency differently. Whereas differential association theory proposes a peer influence or socialization effect (peer delinquency → participant delinquency), the general theory of crime postulates a peer selection effect in which those with low self-control choose to associate with peers who are also low in self-control (participant delinquency → peer delinquency). Both models may be correct, and criminal thinking could be the glue that binds them together. There is now evidence that proactive criminal thinking mediates the peer influence effect (Walters, 2015c, 2016a) and reactive criminal thinking mediates the peer selection effect (Walters, 2016a). The point of differentiation with respect to these sociological antecedents is that while proactive criminal thinking mediates peer influence but not peer selection, reactive criminal thinking mediates peer selection but not peer influence. The point of integration with these sociological antecedents is that proactive criminal thinking appears to clarify differential association with respect to peer influence and reactive criminal thinking may help clarify the general theory of crime with respect to peer selection.

Psychological Antecedents

Developmental psychology is clearly capable of informing theories of criminal thinking. In fact, criminal thinking has its roots in early developmental processes like social perspective-taking and behavioral regulation. Social perspective-taking, or the ability to understand that others may have a perspective different from one's own, can be observed in children as young as 6–8 years of age. Perspective-taking is a building block for future empathy, and children who fail to develop this ability are at increased risk for future antisocial behavior (Davis-Kean, Jager, & Collins, 2009). The fact that weak empathy may be an antecedent to proactive criminal thinking (Walters, 2012a) highlights the role of perspective-taking in a comprehensive theory of criminal thinking. Self-regulation of behavior is another developmental milestone with relevance to criminal thinking. Children who have trouble regulating their behavior encounter high levels of peer rejection (Stocker & Dunn, 1990), school failure (Reeve, 1994), and child–parent conflict (Loeber, Burke, Lahey, Winters, & Zera, 2000). Behavioral dysregulation, which in criminological circles is referred to as low self-control (Gottfredson & Hirschi, 1990), is considered an antecedent to reactive criminal thinking (Walters, 2012a). Problems with peers, school, and parents encourage a child to seek out similarly situated peers, a good portion of whom may be delinquent, thereby providing the child with the opportunity to learn antisocial attitudes and behaviors. This illustrates how the peer selection and peer influence processes interface and reactive and proactive criminal thinking overlap.

Affective Concomitants

Criminal thinking develops in tandem with certain affective, cognitive, and behavioral influences. Affective concomitants of criminal thinking include callousness-unemotionality and weak emotional control/modulation. The affective concomitants derive, in part, from temperament—callous and unemotional traits originating from the fearlessness dimension and weak emotional modulation from the disinhibition dimension. Whereas callous-unemotional traits are more often associated with serious and predatory forms of conduct disorder (Frick, Ray, Thornton, & Kahn, 2014), tenuous emotional control is more often associated with impulsive behavior. Impulsive offending is more frequent and varied than offending based on callous-unemotional traits and is often accompanied by other risk-taking behaviors like drug use, pathological gambling, and reckless driving (Higgins, Kirchner, Ricketts, & Marcum, 2013). Callous and unemotional traits are therefore hypothesized to be concomitant with proactive criminal thinking, and weak emotional modulation is hypothesized to be concomitant with reactive criminal thinking.

Cognitive Concomitants

Crime continuity—the fact that prior criminality is often the best predictor of future criminality—has been explained in several different ways. Gottfredson and Hirschi (1990) contend that time-stable individual differences in criminal propensity account for crime continuity, whereas Sampson and Laub (1993) assert that the past crime–future crime relationship is a function of crime's ability to disrupt informal social control mechanisms. Adopting a middle position, Walters (2012a) holds that crime continuity derives from quasi-time-stable cognitive variables that mediate the past crime–future crime relationship by way of psychological inertia. These variables include criminal thinking styles, hostile attribution biases, positive outcome expectancies for crime, low self-efficacy for conventional behavior, hedonistic values, and short-term goals. Research has confirmed criminal thinking, low self-efficacy for conventional behavior, physically hedonistic values, and short-term goals as mediators of crime continuity (Walters, 2015b, 2015d). The additive postulate of the psychological inertia theorem (i.e., that individual cognitive variables have a cumulative effect) has also received empirical support (Walters, 2016b). The six quasi-time-stable cognitive variables that mediate crime continuity can also be viewed as points of integration with social learning (Akers, 1998) and social cognitive (Bandura, 1986) theories. Positive outcome expectancies, however, appear to align differentially with proactive criminal thinking, and hostile attribution biases appear to align differentially with reactive criminal thinking (Walters, 2007a).

Behavioral Concomitants

In advancing the "worst of both worlds" hypothesis, Walters (2014b) maintains that comorbid criminality and substance misuse predict poorer future crime and drug outcomes better than prior criminality or prior substance misuse alone. This hypothesis has been verified in several studies (Walters, 2014b, 2015e, 2015f) and gives rise to the concept of reciprocal risk whereby prior substance misuse is held to predict future criminality above and beyond the effects of prior criminality, and prior criminality is held to predict future substance misuse above and beyond the effects of prior substance misuse. Research indicates that reactive criminal thinking correlates with substance misuse and mediates the substance misuse–criminality and criminality–substance misuse relationships whereas proactive criminal thinking does not (Walters, 2012b, 2016c). To see whether proactive and reactive criminal thinking enter into opposing countervailing relationships with drug selling, three groups of inmates from the original Walters (2012b) investigation were compared—those with prior convictions for selling drugs but no history of substance misuse, those with prior convictions for selling drugs and a history of substance misuse, and those with no prior convictions for selling drugs. The results revealed that inmates with a history of selling drugs, regardless of drug use, recorded significantly higher proactive criminal thinking scores than inmates without a history of selling drugs. In addition, inmates who had sold and misused drugs achieved significantly higher reactive criminal thinking scores than inmates in the other two groups (see Table 40.3).

Treatment

Proactive and reactive criminal thinking may do more than mediate relationships, they may also moderate them. Nowhere is this more evident than with intervention. Most correctional programs focus on teaching offenders how to control their behavior. Whereas such interventions are highly efficacious in managing reactive criminal thinking, they have minimal impact on proactive criminal thinking. Walters (2009a) found that while a skill-based approach reduced reactive criminal thinking over the course of a 6-week anger management class, it had no effect on proactive criminal thinking. Interventions for proactive criminal thinking must therefore be found, aided perhaps by decision-making theory. Variations in how the two dimensions impact on decision-making is another point of differentiation, whereas the overlap between the two dimensions and rational choice theory (Cornish & Clarke, 1986) is another point of integration between criminal thinking and traditional criminological theory (see Table 40.2). As illustrated in Figure 40.3, reactive criminal thinking, in theory, influences criminal decision-making by stimulating hedonistic emotions and producing

Table 40.2 The Ten Points of Differentiation and Integration

	Proactive Criminal Thinking	*Reactive Criminal Thinking*
Definition	Instrumental (goal-directed)	Responsive (emotions-centered)
Criminal pattern	Planned and predatory (cold-blooded)	Impulsive and irresponsible (hot-blooded)
Temperament	Fearlessness dimension	Disinhibition dimension
Biological antecedents	Reduced amygdala gray matter volume	Reduced hippocampal gray matter volume
Sociological antecedents	Peer influence effect	Peer selection effect
Psychological antecedents	Weak empathy	Low self-control
Affective concomitants	Callousness-unemotionality	Unmodulated emotion
Cognitive concomitants	Positive outcome expectancies for crime	Hostile attribution biases
Behavioral concomitants	Selling drugs	Using drugs
Treatment objectives	Moral decision-making and values	Social, coping, and problem-solving skills

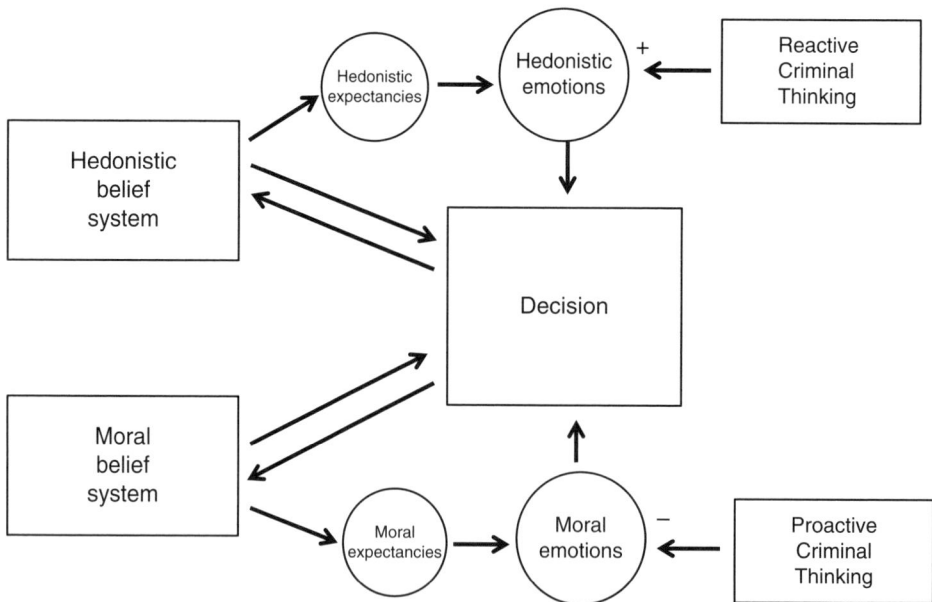

Figure 40.3 Respective roles of proactive and reactive criminal thinking in criminal decision-making. Adapted from Walters (2015g).

decision-irrelevant information, while proactive criminal thinking affects criminal decision-making by inhibiting moral emotions and limiting decision-relevant information. Interventions for proactive criminal thinking should accordingly support moral reasoning and values clarification and reduce well-known cognitive concomitants of proactive criminal thinking like positive outcome expectancies for crime (Walters, 2004).

Table 40.3 Criminal Thinking Scores for Drug Selling, Drug Selling and Using, and Non-Drug Selling Inmates

Dependent measure	*DS* *(n = 622)*	*DS&U* *(n = 1,441)*	*NDS* *(n = 976)*	*Omnibus F* *(2, 3,036)*
Proactive Criminal Thinking	53.01(13.14)$_a$	53.57(13.66)$_a$	50.54(13.72)$_b$	15.00*
Reactive Criminal Thinking	41.98(12.67)$_a$	44.32(13.43)$_b$	41.89(13.50)$_a$	12.37*

Note. Means (with standard deviations in parentheses) are shown; for each row, means with different letter subscripts (a, b) are significantly different from each other ($p < .01$; Scheffe post hoc test); Proactive Criminal Thinking = Proactive Criminal Thinking score from the Psychological Inventory of Criminal Thinking Styles (PICTS); Reactive Criminal Thinking = Reactive Criminal Thinking score from the PICTS; DS = drug selling but not using; DS&U = drug selling and using; NDS = non-drug selling; Omnibus F = overall F-test difference between the three groups.
* $p < 0.01$.

Practice

Assessment

In researching the proactive and reactive dimensions of criminal thinking, I have sometimes had to rely on measures other than the PICTS. The Moral Disengagement scale (Bandura, Barbarnelli, Caprara, & Pastorelli, 1996) and various operationalizations of neutralization theory (Sykes & Matza, 1957) have served as proxies for proactive criminal thinking, and the transposed Impulse Control score from the Weinberger Adjustment Inventory (WAI-IC: Weinberger & Schwartz, 1990) and various operationalizations of impulsive sensation-seeking (Zuckerman, 1996) have served as proxies for reactive criminal thinking. For clinical purposes, however, the PICTS P and R scores should be used whenever possible.

The PICTS interpretation process involves four steps. The first step is to determine whether the profile is valid by ruling out various response styles (i.e., exaggeration, fake bad, minimization, fake good, random responding). Three PICTS scales, Confusion-revised (Cf-r), Infrequency (INF), and Defensiveness-revised (Df-r), and the number of missing items are used to assess profile validity. Problem exaggeration is suggested by a T-score (normative score with a mean of 50 and standard deviation of 10) of 75–94 on the Cf-r and/or a T-score of 60–79 on the INF. A fake bad profile is suggested by a T-score of 95 or higher on the Cf-r or a T-score of 80 or higher on the INF. Problem minimization is implied by a T-score of 60–67 on the Df-r and/or 10–19 unanswered items. A fake good profile is denoted by a T-score above 67 on the Df-r or more than 19 unanswered items. PICTS profiles marked by problem exaggeration and problem minimization are still interpretable but the thinking style scales may be artificially elevated or suppressed, respectively. Fake bad and fake good profiles, on the other hand, are clearly invalid. Random responding is indicated by elevations (T-scores ≥ 60) on both the Cf-r and Df-r, and invariant responding is indicated by 90% or more responses from one of the four response options (e.g., mostly "2" or "uncertain" responses).

Once it has been determined that a PICTS protocol is valid, the next step is to estimate the individual's overall level of criminal thinking. This can best be accomplished by examining the GCT score. T-scores of 50 or higher indicate that general criminal thinking is significant in that the PICTS was normed on low-, medium-, and high-security federal prisoners and the respondent is scoring higher than at least half that group. In situations where one is working with a population vastly different from the one upon which the PICTS was normed (e.g., probationers), it may be better to construct and use local norms. Given the dimensional nature of criminal thinking (Walters, 2009b), any categories we create will be arbitrary. Nonetheless, categorization can have heuristic value for those evaluating an offender's risk of recidivism with the PICTS. One might therefore arbitrarily divide the GCT into the following risk categories: low (T-score ≤ 40), low-moderate (T-score 41–49), high-moderate (T-score 50–59), and high (T-score ≥ 60).

Whereas the GCT provides clinicians with information on general criminal thinking (a process known as trend analysis), the P and R scores supply clinicians with information on patterns of criminal thinking. Pattern analysis entails an idiographic comparison of a client's performance on key dimensions. On the PICTS, the key comparison is between P and R. A difference of at least 10 T-score points with the higher score at T ≥ 55 can be considered evidence of a pattern. A difference of 6–9 points in which the higher score is at T ≥ 50 signals a possible pattern. Research indicates that proactive and reactive criminal thinking are highly correlated such that when P is elevated R is usually elevated as well, and when P is low so usually is R (Walters, 2012a). There are times, however, when one of the scores is significantly higher than the other. Under such circumstances, a P > R pattern denotes that the calculated, callous, and scheming aspects of criminal thinking predominate, whereas an R > P pattern suggests that the impulsive, irresponsible, and emotional aspects of criminal thinking predominate.

Once trends and patterns have been analyzed, the final step in the interpretative process is to examine the eight individual PICTS thinking style scales: Mollification, Entitlement, Power Orientation, Superoptimism, Cutoff, Cognitive Indolence, Discontinuity, and Sentimentality. Scores greater than or equal to a T-score of 60 and scores less than or equal to a T-score of 40 are interpreted. Normally, the top three thinking style scales T ≥ 60 are interpreted, but there are exceptions to this rule. If the T-score of the most highly elevated thinking style scale is in the upper 50s and the Defensiveness scale is elevated at or above 55, then it is permissible to interpret this one thinking style scale as an elevation. In situations where more than three thinking style scales are elevated (T ≥ 60) it is customary to restrict the interpretation to the three most highly elevated scales.

A notable strength of the PICTS is that it fits nicely into Andrews and Bonta's (2010) Risk-Need-Responsivity (RNR) model. For the purposes of assessing risk, the GCT score is the single most important score, given its superior reliability and predictive validity relative to the P and R scores (Walters, 2012a). Moreover, in a study comparing the GCT, P, and R scores in four prison samples, Walters (2007b) determined that only the GCT score achieved incremental validity relative to a participant's response style (as measured by the PICTS Cf-r and Df-r scales) in all four samples. Needs are assessed with the PICTS by examining elevations on the eight thinking style scales, with each scale representing a different need and thus objective for intervention (see Table 40.4). Finally, responsivity is addressed by comparing the P and R scores. Although P and R usually do not differ by more than 5 points, when they do it should be noted. Different treatment protocols, in fact, are required for someone demonstrating a P > R pattern versus an R > P pattern.

Intervention

The treatment protocol for criminal thinking can be broken down into three phases: preparation, action, and follow-up (see Figure 40.4).

Preparation phase

Most offenders do not seek out treatment voluntarily but are instead forced into therapy by a spouse, friend, correctional case manager, probation officer, or judge. Many offenders fear change and most are functioning at either the precontemplation or contemplation stage

Table 40.4 Needs Measured by the Eight PICTS Thinking Style Scales

Thinking style	Needs
Mollification	Taking responsibility for antisocial actions and ability to avoid blaming others for the negative consequences of one's own behavior.
Cutoff	Effectively dealing with frustration, disappointment, and not getting one's own way.
Entitlement	Differentiating between needs and wants and taking inventory of one's priorities and values.
Power Orientation	Emphasizing and developing an internal orientation while de-emphasizing and questioning value and feasibility of external control.
Sentimentality	Challenging the inclination to perform good deeds as a means of excusing past misconduct.
Superoptimism	Accurately appraising the odds of negative consequences in both the short- and long-term from continued involvement in crime.
Cognitive Indolence	Critical reasoning skills, ability to delay gratification, and inhibiting situationally dominant responses.
Discontinuity	Goal-setting, focused attention, filtering out of environmental distractions, and following through on initial plans and commitments.

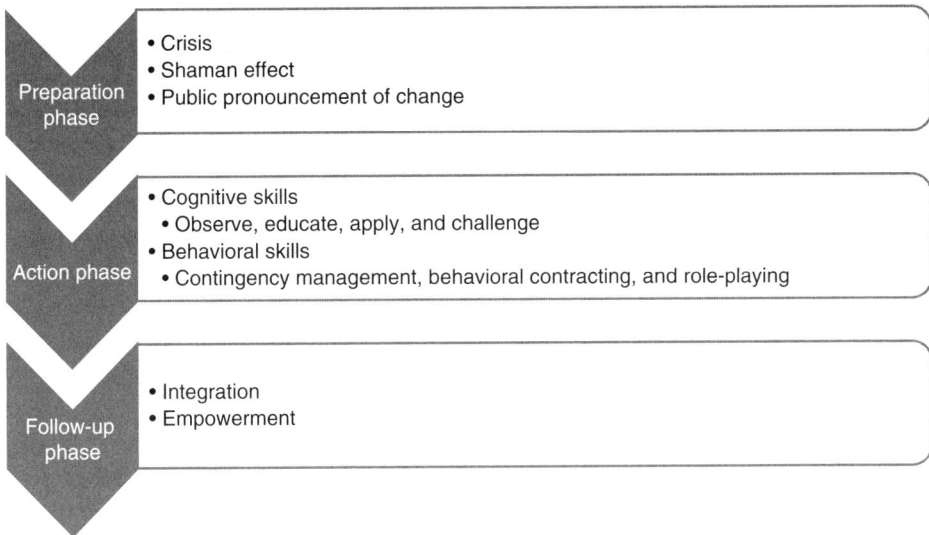

Preparation phase
- Crisis
- Shaman effect
- Public pronouncement of change

Action phase
- Cognitive skills
  - Observe, educate, apply, and challenge
- Behavioral skills
  - Contingency management, behavioral contracting, and role-playing

Follow-up phase
- Integration
- Empowerment

Figure 40.4 Three phases of intervention for criminal thinking.

of change (Prochaska & DiClemente, 1992). They are, at best, ambivalent about change (contemplation) and must therefore be prepared for change. Preparation begins with the development of a crisis. A crisis is the perception that the criminal lifestyle is no longer working and that the negative consequences of the lifestyle are beginning to outweigh the reinforcing aspects. Crises are common in the lives of society's habitual law-breakers. What the therapist or counselor must do is develop one or more of these crises in an effort to temporarily arrest the lifestyle. The therapist does this by asking clients to identify the people they have harmed, the opportunities they have missed, the relationships they have lost, and the embarrassing situations they have encountered as a result of the lifestyle. For the crisis to take

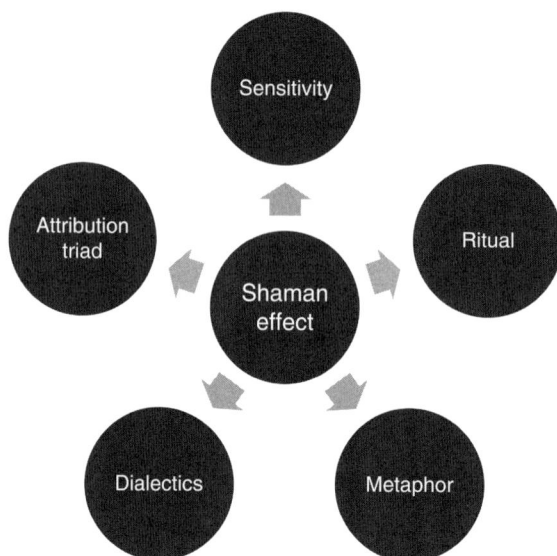

Figure 40.5   Five components of the shaman effect.

root it must be accompanied by the other two components of the preparation stage: the shaman effect and a public pronouncement of change.

   Creation of a shaman effect (Walters, 2001), also known as a working therapeutic alliance or relationship, is the second step in preparing criminal justice clients for change. The five components of the shaman effect are identified in Figure 40.5. Therapists can demonstrate sensitivity to the client's inner world through accurate empathy, interpretation, or prediction. Rituals that foster growth rather than promote a lifestyle are also part of the shaman effect. Enforcing the melodic requirements of speech in one's interactions with clients (metaphor), furnishing the client with a skill to synthesize extreme viewpoints (dialectics), and getting the client to acknowledge that change is necessary, possible, and attainable (attribution triad) are also instrumental in creating a shaman effect. Crisis development and the shaman effect are further reinforced by the third component of the preparation phase; namely, a public pronouncement for change. Research indicates that commitments made in front of an audience, even an imaginary audience, are stronger and more durable than commitments made without an audience (Tice, 1992). The preparation phase of change is designed to reduce resistance to change and encourage the development of self-efficacy for change.

   Action phase

   Lifestyle theory maintains that a person starts acting like a criminal before he or she starts thinking like one, a supposition that has received empirical support (Walters, 2015a). Variable order is reversed, however, when it comes to intervention. When attempting to change criminal behavior, the cognitions that support, maintain, and protect the behavior must be addressed before any meaningful change can be anticipated in the behavior. In concert with contemporary cognitive behavioral theory, the lifestyle approach holds that a change in cognition leads to a change in behavior (Beck, 1979; Ellis, 2007). The action phase of cognitive behavioral therapy (CBT) for criminal thinking consists of two interrelated subphases: the cognitive skills subphase and the behavioral skills subphase.

   The cognitive skills subphase of CBT for criminal thinking is designed to identify and challenge criminal thought processes instrumental in maintaining a criminal lifestyle. This is accomplished using a four-step procedure: (a) because most clients will be unfamiliar with lifestyle theory, they must receive didactic instruction in the thinking styles; (b) because it is easier to see criminal thinking in others than it is to see it in oneself, clients must have the opportunity to observe and identify criminal thinking in others, such as viewing and critiquing taped interviews with notorious criminals; (c) because clients may still have trouble identifying thinking styles in themselves, they must be provided with training exercises and immediate feedback when using the thinking styles; (d) because criminal thinking does not go away simply because one is aware of it, clients must be taught how to challenge criminal thought processes and replace them with non-criminal alternatives by asking themselves two questions: (a) "What is the evidence in support of my belief?" and (b) "How will this thought benefit me in the future?"

As clients progress through the action phase of CBT for criminal thinking there is a shift in emphasis away from cognition alone to a combined focus on cognition and behavior. Through behavioral rehearsal/role-playing and homework assignments the individual tries out new behaviors and gains a sense of accomplishment, satisfaction, and self-efficacy from successfully performing these actions. The role-playing usually occurs first, with support from the therapist and feedback from other group members. Once the skill is learned and practiced under the watchful eye of the therapist, the client graduates to applying the skill in his or her real-life environment through homework assignments. This then is the behavioral subphase of CBT for criminal thinking.

Follow-up phase

Many correctional programs fail for lack of effective aftercare (McCollister et al., 2003). Follow-up sessions may be less frequent than interventions taking place during the preparation and action phases, but they are no less important in bringing about lasting change. The two principal components or subphases of the follow-up phase are integration and empowerment. Integration means pairing the cognitive and behavioral components of the action phase of CBT for criminal thinking by reminding the client of the unity and indivisibility of thought and behavior. Empowerment means enhancing the client's self-efficacy through performance accomplishments (Bandura, 1986), which begins with completion of homework assignments.

Application

The results of several outcome studies have shown that addressing criminal thinking can reduce institutional infractions, recidivism, and related negative behaviors, such as drug use and problem gambling (Walters, 2012a). By using the PICTS to assess areas of need and then addressing these needs with CBT, it may be possible to change the life-course trajectories of even the most hardened criminals.

Conclusion

The main objective of this chapter was to illustrate how criminal behavior can be altered by assessing and challenging criminal thinking. To this end, I reviewed points of differentiation between two higher-order factors (proactive and reactive criminal thinking). From here, I showed how these points of differentiation helped identify points of integration between criminal thought process and other theoretical models and how criminal thinking can be assessed and treated using a CBT framework. Integration also applies to theory, practice, and research: theory informs practice, practice legitimizes theory, and research verifies both. The question for future research is why, despite strong evidence of differentiation between proactive and reactive criminal thinking, do these two dimensions display so much overlap?

Author Note

The author would like to thank Rozanna Tross for sharing information on the South Carolina sexually violent predator treatment (SVPT) program.

Key Readings

Ellis, A. (2007). *The practice of rational emotive behavior therapy* (2nd ed.). New York, NY: Springer.

Kroner, D. G., & Morgan, R. D. (2014). An overview of strategies for the assessment and treatment of criminal thinking. In R. C. Tafrate, & D. Mitchell (Eds.), *Forensic CBT: A handbook for clinical practice* (pp. 87–103). Chichester, UK: Wiley-Blackwell.

Mandracchia, J. T., & Morgan, R. D. (2012). Predicting offenders' criminogenic cognitions with status variables. *Criminal Justice and Behavior*, 39, 5–25.

Walters, G. D. (2014). Applying CBT to the criminal thought process. In R. C. Tafrate, & D. Mitchell (Eds.), *Forensic CBT: A handbook for clinical practice* (pp. 104–121). Chichester, UK: Wiley-Blackwell.

Walters, G. D. (2017). Effect of a brief cognitive behavioural intervention on criminal thinking and prison misconduct in male inmates: Variable-oriented and person-oriented analyses. *Criminal Behaviour and Mental Health*, 27, 457–469.

References

Akers, R. L. (1998). *Social learning and social structure: A general theory of crime and deviance*. Boston, MA: Northeastern University Press.

Andrews, D. A., & Bonta, J. (2010). *The psychology of criminal conduct* (5th ed.). New Providence, NJ: Matthew Bender.

Bandura, A. (1986). *Social foundations of thought and action*. Englewood Cliffs, NJ: Prentice Hall.

Bandura, A., Barbarnelli, C., Caprara, G. V., & Pastorelli, C. (1996). Mechanisms of moral disengagement in the exercise of moral agency. *Journal of Personality and Social Psychology*, 71, 364–374.

Beck, A. T. (1979). *Cognitive therapy and the emotional disorders*. New York, NY: Meridian.

Bureau of Justice Statistics (1994, September). *Fact sheet: Drug-related crime*. Washington, DC: US Department of Justice.

Chambers, J. C., Ward, T., Eccleston, L., & Brown, M. (2009). The pathways model of assault: A qualitative analysis of the assault offender and offense. *Journal of Interpersonal Violence*, 24, 1423–1449.

Cherbuin, N., Windsor, T. D., Anstey, K. J., Maller, J. J., Meslin, C., & Sachdeve, P. S. (2008). Hippocampal volume is positively associated with behavioural inhibition (BIS) in a large community-based sample of mid-life adults: The PATH through life study. *Social Cognitive and Affective Neuroscience*, 3, 262–269.

Chess, S., & Thomas, A. (1977). Temperamental individuality from childhood to adolescence. *Journal of Child Psychiatry*, 16, 218–226.

Cornish, D. B., & Clarke, R. V. (Eds.) (1986). *The reasoning criminal: Rational choice perspectives on offending*. New York, NY: Springer-Verlag.

Davis-Kean, P. E., Jager, J., & Collins, W. A. (2009). The self in action: An emerging link between self-beliefs and behaviors in middle childhood. *Child Development Perspectives*, 3, 184–188.

DeLisi, M., & Vaughn, M. G. (2014). Foundation for a temperament-based theory of antisocial behavior and criminal justice system involvement. *Journal of Criminal Justice*, 42, 10–25.

Dodge, K. A., & Coie, N. R. (1987). Social-information-processing factors in reactive and proactive aggression in children's peer groups. *Journal of Personality and Social Psychology*, 53, 1146–1158.

Ellis, A. (2007). *The practice of rational emotive behavior therapy* (2nd ed.). New York, NY: Springer.

Feeney, F. (1986). Robbers as decision makers. In D. Cornish, & R. Clarke (Eds.), *The reasoning criminal: Rational choice perspectives on offending* (pp. 53–71). New York, NY: Springer-Verlag.

Frick, P. J., Ray, J. V., Thornton, L. C., & Kahn, R. E. (2014). Can callous-unemotional traits enhance the understanding, diagnosis, and treatment of serious conduct problems in children and adolescents? A comprehensive review. *Psychological Bulletin*, 140, 1–57.

Gottfredson, M. R., & Hirschi, T. (1990). *A general theory of crime*. Stanford, CA: Stanford University Press.

Hare, R. D. (1996). Psychopathy: A clinical construct whose time has come. *Criminal Justice and Behavior*, 23, 25–54.

Higgins, G. E., Kirchner, E. E., Ricketts, M. L., & Marcum, C. D. (2013). Impulsivity and offending from childhood to young adulthood in the United States: A developmental trajectory analysis. *International Journal of Criminal Justice Sciences*, 8, 182–197.

Kagan, J. (2010). Emotions and temperament. In M. H. Burnstein (Ed.), *Handbook of cultural developmental science* (pp. 175–194). New York, NY: Psychology Press.

Krueger, R. F., Markon, K. E., Patrick, C. J., Benning, S. D., & Kramer, M. D. (2007). Linking antisocial behavior, substance use, and personality: An integrative quantitative model of the adult externalizing spectrum. *Journal of Abnormal Psychology*, 116, 645–666.

Loeber, R., Burke, J. D., Lahey, B. B., Winters, A., & Zera, M. (2000). Oppositional defiant and conduct disorder: A review of the past 10 years, part I. *Journal of the American Academy of Child & Adolescent Psychiatry*, 39, 1468–1484.

Lykken, D. T. (1957). A study of anxiety in the sociopathic personality. *Journal of Abnormal and Social Psychology*, 55, 6–10.

McCollister, K. E., French, M. T., Prendergast, M., Wexler, H., Sacks, S., & Hall, E. (2003). Is in-prison treatment enough? A cost-effectiveness analysis of prison-based treatment and aftercare services for substance abusing offenders. *Law and Policy*, 25, 62–83.

Mills, J. F., Kroner, D. G., & Forth, A. E. (2002). Measures of Criminal Attitudes and Associates (MCAA): Development, factor structure, reliability, and validity. *Assessment*, 9, 240–253.

Morrison, S. A., & O'Donnel, I. (1996). An analysis of the decision-making practices of armed robbers. In R. Homel (Ed.), *Crime prevention studies, volume 5. The politics and practice of situational crime prevention* (pp. 159–188). Monsey, NY: Criminal Justice Press.

Poulin, F., & Boivin, M. (2000). Reactive and proactive aggression: Evidence of a two-factor model. *Psychological Assessment*, 12, 115–122.

Prochaska, J. O., & DiClemente, C. C. (1992). Stages of change in the modification of problem behaviors. In M. Hersen, R. M. Eisler, & P. M. Miller (Eds.), *Progress in behavior modification* (pp. 184–214). Sycamore, IL: Sycamore.

Reeve, R. (1994). The academic impact of ADD. *Attention*, 1, 8–12.

Sampson, R. J., & Laub, J. H. (1993). *Crime in the making*. Cambridge, MA: Harvard University Press.

Shechner, T., Hong, M., Britton, J. C., Pine, D. S., & Fox, N. A. (2014). Fear conditioning and extinction across development: Evidence from human studies and animal models. *Biological Psychology*, 100, 1–12.

Simourd, D. J. (1997). The Criminal Sentiments Scale–Modified and Pride in Delinquency Scale: Psychometric properties and construct validity of two measures of criminal attitudes. *Criminal Justice and Behavior*, 24, 52–70.

Stocker, C., & Dunn, J. (1990). Sibling relationships in adolescence: Links with friendships and peer relationships. *British Journal of Developmental Psychology*, 8, 227–244.

Sutherland, E. H. (1947). *Principles of criminology* (4th ed.). Philadelphia, PA: J. B. Lippincott.

Sykes, G. M., & Matza, D. (1957). Techniques of neutralization: A theory of delinquency. *American Sociological Review*, 22, 664–670.

Tice, D. M. (1992). Self-concept change and self-presentation: The looking glass self is also a magnifying glass. *Journal of Personality and Social Psychology*, 63, 435–451.

Walsh, A., & Ellis, L. (2007). *Criminology: An interdisciplinary approach*. Thousand Oaks, CA: Sage.

Walters, G. D. (1990). *The criminal lifestyle: Patterns of serious criminal conduct*. Newbury Park, CA: Sage.

Walters, G. D. (1995). The Psychological Inventory of Criminal Thinking Styles: Part I. Reliability and preliminary validity. *Criminal Justice and Behavior*, 22, 307–325.

Walters, G. D. (2001). The shaman effect in counseling clients with alcohol problems. *Alcoholism Treatment Quarterly*, 19(3), 31–43.

Walters, G. D. (2004). Changes in positive and negative crime expectancies in inmates exposed to a brief psychoeducational intervention: Further data. *Personality and Individual Differenes*, 37, 505–512.

Walters, G. D. (2007a). Measuring proactive and reactive criminal thinking with the PICTS: Correlations with outcome expectancies and hostile attribution biases. *Journal of Interpersonal Violence*, 22, 371–385.

Walters, G. D. (2007b). Response style versus crime-specific cognition: Predicting disciplinary adjustment and recidivism in male and female offenders with the PICTS. *Assessment*, 14, 35–43.

Walters, G. D. (2009a). Anger management training in incarcerated male offenders: Differential impact on proactive and reactive criminal thinking. *International Journal of Forensic Mental Health*, 8, 214–217.

Walters, G. D. (2009b). Latent structure of a two-dimensional model of antisocial personality disorder: Construct validation and taxometric analysis. *Journal of Personality Disorders*, 23, 647–660.

Walters, G. D. (2012a). *Crime in a psychological context: From career criminals to criminal careers*. Thousand Oaks, CA: Sage.

Walters, G. D. (2012b). Substance abuse and criminal thinking: Testing the countervailing, mediation, and specificity hypotheses. *Law and Human Behavior*, 36, 506–512.

Walters, G. D. (2014a). Pathways to early delinquency: Exploring the individual and collective contributions of difficult temperament, low maternal involvement, and externalizing behavior. *Journal of Criminal Justice*, 42, 321–326.

Walters, G. D. (2014b). Crime and substance misuse in adjudicated delinquent youth: The worst of both worlds. *Law and Human Behavior*, 38, 139–150.

Walters, G. D. (2015a). Early childhood temperament, maternal monitoring, reactive criminal thinking, and the origin(s) of low self-control. *Journal of Criminal Justice*, 43, 369–376.

Walters, G. D. (2015b). Cognitive mediation of crime continuity: A causal mediation analysis of the past crime–future crime relationship. *Crime and Delinquency*, 61, 1234–1256.

Walters, G. D. (2015c). Proactive criminal thinking and the transmission of differential association: A cross-lagged multi-wave path analysis. *Criminal Justice and Behavior*, 42, 1128–1144.

Walters, G. D. (2015d). Short-term goals and physically hedonistic values as mediators of the past crime–future crime relationship. *Legal and Criminological Psychology*, 20, 81–95.

Walters, G. D. (2015e). Criminal and substance involvement from adolescence to adulthood: Precursors, mediators, and long-term effects. *Justice Quarterly*, 32, 729–747.

Walters, G. D. (2015f). Recidivism and the "worst of both worlds" hypothesis: Do substance misuse and crime interact or accumulate? *Criminal Justice and Behavior*, 42, 435–451.

Walters, G. D. (2015g). The decision to commit crime: Rational or nonrational? *Criminology, Criminal Justice, Law & Society*, 16(3), 1–18.

Walters, G. D. (2016a). Friends, cognition, and delinquency: Proactive and reactive criminal thinking as mediators of the peer influence and peer selection effects among male delinquents. *Justice Quarterly*, 33, 1055–1079.

Walters, G. D. (2016b). Crime continuity and psychological inertia: Testing the cognitive mediation and additive postulates with male adjudicated delinquents. *Journal of Quantitative Criminology*, 32, 237–252.

Walters, G. D. (2016c). Mediating the distal drug-crime relationship with proximal reactive criminal thinking. *Psychology of Addictive Behaviors*, 30, 128–137.

Walters, G. D., & DeLisi, M. (2015). Psychopathy and violence: Does antisocial cognition mediate the relationship between the PCL: YV factor scores and violent offending? *Law and Human Behavior*, 39, 350–359.

Walters, G. D., Hagman, B. T., & Cohn, A. M. (2011). Towards a hierarchical model of criminal thinking: Evidence from item response theory and confirmatory factor analysis. *Psychological Assessment*, 23, 925–936.

Walters, G. D., & Kiehl, K. A. (2015). Limbic correlates of fearlessness and disinhibition in incarcerated youth: Exploring the brain-behavior relationship with the Psychopathy Checklist: Youth Version. *Psychiatry Research*, 230, 205–210.

Walters, G. D., & McCoy, K. (2007). Taxometric analysis of the Psychological Inventory of Criminal Thinking Styles in incarcerated offenders and college students. *Criminal Justice and Behavior*, 34, 781–793.

Weinberger, D. A., & Schwartz, G. E. (1990). Distress and restraint as superordinate dimensions of self-reported adjustment: A typological perspective. *Journal of Personality*, 58, 381–417.

Woodworth, M., & Porter, S. (2002). In cold blood: Characteristics of criminal homicides as a function of psychopathy. *Journal of Abnormal Psychology*, 111, 436–445.

Zuckerman, M. (1996). The psychobiological model for impulsive unsocialized sensation seeking: A comparative approach. *Neuropsychobiology*, 34, 125–129.

41

Schema Therapy in Forensic Settings

David P. Bernstein and Maartje Clercx
Maastricht University, the Netherlands

Marije Keulen-De Vos
Forensic Psychiatric Center de Rooyse Wissel, the Netherlands

Schema therapy (ST) is an integrative therapy for individuals with personality disorders (PD) that combines cognitive, behavioral, psychodynamic object relations, and humanistic/experiential approaches. It is one of the few evidence-based treatments for borderline PD (Farrell, Shaw, & Webber, 2009; Giesen-Bloo et al., 2006; Nadort et al., 2009) and for Cluster C PDs (Bamelis, Evers, Spinhoven, & Arntz, 2014; Gude, Monsen, & Hoffart, 2001). Given the scarcity of evidence-based treatments for forensic patients with PDs, Bernstein and colleagues (Bernstein, Arntz, & Vos, 2007) adapted ST for forensic populations, especially those with antisocial, narcissistic, borderline, or paranoid PDs, which are the PDs most associated with recidivism risk in forensic settings. The forensic adaptation of ST focuses on modifying the repetitive, self-defeating patterns (*early maladaptive schemas*) and emotional states (*schema modes*) that are prevalent in this population—such as states involving anger, impulsivity, aggression, superiority, deceit, and manipulation—and fostering healthy states involving self-reflection, self-regulation, and forming emotional connections with other people. This model also extends to treating psychopathic patients, who have traditionally been considered difficult, if not impossible, to treat (D'Silva, Duggan, & McCarthy, 2004). In 2007, Bernstein and colleagues initiated a 3-year, multicenter randomized controlled trial (RCT) to test the effectiveness of ST compared to treatment-as-usual (TAU) for forensic patients with PDs in seven hospitals (TBS [Ter Beschikking Stellig, treatment on behalf of the state] clinics) in the Netherlands (Bernstein et al., 2012). The study, which was recently completed, provides strong support for the effectiveness of ST with forensic PD patients (see Empirical Support, below). On the basis of these findings, *Erkenningscommissie* ("Recognition Commission") of the Netherlands has officially recognized ST as the first evidence-based treatment for forensic patients with PD (Erkenningscomissie Gedragsinterventies Justitie, 2015). In this chapter we describe the theory and practice of ST in forensic settings, drawing primarily on work conducted with forensic mental health patients. However, the approach also appears to hold promise as a treatment for more general correctional populations, including prisoners and those who are required to attend programs to address their offending behavior.

Clinical studies and meta-analyses indicate that PDs are highly prevalent in correctional settings. PDs are about three times more prevalent among male offenders than in the general

---

The Wiley International Handbook of Correctional Psychology, First Edition. Edited by Devon L. L. Polaschek, Andrew Day, and Clive R. Hollin.
© 2019 John Wiley & Sons Ltd. Published 2019 by John Wiley & Sons Ltd.

population (Rotter, Way, Steinbacher, Sawyer, & Smith, 2002), and prevalence may be as high as 65% of all prisoners (Fazel & Danesh, 2002). In females, the prevalence is slightly lower, with 43% of a female correctional population meeting criteria for at least one PD (Tye & Mullen, 2006), but still much higher than in the general population. PD diagnoses are highly relevant to criminal behavior. Offenders with a PD diagnosis commit more violent and serious crimes (Blackburn, Logan, Donelly, & Renwick, 2003), and show higher recidivism rates, compared to non-PD offenders (Hart, Webster, & Menzies, 1993).

Although treatment is increasingly used to address aggression and recidivism in offender populations, most are based on cognitive behavioral therapy (CBT) and only have modest effects (Ross, Quayle, Newman, & Tansey, 2013; Wong, Gordon, Gu, Lewis, & Olver, 2012). CBT tends to focus on controlling aggressive behavior (Timmerman & Emmelkamp, 2005), but usually does not address symptoms and characteristics associated with PDs. Moreover, offenders with severe PDs, especially criminal psychopaths, are usually considered difficult, if not impossible, to treat (Harris, Rice, & Cormier, 1991), despite the lack of methodologically sound RCTs to test this hypothesis (D'Silva et al., 2004).

Schema Therapy Theory

The theoretical base of ST stems from cognitive, behavioral, psychodynamic, and experiential traditions (Young, Klosko, & Weishaar, 2003). Originally, ST consisted of two concepts: early maladaptive schemas and coping responses. Early maladaptive schemas refer to dysfunctional themes or patterns concerning the self and one's relationships with others, which originate from adverse childhood experiences and the child's own innate temperament. Early maladaptive schemas are linked to unfulfilled or frustrated basic emotional needs that are present in all children: the need for attachment, autonomy, expression of emotions, spontaneity and play, and limit setting. What is important to notice for the purposes of both assessment and treatment is that early maladaptive schemas keep recurring over the course of the person's life: they are self-defeating and self-perpetuating. Maladaptive coping responses reflect three ways in which people behave when early maladaptive schemas are activated. First, they can give in to the schema (surrender); second, they can avoid situations that activate schemas (avoidance); and third, they can do the opposite of the schema (overcompensation; Young et al., 2003).

The concept of schema modes was introduced later because the standard model emphasizing schemas and coping response was of limited effectiveness in treating patients who presented with severe PDs such as borderline, narcissistic, and antisocial PD. Schema modes represent fluctuating states that dominate a person's emotions, cognitions, and behavior. The schema mode is determined by the early maladaptive schema that is activated, the emotional response that is elicited, and the coping response in reaction to the emotion. Typically, four schema mode domains can be distinguished: (a) child modes, which refer to emotional responses that are nearly universal in children, such as fear, sadness, shame, anger, and impulsivity; (b) dysfunctional parent modes, which refer to internalized harsh parental demands or punitive criticism; (c) maladaptive coping modes, which refer to extreme attempts to cope with the activation of schemas, either through surrender, avoidance, or overcompensation; and (d) healthy modes, which reflect healthy self-reflection and feelings of joy and pleasure. Young et al. (2003) hypothesized that patients with certain PDs are characterized by specific patterns of schema modes. Borderline PD, for example, typically consists of five modes: the *Abused and Abandoned* child mode, which encompasses feelings such as fear, helpless, and desperate longing, which are often seen in individuals who experienced abuse or abandonment; the *Impulsive Child* mode in which someone acts on desires and impulses in an uncontrolled manner and with little regard to possible consequences; the *Angry Child* mode, which involves excessive and misplaced anger; the *Punitive Parent* mode, which involves harsh self-criticism and rejection; and the *Detached Protector* mode, which involves feelings of emotional numbness and detachment.

Forensic Theory

Certain emotional states, such as those involving deceit, ruthlessness, and aggression, are very prevalent in offenders but seldom seen in general psychiatric patients. Bernstein and colleagues (Bernstein et al., 2007; Keulen-De Vos, Bernstein, & Arntz, 2014) therefore extended the schema mode model to encompass the emotional states that are often seen in forensic patients. In particular, they observed that these patients often used five modes which involve overcompensation as a coping response. The *Self-Aggrandizer* mode involves dominance, arrogance, and superiority. The *Conning and Manipulative* mode involves deceiving, lying, and manipulation. The *Paranoid Overcontroller* mode involves hypervigilance for threats. The *Bully and Attack* mode involves the use of threats, intimidation, or aggression. The *Predator* mode involves cold, instrumental aggression to eliminate a real or perceived obstacle, threat, or rival. Recent research supports the idea that different patterns of modes are associated with different PDs (Bamelis, Renner, Heidkamp, & Arntz, 2011), that modes are triggered by external stimuli and have both cognitive and physiological correlates (Lobbestael & Arntz, 2010), and that they play a role in criminal and violent behavior (see Empirical Support). Table 41.1 provides an overview of all schema modes and their corresponding domains.

In the forensic ST model, criminal and violent behavior is understood in terms of an unfolding sequence of schema modes (Bernstein et al., 2007; Keulen-De Vos et al., 2014). The events leading up to the crime are often initiated by child modes, for example, situations in which someone feels abandoned, humiliated, lonely, or angry, or acts on his or her impulses. These child modes lead to an escalating sequence of modes, which usually culminate in overcompensatory modes, which occur during the commission of antisocial behavior. For example, a patient's partner refuses to have sex with him or her, leaving the patient feeling inferior (Humiliated Child mode), frustrated (Impulsive Child mode), and angry (Angry Child mode). To cope with these feelings, the patient overcompensates, switching to a Self-Aggrandizer mode in which feelings of sexual arousal and power dominate. The patient walks the streets, searching for a victim (Predator mode). The patient randomly knocks on the doors of houses, until a woman answers. The patient then proceeds to talking his/her way into the house (Conning and Manipulator mode) and violently forces the woman onto the ground and threatens to kills her if she does not cooperate (Bully and Attack mode).

The forensic ST model also provides a framework to understand and treat criminal and violent behavior (Figure 41.1). In this model (Bernstein & Nentjes, 2015) maladaptive schema modes are considered the internal, or psychological, risk factors that increase the likelihood of antisocial behavior, while healthy modes are considered internal protective factors that decrease its likelihood. Schema modes are elicited by the activation of early maladaptive schemas and maladaptive coping responses, which themselves developed in childhood due to the influence of risk factors (e.g., genetic predisposition, childhood abuse, neglect, abandonment, exposure to family or community violence) and protective factors (e.g., genetic predisposition, supportive families and communities, economic opportunities). The likelihood of criminal and

Table 41.1 Schema Modes and Corresponding Domains

Child modes	
Vulnerable Child (Humiliated, Abandoned, and Abused Child)	Feels vulnerable and overwhelmed by painful feelings of fear, depression, sadness, or shame/humiliation.
Impulsive/ Undisciplined Child	Acts like a spoiled child who "gets what she or he wants, when she or he wants it," and cannot accept the frustration of boundaries.
Angry Child	Feels and expresses uncontrollable anger in reaction to real or perceived abuse, abandonment, humiliation, or frustration; often feels treated unjustly; reacts like a child having a temper tantrum.
Lonely Child	Feels alone and empty because no one understands him, comforts him, or reaches out to him.
Avoidant and surrendering coping modes	
Detached Protector	Uses emotional detachment to protect himself against painful feelings; is unaware of his feelings and feels "nothing," seems emotionally distant, subdued or robot-like; avoids closeness to others.
Detached Self-Soother/ Detached Self-Stimulator	Repeatedly uses "addictive" or compulsive behaviors or self-stimulating behavior to calm or soothe the self; uses pleasant or exiting sensations to distance himself from painful feelings.
Complaining Protector	Complains, whines, and places demands in an unsatisfied victim-like manner; expresses dissatisfaction unsympathetically in a manner that hides his real feelings and needs.
Angry Protector	Uses a "wall of anger" to protect himself against others, who are experienced as a threat; keeps others at a safe distance by expressing large amounts of anger; anger is more controlled compared to the Angry Child mode.
Compliant Surrenderer	Readily gives in to real or suspected needs and demands of others who are experienced as more powerful in a fearful attempt to avoid pain and sadness.
Parent modes	
Punitive Parent	Internalized punishing, critical, or harsh parental voices; points strong criticism toward himself; creates feelings of guilt or shame.
Demanding Parent	Sets impossibly high standards and is never satisfied; pushes himself to do and accomplish more and more.
Overcompensatory coping modes	
Self-Aggrandizer	Feels superior, special, or powerful; looks down on others; sees the world in terms of winners and losers and constantly tries to show off. This expresses itself in magnifying behaviors which confirm his own importance; is more concerned with appearances than with feelings or real connections with others.
Conning and Manipulative	Cheats, lies, or manipulates to achieve a specific goal, which can either entail victimizing others or avoiding punishment.
Overcontroller (Obsessive-Compulsive or Paranoid)	Tries to protect himself against real or perceived threat by obsessively checking attention, behaviors, and thoughts. The Obsessive-Compulsive subtype uses order, repetition, or rituals. The Paranoid subtype tries to discover (perceived) hidden threats.

(Continued)

Table 41.1   (*Continued*)

Bully and Attack	Uses threat, intimidation, aggression, and force to get what he wants, which includes revenge on others, and maintenance of dominance; experiences sadistic pleasure from attacking others.
Predator	Eliminates threat, rivals, obstacles, or enemies in a cold, ruthless, and calculating manner.
	Healthy modes
Healthy Adult	Thinks about himself in a balanced, realistic manner. Is aware of his own needs and feelings; realistically evaluates situations and thinks about how he can fulfill his needs in a productive, appropriate, and well-adapted manner.
Happy Child	Acts playful, free, and spontaneous; enjoys having fun and sincerely enjoys people and activities; is open about expressing his happy feelings.

violent behavior at a particular moment is determined by the relative activation of maladaptive and healthy modes. The greater the activation of maladaptive modes, relative to healthy modes, the greater the risk for antisocial behavior becomes. External risk factors in the patient's current environment, such as exposure to antisocial peers, lack of employment opportunities, and discrimination, and external protective factors, such as current social support, interact reciprocally with schema modes. They can influence schema modes, or be influenced by them. For example, exposure to antisocial peers may increase the strength of maladaptive modes, while the presence of maladaptive modes may increase the likelihood that one will seek out antisocial peer groups. These external risk and protective factors can therefore operate on antisocial behavior via their influence on schema modes (i.e., indirect, or mediating factors) or by other mechanisms.

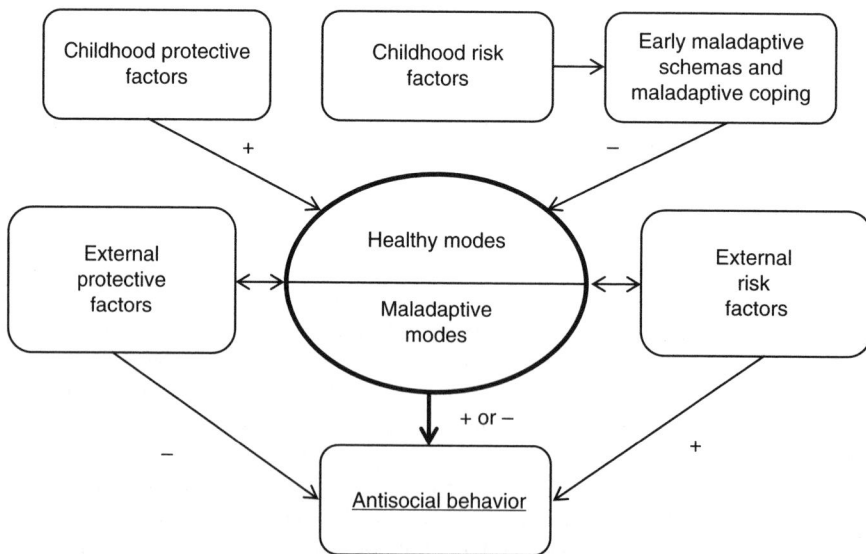

Figure 41.1   Explanatory ST model for criminal and violent behavior. Adapted from Bernstein and Nentjes (2015). *Note.* +: increases risk of antisocial behavior; –: decreases risk of antisocial behavior.

ST Practice

ST Phases of Treatment

ST consists of two broad phases. In the assessment and case conceptualization phase, the therapist uses the concepts of early maladaptive schemas, coping responses, and schema modes to form an understanding of the patient's maladaptive behavior and its origins. During this phase, the therapist also provides psychoeducation, teaching the patient about ST concepts, and helping him or her to apply them to him- or herself. The therapist teaches the patient the "language" of ST, so that the patient can discuss problematic situations that occur inside and outside the therapy sessions in a non-judgmental, accepting way. In the schema change phase, the therapist uses a variety of techniques to reduce the strength of early maladaptive schemas, maladaptive coping responses, and schema modes, with the goal of breaking dysfunctional behavior patterns and initiating healthier forms of coping, so that the patient can get his or her emotional needs met in more productive ways.

ST Techniques

ST utilizes a number of techniques to change early maladaptive schemas, maladaptive coping responses, and schema modes. These techniques are summarized in Table 41.2.

In ST for patients who present with less severe personality disorders, cognitive techniques are often used in the early stage of the therapy to help achieve more intellectual distance from early maladaptive schemas. The patient is able to recognize that she or he has schemas, and that when they are triggered, they distort perceptions of people and situations. Nevertheless, this intellectual distance usually isn't sufficient, as she or he is still liable to become emotionally distressed when the schemas are triggered. ST then turns to emotion-focused, experiential techniques to reprocess the emotional components of schemas. For example, in role-playing techniques, patients can learn to "talk back" to their schemas, counteracting their negative messages. Imagery re-scripting is a powerful experiential

Table 41.2 Schema Therapy Techniques

Limited re-parenting—Providing for some of the patient's unmet or frustrated basic emotional needs, through the therapy relationship.

Empathic confrontation—Confronting the patient in a compassionate way about his maladaptive patterns, as observed both within and outside of the therapy sessions.

Here and now therapy relationship—Carrying out interventions in the "here and now" interactions between the therapist and patient (e.g., empathically confronting a patient about his behavior toward the therapist).

Cognitive techniques—Challenging distorted beliefs (e.g., early maladaptive schemas) through thought records, schema dialogues, schema flash cards, and other exercises.

Experiential techniques—Reprocessing the emotional components of early maladaptive schemas and schema modes through exercises such as role-playing and imagery re-scripting.

Behavioral techniques—Modifying maladaptive behaviors by practicing healthier alternative behaviors both inside and outside of therapy sessions.

Schema mode work—Combining any of the above techniques with an emphasis on schema modes, for example, by using schema mode "language" in carrying out the interventions (e.g., "I see a side of you right now that …").

---

technique, where patients reprocess painful experiences from the past that are triggered by current situations. The patient is asked to close his or her eyes, and vividly re-imagine a current, troubling situation. The therapist then asks the patient to let go of the image of the current situation, but hold on to the emotion associated with it, and allow a situation from childhood to come to mind that felt the same way. The therapist "re-scripts" the childhood situation, altering aversive elements to meet some of the child's basic needs (e.g., warmth, protection, attention). Reprocessing painful childhood memories in this way often leads to decrease in schematic activation, including the emotional components of schemas. Cognitive and emotion-focused techniques lay the groundwork for the introduction of behavioral techniques, which focus on breaking maladaptive behavior patterns. For example, the therapist can have the patient practice new, healthier behaviors through role-playing exercises during sessions, and give behavioral homework assignments between sessions (e.g., facing feared situations).

Adaptation of ST for Forensic Patients

A number of important modifications of ST are needed when working with more severe PD patients, such as those with antisocial, narcissistic, or borderline PD, who are frequently seen in forensic settings (Leue, Borchard, & Hoyer, 2004; De Ruiter & Trestman, 2007). First, we emphasize schema modes, rather than early maladaptive schemas, in our work with forensic patients. Because most forensic patients are unable or unwilling to expose their emotional vulnerability, it is often difficult, particularly early in the therapy, to discuss early maladaptive schemas with the patients. On the other hand, most of them can recognize their schema modes, which are more easily observed in overt behavior. For example, we use the term, "a side of you" or "a part of you" to talk about the patient's tendency to be detached ("the side of you that avoids feelings"), mistrustful ("the side of you that is alert"), or self-aggrandizing ("the side of you that puts yourself above other people"). Second, considerable time and attention needs to be invested in slowly building an emotional bond between therapist and patient. As treatment in forensic mental health settings is usually court mandated, patients often lack motivation for treatment. Also, interpersonal difficulties are common within offender populations, with offenders having higher levels of hostility, self-centeredness, and self-defeating behavior (Ross, Polaschek, & Ward, 2008). These interpersonal difficulties, and the fact that many offenders grew up in insecure environments (e.g., Bohle & de Vogel, 2017) causing insecure attachment (Timmerman & Emmelkamp, 2006; Van IJzendoorn et al., 1997), can obstruct the therapeutic alliance or cause ruptures in the therapeutic bond (Watson, Thomas, & Daffern, 2015). In less severe cases, the patient accepts the therapist's provision of limited re-parenting at face value. She or he experiences it as the therapist's providing something that is needed and was missed out on as a child. Forensic patients, on the other hand, often react with suspicion to the therapist's attempts to form a bond. They keep their guard up, using a variety of modes to keep the therapist at a distance: a *Detached Protector* mode that avoids emotional contact; a *Self-Aggrandizer* mode that devalues the therapist; a *Bully and Attack* mode that keeps the therapist on the defensive; and so forth. The therapist persists in focusing on the patient's unmet emotional needs, and uses schema mode work to empathically confront the modes that are blocking therapeutic progress. The goal of these interventions is to switch, or "flip," the patient from maladaptive modes into ones that are more therapeutically productive: the *Healthy Adult* mode, where the patient can self-reflect and initiate healthier forms of coping, and modes involving painful emotions such as shame, fear, loneliness, or abandonment. The therapist's task isn't easy—it often takes a year or more before more severe patients are beginning to lower their guard, and share their emotional sides more easily. In forensic outpatient settings, where patients often have less severe PD pathology, and in some forensic youth settings, forming a therapeutic bond may occur more quickly, and ST can be implemented over shorter periods of time, with treatment typically lasting from 1 to 2 years.

Although forensic patients are often described as unmotivated (Howells & Day, 2007; Sainsbury, Krishnan, & Evans, 2004), research supports the idea that motivation for treatment is a dynamic, rather than a static, process (Drieschner, Lammers, & Van Der Staak, 2004; Martens, 2000). In ST, we view the patient's fluctuating motivation in terms of the schema modes that block therapeutic progress—for example, a *Detached Protector* mode that blocks feelings; a *Self-Aggrandizer* mode that attempts to dominate and denigrate the therapist; or a *Paranoid Overcontroller* mode that is alert for signs of the therapist's untrustworthiness. There will always be a struggle between the patient's need to preserve his or her dysfunctional modes, which feel safe and familiar, and his or her healthy side, which sees their disadvantages. Similar to motivational interviewing (Hettema, Steele, & Miller, 2005; Miller & Rollnick, 2012), the therapist avoids getting into a struggle with the patient, and instead explores the advantages and disadvantages of the modes, helping the patient to weigh them for him- or herself. The therapist continually monitors the patient's motivation, which can fluctuate throughout the course of treatment, and uses mode work whenever necessary to enhance it.

We view patients' crime scenarios as involving an unfolding sequence of schema modes, often triggered by vulnerable emotions, impulsivity, or anger; usually followed by the use of substances to either soothe painful emotions or reduce inhibitions to criminal behavior; and culminating in criminal or violent acts which often involve over-compensatory coping, feelings of power or aggression to compensate for feelings of helplessness, frustration, or humiliation. We help patients to understand these patterns using a modification of the familiar antecedents-behaviors-consequences (ABC) model of behavioral analysis (Carr et al., 1994). Situations (antecedents) trigger schema modes, which involve clusters of cognitions, emotions, and coping responses (i.e., behaviors), and which in turn lead to certain consequences. For example, a patient whose girlfriend leaves him might first experience painful feelings of abandonment (*Abandoned Child* mode), which lead to drug or alcohol use as an attempt at self-soothing (*Detached Self-Soother* mode). These intoxicated states disinhibit impulses and anger (*Impulsive* and *Angry Child* modes), leading to over-compensatory attempts at coping, for example, by stalking, threatening, and attacking his victim (*Bully and Attack* mode). In these overcompensatory states, the patient no longer feels helpless and abandoned; instead, she or he feels powerful and in control.

Because some forensic patients are emotionally detached (Timmerman & Emmelkamp, 2006), activating their emotions so that they can be reprocessed is of critical importance. In the structured circumstances of forensic settings, patients who use avoidant coping strategies, such as detaching from emotions, are often mistakenly viewed as healthy. For example, they may be able to avoid getting into conflicts with other patients or staff by spending their time in isolated activities, and avoiding people and situations that might trigger them. However, while these strategies have some adaptive aspects, they typically have an all-or-nothing quality; when unable to avoid, these patients can often act out explosively. In forensic ST, the therapist uses experiential techniques to evoke and reprocess the patient's early maladaptive schemas—themes such as abandonment, emotional deprivation, mistrust, shame, and social isolation, that, when triggered, lead to criminality or violence. By decreasing the severity of these schemas, the risk for future crime and violence is diminished.

In the early phase of forensic ST (first year, roughly, in hospitalized forensic patients), the goals of therapy are to assess and conceptualize patients' self-defeating patterns, including criminal and violent behavior, in terms of early maladaptive schemas and schema modes; to educate patients about their schema modes; to enhance their motivation using schema mode work; and to use limited re-parenting to slowly build up the therapeutic relationship. In the middle phase (roughly the second year), the emphasis shifts to using experiential techniques and working within the safety of the therapeutic relationship to reprocess patients' early maladaptive schemas and schema modes. In this phase, cognitive techniques, such as the ABC method (Carr et al., 1994), are also used to help the patient recognize the patterns that lead to criminal and violent behavior. In the final phase (roughly the third year), the emphasis is placed on initiating and maintaining behavioral changes and beginning the process of reintegrating into the community. Techniques like role-playing and behavioral homework assignments are used to practice healthy forms of coping. When patients are triggered in new situations, for example, at work or at home outside of the hospital, these situations are analyzed to deepen the patient's understanding of his or her schemas and modes, and experiential techniques are used to further reprocess his or her emotional triggers. Ultimately, the goal of forensic ST is to reduce the early maladaptive schemas and maladaptive schema modes that represent psychological risk factors for crime and violence, and to build up the patient's healthy schema modes, which represent protective factors.

Empirical Support

There is a considerable body of evidence validating the ST theoretical model in non-forensic populations, including the concepts of early maladaptive schemas and schema modes (Jovev & Jackson, 2004; Lobbestael, Arntz, & Sieswerda, 2005; Lobbestael, Van Vreeswijk, & Arntz, 2008; Nordahl, Holthe, & Haugum, 2005), and supporting the effectiveness of ST in (non-forensic) patients with borderline PD and Cluster C PDs (Bamelis et al., 2014; Giesen-Bloo et al., 2006; Gude et al., 2001; Nadort et al., 2009). More recently, this work has been extended to the forensic field. Chakhssi and colleagues (Chakhssi, Bernstein, & Ruiter, 2014) examined the association of early maladaptive schemas with facets of psychopathy. Personality-disordered offenders (N = 124) were assessed with the Psychopathy Checklist—Revised (PCL-R; Hare & Vertommen, 1991) and the Young Schema Questionnaire (YSQ; Young, 1998). Results showed that the antisocial and lifestyle facets of the PCL-R were significantly related to particular schemas, such as mistrust/abuse and insufficient self-control. Early maladaptive schemas were not related to the affective and interpersonal facets of the PCL-R. A second study (Chakhssi, Ruiter, & Bernstein, 2013) examined the explanatory value of schemas in 23 child sex offenders, 19 sex offenders against adults, and 24 non-sexual violent offenders who were assessed with the PCL-R and YSQ (Hare & Vertommen, 1991; Young, 1998). Results showed that early maladaptive schemas related to abandonment, social isolation, subjugation, shame, and self-sacrifice were more prevalent in child sex offenders compared to non-sexual offenders. Moreover, sex offenders who typically victimized children scored higher on the social isolation schema, compared to sex offenders who typically victimized adults (Chakhssi et al., 2013).

Keulen-De Vos and colleagues (2016) investigated the relationship between schema modes and offense patterns by examining criminal records of 95 offenders with Cluster B personality disorders, including psychopathy. Results showed that (a) criminal behavior was usually preceded by modes involving emotional vulnerability (vulnerable child mode) and loneliness (lonely child mode), as well as states of intoxication (detached self-soother mode); (b) followed by an escalating pattern of anger and impulsivity (angry and impulsive child mode), that is, these modes were present in the events leading up to the crime and increased over time during the crime itself; and (c) criminal behavior was characterized by overcompensatory modes, such as instrumental aggression (Predator mode) and intimidation (Bully and Attack mode), and an absence of emotional vulnerability. Furthermore, schema modes were predictive of institutional transgressions and were associated with facets of psychopathy on the PCL-R (Keulen-De Vos et al., 2016).

A recently completed RCT examined the effectiveness of ST in seven forensic hospitals in the Netherlands (Bernstein, 2016). Male patients (N = 103) with antisocial, borderline, narcissistic, or paranoid PD, or Cluster B PD not otherwise specified (PDNOS; American Psychiatric Association, 2000) were randomly allocated to either 3-years of ST or TAU. Fifty four percent of the patients had significant levels of psychopathy (PCL-R ≥ 25) and 22% were highly psychopathic (PCL-R ≥ 30). Nearly all of the patients were sentenced to forensic treatment for (sexual or non-sexual) violent offenses. Patients were assessed at baseline and repeatedly at 6-month intervals over the course of 3 years, using measures that were not dependent on patients' self-reports for most variables. Results showed that ST patients had significantly superior outcomes compared to those receiving TAU on a broad range of variables, including lowering risks for recidivism and improving strengths and protective factors, improving PD symptoms, reducing early maladaptive schemas, and facilitating the process of reintegrating patients into the community (Bernstein, 2016). Interestingly, there were no differences between treatment conditions with regard to schema modes, which were significantly reduced in both ST and TAU patients. One interpretation of these findings is that ST and TAU both reduce maladaptive emotional states, and improve healthy states, in forensic patients, but through different mechanisms. While patients in both conditions learned healthier coping skills, resulting in improved emotional states, only in the ST patients was this change accompanied by changes in the distorted beliefs about self and others (i.e., early maladaptive schemas) that underlie these states. A 3-year post-treatment follow-up will examine whether ST patients show lower recidivism than patients in the TAU condition.

A recent 7-year case study examined the effectiveness of ST in a psychopathic patient (PCL-R total score = 28.4) who was sentenced to mandatory treatment in a forensic hospital because of a sexual offense. Chakhssi, Kersten, de Ruiter, and Bernstein (2014) report evidence of significant improvement in psychopathic traits, early maladaptive schemas, and risk-related outcomes (i.e., Behavioral Status [BEST]-Index; Reed, Woods, & Robinson, 2000; and HCR-20V2; Webster, Douglas, Eaves, & Hart, 1997) after 4 years of treatment. Improvement was maintained at 3-year follow-up (Chakhssi, Kersten, et al., 2014). Most impressively, the patient's PCL-R score, which was independently and blindly assessed 7 years after the start of treatment, reduced from 28.4 to 14, which is in the non-psychopathic range. At 3-year post-treatment follow-up, he was working, living with his girlfriend and their new baby, and had not recidivated.

Taken together, these findings provide strong support for the theoretical model on which ST is based, and also for the effectiveness of ST in forensic populations of PD patients, including some psychopathic ones.

Future Directions

Recent developments in forensic ST have focused on enhancing its effectiveness when delivered by a multidisciplinary team, such as teams involving psychotherapists, arts therapists, psychiatric nurses, and other professionals. For example, a study (Van den Broek, Keulen-De Vos, & Bernstein, 2011) investigated the integration of ST with arts therapies, such as drama, movement, art, and music therapy, in a pilot study of 10 forensic PD patients. Results found that patients in the ST condition (N = 6) showed significantly more vulnerable child modes in their arts therapy sessions and psychotherapy sessions, compared to patients receiving standard arts therapy and psychotherapy (TAU; N = 4), based on videotaped ratings of 40 randomly selected therapy sessions. These findings suggest that ST may be more effective than treatment as usual at accessing vulnerable emotions in forensic PD patients, when ST is delivered in both psychotherapy and arts therapy forms.

Other recent developments include training psychiatric nurses, prison guards, and other disciplines, which often have the most daily interactions with offenders in forensic settings, to deliver ST-like interventions to improve the climate on the treatment ward. Preliminary findings suggest that forensic personnel can learn to recognize schema modes in forensic patients, and use techniques like limited re-parenting, empathic confrontation, and limit setting to create a therapeutic climate that is warmer and more emotionally supportive, while also enforcing limits in a firm but non-punitive manner.

An important aspect of the implementation of ST on forensic wards is the recent introduction of the iModes cards (Bernstein, 2016), in which schema modes are represented visually in cartoon form—a format that is more congruent with the learning style and capacities of forensic patients and staff, which tend to be more visual and less verbal. A recent study found that college students and individuals who were self-referred via an organization for people with PDs, the Personality Disorders Awareness Network (PDAN; Grogan, 2011), could accurately identify the iModes images in terms of the schema modes that they represent (Clercx, Bernstein, Feddes, & Richter, 2016).

Finally, ST has also been offered to adolescent populations, such as youth with externalizing behavior disorders and emerging PDs. In a recent pilot study, Van Wijk-Herbrink (2016; Van Wijk-Herbrink, Broers, Roelofs, & Bernstein, 2017) and colleagues found that four adolescents in residential treatment with externalizing behavior and PDs showed significant improvement in their early maladaptive schemas and schema modes after a mean of 7 months of ST. An RCT is currently in progress to test the effectiveness of ST in this youth residential care population. These pilot findings hold the promise that ST can be delivered during a developmental period, adolescence, when PDs often first crystalize, preventing the development of more serious later antisocial behavior problems.

Conclusion

Schema therapy holds considerable potential for explaining criminal and violent behavior, and related PD pathology, and has received empirical support for its effectiveness in a major RCT in hospitalized male forensic PD patients. Future studies will shed further light on this promising treatment for offenders with personality disorders.

Key Readings

Bernstein, D. P., Arntz, A., & Vos, M. d. (2007). Schema focused therapy in forensic settings: Theoretical model and recommendations for best clinical practice. *International Journal of Forensic Mental Health*, 6(2), 169–183.

Bernstein, D. P., & Nentjes, L. (2015). *Schema therapy for forensic patients with personality disorders.* Utrecht, the Netherlands: Kwaliteit Forensische Zorg.

Keulen-De Vos, M., Bernstein, D. P., & Arntz, A. (2014). Schema therapy for aggressive offenders with personality disorders. In R. Tafrate, & D. Mitchell (Eds.), *Forensic CBT: A handbook for clinical practice* (pp. 66–83). Chichester, UK: Wiley Blackwell.

Young, J. E., Klosko, J. S., & Weishaar, M. E. (2003). *Schema therapy: A practitioner's guide.* New York, NY: Guilford Press.

References

American Psychiatric Association (2000). *Diagnostic and statistical manual of mental disorders DSM-IV-TR* (4th ed., text revision)). Washington, DC: Author.

Bamelis, L. L., Evers, S. M., Spinhoven, P., & Arntz, A. (2014). Results of a multicenter randomized controlled trial of the clinical effectiveness of schema therapy for personality disorders. *American Journal of Psychiatry*, 171(3), 305–322.

Bamelis, L. L., Renner, F., Heidkamp, D., & Arntz, A. (2011). Extended schema mode conceptualizations for specific personality disorders: An empirical study. *Journal of Personality Disorders*, 25(1), 41–58.

Bernstein, D. P. (2016, July 1). *The effectiveness of schema therapy in forensic practice.* International Society for Schema Therapy annual conference. Vienna, Austria. Keynote address.

Bernstein, D. P., Arntz, A., & Vos, M. d. (2007). Schema focused therapy in forensic settings: Theoretical model and recommendations for best clinical practice. *International Journal of Forensic Mental Health*, 6(2), 169–183.

Bernstein, D. P., & Nentjes, L. (2015). *Schema therapy for forensic patients with personality disorders.* Utrecht, the Netherlands: Kwaliteit Forensische Zorg.

Bernstein, D. P., Nijman, H. L., Karos, K., Keulen-de Vos, M., de Vogel, V., & Lucker, T. P. (2012). Schema therapy for forensic patients with personality disorders: Design and preliminary findings of a multicenter randomized clinical trial in the Netherlands. *International Journal of Forensic Mental Health*, 11(4), 312–324.

Blackburn, R., Logan, C., Donnelly, J., & Renwick, S. (2003). Personality disorders, psychopathy and other mental disorders: Co-morbidity among patients at English and Scottish high security hospitals. *The Journal of Forensic Psychiatry and Psychology*, 14(1), 111–137.

Bohle, A., & de Vogel, V. (2017). Gender differences in victimization and the relation to personality disorders: A multicenter study in forensic psychiatric patients. *Journal of Aggression, Maltreatment & Trauma*, 26, 411–429.

Carr, E. G., Levin, L., McConnachie, G., Carlson, J. I., Kemp, D. C., & Smith, C. E. (1994). *Communication-based intervention for problem behavior: A user's guide for producing positive change.* Baltimore, MD: Brookes.

Chakhssi, F., Bernstein, D. P., & Ruiter, C. (2014). Early maladaptive schemas in relation to facets of psychopathy and institutional violence in offenders with personality disorders. *Legal and Criminological Psychology*, 19(2), 356–372.

Chakhssi, F., Kersten, T., de Ruiter, C., & Bernstein, D. P. (2014). Treating the untreatable: A single case study of a psychopathic inpatient treated with schema therapy. *Psychotherapy (Chicago, Ill.)*, 51(3), 447–461.

Chakhssi, F., Ruiter, C., & Bernstein, D. P. (2013). Early maladaptive cognitive schemas in child sexual offenders compared with sexual offenders against adults and nonsexual violent offenders: An exploratory study. *The Journal of Sexual Medicine*, 10(9), 2201–2210.

Clercx, M., Bernstein, D. P., Feddes, L., & Richter, M. (2016). Content validity of the iModes in a normal and a subclinical sample. Manuscript in preparation.

De Ruiter, C., & Trestman, R. L. (2007). Prevalence and treatment of personality disorders in Dutch forensic mental health services. *Journal of the American Academy of Psychiatry and the Law*, 35(1), 92–97.

Drieschner, K. H., Lammers, S. M. M., & van der Staak, C. P. F. (2004). Treatment motivation: An attempt for clarification of an ambiguous concept. *Clinical Psychology Review*, 23(8), 1115–1137.

D'Silva, K., Duggan, C., & McCarthy, L. (2004). Does treatment really make psychopaths worse? A review of the evidence. *Journal of Personality Disorders*, 18(2), 163–177.

Erkenningscomissie Gedragsinterventies Justitie (2015). *Jaar- en eindverslag Erkenningscomissie Gedragsinterventies Justitie [Annual report of the Ministry of Justice's approval committee for behavioral interventions]*. The Hague, the Netherlands: Ministerie van Veiligheid en Justitie.

Farrell, J. M., Shaw, I. A., & Webber, M. A. (2009). A schema-focused approach to group psychotherapy for outpatients with borderline personality disorder: A randomized controlled trial. *Journal of Behavior Therapy and Experimental Psychiatry*, 40(2), 317–328.

Fazel, S., & Danesh, J. (2002). Serious mental disorder in 23 000 prisoners: A systematic review of 62 surveys. *The Lancet*, 359(9306), 545–550.

Giesen-Bloo, J., Van Dyck, R., Spinhoven, P., Van Tilburg, W., Dirksen, C., Van Asselt, T., ... & Arntz, A. (2006). Outpatient psychotherapy for borderline personality disorder: Randomized trial of schema-focused therapy vs transference-focused psychotherapy. *Archives of General Psychiatry*, 63(6), 649–658.

Grogan, F. (2011). Personality Disorders Awareness Network. http://www.pdan.org

Gude, T., Monsen, J. T., & Hoffart, A. (2001). Schemas, affect consciousness, and Cluster C personality pathology: A prospective one-year follow-up study of patients in a schema-focused short-term treatment program. *Psychotherapy Research*, 11(1), 85–98.

Hare, R. D., & Vertommen, H. (1991). *The Hare Psychopathy Checklist—Revised*. Multi-Health Systems.

Hart, S. D., Webster, C. D., & Menzies, R. J. (1993). A note portraying the accuracy of violence predictions. *Law and Human Behavior*, 17, 695–700.

Harris, G. T., Rice, M. E., & Cormier, C. A. (1991). Psychopathy and violent recidivism. *Law and Human Behavior*, 15(6), 625–637.

Hettema, J., Steele, J., & Miller, W. R. (2005). Motivational interviewing. *Annual Review of Clinical Psychology*, 1, 91–111.

Howells, K., & Day, A. (2007). Readiness for treatment in high risk offenders with personality disorders. *Psychology, Crime & Law*, 13(1), 47–56.

Jovev, M., & Jackson, H. J. (2004). Early maladaptive schemas in personality disordered individuals. *Journal of Personality Disorders*, 18(5), 467–478.

Keulen-De Vos, M., Bernstein, D. P., & Arntz, A. (2014). Schema therapy for aggressive offenders with personality disorders. In R. Tafrate, & D. Mitchell (Eds.), *Forensic CBT: A handbook for clinical practice* (pp. 66–83). Chichester, UK: Wiley Blackwell.

Keulen-De Vos, M. E., Bernstein, D. P., Vanstipelen, S., Vogel, V., Lucker, T. P. C., Slaats, M., ... & Arntz, A. (2016). Schema modes in criminal and violent behaviour of forensic Cluster B PD patients: A retrospective and prospective study. *Legal and Criminological Psychology*, 21, 56–76.

Leue, A., Borchard, B., & Hoyer, J. (2004). Mental disorders in a forensic sample of sexual offenders. *European Psychiatry*, 19(3), 123–130.

Lobbestael, J., & Arntz, A. (2010). Emotional, cognitive and physiological correlates of abuse-related stress in borderline and antisocial personality disorder. *Behaviour Research and Therapy*, 48(2), 116–124.

Lobbestael, J., Arntz, A., & Sieswerda, S. (2005). Schema modes and childhood abuse in borderline and antisocial personality disorders. *Journal of Behavior Therapy and Experimental Psychiatry*, 36(3), 240–253.

Lobbestael, J., Van Vreeswijk, M. F., & Arntz, A. (2008). An empirical test of schema mode conceptualizations in personality disorders. *Behavior Research and Therapy*, 46(7), 854–860.

Martens, W. (2000). *What shall we do with untreatable forensic psychiatric patients?* (Vol. 19). (pp. 389–395) Medicine and Law.

Miller, W. R., & Rollnick, S. (2012). *Motivational interviewing: Helping people change*. New York, NY: Guilford Press.

Nadort, M., Arntz, A., Smit, J. H., Giesen-Bloo, J., Eikelenboom, M., Spinhoven, P., ... & van Dyck, R. (2009). Implementation of outpatient schema therapy for borderline personality disorder with versus without crisis support by the therapist outside office hours: A randomized trial. *Behavior Research and Therapy*, 47(11), 961–973.

Nordahl, H. M., Holthe, H., & Haugum, J. A. (2005). Early maladaptive schemas in patients with or without personality disorders: Does schema modification predict symptomatic relief? *Clinical Psychology & Psychotherapy*, 12(2), 142–149.

Reed, V., Woods, P., & Robinson, D. (2000). *The Behavioural Status Index (BSI): A "life skills" assessment for selecting and monitoring therapy in mental health care*. Sheffield, UK: Psychometric Press.

Ross, E. C., Polaschek, D. L. L., & Ward, T. (2008). The therapeutic alliance: A theoretical revision for offender rehabilitation. *Aggression and Violent Behavior*, 13, 462–480.

Ross, J., Quayle, E., Newman, E., & Tansey, L. (2013). The impact of psychological therapies on violent behaviour in clinical and forensic settings: A systematic review. *Aggression and Violent Behavior*, 18(6), 761–773.

Rotter, M., Way, B., Steinbacher, M., Sawyer, D., & Smith, H. (2002). Personality disorders in prison: Aren't they all antisocial? *Psychiatric Quarterly*, 73(4), 337–349.

Sainsbury, L., Krishnan, G., & Evans, C. (2004). Motivating factors for male forensic patients with personality disorder. *Criminal Behavior and Mental Health*, 14, 29–38.

Timmerman, I. G., & Emmelkamp, P. M. (2005). The effects of cognitive-behavioral treatment for forensic inpatients. *International Journal of Offender Therapy and Comparative Criminology*, 49(5), 590–606.

Timmerman, I. G., & Emmelkamp, P. M. (2006). The relationship between attachment styles and Cluster B personality disorders in prisoners and forensic inpatients. *International Journal of Law and Psychiatry*, 29(1), 48–56.

Tye, C. S., & Mullen, P. E. (2006). Mental disorders in female prisoners. *Australian and New Zealand Journal of Psychiatry*, 40(3), 266–271.

Van den Broek, E., Keulen-De Vos, M., & Bernstein, D. P. (2011). Arts therapies and schema focused therapy: A pilot study. *The Arts in Psychotherapy*, 38(5), 325–332.

van IJzendoorn, M. H., Feldbrugge, J. T. T. M., Derks, F. C. H., de Ruiter, C., Verhagen, M. F. M., Philipse, M. W. G., ... & Riksen-Walraven, J. M. A. (1997). Attachment representations of personality disordered criminal offenders. *American Journal of Orthopsychiatry*, 67, 449–459.

Van Wijk-Herbrink, M. (2016). Weinig vertrouwen in volwassenen: Werk in uitvoering. [Lack of confidence in adults: A work in progress]. *Kind & Adolescent Praktijk*, 15(2), 41–43.

Van Wijk-Herbrink, M., Broers, N. J., Roelofs, J., & Bernstein, D. P. (2017). Schema therapy in adolescents with disruptive behavior disorders and personality pathology in residential care. *Journal of Forensic Mental Health*, 16(3), 261–279.

Watson, R., Thomas, S., & Daffern, M. (2015). The impact of interpersonal style on ruptures and repairs in the therapeutic alliance between offenders and therapists in sex offender treatment. *Sexual Abuse: A Journal of Research and Treatment*, 27, 1–20.

Webster, C. D., Douglas, K. S., Eaves, D., & Hart, S. D. (1997). *HCR-20: Assessing risk for violence (version 2)*. Burnaby, Canada: Simon Fraser University.

Wong, S. C., Gordon, A., Gu, D., Lewis, K., & Olver, M. E. (2012). The effectiveness of violence reduction treatment for psychopathic offenders: Empirical evidence and a treatment model. *International Journal of Forensic Mental Health*, 11(4), 336–349.

Young, J. E. (1998). The Young Schema Questionnaire: Short form. Retrieved from www.schematherapy.com

Young, J. E., Klosko, J. S., & Weishaar, M. E. (2003). *Schema therapy: A practitioner's guide*. New York, NY: Guilford Press.

42

New Developments in Interventions for Working With Offending Behavior

Lawrence Jones
Rampton High Secure Hospital, UK

Innovation in Correctional Intervention

In the 1990s there was a strong movement in the United Kingdom toward standardizing interventions to identify those strategies that were considered to be most likely to be effective. The impact of this was a significant reduction in the range of interventions available. While some of these standardized programs were probably ill thought through, there was at least discussion about what works best. This was an intervention culture that was more focused on individual practitioners developing what they considered to be the most defensible model of intervention. While this resulted in a healthy level of diversity, it was difficult to accumulate knowledge or to justify big differences in practice. In addition, there were variable levels of attention given to evaluating interventions effectively. Standardization led to the equivalent of a dominant paradigm, hegemony, or monopoly, and the plug was pulled on interventions that had not been through the accreditation process. This could be seen as a form of premature closure in thinking about intervention. The relative absence of evidence about many forms of intervention was not evidence of absence of efficacy; it was more evidence of the absence of a culture of evaluation.

More recently, the mixed results of interventions based on meta-analytic summaries of "what works" (e.g., Hanson et al., 2002, for interventions with sex offenders) have encouraged practitioners to explore other forms of intervention. The problems of treatment effects not generalizing to the delivery of interventions in different settings from those in the original study (a problem common to a range of psychological interventions in different fields), and the increasing willingness to work with more complex individuals (who do not fit neatly into diagnoses or categories used by researchers), may have contributed in some degree to this. One impact of these findings has been that a major thrust of recent "what works" literature has moved on to address more specific questions, not just asking whether interventions work, but also asking under which conditions, for whom and how—what psychological mechanisms lead to the onset and maintenance of the problems—they work. Such issues are important for individual-level decision-making, but progress in this area has been very slow.

The Wiley International Handbook of Correctional Psychology, First Edition. Edited by Devon L. L. Polaschek, Andrew Day, and Clive R. Hollin.
© 2019 John Wiley & Sons Ltd. Published 2019 by John Wiley & Sons Ltd.

Evidence-based practice has been the sine qua non of all health and justice-based interventions for some time now. Essentially, the argument has been: (a) it is unethical and economically indefensible to deliver programs that do not have evidence to support their efficacy; (b) the literature needs to be interrogated in order to identify what works best; (c) the strongest design is a randomized controlled trial (RCT); (d) meta-analysis is the most effective way of describing the literature; and (e) clinical governance should center around ending interventions without an evidence base and investing in interventions that do have an evidence base. The approach relies on the assumption that there is a definitive model for measuring outcomes, that the literature is an infinite resource where all possible interventions are compared with all other interventions and the outcome of reviewing the literature provides us with a robust reflection of "reality," that RCTs are an unproblematic reflection of what actually goes on in practice and can be generalized to other settings and client groups, and that pulling the plug on ways of existing working is relatively straightforward. In recent years, all of these assumptions have been challenged (see Barkham, Hardy, & Mellor-Clark, 2010, and House & Loewenthal, 2008, for an exploration of these issues) and there has been growing interest in the idea of "practice-based evidence." Essentially this is a "bottom-up" approach to evaluation that emphasizes the utility of practitioners using their clinical experience to accumulate knowledge. Examples of this approach in the forensic field include the use of single case methodology to explore the real-world implementation of interventions, as well as to better understand models and mechanisms of change (Davies, Howells, & Jones, 2007; Tew, Dixon, Harkins, & Bennett, 2012). Alongside these developments has been a growing sensitivity to and interest in the ethical and cultural issues that are associated with addressing the problems presented by the people with whom forensic practitioners work. This has contributed to an increasing recognition of the potential roles of social injustice, stigma, trauma, and institutionalization in creating the internal and external contexts for a range of types of offending.

When and Why Is Innovation Justified?

Before going on to examine examples of innovative practice (and their associated problems), some criteria for justifying innovation are discussed. These are based on common sense, experience, and pragmatism. In effect, they acknowledge that innovation is, implicitly, an active choice not to use treatment as usual and, as such, needs to be ethically and professionally grounded.

When There Is No Evidence

In circumstances in which there is an absence of evidence of effectiveness (or evidence that an intervention does not work), then developing a new intervention is warranted. Alternative means of justifying the new intervention will be needed (see above), while remembering that absence of evidence is not evidence of absence. And if an evidence-based intervention is available, then any decision not to use it also needs to be justified.

Any decision to use an established intervention (with an evidence base) will require that the individual's demographic and psychological profile maps effectively onto the profile described in the studies from which the evidence base is derived. Moreover, the conditions and expertise of the treatment deliverers will also need to be equivalent. It should not be assumed that findings of studies will be replicated, as the literature is replete with examples of a failure to replicate significant treatment effects (a problem across psychology not just in forensic settings; see Open Science Collaboration, 2012).

When Treatment as Usual Is Costly

An example of when "treatment as usual" is costly is the Dangerous and Severe Personality Disorder services in the United Kingdom. These were criticized on the grounds of cost, and the possibility that more cost-effective ways of delivering the interventions might be possible (Barrett & Tyrer, 2012; Joseph & Benefield, 2012). The selection of adequate measures (and thresholds) for treatment outcome is, however, an issue that impacts on any assessment of cost-effectiveness.

When Evidence-Based Treatment Has Failed to Have an Impact

In cases where an individual has received an intervention that is empirically supported but has not improved, it is justifiable to offer an alternative as long as a clear justification is provided. An example of this has been the development of specialized male personality disorder services at Rampton hospital in the United Kingdom for people who have not responded to interventions delivered in other settings.

When Treatment Effects Are Small

If the treatment impact described in the evidence base is small, then it becomes a political judgment about the extent to which this is considered acceptable.

When There Is Evidence of Possible Iatrogenic Outcomes

An example of when interventions become inadvertently harmful comes from treatment approaches for those with histories of complex and chronic trauma where interventions for simple post-traumatic stress disorder (PTSD) have been inappropriately applied, despite evidence that they are evidence-based when used with other presentations (e.g., Luxenberg, Spinazzola, Hidalgo, Hunt, & van der Kolk, 2001). Jones (2007) has proposed that more care should be taken to collect evidence about iatrogenic interventions. Innovation with medication is often associated with careful monitoring for side effects and adverse responses; psychological interventions should be similarly monitored and evidence from individual cases collated and disseminated.

When the Psychological Change Mechanism Upon Which the Innovative Intervention Is Based Has Empirical Support

Some intervention approaches are explicitly based on clear psychological change mechanisms that have a very significant weight of evidence supporting them. A good example of this is behavior theory. Using behavioral principles in assessment and intervention for any kind of behavior would be justifiable simply because of the weight of evidence supporting the underlying theory. Interestingly, under this paradigm, if the intervention isn't producing change, then it is the formulation that is considered to be lacking, rather than the therapy.

Where Cultural Competence and Sensitivity Becomes Foregrounded as a Critical Issue

If an intervention lacks cultural competence, then innovation may be necessary. The most obvious areas where this has been the case are where interventions for men have been used for women or where those developed for white "Western" people have been used unheedingly with indigenous populations. Work on culturally marginalized and stigmatized groups (e.g., Day, Jones, Nakata, & McDermott, 2012; Day, Nakata, & Howells, 2008) highlights the significance of cultural identity in developing interventions. A lot can be learned from this work about taking culture seriously for all clients. As Tamatea and Day (Chapter 18) note, nobody exists outside of a culture or subculture, and practitioner cultural awareness is likely to be a critical determinant of effectiveness.

Examples of Innovative Practice

Interventions That Use Innovative Methods

Behavioral approaches

The past 20 years have seen a growth in the use of the "third-wave" behavioral interventions with offender populations such as dialectical behavior therapy (DBT and radical openness DBT [RO-DBT]), acceptance and commitment therapy (ACT), and functional analytic psychotherapy (FAP). These developments came out of critiques of earlier versions of behaviorism and cognitive behaviorism concerning their capacity to address key aspects of human nature considered relevant to the task of addressing psychological problems. In particular, problems with language, the role of consciousness, beliefs, attachment, and the relational embeddedness of cognition were variously addressed by DBT, ACT, and FAP. House and Loewenthal (2008) describe these developments as triggering a paradigm crisis in cognitive behavioral therapy (CBT) which was met by a refusal to relinquish core theoretical constructs and a systematic effort to "bolt on" new ideas to make CBT, as a theoretical approach, irrefutable.

Acceptance and commitment therapy

Amrod and Hayes (2014) have developed the ACT approach for working with people in custodial settings. This approach works with six related processes: (a) *cognitive fusion*, a tendency to act on the literal meaning of thoughts, rather than *cognitive defusion*, which entails recognizing that thoughts are "learned, passing and doubtable events that the mind tosses to and fro quicker than we can track" (p. 44); (b) *experiential avoidance*, a tendency to avoid difficult thoughts and feelings, as opposed to *experiential acceptance*, which entails accepting feeling and sensing "in an open and curious way" (p. 44); (c) *loss of flexible contact with the now*, which means ruminating and worrying about the past or the future, as opposed to having a *present moment focus*, which entails placing awareness mindfully in the present in a "flexible, fluid and voluntary way so that the external and internal environment can act as a context for action" (p. 44); (d) *attachment to a conceptualized self*, which involves allowing the dominance of egocentric stories (e.g., as victims or offenders), as opposed to *a perspective-taking sense of self*, which involves developing an experience of self as "grounded in conscious experience and compassionate connection with others" (p. 44); (e) *values problems*, which refers to a lack of chosen meaning in the present, as opposed to *identifying chosen values*, which involves setting "realistic and congruent goals" (p. 44); and (f) *inaction, impulsivity, or avoidant persistence*, as opposed to *committed action work*, which involves preparation to actively take steps to achieve what they want (p. 44). This approach has, however, only just started to be used with people who have offended. It has a clear behavioral theory underpinning it and attends to states of consciousness through its emphasis on mindfulness.

Dialectical behavior therapy for offenders

Perhaps the earliest reported use of DBT with offenders was by Jones (1997). In some ways, however, DBT is not a new intervention but more an integration of a range of behavioral interventions that have been used previously and have their own supporting evidence. Evershed et al. (2003) reported some evidence for the effectiveness of the approach with patients in a high secure forensic setting, and subsequently it has been used with a range of different offenders and adapted for people with intellectual disabilities (Morrissey & Ingamells, 2011). A major strength of this approach is that it was developed by somebody who had expertise by experience. There is much scope for co-working with former offenders to develop new interventions.

Radical openness dialectical behavior therapy

Hamilton (personal communication, 2015) critiques the routine use of the DBT model (i.e., for all individuals), arguing that the problems that some experience are linked with over-control as opposed to under-control. For this group, traditional DBT may be reinforcing a pattern of emotional avoidance as opposed to developing the capacity to experience, communicate, and engage with emotions in an effective way. Lynch, Hempel, and Clark (2016) have piloted this more refined approach with a number of different disorders, and it is currently being piloted with a group of high secure patients.

Functional analytic psychotherapy

FAP (e.g., Kohlenberg & Tsai, 1991) is a behavioral framework for intervention that attempts to integrate a range of other therapeutic models, including, somewhat unusually for behavioral models, psychodynamic techniques. It focuses on three key areas of in-session behavior described as Clinically Relevant Behavior (CRB): CRB1 is any in-session behavior that plays out the target behavior; CRB2 is any in-session behavior that evidences a change in the target behavior; and CRB3 is any evidence of insight and understanding of CRB1 and CRB2. Jones (2004) suggested using this model with offenders, particularly to look at Offense Paralleling Behavior. Shine (2010) has, more recently, developed this approach and advocated its use in a therapeutic milieu, with Newring and Wheeler (2010, 2012) also exploring its use with sex offenders.

Strengths-Based Approaches

Solution-focused and narrative therapy

Narrative and solution-focused approaches are beginning to gain ground in offense-focused work (Jones, 2009). Narrative approaches center people as the experts in their own lives and views problems as separate from people. Emphasis is placed upon the stories of people's lives and the differences that can be made through particular tellings and retellings of these stories. Solution-focused therapy (De Shazer, 1988), for example, aims to identify existing coping and self-regulation strategies and strengthen these. The goal is to work out what has worked well (i.e., situations in which the individual managed to successfully self-regulate, if only in order to avoid going to prison again) and then systematically work toward doing more of this. The approach highlights the importance of individuals' personal beliefs about "what works" and building on these. Strategies that have not worked are explored to identify what can be done to repair or extend them so that they have a better chance of working in the future. The "Good Lives" approach (Ward & Stewart, 2003) is also a strengths-based model. It uses validation and the normalization of needs as a key intervention strategy.

Positive psychology approach

Woldgabreal, Day, and Ward (2014) describe an approach to community-based supervision of offenders that makes use of a positive psychology perspective. This works on building on positive emotional experiences and focusing on strengths, but not to the exclusion of deficits. As an approach, this has much to commend it, as stigmatizing people and undermining confidence in their existing coping skills is potentially unproductive. Again, evidence for this approach is yet to be reported.

Cognitive remediation

Baskin-Sommers, Curtin, and Newman (2015) have pioneered the use of cognitive remediation techniques when working with psychopathy. The approach involves rehearsing very specific cognitive skills that are linked with a clearly defined neuropsychologically framed deficit. A concern with a lack of specification of the mechanisms through which risk factors translate into behavior underpins this approach (see also Ward, 2014). Baskin-Sommers et al. (2015) write:

> In sum, the current results presage a new era of developing specific remediation training regimes to target the cognitive-affective dysfunctions that subvert behavioral control and result in major psychopathology. For decades, mental health professionals have decried the patient "uniformity myth" (Kiesler, 1966) and advocated for an individualized approach to clinical interventions (e.g., Project MATCH; Mattson & Allen, 1991). Unfortunately, investigators have had surprisingly little success in accommodating person-specific dysfunction in treatment research and clinical practice. Perhaps one of the central limitations of previous efforts relates to the failure to integrate definitive research on basic mechanisms with broader treatment development. Ultimately, the success of individualized medicine requires a higher-level integration of these disciplines. The current findings highlight the potential for utilizing a conceptual and multilevel methodological framework to connect particular cognitive-affective mechanisms to the hypothesized action of effective treatments. The present results offer promise for changing neural and behavioral patterns, even for what many consider to be the most recalcitrant treatment population. (p. 53)

Interventions That Look at the Whole Person (Not Just Their Offending)

Schema therapy

Schema therapy (Arntz, Van Genderen, & Drost, 2011; Young, 1999) is a cognitive behavioral approach that developed as a response to a perceived lack of impact of more standard CBT approaches on more distressed and complex individuals. Young (1999) incorporated a range of techniques from other therapies—such as psychodynamic approaches and Gestalt techniques—to work with the problems he encountered in the patients that he was working with, with his methods applied to forensic populations from the late 1990s (e.g., Jones, 1997).

More recently these have been developed to work with people with personality disorder diagnoses who have offended (Bernstein et al., 2012; Chapter 41). A major strength and characteristic of this model is its capacity to assimilate and incorporate aspects of a range of other therapies (e.g., Gestalt, transactional analysis) in a pragmatic manner. This, however, also renders it vulnerable to criticisms such as that leveled by Barnao and Ward (2015) that it is important to have a clear overarching framework for intervention to be useful in a forensic setting.

Cognitive analytic therapy

Cognitive analytic therapy (CAT) is another therapy model developed for working with personality disorder that has been adapted for working with offenders. Pollock, Göpfert, & Stowell-Smith (2006) argue (from clinical experience) that this is an approach that can be effective with offenders of different kinds. It is particularly strong in acknowledging both perpetrator and victim roles as sequelae of trauma and abuse and has the advantage of being a brief therapy (although this can be problematic when used with individuals who present as complex cases). The evidence base for CAT in forensic populations is lagging behind that for schema therapy; however, this may simply be because few RCTs have been reported.

Mentalization-based therapy

Bateman and Fonagy (2006) have developed an intervention, known as mentalization therapy, that aims to address some of the underlying problems linked with poor attachment experiences. They argue that attachment experiences offer the individual the opportunity to explore and understand other people as having minds and, through experiencing being on the receiving end of somebody attending to and caring about what goes on in one's own mind, the capacity to attend to and care about what happens in others' minds then develops. McGauley, Yakeley, Williams, and Bateman (2011) have used mentalization therapy to work with individuals with a diagnosis of antisocial personality disorder and report that this has been effective in reducing self-reported rates of aggressive behavior. From a theoretical perspective, this approach is well thought through and explicitly identifies treatment targets and mechanisms of change. The evidence base is, however, in its infancy.

Interventions that work with the milieu

It is not obvious why forensic practitioners have not developed a natural history of the ways in which individuals respond to the experience of incarceration, given that the evidence that prison increases the likelihood of further imprisonment is strong (Smith, Goggin, & Gendreau, 2002). If, however, simply being in prison is damaging an individual, then it makes sense to systematically offset these mechanisms of harm. Obvious considerations are grief at the loss of liberty (Jones, 2016), skills atrophy (Benn, 2002), learning about new ways of offending, exposure to traumatic abuse from peers, witnessing traumatic abuse, loss of liberty enacting and recapitulating aspects of the individual's trauma history (e.g., being forced to do things), loss of social capital, and not being exposed to key developmental learning experiences. There is a need to research and intervene in the design of regimes that offset or prevent some of these processes. One approach is to design milieu where the whole regime is aimed at the core business of rehabilitation (or habilitation) and where every interaction between clients and between clients and staff is seen as an opportunity either to change or to regress. Therapeutic communities have this kind of aim.

Therapeutic communities (TCs) are probably better thought of as a mode of delivery than as a single model (see Akerman, Chapter 37). The central idea is that it is critical to be working with individuals all of the time, rather than only in discrete therapy sessions. A central tenet is that how the individual lives their day-to-day life in the treatment setting is an ideal forum for addressing the patterns of problems that led to them offending and ending up in prison. TCs use large groups—all residents meet, often as frequently as daily—to learn about being a member of a community and actively seek and offer help to peers. There are three basic models currently being used: the *traditional concept* TC, where residents have a strict hierarchy (they start at the bottom and work their way up based on their behavior); the *traditional democratic* TC, which has a relatively flattened hierarchy and historically used a group analytic therapeutic model; and the *cognitive behavioral* TC, which, while still having a democratic model, utilizes more recently developed psychological models for therapy, such as schema therapy, DBT, and systemic therapy. Originally developed for working with people with diagnoses of personality disorder (Jones, 1997), this model was recently extended to working with people with intellectual disabilities. The adapted TC model (TC+; Taylor, Morrissey, Trout, & Bennett, 2012) has been used in a number of health and prison settings and is currently showing good within-treatment gains (e.g., reductions in infractions).

Recent developments in the political landscape in a number of countries (such as high-profile court cases around clergy and prominent media figures being involved in sexual abuse) have facilitated the collection of evidence that trauma of all kinds is far more prevalent in the offender population than previously acknowledged (Ogloff, Cutajar, Mann, & Mullen, 2012). There is, for example, evidence that traumatic experiences are significant factors in the etiology of sexual offending (Beauregard, Lussier, & Proulx, 2004; Craissati, McClurg, & Browne, 2002; Dube et al., 2001; Heil & Simons, 2008; Jespersen, Lalumiere, & Seto, 2009; Lee, Jackson, Pattison, & Ward, 2002; Marsa et al., 2004; McGee, Wolfe, & Wilson, 1997; Salter et al., 2003; Simons, Wurtele, & Durham, 2008; Simons, Wurtele, & Heil, 2002), with offenders against adults often having a history of violent abuse, and offenders against children often having a history of child sexual abuse. Saradjian (1996) provides similar evidence for the role of abuse in the etiology of sexual offending among female offenders. There is a similar literature on the links between trauma of different kinds and violent behavior (Anda et al., 2006; Brodsky et al., 2001; Gold, Wolan Sullivan, & Lewis, 2011; Kerig & Becker, 2010, 2015; Lansford et al., 2007; McGrath, Nilsen, & Kerley, 2011; Moskowitz, 2004; Sarchiapone, Carli, Cuomo, Marchetti, & Roy, 2009; Widom, 1995).

A common but not exclusive theme here is for violent or physical abuse to be identified as a significant precursor of violent offending. Moskowitz (2004) makes a strong case for a role for dissociation in trauma–violence links. Alongside this there is a literature, also growing, on the association between trauma and different kinds of personality disorder (Afifi et al., 2011; Cohen et al., 2014; Evren, Kural, & Erkiran, 2006; Grilo & Masheb, 2002; Grover et al., 2007; Johnson et al., 2005; Johnson et al., 2001; Johnson, Cohen, Brown, Smailes, & Bernstein, 1999; Johnson, Smailes, Cohen, Brown, & Bernstein, 2000; Kolla et al., 2013; Lobbestael, Arntz, & Bernstein, 2010; Luntz & Widom, 1994; Waxman, Fenton, Skodol, Grant, & Hasin, 2014). Reviewing previous literature, Johnson et al. (2005) identified the following antecedents for the three personality disorders that are most frequently encountered in forensic settings:

a   antisocial PD with a history physical abuse and one or more types of neglect;
b   borderline PD with a history of sexual abuse and either emotional or physical abuse or one or more types of neglect;
c   paranoid PD with childhood emotional abuse in combination with emotional or supervisory neglect.

A similar story is emerging in the substance misuse literature (e.g., Dore, Mills, Murray, Teesson, & Farrugia, 2012; Driessen et al., 2008; Mills, Lynskey, Teesson, Ross, & Darke, 2005; Reynolds et al., 2005) and the literature on psychosis (e.g., Bentall, 2006; Bentall et al., 2014; Moskowitz, Read, Farrelly, Rudegeair, & Williams, 2009; Read, Agar, Argyle, & Aderhold, 2003). This body of work, along with the development of a clinical position that takes a more credulous—but not naïvely credulous—and strengths-based stance with clients, has led to a much stronger recognition that working with trauma is critical to the joint tasks of improving wellbeing and managing safety. The mental health sector has generally been more willing to acknowledge and work with issues relating to trauma, perhaps because it is easier to recognize links between distress and trauma. However, links between offending behavior and trauma are still, at times, viewed as potentially problematic to the extent that they are seen as offering offenders an exculpatory script that allows them to avoid "accepting responsibility." It is clear that issues around personal responsibility can be a concern for those who contextualize their offending in narratives about their own abuse; however, this cannot be a reason to avoid addressing these issues. For example, differences in the sense of injustice that offenders sometimes feel about the perpetrators against them not having been prosecuted render them in a position where they should be *more aware* than others of the harm caused by their own offending.

Ardino (2014; see also Bloom & Farragher, 2013; Levenson, 2014) highlights the requirements of a trauma-informed service and looks at strategies for implementing these, basing her framework on the work of Elliott, Bjelajac, Fallot, Markoff, and Reed (2005). These are summarized in Table 42.1.

Few interventions have directly addressed trauma as a central issue for those who have offended: though arguably more global therapies like schema therapy and CAT (see above) do address this. A few therapies addressing trauma in the etiology of offending have however been developed and some of these have promising outcomes. An example of this is the finding that use of eye movement desensitization and reprocessing (EMDR) with people who have sexually offended against children results in significantly better treatment outcomes than people not doing EMDR in an ad hoc control group (Ricci, 2006; Ricci, Clayton, & Shapiro, 2006). Findings with non-sexual offenders using EMDR have also been promising (see Greenwald, 2002; Soberman, Greenwald, & Rule, 2002). Interestingly, the underlying model of change underpinning EMDR highlights a spontaneous tendency to process information in an adaptive manner and has much in common with strengths-based models that foster the individual's capacity to develop constructive narratives for themselves—rather than supplying these for them. These outcomes offer some evidence that trauma is related to offending, even in the absence of a clear model that specifies the underlying psychological mechanism.

More recent thinking in the field of interventions for trauma highlight the importance of addressing distorted or altered states of consciousness—developing the idea of dissociation—that are related to trauma (see e.g., Frewen & Lanius, 2014). There is clear evidence that these (and/or similar states) are likely to be present in the commission of serious offending. For example, both Kruppa, Hickey, and Hubbard (1995) and Gray et al. (2003) report that a significant proportion of serious offenders have PTSD as a result of their own offending. More recently, Jones (2015) has proposed that addressing trauma-related and offense-related altered states of consciousness is a critical task for those intervening with offending behavior and that the impact of altered states of consciousness on the capacity and willingness to self-regulate needs to be more effectively recognized. Altered states, often characterized by a loss of felt intention to thoughts (i.e., they are experienced as intrusive), rumination, frequent urges to

Table 42.1 Trauma-Informed Forensic Practice

Characteristic of trauma-informed services	*Example of area of practice*
Recognize the impact of violence and victimization on development and coping strategies	Recognition of the difficulties survivors face in seeking services that increase sense of safety and hope. Staff understanding of the effects of traumatic life events on individual development.
Identify recovery from trauma as a primary goal	Offer of specialized services that address past trauma. Integration of trauma care into non-specialized services.
Empower the client and encourage service-user involvement in designing and evaluating services	Support the client to take charge of their life and control over their actions. Collaboration with the client to encourage sense of control over important life decisions. Involvement of service users to design services. Involvement of service users as a part of an ongoing evaluation of those services.
Are based in a relational collaboration and create an atmosphere that is respectful of survivors' need for safety, respect, and acceptance	Recognize the need for healing in a context in which interpersonal relationships are the opposite of traumatizing. Creation of a place perceived as safe and welcoming for survivors who are given clear information which is consistent and predictable.
Emphasize clients' strengths, highlighting adaptations over symptoms and resilience over pathology	Focus on resilience rather than highlighting pathology. Minimize the adverse. Possibilities of effective strategies: intervention approaches that avoid re-traumatizing clients.
Strive to be culturally competent and to understand each person in the context of his/her life experiences and cultural background	Deep understanding of the client's cultural context.

Note. © American Psychological Association. Adapted from Ardino (2014).

act, and memories of past experiences of intense emotion (positive or negative), are key components of these processes. It is not just PTSD that is characterized by this constellation of altered states, but experiences such as intense sexual arousal, euphoric states linked with substance misuse, and some kinds of offending—as are everyday experiences of emotions like love and hatred.

Discussion

Recent years have seen a proliferation in models of intervention for people who have offended. Some of these are well-thought-through integrated models (e.g., FAP and some of the third-wave CBT interventions), but often what clinicians do in practice is assimilate a range of different approaches into a "tool box" of interventions with little heed to an overall integrative model or underlying logic. At best, this is a form of pragmatic eclecticism and, at worse, it is theoretically incoherent.

One approach to conceptualizing the diversity of models available is that proposed by Morton (2004). Morton developed a framework for conceptualizing the way in which causal models identified by different theoretical approaches can be integrated, compared, or evaluated. This framework recognizes that there are different domains constituting different kinds of variable and different kinds of causal accounts: Environmental (developmental or contextual factors), Brain (neuropsychological factors), Cognition (any intra-personal factors including cognition and emotion but also states of consciousness), and Behavior. This model helps to conceptualize the links that exist between neuropsychological mechanisms and behavior that is mediated by psychological processes (see Kinderman, 2005; Kinderman & Tai, 2007; McGuire, 2008). This kind of approach highlights the complex question of how very different kinds of variables—in different Morton domains—impact on each other (how, for instance, does trauma impact on consciousness and on the brain?). Perhaps a weakness of this approach is that it does not provide a narrative account that fits neatly with the individual's own account of how they have arrived at the position they have.

A related issue is the lack of agreement—not just in forensic psychology—about an account of psychological processes and mechanisms driving behavior. Some multilevel models, such as that proposed by Teasdale (1999), offer an architecture of different psychological processes in order to conceptualize how they interact with each other. Examples of this are the Teasdale and Barnard (1993) model, the schematic, propositional, analogical, and associative representational systems (SPAARS) model (Power & Dalgleish, 1997), and the cognitive–experiential self-theory (Epstein, 1994; Epstein & Pacini, 1999). They have been used to explore the process of change in cognition in forensic interventions of different kinds (see Gannon, 2016; Jones, 2002).

Work to identify key mechanisms of change that operate transdiagnostically (e.g., Mansell, Carey, & Tai, 2012) may offer a useful way forward. This approach may ultimately prove more useful than a series of individual program evaluations. Accumulation of evidence about mechanisms of change puts the clinician in a much more versatile position, enabling more sophisticated responses to individual need, as identified in a forensic case formulation (see Sturmey, McMurran, & Daffern, Chapter 29). This scientist-practitioner approach seems a long way away, however, from the ways in which everyday people talk about, make sense of, and explain their behavior. The task of making interventions culturally sensitive and accessible in an everyday idiom is a real challenge to practice. One way in which this can be done is to develop interventions that are better grounded in current experience by working with Offense Paralleling Behaviors and using techniques like behavioral experiments (Polaschek, 2016). Future interventions that are designed to impact on consciousness—perhaps building on the use of meditation techniques developed over centuries for the express purpose of managing consciousness (e.g., pranayama breathing techniques)—would be useful to explore further, as would the application of interventions targeting metacognition (e.g. Dimaggio, Semerari, Carcione, Nicolò, & Procacci, 2007).

Key Readings

Barnao, M., & Ward, T. (2015). Sailing uncharted seas without a compass: A review of interventions in forensic mental health. *Aggression and Violent Behavior, 22*, 77–86.

Bloom, S. L., & Farragher, B. (2013). *Restoring sanctuary: A new operating system for trauma-informed systems of care.* New York, NY: Oxford University Press.

Tafrate, R. C., & Mitchell, D. (Eds.) *Forensic CBT: A handbook for clinical practice.* Chichester, UK: Wiley Blackwell.

References

Afifi, T. O., Mather, A., Boman, J., Fleisher, W., Enns, M. W., MacMillan, H., & Sareen, J. (2011). Childhood adversity and personality disorders: Results from a nationally representative population-based study. *Journal of Psychiatric Research*, 45, 814–822.

Amrod, J., & Hayes, S. C. (2014). ACT for the incarcerated. In R. C. Tafrate, & D. Mithcell (Eds.), *Forensic CBT: A handbook for clinical practice* (pp. 43–65). Chichester, UK: Wiley Blackwell.

Anda, R. F., Felitti, V. J., Bremner, D., Walker, J. D., Whitfield, C., Perry, B. D., & Giles, W. H. (2006). The enduring effects of abuse and related adverse experiences in childhood: A convergence of evidence from neurobiology and epidemiology. *European Archives of Psychiatry and Clinical Neuroscience*, 256, 174–186.

Ardino, V. (2014). Trauma-informed care: Is cultural competence a viable solution for efficient policy strategies? *Clinical Neuropsychiatry*, 1, 45–51.

Arntz, A., Van Genderen, H., & Drost, J. (2011). *Schema therapy for borderline personality disorder*. Chichester, UK: Wiley.

Barkham, M., Hardy, G. E., & Mellor-Clark, J. (2010). *Developing and delivering practice-based evidence: A guide for the psychological therapies*. Chichester, UK: Wiley-Blackwell.

Barnao, M., & Ward, T. (2015). Sailing uncharted seas without a compass: A review of interventions in forensic mental health. *Aggression and Violent Behavior*, 22, 77–86.

Barrett, B., & Tyrer, P. (2012). The cost-effectiveness of the dangerous and severe personality disorder programme. *Criminal Behaviour and Mental Health*, 22, 202–209.

Baskin-Sommers, A. R., Curtin, J. J., & Newman, J. P. (2015). Altering the cognitive-affective dysfunctions of psychopathic and externalizing offender subtypes with cognitive remediation. *Clinical Psychological Science*, 3, 45–57.

Bateman, A. W., & Fonagy, P. (2006). The structure of mentalization-based treatment. In A. W. Bateman, & P. Fonagy (Eds.), *Mentalization-based treatment for borderline personality disorder* (pp. 37–59). Oxford, UK: Oxford University Press.

Beauregard, E., Lussier, P., & Proulx, J. (2004). An exploration of developmental factors related to deviant sexual preferences among adult rapists. *Sexual Abuse: A Journal of Research and Treatment*, 16, 151–161.

Benn, A. (2002). Cognitive behavioural therapy for psychosis in conditions of high security cases 13 (Malcolm) and 14 (Colin): Andy Benn. In D. Kingdon, & D. Turkington (Eds.), *The case study guide to cognitive behaviour therapy of psychosis* (pp. 159–182). Chichester, UK: Wiley.

Bentall, R. P. (2006). The environment and psychosis: Rethinking the evidence. In W. Larkin, & A. Morrison (Eds.), *Trauma and psychosis: New directions for theory and therapy* (pp. 7–22). London, UK: Routledge.

Bentall, R. P., de Sousa, P., Varese, F., Wickham, S., Sitko, K., Haarmans, M., & Read, J. (2014). From adversity to psychosis: Pathways and mechanisms from specific adversities to specific symptoms. *Social Psychiatry and Psychiatric Epidemiology*, 49, 1011–1022.

Bernstein, D. P., Nijman, H., Karos, K., Keulen-de Vos, M., de Vogel, V., & Lucker, T. (2012). Schema therapy for forensic patients with personality disorders: Design and preliminary findings of multi-center randomized clinical trial in the Netherlands. *International Journal of Forensic Mental Health*, 11, 312–324.

Bloom, S. L., & Farragher, B. (2013). *Restoring sanctuary: A new operating system for trauma-informed systems of care*. New York, NY: Oxford University Press.

Brodsky, B. S., Oquendo, M., Ellis, S. P., Haas, G. L., Malone, K. M., & Mann, J. J. (2001). The relationship of childhood abuse to impulsivity and suicidal behavior in adults with major depression. *American Journal of Psychiatry*, 158, 1871–1877.

Cohen, L. J., Tanis, T., Bhattacharjee, R., Nesci, C., Halmi, W., & Galynker, I. (2014). Are there differential relationships between different types of childhood maltreatment and different types of adult personality pathology? *Psychiatry Research*, 215, 192–201.

Craissati, J., McClurg, G., & Browne, K. (2002). Characteristics of perpetrators of child sexual abuse who have been sexually victimized as children. *Sexual Abuse: A Journal of Research and Treatment*, 14, 225–239.

Davies, J., Howells, K., & Jones, L. (2007). Evaluating innovative treatments in forensic mental health: A role for single case methodology? *Journal of Forensic Psychiatry & Psychology*, 18, 353–367.

Day, A., Jones, R., Nakata, M., & McDermott, D. (2012). Indigenous family violence: An attempt to understand the problems and inform appropriate and effective responses to criminal justice system intervention. *Psychiatry, Psychology and Law*, 19, 104–117.

Day, A., Nakata, M., & Howells, K. (2008). *Indigenous men and anger: Understanding and responding to violence*. Annandale, Australia: Federation Press.

De Shazer, S. (1988). *Clues: Investigating solutions in brief therapy*. New York, NY: Norton.

Dimaggio, G., Semerari, A., Carcione, A., Nicolò, G., & Procacci, M. (2007). *Psychotherapy of personality disorders: Metacognition, states of mind and interpersonal cycles*. London, UK: Routledge.

Dore, G., Mills, K. L., Murray, R., Teesson, M., & Farrugia, P. (2012). Post-traumatic stress disorder, depression and suicidality in inpatients with substance use disorders. *Drug and Alcohol Review*, 31, 294–302.

Driessen, M., Schulte, S., Luedecke, C., Schaefer, I., Sutmann, F., Ohlmeier, M., ... & Havemann-Reinicke, U. (2008). Trauma and PTSD in patients with alcohol, drug, or dual dependence: A multi-center study. *Alcoholism: Clinical and Experimental Research*, 32, 481–488.

Dube, S. R., Anda, R. F., Felitti, V. J., Croft, J. B., Edwards, V. J., & Giles, W. H. (2001). Growing up with parental alcohol abuse: Exposure to childhood abuse, neglect, and household dysfunction. *Child Abuse & Neglect*, 25, 1627–1640.

Elliott, D. E., Bjelajac, P., Fallot, R. D., Markoff, L. S., & Reed, B. G. (2005). Trauma-informed or trauma denied: Principles and implementation of trauma-informed services for women. *Journal of Community Psychology*, 33, 461–477.

Epstein, S. (1994). Integration of the cognitive and the psychodynamic unconscious. *American Psychologist*, 49, 709–724.

Epstein, S., & Pacini, R. (1999). Some basic issues regarding dual-process theories from the perspective of cognitive-experiential self-theory. In S. Chaiken, & Y. Trope (Eds.), *Dual-process theories in social psychology* (pp. 462–482). New York, NY: Guilford Press.

Evershed, S., Tennant, A., Boomer, D., Rees, A., Barkham, M., & Watson, A. (2003). Practice-based outcomes of dialectical behaviour therapy (DBT) targeting anger and violence, with male forensic patients: A pragmatic and non-contemporaneous comparison. *Criminal Behaviour and Mental Health*, 13, 198–213.

Evren, C., Kural, S., & Erkiran, M. (2006). Antisocial personality disorder in Turkish substance dependent patients and its relationship with anxiety, depression and a history of childhood abuse. *Israel Journal of Psychiatry and Related Sciences*, 43, 40–46.

Frewen, P. A., & Lanius, R. A. (2014). Trauma-Related Altered States of Consciousness (TRASC): Exploring the 4-D model. *Journal of Trauma & Dissociation*, 15, 436–456.

Gannon, T. A. (2016). Forensic psychologists should use the behavioral experiment to facilitate cognitive change in clients who have offended. *Aggression and Violent Behavior*, 27, 130–141.

Gold, J., Wolan Sullivan, M., & Lewis, M. (2011). The relation between abuse and violent delinquency: The conversion of shame to blame in juvenile offenders. *Child Abuse & Neglect*, 35, 459–467.

Gray, N. S., Carman, N. G., Rogers, P., MacCulloch, M. J., Hayward, P., & Snowden, R. J. (2003). Post-traumatic stress disorder caused in mentally disordered offenders by the committing of a serious violent or sexual offence. *Journal of Forensic Psychiatry & Psychology*, 14, 27–43.

Greenwald, R. (2002). Motivation—Adaptive Skills—Trauma Resolution (MASTR) therapy for adolescents with conduct problems: An open trial. *Journal of Aggression, Maltreatment & Trauma*, 6, 237–261.

Grilo, C. M., & Masheb, R. M. (2002). Childhood maltreatment and personality disorders in adult patients with binge eating disorder. *Acta Psychiatrica Scandinavica*, 106, 183–188.

Grover, K. E., Carpenter, L. L., Price, L. H., Gagne, G. G., Mello, A. F., Mello, M. F., & Tyrka, A. R. (2007). The relationship between childhood abuse and adult personality disorder symptoms. *Journal of Personality Disorders*, 21, 442–447.

Hanson, R. K., Gordon, A., Harris, A. J. R., Marques, J. K., Murphy, W. D., Quinsey, V. L., & Seto, M. C. (2002). First report of the collaborative outcome data project on the effectiveness of psychological treatment of sex offenders. *Sexual Abuse: A Journal of Research and Treatment*, 14, 169–195.

Heil, P., & Simons, D. (2008). Multiple paraphilias: Etiology, prevalence, assessment, and treatment. In D. R. Laws, & W. O'Donohue (Eds.), *Sexual deviance: Theory, assessment, and treatment* (Vol. 2) (pp. 527–556). New York, NY: Guilford Press.

House, R., & Loewenthal, D. (2008). *Against and for CBT: Towards a constructive dialogue*. Ross-on-Wye, UK: PCCS-Books.

Jespersen, A. F., Lalumiere, M. L., & Seto, M. C. (2009). Sexual abuse history among adult sex offenders and non-sex offenders: A meta-analysis. *Child Abuse & Neglect*, 33, 179–192.

Johnson, J. G., Cohen, P., Brown, J., Smailes, E. M., & Bernstein, D. P. (1999). Childhood maltreatment increases risk for personality disorders during early adulthood. *Archives of General Psychiatry*, 56, 600–606.

Johnson, J. G., Cohen, P., Smailes, E. M., Skodol, A. E., Brown, J., & Oldham, J. M. (2001). Childhood verbal abuse and risk for personality disorders during adolescence and early adulthood. *Comprehensive Psychiatry*, 42, 16–23.

Johnson, J. G., McGeoch, P., Caskey, V., Abhary, S., Sneed, J., & Bornstein, R. (2005). The developmental psychopathology of personality disorders. In B. Hankin, & J. Abela (Eds.), *Development of psychopathology: A vulnerability-stress perspective* (pp. 417–465). Thousand Oaks, CA: Sage Publications, Inc.

Johnson, J. G., Smailes, E. M., Cohen, P., Brown, J., & Bernstein, D. P. (2000). Associations between four types of childhood neglect and personality disorder symptoms during adolescence and early adulthood: Findings of a community-based longitudinal study. *Journal of Personality Disorders*, 14, 171–187.

Jones, L. F. (1997). Developing models for managing treatment integrity and efficacy in a prison-based TC: The Max Glatt Centre. In E. Cullen, L. Jones, & R. Woodward (Eds.), *Therapeutic communities for offenders* (pp. 121–157). Chichester, UK: Wiley.

Jones, L. F. (2002). An individual case formulation approach to the assessment of motivation. In M. McMurran (Ed.), *Motivating offenders to change: A guide to enhancing engagement in therapy* (pp. 31–54). Chichester, UK: Wiley.

Jones, L. F. (2004). Offence Paralleling Behaviour (OPB) as a framework for assessment and interventions with offenders. In A. Needs, & G. Towl (Eds.), *Applying psychology to forensic practice* (pp. 34–63). Oxford, UK: Blackwell.

Jones, L. F. (2007). Iatrogenic interventions with personality disordered offenders. *Behaviour, Crime and Law*, 13, 69–79.

Jones, L. F. (2009). Working with sex offenders with personality disorder diagnoses. In A. R. Beech, L. A. Craig, & K. D. Browne (Eds.), *Assessment and treatment of sex offenders: A handbook* (pp. 409–430). Chichester, UK: Wiley-Blackwell.

Jones, L. F. (2015). The Peaks Unit: From pilot for "untreatable psychopaths" to trauma informed care. *Prison Service Journal*, 218, 17–23.

Jones, L. F. (2016). Trauma-informed care and "good lives" in confinement: Acknowledging and offsetting adverse impacts of chronic trauma and loss of liberty. In G. Ackerman, A. Needs, & C. Bainbridge (Eds.), *Transforming environments and rehabilitation: A guide for practitioners in forensic settings and criminal justice* (pp. 92–114). Abingdon, UK: Routledge.

Joseph, N., & Benefield, N. (2012). A joint offender personality disorder pathway strategy: An outline summary. *Criminal Behaviour and Mental Health*, 22, 210–217.

Kerig, P. K., & Becker, S. P. (2010). From internalizing to externalizing: Theoretical models of the processes linking PTSD to juvenile delinquency. In S. J. Egan (Ed.), *Post-traumatic stress disorder (PTSD): Causes, symptoms and treatment* (pp. 33–78). Hauppauge, NY: Nova Science Publishers.

Kerig, P. K., & Becker, S. P. (2015). Early abuse and neglect as predictors of antisocial outcomes in ado-lescence and adulthood. In J. Morizot, & L. Kazemian (Eds.), *The development of criminal and antisocial behavior: Theoretical foundations and practical applications* (pp. 181–199). New York, NY: Springer.

Kiesler, D. J. (1966). Some myths of psychotherapy research and the search for a paradigm. *Psychological Bulletin*, 65, 110–136.

Kinderman, P. (2005). A psychological model of mental disorder. *Harvard Review of Psychiatry*, 13, 206–217.

Kinderman, P., & Tai, S. (2007). Empirically grounded clinical interventions: Clinical implications of a psychological model of mental disorder. *Behavioural and Cognitive Psychotherapy*, 35, 1–14.

Kohlenberg, R., & Tsai, M. (1991). *Functional analytic psychotherapy: Creating intense and curative therapeutic relationships*. New York, NY: Plenum.

Kolla, J. K., Macolm, C., Attard, S., Arenovich, T., Blackwood, N., & Hodgins, S. (2013). Childhood maltreatment and aggressive behaviour in violent offenders with psychopathy. *Canadian Journal of Psychiatry*, 58, 487–494.

Kruppa, I., Hickey, N., & Hubbard, C. (1995). The prevalence of post-traumatic stress disorder in a special hospital population of legal psychopaths. *Psychology, Crime & Law*, 2, 131–141.

Lansford, J. E., Miller-Johnson, S., Berlin, L. J., Dodge, K. A., Bates, J. E., & Pettit, G. S. (2007). Early physical abuse and later violent delinquency: A prospective longitudinal study. *Child Maltreatment*, 12, 233–245.

Lee, J. K. P., Jackson, H. J., Pattison, P., & Ward, T. (2002). Developmental risk factors for sexual offending. *Child Abuse & Neglect*, 26, 73–92.

Levenson, J. (2014). Incorporating trauma-informed care into evidence-based sex offender treatment. *Journal of Sexual Aggression: An International, Interdisciplinary Forum for Research, Theory and Practice*, 20, 9–22.

Lobbestael, J., Arntz, A., & Bernstein, D. (2010). Disentangling the relationship between different types of childhood maltreatment and personality disorders. *Journal of Personality Disorders*, 24, 285–295.

Luntz, B. K., & Widom, C. (1994). Antisocial personality disorder in abused and neglected children grown up. *The American Journal of Psychiatry*, 151, 670–674.

Luxenberg, T., Spinazzola, J., Hidalgo, J., Hunt, C., & van der Kolk, B. A. (2001). Complex trauma and disorders of extreme stress (DESNOS). Part two: Treatment. *Directions in Psychiatry*, 21, 395–414.

Lynch, T. R., Hempel, R. J., & Clark, L. A. (2016). Promoting radical openness and flexible control. In J. Livesley, G. Dimaggio, & J. Clarkin (Eds.), *Integrated treatment for personality disorder: A modular approach* (pp. 325–344). New York, NY: Guilford Press.

Mansell, W., Carey, T. A., & Tai, S. J. (2012). *A transdiagnostic approach to CBT using method of levels therapy: Distinctive features*. (pp. Routledge). London, UK.

Marsa, F., O'Reilly, G., Car, A., Murphy, P., O'Sullivan, M., Cotter, A., & Hevey, D. (2004). Attachment styles and psychological profiles of child sex offenders in Ireland. *Journal of Interpersonal Violence*, 19, 228–251.

Mattson, M. E., & Allen, J. P. (1991). Research on matching alcoholic patients to treatments: Findings, issues, and implications. *Journal of Addictive Diseases*, 11, 33–49.

McGauley, G., Yakeley, J., Williams, A., & Bateman, A. (2011). Attachment, mentalization, and antiso-cial personality disorder: The possible contribution of mentalization-based treatment. *European Journal of Psychotherapy & Counselling*, 13, 1–22.

McGee, R. A., Wolfe, D. A., & Wilson, S. K. (1997). Multiple maltreatment experiences and adolescent behavior problems: Adolescents' perspectives. *Development and Psychopathology*, 9, 131–149.

McGrath, S. A., Nilsen, A. A., & Kerley, K. R. (2011). Sexual victimization in childhood and the propen-sity for juvenile delinquency and adult criminal behavior: A systematic review. *Aggression and Violent Behavior*, 16, 485–492.

McGuire, J. (2008). A review of effective interventions for reducing aggression and violence. *Philosophical Transactions of the Royal Society B*, 363, 2577–2597.

Mills, K. L., Lynskey, M., Teesson, M., Ross, J., & Darke, S. (2005). Post-traumatic stress disorder among people with heroin dependence in the Australian treatment outcome study (ATOS): Prevalence and correlates. *Drug and Alcohol Dependence*, 77, 243–249.

Morrissey, C., & Ingamells, B. (2011). Adapted dialectical behaviour therapy for male offenders with intellectual disability in a high secure environment: Six years on. *Journal of Learning Disabilities and Offending Behaviour*, 2, 10–17.

Morton, J. (2004). *Understanding developmental disorders: A causal modelling approach*. Oxford, UK: Blackwell.

Moskowitz, A. (2004). Dissociation and violence: A review of the literature. *Trauma, Violence & Abuse*, 5, 21–46.

Moskowitz, A., Read, J., Farrelly, S., Rudegeair, T., & Williams, O. (2009). Are psychotic symptoms traumatic in origin and dissociative in kind? In P. Dell, & J. O'Neill (Eds.), *Dissociation and the dissociative disorders: DSM-V and beyond* (pp. 521–533). New York, NY: Routledge.

Newring, K. A. B., & Wheeler, J. G. (2010). FAP with people convicted of sexual offenses. In J. Kanter, M. Tsai, & B. Kohlenberg (Eds.), *The practice of functional analytic psychotherapy* (2nd ed.) (pp. 225–246). New York, NY: Springer.

Newring, K. A. B., & Wheeler, J. G. (2012). Functional analytic psychotherapy with juveniles who have committed sexual offenses. *International Journal of Behavioral Consultation and Therapy*, 7(2), 102–110 Retrieved from http://www.baojournal.com

Ogloff, J. R. P., Cutajar, M. C., Mann, E., & Mullen, P. (2012). *Child sexual abuse and subsequent offending and victimisation: A 45-year follow-up study* (Trends & Issues in Crime & Criminal Justice No. 440). Canberra, Australia: Australian Institute of Criminology.

Open Science Collaboration (2012). An open, large-scale, collaborative effort to estimate the reproducibility of psychological science. *Perspectives on Psychological Science*, 7, 657–660.

Polaschek, D. L. L. (2016). Desistance and dynamic risk factors belong together. *Psychology, Crime & Law*, 22, 171–189.

Pollock, P., Göpfert, M., & Stowell-Smith, M. (2006). *Cognitive analytic therapy for offenders: A new approach to forensic psychotherapy*. Hove, UK: Routledge.

Power, M. J., & Dalgleish, T. (1997). *Cognition and emotion: From order to disorder*. Hove, UK: (Erlbaum, UK) Psychology Press.

Read, J., Agar, K., Argyle, N., & Aderhold, V. (2003). Sexual and physical abuse during childhood and adulthood as predictors of hallucinations, delusions and thought disorder. *Psychology and Psychotherapy: Theory, Research and Practice*, 76, 11–22.

Reynolds, M., Mezey, G., Chapman, M., Wheeler, M., Drummond, C., & Baldacchino, A. (2005). Co-morbid post-traumatic stress disorder in a substance misusing clinical population. *Drug and Alcohol Dependence*, 77, 251–258.

Ricci, R. J. (2006). Trauma resolution using eye movement desensitization and reprocessing with an incestuous sex offender: An instrumental case study. *Clinical Case Studies*, 5, 248–265.

Ricci, R. J., Clayton, C. A., & Shapiro, F. (2006). Some effects of EMDR on previously abused child molesters: Theoretical reviews and preliminary findings. *Journal of Forensic Psychiatry and Psychology*, 17, 538–562.

Salter, D., McMillan, D., Richards, M., Talbot, T., Hodges, J., Bentovim, A., ... & Skuse, D. (2003). Development of sexually abusive behavior in sexually victimized males: A longitudinal study. *Lancet*, 361, 471–476.

Saradjian, J. (1996). *Women who sexually abuse children: From research to clinical practice*. Chichester, UK: Wiley.

Sarchiapone, M., Carli, V., Cuomo, C., Marchetti, M., & Roy, A. (2009). Association between childhood trauma and aggression in male prisoners. *Psychiatry Research*, 165, 187–192.

Shine, J. (2010). Working with Offence Paralleling Behaviour in a therapeutic community setting. In M. Daffern, L. Jones, & J. Shine (Eds.), *Offence Paralleling Behaviour* (pp. 203–214). Chichester, UK: Wiley.

Simons, D. A., Wurtele, S. K., & Heil, P. (2002). Childhood victimization and lack of empathy as predictors of sexual offending against women and children. *Journal of Interpersonal Violence*, 17, 1291–1305.

Simons, D. A., Wurtele, S. K., & Durham, R. L. (2008). Developmental experiences of child sexual abusers and rapists. *Child Abuse & Neglect*, 32, 549–560.

Smith, P., Goggin, C., & Gendreau, P. (2002). *The effects of prison sentences and intermediate sanctions on recidivism: General effects and individual differences.* Ottawa, Canada: Public Works and Government Services, Solicitor General's office.

Soberman, G., Greenwald, R., & Rule, D. (2002). A controlled study of eye movement desensitization and reprocessing (EMDR) for boys with conduct problem. *Journal of Aggression, Maltreatment & Trauma*, 6, 217–236.

Taylor, J., Morrissey, C., Trout, S., & Bennett, C. (2012). The evolution of a therapeutic community for offenders with intellectual disability and personality disorder: Part one – Clinical characteristics. *Therapeutic Communities: The International Journal of Therapeutic Communities*, 33, 144–154.

Teasdale, J. D. (1999). Multi-level theories of cognition–emotion relations. In T. D. Dalgleish, & M. J. Power (Eds.), *Handbook of cognition and emotion* (pp. 665–682). Chichester, UK: Wiley.

Teasdale, J. D., & Barnard, P. J. (1993). *Affect, cognition and change: Re-modelling depressive thought.* Hove, UK: Lawrence Erlbaum.

Tew, J., Dixon, L., Harkins, L., & Bennett, A. (2012). Investigating changes in anger and aggression in offenders with high levels of psychopathic traits attending the Chromis violence reduction programme. *Criminal Behaviour and Mental Health*, 22, 191–201.

Ward, T. (2014). The explanation of sexual offending: From single factor theories to integrative pluralism. *Journal of Sexual Aggression*, 20, 130–141.

Ward, T., & Stewart, C. A. (2003). Criminogenic needs and human needs: A theoretical model. *Psychology, Crime & Law*, 9, 125–143.

Waxman, R., Fenton, M. C., Skodol, A. E., Grant, B. F., & Hasin, D. (2014). Childhood maltreatment and personality disorders in the USA: Specificity of effects and the impact of gender. *Personality and Mental Health*, 8(1), 30–41.

Widom, C. S. (1995). Victims of childhood sexual abuse–later criminal consequences. Washington, DC: National Institute of Justice. NCJ 151525. Retrieved from https://www.ncjrs.gov/pdffiles/abuse.pdf

Woldgabreal, Y., Day, A., & Ward, T. (2014). The community-based supervision of offenders from a positive psychology perspective. *Aggression and Violent Behavior*, 19, 32–41.

Young, J. E. (1999). *Cognitive therapy for personality disorders: A schema-focused approach.* New York, NY: Guilford Press.

Part VIII
Community Interventions

43

Traditional and Innovative Reentry Approaches and Interventions

Marissa Kiss, Sara Del Principel, and Faye S. Taxman
George Mason University, USA

Implementing effective reentry and community-based interventions is important given that of the nearly 11 million people incarcerated worldwide (Walmsley, 2016) most will be released back into the community. Additionally, with nearly 5 million individuals in the United States (Kaeble, Maruschak, & Bonczar, 2015) and over 2 million individuals in Europe (Rhine & Taxman, 2018) on community corrections, there is a great need to develop effective community interventions that promote the transition and reintegration of offenders back into the community (Lawrence, 1991; National Institute of Justice, 2014). As a process of transition, reentry is premised on diversion, advocacy, and reintegration of offenders into the community after a period of incarceration. Within the United States, individuals with a criminal record face many barriers and obstacles to reentry, including obtaining employment, housing, education, public benefits, voting, and substance abuse treatment as well as the stigma of the criminal label (Freudenberg, Daniels, Crum, Perkins, & Richie, 2005; Maruna, 2001; Pager, Western, & Sugie, 2009; US Department of Justice, 2016; Western, 2008). To overcome these barriers, reentry programs, community interventions, and frameworks focusing on housing, employment, substance abuse treatment, treatment matching, and case management have been developed to help facilitate the reentry of offenders back into the community (Visher & Travis, 2003).

Community Interventions

In the following section, we focus on community interventions, primarily those that are not directly administered by the justice system or reentry programming.

Housing

Housing is a critical aspect to successful reentry. Stable housing attainment is one concern and challenge that many offenders face in returning to the community. Stable housing not only provides security and safety, but it impacts an individual's health and wellbeing. It can play a

---

significant role in the reintegration of offenders into the community. Offenders who are homeless or live in shelters or unstable housing are more likely to be reincarcerated. For example, Metraux and Culhane (2004) found that 11.4% of inmates released from New York State prisons entered homeless shelters and nearly one third (32.8%) returned to prison within 2 years after release. Additionally, offenders with substance use or dependence are twice as likely as other inmates to be homeless prior to incarceration, which is a strong predictor to homelessness in reentry (Solomon et al., 2008). In response, reentry programs have been designed to address the housing needs of offenders. In an evaluation of the Washington State Reentry Housing Pilot Program, an initiative which aimed to provide housing and wraparound services for 1 year to returning offenders, Lutze, Rosky, & Hamilton (2014) found that the program was effective in reducing recidivism (new convictions and prison admissions) for program participants. Additionally, an impact evaluation of Washington State's Housing Voucher Program (HVP) yielded similar results. Reentering prisoners who enrolled in the HVP program were provided vouchers to pay for private rent for 3 months after their release. Hamilton, Kigerl, and Hays (2015) found that HVP recipients were less likely to be reincarcerated compared to non-HVP recipients, and HVP recipients also committed fewer crimes when compared to non-recipients. The Returning Home—Ohio (RHO), a supportive housing program whereby participants receive housing, substance abuse, mental health, and additional supportive services in the community, also reported that program participants were 40% less likely to be rearrested and 60% less likely to be reincarcerated compared to non-program participants 1 year post-release (Fontaine, 2013).

Employment

Some research finds that the likelihood of rearrest is greater for offenders who are not employed (Sung and Richter, 2006). But, finding and maintaining employment is a critical dimension of the successful reentry dilemma, with many offenders facing barriers to employment upon release. The stigma of a criminal label and a felony status often deter employers from hiring ex-offenders. Obtaining legitimate and meaningful employment not only provides individuals financial stability and security, but has been linked to a reduction in recidivism. Employment allows for offenders to be productive members of society, provides income for basic needs, and provides structure to daily life to reduce temptation to use drugs or engage in crime (Freudenberg et al., 2005). To help aid offenders in their transition into the community, various employment-focused interventions have been developed. In a recent evaluation of EMPLOY, an employment assistance reentry program facilitated by the Minnesota Department of Corrections for pre-release offenders, Duwe (2015) found that participants enrolled in EMPLOY were less likely to recidivate compared to non-EMPLOY participants. Participants enrolled in EMPLOY were expected to work in a paid position or participate in vocational programming and were mandated to attend Narcotics Anonymous (NA) or some relapse-prevention program if tested positive for substances during random drug testing. EMPLOY participants reported higher rates of finding employment, working more hours, and obtaining higher wages versus participants who did not participate in the program. With regard to long-term benefits, 84% of EMPLOY participants secured employment within the first 2 years of their release, compared to only 45% of non-EMPLOY participants. Similarly, in an evaluation of a Workforce Development Program in the state of Delaware, Visher, Smolter, & O'Connell (2010) found that after 1 year, 61.3% of probationers participating in the program were employed in a part- or full-time job and program participants were less likely to be rearrested or have their probation revoked compared to non-program participants (15 vs. 26%, respectively).

In other studies, Farabee, Zhang, and Wright (2014) evaluated an employment-focused reentry program in California whereby offenders participated in 120 hours of employment assistance programing over the course of 3 weeks. Findings revealed that program participants were slightly less likely to be rearrested 12 months post-release (45.2%) compared to non-program participants (49.4%) and program participants had slightly higher employment rates 1 year after participation in the program (29.9 vs. 27.1%). Graffam, Shinkfield, and Lavelle (2012) also examined the impact of an employment assistance program provided to prisoners on their likelihood of recidivating 2 years after being released. Twelve months prior to their release from prison, offenders received employment assistance, job placement, and employment readiness training. Overall, recidivism rates were lower for participants who participated in the program and even lower for participants who found employment post-release. For example, individuals who were in the program and were employed had a reoffending rate 2-year post-release of 6.5% compared to 7.8% for individuals who were registered for the program but were unable to find employment. Program participants also committed fewer offenses per day compared to non-participants (Fontaine, 2013). While offenders prioritize housing and employment as their primary needs of reentry (Freudenberg et al., 2005), providing substance abuse treatment to offenders who are incarcerated and upon their release is greatly needed due to the fact that 53% of State and 45% of Federal prisoners met *Diagnostic and Statistical Manual of Mental Disorders, Fourth Edition* (DSM-IV) criteria for drug dependence or abuse (Mumola & Karberg, 2006).

Substance Abuse Treatment

Substance abuse treatment both in prison and within the community has been shown to reduce recidivism and drug use. Duwe (2010) conducted a quasi-experimental design to evaluate a prison-based chemical dependency intervention in Minnesota. Offenders were required to attend treatment for 15–25 hours per week. Duwe (2010) found that offenders who received treatment had lower rates of reoffending compared to non-program participants. In addition, offenders who completed the program had lower recidivism rates compared to those who started the program but did not finish. Another in-prison substance abuse treatment program, Forever Free, yielded similar results. Hall, Prendergast, Wellisch, Patten, and Cao (2004) found that 1 year post-release, Forever Free program participants were less likely to be arrested or convicted in comparison to non-program participants. Forever Free participants were also less likely to use drugs at 1-year follow-up (50.5%) compared to non-participants (76.5%). In evaluations of therapeutic communities, Hiller, Knight, and Simpson (2006) found that after 2 years of treatment, program dropouts' recidivism rates were higher than those of program graduates (30 vs. 21%). Additionally, participating in both residential and outpatient aftercare decreased recidivism by 63.3% compared to those who did not participate in any aftercare; those not participating in aftercare had a 47.4% increase in probability of being returned to custody (Burdon Messina, & Prendergast, 2004). However, Inciardi, Martin, and Butzin (2004) found that in an examination of 690 offenders released from prison in the state of Delaware, participation in treatment produced significantly beneficial effects for subsequent drug use but not on subsequent arrests. Just under half of participants who completed treatment and attended aftercare had a new arrest, compared to more than 75% of the group without treatment. Compared to the group with no treatment, offenders in the treatment group were 15–20 times more likely to be drug free. However, the effects of treatment may be short-lived as 58% of treatment graduates had been rearrested and 79%

had relapsed by the 60-month follow-up. Overall, research has shown that long-term treatment in correctional settings can have a major impact on the potential for relapse and recidivism among drug-involved offenders, especially when coupled with aftercare (Inciardi et al., 2004). However, inmates who receive substance abuse treatment programs in prison or jail rarely continue treatment once they return to the community. Thus, prison-based drug treatment is most effective when coupled with aftercare treatment in the community (Gaes, Flanagan, Motiuk, & Stewart, 1999).

With regard to residential treatment interventions, Krebs, Strom, Koetse, and Lattimore (2009) examined the impact of residential and non-residential drug treatment on recidivism for drug involved probationers. Using propensity score matching on a large data set, Krebs et al. (2009) found that probationers who received non-residential treatment were less likely to be rearrested 3 years after placement on supervision. Additionally, an evaluation of the Drug Treatment Alternative to Prison (DTAP) program, which deferred offenders from prison to intensive residential drug treatment for 15–24 months, found that after 3 years, 23% of offenders who completed the program were rearrested versus 47% of non-participants and 52% of program failures. Overall, participating in DTAP reduced rearrest by almost half (56%), and by 60% for new convictions (Herman & Poindexter, 2012). Perez (2009) also examined the influence of participation in residential substance abuse treatment on recidivism rates for high-risk probationers in a southeastern state. Perez (2009) found that probationers who participated in the residential treatment programming were less likely to be rearrested verses the non-treatment group. Lastly, Brown et al. (2001) examined the effectiveness of an aftercare program for probationers and parolees in Baltimore, Maryland, who recently exited court-mandated outpatient treatment. Brown et al. (2001) collected baseline drug use measures as well as 6- and 12-month drug use measures. Participants were randomly assigned either to receive the aftercare services or be placed into a control group who did not receive services. Findings revealed that at 6 months, the non-aftercare group self-reported more weekly and frequent use of opiates (11.8 vs. 4.3%) and other illicit drugs (23.5 vs. 12.8%) and committed more crimes (19.6 vs. 8.5%). Similarly, by 12 months, the differences between groups reduced; however, the non-aftercare group still reported more frequent drug use (11.4 vs. 6.3%), but reported a lower percentage of committing crimes when compared to the aftercare group (15.9 vs. 18.8%).

As illustrated above, substance abuse treatment programs and employment and housing interventions have been developed to benefit offenders in the reentry process and to assist in the transition from prison to the community. The community and community-based interventions are a key component for inmates' success in reentry. Community-based vocational training and work release programs, halfway houses, and some drug treatment programs (intensive plus aftercare) reduced recidivism among participants (Seiter & Kadela, 2003). In addition to these interventions, reentry frameworks and models focusing on case management and the working relationship between offenders and supervising officers have developed over time.

Reentry Frameworks

Petersilia (2004) has argued that for a reentry program to be successful it should take place in the community, include intensive programming, focus on high-risk offenders, utilize cognitive behavioral techniques, and match offenders to the programs that fit their learning styles. Similarly, Bouffard and Bergeron (2006) also point out that effective reentry interventions include assessing individuals' risk and needs and providing them with evidence-based programming that targets their criminogenic needs (e.g., education, employment training, life skills, substance abuse, mental health, and other programs) in the hope of decreasing the likelihood of recidivating. This framework and model is the backbone to the Risk-Need-Responsivity (RNR) principle. The RNR framework outlines a process for using risk and need information in determining individual offenders' risk level and criminogenic needs as well as determining relevant programs, services, and interventions for the offender. The RNR framework aims to target offenders who are at higher risk for recidivating and those with the greatest need of treatment. This is accomplished by utilizing assessment instruments and tools to assess the risk of the client (risk), addressing the specific supervision level needs of the offender (need), and determining the method of delivering treatment (responsivity) (Andrews, Bonta, & Wormith, 2011; Taxman & Caudy, 2015). The use of a risk and needs assessment tool is a means to identify the risk and need factors pertinent to a particular offender. Identification of these factors plays a role in developing the case plan and in determining the types of programs and services that an individual needs through the facilitation of a matching and tailoring process. The RNR framework supports placing clients in services and programs that are known to reduce recidivism such as: *cognitive behavioral programs* (Nagin, Cullen, & Jonson, 2009; Wilson, Bouffard, & Mackenzie, 2005), *therapeutic communities* (Bahr, Masters, & Taylor, 2012; Lipton, 1995; Prendergast, Farabee, & Cartier, 2002), *contingency management or graduated rewards* (Griffith, Rowan-Szal, Roark, & Simpson, 2000; Harrell & Cavanaugh, 1996; Higgins & Silverman, 1999), and *motivational interviewing* (Anstiss, Polaschek, & Wilson, 2011; McMurran, 2009). In addition to treatment matching, another important factor in reducing recidivism is the role of case management and the working relationship between the case manager, counselor, or supervising officer and the offender in community interventions and reentry programs.

Case Management

Traditional case planning and decision-making in correctional settings is generally conducted by authority figures such as counselors, case managers, probation officers, and other key actors. General case management not only includes the development of a case plan, but services are provided to identify needs and treatment programs that are believed to be important to reduce the risk of recidivism. General case management practices were developed by mental health and social service workers over 50 years ago as a service delivery approach to enhance public safety, encourage social reintegration, and address and reduce negative outcomes such as homelessness, unemployment, mental health disorders, infectious diseases, substance abuse, and other conditions. The goal and core component of case management is to engage and link individuals to services in the community (Guydish et al., 2011; Lewis, 2006; Vigilante et al., 1999) and is widely used in justice settings[1] as a process to assign justice-involved individuals to services. Reentry builds on the concepts behind case management to address the unique needs of the individual in three phases: in-prison, transitional, and community (Taxman, Young, & Byrne, 2003a, 2003b). There is a need to include case management in all phases of reentry. A continuity of care model within case management helps identify offenders' needs and assist them in engaging with treatment providers within the community prior to release (Jarrett et al., 2012; Taxman & Bouffard, 2000). A continuity of care reentry model aims to ease the strain placed on returning individuals by ensuring that offenders are linked to services in the community prior to their release (Healey, 1999).

This linkage has been shown to be effective in reducing recidivism and relapse rates (Field, 1998; Inciardi, 1996; Wexler, Falkin, & Lipton, 1988).

Various case management models have been developed and used in reentry not only to assist supervising officers in identifying offender needs and linking offenders to appropriate services (Vanderplasschen, Rapp, Wolf, & Broekaert, 2004), but to foster a positive working and communicative relationship between the offender and the supervising officer (Brun & Rapp, 2001; Jerrell & Ridgely, 1999; Vanderplasschen et al., 2004; Vanderplasschen, Wolf, Rapp, & Broekaert, 2007). These models include the service broker, strength-based, assertive, and a mixed model approach. These various models have been tested in community interventions such as: Case Management through Treatment Alternatives to Street Crime (Anglin, Longshore, & Turner, 1999), Transitional Case Management (Prendergast et al., 2011), and the Serious and Violent Offender Reentry Initiative (Lattimore, Steffey, & Visher, 2009; Lattimore & Visher, 2009).

To combat an increase in offenders in the justice system with substance abuse and use issues in the 1970s, an offender case management model and intervention, Treatment Alternatives to Street Crime (TASC) was developed. TASC was developed to foster treatment and rehabilitation and facilitate/coordinate treatment between the justice system and local drug treatment facilities. Anglin et al. (1999) conducted an evaluation of five TASC programs in five US cities (Birmingham, Canton, Chicago, Orlando, and Portland) to test the effectiveness of the program on services received, substance use, and criminal recidivism. Anglin et al. (1999) found that TASC was effective in identifying and assessing substance abuse problems, making referrals, and helping to deliver services for offenders; however, the effects of TASC on substance use and recidivism varied by site. For example, participation in TASC was effective in reducing drug use in three of the sites and effective in reducing crime in two sites. While results were mixed, TASC is an example of a case management model that involves the coordination of treatment and justice agencies and focuses on the continuity of care of the client from assessment to facilitation of treatment services.

Transitional Case Management (TCM), a strengths-based case management intervention, was developed to provide case management services to substance abusing parolees transitioning from incarceration to the community. TCM aims to increase participation, admission, and retention in community-based substance abuse treatment; improve drug, crime, and HIV outcomes; establish a relationship between the client and case manager; reduce recidivism; and enhance offenders' reentry processes by improving collaboration among correctional, treatment, parole, and other service providers (Prendergast, et al., 2009, 2011). Within the TCM model, the case manager and client work collaboratively to develop, set, and achieve goals for their transition into the community (Prendergast & Cartier, 2008; Prendergast et al., 2009). TCM includes a strengths assessment and screening (pre-release); conference calls with the offender's treatment, supervision, and family network (pre-release); and community case strengths management sessions (post-release). In this model the case manager serves as a bridge by aiding, coordinating, and providing direct services for the client within the community (Prendergast & Cartier, 2008).

In a multi-site randomized evaluation of TCM, Prendergast et al. (2011) found that overall attendance at the weekly meetings declined over time due to reincarceration, the inability to contact offenders, offenders insisting they did not need any further services, or offenders having a lack of trust in their case manager. Overall, Prendergast et al. (2011) found that participation in TCM did not improve behavior outcomes (drug use, arrests, and HIV risk behaviors), treatment participation, or receipt of social services. For example, TCM participants and non-TCM participants received substance abuse treatment at similar rates (62.1 and 65.1%, respectively) and received other services such as HIV/AIDS, medical, mental health, family, employment, and education at similar rates as well (68.8 vs. 64.7%). Comparable patterns emerge for self-report drug use and criminal involvement. Nine months after enrolling in the study, 29.0% of TCM participants and 26.8% of non-TCM participants reported drug use within the past 30 days. With regard to arrest rates, both TCM participants and non-TCM participants reported the same mean number of arrests 9 months after enrolling into the study (0.45). The use of strengths-based case management in TCM revealed few positive effects and outcomes for TCM participants compared to parolees who received standard supervision and referral services.

The Serious and Violent Offender Reentry Initiative (SVORI), a federally funded, multi-site, reentry service brokerage initiative, was developed to improve reentry outcomes in five areas: criminal justice, employment, education, health, and housing (Lattimore & Visher, 2009). Sixty-nine agencies in 14 states were charged with developing comprehensive programs that focused on linkage to targeted services for 2,400 newly released serious and violent adult and juvenile offenders. SVORI aimed to provide a variety of coordinated services (employment, community integration, substance use, mental health, education, family) to returning former prisoners and strived to improve service coordination and collaboration among state and local community organizations (Lattimore et al., 2009). Findings revealed that SVORI participants were more likely to receive an increase in the types and number of services during incarceration and after release than non-SVORI participants, but, overall, participation in SVORI programs did not impact recidivism outcomes. A major reason why this program was not successful was due to the fact that a risk assessment tool was not used, thus, offenders were not appropriately matched to services based upon their needs (Lattimore et al., 2009). Research has shown that programs with positive reentry outcomes are those that are tailored to the needs of the client (Andrews, Bonta, & Hoge, 1990; Bourgon & Gutierrez, 2012; Gendreau & Andrews, 1990). Consequently, effective reentry approaches link and match offenders to services that target their risk and needs.

Working Relationship and a Shared Decision-Making Model

Another reentry approach that is emphasized in community corrections is the working relationship and shared decision-making model. Developing a positive working relationship and supportive and collaborative environment between the supervising officer and the offenders they supervise has been shown to lead to positive changes in the offender's life and is a powerful vehicle for offender change (Clark, 2005; Dowden & Andrews, 2004; Lewis, 2014a; Ross, Polaschek, & Ward, 2008; Taxman & Ainsworth, 2009). The working relationship/alliance is based upon the use of trust, shared goals and tasks, goal setting, and the development of an attachment bond (Bordin, 1979; Lustig, Strauser, Rice, & Rucker, 2002). In community supervision, the working alliance is a collaborative relationship that develops between supervising officers and offenders to help facilitate positive changes and aids in the development of a case plan. If a positive working relationship and rapport is not present, the development of a case plan and case management practices will be hindered. Researchers have shown that a strong working alliance is positively correlated with success while on probation (Florsheim, Shotorbani, Guest-Warnick, Barratt, & Hwang, 2000; Hart & Collins, 2014). Furthermore, Lewis (2014b) found that officer characteristics such as acceptance, respect, support, empathy, reflective listening, and belief can facilitate a positive relationship and can have a powerful impact on the offender, their beliefs, and their behavior. Furthermore, Lewis (2014b) found that supervising officers exhibiting rejection, lack of empathy, respect, support, and belief, and abuse of power can foster a non-collaborative working relationship which can push the offender away. Consequently, a negative relationship or one that is confrontational can be detrimental to an offender's success while on supervision (Bonta, Rugge, Scott, Bourgon, & Yessine, 2008). By promoting a working relationship, the supervising officer is able to encourage the offender to participate in their own case planning, resulting in an increase in motivation and engagement, and the development of a shared decision-making model (Brown & O'Leary, 2000; Polaschek and Ross, 2010; Taft, Murphy, Elliott, & Morrell, 2001; Taft, Murphy, King, Musser, & DeDeyn, 2003).

A shared-decision-making model, seen primarily in physician–patient relationships, includes the involvement of the patient in the treatment planning process (Charles, Gafini, & Whelan, 1999). Charles et al. (1999) and Makoul and Clayman (2006) have demonstrated that the use of a shared physician–patient decision-making process will increase the voice and engagement of the client in developing their treatment plan. Similarly, a shared decision-making approach in community supervision will allow offenders to participate in the case planning process, set goals, and build autonomy and competence, thus resulting in an increase in motivation and engagement. Working with the offender, using risk and needs assessment tools to guarantee treatment-to-needs matching, building rapport and a working relationship, and including clients in the reentry and decision-making process are important steps in building motivation to complete supervision and reduce future recidivism. To test a model that encompasses these elements and the use of the SMART (specific, measurable, attainable, realistic, time-bound) goals framework and shared decision-making model in community corrections, researchers at the Center for Advancing Correctional Excellence! (ACE!) at George Mason University developed and is currently piloting a new reentry initiative: Your Own Reintegration System (YOURS).

Piloting a New Reentry Initiative

YOURS is a guided goal-setting and manualized treatment program provided by supervising officers to facilitate reentry. YOURS is designed to test a system where offenders learn about their own risk-need factors, select their own goals using the SMART goals framework, and work specifically on goal achievement. YOURS is built on the principle of having the offender and the supervising officer jointly develop a case supervision plan through a shared decision-making process model. This model incorporates the offender's conditions of supervision and risk assessment results with the offender's areas of interest to establish agreed upon, tangible supervision goals that are geared toward recidivism reduction. In this model, offenders are included in the decision-making process and provided a voice in their supervision experience. The goal of YOURS is to increase the role of offenders in laying out their supervision goals by getting them invested in their supervision experience, increasing their motivation to work through challenges, building a working and communicative relationship, working with clients on goal-setting skills, helping clients improve their lives in areas they want to work on, and helping clients achieve success while on supervision. The YOURS model will help determine whether or not putting the offender in charge of their own case plan by allowing them to work on the areas that are important to them and teaching methods of goal setting will increase their chances of successful progress on supervision and positive reentry. The YOURS study is currently being piloted in the United States in Baltimore, Maryland, and Allegheny County, in Pittsburgh, Pennsylvania. Supervising officers from both sites were trained in study procedures, officer responsibilities, and the use of the worksheets, client workbook, and officer facilitator manual.

To determine the offender's risk and needs, offenders first complete the YOURS Risk and Need Self-Assessment Tool (O-RNA). The YOURS O-RNA was designed to complement existing agency assessment tools to allow clients to: examine the areas they are doing well in and the areas they need to pay attention to while on supervision, assist in prioritizing their needs, and identify goals using the YOURS Worksheet and YOURS Prioritization Worksheet. The O-RNA helps guide the decision-making process about which goals should be pursued first by having offenders select the areas they are interested in working on while on supervision and select their top two priority goals. Participants enrolled in the study selected employment, education, and housing as the top goal priority areas. Other goal priority areas include work ethics, employment training, finances, and leisure and free time. Upon completion of the O-RNA, clients are provided with a hardcopy version of the Offender (Client) Workbook or with an electronic version (see yours.gmuace.org). The Offender (Client) Workbook is divided up into several chapters, each focusing on various topic areas such as anger management, attitudes toward crime, child custody, criminal associates and peers, education, employment, exercise, family and relationships, healthy eating, housing, leisure and free time, personal finance, substance abuse, and time management. The Offender (Client) Workbook provides a step-by-step guide to assist offenders in setting goals and includes a checklist at the end of each chapter allowing both the offender and the supervising officer to keep track of the progress made in each section of the workbook.

The YOURS Officer Facilitator Manual was created to help supervising officers apply engagement and problem-solving skills to share risk-need information, identify goals, and prioritize which goals should be pursued first. The manual guides the officer as they work through goal-setting processes with their clients. The Facilitator Manual provides guidance on linking client's Level of Service Inventory—Revised (LSI-R) assessment results to tangible supervision goals, encouraging clients to share personally important goals, effectively communicating with offenders, teaching offenders to use meaningful goal-setting processes, and using a shared decision-making process to define goals for the offender to work on between each supervision contact. The Facilitator Manual outlines the steps to complete at each meeting (initial visit, second in-person visit, and follow-up visits) and provides instructions on goal setting via the SMART goal-setting method (Bovend'Eerdt, Botell, & Wade, 2009; Playford, Siegert, Levack, & Freeman, 2009). The SMART goal-setting method is a key component of the YOURS reentry model. This goal-setting method not only assists clients in creating and identifying goals that are specific, measurable, attainable, realistic, and time-bound, but is used as a mechanism for ensuring communication between supervising officers and offenders. The SMART goals framework is predicated on taking a large goal and breaking it down into smaller goals that are achievable. The framework was first introduced by Doran (1981) to help organize, set, and improve goal success and was later utilized as a goal-planning approach by Schut and Stam (1994).

The YOURS model will test if use of SMART goals in conjunction with the YOURS workbook is successful in changing offenders' motivation and attitudes toward supervision, improving goal-setting skills, and overall positive reentry. Goal setting has been tied to increasing an individual's motivation (Latham & Locke, 1979; Locke & Latham, 2002; Wade, 2009; Zimmerman, 2008), aiding in the identification and organization of goal steps, (Latham & Locke, 1979), and monitoring success via self-regulation (Hart & Evans, 2006; Latham &

Locke, 1991; Wade, 2009). Researchers have argued that self-regulation is imbedded in goal setting and goal attainment (Hart & Evans, 2006; Latham & Locke, 1991) and, more importantly, goals are the sine qua non of the regulation process (Locke & Latham, 2006). Self-selection and self-determination of goals are tied to progress monitoring and increasing performance, reward, and commitment (Deci & Ryan, 1985; Latham & Locke, 1991; Phillips & Gully, 1997).

A total of 26 participants enrolled in the study. Eighty-one percent (80.8%) were male, 57.7% were African American, 84.6% were unemployed, and the mean age was 33 years old (SD = 10.8). At the time of the baseline interview, 65.4% of participants reporting living in stable housing and participants had a mean number of 12.5 years of education (SD = 2.0), with 19.2% who did not complete high school and 46.2% who graduated high school or earned their General Education Development equivalency (GED). With regard to criminal history, participants in the study had 12.1 (SD = 13.4) mean number of arrests, 4.8 (SD = 4.1) mean number of convictions, and 3.8 (SD = 3.6) mean years incarcerated. The most commonly reported crimes participants were arrested and charged with include: weapons charges/contempt of court/disorderly conduct/driving while intoxicated (61.5%), violent offenses (57.7%), drug crimes (53.9%), and property offenses (50.0%). With regard to substance abuse, although the majority of the participants had not used any drugs/alcohol within 30 days of the baseline, one participant reported having used alcohol, heroin, and cannabis in the past 30 days, while four participants reported using just alcohol in the past 30 days.

Participants' criminal sentiments (Simourd, 1997), impulsivity (Whiteside & Lynam, 2001), and decision-making skills (Institute of Behavioral Research, 2010) were also assessed. At baseline, while participants generally scored within the middle range on the criminal sentiments scale regarding prosocial attitudes (43.9 on a range of 0–82; the higher the score the greater the criminal attitudes), participants scored lower on the impulsivity scales (67.5 on a potential range of 45–180; the higher the score the more impulsive the behavior), yet, participants' average score on the decision-making scale within the Texas Christian University Adolescent Psychological Functioning Form was slightly higher (36.1 on a range of 10–50; the higher the number the worse the decision-making skills). However, of the participants we interviewed at the 6-month follow-up (*n* = 11), participant's average criminal sentiments (baseline = 43.6; follow-up = 41.2) and impulsivity (baseline = 61.3; follow-up = 58.0) scores on these scales decreased slightly. Additionally, at the 6-month follow-up, there was an 18.2% increase in the proportion of participants who reported stable housing (baseline = 81.8%; follow-up = 100.0%) and a 36.4% increase in the proportion of participants who were employed (baseline = 0.0%; follow-up = 36.4%). Although preliminary, these are promising results that show improvements during a short period of time.

Supervising officers reported that the YOURS intervention changed their supervision practices, case planning, and the way they interacted with their offenders. The intervention served as a communication tool to help facilitate discussions with the offenders about goals and the prioritization of goals and allowed the officers to "look at supervision from the offender's perspective and point of view" (focus group participant). Officers reported that the intervention prompted them to ask offenders questions they had never thought to ask, such as how the offender feels to be on supervision and what their opinions are of their supervising officer. While findings are preliminary, the YOURS intervention has shown signs that as a new reentry initiative and community intervention it will have positive effects for supervising officers and offenders returning to the community.

Conclusion

Reentry is a difficult time, especially for helping individuals to stabilize in the community over basic survival needs such as housing and employment. Various reentry initiatives, approaches, and frameworks focusing on housing, employment, substance abuse treatment, treatment matching, and case management by supervising officers have been developed to help facilitate the reentry of offenders back into the community (Visher & Travis, 2003). Supervising officers promote reintegration and public safety by monitoring behavior for criminal activity; providing assistance, guidance, and program support; and developing case plans. A key component of the role of the supervising officer in reentry, probation, and parole office settings is their relationship with the clients they supervise (Taxman, 2002, 2006). Traditional case planning and decision-making tends to be driven by authority figures such as counselors, case managers, probation officers, and other key actors. An authoritative surveillance and control model is not always effective in producing offender reentry success. A hybrid model that includes both surveillance and treatment and targets criminogenic needs has shown to be effective in correctional rehabilitation (Taxman, Shepardson, & Byrne, 2004). A new approach is shared decision-making, which includes the offender in development of the supervision case plan, open communication, and an emphasis on goal setting in case management. The YOURS intervention focuses on the use of SMART goals, a shared decision-making model, and a client focused workbook in the community corrections setting.

The YOURS model is a new and innovative reentry initiative and community intervention that puts the offender "in charge" of their supervision experience. The goal is to change offenders' motivation and attitudes toward supervision, improve goal-setting skills, and aid in positive reentry. Preliminary data on clients in the YOURS model reported positive changes such as gaining employment and stable housing and not violating conditions of supervision. This is a positive first step but a further evaluation of this approach in reentry is needed. It will be useful to assess whether this pathway fosters a style of supervision and case management that is intertwined to engage both the offender and the supervising officer in using goal setting and prioritization to foster agreement on the components of a case plan.

Note

1   In the United States, various justice settings exist, including prison, jail, community corrections, work release, house arrest, and home detention.

Key Readings

Andrews, D. A., Bonta, J., & Wormith, J. S. (2011). The Risk-Need-Responsivity (RNR) model: Does adding the Good Lives Model contribute to effective crime prevention? *Criminal Justice and Behavior*, 38, 735–755.

Clark, M. D. (2005). Motivational interviewing for probation staff: Increasing the readiness to change. *Federal Probation*, 69(2), 22–28.

Latham, G. P., & Locke, E. A. (1991). Self-regulation through goal setting. *Organizational Behavior and Human Decision Processes*, 50, 212–247.

Petersilia, J. (2004). What works in prisoner reentry? Reviewing and questioning the evidence. *Federal Probation*, 68, 4–8.

Taxman, F. S. (2002). Supervision: Exploring the dimensions of effectiveness. *Federal Probation*, 662, 14–27.

References

Andrews, D. A., Bonta, J., & Hoge, R. D. (1990). Classification for effective rehabilitation: Rediscovering psychology. *Criminal Justice and Behavior*, 17, 19–52.

Andrews, D. A., Bonta, J., & Wormith, J. S. (2011). The Risk-Need-Responsivity (RNR) model: Does adding the Good Lives Model contribute to effective crime prevention? *Criminal Justice and Behavior*, 38, 735–755.

Anglin, M. D., Longshore, D., & Turner, S. (1999). Treatment alternatives to street crime: An evaluation of five programs. *Criminal Justice and Behavior*, 26, 168–195.

Anstiss, B., Polaschek, D. L. L., & Wilson, M. (2011). A brief motivational interviewing intervention with prisoners: When you lead a horse to water, can it drink for itself? *Psychology, Crime & Law*, 17, 1–22.

Bahr, S., Masters, A., & Taylor, B. (2012). What works in substance abuse treatment programs for offenders? *The Prison Journal*, 92, 155–174.

Bonta, J., Rugge, T., Scott, T. L., Bourgon, G., & Yessine, A. K. (2008). Exploring the black box of community supervision. *Journal of Offender Rehabilitation*, 47, 248–270.

Bordin, E. (1979). The generalizability of the psychoanalytic concept of the working alliance. *Psychotherapy: Theory, Research and Practice*, 16, 252–260.

Bouffard, J. A., & Bergeron, L. E. (2006). Reentry works: The implementation and effectiveness of a serious and violent offender reentry initiative. *Journal of Offender Rehabilitation*, 44, 1–29.

Bourgon, G., & Gutierrez, L. (2012). The general responsivity principle in community supervision: The importance of probation officers using cognitive intervention techniques and its influence on recidivism. *Journal of Crime and Justice*, 35, 149–166.

Bovend'Eerdt, T. J. H., Botell, R. E., & Wade, D. T. (2009). Writing SMART rehabilitation goals and achieving goal attainment scaling: A practical guide. *Clinical Rehabilitation*, 23, 352–361.

Brown, B. S., O'Grady, K. E., Battjes, R. J., Farrell, E. E., Smith, N. P., & Nurco, D. N. (2001). Effectiveness of a stand-alone aftercare program for drug-involved offenders. *Journal of Substance Abuse Treatment*, 21, 185–192.

Brown, P. D., & O'Leary, K. D. (2000). Therapeutic alliance: Predicting continuance and success in group treatment for spouse abuse. *Journal of Consulting and Clinical Psychology*, 68, 340–345.

Brun, C., & Rapp, R. C. (2001). Strengths-based case management: Individuals' perspectives on strengths and the case manager relationship. *Social Work*, 46, 278–288.

Burdon, W. M., Messina, N. P., & Prendergast, M. L. (2004). The California Treatment Expansion Initiative: Aftercare participation, recidivism and predictors of outcomes. *The Prison Journal*, 84, 61–80.

Charles, C., Gafni, A., & Whelan, T. (1999). Decision-making in the physician–patient encounter: Revisiting the shared treatment decision-making model. *Social Science & Medicine*, 49, 651–661.

Clark, M. D. (2005). Motivational interviewing for probation staff: Increasing the readiness to change. *Federal Probation*, 69(2), 22–28.

Deci, E. L., & Ryan, R. M. (1985). *Intrinsic motivation and self-determination in human behavior*. New York, NY: Plenum.

Doran, G. T. (1981). There's a S.M.A.R.T. way to write management's goals and objectives. *Management Review*, 70, 35–36.

Dowden, C., & Andrews, D. A. (2004). The importance of staff practice in delivering effective correctional treatment: A meta-analytic review of core correctional practice. *International Journal of Offender Therapy and Comparative Criminology*, 48, 203–214.

Duwe, G. (2010). Prison-based chemical dependency treatment in Minnesota: An outcome evaluation. *Journal of Experimental Criminology*, 6, 57–81.

Duwe, G. (2015). An outcome evaluation of a prison work release program: Estimating its effects on recidivism, employment, and cost avoidance. *Criminal Justice Policy Review*, 26, 531–554.

Farabee, D., Zhang, S. X., & Wright, B. (2014). An experimental evaluation of a nationally recognized employment-focused offender reentry program. *Journal of Experimental Criminology*, 1, 309–322.

Field, G. (1998). From the institution to the community. *Corrections Today*, 60, 94–97.

Florsheim, P., Shotorbani, S., Guest-Warnick, G., Barratt, T., & Hwang, W. C. (2000). Role of the working alliance in the treatment of delinquent boys in community-based programs. *Journal of Clinical Child Psychology*, 29, 94–107.

Fontaine, J. (2013). The role of supportive housing in successful reentry outcomes for disabled prisoners. *Journal of Policy Development and Research*, 15, 53–75.

Freudenberg, N., Daniels, J., Crum, M., Perkins, T., & Richie, B. (2005). Coming home from jail: The social and health consequences of community reentry for women, male adolescents, and their families and communities. *American Journal of Public Health*, 95, 1725–1736.

Gaes, G. G., Flanagan, T. F., Motiuk, L. L., & Stewart, L. (1999). Adult correctional treatment. *Crime and Justice*, 26, 361–426.

Graffam, J., Shinkfield, A. J., & Lavelle, B. (2012). Recidivism among participants of an employment assistance program for prisoners and offenders. *International Journal of Offender Therapy and Comparative Criminology*, 58, 348–363.

Gendreau, P., & Andrews, D. A. (1990). Tertiary prevention: What the meta-analysis of the offender treatment literature tells us about "what works.". *Canadian Journal of Criminology*, 32, 173–184.

Griffith, J. D., Rowan-Szal, G. A., Roark, R. R., & Simpson, D. D. (2000). Contingency management in outpatient methadone treatment: A meta-analysis. *Drug and Alcohol Dependence*, 58, 55–66.

Guydish, J., Chan, M., Bostrom, A., Jessup, M. A., Davis, T. B., & Marsh, C. (2011). A randomized trial of probation case management for drug-involved women offenders. *Crime & Delinquency*, 57, 167–198.

Hall, E. A., Prendergast, M. L., Wellisch, J., Patten, M., & Cao, Y. (2004). Treating drug-abusing women prisoners: An outcome evaluation of the Forever Free program. *The Prison Journal*, 84, 81–105.

Hamilton, Z., Kigerl, A., & Hays, Z. (2015). Removing release impediment and reducing correctional costs: Evaluation of Washington State's Housing Voucher Program. *Justice Quarterly*, 32, 255–287.

Harrell, A., & Cavanagh, S. (1996). *Preliminary results from the evaluation of the DC Superior Court drug intervention program for drug felony defendants.* Washington, DC: National Institute of Justice.

Hart, J., & Collins, K. (2014). A "back to basics" approach to offender supervision: Does working alliance contribute towards success of probation. *European Journal of Probation*, 6, 112–125.

Hart, T., & Evans, J. (2006). Self-regulation and goal theories in brain injury rehabilitation. *Journal of Head Trauma Rehabilitation*, 21, 142–155.

Healey, K. M. (1999). *Case management in the criminal justice system.* Washington, DC: US Department of Justice, National Institute of Justice NCJ 173409.

Herman, P. M, & Poindexter, B. L. (2012). Cost-benefit analysis of Pima County's Drug Treatment Alternative to Prison (DTAP) program. Final Report, 1–12. Retrieved from http://www.pcao.pima.gov/documents/DTAP_CBA_Final_Report%2012%2010%2012.pdf

Higgins, S. T., & Silverman, K. (Eds.) (1999). *Motivating behavior change among illicit-drug abusers: Research on contingency management interventions.* Washington, DC: American Psychological Association.

Hiller, M. L., Knight, K., & Simpson, D. D. (2006). Recidivism following mandated residential substance abuse treatment for felony probationers. *The Prison Journal*, 86, 230–241.

Inciardi, J. A. (1996). *A corrections-based continuum of effective drug abuse treatment.* Washington, DC: US Department of Justice, National Institute of Justice.

Inciardi, J. A., Martin, S. S., & Butzin, C. A. (2004). Five-year outcomes of therapeutic community treatment of drug-involved offenders after release from prison. *Crime & Delinquency*, 50, 86–107.

Institute of Behavioral Research (2010). *TCU Adolescent Psychological Functioning Form (TCU ADOL PSYForm)*. Fort Worth: Texas Christian University, Institute of Behavioral Research Available at ibr. tcu.edu.

Jarrett, M., Thornicroft, G., Forrester, A., Harty, M., Senior, J., King, C., & Shaw, J. (2012). Continuity of care for recently released prisoners with mental illness: A pilot randomised controlled trial testing the feasibility of a critical time intervention. *Epidemiology and Psychiatric Sciences*, 21, 187–193.

Jerrell, J. M., & Ridgely, M. S. (1999). Impact of robustness of program implementation on outcomes of clients in dual diagnosis programs. *Psychiatric Services*, 50, 109–112.

Kaeble, D., Maruschak, L. M., & Bonczar, T. P. (2015). Probation and parole in the United States, 2014. Washington, DC: US Department of Justice, Office of Justice Programs, Bureau of Justice Statistics. NCJ 249057.

Krebs, C. P., Strom, K. J., Koetse, W. H., & Lattimore, P. K. (2009). The impact of residential and non-residential drug treatment on recidivism among drug-involved probationers: A survival analysis. *Crime & Delinquency*, 55, 442–471.

Latham, G. P., & Locke, E. A. (1979). Goal setting: A motivational technique that works. *Organizational Dynamics*, 8, 68–80.

Latham, G. P., & Locke, E. A. (1991). Self-regulation through goal setting. *Organizational Behavior and Human Decision Processes*, 50, 212–247.

Lattimore, P. K., & Visher, C. A. (2009). *The multi-site evaluation of SVORI: Summary and synthesis.* Research Triangle Park, NC: RTI International.

Lattimore, P. K., Steffey, D. M., & Visher, C. (2009). *Prisoner reentry experiences of adult males: Characteristics, service receipt, and outcomes of participants in the SVORI multi-site evaluation.* Research Triangle Park, NC: RTI International.

Lawrence, R. (1991). Reexamining community corrections models. *Crime & Delinquency.*, 37, 449–464.

Lewis, C. (2006). Treating incarcerated women: Gender matters. *Psychiatric Clinics of North America*, 29, 773–789.

Lewis, S. (2014a). Exploring positive working relationships in light of the aims of probation, using a collaborative approach. *Probation Journal*, 61, 334–345.

Lewis, S. (2014b). Learning from success and failure: Deconstructing the working relationship within probation practice and exploring its impact on probationers, using a collaborative approach. *Probation Journal*, 61, 161–175.

Lipton, D. (1995). *The effectiveness of treatment for drug abusers under criminal justice supervision.* Washington, DC: US Department of Justice, National Institute of Justice.

Locke, E. A., & Latham, G. P. (2002). Building a practically useful theory of goal setting and task motivation. *American Psychologist*, 57, 705–717.

Locke, E. A., & Latham, G. P. (2006). New directions in goal-setting theory. *Association for Psychological Science*, 15, 265–268.

Lustig, D. C., Strauser, D. R., Rice, N. D., & Rucker, T. F. (2002). The relationship between working alliance and rehabilitation outcomes. *Rehabilitation Counselling Bulletin*, 46, 24–32.

Lutze, F. E., Rosky, J. W., & Hamilton, Z. K. (2014). Homelessness and reentry: A multisite outcome evaluation of Washington State's reentry housing program for high risk offenders. *Criminal Justice and Behavior*, 41, 471–491.

Makoul, G. M., & Clayman, M. L. (2006). An integrative model of shared decision making in medical encounters. *Patient Education and Counseling*, 60, 301–312.

Maruna, S. (2001). *Making good: How ex-convicts reform and rebuild their lives.* Washington, DC: American Psychological Association.

Metraux, S., & Culhane, D. P. (2004). Homeless shelter use and reincarceration following prison release: Assessing the risk. *Criminology and Public Policy*, 3, 201–222.

McMurran, M. (2009). Motivational interviewing with offenders: A systematic review. *Legal and Criminological Psychology*, 14(1), 83–100.

Mumola, C. J., & Karberg, J. C. (2006). Drug use and dependence, state and federal prisoners, 2004. Washington, DC: US Department of Justice, Office of Justice Programs, Bureau of Justice Statistics. NCJ 213530.

Nagin, D. S., Cullen, F. T., & Jonson, C. L. (2009). Imprisonment and reoffending. *Crime & Justice*, 38, 115–413.

National Institute of Justice. (2014). *Community corrections*. Retrieved from http://www.nij.gov/topics/corrections/community/pages/welcome.aspx

Pager, D., Western, B., & Sugie, N. (2009). Sequencing disadvantage: Barriers to employment facing young Black and White men with criminal records. *Annals of the American Academy of Political and Social Science*, 623, 195–213.

Perez, D. M. (2009). Applying evidence-based practices to community corrections supervision: An evaluation of residential substance abuse treatment for high-risk probationers. *Journal of Contemporary Criminal Justice*, 25, 442–458.

Petersilia, J. (2004). What works in prisoner reentry? Reviewing and questioning the evidence. *Federal Probation*, 68, 4–8.

Phillips, J. M., & Gully, S. M. (1997). Role of goal orientation, ability, need for achievement, and locus of control in the self-efficacy and goal-setting process. *Journal of Applied Psychology*, 82, 792–802.

Playford, E. D., Siegert, R., Levack, W., & Freeman, J. (2009). Areas of consensus and controversy about goal setting in rehabilitation: A conference report. *Clinical Rehabilitation*, 23, 334–344.

Polaschek, D. L. L., & Ross, E. C. (2010). Do early therapeutic alliance, motivation, and stages of change predict therapy change for high-risk, psychopathic violent prisoners? *Criminal Behaviour and Mental Health*, 20, 100–111.

Prendergast, M., & Cartier, J. J. (2008). Improving parolees' participation in drug treatment and other services through strengths case management. *Perspectives (American Probation and Parole Association)*, 32(1), 38–46.

Prendergast, M., Farabee, D., & Cartier, J. (2002). Corrections-based substance abuse programs: Good for inmates, good for prisons. *Offender Substance Abuse Report*, 2, 81–92.

Prendergast, M., Frisman, L., Sacks, J. Y., Staton-Tindall, M., Greenwell, L., Lin, H. J., & Cartier, J. (2011). A multi-site, randomized study of strengths-based case management with substance-abusing parolees. *Journal of Experimental Criminology*, 7, 225–253.

Prendergast, M., Greenwell, L., Cartier, J., Sacks, J., Frisman, L., Rodis, E., & Havens, J. R. (2009). Adherence to scheduled sessions in a randomized field trial of case management: The criminal justice–drug abuse treatment studies transitional case management study. *Journal of Experimental Criminology*, 5, 273–297.

Rhine, E. E., & Taxman, F. S. (2018). American exceptionalism in community supervision: A comparative analysis of probation in the United States, Scotland, and Sweden. In K. R. Reitz (Ed.), *American exceptionalism in crime and punishment* (pp. 367–409). New York, NY: Oxford University Press.

Ross, E. C., Polaschek, D. L. L., & Ward, T. (2008). The therapeutic alliance: A theoretical revision for offender rehabilitation. *Aggression and Violent Behavior*, 13, 462–480.

Schut, H. A., & Stam, H. J. (1994). Goals in rehabilitation teamwork. *Disability Rehabilitation*, 16, 223–226.

Seiter, R., & Kadela, K. (2003). Prisoner reentry: What works, what doesn't, and what's promising. *Crime and Delinquency*, 49, 360–388.

Simourd, D. J. (1997). The criminal sentiments scale-modified and pride in delinquency scale: Psychometric properties and construct validity of two measures of criminal attitudes. *Criminal Justice and Behavior*, 24, 52–70.

Solomon, A. L., Osborne, J., LoBuglio, S. F., Mellow, J., & Mukamal, D. (2008). *Life after lockup: Improving reentry from jail to the community*. Washington, DC: Urban Institute Justice Policy Center.

Sung, H., & Richter, L. (2006). Contextual barriers to successful reentry of recovering drug offenders. *Journal of Substance Abuse Treatment*, 31, 365–374.

Taft, C. T., Murphy, C. M., Elliott, J. D., & Morrel, T. M. (2001). Attendance-enhancing procedures in group counseling for domestic abusers. *Journal of Counseling Psychology*, 48, 51–60.

Taft, C. T., Murphy, C. M., King, D. W., Musser, P. H., & DeDeyn, J. M. (2003). Process and treatment adherence factors in group cognitive behavioral therapy for partner violent men. *Journal of Consulting and Clinical Psychology*, 71, 812–820.

Taxman, F. S. (2002). Supervision: Exploring the dimensions of effectiveness. *Federal Probation*, 66, 14–27.

Taxman, F. S. (2006). What should we expect from parole (and probation) under a behavioral management approach? *Perspectives*, 30(2), 38–45.

Taxman, F. S., & Ainsworth, S. (2009). Correctional milieu: The key to quality outcomes. *Victims & Offenders*, 4, 334–340.

Taxman, F. S., & Bouffard, J. (2000). The importance of systems in improving offender outcomes: New frontiers in treatment integrity. *Justice Research and Policy*, 2(2), 37–58.

Taxman, F. S., & Caudy, M. (2015). Risk tells us who, but not what or how: Empirical assessment of the complexity of criminogenic needs to inform correctional programming. *Criminology & Public Policy*, 14, 71–103.

Taxman, F. S., Shepardson, E. S., & Byrne, J. M. (2004). *Tools of the trade: A guide to incorporating science into practice*. Washington, DC: US Department of Justice, National Institute of Corrections.

Taxman, F. S., Young, D. W., & Byrne, J. M. (2003a). Transforming offender reentry into public safety: Lessons from OJP's reentry partnership initiative. *Justice Research and Policy*, 5, 101–128.

Taxman, F. S., Young, D. W., & Byrne, J. M. (2003b). *Offender's views of reentry: Implications for processes, programs, and services*. Washington, DC: National Institute of Justice.

US Department of Justice (2016). *Roadmap to reentry: Reducing recidivism through reentry reforms at the Federal Bureau of Prisons*. Washington, DC: Author.

Vanderplasschen, W., Wolf, J., Rapp, R. C., & Broekaert, E. (2007). Effectivness of different models of case management for substance-abusing populations. *Journal of Psychoactive Drugs*, 39, 81–95.

Vanderplasschen, W., Rapp, R. C., Wolf, J. R., & Broekaert, E. (2004). The development and implementation of case management for substance use disorders in North America and Europe. *Psychiatric Services*, 55, 913–922.

Vigilante, K. C., Flynn, M. M., Affleck, P. C., Stunkle, J. C., Merriman, N. A., Flanigan, T. P., … & Rich, J. D. (1999). Reduction in recidivism of incarcerated women through primary care, peer counseling, and discharge planning. *Journal of Women's Health*, 8, 409–415.

Visher, C. A., & Travis, J. (2003). Transitions from prison to community: Understanding individual pathways. *Annual Review of Sociology*, 29, 89–113.

Visher, C. A., Smolter, N., & O'Connell, D. (2010). Workforce Development Program: A pilot study of its impact in the US Probation Office, District of Delaware. *Federal Probation*, 74(3), 6–21.

Wade, D. T. (2009). Goal setting in rehabilitation: An overview of what, why and how. *Clinical Rehabilitation*, 23, 291–295.

Walmsley, R. (2016). World prison population list (11th ed.). World Prison Brief. London, UK: Institute for Criminal Policy Research. Retrieved from http://www.prisonstudies.org/sites/default/files/resources/downloads/world_prison_population_list_11th_edition_0.pdf

Western, B. (2008). Criminal background checks and employment among workers with criminal records. *Criminology & Public Policy*, 7, 413–417.

Wexler, H., Falkin, G., & Lipton, D. (1988). *A model prison rehabilitation program: An evaluation of the Stay'n Out therapeutic community*. A final report to the National Institute of Drug Abuse by Narcotic and Drug Research Inc.

Whiteside, S. P., & Lynam, D. R. (2001). The five factor model and impulsivity: Using a structural model of personality to understand impulsivity. *Personality and Individual Differences*, 30, 669–689.

Wilson, D., Bouffard, L., & Mackenzie, D. (2005). Quantitative review of cognitive behavioral programs. *Criminal Justice and Behavior*, 32, 172–204.

Zimmerman, B. J. (2008). Goal setting: A key proactive source of academic self-regulation. In D. H. Schunk, & B. J. Zimmerman (Eds.), *Motivation and self-regulated learning* (pp. 267–295). New York, NY: Lawrence Erlbaum.

44

Recognizing the Importance of Effective Practices in Community Correctional Supervision

Simon Davies
Victoria University of Wellington, New Zealand

Devon L. L. Polaschek
University of Waikato (Te Whare Wānanga o Waikato), New Zealand

In the United States alone there were nearly 5 million adults under community supervision at the end of 2014, about twice as many as were incarcerated in federal and state prisons (Kaeble, Glaze, Tsoutis, & Minton, 2015). One estimate suggests almost 40% of this group will be reconvicted within 5 years (Rhodes, Dyous, Kling, Hunt, & Luallen, 2013), giving community supervision great potential for reducing recidivism.

Community supervision[2] can be conceptualized as having three distinct aspects: (a) monitoring and surveillance with a focus on sentence compliance and early detection of new offenses; (b) social work-type support, including assistance with housing, employment, finances, and accessing mental health treatment, to enhance offender wellbeing and lawful survival; and (c) amelioration of dynamic risk factors through the use of behavioral and cognitive techniques, including interpersonal influence. Arguably, the first two of these have long histories, and community corrections officer (CCO) roles have often been viewed as a mix of each, with that mix varying according to the climate of the day. For example, during the United Kingdom's New Labour government, the emphasis on public protection through punishing and controlling offenders on supervision led in England and Wales to a move away from social work training as a suitable background for probation officers (Deering, 2010). Similarly, consistent with *The New Penology* (Feeley & Simon, 1992), probation officer training in US jurisdictions emphasized frequent face-to-face contacts aimed at controlling supervisee behavior through surveillance, and frequent returns to custody for parole violations (Viglione, 2017).

The third role has become increasingly important as theory and research on what works to reduce reconviction risk has developed over the past 30 years or so (Bourgon, Gutierrez, & Ashton, 2012). The time—often brief—that CCOs may be afforded with offenders during community supervision has come to be understood as a potential rehabilitation resource: a

The Wiley International Handbook of Correctional Psychology, First Edition. Edited by Devon L. L. Polaschek, Andrew Day, and Clive R. Hollin.

valuable opportunity for supporting offenders to move away from a life of crime. Although the exact nature of the sentence may differ—offenders may be attending supervision as a condition of their release from prison (e.g., parole) or as part of a stand-alone community sanction—the nature of community supervision generally remains the same: offenders must regularly report to a CCO and during that time the staff member has the opportunity to influence the future behavior of the offender.

Often these three different roles are directly in conflict with each other. For example, building a good relationship with offenders is very important from both social work and Risk-Need-Responsivity (RNR) perspectives, but it may be difficult if the CCO is also required to drug test offenders, or otherwise check whether they are complying with their sentences or engaging in other offending. An offender with a sentence condition to consume no alcohol is unlikely to be able to seek help from his probation officer if to disclose use results in punitive action such as prosecution. Therefore, the challenge that faces CCOs—and the person being supervised—is to find a way to work together despite these conflicting roles in a way that satisfies practice requirements *and* reduces recidivism. Several small bodies of research suggest community supervision can reduce recidivism, through both the way the CCO behaves toward their client, and the way they use the time they have together.

Background

Community oversight of offenders has a very long history. Probation is said to have begun in the United States in Boston in 1841 (Bonta, Rugge, Scott, Bourgon, & Yessine, 2008) and in the United Kingdom in 1876 as a religious evangelical "soul-saving" enterprise (Whitehead & Statham, 2006). Parole also originated in the mid- to late 1800s (Bonta et al., 2008). These types of supervision of offenders were traditionally viewed as a form of social work (McNeill, 2010; Taxman, 2002). But in the 1970s, community supervision was drawn into the wider debate about whether offender rehabilitation was effective (Martinson, 1974). Although evidence at that time suggested that people released onto parole supervision were less likely to be rearrested and reconvicted than people released from prison without any period of supervision (Lipton, Martinson, & Wilks, 1975; Martinson & Wilks, 1978), this message was not received by law- and policy-makers. Instead, the idea that "nothing works" came to dominate the broader area of offender rehabilitation, including the field of community supervision. The result for CCOs was a move away from social work aimed at rehabilitation and toward a much greater emphasis on sentence enforcement and surveillance (Taxman, 2002).

Two main factors led to another revision of the aims of community supervision in the 1990s. First, the unprecedented growth in the incarcerated population, and the fiscal and physical strain this growth placed on correctional systems across the Western world, forced policy-makers to consider more closely the alternatives to prison (Burrell, 2012). Second, better quality empirical research showing that the "nothing works" movement was misguided reached a critical mass; interventions and services that followed certain psychological principles were shown to be associated with reductions in recidivism (Andrews et al., 1990; Lipsey, 1995). Ironically, although some of Andrews' earliest work on effective correctional interventions was based on understanding the content and process of community supervision (Andrews, 1982), much of the subsequent research on "what works" has largely focused on structured intervention programs, rather than routine community supervision. However, according to Andrews and colleagues' RNR model (Bonta & Andrews, 2017), the key to understanding whether any particular "brand" of sentence is effective in reducing recidivism is to look inside the sentence to gain a functional understanding of the relative contributions of the staff member, the practice, and the offender to the outcome of that sentence.

This issue is well illustrated by Intensive Supervision Programs (ISPs), which emerged as a deterrent sanction in the 1980s, intended to provide an alternative to overcrowded prisons. The main concept of ISPs was that close surveillance in the community through more frequent supervision meetings, random home visits, and regular drug tests would be an effective method of increasing public safety, cheaper than prison, and suitable for high-risk offenders. However, their introduction led to "net-widening"; offenders who would have been previously on lower-intensity supervision were instead sentenced to ISPs (Petersilia, 1998), and these sentences emphasized detecting sentence non-compliance and then imprisoning people for these violations, thus actually *increasing* the prison population. Consequently, they have been found to result in an increase in technical violations with either no corresponding increase in detection of actual offenses, which in any case are unrelated to violations, or a small increase in recidivism (Gendreau, Goggin, Cullen, & Andrews, 2000; Lowenkamp, Flores, Holsinger, Makarios, & Latessa, 2010; Petersilia & Turner, 1993). The overall conclusion about ISPs is that to the extent that they are premised on deterrence theory (i.e., are focused on surveilling, controlling, and threatening to punish offenders), they do not achieve reductions in recidivism. Deterrence approaches in general are ineffective, so this should be no surprise. By contrast, those ISPs offering more treatment services have been associated with reduced recidivism (Lowenkamp et al., 2010). In other words, if ISPs included components with the potential to reduce changeable risk factors for recidivism, they could lead to such reductions. They then join the array of structured interventions that may provide high-risk offenders with help in reducing the strength of dynamic risk factors that otherwise lead to reconviction.

Does Community Supervision/Parole Work?

Global Evaluations of Community-Based Sentences

A group of Canadian psychologists conducted a meta-analysis in the early 2000s, examining the effectiveness of community supervision using studies conducted after the Martinson and Wilks (1978) review. They concluded that an extremely small decrease in recidivism could be attributed to the effects of community supervision, but that overall, "community supervision does not appear to work very well" (Bonta et al., 2008, p. 251). Others reached similar conclusions about the effectiveness of parole supervision (Solomon, Kachnowski, & Bhati, 2005). A key limitation of these evaluations was that information about the content and processes *inside* the interventions they included was not available to be coded. This was a limitation noted much earlier in the process of challenging the "nothing works" doctrine. The same group of Canadian psychologists and researchers led the development of "what works" evidence because they coded services and interventions based not just on "brand names" (e.g., "boot camp," "ISP") but on details from inside the program that could be coded across a wide range of programs (e.g., use of social service trained staff, use of manuals, coverage of strategies of ameliorating alcohol use, skills teaching).

A related approach has been to evaluate the whole sentence, folding a supervision component together with other separate and clearly rehabilitative elements. For example, sentence conditions may require the supervisee to also attend alcohol and drug treatment, or cognitive change interventions (e.g., Paparozzi & Gendreau, 2005; Schram, Koons-Witt, Williams, & McShane, 2006; Veysey, Ostermann, & Lanterman, 2014; Wan, Poynton, Doorn, & Weatherburn, 2014). But the RNR model suggests that in addition to these components that are overtly about helping offenders to reduce risk factors, other aspects of supervisee experience are important, and some of these are relevant to the process of providing supervision itself. Both parole and community supervision usually involve a component of time spent interacting with the supervisee ("reporting in"), which may itself be viewed as an intervention with the potential for influencing positive or negative change in recipients.

The growing body of research on whether practices *inside* the community supervision component itself are likely to contribute to reductions in recidivism has also been oriented to the RNR principles. For example, research has examined the ability of CCOs to accurately assess and then allocate offenders to levels and types of service, based on identifying criminogenic needs (the need principle) and on whether they distribute more of their time or other intervention time to those who are higher risk (Bonta et al., 2008). This trend mirrors the wider offender intervention literature; the risk and need principles have received the lion's share of attention in research.

Responsivity and Community Supervision

Responsivity has remained the least clearly defined and least researched of the RNR principles (Bourgon & Bonta, 2014). One simple definition of responsive intervention has two parts: (a) understanding and factoring in the client characteristics that are relevant to their ability to learn and change, and (b) creating the best environment possible through "skills, language and intervention activities that encourages client engagement in the learning activities and promotes efficient and effective client learning of what is being taught" (Bourgon & Bonta, 2014, p. 5). The latter puts an emphasis on staff practices.

Two principles are considered important for professionals to effectively influence behavior, whether as a therapist, family member, or human service agent in a correctional system. First is the relationship principle: Staff are most likely to influence prosocial behavior when they are "open, warm, enthusiastic, and non-blaming" and when they foster "mutual respect, liking and interest" in the supervisee (Bonta & Andrews, 2017, p. 238). Second is the structuring principle. Effective structuring of interactions includes modeling and rehearsing desired beliefs and behavior, and building related skills, using authority in a firm but fair way, an emphasis on approval for prosocial sentiments and behavior, with occasional disapproval for antisocial equivalents, helping supervisees solve their problems and access resources to do so, and so on (Bonta & Andrews, 2017).

Meaningful increases in the mean effect size of interventions have been observed when correctional practice includes these components (e.g., relationship skills, advocacy and brokerage, effective prosocial modeling, effective authority, effective disapproval) compared to when they are missing, but this research is not specific to community supervision (see Bonta & Andrews, 2017).

Research on CCO Supervision Practice

To better understand how supervision itself may relate to recidivism outcomes, a number of studies have focused in on the interactions between supervisors and supervisees. For example, Bonta et al. (2008) examined whether CCOs in the Canadian province of Manitoba were spending more time with higher-risk offenders (*risk* principle); focusing more on changeable risk factors known to be associated with an increased risk of recidivism (i.e., on criminogenic needs: *need* principle); and using the best approaches for working with offenders (*responsivity* principle), particularly cognitive behavioral techniques and other Core Correctional Practices (CCP).[3] Audiotapes of supervision sessions from three different sentence time points were obtained from 62 CCOs working with 154 different offenders. Analysis of the 211 audiotapes showed moderate adherence to the risk principle, with officers spending too much time on enforcing the conditions of the offender's sentence relative to discussing relevant criminogenic needs. Relationship-building skills (e.g., enthusiasm, encouragement, empathy, openness) were used quite frequently, but specific cognitive behavioral techniques (e.g., reinforcement, modeling, practice) were used relatively infrequently. Time spent discussing criminogenic needs was associated with lower recidivism rates, while time spent on enforcement was associated with higher recidivism rates, though it is not clear whether the latter is actually criminogenic or simply neutral in its effects. They concluded that overall, CCOs' adherence to the RNR principles was low (Bonta et al., 2008).

Similarly, Trotter and Evans (2012) examined the skills used by CCOs in Australia who supervise juvenile offenders. They found that relationship skills were quite strong but other relevant skills such as cognitive behavioral techniques were not being utilized frequently. They did not relate their findings to recidivism.

Raynor, Ugwudike, and Vanstone (2014) investigated the use of skills by CCOs on the British Channel Island of Jersey. An analysis of videotaped sessions revealed that, similar to Trotter and Evans' findings, most CCOs demonstrated good relationship-building skills. However, there was significant variability in the extent to which individual CCOs were using other relevant skills such as problem-solving, prosocial modeling, and motivational interviewing. Offenders supervised by CCOs who used more of the relevant skills were found to be significantly less likely to be reconvicted, even when level of offender risk was taken into account.

Bonta et al. (2008) found that relationship skills alone did not predict recidivism, and noted that this finding would be predicted, given that relationship skills are theoretically conceived of as a necessary but not sufficient condition for prosocial change. However, other studies appear to contradict this assumption. Skeem and colleagues' work on community supervision has approached the issue from the dual role perspective, based on Klockars' (1972) conceptualization of the "synthetic" probation officer who emphasizes equally a therapeutic focus on helping offenders to change behavior, and a focus on compliance, law enforcement, and community safety through risk management.

Skeem, Eno Louden, Polaschek, and Camp (2007) used ratings made by CCOs, supervisees, and trained observers, using a purpose-built tool, the Dual-Role Relationship Inventory—Revised (DRI-R), to examine sentence compliance, supervisee motivation, treatment compliance, and recidivism (technical violations, probation revocation, arrests for new offenses) with mentally disordered offenders. The DRI-R has three factors: caring-fairness (i.e., blending caring with procedural justice orientation), trustworthiness, and toughness. The latter was related to indifference toward the supervisee, an expectation that the supervisee would not rely on the staff member for help, an emphasis on sentence compliance, and a punitive orientation. Interestingly, for caring-fairness, only the probation officer's own ratings were predictive of new probation violations.

A subsequent, more rigorous study was conducted with a mainstream parolee sample (Kennealy, Skeem, Manchak, & Eno Louden, 2012). Total DRI-R scores predicted days to first rearrest. The caring-fairness scale alone was associated with a 25% reduction in risk of rearrest, suggesting that relationship behavior alone may be sufficient. Even after controlling for the supervisees' pre-existing personality traits and static and dynamic factor-based levels of risk—important for attempting to rule out the possibility that CCO behavior is reactive to supervisees' characteristics that are more likely to be driving the effect—the same pattern of results was found.

Finally, based on a brief, eight-item version of the DRI-R, Polaschek (2016) investigated the relationship between ratings of CCO relationship quality made at about 10 weeks into parole for almost 300 men judged to be at high risk of violent and general recidivism. There was some evidence of reactiveness on the part of the CCO: ratings were lower for men with higher risk ratings, who were less motivated and had fewer protective factors and poorer plans for release. But when all of these factors were controlled for, the CCO's own ratings were predictive of reconviction (excluding parole violations) and parolees' ratings of the CCO's behavior were predictive of reimprisonment in the first year after release.

In conclusion, there is some support for the importance of the RNR principles, including those related to CCPs, in the process of community supervision itself. However, the extent to which probation officers implement these principles in their work with parolees or people on community supervision is central to whether the potential of such sentences to reduce recidivism is fully recognized. Even when CCOs have been made aware of evidence, they may resist changing role orientation, finding new ways to continue practices that are oriented to containing offenders or returning them to custody as quickly as possible (Rudes, 2012; Viglione, 2017). Inadequate training can be part of the problem. Even the use of assessment tools that help to identify priorities for intervention does not necessarily lead to the desired change in the service response provided by the CCO (Viglione, Rudes, & Taxman, 2015a).

Training Community Corrections Officers to be More Effective with Supervisees

A combination of (a) research studies suggesting that supervision itself may be effective in reducing recidivism, and (b) the wider body of research suggesting that criminogenic needs-based assessment and referral to services to address those needs reduce recidivism in a wide range of contexts, led to a concentration of activity in some jurisdictions in recent years aimed at improving CCO skills, and implicitly, changing their role orientation away from social work or surveillance alone to something more akin to a psychologically minded case manager.

Although there are differences across jurisdictions, in general, CCO's initial training after recruitment tends to focus largely on the tasks that officers will be required to complete as part of their role, such as report writing, risk assessment, offender and personal safety, sentence enforcement, and other legal requirements relevant to the jurisdiction in question (Annison, Eadie, & Knight, 2008). This focus is justified because most people entering the profession are inexperienced in completing these tasks, although it is sometimes assumed that they will already have other skills that will allow them to work effectively with offenders, particularly if they have qualifications or backgrounds in psychology or social work (Trotter, 2000). For this reason, in the United States at least, initial training has tended to cover only briefly the types of skills known to be effective at managing and changing behavior, such as motivational interviewing and cognitive behavioral techniques (Taxman, 2008).

A number of jurisdictions have responded to recent recognition of the potential to increase the effectiveness of community supervision with training program development (see Table 44.1). Some of these specifically are staff training programs (e.g., Effective Practices in Community Supervision [EPICS], Staff Training Aimed at Reducing Re-arrest [STARR],

Table 44.1   List of Structured, RNR-Based Training Programs Developed for Community
Corrections Officers in Different Jurisdictions

Training program	Acronym	Country	Relevant publications
Strategic Training Initiative in Community Supervision	STICS	Canada	Bonta et al. (2011), Bonta, Bourgon, Rugge, Gress, & Gutierrez (2013), Bourgon & Gutierrez (2012), Rugge & Bonta (2014)
Staff Training Aimed at Reducing Re-arrest	STARR	United States	Lowenkamp, Holsinger, Robinson, & Alexander (2014), Robinson et al. (2012), Robinson, VanBenschoten, Alexander, & Lowenkamp (2011)
Effective Practices in Community Supervision	EPICS	United States	Latessa, Smith, Schweitzer, & Labrecque (2013), Smith, Schweitzer, Labrecque, & Latessa (2012)
Skills for Effective Engagement and Development	SEED	United Kingdom, Romania	Sorsby et al. (2013), Sorsby, Shapland, & Durnescu (2014)
Citizenship[a]	N/A	United Kingdom	Bruce & Hollin (2009), Pearson, McDougall, Kanaan, Bowles, & Torgerson (2011)
Proactive Community Supervision model[a]	PCS	United States	Taxman (2008)

[a] These are broader models or approaches to supervision that include training components for community corrections officers.

Strategic Training Initiative in Community Supervision [STICS]). Others are more complete models or approaches to supervision with a structured CCO training component embedded (e.g., Proactive Community Supervision [PCS], and Citizenship; see Table 44.1). They may also address such factors as the organizational environment, with specific guidelines about how offenders should be managed, from assessment at induction through to the end of the supervision period (Pearson, McDougall, Kanaan, Bowles, & Torgerson, 2011). The development of these programs has been driven by extensive collaboration between researchers and practitioners around the world through the international research network known as CREDOS (Collaboration of Researchers for the Effective Development of Offender Supervision) Below is a description of the general format and structure of these training programs.[4]

Training Program Elements

Format

Training usually has three to four parts: an initial 3- or 4-day training event, a request to submit video or audio recordings of supervision sessions following training, a series of follow-up sessions, and optionally, an individual feedback phase. Although there is some didactic teaching, the initial training event usually has a strong practical focus. Both video and live demonstrations are used to illustrate skills. CCOs then use role-play to practice and receive feedback on their use of the skills. In some programs (e.g., STARR; Robinson et al., 2012), they are asked to bring to the initial training a video or audiotape of a supervision session conducted before the training event. Feedback on that session also introduces the staff member to the new skills. Some programs advocate strongly for officers' regular workplace supervisors to attend the initial training, and be involved throughout, to make it more likely that trainees will continue to receive high-quality, consistent guidance in their work after the initial training has been completed.

After the initial training, trainees submit multiple audio or video recordings of supervision sessions, often including sessions with the same offender in different parts of the sentence, to allow assessment of relationship development between the CCO and supervisee, and progress on the case plan. It also helps program trainers and researchers to evaluate the value of any ongoing coaching the officers are receiving from their regular workplace supervisors (Latessa, Smith, Schweitzer, & Labrecque, 2013).

Group follow-up sessions reinforce initial training. Submitted recordings are reviewed, and the sessions help to embed the trained skills, to enhance "technology transfer" problems (i.e., to address the challenges of transferring knowledge into the real world; Bourgon, Bonta, Rugge, & Gutierrez, 2010). At these sessions, the program trainers often draw on common themes from the recordings that have been submitted to provide overall feedback (Labrecque & Smith, 2015). Follow-up sessions may focus on a particular skill or technique taught at the initial training (Bonta et al., 2011). CCOs may be asked for feedback about how they managed to use that particular skill in their practice since the training. Further role-plays may be used, along with snippets of audio or video recordings, to reinforce the learning.

The frequency and format of follow-up sessions differs between programs: from four sessions, 3 months apart (Robinson et al., 2012), to a session per month for up to 2 years (Latessa et al., 2013), but is usually six or fewer unless implemented at a research site (Labrecque & Smith, 2015). The sessions may be conducted face-to-face, via telephone or video conferencing, or both. In some programs, there may be a refresher between 6 and 12 months after the initial training (Rugge & Bonta, 2014).

Finally, some trainers also provide individual feedback on CCOs' supervision sessions. CCOs are encouraged to complete similar review and coaching sessions at frequent intervals with their regular workplace supervisors.

Content

In general, program content is based on empirical evidence about practices that work to reduce recidivism and can be applied to the community supervision role. The approach taken by each program can be broken down across three main areas: the RNR model, intervention skills, and session structuring.

To address knowledge gaps common in CCOs, training introduces the RNR model—particularly the three most widely known principles of risk, need, and responsivity—and shows how it applies to supervision of individual offenders in the community, and the evidence of its effectiveness in this context (Robinson et al., 2012). Risk/need assessment tools are introduced. Training emphasizes their importance in determining higher-risk offenders and relevant criminogenic needs. CCOs are required to use results of this assessment to inform each offender's case plan.

General Personality and Cognitive Social Learning (GPCSL)-based staff intervention skills are emphasized, as identified by Dowden and Andrews (2004). Consistent with the relationship and structuring principles, training emphasizes both relationship-building skills and effective techniques for supporting prosocial change. Relationship-building skills include the use of a "firm but fair" approach, role clarification, active listening, mutual respect, and open, warm, and enthusiastic communication (Dowden & Andrews, 2004).

Specific behavioral change or management techniques include problem-solving skills, structured learning, and motivational interviewing. Problem-solving skills involve helping offenders to identify a problem, develop a plan to address that problem, and evaluate alternative options (Dowden & Andrews, 2004). Motivational interviewing is a method designed to enhance the motivation of clients to change and includes use of skills such as reflection and summarizing (Miller & Rollnick, 2013). CCOs also learn to model and reinforce prosocial behavior and attitudes, use sparingly disapproval of antisocial behavior and attitudes, and teach offenders the link between thoughts, feelings, and behaviors. The latter point is sometimes referred to as use of the "cognitive model" (e.g., Robinson et al., 2012) and is cited as one of the biggest challenges of these training programs, because training may not be sufficient for officers to understand the model well enough to teach it to offenders (Rugge & Bonta, 2014). Training programs may provide specific tools to assist staff with the use of these different skills (e.g., see Rugge & Bonta, 2014, and Sorsby et al., 2013). In keeping with the GPCSL-related skills, some training programs, particularly Citizenship and the PCS, emphasize the importance of advocacy and brokerage, to encourage offenders to make use of a wide variety of community resources (Pearson et al., 2011).

Teaching CCOs how to structure supervision sessions is another main feature of training programs. Bonta et al. (2008) found that too much time was spent focused on compliance and non-criminogenic needs during supervision sessions. Training programs aim to reduce time spent on sentence compliance and non-criminogenic needs and increase the focus on criminogenic needs relevant to the individual offender. Programs recognize that case management and other statutory obligations are still necessary but can be incorporated into the session in a way that is more consistent with RNR principles (Latessa et al., 2013). Most training programs provide a proposed breakdown for how a supervision session should look, including a check-in, a review of previous work, the teaching of a skill or delivery of an intervention (which should take up the majority of a session), and the setting of a task for the offender to complete or think about before the next session (Rugge & Bonta, 2014). Some programs encourage the mirroring of this structure for coaching sessions between CCOs and their supervisors (Smith, Schweitzer, Labrecque, & Latessa, 2012).

Is Training Effective?

As with other interventions, CCOs must use the practices before it is possible to identify whether they work to reduce recidivism. A number of studies have evaluated the effectiveness of these training programs, and cumulatively they address whether training leads to (a) more effective skills demonstrated by CCOs during supervision sessions, and (b) reductions in recidivism rates of offenders who are supervised by trained officers.

In-session skills

Several studies have examined the impact of these programs on CCO practice. In their evaluation of the STICS training program, Bonta et al. (2011) analyzed 295 audiotapes submitted by CCOs; 33 had been randomly assigned to undertake STICS training and 19 had not. Two trained researchers who were blind to training status analyzed the audiotapes and coded both content of discussion during sessions and the skills or techniques demonstrated by CCOs. Data were aggregated for each officer. STICS-trained officers adhered better to the need principle than untrained officers. STICS officers discussed more often with supervisees all but one criminogenic need, and spent less time discussing offenders' sentence conditions and non-criminogenic needs. The STICS officers also demonstrated better use of relevant skills, including structuring, relationship-building, and cognitive techniques.

In a similar study, 38 CCOs who undertook STARR training were compared with 21 officers who did not (n = 665 audiotapes; Robinson et al., 2012). In a mixed design, a pre-training session for each officer was initially analyzed; these were found to be statistically equivalent. Once training was completed for the STARR group, differences between trained versus untrained officers were similar to those found by Bonta et al. (2011). STARR-trained officers used effective reinforcement and disapproval more frequently during sessions, were more likely to discuss criminogenic needs such as cognitions, peers, and impulsivity, and overall used the cognitive model in talking with offenders (i.e., the link between thoughts, feelings, and behavior) significantly more often than the officers who had not received the training. But Robinson et al. (2012) noted that frequency of skill use even after training was still quite low.

Three published evaluations of the EPICS program found improved practice in trainee CCOs. A small pilot study analyzed 93 audiotapes from 10 CCOs—six had received training and four had not—and found that EPICS-trained officers were more likely to challenge anti-social thoughts or beliefs, reinforce prosocial behavior, assign homework, conduct role-plays, and explore the consequences of an offender's behavior (Smith et al., 2012). Another study found that 21 EPICS-trained officers used evidence-based practices more frequently during supervision than 20 officers who had not been trained (Latessa et al., 2013). A third evaluation, by Labrecque and Smith (2015), found that EPICS-trained officers obtained significantly higher ratings for use of anti-criminal modeling, disapproval, problem-solving, structured learning, cognitive restructuring, and relationship skills. EPICS-trained officers were compared with untrained officers over 18 months post-training, during which they were asked to submit at least one audio recording per month of an interaction with an offender. A composite measure of "skill effectiveness"—based both on quality and quantity of skills used—found that over the entire 18 months, just one session from a single officer in the comparison group (from 190 audiotapes submitted) was rated as "effective," compared to over 30% for EPICS-trained officers immediately after training (34 of 108 audiotapes), and nearly 70% after 1 year (37 of 53 audiotapes). These findings also suggest that ongoing coaching of at least 1 year may contribute to improved skills, although the authors also noted that there was still substantial room for improvement in use of some skills by trained officers.

Finally, Sorsby and colleagues (Sorsby, Shapland, & Durnescu, 2014; Sorsby et al., 2013) evaluated the impact of the Skills for Effective Engagement and Development (SEED) program in England and Romania. Rather than examining recordings directly, they asked 70 UK and 30 Romanian CCOs and offenders about CCO performance 5 months after training. The results were largely consistent with the observation research reviewed above. The responses from offenders—over 300 supervised by officers who had received SEED training in each country, and 150 supervised by officers who had not—suggested that SEED-trained CCOs were more likely to target criminogenic needs, challenge antisocial attitudes, and use relevant skills, particularly structuring skills, compared with untrained officers. That said, most findings were non-significant and there were considerable inconsistencies between the findings in England and Romania.

Two main points can be taken collectively from these studies. First, trained CCOs show better use of skills taught during training than their untrained counterparts. A least one study suggests the quality of skill use increased over time (Labrecque & Smith, 2015), and another showed that skill use did not appear to be due to pre-existing differences in skill between trained and untrained groups (Robinson et al., 2012). Second, despite an increase in the use of relevant skills and techniques, there remained considerable room for further improvement (Bonta et al., 2011; Labrecque & Smith, 2015; Latessa et al., 2013; Robinson et al., 2012; Smith et al., 2012). Findings have been consistent across a large number of recorded sessions, but most studies have included quite small numbers of staff and used short follow-up periods. It remains to be determined how durable these behavior changes are, and which staff and circumstances are most conducive to making them.

Linking training to recidivism

Some studies in the previous section also examined recidivism outcomes (Bonta et al., 2011; Latessa et al., 2013; Robinson et al., 2012). In addition to that research, evaluations of both the PCS and Citizenship models are relevant here. Linking probation officer training to recidivism is ultimately necessary to increase confidence that CCO staff skill is one of the mechanisms by which recidivism is reduced, but linking actual staff practice to recidivism provides a conceptually more rigorous argument in support of this mechanism. Studies vary in the strength of design but collectively do support the importance of staff training and subsequent practice as predictors of supervisee recidivism outcomes.

Evaluations of the PCS and Citizenship models yielded similar findings. Taxman (2008) compared recidivism rates for 274 randomly selected high-risk offenders who had been supervised by CCOs working under the PCS model at four different sites, with a matched comparison sample of offenders—matched on demographic variables, index offense, and supervision type—supervised at sites not operating under the PCS model. Thirty percent of PCS supervisees were rearrested over approximately 9 months on supervision, compared with 42% of the comparison supervisees, indicating the supervision model appeared to have a significant impact on offender recidivism.

Following the promising results of a pilot study, Pearson et al. (2011) conducted a large evaluation of the Citizenship program, comparing 3,819 Citizenship offenders with 2,110 non-Citizenship offenders. The comparison sample was drawn from the same jurisdiction but the offenders were supervised before Citizenship was implemented. The two samples were very similar on most demographic variables, and although there was a slightly higher proportion of high-risk offenders in the comparison group, the average risk level of the two groups was almost identical. After 2 years, 41% of Citizenship model supervisees had been reconvicted, compared with 50% of the comparison sample. Citizenship-supervised offenders were also less likely to have violated the conditions of supervision, and those who had violated their conditions took significantly longer to do so than the earlier cohort of comparison offenders. Comparison with the national recidivism rates for both the comparison and Citizenship samples suggested that these effects could be attributed to the implementation of Citizenship, rather than some form of cohort effect. While neither this study nor Taxman's (2008) evaluation of the PCS model were designed to isolate the effects of the officer training component of their respective initiatives, staff were trained in the implementation of both initiatives, and integrity of implementation was checked in the Taxman study. Together they add to the body of research reviewed earlier in this chapter, suggesting that community supervision can be considered an intervention in its own right. The Taxman evaluation provides further evidence of components of practice that are linked to a reduction in recidivism.

Studies examining the specific impact of training programs have also found significant effects on recidivism. Bonta et al. (2011) found that over a 2-year follow-up period, medium- and high-risk offenders supervised by STICS-trained officers were reconvicted at almost half the rate of offenders supervised by those same CCOs prior to STICS training (25 vs. 47%). This was not a statistically significant difference, but given the small sample of offenders and that officers in that study were randomly allocated to receive training, this is a promising finding that suggests the study may be worth replicating.

Robinson et al. (2012) observed a significant reduction in the recidivism rate for offenders supervised by STARR-trained officers. When Lowenkamp, Holsinger, Robinson, and Alexander (2014) extended the recidivism follow-up length in that study to 2 years, the effect of training was smaller but remained significant. However, the effect observed in both these studies was only present for moderate-risk offenders, with no significant difference in rearrest rates for high-risk offenders. In contrast, the evaluation of the EPICS program in Ohio found a lower recidivism rate for training, but in that study recidivism rates were reduced for high-risk offenders and not for moderate-risk offenders, raising some questions about whether offender risk levels may moderate the potential effectiveness of practices promoted in the training (Latessa et al., 2013).

Trotter (2013b) and Chadwick, DeWolf, and Serin (2015) independently reviewed the accumulating research literature. Chadwick et al. conducted a meta-analysis of 10 studies where CCOs have received structured training in core correctional practices. All of the major training programs and their evaluations (e.g., Bonta et al., 2011; Latessa et al., 2013; Lowenkamp et al., 2014; Pearson et al., 2011; Taxman, 2008) were represented in the meta-analysis, along with work done with CCOs in Jersey (Raynor et al., 2014) and Australia (Trotter, 1996, 2013a). The results indicated that overall, training programs have a small but significant association with recidivism: the average recidivism rate for offenders supervised by trained officers was 36%, while the average rate for those supervised by officers who did not receive training was 50%. The effect remained significant even after controlling for the influence of the large sample in the Pearson et al. (2011) Citizenship evaluation, and its magnitude is very favorable when compared with other types of risk-reducing interventions (Bonta & Andrews, 2017).

Trotter's (2013b) earlier literature review of eight studies included evaluations of STICS, STARR, EPICS, Citizenship, and the PCS model. He concluded that there was an overall trend toward lower recidivism for offenders supervised by CCOs who use certain skills, particularly prosocial modeling, problem-solving, and cognitive behavioral techniques. This review is particularly relevant to the question of whether the training programs are *causing* the observed reductions in recidivism. By focusing on individual skills, an argument can be made that the training programs lead to an improvement in the skills of CCOs, and use of those skills then leads to a reduction in recidivism, as opposed to some other aspect of the training being responsible for the effect. Similarly, Raynor et al.'s (2014) findings that recidivism rates are lower among offenders supervised by officers who demonstrate more skills than among offenders supervised by officers who make less use of the same skills provide further evidence that it is the skills being taught during training that are *causing* the reduction in recidivism. The case is strengthened further by the finding that although Level of Service Inventory—Revised (LSI-R) scores were similar between higher-skilled and lower-skilled groups, supervisees working with more skilled staff had significantly greater changes in their LSI-R scores over time.

Despite this evidence suggesting that these training programs are associated with reduced recidivism, for most studies, the mechanism(s) behind the association remains unclear. How do improved skills of CCOs contribute to offenders' lower recidivism rates? For training to be effective, what has been learned first needs to be demonstrated with supervisees, and while training can help with that, it does not guarantee it. Although not often discussed, it is assumed that training will fit neatly over the top of existing role orientations. But staff do not come to training as tabulae rasae. Traditionally, many trained first as social workers, which probably helps explain why, even after training, their relationship skills may remain stronger than their structuring skills (e.g., Raynor et al., 2014), most notably when the latter require a cognitive behavioral training background. In cases where staff may have been employed during an era when community supervision was oriented to punitive surveillance, staff may not readily make the ideological shift to empirically better-supported practices, especially if training is minimal (Viglione, 2017).

Consistent with the theoretical orientation of the "what works" literature, and *The Psychology of Criminal Conduct* (Bonta & Andrews, 2017), new and improved skills help CCOs (a) develop more influential bonds with offenders, (b) use those bonds to create hope and support a commitment to change, (c) identify the key criminogenic needs underpinning offending more effectively, (d) target these needs for "mini-interventions" they themselves deliver in-session, or (e) through advocacy and brokerage, link offenders to interventions that will target the causes of offending more effectively. A number of studies looked at some of these potential mechanisms as part of evaluating training impacts (e.g., Latessa et al., 2013; Raynor et al., 2014), but future longitudinal research would be helpful in furthering our understanding of how CCOs delivering community supervision actually leads to positive changes in the lives of the people they are supervising.

Future Directions

Research

In addition to the need for longitudinal research—which would also help to establish the long-term sustainability of any training effects—there are some other limitations with the existing research that need to be addressed. In particular, more studies with strong methodologies (e.g., randomized allocation of training and offenders, random recordings of sessions, statistical techniques for nested data[5]) that include larger numbers of CCOs would provide stronger evidence as to the extent to which these training programs significantly reduce recidivism.

Additionally, several studies have found evidence to suggest that the risk level of the offenders being supervised might have an impact on the effectiveness of the training (Latessa et al., 2013; Pearson et al., 2011; Robinson et al., 2012; Taxman, 2008). These findings are particularly interesting because the risk principle in the RNR model explicitly suggests that correctional interventions should target high-risk offenders. The evidence is currently mixed as to which supervisees benefit most from the sorts of CCO interventions reviewed in this chapter, but *these* findings suggest that either the impact of the training or the resulting interventions CCOs can actually deliver or connect with might be relatively weak. As more studies evaluate these programs, moderation analyses that better address the impact of offender risk level will be possible (Chadwick et al., 2015). Examining ways to better measure "dosage" levels or other indirect measures of impact (e.g., time spent on interventions within the interactions) may help to clarify these findings.

Again, with regard specifically to the training, the same people who designed and implemented the training programs have so far been responsible for the majority of the published evaluations. Application of specific models of training, where not run by the designers, would be predicted to be less effective, in line with the typical drop in effect found when programs move from demonstration to routine delivery modes (Bonta & Andrews, 2017). Research evidence from other areas suggests that training programs run by researchers or other experts can be significantly more effective than programs or interventions run by regular service providers (Wilson, Lipsey, & Derzon, 2003). Therefore, evaluations conducted by independent research teams could provide stronger evidence about whether the effectiveness of these programs is generalizable to sites where researchers have not been involved with implementation of the training.

Finally, an examination of the extent to which training can reorient CCOs from their training role orientations (e.g., social work) or untrained identities adopted prior to RNR-oriented training would also be informative, especially given a wider policy commitment to surveillance and control models in both UK and US jurisdictions in recent years. Both social workers and probation officers with a more law enforcement orientation may experience significant ideological resistance to policy changes in how they are supposed to practice (Grant & McNeill, 2015), which, given some of the recent relatively rapid changes at the policy level, may be a good thing!

But on the negative side, the high value given in social work theory and practice to the relationship aspects of the role (Grant & McNeill, 2015), and to actions designed to ameliorate deprivation and inequality (Shapland, Bottoms, & Farrall, 2012), may lead to some resistance in using that relationship to apply the more active ingredients of a change process arising from empirical research that essentially is situated in the discipline of psychology (e.g., supportive challenging of antisocial cognitions). A better understanding of the relevance of staff role identities, their malleability or otherwise, and the most effective ways to integrate old and new, would help with enhancing adherence to effective practices as well (Viglione, Rudes, & Taxman, 2015b). Relatedly, the importance of orienting the wider system (e.g., the key performance indicators) to support the desired practice would also be worth factoring in to evaluations of effectiveness (Shapland et al., 2012).

Practice

The past decade or so has seen a more concerted focus on community supervision itself as a potential rehabilitative (i.e., recidivism-reducing) intervention in its own right, as well as on understanding how CCOs can be conduits to improved uptake of other interventions (e.g., motivational interviewing to increase commitment to change may improve attendance at alcohol and drug treatment). Given heavy demand on rehabilitative services, and scarce resources for such services, especially given high ongoing commitments in several countries to high imprisonment and other non-rehabilitative regimes, ways to make supervision itself more effective are ways to stretch scarce resources further.

Training has been an important part of work to make the supervision process itself more effective. Promising initial findings highlighted earlier have led to wider implementation of some training programs. After being piloted in three Canadian provinces, the STICS program has been fully implemented in both British Columbia and Prince Edward Island. Over 1,300 CCOs and 300 regular workplace supervisors have completed the STARR program, with training still ongoing (S. VanBenschoten, personal communication, April 27, 2016). Other jurisdictions have taken note of these developments and begun to consider the best way of adapting the principles and evidence base behind these programs to their own community supervision practice. Implementation of the STICS program has already commenced in Sweden, and a similar program is being rolled out in Denmark (T. Rugge, personal communication, March 10, 2016).

Even with this expansion, the number of programs that have been developed and the number of jurisdictions in which they have been implemented remains small. The programs discussed here require significant resources and in some cases, serious changes to the approach of a whole organization (Taxman, 2008). However, there is now evidence suggesting these programs can reduce recidivism and some evidence to show that these reductions are sufficiently large to make these programs cost-effective (Pearson et al., 2011). There is also a growing literature providing guidance about how to successfully implement correctional programs on a wide scale. This literature includes Bonta, Bourgon, Rugge, Gress, and Gutierrez's (2013) detailed discussion of some of the challenges they faced when the STICS program was rolled out in British Columbia, in particular, how to ensure both individual CCOs and the wider organization are ready for change. At this point, organizations responsible for community supervision and interested in evidence-based approaches to reducing recidivism will want to consider whether these types of initiatives could be beneficial in their jurisdiction.

If these programs are implemented more widely, bigger questions of how community corrections staff are trained prior to employment arise. At the beginning of this chapter, we noted that the training programs discussed in this chapter generally stand apart from any initial training provided to new CCOs. However, if the psychological skills, techniques, and principles taught during these structured programs are so essential to reducing recidivism, there is a strong case that these skills, techniques, and principles should be taught to CCOs during their initial training, or as part of any community corrections-specific professional qualifications. The skills and techniques are difficult to master, and thus CCOs should be given the greatest possible opportunity to begin learning them. At the same time, we are not suggesting that social work training lacks value as a background for the CCO role, but the emerging research suggests an opening for a more hybrid or blended approach to training that incorporates both the psychology of behavior change and the social activism orientation of social work.

Positive Psychology and Offender Supervision

Finally, as for other forms of offender programs and services, positive approaches to offender supervision that do not focus directly on reducing criminogenic needs have been advocated. For example, it has been argued that, given the importance of an effective working relationship between supervisee and CCO, approaches that offer support to offenders to attain personal goals beyond those directly related to risk amelioration should be considered (e.g., the Good Lives Model; Purvis, Ward, & Willis, 2011; see also Day, Hardcastle, & Birgden, 2012). In our view, these proposals tend to oversimplify what constitutes good practice in existing RNR-based models, by characterizing the related practice as "removing" criminogenic needs (e.g., Woldgabreal, Day, & Ward, 2014). This view tends to suggest that RNR-based practice is understood as a punishment-based approach to behavior change. In contrast, replacement with positive behavior, capabilities, or supporting resources is a far more effective method of gaining enduring change, and this is the conceptual approach that underpins the RNR model. Nevertheless, positive alternatives go well beyond this modest approach. Instead of offense-free survival, they promote a human flourishing approach to supervision that develops and enhances qualities such as optimism, self-efficacy, cognitive flexibility, and hope (Woldgabreal et al., 2014).

It is surely beyond dispute that taking a positive approach to working with offenders will be more effective than deficit-emphasizing, punitive, or authoritarian approaches. The small volume of existing research supports this position. To investigate whether models based on striving to attain optimum wellbeing will outperform the best current approaches, they need an opportunity to be fully implemented and evaluated, both in optimal conditions and in the under-resourced contexts in which much of this practice is currently conducted. The next step in developing these types of practice models requires an agency willing to invest those resources.

Notes

1   In this chapter, unless otherwise noted, the term *community corrections officer* (CCO) is used to refer to staff responsible for the supervision of offenders in the community. The term is used for the supervision of offenders both on stand-alone sentences, such as *probation*, a term used to represent a range of community sentences that are often used as an alternative to prison, and those who are released from prison on *parole*, which is generally a period of supervision designed to ease an offender's transition back into the community after incarceration.

2   General Personality and Cognitive Social Learning (GPCSL)-based staff practices were formally referred to as Core Correctional Practices (CCP). The two terms are used interchangeably throughout this chapter.

3   The brief description draws primarily on the published literature; those wanting more detail should consult the respective training program manuals.

4   Data in these studies are nested (i.e., supervisees are grouped under a smaller number of CCOs who are themselves often grouped across a small number of sites). Modern multivariate techniques can deal with the violations to independence by analyzing data using methods designed for nested data. Existing studies generally do not use these techniques.

Key Readings

Bonta, J., Bourgon, G., Rugge, T., Scott, T. L., Yessine, A. K., Gutierrez, L., & Li, J. (2011). An experimental demonstration of training community corrections officers in evidence-based community supervision. *Criminal Justice and Behavior*, 38, 1127–1148.

Chadwick, N., DeWolf, A., & Serin, R. (2015). Effectively training community supervision officers: A meta-analytic review of the impact on offender outcome. *Criminal Justice and Behavior*, 42, 977–989.

Kennealy, P. J., Skeem, J. L., Manchak, S. M., & Eno Louden, J. (2012). Firm, fair, and caring officer-offender relationships protect against supervision failure. *Law and Human Behavior*, 36, 496–505.

Raynor, P., Ugwudike, P., & Vanstone, M. (2014). The impact of skills in probation work: A reconviction study. *Criminology & Criminal Justice*, 14, 235–249.

References

Andrews, D. A. (1982). *The supervision of offenders: Identifying and gaining control over the factors which make a difference*. Unpublished report to the Research Division of the Ministry of the Solicitor General of Canada (Report 1984-65).

Andrews, D. A., Zinger, I., Hoge, R. D., Bonta, J., Gendreau, P., & Cullen, F. T. (1990). Does correctional treatment work? A clinically relevant and psychologically informed meta-analysis. *Criminology*, 28, 369–404.

Annison, J., Eadie, T., & Knight, C. (2008). People first: Community corrections officer perspectives on probation work. *Probation Journal*, 55, 259–271.

Bonta, J., & Andrews, D. A. (2017). *The psychology of criminal conduct* (6th ed.). London, UK: Routledge.

Bonta, J., Bourgon, G., Rugge, T., Gress, C., & Gutierrez, L. (2013). Taking the leap: From pilot project to wide-scale implementation of the Strategic Training Initiative in Community Supervision (STICS). *Justice Research and Policy*, 15, 17–35.

Bonta, J., Bourgon, G., Rugge, T., Scott, T. L., Yessine, A. K., Gutierrez, L., & Li, J. (2011). An experimental demonstration of training community corrections officers in evidence-based community supervision. *Criminal Justice and Behavior*, 38, 1127–1148.

Bonta, J., Rugge, T., Scott, T., Bourgon, G., & Yessine, A. (2008). Exploring the black box of community supervision. *Journal of Offender Rehabilitation*, 47, 248–270.

Bourgon, G., & Bonta, J. (2014). Reconsidering the responsivity principle: A way to move forward. *Federal Probation*, 78(2), 3–10.

Bourgon, G., Bonta, J., Rugge, T., & Gutierrez, L. (2010). Technology transfer: The importance of on-going clinical supervision in translating "what works" to everyday community supervision. In F. McNeill, P. Raynor, & C. Trotter (Eds.), *Offender supervision: New directions in theory, research and practice* (pp. 88–106). Cullompton, UK: Willan.

Bourgon, G., & Gutierrez, L. (2012). The general responsivity principle in community supervision: The importance of community corrections officers using cognitive intervention techniques and its influence on recidivism. *Journal of Crime and Justice*, 35, 149–166.

Bourgon, G., Gutierrez, L., & Ashton, J. (2012). The evolution of community supervision practice: The transformation from case manager to change agent. *Federal Probation*, 76(2), 27–35.

Bruce, R., & Hollin, C. R. (2009). Developing citizenship. *EuroVista: Probation and Community Justice*, 1, 24–31.

Burrell, W. D. (2012). *Community corrections management: Issues and strategies.* Kingston, NJ: Civic Research Institute.

Chadwick, N., DeWolf, A., & Serin, R. (2015). Effectively training community supervision officers: A meta-analytic review of the impact on offender outcome. *Criminal Justice and Behavior*, 42, 977–989.

Day, A., Hardcastle, L., & Birgden, A. (2012). Case management in community corrections: Current status and future directions. *Journal of Offender Rehabilitation*, 51, 485–495.

Deering, J. (2010). The purposes of supervision: Practitioner and policy perspectives in England and Wales. In F. McNeill, P. Raynor, & C. Trotter (Eds.), *Offender supervision: New directions in theory, research and practice* (pp. 451–470). Abingdon, UK: Willan.

Dowden, C., & Andrews, D. A. (2004). The importance of staff practice in delivering effective correctional treatment: A meta-analytic review of core correctional practice. *International Journal of Offender Therapy and Comparative Criminology*, 48, 203–214.

Feeley, M. M., & Simon, J. (1992). The new penology: Notes on the emerging strategy of corrections and its implications. *Criminology*, 30, 449–474.

Gendreau, P., Goggin, C., Cullen, F. T., & Andrews, D. A. (2000). The effects of community sanctions and incarceration on recidivism. *Forum on Corrections Research*, 12, 10–13.

Grant, S., & McNeill, F. (2015). What matters in practice? Understanding "quality" in the routine supervision of offenders in Scotland. *British Journal of Social Work*, 45, 1985–2002.

Kaeble, D., Glaze, L., Tsoutis, A., & Minton, T. (2015). *Correctional populations in the United States, 2014.* Report No. NCJ 249513. Retrieved from http://www.bjs.gov/content/pub/pdf/cpus14.pdf

Kennealy, P. J., Skeem, J. L., Manchak, S. M., & Eno Louden, J. (2012). Firm, fair, and caring officer-offender relationships protect against supervision failure. *Law and Human Behavior*, 36, 496–505.

Klockars, C. B. (1972). A theory of probation supervision. *The Journal of Criminal Law, Criminology and Police Science*, 63, 550–557.

Labrecque, R. M., & Smith, P. (2015). Does training and coaching matter? An 18-month evaluation of a community supervision model. *Victims & Offenders*, 12(2), 1–20.

Latessa, E. J., Smith, P., Schweitzer, M., & Labrecque, R. M. (2013). *Evaluation of the Effective Practices in Community Supervision model (EPICS) in Ohio.* Unpublished manuscript. Center for Criminal Justice Research, University of Cincinnati, OH.

Lipsey, M. W. (1995). What do we learn from 400 research studies on the effectiveness of treatment with juvenile delinquents? In J. McGuire (Ed.), *What works: Reducing reoffending: Guidelines from research and practice* (pp. 63–78). Chichester, UK: Wiley.

Lipton, D., Martinson, R., & Wilks, J. (1975). *The effectiveness of correctional treatment: A survey of treatment evaluation studies.* New York, NY: Praeger.

Lowenkamp, C. T., Flores, A. W., Holsinger, A. M., Makarios, M. D., & Latessa, E. J. (2010). Intensive supervision programs: Does program philosophy and the principles of effective intervention matter? *Journal of Criminal Justice*, 38, 368–375.

Lowenkamp, C. T., Holsinger, A., Robinson, C. R., & Alexander, M. (2014). Diminishing or durable treatment effects of STARR? A research note on 24-month re-arrest rates. *Journal of Crime and Justice*, 37, 275–283.

Martinson, R. (1974). What works? Questions and answers about prison reform. *The Public Interest*, 35, 22–54.

Martinson, R., & Wilks, J. (1978). Save parole supervision. *Federal Probation*, 42, 23–27.

McNeill, F. (2010). Supervision in historical context: Learning the lessons of (oral) history. In F. McNeill, P. Raynor, & C. Trotter (Eds.), *Offender supervision: New directions in theory, research and practice* (pp. 492–508). Abingdon, UK: Willan.

Miller, W. R., & Rollnick, S. (2013). *Motivational interviewing: Helping people change* (3rd ed.). New York, NY: Guilford Press.

Paparozzi, M. A., & Gendreau, P. (2005). An intensive supervision program that worked: Service delivery, professional orientation, and organizational supportiveness. *The Prison Journal*, 85, 445–466.

Pearson, D. A. S., McDougall, C., Kanaan, M., Bowles, R. A., & Torgerson, D. J. (2011). Reducing criminal recidivism: Evaluation of Citizenship, an evidence-based probation supervision process. *Journal of Experimental Criminology*, 7, 73–102.

Petersilia, J. (1998). A decade of experimenting with intermediate sanctions: What have we learned? *Justice Research and Policy*, 1, 9–23.

Petersilia, J., & Turner, S. (1993). *Evaluating intensive supervision probation/parole: Results of a nationwide experiment*. Washington, DC: US Department of Justice, Office of Justice Programs, National Institute of Justice.

Polaschek, D. L. L. (2016). Do relationships matter? Examining the quality of probation officers' interactions with parolees in preventing recidivism. *Practice: The New Zealand Corrections Journal*, 4(1), 5–8.

Purvis, M., Ward, T., & Willis, G. (2011). The Good Lives Model in practice: Offence pathways and case management. *European Journal of Probation*, 3, 4–28.

Raynor, P., Ugwudike, P., & Vanstone, M. (2014). The impact of skills in probation work: A reconviction study. *Criminology & Criminal Justice*, 14, 235–249.

Rhodes, W., Dyous, C., Kling, R., Hunt, D., & Luallen, J. (2013). *Recidivism of offenders on federal community supervision* (Report No. 241018). Retrieved from https://www.ncjrs.gov/pdffiles1/bjs/grants/241018.pdf

Robinson, C. R., Lowenkamp, C. T., Holsinger, A. M., VanBenschoten, S., Alexander, M., & Oleson, J. C. (2012). A random study of Staff Trained at Reducing Re-arrest (STARR): Using core correctional practices in probation interactions. *Journal of Crime and Justice*, 35, 167–188.

Robinson, C. R., VanBenschoten, S., Alexander, M., & Lowenkamp, C. T. (2011). A random (almost) study of Staff Trained at Reducing Re-Arrest (STARR): Reducing recidivism through intentional design. *Federal Probation*, 75(2), 57–63.

Rudes, D. S. (2012). Getting technical: Parole officers' continued use of technical violations under California's parole reform agenda. *Journal of Crime and Justice*, 35, 249–268.

Rugge, T., & Bonta, J. (2014). Training community corrections officers in cognitive-behavioral intervention strategies. In R. C. Tafrate, & D. Mitchell (Eds.), *Forensic CBT: A handbook for clinical practice* (pp. 227–241). Hoboken, NJ: Wiley-Blackwell.

Schram, P. J., Koons-Witt, B. A., Williams, F. P., & McShane, M. D. (2006). Supervision strategies and approaches for female parolees: Examining the link between unmet needs and parolee outcome. *Crime & Delinquency*, 52, 450–471.

Shapland, J., Bottoms, A., & Farrall, S. (2012). *The quality of probation supervision: A literature review*. Sheffield, UK: University of Sheffield Centre for Criminological Research.

Skeem, J. L., Eno Louden, J., Polaschek, D. L. L., & Camp, J. (2007). Assessing relationship quality in mandated community treatment: Blending care with control. *Psychological Assessment*, 19, 397–410.

Smith, P., Schweitzer, M., Labrecque, R. M., & Latessa, E. J. (2012). Improving community corrections officers' supervision skills: An evaluation of the EPICS model. *Journal of Crime and Justice*, 35, 189–199.

Solomon, A. L., Kachnowski, V., & Bhati, A. (2005). *Does parole work? Analyzing the impact of post-prison supervision on rearrest outcomes*. Washington, DC: Urban Institute Justice Policy Center.

Sorsby, A., Shapland, J., & Durnescu, I. (2014). *External evaluation of the Skills for Effective Engagement and Development (SEED) project in Romania*. Retrieved from http://stream-probation.eu/wp-content/uploads/SEEDS-Study-Fianl-Report.pdf

Sorsby, A., Shapland, J., Farrall, S., McNeill, F., Priede, C., & Robinson, G. (2013). *Probation staff views of the Skills for Effective Engagement Development (SEED) project*. Sheffield, Centre for Criminological Research Occasional paper no. 4. Sheffield, UK: University of Sheffield.

Taxman, F. S. (2002). Supervision: Exploring the dimensions of effectiveness. *Federal Probation*, 66(2), 14–27.

Taxman, F. S. (2008). No illusions: Offender and organizational change in Maryland's Proactive Community Supervision efforts. *Criminology & Public Policy*, 7, 275–302.

Trotter, C. (1996). The impact of different supervision practices in community corrections: Cause for optimism. *Australian & New Zealand Journal of Criminology*, 29, 1–18.

Trotter, C. (2000). Social work education, pro-social orientation and effective probation practice. *Probation Journal*, 47, 256–261.

Trotter, C. (2013a). Effective supervision of young offenders. In P. Ugwudike, & P. Raynor (Eds.), *What works in offender compliance: International perspectives and evidence-based practices* (pp. 227–241). Basingstoke, UK: Palgrave Macmillan.

Trotter, C. (2013b). Reducing recidivism through probation supervision: What we know and don't know from four decades of research. *Federal Probation*, 77(2), 43–48.

Trotter, C., & Evans, P. (2012). An analysis of supervision skills in youth probation. *Australian & New Zealand Journal of Criminology*, 45, 255–273.

Veysey, B. M., Ostermann, M., & Lanterman, J. L. (2014). The effectiveness of enhanced parole supervision and community services: New Jersey's serious and violent offender reentry initiative. *The Prison Journal*, 94, 435–453.

Viglione, J. (2017). Street-level decision making: Acceptability, feasibility, and the use of evidence-based practices in adult probation. *Criminal Justice and Behavior*, 44, 1356–1381.

Viglione, J., Rudes, D. S., & Taxman, F. S. (2015a). Misalignment in supervision: Implementing risk/needs assessment instruments in probation. *Criminal Justice and Behavior*, 42, 263–285.

Viglione, J., Rudes, D. S., & Taxman, F. S. (2015b). The myriad of challenges with correctional change: From goals to culture. *European Journal of Probation*, 7, 103–123.

Wan, W., Poynton, S., Doorn, G. v., & Weatherburn, D. (2014). Parole supervision and reoffending. *Trends and Issues in Crime and Criminal Justice*, 485, 1–7.

Whitehead, P. R., & Statham, R. (2006). *The history of probation: Politics, power and cultural change 1876–2005*. Crayford, UK: Shaw and Sons.

Wilson, S. J., Lipsey, M. W., & Derzon, J. (2003). The effects of school-based intervention programs on aggressive behavior: A meta-analysis. *Journal of Consulting and Clinical Psychology*, 71, 136–149.

Woldgabreal, Y., Day, A., & Ward, T. (2014). The community-based supervision of offenders from a positive psychology perspective. *Aggression and Violent Behavior*, 19(1), 32–41.

45

Integrating Dynamic Risk Assessment Into Community Supervision Practice

Ralph C. Serin and Nick Chadwick
Carleton University, Canada

Caleb D. Lloyd
Swinburne University of Technology, Australia

For more than three decades, correctional psychology has been preoccupied with the creation of risk assessment instruments. Refinements have led to different models of assessment practice (i.e., solely actuarial, combined risk and treatment need scales, structured professional judgment approaches). These approaches have yielded acceptable, and similar, indices of predictive accuracy (e.g., area under the curve [AUCs] indices greater than .70) for general recidivism and for specific subgroups (i.e., non-sexual violence, sexual violence, intimate partner violence). There are notable champions for specific scales, but there is also confusion regarding what should be considered a best practice approach. Empirical guidelines for selecting a preferred risk scale are absent in the published literature, although there have been some attempts to provide assistance to agencies and practitioners (Serin, 2009; Skeem & Eno Louden, 2007; Serin & Lowenkamp, 2015).

Yang, Wong, and Coid's (2010) meta-analysis highlights this conclusion regarding similarities in predictive accuracy across risk measures. Moreover, research by Kroner, Mills, and Reddon (2005) indicates risk measures share similar risk domains. Nonetheless, this proliferation of instruments has arguably masked how little correctional psychology has advanced its *conceptual* knowledge of how risk manifests in offenders' lives and results in the commission of crimes (e.g., Mann, Hanson, & Thornton, 2010). For example, it is a critical weakness that the body of research currently has little to say about how supervision officers (hereafter referred to as POs, i.e., probation or parole officers) can track and manage the evolving risk of offenders under community supervision.

Despite decades of risk assessment research, the field is also limited in its understanding of the immediate features (whether situational or intrapersonal) that influence an individual to take or forego criminal action (Farrington, 2011; Yang & Mulvey, 2012). In light of this, the purpose of this chapter is to review the current state of literature on the dynamic risk factors (DRFs) that may be relatively *proximal* triggers of criminal behavior and discuss how such factors might be integrated into community supervision practice.

The Wiley International Handbook of Correctional Psychology, First Edition. Edited by Devon L. L. Polaschek, Andrew Day, and Clive R. Hollin.

Historical Context

In the early 1990s, Don Andrews and his colleagues' research led to changes in the risk assessment enterprise that dramatically changed the field (see Andrews & Bonta, 2010). Employing meta-analytic findings, they demonstrated that specific correlates of criminal conduct could be identified, some of which were not static. Organizing these findings by the strength of each factor's association with criminal behavior, Andrews and Bonta (2010) presented a hierarchy of risk factors, referred to as the *Central Eight*. In order of greatest effect size for the association with recidivism, these factors are: history of antisocial behavior, antisocial personality pattern, antisocial cognition, antisocial associates, problems in the family, problems in the work domain, problems in leisure and/or recreation domains, and substance abuse. With the exception of history of antisocial behavior, these risk factors can theoretically change in a prosocial direction, and observed changes should be logically associated with an individual's propensity to commit criminal conduct.

Reflecting their goal to identify appropriate targets for rehabilitation programs, and their conceptualization of dynamic risk as relatively slow-evolving features, Andrews and his colleagues referred to these changeable risk factors as *criminogenic needs*. This term came to be considered synonymous with the concept of dynamic risk, but subsequent research has suggested that even though the criminogenic needs in Andrews and Bonta's (2010) *Central Eight* are dynamic, they tend to remain relatively stable across time. For example, change scores on risk and need measures like the Level of Service Inventory—Revised (LSI-R) have demonstrated only minimal effect sizes (Vose, Smith, & Cullen, 2013). This slow pace of change may suggest that criminogenic needs have good utility for risk prediction and long-term case planning, but appreciably less utility for examining intra-individual change in the short term. Moreover, the scoring procedures used to rate these items are typically only sensitive enough to detect change across months, rather than days or weeks.

Defining Dynamic Risk Factors

Within the literature, there remains ambiguity surrounding how to exactly define a truly dynamic risk factor, given some factors may change slowly, some may change quickly, and little research has successfully differentiated between the factors that change at the group level (on average) versus at the individual level (within the same person). In essence, the term *criminogenic need* has become equivalent to changeable factors that are related to offending behavior, but this viewpoint is arguably incomplete. As noted by Yang et al. (2010), a second key feature that should emerge from a set of hypothetically dynamic risk variables (especially *acute* dynamic factors beyond those in the *Central Eight* risk factors) is the ability to identify precipitants of offender outcome; this represents a different task compared to assessing whether risk scores change over time due to intervention. In essence, this refers to the *timing* of the dynamic risk assessment; there should be a closely proximal association between observed change (i.e., specifically increased risk) on an acute dynamic risk factor and an increased risk of imminent recidivism outcome. More generally, changes in either slow- or fast-changing DRFs should prospectively predict recidivism. Thus, all definitions of dynamic risk imply that (a) change is important (i.e., the direction of change, especially movement over a threshold into a different risk band), and (b) a subsequent assessment should be a better signal of future recidivism, compared to previous assessments.

DRFs (particularly relatively stable factors) represent important intervention targets for POs, since reductions in these risk factors are expected to lead to sustained reductions in overall level of risk for future recidivism (Brown, St. Amand, & Zamble, 2009; Caudy, Durso, & Taxman, 2013; Hanson & Harris, 2000; Howard & Dixon, 2013; Jones, Brown, & Zamble, 2009; Lewis, Olver, & Wong, 2012). Additionally, since dynamic factors can purportedly change, it is logically reasonable that POs should regularly incorporate new information about dynamic risk variables into case planning and modify risk management strategies accordingly.

However, most prior studies have been occupied with whether DRFs significantly predict recidivism (with mixed results, especially when researchers first control for static predictors). By contrast, less research has focused on establishing that dynamic risk instruments exhibit the features that are core to the field's conceptualization of DRFs. For example, the majority of research has examined DRFs at one specified point of time. This amounts to treating a dynamic variable as static, and provides no information regarding whether the variable shows change over time, or whether more proximal assessments may serve as improved indicators of imminent risk. To investigate change processes, at least two assessments of risk are necessary to observe differences; to effectively model a change process, experts point out that at least three distinct assessments of dynamic risk are required, since only multiple time points allow researchers to partition measurement error from true change (Brown et al., 2009; Singer & Willett, 2003). Most clearly, a single measurement of a dynamic item (e.g., anger, substance abuse) does not provide the assessor with dynamic information, nor does it allow researchers to argue that the variable exhibits truly dynamic features.

Douglas and Skeem (2005) contributed to the discussion about the temporal relationship between DRFs and outcomes by differentiating between *risk status* and *risk state*. Risk status emphasizes static risk factors that are not expected to change over time, and therefore are of little utility when identifying intervention services or managing correctional clients in the community. Risk state, however, involves an analysis of various factors that could influence change regarding a client's risk. Further, these state variables could change rapidly (e.g., level of anger) or gradually (e.g., antisocial attitudes). Douglas and Skeem (2005) argued that both static and dynamic factors contribute to an individual's risk, suggesting a comprehensive evaluation of an offender's risk is necessary to effectively manage it. Thus, both conceptually and practically, risk state factors are helpful for case conceptualization and management when risk status is already known to be high. This is analogous to a physician taking a patient's temperature when tracking the prognosis of an existing diagnosis, or to attending carefully to the signs that a hurricane may be developing only when one resides along the ocean during seasons when storms occur. Due to their focus on establishing imminence and short-term fluctuations, risk state factors are intriguing because they expand the pool of dynamic factors beyond the traditional *Central Eight* highlighted by Andrews and Bonta (2010).

Earlier, Hanson and Harris (2000) had distinguished between *stable* and *acute* DRFs. They defined stable DRFs as factors that are not expected to change frequently or rapidly, suggesting a time frame of months to years. This is consistent with the traditional viewpoint of criminogenic needs, albeit their work relates specifically to sex offenders. By contrast, acute DRFs are anticipated to change rapidly: over days, sometimes even hours. Accordingly, intervention efforts should be directed at the stable DRFs as these are the factors that, when changed, are anticipated to lead to improvements in the offender's overall level of risk, but the acute risks must be managed to mitigate against reoffending. Perhaps somewhat simplistically, we have mused that static and stable dynamic factors indicate *who* is at risk while acute dynamic factors indicate *when* they are at risk (Serin, Chadwick, & Lloyd, 2016).

Examining the Pool of Dynamic Factors

Traditional (Stable)

Case planning most typically emerges from a standardized risk and need assessment (Offender Assessment System [OASys], Howard, Clark, & Garnham, 2003; Correctional Offender Management Profiling for Alternative Sanctions [COMPAS], Brennan, Dieterich, & Ehret, 2009; The Level of Service/Case Management Inventory [LS/CMI], Andrews, Bonta, & Wormith, 2008; Offender Risk Assessment System [ORAS], Latessa, Smith, Lemke, Makarios, & Lowenkamp, 2009) or a structured case formulaic assessment (Serin & Hanby, in press). In general, an individual showing elevated scores on specific need domains suggests the requirement for intervention; the specific dosage of this intervention is informed by risk level, such that higher-risk clients receive more intensive intervention. Work by Bourgon and Armstrong (2005) provided recommendations for treatment dosage according to client risk level, suggesting that at least 200 hours of structured intervention is required for moderate-risk cases. Despite this, specific and empirical guidelines regarding treatment dosage remain elusive. Unfortunately, the state of the research does not indicate if programs of a lesser dosage can be combined, nor does it indicate how dosage should be defined (e.g., 8 hours per day for 5 weeks; or 4 hours per day, 3 days per week for 16 weeks).

For probation, the issue of dosage is even more obscure. Carter (2014) has attempted to extrapolate the treatment dosage literature to probation supervision standards (i.e., frequency of contact), but her work is not empirically based. Certainly, many probation agencies advocate for an iterative model whereby, with increased successful time in the community, supervision intensity is decreased for a particular client.

Unsurprisingly, the most common needs identified from standardized assessments of DRFs reflect the *Central Eight* factors presented earlier. Accordingly, case planning primarily recommends intervention in terms of criminal thinking, self-regulation and problem-solving, and substance misuse. This is augmented with educational upgrading and employment training. Intervention for special sub-populations (i.e., sex offenders, violent offenders, intimate partner-violent offenders) is also reflected.

These risk and need assessments, however, do not necessarily inform *how* the criminogenic needs relate to criminal conduct, just that they are more or less present for a particular client. The assumption is that higher scores for a particular need or domain relate to its higher ranking as a treatment need. Thus, case analysis requires paying attention not only to the degree to which a risk factor is present but also to the *meaning* of the risk factor within the context of this individual client's prior criminal behavior.

This case analysis can be best accomplished through a detailed review and examination of the sequence of distal and proximal antecedents to the client's criminal conduct. For example, a behavioral offense chain exercise asks clients to consider their overall pattern of crimes. In particular, this exercise considers with whom the client commits crimes, other contextual circumstances, and which locations, internal states, or points in time represent their highest-risk situations.

The results of the behavioral offense chain may indicate certain criminogenic needs (e.g., substance abuse) are commonly present during high-risk situations, but it should also identify additional DRFs that have not been necessarily captured by the *Central Eight* (e.g., access to victims). Creating a comprehensive case planning strategy that addresses all relevant factors will lead to a strategy for improved management efforts. Sometimes researchers conceptualize targeting these additional factors as a method to stabilize clients so they can then extend effort to address criminogenic needs. At other times, the purpose is to address a highly individualized risk factor that appears specifically important within that client's criminal involvement. Thus, the cornerstone of community supervision practice can involve targeting *Central Eight* risk factors, either within sessions or via formalized programs, as well as a consideration of more contemporaneous fluctuations in risk.

Contemporary (Acute)

The review by Douglas and Skeem (2005) expanded the list of potentially important DRFs that deserve consideration during community supervision. In particular, they asserted that changes on these more acute dynamic factors might be prognostic regarding client outcome. Hence, this increased pool of DRFs could be used for more refined case planning and risk management, particularly at the idiographic or case level.

Encouragingly, in the past few years there have been several dynamic risk measures developed that reflect these more acute factors. These include the Short-Term Assessment of Risk and Treatability (START, Desmarais, Nicholls, Wilson, & Brink, 2012; Nicholls, Brink, Desmarais, Webster, & Martin, 2006), the Service Planning Instrument (SPIn, Orbis Partners, 2003), and the Dynamic Risk Assessment of Offender Reentry (DRAOR, Serin, 2007). These are described elsewhere in some detail (Serin, Chadwick, et al., 2016) but only the DRAOR will be discussed here in terms of its application within supervision practice, based on our experience with this measure.

The DRAOR (Serin, 2007) is an empirically informed instrument that considers Stable and Acute dynamic risk and Protective factors. Items are scored but not weighted according to their relationship with client outcome. The DRAOR was developed to assist POs in the assessment, and reassessment, of their clients' circumstances throughout the supervision process. For research purposes, a total score is calculated by summing the Acute and Stable scales and subtracting the Protective scale; however, in practice, a total score for the DRAOR is not calculated. Rather, items in each subscale are totaled to provide a summary of potential problem areas for community supervision officers to address. Client outcome can be improved by decreasing risk factors or enhancing protective factors. Importantly, Cox regression survival analysis has indicated the DRAOR Total score predicts incrementally over a valid static risk measure (the $RoC*RoI$, Bakker, Riley, & O'Malley, 1999; Hanby, 2013; Yesberg & Polaschek, 2014); more proximal assessments are more predictive (Lloyd, 2015), and the measure appears also to have utility irrespective of client gender (Yesberg, Scanlan, Hanby, Serin, & Polaschek, 2015).

Although the DRAOR acute dynamic risks are not necessarily exhaustive, they are representative of similar instruments (Serin, Chadwick, et al., 2016). These acute risks include items such as substance abuse, anger, negative mood, victim access, employment, interpersonal relationships, and living situations. It should be clear that these are distinct from earlier conceptualizations of criminogenic needs, primarily because the DRAOR coding means that these factors could conceivably change between sessions with a client. Increasingly, such factors are proving at the idiographic level to be prognostic of criminal behavior (Babchishin, 2013; Horney, Osgood, & Marshall, 1995; Lloyd, 2015).

As will be discussed in greater detail in subsequent sections, such sensitivity to change between sessions has significant implications for community supervision practice. If a measure can reliably detect change between monthly sessions *and* this change is related to client outcome, then such change derives a newly refined risk management action plan. Hence, it suggests that treatment targets might profitably be expanded beyond those described earlier as stable or traditional dynamic factors. Moreover, it suggests that POs should systematically assess and reassess acute DRFs throughout the supervision period, refining their interactions with clients, partly on the basis of changes in acute dynamic risks.

Dynamic Risk and Protective Factors

Earlier, the term *protective factor* was mentioned, and their inclusion in contemporary dynamic risk measures implies they are important in community supervision practice. Of interest is whether staff at community supervision agencies can increase the incidence or salience of such factors, such that the likelihood that offenders will reoffend when faced with a high-risk situation is reduced. Importantly and until recently, the issue of protective factors has received limited attention from psychological researchers.

To some extent, concern regarding risk assessments that were deficit-specific has led to greater interest in examining the potential importance of protective factors. Three areas of current research are worth highlighting: the application of protective factors in risk assessment (de Vogel, de Ruiter, Bouman, & de Vries Robbé, 2009); positive psychology as it is applied to offender supervision (Woldgabreal, Day, & Ward, 2014); and the desistance literature (Maruna, 2010). Much as contemporary research has begun to expand DRFs beyond the *Central Eight*, each of these areas of research argue that protective factors are conceptually different from risk factors. For example, *high impulse control* as a hypothetical protective factor is not clearly distinct from assessing an individual to have low levels of *impulsivity* (a *Central Eight* risk factor). In this case, impulse control can be easily conceptualized as the opposite of impulsivity. By contrast, a client with a number of prosocial friends may simultaneously have antisocial friends, or may not (i.e., the two types of friends are independent of each other). Thus, the term "protective factors" is only necessary in the risk assessment lexicon if these factors are defined as being distinct, and not simply a reframing of low levels of risk variables.

Under the assumption that protective factors are conceptually distinct, Rutter (2000) proposed two frameworks that each highlight different mechanisms underlying how protective factors may relate to recidivism. According to a *compensatory model*, risk and protective factors are cumulative, with each risk factor increasing the odds of recidivism and each protective factor decreasing the odds of recidivism. Under this model, multiple risk factors are additive, whereas protective factors subtract from the cumulative risk. The second proposed model is an *interactive model* that asserts that protective factors are relevant only depending on the degree to which risk factors are present. Within this model, the impact of protective factors on criminal outcomes varies depending on the level of risk, such that risk is reduced when both risk factors and protective factors are highly present, whereas protective factors have little or no impact on likelihood of recidivism when risk is already low.

Hence, an *interactive model* implies that individual agency is a critical feature of a protective factor, such that when the individual is faced with an opportunity for crime (i.e., at-risk situation), the individual actively selects an adaptive, functional, and non-criminal response. Conversely, criminal action arguably arises when a person chooses to engage in criminal conduct when faced with at-risk situations because a non-criminal response is not considered, valued, or available (i.e., protective factors do not currently exist). If one accepts this conceptualization, then protective factors *moderate* risk but do not *reduce* risk. This contrasts directly with a purely risk avoidance perspective (Mann, Webster, Schofield, & Marshall, 2004) where risk is avoided and therefore is managed by its absence. Unfortunately, avoidance of risk may not be a viable plan for most clients who must interact with others, seek and maintain employment, and deal with an array of affective states.

Elsewhere, dynamic risk and protective factors have been conceptualized to be situated at different points along the age-crime curve (Serin, Lloyd, & Hanby, 2010); DRFs relate to crime acquisition and expression while protective factors reflect crime desistance. Hence, protective factors have been suggested to be important in understanding client success such that their presence may buffer or moderate risk (Jones, Brown, Robinson, & Frey, 2015; Polaschek, 2016; Serin, Chadwick, et al., 2016). These desistance factors (i.e., events and attributions that lead to cessation from crime) encompass what the field refers to as protective factors.

Seminal work by Sampson and Laub (1992, 2005) identified key events such as stable employment and a high-quality relationship that precede or lead to crime desistance. Maruna (2010) nicely summarized the broader desistance literature, identifying numerous desistance factors that reflect a blend of personal and social capital. Salient desistance factors include: getting older and maturing (van Mastrigt & Farrington, 2009); family and relationships (Laub, Nagin, & Sampson, 1998; Maruna, LeBel, & Lanier, 2003); sobriety (Walters, 1998); employment (Uggen, 2000); hope and motivation (LeBel, Burnett, Maruna, & Bushway, 2008); having a place in a social group (Farrall, 2004); not having a criminal identity (Chiricos, Barrick, Bales, & Bontrager, 2007); and being believed in (Rex, 1999). The assumption is that these factors assist in ameliorating risk, thereby leading to cessation from criminal conduct. Much of the desistance literature highlighted here suggests that protective factors may represent some of the internal and external mechanisms that underlie the process of exiting crime (Serin & Lloyd, 2009), making their assessment a critical inclusion to contemporary dynamic risk assessment. Overall, the field has generally embraced the importance of protective factors; however, the lack of clear definitions given to the various terms used to reflect protective factors (e.g., protective, promotive, stabilizers, strengths, and desistance) underscore the field's current confusion regarding how these factors may influence client outcome, and how these factors may be conceptually distinct from known risk factors. For the purpose of this chapter, protective factors are those events or client characteristics that mitigate risk of reoffending. This description is important because clients may have certain strengths (i.e., creativity, artistic skills) that do not mitigate risk. Thus, a lack of impact on recidivism outcomes negates these strength factors from being included in a list of protective factors.

Lösel and Farrington's (2012) conceptual work has been particularly helpful. They define a buffering factor as "a variable that predicts a low probability of offending among persons at risk or interacts with a risk factor to nullify its effect" (p. S9). Specifically, a protective factor is one that interacts with risk, reducing the impact of a negative event (e.g., recidivism), such that the addition of each protective factor further moderates the effect of risk exposure (Fougere & Daffern, 2011; Jessor, Van Den Bos, Vanderryn, Costa, & Turbin, 1995; Lodewijks, de Ruiter, & Doreleijers, 2010). For example, poor parental supervision predicts offending in low-income families; however, high income protects youth in families characterized by poor parental supervision, such that offending likelihood is reduced even in the presence of this risk factor (Lösel & Farrington, 2012). The key distinction for the definition of a protective factor, then, is the interaction between the protective factor and risk.

Alternatively, hypothetically protective factors (i.e., high impulse control, as discussed above) may function as *promotive factors*, which are conceptually and operationally different than protective factors (Jones et al., 2015). Promotive factors are best defined as variables that are negatively correlated with recidivism (and could be considered the opposite of risk factors), such that as a promotive factor increases, the risk of recidivism decreases (Loeber, Pardini, Stouthamer-Loeber, & Raine, 2007). Unlike protective factors, promotive factors directly reduce reoffending, but are not independent of risk (Loeber, et al., 2007; Van der Put et al., 2011). Other examples of promotive factors can include good social skills, good academic achievement, high motivation at school, consistent discipline, and higher family income (Loeber, Slot, & Stouthamer-Loeber, 2008). Note the conceptual overlap between these variables and low levels of the major and minor risk factors (Andrews & Bonta, 2010)

Jones et al. (2015) suggest that a protective factor can co-exist with risk factors, and account for variability in outcome in an otherwise high-risk group of offenders. In an effort to quantify the meaning of protective factors in relation to risk, they propose defining a protective factor as any positive or prosocial facet that would intuitively buffer the risk of a criminal outcome, which is consistent with the earlier definition provided.

Other work has demonstrated that different factors may be protective at different points of release or community supervision. Ullrich and Coid (2011) examined 15 proposed protective factors among a large sample of offenders ($n = 1,396$ at time 1, $n = 813$ after follow-up) who were followed for an average of 5 years. Of the 15 factors examined, results indicated that items assessing social support, emotional support, time spent with prosocial family and friends, involvement in religious activities, and closeness with others demonstrated promotive effects for violence after release from incarceration. After controlling for risk, spare time spent with family or friends demonstrated a significant independent effect on recidivism. In other words, individuals with this strength factor experienced lower rates of recidivism during the follow-up periods, regardless of the level of risk. Notably, the relationship between strength factors and recidivism changed over time; factors that were promotive in year 1 may not have been in year 2 or 3 (Ullrich & Coid, 2011). These findings of the potential temporal effect of DRFs were also emphasized by Brown et al. (2009), suggesting the field needs to consider follow-up time in order to incorporate temporal context into assessments, case planning, and risk management. Of particular note, Jones et al. (2015) provided a rare finding that risk and protective scores significantly interacted, illustrating that high strength scores were particularly effective for attenuating recidivism among higher-risk cases (i.e., fulfilling the *interactive model* definition of protective factor). The DRAOR captures a combination of internal (e.g., responsive to advice, prosocial identity, realistic expectations) and social capital (e.g., social supports, social control) protective factors which appear to lead to lower rates of reoffending (Serin, Gobeil, et al., 2016).

Understanding and Using Static and Dynamic Risk in Community Supervision

With this evolution in risk assessment approaches, it is important to contextualize how static and dynamic risk assessments might be most profitably utilized in community supervision. First, it is important to appreciate that to date the research indicates that static risk measures tend to evidence stronger prediction than dynamic risk measures alone, but dynamic measures are also predictive (Campbell, French, & Gendreau, 2009; Yang et al., 2010). Second, dynamic measures can often provide additional predictive validity (Brown et al., 2009; Hanby, 2013; Lewis et al., 2012; Yesberg & Polaschek, 2014) and are an important supplement in the risk assessment arsenal. Specifically, the use of *both* static and dynamic risk measures should yield the greatest predictive accuracy. Third, primarily static risk measures inform supervision level; high-risk clients are typically assigned more conditions to follow and are seen more frequently by POs and other staff (Cohen, Cook, & Lowenkamp, 2016). In terms of resource allocation, without incorporating the results of a risk assessment it is possible to over- or under-supervise clients, attenuating the potential effectiveness of community supervision. In terms of false negatives, failure to provide a rationale for supervision practices, especially frequency of face-to-face contacts, can be particularly difficult to defend without a valid risk assessment that examines acute risks. Fourth, stable dynamic risk measures can inform case planning (i.e., the identification and ranking of criminogenic needs). Fifth, acute dynamic risk assessments refine this case planning for individual clients over time. For instance, with increases in acute risk (e.g., recent changes in anger, victim access, negative affect), the PO is alerted to determine to what extent such a change increases risk. This is accomplished through their analysis of the client's offense chain, an exercise that can both help bring core problems to light and facilitate an understanding regarding how to change these problems with the client. The PO may also choose to review and establish short-term goals, assign specific home-work, refer the client to a rehabilitation program, and see the client more frequently than their regularly planned session. As always, casework documentation would describe this rationale and practice, thereby affirming the PO's due diligence. Alternatively, the presence of protective factors may mitigate certain risk-based intervention by the PO. In this manner, dynamic risk assessment may lead to the differential community supervision of two clients with a similar crime, similar supervision requirements, and similar static risk estimate. As acute risks and protective factors become noted, different strategies are warranted to manage the case. This approach is depicted in Figure 45.1.

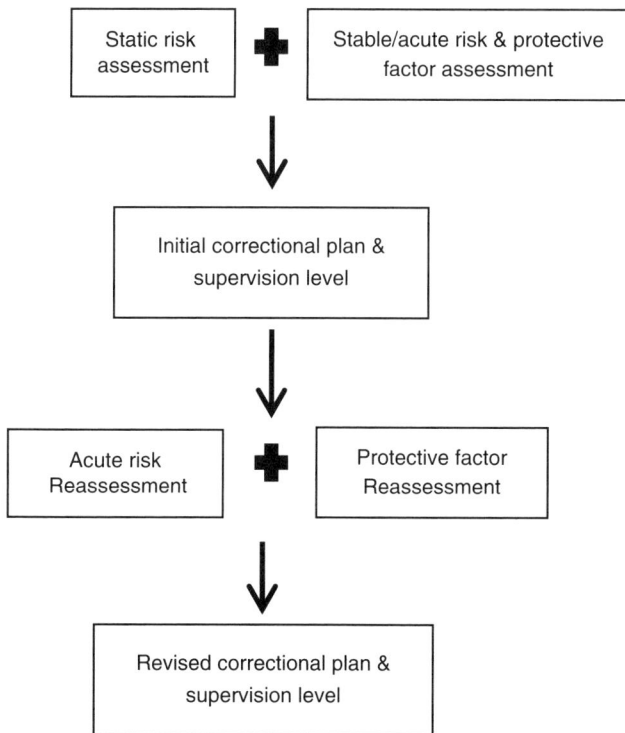

Figure 45.1   Flowchart for risk assessment and case planning.

Using Dynamic Risk Assessment in Ongoing Case Planning

Currently, the most common model in community supervision involves determining a client's initial level of supervision through static risk assessment and/or stable dynamic (i.e., risk and need) assessment. Additionally, for those agencies that use them, stable dynamic risk assessments identify programming or treatment needs. As noted earlier, these treatment needs are most commonly addressed through formal programming; in the community, this programming is usually provided by independent agencies.

Case planning, however, warrants a more comprehensive approach than simply confirming a client abuses substances and then mandating that they attend a self-help program such as Alcoholics Anonymous (AA), or a more structured addictions program. Presumably, assistance such as AA would be reserved for lower-risk clients, given the mixed findings regarding its efficacy (Ferri, Amato, & Davoli, 2006). Case planning requires an assessment of the nature of the relationship (i.e., proximity, severity, and salience) between a particular criminogenic need and criminal behavior. Hence, augmenting a risk and need subscale score with independent measures of substance abuse and criminal thinking should provide greater precision regarding the severity of the issue. In addition to the severity of the criminogenic need, a behavioral analysis would provide clarity regarding the relative rank or importance (i.e., salience) of the various criminogenic needs. For instance, with a client with multiple needs, it would be important in case planning to ascertain the preferred ordering of interventions based on their ranked importance in reducing a client's reoffending. As intervention proceeds, it is important to assess client program participation, degree of change, and level of competency, as well as provide aftercare to maintain treatment gains. The initial case plan would also identify offense-specific program requirements such as counseling for sex offenders. The static risk and/or stable dynamic risk assessment would also be incorporated into a dosage consideration; higher-risk clients would be referred to higher-dosage or multiple, sequential programs. This is only viable for community supervision agencies that have multiple programs reflecting different dosage levels. Of some concern are situations where there is only one program available, since the one program may be insufficient or inappropriate for higher-risk clients. Particularly, mixing lower- with higher-risk clients in the same program leads to poorer outcomes for lower-risk clients (Lloyd, Hanby, & Serin, 2014). As a result, the risk composition of the treatment group is an important consideration when recommending treatment strategies for clients.

Refining Case Planning Using Acute Dynamic Risk Assessment

The reassessment of DRFs introduces the opportunity for caseworkers to refine case planning and risk management. Moreover, with the increasing evidence that the presence of protective factors mitigates risk, it would seem important to include their assessment in supervision practice. The evidence that acute DRFs increase the likelihood and proximity of reoffending highlights the value of incorporating real-time changes in supervision practice. Their assessment provides the opportunity for caseworkers to juxtapose acute risks and protective factors in real time to make adjustments to supervision practice. In the absence of validated decision rules, it seems minimally reasonable that caseworkers should be vigilant for increases in acute risks, targeting elevations within sessions, as well as making referrals to appropriate programs while simultaneously attempting to identify and increase salient protective factors for clients. Since acute dynamic risks can change quickly between sessions, their assessment should be done routinely. For example, regarding acute dynamic risks, imagine a client admits to using cannabis the previous night (elevated risk). In response, the caseworker would be expected to revise the case plan accordingly. Potential changes could include reviewing and targeting triggers for use in sessions, assigning homework regarding relapse prevention, increasing the frequency of office reporting, making a referral to a substance abuse program, and setting up urinalysis testing. However, if one client had stable and meaningful employment, was in a relationship with a prosocial partner, and had been successfully on probation for 14 months, the risk management implications might be different, compared to a client who had just commenced probation, was single, and was unemployed.

What remains absent, at present, are valid decision rules that would permit case workers to refine supervision level based on changes in acute risks and protective factors. For example, how problematic does a certain risk factor need to become to warrant drastic alterations to the supervision approach? Establishing empirically validated decision rules would provide guidance regarding when a PO needs to intervene and at what intensity the given intervention should be provided.

Importantly, the situation described above fails to adequately highlight the body of work described as core correctional practice (CCP; Dowden & Andrews, 2004) that is increasingly being incorporated into community supervision (Bonta, Rugge, Scott, Bourgon, & Yessine, 2008; Robinson, et al., 2012; Chapter 44). CCP reflects a firm but fair approach to client interactions and utilizes key skills to teach offenders how to minimize criminal thinking and increase prosocial behavior. A meta-analytic review indicated that officer training programs operating under the CCP umbrella tended to demonstrate encouraging results, yielding an approximate 13% improvement in client outcomes (Chadwick, DeWolf, & Serin, 2015). Assuming these skills are present, how might a PO utilize the assessment of acute dynamic risks and protective factors in case planning and risk management strategies?

Case Study Example

Case Study

John, aged 26, is a male client with a 12-month probation order for multiple Break and Enter charges (×12) in homes and businesses. John's criminal history began at age 14 (thefts, possession of cannabis) and has continued unabated with an 8-month period of being drug free following completion of a 6-month residential treatment program 2 years ago. He has had five prior short jail sentences and three failed probation orders. His crimes are all acquisitive to get money for drugs, with the exception of one common assault conviction at age 18 for which he received a 30-day jail sentence. He reports the victim was a drug dealer who tried to sell him poor product. His primary group of friends have similar backgrounds; they are constantly unemployed, abusing drugs, and in and out of jail. John has a grade 10 level education through upgrading in prison but virtually no employment history. He rationalizes his crimes by saying his addiction to cocaine is a disease (but he uses any drugs available) and that he is not hurting people because their loss is covered by insurance. He is occasionally depressed and presents with low motivation, other than to say he is tired of his involvement with the courts. He continues to live with his mother, who cannot bear to kick him out onto the street but realizes she cannot positively influence John. A risk assessment places him at moderate-high risk to reoffend in terms of general recidivism and low-moderate in terms of violence due to early age of onset of crime, multiple needs, and overall number of criminal convictions.

Despite brief periods when he is clean, the sequence of events leading to crimes is that he hangs with his friends and uses. Crimes are committed simply for money to pay for drugs or pay drug debts. Sometimes, this is preceded by periods of negative affect (i.e., depressed, feeling life sucks, uncertainty about dealing with things), which he manages through illicit substance use. He is to be seen every 2 weeks by his PO.

Risk-Need-Responsivity Analysis

Considering the Risk-Need-Responsivity (RNR; motivation level, program dosage) principles (Andrews & Bonta, 2010), it is possible to rank John's criminogenic needs, which then can be used to develop a case plan. Despite John's clear drug addiction, it is debatable whether substance abuse intervention alone would be sufficient to reduce reoffending. It may be preferable to consider it a secondary, albeit important need. Given the role of antisocial thinking and criminal peers in John's substance use (both preceding and justifying), we rank these as the primary criminogenic needs, followed by substance use, employment, and use of leisure time. The expectation is that substance abuse cannot be successfully managed without targeting criminal thinking and peers, as well as employment issues and John's use of leisure time. This analysis or ranking of criminogenic needs provides the PO with a rationale for specific program referrals and potentially program sequencing. It is recognized that some agencies may require clients to be "clean" prior to involvement in cognitive behavioral programming, but that seems mainly a policy decision unless the substance abuse impedes program engagement and completion of the program requirements. Given the duration and apparent consistency of criminality and the moderate-high risk estimate, intervention dosage must be greater than simple monthly contacts with his PO. Research by Bourgon and Armstrong (2005) suggests a minimum of 200 hours would be required to mitigate John's risk of relapse and reoffending.

Case Plan

1   Within sessions with the PO, it is mandatory to address criminal thinking. Given the risk assessment, this could be augmented by referral to a treatment group (cognitive behavioral therapy [CBT] approach to criminal thinking).
2   Given duration and seriousness of addiction, residential treatment is preferred. If that is not possible, referral to structured substance abuse program is essential. Self-help groups such as Alcoholics Anonymous are encouraged mainly to remind the client of the substance abuse issues, but the efficacy of some self-help groups may be limited (Kownacki & Shadish, 1999). Urinalysis is used to monitor drug use.
3   Education and employment counseling by PO and referral to agency.
4   Review and lifestyle management assistance by PO, in terms of accommodation and use of leisure time.
5   Review of self-care in terms of awareness and management of negative affect.

Change in Acute and Protective Factors

Imagine the case plan has been implemented, that John has been seen twice monthly, and that he is being reassessed 4 months later regarding his progress:

Through motivational interviewing and goal setting, John has demonstrated improved motivation consistent with someone in the *preparation phase* (suggesting John recognizes his life would benefit from change and is making efforts consistent with this recognition, i.e., the third of five stages within the transtheoretical model of change; Prochaska & DiClemente, 1982). He has joined Narcotics Anonymous and has been regularly seeing a drug counselor as arranged by his PO, with positive reports. In the first month he had two positive urinalysis tests (one for meth and one for cannabis). For the past 3 months his urinalysis tests have been negative and he reports cravings are diminished. He knows this is going to be a long struggle. He is now living with an uncle, thus removing him from his old friends and temptations. In lieu of rent, John has been working as a helper in his uncle's construction company. Reports are that after a couple of weeks to settle in, John has not been absent from work and he is gaining skills. John's uncle has established clear guidelines, including work expectations, choice of friends, and use of leisure time (John has a 9 p.m. curfew). He is also dating a non-criminal young woman, the daughter of a work colleague, which has been going well. She has convinced him to consider seeking trades training or an apprenticeship.

Revised Case Plan and Rationale

Increasingly, there is evidence that the presence of acute risk factors increases likelihood and imminence of problem behaviors while on supervision (Lowenkamp, Johnson, Trevino, & Serin, 2016; Serin, Chadwick, et al., 2016; Yesberg et al., 2015). As well, the presence of protective factors appears to mitigate risk (Jones et al., 2015; Serin, Chadwick, et al., 2016). In the case of John, compared to stable risks, the more recent information *suggests* acute risks have diminished (e.g., negative affect, use of illicit substances, procriminal peer association, employment challenges) and protective factors *may* be present (e.g., prosocial supports), thereby influencing John's behavior. While static risk has not diminished, John's case seems more manageable at 3 months than at the start of his probation. It would seem reasonable to maintain the same case plan but reduce frequency of face-to-face sessions with his PO to monthly meetings.

General Guidelines for Preparing for a Session

While certain acute risks may warrant specific approaches, a PO's key role during face-to-face sessions is to gather information in general regarding changes in acute risk factors, to identify and support protective factors, and to refine their supervision accordingly. Table 45.1 presents some general working guidelines in support of that requirement. In particular, it is important for POs to recognize that risk is fluid; accordingly, changes in risk warrant a change in the case plan and risk management approach. As should be clear from John's case study, there is an increasing expectation that the PO will work with clients to influence change. This requires a clear understanding of risk assessment, an understanding of offending behavior, an understanding of how to motivate and influence clients, an ability to engage clients and develop an effective working relationship, and a purposeful understanding of the PO's role. Many of these areas can be informed by contemporary correctional psychology research.

How Psychology Can Contribute to Community Supervision

It should be apparent that psychology has primarily provided clarity regarding conceptual models for understanding dynamic risk and some recent improvements in measurement. It has

Table 45.1 Utilizing Acute Risk Information

General guidelines for considering changes in acute dynamic risk	
Session	*Following session*
Link acute risks to pattern of crime.	Document case analysis and strategy for management.
Evaluate in terms of current case plan.	Review, examine frequency of contact.
Target specifically to reduce likelihood or recurrence and impact.	Contact other service providers involved in case.
Role-play to improve client skills.	Revise case plan.
Assign homework.	Revise risk management strategy.
Consider referrals to other services.	Discuss case with supervisor.

also informed evidence-based practice in the area of offender programming (i.e., RNR; Smith, Gendreau, & Swartz, 2009). It is less clear that these advances have led to demonstrable practice change in community supervision. This should be an urgent goal for correctional psychology research.

Additional research regarding dynamic risk measures should yield normative data that can be used to further refine community supervision practice. For instance, ongoing research on the DRAOR can provide cutpoints that can be translated into decision rules. Scores exceeding specific cutpoints would initiate increased contact with clients, to mitigate risk. An improved understanding of acute risk factors could help refine POs' understanding of a client's offense chain, informing both case planning and risk management. Finally, an absence of protective factors and their ability to mitigate risk should encourage POs to invest greater effort to increase community supports rather than solely adopting a risk avoidance approach. Psychology can augment this practice approach by increasing the field's understanding of protective factors: definition and measurement, salience for different types of clients, and relationship to risk reduction.

Previously, psychology has had a mainly tangential relationship with many community supervision agencies. Perhaps because of background and training issues, POs may have viewed psychology as too esoteric and thus having limited practical value. This may have been the result of an organization being reluctant to invest in expanded assessments and adhering to a more surveillance approach. Recent interest in POs being agents of change could change the primarily brokering model to one where POs are more actively engaged in change strategies with clients. Psychology has much to offer this new approach to community supervision. Additionally, it appears that few community corrections jurisdictions have dedicated psychological services, and when they do, resources are typically reserved for clinical issues (e.g., diagnosis for mentally disordered clients, oversight for sex offenders and high-risk clients). As the transition away from a law enforcement approach continues toward a more therapeutic model, psychology can be relied on to inform and refine supervision practices. If community supervision is viewed to be only a client surveillance consideration, correctional psychologists will struggle with the "befriend and betray" challenges occasionally present in the dual role embedded within correctional psychology. Of some concern, then, is whether the ethical tenets of psychology allow practitioners to view its role as complementary to community supervision (Day & Ward, 2010). Setting of ground rules (e.g., role clarification) and boundaries will go a long way to clarify expectations and insulate practitioners from ethical misgivings.

Summary

Community supervision practice can be improved by the more formal incorporation of psychological expertise regarding assessment and intervention. The systematic assessment and reassessment of acute dynamic risks and protective factors is a case in point. This requires an approach that extends the current risk and need assessments most commonly utilized in community supervision, by attending to factors that evidence short-term fluctuations and indicate imminence of reoffending. Client change in these factors should alert caseworkers to the need for a modification in both case planning and risk management efforts. Failure to utilize information pertaining to acute dynamic factors in revisions to case planning and risk management could exacerbate client outcomes and place staff in a vulnerable position professionally when attempting to explain client failure. Conversely, attention to and incorporation of protective factors should provide explanatory power to staff in attempting to understand client success and instill hope in clients endeavoring to desist from crime.

Key Readings

Brown, S. L., St. Amand, M. D., & Zamble, E. (2009). The dynamic prediction of criminal recidivism: A three-wave prospective study. *Law and Human Behavior*, 33, 25–45.

Desmarais, S. L., Nicholls, T. L., Wilson, C. M., & Brink, J. (2012). Using dynamic and protective factors to predict inpatient aggression: Reliability and validity of START assessments. *Psychological Assessment*, 24, 685–700.

Jones, N. J., Brown, S. L., Robinson, D., & Frey, D. (2015). Incorporating strengths into quantitative assessments of criminal risk for adult offenders: The Service Planning Instrument. *Criminal Justice and Behavior*, 42, 321–338.

Serin, R. C., Chadwick, N., & Lloyd, C. D. (2016). Dynamic risk and protective factors. *Psychology, Crime & Law*, 22, 151–170.

Ullrich, S., & Coid, J. (2011). Protective factors for violence among released prisoners—effects over time and interactions with static risk. *Journal of Consulting and Clinical Psychology*, 79, 381–390.

References

Andrews, D. A., & Bonta, J. (2010). *The psychology of criminal conduct* (5th ed.). Cincinnati, OH: Anderson.

Andrews, D. A., Bonta, J., & Wormith, S. (2008). *Level of Service/Case Management Inventory (LS/CMI) supplement: A gender-informed risk/need/responsivity assessment.* Toronto, ON: Multi-Health Systems.

Babchishin, K. M. (2013). *Sex offenders do change on risk-relevant propensities: Evidence from a longitudinal study of the Acute-2007* (Unpublished doctoral dissertation). Carleton University, Ottawa, Canada.

Bakker, L., Riley, D., & O'Malley, J. (1999). *Risk of reconviction: Statistical models predicting four types of re-offending.* Wellington, New Zealand: Department of Corrections Psychological Service.

Bonta, J., Rugge, T., Scott, T., Bourgon, G., & Yessine, A. K. (2008). Exploring the black box of community supervision. *Journal of Offender Rehabilitation*, 47, 248–270.

Bourgon, G., & Armstrong, B. (2005). Transferring the principles of effective treatment into a "real world" prison setting. *Criminal Justice and Behavior*, 32, 3–25.

Brennan, T., Dieterich, W., & Ehret, B. (2009). Evaluating the predictive validity of the COMPAS risk and needs assessment system. *Criminal Justice and Behavior*, 36, 21–40.

Brown, S. L., St. Amand, M. D., & Zamble, E. (2009). The dynamic prediction of criminal recidivism: A three-wave prospective study. *Law and Human Behavior*, 33, 25–45.

Campbell, M. A., French, S., & Gendreau, P. (2009). The prediction of violence in adult offenders: A meta-analytic comparison of instruments and methods of assessment. *Criminal Justice and Behavior*, 36, 567–590.

Carter, M. (2014).Dosage probation: Rethinking the structure of probation sentences. National Institute of Corrections. Retrieved from http://wispd.org/attachments/article/272/Dosage%20Based%20 Probation%20Article.pdf

Caudy, M. S., Durso, J. M., & Taxman, F. S. (2013). How well do dynamic needs predict recidivism? Implications for risk assessment and risk reduction. *Journal of Criminal Justice*, 41, 458–466.

Chadwick, N., DeWolf, A. H., & Serin, R. C. (2015). Effectively training community supervision officers: A meta-analytic review of the impact on offender outcome. *Criminal Justice and Behavior*, 42, 977–989.

Chiricos, T., Barrick, K., Bales, W., & Bontrager, S. (2007). The labelling of convicted felons and its consequences for recidivism. *Criminology*, 45, 547–581.

Cohen, T. H., Cook, D., & Lowenkamp, C. T. (2016). The supervision of low-risk federal offenders: How the low-risk policy has changed federal supervision practices without compromising community safety. *Federal Probation*, 80, 3–11.

Day, A., & Ward, T. (2010). Offender rehabilitation as a value-laden process. *International Journal of Offender Therapy and Comparative Criminology*, 54, 289–306.

de Vogel, V., de Ruiter, C., Bouman, Y., & de Vries Robbé, M. (2009). *SAPROF: Guidelines for the assessment of protective factors for violence risk*. Utrecht, the Netherlands: Forum Educatief.

Desmarais, S. L., Nicholls, T. L., Wilson, C. M., & Brink, J. (2012). Using dynamic and protective factors to predict inpatient aggression: Reliability and validity of START assessments. *Psychological Assessment*, 24, 685–700.

Douglas, S. K., & Skeem, J. L. (2005). Violence risk assessment: Getting specific about being dynamic. *Psychology, Public Policy, and Law*, 11, 347–383.

Dowden, C., & Andrews, D. A. (2004). The importance of staff practice in delivering effective correctional treatment: A meta-analytic review of core correctional practices. *International Journal of Offender Therapy and Comparative Criminology*, 48, 203–214.

Farrall, S. (2004). Social capital and offender reintegration: Making probation desistance focused. In S. Maruna, & R. Immarigeon (Eds.), *After crime and punishment: Pathways to offender reintegration* (pp. 57–84). Cullompton, UK: Willan.

Farrington, D. P. (2011). The integrated cognitive antisocial potential (ICAP) theory. In D. P. Farrington (Ed.), *Integrated developmental and life-course theories of offending* (pp. 73–92). New Brunswick, NJ: Transaction.

Ferri, M., Amato, L., & Davoli, M. (2006). Alcoholics Anonymous and other 12-step programmes for alcohol dependence. Cochrane Drugs and Alcohol Group. Cochrane Database of Systematic Reviews, 3, CD005032.

Fougere, A., & Daffern, M. (2011). Resilience in young offenders. *International Journal of Forensic Mental Health*, 10, 244–253.

Hanby, L. J. (2013). *A longitudinal study of dynamic risk, protective factors, and criminal recidivism: Change over time and the impact of assessment timing* (Unpublished doctoral dissertation). Carleton University, Ottawa, Canada.

Hanson, K. R., & Harris, A. J. (2000). Where should we intervene? Dynamic predictors of sexual offense recidivism. *Criminal Justice and Behavior*, 27, 6–35.

Horney, J., Osgood, D. W., & Marshall, I. H. (1995). Criminal careers in the short-term: Intra-individual variability in crime and its relation to local life circumstances. *American Sociological Review*, 60, 655–673.

Howard, P. D., Clark, D., & Garnham, N. (2003). Evaluation and validation of the Offender Assessment System (OASys). London, UK: *OASys Central Research Unit. Report to HM Prison Service and National Probation Service*.

Howard, P. D., & Dixon, L. (2013). Identifying change in the likelihood of violent recidivism: Causal dynamic risk factors in the OASys Violence Predictor. *Journal of Law and Human Behavior*, 37, 163–174.

Jessor, R., Van Den Bos, J., Vanderryn, J., Costa, F. M., & Turbin, M. S. (1995). Protective factors in adolescent problem behavior: Moderator effects and developmental change. *Developmental Psychology*, 31, 923–933.

Jones, N. J., Brown, S. L., Robinson, D., & Frey, D. (2015). Incorporating strengths into quantitative assessments of criminal risk for adult offenders: The Service Planning Instrument. *Criminal Justice and Behavior*, 42, 321–338.

Jones, N. J., Brown, S. L., & Zamble, E. (2009). Predicting criminal recidivism in adult male offenders: Researcher versus parole officer assessment of dynamic risk. *Criminal Justice and Behavior*, 37, 860–882.

Kownacki, R. J., & Shadish, W. R. (1999). Does Alcoholics Anonymous work? The results from a meta-analysis of controlled experiments. *Substance Use & Misuse*, 34, 1897–1916.

Kroner, D. G., Mills, J. F., & Reddon, J. R. (2005). A coffee can, factor analysis, and prediction of anti-social behavior: The structure of criminal risk. *International Journal of Law & Psychiatry*, 28, 360–374.

Latessa, E., Smith, P., Lemke, R., Makarios, M., & Lowenkamp, C. (2009). *Creation and validation of the Ohio Risk Assessment System: Final report*. Cincinnati, OH: Authors Retrieved from https://www.assessments.com/assessments_documentation/ORAS/ORAS_Final_Report_and_Validation.pdf

Laub, J. H., Nagin, D. S., & Sampson, R. J. (1998). Trajectories of change in criminal offending: Good marriages and the desistance process. *American Sociological Review*, 63, 225–238.

LeBel, T. P., Burnett, R., Maruna, S., & Bushway, S. (2008). The "chicken and egg" of subjective and social factors in desistance from crime. *European Journal of Criminology*, 5, 131–159.

Lewis, K., Olver, M. E., & Wong, S. C. (2012). The Violence Risk Scale: Predictive validity and linking changes in risk with violent recidivism in a sample of high-risk offenders with psychopathic traits. *Assessment*, 20, 150–164.

Lloyd, C. D. (2015). *Can a dynamic risk instrument make short-term predictions in "real time"? Developing a framework for testing proximal assessment of offender recidivism risk during re-entry* (Unpublished doctoral dissertation). Carleton University, Ottawa, Canada.

Lloyd, C. D., Hanby, L. J., & Serin, R. C. (2014). Rehabilitation group coparticipants' risk levels are associated with offenders' treatment performance, treatment change, and recidivism. *Journal of Consulting and Clinical Psychology*, 82(2), 298–311.

Lodewijks, H. P., de Ruiter, C., & Doreleijers, T. A. (2010). The impact of protective factors in desistance from violent reoffending: A study in three samples of adolescent offenders. *Journal of Interpersonal Violence*, 25, 568–587.

Loeber, R., Pardini, D. A., Stouthamer-Loeber, M., & Raine, A. (2007). Do cognitive, physiological, and psychosocial risk and promotive factors predict desistance from delinquency in males? *Development and Psychopathology*, 19, 867–887.

Loeber, R., Slot, N. W., & Stouthamer-Loeber, M. (2008). A cumulative developmental model of risk and promotive factors. In R. Loeber, N. W. Slot, P. H. Van der Laan, & M. Hoeve (Eds.), *Tomorrow's criminals. The development of child delinquency and effective interventions* (pp. 133–161). Farnham, UK: Ashgate.

Lösel, F., & Farrington, D. P. (2012). Direct protective and buffering protective factors in the development of youth violence. *American Journal of Preventative Medicine*, 43(2S1), S8–S23.

Lowenkamp, C. T., Johnson, J. L., Trevino, P., & Serin, R. C. (2016). Enhancing community supervision through the application of dynamic risk assessment. *Federal Probation*, 80, 16–20.

Mann, R. E., Hanson, R. K., & Thornton, D. (2010). Assessing risk for sexual recidivism: Some proposals on the nature of psychologically meaningful risk factors. *Sexual Abuse: A Journal of Research and Treatment*, 22, 191–217.

Mann, R. E., Webster, S. D., Schofield, C., & Marshall, W. L. (2004). Approach versus avoidance goals in relapse prevention with sexual offenders. *Sexual Abuse: A Journal of Research and Treatment*, 16, 65–75.

Maruna, S. (2010). *Understanding desistance from crime*. A report for the Ministry of Justice and National Offender Management Services. Retrieved from www.safeground.org.uk/wp-content/uploads/Desistance-Fact-Sheet.pdf

Maruna, S., LeBel, T. P., & Lanier, C. (2003). Generativity behind bars: Some "redemptive truth" about prison society. In E. de St. Aubin, D. McAdams, & T. Kim (Eds.), *The generative society: Caring for future generations* (pp. 131–151). Washington, DC: American Psychological Association.

Nicholls, T. L., Brink, J., Desmarais, S. L., Webster, C. D., & Martin, M. L. (2006). The Short-Term Assessment of Risk and Treatability (START): A prospective validation study in a forensic psychiatric sample. *Assessment*, 13, 313–327.

Orbis Partners (2003). *Service Planning Instrument (SPIn)*. Ottawa, Canada: Author.

Polaschek, D. L. L. (2016). Desistance and dynamic risk factors belong together. *Psychology, Crime & Law*, 22, 171–189.

Prochaska, J. O., & DiClemente, C. C. (1982). Transtheoretical therapy: Toward a more integrative model of change. *Psychotherapy: Theory, Research and Practice*, 19, 276–288.

Rex, S. (1999). Desistance from offending: Experiences of probation. *Howard Journal of Criminal Justice*, 38, 366–383.

Robinson, C. R., Lowenkamp, C. T., Holsinger, A. M., VanBenschoten, S., Alexander, M., & Oleson, J. C. (2012). A random study of Staff Trained at Reducing Re-arrest (STARR): Using core correctional practices in probation interactions. *Journal of Crime and Justice*, 35, 167–188.

Rutter, M. (2000). Resilience reconsidered: Conceptual considerations, empirical findings, and policy implications. In J. P. Shonkoff, & S. J. Meisels (Eds.), *Handbook of early childhood intervention* (pp. 651–682). New York, NY: Cambridge University Press.

Sampson, R. J., & Laub, J. H. (1992). Crime and deviance in the life course. *Annual Review of Sociology*, 18, 63–84.

Sampson, R. J., & Laub, J. H. (2005). A life-course view of the development of crime. *The Annals of the American Academy of Political and Social Science*, 602, 12–45.

Serin, R. C. (2007). *The Dynamic Risk Assessment Scale for Offender Re-Entry (DRAOR)*. Unpublished scale. Carleton University, Ottawa, Canada.

Serin, R. C. (2009). *A correctional agency's consumer guide to the selection of a risk assessment instrument*. Unpublished paper, Carleton University, Ottawa, Canada. Retrieved from http://carleton.ca/cjdml/wp-content/uploads/Correctional-Guide.pdf

Serin, R. C., Chadwick, N., & Lloyd, C. D. (2016). Dynamic risk and protective factors. *Psychology, Crime & Law*, 22, 151–170.

Serin, R. C., Gobeil, R., Lloyd, C. D., Chadwick, N., Wardrop, K., & Hanby, L. J. (2016). Using dynamic risk to enhance conditional release decisions in prisoners to improve their outcomes. *Behavioral Sciences & the Law*, 34(2–3), 321–336.

Serin, R. C., & Hanby, L. J. (in press). Client-based assessment of need and change. In L. E. Marshall, & R. Mann (Eds.), *Treatment of sexual offenders*. Chichester, UK: Wiley.

Serin, R. C., & Lloyd, C. D. (2009). Examining the process of offender change: The transition to crime desistance. *Psychology, Crime, & Law*, 15, 347–364.

Serin, R. C., Lloyd, C. D., & Hanby, L. J. (2010). Enhancing offender re-entry: An integrated model for enhancing offender re-entry. *European Journal of Probation*, 2, 53–75.

Serin, R.C., & Lowenkamp, C.T. (2015). Selecting and using risk and need assessments. Alexandria, VA: National Drug Court Institute. Retrieved from https://www.ndci.org/wp-content/uploads/Fact%20Sheet%20Risk%20Assessment.pdf

Singer, J. D., & Willett, J. B. (2003). *Applied longitudinal data analysis: Modeling change and event occurrence*. New York, NY: Oxford University Press.

Skeem, J., & Eno Louden, J. (2007). *Assessment of evidence on the quality of the Correctional Offender Management Profiling for Alternative Sanctions (COMPAS)*. Davis, CA: Center for Public Policy

Research Retrieved from https://webfiles.uci.edu/skeem/Downloads_files/CDCR%20Skeem%26%20 EnoLouden%20COMPASeval%20SECONDREVISION%20final%20Dec%2028%2007.pdf

Smith, P., Gendreau, P., & Swartz, K. (2009). Validating the principles of effective intervention: A systematic review of the contributions of meta-analysis in the field of corrections. *Victims and Offenders*, 4, 148–169.

Uggen, C. (2000). Work as a turning point in the life course of criminals: A duration model of age, employment, and recidivism. *American Sociological Review*, 65, 529–546.

Ullrich, S., & Coid, J. (2011). Protective factors for violence among released prisoners—effects over time and interactions with static risk. *Journal of Consulting and Clinical Psychology*, 79, 381–390.

Van der Put, C. E., Deković, M., Stams, G. J. J., Van der Laan, P. H., Hoeve, M., & Van Amelsfort, L. (2011). Changes in risk factors during adolescence: Implications for risk assessment. *Criminal Justice and Behavior*, 38, 248–262.

van Mastrigt, S. B., & Farrington, D. P. (2009). Co-offending, age, gender and crime type: Implications for criminal justice policy. *British Journal of Criminology*, 49, 552–573.

Vose, B., Smith, P., & Cullen, F. T. (2013). Predictive validity and the impact of change in total LSI-R score on recidivism. *Criminal Justice and Behavior*, 40, 1383–1396.

Walters, G. D. (1998). *Changing lives of crime and drugs: Intervening with substance-abusing offenders.* New York, NY: Wiley.

Woldgabreal, Y., Day, A., & Ward, T. (2014). The community-based supervision of offenders from a positive psychology perspective. *Aggression and Violent Behavior*, 19, 32–41.

Yang, M., Wong, S. C., & Coid, J. (2010). The efficacy of violence prediction: A meta-analytic comparison of nine risk assessment tools. *Psychological Bulletin*, 136, 740–767.

Yang, S., & Mulvey, E. P. (2012). Violence risk: Re-defining variables from the first-person perspective. *Aggression and Violent Behavior*, 17, 198–207.

Yesberg, J. A., & Polaschek, D. L. (2014). Assessing dynamic risk and protective factors in the community: Examining the validity of the Dynamic Risk Assessment for Offender Re-entry. *Psychology, Crime & Law*, 21, 80–99.

Yesberg, J. A., Scanlan, J., Hanby, L. J., Serin, R. C., & Polaschek, D. L. L. (2015). Predicting women's recidivism: Validating a dynamic community-based "gender-neutral" tool. *Probation Journal*, 62, 33–48.

46

"What Works" in Supervising Probationers with Mental Illness

Sarah M. Manchak
University of Cincinnati, USA

Lydie R. Loth
Pew Charitable Trusts, Philadelphia, USA

Jennifer L. Skeem
University of California, Berkeley, USA

Understanding the Problem: Challenges Posed by Offenders With Mental Illness

Studies of jail, prison, and community corrections populations yield fairly consistent prevalence estimates for offenders with serious mental illness: About one in five offenders qualify for a diagnosis of schizophrenia, bipolar disorder, or major depressive disorder (Steadman, Osher, Robbins, Case, & Samuels, 2009; Teplin 1990, 1994; Watson, Stimpson, & Hostick, 2004). People with these diagnoses often have cognitive, emotional, or social impairments and a range of co-occurring problems that include substance use disorders (Karberg & James, 2005; Kessler, Chiu, Demler, & Walters, 2005), chronic medical conditions like diabetes and hypertension (Cuddeback, Scheyett, Pettus-Davis, & Morrissey, 2010; De Hert et al., 2011), and unemployment and homelessness (Draine, Salzer, Culhane, & Hadley, 2002; Ditton, 1999).

While incarcerated, probationers with mental illness are at high risk for victimization (Blitz, Wolff, & Shi, 2008; Wolff, Blitz, & Shi, 2007) and self-harm (Fazel, Cartwright, Norman-Nott, & Hawton, 2008). For these inmates, symptoms can also interfere with routine prison and jail programming (Ditton, 1999; Feder, 1991; James & Glaze, 2006), frustrating both correctional staff and other inmates. Beyond simple disruptiveness, these inmates are at risk for prison misconduct (Felson, Silver, & Remster, 2012). Unfortunately, most jails and prisons are not equipped to handle the complex and diverse psychiatric, safety, health, and administrative needs of this population.

While supervised in the community on probation or parole, offenders with mental illness face other challenges. Namely, people with serious mental illness are significantly more likely

The Wiley International Handbook of Correctional Psychology, First Edition. Edited by Devon L. L. Polaschek, Andrew Day, and Clive R. Hollin.

to have their community supervision revoked than offenders similarly situated who do not have a mental illness. Revocation often lies downstream from technical violations of the conditions of release (rather than new offenses per se; Dauphinot, 1996; Eno Louden & Skeem, 2011; Feder, 1991; Hartwell, 2004; Lovell, Gagliardi, & Peterson, 2002; McShane, Williams, Pelz, & Quarles, 2005; Porporino & Motiuk, 1995). Revocation sometimes reflects psychiatric symptoms that get in the way of reliably meeting the many technical conditions of community supervision, the increased monitoring and surveillance that supervision officers allocate to this population, or both (see Eno Louden & Skeem, 2006; Skeem, Emke-Francis, & Eno Louden, 2006; Skeem, Encandela, & Eno Louden, 2003; Skeem, Manchak, & Peterson, 2011).

In short, offenders with mental illness do not seem to fare well in the correctional system. In fact, the challenges and adverse outcomes these offenders experience often extend their stay in the correctional system (Feder, 1994; Lurigio, 2001). Deep penetration into the system (see Munetz & Griffin, 2006) is both troubling for offenders and their families and cause for concern among policy-makers. Public health and public safety goals are not being met, as costs for this high-need population skyrocket (Maguire & Pastore, 1997; Torrey, Kennard, Eslinger, Lamb, & Payle, 2010).

There have been many calls to respond to these challenges with innovative approaches (e.g., Council of State Governments, 2002). The principal response to offenders with mental illness in the correctional system is to implement a program that seeks to increase access to mental health services and thereby reduce recidivism. The implicit assumption is that symptoms lead directly to justice system involvement (Skeem et al., 2011). Because most offenders are supervised in the community (Glaze, Kaeble, Minton, & Tsoutis, 2015), many of these programs are implemented directly through probation or work in tandem with probation. The dominant view is that services are more effective when provided in the community than during incarceration.

This chapter has three major sections. First, we review two major "mental health models" for supervising offenders with mental illness—specialty mental health probation and mental health courts. Second, we review a third model of supervision that has recently been proposed (Skeem et al., 2011; Skeem, Steadman, & Manchak, 2015) as an alternative or supplement to the mental health model—the correctional rehabilitation model. This model was developed to manage *all* offenders, regardless of their mental health status. Here, mental illness is a secondary concern that must be addressed to facilitate rehabilitation efforts that target general risk factors for recidivism (i.e., antisocial thinking, antisocial peers, antisocial personality pattern, family and marital conflict, education and employment problems, substance use, and misuse of leisure time; see Andrews & Bonta, 2010). Third, we discuss how the mental health and correctional rehabilitation models might be integrated to best address the diverse psychosocial and criminogenic needs of this population.

Mental Health Models

Mental health courts and specialty mental health probation are perhaps the two most common "mental health model" approaches developed for offenders with mental illness. Both approaches emphasize psychiatric symptoms and treatment. Indeed, in both approaches, psychiatric care—typically in the form of psychotropic medication and also psychosocial counseling—is mandated as a condition of the court or probation supervision. Supervision often focuses on such mental health issues as treatment compliance, coping, functioning, and decompensation (Eno Louden, Skeem, Camp, & Christensen, 2008). Offenders can incur violations or be revoked from the specialty docket or community supervision for non-compliance with treatment. Although these mental health models emphasize treatment and symptom reduction as important goals in themselves, they also implicitly suggest that treatment and symptom control will reduce recidivism (Skeem et al., 2011). Next, we describe each approach and the evidence base supporting it.

Overview of Specialty Mental Health Probation

Many agencies in the United States have implemented specialty mental health probation caseloads. A decade ago, over 100 agencies were implementing such caseloads (Skeem et al., 2006). A national survey revealed significant variability among these agencies; in fact, only one in five agencies that self-identified as "specialty" practiced all core components that were found to distinguish specialty mental supervision from traditional supervision, for people with mental illness (Skeem et al., 2006).

In the survey, prototypic specialty programs differed from traditional agencies in several key ways. Whereas traditional probation caseloads tend to be quite large (100+ offenders per officer) and heterogeneous (in criminogenic and psychosocial needs), specialty mental health caseloads are smaller (<50 offenders per officer) and comprised entirely of offenders with mental illness. Unlike traditional officers, specialty officers tended to have interests, background, or training in mental health. And specialty officers were unique in coordinating community-based services for offenders (rather than simply brokering services or making referrals; Skeem et al., 2006).

Prototypic specialty and traditional probation also differ in their supervision philosophies and strategies. In specialty probation, there is strong emphasis on psychiatric treatment: Officers monitor probationers' symptoms and treatment compliance more carefully than traditional officers (Eno Louden, Skeem, Camp, Vidal, & Peterson, 2012; Skeem et al., 2006). Moreover, prototypic specialty officers place a premium on problem-solving as a response to non-compliance (i.e., identifying any obstacles to compliance, removing them, and agreeing on a compliance plan), whereas prototypic traditional officers tend to rely on sanction threats (Skeem et al., 2006; see also Eno Louden, Skeem, Camp, & Christensen, 2008). In a study of audiotaped meetings between specialty officers and their probationers, Eno Louden et al. (2012) found that specialty officers spent much time discussing mental health issues (e.g., treatment compliance, medication adherence, symptoms; see also Skeem et al., 2003), and tended to use positive reinforcement (e.g., incentivizing; persuasion) more than surveillance and threats.

These prototypic features of specialty probation (Manchak, Skeem, Kennealy, & Eno Louden, 2014) are neither mandated nor necessarily present among programs that self-identify as specialty mental health probation agencies. Nonetheless, they can guide implementation and evaluation of specialty mental health programs. As might be expected, as the number of prototypic features that characterize a specialty agency decreases, they grow more similar to traditional agencies in their approaches to supervising offenders with mental illness (Skeem et al., 2006). In the next section, we provide evidence on the effectiveness of specialty mental health probation.

Effectiveness of Specialty Mental Health Probation on Offenders' Criminal Justice Outcomes

Although few studies have tested whether and how well specialty mental health probation improves criminal justice outcomes for probationers with mental illness, available evidence suggests that it is more effective than traditional probation in doing so. Notably, however, the evidence challenges the widely held notion that specialty supervision is effective *because* of its emphasis on mental health treatment. In fact, only one rigorous study of specialty probation conducted to date has explicitly tested this assumption (described below), and it found not only that it did not significantly impact probationers' symptoms over the course of a year (see Skeem & Manchak, 2009), but that symptom change in probationers had no discernable effect on their criminal outcomes. Instead, specialty mental health probation seems to "work" mostly because it improves how officers interact with probationers (see Lurigio, Epperson, Canada, & Babchuk, 2012, for a review). Specifically, and consistent with prior exploratory qualitative research (Skeem et al., 2003), the quality of the relationship that officers established with probationers and the type of technique officers used to monitor and enforce compliance with the conditions of supervision led to more favorable criminal justice outcomes (e.g., fewer violations, arrests).

In this rigorous study of specialty probation, Skeem and colleagues sought to determine (a) whether specialty probation is more effective (and cost-effective) than traditional probation in reducing recidivism for probationers with mental illness, and (b) what program components explain this greater effectiveness, if found. In this study, 183 probationers with mental illness in a highly prototypic specialty agency were matched on a number of clinical, criminal, and demographic characteristics to 176 probationers with mental illness in a prototypic traditional probation agency. Probationers were interviewed three times throughout the course of a year, and their supervising probation officers completed a brief survey about each probationer on the same schedule. Additionally, 1-year psychiatric treatment records (access, type, and frequency of treatment) and 2-year Federal Bureau of Investigation (FBI) arrest records were gathered. This longitudinal matched trial had four important findings (see Manchak et al., 2014; Skeem, Manchak, & Montoya, 2017).

First, specialty probation officers differed from traditional probation officers in *how* they supervised probationers with mental illness. Both probationer and officer reports indicated that specialty officers met more often with their supervisees than traditional officers, and were more likely to be aware of supervisees' non-compliance with the rules. Moreover, specialty officers demonstrated greater "boundary spanning," as evidenced by officer self-report of contacts with service providers and probationers' evaluations of their supervising officer's knowledge of other social services and assistance with coordinating access to these services. Specialty officers and probationers also endorsed more frequent use of positive (e.g., problem-solving) and less frequent use of negative (e.g., sanctions and threats) compliance strategies. Finally, specialty probationers and officers had higher scores of "dual role relationship quality" (i.e., firm, fair, and caring; see Skeem, Eno Louden, Polaschek, & Camp, 2007) than traditional probationers and officers (Manchak et al., 2014).

Second, specialty probationers accessed more psychiatric services than traditional probationers, even though jurisdictions where probationers were supervised were similarly situated in terms of population size and public expenditures on mental health services (Manchak et al., 2014). Third, specialty probation produced better criminal justice and cost outcomes than traditional probation: Specialty probationers were substantially less likely to be arrested over a 2-year follow-up than traditional probationers (Skeem et al., 2017), and specialty probation was more cost-effective than traditional probation (mostly because of reduced expenditures on crisis- and inpatient-psychiatric services; Skeem & Manchak, 2012). These criminal justice outcomes are consistent with those observed in an independent study of four samples of probationers with mental illness; Wolff et al. (2014) found that, after controlling for age, race, ethnicity, and criminal history, probationers assigned to specialized mental health caseloads had significantly fewer probation violations resulting in arrests and fewer days spent in jail than probationers under general supervision who were receiving mental health treatment.

Fourth, and perhaps most importantly, the effectiveness of specialty probation in reducing arrests was *not* a function of symptom control (see Skeem et al., 2011). As noted briefly above, there was no evidence, for instance, that probationers' symptom reduction protected against rearrest. Instead, mediation tests indicated that the effect of specialty probation on arrest was fully explained by high-quality dual role relationships (see Skeem & Manchak, 2010).

In conclusion, although the evidence base for specialty mental health probation is not vast, it does reflect favorably on the approach. Specialty mental health probation—if well implemented (e.g., adheres to the prototypic features)—seems to be an effective strategy for managing probationers with mental illness. Although its effectiveness as a crime-reduction strategy is not driven by its focus on psychiatric symptoms, it improves correctional practices that "work" with this population. More specifically, specialty probation seems to facilitate higher-quality relationships that protect against arrest (Skeem et al., 2017) and more positive compliance strategies that protect against probation violations (Manchak et al., 2014). Moreover, it also yields better service brokerage—in the form of boundary spanning—which can help probationers access better care for their psychiatric symptoms (e.g., integrated dual diagnosis treatment; see Manchak et al., 2014). Notably, as will be discussed in further detail later in this chapter, all these practices are consistent with the Risk-Need-Responsivity model (RNR; Bonta and Andrews, 2017). In the next section, we discuss the other primary mental health model intervention available to offenders with mental illness on probation.

Overview of Mental Health Courts

In the United States, there are over 300 mental health courts across 44 states (SAMHSA Gaines Center, 2016), making this perhaps the most common program for offenders with mental illness under correctional supervision in the community. The first mental health court was established in Broward County, Florida, in 1997. Like specialty probation, mental health courts emphasize psychiatric treatment as a means to improve offenders' outcomes (Skeem et al., 2011). Of course, mental health courts have a different organizational structure. Whereas the onus of working with offenders falls mostly on probation officers in specialty probation, multiple actors work in concert to supervise and treat offenders in mental health courts.

Specialty mental health courts are modeled after drug courts and serve as an alternative to traditional adversarial court processing. In this model, the prosecution and defense work together, in a collaborative manner, to make decisions about offenders with mental illness. Moreover, these attorneys work very closely with the judge, probation officers, and community treatment providers, typically meeting routinely to make decisions about treatment and, if necessary, about how to respond to offender misconduct. Often (but not always), these courts target first-time, non-violent offenders who are believed to have committed a crime as a result of their mental health problems (see Thompson, Osher, & Tomansini-Joshi, 2007). As a result, the population served by mental health courts will have some overlap with those supervised by specialty probation, but it is likely that mental health court participants are somewhat lower-risk offenders with less serious offense histories.

The National Center for State Courts (2010) provides guidance for the implementation of mental health courts, including performance criteria for assessing their overall effectiveness. Nevertheless, research continues to highlight heterogeneity among mental health courts in (a) eligibility criteria, (b) referral processes, (c) use of sanctions and jail time, (d) how long defendants are required to participate in the court, and (e) requirements the offender must complete in order to graduate from the mental health court (Almquist & Dodd, 2009). Despite this variability, mental health courts share an emphasis on mental health treatment and reducing the amount of time mentally ill offenders spend incarcerated.

Effectiveness of Mental Health Courts

The evidence base examining mental health courts is larger than that for specialty mental health probation. In fact, multi-site, longitudinal studies have been conducted to evaluate mental health courts. The first of these prospective multi-site studies compared recidivism outcomes of newly enrolled mental health court participants ($n = 447$) to those of individuals matched on sex, criminal charges, race, age, and diagnosis who were eligible but not referred to mental health courts ($n = 600$) (Steadman, Redlich, Callahan, Robbins, & Vesselinov, 2011). Based on an 18-month follow-up period, Steadman et al. (2011) discovered that the treatment group (49%) was significantly less likely than the comparison group (58%) to be arrested. More importantly, well-controlled analyses indicated that reductions in annual arrest rates for the treatment group were significantly greater than those for the comparison group, and that the treatment group spent fewer days incarcerated.

Recently, Sarteschi, Vaughan, and Kim (2011) meta-analyzed the effect on recidivism of 18 mental health court evaluations (pre-test post-test, quasi-experimental, or experimental). Although uncontrolled studies were included and several studies had issues with selection bias and attrition, the results indicated a moderate effect (Cohen, 1988) on offender recidivism for the highest-quality studies (−.52). And, although the authors were unable to produce an overall effect on clinical outcomes because the samples varied too much on the clinical indices used, they found that only two of the eight studies examining clinical outcomes made a significant impact, increasing participant functioning and (separately) decreasing the number of inpatient treatment days (Sarteschi et al., 2011).

Most research on mental health courts has focused on outcomes, rather than process. In other words, little is known about the possible active ingredients that drive the effectiveness of mental health courts. Several investigators speculate that staffing, characteristics of the judge, the sanction and reward processes, and quality of treatment services all likely matter, but rigorous tests of most of these potentially mediating variables are not available. A few studies have tested the implicit model underlying the mental health court intervention, that improved psychiatric symptoms are the primary route by which mental health courts "work." Results indicate that symptom reduction is not significantly correlated with reduced recidivism (Steadman, Cocozza, & Veysey, 1999; Steadman & Naples, 2005). Although more research is needed to identify components of mental health courts that effect offender change, there is little support for the notion that symptom control is a key mechanism.

Correctional Rehabilitation Model

Unlike programs reviewed thus far, the correctional rehabilitation model frames mental illness not as a target for recidivism reduction but as a "responsivity" factor to consider while targeting general risk factors for crime. This model is rooted in the work of Canadian psychologists who systematically refuted Martinson's (1974) widely cited finding that "nothing works" to reduce offenders' recidivism. These Canadian psychologists used meta-analysis to statistically summarize effect sizes across controlled studies of correctional treatment, and identified "what works" to reduce recidivism: that is, they identified principles that characterized effective programs.

These principles were distilled in the RNR model (Bonta & Andrews, 2017) of correctional services and supervision. Over the past 25 years, the RNR model has gained traction as an "evidence-based" model of correctional treatment, but it had little influence on policy for offenders with mental illness until recently (see Skeem et al., 2011). Given evidence that symptom control does not reliably translate into reduced recidivism, policy-makers have shifted their gaze from evidence-based psychiatric services (which can improve clinical outcomes like symptoms and functioning) to evidence-based correctional services (which reduce recidivism; Skeem et al., 2015). Recently, researchers have begun to discuss how the mental health and RNR models might work synergistically for justice-involved people with mental illness (Skeem et al., 2011, 2015). As shown next, the RNR model differs from the mental health model in its assumptions about what causes offending for people with mental illness, and how to respond.

RNR Model Overview

Given its theoretically and empirically derived development, comprehensive approach to rehabilitation, and its unparalleled evidence base, the RNR model is currently the dominant model of effective correctional services. Dozens of studies spanning multiple correctional contexts and tens of thousands of offenders suggest that adherence to three key principles can maximize recidivism reduction.

First, the risk principle requires that offenders be assessed for recidivism risk using a validated risk assessment instrument (Bonta & Andrews, 2017). Ideally, the instrument measures both unchangeable (e.g., criminal history) and changeable risk factors that robustly predict recidivism—including antisocial cognition, antisocial peers, substance use, family problems, education and employment problems, and poor use of leisure time. Information about offenders' risk level is used to inform the frequency and intensity of services, such that higher-risk offenders receive more services, more frequently, and for a longer period of time (Bonta & Andrews, 2017).

Second, according to the need principle, correctional services are most effective when they target changeable risk factors for recidivism or "criminogenic needs" (e.g., antisocial attitudes; substance abuse) rather than non-criminogenic needs (e.g., self-esteem or depression; Andrews et al., 1990; Bonta & Andrews, 2017). Correctional practitioners are charged with helping offenders understand and reduce their risk factors.

Third, according to the responsivity principle, services must be responsive to the individual characteristics of offenders, including their learning styles, culture, gender, and so on (Bonta & Andrews, 2017). The principle of general responsivity is well supported; offenders generally respond more favorably to highly structured approaches like cognitive behavioral interventions (where offenders are taught to identify and change their criminogenic thinking patterns). They also may benefit from interventions designed to increase their motivation for treatment

(Andrews, 2012). The principle of "specific responsivity" enjoys less empirical support (Andrews, 2012): It requires practitioners to attend to factors in an individual's life that could act as a barrier to correctional services (e.g., lack of housing or childcare; acute psychiatric symptoms) or influence how an individual may interpret or respond to treatment (e.g., gender, race, or cultural or religious beliefs).

Beyond these three basic principles, the RNR model also emphasizes the importance of staff practices (Bonta & Andrews, 2017). Commonly referred to as "core correctional practices" (Dowden & Andrews, 2004), staff practices consistent with the RNR model place emphasis on *how* officers and providers can interact with offenders to maximize recidivism reduction. Specifically, correctional practitioners are encouraged to use problem-solving techniques and to avoid an authoritarian interaction style with offenders. Instead, practitioners should establish high-quality authoritative (i.e., firm-but-fair) relationships with offenders, where offenders are treated with care, concern, and respect (Skeem et al., 2007; Skeem & Manchak, 2008). When targeting risk factors for recidivism, practitioners are also encouraged to employ a social learning framework, whereby they model desired behavior, facilitate offender rehearsal of new behaviors, and reinforce the offender for exhibiting prosocial behaviors (Dowden & Andrews, 2004).

Effectiveness of RNR

As noted earlier, the effectiveness of RNR largely rests on a number of meta-analyses of controlled treatment studies conducted with general offenders (Smith, Gendreau, & Swartz, 2009). In this section, we briefly highlight findings for general offenders before focusing on evidence about the extent to which RNR principles generalize to offenders with mental illness. Evidence supporting the effectiveness of RNR principles for general offenders is quite strong. Reviews of the risk principle indicate that targeting moderate- to high-risk offenders is significantly correlated with reductions in recidivism rates (Brusman-Lovins, Lowenkamp, Latessa, & Smith, 2007; Lowenkamp & Latessa, 2005; Sperber, Latessa, & Makarios, 2013). One showed a 20% drop in recidivism rates when treatment hours were increased for higher-risk cases (Sperber et al., 2013).

Evidence for the need principle is most robust (Andrews et al., 1990; Bonta & Andrews, 2017; Smith et al., 2009). Meta-analyses reveal a small to moderate effect ($r = .20$ to $.30$) for services that target criminogenic needs (Bonta & Andrews, 2017; Smith et al., 2009). Meanwhile, services that target non-criminogenic needs (factors not strongly tied to recidivism) produce null to negative effects ($r = -.01$ to $.04$; Bonta & Andrews, 2017; Smith et al., 2009).

Consistent with aspects of the general responsivity principle, meta-analyses consistently show more support for cognitive behavioral interventions than other types of treatment (Andrews et al., 1990; Pearson, Lipton, Cleland, & Yee, 2002; Rosenthal & Rubin, 1979; Smith et al., 2009). Some studies revealed a 15% reduction in recidivism for treatments using cognitive behavioral interventions, whereas other modalities (i.e., non-behavioral) were associated with much smaller or null reductions (Gendreau & Smith, 2007; Smith et al., 2009).

A number of studies and meta-analyses indicate that adherence to all three RNR principles moderately to strongly reduces recidivism (Andrews & Dowden, 1999, 2005; Dowden & Andrews, 2000; Latessa & Lowenkamp, 2005; Lowenkamp, Flores, Holsinger, Makarios, & Latessa, 2010; Lowenkamp, Latessa, & Smith, 2006; Smith et al., 2009). In fact, instruments like the Correctional Program Assessment Inventory (CPAI) have been created to distill how well services in a given correctional program or system adhere to the larger set of RNR principles (Gendreau & Andrews, 2001). Lowenkamp et al. (2006) used the CPAI to assess fidelity to RNR among 38 halfway house ("treatment") and parole ("control") programs. The authors compared recidivism rates between the treatment and control groups—as a function of how well programs adhered to RNR—and found CPAI scores moderately predicted various forms of recidivism (r = .35 to .44), explaining 7–18% of the variance in treatment effects. In short, program adherence to RNR corresponded quite closely to program effectiveness.

Because the RNR model ostensibly applies to most kinds of offenders—including those with mental illness—few studies have *directly* examined the utility of RNR principles for offenders with mental illness. In a review of 18 studies that examine how these principles might apply to offenders with mental illness, Skeem et al. (2015) arrived at three main conclusions.

First, with respect to the risk principle, there is strong evidence that instruments that assess general risk factors predict recidivism for offenders with mental illness. Indeed, offenders with and without mental illness share the most robust risk factors for recidivism, and these factors predict recidivism among those with mental illness more strongly than clinical factors like acute symptoms or treatment adherence (Skeem, Winter, Kennealy, Eno Louden, & Tatar, 2014; as cited in Skeem et al., 2015). That said, the more essential component of the risk principle—risk/service matching—has not been examined with this population (notably, this evidence base is somewhat limited in general offenders as well).

Second, with respect to the need principle, several studies have shown that targeting one or more general risk factors in programs for offenders with mental illness can translate into reductions in criminality and violence. For instance, one experiment examined reincarceration rates among inmates randomly assigned to participate in psychiatric "treatment as usual" (TAU) or TAU plus a therapeutic community program that included a focus on criminal thinking (Sacks, Sacks, McKendrick, Banks, & Stommel, 2004): Compared to those in TAU, those in the therapeutic community program were approximately half as likely to return to custody.

Third, although cognitive behavioral treatment that targets antisocial cognition has been shown to reduce criminal thinking among offenders with mental illness (Sacks et al., 2004; Young, Chick, & Gudjonsson, 2010), no studies have examined the specific responsivity principle with this population. Skeem et al. (2015) unpack compelling research questions that must be addressed to determine whether and how the RNR model should be modified to maximize recidivism reduction for offenders with mental illness.

Integrating Models to Improve Outcomes

Historically, there have been two models for supervising and treating probationers with mental illness: a mental health model and a correctional rehabilitation model. Although the two models specify different treatment targets for offenders with mental illness (i.e., mental illness vs. general risk factors), the models also overlap in key ways. Staff practices are explicitly emphasized as part and parcel of the RNR model (Bonta & Andrews, 2017). The mental health model, on the other hand, seems to implicitly encourage these practices via a philosophical emphasis on treatment and behavior change (see Skeem & Manchak, 2009). These practices are viewed as important by practitioners, differentiate the model from traditional community supervision approaches, and appear thus far to be ingredients that drive the effectiveness of specialized criminal justice interventions for offenders with mental illness (Skeem et al., 2006, 2007).

Still, the mental health and correctional rehabilitation models are viewed, in practice, as quite distinct from one another. Indeed, casual conversations with practitioners of either model reveal large gaps in understanding about, and respect for, the opposing model. *If an agency chooses to employ alternative, evidence-based approaches to probation supervision for mentally ill offenders, they often choose one model and ignore the evidence and potential benefits that aspects of the other model can offer.* In some cases, resistance to the potential merits of the opposing model has both stymied research progress and crippled advancements in the management of offenders with mental illness on probation (Skeem et al., 2015).

If the field is to advance and work to increase the potency of interventions for offenders with mental illness on probation, more research is needed in several areas. For instance, it would be beneficial for researchers to conduct direct tests of the applicability of RNR principles to mentally ill offenders (Skeem et al., 2015). Indirect support for their utility with this population simply will not do. Taking this one step further, it would be helpful to determine what aspects of the RNR model (e.g., match service intensity to risk level, use cognitive behavioral therapy interventions, implement good staff practices) yield the strongest effects among offenders with mental illness.

Conversely, more research is needed to understand how mental health treatment can enhance outcomes observed in the correctional rehabilitation model. Psychiatric treatment is seen as a secondary target in the correctional rehabilitation model: an aid to increase responsivity to RNR-based intervention. Yet, no research has yet explicitly tested how offender responsivity is enhanced by psychiatric care or what components of psychiatric care are needed to do so.

Finally, both the correctional rehabilitation and the mental health models would benefit from a more nuanced understanding of how mental health symptoms interact with, influence, and are influenced by criminogenic risk factors. Although a body of evidence suggests quite convincingly that targeting mental health symptoms will not *directly* impact *criminal* outcomes for a majority of offenders (see Skeem et al., 2011, for a review), future research should explore how mental health treatment can influence risk factors for crime or work to improve proximal outcomes that lie upstream from criminal behavior (e.g., improved functioning which enhances work ethic), that can, in turn, reduce criminogenic risks. Practitioners are already being encouraged to integrate these models (Osher, D'amora, Plotkin, Jarrett, & Eggleson, 2012), but research lags behind policy in providing guidance on how and why integration is essential (Skeem et al., 2015). Policy frameworks already suggest (correctly, in our view) that mental health treatment is a necessary but insufficient method to improve justice outcomes for this population (Osher et al., 2012). The challenge is to empirically define *how*—and with what modifications—the correctional rehabilitation model adds value to the traditional mental health focus for this population.

Key Readings

Bonta, J., & Andrews, D. A. (2017). *The psychology of criminal conduct* (6th ed.). London, UK: Taylor & Francis.

Osher, F., D'Amora, D. A., Plotkin, M., Jarrett, N., & Eggleston, A. (2012). *Adults with behavioral health needs under correctional supervision: A shared framework for reducing recidivism and promoting recovery*. Washington, DC: Council of State Governments Justice Center.

Skeem, J. L., Manchak, S. M., & Peterson, J. (2011). Correctional policy for offenders with mental illness: Creating a new paradigm for recidivism reduction. *Law and Human Behavior*, 35, 110–126.

Skeem, J. L., Steadman, H. J., & Manchak, S. M. (2015). Applicability of the Risk-Need-Responsivity model to persons with mental illness involved in the criminal justice system. *Psychiatric Services*, 66(9), 916–922.

754   *Sarah M. Manchak, Lydie R. Loth, and Jennifer L. Skeem*

References

Almquist, L., & Dodd, E. (2009). *Mental health courts: A guide to research-informed policy and practice.* New York, NY: Council of State Governments.

Andrews, D. A. (2012). The Risk-Need-Responsivity (RNR) model of correctional assessment and treatment. In J. Dvoskin, J. L. Skeem, K. Douglas, & R. Novaco (Eds.), *Using social science to reduce violent offending* (pp. 127–156). New York, NY: Oxford University Press.

Andrews, D. A., & Bonta, J. (2010). Rehabilitating criminal justice policy and practice. *Psychology, Public Policy, and Law*, 16, 39–55.

Andrews, D. A., & Dowden, G. (1999). A meta-analytic investigation into effective correctional intervention for female offenders. *Forum on Corrections Research*, 11(3), 18–20.

Andrews, D. A., & Dowden, G. (2005). Managing correctional treatment for reduced recidivism: A meta-analytic review of programme integrity. *Legal and Criminological Psychology*, 10, 173–187.

Andrews, D. A., Zinger, I., Hoge, R. D., Bonta, J., Gendreau, P., & Cullen, F. T. (1990). Does correctional treatment work? A clinically relevant and psychologically informed meta-analysis. *Criminology*, 8, 369–404.

Blitz, C., Wolff, N., & Shi, J. (2008). Physical victimization in prison: The role of mental illness. *International Journal of Law and Psychiatry*, 31, 385–393.

Bonta, J., & Andrews, D. A. (2017). *The psychology of criminal conduct* (6th ed.). London, UK: Taylor & Francis.

Brusman-Lovins, L., Lowenkamp, C. T., Latessa, E. J., & Smith, P. (2007). Application of the risk principle to female offenders. *Journal of Contemporary Criminal Justice*, 23, 383–398.

Cohen, J. (1988). *Statistical power analysis for the behavioral sciences* (2nd ed.). Hillsdale, NJ: Lawrence Erlbaum.

Council of State Governments (2002). *Criminal Justice/Mental Health Consensus Project.* New York, NY: Author Retrieved from https://www.ncjrs.gov/pdffiles1/nij/grants/197103.pdf

Cuddeback, G. S., Scheyett, A., Pettus-Davis, C., & Morrissey, J. P. (2010). General medical problems of incarcerated persons with severe and persistent mental illness: A population-based study. *Psychiatric Services*, 61, 45–49.

Dauphinot, L. (1996). *The efficacy of community correctional supervision for offenders with severe mental illness* (Unpublished doctoral dissertation). University of Texas at Austin.

De Hert, M., Correll, C. U., Bobes, J., Cetkovich-Bakmas, M., Cohen, D., Asai, I., … & Leucht, S. (2011). Physical illness in patients with severe mental disorders. I. Prevalence, impact of medications and disparities in health care. *World Psychiatry*, 10, 52–77.

Ditton, P. M. (1999). *Mental health and treatment of inmates and probationers.* Washington, DC: Bureau of Justice Statistics.

Dowden, C., & Andrews, D. A. (2000). Effective correctional treatment and violent reoffending: A meta-analysis. *Canadian Journal of Criminology*, 42, 449–467.

Dowden, C., & Andrews, D. A. (2004). The importance of staff practice in delivering effective correctional treatment: A meta-analytic review of core correctional practice. *International Journal of Offender Therapy and Comparative Criminology*, 48(2), 203–214.

Draine, J., Salzer, M. S., Culhane, D. P., & Hadley, T. R. (2002). Role of social disadvantage in crime, joblessness, and homelessness among persons with serious mental illness. *Psychiatric Services*, 53, 565–573.

Eno Louden, J., & Skeem, J. (2006). Toward evidence-based practices for probationers and parolees mandated to mental health treatment. *Psychiatric Services*, 57, 333–342.

Eno Louden, J., & Skeem, J. (2011). *Parolees with mental disorder: Toward evidence-based practice.* University of California, Irvine, Center for Evidence Based Corrections. Retrieved from http://ucicorrections.seweb.uci.edu/files/2013/06/Parolees-with-Mental-Disorder.pdf

Eno Louden, J., Skeem, J. L., Camp, J., & Christensen, E. (2008). Supervising probationers with mental disorders: How do agencies respond to violations? *Criminal Justice and Behavior*, 35(7), 832–847.

Eno Louden, J., Skeem, J. L., Camp, J., Vidal, S., & Peterson, J. (2012). Supervision practices in specialty mental health probation: What happens in officer-probationer meetings? *Law and Human Behavior*, 36(2), 109–119.

Fazel, S., Cartwright, J., Norman-Nott, A., & Hawton, K. (2008). Suicide in prisoners: A systematic review of risk factors. *Journal of Clinical Psychiatry*, 69, 1721–1731.

Feder, L. (1991). A comparison of the community adjustment of mentally ill offenders with those from the general prison population. *Law and Human Behavior*, 15, 477–493.

Feder, L. (1994). Psychiatric hospitalization history and parole decisions. *Law and Human Behavior*, 18, 395–410.

Felson, R. B., Silver, E., & Remster, B. (2012). Mental disorder and offending in prison. *Criminal Justice and Behavior*, 39, 125–143.

Gendreau, P., & Andrews, D. A. (2001). *Correctional Program Assessment Inventory (CPAI-2000)*. St. John, Canada: University of New Brunswick.

Gendreau, P., & Smith, P. (2007). Influencing the "people who count": Some perspective on the reporting of meta-analytic results for prediction and treatment outcomes with offenders. *Criminal Justice and Behavior*, 34, 1536–1559.

Glaze, L., Kaeble, D., Minton, T., & Tsoutis, A. (2015). *Correctional populations in the United States, 2014*. Washington, DC: Bureau of Justice Statistics.

Hartwell, S. (2004). Comparison of offenders with mental illness only and offenders with dual diagnoses. *Psychiatric Services*, 55, 145–150.

James, D., & Glaze, L. (2006). *Mental health problems of prison and jail inmates*. US Department of Justice, Office of Justice Programs. Retrieved from https://www.bjs.gov/content/pub/pdf/mhppji.pdf

Karberg, J. C., & James, D. J. (2005). *Substance dependence, abuse, and treatment of jail inmates, 2002*. Washington, DC: Bureau of Justice Statistics.

Kessler, R., Chiu, W., Demler, O., & Walters, E. (2005). Prevalence, severity, and comorbidity of 12-month DSM-IV disorders in the National Comorbidity Survey replication. *Archives of General Psychiatry*, 62, 617–727.

Latessa, E. J., & Lowenkamp, C. (2005). What works in reducing recidivism? *University of St. Thomas Law Journal*, 3, 521–535.

Lovell, D., Gagliardi, G., & Peterson, P. (2002). Recidivism and use of services among persons with mental illness after release from prison. *Psychiatric Services*, 53, 1290–1296.

Lowenkamp, C. T., Flores, A. W., Holsinger, A. M., Makarios, M. D., & Latessa, E. J. (2010). Intensive supervision programs: Does program philosophy and the principles of effective intervention matter? *Journal of Criminal Justice*, 38, 368–375.

Lowenkamp, C. T., & Latessa, E. J. (2005). Increasing the effectiveness of correctional programming through the risk principle: Identifying offenders for residential placement. *Criminology and Public Policy*, 4(2), 263–289.

Lowenkamp, C. T., Latessa, E. J., & Smith, P. (2006). Does correctional program quality really matter? The importance of adhering to the principles of effective intervention. *Criminology and Public Policy*, 5, 201–220.

Lurigio, A. J. (2001). Effective services for parolees with mental illnesses. *Crime and Delinquency*, 47, 446–461.

Lurigio, A. J., Epperson, M. W., Canada, K. E., & Babchuk, L. C. (2012). Specialized probation programs for people with mental illnesses: A review of practices and research. *Journal of Crime and Justice*, 35(2), 317–326.

Maguire, K., & Pastore, A. L. (1997). *Bureau of Justice Statistics sourcebook of criminal justice statistics, 1996*. Washington, DC: Bureau of Justice Statistics.

Manchak, S. M., Skeem, J. L., Kennealy, P. J., & Eno Louden, J. (2014). High-fidelity specialty mental health probation improves officer practices, treatment access, and rule compliance. *Law and Human Behavior*, 38(5), 450–461.

Martinson, R. (1974). What works? Questions and answers about prison reform. *The Public Interest*, 35, 22–54.

McShane, M., Williams, F., Pelz, B., & Quarles, T. (2005). The role of mental disorder in parolee success. *The Southwest Journal of Criminal Justice*, 2, 3–22.

Munetz, M. R., & Griffin, P. A. (2006). Use of the sequential intercept model as an approach to decriminalization of people with serious mental illness. *Psychiatric Services*, 57(4), 544–549.

National Center for State Courts. (2010). Mental health courts resource guide. Retrieved from https://www.ncsc.org/Topics/Alternative-Dockets/Problem-Solving-Courts/Mental-Health-Courts/Resource-Guide.aspx

Osher, F., D'Amora, D. A., Plotkin, M., Jarrett, N., & Eggleston, A. (2012). *Adults with behavioral health needs under correctional supervision: A shared framework for reducing recidivism and promoting recovery*. Washington, DC: Council of State Governments Justice Center.

Pearson, F. S., Lipton, D. D., Cleland, C. M., & Yee, D. S. (2002). The effects of behavioral/cognitive-behavioral programs on recidivism. *Crime and Delinquency*, 48(3), 476–496.

Porporino, F., & Motiuk, L. (1995). The prison careers of mentally disordered offenders. *International Journal of Law and Psychiatry*, 18, 29–44.

Rosenthal, R., & Rubin, D. B. (1979). A note on percent variance explained as a measure of the importance of effects. *Journal of Applied Social Psychology*, 9, 395–396.

Sacks, S., Sacks, J. Y., McKendrick, K., Banks, S., & Stommel, J. (2004). Modified TC for MICA offenders: Crime outcomes. *Behavioral Sciences & the Law*, 22, 477–501.

SAMHSA Gaines Center. (2016). Adult mental health treatment court locator. Retrieved from http://www.samhsa.gov/gains-center/mental-health-treatment-court-locator/adults

Sarteschi, C., Vaughn, M., & Kim, K. (2011). Assessing the effectiveness of mental health courts: A quantitative review. *Journal of Criminal Justice*, 39, 12–20.

Skeem, J. L., Emke-Francis, P., & Eno Louden, J. (2006). Probation, mental health, and mandated treatment: A national survey. *Criminal Justice and Behavior*, 33, 158–184.

Skeem, J. L., Encandela, J., & Eno Louden, J. (2003). Perspectives on probation and mandated mental health treatment in specialized and traditional probation departments. *Behavioral Sciences & the Law*, 21(4), 429–458.

Skeem, J. L., Eno Louden, J., Polaschek, D. L. L., & Camp, J. (2007). Assessing relationship quality in mandated community treatment: Blending care with control. *Psychological Assessment*, 19(4), 397–410.

Skeem, J. L., & Manchak, S. M. (2008). Back to the future: From Klockars' model of effective supervision to evidence-based practice in probation. *Journal of Offender Rehabilitation*, 47(3), 220–247.

Skeem, J. L., & Manchak, S. M. (2009, January). Probation study: Mediation and treatment matching. Paper presented at the MacArthur Network on Mandated Community Treatment meeting, Santa Monica, CA.

Skeem, J. L., & Manchak, S. M. (2010, October). *Final outcomes of the longitudinal study: "What really works!" for probationers with serious mental illness*. Paper presented at the final meeting of the Macarthur Research Network on Mandated Community Treatment, Tucson, AZ.

Skeem, J. L., & Manchak, S. M. (2012, March). *Does specialty mental health probation "fight crime and save money"? A cost-benefit analysis*. Paper presented at the American Psychology-Law Society (AP-LS) annual conference, San Juan, Puerto Rico.

Skeem, J. L., Manchak, S. M., & Montoya, L. (2017). Comparing public safety outcomes for traditional probation vs. specialty mental health probation. *JAMA Psychiatry*, 74(9), 942–948.

Skeem, J. L., Manchak, S. M., & Peterson, J. (2011). Correctional policy for offenders with mental illness: Creating a new paradigm for recidivism reduction. *Law and Human Behavior*, 35, 110–126.

Skeem, J. L., Steadman, H. J., & Manchak, S. M. (2015). Applicability of the Risk-Need-Responsivity model to persons with mental illness involved in the criminal justice system. *Psychiatric Services*, 66(9), 916–922.

Skeem, J. L., Winter, E., Kennealy, P. J., Eno Louden, J., & Tatar, J. R. II (2014). Offenders with mental illness have criminogenic needs, too: Toward recidivism reduction. *Law and Human Behavior*, 38(3), 212–224.

Smith, P., Gendreau, P., & Swartz, K. (2009). Validating the principles of effective intervention: A systematic review of the contributions of meta-analysis in the field of corrections. *Victims and Offenders*, 4, 148–169.

Sperber, K. G., Latessa, E. J., & Makarios, M. D. (2013). Examining the interaction between level of risk and dosage of treatment. *Criminal Justice and Behavior*, 40(3), 338–348.

Steadman, H. J., Cocozza, J. J., & Veysey, B. M. (1999). Comparing outcomes for diverted and nondiverted jail detainees with mental illnesses. *Law and Human Behavior*, 23(6), 615–627.

Steadman, H. J., & Naples, M. (2005). Assessing the effectiveness of jail diversion programs for persons with serious mental illness and co-occurring substance use disorders. *Behavioral Sciences & the Law*, 23, 163–170.

Steadman, H. J., Osher, F., Robbins, P., Case, S., & Samuels, S. (2009). Prevalence of serious mental illness among jail inmates. *Psychiatric Services*, 60, 761–765.

Steadman, H. J., Redlich, A., Callahan, L., Robbins, P. C., & Vesselinov, R. (2011). Effect of mental health courts on arrests and jail days: A multisite study. *Archives of General Psychiatry*, 68(2), 167–172.

Teplin, L. (1990). The prevalence of severe mental disorders among urban male jail detainees: Comparison with the epidemiologic catchment area program. *American Journal of Public Health*, 80, 663–669.

Teplin, L. (1994). Psychiatric and substance abuse disorders among male urban detainees. *American Journal of Public Health*, 84, 290–293.

Thompson, M., Osher, F., & Tomasini-Joshi, D. (2007). *Improving responses to people with mental illness: The essential elements of a mental health court.* Washington, DC: US Department of Justice, Office of Justice Assistance.

Torrey, E., Kennard, A., Eslinger, D., Lamb, R., & Pavle, J. (2010). *More mentally ill persons are in jail and prisons than hospitals: A survey of the states.* Arlington, VA: Treatment Advocacy Center.

Watson, R., Stimpson, A., & Hostick, T. (2004). Prison health care: A review of the literature. *International Journal of Nursing Studies*, 41, 119–128.

Wolff, N., Blitz, C., & Shi, J. (2007). Rates of sexual victimization in prison for inmates with and without mental disorders. *Psychiatric Services*, 58, 1087–1094.

Wolff, N., Epperson, M., Shi, J., Huening, J., Schumann, B. E., & Sullivan, I. R. (2014). Mental health specialized probation caseloads: Are they effective? *International Journal of Law and Psychiatry*, 37, 464–472.

Young, S., Chick, K., & Gudjonsson, G. H. (2010). A preliminary evaluation of Reasoning and Rehabilitation 2 in mentally disordered offenders (R&R2M) across two secure forensic settings in the United Kingdom. *Journal of Forensic Psychiatry and Psychology*, 21, 336–349.

47

Community Treatment: The Need for a Taxonomy

Faye S. Taxman
George Mason University, USA

The offender population is not homogeneous, yet most correctional programs tend to be generic and treat offending as if most offending behavior is similar. Little attention is given to the differences in how individuals commit crimes, why individuals commit crimes, or where individuals commit crimes. This means that the individual-level precursors, community or environmental precursors, or situational factors are often glossed over. Little attention is given to how to tailor a program to meet the unique needs of individuals and/or their crime-producing behaviors. In fact, typically a lot of programs depend on the skills of the counselor or therapist to be responsive to the individual needs or issues that occur during the therapy session(s). The counselor and/or therapist can elect to delve into the specific patterns of offending behaviors, or not. Besides, as noted by many, correctional treatment occurs in environments where the goal is some type of punishment, which has a collateral impact on the context of how treatment is offered. In community settings, treatment may or may not be in correctional space (i.e., probation, parole, pre-trial, diversion programs), but the knowledge that the individual is under correctional control may be sufficient to affect the context of the programming.

While there is general research consensus that behavioral and cognitive social learning approaches are more likely to be effective treatments (Andrews, et al., 1990; Lipsey & Cullen, 2007; Sherman et al., 1998; to name just a few), this finding has been translated into supporting cognitive behavioral therapy (CBT) as the therapeutic orientation which allows for the components of a specific treatment program and/or treatment sessions to be customized to meet the full gamut of dynamic, behavioral needs of individuals involved in the program. As a delivery tool, CBT consists of didactic sessions to help individuals gain skills and knowledge in specific areas, processing groups to practice the skills, and meditation or stress management sessions to further skills in thought processing and managing risky behaviors. The actual components can be tailored to the unique needs of individuals in the groups. Lipsey and Landenberger (2007), in a meta-analysis, identified key components of CBT programs that are more effective in reducing recidivism. Effective CBT programs tend to: (a) occur in community settings, (b) target higher-risk offenders, (c) include an anger

The Wiley International Handbook of Correctional Psychology, First Edition. Edited by Devon L. L. Polaschek, Andrew Day, and Clive R. Hollin.

management component or a cognitive restructuring component, (d) provide supplementary individual sessions, (e) be of sufficient duration, and (f) be well implemented. Landenberger and Lipsey noted that CBT treatment elements of interpersonal problem-solving and anger management appear to approach or be statistically significant predictors of positive findings for CBT treatment. In these meta-analyses examining six curricula, there was not a specific curriculum that had better outcomes than others (partially due to the low number of evaluations of specific curricula or CBT therapy manuals that are available.)

Most evaluations are at the individual program level, and often do not sufficiently measure the programmatic components to allow for a meta-analysis to explore the features that contribute to more positive outcomes. The Landenberger and Lipsey study is one of the few studies that examined, across interventions, the components that are effective in reducing recidivism. However, this meta-analysis and individual studies are hampered by the sheer variety in programming, giving attention to different components, and the lack of a taxonomy to label adequately programs and services (see Crites & Taxman, 2013). This means that a residential program can address a myriad of components with the program title (or description) failing to capture the behaviors that the program is designed to address. The complexity is further impacted by the delivery system. In many places across the world, community programming can be offered by various agencies or organizations with expertise in a given area (i.e., substance abuse, mental illness, vocational training, education, life skills, etc.), including some organizations that have limited experience with those involved in the justice system. Community treatment programming is decentralized, and many of the features of the program are not within the control of the corrections agency. Depending on the funding stream, treatment programming can be offered in-house, at a service provider, or at an inpatient setting. Therefore, there may be limited central authority.

To address the issue of the quality of programming, in the mid-1990s, Canada and many Western European countries started a tradition of accrediting curricula that could be used for offender populations, in both prison and the community. Accredited programs were then allowed to be delivered by a variety of providers—those administered or contracted by justice organizations or those provided by third-party service providers. This was an attempt to ensure that the programs were content-specific to various offender needs and to ensure that the programs were of the highest quality. The accreditation process has not gained favor worldwide, including in the United States, and, within 15 years, many countries have downplayed the use of the accreditation system, which has resulted in fewer accredited programs. In fact, there are few central reviews of programs and services and even fewer standard agreements regarding the nature of the programs and how well they address the specific needs of individuals of varying offending patterns.

The lack of a formal taxonomy for programs and services for those involved in the justice system means that it is unclear what programs offer. The most glaring issue is that inadequate labeling of community programs, coupled with generic content that can be tailored based on the therapist/counselor's perspective, contributes to the difficulty of matching individuals to services (see Polaschek, 2011; Taxman and Caudy, 2015; Warren, 1971). This chapter will review three different conceptual frameworks for classifying programs related to correctional programming. It will also review findings on target behaviors in programming described in meta-analyses, and then identify the key issues in implementing a taxonomy for better matching individuals to services, but also for addressing the precursors and situations that affect offending. This chapter ends with a discussion of a research agenda to advance our knowledge about effective programming in the community.

RNR Framework and Multidimensional Needs

The Risk-Need-Responsivity (RNR) model provides a framework for identifying who should receive what type of programming. The RNR model is most often associated with the use of third and/or fourth generation assessment tools, as well as the use of social-learning cognitive programming, behavioral programming, or CBT in correctional settings. In addition, the RNR model has been recommended as a tool for program design and implementation since its emphasis is on integrating research into practice through addressing risk and need factors (Polaschek, 2011; Taxman & Caudy, 2015; Taxman & Pattavina, 2013). There is an emerging literature linking the RNR framework that translates individual needs to specific aspects of treatment programming, where risk and dynamic needs are assigned to different programs and services (see Crites & Taxman, 2013).

Dynamic (and Static) Risk Factors

Third generation risk and need assessment (RNA) tools—those that include dynamic need factors besides static (criminal history) factors—illustrate that not all offenders are the same. Some individuals have different needs even within various risk levels. The dynamic needs should be used as information to direct the type of programs and/or services that an individual would benefit from. Service allocation should depend on the identification of prominent needs that are directly related to recidivism, such as criminal history, criminal value systems, criminal peer associates or intergenerational family issues related to justice involvement, criminal attitudes, substance abuse, employment, education, family dysfunction, and leisure time activities. By addressing these factors, reductions in recidivism are possible, as evidenced by the supporting literature on the RNR framework. The RNR framework integrates within the responsivity components the different areas where tailoring to individuals is warranted with an emphasis on mental illness, housing stability, social supports, intellectual disabilities, literacy, child of an incarcerated parent, and so on. The use of a third or fourth generation tool provides the capacity to identify individual level precursors of criminal behavior, and combinations of these precursors, as a means to better link an individual to appropriate programs and/or services that should address, and potentially accelerate, desistance.

The upside is that a third or fourth generation risk and need assessment tool provides information, but the downside is that community corrections workers are reluctant to use the information in case or supervision planning. Staff are unsure how to use the information from the instruments due to: (a) a lack of understanding about the different precursors of offending behavior; (b) a lack of understanding of how to interpret the data when an individual has more than one dynamic risk area; (c) a lack of confidence in the instruments; and (d) concerns about the accuracy of the instrument, particularly for individuals that commit certain crimes that are considered high stakes such as sex offenses, alcohol-related crimes, gun violence, and other offenses where individuals may score lower in risk than the officers would expect (Hamilton, Tollefshol, Campagna, & van Wormer, 2017; Miller & Mahoney, 2013; Viglione, Rudes, & Taxman, 2015). Added to the issues regarding the factors affecting the use of information from a risk-need assessment tool is the lack of information that many correctional agencies have to identify how best to place individuals into different programs and services.

The absence of a treatment taxonomy that can assist with assigning to programs and services to address co-occurring conditions adds to the underutilization of risk-need assessment tools.

Community corrections officers have limited strategies on how to deal with the multidimensional needs that people are likely to have. Also, it is unclear whether certain types of needs cluster together. While many interpret the RNR as premised on the notion that the *risk level* should determine intensity of programming (Lowenkamp, Latessa, & Holsinger, 2006), it is actually the needs that should drive placement. Some of this is complicated by the nature of scoring of certain instruments (i.e., Level of Service Inventory—Revised [LSI-R], Ohio Risk Assessment System [ORAS], etc.) where the instrument has a total risk score (one that combines risk and needs). A total score makes it more difficult to disentangle which of the need areas are driving offending behavior. Besides, in many instruments, the total score weights criminal history (see Brame, 2017; Taxman, 2017) more than other areas. The structure of the risk and need assessment tool contributes to how the tool can be used.

The general confusion between risk (for recidivism) and needs (for services/programs) is an ongoing argument in both the research literature and policy discussion. While the risk score identifies those that are higher risk for recidivism, it does not specify the needs that should be addressed to effect desistance. In the presentation of the RNR framework, Andrews and Bonta (2010) emphasize that antisocial values, personality, peers, and criminal history are more important than other need areas, with substance abuse considered of lesser importance. However, Taxman (2014) demonstrate that this may not be the case in all populations or sub-populations, particularly in the United States, where the "war on drugs" uses punishments to address addiction disorders and the correctional population has a high concentration of substance use disorders. Taxman (2014) found that substance abusers with a severe disorder (addicts), as compared to substance users (i.e., more likely to use illicit substances recreationally or not compulsively), are more likely to recidivate—yet few criminal justice third generation risk and need assessment instruments differentiate on severity (and pattern) of the substance use. That is, some substance use is related to recidivism and some is not for those that meet the clinical criteria for substance abuser. Criminal justice instruments do not adequately measure dynamic areas.[2]

Risk, Need, and Program Placement

To further explore the issues related to risk and need for treatment program placement, Taxman and Caudy (2015) conducted a latent class analysis (LCA) of the risk and need profiles of over 18,000 probationers in one state. The analysis identified four main clusters of probationers: those with no major criminogenic needs, those with one or two criminogenic needs, those with predominately substance use disorders, and those with criminogenic needs that are more linked to factors related to a criminal lifestyle (i.e., antisocial personality, antisocial values, antisocial peers). Table 47.1 demonstrates that the allocated Latent Class Analysis (LCA) group does a better job at fitting to the data and identifying risk-need profiles with a greater propensity for identifying recidivism than merely risk alone. The risk alone category would underestimate the role that needs have on predicting recidivism. For example, the minimum risk category's predicted recidivism rate is 12.7%, but when you look at those that are classified in minimum risk, we find that some individuals have no major criminogenic needs (12.7%), 1 or 2 needs (10.5%), severe substance abuse (24.7%), and criminal lifestyle (20.6%). The variation within the category of minimum risk is that while some individuals do not have a serious prior criminal history, within this category a small percentage do have more complex criminogenic needs and these individuals tend to have higher recidivism rates. Another example is LCA 3, where substance abuse has a mix of various risk levels (minimum is 24.7%, low is

Table 47.1 Comparison of Recidivism Rates for Major Categorization of Needs by Assigned Risk Level (%)

	Assessed criminal justice risk level				
Type of needs	*Minimum*	*Low*	*Moderate*	*High*	*1 yr rearrest rate*
No major needs	12.7	21.6	32.2	48.5	21.8
1 or 2 needs	10.5	18.9	28.8	46.1	15.1
Severe substance abuser	24.7	27.1	41.8	53.0	29.9
Criminal lifestyle	20.6	23.0	37.2	51.2	26.7
Rate within risk category	12.7	20.9	33.6	50.1	

Adapted from Taxman and Caudy (2015).

27.1%, moderate is 41.8%, and high is 53.0%). The rearrest rate is high, with 29.9% in 1 year; if only the risk level were being used then there would be an issue with identifying the need factors that relate to recidivism. The clustering of needs illustrates the emphasis on needs which can be a driver for recidivism.

The latent class models identify that criminal justice risk is just one factor, but there are often other factors that should be considered, including the comingling of criminal justice risk with criminogenic needs. Focusing on the latent classes, instead of the number of criminogenic needs, would focus attention on target processes that contribute to offending behaviors. They serve as factors to reduce criminal behaviors. This can then advance the type of programming that a person should be involved in, rather than considering programs to address behavioral issues.

A Taxonomy of Correctional Programming

Determining the appropriate program requires translating the dynamic risk characteristics of the individual into factors that are amenable to change. The offense is often not a good indicator of the drivers of a crime because the conviction offense may actually be different than the factors that contributed to the behavior, the individual may have pleaded to an offense (or have a set of behaviors) that is different than the conviction offense, and there may be situational factors that affect the decisions of individuals. The match between individual level of risk and need factors and programs should be built on a framework that allows for linking dynamic factors to programmatic features. The following are three approaches that have been identified.

Polaschek's *Many Sizes Fit All*

Devon Polaschek (2011) offers a preliminary framework for how to think about CBT programming based on the RNR framework. The framework integrates the following factors: (a) client characteristics including criminal risk and readiness (with responsivity); (b) program characteristics including dosage, treatment targets, delivery methods, change processes, and facilitator-related characteristics; (c) treatment integrity, and (d) change assessments. Using client characteristics, particularly risk level, and program characteristics, Polaschek offers three levels of rehabilitation programming.

1 Basic which is best suited for low-to-medium risk with low-intensity programming.
2 Intermediate which is for those who are medium-to-high risk and should receive a greater intensity of programming. The intermediate level is geared to clients with multi-morbid conditions with interventions that address many of these conditions using a variety of clinical skills. The diversity of clinical skills is needed since these clients are more likely to be resistant to change, and have lower motivation to engage in treatment programming.
3 Comprehensive forensic therapy programs are for high-risk offenders and those involved in interpersonal and violent crimes. These programs are more likely to exist in a therapeutic environment to create a milieu that reinforces new values, attitudes, and behaviors. In many ways, these are combination therapeutic community programming with cognitive behavioral interventions. Clients needing forensic services are those with personality disorders, psychopathy, and those that are often considered untreatable. The staffing for the programs varies, with those with more limited clinical skills administering the basic programming while the forensic programming needs provided by those with PhD level or higher levels of education.

Marlowe's Quadrant Approach

Doug Marlowe (2009) proposes a quadrant approach to programming for individuals with substance use behaviors who are criminally involved. His approach takes advantage of distributing those with various substance abuse needs into programs that are geared to their criminal behavior and the severity of their substance use disorders. This model focuses on who should receive substance abuse treatment and medications, and on consequences for not abiding by program requirements. He defines prosocial habilitation as a means to address criminal thinking which focuses on prosocial roles and responsibilities such as work, school, and parenting. Adaptive habilitation is focused on life skills to improve employability, education, financial management, and homemaking. The tracks are as follows.

1 High substance dependence and high risk: Standard drug court track that involves check-in sessions (referred to as status calendar), substance abuse treatment, prosocial habilitation, adaptive habilitation, and prescribed medication.
2 High substance dependence and low risk: Alternative track with an emphasis on treatment, non-compliance monitoring with visits with judge for any non-compliance, adaptive habilitation, emphasis on treatment, and prescribed medication.
3 Low substance abuse and high risk: Accountability track with status calendar, prevention services, prosocial habilitation, emphasis on abstinence and supervision.
4 Low substance abuse and low risk: Potential for diversion emphasis with a focus on using status hearings to deal with non-compliance behavior, prevention services, and emphasis on abstinence.

Taxman's RNR Simulation Tool

Taxman crafted an adaptation of the RNR into a Simulation Tool (http://www.gmuace.org/tools) that focuses on the broadest range of offending behaviors, and also considers the assignment to appropriate program. The RNR Simulation Tool is designed as a multidimensional methodology to advance the translations of the risk and need framework at three levels: 1) individual client—to match risk, needs, and responsivity to programming; 2) program analysis—to assess what the programs include as well as how they address responsivity; and 3) systems analysis—to advance programming by trying to ensure that agencies /organizations/jurisdictions have the array of programming that meets the actual risk-need profiles of the individuals, based on a review of the range of programs and services that are used in the justice system to address various target behaviors. This was based on a review of the literature including results from meta-analyses. Taxman and colleagues concluded that there are six main domains.

1   Substance dependence: Individuals who have severe substance use disorders that need intensive treatment services fall into this category. It is assumed that providing treatment will reduce criminal behavior because the criminal behavior is a function of factors related to substance use disorders. Individuals may also have comorbid conditions that require attention to maladaptive behaviors and cognitions, self-management, interpersonal skills, and life skills. The needs for these types of additional services will depend on the number of dynamic needs and responsivity factors. If a person has three or more dynamic needs and/or lifestyle destabilizers (i.e., mental illness, housing instability, etc.) then more intensive services of higher dosage are needed.

2   Criminal lifestyle/cognitions: Individuals who present with three or more criminogenic needs (except for substance abuse) are more ingrained in a subculture of crime that is reinforced by cognitive distortions. Individuals in this group do not have substance abuse disorders, but they could be recreational users. The person must have at least two factors that affect cognitive distortions and may impair decision-making, such as antisocial values, antisocial personality, and antisocial peers, and at least one other dynamic need (i.e., education, employment, family). These are more intensive services, and, depending on the number of dynamic needs (>3) and/or responsivity factors, the dosage should be increased. Risk level is less important since placement in this category depends on the number and type of dynamic risk factors. For those with a number of dynamic needs, self-management, interpersonal skills, and life skills may be needed to be added to this mix.

3   Self-management: Self-management programs are typically geared for those who have substance abuse and/or mental illness that are low-to-moderate risk. The emphasis of this programming is on relapse prevention, medication management, disease management, and handling risky situations. The focus is on management of behaviors. Individuals in this category are going to have fewer dynamic risk factors, but they may have a number of lifestyle/(de)stabilizing factors.

4   Interpersonal skills: Conflict management, power and control issues, and social skill development are part of this category of programming. The programming is geared for those who have two dynamic risk factors from offenses that involve relationships such as intimate partner violence, minor assaults, and aggression. These services should be for modest dosage and should include tailoring to meet the needs of the individual. Typically, low-to-moderate-risk individuals are placed in this category with family and peer relationships. (Individuals that are high risk and have more needs who engage in offenses involving relationships should be placed in the criminal lifestyle).

5   Life skills: Programming is geared for those who are low risk, have few to minimal needs, but have deficits in employability and education.

6   Other, including routine punishment: Individuals who are low risk, have no major dynamic needs, and do not present a history or pattern of offending behavior may be suited for no programming. These will typically involve low intensity of punishment, including fines, restitution, community service or work orders, and other efforts.

These categories are based on the individual precursors of offending behaviors (see Crites & Taxman, 2013). However, it should be noted that community precursors such as a hot spot of crime, high concentration of those involved in the justice system, and social disorganization may be used as a basis to increase dosage. Under the RNR Simulation Tool methodology, dosage is the means to intensify services to better meet the needs of the individual but also to provide longer duration of care.

Conclusion About Frameworks

The three frameworks are designed to organize services and interventions as a way to consider service delivery. Given that there are varying risk and need factors that individuals possess and that different programs address, the taxonomy attempts to order services. Each framework uses the RNR framework to organize risk and need factors, with an implicit attention to different precursors of offending behavior. Individuals with more risk and need factors should be targeted for more intensive, structured services. Providing these services, as best described by Polaschek (2011), requires staff with better clinical qualifications. Most importantly, the emphasis on behavioral targets is important to ensure that programs are more directed at their needs.

What Do We Know About Programs in the Community?

The importance of having a taxonomy cannot be understated. Naming conventions in corrections can be misleading. Examples include drug treatment courts that do or do not have status check-in meetings, cognitive behavioral programs that are primarily delivered via correctional officers using workbooks versus programs that are delivered with clinicians offering processing groups, outpatient programming that offers services from one to five times a week, and residential programs that provide bed space versus programs that include clinical groups. The imprecision in naming programs creates problems in understanding what type of risk and need factors a particular program can address. As part of an ongoing series of studies to better understand programming in the community, Taylor, Bhati, and Taxman (2015) explored the differences in how programs can be classified, by examining program targets instead of the name of the programs in a well-cited meta-analysis that was completed by the Washington State Institute for Public Policy (WSIPP) (Aos et al., 2006). The findings are discussed below.

Methods

A team of researchers coded 98 primary studies that were published between 1978 and 2013 and then coded 88 secondary studies of the same main papers to supplement the analysis of key program features, implementation issues, and related material that was not used in the published main study. The primary studies used include 32 for CBT, 7 for correctional education, 5 for domestic violence, 12 for employment training/job assistance, 5 for intensive outpatient programs or outpatient programs, 16 for intensive supervision (ISP), 6 for RNR supervision, and 3 for vocational education. The effect sizes reported by Aos, et al. were used to examine issues related to program category and effect sizes (see Taylor et al., 2015, for a discussion).

The study examined the program quality indicators used as part of a structured tool to identify how the program addresses key factors. The structured program tool encompasses components similar to the Correctional Program Assessment Inventory (CPAI), and other tools used for behavioral health programs (see Crites & Taxman, 2013). The indicators used in this assessment are: (a) use of a standardized, validated risk instrument in determining access to services; (b) use of the dynamic risk scores to determine access to services; (c) ability to identify responsivity factors and use the factors in tailoring programming; (d) implementation factors such as staffing characteristics, funding, quality assurance, technical assistance, integration of services, and so on; (e) dosage or intensity of the program; and (f) the type of structure and punishments used to control behavior. The responsivity factors (c), implementation (d), and dosage (e) are geared to each type of program. For example, one would expect that substance abuse treatment programs would have different features than criminal cognition or life skill programs, given that the programs are designed to develop skills in different areas. While the number of points is similar, the expected components would be tailored to the program category. The total score is given on a scale of 1–100.

Findings

As shown in Table 47.2, of the 98 studies reviewed, the labeling for the meta-analysis varied considerably with the noted target behaviors that are addressed as part of the intervention in programs. In each category, the WSIPP-assigned label was not consistent with the key components of the program. In many WSIPP labels, the key targets were classified as "other" because they did not address factors that are linked to offending or were considered non-clinical programming, including generic, restorative justice, or an undefined range of programming. In terms of the broad, undefined range of programming, the program often took a "kitchen sink" approach where the efforts are spread over a range of topics with generally fewer than three sessions devoted to any topic. Marlowe (2006) reviewed Project Greenlight, one of the CBT-oriented general programs that covered a wide range of topics yet frequently resulted in less attention to cognitive or behavioral skill-building efforts.

Table 47.2 Comparison of WSIPP Label with Behavioral Targets of a Program (%)

| | | | | Behavioral targets of a program | | | |
WSIPP label	SUD	Crim lifestyle	Self-management	Interpersonal skills	Life skills	Other	Total
CBT	2.7	48.6	5.4	0.0	0.0	43.2	100.0
Corr. educ	0.0	0.0	0.0	0.0	28.6	71.4	100.0
DV treatment	0.0	0.0	33.3	66.7	0.0	0.0	100.0
Employment	0.0	0.0	8.3	0.0	66.7	25.0	100.0
IP/OP – community	55.6	0.0	11.1	0.0	0.0	33.3	100.0
ISP	0.0	0.0	0.0	0.0	0.0	100.0	100.0
RNR supervision	0.0	0.0	0.0	0.0	0.0	100.0	100.0
Voc. educ	0.0	0.0	0.0	0.0	66.7	33.3	100.0
Total	11.8	19.4	6.5	2.2	12.9	47.3	100.0

SUD = Substance abuse disorders.

CBT programs covered a range of programming, including substance abuse treatment, criminal thinking and lifestyles, self-management, and other. Many other categories were spread across different target behaviors. Even programs for domestic violence-related behaviors were not consistent; they included programs that ranged in addressing the violent, aggressive, and/or control behavior of clients. That is, it is unclear whether programs are specific as to the criminal behaviors they are trying to reduce or the skills that one is focused on teaching as a means of improving the individual's skills to manage their risky behaviors. The lack of clarity is part of the challenge, since programs that are designed to reduce certain behaviors may be different than those that are focused on building skills, even if the skills might be helpful to the individual, acquiring these skills might not lead to reductions in behaviors of concern. This discrepancy is part of the reason that a taxonomy is needed to further understand the programs and services that are designed to improve certain behaviors (such as reducing recidivism) as compared to skills that are designed to improve an individual's overall ability to function in life. The need for clarity of the part of a program is important because it provides the ability to know not only what the mechanisms of action are but also the non-programmatic factors that affect the ability to deliver quality services, such as staffing, use of manuals, staff training, and so forth (see Miche, Fixsen, Grimshaw, & Eccles, 2009, for a discussion of the need to further describe programs to aid in replication).

Table 47.3 displays the average quality indicator score for WSIPP categories based on the RNR Program Tool. Within each category, the quality indicators illustrate that the programs are not likely to adhere to evidence-based programming or practices, and do not embrace features of sound interventions. For example, for the CBT identified programs, slightly over one third of the programs use risk level to determine eligibility; about half specify the criminogenic needs that they will treat; about one fourth of the programs tailor services to unique features of the treated population (i.e., gender, intellectual disability, developmental issues, etc.); few programs (<10%) have quality assurance measures or were evaluated in the past; most programs scored low in implementation given the nature of the staff, high turnover, little use of standardized curriculum, and other indicators of implementation problems; and 5% of the programs had a dosage level that was appropriate for the risk-need level of individuals that were eligible for the programs. Overall, the quality score for CBT programming is 23% for the required components, which is low, and illustrates that an evidence-based program like CBT

Table 47.3 Distribution of RNR Program Tool Quality Indicator Scores Across WSIPP Categories (%)

WSIPP category	Risk score	Need score	Responsivity score	Implementa- tion score	Dosage score	Structure score	Total score
CBT	36.5	55.5	26.8	7.1	5.5	38.9	22.9
Correctional education	0.0	44.8	12.3	6.3	7.1	28.6	13.4
Domestic violence TX	0.0	44.4	27.8	6.9	13.3	58.3	19.4
Employment	4.2	54.4	24.3	2.2	17.1	41.7	18.8
Intensive IP/OP	10.0	54.1	32.4	0.7	21.7	40.3	21.1
ISP	85.7	35.2	7.5	6.3	2.1	62.5	24.6
RNR supervision	94.0	30.7	16.7	17.6	0.0	52.5	29.0
Voc. education	16.7	55.6	27.8	6.9	13.3	25.0	20.8
Average score	29.7	51.6	23.0	6.3	10.5	40.3	21.6

can be poorly implemented and therefore will not yield the desired results in reducing recidivism, or even addressing specific target behaviors.

As expected, correctional programs place more of an emphasis on restrictions and structure for the individuals assigned to the program than on rehabilitative components. These restrictions include drug testing, curfew restrictions, financial restrictions, and other tools to manage behaviors. The quality indicators illustrate that having sufficient dosage appropriate to the risk-need level of eligible parties is a struggle. Implementation is also challenging, with few clinical staff, high staff turnover, lack of quality assurance methods, lack of curricula that are clear to the users, and failure to evaluate the program. While low scores could be due to the failure to document core components of the program, they are also an indicator that administrators may not be familiar with the features of the program (which is also a quality indicator). That being said, it is clear that we know very little about these programs that are being delivered to those in the community. Even the label of the program does not reassure us that the programs are well structured or focused on attributes that will work to change individuals or reduce recidivism.

Discussion

More and more attention is being paid to the need to better understand how programs deliver services, and what the key mechanisms of action are that work toward fostering individual change. Treatment-oriented programs and services, by their very nature, are designed to facilitate change in certain attitudes and behaviors. For those involved in the justice system, the RNR framework provides the target behaviors that needed to be attended to in order to make progress toward alleviating or modifying those attitudes or behaviors that contribute to offending behaviors. While the RNR framework has been described as atheoretical and based more on empirical factors, it is one way of emphasizing the target behaviors that are related to recidivism. In the community, where there is a myriad of programming, some of which is offered by correctional agencies and some offered by specialty organizations (i.e., substance abuse, mental health, vocational, educational, etc.), a need exists for a taxonomy of programs and services to ensure that individuals are being matched to such services. Polaschek (2011) offers a three-category programming that varies from low intensive services provided by non-clinical staff to high intensive programming provided by forensic clinical staff. Marlowe (2006) articulates the need for four types of programs for substance abusers that range from intensive services for the high-risk/high-need group to minimal services for the low-risk/low-need group. Moreover, Taxman, Perdoni, & Caudy (2013) argue for identifying the major factors that affect offending behaviors and targeting program components to these behaviors. Individuals who have severe substance use disorders and/or criminal lifestyles (with associated distorted cognitions) require more intensive, structured interventions preferably using CBT. Other primary targets are designed to improve the social functioning of the individual.

The need for a taxonomy is further illustrated by looking at a meta-analysis conducted by the WSIPP, an organization that has promoted the use of research to improve practice. WSIPP is unique in that they are funded by the legislature in the state of Washington (United States) and they have conducted return-on-investment analyses to further promote the use of evidence-based programs and practices. Their work uses meta-analyses and then the cost–benefit analysis of these programs along with the effect size. Legislators in Washington State have used these findings to identify programs and services to fund. The methods used by WSIPP are presumed to be based on an assumption that programs in a given category address certain target behaviors that are related to reducing recidivism. That is, programs associated within a category are assumed to be alike and similar. While it is generally acknowledged that programs vary on certain factors, of which we are seldom aware, this analysis has shown that a missing link is that not all programs address a similar behavior. The RNR methodologies that Taxman et al. (2013) developed illustrate that programs in a given category are not the same. The WSIPP-related programs within a given category actually address a broad range of issues, and this may not serve to understand which programs are best suited for actually reducing recidivism. This may serve to make it difficult to replicate. More attention to these issues about program structure and implementation is generally needed to ensure that programs can facilitate positive outcomes.

Using the RNR Program Tool on the studies used in the WSIPP analyses illustrates how difficult it is to apply the RNR model articulated by Andrews and Bonta (2010), including the documentation of these efforts. An underlying component of the RNR framework applied to programs is that the programs need to operate in a human service environment. Yet, the programs in the community that are covered by the WSIPP focus more on structure and restrictions than on being responsive or even applying the needs principle. This represents some of the competing tensions for programs that service justice clients—as to whether there should be a focus on punishment or a focus on habilation and interventions. This tension is reflected in the need to hold individuals accountable, but the quagmire is that the purpose of the habilation services—whether they address cognitive or behavioral issues—is to help individuals learn new skills, understand their behavioral and thinking patterns, and develop new responses to various stimuli or situations. Many correctional programs also must incorporate structure or restrictions on personal liberties along with the clinical components of a program. Often these structures are described as part of the therapeutic process to assist the individual in managing their daily lives. Yet, coupling restrictions with treatment must be accomplished in a milieu that promotes new behaviors, attitudes, and values. This is the major challenge, given that correctional programs have difficulty balancing accountability with clinically oriented services to promote change.

Manualized curricula are generally viewed as a proxy to identify higher-quality programs based on the assumption that staff will use the manual and this will ensure better-quality programming. The manual provides a structure for each session, including content of materials and associated exercises. However, as noted by Landenberg and Lipsey (2006), no one manual appeared to be superior in generating outcomes, and the homegrown curricula did equally well compared to the name-brand curricula. More importantly, the components of the RNR Program Tool only focus on the presence of a manual, but the more important part is the credentials of the staff delivering the curriculum, the hours devoted to various therapeutic tasks and features, the training of the staff, the quality assurance provided by the agency, and the ways in which the manual is tailored to the characteristics of the individual participants. All of this contributes to the quality score, but it also reveals the complexity of community programming.

Collectively, there is a need to develop a taxonomy that is premised on mechanisms of action which specify how programs and/or services facilitate individual transformations. This might begin with meta-analyses where the program features and components are assessed, and with an examination of the impact on effect sizes. In the work described above, we started that process but never fully examined how different program features, implementation factors, and/or program progress are related to effect sizes. This is a pressing agenda since it would generate the core components of effective programs, and it would provide justification for ensuring that community programs include these features. Another research agenda should be devoted to developing the taxonomy, particularly for individuals with multiple conditions and/or needs.

Since many program models tend to either endorse a "kitchen sink" approach (a little of a lot of things) instead of deliberative features, research should assist in defining the dosage that is needed to make progress. Finally, research is needed in the ordering of different program features. Right now, we have limited knowledge about "what comes first," but there is a need for more information to answer this question.

Conclusion

The lack of accreditation standards for different curricula, along with an appropriate taxonomy for programming in the community, essentially leaves the field wide open for well-intentioned but poorly designed and/or implemented programs. The stakes are high because failures from programs contribute to failures on community supervision, with the collateral consequences of potential reincarceration. Furthermore, it contributes to the individuals considering themselves to be failures, which can affect the individuals' willingness, desire, or motivation to participate in programs. This makes a "hard-sell" to corrections, to individuals under correctional control, to policy-makers, and to communities to support programs and services as part of recidivism reduction efforts. The potential for programming that does not serve the greater good exists, and it is the reason that there is a growing need to address the taxonomy, to develop a consensus among target behaviors, to address quality issues, and then to ensure that the programs operate in such a manner to deliver positive outcomes. Much work needs to be done.

Note

1   A recent study by Via, Dezember, & Taxman (2016) examined the content validity of five common major instruments (i.e., Correctional Offender Management profiling for Alternative Sanctions [COMPAS; Brennan & Oliver, 2000], Level of Service Inventory—Revised [LSI-R; Andrews & Bonta, 1995], Ohio Risk Assessment System [ORAS; Latessa et al., 2009], Static Risk and Offender Needs Guide for Recidivism [STRONG-R; Hamilton et al., 2016], and Wisconsin Risk-Needs tool [WRN; Baird, 1981]). The nature of the questions used to define a domain (i.e., substance abuse, attitudes, orientation, employment, value systems, etc.) was reviewed, and across these five instruments there was no consistency in terms of content and construct validity. In fact, the same domain, such as substance abuse, criminal attitudes, and the other domains, could have various meanings across instruments. Few studies even had reliabilities for the domains, again suggesting problems with the instruments. This lack of reliability and predictive validity regarding the needs, and how best to measure them, complicates the utility of using RNA information in case planning.

Key Readings

Landenberger, N. A., & Lipsey, M. W. (2005). The positive effects of cognitive–behavioral programs for offenders: A meta-analysis of factors associated with effective treatment. *Journal of Experimental Criminology*, 1, 451–476.

Marlowe, D. B. (2009). Evidence-based sentencing for drug offenders: An analysis of prognostic risks and criminogenic needs. *Chapman Journal of Criminal Justice*, 1, 167–201.

Polaschek, D. L. L. (2011). Many sizes fit all: A preliminary framework for conceptualizing the development and provision of cognitive-behavioral rehabilitation programs for offenders. *Aggression and Violent Behavior*, 16, 20–35.

Taxman, F. S., & Caudy, M. (2015). Risk tells us who, but not what or how: Empirical assessment of the complexity of criminogenic needs to inform correctional programming. *Criminology and Public Policy.*, 14, 71–103.

Taxman, F. S., Perdoni, M., & Caudy, M. (2013). The plight of providing appropriate substance abuse treatment services to offenders: Modeling the gaps in service delivery. *Victims & Offenders*, 8, 70–93.

Warren, M. Q. (1971). Classification of offenders as an aid to efficient management and effective treatment. *The Journal of Criminal Law, Criminology and Police Science*, 62, 239–258.

References

Andrews, D. A., & Bonta, J. (1995). *The Level of Service Inventory—Revised*. Toronto, Canada: Multi-Health Systems.

Andrews, D. A., & Bonta, J. (2010). *The psychology of criminal conduct* (5th ed.). New Providence, NJ: Matthew Bender.

Andrews, D. A., Zinger, I., Hoge, R. D., Bonta, J., Gendreau, P., & Cullen, F. T. (1990). Does correctional treatment work? A clinically relevant and psychologically informed meta-analysis. *Criminology*, 28, 369–404.

Aos, S., Miller, M., & Drake, E. K. (2006). *Evidence-based adult corrections programs: What works and what does not*. Olympia, WA: Washington State Institute for Public Policy.

Baird, S. C. (1981). Probation and parole classification: The Wisconsin model. *Corrections Today*, 43(3), 36–41.

Brame, R. (2017). Static risk factors and criminal recidivism. In F. S. Taxman (Ed.), *Handbook on risk and need assessment: Theory and practice* (pp. 67–92). London, UK: Routledge.

Brennan, T., & Oliver, W. L. (2000). *Evaluation of reliability and validity of COMPAS scales: National aggregate sample*. Traverse City, MI: Northpointe Institute for Public Management.

Crites, E., & Taxman, F. S. (2013). The responsivity principle: Determining the appropriate program and dosage to match risk and needs. In F. S. Taxman, & A. Pattavina (Eds.), *Simulation strategies to reduce recidivism: Risk Need Responsivity (RNR) modeling for the criminal justice system* (pp. 143–166). New York, NY: Springer.

Hamilton, Z., Tollefshol, E. T., Campagna, M., & van Wormer, J. (2017). Customizing criminal justice assessments. In F. S. Taxman (Ed.), *Handbook on risk and need assessment: Theory and practice* (pp. 333–377). London, UK: Routledge.

Landenberger, N. A., & Lipsey, M. W. (2005). The postive effects of cogntive-behavioral programs for offenders: A meta-analysis of factors associated with effective treatments. *Journal of Experiemtnal Criminology*, 1(4), 451–476.

Latessa, E., Smith, P., Lemke, R., Makarios, M., & Lowenkamp, C. (2009). *Creation and validation of the Ohio Risk Assessment System Final Report*. Cincinnati, OH: University of Cincinnati School of Criminal Justice, Center for Criminal Justice Research.

Lipsey, M. W., & Cullen, F. T. (2007). The effectiveness of correctional rehabilitation: A review of systematic reviews. *Annual Review of Law and Social Science*, 3, 297–320.

Lipsey, M. W., & Landenberger, N. A. (2007). Cognitive-behavioral interventions: A meta-analysis of randomized controlled studies. In B. C. Welsh, & D. P. Farrington (Eds.), *Preventing crime: What works for children, offenders, victims, and places* (pp. 57–72). Berlin, Germany: Springer.

Lowenkamp, C. T., Latessa, E. J., & Holsinger, A. M. (2006). The risk principle in action: What have we learned from 13,676 offenders and 97 correctional programs? *Crime & Delinquency*, 52, 77–93.

Marlowe, D. B. (2006). When "what works" never did: Dodging the "scarlet M" in correctional rehabilitation. *Criminology & Public Policy*, 5, 339–346.

Marlowe, D. B. (2009). Evidence-based sentencing for drug offenders: An analysis of prognostic risks and criminogenic needs. *Chapman Journal of Criminal Justice*, 1, 167–201.

Michie, S., Fixsen, D., Grimshaw, J. W., & Eccles, M. P. (2009). Specifying and reporting complex behaviour change interventions: The need for a scientific method. *Implementation Science*, 4, 40–45.

Miller, J., & Maloney, C. (2013). Practitioner compliance with risk/needs assessment tools: A theoretical and empirical assessment. *Criminal Justice and Behavior*, 40(7), 716–736.

Polaschek, D. L. L. (2011). Many sizes fit all: A preliminary framework for conceptualizing the development and provision of cognitive-behavioral rehabilitation programs for offenders. *Aggression and Violent Behavior*, 16, 20–35.

Sherman, L. W., Gottfredson, D. C., MacKenzie, D. L., Eck, J., Reuter, P., & Bushway, S. D. (1998). *Preventing crime: What works, what doesn't, what's promising.* Washington, DC: National Institute of Justice Retrieved from https://www.ncjrs.gov/pdffiles/171676.pdf

Taxman, F. S. (2014). Substance abuse is sometimes a primary criminogenic need and sometimes a secondary criminogenic need. *Perspectives*, 38(2), 48–56.

Taxman, F. S. (2017). The value and importance of risk and need assessment (RNA) in corrections & sentencing: An overview of the handbook. In F. S. Taxman (Ed.), *Handbook on risk and need assessment: Theory and practice* (pp. 1–20). London, UK: Routledge Press.

Taxman, F. S., & Caudy, M. (2015). Risk tells us who, but not what or how: Empirical assessment of the complexity of criminogenic needs to inform correctional programming. *Criminology and Public Policy*, 14(1), 71–103.

Taxman, F. S., & Pattavina, A. (2013). *Simulation strategies to reduce recidivism: Risk Need Responsivity (RNR) modeling for the criminal justice system.* New York, NY: Springer.

Taxman, F. S., Perdoni, M., & Caudy, M. (2013). The plight of providing appropriate substance abuse treatment services to offenders: Modeling the gaps in service delivery. *Victims & Offenders*, 8(1), 70–93.

Taylor, L., Bhati, A., & Taxman, F. S. (2015). *Exploring program categories among WSIPP meta-analyses.* Fairfax, VA: Center for Advancing Correctional Excellence!

Via, B., Dezember, A., & Taxman, F. S. (2016). Exploring how to measure criminogenic needs: Five instruments and no real answers. In F. S. Taxman (2017, Ed.), *Handbook of corrections & sentencing: Risk and need assessment—theory and practice.* London, UK: Routledge.

Viglione, J., Rudes, D. S., & Taxman, F. S. (2015). Misalignment in supervision: Implementing risk/needs assessment instruments in probation. *Criminal Justice and Behavior*, 42(3), 263–285.

Warren, M. Q. (1971). Classification of offenders as an aid to efficient management and effective treatment. *The Journal of Criminal Law, Criminology and Police Science*, 62, 239–258.

48

Correctional Psychology: Contemplating the Future

Devon L. L. Polaschek
University of Waikato (Te Whare Wānanga o Waikato), New Zealand

Andrew Day
James Cook University and University of Melbourne, Australia

Many factors make, and will continue to make, correctional services particularly challenging settings in which to apply psychological knowledge and to practice as psychologists. This handbook has provided a detailed account of contemporary applications of psychology to both correctional populations and prison environments. But, as is always the case with books of this kind, the content is by its very nature mostly backward-facing, describing where we have come from and what we know today as a result. It falls to this final chapter to reflect on some more forward-facing issues and challenges for psychology in correctional settings.

Politically, at least in the West, correctional policy has been caught up in a partisan law and order political agenda. At times, all political parties have fostered fear in voters about the threats posed by offenders, which translates into legislation that inevitably serves to increase the use of imprisonment. No one, it seems, can afford to be seen as "soft on crime"; there is always pressure to default to interventions that are intended to look punitive, even though they may not work. Sometimes it can seem that anything that even hints at helping offenders to live better, less criminal lives can be justified only in terms of cost savings rather than on the basis of their impact on those individuals who receive the service. Overlaying all of this is a wider discussion about which models of service delivery actually deliver their promised outcomes. And so, in this closing chapter, we consider the future of three core areas of correctional psychological practice: risk assessment, intervention, and research.

Risk Assessment

It is clear that psychologists have made a particularly significant contribution to correctional practice in relation to the assessment of risk of reconviction. Risk assessment nonetheless poses substantial ethical challenges that can—and sometimes should—bring psychologists into conflict with their employers. For example, in a number of jurisdictions legislation has been introduced that enables the detention of people who would formerly have been released at the

The Wiley International Handbook of Correctional Psychology, First Edition. Edited by Devon L. L. Polaschek, Andrew Day, and Clive R. Hollin.

end of their sentence, on the grounds that they will continue to pose a significant risk to others. An example would be civil orders that enable people to be held for long periods after the end of their custodial sentence, or even indefinitely, without ever having committed another offense. Although orders like this have quite a long history in the United States, recent years have seen them implemented in several other Western countries, with psychologists, as risk assessors, assuming a high level of responsibility in assisting legal decision-makers to apply the legislation (Blais & Forth, 2014).

The development of risk assessment tools has, over the past 20 years, formed a large part of correctional psychology research, and an even larger part of everyday practice. We have spent considerable time trying to develop more accurate instruments, and yet there are still many gaps in our understanding of what risk is, and inconsistencies in how this knowledge might apply to particular individuals (e.g., Douglas & Skeem, 2005; Hart, 2016). For instance, questions remain about the validity of conducting an assessment of the types and seriousness of risk posed to the community over many years in the future when an individual has been in custody for two decades. There are also active debates about the validity of assessments across jurisdictions and with different offenders, and about how judgments about the transferability of knowledge should be made. Relatedly, is it professionally acceptable to assess risk solely as if it is a relatively stable person characteristic, as if a person is equally at risk of criminal behavior at all times, and across all situations: to assume that all different sources of risk have an equal influence? Should we be more aware, perhaps, that we are promoting the fundamental attribution error[1] among those who order risk assessments, when years of psychology have documented that interactions between people and their environments are central to determining whether and when events will happen? And so, while we seldom have influence over how risk assessment results are used by others, psychologists have a responsibility to develop their practice around when particular assessments will be conducted and when, instead, they should conclude that there isn't sufficient robust evidence from which to form a scientifically defensible opinion. Taken together, these points suggest the need for more research that can help us to: (a) understand variations in the validity of risk assessments in different contexts and with different people; (b) validate risk assessment tools across a wider range of these contexts; (c) produce clearer professional guidelines to assist judgment about when valid assessments cannot be provided for a particular referral question; and (d) clarify the ethical issues that arise in assessing risk, and provide clear protocols for decision-making, by jurisdiction and referral question.

Intervention

The second major area of correctional practice in which psychological theory, principles, and evidence have proven influential is offender treatment or rehabilitation. In the early years of the "what works" movement, there was considerable enthusiasm, and even confidence, that evidence-based rehabilitation would make a significant contribution to improving the quality of correctional services, and advocates were eager to promote the use of offender services and programs that could be shown to reduce recidivism risk. For example, at the turn of the century, Cullen and Gendreau (2001) said this endeavor would "increasingly construct powerful sets of knowledge about controlling crime that would meaningfully influence policy debates and actual practice" (p. 334). On the face of it, we do now have a large body of empirical research showing that certain types of programs reduce recidivism, and a number of nations' correctional systems have implemented processes to ensure that they only provide programs that are known to work. But is knowledge about effective intervention increasing as this happens? Perhaps what has actually expanded is not so much the knowledge base itself as the incomplete implementation of research knowledge about effective programming. It could be argued, for example, that what has emerged is a predominantly managerial approach to rehabilitation that focuses less on how many offenders have learned how to live a more prosocial life and more on how many have attended programs, how cheaply programs can be run, and whether a sufficient and affordable workforce can be found to deliver programs. In practice, crucial elements of what makes interventions both ethical and effective may often be missing: for example, policies and practices that require staff to use core correctional practices (e.g., build a strong relationship) or to apply the responsivity principle (adapt programs to engage offenders where they are). These omissions damage both the model and the image of psychology. They also result in programs that are much less likely to work, fueling cynicism about what psychology has to offer.

There is still a great need for research that can help us to understand the people with whom we are working. Certain offender characteristics have been well documented, but others that may be very relevant to treatment response (e.g., cognitive functioning and ability to learn, hope and optimism, prosocial support for change in family/social network) are poorly understood. We also need to acknowledge that the volume of research on whether programs work hides the fact that recidivism outcome research alone does nothing to enhance the development of more effective rehabilitative approaches if it is conducted in lieu of research that develops knowledge about the characteristics of particular programs that are associated with optimal outcomes. For example, although there are many variations on sex offender treatment, Biere and Mann (2017) have recently noted "we still hardly have any idea what constitutes the ideal content or process for sex offender treatment" (p. 484). Day et al. (2017) also point to the lack of evidence to support even basic clinical decisions about the optimal duration or timing of treatment. Critical issues arise too in developing ecologically plausible measures of change, and establishing that changes in functioning at the end of a program relate directly to longer-term behavioral change. Since recidivism is an insensitive, delayed, and indirect measure at best, there is an obvious need to develop better short-term measurements of when sufficient change has been made. So, we still have a substantial need to expand evidence about what works for whom and under which conditions, with innovative modes of service delivery and new methods of understanding and measuring relevant change also urgently needed.

Research

As the above discussion clearly illustrates, many of the challenges facing correctional psychology relate as much to the generation of new knowledge as they do to the translation of existing knowledge. There is still much that we need to find out to help correctional managers fulfill their mandates or, as Biere and Mann (2017) have put it, we are missing a considerable volume of the evidence that is needed to decide which programs to fund or provide. As a profession, we need a plan for getting the data needed to be able to answer questions like: "Who does this service work best for?" "How much more effect do we get from a program that is twice as long as another?" "Individual or group?" "What size group is optimal?" "One facilitator or two?" "How should different components be balanced?" "What sort of follow-up is needed to maintain any initial change?" It is hard to argue that we really can offer a truly evidence-based approach until we are able to answer questions like these. And so, our conclusion is that basic research continues to lie at the very center of correctional psychology, even though it can be difficult to find opportunities to systematically run variations on service delivery necessary to address these questions, along with the funding for this sort of research and time for professional psychologists to be involved. Ultimately, it seems, efforts to secure greater commitment to research may rely on psychologists speaking out more about the gaps in current evidence-based practice than about what has already been established to improve correctional outcomes.

New Ways of Working?

Many psychologists complete their training with an (at least implicit) assumption that their work will benefit those whom they encounter in professional practice. This idea is challenged when they arrive in correctional services, where an alternative is proposed: that the community is ultimately a client too, and that they must also find ways to serve potential victims living in the wider community. Correctional psychologists have sought to balance these sometimes competing demands by helping their clients to avoid reconviction through strengthening cognitive and social supports for prosocial behavior, and by teaching skills (i.e., improved communication, relationship skills, affective and behavioral regulation) that reduce risk. According to this logic, offenders' lives will improve in ways that not only reduce the incentive to offend but also offer alternatives to offending when high-risk situations arise. It may also be that the acquisition of these skills will have wider benefits in offenders' lives than simply in relation to their offending (e.g., Coupland, 2015).

There is undoubtedly a rationality in these arguments and, of course, substantial evidence to attest to the effectiveness of psychological intervention that strengthens motivation to change and equips offenders with the skills they need to reduce risk. But recent years have seen increased interest in ways of working with offenders that move beyond addressing individual deficits (Marshall, Marshall, Serran, & O'Brien, 2011). At the heart of many of these is the conviction that helping offenders to develop an understanding of the life goals that matter to them most, and to attain those goals, will lead risk factors, both personal and environmental, to fade into the background. It has been hypothesized that, ultimately, it may prove more effective to start psychological intervention by focusing less on what needs to change and more on what it is that will help the individual to become a competent human being who has no interest in offending. And to achieve this, there is a need to draw on the expertise of those who understand the most about the lives that offenders will live after completion of their sentences, such as those with relevant life experience, family members, and cultural leaders. In our view, these new approaches are particularly well suited to working with those who are compelled to work with psychologists, and reflection on what it means to lead a law-abiding and fulfilling life can only be helpful.

To date, psychologists have had little success in persuading correctional services to embrace these new ways of working, mainly because there is no compelling evidence that these alternative approaches achieve even equivalent results in reducing recidivism. There is, perhaps, even a real risk of undermining the credibility of effective ways of working while at the same time confusing newer psychologists and correctional managers about the value of several decades of evaluation research. Is it time then to get some large-scale trials of more holistic, systemic, or strengths-based approaches underway, and to evaluate their efficacy? Is it time for the proponents of these models to put their case to policy-makers and research funders, rather than just to the profession itself? Perhaps. But undoubtedly the most important contribution of these new ways of thinking will be to stimulate debate about issues that directly relate to the practice of psychology in correctional settings, such as: the importance of post-release support following treatment; whether current rehabilitation increases resilience; and when and how dynamic risk factors stay relevant as offenders age. It is the answers to these types of questions that will persuade correctional services to try new approaches, and it is correctional psychologists who are best placed to make important contributions in these areas.

Chapters in this book on self-harm, solitary confinement, and reducing the violence potential in custodial environments serve to remind us that psychology has other roles to play besides risk assessment and rehabilitation. Correctional psychologists have made some significant contributions to improving standards of offender care and staff safety, and there are new areas of practice and research in these domains as well. But perhaps the biggest challenge is how to break out of the constraints of correctional systems that silo service delivery in ways that are ethically questionable and unlikely to be particularly cost-effective.

To close this handbook, we think it is instructive to re-state the conclusion of Brodsky (2007), who, over a decade ago now, argued that correctional psychologists of previous generations would be flabbergasted to see the essential and valued roles of psychologists in contemporary corrections. Since then, our knowledge base and influence on practice has continued to grow, despite the obvious need to keep strengthening correctional systems in ways that promote the humane, safe, and effective delivery of services. As we have noted elsewhere, correctional psychologists are in a good place to continue to enact professional practice as a thoughtful, analytic, and creative activity: one that defends the interests of all stakeholders across the criminal justice system (Day, 2017).

Note

1 "The fundamental attribution error occurs when we overestimate how much another person's behavior can be explained by dispositional factors. It reflects failing to adequately consider the role of some situational factors that may affect a person's behavior." http://www.psychologyandsociety.com/attributionerror.html.

References

Biere, D. M., & Mann, R. E. (2017). The history and future of prison psychology. *Psychology, Public Policy, and Law*, 23, 478–489.

Blais, J., & Forth, A. E. (2014). Prosecution-retained versus court-appointed experts: Comparing and contrasting risk assessment reports in preventative detention hearings. *Law and Human Behavior*, 38, 531–543.

Brodsky, S. L. (2007). Correctional psychology and the American Association of Correctional Psychology: A revisionist history. *Criminal Justice and Behavior*, 34, 862–869.

Coupland, R. B. A. (2015). *An examination of dynamic risk, protective factors, and treatment-related change in violent offenders* (Unpublished doctoral dissertation). University of Saskatchewan, Sasakatoon, Canada.

Cullen, F. T., & Gendreau, P. (2001). From nothing works to what works: Changing professional ideology in the 21st century. *The Prison Journal*, 81, 313–338.

Day, A. (2017). Current directions in offender rehabilitation. *Forensic Update*. Issue 125.

Day, A., Ross, S., Casey, S., Vess, J., Johns, D., & Hobbs, G. (2017). The intensity and timing of sex offender treatment. *Sexual Abuse: A Journal of Research and Treatment*, 1–13. Advance online publication.

Douglas, K. S., & Skeem, J. L. (2005). Violence risk assessment: Getting specific about being dynamic. *Psychology, Public Policy, and Law*, 11, 347–383.

Hart, S. D. (2016). Culture and violence risk assessment: The case of Ewert v. Canada. *Journal of Threat Assessment and Management*, 3, 76–96.

Marshall, W. L., Marshall, L. E., Serran, G. A., & O'Brien, M. D. (2011). *Rehabilitating sexual offenders: A strength-based approach*. Washington, DC: American Psychological Association.

Index

Page references to Figures are followed by the letter 'f', while references to Tables are followed by the letter 't'. References to Notes are indicated by the page number followed by 'n' and the Note number.